DA

REBIRTH OF THE POLISH REPUBLIC

REBIRTH
OF THE
POLISH REPUBLIC

A Study in the Diplomatic History of Europe,
1914–1920

By

TITUS KOMARNICKI

WILLIAM HEINEMANN LTD
MELBOURNE : LONDON : TORONTO

First Published, 1957

Published by Wm. Heinemann Ltd.
99 Great Russell Street, London, W.C.1

Printed in Great Britain
By The Whitefriars Press Ltd., London and Tonbridge

THIS work is a tribute to the memory of my beloved
brother WACLAW KOMARNICKI (1891-1954), former
Dean of the Faculty of Law and Professor at the
Stephen Batory University of Wilno, Prisoner in
Russia (1939-1941), then Minister of Justice in the
Polish Government in Exile and Professor at the
Polish Faculty of Law at the University of Oxford, a
man of integrity, a great scholar and a selfless friend.

FOREWORD

THE primary object of this book is to ascertain the rôle played by Polish problems in world policy, and in particular in the policy of the Western Powers, France, Great Britain and U.S.A., during the First World War, at the Paris Peace Conference and immediately after; that is to say in the course of the Polish-Soviet War of 1919-20. This study has made necessary a thorough review of the foreign policy of the above-mentioned Powers, as well as that of Germany and Russia, in order to find out the factors determining the attitude of each of them towards Poland. It should be emphasized that so far this page of the history of Western diplomacy has been relatively little known, or simply ignored, although, as the reader will be able to see for himself, the importance of the Polish problem was gradually increasing in the course of the years under review, and the outcome of the Polish-Soviet War of 1919-20 was decisive for the political configuration of Europe between the two World Wars. My researches have been greatly facilitated by the recent valuable publications of diplomatic papers by the British Foreign Office and the American State Department. Unfortunately, there are still big gaps in the documentation because neither France nor Soviet Russia have so far followed the example of the two Anglo-Saxon countries, and it is to be feared that many years may elapse before we shall be acquainted, if ever, with the secret archives of the Quai d'Orsay and the Kremlin. I have tried, nevertheless, to gather as much data on the policy of these two countries as is possible under present circumstances and, moreover, the reader will find many references to Polish sources which throw a new light on many political developments in those years. These sources have been used, however, only incidentally, because the book does not deal so much with local history, as with the general aspects of the Polish problems. I have tried to place myself in the position of a western reader who might be more interested in looking at these problems from the point of view of world affairs than from that of Poland alone. I venture to hope that my book, being based mainly on official sources, will dispose of some preconceived ideas and faulty judgments, due largely to unscrupulous propaganda and the determined pursuit of political ends, using one-sided documentation or distorting the historical truth.

I have worked under particularly difficult conditions, being obliged to carry out extensive researches for more than four years, without having received any grant or subsidy—which I did not solicit, preferring to preserve complete independence of judgment.

The book appears in print thanks to the substantial help of the Jozef Pilsudski Institute of America for Research in the Modern History of Poland, which has greatly encouraged me in my work and arranged a loan to cover a great part of the printing costs.

Moreover, I obtained a personal financial guarantee from a friend who is a prominent member of the General Sikorski Historical Institute in London.

I am very grateful to the above-mentioned as well as to several American, British and Polish friends who have helped me in my researches by drawing attention to some important sources relating to the subject dealth with in this book. I hope that I have not fallen short of their expectations.

In any case I have tried to give a full and unbiased picture of this important page of European history. Although one can look at this period with some detachment after the lapse of more than thirty-five years, one cannot help thinking that many sad experiences we have lived through in the course of recent years could have been avoided if so many errors and ill-advised moves had not been made owing to ignorance, prejudice and lack of courage, unfortunately not so uncommon among statesmen of our times.

1957   TITUS KOMARNICKI

CONTENTS

PART I

WAR AND ARMISTICE (1914–1918)

PART I

WAR AND ARMISTICE
(1914-1918)

MAP 1

Frontiers in Central-Eastern Europe 1815-1918
Frontiers of Poland before the 1st partition in 1772

CHAPTER I

ORIGINS OF THE FIRST WORLD WAR, WAR AIMS, WAR POLICY AND WAR SLOGANS

" In each Government I have visited I have found stubbornness, determination, selfishness and cant. One continually hears self-glorification and the highest motives attributed to themselves because of their part in the war. But I may tell you that my observation is that incompetent statesmanship and selfishness is at the bottom of it all. It is not so much a breaking down of civilization as a lack of wisdom in those that govern ; and history, I believe, will bring an awful indictment against those who were short-sighted and selfish enough to let such a tragedy happen."— (From the letter of E. M. House to President Wilson, 9th February, 1916. House, *Intimate Papers,* II, p. 164).

The origins of the First World War have for a long time remained one of the major controversial issues in modern history. The verdict of the Versailles Treaty, laying the whole burden of responsibility on one country, was given in specific political circumstances (surrender of the Central Powers, the wish to frustrate Bolshevik propaganda inculpating all the capitalist powers including the Tsarist régime, etc.) and cannot be considered wholly unbiased.

To those who at present still exalt the importance of the power factor in international relations we can point out that it was undoubtedly the disposition " to rate material power above moral law," rightly ascribed to the Central Powers but not limited to them, that was one of the main causes of this war. From this point of view, among the remote causes of the war was not only annexation of Alsace-Lorraine and the intrigues of Great Powers in the Balkans, but above all the growth of three imperialistic powers in Central and Eastern Europe at the expense of their weaker neighbours, marked by such events as the rape of Silesia by Frederic II, the partitions of Poland in the eighteenth century and the subsequent condonation by the Western Powers at the Congress of Vienna in 1815 of many acts of spoliation and violation of international law and justice.[1]

The close co-operation between the Western democratic Powers and Tsarist Russia both before and at the outbreak of the First

World War induced public opinion in the West to take more lenient views on the expansion of Russia, the threat of which to peace in Europe weighed so heavily upon many minds in the nineteenth century. The imperialistic policy of the German Reich obscured all other issues and pushed into the background, for some time, the dangers arising from the Russian designs in Europe and Asia. " The cause of peace was damaged by the almost exclusive ascendancy in Europe of a state whose policy was based on material force," says a British historian, A. A. W. Ramsay,[2] and in another place he states that, " the importance of the rise of this new Prussian-German state was due to the fact that it introduced(?) a new element into politics. What that element was has been expressed in various catchwords: ' The State as Power; Might is Right; Bismarck's own poetic Blood and Iron.' "[3]

Some apologists of Russia went very far indeed in justifying Russia's policy, and we find the following enthusiastic outburst of Mr. Edward Foord in an article published in *The Contemporary Review*, November 1916, entitled " The Greatness of Russia ":

> " To conclude, there is, perhaps, no great Empire—not even that of Rome—which has been built without deliberate aggression like that of Russia. And Russia may fairly claim that almost everywhere, even in Poland, her rule has been an improvement, often a vast improvement, upon preceding conditions."(!)

During that war public opinion was led astray by statements coming from the highest quarters, one of the many being that made by Lloyd George in his speech on the 5th January, 1918:

> " Russia accepted war with all its horrors because, true to her traditional guardianship of the weaker communities of her race, she stepped in to protect Serbia from a plot against her independence. It is this honourable sacrifice which not only brought Russia into the war, but France as well."*[4]

Russia's Share of Responsibility for the Outbreak of the War

And yet the verdict of history is almost unanimous: Russia had also her share of responsibility in the outbreak of the First World War, pursuing the same policy of expansion as Germany and aiming to upset the balance of power in Europe. " War came to the West from the East," says the French historian Elie Halévy, " it was

---

* Compare that with a statement made by Lloyd George at the Council of Ten on 12th January, 1919: " We had formally recognized the Tsar's Government although at the time we knew it to be absolutely rotten." *P. R. F. R.*, The Paris Peace Conference, II, p. 491.

forced upon the West by the East." [5] Strangely enough the struggle
between the two main protagonists in the East started not because
of territorial issues involving them directly. " Nobody in St. Petersburg dreamt of conquering German territory; neither did anybody
in Berlin dream of aggrandizing Germany at the expense of Russia.
The two Governments had, in this respect, only one common purpose, which was to keep Poland in a state of disruption and subjection." [6]

Forced for the time being to abandon her dreams of expansion in
the Far East,[7] Tsarist Russia resumed her drive towards the Straits
and South-Eastern Europe, for more than a century considered to
be her historic mission.[8] Was the disruption of Austria-Hungary of
vital interest to Russia? Many prominent Russian statesmen denied it; let us refer, for instance, to the report of General Kuropat-
kin, presented to the Tsar in 1900 and producing many valid arguments against any aggrandizement of Russia at the expense of
Austria-Hungary and Germany.[9] These views were shared by many
Russian statesmen in the subsequent period, as for instance Baron
Rosen who in his memorandum published on the eve of the war, in
1913,[10] asserted that the Pan-Slavic idea " lacked any foundation,
and did not correspond to the real Russian interests." These views
were shared not only by many right-wing leaders, anxious to maintain the old friendship with Germany, but also by the left-wing opposition.[11] Whatever we may think about these disputes between the
advocates of Far Eastern and South-Western expansion of Russia,
we can take for granted that after the annexation of Bosnia-
Herzogovina by Austria-Hungary Russian plans went far beyond
the defence of her interests in the Balkans, aiming for the complete disruption of the Hapsburg monarchy. Undoubtedly the
Russian policy greatly contributed to the state of tension in Europe,
and even such Russian statesmen as Mr. Milyukov, whose " liberal "
outlook never led him astray in defending what he considered vital
Russian interests, admit that the Russian policy in the Balkans
was " insufficiently wise and far-sighted." [12]

The Russian plans for the dismemberment of the Hapsburg
monarchy were well known to western diplomacy even before the
outbreak of the war. Sir George Buchanan, for instance, gives an
interesting account of his conversation with the Tsar on the 14th
April, 1913: [13]

> " The Emperor spoke of Austria without any bitterness, but as
> a source of weakness to Germany and as a danger to peace, owing
> to the fact that Germany was bound to support her in her Balkan
> policy. He further expressed the opinion that the disintegration of
> the Austrian Empire was merely a question of time, and that the

day was not far distant when we should see a Kingdom of Hungary and a Kingdom of Bohemia. ... I ventured to observe that such a recasting of the map of Europe could hardly be effected without general war."

So far as France was concerned, for a long time the prevailing opinion there had been that the existence of Austria-Hungary was a necessary counterbalance to Germany. It was based on the belief that in the course of natural evolution the predominance of the Germanic element in this state would be reduced. This opinion found its best expression in the well known work of André Chéradame, "L'Allemagne, la France et la Question d'Autriche," published at the beginning of this century.[14] We find in the memoirs of M. Paléologue, French Ambassador to Russia during the war, many examples of the difference of opinion between the French envoy and the Russian leaders relating to this question.[15]

The question of Russian mobilization which served the Germans as a major means of defence at Versailles and after, is, in our view, a secondary issue once Austria-Hungary supported by Germany had decided upon the use of force against Serbia,[16] although some historians nevertheless consider that it was one of the immediate causes of the war.[17]

I have made the foregoing remarks not for the purpose of reviving old controversies but for valid reasons which will be better understood in the light of the events described in the following chapters. In my opinion it was necessary to restate some facts relating to the real motives for Russia's participation in the First World War because of much confusion persisting in the West about this subject for nearly a quarter of a century. Public opinion all over the world was more impressed by the " chivalrous " gesture of the Tsar in taking defence of a small Balkan State than by the true aims pursued by Tsarist policy. As the French historiographer Albert Pingaud confesses, the alliance of France with Russia was originally devised as a measure to safeguard peace and eventually turned out to serve " the interests of Slavism in the Orient." [18]

The misunderstanding of the true aims of Russia was greatly increased by the extreme short-sightedness of the Austrian and Hungarian statesmen in dealing with national issues. We agree with the American historian, Fay, who said that it was a great mistake for Berchtold to diminish Serbia and try to destroy her as a Balkan factor, as " a partially dismembered Serbia would have become a still greater source of unrest and danger to the peace of Europe than heretofore. Serbian nationalism would have been intensified by partition," [18a] but we must also agree with the British historian, G. P. Gooch : " It is true that while Austria fought under the banner of self-preservation, Russia, whom nobody threatened, marched out to battle in the name of prestige." [18b]

In view of all this evidence it would be difficult to assert that although the rise of nationalism was one of the forces instrumental in the outbreak of war it was for the vindication of the rights of a small people that two groups of powers came to grips. While due distinction should be made between the expansionist powers who on both sides tried to materialize their imperialistic aims and those who entered the war for the defence of the balance of power, the prevailing cause of the war was the fear that " the nation which did not play its part would be outdistanced in the eternal competition of peoples." [18c] Although the immediate issue concerned only Austria-Hungary and Russia, the crisis was immediately viewed as a " test of strength between the two rival groups of Powers." [19]

War Aims of the Allied Powers

So far as the *war aims of the Allies* were concerned, the following questions should be considered:

1. Had they any general war aims at the beginning, apart of course from winning the war?
2. What changes occurred in the war aims of the Allies in the course of the war, and in what circumstances?

By the Declaration signed on the 5th September, 1914, the Governments of France, Great Britain and Russia pledged themselves not to conclude a separate peace and not to bring forward any terms of peace without previous common agreement.

Apart from this declaration there was no agreement at the beginning on any general problem relating to the reconstruction of Europe after the war.

In his *War Memoirs* Lloyd George writes the following about the initial war aims of the Allied Powers :

> " Once the war started, there were objects which each country resolved to secure as due reward for its sacrifices. France wanted to recover the lost provinces of Alsace and Lorraine. Italy sought to gain the Italian Irredenta of the Trientino and Trieste. The Russian Government wanted Constantinople and the hegemony of the Balkans. ... Britain ... entered the war mainly to defend the integrity of Belgium and *up to the end that was one issue upon which we were not prepared to compromise.*" [20] [My italics.]

It means that each belligerent had his own political aims which he tried to secure in the course of and after the war, usually presenting them as an application of higher general principles, but it would be rash to assert that any one of them was more than a champion of his own cause.

Taking the defence of Serbia, Russia could pretend to take a stand for the cause of oppressed nationalities, but her war aims were purely imperialistic; the disruption of Turkey or the dismemberment of Germany (division of Germany into separate kingdoms) or even the dismemberment of Austria were not dictated by the wishes of the populations concerned (neither the Poles nor the Ukrainians of Galicia desired to be annexed by Russia, and not all the Southern Slavs in Austria-Hungary were yet won to Yugoslav unity). Although in his conversations with Allied ambassadors Sazonov used to call Serbians " little, dear Slav brothers," one of his first steps after the outbreak of the war was to propose to Serbia some territorial concessions to the Bulgarians in Macedonia in order to win the support of the latter, to which the Serbian Government eventually had to agree with many qualifications.[21]

France could claim Alsace-Lorraine in the name of the principle of nationality but, as we have pointed out, she was not interested in the initial stages of the war either in the dismemberment of Austria-Hungary, which on the contrary she wished to preserve as a counterbalance to Germany, nor in the settlement of Balkan problems.

As Lloyd George confessed, Great Britain was prepared to compromise on any issue except that of the independence of Belgium.

To sum up, in the First World War the Allies had not and could not have unity of views on the great problems of the reconstruction of the world after the war. After the desertion of the Allied cause by Russia in 1917, Lloyd George wrote the following in his *Memoirs*: " The fall of Russia . . . would clarify the political aim of the Entente." [21a] In his history of the Russian Revolution [22] Milyukov quotes an interesting correspondence from England, published by the newspaper *Birzhevyie Vedomosti* under the date of 4th May, 1917, in which the British point of view is explained very crudely :

> " Neither the dismemberment of Turkey nor, still less, the partition of Austria-Hungary, are the foundation stones of the English war policy, which would only be glad to throw them overboard should Russia not insist on them any more. Also the question of Alsace-Lorraine and Trient, the autonomy of Czechia and Poland interest England only from the point of view of her allies. If the allies give up their ' interests ' England cannot raise any objections against it."

Another proof that it was the individual war aims of the members of the Western coalition that really mattered, and nothing else, can be found in the fact that all the secret negotiations aiming to find a basis for settlement of the conflict failed exclusively on account of the impossibility of a compromise on the particular issues between the two belligerent blocks. In the peace-feelers and secret negotiations carried out through different channels between Austria-Hungary and the Western Powers in 1917 it was the problem of the Italian claims that constituted the stumbling-block. It is perhaps interesting to observe how little the cause of small nations weighed at that time, for instance, on the minds of some French negotiators. In the account referring to the interview between Prince Sixte and the President of the French Republic (20th May, 1917) we read the following : [23]

" The President, however, considered that as things then stood, Serbia should be quite satisfied with the restoration of her own territory, and in addition such access to the Adriatic as the Emperor specified in his letter, with Durazzo. . . . Mr. Ribot pointed out that Rumania had been completely overlooked. Our obligation was greater to her than to Serbia, as she had only entered the war as our Ally: moreover there was the Polish question. The President answered that *our Allies had come into the war on the strength of promises which he personally considered excessive ; but that the course of events would inevitably mean a curtailment of their aspirations.* ' But it is not for us,' said Mr. Ribot, ' to curtail their aspirations.' " [24]

So far as the possibility of an early peace with Germany was concerned (here we omit for the time being the attempts at a separate peace between Russia and Germany), we are bound to state that the main reason for the failure of these attempts was the stubbornness of German military quarters and many German politicians (among them the future " man of Locarno," Gustav Stresemann), who were unwilling to make any concession in the West.

H. J. Mackinder rightly observed :

" Berlin committed a fundamental mistake ; she fought on two fronts without fully making up her mind on which front she meant to win. You may strike at the two flanks of your enemy, the right and the left, but unless your force is sufficient you must decide beforehand which stroke is to be a feint and which the real attack. Berlin had not decided between her political objectives— Hamburg and overseas dominion or Baghdad and the Heartland— and therefore her stategical aim was uncertain." [25]

The opinion prevails among historians that it would have been difficult for the Western Allies to reject German peace offers if Germany had replied to the Pope's Note of 1st August, 1917, preceded by the conversations of Nuncio Pacelli with the German

Chancellor, in a different way, that is to say on the lines of the Reichstag resolution of the 19th July, 1917. It was the Crown Council held at the Bellevue Castle on the 11th September, 1917, which nipped in the bud the beginnings of a negotiation. At that time Germany was still a formidable power, she expected a decisive success from submarine war and the position of France was particularly critical. It is quite certain that the question of Alsace-Lorraine, so far as the French were concerned, was the only obstacle to peace, but not only was Germany not disposed to sacrifice a portion of her territory but insisted on keeping the coast of Flanders and Liège.[26]

The pacifists in Great Britain were ready to compromise on the problems outside the sphere of immediate interests of the Western Powers. Lord Lansdowne, in his first letter of 28th November, 1917, undoubtedly echoed the opinions of many of his countrymen :

> " Some of our original desiderata became unattainable. Others would probably now be given a less prominent place than when they were first put forward. Others, again, notably the reparation due to Belgium, remain in the first rank ; but when it comes to the wholesale rearrangement of the map of South-Eastern Europe we may well ask for a suspension of judgment and for the elucidation which a frank exchange of views between the Allied Powers can alone afford." [27]

But not only outstanding pacifists held such views. Let us refer here to the opinions of Winston Churchill, noted in Lord Bertie's *Diary* under 26th February, 1918 :

> " I dined at the Ritz, a guest of Sir Charles Ellis, between whom and Winston Churchill I sat. . . . Winston's views are peculiar. At one moment he said that the war ought not to be continued a day beyond what might be necessary to free Belgium and to obtain for France, not necessarily the whole of Alsace-Lorraine, but such part of it as would not enable her to feel and say that she had been deserted by England and justify her in seeking another friend." [28]

Hints that the Western Allies would have welcomed some reasonable proposals from the German side in order to finish the war ordeal were certainly not lacking, and among others we can refer to the well-known speech of General Smuts in Glasgow on 17th June, 1918. While condemning " unhealthy and unwholesome pacifism," General Smuts contested the beliefs of those people who meant " by an allied victory that we must completely smash Germany, cross the Rhine and dictate peace at Berlin. He was not of this opinion. . . . If this war is going to end it will be necessary from time to time for the combatants to try informally to get into touch with one another. ... We shall use diplomacy and all other forces at our disposal in order to bring it to a victorious end. ... The highest objects of peace will be secured not only by the gallantry of our armies but by the weapons of our diplomacy when the time is ripe for obtaining a satisfactory peace for the allies." [29]

We find some explanation of what General Smuts meant by "satisfactory peace" in Lloyd George's *War Memoirs*. Lloyd George mentions there a note General Smuts laid before the British Government on the 29th October, 1918, in which we read the following [30]:

> "The popular cry for justice is very insistent but two governing considerations should be steadily kept in view. Firstly the evil of continuing the war is rapidly beginning to outweigh the good to be achieved by a more complete measure of victory or *justice* at the expense of its own legitimate future." [My italics.]

Quoting these words Lloyd George adds this remark: "The last observation sounds a little cynical. But Smuts doubtless had in mind the advice of Ecclesiastes: 'Be not righteous overmuch. Why shouldest thou destroy thyself.'"

We shall return to this problem in the chapter dealing with the 1918 Armistice; for the time being we limit ourselves to observing that the Western Powers were spared the temptation to make a peace treaty at the expense of smaller nations thanks to the conviction of the German High Command that it could overcome Allied resistance or at least hold on for an indefinite time. Smuts' peace feelers were well understood by von Kühlmann, the German Secretary for Foreign Affairs, who answered by a speech in the Reichstag on the 25th June, 1918, but his attempts failed again owing to the overweening attitude of Ludendorf, and Kühlmann was replaced by Admiral von Hintze.

As Nowak tells in his *Collapse of Central Europe*,[31] in the middle of July the new Secretary for Foreign Affairs asked the Quartermaster whether he was sure of victory over the Western Powers and received from him an unqualified, positive answer. On the 15th September, 1918, the Imperial Chancellor still assured the leaders of the parties represented in the Reichstag that the war could be carried on "to the bitter end." Even after the same party leaders were summoned to a meeting on the 1st October under the presidency of Vice-Chancellor von Payer some eminent Germans refused to believe the catastrophe. Stresemann was one of these, and his biographer, Mrs. A. Vallentin, observes the following about his state of mind :

> "The history of Gustav Stresemann's attitude in the war is the

history of the German people, more especially on the 'Home Front'. . . . 'It is easy,' he said in later years, looking back on his pronouncements in 1918, ' to throw stones on those who believed in a German victory. But anyone who does so must be honest enough to admit that this faith in a German victory was held by the vast majority of the German people, and that, if this faith in victory was a crime, it was one committed by millions of the best German citizens.' " [32]

War Slogans and War Policy

The First World War provides a good example of the discrepancy between war slogans and war policy. From the very beginning of the war Western statesmen stated in many declarations that their main aims went far beyond their purely national interests and that they were fighting also for the rights of the small nations. From the many let us quote the first ones made by Mr. Asquith. On 25th September, 1914, he declared :

" Room must be found and kept for the independent existence and free development of smaller nationalities, each for the life of its history and corporal consciousness of its own. Belgium, Holland, Switzerland and the Scandinavian countries, Greece and the Balkan States, they must be recognized as having exactly as good a title as their more powerful neighbours—more powerful in strength and wealth—exactly as good a title to a place in the sun."

In his famous Guildhall speech on 9th November, 1914, Mr. Asquith declared :

" We shall never sheathe the sword which we have not lightly drawn until Belgium recovers in full measure all and more than all she has sacrificed, until France is adequately secured against the menace of aggression, until the rights of the smaller nationalities of Europe are placed upon an unassailable foundation, and until the military domination of Prussia is wholly and finally destroyed."

In the Allied Note of 30th December, 1916, we read the following:

" Once again the Allies declare that no peace is possible so long as they had not secured reparation of violated rights, recognition of the principle of nationalities, and of the existence of small states."

And yet it would be rash to assume that the Allied policy abided by these principles. We shall deal with this subject more amply in subsequent chapters when we examine the incidence of the Allied policy on the Polish question, but apart from it, all the secret agreements made between the Allies, especially in the first half of the war, clashed with these high-sounding statements. Above all there was the agreement reached in March 1915 between Russia on the one side and England and France on the other, on the partition of Turkey and the enlargement of England's spheres of influence in Persia. There was the Treaty of London of 26th April, 1915,* placing 250,000 Germans and a great number of Slovenes under Italian rule. All these treaties were based on the principle of territorial compensation for the sacrifices in war, and obviously violated the principle of nationalities. In his *Diary* Lord Bertie quotes the point of view on these matters developed by Winston Churchill in a conversation on 7th May, 1915 :

> "Winston Churchill told him (Henri de Breteuil) that Russia is to have Constantinople and the Straits. He defended the arrangement on the pleas that Russia had been of great assistance in the war, had made great sacrifices, and must have her reward: that the Black Sea is a Russian lake, and Russia must have the key to it ; that she will be a great Mediterranean Power and cannot be cooped in the Black Sea." [33]

"Had the French and British Governments," says Wickham Steed, " deliberately set themselves to stultify the principles on which the Allied peoples believed they were fighting the war— respect for the rights of small peoples as opposed to militarism, the idea, in short, of government by consent of the governed as against the imposition of government by force—they could hardly have set their hands to a more effective document than the Treaty of London." [34]

It should be noted, by the way, that these treaties were first published by the Russian Revolutionary Government. They were generally ignored by the Press and the public opinion of the Allied countries. [35]

" Something over two years of the war," writes Macartney, " the belligerents of neither side had adopted the principle of self-determination as a general part of their policy." [36]

But still in 1917 in secret conversations with Prince Sixte strange proposals were put forward by the French negotiators, recalling the schemes of the end of the eighteenth century. In a conversation with Prince Sixte in November 1916, Mr. Jules Cambon made the following suggestions :

> "There is Silesia, the dowry of Maria Theresa. The Silesian nobility is very Prussian ; but, once we have won a defensive vic-

---

* Agreement between France, Russia, Great Britain and Italy signed at London, 26th April, 1915 (*State Papers,* Cmd. 671, 1920).

tory, we shall be free to act. For my part I wish to see but one Imperial Crown, that of Austria, and to reduce Prussia to the limits of its Kingdom. There are dynastic rivalries in Saxony and Bavaria which would be used against Hohenzollern." [37]

This was confirmed by the President of the Republic, M. Poincaré, who in an interview with Prince Sixte on 5th March, 1917, declared : " It is France's interest not merely to keep Austria as she is, but to enlarge her frontiers at Germany's expense by taking in Silesia or Bavaria." [38]

It is in connection with Austrian problems that we can best observe the reappearance of old prejudices, about which we will speak later, relating to the question of small nations and their rights to political freedom. One can state that the disruption of Austria, due to the impact of the national consciousness of the peoples of which the Double Monarchy consisted and the ineptitude of its statesmen in dealing with this problem, took place rather against the inner wishes of many Western statesmen than thanks to any practical steps taken by them.[39] That strange representative of a small nation in the War Cabinet, General Smuts, with rare outspokenness stated the point of view shared at that time by many representatives of big powers [39a]:

" There is a great danger," said Smuts in his memorandum laid before the British War Cabinet in October 1918, " that the bad, but more or less orderly political pre-war system of Europe may give place to a wild disorder of jarring and warring State fragments, such as we now see on a vast scale in Russia. . . . What is going to happen when, as now it seems probable, Austria breaks up and becomes a ' Balkans ' on a vaster scale? With the creation of an ' independent ' Poland, there will be a chain of the discordant fragments right across Europe from Finland in the north to Turkey in the south. No League of Nations could hope to prevent a wild wardance of these so-called free nations in the future." Lloyd George, in spite of his dislike of small nations observed, however, that " the most serious trouble had been created by the rivalries, jealousies and disagreements of the greater powers of Europe and Asia."

Great Powers, Small Nations and the Principle of National Self-determination

As a matter of fact a major war was imaginable only if the interests of great powers clashed, that is to say if there was a danger that a great power wanted to extend its " sphere of influence " to the detriment of another. The great powers had sufficient means to stop a war between small powers, and had often come to agreement at their expense, this rôle having been assumed in the past by the " Concert of Europe." The last conference which succeeded in maintaining peace between the Great Powers was the London Conference held in 1912-13.

It is beyond any doubt that the rise of nationalism and the awakening of many nationalities in Southern and Eastern Europe seemed to offer good opportunities to some great powers to extend their spheres of influence; Russia in particular used the feelings of the Balkan peoples to appear as a protector of their interests. To the Great Powers the national problem appeared exclusively from the point of view of the balance of power, and each national problem was considered not on its merits but in relation to the Great Powers' policy. There was a special political philosophy to justify such a standpoint. We should bear in mind that the last decades of the nineteenth century and the first decade of the twentieth were the heyday of the Great Powers. " In the international architecture of the pre-war period," says Arnold J. Toynbee, " in which the ' Cyclopean blocks ' were represented by the Great Powers, the interstices only left for small ' buffer ' states which, precariously protected by the equilibrium of the vast masses around them from being subjected to a pressure which must have ground them to powder, preserved their poise by maintaining a rigid neutrality." [40] There was a " real cult of the big State during the last decades of the nineteenth century," writes another British author.[41] To E. A. Freeman,[42] for instance, and others of his school, the small State, if not actually (as some thought) an " international nuisance " was apt to multiply temptations to international war. There was no difference between such statements popular in the West and the theories of the German philosopher Treitschke who asserted that " there was something ridiculous in the idea of a small state," and that " morality was the endowment of small men undertaking small things, whereas the state must carry out big things." [43]

For this reason the idea of the liberation of oppressed nationalities which might lead to the formation of new states was quite alien to the Great Powers at the beginning of the war. Masaryk complains, in his work *The Making of a State*,[44] that :

> " Big peoples like the British and the Americans, who are wont to apply continental standards of judgment and are not greatly troubled by questions of language, are wont to look upon the liberation of small peoples and the creation of small States as a bothersome process of political and linguistic Balkanization. Yet circumstances are what they are, determined by Nature and History."

During the whole of the nineteenth century democracy was strictly confined to domestic issues. Let us take, for instance, the attitude of British policy towards the Balkan States from the very beginning of their independent or semi-independent existence (apart from Greece). A British historian observed that [45]:

> "The possibility of using these thriving little states as a barrier to the southward advance of Russia never seems to have occurred to any British statesman. Britain had in the past persistently opposed every attempt at progress apparently not realizing that the stronger these states were the more likely they were to be independent of Russia ... Germany was far more alive than Britain to the importance of the Balkan States. Bismarck lost no opportunity to establish German influence there."

The conclusion which might be drawn from the foregoing is that the national problem in Europe was gradually coming into the foreground, not as a result of a deliberate policy but owing to the necessity for appealing to some forces ignored at the beginning in order to win the war. A characteristic confession in this respect was made by the German Chancellor Bethmann-Hollweg in his speech in the Reichstag on 5th April, 1916 : " Neither Germany nor Austria intended to raise the Polish question; it was the fortunes of the battles that raised it. This question exists and awaits its solution."

It was a young French writer, E. Mantoux, who put the whole question in a nutshell in his brilliant work *The Carthaginian Peace* [46] by saying :

> "For some of the forces that had been instrumental to the outbreak of the war were to assist the Allies in winning it. During the final assault against the Central Empire, the Allies had found in the insurrection of the Slav nations a powerful support ; and only through the hazards of war were the extraordinary conditions manufactured that made it possible, in a moment unique in history, to look forward to a Europe of free nations."

"Alas," wrote Clemenceau, "we must have the courage to say that our programme, when we entered the war, was not one of liberation ... We had started as allies of the Russian oppressors of Poland, with the Polish soldiers of Silesia and Galicia fighting against us. By the collapse of military Russia Poland found herself suddenly set free and recreated, and then all over Europe oppressed peoples raised their heads and our war of national defence was transformed by force of events into a war of liberation. ... A Europe founded upon right ... instead of a dismembered Europe, was a fine dramatic turn of events." [46a]

The rise of national problems in the course of the First World War, unexpected and perhaps even unwanted by the official diplomacy on both sides, is one of the most interesting features of that war, the implications of which were not rightly understood in the post-war period. An English writer, looking at the events of the 1914 war from the perspective of the Second World War, voiced the opinion of many people in the West with little knowledge of the underground forces unchained by the collapse of great multinational empires :

> " Our one agreed aim in 1914 was to break German militarism. It was no part of our original intentions to break up the Hapsbourg and Ottoman Empires, to create Czechoslovakia or resurrect Poland, to make a Russian revolution, to treble the size of Serbia and double that of Rumania, to create Iraq and Estonia and a Jewish National Home, or to give the keys of the Brenner and the Adriatic to Italy. Yet, in the outcome, all these things and much else sprang from the war, while one thing which we promised ourselves, the destruction of German militarism, we failed to achieve." [47]

For a short time, but only for a short time, it might have appeared that Germany had understood the importance of national issues for winning the war, as she took some initiatives which if followed consistently and genuinely could have provided her with great, perhaps decisive, advantages. But all these timid attempts were eventually frustrated by the advocates of German expansionism and by imperialistic lust, although sometimes cloaked by fashionable catchwords, and the German plans unmasked by the too quickly " forgotten " treaties of Brest-Litovsk and Bucharest, stiffened the spirit of resistance both of the belligerents and of the nations fighting for freedom.

Wilson and the European War

The picture would not be complete if we did not take into consideration the growing influence of the United States' policy on the war aims of the Allies. We shall have many occasions to speak about Wilson's policy in connection with Polish problems, both during the war and at the Paris Peace Conference. For the time being we limit ourselves to a few general remarks on the bearing of the Wilsonian policy and ideology on the recognition of the principle of national self-determination in Europe. There is no doubt that there was a fundamental difference of approach to this question between Wilson and the statesmen of the old school.

According to Hartley Notter [47a]:

" Three elements dominated his (Wilson's) policy, which derived from his historical studies, his conception of progress, and his social-religious philosophy. He believed that the modern age was to be moral as defined in Christianity, and that nations as well as individuals must conform to moral laws. ... Belief in the capacity and right of people to rule themselves was another basic element. ... That growth of liberty in the world was to him inevitable by the operation of historical forces. In it he saw the gradual emancipation of mankind from all forms of absolutist governments and in it he saw the effectiveness of the teaching of Christianity and the power of righteousness and of the nobler impulses and aspirations of man. ... The final element of Wilson's foreign policy ... was his conception of America and her mission. ... Each of these fundamental elements of thought which marked Wilson's foreign policy had been determined ... before he entered the White House as President."

One of the most prominent students of Wilsonian policy in the United States, Arthur S. Link, emphasizes that the championing of these ideals " provided the dynamic " for the policy of Wilson and that of his first Secretary of State, Bryan. He further says that " they were both moralists who thought of foreign policy in terms of eternal verities, rather than in terms of expedient." [48] This " missionary diplomacy " failed, however, in Latin America, where it was first inaugurated, as according to the same writer " the years from 1913 to 1921 witnessed intervention by the State Department and the Navy on a scale that had never before been contemplated even by such alleged imperialists as Theodore Roosevelt and William Howard Taft." [49]

With the progressive movement in the United States, however, Wilson shared " the repudiation of the principle of using power as an instrument of diplomacy," and it was the great tragedy of Wilson's life that he failed in his endeavours to obtain peace by persuasion and by appealing to the sense of justice of the belligerent parties. Let us recall Wilson's declaration on the 10th May, 1915, after the sinking of the *Lusitania,* that " there is such a thing as a man being too proud to fight," [49a] and the assurances given by him on many occasions to the German Ambassador, von Bernstorff, that he intended to keep America out of the war. For instance, on the 11th October, 1916, " Wilson gave particular force to his remarks by pointing out that the leaders of the opposition, Roosevelt, Lodge and Co., desired war with Germany, which he was quite unable to understand. His only desire was to remain neutral, and to help to bring the war to an end, as a decision by force of arms seemed to

him out of the question." [50] On the eve of the German declaration
about unrestricted submarine warfare (31st January, 1917), Wilson
still believed in " peace without victory." To this effect we have
not only the evidence of the German Ambassador but also that of
Wilson's closest collaborators. " While Wilson was rent within
himself," writes in his *Memoirs* Joseph Daniels, Secretary of the
Navy, " groping for a way to keep out with honor, Theodore Roosevelt was writing to Lodge : ' If Wilson does not go to war, I will
skin him alive.' " The following scene described by Daniels best
characterizes Wilson's approach to the problem of the war :

> " After reading the text of the Kaiser's declaration of unrestricted
> U-Boat warfare to the listening ten Cabinet members, the Presi-
> dent asked: ' What is the concrete suggestion? What shall I pro-
> pose? I must go to Congress. What shall I say?'
> " One member of the Cabinet—I think it was Lane—asked :
> ' Which side do you wish to see victorious?' That question recalled
> Wilson's speech on ' peace without victory.'
> " ' I do not wish to see either side win. What I most earnestly desire
> is to see all neutrals unite to bring an end to the killing,' replied
> the President." [51]

There is no doubt that the war was imposed on the United States,
that to the last moment Wilson tried to find a peaceful solution to the
conflict. To this effect we have the evidence of his private secretary,
Josph Tumulty : " After recovering from the initial shock of Germany's action, however, Wilson vainly sought alternatives short of
belligerency. Although he gave increasing attention to national preparedness, the war spirit sweeping America frightened him. War
meant the submergence of the principles closest to his heart." [52] It
was rightly observed that although the submarine war was " the
immediate cause of the war," Wilson looked " for a more elevated
and inspiring objective." Professor T. Bailey remarks that in Wilson's way of thinking " the causes began to merge with the objectives, and before the end of the war he seems to have believed—and
he certainly carried a great many with him—that we entered the
conflict to save the world from Prussian autocracy, to make the
world safe for democracy, and to end all wars." [53]

So far as the objectives of the war were concerned, one must keep
in mind that in the early stages of the war Wilson's programme did
not aim to remake the political structure of Europe. Apart from the
Polish problem, the solution of which seemed to Wilson one of the
cornerstones of the lasting pacification of Europe (although no satisfactory solution of it could be found at that time within the framework of a negotiated peace), the programme laid before the
belligerents at the beginning of 1916 by Wilson's special representa-

tive, Colonel House, did not differ very much from the official war
aims of the Western Allies. " Reasonable " terms proposed by
Colonel House at that time were : Complete restoration of Belgium
and Serbia, return of Alsace-Lorraine to France, Constantinople for
Russia, an independent Poland, cession of Italian-speaking regions
by Austria-Hungary to Italy, compensation for Germany outside
Europe, abolition of competitive armaments and guarantees against
military aggression.[54]

But generally speaking Wilson avoided entering into details of the
future European settlement. In his report in cipher of the 28th May,
1916, Bernstorff informed his Government that " the President is
considering a plan of calling together a conference at the Hague, in
which the neutrals will only participate so far as the ' Freedom of
the Seas ' is concerned. . . . (Wilson) is still of the opinion that *the
United States should under no circumstances take part in the actual
settlement of the peace conditions.*" [55]   And on the 13th July, 1916,
he reported : " As far as I know, Mr. Wilson refuses definitely to
take any part in the discussion of territorial questions, but confines
his interest to ' disarmament ' and ' Freedom of the Seas.' " [56]

In his speech of the 27th May, 1916, Wilson limited himself to
expounding the principles by which the world should abide in the
future (" We believe these fundamental things : first, that every
people has a right to choose the sovereignty under which they should
live . . . second, that the small states of the world have a right to
enjoy the same respect for their sovereignty and for their territorial
integrity that the great and powerful nations expect and insist
upon "), but refrained from making any reference to particular
issues. In the same way, while proclaiming in his Message to Congress, 22nd January, 1917, some general principles and proposing
" government by consent of the governed," Wilson mentioned only
the necessity for " united, independent and autonomous Poland," at
the same time adding that " statesmen everywhere were agreed upon
this matter." He denied acting out of a " desire to exalt an abstract
political principle which has always been held very dear by those
who have sought to build up liberty in America, but for the same
reasons that I have spoken of the other conditions of peace which
seem to me clearly indispensable—because I wish frankly to uncover
realities." [57]

This last sentence should be particularly stressed as it denotes the
very cautious and empiric approach by Wilson to particular territorial issues. Bailey rightly said of Wilson that " he respected facts
. . . he did not want opinions from his specialists, he wanted only
facts. And when he was assured that the position he had taken was
based on facts he would fight for that position " agreeably, if we

can, disagreeably if necessary." [58] This feature of Wilson's character does not, of course, tally with the opinion of him spread by his enemies, according to which he was an abstract thinker and wished to shape the face of the world in accordance with some theoretical premises. For instance, Wilson's approach to the question of the nationalities of Austria-Hungary was extremely guarded (although he said in an interview granted to the *New York Times,* 14th December, 1914, that " Austria ought to go to pieces for the welfare of Europe " [58a]), and for a long time he shared the belief of France and Great Britain that Austria-Hungary might be detached from Germany and rearrange her internal structure according to the principle of autonomy for her nationalities. Point X of the Fourteen Points stated that " The peoples of Austria-Hungary whose place among the nations we wish to see safeguarded and assured, should be accorded the freest opportunity of autonomous development." It was generally understood that this implied " the maintenance of the integrity of Austria-Hungary with large internal autonomy." [59] In his memorandum of 24th June, 1918, for the President, Secretary of State Lansing makes the following confession :

> " In the first place we should be perfectly frank with ourselves and admit that, so long as there was a chance of entering into a separate peace with Austria-Hungary, it was wise and expedient to attempt to do so, though it was contrary to the just claim of the nationalities within that Empire which sought independence." [60]

The same observation can be made in relation to Wilson's policy towards the nationalities of Russia. In his Fourteen Points Wilson spoke about Russia and one Russian people, without taking into account the different nationalities of which the Russian Empire consisted. But in the course of 1918 the disintegration of the Empire of the Tsars was quickly progressing. So the interpretative commentary drafted by House at the end of October 1918 and approved by President Wilson takes due account of these realities :

> " Point VI. The first question is whether Russian territory is synonymous with territory belonging to the former Russian Empire. This is clearly not so, because Proposition XIII stipulates an independent Poland, a proposal which excludes the territorial re-establishment of the Empire. What is recognized as valid for the Poles will certainly have to be recognized for the Finns, the Lithuanians, the Letts, and perhaps also for the Ukrainians. Since the formulation of this condition, these subject nationalities have emerged and there can be no doubt that they will have to be given an opportunity of ... This means nothing less than the recognition by the Peace Conference of a series of *de facto* governments representing Finns, Letts, Lithuanians, Ukrainians." [61]

The conclusion can be drawn from the foregoing that while recognizing the general validity of national self-determination in the system of his political philosophy, Wilson as a statesman was never out of touch with realities, and was continuously adapting his decisions to political developments.

Two members of the American delegation to the Peace Conference, Haskins and Lord, in surveying the problems dealt with by the Conference rightly observed that :

> " ' Self-determination,' President Wilson had said, ' is not a mere phrase, it is an imperative principle of action.' But President Wilson had also said that self-government cannot be given but must be earned ; that ' liberty ' is the privilege of maturity and self-control, that some people may have it, therefore, and others may not.' "

Herein perhaps lies the main difference between Wilson's programme based on the recognition of realities and the demagogic, Bolshevik slogans of national self-determination for all peoples whatever might be the degree of their political development. Wilson's entourage was even more cautious in its approach to these issues than the President, as appears from the following passages of a letter by Mr. Lansing, Secretary of State, dated 2nd January, 1918 (to a great extent inspired by memories of the American War of Secession) :

> " If the Bolsheviks intend to suggest that every community can determine its allegiance to this or that political creed or become independent, the present political organization of the world would be shattered and the same disorder would generally prevail as now exists in Russia. It would be international anarchy.
>
> " Though founded entirely on the assertion of loyalty, the right of a community within a constituted federal union to determine their allegiance was denied by the Government of the United States in 1861 and the denial was enforced by military power. We, as a nation, are therefore committed to the principle that a national State may be forced if necessary to prevent a portion of its territory from seceding without its consent especially if it has long exercised sovereignty over it or if its national safety or vital interests would be endangered." [63]

What was the effect of Wilson's theories on the course of war events? The collapse of Germany was due entirely to military defeat, the decomposition of Russia and the disruption of Austria-. Hungary were due to the rise of social and national consciousness of the vast strata of their population. Nevertheless Wilson's pronouncements appeared at the right moment for the Coalition, when national problems in Central, Southern and Eastern Europe were entering a particularly critical stage, and when each belligerent tried to enlist for his own benefit the long pent-up forces reaching breaking point. Wilson had the great merit of seeing some realities sooner than did the Western allies, or rather being free from any political entanglements and previous engagements, he had the necessary courage to state a line of policy agreeing with the trend of opinion of wide masses. It was not Wilson that awakened some forces, but he more quickly became aware of their importance than did the statesmen of the old school. If there is, consequently, some exaggeration in calling Wilson " Messiah," it must nevertheless be recognized that he brought into practical policy what Western Europe most needed at that time : an unprejudiced mind in approaching the complicated national issues in Europe, the sincere conviction that democracy must not be limited to domestic issues only but introduced also into international relations, a deep religious feeling of justice and humanitarian views. As Joseph P. Tumulty [63a] rightly said : " The magical effect of Woodrow Wilson's utterances on all the Allies was due not to his rhetoric but to his sublime gift of seeing and stating a profound truth after which others had been only groping."

After the Second World War it became fashionable to deride such an approach to international relations, and a prominent British historian asserts that " the liberal missionary to the world is rather *viex jeu*," and from this point of view he condemns " the hazy ' internationalism,' the hangover of nineteenth-century liberalism and League of Nations doctrines " because they had allegedly led to " indiscriminate, irresponsible meddling." [64] The alternative is the delimitation of the spheres of interest of the Great Powers, but the history of the world after the Second World War has not produced evidence that this alternative provides more peace, stability and happiness for mankind.

NOTES

[1] E. MANTOUX, *The Carthaginian Peace*, p. 31: " A French preacher once declared that ever since the partition of Poland, Europe had been living in a state of mortal sin. There is indeed much to be said for the view that traces the starting point of national unrest in modern times to the eighteenth-century partitions by which the Great Powers of Eastern Europe had agreed to defer the solution of the newborn Eastern Question. For by allotting themselves equal portions of what Frederic had sarcastically called ' the Eucharistic body of Poland,' Russia, Austria and Prussia had succeeded, as it were, in transposing in space a problem that would inexorably reassert itself in time."

[2] A. A. W. RAMSAY, *Idealism and Foreign Policy*, p. 349.

[3] *Ibidem*, p. 35.

24   REBIRTH OF THE POLISH REPUBLIC

⁴ LORD BERTIE OF THAME (*Diary*, I, p. 1), then Ambassador in Paris, held a different and much more critical point of view towards Russia at that time: " It seems incredible that the Russian Government should plunge Europe into war in order to make themselves the protector of the Servians. Russia comes forward as the protectress of Servia ; by what title except on the exploded pretension that she is by right, the protectress of all Slavs! What rubbish! "

Ibidem, p. 2: " If, however, the Emperor of Russia adheres to the absurd and obsolete claim that she is protectress of all Slavs, however bad their conduct, war is probable."

⁵ E. HALÉVY, *The World Crisis*, p. 28.

⁶ *Ibidem*, p. 29.

⁷ On 1st March, 1903, GENERAL KUROPATKIN, then Minister of War, noted in his *Diary*: " I told Witte that our Tsar has grandiose plans in his head: to capture Manchuria for Russia and to annnex Korea. He is dreaming also of bringing Tibet under his domination. He desires to take Persia and to seize not only Bosphorus but also the Dardanelles."

⁸ KRASNYI ARKHIV, 1926, XVIII. Copy of the memorandum submitted to His Majesty the Tsar by the Minister of Foreign Affairs, 1900: " Zavetnoye istoricheskoye prizvaniye-utvertidsia na beregakh Bosphora. Neobkhodimost i neizbezhnost' etovo sobytiya nastolko ukrepilis' v soznanii vsekh, chto predstavlaetsia izlishnim dokazyvat' vygody dlya Rosii obladaniya Prolivami."

⁹ Report of General Kuropatkin reproduced in his *Memoirs of the Russo-German War*, I, pp. 54-55 (quoted by ALEXINSKY, La Russie et la Guerre, 288): " La frontière politique entre la Russie et l'Autriche ne coïncide pas avec la frontière naturelle, et, pour des raisons stratégiques, il serait peut-être désirable pour la Russie, de la réculer vers l'Ouest jusqu'aux Months Carpathes, en incorporant toute la Galicie à l'Empire Russe. Mais il faut d'abord chercher si une telle augmentation de territoire nous est nécessaire, si elle nous rendra plus forts ou, au contraire, si elle deviendra pour nous une cause de faiblesse et d'inquiétude." " Pour la population slave de la Galicie l'entrée dans l'Etat Russe serait un recul et non un progrès." . ... " Si nous cédions à la tentation d'avancer notre domination en Galicie jusqu'aux frontières naturelles, nous nous créerions, sans doute, un inépuisable sujet de soucis."

¹⁰ *The Memorandum of Baron Rosen*, Ambassador of Russia in Tokio, published in 1913 and subsequently withdrawn from circulation (quoted by ALEXINSKY, o.c., p. 14): " L'idée slave n'est assise sur aucune base réelle et ne correspond pas aux vrais intérêts russes ... la Russie n'a aucune mission dans l'Orient."

¹¹ ALEXINSKY, o.c., p. 291: " Je ne peux que me rallier à cette opinion du général Kuropatkine: Le peuple russe n'a rien à chercher dans ces pays, rien que la haine des aborigènes qui s'indigneraient de lui être asujettis de force."

¹² MILYUKOV, *Istoriya Vtoroi Russkoi Revolutsii*, p. 21.

¹³ SIR GEORGE BUCHANAN, *My Mission to Russia*, I, p. 182.

[14] A. CHÉRADAME, *L'Allemagne, la France et la Question d'Autriche,* p. 227: " Les Russes commettraient une lourde faute en annexant la Galicie " ; p. 232: " La Russie ne peut pas permettre à l'Empire Allemand de porter atteinte, de quelque façon que ce soit, à l'intégrité d'Autriche. Tout ce qui touche l'Autriche présente également pour la France un intérêt extrême. L'existence de la République, en tant que grande puissance, est, en effet, étroitement subordonnée à l'indépendance de l'Etat des Habsbourgs."

[15] PALÉOLOGUE, *La Russie des Tsars,* I, pp. 198 ff. A conversation with the Tsar, 21st November, 1914 ; a conversation with Sazonov, 1st January, 1915. Opinion of Paléologue: " Dans l'épreuve effroyable qui est infligée à la France, les problèmes tchèque et yougoslave me semblent secondaires," and in a dispatch to Delcassé, Paléologue stresses: " Les indisputables avantages pour la France du maintien d'un grand système politique dans la région danubienne."

[16] PIERRE RENOUVIN, *Les Origines Immédiates de la Guerre,* p. 309 : " L'Etat qui mobilise le premier se donne l'apparence de désirer la guerre " ; p. 314: " En juillet 1914 la provocation militaire a été déterminée par une provocation diplomatique: c'est la déclaration de guerre de l'Autriche qui est le lien de l'une à l'autre. Or, l'Allemagne et l'Autriche seules ont voulu cette provocation."

[17] S. B. FAY, *The Origins of the World War,* pp. 479 and 291-2, concerning initial plans for partial mobilization. G. P. GOOCH, *Before the War,* II, p. 289, states that " this decisive step (Russian mobilization) was taken without consulting France whose counsels of caution were ignored."

[18] ALBERT PINGAUD, *Histoire Diplomatique de la France pendant la Grande Guerre,* I, p. 256: " La France se trouvait unie pendant la Grande Guerre à l'Empire Russe par une alliance dont une pratique de plus de vingt années avait fait la base de toute sa politique extèrieure et étendu, peut-être, la portée au delà des intentions primitive de ses auteurs. Elle avait été mise en pratique pendant la paix, la guerre allait fournir l'occasion de la mettre à l'épreuve. Justifierait-elle les espérances parfois démesurées qu'elle avait éveillées en France, dans les sphéres officielles comme dans les milieux populaires? On le désirait d'autant plus ardemment qu'*au début elle y avait été considérée comme une garantie de paix et une sécurité contre l'Allemagne, et qu'on la voyait aboutir à une guerre engagée au nom des intérêts du Slavisme en Orient.*"

B. H. SUMNER, *Survey of Russian History,* p. 434 : " Since the Balkans, not Franco-German or Anglo-German relations, were the immediate origin of War, Russia in the last resort was the deciding partner in the alliance. The issue in July 1914, extremely complicated in detail, was not in doubt once Russia decided that her vital interests compelled her to fight."

[18a] FAY, o.c., II, p. 552.

[18b] GOOCH, o.c., II, p. 369.

[18c] B. E. SCHMITT, *The Coming of the War,* I, p. 481.

[19] GOOCH, o.c., II, p. 369: " Russia's responsibility for the catastrophe

was greater than Sazonov was prepared to admit, for her championship of Pan-Serbian ambitions was Austria's chief anxiety. Yet the ultimate cause of conflagration was the rivalry of two proud empires, which was older than the Austro-Serb feud."

E.VOLKMANN, *Der Grosse Krieg*, p. 13 : " Der Grosse Krieg ist entstanden aus dem ewigen Ringen der Völker um Macht und Weltgeltung.'

[20] LLOYD GEORGE, *War Memoirs*, VI, p. 3232.

[21] A. PINGAUD, o.c., I, pp. 40-1.

[21a] LLOYD GEORGE, o.c., V, p. 2551.

[22] MILYUKOV, o.c., I, p. 139.

[23] *Austria's Peace Offer* (MANTEYR), pp. 159-69.

[24] P. RENOUVIN, o.c., p. 452 : " Dans sa note du 10 janvier l'Entente s'est prononcée en faveur des nationalités d'Autriche-Hongrie ; dans l'hypothèse d'une paix séparée, elle abandonnerait ces minorités nationales ; c'était un changement de front possible mais pénible. Il était plus difficile d'oublier les promesses faites à l'Italie et à la Roumanie lors de l'entrée en guerre."

[25] H. J. MACKINDER, *Democratic Ideals and Reality*, p. 199.

[26] MERMEIX, *Les Négociations Secrètes et les Quatre Armistices*, p. 153. Lettre de M. Briand à M. Ribot, Ministre des Affaires Etrangères, 20 sep., 1917 : " Au point de vue français la seule base admissible est la restitution d'Alsace-Lorraine."

APPUHN, *La Politique Allemande pendant la Guerre*, p. 79 : " Après avoir accepté et même sollicité l'intervention du Pape, le Gouvernement Imperial avait tout fait pour qu'elle demeurât sans résultat. Que serait-il arrivé, si, au Conseil de Bellevue, s'était trouvé un homme de décision, si l'Empereur, si le Kronprinz, si le Chancelier Michaelis, ou seulement le Ministre Kühlmann avaient eu, avec un sentiment plus juste de la situation, le courage de parler net et s'ils avaient réussi à triompher de la résistance opposée par le Haut Commandement ? "

[27] *Documents and Statements Relating to Peace Proposals and War-Aims*, p. 84.

[28] LORD BERTIE OF THAME, II, p. 269.

[29] K. F. NOWAK, *The Collapse of Central Europe*, pp. 328-9.

[30] LLOYD GEORGE, o.c., VI, p. 3308.

[31] NOWAK, o.c., pp. 159 ff.

[32] A. VALLENTIN, *Stresemann*, pp. 33 ff.

[33] LORD BERTIE OF THAME, I, p. 161.

[34] HENRY WICKHAM STEED, *Through Thirty Years*, II, p. 63.

Also C. A. MACARTNEY, *National States and National Minorities*, p. 182 : " Both sides concluded treaties by which they bought the help of new allies, and in each case the price was a concession to national ambitions and thus envisaged a partial adaptation of political to ethnographic frontiers. Yet the purchasers did not scruple to violate ethnographical claims where the seller demanded it. The Treaty of London, by which the Allies brought Italy into the war, promised her the Brenner frontier (which involved presenting her with 250,000 Germans) and ample Yugoslav, Greek and Albanian territory. The Treaty with

Rumania envisaged assigning to her thousands of non-Rumanians. As for the secret treaties between the Allies regarding Turkey, Russia was to have received Constantinople, Eastern Thrace, the Asiatic Bosphorus, Gallipoli, and some of the islands, while the Allies promised themselves, and one another, large concessions in Anatolia."

A. RIBOT, *Journal et Correspondances inédites*, p. 58: In connection with the agreement on the partition of Turkey, Ribot stated the following: "Il faut bien reconnaître que nous sommes loin des préoccupations qu'on avait à l'origine de la guerre. Ce n'est plus à défendre les petites nations qu'on s'applique mais à faire un véritable partage, sans que l'intérêt des populations soit mis en avant."

[35] *Documents and Statements Relating to Peace Proposals and War-Aims*, Introduction by DICKINSON, "The treaties are concerned with partitions of territory calculated to increase the power, the wealth and the strategic security of the Allied Nations while correspondingly weakening the enemy powers, and with this purpose in view they do not hesitate, in many important particulars, to infringe that principle of nationality, which had been advertised from the beginning as a principal war aim of the Entente."

[36] MACARTNEY, o.c., p. 185. See also *Encyclopædia Britannica*, 1945, 14th Edition, under Self-Determination: "As war slogan it was chiefly used by Allied propagandists."

[37] *Austria's Peace Offer* (MANTEYR), p. 23.

[38] *Ibidem*, p. 59.

[39] In his statement on British War Aims, 5th January, 1918, Lloyd George denied that the Western Powers were fighting to destroy Austria-Hungary. See also General Smuts's account of his conversation with Count Mensdorff in Switzerland, 18-19th December, 1917. LLOYD GEORGE, *War Memoirs*, V, pp. 2463 ff. MASARYK, *The Making of a State*, p. 244: "In America, as elsewhere, it was hard to convince people that it would be necessary to break up Austria-Hungary. Unlike Berlin, Vienna was not an object of immediate political enmity ... Austria was generally looked upon as a counterpoise to Germany, as a necessary organization of small peoples and odds and ends of peoples and as a safeguard against ' Balkanization '."

[39a] LLOYD GEORGE, *War Memoirs*, pp. 3307-8.

[40] TOYNBEE, *Survey of International Affairs*, 1926, p. 18.

[41] SIR J. A. R. MARIOTT, *Federalism and the Problems of Small States*, p. 9.

[42] E. A. FREEMAN, *History of Federal Government*, 1863. For the defence of small States, see H. A. L. FISCHER, *The Value of Small States*, Oxford Pamphlets, 1914.

[43] JOSEPH HANČ, *Eastern Europe*, p. 21.

[44] MASARYK, o.c., p. 370.

[45] A. A. RAMSAY, o.c., p. 399.

[46] E. MANTOUX, o.c., p. 35.

[46a] G. CLEMENCEAU, *Grandeur and Misery of Victory*, pp. 179-81.

⁴⁷ H. N. FIELDHOUSE, *Fortnightly*, June 1940, pp. 580-1, quoted by CARR, *Conditions of Peace*, p. 5.

⁴⁷ᵃ H. NOTTER, *The Origins of the Foreign Policy of Woodrow Wilson*, p. 652 ff.

⁴⁸ ARTHUR S. LINK, *Woodrow Wilson and the Progressive Era*, p. 81

⁴⁹ *Ibidem*, p. 93.

⁴⁹ᵃ JOSEPH P. TUMULTY, *Woodrow Wilson as I Know Him*, p. 236: "On May 10th he made a speech in Philadelphia which contained the regrettable and much criticized phrase, 'Too proud to fight.' ... The phrase 'Too proud to fight' was simply expressive of the idea that was close to his heart: a reliance upon means of settling our difficulties with Germany other than a resort to war."

⁵⁰ COUNT BERNSTORFF, *My Three Years in America*, pp. 253-4.

⁵¹ JOSEPHUS DANIELS, *The Wilson Era*, (*Years of War and After*), pp. 17-18.

⁵² JOHN M. BLUM, *Joe Tumulty and Wilson Era*, pp. 130 ff.

⁵³ T. BAILEY, *Woodrow Wilson and the Lost Peace*, pp. 15-16.

⁵⁴ HOUSE, *The Intimate Papers*, II, p. 170 and *Ibidem*,, p. 135: "He (House) was willing to give Germany a chance to accept such terms, for he feared that, if the war went on to a complete smash of Germany, the entire world, victors and vanquished, would go down in economic ruin. Furthermore, he was not convinced that it would be easy to secure a just and permanent peace through the 'knock-out blow,' for he appreciated the extent to which the ideals of the Allies were in danger of taint by selfish aspirations."

⁵ BERNSTORFF, o.c., p. 234.

⁵⁶ *Ibidem*, p. 239.

⁵⁷ H. H. FISHER, *America and the New Poland*, p. 94. "There are several reasons why the President made this specific reference. Poland was a particularly flagrant violation of the right of self-determination, which recent relief negotiations had brought before the world. Finally, both Entente and the Central Powers had given lip-service to the rights of Polish nationality and so perhaps were as near agreement on this issue as any."

⁵⁸ BAILEY, o.c., p. 110.

⁵⁸ᵃ H. NOTTER, o.c., p. 446.

⁵⁹ H. W. TEMPERLEY, *A History of the Peace Conference of Paris*, vol. I, p. 134.

⁶⁰ R. S. BAKER, *Woodrow Wilson, Life and Letters, Armistice*, p. 275: Letter of President Wilson to Senator G. M. Hitchcock, (11th July, 1918) who contemplated submitting a bill for recognizing the independence of Poland: "The Poles may be said to represent a definable territory, but the Czecho-Slovaks and the Yugoslavs do not. It is likely that if they followed their own preference, they would unite in a single state. I should not like in the present circumstances of unrest in the Austrian Empire to throw cold water upon the Bohemians and the Slavs to the south of them, and I fear separate action to Poland would have this effect."

[61] HOUSE, *Intimate Papers,* IV, p. 202.

[62] C. H. HASKINS and R. H. LORD, *Some Problems of the Peace Conference,* p. 14.

[63] *P. R. F. R.* Lansing Papers, II, p. 347.

[63a] TUMULTY, o.c., p. 277.

[64] L. B. NAMIER, *Facing East,* London, 1947, p. 96.

FIRST PHASE OF THE WAR: THE WESTERN POWERS AND PLANS FOR THE "RUSSIAN" SOLUTION OF POLAND'S FUTURE

It is beyond the scope of this book to state all the facts having a bearing on the Polish problem in the course of the First World War. In particular, the policy of the partitioning powers, Russia and the Central Powers, is only broadly outlined so far as was necessary for a better understanding of the policy of the Western Powers towards Poland. For the sake of simplicity we divide our survey into three chapers, although they refer to partly overlapping periods.[1]

10th January, 1917.

" The Allied nations are conscious that they are fighting not for selfish interests but, above all, to safeguard the independence of peoples, right and humanity. .... The intentions of His Majesty the Emperor of Russia in regard to Poland have been clearly indicated by the manifesto he has just addressed to his armies."—(The Allies' Reply to President Wilson's Note of 18th December, 1916).

The Polish Question prior to the War

ON the eve of the 1914 war Western opinion was not prepared for the raising of the Polish issue by any belligerent. A British writer, Phillips W. Alison, who in 1915 published one of the first books on the Polish problem [2] after a long silence on this subject for nearly half a century, observed that while " In Russia, in Germany, in Austria, the Polish problem has remained a living issue "—" in the English-speaking world ... public interest in the Polish question seems to have died away all but completely after the faiiure of the insurrection of 1863."

So far as France was concerned, B. H. Sumner, in his *Survey of Russian History* presents the position in almost identical terms :

" Gradually the Polish question ceased to be the stumbling-block it had been in the past. Poland retained the sympathy of France, especially of the left, but feelings became toned down. Bitter experience has shown how difficult it was to help the Poles in practice even when France was strong and Russia relatively weak and Prussia had not become Germany. Fortunately for the Third Republic, between 1870 and 1914 there was no revolt in Poland and no international raising of the Polish question." [3]

Memories of the failure of the Western Powers in assisting Poland during the insurrection in 1863 were connected with that of a great diplomatic defeat. It was observed that in 1863 " England followed with regard to Poland a characteristic course of practical compromise. Unable or unwilling to enforce her interpretation of the Treaty of Vienna, she was obliged to swallow Russia's confident and humiliating refusal." [4] Older British statesmen still remembered the warning given by Robert, Marquess of Salisbury, in his *Essays* published in the *Quarterly Review* in 1862 and 1863 :

> " It is base to abandon the weak in the moment of their utmost need, and in the presence of a gigantic assailant. But there is a deeper baseness far in the wordy friendship which, implying the promise of aid, without formally pledging it, beguiles the weaker combatant into a fatal trust in his ally, and then deserts him." [5]

Speaking especially about the policy followed on the Polish question in 1863, the Marquess of Salisbury, whose attitude towards all national movements was unsympathetic,[6] and whose opinion of Poland was obviously biased and inspired by German writers, nevertheless condemned in these words the attitude of Lord Russell :

> " Something in point of argument and much in point of sentiment might have been urged in favour of assuming the championship of the cause of Poland. But it was a path in which, when it was once entered, retreat or even hesitation was dishonest."

Influence of German and Russian Historiography on the opinions on Poland in the West

For half a century, after the ruthless suppression of the last Polish insurrection, the Polish problem seemed to the West to become a purely domestic issue of each partitioning power. During that period not only had the official policy of the Western Powers taken only occasional interest in Polish problems but also public opinion in those countries had shown complete indifference to them. The old sympathies for the Polish cause, so much alive in the first half of the ninteenth century, especially among liberals and radicals, were slowly dying except in some socialist quarters. At the same time German and Russian historiographers and political writers were completely distorting opinions on Poland's past. It was so soothing to accept assertions coming from Germany and Russia that the misfortunes of Poland were due exclusively to her own faults and the mismanagement of her affairs by " the Polish aristocracy."

> " A people " [says a British writer] " who show themselves incapable of self-government or unable to develop their national advantages, must inevitably fall the prey of more enterprising and resolute States. To love its liberty and fight for it bravely is not

enough proof that a nation is worthy of independence. If that independence produces only civil strife and internal misgovernment, as in Poland in the eighteenth century ; or the permanent destruction of the natural resources of the country, as in North-West Africa under Mohammedan rule ; or the prevention of the entrance of civilizing influence and the growth of prosperity, as in the Turkish Empire ; it is better for all concerned that the territory in question should be taken by a competent, even if alien government." [8]

This theory seems completely to overlook the historical facts and geo-political realities. As a matter of fact neither Italian unity nor the resurgence of Greece could be achieved without outside assistance. The same can be said about the rise of the Balkan States in more recent times. Moreover, even if we accept the fact that in some historical periods a country may pass through a temporary eclipse (and especially neglect her armaments, a case occurring often even in the history of the Great Powers), a special political and geographical conjuncture is necessary in order that such a country being isolated from its natural allies, might in spite of its most heroic resistance fall a prey to a mighty coalition of its neighbours. But there was a still bigger flaw in this theory: it rested on false historical premises.

On this particular issue let us refer to the statement made by an eminent American historian whose monumental work was based not only on German and Russian sources, as was the case with nearly all the historical books which had appeared in Anglo-Saxon countries before it, but also on Polish ones. Professor Robert Howard Lord summed up in this way his historical researches on the Second Partion of Poland :

" It was the favourite thesis of German and Russian writers that the Poles themselves were primarily responsible for their own downfall." [9] . . . " Poland fell, not at the moment of her deepest degradation, but just when she was beginning to put forth new life to show her greatest patriotism and energy. The work of the Four Years' Diet, the lofty character of its leaders, the generous enthusiasm and high hopes of the period, the Constitution of the Third of May, the effort of the Polish Army in 1792, and the new struggle for liberty under Kosciuszko in 1794—these things brought at least this inestimable advantage that they furnished the nation with a treasure of spiritual goods upon which it could live and maintain its faith in itself and its future after the loss of its independence. From these tragic but ennobling experiences later generations could convince themselves and the unprejudiced outside world that this nation had not deserved to perish." [10]

The fact that for a very long period the views held in Western Europe about the past and present of Central and Eastern Europe were subjected to the very strong, one can even say almost exclusive, influence of German and Russian historiography should be kept constantly in mind by those who wish to reach a proper understanding of the issues having a bearing on this region of our continent. It suffices to look at the bibliography and historical sources used for historical and political studies published in the Anglo-Saxon countries to be convinced of it.[11]

William E. Dodd, an outstanding American scholar who later became Ambassador to Germany, makes pertinent remarks on this subject in his book, *Woodrow Wilson and His Work*, (p. 152).

" For many years American students had been accustomed to study in German universities where indeed the best authorities in the world were to be found. Very many of them returned to their own country unable to distinguish between the good and the bad in German civilization and when the Great War began they promptly took the side of autocracy. Naturally the close connection between American and German universities led to the ready acceptance of the German world propaganda in the elaborate system of exchange professorship that prevailed several years before 1914. The German Ambassador Johann von Bernstorff was justified in the feeling that his country was very close to the academic world when within five years after his appointment to Washington he received the doctorate of laws from ten leading American universities."

This position was realized in France much earlier, as can be seen if we refer, for instance, to the opinion expressed by an eminent French historian, Fustel de Coulanges,[12] who after the Franco-Prussian War of 1870 was shocked by the truly military discipline shown by Germans in all walks of life, which found expression, apart from other ways, in systematic attempts at distorting the whole history of France in order to keep alive feelings of hatred towards that country. If French writers were justified in complaining of these unfair and abusive practices, how much more difficult was the position of the Poles, for more than a century deprived of their own statehood and having only limited opportunities of presenting their case before the world forum. An outstanding Polish historian, Professor O. Halecki, deals with this problem in a well-documented study entitled " Problems of Polish Historiography."[13] He states that

" Previously a strong prejudice existed against Polish historiography and against the cultivation of Polish history. Even in the best books on the writing of history, including those published in the

Anglo-Saxon countries, only a few lines were given to Polish historians, stigmatizing them as 'nationalistic' because they devoted themselves exclusively to the history of their own nation—a nation which was supposed to be of a very limited importance and interest. ... The main reason for this prejudice, which had led even to the neglect of source materials, is to be discovered in the political situation of the nineteenth century and in the leading part which German historiography played at that time in the development of historical science. This development was dominated and directed by a great nation which not only had no sympathy with Poland, but had recently benefited from her partitions."

The position was exactly the same in relation to the influence exercised on Western minds by Russian historiography, about which Halecki says that " There was complete agreement between the leading Russian scholars and the second trend of German historiography, particularly the so-called Prussian school, which instead of merely neglecting Poland treated her with marked hostility."

Impact of the Alliance with Russia on the Policy of the Western Powers

With the gradual crystallization of two adverse political blocks in the period preceding the outbreak of the First World War all issues were, of course, overshadowed by the struggle for power, and once Armageddon had started it was victory which mattered above all other considerations. For the Western Allies it was the maintenance of the common front with Russia against the Central Powers that remained for more than two years of the war the main preoccupation. It is common knowledge that Russia's faithfulness to the West was by no means a foregone conclusion. The Germans had many assets in Russia: influence within the Imperial Court, the sympathy of the high bureaucracy, many representatives of which were of German descent, the aversion of the reactionaries for democratic France and liberal England. It is also common knowledge that for Russia Austria-Hungary was the main enemy, not Germany, contrary to the position taken by the Western Powers. Sazonov's famous " Lâcher l'Autriche et nous lâcherons la France " was not a casual remark but expressed the inmost feelings of the Russian diplomacy.[14]

We wish to recall here in a few words the numerous sacrifices the West had to make in order to keep alive Russian friendship and to maintain the alliance with the Empire of the Tsars :

   (a) To preserve the alliance with Russia before the war France had to subscribe unconditionally to Russian claims in the Balkans, which in the last instance was one of the decisive factors in bringing about armed conflict.[15]

(b) France and Great Britain had to bear the brunt of the first German offensive. Russian strategic plans were well known to the Germans [16] and so in August 1914 seventy German divisions were launched against France while only nine German divisions were available in the East. It is true that the invasion of East Prussia by Rennenkampf and Samsonov is considered by some probably to have saved the Battle of the Marne (the Germans also withdrew some divisions to take Antwerp), but it is also true that the bulk of the Russian army was at that time engaged against the Austrian army. It was only after the retreat of the Austro-Hungarians that the Russian Commander-in-Chief launched the second offensive (or was it rather a counter-offensive?) in the direction of Silesia, which ended about mid-December 1914 after bloody battles near Lodz and Warsaw. But the third Russian offensive was again launched against Austria-Hungary for the purpose of capturing the Carpathian passes and invading the Danubian plain.[17]

(c) The Allies had to accept Russia's claims to Constantinople and some Asiatic territories of Turkey, contrary to their traditional policy of maintaining the integrity of Turkey and not delivering the keys to the Mediterranean to Russia.

(d) The Allies were obliged to agree to Russian methods in negotiations with the Balkan powers, especially with Rumania, thus delaying the entry of the latter into the war and compromising the chances of defending Serbia.[18]

(e) So long as Russia remained on the Entente side any possibility of a separate peace with Austria-Hungary was debarred, and the military and political isolation of Germany was made impossible.[19]

Rumours, ever more insistent after 1915, about negotiations aiming at a separate peace between Germany and Russia secured for Russia an excellent bargaining position which eventually led France, on the eve of the Revolution, to accept the Russian demand for absolute freedom in establishing the future frontier with Germany (February-March 1917), thus giving Tsarist Russia a free hand in dealing with Poland and other countries of Central and Eastern Europe.

It was really a very strange and uneasy relationship, by the way, not very different from that which occurred later, in the course of the Second World War. Whichever might have been the situation of Russia, whether strong, or rather supposed to be strong, or weak, in either case the Western Allies were obliged, or felt obliged, to keep in with Russia. Watching all these moves one cannot help thinking that the Western Powers behaved towards Russia as if they did not possess any bargaining assets or were unwilling to use them.

All these factors explain to some extent the attitude of the Western Powers towards the Polish question in the first stage of the war. Until the outbreak of the Revolution in Russia in 1917 the Western Powers had followed events, but they had not exercised any influence on Russian policy in relation to the Polish cause, in spite of the fact that their passivity could entail far-reaching consequences for the outcome of war in Eastern Europe and therefore for the outcome of the war in general.

On the other side it is very interesting to observe during this period the most persistent efforts of the Russians to keep the Polish problem as a Russian domestic problem—these efforts were bound to fail because of the disruption of the common policy of the former partitioning powers on the Polish question and the natural moves of the Central Powers to enlist Polish support against Russia in order to increase their chances of winning the war. So that if the Polish question became an international issue at the end of this period it was exclusively due to the conditions prevailing in Eastern Europe and not to any deliberate moves of policy of the Entente Powers. The importance of the Polish question grew as the political order established at the Congress of Vienna of 1815 became obsolete.

Proclamation of the Grand Duke Nicholas to the Poles

The first and quite unexpected step taken by Russia at the beginning of the war was the proclamation of the Commander-in-Chief, Grand Duke Nicholas, to the Poles, dated 16th, August, 1914. It was addressed to all Poles, whatever their State allegiance, and was an appeal launched across the frontiers established by the treaties of partition.[20]

It is a debatable matter whether this manifesto announced a real change of heart by the Russians towards the Poles or whether it was conceived at the beginning as a purely tactical move. One should keep in mind that for many months no positive steps were taken by Russia to fulfil the promises foreshadowed by the manifesto.[21] The latter, moreover, was not an act of the Sovereign, as was the Manifesto of the Tsar to the Armenians on the 17th September, 1914,[22] and the Tsar himself later confessed that it was a precipitate step.[23] Moreover at the beginning of the war Russia was prepared to evacuate the Congress Kingdom, and consequently was more anxious that the Poles might not be won by some promises of the Central Powers, especially of much-hated Austria, or organize another rising at the Russian rear according to the secular tradition of the Polish nation, than to enlist the actual support of the Poles. Thus the initial aim of the Manifesto was to forestall any initiative of the Central Powers and check moves for independence.

But the real importance of the Manifesto appears more clearly if we consider it from the point of view of Russia's relations with the Western Allies. It was a clever piece of propaganda cloaking the true Russian war aims with high-sounding words which nevertheless found an immediate response in the public opinion of the Entente countries. What was still more important was that the Manifesto was interpreted as an irrevocable decision of Tsarist Russia to carry on the war unrelentingly not only against Austria-Hungary but also against Germany. This impression appears clearly in the editorial of *The Times* of the 17th August, 1914 :

> " We should deem it rash in the highest degree to predict the consequences of this far-reaching stroke. But of one result we feel sure. The Tsar's offer, if it is effective, makes the quarrel between Russia and the two Central dynasties and nations inexpiable. It is the most signal proof which Russia could give that she means her war with her great neighbours to be war to the knife."

At the same time *The Times* expressed some doubts whether the Poles would " entirely trust the offers made them."

We find the same reaction in the French press. Among numerous voices, and no doubt can arise that there had been very substantial encouragement from the Russian Embassy in Paris to make the utterances as clamorous as possible, we note especially that of the well-known writer and member of the French Academy, Emile Faguet, in the *Annales Politiques et Littéraires* of the 30th August, 1914 :

> " By his appeal to the Poles, the Emperor(?) of Russia denounces the pact (of the three co-partitioning powers) and by this fact he *for ever* puts Russia in a state of hostility towards Prussia and Austria. *For ever* Russia will be the power which has raised Poland against two Germanic Powers. *For ever,* consequently, will Russia remain a hostile power in relation to Prussia and Austria. Inversely and consequently *for ever* Russia will be inevitably the ally of France." [24]

We can see from all these articles that the intentions of Russia towards Poland were considered in the West from the very beginning of the war almost exclusively as a test of Russian reliability as a member of the anti-German coalition. As it was the weakening of Germany and not of Austria-Hungary that was the true aim of the Western Powers, it would be very important for the latter to ascertain whether Russian plans concerning Poland were serious, and not merely tactical moves. But they never made any proposal to make a Joint Allied Declaration on Poland, which might be much more binding on Russia than a unilateral declaration, issued, by the way, by the Supreme Military Commander and not by the Sovereign.

Let us observe first of all that the Proclamation of the Grand Duke took the Allies completely by surprise.[25] Among other evidence on the matter we can quote the testimony of General Yanushkevich, former Chief of the General Staff, before the Extraordinary Investigating Committee on 3rd (22nd) September, 1917 :

> " To the question whether the Allies had anything to do with the issuing of the proclamation, I state that the question of the participation of our allies in this or other form had never been mentioned either before or after the publication, between myself and the Grand Duke or any of our Ministers or military representatives of the Allied powers." [26]

The French Ambassador, Paléologue, confesses in his memoirs that he was informed of the impending action shortly before publication, and the British Ambassador, Sir G. W. Buchanan, seemed completely to ignore the Polish problem and did not refer to it in his memoirs, except casually.

Russian War Aims and the Problem of Poland

There is no doubt that Russia had far-reaching plans to remake South-Eastern Europe in order to transform this region into her zone of influence, but it is also unquestionable that the question of the reunion of the Polish territories was to her a secondary issue. The Manifesto to the Poles was better known in the West than other proclamations made by the Russian generalissimo, such as the proclamation to the peoples of Austria-Hungary, and especially to the Ruthenians of Galicia of the 18th August, 1914, in which it was announced that that province allegedly populated by genuinely Russian population would be incorporated into Russia proper. The first steps of the Russian administration after the occupation of the city of Lwow,[27] and the ruthless measures of the Russian military and bureaucracy provoked great indignation not only in the West but also among Russian liberals.[82] If we compare different Russian moves we can observe that they served to screen the true purposes of Russia, which were : dismemberment of Austria-Hungary and of Turkey.

The Russian war aims were disclosed to the Allies for the first time in a conversation between Mr. Sazonov and the French and British Ambassadors on the 13th September, 1914.[29] Mr. Sazonov then declared that the war should put an end to German hegemony and that the future peace settlement should be based on the principle of nationality. In the first place he mentioned the necessity for annexation by Russia of Eastern Galicia and the lower course of the Niemen (East Prussia). He also mentioned that Poznan, Southern Silesia and Western Galicia should be given to Poland, restored within the framework of the Russian Empire. But he stressed above all the necessity for dismemberment of Austria, which would lose her Slav and Rumanian territories apart from Bohemia, to which autonomy should be granted. The new Hapsburg Monarchy should consist of three parts : Austria, Hungary and Bohemia.

In a conversation on the 1st December, 1914, between the French Ambassador and the Tsar,[30] the latter was much less explicit about Poland. He said that the Russian General Staff advised a " rectification " of the Russian frontier as far as the mouths of the Vistula (the whole of East Prussia). It is true that so far as Poland was concerned the Tsar mentioned Poznan and perhaps Silesia, but he was much more emphatic about the necessity for annexing Galicia and the northern part of Bukovina, which would allow Russia to attain her " natural frontier "—the Carpathians. He was even harsher than his Foreign Minister about Austria, saying that she should be reduced to the old hereditary possessions of the Hapsburgs, German Tyrol and Salzburg.

What was the order of importance of these Russian war aims? [31] A most revealing document from this point of view is the memorandum of three members of the Russian Government who opposed rather moderate schemes for home rule for Poland put forward by Mr. Sazonov. These Ministers, Maklakov (Interior), Shcheglovitov (Justice), and Kasso (Public Education), laid before the Council of Ministers on the 28th November, 1914, a memorandum which presented much more truly the Russian views on the post-war settlement than did the plan adopted by the Council of Ministers and subsequently pigeon-holed. The dissenting Ministers stated, amongst other things, the following [32] :

> " Should the present war, which owing to the extraordinary efforts of the nation is of unparalleled international importance, be ended only by the unification of Poland, although under the sceptre of the Russian Sovereigns, but not materialize our other historical tasks, having much more direct bearing on the life of the Russian nation, such outcome recalling the deplorable result of the Congress of Berlin might arouse deep discontent and acute disappointment among the masses of the Russian people. ...
>
> " So far as the order of importance for Russia of the general State aims is concerned, the following should be kept in mind: (1) So far as possible, the strengthening of the genuine (korrenoi) Russia ; (2) so far as possible, the liberation of other Slav nations from the domination of Germany and Austria-Hungary."

Stressing this point of view the dissenting Ministers advised aiming for the following targets : (1) Incorporation of Eastern Galicia, Northern Bukovina and Carpathian Ruthenia; (2) annexation of Constantinople and the Straits; (3) correction of the frontier in East Prussia and Asiatic Turkey; (4) redistribution of Prussian territories for the benefit of France, Belgium, Mecklenburg, Denmark, and perhaps the restoration of the Kingdom of Hanover; (5) unification and liberation of Poland in the widest possible frontiers, but in any case ethnographic and not historic ones (as it would be contrary to the vital interests and the whole history of Russia); (6) liberation of Austrian Slavs.

To one conversant with the history of Polish-Russian relations there was nothing new in this opposition of the Russian nationalists to the plans giving prominence to the Polish problem in the Russian policy. We should remember the opposition of the Russian ruling class to the Polish plans of Emperor Alexander,[33] and the subsequent reaction of Russian nationalism against the maintenance of the autonomy of the Congress-Poland which provoked the 1830 rising:[34] The fear that the future Poland might become a centre of attraction for the western provinces of Russia seized by the latter in the course of the Partitions explained to a great extent this opposition to any extension of the Polish territories within the orbit of the Russian Empire.

The former leader of the Polish Parliamentary Group in Duma and one of the most prominent representatives of the pro-Entente wing of Polish opinion, Roman Dmowski, in his book, *Polityka Polska i Odbudowanie Panstwa* (Polish Policy and the Rebuilding of the State), p. 231, gives an account of a conversation which took place soon after the retreat of the Russian troops from Poland (1915), between Prince Shcherbatov, then Minister of the Interior, and some Polish political leaders; in this conversation the Minister declared :

" The Polish-Russian problem in Congress-Poland is not a problem. We could easily reach an understanding. The Polish-Russian problem proper, of enormous importance for us, is the problem of the Northern and South-Western lands (former Polish-Lithuanian provinces annexed by Russia by the Partitions of Poland) Herein lies a difficulty of an understanding."

This question was also raised during the debates of the " Council for Preparatory Discussion On the Way in Which Might Be Put Into Practice the Proclamation of the Grand Duke." At the meeting of the Committee with this queer name, of 8th July, 1915, Prince Mirsky drew the attention of those present to this problem :

" In connection with the Polish question in ethnographic Poland also the Polish question in Western Russia should be settled. The Poles should not only forgo their historic claims to Western Russia but also the national and cultural ones. ... The Poles of Western Russia should become faithful and sincere supporters of Russian social feelings and of the Russian economy in these lands."

Different Stages in the Russian Policy towards the Polish Problem until the fall of Tsardom

The extreme caution of the Western allies in relation to the Polish question and some moves of the pro-Entente wing of Polish opinion led by Roman Dmowski can be explained by the fear that the Russians and Germans might resume their old friendship through a new agreement on the Polish question. It was certainly true that a separate peace between Russia and the Central Powers would have rendered impossible the reopening of the Polish question as an international issue. But did the Polish question really stand in the way of Russo-German reconciliation? The answer is absolutely negative. The Polish issue was not the real stumbling-block in Russo-German relations: both parties were forced to outbid each other in Polish affairs because of the impossibility of agreeing on other issues. This new situation was not realized by Western statesmen who relied too much on the experiences of the nineteenth century, during which the Polish problem served to cement the three co-partitioning powers.

We have seen above that Russia had not considered the unification of Poland as her primary war aim and, on the contrary, had been rather reluctant to make attractive to the Poles the prospects of the restoration of Poland on the lines of self-government within the framework of the Russian Empire.

Moreover the military setbacks of Russia in 1915 and 1916 revealed the great inferiority of the Russian armies in comparison with the German, and made it unlikely that Russia could attain her ends single-handed. In his memoirs Sir George Buchanan gives the following account of a conversation with the Tsar which took place in November 1916. First of all I must draw attention to the first of the quoted sentences, as it shows that the British Ambassador from the beginning had had great doubts as to the genuineness of the Russian plans regarding Poland. The following passages of this account prove that at that time Russia had completely lost faith in a decisive victory over Germany and consequently Russian offers to the Poles at that time could not be considered sincere :

" On my asking whether he had ever considered the question of the rectification of Russia's frontier on the side of Germany, His

Majesty replied that he was afraid that he would have to be content with his present frontier, bad as it was. The Germans would have to be driven out of Poland, but a Russian advance into Germany would entail too heavy sacrifices. His idea had always been to create a united Poland under Russia's protection as a buffer state between Germany and Russia, but he saw no prospects at present of including Posen in it." [35]

It is in the light of this frank confession that we should judge all the moves of Russia's policy concerning Poland after the heavy defeats of her armies in early summer 1915. After that time these moves simply pursued the aim of counteracting the moves of the Central Powers and were dictated by the fear which was felt to an even greater extent in the West, in particular in France, that the huge reserves of men in the parts of Poland occupied by Austria-Hungary and Germany might be used on the Eastern Front and a Polish State, closely bound to these two powers, be established. The trend of events in occupied Poland induced Russia to make some further promises to the Poles, apparently going very far at the end of the Tsarist régime, and thus to some extent preparing what was to be one of the first steps of the Provisional Government after the outbreak of the revolution—the recognition of Poland's independence. But, on the other side, the Tsarist Government tried until its inglorious end to exclude the Polish problem from inter-allied conversations and to impose the view that it was a purely domestic Russian issue. Russia did not wish her hands to be tied and was anxious to retain complete freedom of action, undoubtedly also reserving her position in any further dealings with the Central Powers. The same men who opposed any concession to Poland in their inmost hearts desired a reconciliation with Germany.

In accordance with the scope of this book, in giving below the outlines of the Tsarist policy towards Poland I shall confine myself to those issues which may be interesting from the point of view of international policy. Such issues are, above all: the future status of Poland according to Russian views, that is to say the nature of the future relations between Poland and Russia on the one side and between Poland and the rest of the world on the other. In 1914, immediately after the Manifesto of the Grand Duke, so welcomed in the West, the Russians were not disposed to go very far. Very naturally it was Foreign Minister Sazonov who, wishing to forestall any foreign interference with the Polish question, raised the Polish issues within the Russian Cabinet. In his " Reflections " submitted to the Cabinet—October-November 1914—and approved by its majority, he stated that the limits of self-government of Poland should be defined by the Imperial legislation. Foreign relations, including those with the Holy See, and problems of defence should be excluded from the competence of the future Polish authorities. This local self-government should be extended to the Congress Kingdom, Western Galicia and those Polish territories which might be detached from Germany in the event of victory. This draft was eventually pigeon-holed and no immediate measures were taken. After the evacuation of the Congress Kingdom the former Russian bureaucrats kept their posts, and even new appointments *in partibus infidelium* were made.

The second step taken by Mr. Sazonov can be better understood in the light of the exchange of correspondence with Mr. Isvolsky, who complained to Sazonov of the agitation of some radical elements in France and the Polish agents who tried to raise the Polish issue in inter-allied diplomatic exchanges of views, a matter which will be dealt with later. In his telegram to Mr. Isvolsky of 24th February (8th March), 1916, Mr. Sazonov said the following :

> " All suppositions on the future frontiers of Central Europe are for the time being premature, but, it should be kept in mind, that we are ready to grant to France and England complete freedom of action on the moment of determining the Western frontier of Germany, reckoning, in our turn, that they would grant us an equivalent freedom for determining our frontiers with Germany and Austria. It is indispensable, above all, to insist on this point— the Polish question should not be submitted to an international consideration and any attempt to put the future of Poland under a guarantee of Powers should be rejected." [36]

Mr. Sazonov's second draft, of the 17th April, 1916, deserves special attention in view of the arguments used in it and the visible preoccupation of the Russian Foreign Minister with the trend of development of the Polish question in the international field. We give below some of the most striking passages : [37]

> " In Germany and Austria-Hungary some new decisions are being prepared with regard to the future destinies of Poland. Germany in her policy is looking for a new approach to the Polish question, obviously different, to some extent, from the old Prussian traditions."

On the other side, the Poles in France and in England

> " work feverishly to incite the French and English political leaders and public opinion in France and England to take a definite position on the Polish question. So far the governments of the allied countries have been able to oppose successfully such attempts and in particular to influence the press. But in this way the allied governments meet serious obstacles: in the Western Allied countries an idea takes root that the war has been carried on for

'the liberation of nations' and the name of Poland is put in the same line with the names of Belgium and Serbia. At the last allied conference in Paris the Imperial envoy obtained, not without difficulty, the suppression of the proposal made by the very old (*prestarelyi*) radical leader, Léon Bourgeois, member of the Cabinet; although Poland was not expressly mentioned in this proposal, it could nevertheless encourage the attempts to raise the Polish question in the international field."

Sazonov puts the question whether it is proper to maintain a passive attitude which " was taken by the Government after the retreat of the Russian forces from the Congress Kingdom," and he answers in the negative.

" The Polish question in its present stage goes beyond the limits of a private and purely domestic issue of the reorganization, on a more or less wide scale, of the administration of one of the Russian borderlands. It was so as long as there existed alliance and peace among the Powers which once partitioned Poland and each of them supported the others in a policy aiming to deny to Poland the rights to national existence. The war put an end to such a position on the Polish question. . . . The Polish question, which was previously a guarantee of peace with Germany, will become a weapon and object in the Russo-German struggle. . . . To deny the international character of the Polish question would mean closing the eyes to reality. But while recognizing it we should not come to the conclusion that the solution should be left to Europe and submitted to an International Congress. I assume that Russia should not allow the Polish question to be considered an international issue; it should be solved by us only, feeling our responsibility for the past and for the future. The treaty (of peace) should establish only the frontiers of Russia on Polish territory, in accordance with our reasonable interests, the support of the allies for them being taken for granted. Anything else should be left to Russia, but it is precisely in order to avoid this question being raised as an international issue that we should bring its full, clear and unambiguous solution as quickly as possible."

In this way Sazonov wished to deprive the Western Powers of any legal title to intervene in Polish matters, and thus the position of Poland would become even worse than after the Congress of Vienna.[38]

Sazonov further refers to the wish expressed by Tsar Nicholas I during the Polish Rising in 1830, to leave the Poles to their own devices, and he adds that similar wishes recently appeared among many Russians (such a solution, by the way, found numerous advocates at that time, especially among old conservatists who wanted, once and for all, to get rid of any Polish influence on the Western provinces of Russia, detached from the Polish-Lithuanian State by the Partitions of Poland).[39]

Sazonov then examines the three possible solutions of the Polish question: full independence, self-government in union with Russia, and a limited local self-government. He rejects the first solution because an independent Poland might in the future associate herself with Germany and become a " centre of political intrigues against Russia." . . . " Russia should keep a direct and general control of the destinies of Poland and should remain faithful to the historic traditions inherited from Catherine the Second and Alexander the First, and materialized in different forms." Sazonov recommends the second solution, but he proposes to exclude from the competence of the future Polish State the following matters : Dynastic questions, foreign policy, army and navy, Orthodox Church, general Empire expenditure, State Loans, State Bank, Customs, Excise duties, Post, Telephone, Telegraph, railways having importance for the whole Empire, etc. After reading this list one wonders what was the difference in Sazonov's mind between the second solution accepted by him and the third one (limited local self-government). In his *Memoirs* written after the war Sazonov mentions that he always held the view that the Polish question " had to be solved only by the initiative of the Russian monarch." [40] Nor did he show any wish to compromise on issues referring to the position of the old historic provinces of East Poland, the very bone of contention between the Poles and Russians for centuries : " The acquisitions of Russia from three partitions of Poland," asserts Sazonov in his *Memoirs,* " have given her her old heritage(?) and ethnographic unity(?), at the same time assuring her a wonderful frontier, based on the principle of partitions of nationalities." The fear that a free Poland might again become the centre of attraction for the prevailing non-Russian populations of these territories formerly belonging to the Polish-Lithuanian Commonwealth, and that the establishment of a Polish State might be a stepping stone to the incorporation of these territories in Poland was a constant preoccupation of the Russian statesmen, (see above, pp. 40-41).

In the light of these documents it appears clearly that Sazonov, who was considered in the West to be the most liberal-minded member of the Russian Cabinet, in fact did not depart very much from the general line of the traditional policy of the Russian Tsars in regard to Poland.

At the time when Sazonov strongly advised taking the initiative in the Polish question, appeals were also coming from Russian high commanders urging the necessity of reaching some decisions on the subject. General Brusilov, Commander of the South-Western

Front, was particularly insistent in his letter of the 16th June, 1916, in which he expressed the view that " Russia should give the Poles not less than Austria did," and the letter of General Alexeyev to Prime Minister Stürmer (22nd June, 1916) was written in the same spirit. In general the interest taken by the military in this affair shows its importance from the point of view of the war operations. But all these appeals served no purpose, and even Sazonov's plans seemed to Prime Minister Stürmer incompatible with Russian interests and the dignity of autocracy. In his report of the 26th May, 1916, to the Tsar Stürmer goes to the length of asserting :

> " So much had been granted by Your Majesty and Your Most August Ancestors to the Poles living in the Russian Empire but as experience has shown the Tsar's favours and trust have never been able to satisfy Polish political leaders. Their aspirations know no limits and they are incorrigible in their separatist moves."

The plan for the future status of Poland, based on Sazonov's suggestions and prepared by the Under-Secretary of State, Krizhanovsky, was submitted to the Cabinet on 6th June, 1916, and discussed by it on 13th, 16th and 18th June, 1916. It was defeated, only three Ministers (among them the Minister for War) voting for it. Stürmer found supporters among all those who wished for reconciliation with Germany, including the Tsarina, who was strengthened in her opposition by the ill-famed Rasputin and all the evil forces behind him.[41] The Tsar, who at the beginning had seemed to favour Sazonov's plans, dismissed Sazonov and, receiving Count Wielopolski, suggested that he should call on the Empress. The latter in a conversation with Wielopolski did not conceal her hostility to the Polish plans of Sazonov and observed that " Should Poland obtain these rights, it would be necessary to grant similar ones to Courland and other parts of Russia."

The hopes of those who by their opposition to any pledges on the Polish question tried to work a passage to reconciliation with Germany were, however, frustrated and they were not able to stem the course of events regarding Poland. For some time the Central Powers stole the thunder, declaring the independence of Poland on the 5th November, 1916.

At the end of the Tsarist régime, when not only the chances of victory over Germany but even hopes of the reconquest of the lost provinces seemed rather remote, and public opinion became more and more dispirited, an Act issued by the Russian Emperor seemed to foreshadow a complete break with the policy followed so far by Tsardom on the Polish question. In the Tsar's Order of the Day to the Army and Fleet, 25th December, 1916, which stated that the time had not yet come to enter into peace negotiations, the following reasons for this position were given: " The attainment by Russia of the tasks created by the war—the possession of Constantinople and the Dardanelles, as well as the creation of a *free* Poland from all three of her, until now, separated provinces—has not yet been guaranteed." At the audience granted to Count Wielopolski the Tsar authorized him to declare that the word " free " should be interpreted as Poland obtaining a separate constitution, her own Legislative Assembly and her own army. This time also it was the army which supported the initiative on this matter and induced the Tsar to take further steps in this direction. We find very interesting information on this subject in the *Memoirs* of General Basil Gourko, who at that time was acting Chief of the General Staff. He gives the following account of his conversations with the Tsar in winter 1916 [42] :

> " I intended to show the Tsar that the time for half measures had passed, that the Polish question needed a definite decision ; that only such a decision would cut the Gordian knot which for more than two centuries had bound the two Slav nations, and better the position of the Polish nation, who were Russian subjects, as well as the subjects of our enemies.
> " In a few words, I desired that in future the Polish question should be decided in this way: That Russia and Poland should have only one thing in common, a common frontier dividing two independent countries. The other remaining questions which could only concern the Polish nation should be independently decided by the Polish nation itself without any foreign interference."

In relation to the above quoted Order of the Day of the Tsar, Gourko " drew the attention of the Tsar to the fact that the words ' free Poland ' did not comprise the definition of autonomy but meant something much greater and much more definite; that in declaring such a Ukaze the Tsar would take upon himself a certain responsibility from which it would be impossible to withdraw." [43]

A committee was appointed to decide the Polish question, eleven members taking part, the majority of whom were Cabinet Ministers, as well as the former Minister of Foreign Affairs, Sazonov, the President of the Imperial Council, Shcheglovitov, the former Minister of Justice, the President of the Duma, Rodzianko, the former Prime Minister, Goremykin, and others. But this body was unable to reach a unanimous decision. Gourko states that several

> " members understood autonomy as a condition giving Poland the right to have her own troops ; others pictured to themselves a future Dual Kingdom, somewhat like that of Austria-Hungary.

What specially frightened the majority of the people was that Free Poland would fall under Germany's influence, and thus react to the detriment of Russian interests. After three meetings Prince Galitzin took the members' votes—those who were of my opinion, those who were against. The majority was against me." [44]

As we shall see later, no encouragement was given at that time by the Western Allies to the Tsar's initiative in the Polish question, and on the contrary, on the eve of the Revolution in Russia, Russian diplomacy succeeded in obtaining formal recognition of the disinterestedness of France in Polish affairs. The old pillars of reaction in Russia succeeded in defeating the moves of the Army which was well aware of the catastrophic military position of the Empire. Although the word " Free " Poland was undoubtedly ambiguous, we should not underestimate the importance of the evolution which was taking place in Russia under the stress of international developments and which facilitated the declaration on the Polish question by Wilson at that time. This evolution prepared the ground for the further developments in Russia, namely the recognition of the independence of Poland by the Russian Provisional Government after the outbreak of the Revolution. At the same time we wish to note that the argument on the potential danger of Poland's independence to Russia, arising from the possibility of Poland associating herself with Germany, cannot be taken at its face value as it was used by those who in their inmost hearts desired reconciliation with Germany in order to forestall the outbreak of the Revolution.

Whatever it may have been, Russia had to be eliminated more and more from any influence on decisions regarding Poland's fate, and this view was shared by those Poles who at the beginning of the war had put their hopes in a solution of the Polish question through some form of compromise with Russia, supported by the Western Allies.

R. Dmowski and the pro-Entente Wing of Polish public opinion

The most prominent among these Poles was a very gifted leader of the National-Democratic Party, Roman Dmowski, who stressed the importance for Poland of its recovering first of all the old Western Polish provinces which had been the birthplace of the Polish nation, being ethnographically Polish since immemorial times, and in which the Germans pursued a most ruthless policy of denationalization of the native population.

Dmowski believed in the possibility of a compromise between the Russian Empire and reunited Poland, based on the recognition of Poland as a separate political entity. The policy advocated by

Dmowski appealed to many Poles, especially in the Congress King-dom and German Poland, the more so as the Western nations, France in particular, were on the side of Russia. Dmowski's policy tended to bind the Polish cause to the Franco-Russian alliance in a common struggle against German endeavours. He believed that the Polish cause would find the support of the Western Allies at the end of the war, even in the event of Russia holding on without revolution until victory was attained.[45]

Dmowski rendered enormous service to the Polish cause in the latter stages of the war, that is after the withdrawal of Russia from the fighting, and the connections he established with Western statesmen turned out to be extremely valuable, both before and in the course of the Paris Peace Conference, but there is no doubt to-day, in the light of the historic evidence available, that the two above-mentioned premises on which his policy was based at the beginning of the war did not correspond to reality. He himself soon realized that the Tsarist Government could not be moved to break with old methods with regard to the Polish question, and at the beginning of November 1915 he left Russia, establishing his headquarters in London where, as he said, he might have more freedom of movement than in Paris, still very closely following the instructions of the Russian Ambassador Isvolsky.

Developing great political activity, first in Great Britain and France, then in America, Dmowski presented the Polish cause within the framework of a new Central Europe to be rebuilt in accordance with the principle of national self-determination. Dmowski stressed the importance of the Allies putting forward a positive programme appealing to the national feelings of the oppressed nations. One might say that at that time there was a certain parallelism between the views advocated by Dmowski and the Russian programme for the dismemberment of Austria-Hungary. The difference between these two points of view, however, was capital. What Dmowski meant was the true liberation of the oppressed nations, while Russia wanted to transform this area into her sphere of influence, incompatible with the principle of national self-determination. It very soon appeared that Russia could not be won to Dmowski's programme. Proceeding with extreme caution, Dmowski handed his first memorandum to the Russian Ambassador in Paris, Izvolsky, in February 1916. It is very interesting to know the particulars of Dmowski's programme developed in this memorial and the reaction of the Russian Government to it. We quote first some striking passages from this memorial[46]:

" Only a power which will be able to establish its influence in this area (Central and Eastern Europe and the Balkans) populated by several big and small nations settled between the Russians and the Germans will attain its main political aims. ... The Germans were the first who discarded the obsolete ideas and started a new approach to the Polish question. ... The studies made by the Germans on the spot after the occupation of Poland have dashed the annexationist lusts. ... The Germans now take the view that Poland represented a force which might present a danger to the German cause if she is not won for it. ... The Poles, who are a numerous nation and more developed than all other nations in Central Europe and in the Balkans, have the same right to an independent national statehood as other nations and their conscience forbids them to forego this right, which as a matter of fact has been recognized by all other nations. ... We have to state that the enthusiasm for the Allied cause among the nations in Central Europe and in the Balkans has died down and one should not shut one's eyes to the fact that the Allies themselves have lost faith in a great victory. ... The Allies seemed to understand at the beginning of the war that they could oppose to the German conceptions only the ideal of freedom and independence of all nations, but they announced this programme with some hesitation and great qualifications ; their attitude above all in the Polish question allowed the Germans to foster doubts in the sincerity of the Allied plans and they proclaimed themselves the protectors of the oppressed nationalities."

As appears from these lines, Dmowski considered that the liberation of the oppressed nations should be the common programme of all the Allies, which excluded the idea of the subjection of these nations to one country—Russia.

In his report of 25th April, 1916,[47] to Sazonov, Izvolsky, expressly referring to Dmowski's plans, states that they " contain something which is quite unacceptable for Russia, namely the placing of the Polish question on the international agenda." He concludes that " the Poles turn away from us and are ready to accept from the hands of our enemies such solution as would satisfy their national aspiration more than that which they have so far succeeded in obtaining from Russia." Izvolsky nevertheless recommended granting wide autonomy to Poland, to which the Allies might adhere. Even this very moderate and quite unsatisfactory solution recommended by Izvolsky aroused great indignation among the Russian ruling circles, and Stürmer in his report to the Tsar dated 26th May, 1916,[48] asked the following question :

" Has Russia's weight fallen so low in recent times that a moment may come when one of the Allies having ignored mutual rights and duties would take upon himself the responsibility of direct interference in a question which in accordance with the past and present and by its true essence belongs to Russia, and to Russia only."

We know, from our preceding review of Russian policy on the Polish question, that until the very end of Tsardom the Russian Government refused to consider the Polish cause as the common cause of the Allied Powers within the general programme of the European political reconstruction in accordance with the declarations of the Allied Governments that they were fighting for the liberation of the oppressed peoples.

Thus the first premise upon which Dmowski's programme was based at that time, the possibility of a direct Polish-Russian agreement, safeguarding the interests of each party, turned out to be unrealistic, at least so long as the Tsarist régime remained intact.

France and the Polish Question

Let us see now how far the Poles, in this first period of the war, could count on Allied support. Was it possible to obtain a joint guarantee of Poland's independence from the Allies? Did Dmowski's second assumption correspond to reality? [49] First of all we should review the French policy regarding this question, as the traditions of French-Polish comradeship-in-arms, especially in the Napoleonic era, were still alive at that time not only in Poland but also in some French quarters, and the Left Wing in France—which never had much sympathy for the Tsars—continued to show its sympathy for the Polish cause.[49a] Moreover, on the European continent it was France who, on many occasions and in most recent times during the reign of Emperor Napoleon III, appeared as champion of the principle of nationality. One of the most famous French historians, Albert Sorel, who fully understood the bearing of the Polish question on international politics, described the historic rôle of France in the movement for national self-determination.

" C'est un honneur que la France est en droit de revendiquer, d'avoir fondé son droit public sur ce principe qui donne la seule sanction de la conquête, à savoir que les peuples seuls ont le droit de disposer d'eux-mêmes et que, un changement dans leur destinée nationale n'est légitime s'il n'est ratifié par leur suffrage direct, universel et libre." (SOREL, L'Europe et la Révolution Française, Vol. VII, p. 508.)

There were numerous French intellectuals, mostly radicals and socialists but also many Catholics, who since 1914 had predicted the resurgence of Poland as an unavoidable outcome of the war. Jean Herbette, later French Ambassador to Moscow and then one of the leading French publicists, in an article in the Echo de Paris quoted a sentence uttered by a French diplomat even before the outbreak

of the war : " The peace of Europe rests on the half-closed grave
of Poland." [50]   In an article which appeared in *Figaro,* Gabriel
Hanotaux quoted the opinion of Albert Sorel : " All this will finish
by the resurrection of Poland." [51]   Many of these Frenchmen, however, were misled by the high-sounding proclamation of the Grand
Duke, and saw in it the beginning of a new era for the Polish nation.
The pressure of public opinion became particularly strong in the
second half of 1915, after the Russian defeats in Poland and the
growing danger that the Central Powers might win the support of
the Poles in view of Russian reluctance to take any positive steps
towards a true Russo-Polish reconciliation.   At the beginning of
1916 the French Government began to feel great anxiety on account
of Russian ineptitude in the Polish question, and it was more and
more difficult for it to appease the discontent of the advocates of the
Polish cause.   Paléologue notes in his diary under 3rd March :
" The Russian Government continues to keep silence on the restoration of Poland. Paris is worried about it." [52]   Among the elder
statesmen whose influence on the Government was particularly
strong and who insisted on the attention of the Russians being
drawn to the Polish question was Leon Bourgeois; among the
younger we must note the name of the mayor of Lyon, Edouard
Herriot, then at the beginning of his brilliant political career. He
wrote the following about Poland : " Poland should be left to herself. We shall work that Poland may become Polish, not German,
and not even Russian because Russia was wise enough(?) to give
up Poland. Poland will be independent." [52a]   An outstanding
French publicist, Gabriel Séailles, in a series of articles underlined
the international character of the Polish question. In *La Victoire*
Gustave Hervé raised a cry of alarm in his article " Gare à la
Pologne." A French League of the Friends of Poland was formed
in Paris under the chairmanship of Charles Richet, President of the
Academy, and in June 1916 issued a declaration requesting the
restoration of the Polish State.   Among the signatories of this
declaration were Emile Faguet, Charles Gide, Louis Martin, Henri
de Regnier, Pierre Renaudel, Gabriel Séailles, Georges Bienaimé,
and other prominent figures of French political and intellectual life.
The proclamation by the Central Powers of Poland's independence and especially the prospects of raising a big Polish army,
aroused great alarm in the public opinion of the Allied countries.
We shall speak about the real meaning of this proclamation in the
next chapter. For the time being let us note that before the Allied
Governments had taken an official position on this issue the French
papers had widely discussed the new prospects for the Central
Powers arising from the creation of a big Polish army fighting on

their side. *Le Matin* estimated that this army might enlist 700,000 men, and *L'Eveil* stated : " The Poles won't jib, and there will be seven to eight hundred thousand Poles in this army." *Le Temps* published six editorials favouring the Polish cause (5th, 6th, 10th, 13th, 16th and 18th November, 1916), written by André Tardieu who later became one of the closest associates of Clemenceau. The Commission for Foreign Affairs of the French Chamber of Deputies passed the following motion in November 1916 :

> " Germany and Austria, by proclaiming the constitution of an independent Kingdom of Poland consisting of one section of dismembered Poland in order to make of it a tool of their policy, have imprinted an international character on the Polish problem and stressed its military value which commands the attention of the Allies."

H. H. Fisher, in his excellent book *America and the New Poland*, rightly observed that " the restoration of Poland became a war issue for a large public before it was accepted by the foreign offices of Europe." [53] Nowhere else does this remark prove so correct as in regard to France. Which was the French official point of view on Poland's status after the war at that time? Many French statesmen considered that lasting peace in Europe could not be achieved without the restoration of the Polish State, but there were others who took the view that the establishment of an independent Poland might put an end to Franco-Russian collaboration in the future and thus upset the balance of power in Europe. The latter accepted the fact of Russo-German hostility as a permanent feature of international politics, which obviously clashed with many historical experiences and, moreover, seemed to overlook the fact that the Franco-Russian alliance had a rather chequered history, being in some periods directed more against Great Britain than against Germany.[54] Moreover Austria-Hungary was the principal enemy of Russia, and not Germany.[55] Was it wise to leave the Polish pawn completely in Russian hands considering that in the past it had served Russia as a bargaining asset? This was certainly in the mind of Mr. Stürmer and his associates when they opposed any decision on the Polish question which might render more difficult a reconciliation with Germany. Many mistakes of the Western Powers in dealing with the problems of Central-Eastern Europe might have been avoided if the background of Russia's policy in the Polish question had been properly understood. Those Frenchmen who took the view that the restoration of the Polish State might endanger the Franco-Russian alliance in the future were, perhaps, less outspoken on the subject than the partisans of Poland's independence, but it was their views which for a long time prevailed with governmental circles. A phrase coined by a French publicist, Coudurier de Chassaigne, in 1916 perhaps best expresses the feelings of this school of thought : " To give them (the Poles) less than a kind of home rule would be unjust—to give them more would be folly." [56]

The man who at the beginning of the war held the portfolio of Foreign Affairs, M. Delcassé, was by tradition and his whole political outlook one of those French statesmen who were completely devoted to the cause of Russo-French collaboration. His subservience to Russia and unilateral concessions for her benefit, without any reciprocation, had eventually compromised his political career. The British Ambassador, Lord Bertie, notes in his diary under 9th August, 1915 :

> " There is a feeling against Delcassé as being too much at the beck and call of Sazonov and Izvolsky and not having engineered Rumania into an alliance on account of too much deference to Russian susceptibilities: he is also blamed for not protesting against the invasion of Poland (Lwow and Galicia) by a horde of Russian popes." [57]

M. Paléologue, French Ambassador to Petrograd, also showed great caution in all his approaches to the Polish problem. He tried to warn the Poles against any attempt to " internationalize " the cause of their country, and limited himself to vague allusions to the support which France might give to the Polish cause at the end of the war.[58] In his conversations with the Russians he insisted that the French Government desired nothing more than a kind of home rule for a reintegrated Poland, in accordance with the public declarations of the Russians themselves.[59] It was in the middle of 1916, in connection with the departure to Petrograd of a French mission headed by Viviani and Albert Thomas, that the Polish political leaders established in Paris made the first open attempt to win the support of the French Government and asked it to take the initiative in the Polish question. Mr. Erazm Piltz, who later became Under-Secretary of State for Foreign Affairs in independent Poland, handed a note to M. Briand after a conversation with him in April 1916. A sense of deep disappointment pervades this document : " The silence of the Allies who so far have abstained from stating their intentions towards Poland . . . the discouragement provoked by it in the nation as well as deep disquiet among Polish political leaders." Mr. Piltz warned that

> " the negotiations between Austria and Germany relating to the reconstitution of an autonomous Polish State . . . can lead sooner or later to the conclusion of an agreement and to the proclaiming

by the Central Powers of an act which although not solving the Polish question might have harmful consequences. ... In order to obviate the danger arising from the present political situation in Poland it is highly desirable that the Governments of France, Great Britain and Italy break the silence on the Polish problem in which they have persisted until the present, and express their firm purpose to materialize, in agreement with Russia, a plan for reconstitution of a united and free Poland." [60]

The mission of M. Viviani and Albert Thomas, which went with the fixed purpose of " inducing the Imperial Government to sub-scribe to a firm and clear engagement for the benefit of Poland," [61] was warned on its arrival in Petrograd, by M. Paléologue, against raising the Polish issue, and the matter was postponed until the final stage of the negotiations. Mr. Sasonov, receiving the French repre-sentatives before their departure on the 17th May, 1916, in reply to their allusions to the Polish question answered that it would be dangerous for France to raise this issue. [62]

Mr. Piltz was right in warning the French Government against the danger of leaving the whole initiative on Polish questions with the Central Powers. On the 5th November, 1916, the latter pro-claimed Poland's independence. The French and British Govern-ments joined Russia in her protest against this attempt to solve the Polish question. We read in the telegram sent by M. Briand and Mr. Asquith to Mr. Stürmer that the Allied Governments " are pro-foundly gratified to see that Russia, at the very outset of the war, gave to the peoples dwelling in all the Polish lands assurances in conformity with their immemorial hopes." Qualifying the German and Austrian promises as having an " illusory character " they " are happy entirely to concur in the views of which the Imperial Government means to assure the realization for the benefit of the noble Polish people."

In reply to President Wilson's note on the 18th December, 1916, the Polish case was not included among the Allied war aims, and the Western Powers limited themselves to referring to " the intentions of His Majesty the Emperor of Russia in regard to Poland," which they considered " have been clearly indicated by the manifesto he has just addressed to his armies " (see above, p. 47). These docu-ments show beyond any doubt that the Allies were disinclined to do more than acknowledge Russia's moves towards the recognition of the Polish claims, leaving the whole initiative to Russia as to the extent of the freedom which she was prepared to grant Poland.

But in the last months of the Tsarist régime the French Govern-ment realized that the pressure of public opinion in the Polish ques-tion, which could appear rather embarrassing from the point of view of French-Russian relations, might serve as an excellent bargaining asset in securing vital French interests. Such is the background of the exchange of letters Paléologue–Pokrovsky, signed in Petrograd on the 18th February, 1917, and Briand–Izvolsky on the 11th March, 1917, in Paris. On many occasions the Russian Government suggested leaving entire freedom to France in exchange for her disinterestedness in Polish affairs (see above, p. 43). But the negotiations between M. Doumergue and Pokrovsky, Russian Foreign Minister, on the occasion of the visit of the Inter-Allied Mission to Russia consisting of Doumergue, Castelnau, Lord Milner and Scialoja, led only to the recognition of the freedom of France in determining her Eastern frontier and was meant as compensation for previous French concessions to Russia, especially relating to Constantinople and the future frontiers of Russia with Turkey. By the way, the negotiations conducted by M. Doumergue were kept secret from the other allies, and Lord Milner was not informed of what was going on behind his back. Nor were these letters subsequently communicated to the British Government.[63] As M. Ribot, one of the war-time Prime Ministers of France, states in his *Memoirs*, the letters were not communicated even to the President of the French Republic. It was after the exchange of these letters in Petrograd that Mr. Izvolsky called on M. Briand [64] at the Quai d'Orsay and asked for a reciprocal engagement concerning the future Western frontiers of Russia, that is to say both in relation to Germany and Austria. M. Briand was greatly embarrassed by Izvolsky's demand, according to Ribot's information " feeling it inconvenient to abandon to Russia the question of the future frontiers of Poland." [65] He referred to the Cabinet and was eventually authorized by it to agree to Izvolsky's demand. M. Renouvin, an eminent French historian, in his book *La Crise Européenne et la Grande Guerre,* underlines the far-reaching consequences of this decision. It was " a grave declaration, because it allowed the Tsarist Government to oppose the reconstitution of a Polish State and annulled all the preceding attempts of the French diplomacy(?) " [66]

British Policy of Non-interference in Polish-Russian relations

Turning our attention now to the second Western Power allied to Russia, Great Britain, we must keep in mind, first of all, that Great Britain went very far to keep alive the Russian alliance, making great concessions to Russia even on issues of primary importance for British policy, such as the straits and Constantinople. Consequently at the beginning of the war Great Britain was not prepared to do anything which might hurt Russian susceptibilities, the more so as she did not realize the bearing of the Polish problem on the conduct of the war in the East. Therefore the British, although naturally approving any liberal move of the Tsarist policy, did nothing to encourage it. We can say even more, British policy definitely lagged behind, because even at the moment when the Tsar's advisers tried to convince him that the recognition of Poland's independence was inescapable, the British statesmen, viewing the problem exclusively from the balance of power policy, were rather reluctant to concur with this new trend of Russian policy. Looking at British newspapers and periodicals of this period one is rather shocked by the uncritical adulation of everything Russian. The British Ambassador in Petrograd hardly mentions the Polish issue in his *Memoirs*, in spite of its growing importance. Sazonov states in his *Memoirs* that Buchanan had never approached him on the Polish problem.[67] And Lord Bertie mentions his name under the most prominent representatives of the pro-Russian wing in the Foreign Office : " The pro-Russian policy was rampant at the Foreign Office before Harding was there. It was a continuance of Grey, Nicolson and Buchanan which is much appreciated." [68]

Not until the 2nd March, that is nearly eight months after the Proclamation of the Grand Duke, do we find the first official declaration of the British Government on this act, in very reserved terms.

In a written answer to Mr. King given on the 2nd March, 1915 (Mr. King asked whether " the offer of political autonomy to a united Poland, made by the Russian Commander-in-Chief, was communicated to and approved by the French and British allies of Russia before it was proclaimed to the Polish people "), Sir Edward Grey stated the following : " The Proclamation is issued and on record. If the object of the Hon. Member's question is to be assured that His Majesty's Government are not out of sympathy with it, I can assure him that it is so." As we see, the answer was very evasive and non-committal. (*Parliamentary Debates*, Commons, LXX, 2nd March, 1915).

But the importance of the Polish issue, certainly quite unexpectedly for British policy, was nevertheless growing, especially after the retreat of the Russian armies from Poland and the rumours about the plans of the Central Powers began to worry the Allies. On the eve of the fall of Warsaw *The Times,* in its editorial " Tempting the Poles," emphatically assured that the Russian pledges were more solid than the German ones, and even declared that " We welcomed (the Proclamation of the Grand Duke) not only as an engagement between Russia and the Poles, but an engagement between Russia and the Allies." As a matter of fact it was purely lip-service to the Polish cause, because many months later Lord Robert

Cecil, in an oral answer to Mr. Keating as to " whether it is the intention of the Government to recommend a constitution for Poland," stated : " No, Sir, it is not the intention of His Majesty's Government to make any recommendation on a matter of internal policy of another State." (*Parliamentary Debates,* Commons, LXXXV, 23rd August, 1916). After the Proclamation of the 5th November, 1916, *The Times* went a step further, but admitted hardly more than a moral engagement of Russia towards the Allies. We read in this editorial, entitled " The Trap for the Poles " (16th November) :

> " The Proclamation of the Grand Duke Nicholas remains the Charter of all the Polish people. By this document they were promised real freedom and real reunion, but those of them who were Austrian or Prussian subjects were invited to incur the penalties of treason. It therefore constituted in their eyes and in the eyes of the Allies a solemn obligation upon the part of Russia to see harmless all who acted upon it to the utmost of her power. The obligation does not rest upon Russia alone. It is shared at least morally, by her Allies who stood by and crowned the pledge with their heartiest applause. The future of Poland is a European question of the first magnitude, in the solution of which all the Allies are deeply concerned. They agreed that *it must be solved on the Russian lines,* and the overwhelming majority of clear-sighted Poles agree with them."

At the same time the British Government refused to engage itself on the Polish issue, as clearly appears from the answers given to General Sir Ivor Herbert. This Member of Parliament on the 21st November, 1916, raised this question in connection with the Act of the 5th November and wished to know " whether the realization of the hope of the Polish people of a union and autonomy is now placed by His Majesty's Government side by side with the reconstitution of Belgium and Serbia." The Speaker demanded that Sir Ivor should give notice of this question, which was discussed on the 28th November. The Prime Minister then referred to the telegram sent by himself and M. Briand to Mr. Stürmer (see above, p. 55). Sir Ivor persisted and further asked " whether the Right Hon Gentleman is aware that the absence of any definite statement on behalf of His Majesty's Government is creating uneasiness among the Polish people, and is giving point to the German attempts to alienate Polish sympathies from Russia," but the Prime Minister answered that it was " with that in mind " that he jointly with M. Briand sent a telegram to Mr. Stürmer. (*Parliamentary Debates,* Commons, LXXXVII).

The same occurred in the case of the question put by Mr. Ginell on the 4th December, 1916 : " Whether before joining in the Franco-British Note with reference to the formation of a new Kingdom of Russian Poland, the two Governments had agreed to make the restoration of the integrity and independence of entire Poland a condition of peace and to the separate representation of Poland at the International Peace Conference to follow the war; whether Russia concurs; whether a joint declaration of the three Powers to that effect will be made; and whether the same policy will apply to all small nations whose help in the War has been obtained on the promise that it would apply." The Prime Minister answered that he had nothing to add to the published statement on this subject. (*Parliamentary Debates,* Commons, LXXXVIII).

At the beginning of 1917, viewed from Petrograd the problem of the recognition by Russia of Polish independence seemed to be near, as appears from the following passage in *The Times* of 7th February, 1917 (correspondence from Petrograd) in connection with the institution by the Tsar of a special conference to discuss the future organization of Poland (see above, p. 47) :

> " What form the suggestion of the conference will assume on this point remains a matter of conjecture. In the first Russian pledge to Poland, contained in the Grand Duke Nicholas's proclamation issued shortly after the outbreak of the war, it was specified that reunited Poland would remain under the sceptre of the Tsar, but, as the newspapers point out to-day, the international aspects of the Polish question have undergone great changes since then."

And yet, in contrast to the statement of *The Times* that the " future of Poland was a European question of the first magnitude," and in spite of the impact of events the following was said by Lord Hugh Cecil in the House of Commons as late as 22nd March, 1917 :

> " Hon. Members talk loosely about Poland—there is no country which is less an analogy to Ireland—and about what will happen at the Peace Conference. I do not suppose that the question before the Peace Conference will be any question of Home Rule for Poland. I do not suppose that the Peace Conference will trouble its head about Home Rule for any portion of the world. ... I do not suppose that this country will dictate to Russia what form of Home Rule is to be given to Poland, and I am quite sure Russia will not dictate to us what form of Home Rule should be given to Ireland." (*Parliamentary Debates,* Commons, XCI).

In spite of the Russian military defeats and many symptoms of the rottenness of the Tsarist régime, quite obvious about the end of 1916, even progressive circles in Great Britain at that time were unable to break away from the idea that the stability of the world might be better assured by maintaining the big imperial units, and therefore they gave a very qualified support to the claims of the oppressed nations. Working on this principle they favoured not only the maintenance of the integrity of the Russian Empire but even agreed to the enlargement of Russia's frontiers. " Plan for an Allied Peace," published in the *New Statesman* on the 16th September, 1916, is particularly characteristic of this turn of mind. We quote the following passages from this article :

> " If the principle of nationality were to be generally and indis-criminately applied to the whole of Eastern Europe whenever any consciousness of separate nationality is to be found, the Russian Empire would cease to exist. ... The Russian Empire will be sub-stantially enlarged as a result of a complete Allied victory, and so long as that enlargement is confined to the absorption of Slav races there is no particular reason why the Western nations should wish to set any limits to it, provided it is accompanied by a prac-tical scheme of decentralization and local autonomy. ... Prima facie, since our fundamental object is to secure international stability, there are important advantages in having as few units as possible for international purposes, that is to say in the imperial as distinguished from the national solution of race problems. But the conditions of stability cannot be fulfilled by the imperial system un-less it is founded on a basis of common consent. A rebellious Poland would be a permanent weakness to Russia, and a permanent temptation to her Western neighbour."

What is most striking in these passages is a misguided analogy between the British and Russian Empires and complete ignorance of Russian expansionism based on conquests and on the oppression of subjugated peoples. If it is admitted that the Russian frontiers could be moved to the limits of the Western Slavs it means assigning to Russia a controlling position in Central Europe which might hardly contribute to " conditions of stability."

Balfour's " Memorandum on the Peace Settlement in Europe "

But to ascertain what was in fact the real attitude of the British Government on the Polish question at that stage of the war one must look into the confidential State papers, some of which were disclosed in the inter-war period. I have especially in mind the different statements made by Lord Balfour, the Foreign Secretary, in 1916 and 1917. Already in *The Intimate Papers of Colonel House* we have found some allusions to Balfour's views on the future of Poland. On the 14th February, 1916, at a dinner party at the home of the Lord Chief Justice (Reading), attended by House, Lloyd George, Grey, Balfour and Asquith, " the nationalization of Poland was discussed," states House, and he sums up the views expressed by Balfour in the following way : " Balfour thought if

Poland was made an independent Kingdom, becoming a buffer State between Russia and Germany, it would leave France at the mercy of Germany in any future war, for the reason that Russia would not be able to reach Germany without violating the neutrality of Poland. He thought this would be a serious objection from the French point of view, and also from the Russian, and, if it happened, it would probably cause an end of the alliance between Russia and France." [69] This point of view is developed in more detail in a Memorandum prepared by Balfour in November 1916 on " The Peace Settlement in Europe." [70]

In his Memorandum Balfour advises a strategic modification of frontiers and asserts that " the principal object of the war is the attainment of a durable peace " by " the double method of diminishing the area from which the Central Powers can draw the men and money required for a policy of agression " and " some kind of home rule for Poland " (it is very curious in view of what happened at the end of the Second World War that Balfour anticipated transfers of population in order to secure better strategic frontiers. In this connection he said the following : " Of course, such strategic modifications might involve transfers of populations which could not properly be described as negligible.")

> " The point on which there might be most difference of opinion would perhaps be the fate of Poland—since the fate of Constantinople and the Banat is already settled so far as the Allies can settle it. Almost the only thing on which Russia and Germany seem to be agreed is that the status of Poland should be altered by the War, and that while receiving some measure of autonomy, it should remain dependent upon one of its two great neighbours. ... Looking at the Polish question from a purely British point of view, I should like to see the new State include not merely Russian Poland, but as much of Austrian and German Poland as possible. This, of course, is in strict accord with the two principles laid down earlier in the paper. But I should not like to see the old Kingdom of Poland restored. I should fear that the new Poland will suffer from the diseases through which the old Poland perished ; that it would be a theatre of perpetual intrigues between Germany and Russia ; and that its existence, so far from promoting the cause of European peace, would be a perpetual occasion of European strife. Moreover, even if such Poland were capable of playing the part of an efficient buffer State (which I doubt) I am not sure that a buffer State between Germany and Russia would be any advantage to Western Europe. If Germany were relieved of all fear of pressure from Russia, and were at liberty to turn her whole strength towards developing her Western ambitions, France and Britain might be the sufferers: and I am not by any means confident that cutting off Russia from her Western neighbours

might not divert her interests towards the Far East to an extent which British statesmen could not view without some misgivings. The more Russia is made a European than an Asiatic Power the better for everybody.

"I therefore conclude that the solution of the Polish question which would best suit our interests would be the constitution of a Poland endowed with a large measure of autonomy, while remaining an integral part of the Russian Empire—the new State or province—to include not only all Russian Poland but also Austria's and (part at least) of Prussia's share in the plunder of the ancient Kingdom."

The fallacy of these arguments—especially those that the peace of Europe might be better secured by Russia disposing of Poland's resources than by the existence of a completely free Poland (which had been an independent State and a powerful barrier between East and West for eight centuries), and that "the more Russia is a European Power" the better for the world (or rather Great Britain) —was sufficiently proved by subsequent events. The British Government had to revise this point of view in later periods of the war, but Balfour's papers remain as a proof of lack of imagination and survival of old prejudices. Let us, by the way, note that Balfour judges Poland's past according to what was so obligingly presented by German and Russian historian-propagandists, and on this point seems to share the views of Robert, Marquess of Salisbury (see p. 64-5). Moreover, Balfour seems to ignore the history of the nineteenth century, in the course of which Prussia (later the German Reich) and Russia, being neighbours and supporting each other in suppressing the Polish question, were able thanks to their close co-operation to build up two powerful and aggressive Empires menacing the peace of the world.[70a]

It was Colonel House who at that time held more realistic views and saw the shortcomings of Balfour's conceptions. When Balfour went to Washington at the end of April 1917, that is at the time when the restoration of an independent Polish State seemed a foregone conclusion to many statesmen, he still seemed reluctant to part with his old preconceived ideas. House relates in these terms his conversation with Balfour on the 28th April, 1917 :

"We went back to Poland. His objection to a Polish State, cutting off Russia from Germany, was whether it would not hurt France more than Germany, for the reason it would prevent Russia from coming to France's aid in the event of an attack by Germany. I thought we had to take into consideration the Russia of fifty years from now rather than the Russia of to-day. While we might hope it would continue democratic and cease to be aggressive, yet if the contrary happened, Russia would be a menace to Europe and not Germany. I asked him not to look upon Germany as a permanent enemy. If we did this, we would confuse our reasoning and mistakes would likely be made. Balfour, however, was more impressed with the German menace than he was by the possible danger from Russia." [71]

Conclusions

It would be difficult to say what might have happened if Russia had not collapsed in 1917, and how far the Western Powers would have been disposed to support Polish claims had Russia been among the victors at the end of the war. [72] In any case we can state, in the light of the evidence produced in this chapter, that until the outbreak of the Russian Revolution the Western Powers had not taken any step which might be considered as the recognition of the Polish question as an international issue.

There is now no doubt that the Western Allies of Russia were well aware of the true designs of the latter towards Poland. Temperley rightly notes in the *History of the Peace Conference*, when speaking of the political consequences of the Russian Revolution, that " the most important effect was upon the freedom of Poland, on which the utterances of Tsardom had never been convincing." [73]

When the Russian Revolutionary Government published the confidential documents of Tsarist diplomacy the discrepancy between the war slogans of the Allies and their policy towards Poland was brought to light. It certainly put the Western statesmen in an embarrassing position, as clearly appears from the discussion on war aims in the House of Commons on the 19th December, 1917. Mr. Ponsonby, quoting the Russian dispatches insisting on the exclusion of the Polish question from the subjects of international discussions and referring to various statements by British statesmen, said that the latter " did not tally with these (secret) agreements and these interchanges of ideas that were made with the Tsar's Government when that Government was still in existence." Mr. Balfour answered : " The Tsar had declared himself in favour of Poland. We might have wished that declaration had taken a different form, but the declaration was made explicitly and we believed in it." (*Parliamentary Debates*, Commons, Vol. C, 19th December, 1917.)

Indifference to the Polish question and lack of any initiative on it by the Western Powers was widely exploited by the Soviet Government in the inter-war period when it suited its purposes to undermine the confidence of the Polish nation in the West. A very characteristic piece of this propaganda can be found in the preface to the collection of secret documents of the Tsarist diplomacy relating to the Polish question, published by the Soviet Government under the title *Russo-Polish Relations in the Period of the World War*. In this preface we read amongst other things the following :

" In particular the correspondence between the Russian Ambassadors in London and Paris on the one side and the Russian Minister of Foreign Affairs on the other has an exceptional value for the history of the Polish question in the course of the World War," and drawing its conclusions exclusively from the first period of the war, the preface condemns the Western Allies in the following terms :

" So long as the proletarian revolution has not opened the secret archives of the Quai d'Orsay and Downing Street, this correspondence is the only one which throws light on the duplicity, cowardice and cynical selfishness of the Entente Governments, carrying on the war under the banner of the ' freedom of nations.' " [74]

NOTES

[1] Cf. Vol. II of the *Cambridge History of Poland,* From Augustus II to Pilsudski (1697–1935), Oxford University Press, 1941. ROBERT MACHRAY, *Poland 1914–1931,* and the same author, *The Poland of Pilsudski,* London, 1936.

[2] PHILLIPS, W. ALISON, *Poland,* p. 9.

[3] B. H. SUMNER, *Survey of Russian History,* p. 429.

[4] JOHN HOWES GLEASON, *The Genesis of Russophobia.* See the chapter, " The Polish Revolution," pp. 107-34.

[5] LORD SALISBURY'S *Essays,* p. 147.

[6] A. L. KENNEDY, *Old Diplomacy and New,* pp. 8-9. " He (Robert Arthur, Third Marquess of Salisbury) lacked sympathy with popular movements. The sternly practical nature which he extolled in Castlereagh, the scorn with which he denounced those who fail to distinguish between attainable and visionary aims, led him greatly to underestimate the importance of such impalpable forces as race nationalism. He wrote that the hearts of the Poles were already ' parcelled out ' and that an independent Poland was a ' mere chimera ' . . . He referred to the idea of Italian unity as a ' student's dream ' " ; p. 32 : " The nineteenth century had shown a succession of movements—German, Italian, Greek, Serbian and Rumanian—towards national union and national independence. Yet diplomatists set themselves to retake the logic of history and arrest the decay of Turkey. . . . The whole of Lord Salisbury's argument was based on the assumption that the Bulgarians were incapable of asserting their independence."

[7] LORD SALISBURY'S *Essays,* p. 194.

[8] A. A. W. RAMSAY, *Idealism and Foregn Policy,* p. 20.

[9] ROBERT HOWARD LORD, *The Second Partition of Poland,* p. 484.

[10] *Ibidem,* p. 491.

[11] So, for instance, Lord Salisbury based entirely his most harsh and unfair criticism of Poland's past on the assertions of a German historian von Sybel: " With these facts in view, most persons will be inclined to agree with the judgment which von Sybel passes upon the whole case: ' when one weighs these relative conditions one can hardly speak of the Polish nation having been overthrown by the Partitions. What fell in 1793 was the inhuman domination of a few noblemen over the Polish people. These only changed their masters and watched the change which even upon the Russian side could not bring them more harm than good with indolent indifference '." (SALISBURY'S *Essays*, p. 544).

Cf. a similar uncritical acceptance of Russian and German opinions by P. ALISON, o.c., p. 42: " The ultimately determining cause of the downfall of Poland, as the Poles themselves have since recognized(?) was the fact that they had never developed a true national consciousness."

[12] FUSTEL DE COULANGES, *Revue des Deux Mondes*, 1871, Vol. XLI, pp. 21-2: " L'opinion en Prusse à été disciplinée comme l'armée; elle a compris que, pour récolter plus sûrement la victoire, il faut commencer par semer la haine. Ses professeurs se sont attachés à travestir notre révolution française et à dénaturer toute notre histoire pour nous rendre haïssables.'

See also H. E. CARR, *The Twenty Years Crisis*, p. 91: " Theories designed to discredit an enemy or potential enemy, are one of the commonest forms of purposeful thinking. To depict one's enemies or one's prospective victims as inferior beings in the sight of God has been a familiar technique, at any rate since the days of Old Testament. Racial theories, ancient and modern, belong to 'this category; for the rule of one people or class over another is always justified by a belief in the mental and moral inferiority of the ruled."

[13] Published in *The Slavonic and East-European Review*, 1942-3, pp. 223-39.

[14] BETHMANN-HOLLWEG, *Betrachtungen zum Weltkriege*, Vol. II, p. 241: " Der Sazonovsche Wink: ' Lâcher l'Autriche et nous lâcherons la France' hatte doch nur den Wert eines gelegentlichen Aperçu ohne die Möglichkeit politischer Konsequenzen. Osterreich aber wäre in die Lage gekommen neue Freunde zu wählen, es hätte bei den Westmächten offene Arme gefunden."

[15] This is admitted even by a prominent French historian PIERRE RENOUVIN, *Les Origines Immédiates de la Guerre*, p. 305: " Certes, la Russie à la suite des entretiens de M. Poincaré à Petersbourg, et des assurances transmises par M. Paléologue, savait que le gouvernement français ne reculerait pas devant les obligations de l'alliance. Il est possible, il est vraisemblable que ces indications ont eu pour elle la valeur d'un engagement."

The same author, *La Crise Européenne et la Grande Guerre*, p. 183: " Que le nationalisme serbe ait été souvent turbulent et dangereux, que la politique russe ait été imprudente, parfois inquiétante, il n'est pas question de le contester."

[16] There exists much evidence on this point. I wish to refer to that of a prominent Russian war-commander, GENERAL BASIL GOURKO, *Memoirs and Impression of War and Revolution*, p. 15: " The plan of strategical development that began to be realized at the beginning of the mobilization in 1914 was founded on the second idea, namely, that of directing the main blow against Austria, and advancing against Germany afterwards. It can hardly be doubted that Germany knew the fundamental outline of our plan of strategic development. These conditions made the operations of Germany easier and gave her a large scope of freedom in directing the main body of her forces against France."

[17] MAJOR ERICH VOLKMANN, *Der Grosse Krieg*, pp. 51 ff.

[18] A. PINGAUD, *Histoire Diplomatique de la France pendant la Grande Guerre*, Vol. I, about the diplomatic methods of Mr. Sazonov, see pp. 38-9: " Cette précipitation un peu inquiète était de nature à déconcerter la prudence de ses collégues alliés amenés parfois à se demander si l'Entente a trouvé en lui un animateur pour tout entraîner, ou un brouillon pour tout compromettre."

[19] PALEOLOGUE, *La Russie des Tsars*, Vol. I, p. 246. See note 15, Chapter I. PINGAUD, o.c., p. 130: " En transmettant ce nouveau projet à M. Delcassé, M. Paléologue crut devoir en souligner la portée et en indiquer le danger, la réalisation devant entraîner l'écroulement d'une grande puissance qui représentait l'un des élements de l'équilibre européen. Il reçut comme réponse (janvier 1915) la recommandation de ' ne pas prononcer un mot ' de nature à faire croire que la France pourrait peser sur le gouvernement russe pour l'amener à modifier son plan. C'était peut-être de sa part pousser bien loin la complaisance envers les intentions exprimées à Petersbourg."

[20] The Proclamation of the Grand Duke Nicholas: " Poles! The hour has sounded when the sacred dream of your fathers and forefathers can come true. A century and half has passed since the living flesh of Poland was torn in pieces but her soul is not dead. It lives in the hope that the hour will come in which resuscitated Poland will reconcile herself fraternally with Great Russia. The Russian troops bring to you the happy message of reconciliation. May the frontiers disappear that divide the Polish nation, thus making of them a unity under the sceptre of the Emperor of Russia! Under that sceptre Poland will be reborn, free in religion, in language and in self-government. Russia expects from you equal consideration for the rights of nationalities with which history has linked you. Great Russia comes to meet you with open heart and brotherly hand. She is convinced that the sword which struck the enemy at Grunwald is not yet rusted. From the shores of the Pacific to the Northern Seas the Russian regiments are advancing. It is the dawn of a new life for you. May they shine resplendent in that dawn of the Cross, the symbol of Passion and Resurrection of peoples! "

[21] A confidential circular sent by Mr. Maklakov, Minister of the Interior, to his subordinates in December 1914 explained that the Manifesto of the Grand Duke would apply only to the new acquisitions of Russia and not to the Congress-Kingdom and other Polish territories

held by Russia. The first official declaration on the Polish question was made on the eve of the fall of Warsaw, 1st August, 1915, by Mr. Goremykin, Russian Prime Minister. It promised self-government within the framework of the Russian Empire.

[22] The Manifesto of the Tsar to the Armenians of 17th September, 1914, contained the following passage: " Armenians, united to your brethren under the sceptre of the Tsar you will know finally the blessings of freedom and justice.'

[23] RODZIANKO, *Byloye,* 1914-1917, p. 221: states that the Tsar's attitude to the Manifesto of the Grand Duke was later critical. He said: " We made a hasty step " (my potoropilis). Cf. ASKENAZY, *Uwagi,* p. 429.

[24] A collection of the articles which appeared in the French dailies and magazines was published in a leaflet, " Affaires de Pologne. La Proclamation du Généralissime Russe et l'Opinion Française," Paris, 1915. The influence of the Russian Embassy was particularly visible in the article of *Le Matin* which was in close relations with the financial adviser of the Embassy. We quote a passage from this article (6th August, 1914): " Pierre Stolypin, le regretté premier ministre de Russie, était passionément attaché à ce projet de réconciliation polonaise. Mr. Goremykin, son successeur, bien qu'appartenant au parti conservateur, s'était à son tour attaché avec zèle et conviction au grandiose projet impérial. . . . Dans un rapport verbal qu'il addressait au Tsar, le 30 janvier dernier en présence de l'ambassadeur de France, qui était alors M. Delcassé, le Général Skalon, gouverneur de Varsovie, disait: Il y a deux politiques vis-à-vis des gouvernements de Vistule: La politique du Gouvernement allemand dont le but est d'anéantir la nation polonaise, et la politique russe de réconciliation et d'autonomie inaugurée en 1904." It is well known that both Stolypin and Skallon pursued a policy of ruthless denationalization in Polish territories held by Russia and that General Skallon was surprised by the Manifesto of the Grand Duke.

[25] PALÉOLOGUE, *La Russie des Tsars,* I, pp. 78-9 and also 82: " Quand Sazonov me raconte ces détails, je lui cite une parole que le père Gutry prononçait vers 1863: depuis le partage de la Pologne l'Europe est en état de péché mortel."

[26] *Centr.-Arkhiv, Russko-Polskiye Otnosheniya v period Mirovoi Voyny,* p. 141.

[27] FILASIEWICZ, Doc. No. 6. The speech of Lieutenant-General Count Bobrinsky, in reply to the speech of the First Deputy Mayor of the City of Lwow: " Eastern Galicia and the area inhabited by Lemkis have constituted since immemorial times(?) an integrant part of Russia. The native population of these territories was always genuinely Russian ; consequently, their organization should rest on the Russian foundations. I will introduce here the Russian language and Russian administration."

If one takes into consideration that the first steps of the Russian occupying authorities were directed against the Greek-Catholic Church in Galicia, the following outpourings of one of the most

eminent Catholic prelates in France might seem rather surprising:
Alfred Baudrillard, Recteur de l'Université Catholique de Paris, *Revue
Pratique d'Apologétique*: " Que les Polonais de Galicie fassent donc foi
à la parole de l'Empereur, dont les intentions généreuses ne sauraient
pas être mises en doute."

28 LORD BERTIE, *Diary*, I, pp. 138, 154.

Gazette de Lausanne, 1st March, 1915: "La Russie ne serait-elle
pas capable de générosité qu'à l'égard des pays qui ne lui appartiennent pas? ... Il serait rassurant pour l'avenir que la guerre actuelle
entraînât la Russie dans l'orbite des grandes puissances civilisées d'Occident mais pour l'instant, il faut l'avouer la politique russe continue de
s'inspirer des méthodes prussiennes et austro-hongroises bien plus que
des principes anglais et français." (ALEXINSKY, *La Russie et la Guerre*,
pp. 326 ff.).

Maklakov, member of the opposition said at the Duma on 24th April,
1916: " The Government sent to Galicia the scum of bureaucracy and
the methods pursued there by the Russian authorities became an
European scandal. It is not so important that it occurred but that it
could not be otherwise."

29 PALÉOLOGUE, *La Russie des Tsars*, I, p. 198.

30 *Ibidem*, I, p. 198.

31 FRIEDRICH STIEVE, *Izvolsky and the World War*, p. 248 ; Telegram
from Izvolsky to Sazonov, Bordeaux, 30th September–13 October,
1914 ; No. 498: " It seems to me therefore most desirable to acquaint
the Paris and London Cabinets with our view on this question in good
time and with unmistakable clearness. I am letting no opportunity
pass, though speaking for myself only, to point out emphatically here
that it is necessary to make an end of the Hapsburg Monarchy, which
is an entire anachronism, and to summon the various nationalities
which make up the Monarchy, *with the exception of Poles,* to an
independent political existence."

MASARYK, *The Making of a State*, p. 145 ; account of a conversation
with General Alexeyev, Chief of the Imperial General Staff: " At the
beginning of the war he had imagined that Austria-Hungary could be
divided into states serviceable to Russia. Czechs were to extend to
Trieste and Fiume in the Adriatic and thus to take over a large part of
German Austria, including Vienna. ... Serbia was to extend northwards to the Russian frontier as far as Uzhorod. Since the Tsar had
promised to help Serbia, her northern frontier must march with that
of Russia! "

In a leaflet published by the liberal leader Milyukov in 1915: "What
does Russia expect from the War? " we find the following eight Russian
claims: (1) Eastern Galicia and Carpathian Ruthenia ; (2) Western
Galicia and Poznan ; (3) Northern part of Eastern Prussia with Königsberg ; (4) Bosphorus and Dardanelles ; (5) Adrianopol ; (6) Littoral of
Marmara Sea ; (7) Trans-Caucasian territories ; (8) Turkish Armenia.

32 *Russko-Polskiye Otnosheniya*, p. 19.

33 COMMANDANT M. H. WEIL, *Les Dessous du Congrès de Vienne*

d'après les documents originaux des archives du Ministère Impérial et Royal de l'Intérieur à Vienne, Paris, 1917, p. 483: " Les généraux-lieutenants russes, comte Orurk et Zvielinov, qui sont très considérés dans l'armée, que l'empereur à couverts d'honneurs et qui exercent une certaine influence sur l'esprit de l'armée et de la noblesse, sont tellement hostiles au rétablissement de ce Royaume (de Pologne) qu'ils n'ont pas craint de dire que l'Empereur n'a pas le droit aux termes de la Constitution du pays, de détacher de l'Empire une province qui lui a été annéxée. De plus ces Messieurs pensent que la portion dont s'augmentera le duché de Varsovie, est trop petite pour qu'on puisse faire de la Pologne un royaume et que, sans les provinces prussiennes et la Galicie Orientale autrichienne, les Polonais ne seront jamais contents. Le comte Orurk déclare et fait remarquer entre autres que l'intérêt de la Russie lui commande de satisfaire l'Autriche et la Prusse du côté de la Pologne, de renoncer en leur faveur aux deux nouveaux cercles de la Galicie Orientale sur le Dniester et de ne pas songer à des agrandissements de ce côté. La Russie ferait mieux de songer à l'Eglise Grecque et d'accord avec l'Autriche de former jusqu'aux Balkans un seul tout des peuples de la Moldavie, de la Valachie et de la Bulgarie et de placer à la tête de ce nouveau groupement un prince russe qui deviendrait leur roi."

[34] SUMNER, *Survey of Russian History,* p. 215: " But the Constitution was not adhered to by the Russians. They felt—and they were right —that the ' Polish Kingdom ' would be a stepping-stone to the incorporation in it of the ' Western lands.' The Poles had fought for that in 1794 and 1812, and they were to fight for it again in 1830 and 1863."

[35] SIR GEORGE BUCHANAN, *My Mission to Russia,* Vol. II, p. 26.

[36] *Documents Secrets Russes,* (ed. Polonsky), pp. 262-3. See also *Parliamentary Papers,* Cmd. 2169, 1927, Appendix No. 4.

[37] *Russko-Polskiye Otnosheniya,* pp. 85 ff.

[38] Article I, para. 2, of the Treaty of Vienna, 9th June, 1815: " Les Polonais, sujets respectifs de la Russie, de l'Autriche et de la Prusse obtiendront une représentation et des institutions nationales reglées d'après le mode d'existence politique que chacun des governements auxquels ils appartiennent jugera utile et convenable de leur accorder."

It was on this basis, although slender and inadequate, that the Western Powers intervened in the Polish question, on the occasion of the Polish Insurrection in 1863.

[39] Already in March 1915, that is four months before the retreat of the Russian armies from Poland, a considerable group of old conservatists in Moscow headed by Samarin, Prince Obolensky, Prince Golitzin, Tikhomirov, etc., submitted to the Tsar a memorial in which they stated emphatically that the only way of carrying out the promises made by the Grand Duke would be the establishment of an independent Polish State under its own sovereign. They argued that these two nations, Polish and Russian, had nothing in common and were unable to live according to the principle of equal rights under the same monarch and that neither the autonomy of Poland nor even a personal union between

Poland and Russia might give guarantees of stable relations (Dmowski, *Polityka Polska,* pp. 448-9).

[40] SAZONOV, *Vospominaniya,* pp. 371-2.

[41] See the letter of the Tsarina to the Tsar, 4th September, 1916 (original in English): " Do not hurry with the Polish affairs, don't let others push you to do it until we get over frontier. I fully trust in our Friend's (Rasputin) wisdom endowed by the God to council what is right for you and our country " *Pis'ma Imp. Alexandry Fedorovny,* II, 398.

[42] GENERAL BASIL GOURKO, *Memoirs and Impressions of War and Revolution,* p. 203.

[43] *Ibidem,* p. 205.

[44] *Ibidem,* pp. 251-7.

[45] DMOWSKI, o.c., p. 117.

[46] The text of the memorial, Dmowski, o.c., pp. 432 ff.

[47] *Russko-Polskiye Otnosheniya,* p. 95.

[48] *Ibidem,* p. 100.

[49] At a meeting held at Lausanne between 7th and 12th February, 1916, the Polish political leaders, sympathizing with the Entente, stated their political programme in the following terms: " In the case of the defeat of Germany the decision on the fate of Poland would depend not only on Russia, one of the partitioning Powers, but also on England, France and Italy whose interests do not require the subjugation of Poland but on the contrary the reconstitution of an independent and strong Poland " (SEYDA, *Polska na Przelomie,* I, p. 301).

Ibidem, pp. 290-1: " If the pro-Allied circles based their political plans, from the beginning of the war, on the hopes that after the defeat of Germany and her associates, it would be not only Russia but also France and England that would have their say in the settlement of the Polish question, with the course of events, they ever more and more were decided to play this card. The Russian military might was crumbling and the real Russian attitude truly revealed, and especially the Russian wish to reserve for herself the decisions on Poland's fate with the exclusion of the Western Powers."

[49a] The attitude of these French circles was most eloquently defined by George Clemenceau in his book *Grandeur and Misery of Victory,* p. 182: " Let us recall the partition of Poland, the greatest crime in history, which leaves an everlasting stigma on the names of Catherine, Maria-Theresa and Frederick II. No outrage had ever less excuse, no violence perpetrated against humanity ever cried louder for a redress that had been infinitely postponed. The wrong was so great that at no time in the life of Europe, among so many acts of violence for which there was no expiation, could it appear less heinous. It has become a byword in history as one of the worst felonies that can be laid to the charge of our ' civilization '."

[50] JEAN HERBETTE, *L'Echo de Paris,* 16th August, 1914: " Un diplomate français qui joue un rôle fort élévé et fort actif dans la crise actuelle, me disait l'an dernier, quand personne ne pensait aux affaires

polonaises: 'La paix de l'Europe repose sur une tombe mal fermée, la tombe de la Pologne '."

⁵¹ GABRIEL HANOTAUX, *Le Figaro*, 16th July, 1914: " Mais j'entends aussi ceux de le lendemaïn, les historiens au regard profond, comme mon ami Albert Sorel, disant avec l'entêtement: 'Tout cela finira par la résurrection de la Pologne.' Napoléon disait à Sainte-Helène ; ' Le premier souverain qui, au milieu de la présente grande mêlée, embrassera de bonne foi, la cause des peuples, se trouvera à la tête de toute l'Europe et pourra tenter tout ce qu'il voudra '."

⁵² PALÉOLOGUE, o.c., II, p. 206.

⁵²a " La France pour la Pologne," *Enquête de la revue Polonia*, Paris, 1916.

⁵³ H. H. FISHER, o.c., p. 90.

⁵⁴ JACQUES BAINVILLE, *L'Action Française*, 21st September, 1917 (" La Russie et la Barrière de l'Est," pp. 31-2): " L'Alliance franco-russe s'était faite sur un malentendu ou au moins sur une équivoque. . . . La Russie a cherché à nous exciter contre l'Angleterre."

ANDRE CHÉRADAME, *L'Allemagne, la France et la Question d'Autriche*, p. 85: " Sous l'action du travail tendencieux des agences beaucoup de Français ne savent plus très bien si l'alliance avec le Tsar est dirigée vraiment contre l'Allemagne et si elle peut leur être utile contre l'Angleterre, fâcheux état d'esprit qui a permis dans certains milieux et surtout dans les organes parisiens de la presse internationale, de mettre la question de l'existence même de l'alliance."

⁵⁵ JACQUES BAINVILLE, *L'Action Française*, 8 juin, 1917, (o.c., p. 28): " Pour la France, la grande, le seule question, c'était le péril allemand, c'était la sécurité de sa frontière de l'Est. Ni la géographie, ni l'histoire ne montraient ce péril à la Russie. Sauf dans une très petite élite jamais la Russie n'a senti comme nous la menace allemande. . . . Où allaient donc les intérêts et les sentiments de la Russie? Non pas, comme les nôtres, directement contre l'Allemagne. Ils allaient en Orient, et c'est là que l'idée slave se heurtait au germanisme. . . . Les vrais objectifs de la guerre, pour la Russie, c'était Constantinople et les Balkans."

⁵⁶ Quoted by A. GORSKI in his book, *La Pologne et la Guerre*, p. 70. The same author remembers (p. 73) that in 1871 the principal paper of Gambetta, *La République Française,* wrote what follows: " Si la Russie ne peut à aucun prix se séparer de la Pologne, les Polonais de leur côté, doivent bien se persuader qu'ils n'ont rien à attendre de la France pour le rétablissement du Royaume de Pologne. Il est certain, en effet, que par suite des grands événements des ces dernières années, la politique française sera forcément amenée à identifier ses intérêts à ceux de la Russie, et que, par conséquent, elle ne saurait plus favoriser chez les Polonais des tendances d'autonomie particulariste, de nature à diviser au profit de l'Allemagne, la grande race slave."

⁵⁷ LORD BERTIE OF THAME, I, p. 217.

⁵⁸ PALÉOLOGUE, II, p. 206: " Déjeuner avec quelques Polonais. Plater expose que les Allies devraient prendre en main la question polonaise,

de façon à l'internationaliser. Je m'élève avec force contre cette idée. La prétention d'internationaliser la question polonaise provoquerait dans les milieux nationalistes de l'Empire un éclat d'indignation et paralyserait toutes les sympathies qui nous sont acquises dans les autres milieux. .... Mon action sera d'autant plus efficace qu'elle sera plus discrète, plus exempte de tout caractère officiel. .... toutes ces déclarations finissent par constituer une sorte d'engagement *moral* qui en, cas de besoin, permettrait au gouvernment française de parler avec une singulière autorité, quand viendra l'heure de la résolution définitive."

[59] PALÉOLOGUE, II, p. 77: "A ma connaissance, le Gouvernement Français n'a jamais patronné auprès du gouvernement russe autre chose que l'autonomie de la Pologne intégrale. Et, c'est à l'heure actuelle, la volonté de Sa Majesté Impériale."

[60] SEYDA, o.c., I, p. 551.

[61] PALÉOLOGUE, II, p. 260.

[62] *Ibidem*, II, p. 274.

[63] ALEXANDRE RIBOT, *Journal et Correspondances inédites*, p. 92. Albert Thomas, who after the outbreak of the revolution was sent to Petrograd on an official mission got to know the existence of these letters only through Milyukov, the new Russian Minister of Foreign Affairs. *Ibidem*, p. 100: " Le Président de la République me dit que les lettres échangées à Petrograde ne lui étaient pas communiquées."

The declaration of Balfour, Foreign Secretary, in the House of Commons, (19th December, 1917): " This arrangement was not endorsed by Great Britain."

[64] Izvolsky's account of his démarche at the Quai d'Orsay in a telegram to Pokrovsky, 31st January–13th February, 1917 (*Documents Diplomatiques Secrets*, p. 264): Conversation with Cambon: " Je lui ai rappelé que nous avons plus d'une fois déclaré au gouvernement français que nous considérions le statut futur de la Pologne comme une question intérieure de la Russie et que, laissant liberté complète à la France dans la question de l'Alsace et de Lorraine et dans sa future délimitation des frontières avec l'Allemagne nous comptions sur une liberté pareille dans notre délimitation future avec l'Allemagne et l'Autriche ; j'y ai ajouté qu' à présent il ne s'agissait que d'assurer formellement ce qui a été dejà dit et qu'il serait très regrettabledangereux même que cela aboutisse à un différend entre les alliés."

[65] ALEXANDRE RIBOT, *Lettres à un ami*, p. 225.

[66] RENOUVIN, o.c., p. 385. The author states also: " C'est assez dire que la voix de la Pologne ne pourra se faire entendre à la future conférence de la paix."

[67] SAZONOV, o.c., p. 385.

[68] LORD BERTIE OF THAME, II, p. 107. Lord Bertie was among the few British diplomats who from the beginning of the war understood the importance of the Polish question to the allied cause. *Ibidem*, Vol. 1, p. 60: " At the beginning of the war I told Sevastopoulo (Counsellor of the Russian Embassy) that it would be wise for Russia to go in for an independent Poland as a Catholic Slav buffer State between Russia

and Germany and to give to Rumania, as the dot for her alliance, Bessarabia as possessed by her, by the Treaty of 1856; he said that it would be impossible."

[69] HOUSE, *Intimate Papers,* II, p. 181.

[70] E. C. BLANCHE DUGDALE, *Arthur James Balfour,* Vol. II, pp. 436 ff. The famous Polish statesman J. I. Paderewski was completely mistaken in believing in Balfour's declarations that he supported the cause of Poland's independence in the early stages of the war. Paderewski was very much under the influence of Balfour's great intellectual charm and it may explain his confidence in Balfour's utterances. See LANDAU, *Paderewski,* p. 250, a report of a conversation between Landau and Paderewski at the residence of the latter at Rion Bosson, near Morges, Switzerland: "The man for whom I had a very special admiration was Arthur Balfour, and I feel very proud that he should have honoured me with his friendship. He was one of the purest characters I have ever known; one of the most cultured and the most exquisitely mannered men of his time. His knowledge was deep and filled you with real delight. It is very rare to find a mixture of such great refinement, such wonderful education and culture, and at the same time such real simplicity and kindness of heart. If ever there was a gentleman, it was Balfour; and if ever there was a true friend it was he." *Ibidem,* p. 260: "In 1915, when I visited London, Balfour had told me that Poland would be recreated." This statement is repeated in Paderewski's *Memoirs,* p. 240.

[70a] The prominent Czech statesman, Masaryk, in his memorandum on the military situation, circulated in April 1916, in London (SETON WATSON, *Masaryk in England,* p. 196) contests these fallacious deductions: "But it is safe to assume that Germany's pressure on the West will be all the stronger, if she has a huge economic Hinterland easily accessible on her Eastern frontier.

Hence to contend that by liberating Central Europe the Allies would cut off Germany from the East, and thus force her to press the harder against the West, is an argument much more apparent than real. On the contrary, Germany cut off from the East, and no longer having Austria-Hungary and the Balkans at her disposal, would be forced to rely upon her own forces, and would cease to be a danger to the West."

[71] HOUSE, *Intimate Papers,* Vol. III, p. 48.

[72] House's letter to President Wilson (22nd August, 1914): "If the Allies win, it means largely the domination of Russia on the continent of Europe; and if Germany wins, it means the unspeakable tyranny of militarism for generations to come" (HOUSE, *Intimate Papers,* Vol. I, pp. 284-5).

President Wilson's reply (25th August, 1914): "It expresses in a way that was somewhat poignant to my feelings about the possible alternative outcome of the war" (R. S. BAKER, *Woodrow Wilson, Life and Letters,* Vol. V, p. 65.

[73] TEMPERLEY, o.c., Vol. I, p. 185.

[74] *Russko-Polskiye Otnosheniya,* (preface by M. G. Valetsky).

CHAPTER III

SECOND PHASE OF THE WAR : THE UNSUCCESSFUL
ATTEMPTS OF CENTRAL POWERS TO SOLVE THE
POLISH QUESTION WITHIN A FRAMEWORK OF GERMAN-
CONTROLLED "MITTEL EUROPA" [1]

"Without our intention the Polish Problem appeared as the first
consequence of the war."—(Burian, *Drei Jahre aus der Zeit meiner
Amtsführung im Kriege*, p. 71.)

"It was not our or Austria-Hungary's intention to reopen the
Polish question. It was the fate of the battles that reopened it. It
is now on the carpet and awaits a solution. Germany and Austria
must and will solve it."—(Speech of Chancellor Bethmann-Hollweg
in the Reichstag, 5th April, 1916.)

"If we accept anything less than a complete solution of the
Eastern question in its larger sense we shall merely have gained
a respite and our descendants will find themselves under the necessity of marshalling their power afresh for the siege of Heartland."
—H. J. Mackinder, *Democratic Ideals and Reality*, p. 200.)

"The condition of stability in the territorial rearrangement of
East Europe is that the division should be into three and not into
two State-systems. It is a vital necessity that there should be a tier
of independent States between Germany and Russia."—(H. J.
Mackinder, *Ibidem*, p. 205.)

ONLY late in the course of the war, under the impact of events, did
the Western countries begin to realize that the Polish question was a
"living issue" in Eastern Europe, and became aware of the dangers
which might arise from the initiatives and schemes brought forward
on this matter by their enemies. Nevertheless they were very slow
in drawing the proper, practical conclusions, and for some time let
themselves be outdistanced by the Central Powers through fear of
reactions from Russia.

The American Ambassador to Germany at the beginning of the
war, James W. Gerard, although sharing the prejudices against the
Polish past spread by German historians ("The Polish aristocracy
was absolutely incapable of governing its own country which fell an
easy prey to the intrigues of Frederick the Great and the two
Empresses, Maria Theresa of Austria and Catherine of Russia"),[2]
nevertheless notes with amazement in his diary :

"It is a long time since portions of the Kingdom of Poland by

74

various partitions of that Kingdom were incorporated with Prussia, but the Polish question is more alive to-day than at the time of the last partition. The Poles aré of livelier race than the Germans, are Roman Catholic and always retain their dream of a reconstituted and independent Kingdom of Poland. ... Although not so well advertised (as Alsace-Lorraine) the Polish question is as acute as that of Alsace-Lorraine."

Consequences for Germany of the Partitions of Poland

There is perhaps no issue on which German statesmanship has so much failed as in the unsuccessful attempts to solve the Polish question during the war. We can give here only a general survey of these attempts, but I venture to hope that we shall be able to dispose of some unwarranted opinions due to insufficient knowledge of historic sources or to uncritical acceptance of biased accounts. Among such opinions is the assertion referred to in Chapter II (see p. 41) that it was the Polish question which stood in the way of Russo-German reconciliation and prevented the conclusion of a separate peace, a favourite argument also of many German politicians after the First World War. As a matter of fact it was just the opposite which was true. The Polish question arose from the impossibility of maintaining Russo-German relations on the previous basis, the agreement on Poland's subjugation becoming an insufficient link between two Empires pursuing antagonistic aims of expansion. So, rather late but inevitably, the partitions of Poland brought upon the three partitioning powers these dangers which had been sensed even by the arch-enemies of Poland, Frederick II and Bismarck, in moments of lucidity. Professor Lord, author of a remarkable study on the history of Poland at the end of the eighteenth century, describes thus the consequences for Prussia of the II and III partitions of Poland :

" It was also a Prussian interest of equal (to territorial acquisitions) and perhaps even greater importance, that the Republic (of Poland) should be preserved as an effective ' buffer State,' as a real barrier against the great aggressive military Empire in the east. We venture to think that a revived Poland—consolidated and re-invigorated under the Constitution of the Third of May—could never have proved so serious a danger to Prussia as the advance of Russia into the heart of Central Europe to within striking distance of Berlin. At all events, it behoved Prussia to weigh very carefully the advantage of every acquisition in Poland against the perils involved in the aggrandizement of Russia and the necessity of maintaining the existence of the Republic. Frederick the Great appears to have realized this and so did Hertzberg. Whatever charges may be brought against the latter, it must be said in his favour that he planned to make the needed acquisitions on the east with the minimum of loss to the Republic and then to assure the permanent integrity of Poland's remaining possessions. ... In short, while Prussia obtained by the Second Partition the largest acquisitions of territory that she had made down to that time, we think that this was nevertheless one of the most short-sighted, disastrous and morally reprehensible transactions in her history." [3]

Bismarck and Poland

To liberal Germans prior to 1848 the restoration of Poland was one of the principal items of their political programme. To them Russia was a symbol of despotism and barbarism. The reconstitution of Poland appeared to them the logical consequence of the progress of democracy, agreeing with their inmost convictions according to which each nation had the right to be free; moreover, according to their opinions Poland had rendered particular services to humanity as an advanced post of Western civilization. [4] It was Bismarck who, opposing these liberal trends in German political life, established his whole policy on close co-operation with Russian despotism, denying the Poles the right to their own nationhood. But after the Congress of Berlin (1878) and the reappearance of Pan-Slavic trends in the Russian policy, even Bismarck began sometimes to take a longer view on the Polish question. A distinguished Polish historian, J. Feldman, on the eve of the Second World War published a book entitled *Bismarck and Poland* (in Polish—reprinted after the war, in 1945) which threw full light on some plans which had been devised by Bismarck in different epochs of his rule (1882, 1883, 1885, 1887, 1888). Feldman's book is based almost exclusively on German sources and especially on the accounts of persons who had been in constant and direct touch with the Iron Chancellor, such as General Waldersee, then Quartermaster General (*Denkwürdigkeiten*), Lucius von Ballhausen, Minister of Agriculture (*Bismarck, Erinnerungen*), French Ambassador Courcel (*Documents Diplomatiques Français,* ser. I, Vol. I) and others. Some of Bismarck's statements are quite prophetic, as for instance those made to Courcel in 1883 (December) :

> " We shall try to create within the limits of old Poland something which will be able to hold, to defend us, to protect us. We shall certainly not go beyond Smolensk. As a matter of fact, a plan of the reconstitution of the Polish Kingdom under an Austrian archduke is an old plan of Austrian policy. So far as we are concerned, we have no special liking for Poland but if we have to have a rather unpleasant neighbour on our frontier we prefer, of course, a weak to a strong one. A reconstituted Poland will be, in such conditions, less menacing to us than a hostile Russia keeping her present position."

On another occasion Bismarck declared that " it would be better to create Poland between us and Russia than see the Russians in Berlin." "Poland is a weapon which we shall seize against our wishes because we have nothing better available. It is like a hot iron which we shall use to defend ourselves." [5]

Also Bethmann-Hollweg recalls in his *Memoirs* a letter written by Bismarck to Prince Chlodvig Hohenlohe in 1883, in which Bismarck stated that a war with Russia would be a great calamity " because we have nothing to win, not even the war-costs. War would also lead inevitably to the reconstitution of Poland as far as the Dvina (Western) and the Dnieper." [6] It is true that Bismarck thought also that this might be a temporary arrangement, as twenty years later Germany and Russia would again join hands in order to destroy Poland, an argument used by another Chancellor of the Reich, Prince Bülow, against the reopening of the Polish question, [7] but the experiences of 1939-1941 seem to refute these assumptions, as renewed Russo-German " good-neighbour's " policy was short-lived.

German Colonialism in Central Eastern Europe

If we do not take into account a relatively short period at the beginning of the reign of Wilhelm II, we can state that Bismarck's successors preferred to take as patterns the ruthless methods of his anti-Polish policy serving to cement and foster friendship with Russia. Thus Germany entered the war not only without any Polish asset in her hands but with heavy encumbrances arising from the policy pursued by the Prussian Government in the former Polish provinces of Prussia. It suffices to read the outbursts of Prince Bülow in his book *Die Deutsche Politik* to have a general idea of this hatred towards everything Polish, so typical of many of his compatriots, and of the impossibility of reconciling the Polish national idea with this traditional Prussian " colonialism." [8] Taking at their face value the distorted views on Poland's past which the German professors after 1848 impressed on the minds of two German generations, the politicians of Bülow's brand completely lost their bearings once the war with Russia started. They saw the only solution in coming to terms with Russia as soon as possible and making a separate peace with her. This solution, by the way, would have been much preferred by the overwhelming majority of Germans, and if it did not materialize before the outbreak of revolution in Russia it was for reasons which were beyond their control.

There is no doubt that one of the main reasons for German reluctance to reopen the Polish question was the failure of the Prussian policy in its endeavours to denationalize and deprive of land the Poles within the Prussian provinces formerly belonging to Poland, in spite of the most drastic measures which had aroused the indignation of the whole civilized world before the First World War. There was certainly some lack of consistency between disparaging Poland's past and extolling the stubbornness with which the native Polish population defended their nationhood in the provinces of Poznan, West Prussia and Silesia. Even Prince Bülow, who cannot be suspected of tender feelings for the Poles, states in his book that " the energy which the Poles display in the defence against German attacks on their land deserves admiration." [9] and in another part of his book he observes that

> " We must have respect and, as we highly value our own nationhood, also compassion for the faithfulness of the Poles to their national traditions. But this respect and compassion end whenever there appears a tendency to disrupt the unity and cohesion of the Prussian monarchy. All regard for the Polish nationhood must not stop us from taking great care to maintain and strengthen the Germanic elements in the former Polish territories." [9a]

It would go beyond the scope of this book to deal at length with the German efforts to Germanize and colonize with German settlers the former Polish provinces attached to Prussia. Let us refer here to the conclusions of a book written by a notorious enemy of the Poles, Ludwig Bernhard, who studied this problem very carefully : " Only in fifteen districts of the provinces of Poznan and West Prussia have the Germans increased their possessions between 1896 and 1914. In forty-nine districts the Germans were pushed back in spite of all the efforts of the Prussian Government and the extraordinary legislation imposing discriminatory measures." [10]   This vitality of the Polish element was certainly a matter of great worry to those who used to speak of the cultural mission of the German nation in the East, as it deprived them of the argument of the spontaneity of the German " Drang nach Osten." No wonder that many Germans warned against any further acquisition of territories settled by Poles. A well-known military figure and mouthpiece of the German General Staff at the Brest-Litovsk Peace negotiations, General Hoffman, in January 1918 declared to the Kaiser : " I am against any solution of the Polish problem which might increase the number of citizens of Polish descent in Germany. In spite of all the measures taken by the Prussians for some dozens of years, they were unable to stamp out those Poles whom we now have, and I see no advantage in increasing the number of Polish citizens." [11] One of the members of the staff of the Governor-General of occupied Poland, Major Ferdinand Hugo Simon, takes a similar view in a confidential memorandum submitted to General Beseler in November 1915 : " No one can foretell the development of the Polish

question—the Slav tide comes back—with whom the Poles will side
nobody can say. The Germans are already saturated with Slav
blood. We need strong defensive frontiers." [12]

The foregoing remarks should give a better understanding of the
hesitations of German policy and the difficulty for the Germans in
finding the right way between the needs of security on her Eastern
frontier and the secular traditions of Prussian colonialism. What
complicated the task of German policy still more was the fact that
not one of Bismarck's successors was a man of vision and of statesmanlike stature. Moreover, during the war power slipped from the
weak hands of the subsequent chancellors and passed to the narrow-
minded war lords,[13] mostly of Prussian origin and imbued with a
strong anti-Polish bias.[14] It was only natural that in these circumstances the German policy towards Poland was forced upon her by
the trend of events and did not rest on any clear programme. A German historian who devoted a well-documented book to German
policy towards Poland during the First World War criticizes it thus :

> " Instead of proceeding with a clear purpose, the German policy
> let itself be driven by events and one can state that each step for-
> ward which has been taken by it came too late, although half a
> year or one year earlier it might have had some prospects of
> success. This policy created not only a chain of missed opportuni-
> ties but made a pitiful and discrediting impression that the con-
> cessions granted from time to time by the Germans were dictated
> by pure opportunism." [15]

German Aims at the Beginning of the War

It is beyond any doubt that at the beginning of the war the Germans had no clear ideas about their future relations with Russia
and, consequently, had no definite plans for the solution of the
Polish question, although some revival of Bismarck's previous plans
could be seen in the conversation which took place on the 31st July,
1914, between the Emperor and Count Hutten-Czapski, a man who
was rather isolated from his compatriots owing to his Prussian
loyalism. The Emperor declared to Czapski : " It is my firm
decision, if God grants victory to our arms, to restore an independent Polish State bound by an alliance with Germany, and to secure
ourselves for ever in this way against Russia." Bethmann-Hollweg,
Chancellor of the Reich, confirmed the words of his sovereign by
saying that he covered them with his constitutional responsibility.[16]
But this was only one of the variants of the German policy, carried
out two years later. At that time nobody expected that the war
would last so long. The German military plans consisted in first
crushing French military power within six weeks and then throwing
the bulk of their army against Russia in order to impose on her their

terms of peace.[17] For this reason only purely military considerations counted in this first stage of the war. With the outbreak of war the Germans awaited a general rising of the Poles at the Russian rear,[18] and were rather disappointed that the Poles in the Congress Kingdom were unwilling to consider them as their liberators. But on the other hand nothing similar to the Proclamation of the Grand Duke Nicholas to the Poles was issued by the Central Powers, although the German and Austro-Hungarian troops circulated proclamations in which the word "independence" appeared in two places. For two long years Germany hesitated to take any definite step on the Polish question, hoping to come to some arrangement with Russia approximately on the basis of the *status quo* with some substantial corrections of frontiers, allegedly for strategic reasons. But even when the German Government decided to take steps, a legitimate doubt might arise whether such steps were not meant as a means of pressure on Russia in order to induce her to accept an arrangement. We know definitely that after the initial Austrian defeats the Austro-Hungarians and many Germans were ready to make a separate peace with Russia on the basis of the *status quo* or the exchange of a part of Galicia against the southern part of Congress-Kingdom for the benefit of the Austrians, and the Narew line in the north for the benefit of the Germans.[19] The impossibility of reaching a decision on the Western front after the battle of the Marne upset the German military plans and Bethmann-Hollweg advised the limitation of the war aims in the East. It depended then only on the Russians accepting these suggestions, but they were unwilling to accept these terms, being bent on the dismemberment of Austria-Hungary.

The question of the responsibility for the failure of the further attempts before the fall of Tsardom was, after the war, often laid by the pro-Russian wing in Germany entirely on Bethmann-Hollweg and German military leaders, Ludendorff in the first place. The whole matter was deliberately obscured on both sides, but on the strength of the evidence in our possession we are unable to follow those writers who accept at their face value some partisan statements—those of Tirpitz, Helfferich, and Erzberger in the first place. In particular we cannot accept the unwarranted opinion that it was the Polish question and the Proclamation of the 5th November which was the chief obstacle to Russo-German reconciliation, an accusation often brought forward by German politicians, Prince Bülow among others, who in a letter to Stresemann dated 26th December, 1925, stated : "When Nicholas II put Stürmer at the helm in 1916, we could have had an understanding with Russia on the basis of the *status quo ante bellum,* if we had not been lured into the marshes by the Polish will-o'-the-wisp." [20] In exactly the same terms writes a British author, Wheeler-Bennett, in his book *Brest-Litovsk* : " But diplomacy of the clumsiest was forthcoming. Led away by the *mirage* of a Polish army under German officers contributing a much needed addition to the manpower of the Central Powers, the Supreme Command of the German army insisted upon the proclamation of a Kingdom of Poland under the joint protection of the German and Austrian Emperors." [21] On the same note writes P. Frank Chambers, *The War Behind the War*, 1914–1918 : " We have some reasons to believe that such a separate peace in the autumn of 1916 had become a matter of practical politics, but whatever prospects it had instantly vanished on the 5th November." [22] On the other side we have no reason to question the assertions of Bethmann-Hollweg in his *Reflections on the World War* : " Until the early months of 1917 the Czar declined angrily all hints for a separate peace, although he knew perfectly well that Germany would not allow the peace to fail on account of the Polish or Baltic question or that of the freedom of passage through the Straits." [23] And on his side Ludendorff states : " Naturally, also to myself a peace with Russia would have been much more agreeable than the whole Polish army as my attitude towards a Kingdom of Poland was negative considering that I was born in the Province of Poznan." [24]

The danger of an arrangement between the Germans and the Russians at the expense of Poland was acutely felt by Pilsudski, even after the November Manifesto, as appears clearly from his confessions to one of his followers on the 3rd March, 1917 :

> " We have with the Entente even at this stage of the war a common interest and a common programme in relation to Germany and Russia. It is as a matter of fact an interest of the highest importance, namely not to let these two States come to terms at the expense of Poland and the Entente. So long as the Germans raise the problem of independent Poland there cannot be an agreement with Russia, but as soon as they abandon this programme or cease to treat it as a serious issue the separation of Russia from the Entente will become probable. It is not excluded that it will be the Polish question that may serve as blackmail, and therefore I insist so much on a *fait accompli* (that is the formation of the Polish army), as after such *fait accompli* there will be no way of return for Germany." [25]

But it is by following the wavering course of the German policy on the Polish question until the outbreak of the Bolshevik revolution that we can find the most valid arguments for the conclusion that so long as there was a possibility of a separate peace with Russia, Germany was unwilling to play the Polish card, although she was well aware that leaving this problem unsolved might involve for her great trouble in the future. So in 1915, when as we know there were serious prospects of a separate peace with Russia and the Western Powers tried to obviate this danger by making important concessions to their Ally on the question of Constantinople and the Straits, it was a question of frontier corrections that was uppermost in German minds, as appears from numerous memoranda submitted to the Chancellor by the Governor General of Occupied Poland, Beseler, and by other military and political advisers of the German Government.[26] It was only after the failure of these attempts that Bethmann-Hollweg for the first time raised the Polish question in the Reichstag on the 19th August, 1915, in rather vague terms sounding more like a warning to Russia than a definite pledge to the Poles :

> " Geographical and political fate has for centuries forced the Poles and the Germans to fight each other. The memory of these old discords does not diminish the respect for the passion, patriotism and stubbornness with which the Polish people defends its old Western civilization and its love of freedom against Russia, and maintains it amid the calamities of this war. I will not imitate the hypocrite promises made by our enemies, but I hope that the present occupation of the Polish frontiers protecting them from the East will enable a development which will put an end to the old antagonisms between the Germans and the Poles and that that country, liberated from the Russian yoke, will be led to a better future that may secure for it the fostering and development of its national character." [27]

In his second speech at the end of the same year (9th December, 1915) Bethmann-Hollweg confined himself to a sarcastic allusion to Bonar Law's reply to Mr. Trevelyan in the House of Commons on 15th November, 1915. (" Is there any member of this House who believes for a moment that Germany will restore Alsace to France, or will restore Poland to the nationality to which she belongs, unless she is beaten."), and asked whether it meant that Poland belonged to Russia in accordance with nationality. But he did not take any further step on the Polish question and only alluded to the necessity for proceeding with territorial rearrangements in the East and West, closing the gates to future aggression against Germany.[28]

On the 2nd May, 1915, started the great offensive of the Central Powers against Russia by breaking through at Gorlice (West Galicia) ; it lasted until the end of September, with considerable territorial gains but also very heavy sacrifices in men and materials and with no definite result. We know that the aim of this offensive was to force Russia to accept peace offers in order to enable the release of German forces engaged in the East, badly needed for the decisive struggle in the West.[29] There were many attempts by the German side to convince the Russians of the necessity of putting an end to the war between two Great Powers with such a long record of close friendship. The Polish question was often referred to in these conversations as one of the most important issues on which both Russia and Germany should be united, and it also served as a means of pressure as it was argued that the establishment of an independent Polish State would be an inescapable solution in the event of the failure of these attempts. There is no doubt that there were many partisans of Russo-German reconciliation on both sides, but the initiative belonged mainly to the Germans. Thus, for instance, writes Princess Vassilchikova to Emperor Nicholas II on the 27th May, 1915 :

> " There is no inclination here (in Germany) to establish a new Kingdom of Poland as it would constitute a source of discords and such a State would be bound to perish, having no outlet to the sea, considering that neither Germany nor Russia would be disposed to sacrifice to Poland one of their ports on the North Sea " [sic!].[30]

Mr. Nekludov, the Russian envoy in Stockholm, reported to Mr. Sazonov on the 28th July, 1915, that according to information brought to Sweden by Mr. Monkevitz, director of the Deutsche Bank :

> " There are, it seems, two parties in Germany wanting a separate peace, one advocating concessions for the benefit of England, another for the benefit of Russia. . . . The English party wants to push Russia back as far as possible to the East, Poland, Lithuania and the Baltic Provinces being established as Border States. The German Ministry does not share this point of view, being long accustomed to seeing Russia and Germany supporting each other . . . only some rectification of the frontier in Poland (that is Congress Poland) would be needed." [31]

But at the same time negotiations were going on beween Baron von Burian, Austro-Hungarian Foreign Minister, and Bethmann-Hollweg. The Polish question was beginning to be one of the crucial issues in the mutual relations between two allied powers.[32] At the meeting of the 13th August, 1915, the Chancellor of the Reich gave his consent to the union of Poland with Austria-Hungary under some conditions—giving guarantees (change of the electoral law) that the Austrian Germans would not lose their predominant position in the Austrian parliament after the attachment of Galicia to the new Polish State; sixty-nine frontier corrections; economic advantages for Germany in the new Polish State; military convention.[33] This proposal was cold-shouldered by the Austro-Hungarian Government for reasons with which we shall deal in the second part of this chapter. A few months later these concessions were withdrawn by Germany, and at the next meeting on the 14th–15th April, 1916, with Baron von Burian, Bethmann-Hollweg informed him that Germany wanted to create a Polish State depending more on Germany.[34] A few days before, on the 5th April, 1916, Beth-mann-Hollweg had made a momentous speech in the Reichstag announcing the impending decisions on the Polish question. Among other things he said :

"We stood up to defend ourselves. But what had existed is no more. History marched forward with its iron steps ; there is no way back. It was not our or Austria-Hungary's intention to reopen the Polish question—it was the fate of the battles which has reopened it. It is now on the carpet and awaits a solution. Germany and Austria-Hungary must and will solve it. History does not know the *status quo* after such tremendous events. . . .

"In his peace terms Mr. Asquith speaks of the principle of nationality. If he admits it and would put himself in the position of the unvanquished and invincible adversary, how can he admit that Germany might voluntarily deliver the peoples liberated by herself and her comrades-in-arms between the Baltic Sea and the Volhynian marshes to the régime of reactionary Russia, be they Poles, Lithuanians, Balts or Latvians. No, gentlemen, Russia must not for the second time advance her armies to the undefended frontier of East and West Prussia, neither should she once again establish a gate for invasion against undefended Germany on the Vistula with French money." [35]

On the 13th June the German Emperor again called Count Hutten-Czapski and gave him full details of the establishment of a Polish buffer State dependent on Germany, adding that Austria would have been incapable of organizing Poland.[36]

On the 11th–12th August, 1916, an agreement was signed in Vienna between Bethmann-Hollweg and Baron von Burian on the constitu-tion of the Polish State. The main provisions of his agreement were :

"Poland cannot pursue a foreign policy of her own. The limita-tions of Poland's right to diplomatic representations can be left for further consideration. Poland can only be allowed to conclude treaties with other States in so far as the contents of those treaties are not in conflict with the limitations imposed by the agreement between the two Central Powers. For that reason such treaties must be laid down before the two powers. A military convention shall assure to Germany the control and supreme command of the Polish forces. Polish railways should be turned into a limited company. The shares would be divided between the two Central Powers according to the quota of the war indemnity. The two Central Powers would mutually guarantee by special treaty that no part of their former possessions should be surrendered to the State of Poland."

Burian expressed the view that the portions of the former Grand-Duchy of Lithuania with a predominantly Polish population, in particular the city of Wilno, should form part of the Polish State. The German Imperial Chancellor agreed in principle with that view. Both parties reserved to themselves important frontier corrections, Germany in particular the cession of the Government of Suwalki, allegedly indispensable for Germany as a " safety-lock " (Riegel) in the North. Moreover the new State should remain in customs-union with Germany. It clearly appears from these provisions, which were not disclosed until after the war, that the liberation of Poland, or rather of a part of former Russian Poland, actually meant a kind of protectorate and that there was a great discrepancy between the high-sounding words of the Chancellor in the Reichstag and the reality.[37]

But a legitimate doubt can arise as to whether even this limited scheme, which granted no immediate rights to the Poles and had to be followed up by a Proclamation by two Emperors, was not for the time being more than a means of pressure on Russia. In fact the scheme was immediately pigeon-holed in view of various confidential talks with some Russians, carried on more actively especially after the fall of Sazonov on the 20th July, 1916.

The hesitations of Bethmann-Hollweg appear clearly from his correspondence with Hindenburg (telegram to Hindenburg of the 4th October and letter of the 10th October).[38] Delbrück, who knew well many secret German official papers, asserts : " Bethmann wished first to exhaust all chances of peace with Russia." [39] General von Seeckt, an extremely well-informed high-ranking officer (the future organizer of the Reichwehr under the Weimar Republic), who was definitely hostile to this Polish scheme and comforted himself " that it was not for ever and future generations will also have their Polish troubles," notes as early as the 27th August : " For the time being the whole matter is again suspended because we do not wish to bar the way to an understanding with Russia." [40] General von Cramon, chief liaison officer of the German Army at the Austro-Hungarian headquarters, outlines in these terms the plans devised by the Germans at that time in relation to Eastern problems : " Our endeavours are going on in the East to win Russia for the Central Powers. If this plan succeeds Poland would be squeezed into such a powerful region that she would be unable to play the rôle of mischief-maker. It is simply out of the question that he three allied powers, Germany, Austria-Hungary and Russia, could be induced to risk their unity on account of Poland. Should these plans with Russia fail, then it will be possible to keep Poland after her frontiers have been corrected in accordance with the requirements of the Central Powers," and he concludes angrily that unfortunately " it was Poland who was tertius gaudens." [41]

Chelius, one of the intimates of the Kaiser, wrote to Hutten-Czapski on the 16th October, 1916 :

> " The Kaiser takes the view that whatever may be the solution of the Polish question it will always be wrong, because this question cannot be solved, and one has only to choose a ' modus ' which may be least bad. . . . Partition would be by far the best. The other solution is a political monster. . . . I believe that Russia will soon make peace as she has nothing to win and the third war winter would be hard for the country." [42]

Admiral von Tirpitz exclaims in his *Memoirs* : " Never have we had so much to offer to Russia as in 1916." [43]

The well-known conversations in Stockholm in the late summer 1916 between Mr. Protopov, who soon afterwards became Minister of the Interior in Stürmer's Cabinet, and Mr. Wartburg were one of the several attempts to make a separate peace with Russia. Neither the Polish question nor the question of Constantinople were real stumbling blocks in reaching an agreement. The indiscretions to which Erzberger alludes in his *Memoirs* as one of the main reasons for the failure were in fact intentional, aiming to impress the Russian ruling circles by the generosity of the German offers.[44] Sir George Buchanan, British Ambassador to Russia, was extremely alarmed by these offers and correctly reported in his despatch to Lord Grey that should Russia conclude a separate peace with Germany the latter would evacuate Poland (that is Congress-Kingdom) and raise no objections to the surrender of Constantinople to Russia.[45] We know that these indiscretions aroused great indignation among Russian liberals, backed by young officers who some months later started the revolution. This liberal and definitely pro-Western wing of Russian public opinion took the view that the Russian war aims for the dismemberment of Austria-Hungary and the establishment of zones of influence in South-Eastern Europe and the Near East could be materialized only in co-operation with the Allies. Moreover the Russians in general and the Tsar in particular mistrusted Germany and feared that a separate peace with her would be only a temporary solution, and once Germany had overcome the resistance of the West she would be able to withdraw her previous concessions and dictate her terms to Russia. As experience of attempts at a separate peace at the beginning of 1917 had shown it was a risky affair for the Tsarist régime to try to negotiate a separate peace, which according to the views of the Russian intelligentsia would not correspond to the enormous sacrifices made by Russia in the course of the war.

But even after the 5th November Proclamation of Poland's Independence the idea of an arrangement with Russia at Poland's expense was never abandoned by some German statesmen until the complete collapse of Russia. For instance, the so-called " minimum programme " laid down in the Vienna Memoire of the 27th March, 1917, at a meeting between Bethmann-Hollweg and Count Czernin, the new Austro-Hungarian Foreign Minister, referred to the "restoration of the territorial *status quo ante bellum* in East and West." [46]

Bethmann-Hollweg's successor, Reichschancellor Michaelis, in his letter to Count Czernin of the 17th August, 1917, says clearly that should Poland be unwilling to co-operate with Germany it would be more pertinent to leave Poland to " her self-determination even with a possibility of her joining Russia." [47]

As reconciliation with Russia was unattainable, a new approach to the problem of the future relations with Russia and consequently also to the Polish problem became unavoidable. It would be very inaccurate to assert that this new approach was due exclusively to the pressure exercised on the Government by the German war-lords, eager to have a Polish army fighting on the side of the Central Powers. It is quite true that the German war lords pressed for a decision on the Polish question and that their clumsiness and absolute lack of political sense overshadowed all the German schemes relating to Eastern Europe, but the initiative for the revision of the traditional Prussian policy towards Russia and Poland did not belong to soldiers only, being dictated above all by the new realities which began to preoccupy responsible German political leaders.

German plans for frontier rectifications

Side by side with the old conservatists who wished to follow the traditional Prussian policy of friendship with Russia and deeply regretted the clash with her,[48] as well as the anti-British imperialists who saw Germany's future on the Seven Seas—a typical and most prominent representative of this school being Admiral Tirpitz—and who considered that these ends could be achieved only in co-operation with Russia,[49] there was another trend in German public opinion which took the view that Russia should be made harmless for the future by amputations on her Western frontiers and by being debarred from any influence on the provinces conquered in Eastern Europe by German military might. Some of the most rabid annexa-

tionists advised mass expulsion of the native population, thus fore-
shadowing what was done later on a big scale under Hitler in the
course of the Second World War. Thus, for instance, writes a representative of Pan-German circles, Bartels, in his memorandum laid
before the highest political and military authorities and dated 20th
August, 1914 [50]: " Sixteen millions of Poles should be displaced to
the East . . . a forced emigration to Asiatic Russia." We can trace in
this memorandum the origin of the later gigantic plans of Ludendorff on the resettlement, especially by ex-servicemen and Germans
coming from abroad (Auslanddeutsche), of North Poland and the
Baltic provinces.[51]

These ideas were also advocated by the German intelligentsia and
powerful economic organizations. For instance, in the petition of
1,341 intellectuals, among them 352 University professors, laid
before the Chancellor of the Reich in Spring 1915, we read :

> " Military needs and particularly our strategic requirements will
> determine how far Germany's Eastern frontier should be pushed
> forward. Along the Eastern limits of Posen and Silesia, and along
> the Southern frontier of East Prussia a belt of territory must be
> created which, as far as possible, is free from non-German owners
> of land, which would therefore be open for settlement to German
> colonists. This German frontier belt will separate the Prussian
> Poles from the Russian Poles and protect (sichern) them against the
> direct influence of the latter, who may achieve their indepen-
> dence." [52]

Six great economic associations asked the Imperial Chancellor
" with a view to strengthening not only the industrial but also the
agricultural basis of Germany, a comprehensive policy of colonization by German agricultural colonists," and they stressed that " considerable expansion of Germany is needed towards the East "—
" Recreated Eastern Prussia requires more secure frontiers. The
provinces of Western Prussia, Posen and Silesia also must no longer
be allowed to remain in their present exposed position." [53]

The National-Liberals, the party of Gustav Stresemann, the future
" man of Locarno," was particularly clamorous in asking for wide
annexations in the East, and Gustav Stresemann himself in his
speech in the Reichstag on the 6th April, 1916, emphasized the
German character of the Baltic provinces, which in his opinion
should not again be rendered to Russia.[54]

It is also very interesting to know the viewpoint of General
von Seeckt, the future organizer of the Reichwehr under the Weimar
Republic, on the solution of Eastern problems. His ideas, set down
in *Thoughts on Poland* on the 4th December, 1915, were : eliminate
altogether the third partitioning power, Russia, from any influence

on Polish territories and divide the conquered Polish territories between Germany and Austria, roughly on the lines of the Third
Partition of Poland at the end of the eighteenth century.[55]

The idea of annexing what was often euphemistically called the
" security belt " or frontier-zone (Grenzstreifen), in later stages of
the war coupled with the idea of severing any link between Poland
and the Baltic countries, Lithuania in the first place, was never
totally abandoned by the Germans until the very eve of their
collapse, but the extent of these annexations depended on the
fortunes of the war. These requests, to which Bethmann-Hollweg
first turned a sympathetic ear,[56] advocated above all by the war
lords, as we shall see in the following part of this chapter, formed
one of the main obstacles to the so-called Austro-Polish solution, as
such a solution would have obtained German agreement only on the
condition of large amputations of Polish territory for the benefit of
Germany.

But already at that time some more enlightened Germans could see
the unreality and preposterousness of these wild schemes for
colonization of the densely populated provinces of Poland, Lithuania, Latvia and Estonia. In the petition of the " Union of the New
Fatherland " (Bund Neues Vaterland) presented in June 1915 we
read the following : " Congress Poland does not cover its own grain
requirements; having more than eighty inhabitants per square kilo-
metre—it was one of the most densely populated provinces of
Russia. . . . " The petition further recalls that " even before the war
the German economy was obliged to employ big contingents of
foreign labour from Russia, Galicia and Italy, of which at least
400,000 were occupied in agriculture. . . . The colonization of
Poland–Lithuania is bound to fail for the simple reason of lack of
men. The thinly populated North and East of Germany has undergone for many years a process of depopulation which constitutes a
serious preoccupation for economists and politicians." The petition
concluded that " the war has shown the decisive importance of our
policy towards Poland for the outcome of the war." [57]

The discussion on German war aims in the East became particularly lively after the fall of Warsaw and the successes, although not
so decisive as desired, on the Eastern front. A leading German
publicist, Paul Rohrbach, wrote in the magazine *Hilfe* (No. 34) on
the 26th August, 1915 : " If Russia is to be made harmless she
must lose Poland." Hans Sieveking, in a leaflet *Our Tasks* (Unsere
Aufgaben) takes the view that Poland should be made completely
independent. Hans Delbrück in *Preussische Jahrbücher* (September
1915) says that a method should be devised which might put the
brake on the Polish ambitions, either a union with the Hapsburg

Monarchy or some form of link with Germany, but he emphasizes at the same time that " it would be impossible to increase the Polish population within the German Reich."

Poland as member of " Mittel Europa "

Frederick Naumann, the apostle of the idea of " Mittel-Europa," " this loosely federal combination for purposes of offence and defence, military and economic," [58] realized the importance of the proper solution of the Polish question for his wide scheme. Naumann's vision did not lack some greatness : " Our attention must first be directed," he says in his principal work, *Central Europe*, towards that portion of Central Europe which extends from the North and Baltic Seas to the Alps, the Adriatic Sea and the Southern edge of the Danubian plain. Take a map and see what lies between the Vistula and the Vosges Mountains, and what extends from Galicia to Lake Constance! You must think of these stretches of country as a unity, as a brotherhood of many members, as a defensive alliance, as a single economic district." [59] For Naumann it was " the welding together of the German Empire and the Austro-Hungarian Dual Monarchy " that mattered above all, and he was aware of the importance of the solution of the Polish question for the future relations between two great Central Powers. " It may well be," he said, " that the establishment of Poland will be the strongest impulse towards the creation of Central Europe." [60]

Naumann expounded his views on Poland in a leaflet, little known in the West, *Was wird aus Polen?* (What will become of Poland?), published in 1917. " The time has passed," he said in this leaflet, " when Russia and Germany could agree on Poland as on an object since these two powers fell out one with the other. It would be much better if immediately after the cessation of the Alliance of Three Emperors a corresponding change on the Polish question had taken place." [61]

> " Now, when the mist has lifted, one can clearly see the march of the present and of the future ; a long, stubborn and incredibly violent struggle between Eastern and Central Europe. This struggle may, perhaps, be mitigated and interrupted from time to time by peace treaties and agreements but, unfortunately, such desirable periods will be only temporary relaxation breaks. ... The idea of Polish nationhood, the same as any national idea in its first ascent, assumes a superiority over any practical considerations. A truly nationally conscious man will strive for the right to existence of his people even if it should become poorer on this account. Such were the views of our national prophets and so think the Poles." [62]

The following passage from Naumann's book shows that he

rightly understood the very nature of the Polish patriotism and that he fully appreciated the spirit of sacrifice of the Polish nation : " Warsaw, according to my views, would prefer to be destroyed rather than submit voluntarily to a new subjugation. On such an occasion any practical considerations are put aside and old flames rise from the ground." [63]

The German Government also began to feel the necessity for a new approach to the Polish question, although for a long time it delayed any decision for the reasons stated above. Immediately after the fall of Warsaw in August 1915 it sent to Poland a Privy Councillor, Dr. Sering, Professor of Berlin University, entrusting to him inquiries on the spot. In July 1916 Dr. Sering produced a memorandum in which he gave his ideas on Poland's future. He advised the separation from Russia of Congress Poland and the adjoining former provinces of the old Polish Republic in the East, with their mixed Polish-Byelorussian-Ukrainian population, as a necessary living space for the Polish nation. This new State should be closely connected with Germany as " under the protection of a strong Germany which will foster Poland's progress, in her own interests Poland will be able in the highest degree to fulfil her historic mission of a bulwark of Central Europe and its civilization." [64]

Proclamation of the Two Emperors of 5th November, 1916

It was the Governor-General of occupied Congress Kingdom (German zone), Beseler, who became the most fervid advocate of Poland's independence in close connection with Germany. In numerous memoranda to the Emperor, to the Imperial Chancellor, to the Chief of the General Staff, he developed these ideas, and although the plan for the creation of a Polish army was undoubtedly uppermost in his mind, he took a longer view than his military chiefs [65] and he emphasized also the enormous political importance to Germany's future of the creation of a barrier between Russia and Germany—e.g. the following passage from his memorandum, presented to the Imperial Chancellor, No. 1260, on the 20th August, 1916 :

> " What in my view would have been a still more dangerous thing than the delaying of the proclamation of Poland's independence would be the unhappily not yet discarded attempt to reach an agreement with Russia at Poland's expense. It would be a repetition, but on a bigger scale, of the empty truce of Malmö, owing to which Prussia for a long time lost all political credit. Apart from the moral aspect, a sham truce with Russia would be the first step to the regeneration of the latter and the corner stone of such a political system in the East as might one day strangle Germany." [66]

In his memorandum to General von Falkenhayn, Chief of the General Staff, dated 23rd August, 1916, Beseler writes : " It is not liberating or making happier twelve million men that matters to us, but the question of using them to push back the Russian menace further to the East and strengthening our frontier and its defence."

The representative of the German Foreign Office at the General Government of Congress Poland, Gerhard von Mutius (Bethmann-Hollweg's cousin), in his memorandum of April 1916 insists on the prompt solution of the Polish question, as otherwise : " The Russian danger will reappear to the full extent for the German future in spite of all military defeats." . . . " If we come to general peace negotiations with the unsettled Polish problem it can be taken for granted that it will serve as a wedge to split off Germany from Austria and the anti-German patriotism of the Poles will be used by our adversaries. And," he adds angrily, unable to put himself into the position of the Poles, " this nation of political children can so easily be won by pride." [67]

The vacillating Imperial Chancellor Bethmann-Hollweg notes his impressions of the period preceding the November Proclamation in the following way [68] :

> " Whichever form the national aspirations of the Poles might take, the striving for autonomy in Congress Poland, the irridentist moves of the Poles in Prussia, the efforts of Galicia towards political predominance within the Danubian Monarchy—everywhere the aim was the same, the restoration of a united Polish State. . . . Only a drawn battle could lead to the maintenance of the old position. Any other result would fulfil the Polish aspirations at the cost of the defeated party. . . .
>
> " Everywhere in Poland we meet the idea of the restoration of independent Poland. . . . We found very little sympathy for us— as the German has neither the gift nor the inclination to make himself likeable."

There were many flaws in the German schemes relating to Poland, and we shall deal with them while examining the reasons for their failure. For the moment I wish to stress one of them, as it had already appeared at this stage and was subsequently to involve within the framework of Ludendorff's grandiose plans in 1917-18 the biggest German political mistakes in 1918. Taking into account exclusively German interests and considering that it was up to the Poles to adjust themselves to new conditions, these schemes were often combined with the above-mentioned large " frontier rectifications " and plans for wide " colonial " conquests in the Baltic countries. Few Germans were aware of how impossible it was for the Poles to agree voluntarily to such tremendous territorial sacrifices and to the severing of the links with the Baltic countries, above all with Lithuania and her ethnographically Polish part. As a typical example of this strange turn of mind, let us quote some passages from a memorandum produced in 1916 by Major Simon, who served on General Beseler's staff and was one of his close advisers on Polish questions. We find in this memorandum a queer mixture of right observations and wishful thinking.

> " In *each* Polish heart " [writes Major Simon] " I use the term *each* deliberately, lives the desire for Gdansk (Danzig) and Poznan (Posen). ... It would be impossible to create a permanent and solid association with the Polish partners only on the basis of common economic interests. Poland is too developed from the national point of view, perhaps even excessively developed, to sacrifice at a decisive moment her real national interests to Mammon. ... Poland should, after having undergone our training, govern herself in full freedom. But the German arm should be armed. By the annexation of the curve of the Vistula—the Narev (Torun-Modlin-Lomza-Osowiec)—we shall strengthen our position on an endangered spot. ... Poland might move her capital to Lublin and thus replace her centre of gravity in the wanted direction—South-East—towards the Ukraine. ... Should the Poles take Wilno our prospects for a further expansion of our colonial German-Baltic territory would be restrained. And if we give up the strong line Torun-Modlin-Lomza we would be menaced in our possessions. ... We need the security of our Eastern frontier on its so far undefended stretch. The area which we shall win in this way will be made German, and if any need arises will be defended with German blood. Having obtained this security we shall be able to and will help the Poles honestly. Your hopes, Poles, should be directed towards Galicia and the Ukraine. We will help you in that." [69]

But it was the views of the German high commanders that finally distorted any constructive idea in the schemes relating to Poland. After the late summer 1916 the Central Powers began to feel an acute shortage of manpower reserves. Falkenhayn and Ludendorff devoted much space in their memoranda to the dangers arising from the dwindling German reserves.[70]

The Polish territories occupied at that time by the Central Powers possessed very large human resources, due to the fact that the Russians before their retreat had called up only a few annual contingents. These reserves were assessed at about 1,000,000 men between the ages of 17 and 43 in Congress Poland, and about 400,000 in the adjacent former Polish-Lithuanian provinces of Russia; moreover there were about 100,000 Poles in Austrian and German prisoner-of-war camps.[71] The idea of making use of these reserves was strongly advocated by Ludendorff, but it is not true that Ludendorff's and Hindenburg's predecessor, General Falkenhayn, opposed these plans, as is asserted for instance by Mr. Wheeler-Bennet, who also wrongly ascribes to Falkenhayn's opposition the postponement of the Polish plans after the Vienna agreement in August 1916.[72] In a letter written by Falkenhayn on the 29th July, 1916, just the opposite was stated : " If the population of Poland cannot see clearly what its fate will be after joining the Central Powers, the attempt to use Poles apt for military service against Russia will have no chance of success." In his telegram No. 14007 of the 8th August to General Cramon he says : " We have no time to waste," and in his telegram No. 14038 of 9th August in reply to Governor-General Beseler's memorandum, he declared : " I agree with Your Excellency that the organization of the Polish army will be possible only after the clarification of the position relating to the political future of that country."[73] After the war Ludendorff, and to some extent also Hindenburg, tried to shift the whole responsibility for the decisions on the Polish question on to the political leaders, but the documents published by Delbrück in *Ludendorff's Self-Portrait,* as well as other documents, show how impatient was Ludendorff in bringing about a prompt political decision after summer 1915. Of numerous telegrams and memoranda let us quote the most characteristic ones, such as the memorandum sent to the Secretary of State von Jagov on the 2nd September, 1915 : " Should the autocracy on which rests the whole Russian State organization collapse, the total disruption of the Empire is not excluded. If Poland then becomes independent the new order will be established without us, while at present we are able to influence it." In his letter to Secretary of State Zimmermann of the 20th October, 1915, Ludendorff writes : " The more I think over this matter the more convinced I am that Poland should not be rendered to Russia—nor should Poland fall to Austria's share, but should become more or less an independent State under German supremacy." [74]

The brilliant part played by the Polish Legion under Pilsudski's command in Volhynia (especially in the battle of Kostiuchnowka, to the north of the railway line Kowel-Sarny, 4th–5th July, 1916) attracted the attention of the General Commanding on the Volhynian Front, Bernhardi, who sent enthusiastic reports on these actions to the German High Command, pressing for a decision which might provide more of these excellent soldiers. Ludendorff in his letter to Secretary of State Zimmermann of the 17th July sums up his point of view in the following terms :

" The Austrians do not cease to behave like swine. Their troops do not hold any longer, as the sad events of the last days have proved. My eye turns again to the Poles. The Pole is a good soldier. If Austria fails then we must provide new forces for ourselves. ... Let us create a Grand Duchy of Poland with Warsaw and Lublin and immediately after a Polish army under German command. ... This army will be formed in any case, one day, so it would be better to use it now. Perhaps this will involve some political drawbacks, but such arguments should vanish before the prospects of victory which must be ours. Let us act in time."

It was Beseler's Direct Report (Immediatbericht) to the Emperor on the 23rd July which eventually set the ball rolling, followed by ample correspondence between the highest political and military quarters.

The importance of the future Polish army for Germany was emphasized also by the German Emperor in his above-mentioned conversation with Count Hutten-Czapski on the 13th July, 1916. The Emperor spoke in very laudatory terms of the military value of the Polish Legion, on the strength of the reports he had received.[75]

Such is the political and military background of the above quoted Vienna Agreement between Austria-Hungary and Germany of 11th–12th August, 1916 (see p. 84) which for the German leaders was a variant of their policy should the secret negotiations between Russia and Germany bring no positive results. As we know, this Agreement was followed by a three months' lull during which the war lords became ever more insistent on account of the lack of positive results in the attempts at a separate peace with the Tsarist Empire.[75a] Eventually, seeing no way out the Imperial Chancellor agreed to a meeting of Austro-Hungarian and German political and military leaders at Pszczyna (Pless) on the 18th October, 1916, at which the final decisions were taken leading to the Proclamation of the two Emperors on the 5th November, 1916. We have two interesting accounts of this meeting, one by Bethmann-Hollweg and another by Baron Burian, Austro-Hungarian Foreign Minister.

The Imperial Chancellor underlines that the meeting was called on the initiative of the German headquarters and that he agreed to the proposals brought forward with " extreme energy " by the military leaders, having in view the lack of any peace offers from Stürmer, even confidential ones, and the vanishing of the hopes which had appeared in July-August. Moreover, writes Bethmann-Hollweg, " we received information that the Entente promised self-government to the Poles and a separate Polish Government was to be set up in Russia(?)"[76]

The report made by Burian is still more enlightening.[77] According to him it was the soldiers who took the floor, but while Beseler referred in his report to the political and military considerations, Ludendorff viewed the whole problem as a purely technical-military one. Burian warned against undue haste and the one-sided military approach to this highly political question, seeing in such an approach one of the reasons for the subsequent failure of all these schemes. On the other side there was unanimity at the meeting not to set up in the course of the war a Polish State with full attributes but only to give the Poles a " binding " promise. Such is the origin of the November Proclamation, which did not define the frontiers of the future State, nor did it establish a Polish Government and a separate administration. It was a unilateral act, a business concluded without the Poles, as it was not preceded by any agreement with responsible Polish political leaders. Nor did anybody ask the Poles whether they wanted Poland to become a hereditary monarchy closely bound to the Central Powers.[78] Knowing the contents of the Vienna Agreement of the 11th–12th August, 1916, we can now say that the independence promised to the Poles was by no means real independence, but a position of complete subservience to the protecting powers. In any case the Proclamation came too late for the purposes of the Central Powers, only five months before the outbreak of the Revolution in Russia which completely changed the whole political position in that part of the continent.

Underestimating the political maturity of the Polish nation the Germans thought that the Polish army could be formed and the Poles be ready to die for a " common " cause without the establishment of real political authority in Poland.[79] Let us observe that the German war lords insisted on deleting the word " independent " in the Proclamation, which shows the lengths to which their political blindness went.[80] An epic struggle with Pilsudski, the leader of the movement for independence in occupied Poland, was about to begin. We shall speak about these further developments in the third part of this chapter. The Proclamation to the Poles was, nevertheless, the recognition of the fact that the Polish national movement was a reality which had to be taken into account. It was Baron Burian who put the whole problem in a nutshell, writing after the space of a few years :

" It was the first great fact which the war brought about without any deliberate planning, a fact which could no longer be suppressed. All this groping policy which aimed to win the Poles should not cherish any illusions about it ; it was a policy which wanted to use this new-comer, not welcomed everywhere, for the purposes of the war and in order to prepare for him such a position as might be the most favourable to the involuntary liberators within the future European order. And yet the Polish nation, once released from her fetters, was unwilling to put on new ones but wished to make a fresh start in independent life." [81]

We find little understanding for this either in the memoirs of the leading German statesmen and soldiers or in writings devoted to the subject which appeared in the post-war period in Germany. The question of " responsibility " for raising the Polish issue became one of the favourite subjects in German political literature, and Professor Dietrich Schäfer even wrote a special book under this heading. We do not deny that the international repercussions of the November Proclamation were considerable, but the latter only accelerated some processes and, moreover, it was not the Proclamation which started the Polish national movement for independence, for which so many Poles had shed their blood since the Partitions. It was also not on the lines of the November Proclamation and the Vienna Agreement that the new State arose, but in continuous opposition to the policy of the Central Powers and the stubborn resistance of the Polish nation to the imposition on her of new fetters.

War aims of Austria-Hungary and the Polish Question

As the developments in the course of the war showed, the importance of the Polish question for Austria-Hungary also was much greater than the Austrian and Hungarian statesmen were ready to admit at first. There is no doubt that the Danubian Monarchy did not wish for armed conflict with Russia, preparing herself only for a punitive expedition against Serbia without plans for territorial conquests at the expense of the latter. She concentrated her armies against Serbia and her military plans were upset by the further developments.[82] Contrary to the expectations of the Polish political leaders of Galicia, Austria also had no definite plans regarding Poland.

As long ago as the 15th September, 1879, Bismarck wrote to his Emperor that " Austria was a necessary, peace-loving, defensive and conservative power " while " Russia was under the influence of a war-like Slav revolution eager for conquests." [83] For some decades, however, the Russian danger to Austria-Hungary seemed to recede and there were some prospects that Russia and Austria-Hungary might become permanent partners in dividing their spheres of influence in South-Eastern Europe. The conciliatory policy of the two Powers, pursued since 1891 (in 1896 Tsar Nicholas visited Vienna and in 1897 Emperor Francis Joseph revisited the Tsar in St. Petersburg), appeared especially in the " Murzstag Points," 20th October, 1903, signed by Count Goluchowski,

H

Austro-Hungarian Minister of Foreign Affairs, a Galician Pole, and Count Lamsdorff, Russian Foreign Minister. In his above-mentioned book *L'Allemagne, la France et la Question d'Austriche*, André Chéradame wrote in 1902 : " There is a growing tendency in Russia to safeguard the integrity of Austria." [84] It would go beyond the scope of this book to deal in detail with the international developments following the Russian defeats on the Manchurian battlefields in 1904, and the new trends in Russian foreign policy which led to the conflict Izvolsky-Aehrental. Let us observe that neither had Germany (which abandoned the cautious policy of Bismarck) discouraged Austro-Hungarian intransigence, nor had France (the ally of Russia) shown herself capable of checking Russian aggressiveness in the Balkans, as she played a secondary, entirely subservient rôle to Russia in that part of Europe. Without any doubt Austria-Hungary could have saved herself by the right approach to the problem of the Southern Slavs, and missed all opportunities to solve it in accordance with the national aspirations of the latter. Neither the Austrian Germans nor the Magyars understood the whole implications of the problem of nationality. Instead of evolving towards " Monarchic Switzerland," as Chéradame predicted, Austria-Hungary clung to obsolete conceptions, playing off one nationality against another according to the old precept " Divide et impera," in order to preserve her archaic forms. But the programme of foreign policy devised by the leading Austrian political figures in the period preceding the war aimed not at expansion in the direction of Russia—the old plans for the restoration of the Kingdom of Poland united to Austria having been shelved—but on the contrary, anxious to preserve the integrity of the Empire and unwilling to increase the number of her Slav subjects, both the German Austrians and the Magyars would have much preferred the maintenance of the Three Emperors' Agreement based on the *status quo*. Although the Archduke Francis Ferdinand, murdered at Sarajevo on the 28th June, 1914, fostered plans for splitting the old historic crown-lands into smaller units in order to put an end to the supremacy of the Magyars and to the Polish influence in the Austrian part of the Monarchy, he considered Italy and not Russia as the arch-enemy. Similarly Conrad von Hoetzendorff, the very influential Chief of the General Staff, wished to direct Austrian expansion southwards and not eastwards.

Srokowski, a Polish publicist thoroughly conversant with the conditions in Austria both before and during the war, characterizes in these terms the Austrian policy :

" The Austrian policy was groping in the dark among the most important problems of Europe and of its own existence—without knowing what was in fact its 'vital interest' to which the Austro-Hungarian Minister of Foreign Affairs used to refer so often in his speeches before the joint Inter-Parliamentary Committee of Austria and Hungary. Once he emphasized that this vital interest was in the Sanjak of Novi-Bazar, another time—in Albania. Each time it turned out that it was somewhere else. Without the steering and guidance of the State reason the vessel of Old Austria was adrift on the high tides of great times. It was the first sign of decomposition and imminent catastrophe. . . .

" The Austrian policy towards Russia in particular lacked clarity. It consisted in the ingenuous belief that Russia was only bluffing and that she would never herself decide upon war. . . . " [85]

Karol Friedrich Nowak, in his excellent study *The Collapse of Central Europe,* gave a vivid picture of all these internal difficulties of Austro-Hungary which brought doom upon the unhappy Monarchy. With the outbreak of the war the Reichsrat (Parliament) was not called together for three years and the " Austrian Premier, Count Stürgh, gradually built up a system of arbitrary government such as even the Austria of Metternich had hardly known." For three long years, from the 13th March, 1914, the leaders of the Austrian nationalities were compelled to keep silence.[86] But what was still worse was the growing influence of the Austrian military caste, to which passed the decision on the most important issues. The nominal command was given by the Emperor Francis-Joseph to Archduke Ferdinand, but the real power was held by the Chief of the General Staff, Conrad von Hoetzendorff, a most typical representative of this narrow-minded military caste, composed in the great majority of Austrian Germans, mistrusting all national movements and imbued with the old Austrian spirit from the preconstitutional era. This caste was responsible, among other things, for the overthrow of Stürgh's Government, as appears from the Report of the Great Headquarters to the Emperor of the 25th September, 1915, in which was laid down the following programme for the Austrian policy : " The indispensable strengthening of the authority of the State and of the Armed Forces is impossible without the complete extermination of all movements hostile to the Monarchy and the education of all nationalities in the Austrian spirit." For this reason the Supreme Command asked the Emperor to " entrust with the leadership of the kingdoms and lands represented in the Reichsrat a personality that will by his commendable ability and unshaken energy guarantee the happy solution of all the crucial issues for Austria-Hungary." [87]
Against this general political background we are better able to understand the Austro-Hungarian policy on the Polish problem, a

policy characterized by incoherence, muddled thinking and inconsistency. The Austrian chances of winning the sympathies of the Poles, however, seemed the highest among all the partitioning powers, because of the liberal policy of Austria towards the Poles and the leading rôle played by Polish statesmen in the Austrian part of the Empire. When war broke out many Poles in Austria, headed by the Austro-Hungarian Minister of Finance, Bilinski, tried to revive the old plans for the restoration of the Polish State, closely united to Austria-Hungary. They even secured the approval of the Emperor and the Austrian Cabinet for this idea. At a meeting at Count Berchtold's the idea of a Proclamation by the Emperor to the Poles was approved in principle, and the draft of the Proclamation was agreed upon at the meeting of the Austrian Cabinet on the 13th August, 1914. The old Emperor declared that he was ready to sign it. The Proclamation ran as follows :

> " If Almighty God grants victory to the allied armies, your country will be indissolubly united to My States in such a way that jointly with My Land (Galicia) inhabited by your compatriots it will constitute one Polish Kingdom with the administration of which, taking into consideration the supreme interests and needs of the Monarchy, will be entrusted a National Government responsible before the Diet in Warsaw." [88]

One of the most prominent statesmen of Galicia and former Governor of this Crown Land, Bobrzynski, was to be appointed Viceroy in order to organize the new Polish State united to Austria-Hungary. It was the Hungarian Prime Minister, Count Tisza, who at the meeting of the Crown Council on the 22nd August, 1914, opposed this plan, arguing that it might render impossible the conclusion of a peace treaty with Russia when the proper time came. Tisza was a strong personality but without broader vision and he could not understand the importance of national issues in the coming struggle. His parochial and narrow Magyar patriotism [89] was one of the main causes for the inability of the Monarchy to solve the Southern Slav question, one of the principal reasons for the collapse of the Dual Monarchy. Tisza defended his point of view for over three years, as appears from a letter addressed by him to Baron Czernin, dated February 1917 : " The attachment of Poland to the Monarchy should under no circumstances affect the dual structure of the Monarchy," he wrote, further stating that he was " afraid of the future orientation of the Hapsburg Great Power if the Russian-Poles, so little reliable from the point of view of the vital interests both of Austria and Hungary, obtain a predominant position." [90] In January 1917 Tisza advised the cession of the Polish part of Austria to Germany. Tisza wanted no conflicts either with Russia or with Germany on account of Poland, and his liegeman, Berchtold's successor to the post of Austro-Hungarian Minister of Foreign Affairs, Baron Burian, upheld these views during his first tenure of office, completely changing his opinions after he again became Foreign Minister in spring 1918, turning then into the most fervid advocate of the Austro-Polish solution and seeing in it the only way to salvation for the Monarchy.

As a matter of fact Austrian military might was greatly shaken in the first months of the war, which disclosed the whole weakness of the Dual Monarchy. The Austrians, unwilling to make any concessions to the Italians, would have much preferred to make peace with Russia at the end of 1914, possibly through the exchange of part of Galicia for the Southern part of Congress-Kingdom (see above p. 80). In a conversation very characteristic of this turn of mind between Conrad von Hoetzendorff and Count Czernin, then Austro-Hungarian Envoy to Rumania, held on the 26th December, 1914, at Cieszyn (Teschen), von Hoetzendorff stated :

> " If we obtain the *status quo* and have no war costs to pay we should be satisfied, keeping in mind that at the beginning of the war we marched against Serbia only in order to humiliate her and with the more distant aim of attaching her to the Monarchy. From the moment when Russia joined in the war with all her allies and the Great War broke out our war aims became limited and we are concentrated upon the preservation of the Monarchy. One should be happy if one gets through with only a black eye." [91]

As we know from the first part of this chapter, Burian turned down Bethmann-Hollweg's proposals (13th August, 1915) relating to the union of Congress Poland with Austria-Hungary. Perhaps these proposals were but a trap, especially as they were accompanied by requests for large frontier rectifications, making such a solution quite unpalatable to the Poles, and there may have been a legitimate fear that the position of Austria-Hungary would be particularly delicate if hopes for much desired negotiations with Russia should materialize. Moreover, it should be kept in mind that at that time Austria-Hungary was unwilling to pay the price, consisting in partial surrender of her soverignty for the benefit of a Central European Union. The fact is that by her unwillingness to accept German offers the Dual Monarchy let it be understood that her ambitions turned to different parts of the European continent, to the South and South-East and not to the East. In the subsequent period until September 1917 when the Austro-Polish solution was rather belatedly revived, the Polish question served Austria-Hungary only as a bargaining matter. Austria marked her presence, refused to be completely eliminated from decisions on Poland but left the first rôle to Germany, ready even to sell outright the Polish assets for considerable advantages elsewhere.

This tendency appeared most clearly in the first half of 1917 when the Austrian statesmen thought of finding an outlet for their imperialistic lusts in the Balkans and Rumania.

In the Vienna Memoir of the 27th March, 1917, signed by Czernin and Bethmann-Hollweg, relating to the war aims of the Central Powers it was stated that :

> " If the war might have a more favourable conclusion the Central Powers might consider the permanent incorporation of enemy territory in addition to their territorial integrity [sic!]. ... In this connection Germany was thinking principally of the East, and Austria-Hungary mainly of Rumania." [92]

In the memorandum submitted by Count Czernin, Minister of Foreign Affairs, to Emperor Charles of Austria in summer 1917 we read the following :

> " If Germany should emerge from this war with something approximating the status quo ante, I could concede that the Monarchy also should come out of the war with substantially her former frontiers. If, however, as I believe probable in spite of everything, Germany ends the war with territorial gains in the East ... then it is quite impossible in my opinion for the Monarchy to end the war with the status quo, still less a diminution of the Monarchy. ... There are two great territories which may be considered, East and South. ... The Polish State may be built on one of four lines :
>   1. The Austro-Polish solution may be regarded as possible in principle ;
>   2. A ' Germano-Polish ' solution ;
>   3. A ' Russo-Polish ' solution may be envisaged, and finally
>   4. An actually sovereign Polish State, set up in independence of all its neighbours, may be conceived.
> " The first and fourth are purely theoretical ... impossible against the opposition of Germany. ...
> " Unless a new war or a revolution tears Galicia from us, we shall not lose this province, no matter whether the Poles cast longing eyes upon it or not. But to believe that the future will see new wars or national revolutions is to fail to understand the temper of our times. ... I am firmly convinced that this terrible slaughter is likely to be the last war for a period beyond calculation. ...
> " We must have Rumania : we must have Valachia and the whole of Moldavia to the Sereth. ...
> " Only by going to the Balkans and selling Poland to Germany

can the idea of a cession of a part of Alsace-Lorraine assume definite shape." [93]

One of the numerous memoranda originated by the prolific brain of this Bohemian aristocrat, this particular one does not give good testimony either to his far-sightedness or to his comprehension of the needs of modern life. It reads like an indictment against the unscrupulous, tortuous, and idly speculative policy of the decadent Empire.

Czernin's policy found expression in the Kreuznach Agreement between Germany and Austria-Hungary of the 17–18th May, 1917 :

> " 2. If Germany carries through the territorial incorporation of Courland and Lithuania, as well as the solution of the Polish question which is contemplated on the German side, it is agreed that the occupied part of Rumania ... shall form a separate State in Austria-Hungary's sphere of interest, Germany's economic participation in Rumania being guaranteed. ...
> " 3. On the assumption set out in paragraph 2 hereof Austria-Hungary renounces any condominium in Poland and will not be interested in a political and military sense (including the railway question) in the Kingdom of Poland. Germany is conscious of the heavy task she is taking over in Poland." [94]

In a letter addressed to the German Crown Prince from Reichenau on the 20th August, 1917, Emperor Charles referred to a new offer made personally to the German Emperor :

> " I have trustworthy information that we can win France to our side if Germany can bring herself to consent to certain territorial sacrifices in Alsace-Lorraine. If we win over France victory will be ours, and Germany will be able to find ample compensation elsewhere. But I do not want Germany to be alone in making sacrifices ; I will myself give the lion's share, and I therefore explained to H.M. Your Father, that under the conditions mentioned above (unter der vorerwähnten Bedingung) I am prepared not only to renounce all claims to Poland, but also to add Galicia to Poland and to help to incorporate the Kingdom so formed with Germany (Deutschland angliedern to helfen). Thus Germany would gain a Kingdom in the East while in the West she would give up merely a slice of her territory." [95]

What is particularly striking in this offer is that while France was trying at that time to detach Austria-Hungary from Germany, Emperor Charles wanted by selling his Polish assets to withdraw to the South of the Carpathians and leave Germany the undisputed master of Central-Eastern Europe.

Emperor Charles was certainly badly prepared for his difficult position. His small understanding of the Polish question appears

clearly from the following report of General von Seeckt to Ludendorff in late October 1916 :

> " I spoke many times with the Archduke on the Polish question.
> ... The Polish national interests find no response in him. His
> Imperial and Royal Highness is by no means an advocate of the
> incorporation (of Poland) with Austria. . . . I consider that His
> Imperial and Royal Highness, although stressing the Austrian
> prestige, which is only natural, keeps a loyal attitude towards the
> German interests." [96]

This disinterested attitude of Austria in Polish matters certainly
agreed with many Germans who were promoters of the expansion of
Germany towards the East. They considered as the greatest danger
for the future Austro-German relations any increase of Polish influence within the Dual Monarchy, on this point sharing the views
of Magyars and Austrian-Germans, who were unwilling to give up
their predominant position. Bethmann-Hollweg justified the Vienna
Agreement of 11–12th August, 1916, by the argument that the
Austro-Polish solution would make the Poles a decisive factor in the
Danubian Monarchy.[97] The same views were held by Ludendorff,
von Seeckt and the Austrian military caste.[98] Conrad von Hoetzendorff observes in his *Memoirs* :

> " It is clear that France would welcome an Austria with Czech
> or Polish orientation, as such a State would serve her purposes,
> being ready at any time to act as Germany's enemy ... but could
> the Austrian Germans or the Imperial House of German descent
> play such a part? " [99]

So far as the union of Galicia with Poland was concerned German
opinion was divided.

On the one hand we have the following reflections set down by
the above-mentioned Major Simon, of Beseler's staff, dated 30th
June, 1916 [100] :

> " Galicia attached by a thin thread of Cieszyn to Austria has no
> geographical connection with the genuinely Austro-German terri-
> tories. ... It was, certainly, fatal for the development of Austria
> that nine years after the final loss of Silesia (Treaty of Huberts-
> burg, 1763) she pushed out her so exposed tentacles towards the
> Russian colossus from the thus formed narrow passage of Cieszyn.
> How much more would she have been able to devote herself to
> her mission in the Balkans if she had not crossed the protective
> wall of the Carpathians, the more so as at that time the third Italian
> front had then not yet the armour of the Alps (before 1866). ...
> " The economic development of Galicia, although a rich country
> in itself, was rendered impossible not only through political weak-

ness but also owing to the lack of connection with the Austrian motherland (the narrow Cieszyn passage can be called Poland's navel-string). So far Galicia remained a country economically passive for Austria. . . .

" The desire to increase this sub-Carpathian area arises consequently, so far as Austria is concerned, only from her lust for territories and is not a vital question for her.

" From the pont of view of Austria-Hungary as a whole the increasing of Galicia by a part of Congress Poland would have brought about full federalism which so far had remained in a latent stage. . . .

" The increasing of Galicia or even the solution of the Polish question by Austria-Hungary would have been a political catastrophe for the Austro-Hungarian State, and in particular for Austria and her Germans, and last but not least for the well understood Polish interests."

On the other hand in a memorandum submitted by General Beseler to the Imperial Chancellor and dated 12th November, 1917, we read the following :

" The Union of Galicia with Poland will revive the claims to the old Polish territories held by Germany. Should the Austro-Polish solution be carried out I must warn most emphatically against depriving Poland of any possibility of extending to the East. It is the only means by which we can divert her expansion from the West. I am convinced that by the Austro-Hungarian solution the position of Germany in the East will be gravely shaken." [100a]

The Austro-Hungarian attitude towards the Polish question changed unexpectedly and completely in September 1917. Both Emperor Charles and Count Czernin, appalled by the desperate economic and military position of the Monarchy, then saw the only way of salvation for it in a union with Poland. To some extent also they followed the suggestions coming from France and Great Britain to transform the Hapsburg Monarchy into a Federation of States to which Poland might be attached. But while the Entente wished in this way to separate Austria-Hungary from Germany, the Austro-Hungarians were ready, on the contrary, to tighten the bonds between the two Central Powers as the price for the surrender of Poland by Germany. The programme of Austria-Hungary was then a personal union between Poland and the Danubian Monarchy. Count Czernin's new turn of mind appears clearly from a conversation between him and General von Cramon, reported by the latter in his *Memoirs*. The conversation took place during the offensive against Italy in October 1917. Czernin declared to General von Cramon : " Austria cannot exist without Poland and is ready to make concessions to Germany in Rumania " (just the opposite of what this Bohemian aristocrat wished a few weeks before). He would be prepared for a " vassal-relationship " between the Danubian Monarchy and Germany provided the Austro-Polish solution might be obtained at that price.[101]

The conversations between Czernin and Chancellor Michaelis in September 1917 brought no result, Germany insisting on such amputations of the Polish territory that Czernin realized the impossibility of ever obtaining Polish consent to such a solution. The situation changed when Hertling, a Bavarian, took over the post of Imperial Chancellor (9th November, 1917). The German Government became more amenable to Austro-Hungarian plans at the end of 1917, and both Emperor William and the Cabinet agreed in principle to Austrian proposals in spite of the strong opposition of Ludendorff and Hindenburg, who maintained their opposition to the Austro-Polish solution and insisted on very large amputations of the territory of the Polish State. This opposition provoked a great clash between the Emperor and the Great Headquarters and almost to the end there were two different policies in Germany on the Polish question, one pursued by the Cabinet accepting—not without some qualifications—the Austro-Polish solution, and another represented by Ludendorff who tried to reduce Polish national territory and encircle Poland by semi-independent States controlled entirely by Germany, Lithuania with her ethnographically Polish part and the Ukraine with frontiers pushed westwards. We know that the Brest-Litovsk peace negotiations started without a previous final agreement between the Central Powers on the Polish question. If Austria-Hungary had ever had any chances of materializing her Polish schemes she lost them definitely at Brest-Litovsk when Czernin, eager to conclude what was then called a " Bread Treaty " because of the desperate food position of his country, agreed to the cession of a part of the indisputably Polish territory to the then phantom State of the Ukraine, and to the division of Galicia. In his speech before the Austrian Delegation Czernin on the 24th January, 1918, declared : " I hold irrevocably the view that the Polish question should not delay the conclusion of the peace treaty for one day."[102]
The reaction of the Poles to the Brest-Litovsk Treaty, with which we shall deal later, eventually brought about the fall of this misguided adviser of Emperor Charles. It seems strange that after the Brest-Litovsk Treaty the Austro-Hungarian Ministers could have cherished any illusion of winning the backing of the Poles for their plans. The new Foreign Minister Baron Burian (8th April to 24th October, 1918), the same man who in 1915 declined the German offers relating to Poland, appeared now as the most fervid partisan

of the personal union between Poland and the Dual Monarchy. Burian's views had changed radically from those he held during his first tenure of office. In his *Memoirs* Bilinski tells us that in 1915 Baron Burian made the following declaration to him : " The Monarchy wants to create Poland not for the Poles but for itself. Consequently the bases of the new organisms should be worked out by the Central Powers without any influence from the Poles. The Poles will be asked only about the details of the internal organization." The public opinion of Galicia did not impress him.[103] In his *Memoirs* Burian expresses different opinions. He says that the Polish question had a " vital interest " for Austria-Hungary and that any solution of the Polish question which did not meet with the approval of the Poles would be short-lived. So far as Galicia was concerned, he stated that " as soon as the Russian rule ended in Warsaw Galicia felt like a part of Poland and identified itself with the fate of Poland." [104]

Burian, like Czernin at the end of his career, was ready to pay a heavy price for union with Poland.[105] As a matter of fact the various schemes devised in the course of summer 1918 for the establishment of a close organic co-operation between the two Central Powers after the war had been connected with the Polish question, and Burian himself emphasizes this point, saying in connection with the conference at Spa in August, 1918, that " an express junction was made between the question of Alliance and the Polish question," and that " a satisfactory solution of the Polish question was a primary condition of all these arrangements." [106] The German Secretary of State, von Kühlmann, stressed the same point of view in his speech before the Reichstag on the 24th June, 1918 :

> " Turning now to Poland, the mould in which the future lot is to be cast has formed since I have had the honour of being in charge of the foreign office, the object of continual and thorough negotiations, mainly with Austria-Hungary. Both in our discussions at Great Headquarters and in Berlin the future settlement of the Polish question, which is at the same time of the greatest importance for the future arrangement of German-Austro-Hungarian relations, has been the subject of thorough discussions. Not only the great difficulty inherent in this question itself, but the almost inseparable connection existing between this question and the solution of economic questions as between Austria-Hungary and Germany, have so far prevented the attainment of a final result." [107]

The negotiations between Austria-Hungary and Germany in late summer 1918 covered a very wide field. About the agreements signed at Spa on the 14th August, 1918, Nowak says that " the four points signed by Secretary von Kühlmann and Burian . . . provided for an understanding concerning so many political and economic interests of both countries that the two Empires would in future represent a union that went far beyond that of an alliance." [108]

Simultaneously with the negotiations on these matters the question of the future of Poland was discussed. As the chances of victory were vanishing and Poland's right to independence was no longer in dispute, the two Empires tried in this last hour to install on the Polish throne a candidate of their own. These quarrels about the choice of a candidate to the Polish throne and the attempts to impose on the Poles in this last hour a form of government which had not been previously approved by them shows that the rulers of the two Empires had completely lost touch with realities and were living in a fool's paradise. We need not state all the details of these hopeless endeavours, about which Erzberger rightly said : " They quarrelled about the royal crowns and therefore whole countries were being lost." [109]

Austria-Hungary was approaching her final collapse. The Manifesto of Emperor Charles of the 17th October, 1918, came too late to save the Hapsburg Monarchy. The words of the Manifesto— " In accordance with the will of her peoples, Austria will become a Federal State, in which each race within its natural domain shall form its own national State. The union of the Polish territories of Austria with an independent Polish State will thereby in no way be precluded "—found no echo among the Poles, as they did not wish to join the new Federation, to which as a matter of fact none of the nations of Austria-Hungary wished to belong. The peoples of Austria-Hungary were determined to sever all links with the Hapsburg Dynasty, and were already in open revolt.[110] Austria-Hungary was doomed and her catastrophe was largely due to the faults of the Dynasty and the successive governments in the course of the war.

J. Pilsudski and the Polish Legions

The picture given above would be incomplete if we did not take into account the part played by the Poles in the events which took place in Poland in the course of the war. Many capital mistakes made by the Partitioning Powers were due to the fact that in looking after their own interests exclusively they did not consider it necessary to mould, at least to some extent, their policy to Polish interests, and misjudged the motives and the reactions of the Poles to their different initiatives. On that account they were continually surprised and even shocked by the unexpected resistance and stubborn defence by the Poles of their national interests.

It is outside our task to give here the full story of the developments in Poland during the war. We limit ourselves to describing some facts which had a direct bearing on international politics, and in connection with what concerns this chapter, we wish above all to answer the question to what extent the different schemes devised by the Central Powers met the wishes of the Polish nation or arose from the deliberate moves of those Poles who at that time represented in Poland the movement for independence. The central figure in this movement was indisputably Joseph Pilsudski, the future first head of the independent Polish State and one of the leaders of the Polish Socialist Party in the past. Pilsudski considered that unless Russia was defeated the Polish question would not become an international issue. This former leader of the revolutionary movement in Poland in 1905, knew from experience the weakness of Russia and the latent strength of the national and social movements in the Tsarist Empire. From the very beginning of his political career he had thought that the Poles should co-operate with other nationalities of Russia, not only for the purpose of overthrowing Tsarism but also of restoring independence to the oppressed nationalities. His views on the subject were best summed up in a memorandum submitted by him to the Japanese Foreign Ministry on the 13th July, 1904, during his visit to Tokyo, the aim of which was the organization of Polish units, composed of prisoners of war, to fight against Russia on the side of the Japanese army. In this memorandum Pilsudski said that " only the Poles are able to start in Russia an open struggle and give impulse to the other nationalities oppressed by Russia." He said further :

" This driving force which the Poles possess and the importance of the Poles among the component parts of the Empire make us bold enough to set the aim of splitting Russia into her component parts and securing in this way the independence of the countries attached to her by force. We consider it not only as the fulfilment of our cultural aspirations to an independent existence but also as a guarantee of this existence, as Russia deprived of her conquests will cease to be a menacing and dangerous neighbour to our country." [111]

Even before the war Pilsudski began to prepare cadres for a future Polish army, organizing the so-called " Riflemen's Societies " in Galicia, and to some extent enjoyed the support of the Austrian military authorities which, although welcoming the services which the Polish insurrectionist forces might be able to render to the Austro-Hungarian army should war with Russia break out, nevertheless deeply mistrusted Pilsudski and his followers on account of their radical views and revolutionary past. Both sides avoided political commitments, Pilsudski wishing to preserve the independence of the movement and the Austrians looking at these groups of mostly very young men exclusively from the point of view of their military usefulness.

The beginnings of Pilsudski's movement, inspired by old traditions of Polish risings against Russia, read like a romantic story and there were few politicians who believed that this movement might play any significant part in a struggle in which big armies supported by the powerful machinery of their States would be engaged in a deadly struggle. Nevertheless Pilsudski realized the importance of a " token army " at the beginning of the war, hoping that it might develop very soon into a serious force once a part of the Polish territory was cleared of Russians, and he considered that Poland should mark her presence among the belligerents and proclaim her wish for independence by the appearance of forces which would fight only for Polish national aims. In a lecture delivered in Polish in the rooms of the Geographical Society in Paris a few months before the war, in February 1914, Pilsudski stressed the importance which " force " would play in the War from the political point of view. " The development of military preparedness," he said, " constitutes for our country a certain value on the political market, from which the Polish question has been mercilessly banished since the failure of our insurrection in 1863. . . . The movement of military preparedness brings back the Polish problem to the European chess-board. . . . Only the sword weighs in the balance now in the destiny of a nation. A nation which closed her eyes to this obvious fact would irrevocably compromise its future. We must not be such a nation." [112]

Both in his lecture and in several confidential talks with French and Russian émigré socialist leaders Pilsudski predicted that the war would break out very soon and that the two great coalitions would face each other in a struggle in the course of which first Russia would be defeated by Germany and Austria-Hungary, and then the latter would be defeated in their turn by the Western Powers. We have confirmation from many sides that Pilsudski actually made such statements, amongst others from the Russian socialist veteran leader Victor Chernov in his recently published memoirs.[113] Chernov's evidence can be considered as the most reliable, because he gives all the particulars of his conversation with Pilsudski's emissary Jodko and notes his strong disagreement with the views held by Pilsudski at that time, and developed by Jodko in the said conversation. The Russian Social-Revolutionaries, of whom Chernov had been one of the most prominent representatives, disapproved of Pilsudski's decision to side with the Central Powers against Russia, and they did not believe in the possibility of the simultaneous defeat of Russia and the Central Powers. Jodko declared to Chernov that what mattered most to Poland was the possession of a territory on which a Polish army might be formed. After Russia's defeat the turn of the Central Powers would come; the Poles would fight first against Russia and then join France and Great Britain in a struggle against the Central Powers. All this sounded quite fantastic and led to an open clash between Pilsudski's followers and their Russian friends, the Social-Revolutionaries.

The foregoing account enables us to understand Pilsudski's relations and final rupture with the Central Powers. His co-operation with them had a limited scope; he wanted above all that a Polish army under his command might become a factor of power which would necessitate recognition of the political rights of the fighting nation and lead to the reopening of the Polish question as an international issue.

His ideas were quite different from those of the Galician statesmen who advocated a union between Austria-Hungary and Poland. Pilsudski did not care much for Austria, distrusted her and realized her weakness. He therefore did not wish to identify the Polish cause with that of the decrepit Hapsburg Monarchy which was bound to remain Germany's minor partner.

It is true that he was forced at the beginning to co-operate with Austria-Hungary and submit to the ultimatum of 13th August requesting that the Legions take the oath of allegiance to the Emperor of Austria. The Austrian Supreme Command unilaterally decided by its Order of 27th August, 1914, the question of the organization of the Legions, which formally became units of the Austro-Hungarian army. The Austro-Hungarian military authorities, mistrusting Pilsudski, consented to his taking command of one brigade only (the first brigade), while two other brigades were commanded by officers of the Austrian army of Polish descent. (One of them, then Colonel Joseph Haller, afterwards played a prominent part in the revolt of the Legions after the Brest-Litovsk Treaty and eventually became C.-in-C. of the Polish army in France.) All three brigades fought against the Russians on the Eastern front but it was the actions of the First Brigade in Volhyna in 1916 (see p. 94) that in particular drew the attention of the German High Command to the high soldierly qualities of the Polish troops. Pilsudski remained, however, the undisputed political leader of the Legions and his authority was backed by the Council of Colonels which acted on behalf of all three brigades in the critical moments of their existence.

Pilsudski never considered himself a member of the Austro-

Hungarian army and felt himself free from all political obligations towards the Hapsburg Monarchy. Such an independent attitude gave Pilsudski the possibility of seeking a direct approach to the Germans and exploring the differences existing on Polish matters between the Germans and Austro-Hungarians. For this purpose immediately after the outbreak of the war he set up in the southern part of the Congress Kingdom cleared of Russians, a political organization called P.O.N. (Polish National Organization), hoping that it might make him independent of the Austrophile N.K.N. (Supreme National Council) in Galicia, and enable him to reach an agreement—purely tactical—with the representatives of the German army. He realized that without such an agreement he would be unable to reach Warsaw. The representatives of P.O.N.—Sokolnicki, an eminent Polish historian, later Ambassador to Turkey, and Jodko, later Envoy to Latvia—signed two agreements with Colonel Traugott von Sauberzweig, Quartermaster of Hindenburg's army.[114a] The first agreement of the 2nd October, 1914, gave P.O.N. the right to recruit men for the Polish Legion, levy requisitions and carry out propaganda. The second agreement, dated 10th October, provided that one Polish battalion with a strength of 500 men, and one cavalry squadron with a strength of 160 men would take part in the battle of Warsaw and that Polish and German detachments would in turn mount guard at the Royal Castle in Warsaw. These agreements became void on account of further military developments and the retreat of Hindenburg's army, and did not bear fruit until two years later. There is no doubt that the Germans were bitterly disappointed by this first attempt at collaboration with Pilsudski. They expected a general rising in Congress Poland, while the Polish population maintained an expectant and even frankly hostile attitude towards the Central Powers. On the other side the Germans did not at that time wish to have a trained Polish army and required from Pilsudski and his men only some auxiliary services, hoping that the war might finish within six months.[114b]

Pilsudski very quickly drew the practical conclusions from the fact that a general rising against the Russians was impossible for the following reasons :

(1). There was nothing in the past that predestined Germany to play the rôle of Poland's " liberators." The ruthless policy of extermination of the Polish elements in the old historic Polish provinces belonging to Prussia, the heroic resistance of the Polish population in those areas, enjoying full support of all the Poles, the records of the long German-Russian collaboration aiming at the suppression of the Polish question as an international problem, created great psychological obstacles which were very difficult to overcome, and the Germans did practically nothing, at the beginning of the War, to remove the deeply-rooted mistrust of the Polish population in the areas occupied by their military forces.

(2). The Germans and Austro-Hungarians entered those parts of Poland which prior to the war belonged to Russia, without any clear political programme. Furthermore, they were not agreed between themselves on this important issue, the greatness of which they came to realize only gradually. It should be also kept in mind that the Polish nation expected from the War the realization of her hopes of the reunion of all parts of Poland; these hopes were revived at the beginning of the War and many Poles expected that they might be supported by the Western Allies of Russia, especially by France, considered as the traditional friend of Poland. The Central Powers started the occupation of the Congress Kingdom by dividing between themselves what for a century had constituted a homogeneous economic and political unit. It was feared in Poland that it portended a new partition of Poland.

(3). The behaviour of the Central Powers towards the civilians was often ruthless (e.g. the bombardment of the undefended city of Kalisz, which caused many casualties among the civilian population). Moreover, the country was exploited economically in the most vicious way, and its whole economic life was gradually brought to a standstill. " For after confiscating all the stocks of raw materials and manufactured products, after expropriating the bulk of machine-tools, electric motors and other light machines, the Germans proceeded to remove the bronze, copper and nickel parts of the heavy machines. And then, after the machine plant had been rendered useless in this manner, the Germans requisitioned iron— the only metal with which the missing parts could be replaced." [114c] The apostle of Mittel Europa, Frederick Naumann, observing these barbaric proceedings in Lodz, the centre of the textile industry in the Congress Kingdom, judged very severely these wanton destructions, aimed at the " de-industrialization " of Poland, a strange prelude to the peaceful co-operation of the countries of Central and Eastern Europe. " The damage we are causing by proceeding in this way greatly exceeds our benefits (Wir verderben auf diese Weise viel mehr, als wir gewinnen)." [114d]

As a matter of fact, at the beginning the military commanders of the Central Powers deluded themselves that they could win the support of the Poles quite gratuitously, without giving any binding engagements so far as the future of Poland was concerned. To ascertain this turn of mind it suffices to read some cynical outpourings of the Austro-Hungarian and German military commanders. For instance, Conrad von Hoetzendorff writes in a letter to Baron

Arthur von Bolfras, General Aide-de-Camp and Head of the Military Chancellery of the Emperor Francis-Joseph, on the 25th September, 1914 : " General Kummer states that there is no interest in Russian Poland in our liberating abilities. What will happen to our Polish Legion? Cannon-fodder? Well, there is not enough cannon-fodder. Mars is very greedy." They saw in Pilsudski only an undisciplined military commander, a conspirator, and were offended that the Polish Legion wanted to play a political part.[115]

Pilsudski was well aware that neither Austria-Hungary nor Germany wished to raise the Polish question for the time being, and he decided to mark time. He relied more and more on an underground military body, the P.O.W. (Polish Military Organization), organized by himself, and recommended extreme caution in expanding the Legions in spite of the opposition of N.K.N. and in particular the head of the military department of this body, Colonel Sikorski (Prime Minister and C.-in-C. in the course of the Second World War).[116] On the 3rd June, 1915, Pilsudski sent a letter to a meeting organized by the Military Department of N.K.N. protesting against " selling cheaply the Polish business," and taking the view that the Congress Kingdom should keep its ambiguous attitude on account of the alternative : " Either a separate peace will be concluded with Russia and then everything is finished for the time being, or the War will last a long time and in such a case we can wait." [117]

After the capture of Warsaw by the German army Pilsudski went to Warsaw, but a few days later was obliged by the German authorities to leave. It was at a meeting with his followers in Warsaw (15th August, 1915) that he announced his decision to suspend recruitment for the Legion as " to send recruits to the Legion would be contrary to our honour, contrary to our interests "—" Germans have to-day replaced the Russians in Poland. We must resist the Germans." [118]

Nevertheless the Legions continued to take an honourable part in the war operations, and the First Brigade under Pilsudski's command distinguished itself in many battles and especially in the battle at Kosciuchnowka (4th–5th July, 1916, see above, p. 94), which drew the attention of the German Headquarters and Government to the military value of these Polish units.

After this battle Pilsudski tendered his resignation from the post of Commander of the First Brigade of the Legion, and this gesture can be considered as his definite break with Austria-Hungary. Pilsudski had realized for a long time that Poland had nothing to expect from the Danubian Monarchy. In the light of the evidence produced by us in the second part of this chapter we have to state that he was right to cherish no illusions on the subject. In a conversation with one of his confidants in March 1917 he summed up his views on Austria :

"It is necessary for us to separate ourselves from Austrophile schemes and similar nonsense coming from N.K.N., even if such schemes might please the French, which is not to be excluded. I refuse to follow them. I do not wish to associate myself with the dead and I do not see any reason to fortify or revive the Hapsburg Monarchy through injections of Polish blood. But even if Austria is not dead, it is Germany which is the partner with the decisive voice. Austrian schemes can bring about only a new partition of Poland."

Plans for a Polish Army and the causes of failure

The Proclamation of the 5th November, 1916, was certainly an attempt to " buy the Polish business cheaply," underestimating the political maturity of the Polish nation. Immediately after the Proclamation an appeal was launched by the German and Austro-Hungarian Governors—von Beseler and von Kuk—calling on the Poles to enlist in the " Polish army," emphasizing the military deeds of the Polish Legion : " Valiantly and with great glory fought your brethren from the Polish Legion. Follow their example." It was obvious that the Germans wanted to keep full control of this new army. Hutten-Czapski, an intimate adviser of Beseler and a member of his staff with special powers from Emperor William, notes that immediately after the Proclamation Governor-General Beseler wanted to arrest Pilsudski, dissolve P.O.W. and put himself at the head of the Polish army.[119] But the appeal of the two Governors-General was a cry in the wilderness and the Germans realized very quickly that it would be impossible to form a Polish army without Pilsudski.

Pilsudski, of course, welcomed the Proclamation, seeing in it the reopening of the Polish question as an international issue. But to him the Proclamation was only the beginning. He saw in it a great opportunity to form a Polish army, but he wanted such an army to become a political factor. The primary condition for it was the creation of a real State authority on which such an army might depend. The little response from the Poles to enlisting induced the Central Powers to create the embryo of a Polish State authority under the form of a Council of State; the joint order of Beseler and Kuk of the 6th December, 1916, set up this Council, which met for the first time on the 14th January, 1917. It was a step forward, but not sufficient from the Polish point of view because the Council of State was not vested with real authority, having purely advisory functions, while the administration of the country remained with the occupying powers. Nevertheless, Pilsudski joined the Council of State and became the Head of the Military Department of this body.

His views on the conditions under which the Polish army should be formed were summed up in a memorandum submitted to General Beseler on the 15th December, 1916, stating that the Polish army should be formed by the Poles themselves in accordance with Polish national traditions. At that time he was ready to reach a compromise with the Germans, and it was perhaps the only real opportunity for the Central Powers to come to an honest agreement with him, but he wanted a compromise based on clear and explicit agreements : army and enlistment even on a very big scale, but an army submitted to a Polish Government.[120] We know his inmost thoughts from an instruction given to one of his representatives in a neutral country :

" ... The Polish Army should be formed on the Polish territory with the assistance of the Central Powers if the latter guarantee its national character. Such an army could be used only against Russia. ...

" ... We fight together with Austria against Russia but without binding our future in any organic form to this State, having no authorization from our nation for doing it, and striving only after an independent and sovereign Polish State. ...

" ... Poland must not find herself in opposition to the Western countries, with which we have always in history had friendly relations." [121]

This point of view was defended with extreme vigour by Pilsudski within the Council of State. " The Polish nation cannot put up with the Austro-German method of making Poland without the Poles " (Speech at the Council of State on 31st May, 1917). " The army should be a Polish army, depending on a Polish political body, as otherwise it will not be a Polish army but coloured colonial troops " (Speech on 8th June, 1917).

The Central Powers were not eager to have such an army and at no time did they wish to treat the Poles as equal partners. Moreover, some important events led to the final clash between Pilsudski and the Central Powers. On the one hand, Germany, starting a ruthless submarine warfare, hoped to force the Western Powers to surrender before the military and industrial power of the U.S.A. could be felt on the Western front; consequently she considered that she no longer needed the help of Polish troops. Moreover, with Russia in her desperate straits, she cherished illusions of very soon making a separate peace.

On the other hand, the entry into the war of the U.S.A., which by the message of President Wilson stepped forward as an advocate of Poland's independence, and the outbreak of the Russian Revolution followed by the Proclamation of the Provisional Russian Government recognizing Poland's Independence (which seemed to put an end, at least for the time being, to the old Russo-Polish feud) completely changed the political position. Pilsudski tendered his resignation on the 2nd July, 1917, stating " that the Central Powers are mistaken in supposing that it is possible to form a Polish army after their fashion. Since the Council of State can have no legal influence on the formation of a Polish Army, I, as representing that Army, can no longer remain at my post in the Council." In these circumstances the great majority of the Polish Legion refused to take the oath of allegiance to the Central Powers. Pilsudski was arrested by the Germans on the 21st July, 1917, and was imprisoned in the fortress of Magdeburg. As Hutten-Czapski states in his *Memoirs,* this fact weighed heavily not only on the German policy in occupied Poland during the war but also had far-reaching consequences for post-war relations between Germany and Poland.[122] At the time of his arrest Pilsudski had decided to sever all his links with the Central Powers. The plans were fairly advanced for his crossing the front line and going to Russia in order to organize a Polish army on Russian soil.

After Pilsudski's arrest the Polish Military Organization went underground, under the command of Colonel Rydz-Smigly (later Marshal of Poland and C.-in-C. of the Polish Army at the beginning of the Second World War). It played a decisive rôle in the disarmament of German and Austrian garrisons at the moment of the collapse of the Central Powers. The P.O.W. spread its activity to the Ukraine and Russia and established contacts with the Polish divisions formed there from former soldiers of the Russian army.

In spring 1918 Colonel Rydz-Smigly sent his emissaries to Moscow to enter into relations with the head of the French Military Mission, General Lavergne. Rydz-Smigly himself went to Kiev and Jassy, where he conferred with the Allied representatives.[123] The Brest-Litovsk Treaty, which aroused general indignation in Poland, induced the last unit fighting side by side with the Central Powers, the Second Brigade of the Legion, to cross the front line at Rarancza in Bukovina on the 15th February, 1918. From that moment the whole Polish nation was at the side of the Allies, in spite of all the efforts of the Central Powers to maintain the appearance of the existence of an allied Polish State.

After the crisis of July 1917 the efforts of Germany were centred not so much on the formation of a Polish army, which became for them more and more a secondary issue, but on the creation of a *fait accompli* in Poland in order to have at their disposal an important asset at the time of peace negotiations.[124] The Central Powers gradually surrendered some branches of the administration in the Congress Kingdom to the Poles : justice on the 1st September, 1917, schools on the 1st October, 1917, and the rest on the eve of their collapse. On the 14th October, 1917, the two Emperors appointed a Regency Council. The importance of this gradual building up of the Polish State in the course of the war, little known in the West, should not be neglected. A Polish writer who took a prominent part in these activities states : " The views generally held are that the rise of the Polish State was exclusively due to the Entente and that the Polish nation received her statehood as a ready gift. Such opinions are not only false from the historical point of view but they are in contradiction to the well-established notions of constitutional law relating to the formation of new States." [125] There is no doubt that the embryonic Polish State under the occupation was not fully sovereign, but the developments in Poland enabled her to resume her full independence under conditions much more favourable than usually occurs with new States.

*

*   *

The reasons for the failure of the Central Powers to find a solution which might agree both with their interests and with those of the Poles clearly appear from the foregoing. It was not until the end of the War, that is in late summer 1918, that they accepted the idea of a really independent Poland, although insisting on imposing a candidate of their own on the Polish throne. At that moment an independent Poland seemed to all to be an inescapable issue. So far as Germany in particular was concerned, she was unable to find the right way between the needs of security of the German State and the claims of Prussian colonialism. Erzberger was right in saying : " The way to Warsaw leads only through Poznan." [126] Until the end the Prussians did not wish even to abolish the discriminatory anti-Polish measures and the expropriation laws in " Prussian " Poland.

Until the last moment Germany hesitated between different solutions : whether to sell the Polish assets to Russia or accept the fact of the independent Poland or agree to the Austro-Polish solution, previously reducing Polish territory—which made her whole policy towards Poland profoundly insincere and inconsistent.[127] At the time when the German Government was ready to go very far in concessions to Poland, Ludendorff pursued a policy of his own in the East, which at some moments provoked open clashes between him and the Government, as for instance at the beginning of 1918. His idea was to impose on the future Polish State very large " frontier rectifications " and to surround Poland by satellite States of Lithuania and Ukraine, which would inevitably have reduced Poland also to the status of a semi-independent State.[128] This conception was partially carried out, as we know, at Brest-Litovsk. But still at the beginning of July 1918 Ludendorff requested such frontier rectifications as would have deprived Poland of her very valuable possessions and would have required the expulsion of millions of Poles from their native soil.[129] On the eve of the collapse Ludendorff agreed to the surrender to Poland of the undisputably Polish part of Lithuania, but insisted on the very close association of the Polish State with Germany and on separating Poland from Russia by Lithuanian territory.[130] Lithuania and the Baltic States were to be converted, according to his view, into German dependencies to be settled by German colonists. The foolishness of Ludendorff's conceptions consisted in the belief that a constructive policy in the East could be built on purely military arrangements inevitably involving the permanent hostility of all the nations of Eastern Europe.

Effects of the November Proclamation

To the contemporaries the effects of the November Proclamation on the further developments of the Polish question seemed far-reaching. The Germans and Poles agreed on this point. We know that this question became a real obsession in Germany after the War, when the motives and reasons for this initiative were considered from a purely partisan point of view in the heated debate on the causes of the defeat. A German author who wrote a well-documented and rather objective book on the policy of the Central Powers towards Poland during the War wrote : " The November Proclamation raised the Polish question from a Russo-Polish frontier problem to an international issue although Germany opposed it until the end of the War." [131] Burian notes :

> " This act did not fulfil all desires and did not solve all difficulties, but it created a position which could no longer be remade. The restitution of Poland to Russia was thus rendered impossible, the same as the annexation of Poland by the Central Powers, but also the Entente which pretended to fight for the liberation of nations had to accept this event, although with the most unpleasant comments." [132]

We know from the preceding parts of this chapter that Germany and Austria-Hungary in issuing the November Proclamation did not wish to tie their hands, and pursued their own political ends. They certainly did not become the promoters of the principle of national self-determination in Eastern Europe, no matter what may have thought the apostle of the idea of Central-

European Union, Frederick Naumann.[133] Neither Germany nor Austria-Hungary could at that time adhere sincerely to this principle because it meant the loss of the Eastern provinces of Prussia and the dissolution of Austria-Hungary.[134] The plans for remaking the political map of Eastern Europe, carried out by the Central Powers at Brest-Litovsk, show that they acted for purposes of disguised annexations, covered by fashionable slogans. Thus the propagandistic efforts were of short duration.

Were the international repercussions of the November Proclamation on the policy of the Entente far-reaching? Dmowski wrote in his book *Polityka Polska* :

> " The Act of the 5th November rendered great services to our cause. More than anything else it contributed to enlightening the European statesmen on the international bearing of the Polish question. It gave a strong impulse to approaching the Polish question in a more serious way. ... We felt for the first time that we were not only supplying information but that we represented also a force with which one must reckon." [135]

If we examine the effects of the initiatives of the Central Powers on opinion in Western countries we can state that what weighed more heavily than anything else was, above all, the consequences for the military position in Eastern Europe which might have arisen from the appearance of a strong Polish army at the front (see above, p. 52). Pilsudski was right in saying in 1914 that " only the sword weighs in the balance in the destiny of nations." When it became clear that the Poles were unwilling to sell themselves " cheaply." [136] there was a feeling of great relief, and the refusal of the Poles to become simple tools of German policy made the Polish cause more popular in the West than did anything else.

The policy of the Central Powers forced the Russians to revise their policy towards Poland, and was certainly one of the factors instrumental in the issuing of the Order of the Tsar of the 25th December, 1916, and the Proclamation of the Provisional Government of March, 1917.

We saw in the first chapter that in spite of the November Proclamation the Western countries continued to consider the Polish question as depending on the decisions of the Tsarist Government until the outbreak of the Russian Revolution. But even after that and after the congratulations had been sent by the Entente Powers to the Provisional Russian Government on account of its recognition of Polands' independence, there arose in the West some conceptions of promoting the Austro-Polish solution as a price for a separate peace with Austria-Hungary

Secret negotiations with Austria-Hungary

The secret negotiations between Austria and the Western Powers in 1917 bring to light a curious turn of mind of some Western statesmen and their lack of understanding for national issues in Central-Eastern Europe (see above, p. 9). Even before Russia was disabled by revolution, the necessity for preserving Austria-Hungary as a counterpoise to Germany in Central Europe, as an indispensable factor in the European balance of power, had preyed on many minds in Great Britain and France. There was nothing new in this idea, it had been very popular in France about the end of the nineteenth century. We know that the Western Allies of Russia looked with some anxiety at her plans for the dismemberment of Austria-Hungary, but they nevertheless tacitly concurred in them in order to maintain friendship with Russia. There was certainly a grain of truth in the assertions, for instance, of Noel Buxton in the *New Statesman* (20th January, 1917) : " To break Austria-Hungary while the nations embodied in the Russian Empire remain unliberated would destroy the balance of power," and this point of view should be retained for future consideration, as on the one hand the acquiescence in Russian conquests would have made any balance of power in Europe unstable, and on the other hand the integration of the nations of Central-Eastern Europe within the framework of a federal union would be a wise policy; but neither did Austria-Hungary show herself capable of playing the part assigned to her by some Western statesmen nor were the nations inhabiting this area ready to be satisfied with " some internal home-rule."

In the initial stages of the negotiations carried out through Prince Sixte of Bourbon-Parma the Polish question seemed a secondary issue. Making his plans for the conversations on the 15th October, 1916, Prince Sixte observed : " We need not consider for the moment the reconstruction of Poland, which depends on Russia's putting into practice the principles which now prevail." [137] And in a conversation with Prince Sixte at Laxenbourg on the 23rd March, 1917, Emperor Charles " touching on the Polish question, expressed his opinion that its solution would greatly help in removing the difficulties between himself and Russia, in economic matters, questions of boundaries and the like. He relied upon countless ties of sympathy between Austria and Poland, which would be in perfect accord with the traditional affection felt for Poland in France." Emperor Charles " hoped to carry on, in future, the policy of a horizontal alliance between Russia, France, England and Austria." [138] In fact Emperor Charles wished to return to the *status quo,* as appears from the minimum programme laid down at Vienna on the 27th March, 1917, at a meeting between Bethmann-

Hollweg and Czernin. But a few months later Charles and his minister Czernin put Galicia at Germany's disposal and were ready to agree to the surrender of Poland to Germany.

The disruption of Germany was the primary object in the first conversations between Prince Sixte and the French negotiators. On the 5th March, 1917, President Poincaré said to Prince Sixte : " It is in France's interest not merely to keep Austria as she is but to enlarge her frontiers at Germany's expense by taking in Silesia or Bavaria," and M. Cambon made this ridiculous offer, recalling the old diplomatic patterns of the end of the eighteenth century : " There is Silesia, the dowry of Maria Teresa " (see above, p. 13).

The Polish question does not appear in these conversations until the 20th May, being raised by M. Ribot, French Prime Minister, whose attitude was at that time : " Hesitate, procrastinate and then stand still." [139]

We know that it was the question of the need to agree to some important territorial sacrifices by Austria-Hungary to Italy which apparently became the stumbling-block, but in fact the negotiations were based on self-delusion. Neither the Austrian Germans nor the Hungarians would have tolerated these fantastic plans. Czernin was right in saying that carrying out these plans would have provoked civil war in Austria-Hungary. Moreover, Germany was still very strong at that time from the military point of view, and the risks of betrayal were too high for the Hapsburg Monarchy.[140]

The Polish question played a much more important part in the conversations carried out between negotiators less prominent than the preceding ones, namely Major Armand, charged with a mission by the Second Bureau of the French General Staff, on the one side, and Count Nicholas Revertera, an Austrian, on the other. Their conversations began in July 1917 in Switzerland. In the instructions of the French General Staff of the 4th August, 1917, we read the following :

> " The sole enemy of France, the sole danger to Europe is Prussia. . . . The Entente must, therefore, create a power bordering on and irreconcilably hostile to Prussia. We can do this through the Hapsburg Dynasty, if we attach to Austria by ties of a personal sovereignty a federation of those States in which Slavs form a majority, and associate with those States a Poland restored to its frontiers of 1772, that is a Poland extending from Danzig to the Carpathians. . . . Finally, we should directly weaken and exasperate Prussia, by attaching to this union Silesia, as it was annexed by Frederick II. . . ." [141]

There is a curious passage relating to Russia : " Russia will lose no territory which is properly speaking Russian; besides her present position compels us, first and foremost, to overthrow Prussia."

At a conversation on the 7th August during which Major Armand offered to Austria-Hungary : Poland restored to its frontiers prior to the partitions of 1772, the Kingdom of Bavaria and Silesia, which would form one of the hereditary States of Austria, Count Revertera observed rather sarcastically : " I am quite delighted; this is more than we could have hoped for. Some of it is almost too good. They have talked only of dismembering us, so far, and now they want to make us into a great State." He showed as much surprise as pleasure at the suggested federation with Poland, and said that they must first make certain that Bavaria and Silesia would consent to join this new union.[142]

But still more fantastic was the note for Austria communicated by Armand to Revertera on the 22nd August, 1917, especially in the passages containing the anticipations on Russia's future attitude towards all these plans :

> " This federation (in Austria) would allow each of its component States a large measure of autonomy, and would correspond to the democratic aspirations of the peoples. ...
> " The mere fact of such a federation would remove all antagonisms between the new Russia and Austria, and would bridge the gulf which separates Austria from the masses of her Slav population. A liberated and reconstituted Poland, threatened by no risk of hostilities with her Eastern neighbour, would gravitate towards this Danubian Confederation." [143]

Czernin's answer, given on the 19th September, 1917, was " the *status quo* in principle, with the exception of certain exchanges of territory." We know that at that time he began negotiations with Germany for a personal union with Poland, but upon conditions totally different from those advised by the French negotiators : he was ready to agree to Austria entering into very close economic and military relations with Germany, he even consented to the state of " vassalage " provided Germany agreed to the Austro-Polish solution.

A German writer makes the following ironic observations about these negotiations :

> " Thus the Allied and Associated Powers were ready even in summer 1917, at a time when there was no longer a Russian veto (on the Polish question) to offer Poland's independence as the price for a separate Austrian peace, in order to destroy Prussia-Germany." [144]

Illusions on the possibility of detaching Austria from Germany were also shared by some British statesmen, as appears from the conversations between General Smuts and the Austro-Hungarian Ambassador, Count Mensdorff, held in Switzerland late in 1917. General Smuts based his views on Austria-Hungary on completely mistaken analogies between the latter and the British Empire. In a conversation on the 18th–19th December, 1917, General Smuts declared that the British had no intention of " interfering in Austria's internal affairs," and he expressed the view that " if Austria could become a really liberal Empire in which her *subject peoples would, as far as possible, be satisfied and content,* she would become for Central Europe very much what the British Empire had become for the rest of the world." We should keep in mind that it occurred at the time of the Brest-Litovsk negotiations, in the course of which the Austrian attitude was rather dishonourable, at a time when nearly all the nations of Austria were in a state of open revolt against the Monarchy, and the overwhelming majority of Poles were resolved to sever all links with the Hapsburg Dynasty. The readiness of a British statesman acting upon the instructions of his Government to bargain the freedom of " subject peoples " against a mirage of a separate peace which Austria was absolutely incapable of concluding, throws a peculiar light on the state of ignorance and opportunism of the Western countries so far as the affairs of Central Europe were concerned. Mensdorff's views on Poland were much more realistic than those of Smuts. It was very strange that Smuts, who later at the Peace Conference invariably supported the German point of view against the Polish on all vital issues for Poland, at that time had quite unfounded and preposterous fears that the orientation of a new Polish State might be " pro-German." The part of the conversation referring to Poland reads as follows :

> " Mensdorff himself raised the question of Poland which, he said, from its superior culture had rather a Western than an Eastern orientation. I (Smuts) said it was essential from the point of view which we had been discussing that the future Polish State should not have a German orientation He replied that there was little fear of that ; owing to the liberal policy that Austria had followed the future Polish State was much more likely to co-operate with Austria than with Germany. I (Smuts) said that we were pledged to an independent Kingdom or State of Poland *but* that if Austria really broke away and realized the mission sketched out above, the possibility of some link of a personal or a loose union between Austria and Poland was not excluded, and that the addition of Galicia might be a desirable move from that point of view." [145]

It should be emphasized that the attitude of the United States Government was much more correct. That Government also had hopes of inducing Austria to conclude a separate peace. The American attempts to this effect continued almost until the Armistice, but even in the earliest stages, that is at the beginning of 1917, before the declaration of war against Austria-Hungary by the United States, the Government of the latter excluded the Polish question from negotiations with Austria and insisted on the recognition of the full independence of Poland. For instance, in the conversations between the American Ambassador, Penfield, and the Austro-Hungarian Government in February–March 1917,

> " the course of action planned was to say to the Austrians that there was no intention by the Allies to dismember their Empire, except to free Poland, provided conditions did not change and provided the Vienna Government was willing to negotiate with her enemies. ... The United States indicated a willingness, but did not directly offer, to act as intermediary in obtaining a definite assurance from the Allies that they would preserve the integrity of the Austro-Hungarian Empire, always excepting Poland, as a preliminary step to the negotiations." [146]

In the last interview with Count Tarnowski (a Pole, by the way), the Ambassador of Austria-Hungary in Washington, on the 1st May, 1917, Secretary of State Lansing declared that Poland must be free and have an outlet to the sea.[147]

There is no doubt that the Western Powers tried to save Austria-Hungary until the last moment, as appears clearly from Wilson's and Lloyd George's speeches in early 1918 and the whole diplomatic correspondence of that period. The account given by us in the second part of this chapter showed that far from severing or loosening her links with Germany the Danubian Monarchy in the last months of its existence was agreeing to plans which would have led to a German-controlled Central European Union. Lord Balfour's biographer rightly observed :

> " Although Austria was already hysterically anxious for peace, it had to be a peace arranged with both the Central Empires, if Hapsburg domination was to survive. The German elements in Austria in control then, and in control till the end, must cling to Germany as cling they did until the final crash in October 1918." [148]

The disintegration of Austria-Hungary was due to natural causes and was not the result of deliberate moves of policy of the Western Powers; one can even say that it went against their inmost wishes and plans. According to historical traditions, Empress Maria Theresa wept when signing the act of the First Partition of Poland. History justified her gloomy forebodings, as there is no doubt that the growth of two imperialistic empires in the immediate neighbourhood of Austria was one of the main causes of its collapse nearly 150 years later. The Dual Empire became an obsolete form of multi-national State and was unable to adjust its archaic forms to modern requirements and to the new realities. It was impossible to put back the clock of history. Have we not seen the same phenomena in the constitutional development of the British Empire, although occurring by mutual consent and without the use of violence? Professor G. W. Keeton of London University characterized in these terms the process through which the British Empire has passed : "From the constitutional standpoint the transformation of the British Empire has been a process of disintegration into an association of free communities." [149]

In view of the recent and most tragic experience of integration by force, achieved after the Second World War with the acquiescence of the Western Powers, one must wonder at the following words written by Winston Churchill in *The Gathering Storm*, contrary to all historical evidence and profoundly untrue :

" There is not one of the peoples that constituted the Europe of the Hapsburgs to whom gaining their independence has not brought the tortures which ancient poets and theologians had reserved for the damned." [150]

Only by adopting the same methods which prevailed in 1945 could Austria-Hungary have been saved in 1918.

NOTES

[1] There exists an excellent bibliography on Polish-German relations (until 1933): CASIMIR SMOGORZEWSKI, *Abregé d'une bibliographie relative aux relations Germano-Polonaises* (Problèmes Politiques de la Pologne Contemporaine, II (Supplément)), Paris, 1933.

[2] JAMES W. GERARD, *My Four Years in Germany*, pp. 24, 25, 27.

[3] R. H. LORD, o.c., p. 496.

[4] J. FELDMAN, *Bismarck a Polska*, p. 314.

[5] FELDMAN, *Ibidem*, p. 316.

[6] FÜRST HOHENLOHE, *Denkwürdig-Reiten*, II, p. 343. BETHMANN-HOLLWEG, *Die Betrachtungen zum Weltkriege*, 2 Teil, p. 87.

[7] BÜLOW, *Deutsche Politik*, p. 271 : " Fürst Bismarck hat auch wiederholt auf die Gefahr hingewiesen, dass in irgendeiner Form selbständiges Polen der geborene Aliirte von Frankreich, England und jedem anderen unserer Gegner werden könnte."

[8] BÜLOW, *Ibidem*, p. 272: Wir dürfen jedenfalls nicht vergessen, dass die preussische Monarchie durch den Zerfall der polnischen Republik gross geworden ist, und dass der schwarze Adler,

Schwer ist sein Flug,
Er trägt die Weltgeschichte,

stieg im Kampfe mit dem weissen Adler."

Ibidem, p. 282: " Der Kampf um den Boden, der seinem Wesen nach ein Kampf um die ausreichende Durchsetzung des Ostlandes mit deutschen Menschen ist, wird immer das A und O unserer national-deutschen Politik im Osten sein."

Ibidem, p. 259: " Eine Kulturmission ist es gewesen die uns Deutsche einst über die Elbe und die Oder nach dem Osten geführt hat. Als die Polen selbst sich schliesslich ausserstande zeigten, ein staatliches Leben zu erhalten und der starke preussische Rechts- und Ordnungsstaat Teile ehemals polnischer Reichsgebiet unter seine Herrschaft stellte, da war in diesen Gebieten schon seit Generationen deutsche Kulturarbeit geleistet worden."

[9] BÜLOW, ibidem, p. 281.

[9a] BÜLOW, *ibidem*, p. 269.

[10] LUDWIG BERNHARD, *Die Polenfrage*, p. 569. For bibliography on this subject see SMOGORZEWSKI, o.c. Among recent books, R. W. TIMS, *Germanising Prussian Poland*.

[11] GENERAL HOFFMANN, *Krieg der Versäumten Gelegenheiten*, p. 204.

[12] Published from the archives of the former General-Government of Poland by a Polish magazine, *Niepodległość*, Vol. XVIII, pp. 460 ff.

[13] BETHMANN-HOLLWEG, o.c. " Die Diktatur aber, die General Ludendorff anstrebte stiess, indem sie den Reichskanzler zum ausführenden Organ seiner eigenen Entschlüsse machen wollte, unsere staatliche Ordnung um."

[14] E. LUDENDORFF, *Meine Kriegserinnerungen*, p. 57: " Viele Beziehungen verbanden mich mit Provinz und Stadt Posen. Das Polentum hat uns nicht gedankt. Diejenige haben recht, die das deutsche Vaterland immer von seinen Aspirationen gewarnt haben."

[15] DR. PAUL ROTH, *Die politische Entwicklung in Kongresspolen während der deutschen Okkupation*. p. 188 ; see also *P. R. F. R.*, 1918, Sup. I, Vol. I, p. 875. The Minister in Switzerland (Stovall) to the Secretary of State, August 23rd, 1918: " German attitude toward Poland is barometer of condition of German military success. When Germany victorious, Poland is neglected and exploited economically. When situation less advantageous, Germany tries to allure Poland with political concessions."

[16] BOGDAN HUTTEN-CZAPSKI, *Sechzig Jahre Politik und Gesellschaft*, II, p. 145.

[17] VOLKMANN, *Der Grosse Krieg*, pp. 203-4, a letter from Moltke to Conrad, 10th February, 1913: " Bedarf Österreich aller seiner Kräfte, um den Kampf gegen Russland führen, so gilt dasselbe für Deutschland im Kampfe gegen Frankreich. Denn in dem Austrag des Streites zwischen Deutschland und Frankreich liegt meiner Überzeugung nach das Schwergewicht des ganzen europäischen Krieges, und auch das Schicksal Österreichs wird nicht am Bug, sondern an der Seine entgültig entschieden werden."

CONRAD, *Aus meiner Dienstzeit*, III, p. 673: Conversation between Conrad and Moltke at Carlsbad, 12th May, 1914, and Moltke's statement: " Wir hoffen in sechs Wochen nach Beginn der Operationen mit

Frankreich fertig zu sein, oder wenigstens soweit, dass wir unsere Hauptkräfte gegen Osten verschieben können."

[18] KAROL KAUTSKY, *Documents allemands relatifs à l'origine de la guerre*, Vol. IV, No. 876. Le Chef de l'Etat Major Général de l'Armée au Ministère des Affaires Etrangères, Berlin, 5 août, 1914: "L'insurrection en Pologne est fomentée. Elle germera sur un terrain propice, car dès maintenant nos troupes sont accueillies en Pologne comme des amis." Also CONRAD, o.c. IV, p. 197: Account of conversation on 8th and 9th August, 1914, between the Emperor and the representative of the Austro-Hungarian army, General Count Stürgh: "Seine Majestät ... ging sofort auf die Notwendigkeit über deutscherseits Polen, unsererseits Polen und die Ukraine mit allen zu Gebote stehenden Mitteln-Proklamationen, Emissären und viel Geld zu revolutionisiren."

[19] CONRAD, o.c. V, pp. 154-5, 753 and 811: "Der Status quo wäre wohl für uns, aber auch für Russland die annehmbarste Bedingung gewesen, und Russland hätte wohl getan, auf dieser Basis mit uns Frieden zu schliessen. Wäre jedoch Russland auf dem ihm so erwünschten Besitz Ostgaliziens bestanden, so hätte es dafür einen gleich grossen Raum Russisch Polen an uns abtreten müssen, etwa vom Gouvernement Warschau, Praga, Nowo-Georgevsk (Modlin), das Gouvernement Petrikau, Radom mit Ivangorod (Deblin) und das Gouvernement Kielce. Przemysl hätte dabei unbedingt in österreichischem Besitze bleiben müssen."

A letter from von Berchtold to Conrad of 19th December, 1914, *ibidem*, V, p. 848: "Davon bin ich allerdings unterrichtet, dass man an massgebender Stelle in Deutschland den Gedanken erörtert hat, ein Arrangement zwischen Deutschland und Österreich-Ungarn einerseits und Russland andererseits zustande zu bringen, welche den Krieg mit Russland in absehbarer Zeit beendigen und dieses von seinen Alliirten trennen würde. In vager Gestalt scheint eben in Berlin noch immer der Gedanke an einen Zusammenschluss dieser drei Reiche, wiewohl es nicht recht einleuchtend ist, wie die deutsche Ostpolitik sich mit den Aspirationen Russland im Nahen Orient vereinbaren soll." See also BURIAN, *Drei Jahre*, p. 139.

[20] STRESEMANN, *Diaries*, II, p. 291.

[21] WHEELER-BENNETT, *Brest-Litovsk*, p. 10.

[22] P. FRANK CHAMBERS, *The War Behind the War*, p. 470.

[23] BETHMANN-HOLLWEG, o.c., II, p. 99.

[24] LUDENDORFF, *Kriegserrinnerungen*, p. 318.

[25] WLADYSLAW BARANOWSKI, Rozmowy z Pilsudskim, in the magazine *Niepodległość*, Vol. XVIII.

[26] ASKENAZY, *Uwagi*, p. 467.

[27] BETHMANN-HOLLWEG'S *Kriegsreden*, p. 37.

[28] BETHMANN-HOLLWEG'S *Kriegsreden*, p. 79: "Weder im Osten, noch im Westen dürfen unsere Feinde von heute über Einfalltore verfügen, durch die sie uns von morgen ab aufs neue und schärfer als bisher bedrohen."

[29] VOLKMANN, *Der Grosse Krieg*, pp. 59 ff.: "Zur Wiederaufnahme

der Offensive fehlten die Kräfte. Infolge der Niederlage des österreichisch-ungarischen Heeres hatten immer mehr deutsche Truppen nach
dem Osten hierübergezogen werden müssten. Es bestand keine Möglichkeit sie wieder frei zu machen und nach dem Westen zurückzuführen.
Es blieb also nur ein Angriff auf Russland übrig." TIRPITZ, *Erinnerungen.* " Dieser Friedenschluss (with Russia) wurde durch den Beitritt
der Türkei zu unserer Partei und die Nichtausführung des Hinden-
burgschen Feldzuges von 1915 erschweit."

[30] *Documents Secrets.*

[31] *Ibidem,* p. 327. Also the text of an official German memorandum of 26th July, 1915, published by HUTTEN-CZAPSKI, o.c. II,
p. 163: " Die Reichsleitung hat ein lebhaftes Interesse daran, zunächst
keine bindenden Erklärungen hinsichtlich der zukünftigen Zugehörig-
keit der besetzten Gebiete Russlands abzugeben, da sich vorläufig
nicht übersehen lässt, welche politischen Kombinationen bei Friedens-
schluss die für uns güngstigen sein werden."

[32] BETHMANN-HOLLWEG'S *Kriegsreden,* p. 147: " Die mehrfachen
Zusammenkünfte des Reichskanzlers mit dem österreichisch-ungarischen
Minister des Auswärtigen, Baron von Burian, im Laufe des Jahres 1916
haben unzweifelhaft vor allem der polnischen Frage gegolten."

[33] BURIAN, *Drei Jahre,* p. 67. *Bilinski, Wspomnienia i Dokumenty,* II,
pp. 85 ff. In Autumn 1915, Emperor Francis-Joseph made the
following statement to the Polish Archbishops: " Jawohl, der deutsche
Kaiser erklärte mir, dass ganz Polen mir angehören soll." Confirmed
also by Andrassy and German Ambassador in Vienna von Tschirsky.

[34] BURIAN, o.c., p. 71.

[35] BETHMANN-HOLLWEG'S *Kriegsreden,* p. 90.

[36] HUTTEN-CZAPSKI, o.c., II, p. 288: " Seine Majestät entwickelt
ausführlich seinen Plan der Gestaltung der Polenfrage. Ein in der Ver-
waltung vollständig selbstständiger Staat mit engem Anschluss an
Deutschland ; für die Landesverwaltung eine Regierung in Warschau
mit einem Landtage in dem sich die Polen zanken können wie sie es
früher getan. Verträge, die einen Einfluss auf die diplomatische Leitung,
ein militärisches Oberkommando des Kaisers über die Armee, eine
Eisenbahngemeinschaft mit Polen wie diejenige mit Hessen und
Handels-sowie die Schiffahrtsverträge welche letztere Polen ein Absatz-
gebiet über Danzig und andere Häfen sichern, Annexion von
Kalisch . . . "

[37] LUDENDORFF, *The General Staff and Its Problems,* II, pp. 382 ff.
According to BURIAN, o.c., p. 74: " Das deutsche Konzept nicht als
volle Selbständigkeit zu werten war."

[38] BETHMANN-HOLLWEG, II, p. 94. HINDENBURG, *Aus meinem Leben,*
p. 201, declares very cynically that he insisted on the carrying out of the
Vienna Agreement: " Damit wir zum Beginn des nächsten Frühjahr-
kämpfe leidlich ausgebildete Truppen in die vorderste Linie einsetzen
könnten ; möchte dann ein siegreiches Deutschland sich nach dem
Frieden mit der neu aufgerollten polnischer Frage abfinden. Da stiessen
wir, überraschend für mich auf den Widerstand der Reichsleitung. Sie

glaubte in dieser Zeit Fäden für einen Sonderfrieden mit Russland gefunden zu haben, und hielt es für bedenklich die eingeleiteten Schritte durch die Proklamation eines unabhängigen Polens in den Augen des Zares zu kompromittieren. Die militärischen und politischen Rücksichten gerieten also in Widerstreit. Der Ausgang war schliesslich der, dass die Hoffnungen auf einen Sonderfrieden mit Russland scheiterten und in den ersten Tagen des Novembers der Manifest doch veröffentlich wurde."

[39] DELBRÜCK, *Ludendorff's Selbstporträt*, p. 67.

BETHMANN-HOLLWEG, o.c., II, p. 93, confesses himself: "So sind die Wiener Abmachungen von 11 und 12 August entstanden. Sie blieben zunächst interner Vorgang. Die Undurchsichtigkeit der politischen Verhältnisse in Russland machte weiteres Abwarten ratsam, so sehr auch die Zustände in Polen Stellungsnahme hindrängten."

[40] VON SEECKT, *Aus meinem Leben*, I, p. 436: "Kam der Manifest der Selbständigkeitserklärung so könnten und sollten für uns Soldaten im Land aufgehoben werden. Vorläufig ist das Ganze in der Schwebe wieder, da man sich den Weg der Verständigung mit Russland nicht verbarrikadieren will. Meine Lösung ist es nicht."

[41] VON CRAMON, *Unser österreichisch-ungarischer Bundesgenosse*, p. 123.

[42] HUTTEN-CZAPSKI, II, p. 297.

[43] TIRPITZ, o.c., p. 273.

[44] ERZBERGER, *Erlebnisse*, p. 234.

[45] *Documents Secrets*, Dispatch of Sir George Buchanan to Lord Grey, No. 1701.

[46] LUDENDORFF, *The General Staff*, p. 419.

[47] CZERNIN, *Im Weltkriege*, p. 218: "Bei der Gefahr, die nur ein widerwillig angeschlossenes Polen für Deutschland und Österreich-Ungarn bieten würde, es politisch nicht zweckmässiger wäre, dass Deutschland Polen, unter Zurückhaltung der Grenzgebiete, die alsdann zum Zweck des militärischen Grenzschutzes erforderlich erscheinen, seinem vollem Selbstbestimmungsrecht, auch mit der Möglichkeit des Anschlusses an Russland überlässt."

[48] Also many Catholic leaders shared these views, however strange it may appear. So PROF. DR. MARIAN SPAHN, *Im Kampfe um unsere Zukunft*, 1915: "Mit der Ausnahme der Balkanpolitik wo der bestehende Gegensatz unzweifelhaft ausgetragen werden muss, gibt es weltpolitisch wie in der festländischen Politik keinen Punkt, wo sich die Interessen Russlands und unserer Nation unüberbrückbar entgegenstehen. Unser Erbfeind ist Russland sicher nicht. Haben wir beim Friedenschluss militärische Bedürfnisse sicherzustellen, so gibt es kein Zögern. Die Rolle der Völkerbefreier haben bisher andere gespielt, die über mehr Anmut in der Gebärde verfügen. Ergibt sich aus Russlands eigenen Fehlern in diesem Kriege, dass der Traum der polnischen Nation von der Wiederkehr Polens Wirklichkeit wird, können wir Gewehr bei Fuss es geschehen lassen."

[49] TIRPITZ, o.c., p. 141: "Ich weiss nicht ob die Weltgeschichte ein

Beispiel grösserer Verblendung kennt, als die gegenseitige Vernichtung der Deutschen und der Russen ad maiorem gloriam der Angelsachsen."

[50] BARTELS, *Westrussland deutsch Siegespreis*, pol. Denkschrift, quoted by ASKENAZY, *Uwagi*, p. 443.

[51] LUDENDORFF, *Meine Kriegserrinnerungen*, p. 417: " Die erhoffte grosszügige deutsche Siedlungstätigkeit und die Sammlung der Auslandsdeutschen in jenen weiten Ostgebieten, wie sie schon im Jahre 1915 der Reichskanzler für gewisse Grenzstreifen erstrebte, konnte uns in der Zukunft einen weiteren Menschenzuwachs bringen."

[52] GRUMBACH, *Germany's Annexionist Aims*, pp. 40 ff. A memorandum of the University Professor Hoetzsch, December 1914, proposed the annexation of the Government of Courland (Latvia), Suwalki, a part of the Governments of Lomza, Plock, Kalisz and Grodno, coal mines of Dabrowa. A memorandum of a legal adviser of a Berlin group of financiers of December 1915, proposed the annexation of the greater part of the Western and Northern part of Congress-Kingdom, an area totalling 88,000 sq. km. with a population of 9,000,000, leaving to Austria the remaining part with an area of 37,000 sq. km. and population of 3,000,000. A memorandum of the Chamber of Commerce of Upper Silesia requested the annexation of the part of Congress-Kingdom adjacent to Upper Silesia (ASKENAZY, *Uwagi*, p. 467).

[53] GRUMBACH, o.c., pp. 25 ff.

[54] Stresemann's speech in the Reichstag, 16th April, 1916: "Ich sehe in den Ostprovinzen ein deutsches Land, in dem die Balten den deutschen Geist und die deutsche Kultur hoch gehalten haben. Gäben wir dieses Land auf, so würden wir für das um so stärkeres Einsetzen der Russifizierung die Verantwortung vor der Geschichte tragen."

[55] SEECKT, o.c., I, p. 208: Gedanken über Polen: " Soll Polen geteilt werden? . . . Ein neues polnisches Reich soll entstehen aus dem bisherigen Russisch Polen, und mit dem Augenblick, da diese Gründung sich zu gestalten beginnt, schweifen bereits die Blicke zu den " unerlössten Brüdern " . . . " Überall wo die polnische Sprache herrscht, wird sich seine Anziehungskraft fühlbar machen ; für alle Polen von Lemberg bis vor die Tore Wiens, von Thorn und Oberschlesien bis vor die von Berlin gibt es einen gemeinsamen Mittelpunkt ausserhalb des eigenen Staates. So entsteht die Frage: Soll Polen geteilt bleiben? Die wird, soweit Preussen beteiligt ist, wohl von jedem bejaht werden. Nur muss jetzt an die Stelle der Dreiteilung die Zweiteilung treten. Russland in dieser Betrachtung nur Gegenstand, nicht ein mitsprechender Teil. Das ist fast zu bedauern, denn die bisherige Dreiteilung hatte neben manchen Nachteilen auch . . . ihr Gut." *Ibidem*, p. 211: " Wir gelangen dem nach so, wenn wir Rückgabe an Russland, Selbständigkeit und Angliederung an Österreich gleichmässig verwerfen, notgedrungen zu der Einverleibung eines grossen Teils des eroberten Landes in das Königreich Preussen. Die Schaffung einer neuen preussischen Provinz Süd-Preussen-um den historischen Namen wieder aufleben zu lassen-wird also zur zwingenden Notwendigkeit . . . eine gewisse pro-

vinzielle Selbständigkeit und Selbstverwaltung." *Ibidem,* p. 242: "Wenn das Gefühl der Unabänderlichkeit der Verhältnisse hervorgerufen und erhalten wird, dann werden sich die Süd-preussische Polen das Schielen über die Grenze nach Russland und Österreich schnell abgewöhnen."

[56] See note 51.

[57] GRUMBACH, *Das annexionistische Deutschland,* pp. 375 ff. In relation to the Baltic countries the petition observed that: " In den Ostseeprovinzen bildet das Deutschtum nur eine dünne Oberschicht der besitzenden und gebildeten Stände von Gross-grundbesitzern, Kaufleuten, städtischen Gewerbetreibenden und Angehöriger freier Berufe. Man zählt rund 200,000 Deutschen denen fast $2\frac{1}{2}$ Millionen Letten und Esthen gegenüberstehen. Die Grundstimmung dieser Letten und Esthen ist Feindschaft gegen das Deutschtum." Similarly SPAHN, o.c., p. 352.

[58] Preface by W. J. ASHLEY to the English edition of FRIEDRICH NAUMANN, *Central Europe,* London, 1916.

[59] *Ibidem,* p. 3.

[60] *Ibidem,* p. 108.

[61] FRIEDRICH NAUMANN, *Was wird aus Polen?* Berlin, 1917, p. 3.

[62] *Ibidem,* p. 26.

[63] *Ibidem,* p. 34.

[64] PROF. DIETRICH SCHAFER, quoted by SOKOLNICKI, *Polska w Pamietnikach Wielkiej Wojny,* p. 579.

[65] HUTTEN-CZAPSKI, II, p. 291: " Es ist meine persönliche Überzeugung dass Beseler die Errichtung eines selbständigen, mit Deutschland eng verbundenen polnischen Staates im Interesse Deutschland höher bewährte als die von ihm allerdings für sicher gehaltene Schöpfung, eines polnischen Heeres."

Ibidem, II, p. 342. A passage from Beseler's memorandum (end April 1917): " Es handelt sich zunächst nicht darum, ein grosses polnisches Heer zu schaffen, es müsse vielmehr ein Anfang gemacht werden. Es komme darauf an, dass man bei den Friedensverhandlungen sagen könne, der Staat Polen bestehe und hat ein Heer."

[66] The documents are mostly quoted from *Urkunden der ob. Heeresleitung.* Cf. also STEFAN POMARANSKI, " Na Marginesie Niemieckich Planow Organizacji Wojska Polskiego w Czasie Wojny Swiatowej," *Niepodleglosc,* Vol. II, GENERAL JULJAN STACHIEWICZ, " Niemieckie Plany Organizacji Wojska Polskiego w Czasie Wojny Swiatowej," *Niepodleglosc,* Vol. I, M. SOKOLNICKI, o.c.

[67] HUTTEN-CZAPSKI, II, p. 280.

[68] BETHMANN-HOLLWEG, o.c., II, pp. 88-9.

[69] Published from the archives of the former General Government of Warsaw by *Niepodleglosc, V*ol. XIX.

[70] LUDENDORFF, *Kriegserrinnerungen,* p. 241: " Die Lage um die Jahreswende 1916-17: Die zahlenmässige Überlegenheit des Feindes

gewann durch die immer mehr entwickelte Kriegsindustrie der Ententestaaten weiter gefahrvoll an Stärke." An interesting assessment was made during the war by PROF. S. DABROWSKI, (later Under-Secretary of State for Foreign Affairs in independent Poland), printed after the war in a book in French in Paris in 1924: *Les Empires Centraux et la Lutte pour le Recrutement Polonais pendant l'Occupation,* see especially Chapter III, p. 105: " En Autriche-Hongrie, la période annonçant l'épuisement des réserves commencera pour les hommes de 17-45 ans, en janvier 1916, pour les hommes de 17-50 ans en août 1916 ; en Allemagne, l'épuisement des réserves commencera en juillet 1916 pour les classes 17-45." Conclusions, pp. 27-8 : " Les calculs m'amenèrent à conclure que l'automne 1918 serait le moment critique à partir duquel, la guerre continuant, la situation des réserves allemandes irait en empirant rapidement devant l'impossibilité de nouveaux prélèvements dans le pays."

[71] Memorandum of General Beseler to General Falkenhayn, 23rd August, 1916 ; Abt. 16, No. 1271, Geheim: " The assessment that there are about 1,000,000 apt for military service in both General-Governments (that is the German and Austrian zones of occupation in Congress-Kingdom), is probably roughly speaking right. The three intact annual contingents (1895, 1896, 1897) should amount, judging by German standards, to about 60,000 men."

Similarly DABROWSKI, o.c., p. 56: " En décembre 1915, le Chef du Department Militaire, Colonel Sikorski, envoya au Gouvernement de Vienne un rapport confidentiel: ' Combien le Royaume (Congress-Kingdom) possède d'hommes en état de servir et comment les mobiliser '—Déduction faite des individus servant dans l'armée russe et des évacués et des inaptes au service, le rapport évalue à environ 1,040,000 les hommes aptes au service."

[72] WHEELER-BENNETT, *Brest-Litovsk,* p. 104 : " In the summer of 1916 . . . negotiations between Berlin and Vienna, which resulted in an agreement for the creation of an independent Kingdom of Poland with a hereditary costitutional monarchy. The announcement of the agreement had, however, been pigeon-holed, in deference to the representations of Falkenhayn."

[73] J. STACHIEWICZ, o.c.

[74] HANS DELBRÜCK, o.c.

[75] HUTTEN-CZAPSKI, II, p. 289: "-Seine Majestät besprachen ferner die zukünftige polnische Armee, von der Er sich viel verspricht. Die Legionen nach Beseitigung einiger minderwertigen-bewährten sich vorzüglich. Nach den Ihm zugegangenen mündlichen und schriftlichen Mitteilungen hätten sich sogar die jungen Mannschaften wie ausgebildete Soldaten im Kampfe bewährt. Man würde bald einige gute Korps haben."

[75a] Bethmann-Hollweg wired to the German Ambassador in the United States on 2nd September, 1916: " Our West Front stands firm. East Front naturally threatened somewhat by Rumania's declaration of war. . . . Hopes of peace before winter, as result of Russian or

French warweariness, diminished by this development" (BENSTORFF, *My Three Years*).

[76] BETHMANN-HOLLWEG, II, p. 95: "In Verfolg hieran traten auf Antrag der Heeresleitung die deutschen und österreichischen politischen und militärischen Spitzen am 18 Oktober in Pless zu gemeinsamer Besprechung zusammen. Ich habe in dieser Verhandlung, da die im Juli-August verschwomm aufgetauchten Friedensaussichten inzwischen durch keine auch noch so geheime Friedensgeste des Ministeriums Stürmer bestätigt wurden, unumwunden dem mit äusserster Energie gestellten Verlangen der Obersten Heeresleitung zugestimmt ... Wie uns zukommende Nachrichten besagten, standen wir unmittelbar davor, dass die Entente Polen die ersähnte Autonomie versprach und eine polnische Sonderregierung auf russischem Boden etablierte."

[77] BURIAN, o.c., pp. 82 ff.: "Die militärische-politischen Erörtungen führte hauptsächlich General-Gouverneur von Beseler, während Ludendorff streng soldatische Gesichtspunkte mit Lebhaftigkeit vertrat, von denen allerdings nach seiner Auffassung, alle anderen, also auch die politischen Erwägungen zurücktreten und sich den militärischen unterzuordnen hätten" ... "man dürfe nicht der Meinung Nahrung geben, die Mittelmächte seien so schwach, dass sie das Königreich Polen schüfen, nur um eine polnische Armee zu bekommen.".

LUDENDORFF, *Kriegserrinnerungen*, p. 315: "Die ungemein gespannte Kriegslage forderte für den Vierbund mehr als dringend einen Kräfteausgleich. Die oberste Heeresleitung musste pflichtgemäss die Frage nach der Bildung eines polnischen Heeres weiter verfolgen."

[78] DR. PAUL ROTH, o.c., p. 43: "Von demokratischer Seite war einzuwenden, dass es einem neuzeitlichen staatsrechtlichen Empfinden widerspräche, einen Staat durch den Gnadeakt zweier Monarchen, und zwar vor vornherein, ohne Befragung des Volkes, mit vorgeschriebener monarchischer Form ins Leben zu rufen."

[79] VON SEECKT, I, p. 494: 5th November, 1916: "Was sagt Du zu dem Polenmanifeste? Alle Schwierigkeiten sind umgangen und äusserlich unentschieden gelassen. Wann kommt nun wohl der Ruf nach dem Anschluss des preussischen Posens? Dass er kommt und bald so stark wird, dass sehr ernste Folgen entstehen, ist unausbleiblich. Es soll Übereinstimmung bestehen über all noch offenen Fragen. Zunächst wird nun Aushebung die Folge sein, von der man sich hohe Zahlen verspricht."

HOFFMANN, o.c., p. 151: "Ich war zwar skeptisch (in Gesprächen mit Ludendorff), was die polnischen Hilfstruppen anlangte, wir waren aber in der fraglichen Zeit so knapp an Reserven, dass man, rein militärische, jeden Zuwachs mit Freude begrüssen musste."

[80] HUTTEN-CZAPSKI, II, p. 302.

[81] BURIAN, o.c., p. 62-3.

[82] CONRAD, IV, p. 112.

[83] *Die Grosse Politik der Europäischen Kabinette*, p. 477.

[84] CHÉRADAME, o.c., p. 225.

[85] K. SROKOWSKI, *N.K.N.*, p. 38.

[86] NOWAK, o.c., pp. 32-3.

[87] SROKOWSKI, o.c., pp. 365-6.

[88] *Ibidem*, pp. 359-61.

[89] VON CRAMON, o.c., p. 194: " Er(Tisza) betrieb rein ungarische Kirchturmpolitik und beurteilte die Entwicklung der Welt vor allem von dem Standpunkt aus, dass den Magyaren ihre Hegemonie in Ungarn, ihre Stellung in der Monarchie erhalten bleiben müsse. Er gehörte dadurch-darüber kann leider kein Zweifel bestehen-zu den Toten-gräbern des Habsburgerreiches."

SROKOWSKI, o.c., p. 164: " The Emperor (Francis-Joseph) knew Tisza's shortcomings. When once at dinner his qualities were praised he said rather sarcastically: ' Yes, undoubtedly, Tisza is an eminent man —what a pity that he is only a Hungarian.' "

BILINSKI, o.c., II, p. 84: " Bethmann-Hollweg after his conversation in Vienna in Summer 1915 exclaimed to Baron Stürgh: ' Ich begreife den Tisza nicht, der die Zeichen der Zeit nicht kennt! Glauben Sie denn, dass wir Preussen es nicht zu verstehen wissen, dass wir nach dem Kriege unseres Verhältniss zu unseren Polen völlig auf den Kopf stellen müssen? Nur die Ungarn scheinen derartiges nicht zu wissen und zu verstehen.' "

[90] CZERNIN, o.c., p. 274.

[91] CONRAD, V, pp. 910-11. See also note 19.

[92] LUDENDORFF, *The General Staff*, p. 419.

[93] NOWAK, o.c., p. 353.

[94] LUDENDORFF, *The General Staff*, p. 437. CZERNIN, o.c., pp. 197-8.

[95] *Austria's Peace Offer*, (MANTEYER), p. 229.

[96] VON SEECKT, o.c., I, p. 471.

[97] BETHMANN-HOLLWEG, o.c., II, p. 91.

[98] On the occasion of a conversation with Austro-Hungarian states-men in 1917 Ludendorff observed: " The Austro-Polish solution would present a grave danger to German Prussia. The Field-Marshal (Hindenburg) and I were afraid that it meant the disruption of alliance and presented an immediate danger to our Eastern frontier " (*Krieg-serrinnerungen*, p. 352).

SEECKT, I, p. 210: " Ob Österreich in der Lage ist-physisch und moralisch-das neuerworbene Land mit dem eigenen Staatsgedanken zu erfüllen, dass es willig oder unwillig ein zuverlässiges Grenzland bildet, muss bezweifeln werden. ... Die Bundespolitik der Monarchie dürfte im umgekehrten Fall vielleicht wieder einmal auf die Bahnen der Zeit vor 1866 geraten."

Ibidem, p. 575: " Von Seeckt an den Chef des Generalstaabes des Feldheeres, July 1917: ' Mit von den wenigsten Stellen geähnter Stärke haben sich in Österreich selbst die Kräfte hervorgewagt, welche die Durchführung des Nationalitäten- prinzips und damit die Ordnung eines föderalistischen Staates als ihr Ziel erklären. Ein Österreich mit ausschlaggebend slavischem Einfluss wird weder bündnissfähig noch bündnisswillig sein.' "

[99] CONRAD, IV, p. 215.

[100] Memorandum of Major Simon, published from the archives of General Beseler's Chancellery by the Polish review *Niepodleglosc*, Vol. XIX, p. 155.

[100a] CZAPSKI, o.c., II, p. 437.

[101] VON CRAMON, p. 124.

[102] CZERNIN, o.c., p. 400.

[103] BILINSKI, o.c., II, p. 66.

[104] BURIAN, pp. 63 ff.: "Galizien musste entweder das neue Polen heranziehen oder Kongress-Polen in irgendeine nahe Verbindung zur Monarchie zu bringen."

[105] NOWAK, o.c., p. 243: "The Austro-Polish solution was now an axiom to him (Burian) that nothing could upset. Everything must now be done to keep in the good graces of the Poles."

[106] BURIAN, o.c., p. 254: "In einer besonderen, übrigens auch in Spa (12 Mai, 1918), durch ein junktim ausdrücklich betonten Beziehung, stand die polnische Frage. Eine befriedigende Lösung derselben wurde als Voraussetzung der Regulierung des ganzen übrigen Interessenkomplexes erklärt."

[107] NOWAK, o.c., p. 334.

[108] NOWAK, pp, 165-6. BURIAN, p. 244: "Die Verhandlungen in Salzburg 8 Juli, 1918, den ersten politischen Niederschlag der grossen wirtschaftlichen Bewegung bildeten welche drei Jahre vorher mit dem Schlagworte ' Mitteleuropa ' eingesetzt hatte."

[109] ERZBERGER, o.c., p. 183: "Um Königskronen zankte man sich im blutigen Krieg-Länder gingen darüber verloren."

[110] BURIAN, p. 302: "Der österreichische Manifest vom 16 Oktober, welches Österreich zum Bundesstaat erklärte, wurde und wird noch vielfach als Ursache oder Anstoss des Zerfalles angesehen. Diese Meinung überschätzt, wie ich glaube, die Bedeutung dieses Aktes. In dieser Lage griff die österreichische Regierung zu der Massnahme, von der sie hoffte dass durch Anerkennung der nicht mehr zu verhindernenden Selbstätigkeit der österreichischen Völker der Begriff des Gesamtstaates Österreich in der Form eines Bundesstaates gerettet werden könnte."

[111] PILSUDSKI, *Pisma*, II, p. 253.

[112] CASIMIR SMOGORZEWSKI, *Joseph Pilsudski et les Activistes Polonais pendant la guerre*, p. 13.

[113] *Novyi Journal*, New York, Vol. 28.

[114a] SROKOWSKI, o.c., p. 226. HUTTEN-CZAPSKI, II, p. 163. SOKOL-NICKI, o.c., p. 622. Sokolnicki mentions also a visit of Sikorski (later Poland's Prime Minister and C.-in-C. during the Second World War) and Jodko to Berlin, 27th September, 1914. In conversations with the German authorities, two prominent Polish leaders from Prussian

Poland, Korfanty and Trampczynski, also took part. The conversations failed because in spite of the request of the German High Command the Prussian Government was unwilling to abolish the anti-Polish legislative measures and especially the expropriation law. SOKOLNICKI, p. 615.

[114b] SOKOLNICKI, o.c., p. 522: "Soldaten brauchen wir nicht, dazu gehört sechs Monate Übung und bis dann sind wir fertig."

[114c] SMOGORZEWSKI, *Poland's Access to the Sea*, p. 260. See also a well-documented book by W. CZERWINSKI, *Le Problème de l'indépendance économique de la Pologne*, p. 14: "Dans les centres industriels de la Pologne, qui tombent sous leur domination, les autorités militaires allemandes, organisent une destruction systématique de l'outillage industriel, épargné par les ravages de guerre. Sous couvert de réquisitions, l'Administration Militaire des Matières Premières (Militärohstoffverwaltung) démolit les usines, en faisant démonter les machines pour en extraire le cuivre."

Ibidem, p. 79: "Les Allemands ont transporté en Allemagne des centaines de machines tout entières, dont on prétendait avoir besoin. On démontait les autres pour en extraire les pièces en cuivre. Au total: quelques 2,000 moteurs, 6,000 moteurs de toute sorte, plus de 2,500 machines outils."

[114d] F. NAUMANN, *Was wird aus Polen*, p. 20.

[115] CONRAD, IV, p. 375; also IV, p. 877: "Über die lieben Polen sind wir im klaren. Sie kümmern sich gar nicht um uns, hätten nur gewollt, dass wir ihnen mit unserem Blut ein selbständiges Königreich schaffen"; *ibidem*, p. 878: "Die polnische Legion ist tatsächlich ein Kanonen-Futter. Man hat sie mehr aus politischen Gründen akzepiert, übrigens leistet die Legion Pilsudski unserer I Armee sehr gute Dienste"; *ibidem*, pp. 478-9: "Die Polen aber, wenngleich zersplittert in verschiedenen Parteien, sahen doch in der Wiederstellung des selbständigen Königreichs ihr Ideal. Unklar über den Ausgang des Krieges, bemühten sie sich in schmiegsamer Anpassung jeweilig ihren Vorteil zu wahren"; *ibidem*, p. 208: "Die polnische Legionen schlugen sich, insbesondere bei kleinen Unternehmungen in der Regel gut, aber in disziplinären Beziehungen sehr viel zu wünschen übrig und fingen schliesslich an, eine politische Rolle spielen zu wollen."

A. VON CRAMON, o.c., p. 120: "Eine dieser Brigaden führte Pilsudski, das Oberhaupt der gegen Russland gerichteten Militärorganisation-eine ausgesprochene Verschwörer Natur, ehrgeizig, undiszipliniert und unverlässig."

[116] SEYDA, o.c., I, pp. 263-4. DABROWSKI, o.c., p. 56.

[117] SROKOWSKI, p. 340.

[118] *Wspomnienia Legjonowe*, pp. 77-8.

[119] HUTTEN-CZAPSKI, II, p. 314.

[120] BARANOWSKI, "Rozmowy z Pilsudskim," *Niepodleglosc*, Vol. XVIII, p. 31.

[121] *Ibidem*.

[122] HUTTEN-CZAPSKI, II, p. 377: " Die Verhaftung Pilsudskis war die Schicksalsstunde der deutschen Politik in Polen. Nicht nur die nächste Zeit stand unter dem Zeichen dieses Ereignisses. Auch später lastete es auf den politischen Beziehungen zwischen beiden Ländern."

[123] SMOGORZEWSKI, *Joseph Pilsudski et les Activistes Polonais*, p. 59.

[124] See note 65.

[125] STANISLAW BUKOWIECKI, " Rola czynnikow wewnetrznych w tworzeniu nowej panstwowosci polskiej," *Niepodleglosc*, Vol. II, p. 1930.

[126] ERZBERGER, o.c., p. 171.

[127] CZERNIN, o.c., p. 279: " In der weiteren Entwicklung hat der deutsche Standpunkt verschiedene Varianten durchgemacht. In allgemeinen hat er stets zwischen zweien geschwankt: entweder müsse sich Polen an Deutschland angliedern-Germano Polnische Lösung-oder aber grosse Teile seines Gebietes unter dem Titel von Grenzrektifikationen an Deutschland abreten, der Rest werde uns oder sich selbst überlassen werden."

[128] ROTH, o.c., p. 187: " Die Idee der Isolierung Polens kann nur bezeichnet werden als unglückliche Ausgeburt militärischer Politik ; sie hatte ihre Wurzel in den Kreisen rechsstehender Parteien und der Politik treibender höheren und höchsten Militärs. Sie war in diesem Zusammenhange ein Teil des Planes die russischen Randstaaten vom Russischen Reich abzulösen, insbesondere an der Ostsee einen Kranz baltischer Staaten in enger Verbindung mit Deutschland aufzurichten."

[129] HUTTEN-CZAPSKI, II, p. 491. A conversation with Beseler, 18th July, 1918: " Vor ihm lag ein mit dem Kopf ' Chef des Generalstabes des Feldheeres ' versehenes an den Reichskanzler gerichtetes Schriftstück, datiert vom 5 Juli, welches er mir langsam und deutlich verlas: Deren Inhalt war einen polnischen ' Grenzstreifen ' von 20,000 Quadratkilometer abzutrennen, der entgegen den noch nach der Januarkrise von der Obersten Heeresleitung gemachten Zugeständnissen auch Kalisz und Kolo übergriefen sollte. Von diesem Gebiete sollte ein 8,000 Quadratkilometer umfassender Teil unverzüglich von der ganzen polnischen Bevölkerung geräumt und mit deutschen Kolonisten besiedelt werden. Wie sich ergab rechnete man mit 300,000 Familien, dass heisst etwa ein und halb Millionen Köpfen deutscher Rückwanderer aus Russland, die hier unterbracht werden sollten. Auf diese Weise hoffte man, den ' grosspolnischen ' Traum zu vernichten und für alle Zeiten das Bestreben der polnisch sprechenden Gebiete Preussens, mit dem neubegründeten polnischen Staat vereinigt zu werden zu vereiteln."

[130] LUDENDORFF, *The General Staff*, pp. 597-8. Ludendorff's letter to the State Secretary von Hinze, dated 31st August, 1918: " I can give my sanction to the Warsaw-Wilno solution on condition that it will give us definite guarantees of close association with Germany. ... It would be no disadvantage for the development of Lithuania if it lost districts which had a preponderance of Poles. ... If Greater Lithuania no longer serves the purpose of a safe-concentration area, the bridgeheads at Ostrolenka, Lomza and Ossowiec are an indispensable military requirement. ... In order to render impossible the Austro-Polish solu-

tion so far as it can be done, I advise Your Excellency to push the correction of the Polish-German frontier as far as possible, for instance, to the line Pilica-Rawka-Bzura-Narew. Neither should there be any doubt that in the case of the Austro-Polish solution Poland in no case should have a common frontier with Russia, but should be separated from Russia by Lithuanian territory."

[181] ROTH, o.c., p. 44.

[182] BURIAN, o.c., p. 87.

[133] FREDERICK NAUMANN, *Was wird aus Polen?* p. 56: " Als die Proklamation erschien war sie ein internationaler Akt der Mittelmächte. In der ganzen weiten Welt wurde mit Befriedigung oder Zweifel festgestellt, dass die Zentralmächte, von deren Brutalität die Ententeblätter nicht genug erzählen können, eine Befreiungstat begonnen hatten. In Deutschland und Österreich schrieb man: Während die Engländer sich mit der Bedrückung Griechenlands beschäftigen, befreien wir Polen! Am meisten aber hörten die West-und Südslaven diese neue Botschaft. Leuchtete hier nicht ein weitgehender, verheissungsvoller politscher Gedanke auf? ... Ein wirklich mit Hilfe der Zentralmächte aufgerichtetes antirussisches Königreich Polen verändert das Angesicht aller Nationalitätenstreitigkeiten zwischen Weichsel und Adriatischem Meer. Man bekam eine Ahnung welche heilsamen weltgeschichtlichen Folgen die Beselersche Idee gewinnen konnte-konnte und sollte!"

[134] HELFFERICH, *Der Weltkrieg*, III, p. 256: "Ich habe die undefinierte und damit uneingeschränkte Annerkennung des Selbstbestimmungsrechts der Nationalitäten stets für eine Gefahr gehalten, nicht nur für das Deutsche Reich hinsichtlich seiner Grenzmarken im Osten, Westen und Norden, sondern vor allem auch für die Habsburgische Monarchie, für die es kein stärkeres Sprengstoff geben konnte."

[135] DMOWSKI, *Polityka Polska*, p. 272. SEYDA, o.c., pp. 344, 399. Declaration of Mr. Piltz to Mr. Ronikier on 17th July, 1917. " Only the November Proclamation put the Polish question on international ground not only in the Western countries but also in Russia where it became an *idée fixe* of the Tsar " (SEYDA, I, p. 602).

[136] ERZBERGER, p. 17, derides Ludendorff's assessment of the strength of the future Polish army at 350,000: " So viele Selbstmörder gibt es im Königreich Polen nicht."

[137] *Austria's Peace Offer* (MANTEYER), pp. 20-21.

[138] *Ibidem*, p. 75.

[139] See Ribot's account of negotiations in A. RIBOT, *Journal et Cor. In.*, pp. 62 ff.

[140] CZERNIN, o.c., p. 29: " Die Vorstellung, als ob eine solche Trennung der beiden Armeen sich in gegenseitigem Einvernehmen hätte vollziehen können auf volständig falschen Voraussetzungen beruhe, und um damit zu beweisen, dass hier der erste Moment vorliegt, welches ergibt, dass wir durch einen Separatfrieden den Krieg nicht beendet hätten, sondern in einen neuen Krieg verwickelt werden wären. ... Was sich aber an der Front abgespielt hätte, da hätte sich in verstärktem Masse in dem gesamten Hinterland wiederholt: der Bürgerkrieg wäre

unaufhaltsam gewesen."

[141] *Austria's Peace Offer*, p. 219.

[142] *Ibidem*, pp. 222-3.

[143] *Ibidem*, p. 263 ; also MERMEIX, *Les Négociations Secrètes*, p. 165.

[144] P. ROTH, o.c., p. 35.

[145] LLOYD GEORGE, *War Memoirs*, V, pp. 2463 ff.

[146] ROBERT LANSING, *War Memoirs*, p. 247.

[147] *Ibidem*, p. 254.

[148] DUGDALE, o.c., II, p. 248.

[149] PROF. KEETON, *National Sovereignty and National Order*, p. 162.

[150] WINSTON CHURCHILL, *The Gathering Storm*, p. 10.

THIRD PHASE OF THE WAR : THE ALLIED GOVERN-MENTS RECOGNIZE THE NECESSITY FOR A UNITED AND INDEPENDENT POLISH STATE

" It requires something more than a merely parochial outlook to see our highest interests ; but our highest moral and national interests, our noblest aspirations, are bound up with the fate of countries whose language we cannot speak and with whose history I dare say a good many of us here are very imperfectly acquainted." —(Speech of the Foreign Secretary, A. J. Balfour, in Edinburgh, 11th January, 1918.)

" The creation of a united and independent Polish State, with free access to the sea, constitutes one of the conditions for just and durable peace and of the rule of right in Europe."—(Declaration of the Heads of the Allied Governments (Clemenceau, Lloyd George and Orlando) at Versailles, 3rd June, 1918.)

SINCE the beginning of 1917 the Polish question had made steady progress in the West, but eighteen months were to elapse before a joint declaration was issued by the Allied Governments stating that the creation of the Polish State was one of the conditions of a just and durable peace. Several important events conduced to this success-ful result : the intervention of the United States of America, the out-break of the Russian Revolution and the Proclamation of the Pro-visional Russian Government of 29th March, 1917, the outbreak of the Bolshevik Revolution, and the Brest-Litovsk negotiations, which revealed to Europe to the full extent the danger of German supremacy in Eastern Europe. But without the collapse of the Central Powers in November 1918 the Poles would probably have been unable to recover their Western provinces. During this period many factors interfered with the progress of the Polish question in the international field, and the final result was to a great extent the result of the endeavours of the Poles themselves, both in the home-land and abroad.

Paderewski and Wilson

The background of Wilson's interventions in Poland's favour con-stitutes, perhaps, one of the most interesting pages of the Wilsonian policy. No unbiased study on this matter, based on historical sources, has yet been published; the attitude of writers has so far moved between two extremes—either adulation of Wilson, uncritically ascribing to him nearly all the merit for the restoration of the Polish State, or the debasement of Wilson as the man responsible for the betrayal of the realistic and isolationist traditions of American policy. It is extraordinary to note the extent to which political passions continue to blur the views of many writers, amongst whom one can find, especially in recent times, advocates of American non-interference in what is considered the legitimate sphere of interest of another Great Power, Russia.

In fact it was a strange coincidence that Wilson, who as we stated in the first chapter, entered the White House with the " fundamental elements of thought which marked his foreign policy " well determined, met on his way a man—J. I. Paderewski—who was able to present to him the Polish problem as the test case of the practical application of the principles cherished by the President. It was also very fortunate for Paderewski that he found in the White House a man who had full understanding of the importance of nationalist problems in our times.

Let us state, first of all, that interest in Polish problems was fairly common among the Americans and was not limited to the Americans of Polish descent—the Americans were not so ignorant of European affairs at that time as is sometimes assumed. Paderewski wrote in his *Memoirs* that during his tour as pianist in the States in 1907 he was invited to the White House by Wilson's predecessor, Theodore Roosevelt, and after the concert had a talk with the President, " a strong, brilliant and exceptionally well-informed man, knowing a great deal about European conditions, and particularly acquainted with my own country, which was chiefly due to his love of our remarkable writer Sienkiewicz, who wrote those world-famous novels, *By Fire and Sword, Children of the Soil*, and *Quo Vadis*. " He told me," writes Paderewski, " that he travelled for years with Sienkiewicz's trilogy. Certain opinions about my country expressed by President Roosevelt were extremely encouraging to me and I still gladly and gratefully remember every word he said on that subject." [1]

Wilson's Secretary of State after Bryan's resignation, Robert Lansing, often disagreeing with his chief's policy, shared nevertheless the views of the latter on Poland as appears from the following passage of his book *The Big Four* : " The dismemberment of so large and populous a territory, possessing solidarity in race, language and religion, such as Poland possessed was an international crime which hardly finds a parallel in the annals of the past four hundred years." [1a]

On the other hand, on many occasions in the course of the War the Republican Party showed its lively interest in Poland's future, and advocating a much harsher policy towards Germany was often ahead of Wilson in upholding the claims of Poland (see below, pp. 207-8, Senator Lodge's resolution on Poland, 18th November, 1918).

There are many reasons to suppose that it was in the case of Poland that Wilson was forming his ideas on the possibility of putting into practice the fundamental elements of his foreign policy. In fact at the very beginning of the War he received a letter from the American Ambassador in London, Page (dated 29th October, 1914), in which the latter expounded the view of General French on the probable end of the War in the next summer or autumn. According to this letter,

> " General French believed that each country must retain its nationality in the end, and that the several parts of the Central Powers should be allowed to choose their future allegiance : Alsace-Lorraine to be French, Schlesvig-Holstein to be Danish, Poland to be Polish, and the Slav peoples of Austria to be Russian if they so desire."

On the 10th November Wilson replied stating that what interested him in this connection was not the details " but the general judgment as to the prospects of the War and the general principle involved in the outlined settlement." Relating this, Notter observes that it was " the principle of ' nationality ' or ' self-determination ' which became fundamental in Wilson's programme for World Order and which was already defined and developed in his political philosophy." [1b]

The American approach to the Polish problem in the early stages of the War was in the first instance humanitarian, as it was the question of relief for Poland that aroused American sympathy for the starving Polish people, whose position had become critical after the retreat from the Congress Kingdom of the Russian armies, accomplished according to the " scorched earth " method, and the subsequent exploitation by the German and Austrian armies of occupation. (Those interested in the question of American relief for Poland can find the relevant details in H. H. Fisher's book entitled *America and the New Poland*.) Neither was the British Government willing to lift the blockade for this specific purpose, nor were the Central Powers ready to give definite pledges to stop food requisitioning in the parts of Poland occupied by their troops. When diplomatic steps failed, Wilson himself addressed a pathetic letter to the Heads of the Governments concerned, but he received very unsatisfactory answers (a very characteristic answer came from Emperor

Francis-Joseph, that there was " no talk of famine where his armies were standing " [1c]).

H. H. Fisher is right in observing that

> " the propaganda of relief inevitably directed attention to Poland's political situation, and sympathy for the war sufferings of the Poles merged with sympathy for their demand for the unity and independence of their nation. In this way the restoration of Poland became a war issue long before it was accepted by the foreign offices of Europe." [1d]

Such was in fact the view of many prominent Americans, as witnessed by the following account by Mr. J. Daniels, Secretary of the Navy :

> " I never saw Paderewski until he called at my office in the Navy Department during the World War to request co-operation to help his suffering countrymen in Poland. With eloquent words on his tongue and tears in his eyes, he related the story of the dismemberment of his country as if it were a fresh tragedy, and the present hopes and needs of his countrymen. With an audience of one, he was as much moved as if he were speaking to a multitude. He opened his heart to me and from that moment I was an ardent advocate of the ambitions of the Poles." [1e]

Mrs. Wilson, the President's wife, recorded in these words the impression made on her by Paderewski's pleading for his country.

> " On Monday, 6th November, 1916, I find recorded in my ' Line-a-Day Book ': ' At 2.30 a delegation headed by Mr. Paderewski arrived to ask to set aside a day to help the Poles. I knelt in the hall above and heard all they said. Mr. Paderewski ended with a beautiful tribute to my husband and expressed his utmost faith in him and his sincere desire to help this suffering people.' I shall never forget Mr. Paderewski's face as he stood pleading the cause of his country. It was so fine, so tragic, so earnest. As I knelt there above them I felt I was witnessing through his eyes all the suffering and degradation of his countrymen. His hair was like a nymbus around his head. To have seen together these two men who were making the world better and happier is a memory I shall always cherish." [1f]

But it was the friendship between Paderewski and Colonel House, the most intimate counsellor of President Wilson, a friendship that lasted until the end of House's life, that contributed the most to drawing the attention of the responsible American quarters to the importance of the settlement of the Polish case within the framework of the Wilsonian policy. Paderewski became acquainted with House on 12th November, 1915, as appears from House's

Diary,[1g] consequently soon after Paderewski's arrival in America during the War. This friendship bore fruit very quickly because as early as February 1916 Colonel House put the question of Poland on the international agenda while drafting his " reasonable " peace terms (see p. 20). Landau in his Paderewski biography writes that it was House who introduced Paderewski to Wilson, and he gives a vivid account of the evening party at the White House in summer 1916 at which Paderewski played " Chopin, nothing but Chopin." After the concert, in a conversation between Paderewski and Wilson, Poland was the only subject and " Wilson's keen sense of justice and of the rights of men was deeply shocked by the historic crime committed on the Polish nation. It was the sort of cause that appealed to him, its political aspect was for him less important than the larger moral issue. The idea of the rehabilitation of Poland had acquired the attraction of a moral task." [1h]

What Wilson thought of Paderewski was told the best by himself during the Paris Peace Conference, after a lunch with the Secretary of the Navy, J. Daniels [11] :

> " I wish you could have heard Paderewski's speeches for his country. They compared with Patrick Healy's speeches, ' Give me liberty or give me death,' and I could understand how the self-contained Jefferson was so moved as to light a fire of liberty in his heart that was never extinguished. I knew Paderewski was a master of harmony, but as we heard his eloquent appeals for his country I felt that it was in victory that he had touched chords more sublime than when he moved thousands as he commanded harmony from the piano." *

* Louis L. Gerson in his recent book, *Woodrow Wilson and the Rebirth of Poland* (Yale University Press, 1953), abounding in misleading data and information, calls Paderewski " aristocrat " (see p. 105 of Gerson's book; many Poles whose political views are disliked by Mr. Gerson appear in his book as aristocrats, for instance, Bilinski, Austro-Hungarian Minister of Finance, *ibidem*, p. 15), although it is well known that Paderewski was the son of a humble employee in Count Potocki's estate at Szepietowka. Gerson's general attitude to the Polish problem appears the best in the deriding of the Polish propaganda in America during the War which allegedly " tortured history to prove that the partitions of Poland were the greatest crime in history." As a matter of fact it is Mr. Gerson who tortures history (we would not have dealt with his book at all but for its being published by the Yale University Press), and we shall return to this matter on other occasions in order to prove the unreliability of Gerson's account.

One of the most preposterous assertions of Mr. Gerson is that on p. 79, that " the pressure from the United States increased, the Polish question assumed greater importance in Great Britain " because " there as well as in the United States, the naturalized Poles and their sympathizers were strongly organized." As a matter of fact the number of Polish immigrants in Great

The Proclamation on the 5th November, 1916, by the Central Powers of Poland's independence drew the attention of the Western world to the importance of the Polish problem, and certainly impressed Wilson, encouraging him to take the first official step regarding the Polish question a few months later without prejudice to his neutral standpoint. The Proclamation, as reported by the German Ambassador in the United States, von Bernstorff, was however, " to say the least, received with scepticism by the American press, which is comparatively well informed on the Polish question "; " the words of the virtuoso Paderewski," continues von Bernstorff in his report, " who is working here in the interests of the Polish sufferers through the war : ' This means only more suffering for my people; it means that another army will be raised, and that there will be more killing and devastating,' were reproduced by many newspapers and regarded as an authoritative statement of what might be expected from the German-Austrian proclamation." But the weekly paper *Free Poland,* published by the Polish National Council of America, showed a better understanding for the meaning of this act, again putting the Polish question on the international agenda : " Though this move on the part of Germany will at least draw the world's attention to the inalienable rights of Poland as a nation, and make of the Polish question an international one, yet it must not be forgotten that the Poles in Europe will vehemently protest against any curtailment of their national aims and aspirations." [1k]

Paderewski saw Wilson, for the third time, on the 6th November, 1916, that is on the day following the Proclamation by the Central Powers. It was also the day on which the Presidential election was in progress. According to Paderewski's statement Wilson gave him solemn assurance that Poland would be resurrected, and he showed a special interest for Paderewski's arguments referring to the problem of Poland's access to the sea.[11] It is a matter of doubt whether the question of winning Polish votes in his re-election played any rôle in Wilson's policy.[1m] President Wilson was re-elected above all on account of his policy of aiming at preserving America's neutrality. " The pacifist tendency in the United States has won," wired von Bernstorff to his Government on 20th October— " for the

Britain was insignificant (until 1939) and still less the number of naturalized Poles.

On p. 48 of his book Gerson asserts that " the man who ' united ' the Poles in favour of the rebirth of Poland was Ignace Jan Paderewski," and on p. 50 " to the majority of American Poles, Paderewski was not a representative of Poland; he was only an agent of the pro-Russian bloc." Similar inconsistencies occur all through the book.

battle was under the watchword that Mr. Wilson had preserved peace for the United States." He refers in his telegram to the accusations of the Germans from the Eastern States that " Wilson's re-election was due to the German vote in the West which had obeyed a more or less clear order from the German Embassy." While denying these accusations von Bernstorff stated, nevertheless, that " I never for a moment denied that I personally should be glad to see Mr. Wilson re-elected, as I was convinced that he had the determination and the power to bring about peace." [1n]

Wilson's sympathies were certainly on the Allied side, and Arthur S. Link rightly stated that " before the summer of 1916 the President's policy, on the whole, constituted a differential neutrality favourable to the Allies." But the replies to his appeal to the belligerents to state their peace terms (18th December, 1916), convinced him " that the Allied Governments did not want a reasonable peace " and he began to change differential neutrality into impartiality.[1o]

On the other side we know that he was most reluctant to enter into any discussions on the specific territorial problems, and in this he was nearer at that time to the point of view of the German Government than to that of the Allied Powers. This is clear from the telegrams of Count Bernstorff, e.g. 5th October, 1916 :

> " The Imperial Government desired that the territorial questions should be regulated by direct negotiations between the combatant Powers. Mr. Wilson, as Colonel House told me, was in agreement with this. ... In my conversations with Colonel House, we never spoke of the evacuation of any German territory. We always confined ourselves exclusively to a real peace by negotiation on the basis of the *status quo ante*. With such a peace Germany's position in the world would have remained unimpaired." [1p]

And still on 27th January, 1917, he reported :

> " House suddenly invited me to visit him on behalf of Wilson, and told me the following as an official message from the President. First of all, Wilson offers privately to mediate the peace on the basis of his appeal to the Senate, i.e. therefore without interference in territorial terms of peace." [1r]

Wilson's Address of 22nd January, 1917

In view of the unsatisfactory replies to his Note to the belligerents of 18th December, 1916, Wilson decided to take a further step in order to save the last possibility of preserving America from the war, which seemed unavoidable should the Germans proceed to unrestricted submarine warfare. He consulted House in the beginning of January 1917 about a declaration which he intended to make in the Senate on the general terms of settlement, " making the keystone of the settlement arch the future security of the world against wars, and letting territorial adjustments be subordinate to the main purpose." As Colonel House states : " To avoid blurring the main principle of the address, Wilson decided not to include any statement of a desirable territorial settlement : he mentioned merely the necessity of a united independent Poland." [2] In fact Wilson " narrowed his discussion of specific territorial claims to Poland," [3] but we know that he had in mind at that time, as appeared from his conference with House, that Belgium and Serbia should be restored, Turkey should be eliminated from Europe, Russia should have an ice-free port, and Poland should be " free." He was uncertain what should be done with Alsace and Lorraine.[3a] Strangely enough the Polish issue seemed to be one on which both sides seemed to agree to some extent in view of the Proclamation of 5th November, 1916, by the Central Powers and the Tsar's Order of the Day of 25th December, 1916, announcing that " the creation of free Poland from all three until now separated provinces " was one of Russia's war aims.

Wilson received also additional assurances on the German part that Germany stood by the principle of Poland's independence. Count von Bernstorff called on Colonel House and let him know that German war aims were moderate. House informed Wilson by a letter of 15th January that according to his conversations with Bernstorff, " Germany would not take any part of Belgium, wished to make Poland and Lithuania independent." [3b]

Bethmann-Hollweg authorized von Bernstorff to tell Wilson " for his own private information " the terms on which Germany was prepared to take part in peace negotiations with the Entente : " The restitution to France of that part of Upper Alsace occupied by her. The acquisition of a strategical and economic safety frontier-zone separating Germany and Poland from Russia." [3c]

Encouraged by this attitude of the partitioning Powers, who seemed agreed on the question of the principle of an independent Poland, Wilson entrusted House with preparing an appropriate text on Poland. House called on Paderewski in New York and asked him to present a memorandum on the Polish problem. According to Landau's biography of Paderewski, the latter " shut himself up and worked for thirty-six hours on end." House, leaving New York for Washington on 11th January, had Paderewski's memorandum in his pocket. Asked by Paderewski a few days later about the memorandum he answered : " On my way to Washington I read your text four or five times. I practically learned the essential passages by heart. In the course of the following few days I constantly mentioned your arguments to the President during lunch and dinner. On a number of occasions he declared that he absolutely agreed with them. To-day the President withdrew to his room. In solitude he is preparing his message. The bomb will explode in a few days' time." [3d]

In his article, " Paderewski : The Paradox of Europe " (*Harper's Magazine*, December 1925, pp. 30-6), House tells that " about this period of my career I came in intimate and constant touch with him (Paderewski). We pored—over his maps and mine—of Central and Eastern Europe, and together we traced what we thought should be a homogeneous Poland."

But it was not the details that mattered in January 1917. The most important was the fact that the President of the United States proclaimed the necessity of a united and independent Poland while the Allied Powers in their reply to him merely accepted as their own the Russian terms of the solution of the Polish problem as expressed in the above-mentioned Order of the Day of the Tsar of 25th December, 1916 (see p. 47).

Wilson's address to the Senate of 22nd January, 1917, apparently used the same phraseology as the previous declarations of the Western Powers on the rights of small nations, but the latter in practice considerably narrowed the field of application of the principles proclaimed by them, which was particularly striking in relation to the Polish problem.

Moreover, Wilson spoke for the first time of " a united," and not only independent and autonomous Poland and he took the view that the Polish problem, the only territorial problem referred to by him, was a test case of application of the principle of national self-determination. " The Governments," he said, " derive all their just powers from the consent of the governed," and " that no right anywhere exists to hound them about from potentate to potentate as if they were property."

There was of course a big flaw in Wilson's reasoning. Being the representative of a then neutral country, he believed at that stage that these ends might be secured without the use of force and that all the belligerents might be induced to concur voluntarily in carrying out their policy in accordance with these principles. Namely he stated in the further part of his address that it must be " a peace without victory. . . . Victory would mean peace forced upon the loser, a victor's terms imposed in humiliation. . . . Only a peace between equals can last."

Lloyd George once remarked about Wilson's policy : " The de-

fect characterized Wilson's conduct before and after the war. He
had an implicit faith in the efficacy of words. Diamond does not
break glass; its impress has to be followed by adequate pressure." [4]
These words are certainly unfair and ungenerous to Wilson, especially considering the great part played by the United States of
America in winning the common victory, but they seem to me particularly appropriate in relation to this stage of Wilson's great
crusade for a democratic peace.

It suffices to look at the reactions of the Germans to be convinced
of the impossibility of achieving Wilson's ends without the use of
force. The following conversation between the American Ambassador in Berlin and the German Chancellor relating to Wilson's
Address of 22nd January provides the best proof. It appears also
from this conversation that the American representatives abroad did
not rightly understand at that time the real meaning of the President's message which proclaimed some principles without entering
into details of the future settlement. Ambassador Gerard's report
runs as follows :

" He (the German Chancellor) spoke particularly of the President's speech of 22nd January, and said that in that speech the
President had made it plain that he considered that the answer of
the Entente Powers to his Peace Note formed a basis of peace
which was a thing impossible for Germany even to consider ; and
said further—and this was a criticism I heard not only from him
but also from many Germans—that when the President spoke of a
united and independent Poland he evidently meant to take away
from Germany that part of Poland which had been incorporated in
the Kingdom of Prussia, and give it to this new and independent
Kingdom thereby bringing the Eastern frontier of Germany within
two hours by motor from Berlin, and that, further, when the President spoke of giving each nation a highway to the sea he meant that
the German port of Danzig should be turned over to this new State
of Poland, thereby not only taking a Prussian port, but cutting the
extreme Eastern part of Prussia from the remainder of the country.
... I said that these objections appeared to me very frivolous. ...
The President was in favour of a peace without victory, which
meant, of course, that Germany should be secured from crushing
and dismemberment which Germany's statesmen stated so often
that they feared. I said further that I was sure that when the President spoke of the united and independent Poland he had not, of
course, made reference to Poland at any particular period of its
history, but undoubtedly to Poland as constituted by Germany and
Austria themselves ; and that, in referring to the right of a nation
to have access to the sea, he had in mind Russia and the Dardanelles, rather than any attempt to take a Prussian port for the benefit
of Poland." [5]

If we now wish to know the inmost thoughts of a typical representative of the German military caste at that time, we have to
turn to General von Seeckt, later the organizer of the new German
Army under the Weimar Republic. Under the 22nd January he
notes :

> " A comical draft the last note of Wilson? Does the man really
> believe it? That a nation which still has some force and honour
> might not seize the sword when her vital interests are at stake?
> Shall then the police under American leadership intervene with a
> big stick and anyway launch a war in order to secure peace? " [6]

In an earlier letter written on the 29th November, 1915, to his
friend von Winterfeld-Menking, Seeckt anticipated the following :

> " We shall conclude such a peace as will make us stronger for the
> next war. ... What do we need for such a purpose? Frontiers
> which might be well defended ... frontiers which are good for
> defence but from which one could also go ahead. ... America
> itself is unassailable for us so long as techniques do not provide us
> with new weapons, against England too. ... Our dominion should
> extend from the Atlantic Ocean to Persia." [7]

Wilson himself soon realized the impossibility of carrying out his
programme without the use of force. At the moment of the Declaration of the State of War to Germany by the U.S.A., Wilson declared
in the Congress on the 2nd April, 1917 :

> " We are glad that we see the facts without the veil of false
> pretence about them, to fight thus for ultimate peace of the world
> and for the liberation of its peoples, the German people included ;
> for the rights of nations great and small and the privilege of men
> everywhere to choose their way of life and obedience. The world
> must be safe for democracy." [8]

The address of President Wilson of the 22nd January, 1917, was
certainly a great event from the Polish point of view. From then on
Wilson appeared as the champion of Poland's independence and
nobody could deny that he loyally abided by his pledges so long as
he retained real power in the United States. From the distant Polish
capital, Warsaw, the newly installed Provisional Council of State
(at that time Pilsudski and his followers were members of the Council), in spite of the foreign occupation had the courage to send the
following telegram to the President :

> " It is in fact for the first time during this war that a Head of a
> powerful neutral State and the highest representative of a great
> nation has officially declared that according to his conviction an
> independent Polish State is the only fair solution of the Polish

question and the indispensable condition for a just and durable peace." [9]

There is no doubt that Wilson's declaration promoted the Allied cause much more in occupied Poland—strengthening her resistance to the Central Powers—than did the hesitating and ambiguous policy of Great Britain and France. The " idealistic " policy of Wilson took more account of the realities of the modern world—the force of national movements as factors of international policy—than the policy of the West European countries, embedded in old prejudices.[10]   " The winged words of Woodrow Wilson were worth armies," writes an American historian.[10a]

Russian Revolution and the Proclamation of the Provisional Russian Government of 29th March, 1917

The outbreak of the March Revolution in Russia brought about many important changes in the attitude of Russia towards the Polish question. In the light of all the evidence in our possession there is no doubt that the momentous decisions taken at the end of March 1917 were caused not by any external influence but arose from the general trend of events in Russia herself and from the very opportune initiatives taken in the Russian capital by those Poles, A. Lednicki in the first place, who had long been in close relations with Russian democratic circles.

It should be kept in mind that the first Minister of Foreign Affairs in the Provisional Russian Government, Milyukov, belonged to the Party of Constitutional-Democrats (Cadets) who represented an imperialistic wing of the Russian opposition to the Tsarist régime. Milyukov's programme did not differ substantially from that of Sazonov in the first two years of the War.[11] He did not forswear any of the war aims proclaimed by the Tsarist régime at the beginning of the War, and he intended to defend all the rights acquired by Russia by virtue of secret treaties with the Allies. On the 5th April Milyukov declared to press representatives that " Russia looked for confirmation of its claims to the Ukrainian lands of Austria-Hungary, to Constantinople and the Dardanelles, the acquisition of which had always been an ancient national problem of Russia. [12] In a note sent to the Allied Governments Milyukov took the same standpoint. A clash between Milyukov's programme and that upheld at that time by the Petrograd Soviet of Workers' and Soldiers' Deputies was one of the first big clashes between two wings of the Russian Revolution. Milyukov's resignation on the 16th May, 1917, was also one of the first victories of the Soviet, which demanded " peace without annexations and indemnities " in conformity with the decisions of the Left Wing of the International Socialist Congresses at Zimmerwald (5th December, 1915) and at Kienthal (5th September, 1916) in Switzerland.[13] Stalin in *Pravda* commented at that time on Milyukov's programme in the following words :

> " The readers of *Pravda* know that these aims are imperialistic : the conquest of Constantinople, the acquisition of Armenia, the dismemberment of Austria and Turkey, the acquisition of Northern Persia. ... It turns out that Russian soldiers are shedding their blood on the battlefields not to ' defend their fatherland ' nor ' for liberty,' as the venal bourgeois press assures us, but for the conquest of foreign lands." [14]

So far as the Polish question was concerned, the Cadets on the eve of the Revolution still maintained the traditional imperialistic point of view, as clearly appears from the article published in the *Ryech,* their press organ, 1st (14th February), 1917, in which it was stated that " Russia should not allow the establishment on the Russian frontier of a new sovereign Polish State." The representative of the Cadets, President of the Duma, Rodzianko, voted against General Gourko's proposals at the meetings of the special commission appointed by the Tsar for the purpose of carrying out the promises made by the latter in his Order of the Day to the Army and Fleet on 25th December, 1916 (see pp. 47 ff.).[15]

On the other side there existed among the democratic circles of Russia some trends sympathizing with the Polish claims to independence.[15a] In 1916 was founded there the Circle of the Friends of Polish Independence, with Prof. Kuzmin-Karayev as chairman, and to which belonged some future prominent leaders : Kerensky, Nekrasov, Chkheidze. In 1916 Samarin, chairman of the Nobility of Moscow, handed to the Government a memorandum in which he emphasized the necessity for the recognition of Poland's independence. The most active Poles in Russia who had close contacts with circles of the Russian opposition were : A. Lednicki in Moscow, A. Babianski in Petrograd, and A. Wieckowski, who was specially active among the socialists. It was indisputably Lednicki who was the most prominent among them. He was a lawyer with a very wide practice, a brilliant orator and a great master of the Russian language, long established in Moscow; he joined the K.D. Party in 1905 in agreement with the Polish Progressive Party, of which he was one of the leaders. Elected to the first Duma from Minsk he signed the famous Viborg Manifesto of the Russian opposition after the dissolution of the Duma. He belonged at the same time to the K.D. Parliamentary Group in the Duma and the Circle of Polish

Deputies from Lithuania, White Russia, the Ukraine and Podolia, thus becoming a natural link between the Poles and democratic Russians. His rôle became particularly important after the outbreak of the War when he was elected, first, chairman of the Polish Committee in Moscow, and then chairman of the Joint Committees of the Polish Associations in Russia. In his flat in Moscow the Russian delegates used to meet many Poles of all political shades. Among the Russians there were such prominent personalities as Prince Lvov, later President of the First Provisional Government after the outbreak of the Revolution, Prince Dolgoruky, Prince Trubetzkoy, V. Maklakov, Kokoshkin, Milyukov, Rodichev, Nabokov, etc. In 1916, after Sazonov's dismissal, Lednicki left the K.D. Party whose position on the Polish question did not satisfy him. Lednicki, however, did not stop his political activity. In a memorandum submitted to the Government in 1916 and published by the *Russkoye Slovo* he wrote :

> " It would be a reasonable policy on the part of Russia and the Coalition to grant the same guarantees to Poland as those received already by Belgium and Serbia, that is to say, to recognize that independence of Poland should be one of the war aims."

After the Proclamation of 5th November, 1916, by the Central Powers Lednicki wrote (12th November, 1916) :

> " There is nothing that might put into doubt the importance of this event. It was publicly recognized by the German and Austrian Governments that the Polish Nation had the right to an independent existence. The Polish question ceased definitely to be a domestic issue of the Partitioning Powers, that is to say it was put on the international agenda."

The outbreak of the Russian Revolution united all the Poles in Russia in the request for Polish independence. Many meetings of Polish refugees (very numerous then in Russia) and Poles settled in Russia were held all over the country and resolutions were adopted unanimously requesting from the Provisional Government a prompt recognition of Poland's independence. There were also many prominent Russians who expressed their sympathy and support for the Polish claims. Kerensky, at a meeting of the Polish Democratic Club on 7th(20th) March declared that " his position on the Polish question remained unchanged and that he would do his best in order that the official recognition of Polish independence be made as soon as possible." In a telegram sent to the Polish Democratic Club in Moscow, and read at the meeting of the Club on 10th(23rd) March, Kishkin, representative in Moscow of the Provisional Government, expressed his hopes for " an alliance between an independent Poland and Great Russia." In a moving telegram sent from Moscow to the Committee of the Duma in Petrograd and signed by the representatives of different Polish political parties, we find a sentence that proved that the democratic Poles expected the obliteration of the past and an understanding with democratic Russia : " Let us forget yesterday. We salute the rising day (Dniu vcherashnemu zabveniye—dniu griadushchemu privet)."

On the 24th March, Lednicki was called to Petrograd by telegram and was received the following day by Prince Lvov, President of the Provisional Government, whom he asked when the Provisional Government would issue an official proclamation on Poland's independence. According to some information Prince Lvov referred to the fears expressed by the British Ambassador, Buchanan, and the French Ambassador, Paléologue, that in the event of Russia giving up her claims in Poland she might lose interest in the continuation of the war. Lednicki called on Milyukov on the 26th March. The latter expressed some doubts whether the Provisional Government possessed the necessary authority to decide a question which in his opinion was within the province of the Constituent Assembly, but eventually he had to agree without giving any pledges on the future frontiers, about which the final decision was to be left with the future Constituent Assembly.

On the 27th March the Petrograd Soviet published its appeal to the Peoples of the World, in which " it called on the proletarians of all the belligerent countries to commence the decisive struggle with the grasping ambitions of their governments and take into their own hands the decision of questions of war and peace." [16]

It was a logical conclusion from the above appeal that the Soviet also carried a resolution on the 28th March on the recognition of Poland's independence.

Some writers affirm that it was this appeal of the Petrograd Soviet that gave the last push to the hesitating Provisional Government to state its views on Poland's independence.[17] Such was later, in fact, the claim of the Bolshevik propaganda, but as one can see from the preceding account the question was virtually settled between Lednicki and Milyukov at that time and Lednicki's draft relating to the establishment of the Commission of Liquidation was approved by the Council of Ministers on 28th March, (Lednicki was appointed its chairman). The Petrograd Soviet did not then possess the authority which it acquired in the latter stages of the Revolution. Milyukov himself denied these rumours in Lednicki's biography published by a Polish review, *Przeglad Wspolczesny* : " There was no dualism of power at that time in Russia and the resolution of the

Soviet was unknown to me in those days." (This assertion seems quite plausible.)

It was Milyukov who drafted the text of the Proclamation of the Provisional Government (with some corrections introduced by Lednicki, who was, however, surprised in reading the final text of the declaration in the newspapers in which he found some passages which did not appear in the original text shown to him by Milyukov). Milyukov denied also (which was less true) that he had changed his opinions on Poland's independence under the stress of events. In a reply to the address of the Polish Democratic Club whose representatives called on him after the Proclamation to express to him its thanks, Milyukov stated :

> " My political opinions did not change. A realistic politician must realize that words are binding and that they should be followed by acts and the acts were beyond our control at that time ; we had, consequently, to wait until the moment when by the decision in our own power we should be able to carry out the will of the Russian nation and follow the voice of our conscience."

The Proclamation of the Provisional Government on 29th(16th) March, 1917, started by a phrase which branded the previous policy of the Tsarist Government on the Polish question : " The old authority gave you only hypocritical promises which it could have fulfilled but which it did not fulfil." The next passage shows that the question of the formation of a Polish army by the Central Powers was one of the reasons for the Russian decision : " The Polish army will not now fight for the oppression of freedom, for the division of its country under the command of its secular enemy."

The following passages of the Proclamation refer to the recognition of Poland's independence :

> " The Russian Provisional Government considers that the creation of an independent Polish State from all the territories where the Polish people constitute a majority of population is a certain guarantee of durable peace in a future unified Europe. *United to Russia by a free military alliance,* the Polish State will become a strong bulwark against the pressure of the Central Powers against Slavism. ... Russia believes that the nationalities attached to Poland by the secular bonds of common life will obtain guarantees of their civic and national existence ... *it will be for the Russian Constituent Assembly finally to ratify the new brotherly alliance* and give its consent to the changes of the Russian State territory, which will be required for the constitution of an independent Poland from all her three parts, now divided. ... May the union of our feelings and hearts prepare the future alliance of our States." [18]

There were important objections on the Polish part to some

passages of this Proclamation. Some of them were laid down in the statement of the Provisional Council of State in Warsaw (to which Pilsudski and his followers still belonged at that time) which appeared on the 6th April, 1917. The Provisional Council of State observed :

> " that the secular Russo-Polish dispute on the question of the vast countries between ethnographic Poland and Russia, countries which had for centuries shared the destinies of Poland, has not been settled by the Proclamation of the Russian Government. We cannot leave the solution of this dispute to a unilateral decision of the Russian Constituent Assembly. The fate of these countries should be settled for the benefit of Poland, respecting the wishes of the peoples inhabiting these areas." [19]

In fact the Proclamation did not annul the Treaties of Partition, which was not done until the following year. Moreover, the Proclamation took for granted that the future Poland would wish to remain in some indefinite military alliance with Russia (although reached by free agreement, the word " free " being introduced on Lednicki's demand). Does it mean that we should minimize and depreciate this first effort of the Russian and Polish democrats, whatever might have been their illusions that Russia would remain a democratic country, an illusion which was not shared, by the way, by Dmowski? It might have become a starting point for a lasting understanding under certain conditions.

A British writer who rather dislikes the liberal trends in the Russian political thought, Prof. E. H. Carr, takes a disparaging view of the Proclamation, ascribing it to sheer opportunism :

> " Poland was by this time wholly under German occupation and the Central Powers were already offering independence to a puppet Polish State. The Russian Provisional Government could hardly do less, and was in a position to promise without any immediate obligation to perform." [20]

Milyukov himself in his *History of the Second Russian Revolution* recalls that the Proclamation was not a formal juridical act but drafted in the form of an appeal to the Poles, the text of which was not couched in precise juridical language as had been the case with the recognition of the national freedoms of the Finns (but not of the independence of Finland recognized only later by the Soviet Government). Milyukov admits also that the fear of the formation of a Polish army which might appear on the front and the establishment of close links between Poland and the Central Powers was uppermost in his mind. [21]

In his biography of A. Lednicki, Milyukov gives an explanation which in our view corresponded to the opinions prevailing at that time within the Russian democratic front.

> " It was natural [he writes] that the Polish question could be settled only after a victorious war in an international way ; thus the decision of the Provisional Government could not be final ; for this reason the Proclamation could express only some desires so far as the domestic and foreign policy of the future Polish State was concerned, without giving the form of a binding nature to these desires as it would have meant an interference with the problems of policy of the independent State which had just been constituted. The only, purely moral, ground for fostering the hope that these desires would find a response on the Polish side rested on the identity of the political aspirations of the Russian and Polish political parties, which by way of a mutual understanding agreed to the settlement of the problem."

As we have stated above, the Proclamation could be only a starting point for a lasting understanding between an independent Poland and a regenerated Russia, but the future of Polish-Russian relations depended on Russia becoming a real democracy, that is to say forswearing compulsion in her policy towards the subjugated nationalities. Was the new Russia ready to recognize the validity of the principle of national self-determination so far as the other alien nationalities of Russia were concerned? Or did she wish to follow the policy of Jacobins and insist on the principle of " one and indivisible Russia?" In this connection another question arose : was Russia ready to fight on the side of the democratic powers and put into practice the ideals she proclaimed, or come to terms with the imperialistic Central Powers? In the latter case the Proclamation to the Poles would be empty of meaning and without any immediate political significance. While the K.D. party and the right wing of the new Government were rather reluctant to admit the principle of national determination, but were ready to continue the war, those who insisted on recognition and on carrying out the principle of national self-determination were at that time divided into two camps : some members of the Petrograd Soviet, mostly belonging to the Mensheviks, wished to continue the " war of liberation," others, the Bolsheviks, above all insisted on the quick termination of the war on the basis of " no annexations and no indemnities," which would have left unsolved the most important national issues in Central Europe and might have saved the Central Powers from impending disaster. They believed, or pretended to believe, that all the problems would be solved by a proletarian revolution and not by the continuation of the War. After Wilson's speech of the 7th June, in which he insisted on the impossibility of maintaining the *status quo* after the War, and declared that nations must not be subjugated, the following answer was given in *Izvestia* :

> "President Wilson is mistaken if he thinks that such ideas can enter the heads of the revolutionary people of Russia ... the road to the passionately longed for universal peace lies only through the united struggle of the toilers all over the world against world imperialists. It cannot be misled by hazy and high-flown phrases." [22]

At the time of Milyukov's dismissal the Petrograd Soviet demanded :

> "A vigorous foreign policy aiming at the speediest attainment of a general peace on the principle of the self-determination of nationalities, without annexations or indemnities, in particular the preparation for negotiations with the Allies with the object of securing a revision of treaties on the basis of the Provisional Government's Declaration of the 9th April." [23]

The history of the Declaration of the 9th April is rather interesting, showing that the Provisional Government had to make important concessions to the claims of the Petrograd Soviet. In his *History of the Second Russian Revolution* Milyukov says that being pressed by the representatives of different nationalities of Russia (Lithuanians, Ukrainians) to recognize their national rights, he took the view that the matter " was not urgent and could be postponed until the Constituent Assembly." [24] According to the information of Mr. Wilcox, then correspondent of the *Daily Telegraph* in Petrograd, the text " of the declaration was agreed to only after long and painful debate, both among the Ministers themselves and between the Cabinet and the Control Commission of the Soviet. An influential element in the Government wished to give unresistingly before the rising wind of popular clamour and to accept without reservation or qualification of any kind the current formula ' peace without annexations or indemnities ' on the basis of self-determination of nations." [25] In the Declaration of the 9th April, 1917, the Provisional Government was forced, nevertheless, to recognize the general validity of the principle of national self-determination, of which the case of Poland was one of the most striking and indisputable :

> "The Provisional Government deems it its right and duty to declare here and now that free Russia does not aim to dominate other peoples and deprive them of their national patrimony, to occupy foreign territory by force, but to establish a firm peace on the foundation of the right of peoples to determine their own destiny. The Russian people do not covet any accession of power

at the expense of other peoples, do not aim to subjugate or degrade anyone. In the name of the higher principles of equity it has removed the shackles that weighed down the Polish nation." [26]

The second trend in the Russian revolutionary movement was making steady progress, and finally triumphed when the Second Russian Revolution gave power to the Bolsheviks.

The Allied representatives in Petrograd viewed with growing anxiety the developments in Russia. Losing her imperialistic drive Russia was at the same time losing all interest in the War. It was a strange and tragic coincidence that the representatives of Western democracies had to deplore the eclipse of Russian imperialism and centralism.

In a telegram of the 11th April, 1917, the French Ambassador Paléologue noted his apprehensions on account of the disinterested-ness of a part of Russian opinion in matters regarding Poland and even Lithuania.[27] The beginning of the disintegration of Russia owing to the growing unrest of her subjugated nationalities preoccupied to the highest degree the Allied representatives. Palé-ologue noted in his diary under 30th March : " The most dangerous germs. . . . Finland, Livonia, Esthonia, Lithuania, Ukraine, Georgia, Siberia raise claims to independence . . . " and unable to understand the difference between national problems in Western Europe and in Russia he exclaimed :

" The present movement is much more separatist than regional, more secessionist than federalist ; it aims at nothing less than a national disintegration. So, the Soviet favours it as much as it can and the fools of the Tauride Palace (the seat of the Soviet) try to destroy in a few weeks the historical work of ten centuries! The French Revolution started by proclaiming one and indivisible Republic. It sacrificed for the sake of this principle thousands of heads, and so French unity was saved. The Russian Revolution abides by the principle: A disrupted and dismembered Russia." [28]

*
*   *

In connection with these developments in Russia the question arises : what was the part played by the Western Allies of Russia in the issuing of the Proclamation to the Poles by the Provisional Government? The account given above reduces the rôle of the Western envoys to that of observers who viewed with some appre-hension the trend of events in Russia, and even at the beginning raised some objections to the Provisional Government taking initia-tives which might clash with the war effort of the Russian Empire. Nevertheless there exist different versions of events, and for the sake of historical truth we feel obliged to deal with them. So, according to some assertions, the Proclamation to the Poles was issued, thanks to the intervention of the British Ambassador, Buchanan, upon an instruction from Arthur Balfour. Let us state that we find no confirmation of it in Buchanan's *Memoirs*, although it seems rather strange in view of the importance of such a step. It was an English writer, E. J. Dillon, who first published this information in his book *The Peace Conference*. He says that at the request of the Polish representatives " the Foreign Secretary (Balfour) despatched at once a telegram to the Ambassador in the Russian capital to lay the matter before the Russian Foreign Minister, and urge him to lose no time in establishing the claims of the Polish Provisional Government (it did not exist at that time!) to the sympathies of the world, and the redress of its wrongs by Russia." Milyukov refused; he " regretted his inability to deal with the problem at that conjuncture, owing to its great complexity and various bearings, and also because of his apprehension that the Poles would demand the incorporation of Russian lands in their reconstituted State." Balfour allegedly telegraphed again to the British Ambassador, instructing him to " insist upon the recognition of Poland, as the matter is urgent, and to exhort the Provisional Government to give in good time the desired proof of the democratic faith that is to save Russia." At Buchanan's second call on Milyukov the latter " gave way, drafted and issued the proclamation." [29]

The whole account sounds rather fantastic and was refuted by Prince Lvov and Milyukov, as appears from a letter published in Warsaw by Milyukov's friend, Mr. F. Rodichev, who approached the two Russian politicians in connection with Dillon's story, (*Tygodnik Polski*, No. 20, 29th August, 1920).

> " Prince Lvov [wrote Rodichev] emphatically denied any sort of intervention by Buchanan ... the proclamation was a natural consequence of the events and was uppermost in all minds simultaneously, the same as the proclamation of equal rights for all nationalities, abolition of restrictions on the Jews, etc." " Milyukov [continues Rodichev] sent a letter to Warsaw, authorizing me to publish it in the papers, in which he categorically denied Dillon's assertions. It was not Buchanan who informed him but he who informed Buchanan of the Act of the Provisional Government. Buchanan did not demand anything and only took notice of his communication."

In Lednicki's biography quoted above Milyukov wrote :

> " Neither the intervention of the foreign Powers, nor the suggestions of the Soviet, had any influence on my initiative and the

decision of the Provisional Government. So far as the first item was concerned Lednicki made interesting disclosures to us. It was well known that the decision of the Provisional Government did not find an enthusiastic response either in the British or in the French Embassy as they feared that Russia renouncing Poland would lose one of the possible war-aims and thus her interest for the continuation of the War might be weakened."

In fact Dmowski called on Balfour on 25th March and handed him a Pro-Memoria in which he emphasized the necessity for *joint* recognition by the Allies of Poland's independence as an indispensable factor of the European balance of power. According to Dmowski the new State should be :

(1) Big and strong enough; (2) enjoy economic independence; and (3) have its own foreign policy. So far as the territory of the future Polish State was concerned, Dmowski did not maintain the claims to all the historical Polish territory, but insisted that Poland should have a territory " in which the masses speak Polish, have the consciousness of belonging to the Polish nationality, and are attached to the Polish cause." These points were elaborated in detail in Dmowski's subsequent memoranda and we shall deal with them later. In fact Dmowski asked Balfour to give instructions to Buchanan in order to induce the Provisional Government to join the Allies in issuing a *common* declaration on Poland's independence. Dmowski's version of events can be found in his book *Polityka Polska* [30] and in more detail in a report from the American Ambassador in France to the Secretary of State of the 19th October, 1917.[31] We produce below the corresponding passage of this report on a conversation with Dmowski in Paris :

" When the Provisional Government was established last spring in Petrograd he (Dmowski) went over to London to press the question of the recognition of the independence upon Balfour, stating that the time was most favourable for such action. Balfour entirely agreed with him and instructed the British Ambassador, Mr. Buchanan, at Petrograd, to urge this matter for favourable consideration upon the Russian Government ; a few days later he received an answer that it did not appear as though such a movement would be successful, as it was not looked upon with favour by the Russian Government. However, Dmowski told me, very soon after that the instructions were again sent to the Ambassador to vigorously push the matter, representing that that action be taken, and a few days later the Provisional Government at Petrograd proclaimed the independence of Poland."

Let us observe first of all that Dmowski called on Balfour on the 25th March and that the Proclamation to the Poles was issued on the

29th March, and it is hardly possible that all the events described by Dmowski could have taken place within four days. Moreover, as appears from the text of the Pro-Memoria and the statements of Lord Balfour quoted below, Dmowski asked for a joint declaration by the Allies, while the Proclamation was a unilateral act in which the Allies had not concurred. Although we do not know the text of the instructions sent by Balfour and Buchanan's replies, we possess a document of great importance for the matter under consideration, namely Balfour's Statement on Foreign Policy to the Imperial War Council made on the day following Dmowski's visit to Downing Street.[32] In this statement we read the following on Balfour's views on the Polish problem at that time :

" Galicia is not part of historic Austria, and might and ought to go to Poland of the future. . . . But what is Poland of the future? That I think is now as it has been ever since the great crime of partition was accomplished, the greatest crux of European diplomacy. A very distinguished Pole came to see me yesterday, whose name I will not venture to pronounce (Lord Robert Cecil: Mr. Dmowski), but he is a man of high character and great position. . . . He said . . . you cannot precisely follow these old frontiers . . . part of what was then Poland is more Russian than Polish—the Eastern part of it. . . .

" He (Dmowski) urged me very strongly to make a public appeal now on behalf of Poland, ' Now,' he said, ' that the Tsar has gone, the Entente nations ought to announce publicly that they are going to establish an independent Poland, and if you do not do that,' he said, ' there is a great danger that the Germans may succeed in the future in doing what they have failed to do in the past, which is to raise a Polish army.'

" Germany . . . might succeed in producing this great addition to her manpower. If it did, the effect upon the Allied cause would undoubtedly be most serious. He put the numbers down at between 700,000 and 1,000,000. Supposing Poland came in, in that way, on the side of the Central Powers, and supposing Russia fell into disorganization and military chaos, the whole of the position in the East would be changed disastrously for the worse. *Whether we are now in a position to proclaim our intentions with regard to Poland and whether if we did, it would have the effect which he says, I do not know : I think very likely it would. . . .*

" *I am sending an account of these conversations to Sir George Buchanan and I shall be interested to hear what he says about it.*

" Personally, from a selfish Western point of view, I would rather that Poland was autonomous under the Russians, because if you make an absolutely independent Poland lying between Russia and the Central States, you cut off Russia altogether from the West. Russia ceases to be a factor in Western politics, or almost ceases. She will be largely divided from Austria by Rumania. She will be divided from Germany by the new Polish State ; and she will not be coterminous with any of the belligerents. And if Germany has designs in the future upon France or the West, I think she will be protected by this new State from any action on the part of Russia and I am not at all sure that that is to the interests of Western civilization. It is a problem which has greatly exercised my mind, and for which I do not see a clear solution. These are disjointed observations in regard to Poland ; they lead to *no clear recommendation on my part*. I am not pleading for a cause ; I am trying to lay before the Cabinet the various elements in the problem as they strike me."

The following conclusions can be drawn from these " disjointed observations," reflecting Balfour's sceptical turn of mind (so far as the substance of these observations is concerned we can refer to our remarks on pp. 61 ff. in connection with Balfour's memorandum drafted in November 1916) : no positive instructions were sent to Sir George Buchanan, who had been asked only to state his views (his marked Russophilism was well known), and the British Government at that time had not made up its mind whether the severance of all links between Poland and Russia would be desirable from the point of view of British interests, but was rather inclined to think it was not.*

* There is another document much more sympathetic to Poland, prepared by the Foreign Office in autumn 1916 and published by Lloyd George in his book *Truth About the Peace Treaties*, I, pp. 31 ff.: " This remarkable document," says Lloyd George, " was prepared and signed by two prominent officials of the Foreign Office. It was circulated to the Cabinet without any covering recommendation or comment from Sir Edward Grey." But even this document, showing much deeper knowledge of European realities than Balfour's memoranda, recommended a personal union between Poland and Russia, although otherwise it insisted on the full independence of the Polish State. Since the document cannot be considered a statement on British policy, and in fact advised a much wider recognition of the principle of national self-determination than the British Government was ready to admit at that time, and since many of the recommendations of the authors (dismemberment of Austria-Hungary) stood in direct opposition to official British policy, the passages referring to Poland reproduced below can interest us only as the expression of the personal views of two prominent officials of the Foreign Office :

" On Poland it mentions three alternative suggestions but declares finally in favour of the ' creation of a Polish Kingdom under a Russian Grand Duke.' This Kingdom would be merely connected with Russia by the personal link of its ruler, but would in every respect enjoy complete independence. The grant of independence under such conditions would satisfy to the full the national aspirations of the Polish nation, and if it could be coupled with the acquisition of a commercial outlet for Poland in the Baltic, it would lead to the establishment of a State that from the point of view of

After the Proclamation was issued by the Provisional Government, the Allied Governments singly (the first telegram was sent by the Italian Prime Minister, Boselli, as soon as the 2nd April) and collectively (a joint telegram from the Governments of France, Great Britain and Italy was sent on the 14th April, 1917) expressed their sympathy for and approval of this act, promising also their support in vague and general terms.[33] In the House of Commons on the 26th April, that is nearly a month after, the Chancellor of the Exchequer, Bonar Law, in answer to a question from Mr. Asquith made a statement in regard to Poland, ending by the following warm words :

> " I am confident that I rightly interpret the feeling of this House when I say that we welcome that declaration and look forward to the time when, thanks to the liberal and statesmanlike action of the

national feeling and economic interests promises stability. Given the strong race antagonism of Poland to Prussia, which had secured during the war the open adhesion of the Russian Poles and the tacit support of what is best in Galicia and the Duchy of Posen, there is every reason to expect that the future Polish State would become a buffer State between Russia and Germany, in the best sense of the word, that is to say it would secure for Russia a Poland that would be most unlikely to be found in league against Russia, as long as Russia remains faithful to the programme of the Allies, which is respect for the independence of small nations. This new Polish State would be one of the most powerful units among the independent countries which are expected to come into existence upon the dissolution of Austria-Hungary. From the point of view of England and France, this conglomeration of States would prove an efficient barrier against Russian preponderance in Europe, and German extension towards the Near East, because these States would be happy and contented in the realization of their national aspirations, and strong as regards their economic future, which would be secured by the possession of their natural commercial outlet to the sea. ... We are quite alive to the opposition such a programme may encounter at Petrograd; we also realize that it is not likely to be overcome unless the military situation should oblige Russia to require Anglo-French co-operation in order to secure the evacuation of her territory, which is now in the hands of the enemy ... the solution which we have submitted is the best in the interests of the Allies, as it will preserve for them the reputation of good faith, and constitute a great asset to be created by their victory; it will seriously weaken Prussia by withdrawing from her a very capable and prosperous population, together with the loss of considerable coalfields in Silesia."

So far as Bohemia was concerned the document was a curious anticipation of the future, because it recommended linking Bohemia with the Kingdom of Poland, according to the authors a solution " desired both by farseeing Czechs and Poles " ... " the latter realize fully that the addition of Bohemia to Poland would afford and promote very considerably the economic development of Poland. The Czechs, on the other hand, fully appreciate that they would benefit by the superior culture and civilization of the Poles." Plans for Czech-Polish Confederation were topical during the Second World War and eventually failed owing to Russian pressure on the Czechs.

Provisional Russian Government, Poland will appear again in international life and take her share with other nations in working together for the common good of civilization. Our efforts in the War will be directed towards helping Poland to realize her unity on the lines described in the Russian proclamation, that is to say, under conditions which will make her strong and independent. We hope that after the War Great Britain will remain reunited to Poland in bonds of close friendship." [34]

It was certainly great progress in comparison with previous elusive statements in the House of Commons on the Polish question, but is it possible to say that " the programme of Poland's independence and unity became a part of the programme of the whole coalition?" [35] Did this issue become a common war aim of the Entente? So far the Polish question had been a specifically Russian war aim, and as we see from the above declaration the Western Allies, while expressing their sympathy and promising some measure of assistance, made no formal pledges and obviously did not wish to commit themselves to any specific formula for the solution of Polish political and territorial status after the War. There were many reasons for this, of which the unsettled political situation in Eastern Europe and the vanishing authority of the Russian Provisional Government were of primary importance. Moreover at that time the military position of the Allies was by no means brilliant; France, after the failure of the offensive on the Aisne in which she lost 120,000 men, showed signs of utter exhaustion, and for some months of 1917 was near to total collapse. There is no doubt that the Entente was saved by British undaunted vigour.[36] Among various peace moves the secret negotiations with Austria (see above, pp. 121 ff.) were certainly of the highest importance. So long as France and Great Britain believed that Austria-Hungary might be preserved as a counterpoise to Germany, thus replacing the pre-war Russia in the new balance of power system, the Polish question was relegated to the background, in spite of the efforts of the Polish leaders staying in the West.

In the meantime it was ever more obvious that Russia's participation in the War was nearing an inglorious end. In July 1917 the programme of peace " without annexations or indemnities " prevailed within the Soviet, although the new Government headed by Kerensky (23rd July) wished to continue the War at the side of the Allies. In all successive governments after Milyukov's resignation it was Tereshchenko who occupied the post of Minister of Foreign Affairs, being at the end the last representative of non-Socialist elements within the Cabinet. Tereshchenko was in an unenviable position, as he had to fight on two fronts : on the one side, Russia's voice in the Allied councils did not carry the same weight as before the Revolution in view of the military disasters and the growing demoralization of the army; on the other, he had to defend the principles of the traditional Russian policy against the vigorous attacks of the Soviet, the programme of which involved apparently not only the loss of Poland but of other vast territories with non-Russian population, and the discontinuance of the War, that is to say an open breach of the international engagements of Russia. Tereshchenko until the end defended the programme of the territorial integrity of Russia, and according to Milyukov's definition " adapted the democratic slogans to the Russian State interests." [37] The debates in late October and early November 1917, on the eve of the Bolshevik Revolution, on the text of the instructions for Skobelev, appointed Russia's representative at the Inter-Allied Council which had on its agenda the discussion of the revised war aims of the Entente, provide the best example of the impossibility of reconciling the two antagonistic outlooks in Russian foreign policy : one represented by the Government and the other by the Soviet. The programme of the latter was very near to that proclaimed by the Stockholm Conference of the Socialists of the neutral countries : peace without annexations and indemnities. So far as Poland was concerned it left to further international agreements the fate of Poland's Western provinces, held by Germany and Austria. On the other hand the Soviet apparently admitted a very wide application of the principle of self-determination in relation to non-Russian nationalities, and in particular to the Baltic countries. Tereshchenko insisted on the maintenance of Russian territorial integrity and was unwilling to extend the principle of national self-determination to the Baltic countries. He was particularly emphatic on this point, exclaiming in the course of the debate : " A Russia without the ice-free ports of the Baltic Sea would return to the times before Peter the Great." [38] So far as Poland was concerned Tereshchenko insisted on the necessity for Poland regaining her Western provinces, but he wanted a Poland formed on strictly ethnographic lines, seeing the danger in the plans developed at that time in the Western capitals by Dmowski, especially in the memorandum printed in July 1917 by Dmowski, *Problems of Central and Eastern Europe,* with which we shall deal later (see p. 177) and in which Dmowski proposed the formation of a Polish State from all the territories in which the Polish element held the predominant position, that is to say a State consisting not only of the Congress Kingdom but also of a part of the former Polish-Lithuanian provinces (and of course also of the Polish provinces of Austria and Germany). Tereshchenko wanted the Allies to accept the Russian point of view on the solution of the Polish question, and this explains many of the steps taken by him in the international field. His point of view on Poland was best summed up in his statement of the 28th September, 1917, in connection with the replies of the Central Powers to the Pope's Peace Note :

> " Russia opposes to this policy (the policy of the Central Powers) the principle of national self-determination proclaimed by her. The Provisional Government confirms its unshakable determination to realize the principles announced by it in the appeal to the Poles of 29th March—that is the restoration on the basis of the free self-determination of the Polish people and with the maintenance of ethnographic principle—of an independent Polish State formed by the unification of all lands containing a Polish majority of population. The Provisional Government has suggested to the Allied Powers the consideration of the question of the publication by the Allies of a special act sanctioning the fundamental principle laid down in respect of Poland by our Manifesto of 29th March." [39]

The Bolshevik Revolution brought about a complete change of the political position in Eastern Europe. From that moment the Western Allies were able to view the Polish question from a new angle, taking into account the new realities in Eastern Europe, and under conditions quite different from those under which the last proposal of the Russian Provisional Government had been made.

Polish Army in France

The next stage of the development of the Polish question was marked by some important events with far-reaching consequences for the post-war settlement in Central-Eastern Europe. These were : the withdrawal of Pilsudski from the Council of State and his subsequent arrest by the Germans (21st July, 1917) (see above, p. 117), the Decree of the 4th June of the President of the French Republic on the creation of an autonomous Polish Army, the attempts of the U.S. Government to set up a Polish Government on American soil, and the constitution of the Polish National Council at a meeting of Polish political *émigré* leaders at Lausanne on the 15th August, 1917.

The arrest of Pilsudski practically put an end to the plans of the Central Powers to win the Poles and to enlist a Polish army to fight on their side, although all the implications of this fact were not properly understood by the German authorities at that time. From that moment, apart from some insignificant groups, all the active elements in Poland linked the fate of their country with the Allied victory.

The Decree of President Poincaré had rather obscure origins, which could be brought to light if we knew all about the diplomatic negotiations which led to the issuing of this act. The fact is that it was not preceded by any conversations with responsible political leaders abroad (apart from Mr. Piltz in Paris). There is a strong suspicion that the Decree, if not entirely due to Russian initiative, was at least the outcome of secret negotiations with the Russian Embassy. The concurrence of the latter appears clearly from the text of the Decree :

> " On the other side the intentions of the Allied Governments and in particular of the Provisional Russian Government relating to the restoration of the Polish State cannot assert themselves in a better way than by allowing the Poles to fight under their national banner." [40]

The choice of the first organizers of this army having close connections with the Russian Military Attaché in Paris and unknown amongst the Poles corroborates the suspicion that it was an attempt from the Russian side to pass control of Polish matters in the West to the French Government, the most reliable from the Russian point of view, considering the Russo-French Agreements of February–March 1917 (see above, p. 56).

A Polish observer in the United States at that time characterized in these terms the policy of the Russian Ambassador in Paris towards Poland :

> " Izvolsky's aim was: to divert the attention of the Poles from the East, to accumulate all their energies on the Western Front, to centre all political endeavours on France on which Russia can rely, having agreed to the establishment of the French frontier on the Rhine ; to force the Poles to base their political future on an agreement with the French plans ; to oppose the French influence to the Polish influence in the United States and to fence off the Poles from the Americans with a French diplomatic wall, and so to render impossible an independent Polish policy in the future." [41]

To this effect we have another, much more authoritative testimony, that of one of the closest advisers of R. Dmowski, M. Seyda, who in his well-documented book based on papers from the archives of the Polish National Council, states approximately the same :

> " The initiative of the French Government was not free, nevertheless, from serious mistakes, being insufficiently prepared and hastily carried out. So, the Decree has created an autonomous Polish Army but it did not specify in what this autonomy should consist. The Army was organized but did not possess its own military statute as a basis for its organization. ... One was under the impression that it was an attempt to face the United States with an

accomplished fact, and for this reason the Polish Army was created in France by a unilateral French act." [42]

American Plans for a Polish Government in the U.S.A.

The official American documents since published by the Department of State fully confirm the last remark in Seyda's book. It was natural that the U.S. Government, in view of President Wilson's initiative on Polish questions, prepared plans to implement the principles laid down in the speeches of the President. We find there an interesting note submitted by the Secretary of State, Robert Lansing, to President Wilson on the 21st June, 1917. In view of the importance of this document we reproduce below the main points in it :

> " I have been turning over in my mind in what way we can best utilize the intense longing of the Poles for the restoration of Poland as an independent nation. ... To gain the full benefit of the loyalty of the Poles to their country it seems to me that, in the first place, this Government and those of the Allies should announce in separate but identical declarations that they recognize the legitimate nature of Polish desires for self-government and that they purpose to devote their energies to free Poland and restore the nation to full sovereignty, in contradistinction to a nation under the protection or control of any neighbouring power. In the second place, the matter of financing the Polish military establishment is most important. Of course it will have to be done by this country. My suggestion is that a Polish Provisional Government be set up in this country, that it be recognized by this Government and the Allied governments and that it send diplomatic representations to all the Powers with which it is associated in the War. After formal recognition of this Government of an independent Poland we could legally loan the Government for military purposes the necessary funds secured by Polish bonds underwritten by this country and the Allies.
> " I have carefully considered the plan where the Provisional Government should be located and have come to the conclusion that to avoid all suspicions as to the genuine purpose of this step looking to the rebirth of Poland this country is the only place. Furthermore, in view of the fact that this country will have to supply the money for this enterprise, I believe that the Government should be where we can keep a watchful eye on the expenditure." [43]

It is very interesting that a few weeks later the Department of State received a memorandum from the British Embassy in Washington, dated 23rd July, in which it was stated that :

> " His Majesty's Government are of the opinion that the efforts of the Polish people to obtain their freedom and their independence should be supported in every possible way, and that they should be similarly discouraged from listening to the specious assurances of

the enemy of a spurious independence. . . . His Majesty's Government proposes . . . that all Poles should be granted open recognition as friends and potential allies. . . . Such a step would crystallize the idea of a separate and free Polish State and people in the minds of the public in the countries of the Allied Governments, and it would be in the nature of a guarantee to the Polish people themselves that their claims to independence were being backed by the Allies. . . . As a corollary to such action it would be highly desirable to establish a committee to represent the Polish community in each of the Allied countries." [44]

The following can be observed in connection with this memorandum : there is no doubt that the British Government began to realize the importance of winning the sympathies of the Poles, especially in view of the military collapse of Russia and the German endeavours in Poland. [45] The British proposals were, however, much more modest than the American ones : no formal guarantee, but only an implicit one, no central political body representing Polish interests abroad but only a committee in each Allied country.

In spite of this British memorandum Lansing sent an instruction to the American Ambassador in Great Britain on 27th August in which he repeated his proposal relating to the establishment of a Provisional Government in the U.S. It proves that in the meantime Lansing had secured the approval of the President for his Polish scheme. At that time Lansing used to receive in his office a Pole without special political connections, a certain Mr. Sosnowski, who tried to win him to the idea of establishing a Polish Government in the U.S. [46] In any case we are not quite sure whether Mr. Paderewski, a prominent figure among the Poles in America and a close friend of Colonel House, was fully conversant with these plans, and it is more than probable that he was not, as may appear from the steps he took soon afterwards on behalf of the Polish National Committee set up in Lausanne on the 15th August, 1917.

Moreover, while during the Peace Conference in Paris Lansing held Paderewski in very high esteem, this was not the case at the beginning of their acquaintance. In his brilliant sketch of Paderewski in the book *The Big Four and Others at the Peace Conference* (pp. 200-10), Lansing says that " to-day he can think of Paderewski only as the zealous advocate of Polish independence, as the sagacious statesman, as the tactful negotiator, as the unselfish public servant who thought only of the welfare of his country and of its people," but he confesses that such were not his views on Paderewski in the earlier stages of the War :

"When the famous musician came to see me in my office at the Department of State, as he did on many occasions after the United

States had entered the War ... I could not avoid the thought that his emotions were leading him into a path which was wholly unsuitable to follow. My feeling was that I had to deal with one given over to extravagant ideals, to the visions and fantasies of a person controlled by his emotional impulses rather than by his reason and the actualities of life. I was impressed by his fervid patriotism, and by his intense devotion to the cause of Poland, but it was not unnatural to think that so temperamental a nature would be swayed by sentimentality in the advocacy of a course of action and would give passionate support to his ideas with little regard to logic or practical considerations. Holding this impression of Mr. Paderewski, an impression which I believe was shared by many of those with whom he came in contact in those early days of his active work for his country, I confess that I was not disposed to give the weight to his opinions that I did later."

Constitution of the Polish National Committee

The constitution of a Government in exile of a country which has no legal representation abroad and the legal continuity of which has been interrupted is always a difficult and delicate task, and in this case it was a particularly intricate one, because apart from Austria the Poles had not shared in the responsibilities of a Government since the failure of the insurrection of 1830–1831. Mr. Lansing was well aware of this difficulty and, asking Ambassador Page to " sound informally and orally the British Government to ascertain whether the present time is considered opportune for action," he awaited also " any suggestions " from this Government " as to the method to be adopted to secure proper representation of the Polish people in any government to be established in this country."

Meanwhile the Polish National Committee was set up by Polish *émigré* leaders in Lausanne. This Committee established its seat in Paris and enjoyed the obvious protection of the French Government, which was the first to recognize it (20th September). The Committee did not include all shades of Polish political opinion, it consisted mostly of members of the National-Democrat Party (which had branches in all parts of Poland), and some conservatist leaders who from the beginning of the War had linked the cause of Poland with that of the Allies. The Left Wing, which at that time followed Pilsudski, was consequently not represented in the Committee. Notifying its establishment to the Allied Governments on the 28th August, 1917, the Committee in the following terms censured the Tsarist policy towards Poland :

" The links existing between Poland and the Allies could not come fully to light in the first three years of the War owing to the policy of the Russian Government under the old régime with which the Allies were forced to reckon. The attitude of Russia gave the enemy the opportunity to take the Polish question in its hands in order to make of it a tool of its policy." [47]

From its very beginning the Polish National Committee raised a natural claim to the political control of the Polish Army in France constituted, as we have said above, by the Decree of the President of the French Republic of 4th June, 1917, but its request was granted only on 20th March, 1918, when the rights of the Committee were recognized in a general manner by a letter of the Minister of Foreign Affairs of France. Those rights did not extend to military matters. The position of the Polish Army in France was more clearly defined by another Decree of the French President of 31st May, 1918. But it was not until the 28th September, 1918, that an agreement was signed between the National Committee and the French Government by which the Polish Army in France was put under the supreme control of the Committee, which appointed General J. Haller the Commander-in-Chief on 4th October, 1918.

This circumspection of the French Government in dealing with the Polish forces in France may seem surprising, and confirms the suspicions that the Russian Embassy continued to interfere in these affairs and that the French Government did not wish to proceed without agreement with the Russians in spite of the Proclamation of the Provisional Russian Government recognizing Poland's independence. It should be noted that the Czecho-Slovak Army in France enjoyed a more privileged position because it was put under the political control of the National Committee of Czech and Slovak Lands as early as the 16th December, 1917.[47a]

The constitution of the National Committee obviously surprised the Government of the United States. An interesting exchange of views between the British and American Governments took place in connection with this event. By a note dated 3rd September, 1917, the British Embassy in Washington informed the State Department that His Majesty's Government had " received an official notification of the constitution of a National Polish Committee the seat of which is to be in Paris " and the scope of which is " to represent the Polish interests in Allied countries arising out of a Polish Army to fight on the side of the Allies " and " the protection of persons of Polish nationality." The Embassy further informed the State Department that " His Majesty's Government is inclined to recognize this Committee but would be glad of the views of the U.S. Government on the proposals, before they take any action, in view of a recent suggestion by the United States Ambassador in London that His Majesty's Government should recognize a Polish Provisional

Government in the United States." [48] On the 4th September the American Ambassador in Great Britain informed the State Department that the Committee would " do practically what the proposed Provisional Government in the United States would do and this Committee is represented to the British Government as being more completely representative than any other as having working relations with bodies of Poles in Poland. ... Lord Robert Cecil is disposed to see what the Committee can accomplish before committing himself to the appraisal of your plans." [49]

In view of the hesitations of the American Government the representative of the Committee in America, Mr. Paderewski, sent a telegram from Chicago to President Wilson in which he informed him that " both the British and French Governments in order to put an end to the nefarious pro-German intrigue agreed to recognize (in fact the French Government already recognized the Committee, and the British Government did not recognize it until the 15th October) the Polish National Committee recently formed in Paris as official experts and unofficial representatives of the Polish nation provided that the United States would recognize it as well." Paderewski ended this telegram by an emphatic appeal to Wilson, in his usual flowery style calling Wilson " a foster-father of a chiefless land " and " Poland's inspired protector." " For many a month the spelling of your name has been the only comfort of a starving nation. For many a month among the ruins of a devastated country millions of people have been feeding on you." [50]

The Secretary of State asked the U.S. Ambassador in France, by a telegram of the 8th October, 1917, to supply information on : " (1) Purpose of the Committee, (2) factions represented by the Committee, and (3) nature of recognition desired." [51] In reply to this telegram the U.S. Ambassador in France, by a telegram of the 11th October, informed the State Department that he had received " a written statement given by Mr. Piltz, in which it was said that ' the Committee holds its authority from a secret mandate of the Polish continental organization forming the great majority of Poland '." So far as the Socialist Party was concerned, Mr. Dmowski told the U.S. Ambassador that " while the Socialist Party was not now represented on the Committee yet he hoped soon that it would have such a representation." He said that the Socialist Party in Poland championed very much the same principles as the socialist party groups of Germany, and had, until the revolution in Russia, been in favour of the Central Powers due to their hatred of that country. He stated that owing to this revolution the socialists had now changed in favour of Russia and for that reason he hoped consequently that they would soon be represented on the committee.

However, they had never as a party been strong enough to elect a member of the Duma. The Ambassador ended his telegram by stating that " Mr. Dmowski and Mr. Piltz . . . impressed me as men of a high grade of ability and as deeply earnest in their rôle. They evidently belong to the best class of Polish statesmen and are men who have a long and valuable experience in the political affairs of that country." [52]

In spite of this favourable report of the Ambassador in Paris a quite unexpected event delayed the recognition of the Committee by the U.S. Government. After a conversation with the Russian Ambassador in Washington some doubts arose in Lansing's mind, and he decided to get into touch with the Russian Government. As Mr. Lansing said in his telegram of the 15th October, 1917 : " The Department cannot but feel that failure to consult Russia in a matter that concerns her so intimately could not but affect adversely the success of the whole movement, a movement that has the hearty sympathy of this Government." It may seen strange that the American Government felt it necessary to ascertain the views of the Russian Government on the creation of a body with limited authority, while not long before it had been ready to grant its hospitality to a Provisional Polish Government with the full statute of an Allied Government. We can only suppose that the U.S. Government was disappointed at being deprived of the control over the activities of a body established on foreign soil. Moreover it was certainly approached by some Poles in the U.S. having more radical views than Mr. Dmowski and his followers and who, having at that time closer links with the Revolutionary Government in Russia than the latter, expected some changes to be made in the composition of the Committee under Russian pressure. Asked by the U.S. Ambassador Francis, the Russian Government nevertheless declined to interfere in this matter, declaring that the recognition by it of the Committee " would be prolific of great dissensions " (among Poles) but did not object to its recognition by the Allies.

Another exchange of views between the American Ambassador in Paris and Mr. Dmowski took place on the 19th October. To the question why the " Ludowe or Peasant Party had no representation on the Committee," Mr. Dmowski answered that he expected soon to have some representatives of this party coming from Petrograd, but he added that " as a matter of fact he himself represented a great majority of the Peasant Party in Poland." Mr. Dmowski further declared that he had " no desire to ignore Russia in the matter of securing recognition of the Committee," but at the same time he expressed the opinion that " the Russian Government would be glad to see (a socialist) on the Paris Committee, one that would be more in sympathy with revolutionary tendencies, but that to have a committee representing Poland so constituted would be to plant the seeds of a future revolution in Poland, which neither he nor his co-members would want to see brought about." [53]

Eventually, by a telegram of the 10th November, the U.S. Government instructed its Ambassador in France to extend its recognition to the Polish National Committee in Paris.

There is no doubt that the constitution of the Polish National Committee in Paris and its recognition as a Polish representative body by the Allied Governments mark an important date in the history of Polish diplomacy. For the first time for many years Poland had a body abroad which could defend her interests and officially present Polish claims. It is true that the Committee, consisting almost exclusively of the Right Wing, was not fully representative, but the difficulties appeared only in later stages as the differences of views concerned issues which were not then topical : problems of the Eastern frontier of Poland, social and constitutional issues. The primary task of this political body in 1917–18 was to defend Polish interests in the West and to present the Polish views on the post-war settlement in the event of the defeat of the Central Powers. It had the privilege of having two outstanding figures in its ranks : Mr. Dmowski, leader of a big Polish party, a shrewd negotiator with a dynamic nature, but unfortunately not very disposed to collaborate with other political parties; and Mr. Paderewski, an inspired artist and a man of great intellectual gifts who, as we know, enjoyed a special position in the United States [54]

Polish attempts to obtain from the Allied Powers a declaration on Poland's independence

By the constitution of the Polish National Committee and the recognition of it by the Great Powers an important point was scored by Polish policy, but a much more difficult task faced Polish statesmen abroad : to obtain from the Allies formal pledges regarding the reconstitution of the Polish State and securing to it the position of a party in the post-war settlement. Dmowski rendered a great service not only to his own country but also to the Allied cause in warning the Western countries against the consequences which would inevitably follow if Germany was allowed to keep her old and new conquests in Central and Eastern Europe; he drew the attention of Western leaders to the necessity of liberating the subjugated nationalities in this area and opposing their dynamic forces to the endeavours of German imperialism. Many months elapsed, however, before Western statesmen realized the full meaning of the events taking place in Eastern Europe after Russia's collapse, and only some time after the Brest-Litovsk Treaty was the Polish point of view properly understood and the necessity for a total reconstruction of Central Europe on the basis of self-determination became an avowed programme of the Entente.

We spoke above of a memorandum submitted by Dmowski to Foreign Secretary Balfour in March 1917, before the latter's voyage to the United States (see above, p. 162). At that time Balfour was not yet convinced by Dmowski's arguments, and while House in Washington " warmly advocated a Poland big enough and powerful enough to serve as a buffer State between Germany and Russia." [55] Balfour maintained the point of view expressed in his previous memoranda and statements. In spite of all the arguments used by President Wilson in favour of Poland, Balfour shrank from the consequences involved by remaking the map of Europe. His point of view was quickly known in the United States from correspondence published by the Associated Press. The Polish Press in the U.S. was particularly offended by Balfour's definition of Poland as a " medley of nationalities," reaching deep into the heart of Germany and Austria and cutting off Eastern Prussia from the rest of Germany.[56] We note this point in view of the complete reversal of Balfour's position after the Brest-Litovsk Treaty.

Dmowski more amply developed his ideas in a privately printed leaflet which appeared in July 1917 under the title " Problems of Central and Eastern Europe." Dmowski in this leaflet warned against the consequences of a " negotiated peace " based on the *status quo* in the West and leaving Germany the free space in Eastern Europe, as such a peace would mean a German victory. He was fully aware of the danger of slogans, " no annexations or indemnities," as the creation of a chain of semi-independent States under German control in Eastern Europe would immensely increase the military and economic potential of the Central Powers, endangering the peace of the world. The total rebuilding of Central Europe in accordance with political realities and democratic ideas was in his opinion the key problem of a durable peace in Europe. Germany should be reduced to the area inhabited by the German race, and Austria-Hungary dismembered, as she could only be a German satellite facilitating the German expansion in the Near East. Dmowski was most emphatic about the necessity for the creation of a State uniting the Czechs and Slovaks, saying that :

> " The Czechs are among the most energetic and best organized races in Europe, and they will be able to erect a strong national State immune against all inside influences. It should be added that, as regards natural resources, Bohemia and Moravia rank among the richest territories in Europe and are also among the most

advanced in industry, agriculture and popular education. Between
the Poles and Czechs no serious antagonisms exist ... there has
been a marked inclination to friendship ... those countries, moreover, have economic as well as political interests in common, and
the Polish port of Danzig would serve as an outlet also for
Bohemia."

So far as the territory of the future Polish State was concerned,
Dmowski took the view that only a Poland having an area of
200,000 square miles and a population of about thirty million would
be able to play the part of an efficient barrier between Germany and
Russia and frustrate German plans in Russia. The Polish State
should include in the West : Poznan Province, West Prussia
with Danzig, and the whole of Upper Silesia.   East Prussia could
become either an autonomous province of Poland or a small independent republic having a customs union with Poland. In this way
all " colonial " possessions of Germany in the East having a majority
of Polish population would pass to Poland. In the East : the frontiers traced by Dmowski were approximately the same as Poland
received by virtue of the Treaty of Riga in 1921 (except for Minsk
Litovsk and some districts of Podolia). Thus Dmowski did not
claim the return of all Polish-Lithuanian provinces detached from
the old Republic, wishing to take only the Western part of them,
basing himself on the line of the partition of two civilizations.   In
these provinces the number of Poles was considerable, and the
Polish and Catholic influence predominant. He believed at that
time that the Poles and Lithuanians could reach an understanding,
considering the old political and cultural bonds and the memories of
the union between the two countries which had lasted five centuries.
So far as the Ukrainians were concerned, he did not consider that
they had developed sufficiently from the national point of view, and
he recommended that the Ukraine should remain with Russia.
Dmowski believed that only Poland would be able to assure the
cultural and economic development of the Eastern territories, which
he claimed for Poland. He considered that the partitions of Poland
were a great mistake from the Russian point of view and that it was
neither in Russia's interest nor in that of the world that Russia's
frontiers had been advanced into the heart of Europe, far beyond the
ethnographic frontiers of the Great-Russian race. He hoped that
Poland might remain in friendly relations with Russia under these
conditions, and believed that Russia would disintegrate and that we
were witnessing " the downfall of Russian power." Consequently
he anticipated that " Russia will not reappear on the stage of history
as an Empire organized for conquest."

For the moment we leave Dmowski's programme relating to the

Eastern frontiers of Poland, as we shall deal amply with this matter in the second part of this book, in which we shall stress in particular the differences between Dmowski's and Pilsudski's programme. It was the problem of the Western frontiers of Poland on which all the efforts of Dmowski and the Polish National Committee were concentrated in the years 1917–18.

It was evident that Dmowski's plans could materialize only in the event of the total defeat of Germany, and this probability seemed rather remote in 1917. Although Austria-Hungary already showed signs of disintegration at that time Germany was still very strong and believed in her victory.[57] On the other side there were many forces in the world working for a settlement based on the maintenance of the *status quo* in the West, leaving the main problems of Central Europe unsettled. Although in Germany Bethmann-Hollweg, whose relations with the Great Headquarters had been strained, resigned on the 13th July, 1917, and his sucessor, Michaelis, was a liegeman of the German military clique and of the Ring Wing (Stresemann was one of the principal politicians responsible for Bethmann-Hollweg's downfall), on the 19th July, 1917, the German Reichstag voted a peace resolution claiming peace " without annexations and indemnities." On the 1st August the Pope addressed a note to all the belligerents, suggesting a settlement of the War upon the principle of complete restoration of occupied territory, disarmament and international arbitration. The main points of the note were well known to Germany before it was issued, and to a great extent were due to the initiative of the Central Powers. According to Mr Temperley the Pope's note " showed a desire or belief that Europe could resume not only approximately its old frontiers but even approximately its old life." The passages referring to Poland seemed to indicate that Poland's future [58] could be decided by way of mutual compromises at the table of a Peace Conference.

> " The same spirit of equity and justice should direct the examination of the other territorial and political questions, and more especially those relating to Armenia, the Balkan States, and the territories forming *part* of the ancient Kingdom of Poland, for which in particular the sympathies of the nations should be enlisted on account of its noble historical traditions, and the sufferings endured during the present war."

It appears from the text that the Holy See did not think at that time of an integral solution of the Polish question, and there is every reason to assume that it had in mind the Austro-Polish solution.

It was Wilson who took the right line in answering the Pope's Note on the 27th August :

" His Holiness in substance proposes that we return to the *status quo ante bellum,* and that then there will be a general condonation, disarmament and a concert of nations based upon an acceptance of the principle of arbitration ; and that the territorial claims of France and Italy, the perplexing problems of the Balkan States, and the restitution of Poland be left to such conciliatory adjustments as may be possible in the new temper of such a peace, due regard being paid to the aspirations of the peoples whose political fortunes and affiliations will be involved."

We know that the conciliatory moves of the Central Powers were of short duration and no serious negotiations could start in these conditions (see pp. 9 ff.).

But the possibility of negotiations was by no means debarred in autumn and early winter 1917 by Western statesmen, and some hopes were also set on breaking up the alliance between the Hapsburgs and Hohenzollerns. This explains to a great extent the caution of the Allied diplomacy which also had to reckon with pacifist trends in their own countries.[59] The knock-out blow policy was the main target of the attacks of those who wished to limit the war aims to the issues of immediate concern to the Western nations. Even on the 13th February, 1918, Lord Henry Cavendish-Bentinck, speaking in the House of Commons, stated that :

" perhaps if a poll were taken to ascertain the ideal war-aims of the people of this country, 90 per cent. would say that if Germany were to evacuate Belgium, France, Serbia, and Rumania, they would be satisfied to leave everything else to the international conference that is to assemble." [60]

In these circumstances the Allied Governments were unwilling to commit themselves to a definite line of policy on any particular issue and were unable to reach an agreement on their war-aims until the early months of 1918 and the conclusion of the Brest-Litovsk Treaty. The Inter-Allied Conference held in Paris from 29th November to 3rd December, 1917, did not make known the Allied war-aims in spite of the efforts of Colonel House. " Had I been successful," wrote Colonel House a few years later, " I should have endeavoured to include a declaration favourable to an independent Poland." [61] In fact such efforts were made at that time by Dmowski who on the occasion of the said conference made an unsuccessful attempt to obtain formal pledges from the Allied and Associated Governments on the reconstitution of the Polish State. On 13th November he proposed a convention between the Polish National Committee and the above-mentioned Governments by which the latter should agree to the " re-establishment of an independent Poland containing all the Polish territory belonging at the moment to Russia, Germany and

Austria." The convention should also state "that some of the Baltic coast-line, with the mouths of the Vistula and the Niemen, should form part of the Polish State." [62]

The idea of the convention had to be abandoned, although it was vigorously supported by the French, mainly because of the opposition of Lloyd George. Also the subsequent proposal of a unilateral declaration by the Allied and Associated Powers suggested by the French was not retained because difficulties arose in connection with the text proposed by Dmowski on 27th November. Colonel House held the view that it would be inappropriate at this stage of the war to state that Poland's independence was one of the war-aims as it would be sufficient to declare that " it was a condition of a sure and lasting peace." Dmowski agreed to this modification but this new draft was not accepted by Lloyd George who stated that " the Allies must not precisely define their attitude on any question, especially one which would risk the prolongation of the war." The formula proposed instead by Lloyd George was rather ambiguous (" the formation of an independent and indivisible(?) Poland under conditions which would ensure her free political and economic development constitutes one of the conditions of a sound peace and the rule of law in Europe "). At their last meeting the Western Governments left the question to individual declarations by the Powers. Such declarations were actually made in January (Lloyd George's speech on 5th January, 1918, and Wilson's Fourteen Points Message on 8th January). No joint declaration by the Allies was made until 3rd June, 1918.[63]

Bolshevik Revolution and the problem of nationalities of Russia

The trend of events in Eastern Europe at the end of 1917 and beginning of 1918—the Bolshevik Revolution, the Brest-Litovsk negotiations and the different interpretations of the principle of national self-determination—eventually forced the Governments of the Allied Powers to state their terms for the post-war political settlement.

There was complete incompatibility between the two main items of the Bolshevik programme and the war-aims of the Entente : immediate peace without contributions and annexations, and the extension of the principle of self-determination to all parts of the world. In the first instance let us state that the first issue had absolute precedence over the second in the views of the Bolshevik leaders, which shows that the second was above all a propaganda slogan serving the purposes of world revolution and not an immediate object of their policy.

In his appeal to the toiling, oppressed and exhausted peoples of Europe, Trotsky, then People's Commissar for Foreign Affairs, stated frankly :

> "Belgium, Serbia, Rumania, Poland, the Ukraine, Greece, Persia and Armenia, can only be liberated by the workers in all belligerent and neutral countries in the victorious struggle against all imperialists and not only by the victory of one of the imperialist nations." [64]

In the twenty-one theses for peace proclaimed by Lenin on the 20th January, 1918, we find the following passage [65] :

"A truly revolutionary war at this moment would be a war between a socialist republic and the bourgeois countries. Such a war would have to be fully approved by the socialist army and have as its object the overthrow of the bourgeoisie in other countries. For the time being, however, we cannot make this our object. In reality we should be fighting now for the liberation of Poland, Lithuania and Courland. There is not a single Marxist who, while adhering to the foundations of Marxism and Socialism, would not say that the interests of socialism are above the right of nations to self-determination. . . . Peace on condition of the liberation of Poland, Lithuania and Courland would be a 'patriotic' peace from the Russian point of view, but it would be none the less a peace with annexations and with the German imperialists."

In a frank exchange of views between Mr. Bruce-Lockhart, a British agent in Petrograd, and a prominent Bolshevik, Rothstein, the latter

> "pointed out that if he were Lloyd George he would accept Trotsky's offer of a (peace) conference unconditionally. England would be the chief beneficiary. The Russian stipulations about self-determination would fall through with an ineffective protest from Trotsky, and England and Germany could arrange the colonial question between them. Germany would agree to almost all other terms—that is, no annexations and no contributions. She might even be prepared to compromise on the Alsace-Lorraine question. In any case it was absurd for England to prolong the war for the sake of Alsace-Lorraine. Nothing was easier to destroy than sentimental causes which are not rooted in a people itself and we should consider very seriously whether we should get a better peace nine months hence." [66]

Such a programme could at that time appeal to some uncritical minds in the West, but its acceptance by the West would mean suicide. German power would have remained intact, and it was by no means a foregone conclusion, as the Bolsheviks seemed to believe at that time, that a revolution would have broken out in Germany bringing to power a Communist government. It is obvious that the Bolsheviks neither believed in the Allied victory nor considered it desirable for their purposes.

So far as the doctrine of national self-determination was concerned, it had two aspects for the Entente Powers. They were, of course, absolutely opposed to its indiscriminate and general application. On the other hand they did not realize the importance of the national issues in Russia. Judging by their own standards, they saw in the application of this doctrine to Russia only a sinister plot between the Bolshevik leaders and Germany, and considered the whole problem only from the point of view of the balance of power policy. We shall deal with the Bolshevik doctrine of national self-determination more fully in the second part of this book. For the time being let us observe that it was by no means appropriate to consider this problem from the point of view of a political intrigue between the Germans and the Bolshevik leaders. The Bolsheviks were forced to raise the national issue in order to bring the revolution to a successful end. From his point of view Lenin was right when, opposing within his own party the advocates of " democratic centralism," among whom Rosa Luxemburg was the most prominent, he decided to avail himself of this issue as " an important weapon of anti-imperialist struggle."

> " In Russia [wrote Lenin] where no less than 57 per cent. that is over 100,000,000 of the population, belong to oppressed nations, where those nations mainly inhabit the border provinces, where some of those nations are more cultured than the Great Russians, where the political system is distinguished by its particularly barbarous and medieval character, where the bourgeois-democratic revolution has not been completed—the recognition of the rights of the nations oppressed by Tsarism to free secession from Russia is absolutely obligatory for Social Democracy in the interests of its democratic and socialist tasks. Russian socialists who fail to demand freedom of secession for Finland, Poland, the Ukraine, etc., etc., are behaving like chauvinists, like lackeys of the blood- and mud-stained imperialist monarchies and the imperialist bourgeoisie." [67]

As has been observed by the author of an interesting study, *The Right of Self-Determination and the Soviet Union*, Mr. A. A. Kristian :

> " Wishing for the political support of the national minorities, Lenin wanted to prevent their opposition to his usurpation of power in Central Russia and to ensure that they would let events there take their course. If the minorities seduced by Communist propaganda had actively supported the *coup d'état*, Lenin's

chances would have been much better. The unanimous support of the minorities would have made it possible to plan not only a successful *coup d'état* but also, which was the final aim, a more rapid achievement of all the goals of the projected social revolution." [68]

But, of course, even in Lenin's mind, the liberation of the oppressed nations was only a temporary solution, valid for the transition period and leading eventually to the abolition of national States, to " be effected through the fusion of nationalities within a single Soviet State." [69] Moreover this doctrine was affected by the doctrine of the dictatorship of the proletariat. The right of self-determination had to be exercised only by the " toiling and oppressed classes " of the population.

At Brest-Litovsk the Bolsheviks apparently used democratic language, but the meaning of the terms used by them was already then quite different from Western concepts of nation, democracy and freedom. For instance, the wish of the Polish nation to become really independent was not yet, in Bolshevik views, clearly manifested, and Poland's independence had to be decided by a plebiscite. At the meeting of the Conference at Brest-Litovsk on the 28th December the Russian delegation made the following proposal :

> " Withdrawal by both parties of their troops from occupied territories (Poland, Lithuania, Courland and other regions of Russia) ... the population of these districts will be given an opportunity within the shortest possible time of deciding entirely freely the question of their *union* with one or another empire or of *formation into independent States.* In this connection the presence of any troops apart from the national or local militia in the territories which are voting is not permissible. Until the question is decided the Government of these regions will remain in the hands of the representatives of the local population elected democratically." [70]

At the session of the 12th January, 1918, the Russian delegation declared the following :

> " From the fact that the occupied territories belonged to the former Russian Empire the Russian Government draws no conclusions which would impose any constitutional obligation on the population of these regions in relation to the Russian Government. The old frontiers of the former Russian Empire, frontiers formed by acts of violence and crimes against peoples, especially against the Polish people, have vanished with Tsarism. The new frontiers of the *fraternal* League of the Peoples of the Russian Republic and of the peoples which desire to remain outside its borders must be formed by free resolution of the peoples concerned."

What the Russians expected from these *democratic* plebiscites appears clearly from Trotsky's press interview of the 2nd January, 1918 :

> " We do not for a moment doubt where the sympathies of the propertied classes of Poland, Lithuania and Courland lie. But for us the real will of those countries is expressed not by the vote of their landlords, capitalists and bankers—not, that is, by these sections of the nation which oppress the entire working people. We wish, and demand, that the question of Poland's fate should be decided by the Polish workers and peasants—and, moreover, throughout the whole of Poland."

Let us note also that the Commissar of Nationalities, Stalin, called upon to put into practice the principle of self-determination in relation to the nations oppressed by Russia, was much nearer to the programme of Rosa Luxemburg than to that of Lenin, that is to the programme of centralism and the solidarity of working people all over Russia, overriding national issues. So far as Poland was concerned, there was only one small party on Polish territories belonging to Russia before the war, the Social-Democratic Party of the Congress Kingdom and Lithuania, led by a few Russified Poles and Jews, that backed the programme of Rosa Luxemburg. It stressed the importance of the economic bonds between all parts of Russia, including Poland, and considered that the severance of the political links between Poland and Russia would be very harmful to the interests of the Polish working people. The Bolshevik leaders only later had occasion to ascertain that the overwhelming majority of the Polish working people was opposed to this programme and was ready to shed their blood for the independence of their country. Lenin himself publicly recognized the mistakes of the Bolshevik policy during the Polish-Soviet war in 1919–20.

Stalin had already showed, in his *Marxism and the National Question,* first published in the magazine *Prosveshcheniye* in 1913, that he sympathized with the views of the small minority of the Polish workers represented by the above-mentioned party. In this article he complained, however, that " a considerable proportion of the Polish workers are still in the intellectual bondage of the bourgeois nationalists," and awaited " the emancipation " of the Polish working movement from nationalist influence.[71] Of the solution of the Polish question he says the following :

> " In the middle of the nineteenth century Marx was in favour of the separation of Russian Poland ; and he was right. ...
> " At the end of the nineteenth century the Polish Marxists were already declaring against the separation of Poland ; and they were

also right, for during the fifty years that had elapsed profound changes had taken place, bringing Russia and Poland closer economically and culturally.

" Moreover, during this period the question of separation had been converted from a political matter into a matter for economic disputes, which excited nobody except, perhaps, the intellectuals abroad. This, of course, by no means precludes the possibility that certain internal and external conditions may arise in which the question of the separation of Poland may again become actual." [72]

But what was most significant for the attitude of the Bolsheviks towards the question of Poland's independence was the presence among the Russian delegates at Brest-Litovsk of two representatives of the Social-Democratic Party of Congress Kingdom and Lithuania, Comrades Radek and Bobinski, who pretended to be the representatives of the Polish working masses and consequently of the whole Polish nation. At the meeting of the Brest-Litovsk Conference on the 7th February, 1918, it was Bobinski who took the floor, and declared that he spoke on behalf of the working classes of Poland. He finished his speech in the following way :

" In the name of the Polish proletariat we now already solemnly declare that so far only revolutionary Russia protects the interests and freedoms of the Polish people and but for the German-Austrian occupation Poland would already have enjoyed the same liberty which the nations of Russia possess. The refusal of Germany to evacuate her troops from Poland and the plan which lies behind this refusal is a disguised annexation and interference with the internal problems of Poland."

A great part of the provinces of Poland before the partitions was for the time being out of reach of the Bolsheviks, as these vast territories were under the occupation of the Central Powers, wishing to establish their zone of influence there. Only after the German collapse was Poland faced with the practical consequences of the Soviet interpretation of the doctrine of self-determination. Other nationalities of the former Russian Empire much sooner learned the difference between Soviet theories and practice. Stalin, the first Commissar for Nationalities, gave Soviet doctrine his own interpretation, which led to the ruthless suppression of national movements in Russia. In his article, which appeared in the *Proletaryi* of the 13th August, 1917, Stalin wrote the following :

" We are not against the union of nations in one State organization. We are not at all for the division of big States into small ones. It is obvious that a union of small States is one of the conditions making possible the achievement of socialism. But we are unconditionally for the carrying out of the unification by free will, as only such union could be a real and enduring one. .... To deliver power into the hands of the proletariat and revolutionary peasants means to achieve the full liberation of the nations of Russia from national oppression." [73]

In Stalin's opinion " the principle of self-determination should be used as a means of struggle for socialism, and it should be subordinated to the principles of socialism." [74]

So the freedom of the nations of Russia, so much advertised by the Bolsheviks at Brest-Litovsk, in practice was given an interpretation which destroyed its entire meaning. In December 1917 the Soviet leaders decided " to crush the two main centres of opposition to their régime, in the Don and in the Ukraine," [75] and invaded the Ukraine, capturing Kiev on the 9th February, 1918, that is about the time when the Ukrainian delegation was signing a separate treaty with the Central Powers.

While at Brest-Litovsk the Bolsheviks proclaimed that " the union by violence of territories conquered during the war will not be tolerated," [76] it was by the might of the Red Army, supported in some countries by a part of the town proletariat, that the Bolsheviks tried to extend their power. " Among the contradictions of Bolshevism," writes Souvarin, " there is none more violent than that between theory and practice in regard to nationalities." ... " What the Red Army could not accomplish in Finland and Poland it did accomplish first in the Ukraine and then in Caucasus." [77]

The whole implication of the Bolshevik policy towards nationalities in Russia was completely misunderstood at that time in the West : while the labour leaders and Left-wing politicians were attracted by the high-sounding slogans and the democratic phraseology of the Bolshevik Revolution, the governments and conservatists in Europe were appalled by the consequences of the disruption of Russia, and tried to preserve Russian territorial integrity, menaced by a revolutionary doctrine destroying it. They considered it a temporary disease, and hoped for the restoration of the old Empire as a factor in the European balance of power.

Germany and Bolshevism

The outbreak of the revolution in Russia and her military collapse provided Germany with a chance to end the war with great advantages for herself, had she at the same time pursued a policy of moderation and self-restraint towards the West,[78] and not been allured by the mirage of empty space in the East. But Germany missed this opportunity, opting for a policy which brought upon her unprecedented disaster. Three ways were open to Germany in relation to Russia :

(1). To win for her policy the new Russian Government, or in later stages to install in Russia a government favourable to the Central Powers, at the same time limiting the programme of German territorial expansion in the East;

(2). to protect herself by a belt of really independent States, rising on the ruins of the Russian Empire—that is to say to pursue a policy of liberating the oppressed nations of Russia, a policy of genuine self-determination;

(3). to pursue a policy of more or less disguised annexations and after the division of the spheres of influence with Bolshevik Russia to establish collaboration with new rulers.

The first and third ways debarred the possibility of a compromise with the West, because they meant the continuation of the war against the West, with open or implicit Russian backing.

So far as the first method of dealing with the problem of Russia was concerned, immediately after the outbreak of the March Revolution some German politicians recommended a policy of assisting Russia in consolidating the new régime, so that Russia might become not only Germany's friend but even an ally. Such were, for instance, the views of Erzberger and Helfferich.[79] When Kerensky became head of the Russian Provisional Government the German Foreign Office expected to reach an understanding with him.[80] This policy would, of course, have required a limitation of the German war aims in the East. In spite of the Emperor's approval of this change of policy towards Russia, the Pan-German elements—among whom Stresemann was one of the most prominent—required the wide annexations in the East and, playing into Ludendorff's hands, brought about the dismissal of Bethmann-Hollweg, the protagonist of this new programme of limitation of war aims in the East.

After the Brest-Litovsk Treaty, followed by some months of uneasy relations with the Bolsheviks, prominent Germans recommended the overthrow of the Bolshevik régime and the restoration of Tsardom in Russia. For instance, General Hoffmann, well known from the Brest-Litovsk negotiations, at that time outlined the following plan :

" Create clear conditions in the East, that is to say denounce the peace treaty, go to Moscow, set up a different Russian Government, giving it better conditions than those provided by the Brest-Litovsk Treaty—it is possible, for instance, in the first place to give it back Poland, and enter into alliance with this new Russian Government." [81]

Hoffmann's choice for the post of Regent of the Empire (Reichs-verweser) was Grand Duke Paul, with whom the Headquarters in the East remained in touch through his son-in-law, Colonel Durnovo.

It might seem that after the murder in Moscow of the German Ambassador, Count Mirbach, the German policy towards the Bol-sheviks would undergo a radical change. Helfferich, who advised such a reversion of policy, states that many Russian anti-Bolshevik leaders, even " liberal " Milyukov, were ready at that time to collaborate with the Germans. [82]

There is no doubt that all these plans were contrary to the interests both of the Western Powers and of Poland, as they meant the surrender of Poland to Russia and the strengthening of the Ger-man military position. The readiness of some Russian politicians who were considered to be Western-minded to collaborate with reactionary Germany proves, moreover, that their allegiance to the Western cause was not very deeply rooted in them.

Some Western statesmen realized the danger to the Entente of the restoration of the old régime, which would inevitably have collaborated with Germany. In a memorandum submitted to Lloyd George on the 16th July, 1918, Balfour says the following :

> " The fact is that an autocratic system is not only repulsive to Englishmen of all shades of opinion, but that the re-establishment of the Russian autocracy would, so far as I can judge, be a mis-fortune for the British Empire. Autocracy and militarism go to-gether ; and it is almost inconceivable that, if the Tsar should be re-established, Russia would not again become a purely military Empire. If so, she would inevitably be a danger to her neighbours as much as to ourselves. In my opinion, moreover, a restored Tsardom would be more dangerous to British interests than the Tsardom which has just vanished ; for it would almost certainly be dependent upon Germany." [83]

There is no doubt that the Germans could have found allies in all Russian political parties opposed to Bolshevism, especially after the dissolution of the Constituent Assembly on the 18th January, 1918, when, as Wheeler-Bennett rightly states, the Bolsheviks " had abandoned whatever moral basis they had ever had at Brest-Litovsk." [84] Consequently the Germans had a free choice, and the fate of Bolshevism which they helped to install in Russia depended entirely on their decisions. The German Government opted for collaboration with Bolshevism. The signing of treaties additional to the Brest-Litovsk Treaty in August, 1918, by which Russia renounced her sovereignty in Esthonia and Livonia and recognized Georgia as an independent State, while Germany pledged herself not to interfere in " the relations between the Russian Empire and parts of its territory " and " neither cause nor support the formation of independent States in those territories," gave the Soviet régime a much-needed breathing space, and helped it to overcome one of the most critical periods of the civil war. So began the strange although very uneasy collaboration between capitalist and militarist Germany and a " socialist " régime, which with some interruptions was to continue for many years between the two wars. Many Germans were puzzled at that time by this strange policy, and Helfferich, Count Mirbach's successor as German Ambassador to Russia, observed that " German policy had assisted Bolshevism to pass through its most critical period." [85] Erzberger, who also criticized this policy and especially the condonation of the expropriation of private property, states that Germany betrayed the principles of Western civilization and behaved " like Judas among the Great Powers." After a conversation with the Soviet representative in Berlin, Joffe, Erzberger observed that since the signing of the additional treaties Germany was marching hand in hand with Bolshevism and that in the opinion of the Russians opposed to Bolshevism, Germany and Bolshevism were pursuing the same policy.[86] By these acts Germany definitely forfeited all moral titles to represent the principles of Western civilization in the East and, awakening the vigilance of the Western world, she sealed her doom.[87]

The Poles were the first to bear the brunt of the Bolshevik-German collusion. Important Polish units composed of former soldiers of the Russian army (the First Polish Army Corps) were concentrated in the area of Bobruisk, in White Russia. Being hard-pressed by the Bolsheviks, they submitted to the Regency Council in Warsaw and on the 26th February, 1918, signed an agreement with German Headquarters in the East, which recognized the autonomy of these forces and declared the three districts occupied by them as a neutral zone. The soldiers belonging to these units had known all the horrors of the Bolshevik revolution and were resolutely opposed to the régime of terror introduced by it. But a few months later, on the 8th May, Beseler, Governor-General of the German zone of occupation in the Congress Kingdom, informed the Regency Council that these units should be disbanded and the soldiers sent home. Although some officers advised resisting and breaking through in order to join other Polish units in the Ukraine, the commanding General Dowbor-Musnicki did not wish to take such risks and eventually surrendered to the Germans on the 21st May. A German writer observes in this connection that from then on those Poles who were opposed to Bolshevism could find their place only at the side of the Entente.[88]

Also those Poles who, belonging to the socialist or radical parties and wishing to fight against the Germans, saw in revolutionary Russia a potential ally against German imperialism, passed through most bitter disappointments. One of them, a prominent writer and politician, Mr. T. Holowko, describes in these terms the hopes awakened by the Russian revolution :

> " Soviet Russia, accepting a most humiliating peace treaty with Germany, could not in fact tolerate the terms of this treaty, the more so as the reactionary imperialistic Germany and decaying Hapsburg Monarchy were in fact the mainstays of the old social order. Consequently all those who were ready to fight against the Germans should be treated by Russia as allies." [89]

These hopes were quickly dispelled. The Bolsheviks wished only to have at their disposal those Poles who would be willing to join the Red Army and serve as the advanced guard of the future revolution in Poland, and they distrusted all other " reactionary " Poles.

Thus the Polish soldiers who tried to escape either to the North or to the South to join the Polish units were considered counter-revolutionaries. By virtue of a secret agreement between the German Ambassador in Russia and the Soviet authorities, all Poles who tried to escape to the Polish or Allied Forces were to be executed on the spot, and many of them paid with their lives for such endeavours. Inevitably, all the Poles in Russia who were not under the influence of the Bolshevik doctrine could only find a place in the units fighting against the Bolsheviks.

German policy in Eastern Europe after the Brest-Litovsk Treaty

Let us see now how Germany interpreted the principles of self-determination, on which she allegedly based the new political order west of the frontier traced by the Brest-Litovsk Treaty and the Additional Treaty of August 1918. These treaties eliminated Russia from any influence on the fate of the population of the territories surrendered by her. We know that the German High Command and Right-Wing politicians at that time requested a policy of wholesale annexations, and General Hoffmann complains in his *Memoirs* that it was State Secretary von Kühlmann who obtained the approval of the Crown Council on the 2nd January, 1918, for a more subtle policy of the interpretation of the doctrine of self-determination in accordance with German interests.[90] Germany claimed that she would settle the fate of the detached provinces of Russia in accordance with the wishes of the population.

In the Reichstag the German Chancellor Hertling tried to appear as the advocate of the principle of self-determination, and represented Germany as the liberator of Poland and other border nations of Russia. Answering the famous Fourteen Points message of President Wilson of the 8th January and Lloyd George's speech of the 5th January, 1918, Chancellor Hertling said in the Reichstag on the 24th January :

> " It was not the Entente, which had only empty words for Poland, and before the war had never interceded for Poland with Russia, but the German Empire and the Austro-Hungarian Monarchy which liberated Poland from the Tsarist régime crushing her national individuality. It may thus be left to Germany, Austria-Hungary and Poland to come to an agreement on the future shaping of this country."

In his speech of the 25th February the German Chancellor tried to be even more explicit on the Polish question :

> " A word regarding Poland, on behalf of whom the Entente and President Wilson recently appeared very specially to interest themselves ... the country was liberated from oppressive dependence on Tsarist Russia by the united forces of Germany and Austria-Hungary for the purpose of establishing an independent State which, in the unrestricted development of its national culture, will at the same time become a pillar of the peace of Europe."

Nevertheless the Imperial Chancellor was obliged to speak about some frontier corrections, but he assured that " only the indispensable will be demanded on Germany's part."

How was self-determination carried out in practice by Germany? We investigated, in the preceding chapter, the background and aims of the German policy relating to Poland. Let us say a few words about the general features of the German plans relating to the post-war settlement in Eastern Europe. We leave aside the problem of the two Baltic countries, Latvia and Esthonia, as it is a matter of common knowledge that the German policy there was directed against the native population, the Latvians and Esthonians, and above all supported the German minority composed of landlords and upper strata of the town population. In the representative bodies constituted by Germans the German minority had exclusive influence. If we now pass to the vast areas of the former Grand Duchy of Lithuania, which for five centuries had been united to Poland, we must observe that although the Germans had been obliged for the time being to abandon some earlier plans for converting this area as soon as possible into a German province to which about three million Germans were to be transferred,[91] they were nevertheless firmly decided to establish there their exclusive political, cultural and economic influence. To achieve their ends the Germans tried to disrupt the unity of the country, in which for centuries many races had peacefully lived together, and to sow seeds of hatred between the different national groups. After the occupation of these provinces, which were put under the military administration of the German Headquarters in the East (Ober-Ost) the Germans became aware that the Polish element was the only one there which could offer effective resistance to their plans. They realized that the pre-war Russian statistics gave a very blurred picture of the real conditions of the country, and they carried out a census of population which opened their eyes to the numerical and cultural importance of the Polish element there. According to this census, of the thirteen districts of the area Wilno-Grodno, the Poles had an absolute majority in seven, a relative majority in one, and in four districts they constituted 30 per cent. of the population. Even in Lithuania proper, that is the ethnically Lithuanian part of the former Grand Duchy of Lithuania, in two districts—Kowno (Kaunas) and Kiejdany—25 per cent. of the population stated their nationality as Polish.

The head of the administration of the city of Wilno, von Beckerath, in a memorandum submitted to the German Great Head-quarters and dated 3rd January, 1917, wrote the following :

> " The Poles constitute a compact majority in Wilno and the neighbouring district. In other districts they constitute an impor-tant minority. Not only numerical importance but also its political and economic weight is underestimated in Berlin. Russian official statistics ... were undoubtedly falsified to the detriment of the Poles. Our census of 1916 showed that the importance of the Polish element in Lithuania is considerably greater and that only Poles had previous political and organizing ability. If it is even possible to rule there without them during the war, it seems to me that it would be a difficult and even dangerous task to do so in peace-time, as all other elements lack a real and stable supporting base." [92]

Ludendorff, the most prominent figure in these grandiose plans of German expansion in Eastern Europe (but it would be quite mis-taken to lay the whole burden of responsibility on his shoulders, as he had the support of vast strata of the German nation and of many politicians), stated with disappointment in his *Memoirs* that many cities and districts in the former Duchy of Lithuania had a majority of Polish population.[93] He observes also that should Lithuania have Wilno as a capital she would inevitably fall under Polish influence unless the Germans safeguarded their position by special provisions.[94]

Consequently the Germans decided to follow the policy of *divide et impera* and while the Poles tried to save the unity of the country and to establish a common front of all nationalities of the former Grand Duchy, appealing to the glorious traditions of the Polish-Lithuanian union, the Germans strove to arouse the young nationalism of Lithuanians against the Poles for the purpose of making all the peoples inhabiting this area the tools of their imperialistic policy. We know that on the eve of the Armistice Ludendorff agreed to surrender to Poland the districts with prevalently Polish population in order to make of the rest of the Grand Duchy an area entirely submissive to Germany (see above, p. 119).

The Germans could not pretend that they were protecting the Byelorussians and Lithuanians against the Poles in order to safeguard the interests of smaller nationalities. As a matter of fact they very quickly lost interest in the Byelorussians [95] and Ludendorff sarcastically observed about the failure of his attempts to raise the Byelorussian problem : " One cannot create States fit to live or maintain them in life only by means of political slogans." [96] The Germans preferred to stake their all on the reconstitution of a Great Lithuania submissive to them and encircling Poland from the North-East.

So far as the Lithuanians were concerned, the National Lithuanian Council, called " Taryba," was forced by the Germans to issue a declaration on the 11th December, 1917, in which jointly with the proclamation of the independence of the Lithuanian State with its capital in Wilno, and the severance of all historic links with other nations, it was stated that the new State would enter into close constitutional relations with the German Empire by concluding with the latter four conventions relating to defence, communications, customs and monetary union. The Lithuanians fully realized that this declaration meant a disguised annexation of their country. When, therefore, Taryba issued another declaration on the 16th February, 1918, since considered by all Lithuanians as the Lithuanian Independence Act, in which no mention was made of the future links with Germany, the Germans considered it a breach of the former undertaking. Chancellor Hertling on the 21st February, 1918, addressed a letter to the Taryba in which he peremptorily stated that the Lithuanians should abide by the Declaration of the 11th December, 1917. Only the Declaration of the 11th December, 1917, was considered valid by the Germans until the end of the occupation. [97]

After the conclusion of the Brest-Litovsk Treaty the territory of the future satellite Lithuanian State was enormously increased; it included many purely Polish and Byelorussian districts in which there was no Lithuanian-speaking population. It was obvious that in the German plans Lithuania was assigned the rôle of a bridge to the Baltic countries and that together with them she was to become an area of German economic, demographic and cultural expansion. Only the collapse of Germany in November 1918 saved for twenty years the Baltic nations from gradual absorption by a greater and aggressive neighbour.

The policy pursued by the Germans in the Ukraine has been dealt with in many special studies and we need not say much about it. It is common knowledge that it was a policy of ruthless exploitation of the resources of this rich country for war purposes, and that the Germans based their policy there on some puppets without any real backing from the people. The concessions granted to the Ukraine by the first Brest-Litovsk Treaty signed with the Ukraine on the 9th February, before the Treaty with Soviet Russia (3rd March, 1918), in the first instance served to face the Bolsheviks with an accomplished fact and force them to accept peace terms, and in the second instance to weaken Poland by depriving her of a valuable part of the Congress Kingdom in order to establish a junction between a greater Lithuania and the Ukraine, shutting off Poland from any territorial contact with Russia.

General Hoffmann, the German negotiator in Brest-Litovsk, frankly confesses in his book that the cession of the Chelm (Kholm) district of the Congress Kingdom was a violation of the principle of self-determination,[98] stating at the same time that he considered an independent Polish State a utopian conception.[99] His attitude to the Ukrainians was by no means more positive. He said of the Ukrainian negotiators at Brest-Litovsk that they should have been aware that without German backing they would not exist and that their government was a fiction.[100]

The Polish Group in the Vienna Parliament, in its message published immediately after the conclusion of the Treaty with the Ukraine, boldly unmasked the true German aims in the East :

" The first Peace Treaty, signed on the 9th February, 1918, at Brest, struck us like lightning, a sinister warning that the German militarists together with the wicked and clumsy diplomacy of old Austria wish to amputate the Polish land and make the Pole an outcast and slave in his own country. The German-Ukrainian friendship which will be based on the corpses of Poland and Lithuania aims to sow hatred between the Polish and Ukrainian nations, aims to deprive Poland of any political and economic significance and make her a slave of the German State, industry and trade, guarded in the East by a Ukrainian State controlled by Germany. Instead of freedom we must expect enslavement, instead of a just

peace based on free, independent and united nations, this peace
foreshadows new fratricidal struggles, new victims and new misery
of the Polish nation."

One can see in all these grandiose plans of the German Great
Headquarters, in which the German Government had to concur,
more or less reluctantly, the revival of Prussian colonialism, based
on the preposterous assumption of empty space in the East which
should become living space for the German race, being filled by German settlers and impregnated with German Kultur. It is no wonder
that these plans were in the first place directed against the Poles as a
nation with long historical traditions and great vitality. In relation
to Poland the principle of self-determination has always been a
double-edged weapon, the Germans never thought of applying it
to the provinces raped by them in the partitions of Poland. It was
fear for the maintenance of these older colonial possessions of
Prussia that dictated many steps taken by German policy in the
East. " A Poland," confesses Ludendorff, " spreading along
Eastern and Western Prussia cannot be considered as compatible
with German security. The Commander-in-Chief in the East
had to rely, consequently, on the Lithuanians and Byelorussians."[101]
For this reason the German Great Headquarters began to carry out
the plan of encircling Poland's Eastern frontier by Lithuania in the
North and the Ukraine in the South, both these States being considered as future semi-independent German appendages.[102] For this
reason the frontier of a Greater Lithuania had to be pushed far to
the South, across districts purely Polish or Byelorussian, and the
frontier of the Ukraine moved northwards across the Eastern part
of the Congress Kingdom. It was this conception that triumphed at
the Brest-Litovsk Treaty and was subsequently to be followed by
territorial rearrangements in the East. It was the idea of a small, en-
compassed Poland with amputated frontiers in the North and West
for the benefit of Germany, a Poland with a limited military and
economic sovereignty.[103] It was the idea of an " isolated " Poland,
as expounded in an article by Richard Schmidt in 1918.[104] Poland
was mistrusted by the Germans as the bulwark of Western influence
in the East, and the Germans realized that she would always remain
a stumbling-block on the way to their complete domination of
Eastern Europe detached from Russia by the Brest-Litovsk Treaty.

So in practice appeared the last stage of the " liberation " of
Poland by Germany. It is really quite astonishing in these circumstances that after the War many Germans used to speak of Poland's
ingratitude and the Poles' utter disregard of the alleged services
rendered by the Germans to the Poles in the course of the war (even

General Ludendorff says so).[105] As a matter of fact the case of Poland is the most striking example of this " Machtpolitik," perverting the principle of self-determination.[106]

Even a German writer admits that in the event of a German victory all the resolutions of the Reichstag on a peace without annexations, a peace based on the principle of self-determination, would have remained a dead letter.[107]

Allied intervention in Russia

The early intervention of the Western Powers in Russia from the outbreak of the revolution in November 1917 to the Armistice with Germany in November 1918 was represented " not very ingeniously in some cases," according to W. H. Chamberlin, " as part of the war effort." [108] This point of view was often stressed, especially by British statesmen. In his dispatch to Bruce-Lockhart, the British agent in Petrograd, of the 7th February, 1918, Balfour stated the following :

> " We are in no way concerned with the internal affairs of Russia as such ; our sole interest in them is how they affect the war. Should it be the case that extensive areas of the country favour the Bolshevik form of Socialism that is the concern not of Britain but of Russia, and it does not seem to us to have anything to do with the issue whether we recognize the Russian Government diplomatically. ... With the Bolshevik Government at Petrograd we are prepared to enter into relations in just the same way as we have done with the *de facto* governments of the Ukraine, Finland and elsewhere." [109]

That means that Great Britain was prepared to treat simultaneously with all *de facto* governments or administrations which controlled parts of the territory of the former Russian Empire so long as they were prepared to continue the war against Germany. But, since the Bolsheviks stopped military operations against the Central Powers, concluded a peace treaty with them and eventually entered into close collaboration with Germany, the Western Powers considered it necessary to extend their assistance to the *de facto* governments and administrations resisting the Bolshevik aggression. Lloyd George explains the position arising from this assistance against the Bolshevik endeavours in the following way :

> " We were not concerned to overthrow the Bolshevik Government in Moscow. But we were concerned to keep them, so long as war with Germany was afoot, from overthrowing those non-Bolshevik administrations and movements outside Moscow which

were prepared to work with us against the enemy. And it was inevitable that before long our co-operation with these allies should give our Russian activities an appearance of being aimed at over-throwing the Bolshevik Government. That was certainly not their original intention." [110]

Allied intervention in Russia at the end of the war consequently had a limited and temporary scope. The landings of small Allied forces in Murmansk and Archangelsk in April 1918 were only for the purpose of not letting the huge stores of arms and ammunition fall into the hands of the Germans or Bolsheviks. The Allies made no attempt to march on Leningrad or Moscow, since so long as the war against Germany was carried on they had no available forces for such an enterprise. [111]

Much greater prospects were open to the Allies in the South, but the position there was infinitely more delicate from the political point of view. The Convention of the 23rd December, 1917, be-tween France and Great Britain regulating the future operations of British and French forces in Russia concerned some territories there in which national separatist movements had suceeded in taking control of the administration. The French zone included Bess-arabia, the Ukraine and Crimea, and the British one the Cossack territories, Caucasus, Armenia, Georgia and Azerbaijan. [112] But it would be a hasty conclusion to say that the Allies pursued there more than a policy of " exploratory opportunism prompted by mili-tary considerations." [113]   Chamberlin rightly states that " the lively British interest in the security of Georgia, Azerbaijan and Armenia can scarcely be attributed to abstract zeal for the rights of small nations." [114]

So far as the Ukraine was concerned the Allied Governments recognized the *de facto* Government of the Ukrainian Rada (by its III Universal of 7th(19th) November, 1917, the Rada proclaimed a democratic Ukrainian Republic without severing, however, the links with Russia, and by its IV Universal of 22nd January, 1918, pro-claimed a complete independence which had existed in fact for several months already). [115]   On 29th December, 1917, General Tabouis was appointed Commissioner of the French Republic in the Ukraine and by a letter of 3rd January he formally notified his nomi-nation to the Ukrainian Government: the nomination of Mr. Picton Bagge, British Consul, as representative of Great Britain was notified in the same way.   But as an Ukrainian historian rightly observed, " what was granted was not recognition but a qualified acknowledg-ment which was later withdrawn." [116]   In fact it appears clearly from the declarations of the above-mentioned Allied representatives that the participation in the common struggle against the Central Powers was an imperative condition of the Entente maintaining relations with the Ukrainian Republic.[116a]

Shulgin, then Minister of Foreign Affairs, assured the Allied representatives that so long as he remained in power the Allied representatives would not be faced with any accomplished fact and no separate treaty with the Central Powers would be signed by the Ukraine.[116b] He kept his promise because he resigned after the signature of the Peace Treaty at Brest-Litovsk by the Ukrainian Delegation. This signature on the part of an administration which lived under a double threat of invasion was an ill-advised step as it did not save the existence of a democratic Ukrainian Republic and alienated that country from the Western democracies. The new Ukrainian State associated itself with the Central Powers in the perversion of the principle of national self-determination and rendered more difficult the collaboration between Poland and the Ukraine later.

In this early stage of intervention the Entente Powers did not follow any definite political programme; they considered Bolshevism a temporary illness, and although securing some military bases on the soil of the Russian Empire they neither believed in nor desired the dismemberment or permanent weakening of the future Russia. There is a grain of truth in the words of von Solf, German Colonial Secretary, in his speech of the 20th August, 1918 :

> " The problem of foreign races, even the entire Russian problem, is regarded by England entirely from the point of view of assisting British warfare. England is satisfied with any kind of constitution which maintains Russia as a serviceable piece of war machinery, and were Ivan the Terrible to rise again to weld Russia together for renewed fighting, he would be a welcome ally to England in the crusade for freedom and right." [117]

It is true that Germany, closely collaborating with Bolshevism at that time, was the last country in the world to make such criticism.

Intervention in Russia had, moreover, no American backing. We know that President Wilson was opposed in particular to the intervention in Siberia with the participation of Japan, as he distrusted the intentions of that country regarding the mainland of Asia.[118] President Wilson was in favour only of intervention with the approval of the Soviet Government, as he was to some extent under the influence of Raymond Robins, Head of the American Red Cross Mission in Russia. Bruce-Lockhart says about Robins that " Lenin captured his imagination," and that he knew no Russian and very little about Russia, but he " set himself the task of persuading President Wilson to recognize the Soviet Government." [119]

Other junior Entente agents in Russia set themselves the same

task, including Bruce-Lockhart himself and Captain Sadoul of the
French Military Mission. It would have been difficult and even
dangerous for the Entente to follow such a policy. It would have
forced all anti-Bolshevik forces and national movements in Russia,
for which Bruce-Lockhart had very slight regard as appears from
his disparaging and most unfair remarks about the Poles,[120] to
collaborate with Germany. Moreover, it was not Trotsky, wishing
to fight the Germans, but Lenin who was the decisive figure in the
Bolshevik Government. Lenin realized that without a peace and
even collaboration with the Germans, Bolshevism would not have
been able to survive. At one moment early in 1918 the Bolsheviks
took fright that the Germans might wish to foster the restoration of
the old order in Russia. We know that such plans were fostered by
some German militarists (General Hoffmann, see above, p. 188).
Only in the event of reversal of the German policy would the Bolsheviks have needed Allied support, but they were aware that such
support could not have been very effective as the Entente had no
available forces. But even in such a contingency the Bolsheviks were
not prepared to make common cause with the Allied Powers, as
appears from the words of Lenin in the interview with Bruce-
Lockhart on the 29th February, 1918 :

> " If the Germans forced their hands and tried to install a bour-
> geois government, the Bolsheviks would fight even if they had to
> withdraw to the Volga and the Urals. But they would fight on
> their own conditions. They were not to be made a cat's paw for
> the Allies. ... To the Bolsheviks, Anglo-American capitalism was
> almost as hateful as German militarism, but for the moment Ger-
> man militarism was the common menace." [121]

One reads with astonishment the statement of a British historian
who regrets that the Allies did not take a decision on the lines proposed by Lockhart :

> " The Allies at this moment were more afraid of Bolshevism
> than of Germany, yet it is more than probable that adequate inter-
> vention at this moment would have hampered the mighty concen-
> tration of troops which Ludendorff was preparing in the West and
> which was so soon to be loosed against the British Fifth Army." [122]

We can hardly subscribe to this opinion. Many illusions about
the advantages of collaboration between the Western countries and
Bolshevism had been dispelled since these early attempts to strike
up a friendship with Communist Russia. We leave aside the moral
aspects of such collaboration, the open betrayal of principles of
liberty and democracy in the name of which the Entente pretended
to fight—it suffices to remember that the Bolsheviks were able to

stay in power in Russia only thanks to the régime of Red Terror ruthlessly carried out through the so-called Extraordinary Commission for the Suppression of Counter-revolution, or Cheka, set up by Lenin on the 20th December, 1917; that the Constituent Assembly with its non-Communist majority was disbanded by military force in January 1918, and with that " all shadow of hope for democracy in Russia " vanished altogether.[123]

Moreover, Lenin expressly said to Bruce-Lockhart that he would welcome Western help only in the event of the Germans wishing to restore the old régime in Russia. The Germans preferred to collaborate with the Bolsheviks, and this collaboration was much more precious to the Bolsheviks than any limited Western assistance.

It was certainly much better that the West defeated the Germans alone, and events proved that it was able to do so without making any pledges to the Bolsheviks.

It is true that Allied intervention in Russia did not achieve its ends, but as Chamberlin rightly stated it had " a retarding, defensive value against the very real threat of widespread social upheavals in 1919." [124] Thanks to that intervention, which in fact cost very few lives on the Entente side, another unexpected result was achieved : a barrier of independent and thriving States separated Soviet Russia from Germany and Hungary, where the régime of Bela Kuhn could not survive owing to its isolation. The position of Europe would have been infinitely worse at the end of 1918 if the Western countries had supported the Bolsheviks.

Lloyd George's speech and Wilson's fourteen points

Against this general political background we can understand the meaning and aim of the important declarations on the future peace terms made by two Anglo-Saxon leaders in the course of January 1918, Lloyd George's speech to the Trade Unions on the 5th and Wilson's Message to Congress of the 8th. The Bolshevik appeals for convening a general peace conference, the deadlock in the Brest-Litovsk negotiations and the strain of a long war on the peoples explain the great moderation of both speeches, addressed to public opinion not only at home but also in the enemy countries and Russia. Apart from minor details the programmes outlined in the two declarations were almost identical. No far-reaching changes of territorial status in Europe were proposed, the rearrangements envisaged did not essentially affect the pre-war European political order, the status of all great powers, whether Allied or enemy, was to be maintained. Apart from Poland, whose right to independence was once more recognized, the principle of national self-determination received rather limited application.

In reading the passages relating to Russia one should keep in mind that one of the main purposes of the declarations was to stiffen Russian public opinion against the wide German plans for annexations and to bring about the failure of the Brest-Litovsk negotiations. This explains the use of the most flattering remarks about the part played by Russia in Europe in the course of the War. While the principle of Russian territorial integrity is strongly stressed, the existence of national separatist movements in Russia is practically ignored, the only exception being made for Poland. This feature is particularly striking in Lloyd George's speech : " Whatever phrases she (Germany) may use to delude Russia she does not mean to surrender one of the fair provinces or cities of Russia now occupied by her under one name or another." We know also that President Wilson considered it a matter of personal loyalty to stand for the maintenance of Russian integrity. In connection with the Japanese intervention in Siberia, Wilson's reply on the 28th May, 1918, to General Bliss's request for instructions was : " The President's attitude is that Russia's misfortunes impose upon us at this time the obligation of unswerving fidelity to the principle of Russian territorial integrity and political independence." [125] In spite of Wilson's reference in his speeches to the principle of self-determination, Americans at that time distrusted the separatist national movements in Russia, arguing from the analogy of the War of Secession in 1861 (see above, p. 22).

In relation to Germany, both declarations state that her unity should be preserved and that the disintegration of that country was not aimed at; only the reparation of some more recent wrongs are explicitly requested (Alsace-Lorraine), and Poland's case is mentioned not in connection with the German problem but with the Russian one. The same conciliatory mood prevails towards Austria-Hungary. It is denied that the Allies are fighting to destroy the Hapsburg Monarchy. Lloyd George, more than Wilson, stresses the necessity for granting " a genuine self-government on true democratic principles " to the peoples of the Monarchy, but no breaking up of Austria-Hungary is envisaged by either; this fully agrees with what was stated above about the secret negotiations between the Entente Powers and that country (see above, pp. 121 ff.). On a previous occasion, namely in his address to Congress delivered on the 4th December, 1917 (Declaration of War on Austria-Hungary), Wilson went even further in his desire to preserve intact Austria-Hungary. He stated then that " it is no affair of ours what they do with their own life, either industrially or politically. We do not propose or desire to dictate to them in any way. We only desire to see that their affairs are left in their own hands, in all matters great and small." The conclusion could be drawn from this statement that it was the severance of the links with Germany that was requested above all from Austria-Hungary, the question of constitutional changes being left to the trend of natural internal evolution.

In a report by a group of experts appointed by Wilson to advise him on the post-war settlement—the so-called " Inquiry "—submitted to the President before he delivered his Message on the 22nd December, 1917, we read the following opinion about the Double Monarchy : " We see promise in the *discussions* now going on between the Austro-Hungarian Government and the peoples of the Monarchy . . . ," and the report recommends : " to *encourage* the present movement towards federalism in Austria which, *if it is successful,* will break the German-Magyar ascendancy." [126] We know that this attitude towards Austria-Hungary did not change until late, almost on the eve of the Armistice, and in the Declaration of the Prime Ministers of three Allied countries on the 3rd June, 1918, which was most emphatic about the necessity for " a united and independent Poland," only sympathy was expressed " for the nationalistic aspirations towards freedom of the Czecho-Slovak and Yugo-Slav peoples."

As a matter of fact, just as it was reasons of political opportunism and above all the desire to safeguard the balance of power in Europe which dictated to the Great Powers their conservative policy towards the Hapsburg Monarchy, so the reversal of this policy was due more to the changes occurring in Eastern Europe than to ideological reasons. We find a most revealing document in this connection in the Lansing Papers, namely his letter to President Wilson dated 10th May, 1918, in which Lansing put to his chief the following question : " Should we or should we not favour the disintegration of the Austro-Hungarian Empire into its component parts and a union of these parts, or certain of them, based upon self-determination? " At the same time he states his own point of view :

> " I do not think in considering this subject we should ignore the fact that the German Government has been eminently successful in the disorganization of Russia by appealing to the national jealousies and aspirations of the several peoples under the Tsar's sovereignty. *Whether we like the method or not,* the resulting impotency of Russia presents a strong argument in favour of employing as far as possible the same method in relation to Austria's alien provinces. I do not think it would be wise to ignore the lesson to be learned from Germany's policy towards the Russian people." [127]

It follows from our foregoing general remarks about the spirit with which both declarations were imbued that at the moment when they were delivered hope had not been abandoned that a future peace settlement might be a settled peace and not a peace imposed by the victors on the vanquished.

Conciliatory moods towards the Enemy Powers and the desire to take into account the Russian State interests are reflected in the passages of both declarations referring to Poland. They are couched in the following terms :

WILSON'S MESSAGE Art. XIII	LLOYD GEORGE'S SPEECH
An independent Polish State should be erected which should include the territories inhabited by indisputably Polish populations, which should be assured a free and secure access to the sea, and whose political and economic independence and territorial integrity should be guaranteed by international covenant.	An independent Poland, comprising all those genuinely Polish elements who desire to form part of it, is an urgent necessity for the stability of Western Europe.

There are obvious differences beween the two drafts, but they have some important features in common. In neither do we find the adjective " united " which appeared in Wilson's previous speech of the 22nd January, 1917, and was to reappear in the Declaration of three Allied Governments of the 3rd June, 1918. Moreover, there is no mention of making good the old historic wrongs, as in the case of Alsace-Lorraine, of restoring a State which fell a victim to the sinister plots of its neighbours. One might think that Poland should " be erected " as a quite new State without links with its historic past. The application of the exclusively ethnographic principle to the new Poland only while her neighbours should keep the areas with mixed populations could be understood as a reassurance to Russia that the old dispute between her and Poland about the fate of Poland's Eastern provinces should be solved to the advantage of Russia, in spite of the fact that the population of these provinces was non-Russian. Both declarations seem to accept the standpoint of the Proclamation of the Provisional Russian Government of the 29th(16th) March relating to Poland's independence, and the subsequent statements of that Government insisting on a strong application of the ethnographic principle to the new Poland (see above, pp. 167 ff.). In Lloyd George's speech the request that the ' genuinely ' Polish elements should expressly manifest their desire to join the new State bears the mark of the Bolshevik proposals at Brest-Litovsk on holding plebiscites in order to ascertain the true wishes of the population.

Also in relation to the future German-Polish delimitation the terms used in the declarations, and above all the omission of the adjective " united," might arouse strong suspicions that both Anglo-Saxon countries had not yet made up their minds about the future of the former Poland's Western provinces, detached by partitions. Moreover, should the future German-Polish delimitation follow exactly the principles laid down in the declarations, Prussia might reap all the benefit from her ruthless methods of Germanization of the Polish provinces in her possession, methodically pursued since the partitions. We find confirmation of our interpretation of some ambiguous terms in the Message in a document submitted to President Wilson by the " Inquiry " on the 22nd December, 1917. Colonel House says of the recommendations of the Inquiry that " Mr. Wilson studied them with care, especially those relating to the settlement of territorial issues, discussed them with Colonel House and wrote shorthand annotations on the margin of the report, some of which he later embodied in his speech." [128] Consequently, although we cannot take for granted that Wilson shared all the views of his experts, we must consider the above-mentioned report of the Inquiry an important document which to some extent explains the cautious terms used in the final draft of the message to Congress. We find the following remarks about Poland in this document :

" *Poland.*
        " An independent and democratic Poland shall be established. Its boundaries shall be based on a fair balance of national and economic considerations, giving full weight to the necessity for adequate access to the sea. The form of Poland's government and its economic and political relations should be left to the determination of the people of Poland through their chosen representatives.
        " The subject of Poland is by far the most complex of all the problems to be considered. The present distribution of Poles is such as to make their complete unification impossible without separating East Prussia from Germany. This is probably not within the bounds of practical politics. A Poland which consists *essentially* of *Russian* and *perhaps* Austrian Poland would probably secure its access to the sea through the Vistula river and the canals of Germany which run to Hamburg and Bremen. The relationship would very probably involve both the economic subjection of Poland and the establishment of an area of great friction. If Russia is to remain weak the new Poland will be in an exceedingly exposed position." [129]

Some months later, in a Report on Inquiry (Its Scope and Method) of the 20th March, 1918, the following three possible solutions of the Polish question were outlined :

"(*a*)   The creation of an independent and united Poland with complete right of self-determination ;

(*b*)   the exclusion of Prussian Poland, or Galicia, or both ;

(*c*)   the inclusion of Lithuania and Kurland." [130]

On the basis of these documents one can state that a complete solution of the Polish question fully agreeing with the complete right of self-determination was not yet a foregone conclusion at the beginning of 1918 so far as the Anglo-Saxon leaders were concerned, and it required great efforts on the Polish side to dispel many preconceived ideas on Poland and her national claims. All these efforts would have been in vain but for the changes in the general political position arising from the German policy in Eastern Europe, and the final military collapse of the Central Powers.

Wilson's caution at the beginning of 1918 can be considered a temporary retreat from his previous standpoint, undoubtedly due to the rather precarious position of the Allies caused by the Russian collapse and the Bolshevik revolution. Hopes for total victory were certainly in eclipse in many quarters in the West.

House says of the discussions with Wilson that led to the final draft of Article XIII :

"Wilson spent some time on Poland. I gave him the memoranda which the Polish National Council in Paris had given me, containing a paragraph which they wished the Inter-Allied Conference to adopt (see above, p. 180), but which was refused. We read this over carefully and both concluded that it could not be used in full, but the paragraph as framed came as near to it as he felt was *wise* and *expedient.*" [131]

The great enthusiasm aroused by Wilson's Fourteen Points Message among the oppressed nations in Central and Eastern Europe, in particular in Poland, made Wilson the hero of the hour, and Bolshevik propaganda had to take great pains to counteract the impact of the Wilsonian words on the masses. And yet one can hardly say that a peace which might have been signed immediately after the delivery of this message would have been a peace based on the principle of self-determination, even so far as Poland was concerned.

After the two speeches were made by the Anglo-Saxon leaders, almost simultaneously and following the same general lines, a marked difference nevertheless began to appear between these two countries in relation to Germany. Wilson's attitude continued to be rather lenient in this respect, and almost to the end he held the view which he had expressed in his speech at the Washington Monument on the 14th June, 1917, that the German people " did not originate or desire the hideous war " and that they were " in the grip of the same sinister power that had stretched its ugly talons out and drawn blood from us." As Mr. Wilson's friend, Mr. Dodd, observed : " It is the idealist and democratic waging war upon autocracy. . . . To him the German people was a helpless, deluded race, unconvinced of the great wrong it was doing the world." [132]

It is true that Wilson realized the impossibility of agreeing to the terms imposed by Germany on the nations of Central and Eastern Europe, but he laid the whole burden of responsibility on Germany's " military masters." In his Baltimore speech on the 6th April, 1918, he said that " if Germany's military masters propose favourable and equitable terms with regard to Belgium and France and Italy, could they blame us if we concluded that they did so only to assure themselves of a free hand in Russia and in the East " . . . " they fancy that they can erect an Empire of gain and commercial supremacy "; and he stated that " in such a programme our ideals, the ideals of justice and liberty, the principle of the free self-determination of nations upon which all the modern world insists, can play no part."

Awaiting the emergence of liberal leaders in Germany with whom a reasonable agreement could be made, and being in principle opposed to the knock-out blow policy, Wilson for a long time avoided any commitment on the territorial issues between Germany and Poland. A member of the Polish National Committee who was on an official mission to the United States in June and July 1918, Mr. M. Seyda, noted that the American Government expected a " sufficient victory " before winter 1918, which would put an end to the war. He was also informed of the plans prepared by the Inquiry, excluding the Polish provinces of Prussia and Eastern Galicia from the future Polish State.[133] Dmowski went to the United States in September 1918. He discussed with Wilson the Polish claims in the West and gave him ample documentation on this matter.[134] Wilson, although much more amenable to the Polish point of view, had in mind the neutralization of the Vistula and the establishment of a free port in Danzig. When Dmowski mentioned the necessity for taking strategic reasons into account in connection with the future delimitation, Wilson denied that strategic reasons might play any part after the War because of the system of collective security within the framework of the League of Nations. It was not until October 1918, that is on the eve of the Armistice, that the Inquiry was told to prepare plans in connection with the envisaged inclusion of the Polish provinces of Prussia in the future Polish State.[135]

It was the Republican Party which insisted on Germany's unconditional surrender and took a more favourable standpoint to the

Polish rights than Colonel House's body of advisers. A resolution of Senator Lodge was voted by the U.S. Senate, 18th November, 1918 (*Congressional Record*, Vol. 56, No. 259, p. 12678) against attempts at curtailing Polish claims at the future Peace Conference. Lodge's draft resolution said :

> " It will be very well at this time for the Senate to join itself with the President in the statement on that point in regard to Poland.
> " The reason why I say it is this. You will observe that the President speaks of access to the sea. The access to the sea can only be at Danzig at the mouth of the Vistula. The Vistula is inhabited entirely along both banks by Poles, but Danzig is a German city and I have already seen attempts to say that as a German city they must continue to hold it and give certain rights to the Poles. The access to the sea that the Poles will get if Danzig is held will be not worth having. Guaranties can be given to the people of Danzig. I think nothing is more important than the President's propositions about access to the sea." [135a]

Reactions in the West to the Brest-Litovsk Treaty

A much stiffer attitude towards Germany was taken at that time by France and Great Britain. To the vital interests of both countries German expansion in Eastern Europe, the enormous increase of Germany's economic and demographic resources as well as the prospects of close collaboration between Germany and Bolshevik Russia presented the immediate danger.

Balfour, the Foreign Secretary, in his great public speech in Edinburgh in January 1918 opposed all moves for a premature peace and stated that the war should continue, not only to bring about the redress of recent wrongs but also " to prevent another great wrong done, not in 1871 but in 1772 by a predecessor of the present Emperor of Germany, the great wrong of the partition of Poland, from not being set right." [136] He was still more explicit on Polish territorial claims in the West in the House of Commons on the 27th February :

> " The Hon. gentleman talks as if it was the desire of Count Czernin to establish the ancient Kingdom of Poland as far as that really was a Polish nationality upon independent basis. ... You cannot confidently, completely or adequately carry out any policy of that kind without restoring to Poland those provinces ravished from her by Germany at the time of the partition or since and which are to a very great extent at the present time inhabited by Poles." [137]

The conclusion of the first Brest-Litovsk Treaty with the Ukraine induced the British Government to take a step which amounted to recognition of the status of Poland as that of an allied country. In a note of the 18th February, 1918, the Foreign Office informed the representative of the Polish National Committee in London that :

> " His Majesty's Government have instructed their agent at Kiev to make a declaration to the effect that they do not recognize the peace treaty recently concluded between the Ukraine and Central Powers.
> " In making this communication to you as representative in London of the Polish National Committee I am to inform you that Great Britain will not recognize any peace without previous consultation with that country." [138]

First Joint Allied Declarations on Poland's independence

It was Polish soldiers on a distant front in Bessarabia who received the first joint official declaration of the representatives of the Allied and Associated Powers, drafted in a clear and binding manner. It is little known, but a very interesting story.

The conclusion of the first Brest-Litovsk Treaty led to undeclared war between the Central Powers and the Polish nation (p. 117) carried out in the homeland by a secret Polish military organization (P.O.W.), and outside Poland everywhere where Poles could gather sufficient strength and form special national units. The last unit of the Polish Legion under Colonel Haller's command crossed the front line at Rarancza in Bukovina on the 15th February, 1918, moving to the south-east to join the Polish forces in Bessarabia. There (at Soroki in Bessarabia) at that time was the Second Polish Army Corps—the former soldiers of the Ninth Russian Army on the Rumanian front. It was the Second Polish Army Corps increased by Haller's units that a few months later, surrounded by the German troops of General Eichorn at Kaniow (Ukraine), fought a desperate and lonely battle. But before the Second Polish Army Corps left Bessarabia to move to the Ukraine important negotiations took place between the representatives of the Allied and Associated Powers at Jassy and the representatives of the Polish soldiers on the Rumanian front. The Poles wished to know the true intentions of the Entente towards Poland. In fact they distrusted the Entente, being influenced by the secret documents published a few months before by the Soviet Government, and from which it appeared that the Entente had agreed to give a free hand to Tsarist Russia in solving the Polish question. The delegate of the Polish soldiers of the Rumanian front carried out the negotiations with the Allied representatives on the lines approved by the Polish Executive Committee. The respecive resolution of this Committee, very characteristic of the turn of mind of these men, ran as follows :

> " Stating that in her moves for independence and union of the

Polish territories the Polish nation is forced by the course of events to carry on an active struggle against the Central Powers and that therefore the common action of the Polish nation with the Entente Powers becomes possible, the Polish Executive Committee of the Rumanian front declares that the following conditions are indispensable for such common action:

(1) The Entente Powers should pledge themselves by an official declaration addressed to the Polish nation that one of their war aims is the restoration of an independent united Poland with access to the sea through her own littoral.

(2) The Entente Powers should guarantee that a Polish representation entitled to vote on an equal footing with the representatives of other States and Powers will be admitted to the International Congress called for the final liquidation of the present war and to take decisions on matters concerning the Polish nation."

These proud soldiers, enlightened by the experiences of the war, were ready to die, but for Poland only and not for the interests of foreign Powers which so far had done little for Poland. They were rewarded for their efforts in the form of a collective declaration dated 2nd March, 1918, in which in reply to the request of the Polish Executive Committee the envoys of Great Britain, France, the U.S.A, and Italy stated :

" The undersigned ministers, on the basis of the solemn declarations of the heads of the Allied governments, declare:

(1) That any treaty of peace concluded outside the Entente countries and contrary to the principle of nationality is null and void ;

(2) that one of the principal aims of the Entente in the present war is the restoration of Poland, in her *geographical* and *historical limits*, having all necessary elements for a free national existence as well as for her economic development ;

(3) that such restoration will be for the Entente in the event of victory an essential condition for the conclusion of peace." [139]

The terms of this declaration were much more satisfactory from the Polish point of view than the terms used in Article XIII of Wilson's Message, and even more so than those in Lloyd George's speech of the 5th January.

This declaration, having a local character but following the new lines of policy of the governments whose representatives signed it, was one of the first consequences of the Brest-Litovsk Treaties and German attempts to face the world with a series of accomplished facts in Eastern Europe. Great Britain and France reacted very violently to these arbitrary and iniquitous acts. In the House of Commons on the 27th February, 1918, Balfour branded the Treaty with the Ukraine as a " gross violation " of the principle of self-determination so loudly proclaimed by the Central Powers which, settling the boundaries of the Ukraine, " had handed over a portion of an undoubted Polish territory to the new republic." [140] On the 8th August in the House of Commons, arguing with the partisans of a " peace of restoration," Balfour presented the case for Poland as a test case of German imperialistic lusts and dreams of further expansion :

> " The true obstacle to any legitimate peace is what has been concisely described as ' German militarism,' a policy of universal domination ... so determined is she (Germany) to keep these nations under her heel that, having absolutely in her power to rearrange the map of this part of Europe as she pleases, she has been careful not to arrange it according to national or ethnic limitations. ... I cannot conceive any peace being tolerated, any peace being assented to by the Powers of the Entente which leaves that state of things unremedied. If it were unremedied future wars would be an absolute certainty, and Germany's power of waging those would be, as she herself openly admits, enormously increased." [141]

For France the Brest-Litovsk Treaties were a turning point in her policy towards Poland. At the beginning of the War France had been ready to agree to Russia's plans relating to Poland. Then she supported the Austro-Polish solution with the return of Poland to her 1772 frontiers in the West. Eventually, with the Brest-Litovsk Treaties and the state of revolt of all Poles and other nationalities of Austria-Hungary against the Hapsburgs, all hopes of winning Austria-Hungary had vanished, and Poland remained the only reliable friend of the Western Powers in Eastern Europe. It was France then that pressed the other allied powers to make definite promises to the Poles, as the fulfilment of these promises meant the permanent weakening of her most dangerous adversary, Germany. It was certainly to a great extent thanks to French initiative that the Declaration of the three Allied governments was issued on the 3rd June, 1918, a declaration awaited for such a long time by the Polish National Committee, which had tried for so many months, since the outbreak of the Russian revolution, to induce the Entente Powers to take this binding step. The direct link between the declaration of the 3rd June, 1918, and the outcome of the Brest-Litovsk negotiations can be established by the note, quoted below, from the French Ambassador in the United States, Jusserand, to the Secretary of State, dated 8th March, 1918. This note was the first French move which led eventually to the said Declaration, and in it we read the following :

> " My Government has just informed me that, in its opinion, the Allied Powers should not, without uttering a joint protest, witness the events which tend to culminate in another partition of Poland and deliver to Austro-German domination *integrant parts of that ancient Kingdom*.
>
> " Continued silence on this point would be contrary and harmful to the rights of the peoples which we have ceaselessly affirmed and to the fundamental requirements of a just and lasting peace. Again we should not turn a deaf ear to the appeals that come to us from the Polish patriots.
>
> " It is, to my Government's mind, the duty of the Allies to uphold the claims that have ever been formulated with respect to Poland and have been particularly formulated with so much eloquence and accuracy by the President of the United States. It is likewise advisable in every respect to promote and *encourage the resistance of a people whose rôle in the midst of our enemies may prove of the highest importance for the very outcome of the war*.

.   .   .   .

" DRAFT OF A DECLARATION CONCERNING POLAND

> " The Government of ...... and of ...... continue to consider the constitution of an independent Polish State as one of the prime conditions of the organization of a Europe constituted in accordance with the principle of nationalities and secure from the surprise of another war ; they regard as null and void peace treaties imposed by force which ignoring the right of peoples to dispose of themselves, assign to Ukraine or to the Central Powers *territories that are unquestionably Polish from the ethnographic as well as from the historic standpoint*. They again proclaim their resolution to pursue the creation of an independent, autonomous Poland capable of insuring its economic, political and military development, with access to the sea." [142]

The final text adopted by the heads of the three Allied Powers (consequently without America) on the 3rd June, 1918, was much shorter than the foregoing but was quite satisfactory from the Polish point of view. There reappeared the adjective " united ", and " free access to the sea " was expressly guaranteed; although the word " creation " might arouse some objections there was nothing in the text which imposed limitations on the future territorial status. (The text was quoted at the beginning of this chapter.)

The Declaration of the 3rd June, 1918, crowned the efforts of the Poles on both sides of the front line to obtain from the Western Powers recognition of the international character of the Polish question and the necessity for the restoration of the Polish State. This recognition came rather late, and certainly did not arise from abstract speculation or from the sudden awakening of the sense of justice or from ideological slogans, but from the impact of events and the understanding of political realities in Central and Eastern Europe. The old political order established in that part of the continent on the division of the spoils of Poland collapsed. The disappearance of the Polish State, which for centuries had been a most important bulwark of the West against invasions from the East, and which at the same time had held in check the aggressive Prussian colonialism, hotbed of German imperialism of the nineteenth and twentieth centuries, eventually brought upon Europe one of the worst calamities in her long and chequered history.

For the Western statesmen who had displayed extreme caution in the course of the War in any approach to the problems of Central and Eastern Europe, who would have much preferred to leave intact the pre-war political order, who parted most reluctantly with old prejudices and preconceived ideas and whose knowledge of history and geography were rather scanty, the new policy might seem a leap in the dark. For the time being they stated their views on Poland's future only, but everyone felt that Europe was approaching a total remaking in view of the impact of national passions released all over Central and Eastern Europe.[143] Western statesmen were left with no alternative, because they had to oppose the grandiose plans for remaking the map of Europe in accordance with German requirements, their own plans enlisting the support of the oppressed nations for the Allied cause.

It was natural that all those who wished for a " peace of restoration " and were opposed to the knock-out blow policy saw in these new political commitments an obstacle at an early peace. Voicing this opinion, Mr. Dillon said in the House of Commons on the 1st August, 1918 :

> " Two months ago a meeting took place in Paris of the Prime Ministers of this country, France and Italy, and they sent a dispatch to the leaders of the Polish people that they now solemnly declare it to be a prime object of the Allies that Poland should be reunited and constituted an independent State. That, of course, is a gigantic change. It involves taking from Germany one of her richest provinces and taking from the Austrian Empire the greatest province of Galicia. It is a very great change in our whole commitments in this war." [144]

But apart from pacifists, whose influence on the action of Governments was very limited at that time, especially in Great Britain, there were some men enjoying considerable authority whose policy aimed to preserve the old political order in Europe, and who were afraid of the consequences of the collapse of great Empires. If now we wish to answer the question whether the fears that the new Allied policy relating to Central and Eastern Europe might delay the conclusion of hostilities were justified, we can state most emphatically that they were not. The collapse of Austria-Hungary did not come because of the encouragement given at the last moment by the West to the disintegrating national forces in the Double Monarchy; the military collapse of Germany had nothing to do with the new trends in the policy of the Entente, because Germany had to abandon simultaneously *all* her war aims in the West and the East. It occurred as it had been predicted nearly two years before by a British periodical, *New Statesman,* which in its leader of the 20th January, 1917, arguing with Noel Buxton's views in his letter to the Editor, stated :

> " We entirely agree with him (Noel Buxton) in feeling that this country is not called upon to sacrifice half a million lives for the independence of the Czechs or of any other of the subject peoples of Eastern and Central Europe ... but does he, or anyone else, believe that by the time Germany is beaten to the extent, say, of being willing to restore Alsace-Lorraine to France, she will fight another hour to save Bohemia for Austria. The idea is incredible." [145]

What was then said about the nations of Austria-Hungary could be said about all the other issues at stake between the Entente and the Central Powers. No half-victory was possible in such gigantic struggles. The War stopped when the adversary lost all hope in victory and was unable to endure any longer the stress of war. Hostilities did not last one day longer on account of the commitments of the Entente towards Poland or any other nation of Central and Eastern Europe, and no additional sacrifice in human lives was needed on the Entente side for these purposes. On the other hand, as we shall see in the following chapter, the terms of the Armistice might arouse grave suspicions that the Entente had no definite programme in relation to the problems of Central and Eastern Europe.

NOTES

[1] J. I. PADEREWSKI, *Memoirs,* p. 369.
[1a] R. LANSING, *The Big Four,* p. 197.
[1b] H. NOTTER, *The Origins,* p. 359.
[1c] *Ibidem,* p. 551.
[1d] H. H. FISHER, o.c., p. 90.
[1e] J. DANIELS, *The Wilson Era (Years of War and After),* p. 399.
[1f] MRS. WILSON, *My Memoir,* p. 113. The Polish Delegation was received at Shadow Lane. (" Paderewski," p. 114.)

[1g] And not at the beginning of 1916 as wrongly asserted by Landau and following him by SMOGORZEWSKI, *Poland's Access to the Sea*, p. 92. Paderewski often called on House at different hours, even at night and early morning. See BONSAL, *Unfinished Business*, under the date of 30th March, 1919. " Paddy is the Colonel's pet," I once heard a yeoman of the guard explain. " We boys think he likes ' Paddy ' better even than the ' Tiger '."

[1h] LANDAU, *Paderewski*, pp. 113-14.

[1i] J. DANIELS, o.c., p. 399.

[1k] COUNT BERNSTORFF, *My Three Years in America*, pp. 298-9.

[1l] SMOGORZEWSKI, o.c., p. 92.

[1m] As asserted by Gerson, o.c., p. 66.

[1n] BERNSTORFF, o.c., pp. 255 ff.

[1o] A. S. LINK, *Woodrow Wilson and the Progressive Era*, p. 280.

[1p] BERNSTORFF, o.c., pp. 248 ff.

[1r] *Ibidem*, p. 319.

[2] HOUSE, *Intimate Papers*, II, pp. 434 ff.

[3] H. H. FISHER, o.c., p. 94.

[3a] H. NOTTER, o.c., p. 594.

[3b] *Ibidem*, pp. 599-600.

[3c] BERNSTORFF, o.c., p. 321.

[3d] LANDAU, o.c., p. 117.

[4] LLOYD GEORGE, *The Truth About Peace Treaties*, p. 228.
A similar point of view was expressed by a British pacifist, Mr. Holt, in the House of Commons on 13th February 1918 : " But the war has some very different objects. It was a war made for the destruction of Prussian militarism ; it was a war for the restoration of public law in Europe ; it was a war in order that regard should be had to the rights of small nations, and it was a war to establish a League of Nations. *All these objects cannot be attained by force*."

[5] JAMES W. GERARD, *My Four Years in Germany*, p. 268.

[6] HANS VON SEECKT, o.c., I, p. 545.

[7] *Ibidem*, I, p. 258.

[8] R. LANSING, *War Memoirs*, II, p. 241.

[9] FILASIEWICZ, o.c., p. 135.

[10] R. DMOWSKI, o.c., p. 442, from a Pro-Memoria left by Dmowski for Balfour on 25th March, 1917 : " In vain a clear declaration (of Western Powers) on Poland's future has been expected in Poland. The answer of the Allied Governments to President Wilson was exploited by agitators for the benefit of Germany, as a proof that the Western Powers were leaving to Russia the decision on the Polish question."

[10a] T. BAILEY, *Woodrow Wilson and the Lost Peace*, p. 28.

[11] See p. 68, note 31.

[12] W. H. CHAMBERLIN, *The Russian Revolution*, I, pp. 107 ff.

[13] DE BASILY, *Russia Under Soviet Rule*, p. 71. From 5th to 12th September, 1915, an International Socialist Congress met at Zimmerwald and its Left Wing—the Russian one—voted a resolution according to which the outcome of the war should not be a nationalist victory,

but a ' peace without annexations, based on self-determination of peoples, and the fight for socialism.' A second Congress held in another Swiss town, Kienthal, from 5th to 9th February, 1916, went further and called for a struggle, ' by every means,' for an immediate peace without annexations."

[14] J. STALIN, *Sochineniya*, III, translation by Deutscher in his book *Stalin*, pp. 133-4. See also Deutscher's remark : " It could have hardly occurred to the writer (Stalin) that nearly thirty years later he himself would rehash some of Milyukov's war-aims and that Milyukov himself would then, from his deathbed in his Parisian exile, generally applaud his former critic."

[15] SEYDA, o.c., I, p. 458.

[15a] This account is based mainly on two sources : L. KOZLOWSKI, *Russkaya Revolutsiya i nezavisimost' Polshi* (translated from Polish), Paris, 1922, and P. MILYUKOV, " Aleksander Lednicki," *Przeglad Wspolczesny*, Warsaw, 1939 (Vol. XVIII—series LXVIII, January–March).

[16] E. W. WILCOX, *Russia's Ruin*, p. 167.

[17] As asserted, for instance, by a Polish historian, S. ASKENAZY, *Uwagi*, pp. 457 ff.

[18] FILASIEWICZ, o.c., p. 151.

[19] *Ibidem*, p. 154.

[20] E. H. CARR, *The Bolshevik Revolution*, I, p. 287.

[21] MILYUKOV, *Istoriya Vtoroi Russkoi Revolutsii*, I, p. 64-5.

[22] MRS. HAROLD WILLIAMS, *From Liberty to Brest-Litovsk*, p. 100.

[23] WILCOX, o.c., p. 183.

[24] MILYUKOV, o.c., I, p. 65. Milyukov remained centralist in his inmost heart until the end of his life. See a very characteristic declaration given by him to the French newspaper *Le Temps*, 26th December, 1918. In this declaration Milyukov, defending himself against the accusations of the " betrayal " of the Allied cause in the course of the conversations with the German respresentatives at Kiev after the conclusion of the Brest-Litovsk Treaty, states that he insisted there on the recognition by the Germans of the Russian unity and the return to Russia of newly-constituted limitrophe States : " Il faut que l'unité de la Russie soit reconstituée ... que les Etates artificiels ébauchés sous la protection allemande le long frontières russes lui fussent restitués."

[25] WILCOX, o.c., p. 168.

[26] *P. R. F. R.*, 1917. Sup. 2, Vol. I, p. 54.

[27] A. RIBOT, *Journal et Correspondances inédites*, p. 68.

[28] PALÉOLOGUE, o.c., III, p. 193.

[29] E. J. DILLON, *History of the Peace Conference*, pp. 226-7.

[30] DMOWSKI, o.c., pp. 255 ff. KOZICKI, *Sprawa Granic*, p. 18. Dmowski's friend and close associate during the war, Mr. M. Seyda, speaks more cautiously in his book (o.c., I, p. 502) : " Buchanan, as it seems, received in fact an instruction of his Government and proposed to Milyukov the issuing by the Entente of a joint declaration on the unification and independence of Poland but Milyukov refused."

[31] *P. R. F. R.*, 1917, Sup. I, Vol. I, pp. 771-5.

[32] *P. R. F. R.*, " The Lansing Papers," II, pp. 19 ff.

[33] FILASIEWICZ, o.c., pp. 156 ff.

[34] *Parliamentary Debates,* House of Commons, 1917, Vol. XCII, 26th April, 1917.

[35] SEYDA, o.c., I, p. 468.

[36] VOLKMANN, *Der Grosse Krieg*, pp. 132 ff. See p. 134: " Nie war Englands Politik grösser als in dem traurigen Jahre 1917."

[37] MILYUKOV, o.c., p. 132.

[38] *Ibidem*, p. 161.

[39] *Documents and Statements Relating to Peace-Proposals and War-Aims*, pp. 60 ff.

[40] FILASIEWICZ, o.c., No. 97.

[41] J. J. SOSNOWSKI, *Prawda Dziejowa*, p. 690.

[42] SEYDA, o.c., II, p. 162.

[43] *P. R. F. R.*, " The Lansing Papers," II, pp. 35 ff.

[44] *P. R. F. R.*, 1917, Sup. II, Vol. 1, p. 759.

[45] LLOYD GEORGE, *War Memoirs*, V, pp. 2350-1. " The military Conference which met on 26th July, 1917, was attended by Generals Cadorna, Robertson, Pershing, Pétain and Foch. Their statement was an indication of the grave consequences which they apprehended would ensue from the desertion of the Allied cause by Russia. ... The fall of Russia would entail the following consequences: *Political*. It would clarify the political aims of the Entente. It is therefore suggested that the Governments should at once consider and decide the new political aims to be pursued."

[46] J. J. SOSNOWSKI, o.c., pp. 691-700.

[47] SEYDA, o.c., II, *Documents.*

[47a] E. VON GLAISE-HORSTENALL, *The Collapse of the Austro-Hungarian Empire*, p. 3.

[48] *P. R. F. R.*, 1917, Sup. Vol. I, pp. 761-2.

[49] *Ibidem*, p. 762.

[50] *Ibidem*, pp. 763-5.

[51] *Ibidem*, p. 765.

[52] *Ibidem*, pp. 766-9.

[53] *Ibidem*, pp. 771-5.

[54] HOUSE, *Intimate Papers*, IV, p. 272.

[55] HOUSE, *ibidem*, III, p. 45.

[56] J. J. SOSNOWSKI, o.c., p. 69.

[57] APPUHN, *La Politique Allemande*, p. 37. " Outre qu'en 1917 la force de l'Allemagne aparaissait très grande, la coalition de ses ennemis n'ayant pu l'abattre, elle restait formidablement armée et conservait intact son outillage ; ses régions industrielles n'avaient pas souffert de la guerre ; elle fût devenue en quelques années de paix ce qu'elle était ou tendait à être avant le guerre: la première puissance du monde dans l'ordre économique et dans l'ordre politique."

[58] TEMPERLEY, o.c., Vol. I.

[59] APPUHN, o.c., p. 57. " Il eût été difficile au gouvernement britan-

nique de résister au courant pacifique dejà fort en Angleterre si l'Allemagne avait l'habileté de répondre à la note du Pape comme l'espérait
le cardinal Gasparri."

[60] *The Parliamentary Debates,* House of Commons, Vol. 103, 13th
February, 1918. See also APPUHN, o.c., p. 47: " Pour l'Angleterre
l'intégrité territoriale et l'indépendance de la Belgique est de beaucoup
ce qui importe le plus, peut-être la seule condition essentielle. Voici le
texte anglais de la déclaration du ministre d'Angleterre après l'entretien
du 24 août avec le Cardinal Gasparri." " I replied, that a declaration
on the question of Belgium appeared to be desirable. He should remember that this was only one of the many issues between the belligerent
powers ; it was, however, of special importance to us." See also Chapter
I, p. 8.

[61] HOUSE, " Paderewski: The Paradox of Europe " (*Harper's Magazine,* December 1925).

[62] DMOWSKI, o.c., p. 502 ; SMOGORZEWSKI, *Poland's Access to the
Sea,* pp. 107-8.

[63] SEYDA, o.c., II, p. 223.

[64] JANE DEGRAS, *Soviet Documents on Foreign Policy,* p. 20.

[65] WHEELER-BENNETT, *Brest-Litovsk,* p. 390.

[66] R. H. BRUCE-LOCKHART, *Memoirs of a British Agent,* p. 201.

[67] LENIN, *The Attitude of the Russian and Polish Social-Democracy
and of the Second International,* Selected Works. See RUTH FISCHER,
Stalin and German Communism, p. 26.

[68] A. A. KRISTIAN, *The Right to Self-Determination and the Soviet
Union,* p. 20.

[69] T. A. TARACUZIO, *The Soviet Union and International Law,* p. 33.
" Lenin believed that just as the achievement of the abolition of classes
was possible only by passing through a period of the dictatorship of the
once oppressed classes, so also the inevitable abolition of nationalities,
to be effected through the fusion of nations, could be attained only by
passing through a transition period characterized by the complete liberation of oppressed nationalities within the State."

[70] *Proceedings of the Brest-Litovsk Peace Conference,* p. 44.

[71] STALIN, *Marxism and National Question,* English Edition, p. 18.

[72] *Ibidem,* p. 21. Also some " western-minded " Russian socialists
took the same view during the War. See ALEXINSKY, *La Russie et la
Guerre,* p. 164: " Il y a longtemps que les ouvriers conscients ont
abandonné l'idée d'une lutte pour l'indépendance nationale et lui ont
substitué celle d'une lutte de classes. Seul, un tout petit groupe de
socialistes est en désaccord avec eux sur ce sujet, et même avant la
guerre, if fomentait une insurrection nationale contre la Russie."

[73] STALIN, *Sochineniya,* III, pp. 208-9.

[74] I. DEUTSCHER, *Stalin,* pp. 184-5.

[75] CHAMBERLIN, *The Russian Revolution,* I, pp. 373 ff.

[76] Soviet proposals presented at the meeting of 22nd December, 1917,
of the Brest-Litovsk Peace Conference. *Proceedings,* p. 38.

[77] BORIS SOUVARINE, *Stalin,* p. 300.

[78] DELBRÜCK, *Ludendorff's Selbsporträt*, p. 32. " Dass, wenn Deutschland nach Osten auf gewaltigste angriff, es im Westen umso zurückhaltender und nachgiebiger hätte sein müssen, um sich wieder in die Weltpolitik einzupassen, das war ein Gedanke, der, so einfach er ist, doch schon ausser Ludendorff's Horizont lag."

[79] ERZBERGER, o.c., p. 235. The letter to the Imperial Chancellor of 27th March, 1917: " Wer jetzt Russland helfe sich im Innern zu konsolidieren habe den grossen Trumpf für die Zukunft in der Hand. Das neue Russland dürfe in Deutschland nicht seinen Feind erblicken ; es müsse vielmehr unser Freund und Verbündeter werden. ... Das russische Kriegsziel sei erreicht durch die Beseitigung der Autokratie."

[80] HOFFMANN, o.c., p. 168. DELBRÜCK, o.c., p. 82.

[81] HOFFMANN, o.c., p. 223.

[82] HELFFERICH, *Der Weltkrieg*, III, 474.

[83] LLOYD GEORGE, *War Memoirs*, VI, p. 3190.

[84] WHEELER-BENNETT, *Brest-Litovsk*, p. 183.

[85] HELFFERICH, o.c., III, p. 493: " Die deutsche Politik hatte in eigensinniger Verkennung der Sachlage dem Bolschevismus über seine schwerste Krise hinausgeholfen."

[86] ERZBERGER, o.c., pp. 248-9.

[87] WHEELER-BENNETT, o.c., XVIII. " Should Germany succeed in re-establishing the situation which existed for a brief moment after Brest-Litovsk, the results would be even more threatening than they were then. For an industrialized Russia exploited by the organizing genius of Germany conjures up a vision which no Western European can contemplate with equanimity."

[88] P. ROTH, *Die politische Entwicklung*, p. 108.

[89] T. HOLOWKO, *Przez Dwa Fronty*, p. 9.

[90] HOFFMANN, o.c., LOUIS FISHER, *The Soviets in the World Affairs*, I, p. 39.

[91] The German plans relating to Kurland and Lithuania were laid down in a leaflet written in 1915 by Silvio Broederich-Kurmahlen, " Das neue Ostland." The Deutsch-Baltische Gesellschaft, under the chairmanship of Prince Johann von Mecklenburg, had to carry out the plans for Germanizing Kurland and Lithuania by transferring there 3,200,000 Germans. All land transactions in Lithuania were forbidden by the Decree of 12th July, 1916, as the land was reserved for the future German settlers. See WIELHORSKI, *Polska a Litwa*, p. 260.

[92] K. OKULICZ, *Podzial Ziem Wielkiego Ksiestwa Litewskiego*, p. 103.

[93] LUDENDORFF, *Kriegserrinnerungen*, p. 375. " Wilno, Grodno und andere Städte waren polnisch."

[94] *Ibidem*, p. 428. " Lithuania with Wilno as capital " war auf dem besten Wege den Polen zu verfallen, wenn die Konventionen nicht Bedingungen angenommen wurden, die den Einfluss Deutschlands sicherstellten."

[95] *Ibidem*, p. 145. " Ich wollte mir im Herbst 1915 ein Bild über die Verteilung der Weissruthenen machen. Sie waren buchstäblich nicht zu finden. Später erst zeigte es sich, dass sie ein ganz verbreiteter, aber

äusserlich polonisirter Stamm sind, der auf so niedriger Kulturstufe steht, dass ihm nur bei langer Einwirkung geholfen werden kann."

[96] *Ibidem*, p. 428.

[97] WIELHORSKI, o.c., pp. 263 ff.

[98] HOFFMANN, o.c., p. 211. "Das Abtreten des Cholmer Gebietes ohne Befragen der Bevölkerung gerade dieses Selbstbestimmungsrecht durchbrach."

[99] *Ibidem*, p. 210. "Da ich einen selbständigen polnischen Staat für eine Utopie hielt und halte, hatte ich kein Bedenken, den Ukrainern meine Unterstützung in Bezug auf das Cholmerland zuzusagen."

[100] *Ibidem*, p. 213. "Ich habe in jenen Tagen die jungen Ukrainern bewundert. Sicher wussten sie genau, dass ausser der eventuellen deutschen Hilfe nichts mehr hinter ihnen stand, dass ihre Regierung ein fiktiver Begriff ist."

[101] LUDENDORFF, o.c., p. 374.

[102] ASKENAZY, *Uwagi*, pp. 291 ff.

[103] ROTH, o.c., p. 87. "Als aber die oberste Heeresleitung durch ihre bestimmte Einwirkung auf die Brester Friedensverhandlungen, wie sie in dem Eingreifen des Generals Hoffman zum Ausdruck kam, ihren politischen Einfluss gerade in der zukünftigen Gestaltungen der östlichen Gebietsfragen stark geltend zu machen begann, trat eine andere Konzeption der polnischen Frage in den Vordergrund: die Idee eines kleinen, eingeengten Polen, dem Grenzstreifen im Norden und Westen als militärische und wirtschaftlich Sicherungen wegzunehmen wären und das ringsum, auch gegen Grossrussland hin, durch Nachbarstaaten eingeengt und abgeschlossen sein sollte."

[104] RICHARD SCHMIDT, "Die neuen Richtungen der Organisation Polens," *Zeitschrift für die Deutsche Politik*, 1918, Heft 3.

[105] HELFFERICH, *Der Weltkrieg*, III, pp. 342-3. "Dieses edle Volk (Polen), dass lediglich den Waffenerfolgen Deutschlands und seiner Verbündeten und dem Blute vieler Tausenden von Deutschen und Österreichern die Aussicht auf seine staatliche Wiederaufstehung verdankte, das für dieses grosse nationale Ziel keine Hand gerührt und keinen Tropfen Blut vergossen, sondern in diesem grössten Krieg aller Zeiten abwartend beiseite gestanden hatte, wandte sich, nach dem von Russland nichts mehr zu befürchten hatte, immer deutlicher gegen seine Befreier. Die polnische Frage, das schwierigste aller östlichen Probleme, wurde also durch die Brester Friedensverträge, nicht nur nicht gelösst, sondern geradezu verschärft."

[106] WHEELER-BENNETT, o.c., p. 164. "Germany as the champion of Western civilization protecting the border State from civil war, rapine and bloody murder, as a bulwark against the spread of Bolshevism, would have been in an infinitely stronger position both within and without, than Germany, the apostle of Machtpolitik, deliberately perverting the principle of self-determination to cover a policy of annexation. The propaganda of the Entente would have been robbed of one of its most effective weapons."

[107] ROTH, o.c., p. 100. "Dass die polnische Frage einen derartigen

schwankenden Charakter zeugte und über dies nicht vom Fleck kam, war ja durchaus nicht Schuld der Militärs allein. Aber ihr Einfluss in den ganzen östlichen Problemem war doch unverkennbar, und wenn der Ausgang des Krieges für die Zentralmächte siegreich gewesen wäre würde wohl die Reichtagsresolution vom 22 März, 1918, die Berücksichtigung des Selbstbestimmungrechtes Polens, Lithuaniens und Kurlands forderte, so wenig positiven Erfolg gehabt haben, wie die bekannte Friedensresolution vom 19 Juli, 1917."

[108] W. H. CHAMBERLIN, o.c., II, p. 150.

[109] LLOYD GEORGE, *War Memoirs*, V, p. 2592.

[110] *Ibidem*, VI, p. 3191.

[111] WILLIAM C. BULLITT, *The Great Globe Itself*, p. 54

[112] CHAMBERLIN, IV, p. 153. L. FISHER, *The Soviets in World Affairs*, I, pp. 154-5 and II, p. 636.

[113] JOHN S. RESHETAR, JR., *The Ukrainian Revolution*, p. 100.

[114] CHAMBERLIN, II, p. 168.

[115] CHOULGINE, *L'Ukraine contre Moscou*, pp. 146-7.

[116] RESHETAR, o.c., p. 100.

[116a] Allocution by General Tabouis on 4th January, 1918: "Je vous apporte l'assurance formelle que la France qui est la première à faire ce geste décisif soutiendra de toutes ses forces morales et matérielles la République Ukrainienne dans les efforts qu'elle accomplira pour continuer à marcher dans la voie que se sont tracée les Alliés et qu'ils poursuivront sans hésitation à l'avenir en pleine connaissance de leurs droits et de leurs devoirs, devant la démocratie du monde entier et de l'humanité" (CHOULGINE, o.c., p. 174). A letter by M. Bagge: "Mon Gouvernement m'a chargé de vous donner l'assurance de sa bonne volonté. Il appuiera de toutes ses forces le Gouvernement Ukrainien dans la tâche qu'il a entreprise de faire oeuvre de bon gouvernement, de maintien de l'ordre et de combattre les puissances centrales, ennemis de la démocratie et de l'humanité" (*Ibidem*, p. 176).

[116b] CHOULGINE, o.c., p. 170.

[117] *Documents and Statements Relating to Peace Proposals and War-Aims.*

[118] LLOYD GEORGE, VI, p. 3183.

[119] BRUCE-LOCKHART, pp. 222-3. Wilson's Message to the Congress of Soviets, meeting in Moscow, BAKER-DODD, *The Public Papers of Woodrow Wilson*, Vol. I, p. 191. See also JACQUES SADOUL, *Notes sur la Révolution Bolchevique*.

[120] *Ibidem*, p. 148. "Yet these people (Poles), who have never been able to help themselves and who certainly contributed little to the Allied cause in the war, have been rewarded with the largest slice of territory granted to any nation under the Treaty of Versailles."

[121] BRUCE-LOCKHART, p. 239. L. J. STRAKHOVSKY, *The Origins of American Intervention in North Russia*, p. 105: "The fundamental difference between the Allied and Bolshevik policies was that the former wanted to re-establish the Eastern Front, although even in this purpose there was no common understanding nor efficient co-operation, while

the latter, fearful of their own position, afraid of the Allies and Germany alike, wanted to gain time and gather forces for their support. They therefore chose a policy of playing off the two adversaries against each other ... "

[122] WHEELER-BENNETT, o.c., p. 298.

[123] JOHN REED, *The Days that Shook the World*, p. 139. BULLITT, o.c., p. 49.

[124] CHAMBERLIN, II, pp. 395-6.

[125] R. S. BAKER, *Woodrow Wilson, Life and Letters*, p. 175.

[126] The Paris Peace Conference, I, p. 52.

[127] Lansing Papers, II, pp. 126 ff.

[128] HOUSE, *Intimate Papers*, III, p. 330.

[129] The Paris Peace Conference, I, p. 31.

[130] *Ibidem*, p. 66.

[131] HOUSE, III, p. 340.

[132] WILLIAM E. DODD, *Woodrow Wilson and His Work*, pp. 131-2.

[133] SEYDA, o.c., II, p. 397.

[134] BAKER, *Woodrow Wilson, Life and Letters*, Armistice, p. 398. " September 13th. Ignace Paderewski presented Roman Dmowski of the Polish National Committee. (On 8th October, Dmowski, in accordance with the President's wish, sent him a number of historical maps of Polish territory, also one showing the proposed frontier of Poland.")

[135] R. DMOWSKI, o.c., pp. 333 ff.

[135a] H. H. FISHER, o.c., Document No. 11.

[136] *The Times*, 11th January, 1918.

[137] *The Parliamentary Debates*, House of Commons, 27th February, 1918.

[138] FILASIEWICZ, o.c., p. 359.

[139] RUPNIEWSKI, Umowa Komitetu Wykonawczego Wojskowych Polakow Frontu Rumunskiego z przedstawicielami Koalicji (*Niepodleglosc*, Vol. II). W. LIPINSKI, *Walka Zbrojna o Niepodleglosc Polski*, pp. 326 ff. HOLOWKO, o.c., pp. 221 ff.

[140] *The Parliamentary Debates*, House of Commons, Vol. 103.

[141] *The Parliamentary Debates*, House of Commons, Vol. 109.

[142] P. R. F. R., 1918, Sup. I, Vol. I, p. 871.

[143] The Declaration of 3rd June has disappointed the Czecho-Slovaks and Yugoslavs. See *ibidem*, p. 811: " Ambassador in Italy (Page) to the Secretary of State, 9th June, 1918. Conversation with Mr. Trumbic, who expressed ' great disappointment because clear line of division between Poland's and Yugoslav aspirations.' I pointed out that Polish independence had long been declared to be one of the war aims of the Allies whereas the Yugoslav movement is comparatively recent."

[144] *The Parliamentary Debates*, House of Commons, Vol. 109, 1st August, 1918.

[145] *New Statesman*, 20th January, 1917.

CHAPTER V

ARMISTICE

" At the moment when the conclusion of Armistice with Germany has set the seal on the united efforts of the Allies in the cause of freedom. His Majesty's Government are more than ever conscious of the loyal co-operation which they have received from the Polish nation in the course of this cruel war."—(Balfour's letter to the representative of the Polish National Committee in London, dated 12th November, 1918.) [1]

" I remember that when I was still in the Magdeburg (prison) I read the terms of the Armistice and noticed with extreme anguish that no mention of Poland had been made in the Armistice terms and that she was to remain for the time being in the same position."—(From a speech of J. Pilsudski on the 27th December, 1921, on the occasion of the third anniversary of the Poznan rising.) [2]

German military collapse and the terms of the armistice

ALTHOUGH the circumstances in which the Armistice with Germany was signed have been amply described in special studies, of which one of the most recent, by Mr. H. Rudin, is particularly instructive, [3] we find in these relatively little about the attitude of the Western Powers towards the problems arising on the East European front with the collapse of German military power. As a matter of fact their attitude denotes the wish to evade decisions on the most important issues relating to that part of Europe and to postpone them until the Peace Conference. We can better ascertain the position of Central and Eastern Europe as it appeared in the outcome of the Armistice by stating what was left out than by what was actually stipulated by this international instrument. The omissions are particularly characteristic in relation to Poland, the name of which does not even appear in the text. The gap between the requests of the Polish representatives and the provisions of the Armistice was very wide indeed, and one can consider this fact as early evidence of the lack of an agreed Allied programme on the problems of Central and Eastern Europe.

From the middle of August the German Great Headquarters began to press the German Government to start negotiations for peace, [4] and on the 29th September, 1918, Hindenburg and Ludendorff informed the Emperor that Germany was unable to carry on

the war and demanded an armistice within twenty-four hours. It
came as a complete surprise not only to Allied but even to German
statesmen (see above, pp. 11 ff.). It is common knowledge that the
Western countries were preparing for a new winter campaign, did not
expect a decisive victory for a long time, if ever,[5] and when the news
of the German peace offer arrived there was a feeling of relief in
many quarters in the West. Nevertheless there was no unity of
views in the West. about the nature of the conditions which were to
be imposed on Germany. Above all there was a dispute in the
United States between the advocates of Germany's unconditional
surrender, among them General Pershing, Commander-in-Chief of
the American forces in France,[6] Senator Lodge and Theodore
Roosevelt at home (a very characteristic passage from Roosevelt's
telegram of 24th October : " Let us dictate peace by the hammer-
ing guns and not chat about peace to the accompaniment of the
clicking of typewriters "),[7] and the point of view represented by
President Wilson who accepted an armistice on the basis of the
fourteen points of his Address of January 1918. The final conditions of the Armistice were, however, rather severe, rendering
impossible any further resistance by the German forces, the main
proposals of Marshal Foch having been accepted. Field-Marshal
Haig even took the view that " the only difference between his
(Foch's) conditions and a general unconditional surrender is that
the German army is allowed to march back with its rifles, and
officers with their swords." [8] But Haig's views were based on the
terms imposed on Germany in the West, as he advised his Government not to interfere with the problems of Eastern Europe. Yet
even from the general point of view the Armistice cannot be considered an unconditional surrender. Erzberger obtained some
amelioration of the original terms presented to him by Foch,
enabling an orderly retreat of the German forces and a valuable
addition to Article XII.[9] Moreover, the Germans very soon became
aware that the Allies had no clear ideas about the problems of
Eastern Europe, and that there remained a wide margin for bargaining. From the fact that Poland had not been mentioned in the
Armistice clauses they drew the conclusion that she did not belong
to the Entente at the moment of signing the Armistice,[10] although
the Polish army had been recognized as an autonomous, Allied and
co-belligerent army, not only by France but also by the other Allies
(Great Britain on the 11th October, 1918, the United States on the
1st November, 1918).

What were the reasons for the reluctance, especially on the part
of the British, to lay down in the Armistice Agreement some
political clauses relating to Eastern Europe analogous to those stipu-

lated for the West? Was it the fear that Germany might not sign such an Armistice? The Allies actually " considered the possibility of Germany's refusal of Armistice terms, a week before the signatures of armistice," according to Colonel House's information. This fear, arising exclusively from the terms established for the West, seemed legitimate to some extent, considering that the internal state of Germany was little known at that time. But a Germany which was forced to accept the terms proposed by Foch, with the occupation of the Rhineland and the surrender of nearly all available war material, would have accepted any other conditions, especially after the collapse of Turkey and Austria-Hungary. Whatever it may have been, if there were any risks of Germany refusing to sign the Armistice they were not incurred on account of provisions referring to Eastern Europe. Field-Marshal Haig, supported in the War Cabinet by General Smuts, wished to limit even more the objects which Great Britain might secure by armistice. Haig expounded his views at a meeting at 10 Downing Street on the 19th October. He believed at that time that the German army was " capable of retiring to its own frontier and holding that line if there should be any attempt to touch the honour of the German people, and make them fight with the courage of despair "; and on the other side considered that " the French and American armies are not capable of making a serious offensive now," reaching the conclusion that " the British alone might bring the enemy to his knees. But why expend more British lives—and for what? " Consequently he recommended that the terms of the Armistice should be limited to the request for the immediate evacuation of Belgium and occupied French territory, to the occupation of Metz and Strasbourg by the Allied armies, the evacuation of Alsace-Lorraine and the restoration of the French and Belgian rolling stock, as well as the inhabitants of the occupied territories in the West. " The British Army," stated Haig, " has done most of the fighting latterly, and everyone wants to have done with the war, provided we get what we want. I therefore advise that we only ask in the armistice for what we intend to hold, and that we set our faces against the French entering Germany to pay off old scores. In my opinion, under the supposed conditions, the British Army would not fight keenly for what is really not its own affair." When in the discussion which followed Mr. Balfour spoke about deserting the Poles and the peoples of Eastern Europe, the Prime Minister (Lloyd George) " *gave the opinion that we cannot expect the British to go on sacrificing their lives for the Poles.*" [11]

This inside story together with two memoranda submitted to the Cabinet by General Smuts in which he warned against " trying to defeat Germany, as that might mean dragging on the war for another year " (see pp. 11 ff.), provide valuable clues for understanding the British attitude in the course of the negotiations among the Allies leading to the establishment of the terms of the Armistice.

In the first report submitted by Foch to Clemenceau on the 8th October there were no provisions relating to the Eastern Front.[12] The same remark applies to the Draft of the Military Clauses of the Armistice adopted at the meeting of the Allied Commanders—Haig, Pershing, Pétain—under the chairmanship of Foch at Senlis on the 25th October.[13] This draft was discussed at the Supreme Council which met on the 1st November in Paris.[14] It was Clemenceau who objected to the lack of any reference to Russia and proposed to demand the abrogation of the treaties of Brest-Litovsk and Bucharest. Lloyd George then made the proposal to state the conditions for the Eastern Front, and Marshal Foch was instructed to propose a text on this subject. Foch asked for the ideas of the Allied Governments : " Evacuation of the Eastern countries, Russia, Poland, Rumania, is all very well," he said, " but are we going to take these countries over on our own account? Rumania may be able to extricate herself from the affair alone, but what about the others? Are we to abandon them to themselves? " Foch did not receive a clear answer to this question until the end of the discussions, which lasted until the 4th November. At the meeting on the 1st November Colonel House stated that " it is a very delicate question, for the retreat of the troops would be followed by a Bolshevist régime," but he proposed no remedy. Clemenceau gave proof of his poor knowledge of the conditions prevailing at that time in Eastern Europe because he stated that " to believe in the Bolshevist danger in those territories is to let oneself be lured by German propaganda." At the next meeting it was Balfour who expressed fears that in the event of the evacuation of these regions by the Germans they would become the " prey of Bolshevism." But the only remedy which he proposed was " to allow the people certain arms so that they will not give in without resisting the first invader who comes." The following text was submitted by Balfour at the meeting on the 2nd November :

> " When the Germans, according to this agreement, shall evacuate the territories on their Eastern frontier, they must leave a third of their arms in the hands of legal authorities to be designated by the Allies, in order to permit the population to defend itself against all disorders and aggressions."

This proposal eventually fell through at the meeting on the 4th November. It met with opposition from Pichon, French Foreign

Minister, as according to his views " the arms which you will leave in these countries if the Allies are not there will serve the Bolshevists only, and other Governments in which we cannot have any confidence." Some speakers expressed fears that the arms might serve for carrying on the civil war in Russia, and a Serb representative, Mr. Vesnich, declared that " we all wish to see the Russia of other days revive," to which Balfour retorted that he was not " thinking of Russia at all in making this proposal, but of the small peoples who aspire to autonomy, such as the Esthonians and the Letts." As Marshal Foch also joined the opponents and expressed the view that it was " an unrealizable prescription," Balfour withdrew his proposal.

Consequently there was no provision in the Armistice specifying what was to become of the territories in Eastern Europe occupied by Germany once the German armed forces had withdrawn from them, nor were arrangements made for the purpose of helping these countries to organize their defence against the Bolshevik invasion. On the other side we look in vain in the terms of the Armistice with Germany relating to the Eastern Front for a clause similar to that contained in Articles III and IV of the Protocol of Armistice of the 3rd November with Austria-Hungary, by virtue of which the Allied and American forces were granted the right to occupy some disputable areas and to move freely all over the territory of Austria-Hungary.[15]

Very disappointing from the Polish point of view was the decision of the Allies that the Germans must return within their frontiers as they were before the month of August 1914, as it meant that the German sovereignty was maintained until the decisions of the Peace Conference over all the old Polish provinces in Prussian possession. At the meeting on the 2nd November Marshal Foch proposed the evacuation of the German forces on a much bigger scale :

> " Clause II. Evacuation of German troops in a period of (fifteen days) of all the territories of Poland, including old Poland, as she existed before the first partition, with Danzig."

This proposal was supported by the French Foreign Minister, Pichon, who said :

> " I wish to insist that, in the evacuated territories, all territories are clearly included which formed the Kingdom of Poland before the first partition of 1772. Moreover that springs from the declarations and original agreements of all the governments at the beginning of the war ; the United States has accepted it. I desire the restoration of old Poland with access to the sea. It is one of the war aims of the Allies and President Wilson has entirely approved

of it. The Poles who have remained on the spot, the Polish Committee of Paris, which we have recognized, consider that we owe
them this pledge. There is need for mentioning this clause in the
armistice conditions in order to avoid all discussions at the time of
the examination of the peace terms."

This proposal met with opposition from Mr. Balfour, who stated
that he listened to it with " anxiety ":

> " The Poland of 1772, you say, must be the Poland of 1918. It is
> not to that that we pledged ourselves. We pledged ourselves to
> restore a Poland composed of Poles. That of 1772 did not corres-
> pont to this aim ; it was not composed solely of Poles. Non-Polish
> territories were included while Polish ones were not included. This
> formula would therefore offend by its insufficiency as well as by its
> excess. The exact delimitation of the frontiers of this new Poland
> is such a complicated subject that I entreat you not to introduce it
> into the armistice clauses. I propose to sum up in one sentence,
> taking the whole Eastern Front, what Marshal Foch said: 'All the
> German forces in the East must return within their frontiers as
> they were before the month of August 1914.' We shall leave the
> task of studying this question to the Inter-Allied Conference, which
> must necessarily meet before the Peace Conference."

Colonel House accepted Balfour's proposal and Mr. Pichon withdrew his own, stating that he wished it might be " clearly understood
by the Polish people that we are not renouncing anything which we
have promised to them."

It is true that as Foch stated in his *Memoirs* the Armistice was
neither a peace treaty nor even the preliminary to peace,[16] and at
that time it was a foregone conclusion that the Germans would
eventually be forced, by virtue of the Peace Treaty, to surrender
important portions of their territory in the East to the Polish State.
But the fact that Germany was left for such a long time, much
longer than had been anticipated at the time of the Armistice,[17]
with the possession intact of her Eastern provinces, rendered more
difficult the initial tasks of the Polish State and left much room for
abuses by the German administration in relation to the Polish population in Prussia, leading eventually to the outbreak of uprisings in
Poznan Province and Silesia. Moreover, the retrocession by virtue
of the Peace Treaty of the Polish provinces by Prussia produced
more ill-feeling in Germany than would have been the case if the
contested area had been occupied by the Allied or Polish forces
immediately after the Armistice; it would also have saved many
precious lives and facilitated the organization of Polish resistance
to the Bolshevik invasion.

The Germans were also left a free hand in exploiting economically those parts of their territory which they had eventually to surrender. From Article XIV of the Armistice, which enjoined " cessation of requisitions by Germany in Rumania, Poland and Russia in the boundaries before 1914," the word " Poland " was deleted on the proposal of Balfour, who on that occasion made the rather astonishing remark that " this country was included in the Russia of 1st August, 1914." It goes without saying that the restrictions imposed on Germany, such as blockade, etc., applied to her whole pre-war territory, and so the Poles within the Eastern provinces of Prussia had to endure the same privations as the rest of Germany, which was neither fair nor reasonable. The only clause which safeguarded Polish interests to some extent was that proposed by Balfour at the meeting on the 2nd November :

> " If we do not consider a special clause [said Balfour], the Allies will be cut off from Poland and the neighbouring countries. We ought to insist upon keeping contact with them, by Danzig for instance, or by any other means of access which would allow us to send to those countries arms and police, if a special need became apparent, or food supplies if tonnage permitted us."

Such is the origin of Article XVI of the Armistice. The final wording of this Article was less peremptory than Balfour's suggestion, and gave rise to some misunderstanding with Germany as we shall see later. It ran as follows :

> " The Allies shall have free access to the territories evacuated by the Germans on their Eastern frontier, either through Danzig or by the Vistula, in order to convey supplies to the population of these territories or for the purpose of maintaining order."

Requests of the Polish National Committee

Let us see now how far the terms of the Armistice prepared in Paris agreed with the wishes and requests of the Polish National Committee, which at that time had charge of Polish interests in the West. Thanks to the efforts of this Committee the Polish Army in the West, which had so far been recognized only by France as an Allied and co-belligerent army, was recognized as such also by Great Britain on the 11th October, and by the U.S.A. on the 1st November; this meant that at the moment of signing the Armistice Poland was formally a member of the Entente. Balfour's note of the 11th October, 1918, was couched in particularly warm terms; he stressed the importance to the Allied cause of the Polish resistance to the German plans :

> " His Majesty's Government have repeatedly announced their

desire to see the creation of a united and independent Polish State,
and they were glad to join in the declaration by the Great Powers
at Versailles on 3rd June, 1918, that the creation of such a State
with free access to the sea constitutes one of the conditions of a
solid and just peace.

" I need hardly assure you that the sympathies of this country
have been and are with the people of Poland, of whatever politics,
class or creed, in all the sufferings to which they have been subjected during the War. It admires their firm refusal to allow Germany
and Austria-Hungary to dictate the future status and boundaries
of their country, and it looks forward to a time when the present
provisional arrangements will come to an end and a Poland free
and united will shape its own constitution according to the wishes
of its people." [18]

The President of the Polish National Committee, R. Dmowski,
while in Washington asked the Secretary of State by a note dated
25th October " to recognize the Polish Army, under the supreme
political authority of the Polish National Committee, as autonomous, allied and co-belligerent." Mr. Lansing, by his letter of the
1st November, 1918, on behalf of the U.S. Government granted
this recognition on the terms specified by Mr. Dmowski.[19]

The Polish National Committee was less successful in its
démarches, started on the 13th October, aiming to obtain recognition by the Allies as *de facto* government with regard to : (1)
foreign representation; (2) political direction of the Polish Army;
(3) civil protection of Polish nationals abroad. Recognition was
granted to the Committee by the French Government only, on
15th November. The latter supported this demand before the other
Allied Governments, but the British Government refused on 30th
November and the American Government followed this example.

Important events were taking place at that time in Poland : the
German garrisons were disarmed in the Congress Kingdom, and
Pilsudski, after his release from Magdeburg prison by the Germans
on the eve of the Armistice, assumed power in Warsaw. Neither
Great Britain nor the United States considered it wise to give any
decision on the matter raised by the French Government before
ascertaining the true wishes of the Polish people. We shall deal later
with this problem; for the time being let us observe that it seems
most unlikely that even if such recognition had been granted and
Polish representatives invited to attend the meetings of the Allied
Council preparing the Draft of the Armistice, the final text would
have been much different from that adopted in Paris. A prominent
member of the Polish National Committee, Mr. M. Seyda, states
in this connection that

" the propositions of the Committee aiming to create a clear and definite position from the very beginning clashed obviously with the policy pursued by the majority of the Allies, a policy of temporizing, dictated by fear of an immediate and too fast contact with Eastern Europe, and above all avoiding any commitments in the difficult question of the Polish territories belonging to Prussia." [20]

What were the propositions of the Polish National Committee when the question of the armistice with Germany became topical?

We have the account of one of the first conversations devoted to this subject, between Mr. Dmowski who was at that time staying in Washington, and Mr. Phillips, Assistant Secretary of State. In this conversation Mr. Dmowski took the view that " the position will be desperate unless Allied troops could come in and take the place of the German troops, who at least were keeping the Bolsheviks from gaining the upper hand throughout Poland." [21] We find concrete proposals in the memorandum submitted under the signature of Mr Wielowieyski, Head of the Military Department of the said Committee in Paris, to the Allied Governments and dated 12th October. The memorandum deals with " the evacuation of the Polish territories by the Austro-Germans and the occupation of these territories by Polish and Allied troops." It advises the signing of a special agreement relating to sending Allied and Polish troops through Bulgaria and Rumania, a route which it was anticipated would be negotiable within a very short time. " As soon as a sufficiently important part of the Polish territory has been evacuated by the enemy troops a national government will be proclaimed there." The authors of the memorandum hoped to win the support of Pilsudski for the common cause once he had been released from German captivity, and they took the view that he might be willing to collaborate with General Haller, Commander of the Polish Army in France. The expeditionary corps was to consist of Polish and Allied battalions transferred to the Balkan Front and directed to Galicia across Rumania. The number of recruits enlisted in Poland after the occupation of the Polish territory would allow the early release of French or British battalions, which would be used for the occupation of three important strategic objectives : Brest-Litovsk, Kamienietz-Podolsk and Kovno (Kaunas). The occupation of these places would guarantee the security of Poland in the East and might serve for future military action by the Allies in Russia. [22]

General E. L. Spears, Head of the British Military Mission in France, transmitted this memorandum on the same day (12th October) to General Sir Henry Wilson, Chief of the Imperial General Staff, stating that according to the views of the Quai d'Orsay it seemed to be " unrealizable for the time being." [23]

In a telegram sent to the National Committee in Paris on the 28th October Dmowski gives an account of his conversations with Mr. Lansing, Secretary of State, in the course of which he stressed the same point.[24]

But the most complete statement of the views of the Polish National Committee can be found in the note handed by Mr. E. Piltz at the Quai d'Orsay on the 4th November. The most important passages of this note run as follows :

" It is necessary that:
(1) The evacuation of the Polish territories by the German forces be followed by the entry in Poland of the Allied Armies, and simultaneously of the Polish Army which is at present in France. . . .
(2) The evacuation by the German armies and authorities not only of the territories occupied during the War, but also of the Polish territories the restoration of which by Prussia will be, according to the Versailles Declaration of the 3rd June, 1918, one of the points of the peace treaty."

The following territories were specified in the note :
Poznan Province,
West Prussia,
District (Regierungsbezirk) of Olsztyn (Allenstein) in East Prussia,
District (Regierungsbezirk) of Opole (Upper Silesia).

In addition the occupation of a strategic line passing through Koslin, Landsberg, Glogau, Wroclaw (Breslau) and Neisse, as well as the occupation of the fortresses of Grudziadz, Torun and Poznan was considered necessary.[25]

The same day (4th November) General J. Haller, Commander-in-Chief of the Polish Army in France, addressed a letter to M. Georges Clemenceau in which he indicated various routes for sending the Expeditionary Corps to Poland (through Hungary, Rumania or Odessa).

But at that time the draft of the Armistice with Germany was already approved by the Supreme Council and, as we stated above, none of the Polish requests was taken into consideration. The Germans had to evacuate only former Russian territories, and no occupation of the Polish territories by mixed Allied and Polish forces was announced by the clauses of the Armistice. It is particularly striking because at the same time the Allies envisaged the use of Czecho-Slovak forces in the event of Germany refusing to accept the Armistice. According to Colonel House's telegram of the 4th November to the Secretary of State, a meeting was held at his headquarters on that day, attended by the heads of the principal Allied

Governments, Marshal Foch, and the Allied naval and military advisers. To this meeting Dr. Beneš also was invited. A resolution was approved referring to the plan of operations against Germany through Austria. The possibility had to be examined of " taking immediate steps to send a force which shall include the Czecho-Slovak forces on the French and Italian fronts to Bohemia and Galicia." [26] Had these plans been carried out Czecho-Slovak troops would have appeared in Galicia, a Polish province of Austria, before Polish units.

Articles XII and XVI of the Armistice with Germany

At the Armistice negotiations Erzberger, Head of the German delegation, made some interesting remarks in connection with the clauses relating to the Eastern Front. First of all he drew the attention of Marshal Foch to the fact that while the evacuation of the territories so far belonging to Austria-Hungary, Rumania and Turkey could take place at once, " an immediate evacuation of former Russian territories, now occupied by German troops, would deliver the defenceless population of those territories to the atrocities of Bolshevism." [27] This observation was taken into account by the Allies, and the new text of Article XII ran as follows :

> " All German troops at present in any territory which before the war formed part of Austria-Hungary, Rumania or Turkey shall withdraw within the frontiers of Germany as they existed on the 1st August, 1914, and all German troops at present in territories which before the war formed part of Russia must likewise return to within the frontiers of Germany as above defined *as soon as the Allies shall think the moment suitable, having regard to the internal situation of these territories.*"

There is no doubt that since the Allies did not wish to send their own troops to Eastern Europe some provisional arrangements were necessary in order to enable the populations of the former Russian Empire which neither desired to remain with Russia nor had any liking for the Bolshevik doctrine, and especially for Bolshevik methods, to organize their life and prepare defensive measures against invasion from the East.

It was obvious that in proposing some changes to Article XII the Germans had actually in view their own interests and not those of the populations of the said territories, as they stated themselves in a memorandum of the 13th January, 1919 :

> " Articles XII and XIII of the Armistice Agreement stipulated at first the withdrawal of German troops from the territories which,

before the war, belonged to Russia. At Germany's instigation the wording of Article XII was altered. This alteration did not, how-ever, make it an obligation for Germany to care for the mainten-ance of order in those territories, but simply conferred on it the right to evacuate the same gradually." [28]

It is a debatable matter whether the Germans carried out this clause of the Armistice in a satisfactory way from the point of view of the interests of the populations concerned, and whether the German atti-tude towards Bolshevism was always irreproachable from the Western point of view. The German authorities, of course, defended them-selves against accusations of the Allies that they favoured the Bol-shevik plans.[29] In any case they had much more room for political manœuvres than had been initially anticipated, because the Entente Powers were unable to make clear which rôle they assigned to the Germans in the East,[30] having no agreed policy on the problems of Eastern Europe.

The Allies' consent to the alteration of Article XII, due to the German initiative,* shows that the Allies realized that they were on the point of committing a capital mistake. In fact, the original demand of the Allies for the immediate evacuation of the former Russian territories by the Germans without providing for the defence of the populations can be qualified as an irresponsible policy. If carried out it would have led to unprecedented disaster, not only for the countries on the Western borders of Russia but for Europe as a whole.

The second German observation relating to the armistice clauses having a bearing on the Eastern front was made in regard to Article XVI, drafted as we mentioned above (p. 229), in rather vague terms. The Germans availed themselves of the ambiguity of this Article and, stressing that the transit through Danzig could concern only transport to the former Russian territories, wished to obtain the assurance that only food supplies would be directed via this port.[31]

Apparently they received no satisfaction, because in their reply the Allies insisted on the maintenance of the original text, but on the other hand the latter did not make it clear that they were

---

* Dmowski's account of this particular point is misleading, as he ascribes to himself the initiative of the alteration of Article XII. He was probably misinformed; his démarche, made at the last moment, might nevertheless have had some influence on the eventual decision of the Allies to accept the German suggestions. (See R. DMOWSKI, o.c., p. 341: "I went immediately to Lansing and requested the completion of this Article by a reservation stating that in the East the evacuation of the German troops would take place only when the Allied Powers demanded it.")

resolved to use the port of Danzig without any restrictions, which led to serious misunderstandings a few months later.

The solution adopted in the Armistice Agreement obviously disregarded the most vital needs of Poland, as only the occupation of the port would have guaranteed to Poland regular supplies from the West.

It was Marshal Foch who on the 12th January, 1919, drew the attention of the Council of Ten to the necessity for the enforcement of the provisions contained in Article XVI of the Armistice. He proposed the inclusion of the question of Poland in the new terms of Armistice, and took the view that " all powers required were covered by Clause XVI of the Armistice." [32] In his " Note on the situation in Poland," submitted to the Council, he stated that

> " At the moment when the Armistice is about to be renewed, it is necessary to profit by the German plenipotentiaries being assembled to ensure the settlement of a highly important question : namely the situation on the Eastern frontiers of Germany.
>
> " As a matter of fact, hostilities never altogether ceased there, owing to the Bolsheviks or the Germans. The disturbances which exist in those regions are a danger for the whole of Europe ; *the situation of the Polish population is not in keeping with the promises made by the Allies in regard to Poland.*
>
> " This situation must be altered without delay."

Consequently he proposed sending one division each of Americans, British, French and Italians, and to secure the Danzig base with the Danzig-Torun railway. [33]

The proposed clause for renewal of Armistice ran as follows :

> " With a view to enable the Entente Powers to bring home the Polish troops which are at present in France and Italy, to ensure Poland's being furnished with supplies and to help that country in the task of re-establishing order on its territory, the Allies decide to put into immediate execution the clauses of Article XVI of the Armistice Convention." [34]

Unfortunately this question was linked with much wider issues, such as the Allied intervention in Russia and various Polish territorial claims, questions with which we deal in another place, and strong objections were raised to the proposal of Marshal Foch when it came under discussion by the Council on the 22nd January. It was decided to send only a Commission to Poland, to study the whole position on the spot, and this caused new delays against which Foch warned in his speech, saying that " Poland might be suffocated before its birth. It had no bases, no outlets, no supplies, no army." [35]

Presenting the Polish point of view before the Council of Ten on the 29th January, 1919, Dmowski stated that Article XVI was a dead letter, and he in vain repeated the Polish request for " the temporary occupation by Allied troops of Danzig and of the railway line between Danzig and Poland " as well as sending arms and ammunition along this line, warning the Allies that " if Poland could not be assisted and assisted quickly, she must be crushed and submerged by Bolshevism." [36]

Although the Allies in their note to the German Armistice Delegation of February 1919 on the third renewal of the Armistice observed that " contrary to the terms of Article XVI the Germans refuse to guarantee the security of the food supplies for the Polish populations," [37] they made no reference to the transport of other items such as arms and ammunition, and still less to the transport of troops.

Transport of Haller Army to Poland

But it was the question of the transport of the Polish Army from France (Haller Army) to Poland that revealed that Poland's access to the sea, so loudly proclaimed by recent Allied declarations, still remained a dead letter in spite of the most critical position of the new State facing Bolshevik aggression. When the Chairman of the Allied Commission in Poland, Ambassador Noulens, informed the German representative in Bydgoszcz, Freiherr von Rechenberg, by a note of the 5th March that an Allied mission intended to go to Danzig to make the necessary arrangements for the transport of the said troops via this port, the Germans raised a very strong protest. Erzberger instructed General Freiherr von Hammerstein, Chairman of the German Military Delegation, to declare that " Germany declined any responsibility for the bloodshed that would come about and for any further consequences." Freiherr von Hammerstein in his note to the Allied Delegation of the 7th March alleged that the transport of the Haller Army through Danzig " would endanger the rear of the German Front against Russian Bolshevism," although at that time the Germans were already quickly withdrawing from the East and, moreover, had at their disposal other ports nearer the front line, such as Königsberg, Memel and Libau. In a second note of the 8th March he pointed out that Article XVI did not give the right to land Polish troops in Danzig. [38]

Although the Allies did not hesitate to introduce many drastic changes to the original clauses of the Armistice Agreement, they were unable at that time to agree amongst themselves on a firmer line of policy on this matter, the more so as the whole question of the future of Danzig was at that time under discussion. Consequently the Allies accepted the German suggestion to transport this army by rail, and the respective Protocol with Germany was signed on the 4th April (route Koblenz-Halle-Cottbus-Leszno).

Poland partly liberated

Although the Armistice clauses left all the problems of Eastern Europe in abeyance and the Allied Powers reserved for themselves the right to decide when the German troops would be allowed to evacuate the occupied territories, the developments taking place at that time in this area very soon rendered obsolete some provisions of the Armistice. At the same time all the plans of the Central Powers to face the Peace Conference with accomplished facts collapsed,[39] as they found no real backing from the population, which was impatient to be completely free and to get rid as soon as possible of its " protectors." These spontaneous moves were particularly rapid in Poland. It would go beyond the scope of our study to relate the full story of the end of the Austro-German régime in Congress Kingdom and in Galicia. But an important circumstance should be noted, that Poland at that time was passing through not only a national revolution but also social upheavals which for the first time brought to power in Poland the representatives of workers and peasants supporting Pilsudski. We shall deal with this side of the problem later, as it had important repercussions in international politics. What interests us in the first instance is the fact that the Austrian and German occupation ended in Poland much more quickly than had been anticipated in the West, and that this was possible only thanks to the fact that all strata of the population joined in a movement for liberation; soldiers from the armies of the partitioning powers, factory workers, intelligentsia, peasants and town population. The Polish Underground Organization (P.O.W.), consisting of Pilsudski's followers, with marked radical sympathies, also played an important part in these events, especially in the Congress Kingdom.

As soon as the news of the German demand for peace reached Poland the Regency Council in Warsaw took some steps which in practice meant an attempt to take control of the country, although the German and Austrian authorities still kept effective power. The patriotic appeals of the Regency Council, however, found little response among the Left-Wing parties, unwilling to co-operate with the authority installed by the occupying Powers, and the Cabinet appointed by the Council under Mr. Swierzynski's presidency consisted exclusively of moderate parties closely connected with the Polish National Council in Paris. This Cabinet failed to obtain from the occupying Powers the handing over of the administration, and trying to make itself independent of the Regency Council was eventually dismissed by it.

It was the Austrian part of Poland that was the first to become free. In Cieszyn (Teschen) Silesia the Polish National Council was constituted as early as the 19th October, and, basing itself on the will of the people, took power on the 31st October after the Austrian garrison had been disarmed by Polish soldiers from the Austrian Army. At the end of October a Polish Commission of Liquidation was constituted in Galicia, and on the 31st October the Austrian garrison was disarmed in the old Polish capital, Cracow. A great part of Galicia was liberated from the Austrian troops, but not in the East where owing to the connivance of the Austrian Military Command the Ukrainians were able to seize a part of the city of Lwow and occupied important portions of territory, meeting stubborn resistance from the Polish population which led to heavy fighting for some months until the complete liberation of this province by Polish troops (see Part II).

The Austrian zone of occupation in the Congress Kingdom was also liberated from the Austrian troops in the first days of November, and on the 7th of that month a radical government was constituted in Lublin with the old socialist leader Daszynski at its head. From the beginning this government took a very hostile attitude towards the Regency Council.

Pilsudski, released by the Germans without any conditions (in the last weeks of his captivity they tried in vain to obtain from him some reassurances that he would not support the Polish claims to Danzig), arrived in Warsaw in the early morning of 10th November, and on the same day the population began to disarm the German troops. In order to avoid unnecessary bloodshed Pilsudski made an agreement with the German Soldiers' Council, by virtue of which all the Germans were allowed to leave the territory of the Congress Kingdom with their arms, which they were to surrender only at the frontier. This agreement was faithfully carried out by both parties, and on the 19th November the whole Congress Kingdom (except some small Eastern parts) was free from foreign occupation.

On the 14th November the Regency Council dissolved itself and handed over all power to Pilsudski who, after the dissolution of the Lublin Government, appointed his first government, mostly consisting of representatives of radical parties, with socialist Moraczewski as its leader (18th November).

The position of Pilsudski and his first government in relation to the Entente was very difficult and delicate. The Allied Governments maintained relations with the Polish National Committee in Paris and recognized it as the supreme political authority for the Polish Army in the West. The French Government had even recognized it as *de facto* Government. As a matter of fact Moraczewski's Government was never recognized by the Allied Powers, which means that until the constitution of Paderewski's Cabinet on the 16th January, 1919, there were no official relations between Poland and the Entente Powers, and, still more important, Poland was for some time left to her own devices in organizing the national defence.

Growth of the Polish Army

Much precious time was lost owing to this delay, but in spite of that Poland in that period laid the foundations of her system of defence, thanks to which she was able to survive and bring to a victorious end the war against Bolshevik Russia. According to a Polish writer :

> " One can say without exaggeration that the first stage of the organization of the Polish Armed Forces started in the first days of November, and lasting more or less until April 1919 was a great and splendid improvisation, particularly remarkable because done by its own forces. The assistance of the Allied Powers in supplies of war material came later, and still later the assistance in organization and training."

The same author gives a rough idea of the size of the effort :

On the 11th November, 1918, Poland had :

    24 infantry battalions

    3 cavalry squadrons

    5 batteries.

Two months later, that is to say in mid-January 1919, Poland had :

    100 infantry battalions

    70 cavalry squadrons

    80 batteries.

In mid-March 1919, that is to say two months later, after calling up six yearly contingents by the Constituent Assembly, the Polish Armed Forces already numbered 170,000 men, of which 80,000 were at the front.[40] Only this gigantic effort, made by a country ruined by war and long occupation, allowed Poland to play the rôle of an important factor at this critical time for all Europe. She was to be judged according to her achievements in this initial period, as appears from the following passage of the instruction for the Delegates of the Allied Powers in Poland, adopted by the Council of Ten on the 29th January, 1919 :

> " The Delegates should inquire how far the Polish Government possesses the means to maintain order within their existing territory and of preserving it from external aggression whether carried out

by Bolshevists or any other forces, and study and report on the measures necessary to supply any deficiencies which may be found to exist." [41]

For different reasons, in this first very important stage the Allies behaved more as observers, making their future assistance dependent on the achievements attained by the Poles by their own efforts.

On the other side, the building up of a strong Polish army, a necessary factor for Poland's security, aroused many unfavourable comments, especially among those who refused to see in Bolshevism a danger to international peace and did not believe that the Bolsheviks could present a serious danger to their neighbours. These initial illusions were shared also by President Wilson, who at the meeting of the Council of Ten on the 12th January said " that there was room for great doubt whether the advance of Bolshevism westwards could be checked by arms." [42] Poland had to create her army and expand her war potential at the moment when Western countries were eager.to disarm. Those who were little conversant with the true position in Central and Eastern Europe jumped to the conclusion that Poland was a militarist country, and they were joined by all those who disliked the prospect of a strong, that is really independent, Poland.

Rising in Poznan and the Allied intervention

A wave of patriotic feeling sweeping over all Poland within two months rendered obsolete another clause of the original Armistice Agreement. As we mentioned above, the French proposal relating to the evacuation by German troops of the former Polish provinces held by Prussia was not introduced into the terms of the Armistice. It created a strange and extremely painful position for the Polish population of those provinces which witnessed one Polish territory after another shaking off the foreign yoke while it had to endure servitude for an indefinite time, in any case much longer than had been anticipated even by the Western Powers at the time of signing the Armistice, when the final settlement seemed to be only a few weeks ahead.

As early as 15th October, 1918, that is to say even before the conclusion of the Armistice, the national claims of the so-called Prussian Poles were presented at the meeting of the Reichstag by the well-known Silesian leader W. Korfanty. The Polish deputies ceased to take part in the work of the Reichstag, declaring that they considered themselves already citizens of the Polish State. The Poles in Prussian Poland organized their own political representation, the Provincial Diet, which held its meetings in Poznan from 3rd to 6th December, 1918, having elected the Supreme People's Council as the highest Polish political authority in Prussian Poland, with the Commissariat in Poznan as its executive organ. The revolutionary outbreak in Germany had its repercussions also in Polish parts of Prussia owing to the presence there of numerous German units, but in the Soldiers' and Workers' Council in Poznan the Poles won the majority (its Praesidium in Poznan consisted of two Poles and one German).

Most of the political leaders in Prussian Poland belonged to the Right Wing and moderate parties and therefore they were much nearer to the Polish National Committee in Paris than to the Socialist Government under Moraczewski in Warsaw. Putting all their hopes in a prompt liberation from the Prussian yoke by virtue of a decision of the Peace Conference thanks to the endeavours of their friends in Paris, they were against any revolutionary move, advising their countrymen to preserve self-control and calm in spite of many German provocations. It should be observed that the German authorities did not facilitate such an attitude on the part of the Poles—the formation of special volunteer units such as Heimat-schutz-Ost, (renamed afterwards Grenzschutz), for the purpose of repressing all Polish separatist moves, the retaining of former soldiers of the German Army of Polish descent inside Germany, refusal to admit the Poles to the administrative bodies—all this created an atmosphere of growing tension between the Poles and Germans and forced the Poles to take measures of self-defence.

In these circumstances Paderewski's arrival in Poznan on 27th December on his way from England to Warsaw and the patriotic manifestations which followed it gave rise to the fighting between the German troops stationed in the city and the hastily organized Polish volunteers. It led to the liberation of Poznan and of a great part of the province.[43]

This uprising was quite spontaneous, as appears from the account given in the *History of the Paris Peace Conference* (ed. H. W Temperley), based on the information of members of the British Military Mission which accompanied Paderewski on his journey to Poland :

> "The occasion provoked patriotic demonstrations on the part of the Polish-speaking inhabitants, which led to reprisal by the Prussian troops stationed in Posen. As the General commanding the German troops had declared that he had lost control over them, order was restored by the National Guard of Posen with the aid of volunteer Polish formations." [44]

The Poznan rising was a revolt by the younger generation, more impatient than their elders to put an end to the German occupation and unwilling any longer to endure the numerous German provocations.

The tension between the Polish majority and the German minority, enjoying all the old privileges of a ruling class and the protection of the Prussian administration, reached breaking point, and no one could have stopped it. The spontaneous character of the rising appears also from the fact that the Warsaw Government was not able to give any substantial support to this movement as it had very small forces at its disposal and these were fully engaged in defensive fighting in Eastern Galicia, occupying the Eastern outskirts of the Congress Kingdom and maintaining order in a country passing through a hectic period. It was left to the natives of this Polish province to fight alone and unaided by their countrymen from other parts of Poland (apart from some volunteers). Temperley's account confirms this fact : " These forces were drawn from the Prussian Poles alone, not from the Russian or Austrian Poles, so that the question of Polish interference from outside did not arise."

But even after the Poznan events the Polish leader Korfanty declared to the German representatives on the 30th December :

> " We do not wish to forestall the decisions of the Peace Conference. We request what is due to us on the ground of equality of rights—that is to say participation in the administration of the country and judicature. . . . Now you have to face the facts. If you do not reach an understanding with us you must use your imagination and think about such problems as food supplies. Think about what might happen in Upper Silesia. One word would suffice and all the mines would be at a standstill. . . . It would not be beneath the dignity of the German State if it recognized the equality of rights of the Poles. . . . "

In spite of these very moderate demands and the position of the Germans being considerably weakened in view of the spread of the Polish movement for liberation, in spite of the support given to these demands by the local German Volksrat, warlike trends prevailed at the joint meeting of the German and Prussian Cabinets on the 2nd January, 1919, under the influence of the Socialist leader Noske, and in these circumstances the continuation of the Polish-German fighting became unavoidable.

The liberation of Poznan and a great part of that province as well as maintaining the front line was a remarkable achievement because of the presence there of many German units returning from the East. The Poles were able, however, to withstand the pressure of numerous German forces pouring in from other parts of Germany (German Great Headquarters were moved for this purpose from Kreuznach to Kolobrzeg (Kolberg) in Pomerania, and the headquarters of the Fifth Army Corps were established in Frankfurt-on-Oder). The fighting revealed fully the weakness of the German element in that part of Poland, and also the extent of the demoralization of the German army.

There is no doubt that the Poznan rising caused great embarrassment to the Great Powers, as the Supreme Council saw in it a direct challenge to its authority. Nevertheless in the long run they could not deny to the Poles in Prussian Poland the same rights as had been recognized in other parts of Poland.

As we have said above (p. 235), it was Foch who at the meeting of the Council of Ten on 12th January insisted on the urgency of the settlement of the question of the Western frontiers of Poland. The Polish question was further discussed at the meeting of the Council on 22nd January, at which it was decided to send an Allied Commission to Poland under the chairmanship of Ambassador Noulens. In the course of the discussion suggestions were made that the Poles should confine their activities to resisting the Bolsheviks (Marshal Foch, Sonnino). At the meeting on 23rd January Clemenceau declared that " the Allies would always be considered the supporters of Poland but that they could not at the same time support the Poles in breaking Germany and ask the Germans to disarm." Moreover, the Council seeing its authority challenged, transmitted to all parts of the world a communication in which it drew attention to " many instances in which armed force is being made use of, in many parts of Europe and the East, to gain possession of territory, the rightful claim to which the Peace Conference is to be asked to determine," and issued the " solemn warning that possession gained by force will seriously prejudice the claims of those who use such means." [45] When the question arose of sending troops and arms through Danzig to Poland, Lloyd George showed his strong anti-Polish bias. Although stating that " we do not know enough about the facts of the situation in Poland," he nevertheless added that he

> " could not see any great difference between conveying armed men and conveying arms over the Danzig-Torun railway. We could not expect the Germans to allow arms to go through if they were to equip a Polish army to attack them. This would be asking more than was laid down in the Armistice. Fairness was due even to the enemy. He was not prepared at the present moment to make any declaration concerning the rights to Posen (Poznan) which the Poles were attempting to conquer by force and thereby to prejudge what the Congress was assembled to do." [46]

Nevertheless it was impossible for the Allies to maintain a passive attitude for a long time, and very soon wiser counsels prevailed when the facts became better known thanks to reports coming from the

Allied Commission sent to Poland. Let us note, by the way, that it was the British representative, Mr. Balfour, who at the meeting of the Council of Ten on 22nd February was the first to propose " the sending of (Polish) troops to Poland " in view " of very strong recommendations which had been received on this subject from the British members of the Allied Commission in Poland." [47] The continuing fighting between Poles and Germans in Poznan province induced the Supreme Council at its meeting on the 7th February, 1919, to reconsider the whole question when the third renewal of the Armistice Agreement became topical, especially as while the Poles abstained from any further aggressive actions the Germans refused to comply with the injunctions of the Allied authorities. Clemenceau raised this issue before the Council, observing that

> " the Poles had stopped the further advance of their troops at the request of the Allies, but the Germans had treated a similar request with a blank refusal." . . . " The Allies would be exposed to a great danger unless they menaced the Germans now. There was need of a strong Poland. Furthermore President Wilson had, as one of his fourteen points, assumed the obligation of reconstituting Poland. The League of Nations was a very fine conception, but it could not be constituted without nations. As one of the nations concerned, Poland was most necessary as a buffer on the East, just as France formed a buffer on the West. If the Germans were formally told that any attack by them on the East would mean an advance by the Allies on the West, he knew that such language would be understood by the Germans and would command immediate compliance." [48]

In the outcome of this discussion Marshal Foch was authorized to send the respective orders. General Nudant, of the Allied Armistice Commission, was informed that :

> " The Marshal is communicating to the German authorities in German Poland the injunction of the Associated Powers that they should henceforward abstain from any use of force in that province and from interference in its public life pending the completion of the Peace Conference." [49]

The Allied note on the renewal of armistice of 14th February emphasized that the Allies were decided to tolerate no longer the concentration of German forces against the Poles in Poznan as well as the further actions of the Poles, and demanded that the Germans should stop all operations against the Poles and not pass the line marked on a map enclosed with the note.[50] At the meeting of the Armistice Commission on 14th February Erzberger raised a strong protest against the Allied demand, calling the Polish action " an invasion of parts of the German Empire" and qualifying as "exorbitant" the Allied demand that the German authorities should refrain from interference in the public life of the former Polish provinces held by Prussia. There is no doubt, however, that the Germans, being well aware of the weakness of their position in Prussian Poland, took into account the loss, if not of all, at least of a great part of their Polish possessions in the event of a defeat. This appears clearly from all their reactions to Wilson's declarations.

In the *Memoirs of Prince Max of Baden,* Chancellor of the Reich at the time of the Armistice, we find indisputable proof that the implications of acceptance of Wilson's programme were well understood by the German statesmen, and only the German war leaders refused to bow to the facts :

> " The Supreme Command had probably no clear idea at first as to the fateful conditions to which the Fourteen Points must in any case commit Germany. They probably saw in Wilson's programme a mere collection of phrases which a skilful diplomacy would be able to interpret at the conference table in a sense favourable to Germany. I had put them the question whether the Supreme Command was aware that the course they were entering upon might lead to the loss of colonies and even of German soil—in particular of Alsace-Lorraine and of the *purely-Polish* districts of our Eastern provinces. I received an evasive reply: ' The Supreme Command is ready to consider the cession of some small French-speaking parts of Alsace-Lorraine, if that is unavoidable. The cession of German territory on the Eastern frontier is for them out of the question.' " [51]

Stresemann also foresaw the consequences of acceptance of the Wilsonian programme, as clearly appears from his letter to a friend, Dr. Friedberg, on the 26th February, 1918 :

> " As far as I can see, Wilson's Fourteen Points already present the possibility of the loss of Alsace-Lorraine, Upper Silesia, Posen and parts of West Prussia. . . . The loss of the ironworks in Alsace-Lorraine and the coal mines in Upper Silesia would strike at the very vitals of our economic system." [52]

The lack of any provisions relating to Poland in the Armistice conditions, and the postponement of all territorial issues until the Peace Conference, jointly with the maintenance of the *status quo* in Eastern Germany, while Alsace-Lorraine was evacuated by the Germans immediately, stiffened German resistance to the Polish claims for the restitution of the territories once torn from Poland and eventually made the severance of these territories from the Reich a much more painful operation for German national pride than might have been the case if a clear position had been created in respect of these provinces by the terms of the Armistice.

In the above-mentioned speech of Erzberger at the meeting of the Armistice Commission on the 14th February we find a curious interpretation of the Wilsonian doctrine adapted to German national interests :

> " The German people cannot and will not admit that it might be deprived of the right to defend itself with all means at its disposal against impudent (*frech*) encroachments of the Poles upon its own territory. Germany has accepted Wilson's Fourteen Points, but so did the Allies. Point XIII does not state, however, that Germany made an undertaking to stand by while the Poles try to tear off portions of the German territory. Point XIII does not, either, give the right to the Allies to forbid the German people to repel such encroachments. *The right of the German people to the intact preservation of its unity within the framework of the Wilsonian Points* as well as to repulse all attacks against this unity remains eternal and inviolable."

Foch was obliged to issue an ultimatum to the Germans and they were eventually forced to sign the Convention of the 16th February at Trier on the suspension of hostilities. Nevertheless the Germans obtained important satisfaction in the final terms of the Convention, as it left Upper Silesia outside the demarcation line and secured to the Germans temporary possession of some places in which the military position was still unsettled.[53] After the signing of the Convention of 16th February an agreement was signed in Poznan in March between the Allied and German delegations, assuring the protection of the Poles in some provinces of Germany and of Germans in Poznan province.[54] This agreement remained in force until the ratification of the Peace Treaty. The German accusations that the Poznan rising was due to Allied instigation and encouragement lack any foundation and cannot be supported by serious evidence.[55] On the contrary the Germans themselves admit that in the course of the second renewal of the Armistice Convention on the 16th January the attitude of the Allies remained passive.[56] The successful outcome of the Poznan rising, that spontaneous move by the Polish population, the increasing German aggressiveness and lack of any spirit of compromise on the German side eventually induced the Allies to intervene and impose the suspension of hostilities. It is of course a matter for regret that many lives had to be sacrificed in stubborn fighting between Poles and Germans after the conclusion of a general armistice, as it could have been prevented if the Entente Powers had shown more foresight at the end of the war and taken the necessary measures to give satisfaction to the natural urge of an oppressed nation to begin as soon as possible the new life. Leaving without protection the native population in the disputable area the Entente Powers to a great extent assumed responsibility for the outbreak of the rising, in that much more time had to elapse before the fate of this area was decided at the conference table than had originally been assumed.

Political developments in Poland until the constitution of Paderewski's Cabinet

The difficult international position of Poland in the early months of her independence was due not only to the unsatisfactory terms of the Armistice Agreement, the lack of any programme on the Allied part relating to Eastern Europe, and to external dangers from West and East menacing the very existence of the young republic, but also to the fact that, surprised by the turn of events in Poland after the Armistice and the emergence of a radical government in Warsaw, the Allies for more than two months avoided any official contacts with that government. Being unable to agree on a common policy towards the Warsaw Government, the Entente Powers left Poland to her own devices in the most difficult initial period of her existence, although they were well aware of the worsening of the political situation of Eastern Europe due to the quick withdrawal of the German forces and the progress of the Bolshevik invasion. On his return from German captivity Pilsudski found the country at boiling point; on the one side there was the Regency Council in Warsaw and the radical government in Lublin, presided over by the old Socialist leader Daszynski, displaying a very advanced social programme and claiming all power for the parties of the Left. Pilsudski's authority ranked so high at that moment that he was able to liquidate this duality of power within a few days : the Regency Council tendered its resignation and transmitted all its powers to Pilsudski, while the Lublin Government agreed to submit itself to Pilsudski and dissolved itself. Pilsudski could have become dictator at that moment, but he preferred to solve the crisis in a democratic way. He tried to form a coalition Government under Daszynski, but neither Right nor Left showed any inclination to compromise. Being obliged to take into account popular passions, Pilsudski eventually appointed a government under another Socialist leader, Moraczewski, his close friend, with socialists, radical intelligentsia and peasants playing a prominent part in it. Such a government was most certainly a necessary stage at the beginning, as even one of its most resolute adversaries, Dmowski, recognized it, stating at the meeting of the Council of Ten on the 29th January, 1919 : " The National Council felt that a Socialist Government situated between two extreme socialist governments was necessary for the safety of Poland at the time." [57]

Moraczewski's Government was far from being fully representative; one may even say, in the light of subsequent elections, that it was a government of a minority, but it was nevertheless a government professing truly democratic principles and ready to stand the test of parliamentary elections. On the 28th November, 1918, it issued a decree introducing a democratic electoral law (the franchise was to be equal and direct; to include both sexes, the voting age being fixed at 21; to be secret, and based on the system of proportional representation). [58] Pilsudski himself in many declarations emphasized that he wished to leave all the decisions on the future policy of the country entirely to the future Diet. Receiving a delegation of the Polish Socialist Party and of the Peasant Party on the 8th December, 1918, he said :

> " My most important task at this moment is the calling of the Diet. Every group now claims that it possesses the majority. Only the Diet will clarify this position and state where is the majority and what this majority desires. I have decided to submit myself and the army to the will of the nation as expressed by the Diet." [59]

Both Pilsudski and Moraczewski kept their pledges and completely free elections were held on the 26th January, 1919. At the third meeting of the Diet Pilsudski made the following declaration :

> " Amid great upheavals, at a time when millions of men settle all issues by violence and force, I maintained the view that in our country the necessary and unavoidable social disputes should be solved in a democratic way—that is to say by the representatives of the people elected to enact laws. I tried to attain this aim as quickly as possible." [60]

The accusations spread by the adversaries of Moraczewski's government, both at home and abroad, alleging that it was infected by Bolshevik influences or had a pro-German bias, were absolutely unwarranted, although its approach to some problems of domestic and foreign policy was unquestionably different from that of the National Committee in Paris.

The foreign policy programme of that Government was imbued with noble idealism and the sincere belief that all international disputes could be solved in a peaceful manner by mutual understanding between democratic peoples without any outside interference. It proclaimed that " the democracies of Poland, Lithuania, Byelorussia, the Ukraine, Bohemia, Slovakia, Hungary and Germany will find a common basis for establishing the conditions of co-existence of free and equal peoples." The organ of the Polish

Socialist Party, *Robotnik* (*The Worker*), in an article of the 20th December, 1918, assured that " a realistic policy consists in a movement towards a union of nations—although such a policy would be carried out completely and with all guarantees only by Socialist republics."

It must be observed on the other side that Moraczewski's Government took the first diplomatic steps to defend the Polish population in the Eastern provinces of Poland invaded by the Red Army (see the exchange of correspondence with the Soviet Government in this matter in Part II, Chapter IV, of this book), and showed full understanding of the need to build up quickly the Polish armed forces under Pilsudski's command, being in full agreement with the Chief of State on this point.

A more controversial question might seem that of the admission of a German representative, Count Harry Kessler, who came unasked to Warsaw on an extraordinary mission on the 19th November. The presence of this diplomat in the Polish capital naturally roused some bitter criticism amongst many Poles and in the Entente countries. One must bear in mind, however, that the Polish Government was in an awkward position, as it had to negotiate with a qualified German representative the question of evacuating German troops from the East in such a way that they might bypass the Congress Kingdom. Poland was not protected by any clause of the Armistice, and she might have been overrun and reduced to famine by these big withdrawing armies. An agreement was reached with Count Kessler on this point, but he was eventually obliged to leave Warsaw on the 16th December (his whole mission lasting less than a month) as his presence in Warsaw could no longer be tolerated by Polish public opinion.[61] Thus Poland fell into step with the general Allied policy. There is no doubt that in sending this diplomat to Warsaw, Germany had some more far-reaching scheme in mind than simply the negotiating of the question of withdrawing German troops from the East, a question in which Poland was more interested than Germany. She wanted above all to create the impression abroad that under Moraczewski's Government Poland pursued a policy of neutrality, as in such a case there would be no title for Poland to participate in the Peace Conference. On this point some German writers tried to see a capital difference between two trends of Polish public opinion, alleging that the Left was inclined to neutrality.[62] This assertion can easily be refuted, because Moraczewski's Government, by its Decree of the 29th November, 1918, proclaimed that the elections should take place in all Polish territories including those held by Germany. This provision could not, of course, be materialized before the ratification of the Peace Treaty.

Count Harry Kessler seemed particularly suitable for the schemes pursued at that time by Germany. It was he who liberated Pilsudski (together with his Chief of Staff, then Colonel K. Sosnkowski), from Magdeburg prison in November 1918. Before that he paid a visit to Pilsudski in prison, in October 1918, and tried to put some conditions for his liberation, namely an undertaking not to fight against Germany and the limitation of the Polish territorial claims. At that time Kessler realized that Prussia could no longer avoid the loss of Poznania, but he emphasized to Pilsudski that Prussia would never give up Danzig. Pilsudski flatly refused to bind himself, saying that so long as he remained in prison he could not accept any condition and that in any case Poland would always be ready to accept what might be given to her.[63] Owing to the outbreak of revolution in Germany Pilsudski was released without any condition, but it was Count Kessler who served as intermediary. In an interview published by a French newspaper, *Le Petit Parisien,* on the 16th March, 1919, Pilsudski himself stated, in reply to the question : " Why has von Kessler liberated you? ":

> " I knew him personally and had some contact with him when I commanded the Legion (on the Volhynian front when von Kessler served as a German liaison officer). He knew that the revolution would liberate me and he wished to create the impression that he rendered me a service ; he thought, without any doubt, to discredit me in the eyes of the Entente and to obliterate the memory of my staying in a German prison for two years." [64]

Although his mission in Warsaw had failed, Kessler was used later by the German Government as a propagandist, to spread various fantastic stories about Pilsudski, abusing the credulity of the Anglo-Saxon public. In his lectures in America, published in 1923, he asserted that the purpose of his mission was to reach an agreement with Poland on the internationalization of the Vistula, and he alleged that Pilsudski sympathized with such schemes. Here is the core of the proposals which according to Kessler were submitted to the Polish Government at that time :

> " This is what I myself, who was at the time German Minister to Poland, was prepared on the instructions of my Government to propose or to accept. A right of way on land, coupled with a railway neutralized and guaranteed by international agreement and a port on the Baltic next to Danzig under Polish sovereignty, could have completed the arrangement and given Poland a perfectly free and direct access to the sea." [65]

The assertion that Pilsudski was ready to agree to such proposals does not rest on any historical evidence, and we have to quote only his interview published in a Paris newspaper, *Le Matin*, on the 19th February, 1919 :

> " An extraordinary thing is occurring at present: a tiny army fights victoriously on three fronts. But if one says to these soldiers: ' The Vistula will not belong to you completely, your enemies will for ever have her mouths and you will for ever be subjugated and surrounded by your enemies,' these men fighting with such heroism may lose the courage to endure." [66]

The tragedy of Moraczewski's Government lay in the fact that it could not count on any substantial support abroad. The Western Governments were at that time dominated by the parties of the Right, and this applies in particular to the Clemenceau Government in France. They were faced by labour unrests and the opposition of socialist parties in their own parliaments. They considered the social programme of Moraczewski's Government much too advanced, and saw some analogy between it and Kerensky's Government in Russia before the outbreak of the Bolshevik revolution. The illusions cherished by Polish radicals that they might win the sympathy of the democratic West without coming to terms with the National Committee in Paris were quickly dispelled owing to the adamant policy of the French Government. Nor could they find partners among the German socialists for a policy of peaceful settlement of territorial disputes dividing the two neighbouring countries. The German socialists were following the lead of the German militarists so far as the question of relations with Poland was concerned. It suffices to quote an article published by the main socialist organ, *Vorwärts*, regarding the outbreak of the Poznan rising : " It is about time " [wrote *Vorwärts* at the beginning of January 1919] " to advance to the East purely German troops, sufficiently strong. Their mission should consist not only in containing the Poles but also in disarming and disbanding their organizations." [67]

It would be a great mistake to identify Pilsudski himself with the government appointed by him, although this consisted of his old friends and associates. Pilsudski's approach to international politics was much more realistic than that of his government, he was well aware of its shortcomings and limitations and he understood what many of his partisans refused to see: that a compromise with the National Committee was unavoidable owing to the insufficient support given to the government by public opinion all over Poland, and the position taken by the Western Powers, France in particular, giving full backing to the Paris Committee. There are two major reasons why a compromise between the two wings of Polish public opinion was urgent and could not be postponed until after the elections to the Diet : the Peace Conference was to meet at the beginning of January, and it was necessary to present a united diplomatic front at that Conference, and secondly, owing to the quick withdrawal of the German forces and the advance of the Bolshevik forces, developments in the East were taking a dramatic turn and quick Allied assistance for building up the defensive system and for the economic rehabilitation of the country could no longer be delayed. So far as the first question was concerned, it was obvious that only the Paris Committee, enjoying the full support of the French Government, could negotiate a satisfactory solution of the problem of Poland's Western frontiers. There remained, of course, big differences between Pilsudski's views and those of the Committee, and above all on the problem of the future organization of Central and Eastern Europe, but it was an issue which Pilsudski considered could hardly be solved by the diplomats in Paris. Pilsudski did not believe that the Entente would be able to agree in Paris on a common programme in relation to the problems of Eastern Europe. In his opinion these issues could be solved only by Poland's own efforts. Nor did he wish for direct intervention by the Allies using Polish soil. He expressed this point of view in his first telegram to Foch on the 16th November, 1918 :

" Basing myself on the Polish Army under my command, I hope that from now on no foreign army may enter Poland before we have expressed our formal wish."

Pilsudski's point of view was well summed up by M. Sokolnicki, one of his envoys to Paris (subsequently Secretary-General of the Polish Delegation at the Peace Conference), in a conversation with the American Chargé d'Affaires in Paris, Mr. Dawson, on the 23rd January :

> " There is no question of an intervention in Poland ; even less is the question to provoke an Allied intervention in Russia ; Poland does not ask that the forces of the Entente take her place in the defence of her frontiers. All that we demand, and we demand it from all, is to help Poland to defend herself and to defend Lithuania against the Bolshevik invasion ; our army defends itself vigorously and stubbornly, but it does not suffice on account of simultaneous actions by the enemy in Poland, in the South and in the East. The assistance of the Allied Powers should consist in: (1) sending the Haller army (from France) ; (2) sending munitions, arms, equipment and rolling stock ; (3) limited military contingents." [68]

So far as the policy of the Entente towards the constitutional developments in Poland was concerned, there had been from the beginning some difference between the rigid attitude of the French

Government and the more flexible attitude of the other Allies, but the fact is, for more than two months there were no official relations between the Warsaw Government and the Allied Governments.

In the notes sent by the French Government on the 15th November, 1918, to the other Allied Governments a demand was put forward to recognize the Paris National Committee as a *de facto* Government in questions relating to foreign policy, to the political direction of the Polish Army and to the civil protection of Polish nationals abroad. In the view of the French Government such recognition seemed necessary " in the interests of the Poles and ourselves to strengthen the parties of order " [69] and in order to strengthen the position of the National Committee which " would create a central organization around which some elements in the country favourable to the Allies could group themselves." [70] Thus the French Government took sides in the political struggle in Poland, which could be decided only by the Poles themselves. Moreover, it was hardly necessary to group in Poland the " elements favourable to the Entente." A more reasonable attitude was taken at that time by the prominent French paper *Le Temps*, which devoted many editorials to this question. So for instance, it stated on 28th December :

> " There are at present two Polish governments: one which cannot go out of its country, the other which cannot enter it.
> " . . . French diplomacy boasts of working for a reconciliation. But if one wishes to play the part of mediator one must keep the balance between the different camps. Are we doing so? ... For such a purpose it would be necessary to listen to two sources of information. What really happened? While the members of the National Committee have daily access to the Quai d'Orsay, France has not sent any diplomatic representative to Warsaw. ... Should we enter into the merits of the question, in order that the French public may choose between the policy embodied by General Pilsudski and that represented by the National Committee? We do not desire such discussion because we do not think it would be proper to intervene in the internal affairs of Poland. ... "

The point of view defended by the French Government, which amounted to an attempt to impose on Poland an emigré government, was not shared by other Governments. The British Government was the first to refuse to comply with the French request, and replying to the French note on the 30th November stated, among other things, that :

> " H.M. Government entirely share the opinion expressed by M. Pichon as to the fidelity of the Polish National Committee to the

Allied cause, and ever since the constitution of that body H.M. Government have consistently supported them in their work.

" The present suggestion, however, appears to H.M. Government to attribute to the Polish National Committee functions which are in reality those of a Government of a recognized independent State. They therefore feel that it would be premature at the present moment, and until more precise information as to the political situation in Poland is available, to accord to the Polish National Committee the formal measure of recognition which they now seek. Such a step might risk the definite alienation of general opinion in Poland whose wishes have never reached the Allied Governments in any substantial form."

The refusal of the British Government to accede to the French demand to grant to the National Committee the status of a *de facto* government upset the plans devised at the Quai d'Orsay jointly with that Committee. The latter was induced to send its representative, Mr. S. Grabski, to Warsaw, where he arrived on the 4th December. The conversations between Pilsudski and Grabski served to establish the community of views on many political problems. Pilsudski was quite prepared to recognize the National Committee as a diplomatic representation of Poland to the Allied Governments, seeing in this obvious advantages for the attainment of the aims on Poland's Western frontier. Nor did the problem of the Eastern frontiers present insuperable difficulties, although Pilsudski wished to extend even further than did the National Committee the Polish influence in the East, and did not like the idea of dividing the former Polish-Lithuanian provinces between Poland and Russia. However, both parties were in agreement on the necessity for checking the advance of the Red Army.

Nevertheless there remained a grave constitutional issue : the formation of a coalition government; unfortunately no satisfactory solution could be found at that time. Pilsudski proposed the formation of a Cabinet composed of non-party men, specialists in different branches of administration, while Grabski insisted on the parties represented in the National Committee sharing the governmental responsibilities. Pilsudski was unable to accede to this demand, as passions ran very high in the country and he was afraid of provoking social troubles.[71] Moreover, the parties of the left flatly refused this. Only the formation of Paderewski's Government brought an end to these differences.

The French Government adopted as its own the request of the National Committee to assign to the parties represented in it a share in a coalition government in Warsaw, and refused to have any official contacts with the delegation sent by Pilsudski in his capacity as Chief of State, which arrived in Paris on 4th January. M. Pichon, Minister for Foreign Affairs, refused to receive the delegation so long as no agreement had been reached between it and the National Committee.

A considerable part of French public opinion saw great danger in the policy followed in Polish matters by the Government from the point of view of Allied policy in Eastern Europe. Such preoccupations were particularly alive in those quarters which advised a vigorous policy in Eastern Europe.

We find very characteristic remarks on this point in an editorial in *Le Temps* on 26th December :

> " The Armistice was signed on the 11th November. To-day it is the 25th December. How does it happen that the Polish troops from the Western Front have not yet left for Danzig? They are for the Allies an instrument ready to use. Poland is a base ready for Allied policy. Why do we wait? "

Similar views were expressed in the debates at the Chambre des Députés on 29th December,[72] by M. Franklin-Bouillon. He said that the French Government had no definite policy in Russia, nor had the Allies, which by the way should not serve as an excuse for the French Government, France being particularly interested in the problems of Eastern Europe. He put the question whether France should strive for the reconstitution of a united Russia or of a federated one, and strongly advised supporting the nationalities of Russia struggling for liberation.

> " Without mentioning Finland and Poland " [he declared], " there are Esthonians, Latvians, Lithuanians and Ukrainians who should be supported and organised. They could become a most solid barrier against Germany and at the same time be centres of action for the purpose of reviving Russia proper. But this double action should be taken simultaneously, otherwise all our efforts are bound to be futile. . . .
>
> " It is not properly understood that the most efficient means in the struggle against Bolshevism in Russia is to foster the national feelings, particularly of the alien nationalities. There are forces offering themselves to us and which we allow to disintegrate."

He severely criticized the reactionary spirit of the French Foreign Office " which pretends to have the exclusive right to deal with the problems of foreign policy."

Still more violent was a representative of the Socialist Party, M. Ernest Lafont, who stated that " the French policy both in Russian and Polish matters was distorted by the personal likings, or rather ignorance, of those officials who had charge of supplying the

Minister of Foreign Affairs with information." Taking his bearings from the opinions of Polish radicals on the National Committee in Paris, he criticized the " reactionary " officials at the Quai d'Orsay grouped around M. Berthelot, de Margerie and Kammerer, who listened to the members of the National Committee and White Russians.

The reply of M. Pichon, French Foreign Minister, contained many inaccurate statements. He declared that the National Committee had been recognized as a " regular Polish Government " not only by France but also by Great Britain, Japan, the United States and Italy, which was untrue. He further said that the arrival of the Delegation sent by Pilsudski was " provoked " by the French Government, which also did not agree with the facts. Replying to M. Lafont, he declared emphatically that it would be up to the Government constituted by the National Committee to bring Poland to life again as a necessary counterweight to Germany.

The Socialists' undisguised hostility to the National Committee and the biased attitude of M. Pichon towards Pilsudski personally and towards the Warsaw Government characterized these passionate debates, which served no useful purpose. Neither party had full information about the developments in Poland, and had to rely on that supplied by Polish friends, so it would be mistaken to take at face value anything that was said in the House about the internal situation of Poland. The French Government stuck to its point of view in relation to Warsaw until the formation of Paderewski's Government. On the eve of Paderewski's appointment as Prime Minister of Poland the French Government sent a note *to the National Committee* asking it to designate two delegates to the Peace Conference,[78] thus trying to eliminate from that Conference the government installed in Poland. There is no doubt that the rigid attitude of the French Government towards Warsaw was not dictated by purely personal considerations but depended on the line of policy adopted in matters concerning Eastern Europe. In France at that time many hopes were put in bold schemes for intervention in Southern Russia, and Foch was preparing grandiose plans for sending an expeditionary corps to Poland and Rumania for that purpose. The Haller Army, remaining under Allied command was assigned a considerable part in these plans, and France was not willing to pass it over to the Warsaw Government. We shall deal more amply with these matters in the second part of this book. For the time being let us state that in these circumstances France would have much preferred to have in Poland a government which in her opinion might have been much more amenable to her policy. Knowing the hostility of their own Socialists to the plans, which were based on collaboration with the White Russians, the French Government were not disposed to collaborate with Socialists in Warsaw. Pilsudski himself was distrusted on account of his revolutionary past and the part he had played in the struggle against Russia. But it was with Pilsudski that France eventually had to collaborate, and from this point of view M. Lafont was right in saying in the Chamber of Deputies : " I confess that I am unable to understand the stubborn hostility of the French Foreign Minister towards the Polish Government, which he will be forced to recognize to-morrow: they are the utterances of a polemist but not the statements of a member of the Government."

An agreement was eventually reached between Pilsudski and Paderewski in spite of all the psychological and social obstacles, and the country went to the polls without any disturbances. The French interference in Polish domestic policy greatly contributed, nevertheless, to the initial confusion. If France wished to play the part of a conciliator, she should have appointed at the beginning a diplomatic representative in Warsaw, as was suggested on many sides.

We find confirmation for our assumptions regarding the ends pursued by France in Poland at that time in the fact that it was Ambassador Noulens, who had just left Russia, who was designated Chairman of the Allied Commission in Poland, sent to that country by virtue of the decision of the Supreme Council of 22nd January. M. Noulens, on leaving Archangel at the end of December, 1918, declared to press representatives that he considered himself only on leave and that he intended to follow his mission in other places.[74] So France was sending to Poland the most fervid partisan of Allied intervention in Russia.

Following the example of the British, the American Government refused to commit itself to a definite line of policy in the matter of recognizing either the National Committee in Paris or Pilsudski's Government in Warsaw.[75] We find some interesting views of an observer of that Government on the situation in Poland in a memorandum written by an American expert, Major Julian C. Coolidge, on the 11th December, 1918 :

"The first Polish division in France is a well-organized unit under the command of the capable French General Vidalon. ... Such a division may be of great value in maintaining order in Poland, but the question is beset with political difficulties. ... *De facto* Government of Poland is that of Pilsudski. ... On the other hand, is the Polish National Committee recognized by the Allied Governments as the basis for the constitution of the future Polish State ... It is recognized by all intelligent Poles that unless unity of action can be found the Peace Conference will deem Poland incapable of self-government and will be little disposed to aid the Polish cause, but it is easier to approve of unity in theory than to carry it out in practice. ... If the first Polish Division is going to Poland, shall it go as a Polish or an Allied Army? ... The question of sending this Polish Division to Poland cannot be separated from that of the transfer of the Polish National Committee to that country. ... If the soldiers go before the National Committee, they are cut off from the authority upon which they depend. ... If the National Committee goes before ... they are without reliable backing. ... If the National Committee and the troops go at the same time there is danger that it will seem as though the Committee were entering the country accompanied by an armed force in order to suppress their political rivals." [76]

At that time many reports on the situation in Poland were reaching the State Department in Washington. One of these reports, written by Mr. A. W. Dulles from Berne and dated 30th December, gives a fairly exact picture, although it does not take sufficiently into account the personal influence of Pilsudski, thanks to which the political crisis in Poland was eventually solved without provoking any major social unrest :

" The Pilsudski Government has, up to the present, succeeded in maintaining the support of the Socialist elements (which appear to-day to be all powerful in Poland) without, however, committing itself to radical socialism or Bolshevism. Much as Pilsudski personally would like to reach an agreement with Dmowski and the National Democrats, he is unable to do it in view of the socialist opposition, as it would cost him his position in case the socialists would charge him with negotiations with either Dmowski or the National Democrats, whom the Polish socialists regard as reactionary and imperialistic." [77]

The imminent opening of the Peace Conference was unquestionably one of the incentives to those Poles who realized the necessity for a political truce in Poland in order to present a united political front. Pilsudski sent a letter dated 21st December to Dmowski (delivered by his delegates in Paris on 6th January) in which he said among other things : " Believe me that I wish above all to avoid Poland being represented by two different missions to the Allied Governments; only one representation can secure the acceptance of our requests." [78] How imperative was this truce appears clearly from the following passage of the " Skeleton Draft of the Peace Treaty," presented by technical advisers to the American Commission to Negotiate Peace :

" The existence of a Polish State is certain to be recognized by the Peace Conference. The only difficulty in including Poland among the signatories to the Treaty of Peace will arise out of the disturbed political situation among the Poles. It may be necessary to insist that the various political parties in Poland should take part in a choice of the representatives who will bind the new State by executing the Treaty of Peace." [79]

Eventually the truce came about, and it was due to the collaboration of two men : I. Paderewski and J. Pilsudski, Chief of State, who held in his hands the ultimate decision on the change of administration. Paderewski's arrival in Poland precipitated the solution of the political crisis in Poland. Being extremely popular throughout Poland, known as a man of great integrity and ardent advocate of the Polish cause in the United States during the War, he was unquestionably the most suitable candidate at that time for the post of Prime Minister of Poland, whatever one might think about his gifts as administrator and political leader.

It is worthy of note that his journey to Poland was due to British initiative, as he left Paris after having received a suggestion made by that Government in a telegram sent from London, a British plane was put at his disposal and he eventually made the voyage in a British cruiser, *Condor*. He was accompanied by Colonel Wade, head of the British Mission to Poland (the first official Allied Mission to Poland, closely followed by the American one). He arrived in Danzig on 25th December, and passed through Poznan where his arrival started big patriotic manifestations followed by German reprisals, which as we have said provoked the Poznan rising, leading to the liberation of a great part of Poznania.

On arrival in Warsaw he took a very critical view of Moraczewski's Government. Having stayed outside the country for a long time and collaborated with the parties of the Right in the National Committee, he was obviously prejudiced against the radical movement in Poland and was prone to exaggerate the influence of Bolshevism on the parties of the Left in the home country. Moreover, at the beginning he took a rather casual view of the efforts made by the Government in the matter of national defence and, underestimating Poland's potentialities, believed that Poland would perish without direct armed assistance from the Allies. Only gradually did his views evolve, as may appear from various telegrams sent to Paris.

On 4th January, that is immediately after his arrival in Warsaw, he sent a telegram to Colonel House in which he described the situation in Poland in extremely sombre colours :

"Situation most critical. Bolshevik invasion of former Polish territory still in progress. . . . Vilno, Minsk, even Grodno menaced.

... Present Polish Government too weak to organize any resistance; human material still considerable, but no arms, equipment, munitions. Disaster imminent. At this tragic hour my country appeals to her best, most generous friends asking for help, for salvation. 50,000 Americans, one division of French and one of British troops if sent immediately with necessary material for a large Polish army will certainly stop further progress of this barbarous movement. If action is delayed our entire civilization may cease to exist. The war may result in establishment of barbarism all over Europe." [80]

The influence on Paderewski of the opinions prevailing at that time within the National Committee in Paris is particularly striking in this telegram. This point of view gradually changed after conversations with Pilsudski, and in the next telegram to House Paderewski asked only for arms, munitions, food and uniforms to be sent, and he no longer insisted on the sending of Allied contingents. His negative attitude to Moraczewski's Government did not change, however, as appears from the telegram of the 12th January, 1919, to House :

"We have no food, no uniforms, no munitions. We have but men, at best 500,000, willing to fight to defend the country under a strong government. The present government is weak and dangerous, it is almost exclusively radical-socialist." [81]

At a meeting of the Council of Ten on 22nd January, President Wilson, mentioning this letter from Paderewski, added that the latter " only suggested that the Allies should supply him with weapons." [82]

We also know the opinions of Paderewski at that time from a telegram sent by Colonel William R. Grove (of the Food Administration Mission to Poland) to General Marlborough Churchill, dated 9th January, 1919 :

"On the afternoon of 7th January, Dr. Vernon Kellog, Chief of the Food Administration Mission to Poland, and I called on Mr. Paderewski, who spoke frankly about the political situation here. He considers that Pilsudski is a good man, but that he represents a party only, and not the whole of Poland; that what is necessary is a National Council, which would include Galicia and Poznania; that certain members of the Ministry are impossible, having no training whatever for the work at hand, and apparently having been put solely to placate certain interests, these interests being in the main either socialistic or bolshevistic." [83]

The question arises as to the extent to which American influence was instrumental in bringing about the change of Government in Poland. We find an allegation in the *Memoirs* of the former President of the United States, Mr. Hoover, then head of the Food

Administration, that this influence was decisive. Mr. Hoover says in his *Memoirs* :

> " On his arrival (in Poland) Dr. Kellog advised me of the impossible political situation. He felt that there was only one hope and that was for Pilsudski, who had the army's backing, to be put on ' a pedestal.' To close up the factions, he recommended that Ignace Paderewski, the favourite of all Poles, should be placed at the head of a stronger Cabinet as Prime Minister and take complete control of the civil Government. Not only did Paderewski hold the imagination of all the people, but was a man of superlative integrity, deeply imbued with democratic ideals. Dr. Kellog asked that he be authorized to inform Paderewski that unless this was done, American co-operation and aid were futile. I did so and got the hint reinforced from President Wilson. As a result Pilsudski was elevated to the position of ' Chief of State ' and Paderewski became Prime Minister on 16th January." [84]

It seems to me that Mr. Hoover's memory has failed him. In the first instance, let us state that Pilsudski had been from the beginning " Chief of State " and not head of the Government, and that he also at that time considered Moraczewski's Cabinet incapable of coping with the great tasks ahead. Moreover, Paderewski's Government was not a coalition government, properly speaking, but was formed according to a formula proposed many times by Pilsudski to the National Committee of Paris : a Cabinet consisting mostly of specialists with no definite party allegiance.[85] We know the inmost thoughts of Pilsudski about the events which brought about the change of Government from his confidential letter to Mr. K. Dluski, Chairman of the Mission sent by him to Paris, written on the 17th January, that is immediately after the constitution of Paderewski's Government. We quote below the relevant passages from this letter :

> " The following were the reasons for the change of Ministry:
> " Shortage of technical means and the impossibility of producing them at home made it imperative for foreign policy to concentrate all efforts on obtaining the assistance of the Entente in money and food, as well as arms supplies.
> " This aim could be most easily attained by reaching a compromise with the National-Democrats (the party headed by Dmowski).
> " What I considered the most important in internal policy was to hold on till the meeting of the Diet without too violent domestic struggles, as they might lead to bloodshed.
> " It was possible to attain this aim by having the backing of a part of the Left (Peasant Party and Socialists), which brought about the

scission of the Left into two camps and weakened its striking power in opposition.

" The difficulty consisted in agreeing and keeping parallel these two lines, one leaning to the right on account of the requirements of foreign policy, the other leaning to the left for reasons of internal policy.

" The difficulties became formidable as contrary to my previous anticipations that the Germans would vacate the territories of the Ober-Ost (Eastern Command) only in March, the evacuation started much earlier and the danger of the Bolshevik invasion consequently became much nearer. The Germans withdrawing from the East are neither demoralized nor disorganized, they constitute a force with which one has to reckon. They collaborate with the Bolsheviks and Poland has to face a war against this German-Bolshevik alliance, a war the burden of which Poland alone in all Europe will assume.

" All the foregoing facts caused the question of the assistance of the Entente to become most urgent and hence the necessity of constituting Paderewski's Government, through which I believe this assistance may be granted. . . . The present Cabinet, consisting of specialists, above all must obtain the assistance of the Entente, which so far has made only promises, and moreover in inadequate measure ; secondly it must find an issue from financial difficulties. . . .

" . . . the moral gain of the change is that Paderewski in taking power from my hand recognized me as the Chief of State ; secondly, by addressing his thanks to the retiring Cabinet he recognized what had been done before in the Polish policy, consequently finding himself in opposition to the violent and unrestrained criticism of the Cabinet by the National Democrats who condemn everything that has been done until now. . . . The appointment of a Cabinet consisting of specialists will provoke many difficulties on the Left. It is important that the Polish Socialist Party may successfully resist the pressure of the opposition from below. This will be rather difficult because from the beginning it has stuck to a dogma: A government of peasants and workers. The strike proclaimed by the Polish Socialist Party as a protest against the dismissal of Moraczewski's Government will be limited to one day. I hope that the near date of the elections will provoke a fever which will absorb a great deal of energy and this will not allow it to expand in other directions." [86]

It appears from the above quoted passages of Pilsudski's letter that in this occurrence he showed himself to be a statesman free from partisan spirit, capable of dissociating himself from his old friends and followers when the interests of the State were at stake. It should also be noted that it was only thanks to his close links with a part of the Left which trusted him that this ministerial crisis, which was not an ordinary one, could find a peaceful solution. One must keep in mind that it took place during a hectic period when many countries were rent by internal upheavals and revolutionary outbreaks were spreading in two neighbouring countries, Germany and Russia. Poland also owed very much to the patriotic spirit of the working masses, to their self-imposed discipline, these civic virtues of the Polish people enabling it to go through the most difficult trials in 1919 and 1920.

This suffices as proof that Poland did not need any American ultimatum in her hour of danger.[87] The moral position of the United States ranked, of course, very high in Poland at that time, and the assistance given by the Hoover Mission to the starving population, and especially to poor children, is held in grateful memory by the Polish nation. It would have been monstrous if that Mission had tried to bargain the assistance to the distressed population against any political advantages and exercised undue pressure on the Polish political leaders.

H. H. Fisher in his book quoted before, *America and the New Poland*, based on a direct access to the American Food Mission's reports, underlines that the catastrophic position of the Polish population (see o.c., pp. 126-30 : " Out of a population of 27,000,000 in territories claimed by the Polish Government more than one-third, or about ten million, were unable to provide themselves with enough food to maintain health,") was relieved only thanks to the " swiftness and directness " of Hoover's action. " Within a few weeks from the time the first mission arrived in Warsaw and had reported back to Hoover the terrible situation of the Polish people, the relief food was flowing to Poland through Danzig " (*Ibidem*, p. 264). Fisher refutes categorically any direct interference of the Food Mission in the political problems :

> " Kellog and Grove reached Warsaw on 2nd January, 1919, while the conferences between Pilsudski and Paderewski were going on. Without waiting for the outcome of these conversations and without attempting to bear any tremendous pressure which their position placed in their hands, they began discussions of the food situation with the Chief of Staff, the Prime Minister, the Ministers of Approvisation, Agriculture, Railways and Finance, the President of the City of Warsaw and various delegations of citizens."

In the article written by Mr. Vernon Kellog himself under the very significant heading " Paderewski, Pilsudski and Poland. Two compatriots who sank their political differences to save their country " (*The World's Work*, May 1919), a few months after the constitution of Paderewski's Cabinet, we find some allusions to the shortcomings of Moraczewski's administration and to the suggestions of the mission to set up a more representative government, but as we have seen above Pilsudski himself was well aware of the inefficiency of Moraczewski's Cabinet and of the necessity for calling on more capable administrators. Vernon Kellog writes in his article :

> " One point in all the negotiations was emphasized. It was a *suggestive* point. It was plainly indicated that no food could come from America or the Allies on a wholesale scale if there was any serious danger that it could not be properly controlled, so that it could be kept out of the hands of speculators, and prevented from leaking across the borders into Germany or Russia. This all meant that food relief—imperatively needed to keep Poland alive and free from that push of misery that meant revolution and bolshevism—could only be hoped for in the presence of a government—so strongly representative, and so universally accepted by the people that it could be relied on by America and the Allies to keep order and maintain a safe control of the imported foodstuffs. The Food Mission concerned itself with no politics. But after all food and politics have had an inevitable and inseparable connection ever since the beginning of the war ; and they have it still."

Without, therefore, denying some " suggestions " which could only be welcomed by Pilsudski at that time, Vernon Kellog most emphatically states that " the new government was the result of the statecraft and diplomacy of the greatest pianist in the world—whom we must forget as a piano-player and remember as a statesman, an orator, and a patriot—" and the good sense and shrewdness of a one-time nihililist(?) and present extreme socialist(?)." The words provided by me with question marks prove with what prejudices against Pilsudski Vernon Kellog came to Warsaw. And yet after a short contact with the Chief of State he was captivated by his personality as appears from the following lines : " Pilsudski himself is a patriot, a good soldier, a man of much shrewdness and native capacity, withal he has individual color and rather an attractive personality. Despite a serious mien, plain face, and bristling roached hair, he has a quick smile and eyes of such a kindly twinkling when one dares lightness of speech that one leaves an audience with him with the impression of having had a pleasant conversation with a man of swift intelligence and a sense of humour " (p. 109). And in another place Vernon Kellog writes : " Pilsudski himself is a patriot. He loves his country and his people. He saw the importance of a united front before the world. He knew that his Cabinet was not only non-representative but weak " (p. 112).

*
*   *

The Paderewski Cabinet was recognized within a few days by the Allied and Associated Powers. But the latter did not keep step with the quick and dramatic developments in Eastern Europe owing to the lack of agreement between them on the line of policy to be pursued towards Eastern Europe in general and Bolshevism in particular.

In an interview granted to the correspondent of a Paris newspaper, *Le Petit Parisien,* on the 27th January, 1919, Pilsudski stated :

> " Only actions count. The best wishes remain inefficient if they do not involve practical consequences. We are cut off from the outside world. I do not believe that it would be possible to receive any assistance within a short time." [88]

Mr. Sokolnicki, a member of Pilsudski's Mission in Paris, describes in his diary the disappointment caused in Poland by the dilatory policy of the Allied Supreme Council :

> " For twenty days, since the special Delegation sent by Pilsudski arrived in Paris, we have asked for arms, munitions and equipment ; we have obtained what could have been granted to us three months ago—an exploratory mission. It is, perhaps, something, but it is not sufficient and above all this is neither real nor immediate assistance. The Conference seems to have no idea of time." [89]

Dmowski, whose pro-Entente feelings cannot be questioned by anyone, in his book *Polityka Polska* speaks in bitter terms [90]:

> " No country after the end of the war was in such a dangerous position, and was left to such an extent to its own devices ; none of them met with so many obstacles put by the Allies in the way of the organization and use of its forces."

Did the internal position in Poland after the Armistice justify the policy of aloofness from the authorities established there? Would it not have been wiser if the Allies had marked their presence in Warsaw immediately after the Armistice, as they might then have dispelled many misgivings about their intentions, and ascertained the needs of the country instead of relying on the unwarranted allegations according to which the new régime in Poland was infected by Bolshevism and pursued a policy hostile to the Allies? In its editorial of 27th December, entitled " When shall we have an Eastern policy? ", *Le Temps* made these very relevant remarks :

> " Everybody agrees that it is necessary to help Poland. It remains to know why we have not helped her until now? ... The Allies cannot solve the Polish question if they have no common policy on the whole problem of Eastern Europe. Have they one? The first duty of the Allies (after the Armistice) was to send missions

to the spot in order to obtain information on the internal situation, to enter into relations with the Governments or groups capable of exercising power, and lastly to arrange the withdrawal of the German forces, at the same time trying to provide the local authorities with the necessary means—arms, munitions, credits, food—in order to maintain order after the withdrawal of the Germans. ... What really happened? One fact illustrates the situation: at the time when public opinion insists on assistance to Poland, the Allied Governments have not yet diplomatic representatives in Warsaw. ... Thus, during six weeks which have elapsed since the signing of the Armistice, the Allied Governments have seen the invasion by Bolsheviks of vast areas. ... So, when there is so much talk about economizing Allied forces in Russia, we allow to perish peoples which would have been able to provide the bases and the soldiers. A nice preface to the League of Nations! A nice guarantee for the peace of to-morrow! "

All the facts related in this chapter rouse legitimate suspicions that the initial and quite natural internal difficulties of Poland served as a convenient pretext for postponing decisions relating to Eastern Europe. We shall deal with the grave consequences of this policy in the Second Part of this book.

NOTES

[1] FILASIEWICZ, o.c., p. 581.

[2] J. PILSUDSKI, *Pisma*, V, p. 231.

[3] HARRY RUDIN, *Armistice*.

[4] SIR FREDERICK MAURICE, *The Armistice of* 1918, p. 4.

[5] LLOYD GEORGE, *War Memoirs*, Vol. VI, pp. 3110 *et seq.* Memorandum of the Chief of the Imperial General Staff, General Sir Henry Wilson, presented to the Imperial War Council assembled in London on 31st July, 1918 ; among five possibilities two in particular show the extent of Sir Henry's pessimism: " (2) The British Army may be forced to abandon the Channel ports. ... (3) The enemy may capture Paris. ... " "We should fix the culminating period of our supreme military effort on the Western front not later than 1st July, 1919, but even then he *could not hold out hope of achieving more than substantial military success.*"

[6] GENERAL PERSHING, *My Experiences in the World War*, pp. 675 *et seq.* SIR FREDERICK MAURICE, o.c., p. 47.

[7] BAKER, *Woodrow Wilson, Life and Letters, Armistice*, p. 510.

[8] DOUGLAS HAIG, *The Private Papers*, p. 330.

[9] RUDIN, o.c., pp. 343 *et seq.*

[10] *Der Waffenstillstand*, Herausgegeben im Auftrage der Deutschen Waffenstillstands-Kommission, Vol. III, p. 126. " Da bei Abschluss des Waffenstillstandes vom 11 November, 1918, Polen nicht zur Entente rechnete, sind besondere Bestimmungen betreffs Polen nicht gemacht worden."

¹¹ HAIG, o.c., pp. 333-4. See also his conversation with Lloyd George on 29th October. (*Ibidem*, p. 338) in which he advised " to insist on strong naval terms," and, although the collapse of Austria made Germany's position hopeless, " more lenient terms on land."

¹² COMMANDANT LHOPITAL, *Foch, Armistice et la Paix*, p. 14. Note sur les conditions d'un armistice avec l'Allemagne.

¹³ *Ibidem*, p. 60. Le projet des conditions militaires d'armistice.

¹⁴ The account of the meeting is based on the proceedings of this conference published by Mermeix, *Les Négociations Secrètes et les Quatre Armistices*. English translation in RUDIN'S *Armistice*.

¹⁵ Protocol of the Armistice between the Allied and Associated Powers and Austria-Hungary. Article III: Evacuation of all territory invaded by Austria-Hungary since the beginning of the War, and withdrawal of Austro-Hungarian forces, within a space of time to be laid down by the Generals-Commanding-in-Chief of the Allied forces on the different fronts beyond a line fixed as follows. ... All territories thus evacuated will be occupied by Allied and American troops. Article IV: Allied armies have the right of free movement over all road and rail and waterways in Austro-Hungarian territory which shall be necessary.

¹⁶ F. FOCH, *Memoirs pour servir à l'histoire de la guerre de* 1914-1918, Vol. II, p. 321. " L'armistice signé par le commandant en chef des armées alliés n'était ni un traité de paix, ni même des préliminaires de paix. ... Bien que le texte comportât certaine clauses politiques ou financières d'une réalisation immédiate, il ne fixait pas la situation des Etats belligérants à l'issue de la lutte. Les gouvernements alliés s'étaient réservés cette tâche importante: le traité de paix."

¹⁷ SIR FREDERIC MAURICE, o.c., p. 60. " The general impression in December 1918 was that the main lines of the peace treaty with Germany could be drawn up and agreed upon in a few weeks. Actually it was seven and a half months before this treaty was signed, and more than a year before it was ratified."

¹⁸ FILASIEWICZ, o.c., p. 560.

¹⁹ *P. R. F. R.*, 1918, Sup. I, Vol. I, pp. 879 *et seq.*

²⁰ M. SEYDA, o.c., II, pp. 488-9.

²¹ *P. R. F. R.*, etc., *ibidem*, p. 878.

²² CASIMIR SMOGORZEWSKI, *L'Union Sacrée Polonaise*. Le Gouvernement de Varsovie et le " Gouvernement " Polonais de Paris, p. 11.

²³ *Ibidem*, p. 12.

²⁴ *Ibidem*, p. 7.

²⁵ *Ibidem*, p. 14 *et seq.*

²⁶ *P. R. F. R.*, 1918, Sup. I, Vol. I, p. 466. See also HOUSE, *Intimate Papers*, IV, p. 110. " The political chiefs approved the Generals' plan and authorized them to study the following question: The possibility of taking immediate steps to send a force which shall include the Czecho-Slovak forces on the French and Italian fronts to Bohemia and Galicia with the following object: to organize these countries against invasion by Germany."

[27] *Der Waffenstillstand,* I, p. 36. H. KRAUS and G. RÖDIGER, *Urkunden zum Friedensvertrage,* I, p. 38.

[28] *P. R. F. R.,* The Paris Peace Conference, II, p. 65.

[29] *Der Waffenstillstand,* III, p. 19. " Unverständlich erscheint unter diesen Umständen die in offiziellen Noten der Gegner immer wiederholte Behauptung, die deutsche Regierung oder die O.H.L. oder andere amtliche deutsche Stellen unterstützten die russischen Bolschewisten oder hätten entgegen dem Verbot des Artikels XIII Agenten und Instrukteure im russischen Heere oder in Finland oder anderswo."

[30] *Ibidem.* " Die Entente war sich über das einzuschlagende Verfahren anfänglich offenbar nicht klar. Die Fragen waren eben, wie General Weygand bei einer Gelegenheit dem General von Winterfeld erklärte, für die Alliirten ' sehr dornig ' (épineuse). Anscheinend spielten innere Schwierigkeiten der Entente eine grosse Rolle wie Unaufrichtigkeit, Hass und Furcht."

[31] *Der Waffenstillstand,* I, p. 39. Bemerkungen der deutschen Waffenstillstands-Kommission. " Eis wird um Erläuterung gebeten, was mit Art. XVI gemeint ist, da die Weichsel kein schiffbarer Fluss ist. Deutschland ist bereit, den Alliirten und den Vereinigten Staaten die freie Durchfuhr von *Lebensbedürfnissen nach den früheren russischen Gebietsteilen zu ermöglichen."*

[32] *P. R. F. R.,* The Paris Peace Conference, III, pp. 471 *et seq.*

[33] *Ibidem,* p. 478.

[34] *Ibidem.*

[35] *Ibidem,* p. 674.

[36] *Ibidem,* pp. 772 *et seq.*

[37] *Der Waffenstillstand,* I, p. 198.

[38] *Ibidem,* II, pp. 337 *et seq.* See the discussion at the meeting of the Council of Ten on 21st March, 1919 (*P. R. F. R.,* Paris Peace Conference, IV, pp. 430 *et seq.*) President Wilson declared among other things : " To send troops by another route than Danzig would constitute an entire yielding to German demands." The resolution proposed by Lloyd George: " That Marshal Foch shall receive full authority to demand from the Germans that Clause XVI of the Armistice of 11th November shall be so interpreted as to permit the free passage of General Haller's army, as part of the Allied Army, to Poland through Danzig to maintain order in Poland ... ", and his declaration: " He could not believe the Germans would refuse to allow the troops free passage along the Danzig-Thorn railway line ... such an outrage would lead at once to the Allied troops marching into Germany, or to the renewal of a strict blockade."

[39] See a report on the military situation written by Major Alfred Niemann (General Staff officer attached to the Kaiser) 20th July, 1918: " Definitive settlement of the question of territories attached to us (Angliederungsfragen) in the West and in the East will give the impression of our strong determination. We must confront our opponents with accomplished facts " (RUDIN, o.c., pp. 17-18).

[40] A. Przybylski, *Wojna Polska,* 1918-1921, pp. 35 *et seq.*

[41] *P. R. F. R.,* The Paris Peace Conference, III, p. 779.

[42] *Ibidem,* p. 471.

[43] Z. Wieliczka, *Od Prosny po Rawicz.* Poznan, 1931, p. 355. " The Supreme People's Council awaited the results of the uprising, unwilling, probably, to engage itself too early, and its co-operation with the insurgents dated from the moment when two points became certain : (1) that no intervention or truce would be able to stop the uprising, and (2) when the success of the uprising was nearly assured " ; the same author, *Wielkopolska a Prusy.* pp. 51 ff.

[44] H. W. Temperley, o.c., Vol. I, p. 339.

[45] *P. R. F. R.,* The Paris Peace Conference, III, p. 715.

[46] *Ibidem,* p. 674.

[47] D. H. Miller, *My Diary at the Conference of Paris,* XV, p. 21. *P. R. F. R.,* The Paris Peace Conference, IV, p. 97.

[48] *Ibidem,* The Paris Peace Conference, II, p. 903.

[49] *Ibidem,* pp. 924-5.

[50] *Der Waffenstillstand,* I, p. 204. " Les Allemands devront renoncer immédiatement à toutes opérations offensives contre les Polonais dans la région de Posen ou dans toute autre région. Dans ce but il leur est interdit de faire franchir par leur troupes. . . . "

[51] *Memoirs of Prince Max of Baden,* Vol. II, p. 24. Sir Frederic Maurice, o.c., p. 29.

[52] Stresemann, *His Diaries, Letters and Papers,* I, p. 17.

[53] *Der Waffenstillstand,* III, p. 22. " Von 14 bis 16 Februar fanden die Verhandlungen in Trier statt, in denen Deutschland zur Annahme der Demarkationslinie im deutschen Osten gezwungen wurde. Es war nur ein geringer Trost, dass es wenigsten gelungen war, Oberschlesien vorläufig zu retten und auch sonst entsprechend der damaligen Kriegslage-einige Verbesserungen gegenüber dem ursprüglichen Entwurf zu erlangen."

[54] *Der Waffenstillstand,* III. " Accords conclus à Posen entre les Délégations Interalliée et Allemande pour l'application de l'article I de l'Armistice du 16 Février, 1919, pour les règles de protection des citoyens polonais dans certaines provinces de l'Allemagne et des Allemands en Posnanie et pour la reprise des relations entre les deux pays."

[55] *Ibidem,* p. 407. " Der Waffenstillstand enthält nichts über die Abtretung der deutschen Gebiete an Polen. Die Alliirten und Assoziirten Regierungent haben es aber nicht nur zugelassen, sondern begünstigt und schliesslich vertraglich sanktioniert, dass sich die Polen während des Waffenstillstandes weite Gebiete des deutschen Reiches mit rechtswidriger Gewalt aneigneten."

[56] *Ibidem,* III, p. 22. " Die polnische Frage im deutschen Osten wurde akut durch den Aufstand in Posen Ende Dezember 1918. Der Waffenstillstands Kommission wurde damals jedoch kaum von der Angelegenheit berührt, da *die Alliirten zunächst nicht versuchten sich einzumischen.*"

[57] *P. R. F. R.,* The Paris Peace Conference, III, p. 775.

[58] ROBERT MACHRAY, *The Poland of Pilsudski*, p. 74.

[59] J. PILSUDSKI, *Pisma*, V, p. 35. See also a telegram published by *Le Temps* on 3rd January, 1919: " Pendant son séjour à Cracovie, le général Pilsudski a déclaré aux représentants de la presse que sa politique se résumait en un mot: Constituante. Après les élections, on pourra voir qui a la majorité dans la pays." Mr. Wasilewski, Minister of Foreign Affairs, declared at the same time: " Le ministère actuel s'inclinera devant la volonté de la Constituante quelle qu'elle soit."

[60] *Ibidem*, p. 60.

[61] *Le Temps*, 18th December, 1918. " Dans la matinée du 16 décembre une note à été remise au comte Kessler, représentant de l'Allemagne à Varsovie. Le Gouvernement polonais s'appuyant sur la situation qui règne dans les territoires de l'ancien Commandement de l'Est Supérieur où les autorités allemandes commettent des actes contraires aux intérêts de l'Etat polonais et qui font cause commune avec les bolchevistes, exprime dans cette note la conviction qu'il est inutile de poursuivre des négociations avec le Gouvernement allemand et pense même qu'elles sont préjudiciables à l'ordre intérieur du pays comme aux relations futures des deux Etats."

[62] P. ROTH, *Die politische Entwicklung*, p. 130. " In der äusseren Politik drängte der Interparteiliche Klub den rückhaltlosen Anschluss Polens als eines verbundenen Staates an die Entente, während die Sozialisten die Neutralität Polens durchsetzen wollten."

[63] M. SOKOLNICKI, " W sluzbie Komendanta," published in the Paris review *Kultura*, No. 12/74, p. 77.

[64] J. PILSUDSKI, *Pisma*, V, p. 66.

[65] COUNT HARRY KESSLER, *Germany and Europe*, p. 33.

[66] J. PILSUDSKI, *Pisma*, V, p. 59.

[67] Quoted from *Le Temps*, 5th January, 1919. The following remark was added by the editor of the French newspaper: " C'est ainsi qu'on interprète à Berlin la clause du programme wilsonien qui promet l'indépendance à tous les territoires incontestablement polonais."

[68] M. SOKOLNICKI, article quoted above, p. 95.

[69] *P. R. F. R.*, The Paris Peace Conference, II, p. 412.

[70] FILASIEWICZ, o.c., No. 286.

[71] See the details on Grabski's mission in SOKOLNICKI, o.c., p. 80 *et seq.*, SMOGORZEWSKI, o.c., p. 28 *et seq.*, SEYDA, o.c., II, p. 533.

[72] *Journal Officiel*, 30th December, 1918. Chambre des Députés, 2-ième séance du 29 décembre, 1918.

[73] The note of M. Pichon to M. Piltz, representative of the Polish National Committee in Paris, dated 15th January, 1919 (FILASIEWICZ, o.c., No. 291).

[74] *Le Temps*, 20 décembre, 1918. Declaration of Ambassador Noulens before leaving Arkhangelsk: " Le congé que je prends ne suspendra la tâche qui m'a confiée le gouvernement français et qui s'inspire à la fois de nos intérêts nationaux en Russie et de la nécessité d'aider notre ancienne alliée à sortir de l'anarchie pour retrouver sa puissance sous un régime d'ordre et de liberté. Ni la France ni les autres

nations alliées ne songent à abandonner le peuple russe aux excès des bolchevistes. Elles se considèrent comme engagées par leurs intérêts solidaires, leurs affinités réciproques et leurs souvenirs communs à préparer le relèvement d'un pays auquel sa population, ses richesses naturelles assureront toujours un rôle politique et économique de premier ordre dans l'histoire mondiale."

[75] The United States Government replied to the French note of 15th November in the matter of recognition of the National Committee in Paris as *de facto* Government, only on 24th December, stating that " as soon as the position of the United States on this question is determined you will be promptly informed." (*P. R. F. R.*, The Paris Peace Conference, I, p. 264.) On 21st December, the Acting Secretary of State sent the following instructions to the Ambassador in Paris : " Investigate carefully and report promptly exact relation between Polish National Committee and Polish officers in charge of affairs in Poland " (*Ibidem,* II, p. 416).

[76] *Ibidem,* II, pp. 414-5.

[77] *Ibidem,* II, p. 482.

[78] J. PILSUDSKI, *Pisma,* V, p. 45.

[79] *P. R. F. R.,* The Paris Peace Conference, I, p. 312.

[80] *Ibidem,* II, pp. 424-5.

[81] HOUSE, *Intimate Papers,* IV, pp. 273-4.

[82] *P. R. F. R.,* The Paris Peace Conference, III, p. 673.

[83] *Ibidem,* II, p. 427.

[84] HERBERT HOOVER, *The Memoirs,* p. 356.

[85] A few days before the constitution of the Paderewski Cabinet, on 8th January, the United States Chargé d'Affaires in Paris reported to the Secretary of State : " The Committee (Polish National Committee) is however disposed, he (Dmowski) says, to recognize Pilsudski in any official position, even that of President, if necessary, provided he will appoint a coalition government and that he is disposed to accept this proposal, but his (Pilsudski's) party is obdurate " (The Paris Peace Conference, II, p. 426).

Landau in his biography of J. I. Paderewski stresses (p. 139) that " Paderewski was determined not to form a party cabinet. He endeavoured to form a cabinet of experts." The reason for this decision was not only the fear of serious disturbances on the part of socialists and radicals should any prominent Right-wing politician enter the cabinet, but above all the necessity for awaiting the results of the elections to the Constituent Diet.

[86] The passages quoted are taken from a photostat copy of the document kept in the archives of the Jozef Pilsudski Historical Institute of America. See a very interesting commentary in an article of W. Jedrzejewicz, published in the Polish weekly of London, *Wiadomosci,* 11th January, 1953, No. 2, p. 354.

[87] L. L. GERSON, o.c., p. 109, although observing that " no records of the conversations between Paderewski and Pilsudski survived," asserts that Paderewski had shown to Pilsudski a letter from Hoover " endorsed

by Wilson " in which it was categorically stated that the aid would
be extended to Poland *so long as he was in charge* [my underlining].
But it is quite clear from his own note 24 that the letter was written in
May 1919(?). Moreover, the words underlined by me confirm that such
a letter could not have been written before Paderewski assumed his
charge. But it is the following passage in Gerson's book that shows the
extent to which he abuses his readers' ignorance of the Polish sources.
He states namely (p. 106), that it appears from Pilsudski's article
" Historical Corrections " (see PILSUDSKI, *Pisma*, Vol. IX, p. 313) that
" it was quite plain that he (Pilsudski) did not at the first meeting with
Paderewski offer him the premiership." First of all the passage in Pilsudski's article did not refer to J. I. Paderewski, but to a quite different
Paderewski, namely Dr. Paderewski (it is said expressly in Pilsudski's
article " Doctor Paderewski "), member of the N.D. Party and former
deputy to the Russian Duma from Piotrkow circumscription. Moreover, the article deals with the events which took place in November
1918 during the formation of Moraczewski's Government.

88 J. PILSUDSKI, *Pisma*, V, p. 53.
89 M. SOKOLNICKI, article quoted above, p. 99.
90 R. DMOWSKI, o.c., p. 349.

PART II

STRUGGLE FOR THE FRONTIERS OF THE RESTORED POLISH STATE (1918-1920)

THE PARIS PEACE CONFERENCE : ATTITUDE OF THE PRINCIPAL POWERS TOWARDS THE SMALL* STATES

" Altogether, a plenary session of the Conference as the Preliminaries of Peace was a farce. It was never a deliberative assembly which reached an agreement by a frank exchange of views. The delegates were called together to listen, not to criticize or object, to the programme of the Council of Ten. They were there to go through the formality of registering their approval, whichever their real opinions might be. It was medieval rather than modern ; despotic rather than democratic. It was in one sense a farce, but in another it was a tragedy."—(ROBERT LANSING, *The Big Four and Others of the Peace Conference,* pp. 19-20.)

" Mr. Lloyd George urged that the Great Powers should not allow the small States to use them as cats-paws for their miserable ambitions."—(Meeting of the Council of Four, 22nd May, 1919. *P. R. F. R.,* The Paris Peace Conference, V, p. 904.)

Position of small States at the Peace Conference

THE critics of the 1919 Peace Treaties, and there were very many in the inter-war period, seem to have used for their special purposes a quite distorted picture of the Paris Peace Conference and of its political background. It was often alleged, for instance, that the interests of the absent Great Powers (one just defeated and another disintegrating) were utterly disregarded there and the interests of small States specially favoured, all this owing to the indiscriminate application of some abstract principles such as the principle of national self-determination. It was this deliberate policy that allegedly brought about the breaking-up of great imperial units " in an age which called for larger and larger units," according to the words of Prof. E. H. Carr.[1]

* We use the term " small " States for the sake of simplicity, being fully aware of its inadequacy, as it embraces all States of whatever size or political and economic importance but having no recognized status as a Great Power. We also use the term " New States " in accordance with official terminology of the Peace Conference, although this term can hardly be applied to Poland, restored to her old sovereignty, or to such States as Rumania, Hungary or Yugoslavia, whose legal continuity cannot be disputed by anyone.

Little care has been taken by all these critics to ascertain the historical truth and they are themselves victims of their own preconceived ideas on what seemed to them to be "a better international order." †

Had the peace-makers in Paris a choice of an alternative solution : preserving bigger units at that time in full decomposition or backing the national movements? So says, for instance, Professor T. Bailey:

> "But on the whole the Paris settlement was a victory for the principle of self-determination. ... The result was the closest approximation that modern Europe had ever had to an ethnographic map coinciding with a political map. This raises the question whether an ethnographic map was what Europe needed; whether it would have not been better to have fewer States rather than more, whether it would have not been better to have more economic self-sufficiency and less self-determination, less abstract justice and more economic viability. Man does not live by bread alone, but one cannot live without bread." [1b]

We shall deal on another occasion with the question whether it was true that the Paris settlement was mainly responsible for the economic crises in the world, an assumption which does not stand the test of the facts. What does interest us in this connection is the idea, mistaken in our view, that the peace-makers in Paris were faced with the alternative referred to by Professor Bailey. Or was it not rather an alternative between backing the movements for national self-determination, very strong in Central and Eastern Europe, and the Bolshevization of half Europe, an alternative which still exists in this part of the old continent, and perhaps also elsewhere?

Is it true that there were in Paris statesmen who, as asserts Mr. Keith Feiling, biographer of Neville Chamberlain, " disregarded revolutionary Russia " and " assigned to others " territories " which she

---

† According to the views of many critics of the Versailles settlement there exists a basic contradiction between the independence of small States and the need for the economic and social integration. Such assertions appear quite obsolete at the time of the gradual disintegration of old colonial empires and the recognition of the right to independence, respectively self-government, of many Asiatic and African peoples. The " international planners " seem to take their patterns exclusively from the Soviet Empire where such an integration is achieved by compulsion, but outside this Empire, historical evolution follows quite a different path in conformity with the traditions of Western civilization. Is the Western bloc doomed because it does not follow the lines of evolution foreshadowed by international planners? Paul Bonsal was right when in his excellent book *Versailles, Twenty Years After*, he called such an approach "intellectual nihilism" and the " disillusioned liberals " who professed such ideas " unwittingly allies of the cynical advocates of physical force as the only conceivable basis for world politics." [1a]

had for a hundred or two hundred years "? Is it true, as he further asserts, that it was by the action of the statesmen in Paris that " the Hapsburg Monarchy together with provinces of Germany, Russia and Turkey were redistributed among thirteen little States," and that thus France was able to create " a circle of vassal countries "? [2] Is it true, as for instance Professor Carr asserts in his book *Conditions of Peace,* that there were statesmen in Paris who " fostered the disintegration of existing political units and favoured the creation of smaller units "? [3] We leave aside, as being beyond the scope of this historical work, the question as to whether the fostering of the creation of bigger units, as advocated by these critics of the Peace Treaties, assured a more lasting peace to mankind after the Second World War. We will limit ourselves, in the first instance, to the investigation of the question whether the small States were " pampered " in Paris, obtaining undeserved advantages at the expense of Germany and Russia.

Let us state in the first instance that at the bottom of many misguided opinions about the world settlement after the First World War lies the idea that the political status of Europe was an artificial creation of the statesmen of the so-called Principal Allied and Associated Powers, and that the peace-makers in Paris had an absolutely free hand in shaping the destinies of European nations. As a matter of fact the post-Versailles Europe was the outcome of the war and of some forces which were instrumental in the final victory of the Allies. Mr. Shotwell, a prominent member of the American delegation to the Peace Conference, devoted some very pertinent remarks to this " over-simplification " in judgments on the post-war developments prevailing in many quarters in the period between the two World Wars :

> " When diplomacy succeeded to war, the unreconciled nations drew from the treaties their slogans of discord, and the settlements made by the Paris Peace Conference imposed themselves upon the imagination of a whole generation as the cause of most of the evils from which the post-war world was suffering. That this was an oversimplification even for Germany was clear to all judicious students of contemporary Europe. The war was chiefly responsible for much that was attributed to the treaties, and pre-war Europe was responsible for the issues of the war. ... The post-war years witnessed the creation of a myth in which the Peace Conference figures as a sinister thing, sowing dragon's teeth, vindictively, subtly, while high-minded idealists looked on confused and frustrated. Myths like this do not die readily, especially while the attitude of mind which produced them still persists." [4]

Let us remember here some historical facts which are easily overlooked or deliberately ignored by those who, obsessed by some preconceived ideas, are unable to see the historical processes in their true perspective. The eminent British historian, Professor Arnold Toynbee, speaking about the situation which had arisen in Central and Eastern Europe at the end of the First World War, says that " the new map had been brought into existence by a sudden, violent explosion of long-pent-up forces." [5] A. L. Kennedy, in his book *Old Diplomacy and New,* recalls the well-known facts :

> " The races of the Hapsburg Monarchy, previously exploited by an Austro-Hungarian oligarchy, were freed. Poles were liberated from subjugation to Austria, Russia and Germany and have already constituted themselves into an independent State. When the Paris Congress assembled, Poland, Czechoslovakia and Yugoslavia had already existed as free States for three months. This is important to remember as it is often loosely said that the Treaty of Versailles ' created ' these States. The treaty ratified their independence, of which they could certainly have only been deprived by force." [6]

C. A. Macartney stresses that " it would not have been possible to put the clock back and re-establish the old Austria or the old Hungary." [7] This was also the general opinion in the New States. Joseph Hanc describes in these terms the position of the new national States at the end of the war :

> " Nationalities in 1918 represented living realities demanding political body. By the time the Armistice was signed in November 1918 the liberation of each Eastern European people was in fact an accomplished reality. Throughout the years of 1917 and 1918 the individual nations proclaimed their independence, and before the Peace Conference began its sessions they had established their governments, occupied the territories they claimed, and in several instances passed provisional constitutions. Their delegations came to Paris not for the purpose of asking for independence, which they had already attained, but to demand the recognition of their specific territorial claims. They appeared at the Peace Conference not in the rôle of supplicants with cap in hand, but as delegates of States, some of which had been previously recognized as allies and cobelligerents." [8]

Lloyd George, whom nobody can accuse of tender feelings towards the small States, in the following words refutes " the cheap stuff written by sensational economists," and gives a totally different picture from that used by the critics of the post-war settlement :

> " Ere the Powers came to consider the Austrian peace they were confronted with accomplished facts. ... There was not an area in the whole Austrian Empire which had not been parcelled out

amongst the various claimants and occupied by their troops before the Powers ever met in Conference to consider the terms of the Treaty of Peace with Austria. The task of the Parisian Treaty-makers was not to decide what in fairness should be given to the liberated nationalities, but what in common honesty should be freed from their clutches when they overstepped the bounds of self-determination." [9]

The last remark of Lloyd George, whose influence on many decisions of the Peace Conference was paramount, throws a peculiar light on what really happened there and the rôle of the Great Powers as self-appointed arbiters in the territorial disputes which had arisen after the end of the war. As we have said before, the liberation of the subjugated nationalities of Central and Eastern Europe (Chapter I, Part I) may be called a by-product of the war and not a result of a deliberate policy of the Entente Powers.

Nevertheless the representatives of the Great Powers tried to base the authority of their decisions on the sacrifices borne by them for the cause of small nations. Even before the Conference was opened, in the debates at the French Chambre des Députés on the 29th December, 1918, one of the prominent members, M. Franklin-Bouillon, exclaimed : " We have agreed to the heaviest sacrifices in order to reconstitute Poland, dismembered fifty years before 1815(!)," [10] although one may fairly say that not one French soldier fell in the cause of Poland's independence in the 1914-18 war.

At the meeting of the Council of Ten on the 5th June, 1919, Lloyd George declared : " We won freedom for nations that had not the slightest hope of it—Czechoslovakia, Poland and others. Nations that have won their freedom at the expense of the blood of Italians and Frenchmen and Englishmen and Americans." [11] Let us remember here the words of the same Lloyd George when the question of the German Armistice was discussed : " We cannot expect the British to go on sacrificing their lives for the Poles " (p. 225).

In connection with the discussion on the terms of the special treaty with Poland (minority clauses and others) at the meeting of the 1st May, 1919,[12] Lloyd George developed a rather interesting idea, clashing with the theory of international law [12a] and the principles of logic :

> " *Lloyd George* said the difficulty was that the New States had already been recognized, but they had not been created.
> " *President Wilson* asked what was the act of creating a New State?
> " *Lloyd George* said that the treaty would be the act of creation, since, until the Treaties were signed, they would be a part of Germany or Austria."

In a letter from M. Berthelot, on behalf of the Commission on New States, to Sir Maurice Hankey, we find the following passage : " Poland . . . owes her liberation entirely to the efforts and sacrifices of the Powers." [13]

In the preamble to the Treaty with Poland of the 28th June, 1919, we read the following statement :

> " Whereas the Allied and Associated Powers have by the success of their arms restored to the Polish nation the independence of which it had been unjustly deprived . . . "

and in the covering letter addressed to Mr. Paderewski in transmitting the Treaty to him, Clemenceau, acting in his capacity as Chairman of the Peace Conference, in the following words justifies the limitations imposed on Poland's sovereignty :

> " I must also recall to your consideration the fact that it is to the endeavours and sacrifices of the Powers in whose name I am addressing you that the Polish nation owes the recovery of its independence."

In this connection C. A. Macartney observes that the Powers " were interpreting their own contribution generously, to say the least of it." [14] In his opinion, although the argument was stronger in the case of Czechoslovakia, it was inapplicable to the case of many other States. For his part, Masaryk in his *Memoirs* stresses that " generally speaking our independence is a fruit of the fall of Austria-Hungary and of the world conflagration. . . . It was only by our resistance to Austria-Hungary and by our revolt against her that we earned our independence." [15] So far as concerned the States constituted on the ruins of the Russian Empire, Macartney observes that : " In the case of Finland, the Allied and Associated Powers had to bear practically no responsibility, either for its existence or for the determination of its frontiers," . . . " Estonia and Latvia separated similarly from Russia in conformity with the Bolshevik doctrine of self-determination," and in the same way " the independence of Lithuania was the work of the Lithuanian nation." [16]

It may be added to these words that all the neighbours of Russia were able to maintain their independence against Soviet aggression only thanks to their own sacrifices, with a certain material contribution from the Allied and Associated Powers.

Another justification for the authority of the decisions of the Great Powers was that they pledged themselves to guarantee the treaties and that the small powers could not exist without the support of the big ones. So, for instance, said Lloyd George at the meeting of the Council of Four on the 17th June, 1919 : " Poland

and Czechoslovakia had been called into existence by the Great Powers and could not live without these Powers." [17] To this argument one might easily object that under the conditions of modern warfare, when wars are carried on between mighty coalitions, no State either big or small can defend itself single-handed, and has to rely on the assistance of its allies.

A very characteristic discussion from this point of view took place at the meeting of the Preliminary Peace Conference on the 31st May, 1919. Wilson declared that

> " we are trying to make an equitable distribution according to the race, the ethnographic character of the people inhabiting them. And back of that lies an important fact, that when the decisions were made the Allied and Associated Powers guaranteed to maintain them ... we must not close our eyes to the fact that in the last analysis the military and naval strength of the Great Powers will be the final guarantee of the peace of the world."

The answer given by the Rumanian representative Bratianu was the most pertinent :

> " It is undeniable that the Great Powers, by their sacrifices, have made certain the victory of the great cause common to us ... but I will add that the responsibility of each State in matters of independence and security, nevertheless, remains just as entire, whatever be its extent ... even though the Great Powers have a more important part to play, in proportion to their size, the responsibilities and duties of independent States, whatever their size, remain undiminished." [18]

No doubt can exist as to the sincerity of Wilson's endeavours to secure the assistance of the Great Powers in the event of aggression against the member States of the League of Nations. According to Wilson Article X of the Covenant (guarantee of the political independence and territorial integrity of all members of the League) should become the very backbone of this solemn agreement. Some of the statements Wilson made during his campaign in the United States for the ratification of the Versailles Treaty by the United States sound quite prophetic in the light of the events of the Second World War. For instance, he said in his speech at Indianopolis on the 4th September, 1919 :

> " If the nations of the world do not maintain their concert to sustain the independence and freedom of these peoples, Germany will yet have her will upon them, and we shall witness the very interesting spectacle of having spent millions upon millions of American lives ... to do a thing which we will then leave to be undone at the leisure of those who are masters of intrigue, at the

leisure of those who are masters in combining wrong influences to overcome right influences, of those who are the masters of the very things we hate and mean always to fight. For, my fellow citizens, if Germany should ever attempt that again, whether we are in the League of Nations or not, we will join to prevent it. We do not stand off and see murder done."

In his address at St. Louis on the 5th September, 1919, he said :

" All the nations that Germany meant to crush and reduce to the status of tools in her own hands have been redeemed by this war and given the guarantee of the strongest nations of the world that nobody shall invade their liberty again. If you do not want to give them that guarantee, then you make it certain that ... the attempt will be made again, and if another war starts like this one, are you going to keep out of it? "

We do not need to prove here, however, that the system of collective security devised in Paris was still-born and that, especially after the refusal of the United States to ratify the Treaty of Versailles, all promises to guarantee the new international order by the Great Powers seemed fallacious. Consequently one of the main reasons on which they based their authority to decide the fate of other nations lacked moral and legal foundation, being based simply on their superior material strength.

Even before the Peace Treaty had been signed, in one of the crucial moments of the Paris Conference, when the revision of the Draft Peace Treaty was under discussion, Lloyd George justified his demands for substantial concessions to Germany's benefit, by the unwillingness of the British nation to assume responsibility for the settlement proposed in Paris. At the meeting of the Council of Four on the 2nd June, 1919, he declared : " So far as the British public was concerned, it had made up its mind that it wanted to get peace and was not so much concerned about the precise terms. British public opinion would not support a Government that went on with war without very substantial reasons." [20] So before the final text of the treaty was ready began a series of concessions which undermined the political structure of the new Europe.

Promises to guarantee the provisions of the Treaty once all the parties concerned reached an agreement served as a convenient weapon for the Great Powers in wringing the far-reaching concessions from small States. The promises remained unfulfilled, the concessions were not reciprocated.[21]

*

* *

It is well known from many special studies devoted to the Paris Peace Conference that the Great Powers, within the above-stated limits, were practically responsible for the political and economic provisions of the treaties. The Council of Ten, the Council of Four, the Council of Foreign Ministers of the Allied and Associated Powers, the commissions dealing with the redistribution of enemy territories, consisted exclusively of representatives of the principal powers. H. W. Temperley observed that

> " as events turned out, the Great Powers kept matters in their own hands to a much greater extent than was at that time anticipated and the bulk of the Treaty was made by them alone, and only presented to their smaller allies when the time came for signature." [22]
> " The full text of the Treaty was not presented to the plenary Conference until the day before it was presented to the Germans. Though no formal vote was taken, their assent was obtained, but much indignation was expressed at the almost total exclusion of the smaller powers, including the British Dominions, from the final decisions." [23]

Thus the Conference followed the patterns of the " Concert of Europe," although it may be questioned whether the maintenance of the privileged position of some Great Powers was fully justified by the economic and political developments after the 1914 war. Professor Arnold J. Toynbee and Harold Nicolson, reviewing the work of the Conference, agree on this point, that there were two main reasons why the privileged position of the Great Powers was obsolete at that time. First of all, the economic progress of the world :

> " In January 1920 " [writes Professor Toynbee], " the authority of the Allied and Associated Powers was not proving a satisfactory substitute for the defunct Concert of the Powers in those regions where the war produced the greatest dislocation, and where the need for some constructive principles of international law and order was proportionately great." [24] ... " In fact, the progress of the Industrial Revolution had made even the greatest of the previous units inadequate from the economic point of view, and was merging them all into one single economic system co-extensive with the world itself. Thus the economic reason for the existence of the Great Powers had partly disappeared." [25]

Nicolson stresses the same point, saying that " the industrial system, in terms of Europe as expanded from 1870 onwards, diminished the self-sufficiency of the Great, as compared to the lesser Powers. Economically, such countries as Sweden or Rumania, assumed an importance in excess of their military, political or territorial strength." [26]

Another reason was the disclocation of multi-national empires and the impact of the doctrine of nationality on the political life of Europe. As Nicolson observed, this dislocation was bound to undermine the Great Powers' system, and in fact, " in 1914, for instance, the autocracy of the Great Powers was already less unquestioned than it had been in 1874. A final dislocation was precipitated by the World War of 1914-18. This dislocation can best be defined in terms of the collapse of the Concert of Europe." [27]

The bearing of these processes on political life seemed to be ignored by most delegates of the Principal Powers to the Peace Conference. Instead of adjusting themselves to the new reality they tried to revive the obsolete methods of the Concert of Europe, without being prepared to assume full responsibility for maintaining the new international order. This appears most strikingly in the attitude of some delegates towards lesser States, which was often imbued with old prejudices, distrust and even disdain, and in the tendency to leave some important questions open or decided upon to the detriment of lesser States in order to safeguard the future position and interests of Germany and Russia. Many clashes at the Conference between Lloyd George and Wilson were often due to their different approach to the problem of small nations. Wilson's views on this matter are known from his many speeches, amongst them one which should be specially recorded here, that of the 11th February, 1918 :

> " The War had its roots in the disregard of small nations and of nationalities which lacked the union and the force to make good their claim to determine their own allegiance and their own forms of political life."

The British standpoint was defined by R. S. Baker in the following terms :

> " As for the British, their attitude towards the small States—the note oftenest sounded in the Peace Conference—was one of sharp impatience with the small powers because they were trouble-makers and costly, and so long as they would not settle down there could be no return to peace, and no revival of normal trade and commerce in which the British (and to a lesser degree the Americans) were vitally interested." [28]

To Lloyd George the ambitions of small States were " miserable," as he said on one occasion.[29] Dr. E. J. Dillon, a contemporary witness, in his work, *The Peace Conference*, deals amply with the " sharp methods " applied by the Principal Powers in discharging their " self-set " functions and he records a characteristic confession of a delegate of a small State after the signature of the Treaty with Germany :

" The Big Three are superlatively unsympathetic to most of the envoys from the lesser belligerent States. And it would be a wonder if it were otherwise, for they make no effort to hide their disdain for us. In fact, it is downright contempt. They never consult us. When we approach them, they shove us aside as importunate intruders. They come to decisions unknown to us and carry them out in secrecy as though we were enemies or spies. If we protest or remonstrate we are imperialists and ungrateful." [30]

The Chairman of the Conference, M. Clemenceau, was, according to Mr. Lansing the American Secretary of State,

" the believer in the primacy of the Great Powers. ... To be the executive of such an oligarchy in the Peace Conference he was specially equipped by experience, by temperament, and by resourcefulness. His nature was that of a despot." [30a]

But even the attitude of the American delegates, although as a rule more benevolent to lesser States, at least so long as President Wilson attended the Conference, was marked by a kind of patronizing paternalism which hurt the feelings of self-respect and national pride of civilized peoples. This feature appeared, for instance, in the first American drafts of the Covenant of the League of Nations. In his letter dated 14th July, 1918, to President Wilson, House explained the spirit in which he wrote his draft :

" It is written with the view of not hurting the sensibilities of any nation either in the Entente or Central Powers. It is written also with a view that the League might be confined to the Great Powers, giving the smaller powers every benefit that may be derived therefrom. If the smaller nations are taken in, the question of equal voting power is an almost insurmountable obstacle. ... These smaller nations might become neutralized as Belgium and Switzerland were, with representation without voting power, just as our Territories have had representation in Congress without votes." [31]

Wilson's first draft of the Covenant submitted to the Supreme Council tried to make permanent the oligarchy of five Great Powers, and was contested by his own Secretary of State, R. Lansing, on the ground of its incompatibility with the principle of equality. It is worthwhile to remember here some of Lansing's remarks in view of the present structure of the United Nations, some features of which are similar to the original drafts of the Covenant, proposed by Wilson, General Smuts and Lord Robert Cecil :

" Equality in the exercise of sovereign rights in times of peace, an equality which is imposed by the very nature of sovereignty, seems to me fundamental to a world organization affecting in any way a nation's independence of action or its exercise of supreme authority over its external or domestic affairs. In my judgment any departure from that principle would be a serious error fraught with danger to the general peace of the world and to the recognized law of nations since it could mean nothing less than the primacy of the Great Powers and the acknowledgment that because they possessed the physical might they had a right to control the affairs of the world in time of peace as in time of war. For the United States to admit that such a primacy ought to be formed would be bad enough, but to suggest it indirectly by proposing an international organization based on that idea would be far worse." [31a]

General Smuts's and Lord Robert Cecil's plans did not disguise their purposes : perpetuation of the War Council composed of Five Great Powers " based on the power to compel obedience, on the right of the powerful to rule." As Lansing stated, " there was nothing idealistic in the plan of Lord Robert Cecil, although he was reputed to be an idealist favouring a new international order." [31b]

Plans for limitation of armaments of small States

A further interesting attempt at the drastic limitation of the sovereignty of the small States, in which President Wilson concurred to some extent, was that arising in connection with the plans for limitation of armaments of these States. The discussion on this matter within the Council of Four shows that the representatives of the Great Powers, perhaps drawing some mistaken analogies from the conditions prevailing in the Balkan countries at the beginning of the century, took the view that the peace of the world was most likely to be endangered by the small States.

It is difficult to find a bigger perversion of the historical truth than this strange assertion contained in the following passage from Lloyd George's speech in the House of Commons on the 16th April, 1919 :

> " It was the quarrel for small States that made the Great War. The difficulties of the Balkans—I believe they disturbed Europe, they created the atmosphere of unrest which began the trouble, they aroused the military temper, and I am not at all sure they did not excite the blood lust in Europe." [32]

No one who has studied the history of modern imperialism could agree with this rather simple theory, which throws the whole burden of responsibility for the outbreak of modern wars on the small States.

The question of the limitation of armaments of small States was raised by Lloyd George at the meeting of the Council of Four on the 15th May, 1919, when the military clauses of the Treaty with Austria were discussed.[33] Lloyd George observed then that " should it be decided that each of these little States, including Rumania, Czechoslovakia, were each allowed to maintain comparatively large armies, nothing would keep them from going to war with one another." In the course of the further discussion Lloyd George proposed that the military representatives at Versailles " should be instructed to consider what forces should be allowed to Austria, Hungary, Rumania, Czechoslovakia, Yugoslavia, including Serbia and Montenegro, Poland and Greece." He was supported by the Italian representative, M. Orlando, and President Wilson who added, however, that " the calculation should not be carried out on a strictly mathematic basis but the military régime applied to Germany should be taken as the standard, making the exception in the case of Poland." [34]

The report of the Military Representatives of the Supreme War Council was submitted to the Council of Four on the 23rd May.[35] General Bliss in presenting this report observed that the question should be settled " chiefly on political grounds," and he added that he " felt strongly that by radically reducing the forces of Austria-Hungary, Czechoslovakia, Yugoslavia, Rumania, Bulgaria and Greece, as proposed, *these States would be converted into mere vassals of the two continental powers of the Entente.* Should disorders then occur, and the States be unable to cope with the same, through want of forces, the inevitable result would be that stronger armies would have to be maintained by France and Italy, following in the occupation from time to time of the territories in question for the purpose of quelling disorders." He did not think that such a situation pointed to the maintenance of the peace of Europe in the future, but at the same time he expressed the fear of the possibility of " the future combination between Germanic, Slavonic and Asiatic races, which might eventually sweep the civilization of Western Europe out of the way." There is no need to say how preposterous was the idea of these States, which mostly belonged to the Western civilization, and were closely connected with the Western Powers, of their own free choice casting their lot with their former oppressors.

The future effective strength proposed by the Military Representatives amounted in the case of Poland to 80,000 men, of Czechoslovakia 50,000, Yugoslavia 40,000, etc.

President Wilson then drew the attention of the Council to the following passage of the report of the Military Representatives :

" On their Eastern frontier these two nations, Poland and Rumania, are in contact with Bolshevist Russia. Not only are they themselves directly menaced by this, but they in fact constitute a barrier which defends Europe against Bolshevism. They must therefore be left in a condition to continue war against the Russian Maximalists with all possible means at their disposal. It is indispensable that Poland and Rumania should be authorized to keep all their forces mobilized under the control of the League of Nations until the Russian question is definitely settled."

Lloyd George, insisting on the necessity for the limitation of the armaments of small States, also alluded to the danger mentioned by General Bliss of an offensive alliance between Germany and the Balkan States " aimed at the Western Powers."

The discussion was resumed at the second meeting held on the 23rd May.[36] Lloyd George " urged that the Great Powers should not allow the small States to use them as cat's-paws for their *miserable ambitions*." Clemenceau proposed " to hear what these small nations themselves had to say," and observed that " one of the strongest guarantees against German aggression was that behind Germany, in an excellent strategic position, lay these independent States—the Poles and the Czechoslovaks . . . his military advisers were opposed to reducing the Polish army owing to the danger to Poland from Russia. The same applied to Rumania." The question was adjourned, and the discussion was resumed on the 4th June,[37] on which day it was decided to hear in the afternoon the representatives of the small States. An interesting remark was made by President Wilson on this occasion :

> " One argument which the Principal Powers might find embar-rassing was if they were asked whether they intended to impose a limitation of armaments on themselves. The reply would be ' Yes, if the Council of the League of Nations is to present a plan.' To this the representatives of the small States would reply, ' Are you bound to accept it? ' and the Principal Powers would have to reply ' No '."

This question was not actually asked by the representatives of the small States at the meeting of the Council of Four on the 5th June, but the arguments used by them in their statements greatly impressed the members of the Council.[38]

Mr. Vesnitch, on behalf of the Serbo-Croat-Slovene State, said that " he must confess the proposals came quite as a surprise. His Delegation felt bound to put the question of how matters of such importance for Allied States who fought side by side with the larger Powers could be decided as part of settlement with the enemy. This gave him serious preoccupation. A second and equally important point was the tendency to diminish and even to annihilate the sovereignty of the smaller States. In entering the war, one of the things for which his country had fought was to obtain for small States the same freedom, the same right of organization and the same juridical equality as had been recognized as just ever since international law had existed." Mr. Bratiano, speaking as a representative of

Rumania, a country which for the time being did not know " whether she would have as neighbour the Ukraine or a great united Russia," declared that the Rumanian effectives " could not be considered until an answer could be given as to what would be the status of Russia, the strength of her forces and her relation to the League of Nations."

Mr. Paderewski drew the attention of the Council to the " peculiar position of Poland. ... Poland was greatly menaced by Germany, not only on the West and on the North-West, but in the country itself. From 300,000 to 350,000 German soldiers were concentrated round Poland in Upper Silesia, Poznania, East Prussia and Lithuania. ... On the other side Poland was not menaced but forced by circumstances to be at war with Bolshevik Russia and the Ukraine. On the Eastern side of Germany the German forces were not yet entirely controlled by the Allied and Associated Powers, and on the Eastern frontiers of Poland the Peace Conference exercised no authority whatsoever. Hence, he was obliged to ask that the Principal Powers in the case of disarmament would undertake to protect Poland against Russia and Germany." The last demand was rather insidious because it was well known at that time that the Great Powers were unwilling to send any troops to Eastern Europe.

After these declarations it became obvious that it would be most unwise for the representatives of the Principal Powers to insist on their misguided plans. President Wilson was the first to state that " all recognized the danger of present circumstances to the States of Central Europe. He felt that after hearing these views he would have to think the whole matter over again." Lloyd George, agreeing on this point with President Wilson, observed that " the argument presented by the statesmen present had been very powerful and clever, but he and his colleagues had no idea of any interference with sovereignty(!). Moreover they would not impose conditions they were unwilling to accept themselves. After peace was signed there would be a great reduction in the military forces of the British Empire. The Rumanian army would almost certainly be larger than the British, and probably the same could be said of the Polish." To the latter remark Mr. Paderewski retorted that " Great Britain did not have to ' fight water ' on its frontiers." M. Clemenceau associated himself with the point of view presented by the representatives of small nations and concluded that " the best plan would be to decide to take a mutual obligation by the great and little powers to settle these questions when the right time came," and the whole plan was eventually dropped, but over and over again in the inter-war period it was asserted that the defensive armaments of the small States might endanger the peace of Europe.

We wish to mention in a few words another proposal to interfere with the sovereignty of small States, due to General Smuts whose lack of sympathy for the cause of freedom of the nations of Central and Eastern Europe, side by side with his marked pro-German bias, is astonishing in one who was such a prominent figure in defending and advocating the cause of his own nation. General Smuts obviously saw all the nations of that area through German eyes and did not believe in their maturity and capacity for independent life; he made some very definite proposals, although his knowledge of these problems was extremely limited. This appears clearly from his " Practical Suggestion " for a League of Nations [39]:

> " The peoples left behind by the decomposition of Russia, Austria and Turkey, are mostly untrained politically: many of them are either incapable of or deficient in power of self-government; they are mostly destitute and will require much nursing towards economic and political independence. ... That, so far at any rate as the peoples and territories formerly belonging to Russia, Austria-Hungary and Turkey are concerned, the League of Nations should be considered as the reversionary in the most general sense and as clothed with the right of ultimate disposal in accordance with certain fundamental principles. Reversion to the League of Nations should be substituted for any policy of national annexation."

The proposal to apply the same treatment to the old historic nations of Central and Eastern Europe and to the backward countries outside Europe was too preposterous to be fully retained by the Allied statesmen, although these ideas were to some extent applied to Poland in the Austrian Peace Treaty, as we shall see later (see Chapter III). It is interesting to note that Smuts, admitting the case of disannexation in the return of Alsace-Lorraine to France, did not see any analogy between this case and that of the old provinces of Poland seized by Prussia, Austria and Russia.

> " In the first place, if Alsace-Lorraine is annexed to France, that would be a case of disannexation, as it has been put ; that is to say, it is a case of restoration to France of what was violently and wrongfully taken from her in 1871, against the protests not only of France but of the population of Alsace-Lorraine speaking through their elected representation. It is a restitution in integrum on moral and legal grounds, and only in a secondary or consequential sense a territorial annexation. Its restitution to France would therefore satisfy instead of violating, the moral sense of the world."

But the tables were turned on General Smuts in that occurrence, because the idea of mandates was taken over by Wilson from Smuts and applied to German colonies as well as to former Turkish territories, to the great confusion of the General and his compatriots.

General Smuts excluded from his proposal the German colonies : did he consider his nation more civilized than the old European nations? In any case it was Smuts's good friend Lloyd George who went straight to the point in a letter to him of the 3rd June, 1919, in reply to his criticism of the Versailles Treaty.[40] " The Germans," wrote Lloyd George, " repeatedly request the return of colonies. Are you prepared to allow German South-West Africa and German East Africa to be returned to Germany as a concession which might induce them to sign the peace? " Smuts's reply on the following day shows that he felt himself in an awkward position : " Please do not have the impression," he wrote, " that I would be generous at the expense of others so long as the Union gets South-West Africa."

Minority clauses and the Jewish question in Poland

Another issue on which the sovereignty of new States underwent drastic limitations was that implied by the minority clauses contained in special treaties with new States and to which, so far as Poland was concerned, referred Article XCIII of the Treaty of Versailles :

> " Poland accepts and agrees to embody in a Treaty with the Principal Allied and Associated Powers such provisions as may be deemed necessary by the said Powers to protect the interests of the inhabitants of Poland who differ from the majority of the population in race, language or religion."

We cannot go more fully either into the historic background or the merits of the Minorities Treaties,[40a] to which many special studies were devoted in the inter-war period and which gave rise to many heated polemics between the partisans and adversaries of these Treaties.[41] We know that the provisions referring to the protection of racial or national minorities were imposed on the so-called new States owing above all to the insistence of some Jewish organizations.[41a] While old and powerful Jewish organizations such as " Alliance Israélite Universelle " established in Paris, and " The Joint Foreign Committee " in Great Britain claimed only the abolition of all the restrictions on Jews which had existed before the war in Russia and Rumania and which might have been introduced in Poland, as well as equality of treatment and autonomous management of Jewish religious, cultural and charitable institutions, the American Jewish organizations under the influence of the émigrés from Central and Eastern Europe asked for infinitely more, namely, for the régime of personal autonomy which would have preserved the Jews from any attempts at assimilation. It was the latter trend, marking the revival of Jewish national ambitions, that eventually prevailed, not without great opposition within the " Committee of the Jewish Delegations at the Peace Conference." The draft presented by this body on 19th April, 1919, and later only slightly amended, asked for automatic right of citizenship, equality of civil, religious, political and national rights, the right for all minorities comprising at least one per cent. of the total population to constitute an autonomous body political with the right of establishing their own national, religious, cultural, charitable and social institutions, separate electoral colleges in all elections, representation proportional to the number of the minority in the State, a share proportional to the number of minority in the State from the public funds to cover their expenditure, so far as this involved the exercise of governmental functions. These far-reaching demands were backed to a great extent by the American legal adviser, D. H. Miller.

The matter was brought before the Council of Four on the 1st May [42] by President Wilson, who remarked that " the Jews were somewhat inhospitably regarded in Poland."

Two clauses proposed by Wilson himself were of a quite general nature and concerned equality of treatment and " the free exercise of any creed, religion or belief whose practices are not inconsistent with public order or public morals," but the draft submitted at the same time by Mr. David Hunter Miller, Legal Adviser to the American Delegation, met many Jewish demands,[43] proposing the recognition by Poland of several national minorities " as constituting distinct public corporations, and as such having the right to establish,. manage and control their schools and their religious, educational, charitable or social institutions."

According to another clause, which had two variants, the national minorities should be " allotted a proportion " of the funds from the State, departmental, municipal and other budgets " for the maintenance of schools or religious, educational, charitable or social institutions."

Moreover, Poland was to adopt " the principle of proportional minority representation in all sorts of elections, based upon the ratio of its members in the respective electoral areas to the entire population therein."

The Supreme Council on 1st May appointed a small committee known as " The New States Committee " under the chairmanship of the French representative, M. Ph. Berthelot, which was to deal with the minority and economic clauses to be inserted into special treaties with the new States. The Committee presented its report on 16th May, rejecting the request for national-cultural autonomy claimed by the Jews. " It was unanimously agreed," stated the report, " that these claims could not be accepted, for they would seriously undermine the authority of the Polish State." It was on the insistent request of the British delegate that an article on the " Sabbath " was inserted into the draft against the opposition of the American and Italian delegates which considered it as an inadmissible restraint on Poland.[43a]

In the final provisions of the Treaties with Poland and other new States these clauses were still more toned down. For instance, in Article VIII of the Treaty with Poland the latter had to grant to the minorities the right " to establish, manage and control *at their own expense* charitable, religious and social institutions with the right to use their own language and to exercise their religion freely therein." In Article IX of the said Treaty only " in *primary schools* the instruction shall be given to the children of such Polish nationals through the medium of their own language. This provision should not prevent the Polish Government from making the teaching of the Polish language obligatory in the said schools." And the subsequent paragraph of this Article speaks only of " an equitable share in the enjoyment and application of the sums which may be provided out of public funds," and this only " in towns and districts where there is a considerable proportion of Polish nationals belonging to racial, religious or linguistic minorities." No provision was made as to the proportional representation of the minorities in all sorts of elections.

These changes were due to some extent to the opposition of the representatives of the small States. A very characteristic exchange of views between Wilson and Lloyd George took place at the meeting of the Council of Four on the 17th June, 1919,[44] after the reading of the memorandum of Mr. Paderewski of the 15th June. President Wilson remarked that " it was a serious indictment that we were claiming more for the Germans in Poland than for the Poles in Germany," and he pointed out the danger arising from " imparting to the Jews a corporate capacity." Lloyd George also had some misgivings. He said that " there was somewhat in the contention that a separate organization for the Jewish schools would tend to create a separate nation of the Jews in Poland rather than unity." [44a]

The Polish point of view was summed up in the memorandum of Mr. Paderewski of the 15th June.[45] He presented the objection " from the point of view of the sovereign rights of Poland," which should find confirmation by a treaty between the Polish State and the Principal Powers, and referred to the " nefarious consequences which may result from the protection exercised by Foreign Powers over ethical and religious minorities. The Polish nation has not forgotten that the dismemberment of Poland was the consequence of the intervention of foreign powers concerning her religious minorities, and this painful memory makes Poland fear the external interference in internal matters of State more than anything."

Dealing in particular with Polish-Jewish relations, Mr. Paderewski recalled that " it was the former Polish State which outdistanced others in the matter of assuring equality of political rights to all its citizens, without distinction of origin, language, or creed, and had opened its doors to sects persecuted in neighbouring States and had assured a refuge to the Jews banished from the West." He admitted that the " relations between the Jewish and Christian population in Poland have lately become strained. To those who are acquainted with the evolution of the Jewish question in Poland, this is rather a surprising phenomenon. The Polish nation with whom the Jews, chased from Germany, had found refuge for several centuries and all facilities for organizing their religious life, wished towards the end of the eighteenth century to emancipate these Jews, relegated to their ghettoes, and even after the loss of its independence attempted to grant them the full measure of civil rights. Polish-Jewish relations during the whole of the nineteenth century were distinguished by good understanding." He attributed the recent misunderstandings to the fact that on many occasions the Jews considering the Polish cause lost, sided with Poland's enemies, a matter with which we deal later in connection with the reports of the American and British observers in Poland. According to Mr. Paderewski there was no doubt that the Polish Constitution would safeguard equal rights for all Polish citizens, but there were great dangers in " transferring the question on to international ground."

The Polish memorandum " expressed the desire that the principles of freedom should be universally applied to minorities. Poland promises to realize the stipulations concerning their rights which the League of Nations will recognize as being obligatory for all States belonging to the League, in the same way as with regard to the protection of labour." It should be noted that this demand for the general application of the basic principles of equality of rights of all men without regard to their origin and race put the Great Powers in a rather awkward position, considering that a very moderate Japanese proposal submitted by Baron Makino to the Peace Conference (addition of a clause to Article XXI of the Covenant of the League of Nations) had been discarded in view of the opposition of the United States and the British Dominions which feared the consequences which might follow from its application in relation to their immigration laws. Thus the Principal Powers were imposing on Poland some rules which they were unwilling to accept for themselves.

" It was an error of principle in the Peace Treaties " [stated Professor Gilbert Murray, in his preface to the book of L. P. Mair, *The Protection of Minorities*], " to impose the clauses for the due protection of Minorities upon the new nations alone. The same obligation should have been accepted by the Great Powers, and made part of the common law of Europe." " . . . the whole principle of exempting the Great Powers is indefensible. As it is, the new nations do not accept the minority clauses as a part of the natural duties of a civilized State, but resent them as a limitation of their independence."

The Polish memorandum referred further to another valid argument, which later events fully justified, namely that the treaty did not guarantee the rights of Poles in Germany. Mr. Paderewski's memorandum contained the following remarks on this subject :

" After conclusion of the Peace a large proportion of the Polish population will remain within the German Empire. Formerly, the Polish population in Germany was not only deprived of equality of rights, but was submitted to a rigorous system of exceptional laws and administrative decrees, aiming at the extermination of the Polish element. The Peace Treaty does not impose on the Germans any obligation to grant equality of rights to the Poles of the Empire. . . . The treatment of the Polish minorities in Germany and of the German minorities in Poland cannot therefore be considered on the basis of reciprocity."

Such reciprocity was partially assured later only in the German part of Upper Silesia, and this only for a limited period.

M. Berthelot's letter of the 19th June to Sir Maurice Hankey, referring to this Polish demand for reciprocity, stated inaccurately that there would remain very few groups of Poles in Germany.[46]

Mr. Paderewski repeated his demand for reciprocity in a letter addressed to M. Clemenceau and dated 26th June, and the question was discussed in his presence at the meeting of the Council of Four on the 27th June.[47] The answers given there by the members of the Council were completely unsatisfactory. Lloyd George suggested that " the best plan would be for Poland to make an appeal to the League of Nations on the subject," forgetting that such an appeal would have lacked any juridical basis, as no legal obligation was binding on Germany. President Wilson " suggested that the League might be asked to insist on corresponding treatment to the Poles in German territory as a condition for Germany's entering into the League of Nations. He regretted that provision for just treatment of Poles in Germany had not been made in the German Treaty and that it would be necessary to postpone the matter for the present, but, in the circumstances, he thought this was the best plan." This suggestion was never implemented, as at the moment of Germany's entry into the League of Nations the Great Powers were too eager to accept German candidature, and so Germany was left entirely free from any foreign interference in her internal affairs.

The greatest defect of the Minorities Treaties, as will appear in the later stages, was that all the minority questions were submitted in the first instance to the Council of the League of Nations, a political body the members of which were always inclined to consider them not on their merits but from the point of view of the general policy of the States which they represented. To obtain some advantages in the other field the delegates to the Council of the League were often induced to make far-reaching concessions to German minorities supported by the German Reich. Thus the German minorities enjoyed a privileged position within the new States, being always ready to serve the interests of their country of origin against the State to which they owed allegiance.

So the German minorities problem became an important element in the general appeasement policy of the Great Powers in relation to Germany, considerably weakening the position of the new States, Poland in particular.

The whole problem can also be considered from the point of view of the policy of the Principal Powers towards the new States. It showed the tendency to put them in an inferior position in the international community, in spite of all the sacrifices borne by them for the cause of their freedom, and consequently for the common cause of the Allied and Associated Powers. The position of these States was even worse than that of neutral States. Their début in international life began with a serious handicap. Mr. Paderewski was right when he stated in his above-mentioned letter that

> " to place one special part of the Polish Constitution under the protection of the League of Nations ... is equivalent to regarding the Polish nation as a nation of inferior standard of civilization, incapable of ensuring to all its citizens the rights and civic liberties and ignorant of the conception of the duties of a modern State."

A contemporary observer, Mr. Dillon, makes the following remark in his book, *The Paris Peace Conference,* which appeared immediately after the Conference closed :

> " We behold her (Poland) about to begin her national existence as a semi-independent nation, beset with enemies domestic and foreign. For it would be an abuse of terms to affirm that Poland, or indeed, any of the lesser States, is fully independent in the old sense of the word." [48]

And in another place in his book he says :

> " The minority treaties tend to transform each of the States on which it is imposed into a miniature Balkans, to keep Europe in continuous turmoil and hinder the growth of the new and creative ideas from which alone one could expect the union of collective energy with individual freedom, which is essential to peace and progress. Modern history affords no more striking example of the

force of abstract bias over the teaching of experience than this amateur legislation which is scattering seeds of mischief and conflict throughout Europe." [49]

Before leaving this problem it would be proper to answer the question whether, at least so far as Poland was concerned, the information in the possession of the representatives of the Principal Powers relating to the alleged ill-treatment of the Jewish population in Poland (with tacit or express approval of the authorities), and which might to some extent have justified the steps taken by them in order to safeguard the rights of the Jewish population in that country, agreed with the facts? As soon as Poland was liberated the news spread all over the world of mass pogroms of the Jewish population in that country. One may say, reading American, English, and French newspapers of that epoch, that the *only* news reaching the West from Poland, especially at the end of November 1918 and the beginning of December 1918, was that concerning the ill-treatment of the Jewish population in that country. It seems the more astonishing since the first Government in liberated Poland consisted—as we have said in Chapter V of the first Part of this book—exclusively of Socialists and Radicals whose parties numbered many persons of Jewish descent in their ranks, some of them reaching the highest posts in the party hierarchy. Moreover Pilsudski himself was entirely free from racial prejudices, and in the Polish Legions many Poles of Jewish origin served with great distinction, even as officers of high rank.

The proceedings of the House of Commons at that period also show that many questions to the Government were devoted to the alleged Polish atrocities against Jews.

Only gradually, but *after* Poland had signed the Minority Treaty, it appeared that much of the information about the alleged pogroms against the Jews in Poland was based on gross exaggeration. As a matter of fact the results of two great inquiries into the conditions of Jews in Poland, carried out on the spot, were published *after* the signature (the report of Sir Stuart Samuel's Mission to Poland, dated 2nd June, 1919, and the report of the Morgenthau Mission still later, namely, 3rd October, 1919). Thus the provisions of the Minority Treaty were drafted on the basis of biased information. In fact the report of the " New States Committee," dated 15th May, based its findings on the assumption that the Jews were persecuted in Poland, as appears from the following passage of the said report : " It is strong evidence of a deliberate purpose to submit them (the Jews) to a cruel and calculated moral and physical persecution. This throws upon the Allies an obligation to provide safeguards which, it is hoped, will not be necessary for other minorities." And yet even before the reports of the Special Commission sent by the British Government could reach it, the British representative in the Inter-Allied Commission to Poland, Sir Esme Howard (later Lord Howard of Penrith, Ambassador to Rome and Washington) warned his Government against the one-sided and biased information on the position of the Jews in Poland, in his report to Lord Balfour, dated 26th March, 1919.[49a] Stating that " there are several divisions amongst the Jews in Poland " and that " the assimilated Jews are openly pro-Polish and desire no privileges," that " the orthodox Jews forming nearly one-half of the Jewish population ... desire only special confessional schools," he deals in the third instance with the Zionists and the party of the Jewish Bund, " whose desires range from a sort of educational autonomy down to having their own budget, their own police and their own military." Sir Esme Howard found also that " a great number of Jews unquestionably sided with the Germans and openly declared their anti-Polish and anti-national sentiments. Their main object indeed seems to have been to destroy the possibility of a Polish State, and it is largely owing, I am inclined to think, to their propaganda that the belief in the Poles as a persecutionary race has sprung up. I noticed in an article in the *Manchester Guardian* of the 19th March, for instance, the following question : ' Who dreams that Poland of her own motion will do aught but continue to persecute the Jews?' "

It appears from the reports of two special commissions sent to Poland, the details of which are given below, that although there were some sporadic excesses in Poland they were far from being on such a large scale as in other East European countries and, moreover, the Polish authorities took the steps necessary to prevent the recurrence of such reprehensible acts which were due to the chaotic initial conditions and the war.

It was on the strength of this revised information that the Western Governments were obliged in the later stages to take the defence of the Polish Government, which continued to be accused of many acts of violence. As an example we reproduce below passages from two characteristic debates in the House of Commons dealing with the alleged " Jewish massacres " in Poland.

At the meeting of the 2nd July, 1919, answering the question of W. Seager about the " atrocities perpetrated by the *new* Polish nation upon Jews," Mr. Harmsworth stated :

> " The information which we have received with regard to these Jewish pogroms is much more favourable to the Polish authorities than some accounts give the public to understand " (*Parliamentary Debates*, House of Commons, Vol. 117).

At the meeting of the 9th July, 1919, Sir Kinloch-Cooke referred to the " indignation prevailing in Jewish circles in this country at the continued massacres of the defenceless Jewish population in Polish towns." On behalf of the Government, Mr. Harmsworth answered that " the Polish Government are determined to prevent anything in the nature of organized attacks upon the persons or property of Jews."

Mr. Raper then asked : " Is it not a fact that in every case for some time after these massacres were reported a Mission was sent to inquire into them, and does not their report prove that many of the accounts were exaggerated? " To this question Mr. Harmsworth answered : " I have already stated in the House that later reports indicate that there has been exaggeration " (*ibidem*).

The first of the Missions sent to Poland was the British Mission headed by Sir Stuart Samuel (*State Papers*, Cmd. 674, Miscellaneous No. 10 (1920). The Mission was unable to agree on an unanimous report and we have thus two reports, one signed by Sir Stuart and another by Captain P. Wright. Nor did the British Envoy in Warsaw (Sir Horace Rumbold) share all the views held by Sir Stuart. In his covering letter addressed to Lord Curzon he stated :

> " The excesses against the Jews were described as pogroms in the Press of Western Europe, but it can be here remarked that the word ' pogrom ' is used in a different sense in Poland from what it is understood to convey in Western Europe. The word ' pogrom ' conveys to the inhabitant of Western Europe massacres or excesses against a portion of the population which are either organized or countenanced by the authorities. In Poland the word is applied to disturbances in which lives are not necessarily lost."

Examining the figures stated in Sir Stuart's report (" The excesses in Poland proper, in the course of which eighteen Jews lost their lives ... those which took place in the war zones which, in November 1918, included Lemberg, and where the majority of the murders occurred ... Sir Stuart Samuel estimates the total number of lives lost at not less than 348, so that 330 Jews were killed in the war zone "), Sir Horace concludes that " in view of the weakness of central administration and the original want of discipline in the Polish army, it would appear that the authorities could not be held responsible for the excesses, and therefore they lose the character of pogroms." Sir Horace explains further that the anti-semitic feelings in Poland were due to the Russian special anti-Jewish legislation which had driven thousands of Jews outside the so-called Pale of Settlement creating big competition between the Poles and the Jews. He notes also the fact that " the Germans employed a large number of Jews during the occupation of Poland while the Poles served the

Germans by compulsion only." Sir Horace states that as appears from Sir Stuart's report, the conditions of the Jews in Poland " have been far better than in most of the surrounding countries." " It is giving the Jews very little assistance to single out as is sometimes done, for reprobation and protest, the country where they have perhaps suffered least."

Although Sir Stuart Samuel's report is somewhat more severe on the Poles, which to a certain extent can be explained by the Jewish origin of its author, it emphasizes nevertheless that " every assistance was rendered by the Polish Government to the Mission in prosecuting its inquiries."

Captain P. Wright starts his report by a very pertinent remark : " The Poles complained bitterly of foreign commissions meddling with their national affairs without any acquaintance with the history of their past, as if they were savages without any past history at all. This complaint seemed to me reasonable and just; for our own domestic questions, like the Irish question, for example, could hardly be understood by foreigners ignorant of and indifferent to our past history."

" Inquiring into the nature and origin of the animosity," Captain Wright draws attention to the fact that " nothing less than half the Polish Jews is not only far from European, but it is also very primitive ... they are not civilized in our sense of the word and it is impossible for Poles to amalgamate with them, and difficult to mix with them, or even to frame common laws for them." In the past Poland was called " Paradisus Judærum." " When one thinks," he says, " of what happened to the other ' racial, religious and linguistic minorities ' of Europe in modern times, say the French protestants, or the Irish catholics, to take the first of numberless examples that come to hand, the Jew appears not as the most persecuted, but as the most favoured people of Europe." The situation changed in the nineteenth century when " the Jews had become, more and more, not only a separate body as in the previous ages, but a body politically claiming an independence as much as the Poles, and socially complete equality ... but the Jews in Poland have not only been Polonized they have been Russified and Germanized. So that the Jews appear to the Poles as the representatives of their oppressors. ... The Tsarist Government drove the Jews out of Russia and tried to make ' one great ghetto of Poland.' ... The ' Litvaki ' openly professed themselves the partisans of conquering Russia, deliberately talked Russian."

Wright then refers to the special conditions which have arisen during the German occupation of some Polish territories : " But the high day and triumph of the Jews was during the German occupation. The Jews in Poland are deeply Germanized and German carries you over Poland because Jews are everywhere. So the Germans found everywhere people who knew their language and could work for them. It was with Jews that the Germans set up their organization to squeeze and drain Poland—Poles and Jews included—of everything they had; it was in concert with Jews that German officials and officers toward the end carried on business all over the country."

Captain Wright's conclusion recalls that reached by Sir Horace Rumbold : " The Jews have suffered very much during the last year, and unfortunately there is no exact measure of suffering. However, I estimate that no more than 200 or 300 have been unjustly killed. One would be too many, but taking these casualties as a standard with which to measure the excess committed against them, I am more astonished at their smallness than their greatness. At least a hundred times as many have been slaughtered during the same period in the Ukraine, and perhaps quite as many in Hungary or Czechoslovakia."

Still more explicit and favourable to Poland are the conclusions reached by the American Mission to Poland headed by the distinguished American statesman, himself of Jewish origin, Mr. Morgenthau. Let us remember in this connection that the American representatives were among the foremost advocates of the Jewish cause at the Peace Conference. The report of Mr. Morgenthau, to the American Commission to Negotiate Peace, is dated 3rd October, 1919.[50] This very interesting and exhaustive document starts by the following statement :

" Just as the Jews would resent being condemned as a race for the action of a few of their undesirable coreligionists, so it would be correspondingly unfair to condemn the Polish nation as a whole for the violence committed by uncontrolled troops or local mobs. These excesses were apparently not premeditated, for if they had been part of a preconceived plan, the number of victims would run into thousands instead of amounting to about 280."

Still more interesting are the enclosed reports of General Edgar Jadwin and Mr. Hoover H. Johnson of the Mission to Poland, dated 31st October, 1919.[51] They also inquire into the causes of the Polish-Jewish friction in recent times, which arose from the rigid enforcement by the Tsarist Government of the Pale of Settlement pushing from Central Russia towards Poland the masses of Russified Jews; and later, in the period of the occupation of Poland by the Central Powers, from the German policy towards the Jewish community, some members of which were used by Germany as " agents for various purposes " in view of " the readiness of certain Jewish elements to enter into relations with the winning side." Referring in particular to the unrest in Lwow, provoked by some individuals in connection with the fighting between Poles and Ukrainians, the report makes interesting disclosures on the motives of this anti-Polish propaganda spread in the West :

> " The disorders of 21st to 23rd November, 1918, in Lemberg (Lwow) became, like the excesses in Lithuania, a weapon of foreign anti-Polish propaganda. The Press Bureau of the Central Powers, whose interest is to discredit the Polish Republic before the world, permitted the publication of articles like that in the *Neue Freie Presse* of 30th November, 1918, in which an eye-witness estimated the number of victims between 2,500 and 3,000 although the extreme number furnished by the local Jewish committee was 76. ... The Jewish question is rendered more difficult by the efforts of certain malicious German influences to further their Eastern projects by discrediting Poland financially and otherwise. It is not in the interest of the German State to allow Poland to become a powerful and prosperous competitor, since Poland is more favourably situated to act as centre of exchange between Russia and the West. There are also conservative elements among Russian statesmen who are equally anxious to prevent foreign financial aid to Poland and are using criticism of the Polish State as a weapon to forestall the assistance of the Allied and Associated Powers. If Poland is to become a firmly established State, the needs of the Republic must be considered from the angle of Polish national aspirations and rights, and not simply on the basis of the purposes of its temporarily paralysed neighbours to the East and West."

The report of the first American envoy to Poland, Mr. Gibson, to the State Department of the 2nd June, 1919, dots the i's and crosses the t's [52]:

> " The present campaign abroad is largely based on agitation fomented outside Poland. ... I learn from Lieutenant-Colonel Dawley, of the General Staff, that there is a German news agency established at Kovno (Kaunas) which is in German hands and that this agency is pouring out (to Berlin) a stream of stories as to what is happening in the neighbouring regions under Polish occupation. ... The Germans are clearly doing this with a purpose: (*a*) to stir up as much dissension as possible inside the country so as to keep it in a weakened condition, and (*b*) to create the impression throughout the world that Poland is a country unworthy of our sympathy and support, thereby weakening her as a possible rival or enemy. The German propaganda is certainly not undertaken for the altruistic purpose of helping the Jews." [53]

There is no doubt that some Jewish organizations abroad fell victims in 1918-19 to this German propaganda, supported by German Jews who were eager to serve the interests of the country to which they owed allegiance.[53a] On the other side one should keep in mind that so far as the Eastern provinces of Poland were concerned it was no wonder that a part of the Jewish population there (especially the younger generation), consisting mostly of destitute town proletariat, felt strongly the appeal of the Bolshevik slogans promising equal chances to all men irrespective of race and origin. It is common knowledge that many Jews held the highest posts in the Soviet hierarchy in the first years of the Bolshevik Revolution and that the Bolshevik delegation to the Brest-Litovsk Conference consisted almost exclusively of Jews (even Radek, who acted there as the mouthpiece of the Polish nation, was a Galician Jew). But later developments have shown that it was the biggest mistake of Jewish history to side with Germany or Soviet Russia. In any case, the main body of Jews in Poland continued to live undisturbed, and remained aloof from foreign inspirations. Nobody can deny that there unfortunately existed in Poland as well as in other Central and Eastern European States an anti-Semitic agitation in some nationalistic quarters, but no outside interference could have removed the deep roots of existing frictions. It would be beyond the scope of this book to deal at length with all the aspects of the Jewish question in Poland and other Central European countries.[53b] The fact is that in spite of all the dark sides of Jewish life in the Central European diaspora, in Poland there had arisen the most flourishing Zionist centres and the number of the most prominent leaders of the new State of Israel who came from Poland is astonishingly high. It was Germany, in which so many Jews put their hopes in 1914-18, that eventually ruthlessly liquidated the Jewish population in Poland as well as in other countries of Central and Eastern Europe. Soviet Russia in its own way liquidated the Jewish question in the territories occupied by it by forcibly merging the Jews with the rest of the population, at the same time depriving them of their secular traditions, of which the Jewish nation could be legitimately proud.

It appears clearly from the foregoing that the decisions of the principal statesmen in Paris were based, in this as in other questions, on one-sided and biased information. Dillon was right in calling many decisions taken by these statesmen " improvisation and haphazard conclusions," [54] and Temperley, in his quoted book, speaking about the " secret and speedy decisions " of the principal statesmen, draws attention to the disadvantages of this procedure which " threw greatly increased power into the hands of those who formed the personal staff of the chief statesmen. Neither the Chiefs nor their immediate following could be fully informed as to the many questions on which the decisions were made, yet advice is sought from subordinate officials and irresponsible sources which would have been of greater value if checked by the machinery already established in Paris." [55]

Reparations, War debts and Polish claims

Another issue on which the " new " States, Poland in the first place, were treated in a discriminatory manner was that of the reparations and financial clauses contained in the Treaties of Versailles and St. Germain. It is well known that it was on Polish soil that the biggest battles were fought in Eastern Europe, and the damage through military operations and the systematic exploitation of that part of the country which had been occupied by the Central Powers were estimated at 75 billion francs. [56]

" Western Europe and America never realized the savage devastation visited on Poland in 1914-15," exclaims an American writer, H. H. Fisher, who has very thoroughly reviewed the data referring to war damage in Poland. [56a] (We stated above some figures referring to the policy of " de-industrialization " of the Congress Kingdom carried out by the German occupying authorities, see p. 113). Another American writer who visited Poland and became acquainted with the respective statistical figures, R. L. Buell, stated that " except for Belgium, Poland had suffered greater devastation than any other European nation," and quoted some very impressive figures :

" ... 1,800,000 buildings in cities and villages destroyed ... 11 million acres of agricultural land put out of use ... the losses in livestock amounted to 2 million head of cattle, 1 million horses, and 1,500,000 sheep and goats ... within the area of war operations 6 million acres of forest ... were totally destroyed and devastated by alien armies, who removed 4,661 million cubic feet of timber from the country ... invading belligerents carried away from Poland 4,259 electrical motors and engines and 3,844 tooling machines ... before leaving Poland at the end of the war, the Austro-German forces blew up 7,500 bridges and destroyed 940 railway stations." [56b]

Yet from the beginning the view was taken by the Allied experts, [57] subsequently approved by the Council of Four, that Poland and Czechoslovakia should not be entitled to claim reparations, on the ground that they constituted a part of enemy countries. When the suggestion was discussed at the meeting of the Council of Four on the 23rd April, [58] Lloyd George justified this point of view in a rather curious manner : " there had been considerable devastation in Poland, but Poland had nominally been at war against us even though it had been against the will of the Polish people. Poles had actually taken part in the devastation of France." On the other hand, the question arose whether Poland should bear any part of the costs of the war in connection with the Austrian and Hungarian Treaties. It was Wilson who then tried to defend the Polish interests. At the meeting of the Council of Four on 10th May he said [59] " his first and sentimental idea was that Poland ought to be let off altogether. Poland had been caught, as it were, in three nets —the Austrian, the German, and the Russian, and had in consequence suffered dreadfully. It seemed only common justice to leave her out from any costs of the war or reparations." At the meeting of the Council of Four on the 14th June,[60] when the question was discussed as to the position in regard to reparation of territories which were German at the beginning of the war (Danzig, Upper Silesia), President Wilson again remarked :

> " Whatever views anyone might hold about Poland, the Polish people had been compelled to fight for the Central Powers. They had no choice. Their territory had been devastated by Russia as well as by Germany. They had suffered as hard a fate as any nation in the war."

So far as Lloyd George was concerned, he stuck to his original ideas and refused to make any concessions to Poland and the other new States. At the meeting of the Council of Four on the 10th May he repeated his previous objections, adding that there was another valid reason : the sacrifices borne by the Principal Powers for the cause of small nations :

> " All the Allied Powers had incurred heavy debts for the emancipation of these races. They had been freed not by their own efforts, but by those of the Allies. Their only share in the war had been to fight against us. Without taking any final decision as to the case of Poland he thought that the inquiry should be extended to Poland." [61]

Even if one accepts the point of view defended by Lloyd George that formally a part of Poland was an enemy country during the war, this should not apply to another part of Poland which before the war belonged to the Russian Empire. But the rights of Russia were safeguarded by Article CXVI of the Versailles Treaty which stipulated that " the Allied and Associated Powers formally reserve the right of Russia to obtain from Germany restitution and reparation based on the principle of the present Treaty." While Poland was not admitted to the benefits under this clause, she was on the other hand bound to recognize her liability for a part of the Russian debt. Article XXI of the special Treaty with Poland provided that " Poland agrees to assume responsibility for such proportion of the Russian debt and other Russian public liabilities of any kind as may be assigned to her under a special convention between the Principal

Allied and Associated Powers on the one hand and Poland on the other, to be prepared by a Commission appointed by the above States." The injustice of this provision is the more striking if one keeps in mind that the Polish provinces of Russia had been systematically exploited by the Russian authorities, and the Congress Kingdom in particular paid considerable sums to the Russian budget, sums greatly exceeding the expenditure for the special purposes of this province. This unfavourable position of the Congress Kingdom in the pre-war years was expressly recognized in the Treaty of Riga with Soviet Russia.

The general clauses of the Versailles Treaty relating to reparations were redrafted for a special purpose, that of excluding Poland from the claims to reparations, as clearly appears from the letter addressed by Sir Maurice Hankey, Secretary of the Supreme Council, to Mr. Dutasta, Secretary-General of the Peace Conference, dated 3rd May [62]:

> " At a meeting between President Wilson, Mr. Lloyd George and Mr. Loucher, with Financial Experts this morning, the question was raised as to whether the Reparation Chapter as now drafted did not give Poland a claim for damages against Germany.
>
> " It was decided that this was not intended, and should be dealt with by the introduction in the appropriate place of words to the effect that the claims against Germany by Allied and Associated Powers should only rank if damages were incurred at a date at which a given power had been acknowledged as an Allied and Associated Power belligerent."

These words were actually inserted in Article CCXXXII, para. 2 of the Versailles Treaty.

We cannot deal with all the provisions of the Versailles and St. Germain Treaties referring to Poland's special position in the matter of reparations and her share in a part of the public debts of the enemy countries,[63] dealing here only with the political aspects of the problem. How Poland felt about the unjust treatment to which she was subjected appears clearly from a letter from the Polish Delegation to the Organization Committee of the Reparations Commission dated 5th December, 1919, in which we read among other things [64]:

> " ... there is also a political side which the Commission might not consider but to which the Polish Government believes it important to draw the French Government's attention.
>
> " A decision which would deprive Poland of all claims to reparation would produce profound disillusion, it would alarm Polish public opinion in the extreme, and might be interpreted by the public as a change of Allied policy in regard to Poland. For it would not understand why Russia, whose territory has suffered

only slightly as a result of the war, should benefit by a right to reparations (paragraph 116 of the Peace Treaty) while Poland is deprived of them, particularly as Poland has been almost exclusively the battleground of military operations in the East, and has been subject to devastation not less than Belgium or Serbia, and who, finally, had agreed to assume part of the Russian debt.

"According to the Treaties of Versailles and Saint Germain, Poland is to contribute to the mutual reparations fund considerable amounts to the credit of Germany and Austria. If the Polish claims are recognized, if only in part, the liabilities which Poland assumes in this way would be balanced. If the contrary should take place, not only would Poland be deprived of all reparations, but would be obliged to contribute to those of the others. The need of reconstituting the industrial and agricultural life of the devastated countries, as well as the precarious condition of Polish finances, so harmed by the war, a war defensive in the East against the Bolshevist danger which is threatening all Europe, make it absolutely impossible for the Polish Government to assume any new charges."

The foregoing account should dispose of the legend of a privileged position conceded by the Great Powers at the Peace Conference to a country which was among those that were most affected by the evils of war. Poland was practically left to her own devices to start political and economic life; she was moreover burdened with considerable liabilities undermining her credit and hampering her economic reconstruction. The same Mr. Keynes who, in his capacity of financial expert to the British Delegation at the Peace Conference was the first to insist on the inadmissibility of the Polish claims to reparations, sarcastically observed in his book, *The Economic Consequences of the Peace*, that " Poland is an economic impossibility with no industry but Jew-baiting." [65]

This most unfair remark shows how exclusively Keynes took his bearings on matters referring to Central and Eastern Europe from the Germans. It was, in fact, the Germans who tried at that time to convince the whole world that only they were capable of organizing this area. " What are these states of Poland, Czechoslovakia and Yugoslavia which you have created? " said Walther Rathenau to Stephen Bonsal on 26th September, 1919. " Let me tell you : nothing will last except the shame of them; nothing that will advance humanity; nothing that will redound to the credit of civilization."[66]

As a matter of fact, before the 1914 war Poland was not the master of her destinies, and Mr. Keynes should have known it. What was true was that in German Poland the Germans developed exclusively the agriculture without installing any industry there; that Galicia was exploited by Austria who " deliberately retarded the economic development of certain of its provinces for the benefit of others; thus Galicia during the nineteenth century was one of the poorest and worst-treated provinces, economically speaking, in the Austro-Hungarian Empire." [67] It was observed that " on the eve of the War the province represented an annual balance of profit of six million golden pounds in the Austro-Hungarian budget " [68] arising from the fact that practically no money was invested by the Austro-Hungarian Government in the province considered as peripheral; but, on the other hand, in the Congress Kingdom, in spite of all the restriction put by the Russians on private initiative, industry had greatly developed since 1860, the production of coal having risen in million pounds from 3,6 in 1860 to 150,8 in 1890, of pig iron from 0,7 in 1860 to 7,4 in 1890, and the number in thousands of spindles in the cotton industry from 116,2 in 1863 to 600. The total number of workers in the industry of the Congress Kingdom rose from 76,000 in 1876 to 400,000 on the eve of the 1914 war.[69] As we have stated above, the Germans tried to " de-industrialize " Poland by their policy of wanton requisitions during the occupation (see above, p. 113), doing exactly the opposite to what one might expect from the " organizers " of Mittel-Europa, but the progress of the economic rehabilitation after the war, due almost exclusively to Poland's own efforts, gave the lie to all the gloomy anticipations by Poland's enemies. H. H. Fisher in his book, *America and the New Poland*, was able to state a few years after the Paris settlement that " the rapidity with which major branches of industry were brought into production was an admirable proof of the will and the capacity of the Polish people towards work." [70]

NOTES

[1] E. H. CARR, Twenty Years Crisis, p. 294.

[1a] P. BIRDSALL, *Versailles, Twenty Years After*, p. 289.

[1b] T. BAILEY, *Woodrow Wilson and the Lost Peace*, p. 316.

[2] KEITH FEILING, *The Life of Neville Chamberlain*, p. 245.

[3] E. H. CARR, *Conditions of Peace*, p. 49.

[4] JAMES T. SHOTWELL, *At the Paris Peace Conference*, preface.

[5] ARNOLD J. TOYNBEE, *Survey of International Affairs*, London, 1925, p. 204.

[6] A. L. KENNEDY, *Old Diplomacy and New*, p. 29. Similarly G. M. TREVELYAN, *History of England*, p. 729. " Upon the whole, the drawing of the European boundaries was not ill done at Versailles. The new Europe consisted of a number of States based on the real principle of nationality. Indeed Poland, and the States that became heirs of Austria-Hungary, had been formed by the act of their own populations, as a result of the last stage of the War, before ever the statesmen met at Versailles to confirm the change. It was the War, not the Peace, that destroyed the Empire of the Hapsburgs." It was Arthur Balfour who

gave the most pertinent answer to the critics of the Peace Settlement in Paris. See *Parliamentary Debates*, House of Commons, Vol. 125, 12th February, 1920: " My right honourable friend opposite, although he dwelt upon these evils forbore to say what seemed a logical conclusion of his criticisms, that we ought to have pursued political economy and left the Austrian Empire in its original form. But he did not say that and I imagine he does not think it. Then what is the use of criticism? If we are at the same time to establish these new States with their populations which, if not homogenous, are as homogenous as we can make them, are we going to try to make their foreign policy, their foreign fiscal policy, the mere subservient tools of the Great Powers? "

[7] C. A. MACARTNEY, *National States and National Minorities*, p. 193.

[8] J. HANC, *Eastern Europe*, p. 22.

[9] DAVID LLOYD GEORGE, *Truth About the Peace Treaties*, I, pp. 89 ff.

[10] *Journal Officiel* du 30 décembre, 1918, Chambre des Députés, 2-ème séance.

[11] *P. R. F. R.*, The Paris Peace Conference, VI, p. 198.

[12] *Ibidem*, V, p. 395.

[12a] PROFESSOR D. ANZIOTTI, *Corso di Diritto Internazionale*, Roma, 1923, p. 126. " Un potere giuridico degli Stati di creare un nuovo Stato è tanto inconcepibile quanto un potere giuridico degli uomini di dar vita ad un altro uomo."

[13] *Ibidem*, VI, p. 571.

[14] O.c., pp. 288-9.

[15] MASARYK, *The Making of a State*, p. 333.

[16] O.c., pp. 195-6.

[17] *P. R. F. R.*, The Paris Peace Conference, VI, p. 530.

[18] *Ibidem*, III, pp. 395 ff.

[20] *P. R. F. R.*, The Paris Peace Conference, VI, p. 139.

[21] See a Memorandum of the Governments of Poland, Greece, Czechoslovakia, Rumania and Yugoslavia, submitted to the League of Nations in 1929 (*C.8.M.5.*, 1931): " As it is known, the promised guarantees have, in fact, not yet been furnished. The States which accepted the rules for the protection of minorities, have, consequently, found themselves in a position different from that which they were entitled to expect."

[22] H. W. TEMPERLEY, o.c., Vol. I, p. 249.

[23] *Ibidem*, p. 269.

[24] A. J. TOYNBEE, *The World After the Peace Conference*, p. 45.

[25] *Ibidem*, p. 25.

[26] H. NICOLSON, *Curzon : The Last Phase*, p. 153.

[27] *Ibidem*, p. 154.

[28] R. S. BAKER, *Woodrow Wilson and World Settlement*, I, pp. 398-9.

[29] See p. 288.

[30] DR. E. J. DILLON, *The Paris Peace Conference*, p. 173.

[30a] R. LANSING, *The Big Four*, p. 21. It was at the meetings of the Supreme Council held in Paris on 12th to 14th January that the decision of leaving all important problems to the Great Powers was taken on

Clemenceau's proposal. See GENERAL MORDACQ, *Le Ministère Clemenceau*, Vol. III, p. 85-6.

[31] HOUSE, IV, p. 23. R. S. BAKER, *Woodrow Wilson, Life and Letters, Armistice*, p. 279.

[31a] R. LANSING, *The Peace Negotiations*, p. 53.

[31b] *Ibidem*, p. 79.

[32] *Parliamentary Debates*, Vol. 114.

[33] *The Paris Peace Conference*, V, pp. 627 ff.

[34] Wilson's views had changed since 30th January, 1919, when he observed: " Mr. Dmowski had said that Poland must be a barrier between Russia and Germany. Did that mean a barrier based on armaments? Obviously not, because Germany would be disarmed and if Germany was disarmed Poland could not be allowed to arm except for police purposes " (D. H. MILLER, *Diary*, XIV, p. 80).

[35] *The Paris Peace Conference*, V, pp. 877 ff.

[36] *Ibidem*, p. 904.

[37] *Ibidem*, VI, pp. 182 ff.

[38] *Ibidem*, pp. 202 ff. Similar ideas were developed by General Smuts in his *Practical Suggestion for a League of Nations*: that the new States arising from the old empires shall not be recognized or admitted to the League unless on condition that their military forces and armaments shall conform to a standard laid down by the League in respect of it from time to time " (D. H. MILLER, *Diary*, III, p. 47).

[39] *Ibidem*, pp. 37-8.

[40] SARAH GERTRUD MILKIN, *General Smuts*, II, pp. 241 ff.

[40a] See in particular: O. I. JANOWSKI, *The Jews and Minority Rights, 1898-1919*, London, 1933 ; N. FEINBERG, *La Question des Minorités à la Conférence de la Paix*, 1919-20, Paris ; C. A. MACARTNEY, o.c. ; D. H. MILLER, *My Diary*, especially Vols. I and II.

[41] One of the last books devoted to this problem and published when the tragedy of Central European Jewry was not yet known to the authors was: *Were the Minority Treaties a Failure?* by Jacob Robinson, Oscar Karbach, Max M. Laserson, Nehemian Robinson, Marc Vishniak (Institute of Jewish Affairs of the American Jewish Congress and the World Jewish Congress), New York, 1943.

[41a] About Archibald Cary Coolidge's initiative, see D. H. MILLER, *My Diary*, Vol. VII, pp. 366-7, and A. C. COOLIDGE, *Life and Letters*, pp. 231-2.

[42] *P. R. F. R.*,The Paris Peace Conference, V, p. 393. See also Wilson's statement at the meeting of the Council of Four of 3rd May, P. MANTOUX, *Les Délibérations*, Vol. I, p. 475: " L'antisémitisme en Pologne est très aigu ; je vous rappelle à ce sujet l'attitude personnelle de M. Dmowski."

[43] *P. R. F. R.*, The Paris Peace Conference, V, pp. 397 ff.

[43a] P. MANTOUX, *Les Délibérations*, Vol. II, p. 93, meeting of 17th May, 1919. M. Headlam-Morley: " L'article en question a été rédigé après consultations de représentants des Juifs d'opinion modérée, et d'experts impartiaux, tels que M. Namier."

[44] *P. R. F. R.*, The Paris Peace Conference, VI, pp. 529 ff.

[44a] See also the discussion at the Council of Four of 23rd June, 1919 (P. MANTOUX, *Les Délibérations*, Vol. II, pp. 490 ff.), and especially the statement of Arthur Balfour: " Je crains fort que le problème juif ne devienne dans l'avenir un des plus graves. Cette idée de constituer à l'intérieur de la Pologne une nation juive est très dangereuse. Nous ne devons rien stipuler pour les Juifs, mais seulement pour les personnes de religion juive. Il est dangereux de paraître légiférer en faveur d'une race."

[45] *P. R. F. R.*, The Paris Peace Conference, VI, pp. 533 ff.

[46] *Ibidem*, p. 572.

[47] *Ibidem*, p. 723.

[48] O.c., p. 224.

[49] *Ibidem*, p. 432. This fact is partially admitted even by the authors of the above-mentioned book, *Were the Minority Treaties a Failure?*, see p. 260: " In retrospect, it is clear that, with due allowance to differences among the various nationalities, they were themselves not completely innocent parties in the breakdown of the international system of protection. Those groups which permitted themselves to be used as tools for the disruptive plans of their powerful co-nationals, unwittingly sacrificed their own interests as well as the cause of all minorities."

[49a] SIR ESME HOWARD, *Theatre of Life*, Vol. II, Appendix C.

[50] *P.R.F.R.*, 1919, Vol. II, pp. 774 ff.

[51] *Ibidem*, pp. 786 ff.

[52] Pp. 746 ff., 758 ff.

[53] See also a very objective article by a prominent French radical writer, Charles Rivet, " Les rapports polono-juifs," in *Le Temps*, 8th January, 1919.

[53a] K. SMOGORZEWSKI's book, *La Pologne Restaurée*, contains much valuable information about the pro-German attitude of the Jews of Central-Eastern Europe in the course of the First World War. See, in particular, p. 217, with a quotation from a leaflet, " Der Krieg, eine Schicksalstunde des Jüdischen Volkes," published at Bonn in 1915 by W. W. Kaplan-Kogan: " Il n'y a pas de peuple à l'Est qui ait des raisons si profondes que les Juifs de sympathiser avec les Allemands. Ces sympathies sont d'un caractère durable. Aussi les Juifs seront les pionniers les plus sûrs du germanisme dans l'Europe orientale."

The German policy favouring the Jews in Congress Kingdom during the occupation gained many friends for Germany amongst the Americans, as appears from the following report of the German Ambassador in Washington, dated 11th December, 1916 (BERNSTORFF, o.c., p. 299): " The impression, on the whole unfavourable, made by the Polish measures on the American press was gradually in part balanced by the announcement that the Polish Jews had been recognized as an independent religious community. Since it was thought in many quarters that this might be taken to be the first step towards the cultural and political emancipation of the Eastern Jews, it was discussed with great interest, in view of the strong influence exerted by the American Jewish community, in an important section of the American press, particularly that of New York."

[53b] See the remarks of an American observer, RAYMOND LESLIE BUELL,, *Poland : Key to Europe*, p. 297: "The foreign observer is nevertheless struck by the readiness of the ordinary Poles to accept the assimilated or baptized Jew as an equal. In government departments, in the army, in the banks, and in newspapers, one finds baptized Jews occupying important positions. This class, which in Nazi Germany is subjected to bitter persecution, has been freely acrepted in Poland. With the growth of nationalist spirit among both Jews and Poles, the trend toward assimilation seems to have been arrested. It remains true, however, that the Polish attitude toward the Jew is governed by racial considerations to a lesser degree than the attitude of other peoples."

[54] O.c., p. 124.

[55] O.c., I, pp. 263 ff.

[56] Memorial establishing Poland's claims to the reparations can be found in D. H. MILLER, *My Diary*, VIII, Document 750. See also a leaflet entitled " La Part de la Pologne dans les indemnités devant être payées aux alliés par l'Allemagne," Paris, 1919. See also PHILIP MASON BARNETT, *Reparation at the Peace Conference*, 2 vols.

[56a] H. H. FISHER, o.c., p. 80.

[56b] R. L. BUELL, o.c., p. 86. DR. ROMAN GORECKI, *Poland and Her Economic Development*, p. 21. W. CZERWINSKI, o.c., pp. 77 ff.

[57] J. M. KEYNES, *Revision of the Treaty*, p. 118. "The aggregate of the claims for material damages in relation with the final assessment of the Reparation Committee ... there are omitted from this table Poland and Czechoslovakia, of which the claims are probably inadmissible." The British Government defended an opposite point of view on the eve of the Peace Conference. See BARNETT, o.c., I, p. 383. Extract from British Memorandum on Wilson's speech as a Basis of Negotiation, 12th October, 1918: "The statement will probably be considered, from the point of view of the Allies, as seriously unsatisfactory in that it included no reference to reparation: this, as has been pointed out, is omitted in dealing with Belgium and France, it is also omitted in dealing with Poland."

[58] *The Paris Peace Conference*, V, p. 374.

[59] *Ibidem*, p. 561.

[60] *Ibidem*, VI, p. 454.

[61] *Ibidem*, p. 562.

[62] *Ibidem*, V, p. 450.

[63] See in the Versailles Treaty with Germany the Articles XCII, CCLIV-VI.

[64] *D . B . F . P .,* 1919-1939, First Series, Vol. II, p. 512.

[65] J. M. KEYNES, *The Economic Consequences of the Peace*, p. 272.

[66] S. BONSAL, *Unfinished Business*, p. 227.

[67] BUELL, o.c., p. 156.

[68] C. SMOGORZEWSKI, *Poland's Access to the Sea*, p. 237.

[69] W. CZERWINSKI, o.c., p. 73.

[70] H. H. FISHER, o.c., p. 343.

CHAPTER II

THE PARIS PEACE CONFERENCE :
SELF-DETERMINATION AND THE SETTLEMENT OF
THE POLISH-GERMAN FRONTIER

" I had had little to do with the actual Peace Conference work except the Polish-German frontiers, which have been much criticized since by those who have never studied the history, economy and ethnology of those parts."—(LORD HOWARD OF PENRITH, *Theatre of Life*, Vol. II, p. 393.)

" In the settlement of territorial rights and of the sovereignty to be exercised over particular regions there are several factors which require consideration. International boundaries may be drawn along ethnic, economic, geographic or strategic lines. One or all these elements may influence the decision, but whatever argument may be urged in favour of any of these factors, the chief object in the determination of the sovereignty to be exercised within a certain territory is national safety. National safety is as dominant in the life of a nation as self-preservation is in the life of an individual."—(R. LANSING, *The Peace Negotiations*, p. 91.)

Different interpretation of the principle of national self-determination
THERE had been no more fashionable slogan during the Paris Peace Conference than that of national self-determination. Major fights at the Conference, and above all within the Supreme Council, were fought under this banner. There were even quite unexpected conversions to the doctrine of self-determination. Thus, Brockdorff-Rantsau, the representative of a nation who had pursued a policy of imperialist expansion and contributed the most to the perversion of the principle of national self-determination in the ill-famed treaties of Brest-Litovsk and Bucharest, appeared at Versailles as its most fervent protagonist. In his speech of the 7th May, 1919, at the plenary session of the Peace Conference he said : " During the last fifty years the imperialism of all European States has chronically poisoned the international situation. The policy of retaliation and that of expansion as well as disregard of the rights of peoples to self-determination, contributed to the disease of Europe, which reached its crisis in the world war." [1] The observations of the German delegate on the " Conditions of Peace " of the 29th May, 1919, were based entirely on a specific interpretation of the principle of " self-determination."

THE POLISH-GERMAN FRONTIER.

—·—·— 1914 frontiers.

— — — Boundaries proposed by the Polish Delegation.

••••••• Boundaries proposed by the Commission on Polish Affairs.

▨ Plebiscite areas.

▬ Final Polish-German frontier.

⬭ Areas incorporated with Poland.

⬭ Area of the Free City of Danzig

J.T.M.

So far as the Allies were concerned their attitude in the course of the war to the self-determination of nations has been expounded in Chapter I of Part I of this book. On this point our opinion agrees with that of Professor Gilbert Murray, who in his illuminating study " Self-determination of Nationalities " [2] said : " It was quite late in the war when we discovered that we were fighting for the independence of the Czechoslovaks, and General Smuts confessed that it came to him as a surprise."

This unanimity of views apparently prevailing in 1919 on the necessity for shaping international life in accordance with the concept of self-determination, obviously covering different political outlooks and serving different interests, must give rise to the legitimate suspicion that there were different interpretations of the concept itself. Great confusion in the opinions prevailing in the interwar period on the way in which this concept had actually been carried out at the Paris Conference, was due to a biased and partisan approach to the whole problem of the territorial settlement made in Paris, caring little for historical truth and making Wilson mainly responsible for what critics considered as an application of the abstract principle to the living international issues.

In the first instance, let us state that according to the greatest authorities on international law and international relations the concept of self-determination is not a legal but a political one. Professor Clyde Eagleton, in his recent article " Excesses of Self-determination," published in the American review *Foreign Affairs* (Vol. 31, No. 4, July 1953), says that the " concept of self-determination is not a simple one, and it had always defied legal definition. ... The textbooks of international law do not recognize any legal right of self-determination, nor do they know any standards for determining which groups are entitled to independence." [3]   In his above-quoted study Professor Gilbert Murray also says that " the formula is a political formula and has to be judged in the light of political circumstances in which it was first or chiefly used." [4]

Was Wilson an abstract theorist, or having raised this issue in the course of the war had he in mind a definite political programme? James T. Shotwell, who attended the Paris Peace Conference in the capacity of an expert, strongly opposes " a highly superficial view of Wilson's statesmanship which presents him as a mere doctrinaire incapable of appreciating the intricacies of economics or politics," and calls it " a tainted picture " due to the " cleverest of journalists among the economists, Mr. John Maynard Keynes." [5]

As we have said in the first chapter of Part I of this book (see pp. 17 *et seq.*), Wilson's approach to the problem of self-determination was very cautious, realistic and experimental. He spoke only of " well-defined national aspirations," and while from the very beginning of his campaign for peace in Europe based on democratic principles he proclaimed the necessity for an independent and united Poland, he was much more cautious in recommending definite solutions for other nations of Central and Eastern Europe, only gradually extending the field of application of this principle when the trend of events proved that there were " well-defined national aspirations " which might eventually lead to a disruption of multi-national States, Austria-Hungary in the first instance. Professor Eagleton rightly states that " if one thinks back to earlier stages of the term one finds that ' self-determination ' applied only to nationalistic minority groups, such as Czechoslovakia and Poland." Wilson and his colleagues, among whom were some wise experts and some wise statesmen, were thinking in terms of European minorities, not of colonies. Herein lay the main difference between Wilson's programme and the one preached at that time by the Bolsheviks, for whom this doctrine was simply one of the means for the total destruction of the existing social fabric all over the world.

The Bolsheviks realized much more quickly than many Western statesmen that the nationalist issue might become one that would wreck their plans of expansion in Central and Eastern Europe. Such was also the opinion of many Western observers sent to inquire into political and social conditions on the spot. We can refer, for instance, to the evidence of Sir Esme Howard, the British member of the first Inter-Allied Commission to Poland sent to that country in spring 1919 : " Apart . . . from my personal sentiment in favour of the freedom of all the subject nations," he wrote in his personal recollections of his life, " I was strongly convinced that their national spirit formed the best bulwark against Bolshevik fanaticism which, had it then gained Germany, might have swept away our civilization, Mr. Lloyd George included." [6] The Bolshevik leaders tried, consequently, to outbid Wilson and frighten the Western statesmen by proposing to extend the application of the principle of national self-determination to all countries of the world whatever might be the degree of maturity of the populations concerned and whatever might have been the immediate political implications involved by such a policy. Louis Fischer in his diplomatic history of the Soviet Revolution, *The Soviets in World Affairs*, remarked that the Bolshevist leaders " sought to dispel the ' Wilson illusion ' which might, the Communists thought, check that spirit from which revolutions spring." [6a] We read, for instance, in Lenin's famous message : " You demand the independence of Poland, Serbia, Belgium, and freedom for the peoples of Austria-Hungary. . . . But strangely we do not notice in your demands a mention of freedom for Ireland, Egypt, India, or even the Philippine Islands." We have dealt with this aspect of the Bolshevik programme in its initial stage in Chapter IV of Part I of this book (pp. 181 *et seq.*), and we shall have more to say about it in connection with later developments. For the time being it is important to keep in mind the difference of approach to the problem of self-determination between Wilson and the Bolsheviks. We cannot agree with Professor Carr, who says that "Wilson assumed, with an unquestioning readiness which seems incomprehensible to-day, that *the universal recognition* of the right of national self-determination would bring universal peace." [7] Nothing is further from the truth!

Wilson took the view that a nation whose right to self-determination should be recognized, must have proper conditions of life ensuring her economic progress and placing her in a position which would enable her to defend herself against stronger neighbours. So far as the last issue was concerned, Wilson rather reluctantly admitted the necessity for strategic boundaries, believing that the League of Nations would render strategic considerations less important. But he did not go so far as to exclude altogether the necessity for taking into account the adjustment of national frontiers to the requirements of national defence. In a letter to Secretary of State Lansing, dated 29th January, 1918, Wilson stated :

"While, as you know, I am strongly inclined to nationality as the basis for territorial limits, I believe that it cannot be invariably adopted, but that in certain cases physical boundaries must be considered and modify boundaries based on nationality." [8]

There is no valid reason why the new States should have been placed in a less advantageous position than the old ones. Professor Gilbert Murray, referring to the case " where the strategic interest of a large nation clashes with the desire of a small homogeneous group," states: " If we answer this question in one way we shall be asking Great Britain to evacuate Gibraltar, Malta, Cyprus, the Suez Canal, Aden and much more . . . clearly it is a matter of degree." [9]

Wilson's concept of self-determination applied to nations as distinct ethnic entities, and there is no doubt that in the specific cases to which he extended this concept, such as Poland, Czechoslovakia, etc., he had to deal with nations whose aspirations by Western standards were well defined, the more so as some of these nations brought immense sacrifices to the cause of their freedom. But this conception was challenged by the theory that " self-determination is not a right of certain recognized nations but a right of individual men and women." [10] This theory, lately presented in an attractive form by Professor Carr, was already presented in Paris by the German

Delegation to the Peace Conference and served to justify many plebiscites in the disputed areas. Professor Carr's theory rests on the assumption that the concept of nationality " applicable in the Western world of closely integrated communities " is " irrelevant elsewhere." [11] In fact this whole theory clashes with the historic evidence and is a product of theoretical speculation pursuing definite political purposes. It rests on the assumption that an individual " wants to belong to a group powerful and strong enough to play a significant rôle," but in fact it had little regard for this individual because, as Professor Carr states : " If the individual himself is incapable of making this adjustment it may occur readily enough in the next generation." [12] Obviously Professor Carr wishes—at any price, even at the cost of individual and national freedoms—to keep intact the existing political and economic units, but it suffices to stress that his theory clashes primarily with the experiences of the British Empire, about which Professor Keeton says that " from the constitutional standpoint the transformation of the British Empire into the British Commonwealth of Nations has been a process of disintegration from a unitary State into an association of free communities." [13]

It is necessary to stress the difference between the Wilsonian concept of self-determination based on political realities, and the concept of self-determination as the right of individual men and women, because in fact it was the latter concept that prevailed in the settlement of the Polish-German frontier in Paris. It is very strange that this circumstance escaped the notice of the critics of the Treaty of Versailles. Important changes in the provisions relating to the Polish-German frontiers were introduced on the initiative of Lloyd George despite the opposition of Wilson and Clemenceau. Criticisms should consequently be addressed to Lloyd George and his Balance of Power policy appearing under the cover of the doctrine of national self-determination reduced ad absurdum.

The Big Three and the territorial settlement in Europe

As we can see from the debates at the Peace Conference dealing with the settlement of the Polish-German frontier, the French and Americans agreed on this point, that it was necessary to build in the East a strong barrier between Germany and Russia by granting to the Eastern neighbours of Germany adequate living conditions and depriving Germany of the possibility of pursuing an aggressive policy in the future. " It was not only sentiment which prevailed with President Wilson," the Earl of Birkenhead rightly observed, " there came in considerations of Realpolitik which no less directly affected Clemenceau." [13a]

France wanted to force Prussia to abandon her relatively recent

conquests in the East, made at the expense of Poland, first by backing the Russian plans for a united Poland within the orbit of the
Russian Empire and then by proposing the extension of the frontiers
of the Dual Monarchy to the old frontiers of the Polish Republic of
1772. It was the third solution, that of a totally independent Poland
as a strong bulwark in Central and Eastern Europe against German
expansionism, that eventually became the only one which remained
possible. Let us observe that to some extent many British statesmen,
namely those who above all feared the renewal of German expansionism in the future, concurred eventually with this French conception. It was for this reason that the French statesmen (and also
Arthur Balfour, for instance, as appears from his speech in Edinburgh in January 1918, see pp. 208 *et seq.*), insisted on the necessity
for redressing the old historic wrongs done by Prussia to Poland.
Clemenceau stated his views on this matter in a letter addressed on
the 5th September, 1918, to the Polish National Committee in Paris,
in which we read : " France, faithful to her historic traditions and to
her programme, and acting in agreement with her allies, will not
spare any effort in order to restore Poland in *accordance with her
national aspirations and within her historic limits.*" [14] Such also
were the motives which dictated the French proposals in the course
of the discussion on the terms of the armistice with Germany, made
on the 2nd November, 1918 (see p. 227). In the " Proposed Basis for
the Preliminaries of Peace with Germany " submitted by the French
Government to the other Allied Governments in the beginning of
December 1918 we find the following proposal relating to Poland :

> " II.   Complete restoration of Poland (for she is irreconcilable
> with the Kingdom of Prussia) ... (territorial changes : (*b*) Surren-
> der to the reconstituted State of Poland of the Polish districts of
> Prussia, of Posnania and Upper Silesia, as well as access to the
> Baltic ... all the Southern districts of Eastern Prussia which are
> by language or race Polish." [15]

Since the concept of self-determination is pre-eminently political,
it is necessary to look into the political programme of the First
British Delegate to the Peace Conference, Mr. Lloyd George, the
principal opponent of the Wilsonian and French programme on the
Polish issues at that international gathering. All who have written
about the Paris Peace Conference agree on this point, that the
British Prime Minister was very badly prepared for his task as
peace-maker. He was a man " of autocratic habit of mind," [16]
acquired in parliamentary life, his attitude towards the representatives of other nations, and in particular of the small ones, would
often appear haughty and overbearing; his knowledge of inter-

national affairs was very restricted and tainted by many prejudices.
" Obscurantism and improvisation " are the words used by Nicolson
to characterize Lloyd George. A. L. Kennedy says of him that " he
might have taken Mr. Arnold Bennett's dictum ' The present is just
as important as the future ' for his motto; and he seems not only to
forget, but to dissociate himself from his own previous declarations. He is without persistent convictions; he looks neither forward
nor back; he lives in the present and for the moment." [17] Dillon
devotes the following lines to Lloyd George :

> " Guided by no sound knowledge and devoid of the ballast of
> principle, he was tossed and driven hither and thither like a wreck
> on the ocean. Mr. Melville Stone, the veteran American journalist,
> gave his countrymen his impressions of the First British Delegate:
> ' Mr. Lloyd George,' he said, ' has a very keen sense of humour
> and a great power over the multitude, but with this he displays a
> startling indifference to, if not ignorance of, the larger affairs of
> nations.' ... To sum up: the First British Delegate, essentially a
> man of expedients and shifts, was incapable of measuring more
> than an arc of the political circle at a time. ... He relied upon
> imagination and intuition as substitutes for precise knowledge and
> technical skill."

Robert Lansing said about Lloyd George that " inconsistency
never seemed to disturb him or to cause him to hesitate ... it
apparently was a trivial matter to him to change his mind once or
twice on a proposed settlement." [17a] Professor T. Bailey confirms this
judgment saying that in Lloyd George's views " consistency was
the mark of a small mind and strict truth an insuperable handicap
to political preferment. He once quoted to Lord Riddell the cynical
adage : ' If you want to succeed in politics, you must keep your
conscience well under control.' " Professor Bailey adds : " Lloyd
George was as reliable as quicksilver, as direct as a zigzag, as un-
wavering as a weathercock." [17b]

Although Lloyd George did not possess the necessary qualifications for international negotiations on such big issues, involving the
fate of so many nations, nor had he a sound knowledge of history,
geography, economics or politics (see for instance his speech in the
House of Commons on the 16th April, 1919 : " How many Members
have heard of Teschen? I do not mind saying that I have never
heard of it "),[18] he relied very little on the advice and information
of his own experts when they clashed with his preconceived ideas,
as actually occurred on many occasions in relation to the Polish
and East-European issues.

Sir Esme Howard (later Lord Howard of Penrith) complains in
his diary : "Though I was head of the Department whose business

it was to deal with the present condition of Russia and which had collected a mass of evidence on the situation, I cannot remember that I was once asked to discuss with the Prime Minister any single matter connected with Russia and her attitude to her neighbours." [18a]

As we have said before (p. 303) owing to the secrecy of the proceedings within the Council of Four, the influence of the personal staff of the principal peace-makers was greatly increased, and the British Prime Minister was much more prone than anyone else to listen to the information and advice reaching him from " subordinate officials " and " irresponsible sources." On the contrary (see above, p. 20), " trained as a specialist Wilson respected specialists —academic specialists. They were ' his kind,' they spoke the language he understood. He also respected facts " [18b]; " thirsting for and respecting facts, he largely ignored his fellow commissioners, except Colonel House, but sought information from experts, who frequently sat on a cushion behind him and whispered promptings into his ear." [18c] The judgment on Wilson by the distinguished American historian whose words we have reproduced above is certainly correct : " Clemenceau knew more about French interests than Wilson, but Wilson probably saw the overall picture better than any of the other members of the Big Four." It must be added that according to Professor Seymour " the American representatives found themselves as well-equipped with exact facts as any of the foreigners," and he recalls a very characteristic incident at a meeting of a commission of the Peace Conference when " the American delegate asked permission to introduce an amendment to the boundary line, stating that he had with him statistics which would, in his opinion, justify the change. A foreign delegate said at once : ' I suggest that we accept the amendment without asking for evidence. Hitherto the facts presented by the Americans have been irrefutable; it would be a waste of time to consider them.' " [18d]

As gradually appeared in the course of the peace negotiations, Lloyd George had quite opposite views on the merits of the new international order in Central and Eastern Europe. His programme was deeply rooted in the traditional British policy of the balance of power on the European continent, and from that point of view he represented the methods of old diplomacy much more than Wilson and Clemenceau who thought that peace in Europe might be better assured by appealing to the national feelings of the so-called small nations. The traditional line of the British policy required more than one strong Power on the Continent, and hence Lloyd George's tendency to restore Germany to her pre-war status of a great Power and safeguard the position of Russia for the future.

On the eve of the Conference Colonel House warned Clemenceau, in a " heart-to-heart " talk (7th January, 1919), of the imminent danger of Great Britain resuming her old policy.   House considered that the only remedy could be France's wholehearted support of the American schemes for a League of Nations.

> " To-day," [said House], " there was only one military power on the Continent of Europe, and that was France. There was no balance of power as far as the Continent was concerned, because Russia had disappeared and both Germany and Austria had gone under. The thing that was apparent to me and to him must necessarily be apparent to England. The English had always thrown their weight first in the one direction and then in the other, to establish an equilibrium. The English would not look with favour upon the present situation." [19]

The idea of a solid barrier between Germany and Russia, implying the weakening of Germany through assuring proper living conditions to her neighbours, was consequently repulsive to Lloyd George, who as we have seen had little sympathy for the small nations and their " miserable ambitions." It agreed much better with his imperial vision to look upon these nations as an " international nuisance," and he did not hesitate when the need arose to use the most offensive language in speaking about them, or to avail himself of German propaganda slogans on their incapacity for self-government and independent life, allegedly proved by their historic records tainted by German and Russian historiography. Lloyd George expounded his views very outspokenly in a memorandum dated 25th March, 1919, entitled " Some Considerations for the Peace Conference before they finally draft their Terms " [20] :

> " I cannot conceive any greater cause of future war than that the German people, who have proved themselves one of the most vigorous and powerful races of the world, should be surrounded by a number of small States, many of them consisting of peoples who have never previously set up a stable government for themselves, but each containing large masses of Germans clamouring for reunion with their native land. The proposal of the Polish Commission that 2,100,000 Germans should be placed under the control of a people of different religion and which has never proved its ability for stable self-government throughout its history must, in any judgment, sooner or later lead to a new war in the East of Europe."

Another argument used by Lloyd George was that Germany might throw in her lot with Soviet Russia and thus upset the whole international order. His above-mentioned memorandum states the following in this connection :

" The whole existing order in its political, social and economic aspects is questioned by the masses of the population from one end of Europe to the other. In some countries, like Germany and Russia, the unrest takes the form of open rebellion ; in others, like France, Great Britain and Italy, it takes the shape of strikes and of general disinclination to settle down to work—symptoms which are just as much concerned with the desire for political and social change as with wage demands ... the greatest danger that I see in the present situation is that Germany may throw in her lot with Bolshevism and place her resources, her brains, her vast organizing power at the disposal of the revolutionary fanatics whose dream is to conquer the world for Bolshevism by force of arms. ... If Germany goes over to the Spartacists it is inevitable that she should throw in her lot with the Russian Bolshevists. Once that happens all Eastern Europe will be swept into the orbit of the Bolshevik revolution. ... If we are wise, we should offer to Germany a peace which, while just, will be preferable to the alternative of Bolshevism."

At the end of the memorandum were set out the " Outlines of Peace Terms," which stated among other things that one of the conditions for the admission to the League of Nations of the lesser States should be : " to accept the limitation of armaments and the abolition of conscription " ... and that : " Poland be given a corridor to Danzig, but this to be drawn irrespective of strategic or transportation considerations so as to embrace the smallest possible number of Germans."

Better than anything else this memorandum explains nearly all the moves of Lloyd George in relation to the Polish-German frontier. For the moment let us state that Lloyd George made two capital mistakes in his memorandum, as proved by historic experience : one was the belief that Germany might be appeased by some concessions at the Polish expense and abandon all dreams of further expansion, and the second that the removal or weakening of the barrier between Germany and Russia might serve the interests of world peace better than the building up of an intermediate zone consisting of vigorous and prosperous nations. Actually it was Poland, not Germany, that saved Europe from the Bolshevik invasion in 1920.

Clemenceau immediately replied to Lloyd George, and his answer is striking for its forceful logic and prophetic warning :

" The note of Mr. Lloyd George fears that too severe territorial conditions will be playing the game of Bolshevism in Germany. Is it not to be feared that the method suggested will have precisely this result?

" The Conference has decided to call to life a certain number of new States. Can the Conference, without committing an injustice, sacrifice them out of consideration for Germany, by imposing on them inacceptable frontiers? If these peoples, especially Poland and Bohemia, have been able to resist Bolshevism up to now, it is because of a sense of nationality. If violence is done to this sentiment, Bolshevism will find these two peoples an easy prey, and the only barrier which at the present moment exists between Russian Bolshevism and German Bolshevism will be shattered.

" The result will be either a confederation of Eastern and Central Europe under the domination of a Bolshevist Germany or the enslavement of the same countries by a reactionary Germany, thanks to the general anarchy. In both cases the Allies will have lost the war. On the contrary, the policy of the French Government is resolutely to aid these young peoples with the support of the liberal elements in Europe, and not to seek, at their expense, ineffectual attenuation of the colonial, naval and commercial disaster inflicted upon Germany by the Peace. If one is obliged, in giving to these young peoples frontiers without which they cannot live, to transfer to their sovereignty the sons of the very Germans, it is to be regretted and it must be done with moderation, but it cannot be avoided.

" Moreover, while one deprives Germany totally and definitely of her colonies, because they maltreated the indigenous population, by what right can one refuse to give Poland and Bohemia normal frontiers because the Germans have installed themselves upon Polish and Bohemian soil as guarantors of oppressive Pan-Germanism." [21]

General Smuts went even further than Lloyd George in his wish to appease the Germans. In his letter to Lloyd George of the 26th March, 1919, he said among other things :

"How could Germany with an army of a hundred thousand men maintain internal order and stem the Bolshevik wave from the East? How could there be even talk of Danzig going to Poland and the Saar to France?

" ... Instead of dismembering and destroying Germany she ought in a measure to be taken into the scope of our policy, and be made responsible for part of the burden which is clearly too heavy for us to bear. Are we going to defend Poland and Bohemia as we have defended the Ukraine against the Bolsheviks? ... We cannot save Europe without the co-operation of Germany."

He advised the revision of the following clauses of the Versailles Treaty : the occupation, reparation and punishment clauses; matters of the Saar Basin and Germany's Eastern frontiers. [22]

Smuts' biographer, Mrs. Sarah Gertrude Milkin, says that " of all the people at the Peace Conference, even including Germany's allies (ruined, they felt, for Germany's ambitions), only two men

knew any real sympathy for Germany : the two Boers who had lost
the war themselves : Jan Christian Smuts and Louis Botha." [23] His
pro-German feelings can be explained not only by the attitude of a
good sportsman, but above all by his fear of Russia. His " bogies
were Russia and France." As Mrs. Milkin states : " He had
Moscow on the brain : he saw everywhere, and particularly in the
future, the red hand of Moscow; even his pleas on behalf of Germany were largely grounded in his fear of Moscow." [24] But his
views on Bolshevism do not prove either his farsightedness or wide
vision. In his farewell message on leaving England after the Peace
Conference he offered this advice :

> " Leave Russia alone, remove the blockade, adopt a policy of
> friendly neutrality, and Gallio-like impartiality to all factions. It
> may well be that the only ultimate hope for Russia is a *sobered,
> purified Soviet* system ; and that may be better than the Tsarism
> to which our present policy seems inevitably tending. If we have
> to appear on the Russian soil at all, let it be as impartial, benevo-
> lent friends and helpers and not as military partisans. Be patient
> with sick Russia, give her time and sympathy, and *await the results
> of her convalescence.*" [25]

Smuts knew as little of Central and Eastern Europe as he knew of
Russia, and what he knew was provided by German propaganda
books, in which he readily believed. His contempt for all nations
beyond Germany's Eastern frontiers went even further than that of
Lloyd George, as appears from this outburst : " Poland is an
historic failure, and will always be a failure, and in this treaty we
are trying to reverse the verdict of history." [26] It was on such biased
opinions that he based his disapproval of the Versailles Treaty,
having little suspicion that it would be at the gates of Warsaw that
the advance of Bolshevism would be stopped.

This was too much even for Lloyd George, who replied on the spur
of the moment (letter of 3rd June, 1919). The letter should be
remembered in view of the attitude of Lloyd George in subsequent
years. " Am I to understand," he wrote, " that it is your proposal to
depart from the principle of nationality and have great numbers of
downtrodden Poles under Prussian rule? That is the only way in
which the Eastern boundaries of Germany can be thoroughly
revised." [27]

Polish–German frontier discussions in the Council of Ten

The handling by the Peace Conference of the question of the
settlement of the Polish-German frontier can be compared to
nibbling at a cake, as through the successive interventions of the
British First Delegate the original territory which was to have been
assigned to Poland was continually dwindling. One may say that

nearly all the concessions to German interests were made at the Polish expense. Such was the opinion expressed by Wilson at the meeting of the Council of Four on the 11th June.

The Polish claims were presented first by Dmowski at the meeting of the Council of Ten on the 29th January. He demanded for Poland in the West the historic boundaries of 1772 together with Upper Silesia and those districts of East Prussia which were Polish by race. Comparing the Polish interest in free access to the Baltic sea with that of a small island of Germans (East Prussia) which would be cut off from the rest of Germany in the event of Polish claims being satisfied, he took the view that the first should prevail over the other. He also suggested that this small island of German people should be made a republic with its capital at Königsberg.[28]

On 12th February the Supreme Council appointed a commission to work out the future frontiers betwen Poland and Germany. Following his speech on 29th January Dmowski, on behalf of the Polish Delegation to the Peace Conference, sent to the Commission on Polish Affairs on 28th February a detailed scheme of the future frontier of Poland including all Western Prussia, a great part of Eastern Prussia (Warmia and the Mazurian Lake District, inhabited by two million Polish speaking Protestants) and the whole of Upper Silesia with some fractions of Middle Silesia.

The British and American experts had already started their work at the beginning of February as appears from a note in Sir Esme Howard's Diary : " February 3rd. In afternoon started work on Polish-German frontier with my American counterpart, Professor Lord, who is very well informed." The British diplomat adds that both himself and Professor Lord kept in view that " Poland was to be re-established within her *old* ethnographical frontiers." One might assume from these words that the Anglo-Saxon experts were to disregard the consequences of the German colonization in Eastern Europe backed up since the partitions of Poland by the whole might of the Prussian State. They did not go so far, however, basing themselves on the Prussian statistics of 1910, that is to say the most recent ones. Sir Esme Howard states that Professor Lord and himself " worked out independently the frontier of West Prussia and Poland on the basis of the *last* [my italics] Prussian census of 1910 which gave the fullest and most accurate details on every possible subject." " It is quite misleading to say," states Sir Esme Howard, " that this was based on Polish data. Our data was taken wholly from the Prussian census of 1910." [28a] It should be emphasized, by the way, that it was well known at that time that the German 1910 Census was less reliable than that of 1900. Thus the decision of the Allied experts allowed Germany to raise claims to some disputable areas (Marienwerder, Upper Silesia) in the later stages of the Peace Conference and prompted some initiatives taken by Lloyd George to the prejudice of the Poles.[28b]

Giving primary importance to the ethnic factor the Commission on Polish Affairs reduced by one-third the Polish claims. The most important change proposed by the Commission concerned the " Regierungsbezirk " of Allenstein in which a plebiscite was to be held to decide the fate of this area. This plebiscite was actually held there under most unfavourable conditions for the Poles as it coincided with the Russian advance on Warsaw in summer 1920. Moreover, the Prussian administration remained there. The Polish population of this area was economically weak and its national renaissance was not in such an advanced stage as it was the case in a great part of Upper Silesia, for instance. This first important reduction of the territory which was to be assigned to Poland without restriction foreshadowed a considerable narrowing of the Polish connection with the seaport of Danzig which the Commission proposed, however, to give Poland with the area on two banks of the Vistula and two railway lines from Warsaw to the Baltic coast. The strategic consequences for Poland's access to the sea in the event of the unfavourable outcome of the plebiscite in the Warmia and Mazurian Lakes District (Allenstein) were far-reaching. Without this area East Prussia would have become a tiny island and the possibility of pursuing any aggressive action by Germany against Poland would be greatly reduced. We know that thanks to the possession of East Prussia, Germany was capable of launching a great pincers movement manœuvre against the Polish armies in 1939. " Should this region be assigned to Poland," states *A History of the Peace Conference of Paris* (ed. H. W. V. Temperley), " her Northern frontier would be within fifty miles of Königsberg (instead of twice that distance), while the (militarily speaking) difficult terrain of the Mazurian Lake District would be situated behind the Polish frontier instead of immediately before it." [28c]

As we know from our previous account, there was some hesitation in American quarters in 1918 as to whether Danzig should go to Poland, but this hesitation vanished early in 1919. In their " Proposal for New Boundaries of Poland " the American experts were of the opinion that " Danzig should be included in Poland." [29] We find confirmation of this fact in the account given by House of his conversation with Clemenceau on the 23rd February. We find there also one of the first hints at the difference of views on this question between the British Government and its experts at the Peace Conference. House says that " in the East Clemenceau thinks that Danzig should go to Poland. Our experts also believe this to be the best solution and they are joined by the British experts, but the British Government disagrees on this point." [30]

Report No. 1 of the Commission on Polish Affairs, *unanimously* adopted on the 12th March, laid down in the following terms its recommendations for the Polish-German frontier :

> " (a) that primary consideration be given to the line of ethnic separation in such a way as to secure the fairest possible settlement between the two peoples concerned. ...
>
> " (f) that account be taken of the exposed situation of Poland between Russia on the one hand and Germany on the other, and that after all the above factors have been duly taken into consideration, attention be paid to the strengthening of the defensive frontiers of the new Polish State. While such strengthening in no case gives Poland any advantage for offensive action, it diminishes to some extent the danger which threatens her, exposed as she is to attack on the East, the West and the North over unobstructed plains which offer but insignificant natural defences. ... The ' Schneidemühl ' region is inhabited chiefly by Germans, but it is included within the proposed Polish frontier because ever since the First Partition and especially since the time of Bismarck, it has been a region of unfair discrimination on the part of the Prussian Government against the Polish subjects. ... The artificial colonization plan of the German Government had produced its most marked effect, so as almost to cut off the Polish corridor to the Baltic from the solidly Polish area in the South. ... Danzig, both port and town, should be given to Poland, in *unrestricted ownership*." [31]

The report of the Commission on Polish Affairs was discussed at the meeting of the Council of Ten on the 19th March.[32] The Chairman of the Commission, M. Cambon, commenting on the report, said among other things :

> " The Commission had followed so far as possible the ethnological principle, but it had been impossible to draw any lines that did not include alien population. Economic and strategic requirements had also been taken into account, in order that the new State should be so delimited as to be capable of life. At all points save one, the frontier adopted by the Commission gave the Poles less than they asked for. The exception was in the region of the river Bartsch. The reason in this case was of a military nature. Without this line of frontier Posen would be exposed, at the very outbreak of war with Germany, and captured at once. It was to render its defence possible that the Committee had placed the frontier further West than the Poles themselves had suggested. Further North the Committee had adopted a line considerably more to the East than the Poles. This region was sparsely populated and was the scene of the intense German colonization that had been pursued of late

years. In 1905 Prince Bülow, who was then Chancellor, had obtained legislation for the forcible expropriation of the Poles in this region. ... Danzig had been Polish until the first partition, and the possession was a matter of life and death to Poland. ... It was true that the townspeople themselves were mostly of German race, but the surrounding population was Polish. Danzig had communication with the interior by two railways, one leading to Thorn and the other Mlava. The Committee proposed to give both these lines to Poland."

Only Lloyd George attacked the findings of the Commission, and he did it in a very insidious and clever way. As Dmowski states in his book *Polityka Polska* [33]:

"Lloyd George, setting his hand to the rejection of the findings of the Commission, chose a very curious procedure. First, he did not dispute all the findings at once, as it might have aroused too big a scandal. He began with the smaller items, which it was much easier to question, and having secured one position he immediately aimed at the second, much bigger one. Secondly, he decided to be more Wilsonian than Wilson himself. He began by questioning the Kwidzyn (Marienwerder) area, that is to say the four districts on the right bank of the Vistula."

In fact Lloyd George did not at that meeting raise his biggest objection relating to the handing over of Danzig, but started by trying to deprive Poland of the railway lines to Danzig. He observed at the beginning of his speech that " the bulk of the recommendations of the Committee represented views that had secured general agreement," but immediately after raised objections to the surrender to Poland of more than two million Germans, and expressed fears that " the Germans might hesitate to sign any treaty containing such a provision."

Cambon replied to Lloyd George's objections that the Committee

"had been asked to examine the means of setting up a Polish State with some prospects of continued life. The Committee had tried to approximate to the Polish State as it existed before the first partition. After examination they had made recommendations of far more modest character. ... It was no use to set up a Poland deprived of access to the sea as it would inevitably be the prey of Germany or Russia. Not only must Poland have a seaboard, but full and free communication with Danzig. If he had to choose between protecting German populations largely imported since the eighteenth century and protecting the Poles, he preferred the latter alternative."

Wilson also vigorously defended the findings of the Commission. He stressed that " it was necessary to consider not only the economic but the strategic needs of this State which would have to cope with Germany on both sides of it (corridor), the Eastern fragment of Germany being of a most aggressive character." He also pointed out that there was some reciprocity on both sides of the proposed frontier, as " many Poles in areas historically Polish were to be left within Germany." " Everywhere in Europe," he said, " blocks of foreign people would be found whose possession of the country could be justified by historic, commercial and similar arrangements." He also corrected inexact information on which Lloyd George had based one of his arguments (the latter said that " the Vistula was a navigable river, and must remain the principal artery to commerce ") by observing that " Lloyd George was misinformed in saying that the river carried the largest proportion of commerce. He would find that the railroad along the river carried the greater, or at least an equal amount of the traffic " (see note 31 to Chapter V of Part I of this book, in which we referred to the observations of the German Armistice Delegation on Article XVI of the Armistice : " the Vistula is *not* a navigable river "). Cambon added to Wilson's remarks that " Marienwerder dominated the Vistula as well as the railway lines, and anyone holding that place commanded the valley."

The Committee on Polish Affairs, asked to reconsider its recommendations in the light of the discussion in the Council of Ten on the 19th March, maintained its previous proposals. One of the most important passages of the new report, dated 20th March,[34] ran as follows :

> " One general fact therefore becomes clear—that the large number of Germans assigned to Poland is primarily the result of the intimate racial distribution in this part of Europe, and not of any neglect on the part of the Commission to consider ethnographical facts. Before Poland was partitioned there were large German minorities permanently settled on Polish territory. Since the partitions, and more especially since the creation of the German Empire, the immense energy of one of the most efficient of modern States has been directed towards the Germanization of this area by all possible means, and the most extreme measures have been taken to maintain and to increase the proportion of Germans to Poles."

It should be added that the Central Territorial Commission of the Peace Conference endorsed the conclusions of the Commission on Polish Affairs and that the Inter-Allied Commission to Poland registered the following conclusions (17th April) :

> " The Commission is *unanimously* of the opinion that Danzig should go to Poland, together with the Danzig-Mlava-Warsaw

railway and that Poland should have a sea-frontage of 100 kilometres." [35]

The intervention of Lloyd George against the unanimous conclusions of the Committee on Polish Affairs immediately became
known through the indiscretion of the Press, and provoked one of
the major crises within the Supreme Council. Alluding to this crisis
Temperley says that " the publicity which this drastic action
obtained in the Press did not contribute to the harmony of the Conference." [36] Lloyd George's attitude aroused some indignation even
among his compatriots, as shown by these remarks of the British
Ambassador in Paris, Lord Bertie, in his Diary :

> " Lloyd George, because his views on the Polish question do not
> find favour with experts and the French public and Press, threatens
> to have the Conference transferred to a neutral country—which is
> a ridiculous pretension on his part. ... Poland to live must have
> territorial access to Danzig—and broad territorial access, not a
> wayleave nor a narrow corridor—and she must not be left to look
> to Russia or to Germany or Prussia as a species of protecting
> power ; she must be a real buffer State in alliance with the other
> States to be detached from Russia and Austria, and, of course,
> Germany." [37]

In the House of Commons during the debate on the 16th April,
Lieutenant-Colonel W. Guinness, criticizing Lloyd George's attitude
on the Danzig question, said :

> " One cannot fail to notice that we bore with equanimity the
> position under which millions of Poles were subjected to a very
> harsh German rule, but when the question arose of putting a
> smaller number of Germans under the Poles, we find our repre-
> sentatives invoking the principle of self-determination. This matter
> is, unfortunately, only one of the several parallel cases, and it is
> to be hoped that the Government will see their way to remove their
> veto on this solution of a strong Poland, and that they will extend
> the same principle to Czechoslovakia and to Yugoslavia, and the
> other small States which are being built in Europe. It seems to me
> that the creation of these States in a self-supporting condition is a
> matter of enormous importance to this country, and in the creation
> of each one of these small States we shall have to strike a balance
> between national security and this principle of self-determin-
> ation." [38]

Complaining about the " garbled accounts " of his speech concerning Poland, Lloyd George made a curious observation (at the
meeting of the Council of Ten on the 21st March) : " The occurrence of such incidents only tended to encourage the Germans to
give the public the *wrong* impression that the Allies were only fight-

ing each other for individual advantages." [39] It should be observed that the delegation concerned, the Polish, was not officially advised at this stage of the solutions proposed by the Supreme Council, and as it was not admitted to state its views on the question it could rely only on some indiscretions. Mr. Balfour observed at the same meeting of the Council that " the same leakage was taking place in regard to Commissions and Committees, with the result that the members who had expressed an opinion on any question were subsequently lectured by *outside parties*. For instance, he himself had mentioned at one of the meetings that the port of Danzig constituted a difficult problem. In consequence Mr. Dmowski had called on him and talked to him for a considerable time on his supposed anti-Polish feelings; though, as a matter of fact, he was a great supporter of the Poles." [40] Could Poland be considered an " outside party " in this case, and was it so astonishing that the Polish delegate tried to approach one of the delegates and defend the Polish claims? Was it not a typical case of the total exclusion of small States from any concurrence in the decisions which concerned their most vital interests?

Faced with a second report of the Committee on Polish Affairs, fully maintaining its previous conclusions, Lloyd George said at the Meeting of the Council of Ten on the 22nd March that : " He did not wish to criticize the Polish Committee which had worked in a *perfect spirit of impartiality* and which had had to solve serious difficulties. Poland had to be given a corridor to the sea with every guarantee of security(?) . . . He was inclined to accept, provisionally, the solution proposed by the Committee . . . with the clear understanding that the Supreme Council reserved the right of revision when it came to consider the total effect of all these proposals." [41] It was on the 25th March that he stated his views on Danzig and other Polish claims in a memorandum quoted above (see pp. 322 ff.), " Some Considerations for the Peace Conference."

On 24th March appeared the last communiqué of the Council of Ten. " Quietly and unostentatiously," observes G. B. Noble, " the Council of Ten was dethroned and the Council of Four assumed supreme command." [41a]

Isaiah Bowman, chief Territorial Adviser to the American Peace Commission, gave the most vivid description of Lloyd George's interventions on the Danzig question. He speaks of " his aggressive participation " in the debates and that he " never relaxed his interest or his control." Bowman stresses also purely political motives behind Lloyd George's defence of the principle of self-determination. " Directly thereafter the Council of Four was organized," he writes in his most interesting article, "where decisions could be reached without the bother of territorial experts, with whose facts, or any other kind of facts except purely political ones, Lloyd George had no patience whatever. The next we hear of the Danzig question Lloyd George and President Wilson have agreed to make it a free city." [41b]

The Council of Four and the problem of Danzig

One of the first items put on the agenda of the Council of Four was in fact the question of Poland's Western frontiers and the future of Danzig. At the meeting of 27th March,[41c] the memorandum of Lloyd George of 25th March, about which we have spoken above, was discussed by the Western statesmen. It was Clemenceau who raised the strongest objections to Lloyd George's disregard for the strategic needs of the restored Polish State, especially in relation to the communications between Poland and the Baltic Sea. " Should we follow this advice," he said prophetically, " we would leave a sad heritage to our successors."

It was in the course of the following days that Lloyd George succeeded in converting Wilson to his point of view. We do not know which kind of arguments were used by Lloyd George in these intimate talks. There are some reasons, however, to assume that the question of the Italian claims to Fiume to which Wilson was strongly opposed on ethnographical grounds, and probably also some provisions relating to the future Covenant of the League of Nations, provided Lloyd George with valid arguments for Wilson's conversion. We find, nevertheless, some discrepancies in the views expressed by Wilson at the morning meeting of the Council of Four on 1st April, and those stated by him on the same day in the afternoon. He said at this first meeting : " The majority of experts agree on this point that the Poles should dispose of Danzig. Bismarck said to Crispi : ' A restoration of Poland is impossible without depriving Prussia of Torun (Thorn) and Danzig and without dismembering the German Empire! ' " [41d] But on the same day, in the afternoon, at a meeting which was decisive for the future of Danzig,[41e] Wilson opened the debate by summing up four proposals relating to Danzig; the first of them recommended the status of free city for Danzig, the second and the third advised the cession of Danzig to Poland, in accordance with the unanimous proposals of the Commission on Polish Affairs, while the fourth, put forward by an expert of the British Delegation, Headlam-Morley, provided for the cession of Danzig to Poland, through the League of Nations, but under the condition of Poland granting to Danzig an autonomous status. Lloyd George declared then the he favoured a combination of the first and fourth proposals, choosing from each those provisions which encroached the most on Poland's rights.

According to him an " independent " City of Danzig should be

included into the customs frontiers of Poland, and thus the inhabitants of Danzig would be gradually induced to realize that their
interests and prosperity entirely depended on the strengthening of
the economic ties with Poland. At the same time Lloyd George proposed to leave the Marienwerder district with Germany, eventually
agreeing to Wilson's suggestion to hold a plebiscite there. Wilson
remained impassive on hearing these radical proposals with which
he seemed to be well conversant, only expressing fears that the Poles
might be shocked by them in view of their well-known opposition to
the idea of constituting Danzig a free city. Clemenceau remarked
only that no definite decision could be taken in the absence of the
Poles, to which Wilson retorted that the four could, nevertheless,
agree among themselves before hearing the Polish delegate. Lloyd
George took the view that it was vain to hope to satisfy the Poles.
Then Wilson asked the Council whether it accepted in principle the
solution proposed, namely the idea of " forming a free State around
Danzig," to which Lloyd George added, " under the authority of
the League of Nations." He explained that he understood by it the
appointment of a High Commissioner of the League of Nations in
Danzig, similar to the posts of British High Commissioners in Canada
and Australia whose presence in those countries did not prevent their
inhabitants from governing themselves freely. Thus the idea of
entrusting the League of Nations with a kind of mandate in Danzig
and the establishment of a High Commissioner of the League of
Nations in Danzig were due entirely to the British initiative. The
Council agreed also to Lloyd George's proposal to hold a plebiscite
in the Marienwerder area. Both decisions were welcomed by Lloyd
George, who justified them by the fact that " we have no obligations
towards the Poles who fought as well against us as for us." Only
Clemenceau had some doubts about the wisdom of these decisions,
stating that it should not be taken for granted that the Germans
would be " coaxed " (amadoués) by these concessions. It is worth-
while to note Lloyd George's conclusions, as they were to be completely belied by the events preceding the outbreak of the Second
World War. " What I ask," he said, " is that we might not put into
the Peace Treaty the provisions for which we would not be ready to
declare war. France will fight to-morrow for Alsace if her rights to
this province were challenged. *But would we carry out a war for
Danzig?* " Wilson's two interventions in the course of the debate
showed that this time his sympathies were not on the Polish side.
Clemenceau's agreement was qualified, but he had to yield in view
of the united front of the two Anglo-Saxon Powers, the Italian delegate remaining silent; he advised only to be cautious in order not
" to throw the Poles into disorder."

At the meeting of 3rd April,[41f] Wilson informed the Council that a Committee composed of Professor Haskins (U.S.A.), Headlam-Morley (Great Britain) and Tardieu (France) unanimously adopted the plan of establishing a free City of Danzig and holding a plebiscite in the Marienwerder district.

The whole problem was again reviewed by the Council on 9th April,[41g] and the draft of the respective articles of the Treaty approved. Then Mr. Paderewski was introduced, to whom Wilson explained the nature of the settlement proposed by the Council. As was expected, Paderewski raised the strongest objections against the proposals, saying that even the biggest concessions would not prevent the resurgence of Germania irredenta. The Western statesmen tried to persuade the Polish delegate that the provisions put forward fully safeguarded the Polish interests. As the subsequent developments were to show, these verbal assurances did not correspond to the interpretation of the respective provisions of the Peace Treaty as laid down later in the special treaties imposed on Poland and relating to the Polish rights in Danzig. Wilson said that " Danzig will be within the customs frontiers of *Poland who from all points of view will have the same rights in the Port of Danzig as if she were sovereign there.*" When Paderewski rightly observed that " Danzig will remain in German hands, consequently in the hands of Germany to which it will eventually return," Wilson emphasized the economic interest of the population which must " foster the leaning towards Poland." Paderewski by his answer showed that he had a better understanding for the priority of nationalistic feelings over economic interests and warned the Council against the revival of German expansionism.

When the whole problem reappeared again on the agenda of the Council on 12th April,[41h] Clemenceau made a last attempt to save the Marienwerder area for Poland, but met with Lloyd George's rebuttal. " After all," said the Prime Minister, " the Poles are assured of independence after one and a half centuries of servitude. They should not pretend to be unable to live because we refused them a small territory which is populated by 150,000 Germans." Without raising the question of the exactitude of the statistical data based on the German census of 1910, the reliability of which was disputed even by a British official publication (see Note 28b), we wish to observe that the value of some territories cannot be measured by their area or number of inhabitants. The importance of Gibraltar or Malta or Cyprus for Great Britain does not arise from the number of their population but from the geographical position of these key points; the same occurs in the case of Danzig and the areas around it, as on their possession by the Poles depended the free access to the

Baltic Sea of a great country numbering at that time about twenty-five million inhabitants.

The last meeting of the Council of Four, which dealt with Poland's Western frontiers, was held on 18th April,[411] when the amended articles of the Peace Treaty were definitely approved. Clemenceau limited himself to the remark that he would have preferred a different solution but realized that it was quite impossible.

The best proof that Great Britain pursued her own political and economic advantages in the settlement of the Danzig question was the fact of her subsequently taking real control of the affairs of the Free City, for a certain period, through the international agents formally representing the League of Nations. Seymour alludes to this occurrence in the following passage of his article :

> " Six months after, and against the protest of the American representative on the Supreme Council, Sir Reginald Tower was appointed High Commissioner at Danzig. His stormy course there could have been predicted with mathematical accuracy by any interested enough to see why Lloyd George laboured for a free city on the shores of the Baltic, where British shipping and capital were to be rapidly increased, and why Sir Reginald was chosen on the basis of a record in South America quite unfavourably known to many American merchants. In this and in many other matters the British knew just what they wanted and how to get it."

The constitution of the Free City of Danzig and the arranging of the plebiscite in the Marienwerder (Kwidzyn) area, inhabited by many German colonists, both measures taken on Lloyd George's initiative and passed owing to his insistence, eventually reduced Poland's connection with the sea-coast to a narrow corridor, an ideal target for the future revisionist propaganda of Germany whose " Drang nach Osten " policy was revived thanks to the unexpected encouragement given by this decision of the Big Four.

Lord Birkenhead, by no means a friend of Poland and for some time a supporter of German revisionist aims, gave, however, very sound judgment on the merits of the question of Poland's access to the sea. Observing that by " cutting down Poland's territorial claims to the indisputably Polish element " Lloyd George " originated the ' corridor ' idea," he states the following :

> " Thus Danzig and the Corridor were the offspring of Idealism mated with Machtpolitik. Danzig instead of being given to Poland outright was made a free city under the protection of the League of Nations, and tacked on to Poland by a strip of territory. Here was to be found a crop of troubles for the future peace of Europe. Half-measures at the time may offer a refuge from action but action must sooner or later be faced, and if the course be right there is

seldom any advantages in postponing it. Thoughtful men have soberly considered that it would have been well to give Danzig and its hinterland outright to Poland. Germany could hardly have complained ; she would have bowed to the fortune of war and an application of her own doctrine of *vae victis*. But she can scarcely acquiesce cheerfully in the settlement of to-day."[41]

There were some historic precedents for such an unfriendly attitude of Great Britain on the question of the possession of Danzig by Poland : first, before the Second Partition of Poland, when the British Ambassador in Warsaw exerted pressure on the Polish Government to the effect of it surrendering Danzig to Prussia; secondly, at the Congress of Vienna in 1815, when as the prominent Polish historian S. Askenazy recalls in his book *Danzig and Poland :*

" Lord Castlereagh, the Secretary of State for Foreign Affairs, took a most perverted view of the Danzig question, as indeed of that of Poland as a whole. Castlereagh, on the suggestion of the Prussian Cabinet, was daily kept in dread of the Russian peril, and recalling the mistaken and now out-of-date initiative of Pitt, twenty years previously, declared himself favourable to the restoraation of Danzig to Prussia." [42]

Dmowski echoed the opinion of all Poland when he said of the decision of the Peace Conference on Danzig : " A wound was inflicted on our State in a most vital spot." [43]

In spite of his concurrence in the decision wrung from the members of the Supreme Council by Lloyd George, Wilson said in the course of the debates on the Fiume question (Council of Four, 19th April, 1919) :

" All the economic and strategic arguments had been in favour of uniting Danzig with Poland, yet, in order to give effect to the general principle on which the peace was based an *unscientific method* had been adopted and a rough line had been drawn and the principle of plebiscite had been accepted which will probably result in a line of railway connecting Danzig with Poland traversing German territory. The *strategic and economic reasons had therefore been ignored.*" [44]

Lord Bertie joined those who condemned the verdict of Four :

" Notwithstanding the reaffirmation by the experts of their recommendation that Danzig should go to Poland with a broad Polish approach to it, the Conference has passed *outre* and obtained for Danzig a free city, with customs union with Poland ; a very foolish and wrong proceeding." [45]

The meaning of this momentous decision appears clearly from the following words of the well-known British writer, H. J. Mackinder :

> " By some means new Poland must be given access to the Baltic
> Sea, not only because that is essential to her economic indepen-
> dence, but also because it is desirable to have Polish ships on the
> Baltic, which stategically is a closed sea of the Heartland, and
> further, there must be a complete territorial buffer between Ger-
> many and Russia." [46]

History has fully vindicated the truth of these words. When the
Second World War started the defensive position of Poland, than an
ally of Great Britain, was jeopardized from the very beginning, which
caused the collapse of the Polish front, leading to the defeat of France
and to Dunkirk in the following year. Lloyd George proved by his
handling of the Danzig question that he " lived for the present and
for the moment," looking " neither forward nor back."

Revision of the Draft Treay and the problem of Upper Silesia

This was not the end of the concessions made by the Principal
Powers to Germany at Poland's expense. The Germans understood very early that if they concentrated their attacks against the
proposed terms of the Peace Treaty on the provisions relating to
Poland they might have a chance of obtaining considerable allevia-
tions, being well informed of Lloyd George's unfriendly attitude
towards Poland. In their attacks against these provisions they
brought forward their own interpretation of the principle of self-
determination, considerably reducing its field of application so far
as Poland was concerned (according to their views it should be
carried out only in territories with compact Polish population);
wherever this principle went against German interests they alleged
that the economic considerations should override it, and the same
should occur for the sake of safeguarding the communications
between East Prussia and the rest of Germany.

The line of policy adopted by the German Government on Polish
claims appears clearly from the following instructions given to the
German plenipotentiaries (drawn up by the German Foreign Office
in April 1919 under the title " Richtlinien für deutschen Friedens-
unterhändler ") [47] :

> " *Poland*. Disputes as to which territory is to be considered
> Polish, according to these principles, can be settled only by a non-
> partisan tribunal, whose decisions must be governed by a popular
> plebiscite. The plebiscite is to be limited to the province of Posen
> (Poznan) beyond the line of demarcation, because it is only there
> that an area which linguistically is almost solidly Polish can be
> found. We should endeavour, if possible, to push the line of

demarcation further back. It would be unjustifiable to include West Prussia and Upper Silesia, because in that case East Prussia would be separated from the Reich, and because the possession of Upper Silesia, which produces 22 per cent. of Germany's coal, is indispensable to the life of Germany ; and furthermore, union with Poland would not be in the interests of the population of Upper Silesia. ... Free access to the sea must not be created by a Polish corridor to Danzig. ... Polish interests are rather to be safeguarded by economic measures."

The Draft Peace Treaty was presented to the German plenipotentiaries at the plenary session of the Peace Conference on the 7th May. The German counter-proposals were presented on the 29th May and the Allies replied on the 16th June. So far as the spirit of the German counter-proposals was concerned, Temperley observed that it was especially in dealing with Poland that " it became apparent that the German mentality had changed little. ... Every possible concession to Poland was refused, every possible claim denied, every possible attempt made to depreciate Polish civilization and capacity." [48]

We will not go into the merits of the specific interpretation of the principle of self-determination by the German delegation, as it was best refuted by the Reply of the Allied and Associated Powers. We reproduce some characteristic passages from the Reply, in view of the astonishing allegations often put forward in the inter-war period in the West regarding the violation of the principle of self-determination by the Versailles Treaty in its provisions relating to Poland :

" Accordingly the Allied and Associated Powers have provided for the reconstitution of Poland as an independent State with ' free and secure access to the sea.' All territories inhabited by ' indubitably Polish populations ' had been accorded to Poland. All territory inhabited by German majorities, save for a few isolated towns and for colonies established on land recently forcibly expropriated and situated in the midst of indubitably Polish territory, have been left to Germany. Wherever the will of the people is in doubt, a plebiscite has been provided for. ... The German counter-proposals entirely conflict with the agreed basis of peace. They provide that great majorities of indisputably Polish population shall be kept under German rule. ...

" In dealing with the problem of the Eastern frontiers of Germany, it is desirable to place on record two cardinal principles.

" First, there is imposed upon the Allies a special obligation to use the victory which they have won in order to re-establish the Polish nation in the independence of which it was unjustly deprived more than one hundred years ago. This act was one of the greatest wrongs of which history has record, a crime the memory and the result of which has for long poisoned the political life of a large portion of the continent of Europe. The seizure of the Western provinces of Poland was one of the essential steps by which the military power of Prussia was built up, the necessity of holding fast these provinces has perverted the whole political life, first of Prussia and then of Germany. ... The second principle, which has been proclaimed by the Allies and formally accepted by Germany, is that there shall be included in the restored Poland those districts which are now inhabited by an indisputably Polish population.

" These are the principles which have guided the Allies in determining the Eastern frontiers of Germany, and the Conditions of Peace have been drawn up in strict accordance with them. ...

" When the partition took place these portions of Poland (Provinces of Poznan and West Prussia) were predominantly inhabited by Poles ; except in some towns and districts to which German colonists had made their way, the country was completely Polish in speech and sentiment. Had the Allies and Associated Powers applied the strict law of historic retribution, they would have been justified in restoring to Poland these two provinces almost in their entirety. They have in fact not done so ; they have deliberately waived the claims of historic right because they wished to avoid even the appearance of injustice, and they have left to Germany those districts on the West in which there is an undisputed German predominance in immediate contiguity to German territory."

Speaking about the specific Prussian " methods by which German preponderance in certain districts has been established," the Reply states that " to recognize that such action should give a permanent title to the country would be to give encouragement and premium to grossest acts of injustice and oppression."

The German counter-proposals greatly exaggerated the consequences of the separation of the Polish provinces from Germany for the German economic life. We can say " exaggeration " because as experience has shown this separation had in fact very limited consequences for the German economy. Yet this point cannot be over-emphasized because of its impact on some quarters in the West, anxious about the disruption of European economic life. The German counter-proposals, for instance, emphasize that :

" By putting into force the territorial clauses of the Treaty of Peace, Germany would lose to the East the most important regions for the production of corn and potatoes, which would be equivalent to the loss of 21 per cent. of the total crop of those articles of food. ... At the end of a very short time Germany would, therefore, not be in a position to give bread and work to her numerous millions of inhabitants ... these persons would have to emigrate ... the putting into execution of the conditions of Peace would, therefore, logically bring about the loss of several million persons in Germany ... deaths *en masse*."

It was in relation to Upper Silesia that the Germans touched the most sensitive spot because of the alleged connection with the German capacity for the payment of reparations :

> " Only with Upper Silesia can Germany fulfil the obligations arising from the war, but without it never. On this basis, if on no other, Germany could not acquiesce in the cession of Upper Silesia."

A distinguished British writer, Mr. H. J. Paton, in a paper read on the 20th December, 1921, at a meeting of the British Institute of International Affairs, refuted these allegations in the most pertinent way :

> " You cannot bandy about a couple of human beings in defiance of their wishes in order to avoid temporary inconvenience to other people. ... It is indeed obvious that the loss of so important a mineral area must result in a considerable reorganization of German industry and a considerable diminution of German wealth, but there was no evidence that it would result in the economic ruin of Germany." [49]

The best proof of the bad faith on the German side was a series of arguments on the alleged incapacity of Poland to organize the industries of Upper Silesia. Such for instance was the following allegation : " The cession of Upper Silesia to Poland would mean ' industrial decay ' for conditions of life, sanitary regulations and social amelioration were incomparably better in Upper Silesia than in the adjacent Kingdom of Poland, whose legislation for the benefit of the working classes has scarcely begun." Similarly in the Labour Section of the German counter-proposals we read that " States like the future Poland possess no, or insufficient, qualifications for the welfare of workers." These arguments completely overlooked the fact that in the former Russian Poland it was the Russian Government that was solely responsible for industrial and social legislation. The restored Polish State had immediately started a series of important social reforms, and Poland could be proud of having one of the most progressive social legislations in Europe before the 1939 war. So far as the industrial capacity of Poland was concerned, it is well known that Upper Silesia maintained its high industrial standard under Polish rule. Moreover at the time when the counter-proposals were drawn up it was common knowledge that the Poles had played a prominent rôle in the organization of the industries all over the Russian Empire. An unbiased British writer observed in this connection :

" The war and the German occupation have given all this industry a terrible setback, and Poland, like other Central European
countries, finds it difficult to get the raw materials to restart her
industries. Yet, in view of *the very great ability in industrial and
engineering enterprises which the Poles were manifesting before
the war* it is not unreasonable to hope that, if once successfully
restarted, Polish industry might develop in a very remarkable and
rapid way " [my italics].[50]

In the first days of June, when the German counter-proposals had
been examined by the delegates of the Principal Powers, Lloyd
George began to advocate further revisions of the important clauses
of the Draft Peace Treaty to meet some German objections. His
main targets for attack were again the provisions concerning Poland,
as he announced unexpectedly to the other members at the meeting
of the Council of Four on the 2nd June, 1919.[51] He referred to the
opinions of all sections of the British Cabinet who " unanimously
agreed that unless certain defects in the Treaty were put right they
could not advise that the British Army should be allowed to march
or that the Fleet should take part in the blockade." Was the fear
expressed by Lloyd George that Germany would refuse to sign the
Peace Treaty unless it was revised fully warranted by the facts? Did
Lloyd George in this case act in good faith? It is difficult to answer
with certainty. It is true, as Nicolson says, that the public opinion
in Western countries in 1919 " was passing through an illogical
phase," as on the one hand " the democracies of Europe were determined now that the victory had been achieved to renounce all
further physical effort," and on the other hand they " expected their
statesmen to obtain and preserve for them the most triumphant
spoils." [52] As Nowak states, Haig pressed Lloyd George to terminate the state of war as soon as possible and he adds that " this was,
obviously, the only possible line for the British Premier to take,
quite apart from the fact that one of Mr. Lloyd George's pet aver-
sions was the remote, alien and unprepossessing Polish nation." [53]
This may absolve Lloyd George from a part of the responsibility,
but we can take it for granted that he carried out his mission
of destroying an important part of the Draft Peace Treaty with
some relish. As a matter of fact the fears that unless they were
revised the terms of the Peace Treaty would have to be enforced
on the Germans were exaggerated. The Germans could not offer
any serious resistance to the Allied demands. Such was the opinion
of Hindenburg himself, who in reply to Noske, Minister for War,
stated that the Germans had no chance of resisting the march of the
Allied Armies in the West.[54]

At the meeting of the 2nd June Lloyd George advised that so far as the Eastern frontiers were concerned a plebiscite should be held in Upper Silesia, although " his personal views were that Upper Silesia would vote for Poland." Another frontier correction proposed by Lloyd George concerned the district of Guhrau and Militsch, the districts of Schneidemühl-Konitz, and a small district in the extreme north of Pomerania. All the proposed frontier corrections reduced the width of the Polish corridor and still further diminished its defensibility.

It was Clemenceau who showed all the political implications of the changes proposed by Lloyd George, and history proved that he was right.

> " When we spoke of re-establishing Poland " [he said], " it must be remembered this was not done merely to redress one of the greatest wrongs in history. It was desired *to create a barrier between Germany and Russia.* He would emphasize this by referring to the statement attributed to Erzberger and reproduced in the Paris edition of the *Chicago Tribune.* He was alleged to have said that the principal aim of Germany would be to weaken Poland. If Poland were weak, she would be at the mercy of Germany. If she was strong she would provide a barrier between Germany and Russia. If Poland fell to Germany, the Allies would have lost the war. Germany would be stronger than ever and would be able to renew the advance of 1914, and as Erzberger had put it, ' resume her march on Paris '."

President Wilson observed that " the objections raised to the Peace Treaty were of such importance " that he was forced to propose the postponement of the date of the next meeting in order that he might consult the American group of plenipotentiaries and experts and hear their views. Such consultation took place in the morning of the 3rd June, but was not conclusive. While the experts conversant with Polish matters, such as Professor Lord, defended the provisions of the Treaty except for some minor corrections, " the majority of the American experts advocated a plebiscite in Upper Silesia, or a rectification of the Eastern frontier in some way." [55] The opinion of the majority was not shared by Wilson so far as Upper Silesia was concerned, but it had considerably weakened his resistance and he eventually agreed both to some frontier corrections and to the holding of a plebiscite in Upper Silesia. However, he stated that the " people in Upper Silesia were entirely dominated by a small number of magnates and capitalists," and that his experts " did not believe that a free plebiscite was possible in these conditions." [56]

Lloyd George again appeared as an advocate of self-determination, and declared that he was " simply standing by President

Wilson's Fourteen Points " and " fighting them through," to which
Wilson retorted that he " could not allow Mr. Lloyd George to
suggest that he himself was not in favour of self-determination. All
he wanted was to be sure that it was a *genuine* self-determination,"
and he was " less concerned with the question of whether Germany would or would not sign than with ensuring that the arrangements of the Peace Treaty were sound and just. He was not moved
by the arguments that the Germans would not sign unless it could
be shown by them that the Allied and Associated Powers had
adhered to the principles on which they had agreed to make peace."
Opposing Lloyd George's interpretation of No. 13 of his Fourteen
Points he said that " we know the ethnographical facts, and there
was no need to add a plebiscite, which was not imposed by the
Fourteen Points." Nevertheless he agreed to the plebiscite, although
only on the condition " that an agreement should be extracted from
Germany to accept a plebiscite under safeguards to be laid down
by an International Commission."

Thus Lloyd George won again, in spite of the opposition of all his
colleagues in the Supreme Council. Wilson stated expressly at the
meeting on 14th June that " he was not obliged under the Armistice
to agree to a plebiscite in Upper Silesia at all, as No. 13 of the
Fourteen Points was perfectly clear on the subject. He had only
conceded the plebiscite to meet Mr. Lloyd George's proposals." [57]
On the 11th June Clemenceau said that " he himself was opposed
to the idea of a plebiscite, but to meet his colleagues he had accepted
it." [58]

Apart from the plebiscite, it was decided to impose on Poland
certain additional obligations in the event of Upper Silesia going to
Poland.

The decisions of the Supreme Council were conveyed to the
First Delegate of Poland on the 5th June.[59] President Wilson,
speaking on behalf of the Council, stated that " my own judgment
is that nothwithstanding the fact that the Germans admit that
(Upper Silesia) has an overwhelmingly Polish population the very
great mineral riches of Silesia are of great concern to them." Mr.
Paderewski, obviously aggrieved by this announcement, objected to
the holding of the plebiscite. He pointed out the influence of the
Catholic clergy in the agricultural part of Silesia, this clergy being
" brought up in a very strong German spirit by the Archbishop
of Breslau," and declared that from his point of view " a plebiscite
is absolutely impossible." This danger, by the way, was referred
to a few days later by President Wilson on the strength of information obtained by a member of the American delegation, Mr. White
(The Council of Four, 11th June).[60] But this point also was dis-

puted by Lloyd George, who said that "the Poles like the Irish were especially good at propaganda," to which Wilson retorted that "as a matter of fact the Germans were far more subtle propagandists than the Poles. No one could induce him to believe that the Poles, who were in no political position, would be better propagandists in Upper Silesia than the Germans, who were. *As against the Germans he was pro-Pole with all his heart.*" * This exchange of arguments is the best proof that Lloyd George did not disdain any means in order to attain his principal aim, which was to render the position of the Poles far more difficult in the future plebiscite than that of the Germans. The latter had great advantages over the Poles owing to their exclusive influence over the local administration, police, clergy, industry, etc., in that area. And further, the provisions concerning the plebiscite placed the Germans in a much more favourable position than the Poles.

Let us see what an unbiased British writer, Mr. H. J. Paton, says about the ethnographic position in Upper Silesia :

> "There could, of course, be *no shadow of doubt that, in one sense, Upper Silesia was inhabited by an indisputably Polish population,* and this was the view strongly upheld by President Wilson himself. The area had been inhabited by people of Polish race and language since the early Middle Ages and the German minority consisted of either Germanized Poles (*as indeed is the case in Middle Silesia also*), or of Germans who entered the country for purposes of trade and industry, some of them at least in comparatively recent times" [61] [my italics].

Lloyd George won fame at home as a bold social reformer and champion of the cause of democratic progress. In Upper Silesia he appeared as a protagonist of capitalism and international finance

---

* Although it is quite unscientific to assert, as Mr. Louis Gerson does, (o.c., p. 8) that "a united, independent, and free Polish nation could not have been resurrected without the intervention of the United States and President Wilson and the diplomacy used at the Peace settlement," because, firstly, Poland was not "created" by the Versailles Peace Treaty, and secondly, she owed her resurrection above all to the undaunted patriotism of her people, the name of Wilson is remembered in Poland with deep gratitude. This great statesman fully realized the importance of a strong barrier between Germany and Russia, as the factor for the preservation of peace and checking the aggressive aspirations of her neighbours. Unfortunately, he made important concessions to Lloyd George (Danzig, Upper Silesia) which had such evil consequences for Poland. Wilson was well aware of the feelings of the Polish nation towards him and the only foreign decoration accepted by him was the Order of the White Eagle. Mrs. Wilson writes in her *Memoir* (p. 343) that her husband received the Order of the White Eagle in 1922, and that he wore this decoration on 5th January, 1923, at a family dinner in honour of her mother-in-law's birthday.

against the interests of the Polish working people. Dillon, in his history of the Peace Conference, alludes to this obscure influence :

> " the authorship of the powerful and successful opposition to the allotting of Danzig to Poland was rightly or wrongly ascribed not to him but to what is euphemistically termed ' international finance ' lurking in the background, whose interest in Poland was keen and whose influence on the Supreme Council, although less obvious, was believed to be far-reaching. The same explanation was currently suggested for the fixed resolve of Mr. Lloyd George not to assign Upper Silesia to Poland without a plebiscite." [62]

The standpoint taken by Mr. Keynes, delegate of the British Treasury and a man closely connected with the City, and his strong anti-Polish bias might confirm these legitimate suspicions. " Poland too," he says in his book *A Revision of the Treaty*,[63] " must be given a possible problem, but *it is not easy to be practical with so impraticable a subject*. Her main problem can be solved only by time, and the recovery of her neighbours." Mr. E. Mantoux, in his excellent book *The Carthaginian Peace*, showed that even where all the economic factors had been taken into account in the delimitation of the frontiers the future political complications could not always be avoided :

> " A minority of some three million German-speaking people was included in Czechoslovakia. Here was the clear instance where ' economic considerations ' had prevailed over the strictest application of the principle of self-determination. Perhaps, for this very reason, Mr. Keynes was satisfied with the solution arrived at, for he made no critical reference to it: And yet it was precisely the problem of the Sudeten Germans that brought Europe to the brink of war in September 1938. Thus even when food, coal and transport were given their due share of attention, frontiers and sovereignties would still be inviting trouble." [64]

Was Lloyd George consistent in his interpretation of the doctrine of self-determination at the Peace Conference? It is enough to mention here the problem of the Brenner frontier, where strategic considerations prevailed over the principle of self-determination, the denial of the right of German Austrians to join the Reich, and above all the whole attitude of Lloyd George in the question of the Greek claims to Asia Minor. Once when speaking to Winston Churchill he said :

> " The Greeks are the people of the future in the Eastern Mediterranean. They are prolific and full of energy. They represent Christian civilization against Turkish barbarism. ... A greater Greece will be an invaluable advantage to the British Empire ...

they are now a nation of five or six millions, and in fifty years, if they hold the territories which have been assigned to them, they will be a nation of twenty millions." [65]

On many occasions, to some of which reference has already been made, Lloyd George showed his antipathy to the Poles, and this fact is confirmed by all those writers who devoted their studies to the Paris Peace Conference.[66] Lloyd George did not disguise his intensely unfriendly feelings towards the Poles either in conversation with his intimate friends or at international gatherings. He continued to slander Poland in his books after he retired from office, and retained these feelings until his death. For instance, speaking to Lord Riddell on the 28th March, 1919, he said :

> " We must make, if we can, an enduring peace. That is why I feel so strongly regarding the proposal to hand over two million Germans to *the Poles who are an inferior people* so far as concerns experience and capacity for government." [67]

At the meeting of the Supreme Council on the 11th March, 1919, when the question was discussed of appointing General Henrys as Chief of Staff to the President of the Polish Republic (we deal with this question later, see p. 401), he said : *The Poles have no idea of organization, they have no capacity to direct or govern."* [68]

We think the best explanation of this prejudiced judgment is that the conception of Poland as a strong barrier between Russia and Germany did not agree with Lloyd George's plans for rehabilitating Germany as a counter-weight to France. Poland stood in the way of these plans, so he chose the well-known method of denigrating the adversary, accepting at their face value all the anti-Polish propaganda slogans spread either by Germans or Russians, who tried to justify their previous policy towards Poland by stressing the alleged incapacity of the Poles for independent life. Lloyd George wished to appear a righteous and honest man, and this explains his repeated assertions that anything he was doing agreed with the principles of fair dealing and justice.

In a speech introducing the Versailles Treaty to the House of Commons on the 3rd July he defended his policy as farsighted statesmanship which might help to avoid any war in the future, owing to the concessions made for Germany's benefit. This speech, a brilliant piece of oratory and full of prophecies belied by subsequent events, shows clearly, should further proof be required, that whenever a doubt had arisen in his mind he gave the benefit of it to the Germans and not to the Poles. This point should be remembered in view of the fact that the campaign against the Polish-German settlement, in which Lloyd George himself later shared, never stopped in the inter-war period. Even the judgment of usually objective and unprejudiced minds was often distorted owing to the inadequate knowledge of the circumstances in which the settlement had been worked out. So said, for instance, Professor Gilbert Murray in his preface to L. P. Mair's book *The Protection of Minorities* : " It is easy to criticize the statesmanship of the Peace Treaties and to point out that *in almost all disputed cases the victorious legislators gave the benefit of doubt to their friends*" [my italics], while just the opposite was true so far as the Polish issues were concerned.

In the above-mentioned speech Lloyd George after having paid a tribute to the efficient and skilful work of the experts (whose advice he largely ignored in Paris), said in relation to the territorial clauses of the Versailles Treaty, which he called " stern and just," the following [69]:

> " Take the territorial clauses. In so far as territories have been taken away from Germany, it is a restoration. ... This Treaty has reknit the torn flag of Poland, which is now waving over a free and united people ; and it will have to be defended, not merely with gallantry, but with wisdom. For Poland is in a perilous position, between a Germany shorn of her prey and unknown Russia which has not yet emerged. All these territorial adjustments of which we have heard are restorations. Take Danzig—a free city, forcibly incorporated in the Kingdom of Prussia. They are all territories that ought not to belong to Germany, and they are now restored to the independence of which they had been deprived by Prussian aggression. ... However unjust it was to take Polish population and place them under German rule, it would have been equally unjust to take German population and place them under Polish rule—it would have been equally foolish. Whether for strategic or economic reasons, it would do nothing but produce mischief in Europe. ... It would have been wrong not merely to Germany but to Poland ; it would have been a wrong to Europe. Perhaps in fifty years' time Poland would have to pay the penalty of the blunder committed by the Allies in this year. For that reason the British Delegation—and I have no hesitation in claiming a share in it—resolutely opposed any attempt to put predominantly German population under Polish rule. *I think Poland will have good reason to thank us for the part which we took in that action.* But take all these territorial adjustments. I ask anyone to point to any territorial change we made in respect to Germany in Europe which is in the least an injustice, judged by any principle of fairness."

This point of view was at that time entirely shared by Winston Churchill, who said in *The Aftermath* [70]:

> " But a fair judgment upon the whole settlement, a simple

explanation of how it arose, cannot leave the authors of the new map of Europe under any serious reproach. To an overwhelming extent the wishes of the various populations prevailed. ... The moulds into which Central and Southern Europe have been cast were very hastily and in parts roughly shaped, but they conformed for all practical purposes with much exactness to the general design ; and according to the lights of the twentieth century that design seems true."

A similar opinion was expressed by Ian F. D. Morrow, who (assisted by L. M. Sieveking) carried out an extensive inquiry on the Polish-German settlement, summed up in a book published under the auspices of the Royal Institute of International Affairs in 1936 [71]: "Whatever may be thought of the actual settlement effected in North-West Europe," he says, "it is unquestionable that it does represent a sincere attempt to do—in Lord Howard of Penrith's words—'what seemed just and fair'."

But at the same time we subscribe to the other statement that "the settlement was inspired by the hope—if not by a confident belief—that the nations would profit by the lesson of the World War and co-operate among themselves for their common good. At the close of the second millenary of the Christian era it is tragic to have to admit that this hope has hitherto proved illusory."

From this point of view it would have been much wiser if clear-cut solutions had been adopted by the peace-makers in Paris, depriving the aggressive nations of all the spoils of their previous aggressions and securing to the liberated nations better chances of survival in proper strategic and economic conditions. It was Arthur Balfour who as early as 1916 (see p. 61) advised transfers of population "which could not properly be negligible," for strategic reasons which might safeguard the peace of the world. It was H. J. Mackinder, a profound thinker whose book *The Democratic Ideals* has an imperishable value, who said in speaking about transfers of populations which in his meaning should have been carried out after 1918 : "Would it not pay Humanity to bear the cost of a radical remedy, a remedy made just and even generous towards individuals in every respect." [72]

NOTES

[1] *P. R. F. R.*, The Paris Peace Conference, III, p. 417.

[2] GILBERT MURRAY, "Self-Determination of Nationalities." *Journal of the British Institute of International Affairs,* Vols. I and II, 1922, p. 8.

[3] O.c., p. 593.

[4] O.c., p. 10.

5 O.c., p. 26.

6 LORD HOWARD OF PENRITH, *Theatre of Life*, Vol. II, p. 298.

6a Vol. I, p. 147.

7 CARR, *Conditions of Peace*, p. 47.

8 WOODROW WILSON, *Life and Letters* (ed. by RAY STANNARD BAKER),
p. 506.

9 O.c., p. 12.

10 CARR, o.c., p. 47.

11 *Ibidem*, p. 43.

12 *Ibidem*, p. 60.

13 KEETON, *National Sovereignty and International Order*, p. 162

13a THE EARL OF BIRKENHEAD, *Turning Points in History*, p. 263.

14 FILASIEWICZ, No. 251.

15 *The Paris Peace Conference*, I, p. 372.

16 H. NICOLSON, *Curzon : The Last Phase*, p. 400.

17 A. L. KENNEDY, *Old Diplomacy and New*, p. 282.

17a R. LANSING, *The Big Four*, p. 78.

17b T. BAILEY, *Woodrow Wilson and the Lost Peace*, pp. 157-8.

18 *Parliamentary Debates*, Commons, Vol. 114.

18a LORD HOWARD OF PENRITH, o.c., p. 296. In this connection it is
interesting to note that the first Inter-Allied Commission to Poland
appointed by the Council of Ten on 22nd January, 1919 (*The Paris
Peace Conference*, III, p. 675), on its return to Paris was unable to
present its conclusions to the Peace Conference. See DILLON, o.c.,
p. 139: " The Commission was accordingly appointed. Among its members were Sir Esme Howard, who has since become Ambassador in
Rome, the American General Kernan and M. Noulens, the ex-
Ambassador of France in Petrograd. The envoys and their colleagues
set out for Poland to study the problems on the spot. They exerted
themselves to the utmost to gather data for a serious judgment and
returned to Paris after a sojourn of some two months, legitimately
proud of the copious and well-sifted results of their research. And then
they waited. Days passed and weeks, but nobody took the slightest
interest in the envoys. They were ignored. At last, the Chief of the
Commission, M. Noulens, taking the decision, wrote direct to M.
Clemenceau informing him that the task entrusted to him and his
colleagues had been achieved and requesting to be permitted to make
their report to the Conference. The reply was an order to wind up the
Commission."

18b T. BAILEY, o.c., p. 110.

18c *Ibidem*, p. 150.

18d HOUSE–SEYMOUR, *What Really Happened in Paris*, p. 96.

19 HOUSE, *Papers*, IV, p. 280.

20 *Parliamentary Papers*, Vol. XXIII (1922), Cmd. 1614.

21 R. S. BAKER, *Woodrow Wilson and World Settlement*, III,
pp. 249 ff.

22 SARAH GERTRUDE MILKIN, o.c., II, pp. 210 ff.

23 *Ibidem*, p. 208.

[24] *Ibidem*, p. 200.

[25] TEMPERLEY, o.c., III, p. 74.

[26] At the meeting of the British Empire delegation before the signing of the Versailles Treaty (see MILKIN, o.c., II, p. 237).

[27] *Ibidem*, II, pp. 241-2.

[28] *The Paris Peace Conference*, III, pp. 777 ff., D. H. MILLER, XIV, pp. 55 ff.

[28a] LORD HOWARD OF PENRITH, o.c., p. 307.

[28b] See handbooks prepared under the direction of the Historical Section of the Foreign Office, No. 40, *Upper Silesia*: " It is, however, clear that the most recent census (1910) figures cannot be relied upon, a fact due to the political bias of the enumerators and local officials. It may be concluded that the proportion of Poles to the total population has not fallen in the period, but was in 1910 at least as high as in 1900, and probably rather higher. The figures for 1900 are thus the best available means of determining the proportion of Poles both in the whole area and in the different districts.

[28c] H. W. V. TEMPERLEY, o.c., Vol. II, p. 211.

[29] *Ibidem*, VI, Document 441. R. LANSING, *The Peace Negotiations*. A memorandum of my views as to the territorial settlement, 21st September, 1918. " An independent Poland . . . in the possession of the port of Danzig."

[30] HOUSE, IV, p. 345.

[31] D. H. MILLER, VI, Document 498.

[32] *The Paris Peace Conference*, IV, p. 413. D. H. MILLER, XV, pp. 422 ff.

[33] O.c., pp. 385 ff.

[34] D. H. MILLER, VII, Document 570.

[35] *Ibidem*, XIX, p. 85.

[36] O.c., Vol. I, p. 262.

[37] LORD BERTIE, o.c., II, p. 322.

[38] *Parliamentary Debates*, Commons, Vol. 114.

[39] *The Paris Peace Conference*, IV, p. 444.

[40] *Ibidem*, p. 446.

[41] *Ibidem*, p. 449.

[41a] G. B. NOBLE, *Policies and Opinions of Paris*, 1919, p. 346.

[41b] HOUSE-SEYMOUR, o.c., pp. 160-2.

[41c] P. MANTOUX, *Les Délibérations*, Vol. I, pp. 44 ff.

[41d] *Ibidem*, pp. 105 ff.

[41e] *Ibidem*, pp. 109 ff.

[41f] *Ibidem*, pp. 125 ff.

[41g] *Ibidem*, pp. 197 ff.

[41h] *Ibidem*, pp. 230 ff.

[41i] *Ibidem*, pp. 271 ff.

[41j] LORD BIRKENHEAD, o.c., p. 265.

[42] S. ASKENAZY, *Danzig and Poland*, p. 74.

[43] R. DMOWSKI, o.c., p. 383.

[44] *The Paris Peace Conference,* V, p. 86. TEMPERLEY, II, p. 210. " The strategical aspects of the Plebiscite in the Allenstein and Marienwerder Areas ... a considerable bearing on the vulnerability of the Polish ' corridor.' ... The Marienwerder plebiscite will directly affect the width of the corridor, and will further decide whether the latter is to include that section of the important Danzig-Mlava railway which lies between Marienwerder and Deutsch-Eylau."

[45] O.c., II, p. 326.

[46] H. J. MACKINDER, *Democratic Ideals and Reality,* p. 208.

[47] ALMA LUCKNAU, *The German Delegation at the Paris Peace Conference,* p. 200.

[48] TEMPERLEY, II, p. 4.

[49] H. J. PATON, " Upper Silesia " (Paper read on 20th December, 1921. *Journal of the British Institute of International Affairs,* Vols. I-II, 1922-3, p. 15.

[50] TEMPERLEY, VI, p. 281.

[51] *The Paris Peace Conference,* VI, pp. 139 ff.

[52] NICOLSON, o.c., p. 68.

[53] KARL FRIEDRICH NOWAK, *Versailles,* p. 41. See also Professor Howard Lord in HOUSE–SEYMOUR, o.c., p. 70. " Rather different was the tendency of England. While committed to, and doubtless sincerely anxious for the restoration of an independent Poland, she did not appear to be particularly concerned that it should be a large, or strong one. ... England regarded Poland as a liability rather than an asset. ... England seems to have little desire to increase her responsibility unnecessarily on behalf of a State that was a natural client of France, but of no special interest to herself."

[54] NOWAK, o.c., p. 266.

[55] See Stenographic Report of Meeting between the President, the Commissioners and the Technical Advisers of the American Commission to Negotiate Peace, 3rd June, 1919, *The Paris Peace Conference,* Vol. XI, pp. 205 ff. A. LUCKNAU, o.c., p. 88.

[56] *The Paris Peace Conference,* VI, pp. 147 ff. See also GENERAL MORDACQ, *Le Ministère Clemenceau,* Vol. III, p. 303. " M. Clemenceau passa l'après-midi de la journée du 3 juin au Conseil des Quatre et, le soir, je le trouvai assez soucieux. Cette séance fut consacrée, en effet, en très grande partie, à la Pologne et surtout à la question du plébiscite pour la Haute-Silésie. Au dire du Président, jusque-là il avait cru compter, pour cette question, sur l'appui de M. Wilson et avait espéré ainsi venir à bout de l'intransigence de M. Lloyd George. Mais, hanté depuis une quinzaine de jours par l'idée que les Allemands ne signeraient pas le traité, ce dernier saisissait maintenant toutes les occasions pour essayer de faire adoucir les conditions concernant l'Allemagne. Au cours de cette discussion du 3 juin, M. Clemenceau se rendit très bien compte que M. Lloyd George avait certainement agi sur M. Wilson, qui semblait maintenant accepter en principe cette idée de plébiscite pour la Haute Silésie. ' Encore une désillusion de plus ' me disait ce soir-là le Président en me narrant la discussion."

For the reactions of the French Press see G. B. NOBLE, o.c., pp. 367 ff. In particular *Le Temps* warned against any concession: " The weakening of Poland ... would be a danger for the peace of the world. Importunate and indefatigable, the voice of France repeats to the Four: ' Do not yield in the East.' "

[57] *The Paris Peace Conference*, VI, p. 456.

[58] *Ibidem*, p. 303.

[59] *Ibidem*, p. 191. See also a vivid description of the meeting in CONTE LUIGI ALDROVANDI DI MARESOTTI, *Nuovi Ricordi e frammenti*, pp. 35-6. " Paderewski difende strenuamente il punto di vista polacco. Wilson e Clemenceau appaiono indifferenti, Lloyd George invece molto interessato. Rispondendo a Paderewski accusa la Polonia di imperialismo. Paderewski, contrariamente all'uso fra i Quattri, si alza in piedi per replicare. Parla bene e forte, con onesto patriotismo e commossa indignazione.

" Orlando (a me, mezza voce): Ma guarda come questo suonatore ha il senso politico.

" Lloyd George che dapprima era molto eccitato, si rabonisce, e finisce per invitare Paderewski a colazione."

[60] *The Paris Peace Conference*, VI, p. 303.

[61] PATON, o.c., p. 15.

[62] DILLON, o.c., p. 161. The same opinion was expressed by B. JOUVENEL, *D'une Guerre à l'autre*, p. 234. " Nous avons vu que la finance britannique, intéressée à tous les mouvements internationaux de marchandises souhaitait vivement que l'Allemagne se relevât. Les attaches de M. Lloyd George avec la Cité étaient fort étroites. ... Certes, ce n'est pas seulement la finance britannique qui prenait le parti de l'Allemagne. En faveur de Berlin militaient aussi cités par ordre d'importance, premièrement l'humanitarisme puritain, absolvant le peuple allemand des fautes de ses dirigeants, complaisant envers l'ennemi abattu, attendri sur la misère des femmes et des enfants, deuxièmement le personnel du Foreign Office attaché à cette tradition qu'aucune puissance ne doit dominer sur le continent, la France d'aujourd'hui, pas plus que l'Allemagne hier, troisièmement certains milieux mondains qui, au fort même de la guerre, avaient conservé leurs préférences pour le pays aristocratique d'Allemagne."

[63] KEYNES, *A Revision of the Treaty*, p. 179.

[64] E. MANTOUX, o.c., pp. 40-1.

[65] W. CHURCHILL, *The Aftermath*, p. 390.

[66] See, for instance, MERMEIX (Gabriel Terrail), *Le Combat des Trois*, p. 233. " Au cours de toute la négociation, les Français et les Américains avaient remarqué chez le premier britannique un ton peu bienveillant chaque fois qu'était abordée une question touchant la Pologne. Contre les Polonais, il avait visiblement des préventions: il participait sans satisfaction, sans confiance à la reconstitution d'un Etat qui avait péri parce que l'esprit politique lui avait manqué. Il se demandait si entre l'Allemagne qui voudrait un jour se refaire, et la Russie, qui tôt ou tard sortirait de l'abjection où les Bolcheviks

l'avaient mise, il n'était pas imprudent de replacer une nouvelle Pologne qui ressemblerait, peut-être à l'ancienne par son inconsistence."

[67] LORD RIDDELL'S *Intimate Diary*, 28th March, 1919.

[68] *The Paris Peace Conference*, IV, p. 316. D. H. MILLER, XV, p. 314.

[69] *Parliamentary Debates*, House of Commons, Vol. 117, 3rd July, 1919.

[70] W. CHURCHILL, o.c., p. 231.

[71] IAN F. D. MORROW, *The Peace Settlement in the German-Polish Borderlands*. A study of conditions to-day in the pre-war Prussian provinces of East and West Prussia, Oxford, 1936.

[72] H. J. MACKINDER, o.c., p. 209.

CHAPTER III

DISINTEGRATION OF THE AUSTRO-HUNGARIAN EMPIRE; THE PROBLEMS OF CIESZYN (TESCHEN) SILESIA AND GALICIA

THE questions arising from the disintegration of the Austro-Hungarian Empire were totally different in character from those of fixing the new frontiers of Germany. As Seton-Watson rightly observed, " the Allies in concluding the armistice of Villa Giusti on 3rd November were negotiating with men, alike civil and military, from whose hands authority was slipping hour by hour." [1] A great part of the former territory inhabited by non-Magyar or non-Germanic races was passing under the control of the liberated nations, and one may say that the Austro-Hungarian Empire at that time was a legal fiction. It was particularly true in relation to the two former Austrian provinces, Silesia and Galicia, the fate of which is the subject of this chapter.

I
TESCHEN SILESIA *

" There is little probability that the noble aim of the Supreme Council to put an end to the conflict and establish normal and friendly solutions between the Republic of Poland and the Republic of Czechoslovakia might be attained in this manner. The decision reached by the Council of Ambassadors opened a gulf between the two nations, and nothing could fill it. The Polish Government signed a formal pledge which must be carried out. It is with overwhelming sorrow that I put my signature to a document which deprives us of such a worthy, such a precious, so dear to our hearts a part of our nation. Before doing this I have to declare, Mr. Chairman, that the Polish Government sincerely wishes to abide by its signature, but it would be impossible for it to convince the Polish nation that justice has been done."—(Declaration of J. I. Paderewski before the Council of Ambassadors on the 28th July, 1920.)

---

* In this account we use the name of Teschen Silesia according to the official nomenclature of the Peace Conference, although this name is neither Polish (Cieszyn) nor Czech (Tešin), but German.

We deal only incidentally with other minor territorial problems dividing Poland and Czechoslovakia, such as the questions of Spiesz and Orava, as from the political point of view they do not introduce any new elements.

While in the Polish-German territorial settlement the Principal Allied and Associated Powers, following the lead of Great Britain, professed to adhere strictly and punctiliously to the ethnological and linguistic criteria, a quite different policy prevailed in the partition of the former Duchy of Teschen between Poland and Czechoslovakia.

Ethnic conditions in Teschen Silesia

There was no doubt whatever that the majority of the native population of the Duchy was Polish in all districts but one, agricultural, mining and industrial. A fair partition on ethnographic and linguistic lines was very easy since the Czechs lived in a compact mass in one district only, adjoining Bohemia, namely the district of Friedek, while the four remaining districts of Friestadt (Frysztat), Bielitz (Bielsko), Teschen (Cieszyn) and Jablonkau (Jablonkow), were inhabited by an an overwhelmingly Polish population.[1a] This fact is not disputed even by pro-Czech writers. For instance, Seton-Watson in *A History of Czechs and Slovaks* says : " In 1910 the Duchy . . . had a total population of whom 233,000 were Poles, 115,000 Czechs, and 76,000 Germans." [2] Nor were the historic arguments stressed by the Czechs very pertinent, and an American writer, S. Harrison Thomson, in his recent book *Czechoslovakia in European History*, although stating figures much too high for the Czech population drawn from Czech statistics, admits :

> " Ethnographically mixed—Poles 54·8 per cent., Czechs 27·1 per cent., Germans 18·1 per cent.—the territory around Teschen had had a chequered history, having belonged at various times to Poland, Bohemia, and Hapsburg Austria." [3]

At the moment of the disruption of Austria, the Polish Group in the Austrian Parliament and the Polish National Council proposed to the Czechs a partition of the territory in accordance with ethnographical and linguistic criteria.[4] " In this way the cause of friction would be removed and both nations could live in perfect friendship, bound by an alliance, an economic and military convention. The frontier should be established on mutual understanding "—such was the programme advocated by Dmowski, whose friendly feelings towards the Czechs had been manifested on many occasions (see, pp. 177-8). In his *Memoirs* Masaryk also stressed Dmowski's friendliness towards the Czechs : " With the Poles," he says, " and notably with Dmowski, we frequently discussed in detail the post-war relationship of our peoples. Dmowski himself favoured the closest relations and often advocated federation." [5]

On the 5th November, 1918, when the Austrian garrisons were disarmed in Teschen Silesia, an agreement was reached at Teschen between the Polish National Council of Austrian Silesia and the

Czech National Committee of that province (Narodni Vybor) establishing a provisional demarcation line, leaving on the Czech side a territory of 519 square kilometres with 140,000 inhabitants of whom 70 per cent. were Czechs, 20 per cent. Poles and 10 per cent. Germans, while on the Polish side remained 1,762 square kilometres with a population of 293,000 of whom 73 per cent. were Poles, 22 per cent. Germans and 5 per cent. Czechs. It should be emphasized that the Polish population of the Duchy had a highly-developed national consciousness, before the war used to elect Poles to the Austrian Parliament, and had numerous cultural and social organizations. It was very natural, if only because of the proximity of Cracow, the old centre of the Polish civilization.

The Czech politicians in exile had quite different plans, and were preparing diplomatic support abroad for their "historic" claims. Taking advantage of the ignorance of foreign statesmen (Beneš himself confessed that the French did not know that Austrian Silesia was inhabited mainly by Poles), they obtained formal recognition of their "historic" rights from the French Government. In a note addressed to Beneš on the 30th June, 1918, M. Pichon, the French Foreign Minister, pledged himself to "support with all solicitude the realization of your aspirations to independence within the historic boundaries of your territories." [6] We cannot say whether at that stage the Czechs had already given binding promises of far-reaching concessions to the French in the mining and steel industry of Teschen Silesia, which played an important rôle in the final decision on the fate of this rich area. It should be added that the diplomatic position of Czechoslovakia was much stronger in the initial period because the Provisional Czechoslovak Government had obtained a *de jure* recognition, first by France on the 15th October, 1918, and soon afterwards by other Principal Allied and Associated Powers, consequently much earlier than the Polish Government.

In the beginning of December 1918 news reached the Warsaw Government that the Czechs were preparing a *coup de force* in Teschen Silesia. The Polish Government decided to send a personal letter by the Chief of State, Pilsudski, to President Masaryk, proposing the setting up of a mixed Czecho-Polish Commission to review and settle by mutual understanding all the outstanding questions between the two neighbouring States. A mission was headed by Mr. Gutowski, who had known well Prime Minister Kramar before the war and had attended the Slav Congresses, one of which had been held in Prague. We have a detailed account of the negotiations carried out by this Mission from an article written by a member of this delegation, Mr. Damian S. Wandycz, and published in 1953 by a Polish weekly in London.[7] It appears from this account that the Polish Mission was cold-shouldered in Prague, where it arrived on the 16–17th December, 1918. In a first conversation with Mr. Gutowski, Mr. Kramar declared that the Czech Government did not recognize the agreement signed on the 5th November between the Polish and Czech National Councils in Silesia, and stated that the latter had no authority to sign it. Nor did a conversation with the recently arrived President Masaryk give a satisfactory result, although he received the members of the Mission in a more friendly way than the other leading Czech statesmen. On its return to Warsaw the Mission reported that a *coup de force* by the Czechs was imminent in Silesia, and that steps should be taken immediately in Paris, where the Polish proposals for a peaceful settlement of the Polish-Czech difficulties should be favourably received by the Peace Conference.

However, the Polish authorities were reluctant to believe that the Czechs would dare to challenge the authority of the Peace Conference, and Prime Minister Paderewski, speaking in Cracow in mid-January 1919 to the delegates from Teschen Silesia, assured them that the fears of Czech invasion were exaggerated and that " any accomplished facts would have no importance " as " it would be the ethnographic principle which would prevail in Paris."

Czech invasion of Teschen Silesia

At the moment most critical for Poland in view of the Polish-German fight for Poznan province, and the conflict in Galicia, the Czechs, wishing to prevent the holding of elections to the Polish Seym (due on the 26th January), which would have stressed the Polish character of that area, decided to create a *fait accompli,* and their armed forces crossed the demarcation line of the 5th November, invading nearly the whole of Teschen Silesia. Their advance was eventually stemmed at the battle of Skoczow by a small Polish garrison, but much of the Duchy was occupied by the invaders.

The developments in the former Austro-Hungarian territories were closely watched at that time by the American Mission in Vienna headed by Professor Archibald Cary Coolidge, a man of great science and impartiality. His staff was composed of the best specialists in Central-European affairs that the United States could produce. In Professor Coolidge's views " Teschen Silesia contained, indeed, very few Czechs, but a great deal of coal." As soon as the news of the invasion of Teschen Silesia by the Czechs reached him, he ordered the necessary inquiries, the more so as it was asserted that " the Czech coup was being done by orders of the Peace Conference and under the direction of an inter-allied commission."

Professor Coolidge's "extremely active and efficient agent in Poland," Lieutenant Reginald Foster, "hurried down" to Czechoslovakia, visited the front line in Teschen Silesia and called on President Masaryk and the Cabinet Ministers in Prague. The results of these inquiries led to the discovery of one of the greatest impostures in the after-war period.

> "He had found that there were, indeed, officers of all the four chief Allied powers with the Czechoslovak troops, but they did not form in any sense an inter-allied commission and had no orders whatever from Paris. They had, however, been persuaded by the Czechs to lend their services towards facilitating the seizure of Teschen. In the hope of bluffing the Poles into passive submission and thus averting bloodshed, the Allied officers had posed as an official commission, ordered the Polish authorities to evacuate the territory, allowed placards to be posted and notices to be printed in the newspapers to the effect that the Czechoslovak occupation was being carried out by orders of the Entente. Worst of all, the United States' representative in this ' Commission,' an American lieutenant of Czech extraction, had actually taken part in leading Czechoslovak units in the forcible occupation of various towns and villages, and he showed Foster two empty cartridges which he had fired against Allied Polish troops."

Members of the Coolidge Mission used to tell afterwards a rather amusing story, that their chief on receiving this report " said nothing but in silence and dignity smashed everything in his office."

The reports sent by Coolidge to Paris on the Czech invasion of Teschen Silesia were, according to his biographer, "exceedingly vigorous and most usefully clarifying to the authorities there." [7a]

Nor was the British Delegation to the Peace Conference kept in the dark about the Teschen incident as appears from Sir Esme Howard's Diary :

> "February 2nd, 1919 ... a long talk to Rowland Kenney who had just returned from Warsaw with dispatches showing that Czechs had behaved very badly in pretending the Entente Powers had authorized their attack on the Poles in Teschen." [7b]

Discussion in the Council of Ten on the future of the Principality

In the light of this evidence the leniency shown by the Supreme Council in relation to the Czechs is most astonishing, particularly as it was the first direct challenge to the authority of this body.

The question was brought before the Council of Ten on the 29th January. The Polish Delegate, Dmowski, declared that " this was not only an act of violence but it was dangerous because if the Czech troops continued to remain there bloodshed must follow." [8] Dr. Kramar, appearing on behalf of the Czech Government, tried to lay the burden of responsibility on the Poles, and even alleged that it was the Poles who had committed the act of aggression. But the facts were too obvious, and in spite of his pro-Czech attitude Ambassador Noulens was obliged to state that it was the Czechs who had invaded the territory of the Duchy. In spite of this statement the reaction of the Council of Ten was rather mild, as appears from the report of Ambassador Noulens, submitted to the Council of Ten at the next meeting :

> " The Czechoslovaks had been asked *whether they would consent to the immediate withdrawal of their troops* (from Teschen to Jablunkau), leaving the final settlement of the question to the Peace Conference. ... The Czech delegates maintained that the authority of Mr. Masaryk and Mr. Kramar would be compromised by the acceptance of this proposal. ... The Czech delegates had also maintained that the Poles were incapable of maintaining order in the mining districts, and that as a result Bolshevism would spread into Czechoslovakia." [9]

The Commission headed by Ambassador Noulens nevertheless recommended the *status quo of* 5th November, and also that " the railway should be handed over to the Inter-Allied troops representing a force of three battalions, if the Associated Governments so decided." The Supreme Council eventually decided that the railway line occupied by the Czechs should remain in their possession, as well as the whole part invaded by Czech troops. Although at the same time it was decided to send immediately a Commission to the spot, the authority of this body was greatly impaired by the fact that no allied troops were sent to Teschen. Consequently the Czechs were allowed to keep the spoils of their aggression. It had far-reaching consequences for relations between Czechoslovakia and Poland, and greatly undermined the authority of the Peace Conference in Central Europe.

The agreement of the 1st February imposed on both parties ratified the act of violation committed by the Czechs and stated that " pending the decision of the Peace Conference as to the definite assignment of the territories that part of the railway line to the North of Teschen and the mining region will remain in the occupation of the Czech troops," but adding that " No measure implying annexation of all or of a part of the said principality either to the territory of Poland or of Czechoslovakia taken by the interested parties shall have binding force." [10]

Besides false accusations against the Poles that they invaded the territory under Czech occupation, the Czech delegates alleged that " the Czechoslovak Republic could not exist without the large coal area which was within the disputed area " (Kramar, at the meeting of the 29th January), and that " the people as a whole, if given the choice, would elect to join the Czechoslovaks rather than the Poles, as being the richer of the two and one which offered the greater likelihood of order and freedom " (Beneš, at the meeting on the 3rd February). But, as subsequent events showed, the Czechs actually feared a popular consultation in Teschen Silesia.

The Inter-Allied Commission arrived in Teschen on the 12th February, and from the beginning met with great obstacles from the Czech authorities, who treated all its orders as proposals which they were free to accept or reject. Although at first the Commission was rather prejudiced against the Poles it very soon found that the country was predominantly Polish. Its first proposal to constitute Teschen Silesia as an independent Country was certainly ill-advised, and was rejected by the Powers. Then the Commission proposed a division of the area, assigning to Poland the mining district and steel works at Trzyniec, and to Czechoslovakia the railway line. The report of the Commission stated that " the population of the Principality of Teschen is undoubtedly Polish by national conscience, civilization and language." The question was submitted to the Joint Czechoslovak and Polish Commission of the Peace Conference, the report of which was presented to the Council of Foreign Ministers of the Principal Powers on the 23rd April, 1919, by Mr. Laroche.[11] The report made a proposal much more favourable to the Czechs than the report of the Inter-Allied Commission in Teschen, although Mr. Laroche was obliged to admit that " the districts of Friedek, Freistadt and Teschen were mainly Polish " and that " the Teschen Commission had proposed a line ethnographically more accurate." The Italian Delegate, Martino, objected to the report of the Joint Commission and proposed a solution " much more corresponding to the ethnographical position, leaving only 50,000 Poles to the Czechs instead of 167,000." In view of the lack of unanimity within the Council the Polish Delegation proposed that a plebiscite should be held, and when this proposal was not accepted suggested direct conversations between the two Governments concerned. The American Delegation shared the Italian views as to the predominantly Polish character of the area, as appears from the following words of President Wilson at the meeting of the Council of Four on the 17th May : " In any case most of the coal basin, of which the Teschen coal mines formed a part, must form a part of Poland." [12]

Direct conversations between the two Governments concerned took place in Cracow (20th–23rd July), but produced no result, the Czechs rejecting the Polish proposal for a plebiscite and the evacuation by Czech troops of the indisputably Polish districts.

In view of the failure of the direct negotiations the question was again brought before the Supreme Council on the 22nd August.[13]

The Council was in possession of an *unanimous* report of the Joint Czechoslovak and Polish Commissions of the Peace Conference. The report stated that " from the ethnographic point of view the Polish claims to the districts of Friedstadt, Teschen and Bielitz are fully justified," and it " saw no possibility of inducing the Polish population, whose national feelings are very ardent, to live peace-fully under Czechoslovak domination." It proposed a partition line, however, which did not fully agree with the ethnographical point of view, giving considerable advantages to the Czechs, namely assigning to Poland an area inhabited by 171,770 Poles and 10,443 Czechs, and to Czechoslovakia an area with 105,161 Czechs and 62,080 Poles. The division of the mining district also gave the lion's share to the Czechs (coal : 3,000,000 to the Poles and 4,595,000, that is to say 60 per cent. to the Czechs; coke : 520,000 to the Poles and 1,198,000, that is 69 per cent. to the Czechs).

Only Clemenceau refused to accept the unanimous report of the Commission, and the Council decided to hear the Czech and the Polish Delegates at one of the following meetings.

The Supreme Council heard Mr. Beneš on the 4th September.[14] The Czech Delegate disputed the accuracy of the Austrian statistics referring to the ethnographical composition of the disputed area. We need not deal with his arguments on this point, considering the above-quoted opinions of impartial international bodies on the matter. We wish only to stress an astonishing allegation of Mr. Beneš, that the population in Teschen did not speak the proper Polish language but a dialect which was a mixture of Czechoslovak and Polish. As a matter of fact, according to linguists the purest Polish dialect was preserved in Teschen Silesia, and there is no such thing as a Czechoslovak language, Czech and Slovak being different Slavic languages. Nor were the economic arguments brought for-ward by Beneš convincing, as the close collaboration between two neighbouring countries so strongly advocated by Dmowski could have prevented any drawbacks of partition. Mr. Beneš tried, more-over, to present his country as the main pillar of Western policy in Central and Eastern Europe, taking a rather disparaging view of Poland's future rôle in this area. Beneš said that :

> " he had desired to see his country reconstituted on a firm economic basis as rapidly as possible, in order that he might make it a sort of rallying point for the political aims of Western European policy. By so doing he had hoped that her neighbours would gather round her, and that the Western Powers would find a support for their policies in Czechoslovakia. Poland was neces-sarily involved in the politics of Eastern Europe. She was faced with all the difficulties of the Russian situation, in which she would

be involved for a long time to come. For this reason, Poland would require the collaboration of Czechoslovakia, but this could not be given if the last-named country was deprived of Teschen, which was regarded as essential to her economic existence. . . . He desired in conclusion to ask the Conference to consider with the utmost care all the arguments that he had brought forward, to weigh the grave political consequences which might follow a decision contrary to the wishes of the Czechoslovak population and to take into account the immense sacrifices which Czechoslovakia had made in supporting the Entente throughout the war."

The Polish Delegates were heard by the Supreme Council on the 5th September.[15] Dmowski spoke first, then Paderewski, both stating the Polish case in the Teschen area with great self-restraint and in a very conciliatory way. Dmowski reminded the Council that

" he himself had always defended the Czechoslovak case as if he had been a Czechoslovak himself. . . . He would continue to do so. He would always endeavour to secure a friendly agreement between the two neighbouring countries. He thought that the worst cause of conflict between neighbours was the subjection of one nationality to another. . . . Statesmen established their claims on the national sentiments of the populations in question. The population of Teschen was literate. It could not be treated like an inarticulate mass. Each man knew what his national feeling was. In the first Slav Congress at Prague in 1848, the representative of Teschen had joined the Poles, and the first newspaper published in Teschen during the nineteenth century had been written in Polish and not in Czech or in German.. . . The Polish Delegation maintained that the balance should be in favour of the national sentiment of the population. By a very strict application of this principle Poland had been deprived of Danzig, which was the lungs of Poland. Danzig represented far more for Poland than the mines of Teschen for Bohemia. It would not be possible to deprive the Poles of the advantage of a rule which had been made to operate against them in favour of defeated Germany."

Dmowski showed that economic arguments could also be used in Poland's favour, since Poland had no coal convertible into coke. He also objected to the Czech arguments referring to the necessity for maintaining by Czechoslovakia the railway line from Oderberg to Kaschau, as this line " carried coal from Upper Silesia to Hungary and the Balkans " and " the Czechs had four other lines connecting Bohemia and Slovakia." He was not satisfied with the partition line proposed by the Joint Commissions as " in order to attribute to Czechoslovakia the southern part of this railway, the Commission had handed over to Czechoslovakia the most Polish of the

Polish areas in Teschen—he might almost say the most Polish
population in Poland (Jablonkow). There were few parts of Poland
in which the population was 100 per cent. Polish : in this area it
was."

For his part Paderewski declared that

> " no one more than himself desired good relations with Czecho-
> slovakia. ... Was coal so important a matter as to justify the
> subjugation of an unwilling population and the estrangement of a
> country four times as big as Czechoslovakia? On the same line,
> what should Italy do, seeing that she had neither coal, oil nor
> forests? In reality, was Czechoslovakia so poor in coal? Out of
> a production of 26½ million tons of lignite throughout the former
> monarchy, 83 per cent. had been produced in Bohemia and 86 per
> cent. of Austrian and Hungarian coal came from Bohemia. These
> figures proved Bohemia to be one of the richest coal-producing
> countries in the world, after Great Britain, America and
> Germany."

The Teschen question was again discussed by the Supreme
Council on the 10th September.[16] The British, American and Italian
delegates defended the proposals of the Joint Commissions, and
Balfour said :

> " The Poles regarded the Karwin Basin as a Polish district, as
> indeed it was. There was no serious objection to cutting the coal-
> field into two halves, because the geological formations in other
> portions of the world were frequently divided politically. ... His
> conviction on this point was not only that of the Expert Commit-
> tees of the Peace Conference, but also that of the International
> Committee in Teschen, who had studied the question locally. It
> was very dangerous to improvise another solution, more particu-
> larly as the line proposed by the Joint Polish and Czechoslovak
> Committees was really favourable to the Czechs, to whom it
> granted 60 per cent. of the coal produce, and 40 per cent. to the
> Poles. It could not possibly be said that, under such a solution, the
> Czechs were being deprived of coal."

Balfour also strongly objected to drawing any analogies between
the problems of Teschen and of Eastern Galicia, stating that " the
decision on the subject of Galicia had been arrived at because the
Ruthenian population in that country could not stand alone. It was
inevitable that the Ruthenians should eventually be placed under
the rule of a non-Ruthenian State. Nothing parallel, or similar, to
these considerations arose in the Teschen problem." In spite of the
fact that the report of the Joint Committees had been adopted
unanimously, which means that the French experts voted for it, the
French Delegates—Clemenceau, Pichon, Cambon and Berthelot—

demanded the revision of the findings in favour of Czechoslovakia, and after a long discussion within the Council the whole problem was again referred to the Joint Committees for a report on the following day. The Committees were, however, unable this time to reach an unanimous decision owing to the changed attitude of the French member under pressure from his Delegation. Two opinions were consequently submitted to the Supreme Council, one of the majority, signed by the American, British, Italian and Japanese members, and another signed only by the French member.[17] The majority reminded that " from the ethnographic point of view the report of the 22nd August is more favourable to Czechoslovakia than to Poland, the whole Czech population of the principality except 10,400 inhabitants being assigned to Czechoslovakia while 62,000 Poles are lost for Poland."

In its conclusions the majority of the Committee stated that they " saw no possibility of proposing a boundary more favourable to Czechoslovakia than that proposed by the report of the 22nd August; in their views *any proposal in another sense would have been a great injustice to Poland's detriment* and would entail permanent hostility between the two countries."

The Supreme Council eventually decided at its meeting on the 11th September [18] that a plebiscite should be held in the Duchy of Teschen and in the districts of Spiesz and Orava. Balfour, commenting on this decision, said that he

> " feared the result of the plebiscite in Teschen would be to deprive Czechoslovakia not of 40 per cent. of the coal, but of 100 per cent. The territory was Polish and the Commission had attributed it to Czechoslovakia because of the railway running through it, connecting Bohemia and Slovakia. This railway would almost certainly become Polish property. Surely this was far more contrary to the interests of the Czechoslovaks than anything that the Commission had proposed. Nevertheless, as Mr Beneš appeared to accept a plebiscite, it must be assumed that he knew his own business best."

It was at the Conference at Spa (5th–16th July, 1920), at a tragic moment in modern Polish history when the very existence of Poland was endangered that the Principal Allied Governments imposed on Poland, as one of the conditions of their assistance, the acceptance of a verdict of the Allied Governments on Teschen Silesia, without holding a plebiscite. This verdict was given by the Ambassadors' Conference on the 28th July, 1920, depriving Poland of a major part of Teschen Silesia and assigning to Czechoslovakia a population predominantly Polish (190,000).[18a]

At the beginning of this chapter we quoted the pathetic declaration of Paderewski at the moment of signing this agreement. These words were echoed in Poland by the Prime Minister of Poland, the peasant leader Witos, who said : " The decision on the Teschen question is a hard blow for Poland, and it will weigh heavily on relations between Poland and Czechoslovakia. The Polish nation cannot endure this injustice."

A pro-Czech writer, R. W. Seton-Watson, although stating that " this settlement was the fairest attainable and represented a reasonable compromise "(?), adds that the grievance of the Poles, " it is fair to say, was augmented by the feeling that the Czechs had taken advantage of their weakness during the Russo-Polish war of 1920 to extract concessions and decisions which could not have been obtained in times of peace." [19]

It should be remembered that the verdict of the Principal Powers was given at a time when Poland was defending the whole of Europe against the Bolshevik invasion, while Czechoslovakia loudly proclaimed her desire to remain neutral both in relation to Soviet Russia and to Germany.[20]

How little regard is sometimes shown for truth in the West when problems of Central and Eastern Europe are concerned may appear clearly from this strange statement by Mr. Hoover, former President, in his *Memoirs* : " They (the Poles) secured entirely too many fringes of Germans, Czechs, Russians and Lithuanians for the good of Poland." [21] As a matter of fact the number of Czechs incorporated into Poland was negligible, and the truth was quite the opposite.*

The foregoing account recalled some facts mostly forgotten in the West, the whole importance of which was suddenly revealed in the course of the tragic events leading to the dismemberment of the Czechoslovak State in 1938–39. France played a sad part in this whole story. The Teschen area might easily have become a link between two neighbouring countries if France had pursued a more far-sighted and constructive policy in that part of Europe.

There is much evidence that the policy of the annexation of the ethnographically Polish part of Teschen area was due above all to the policy carried out by the Czech statesmen in exile, and that it did not entirely agree with the wishes of the local Czech population, desiring to live in harmony with its Slav kinsfolk. The best proof of it is the agreement of the 5th November concluded between two national committees in Silesia, the Czech and Polish, establishing

---

* According to Louis L. Gerson (o.c., p. 31), " Poland prior to the partition was inhabited by Czechs, Slovaks, Slovenes(!), Ukrainians, Lithuanians and other Slavic peoples." He seems not to know that the Slovenes live in a quite different region of Europe (now Yugoslavia) !

a provisional frontier in accordance with the ethnographical principle. But still earlier, in April 1918, that is during the war, a Czech meeting held in Friedek passed the following resolution :

> " The members of the meeting state that they wish to remain in good and friendly relations with the Poles, as the only Slav neighbour. We recognize that both Slav nations have their natural rights to Teschen Silesia, the Czechs having besides a historical right. The establishment of the future frontier should be based on the ethnographical principle in such a way that the Eastern part of the area should be assigned to Poland and the Western to Bohemia." [22]

As a matter of fact nothing had been done by the Western Powers to encourage those trends in the Czech policy which aimed at a closer collaboration with Poland. Such trends had undoubtedly existed on the eve of the Peace Conference. Masaryk himself spoke of " the beginning of a free federalization of Europe in place of the absolutist mastery of one Great Power or alliances of Great Powers over the Continent," [23] and he predicted the grouping of small States. " If the Poles were included," he said, " there would be more than 100,000,000 inhabitants in the zone of small nations." [24]

In a conversation with Mr. Frazier, diplomatic liaison officer of the U.S. to the Supreme War Council, on the 28th May, 1918,

> " Dr Beneš assured him that the Czechoslovak, Yugoslav and Polish movements were essentially democratic in spirit and he anticipated the formation of independent States in Bohemia, Poland and the territory occupied by the Yugoslavs. All of these could be united by close alliance, especially Poland and Bohemia, which have a common frontier and which comprise a total of 40,000,000 inhabitants." [25]

We find still more interesting details in an interview granted by Beneš to a Swiss newspaper, *Tribune de Genève,* on the 3rd August, 1918. Beneš then developed an idea of a Slav Mittel-Europa, grouped around Bohemia as the richest and most industrialized country of this area, which, moreover, had suffered little in the course of the war. Beneš asserted that

> " the future Czech State would not incur any risks of being crushed thanks to the policy of neutrality. But neutrality could not give sufficient guarantees as it did in the past. The Czechs now look for natural allies: an alliance in the East with the Poles and in the South with the Yugoslavs. These alliances will be close and can even lead to an economic union (which means a federation) and a united Poland and Bohemia will have a common port on the Baltic Sea. ... Speaking about Poland we have also in mind her

possible prolongation: Lithuania, Latvia, Estonia, etc. It makes us say that in a natural way and owing to geographic necessity Bohemia can become the axis of Slav Mittel-Europa, the only one which can save us from the nightmare of a German Mittel-Europa."

For what reasons were these plans eventually discarded by the Czechs? They may be found in the final decisions of the Peace Conference, due to Lloyd George's policy depriving Poland of her natural outlet to the sea in Danzig and denying Poland proper economic and strategic conditions. Nor did Poland's policy towards Russia find proper understanding in the West, and Poland had to fight a lonely battle. By weakening the barrier between Germany and Russia the Principal Powers discouraged the Czechs from casting their lot with Poland, a State beginning her life in particularly difficult conditions.

On the other side France preferred to deal separately with each new State, pursuing different and often contradictory policies in Poland and Czechoslovakia, with no coherent plan.

Pro-Russian and neutralistic trends in Czechoslovak policy

The disruption of a common front between two neighbouring States equally menaced by Germany induced in the Czechs false beliefs that they were much more secure than the Poles so far as the German endeavours were concerned. One reads with astonishment this strange statement by Masaryk :

> " Yet, if we owe the restoration of our independence to France, England, America and Italy, our policy is nevertheless *untrammelled* in regard to Germany. The relation between France and Germany is painful, but it will improve." [26]

The persistence with which Beneš pursued his plan of wanton annexation of Teschen Silesia proves that in fact he counted very little on co-operation with Poland and relied much more on a hypothetical support from some Great Power than on the joint efforts of the liberated States of this European zone. These assumptions gave the Czechoslovaks, from the very start of their independent life, an exaggerated feeling of self-confidence which subsequent events did not justify. Very curious evidence of this turn of mind can be found early in the course of the war in an article obviously inspired by the Czechs, published by the *New Statesman* on the 9th December, 1916 :

> " When once a free Bohemian land emerges in the heart of Central Europe we shall know that the flood of German-Magyar aggression is receding, never to start again. . . . *There is not a single*

*State among the Allies whose interests clash with those of the
Czech nation. ...* Bohemia re-created shall never again be over-
whelmed, and by her very existence will destroy the nightmare of
German-Magyar hegemony of Europe."

We know that at the beginning of the 1914-18 war Czech public
opinion " was uncritically pro-Russian in the expectation that the
Russians would set us free," as Masaryk tells in his *Memoirs.*[27]
Although he adds that he did not share these feelings and
" expressed his fears of the Russian dynasty and even of a Russian
Governor, since Russian absolutism and indolence, as well as
Russian ignorance of things and men among us, would soon
demolish our Russophilism," it may be taken for granted that he
reached these conclusions at a later stage of the war, in any case
only after the Russian defeats in summer 1915, because in a memorandum submitted early in 1915 to Edward Grey in which he stated
the Czech territorial claims (Bohemia, Moravia, Silesia, the Slovak
district of Northern Hungary. ... " The Slovaks are Bohemians in
spite of their using their dialect "), Masaryk asserted that " The
Bohemian people, that must be emphasized once more, are
thoroughly Russophile. A Russian dynasty in whatever form would
be most popular. ... Russia's wishes will be of determining influence." [28] Because of that it would be difficult for us to take at their
face value Masaryk's assertions that " the pro-Slav twaddle "—as
Neruda once called it—was repugnant to him.[29] There had been
two trends in Czech national opinion since the national reawakening of Bohemia : the Western and the Pan-Slav, or more correctly
Pro-Russian. In a memorandum presented by Ruger to Napoleon
III we read these proud words : " A Slavic Bohemia would never
be a Russian pawn. Her historic pride, independence, language and
culture are too individual for that." [30] If the pro-Russian trend had
the upper hand in the twentieth century in Czechoslovakia it was
certainly due to the indifference in the West to the fate of the
nationalities of Austria-Hungary and the desire so often manifested
by the Western Powers to maintain the integrity of Austria-Hungary
as an element of the European balance of power, a desire deeply
rooted especially in France (see p. 6). This alternative solution
reappeared in Czechoslovakia on many occasions in her chequered
history, and the Czech nation often looked for salvation from
distant Russia in difficult hours, in spite of the Western character
of her civilization. Much disillusionment awaited the Czechs on
this path, but the burden of responsibility should be laid above all
on the Western peoples and to a much lesser degree on the Czech
nation, so stubbornly fighting for her national self-determination.

It was certainly a great historic merit of Masaryk that he realized relatively early in the course of the war that Bohemia could not expect everything from Russia, at least for the time being, because of the inherent weakness of Tsarism, and that it was necessary to arouse also the sympathies and interests of the West for the cause of Bohemia's independence. He was right in stating in his *Memoirs* :

> " I think that one of my soundest political judgments was in not staking our national cause on the Russian card *alone* and in seeking, on the contrary, to win the sympathies of all the Allies instead of sharing the mood of uncritical and passive Russophilism then prevalent." [31]

The word " alone " is in italics because as a matter of fact Masaryk and his disciple Beneš assigned to the future Russia a rôle in their plans which was hardly compatible with the independence of other nations of Central and Eastern Europe. When the March Revolution broke out in Russia Masaryk sent a telegram to Rodzianko and Milukov in which he urged the provisional government to proclaim the freedom of the Slavs. According to his own words : " The Slav programme I stated briefly as follows : the unification of the Poles in close association with Russia; the unification of the Serbs, Croats and Slovenes; and equally, the unification and liberation of us Czechs and Slovaks." [32] Thus, while claiming liberation for the Czechs and Slovaks he was much less generous to the Poles, for whom in his opinion unification should suffice. This occurred at a time when the Russian Provisional Government itself recognized the necessity for Poland's independence.

Masaryk was still more explicit in a memorandum written on the 10th April, 1918, in Tokio and destined for President Wilson.[33] Apart from a curious prediction that " the Bolshevists will hold power longer than their adversaries suppose. Like all the other parties they will die of political dilletantism," we find an assertion that the peoples of Central and Eastern Europe needed Russia against Germany. Consequently Masaryk took for granted that the new Russia would necessarily become anti-German, an illusion shared by so many Westerners : " All the small peoples in the East of Europe (Finns, Poles, Esthonians, Letts, Lithuanians, Czechs and Slovaks, and Roumanians) need a strong Russia lest they be at the mercy of the Germans and the Austrians." Masaryk also defended Russia against accusations of imperialism, and in his lecture on the 22nd February, 1916, he tried to prove " that among the Slavs and in Russia there was no imperialism of pan-German sort." [34]

In a leaflet published for private circulation in 1918, " The New Europe," Masaryk supported the plans of Russian expansion in

Central and Eastern Europe and saw the future of Russia as a great
federation of peoples :

> " 14.   The Ukrainians in Galicia, Bukovina, Hungary, will
> become a part of the Russian Ukraine. . . .
> " 24.   Russia will organize itself in accordance with the principle
> of self-determination of nations into a federation of nations. In
> this federation there could in the West (outside of the Poles) be the
> Estonians, Letts and Lithuanians ; the Ukraine will be an autono-
> mous part of Russia—their attempt to be entirely independent
> would sufficiently convince the Ukrainians that separation from
> Russia will turn them into slaves of the Germans. . . . Finland may
> be independent if it reaches an agreement to this effect with
> Russia." [35]

Masaryk took the view that only Germany could menace the
territorial integrity and political independence of the States of the
Central and Eastern European area; he was unable to understand
the dangers of Russian imperialism for Europe and for his own
country, and being a man of the nineteenth century he shared all
the optimistic beliefs of his generation in the final triumph of
reason and human principles :

> " Not only the Ukraine " [he said], " but Poland and the other
> small nations in the East need the support of a strong Russia :
> otherwise they could easily come under the deciding economic and
> even political control of Germany. . . . The relation of Germany to
> Russia is the relation of Prussia to Tsarism. . . . Europe and
> humanity need an independent and strong Russia. . . . Russia can-
> not for some time make herself felt as a military force ; Napoleon's
> prophecy of a Cossack Europe has not been fulfilled ; Europe is
> marching towards liberty and humanity." [36]

Masaryk himself summed up his belief in the future political
rôle of Russia in this characteristic passage in his *Memoirs* [37] :

> " I believe that Russia will come to her senses, consolidate her-
> self and once more play a great political rôle, greater than under
> Tsarism. We and the other Slavs need her, nay, the whole world
> needs her. Russophile we remain, but in future we shall be so
> more thoughtfully, more practically."

In the light of these statements we understand the Czech
endeavours to secure a common frontier with Russia. In the question of Eastern Galicia the Czechoslovaks took a distinctly pro-
Russian attitude against the wishes of nearly the whole population
of that area, because neither Poles nor Ukrainians desired to
belong to Russia. The claims of the Czechoslovaks to the possession

of Carpathian Ruthenia, a country to which the Czechoslovaks had neither ethnographical nor historical rights, can be explained for the same reasons. Seton-Watson admits that " Ruthenia's main importance was strategic." The Principal Powers, who owing to Lloyd George's insistence refused to recognize the validity of this argument in relation to the Polish-German frontier, nevertheless agreed to the cession of Ruthenia to Czechoslovakia. Nor did they protest against the Czech violation of the provisions of the Treaty between Czechoslovakia and the Principal Allied and Associated Powers signed at St. Germain on the 10th September, 1919, which promised self-government to that province (Article X) :

> " Czechoslovakia undertakes to constitute the Ruthene territory South of the Carpathians within frontiers delimited by the Principal Allied and Associated Powers as an autonomous unit within the Czechoslovak State, and to accord to it the fullest degree of self-government compatible with the unity of the Czechoslovak State."

It is beyond the scope of this book to dwell upon the consequences of the pro-Russian attitude of the Czechoslovak State in the inter-war period for the Czechoslovaks themselves. The assumption that Czechoslovakia would incur no risks in the event of the reappearance of Russia on the European stage turned out to be a great illusion. Nor did it help Czechoslovakia that on many occasions she tried to defend Russian interests in Central and Eastern Europe, and that Czech statesmen often offered their services to Western Powers as unwanted intermediaries in dealing with Russia.[38]

To the West, little conversant with the intricacies of the political problems of Eastern Europe, the Czechoslovak policy seemed more reasonable and understandable, more agreeable to " wishful thinking," than the policy of Poland who, owing to her geographical position, had primarily to resist Russian expansionism towards Central Europe, endangering the independent existence of all the nations of this area. This to a great extent explains the pro-Czech bias in some Western quarters and particularly in France, who like Czechoslovakia, had illusions that a new Russia soon emerging on the ruins of Bolshevism might become a factor of European stability and restored balance of power. For this reason France saw in Czechoslovakia a valuable link with the future Russia, without realizing the fact that it rendered impossible any constructive policy, which could be achieved only through close collaboration between Poland and Czechoslovakia, around which other independent States of this area could be grouped.

II
LIBERATION OF GALICIA

" The Bolsheviks are attacking Galicia and gaining successes, and the Allies, on the other hand, were hampering the action of the Poles."—(A. Balfour, Meeting of the Council of Foreign Ministers, 18th June, 1919.)

" We are not imperialists and we do not want to annex any country or any people. We have never imposed upon any nation or foreign language. We never persecuted any religion. We never imposed upon the peoples different customs, and the proof of this is this, that after six hundred years of common life with peoples like the Lithuanians, like the Ruthenians, even like the Ukrainians, these peoples are still existing and even with our assistance, with our practical help, are regaining their individual character."— (J. I. Paderewski, Meeting of the Council of Four, 5th June, 1919.)

It was in reference to the methods of dealing with the problem of Eastern Galicia that Dillon said in his book *The Peace Conference* :

" Neither the Supreme Council nor the agents it employed had a real grasp of the East European situation, or of the rôle deliberately assigned to Poland by its French sponsors—that of superceding Russia as a bulwark against Germany in the East—or of the local conditions. Their action, as was natural in these circumstances, was a sequence of groping in the dark, of incongruous behests, exhortations and prohibitions which discredited them in the eyes of those on whose trust and docility the success of their mission depended." [39]

Polish-Ukrainian relations in Galicia

It is of course impossible to present in full in this book the intricate relations between two main ethnic groups, the Poles and the Ukrainians (often called Ruthenians at that time) in Galicia. But let us state some indisputable facts which may help us to understand the events occurring in Galicia at the time of the Conference.

The Poles and Ukrainians have lived side by side in this province since time immemorial, mixing their blood in very frequent intermarriages to such an extent that the witty remark was made that the boundary between the two nationalities in Eastern Galicia passed down the middle of the marriage-bed. It often happened that one part of the family was Polish and the other Ukrainian, the best example being that of the Szeptycki family, one member of which was the Metropolitan of the Greek Catholic Church in Lwow and an advocate of Ukrainian nationalism, and his brother a prominent Polish general. The two nationalities were united by a common Western civilization and religious beliefs (allegiance to the Church of Rome).

The Polish rule extended to the whole province in the fourteenth century (1340), and the population lived under Polish rule until the partition of Poland, when it came under Austrian rule, the Poles occupying the leading position in the administration of this province, since it was granted fairly wide autonomy (a provincial Diet).

The term Eastern Galicia, often used in relation to the Eastern part of the province, did not correspond to any administrative division,[40] and the Committee for Polish Affairs was greatly embarrassed when called upon to establish a boundary. For instance, in its report of the 17th June it considered two possible lines, one going more to the West, the so-called Line A, and the other, Line B, further to the East and leaving Lwow (Lemberg) and the oil districts of Drohobycz on the Western side.[41]

It is also unquestionable that in the Eastern part of Galicia the Ukrainians were in the majority, but that part of the population which used Polish as its mother tongue constituted an important minority (in the 1910 census 37·10 per cent. of the inhabitants stated their mother-tongue as Polish, and 61·3 per cent. Ukrainian).[41a] From the confessional point of view there were 23 per cent. Roman Catholics, 64 per cent. Greek Catholics and 13 per cent. Jews. It should be stressed that not all the Greek Catholics were Ukrainians. There were few Ukrainians living in towns, and this was particularly striking in Lwow and other bigger cities, although the number of the Ukrainian population in the towns was steadily increasing in the years preceding the outbreak of the First World War. An impartial judge, the American Secretary of State, Lansing, characterized in the following terms the Ukrainian population of Galicia at that time (Meeting of the Council of Foreign Ministers, 18th June, 1919): " Lansing said that his view of the question was based largely on the condition of the Ruthenian population. It must be recognized that this population was 60 per cent. illiterate, and therefore unfit for self-government." [42] In a note presented by Balfour on the 18th June, 1919, we find a similar opinion : " The Ruthenian majority is backward, illiterate, and at present incapable of standing alone. The urban and educated classes are largely Polish, and when not Polish are Jews." [43] It was for this reason that the Supreme Council rejected the idea of constituting an independent State from Eastern Galicia, moreover such a small State not having conditions for survival. The concept of self-determination applied to such a limited area would necessarily have a meaning different from that in relation to the " well-defined national aspirations " of larger ethnic groups living in more or less homogeneous territories. As Professor Eagleton explains in his previously quoted study on the problems of self-determination :

" More broadly, self-determination had been defined as the right of a people to determine their own political destiny : this might mean incorporation into a State, or some measure of autonomy within a State, or a somewhat larger degree of freedom in a federation or commonwealth, or union; or it might mean complete independence." [44]

Origin of the Polish-Ukrainian hostilities

As the complete independence of Eastern Galicia was unthinkable, two problems arose in connection with the mixed character of the population of this area : incorporation into one of the neighbouring States, and the satisfaction of the legitimate aspirations of both ethnic groups by a national legislation of the country to which the area was assigned. Even before the war many prominent Poles of Galicia realized the necessity for making large concessions to the Ukrainian part of the population and assigning to it a larger share in the administration of the country. It was above all the Conservative Party of Galicia, then the party having a predominant influence in Galicia and within the Polish parliamentary group in Vienna, that took the initiative of negotiations with the Ukrainian political leaders in order to establish a reasonable *modus vivendi* between the two national groups of Galicia. This policy met with the opposition of the nationalistic wing of Polish opinion, but the latter could not prevent the reform of the electoral law to the provincial Diet, which greatly increased the number of Ukrainian deputies. It should be emphasized that the policy of the Polish-Ukrainian *rapprochement* was viewed with marked hostility by some influential German quarters in Austria, including those members of the Hapsburg dynasty who remained faithful to the traditional principle of *divide et impera*. The predominant position of these elements in the Austro-Hungarian Supreme Command, supported by the German Great Headquarters, was to a great extent responsible for frustrating the plans for a durable *rapprochement* between the Poles and Ukrainians in Galicia, a matter which would require a special study. The Germans favoured the Ukraine as a satellite State expanded to the detriment of Poland at the time of the Brest-Litovsk Peace negotiations (see pp. 195 *et seq.*).[45]

When the military collapse of Austria-Hungary appeared imminent, a plan was devised at the Austrian Headquarters to help the Ukrainians in gaining control over the Eastern part of Galicia. There is no evidence of direct connivance by the Vienna Government, but there is no doubt of the initiative of the Austrian and German military authorities and of the support given to it by some members of the Hapsburg dynasty (Arch-Duke Wilhelm, known by the Ukrainian name of Vasil Vyshyvany).

In the last weeks of October 1918 were grouped on the territory of Eastern Galicia those Austrian regiments and units in which the Ukrainian element was in the majority, while the units which numbered many Poles were left in other, more distant provinces of Austria although they had been normally stationed in Eastern Galicia. All the units which had been transferred to Eastern Galicia occupied even the small towns which had never before had military garrisons, and, what is still more important, they played a big part in the military *coup de force* in Galicia.[46]

On the 1st November, 1918, these units occupied the main points in Lwow and took control of most towns in Eastern Galicia. The heroic defence of Lwow by the predominantly Polish population of that city, in which women and children played such a prominent part, will remain for ever one of the most moving pages of Polish modern history.[47] Lwow was relieved by the 20th November, but it had to endure a regular siege and fighting went on in Eastern Galicia for several months.

Such was the genesis of this short local war, which could be considered more as a civil war than an international one but for the participation of many former Austrian officers, mostly of German descent, in the ranks of the improvised Ukrainian army.

How one-sided was the information about what was going on in Galicia may be seen from the fact that as soon as the 8th November, 1918, the representative of the Polish National Committee in London received the following note from the Foreign Office :

> " The Secretary of State for Foreign Affairs desires to inform the Representative of the Polish National Committee in London that His Majesty's Government would view with serious displeasure any military or other action of the Polish Government in East Galicia or elsewhere, of a nature to prejudice or forestall the decisions of the Peace Conference." [48]

Should the Polish population in Galicia have endured the acts of violence of the undisciplined troops who, as confirmed by many Allied observers on the spot, committed numerous atrocities? Should the Warsaw Government have remained impassive in face of the attempt to create an accomplished fact, and admit all the consequences of this fact for the defence of its country against Bolshevist invasion? Was the British Government in this case prompted by the principle of self-determination, or did it rather wish above all to prevent the Poles from winning control of this old Polish province in order that the Powers might dispose of it in the future in a manner best suited to the aims pursued by British policy in Eastern Europe? It can be answered with certainty that at the beginning the Allies knew very little about the state of mind of the population in Galicia and cared little for its feelings.[48a] (How little Lloyd George knew about Galicia, nevertheless making many emphatic declarations on the subject and accusing the Poles of imperialism, may appear from the following, very characteristic confession at the meeting of the Supreme Council on the 5th June : " I only saw a Ukrainian once. The only Ukrainian I have ever seen in the flesh was upstairs. I haven't seen another, and I am not sure that I want to see any more. That is all I know about it." *D.B.F.P.,* First Series, Vol. III, p. 353.) At the end, when the true position in Galicia was known, quite opposite opinions prevailed in the Supreme Council, as appears from the following exchange of views at the meeting of the Council of Foreign Ministers on the 25th June, 1919 [49] :

> "*Mr. Pichon* said that the information received by the French Foreign Office positively indicated that no feelings of hostility existed between the Ruthenians and the Poles. On the contrary, a good understanding appeared to exist between them. Further, the views expressed by the *American Ambassador,* Mr. Gibson, appeared to bear out these reports.
>
> "*Marquis Imperiali* said that his information fully confirmed that received by Mr. Pichon. The largest part of the population was indifferent and all signs of disturbance were undoubtedly due to external causes. On the other hand religious sentiments turned towards Poland rather than towards the Ukraine, the latter territory being fully Orthodox."

In order to understand what was really at the back of the minds of some British statesmen we should remember that there was one factor which played a considerable part in all the proposed solutions of this matter, a factor which had nothing to do with the principle of self-determination, and one can say was even a negation of this principle so far as all the strata of the Galician population were concerned. Namely it should be remembered that at the beginning of the war Russia intended to annex the Eastern part of Galicia, alleging that its population was Russian. The Russian émigrés in Paris developed a feverish activity to win the support of the Allied statesmen for the Russian claims. From this point of view there is no more revealing document—incidentally throwing light on the Czech plans at that time—than a memorandum submitted to the Peace Conference by the Russian Political Conference (Suggestions with regard to the Treaties with Austria and Hungary) dated 10th May and signed by Prince Lvov, Sazonov, Tchaykovsky and Maklakov :

> " In Eastern Galicia the Russians have a powerful majority in almost all regions, with very few exceptions. Moreover, Lemkov-

shtchisna, which is part of Western Galicia, has in certain cantons a purely Russian character. ... Moreover, in view of the fact that in the Western part of Russia industry is very little developed, it is exceedingly important that immediate contact be established between these districts and the great industrial centres of Bohemia and Moravia. To this end it is absolutely necessary that the Russian territory has a common frontier with Czechoslovakia." [50]

On more than one occasion British delegates disclosed the reasons for the policy of their Government. For instance, at the meeting of the Council of Five on the 19th September, 1919, Sir Eyre Crowe said :

" The main idea which had guided the Council in all its discussions on the autonomy of Eastern Galicia had been that a people was being dealt with who had retained marked sympathy for certain of its neighbours, more particularly Russia. ... No obstacle should be placed in the way of an ultimate union of Eastern Galicia with Russia, and it therefore should not be made impossible for this province to separate itself from Poland." [51]

One wonders that such opinions could be expressed by a member of the Supreme Council, since both parties, Poles and Ukrainians, did not hide their feelings towards Russia. During the hearing of the Ukrainian Delegates from Galicia on 21st May, Sydorenko stated unequivocally that the Ukrainians " regarded the Bolshevists as their worst enemies," and that " the Russians had always only used Ukrainia for their own interests." The belief that the Ukrainians constituted a part of a Great-Russian nation, due to Russian propaganda, was as we see deeply rooted in some Western minds.

In all subsequent stages of the question of Eastern Galicia the Principal Powers had to retract their decisions and finally admit that the point of view defended by Poland was justified by the local conditions and the general political situation. In the first period the endeavours of the Principal Powers aimed at the suspension of hostilities between the Poles and Ukrainians, which meant that the latter could retain the advantages of their *coup de force* and render impossible a real pacification of the province, at the same time being unable to assure the defence of Galicia against the Red Army. When attempts through the members of the Military Mission to Poland failed to bring agreement between the two combatants, the Supreme Council had to review the situation in the light of the events taking place at the end of March in Hungary (Bela Kuhn Communist Government in Hungary) and in the Soviet Ukraine where the Red Army was quickly advancing towards the old Austro-Russian frontier. It was Marshal Foch who first realized the military and poltical implications of the events occurring in Galicia. Unfortunately his plans aroused great suspicion among some members of the Council, who saw in them an attempt at Allied intervention in Russia, already discarded by the Supreme Council. Marshal Foch brought the question before the Council of Ten on the 17th March, 1919,[52] pointing out " the most imminent danger related to the town of Lemberg (Lwow) which was infested by the Ukrainians and whose fall would entail that of the Polish Government." Foch proposed

" the transport to Lemberg of a part of the Polish troops at Odessa if the situation in that region made this possible and the transport to Lemberg of the Polish regiments from France. The force thus made available would, however, be largely strengthened by the support of the Rumanian Army, for which purpose a force of ten to twelve divisions at least could be obtained, of good physique and morale. . . . To sum up, the two countries, Poland and Rumania, with whom the Allies were tied, offered sufficient forces for the purpose required, provided that these troops received guidance and material assistance. Their combined action would constitute a most solid barrier against Bolshevism, which would otherwise triumph."

This intervention immediately provoked an outburst of anti-Polish feeling by Lloyd George, who at that time was particularly aroused against the Poles in connection with the question of Danzig and the Polish-German territorial settlement in general. Lloyd George said among other things :

" The Poles were starving and unable to defend Lemberg against an untrained mob of Ukrainian rebels, unless they were organized, furnished with supplies and paid by the Allies. He, therefore, personally would have nothing to do with the proposal which merely being interpreted, meant that in the first place the Rumanians and the Poles would be established in Galicia and under the guise of relieving Lemberg, Russia would be invaded. . . . Had the Poles felt very strongly on this question he thought they would have been able to defend themselves."

Lloyd George seemed to forget that at that time Poland had to earmark a great part of her troops for unforeseeable contingencies on the Western Front should the Germans refuse to sign the Peace Treaty, that she was faced with Russian invasion in the North, and that the question of establishing a junction with Rumania was a most vital question for her, as this might be the only free channel of communication with the Allies if the Germans refused the transit facilities through Danzig. Moreover, it was to be the British delegate, Arthur Balfour, who in later stages was to insist on the dangers arising from hampering the Polish advance in Galicia, menaced by the invasion of Bolshevists.

Consequently the Supreme Council decided to continue the endeavours for the conclusion of the Armistice in Eastern Galicia, Marshal Foch being authorized to study the possibility of transporting the Polish troops from Odessa and France to Poland. By the decision of the Council of the 3rd April a Commission was set up under the Boer General L. Botha to negotiate an armistice between Poland and the Ukraine. The plan of the Armistice prepared by this Commission left Lwow on the Polish side and the oil district of Drohobycz on the Ukrainian side. This plan could not be accepted by the Poles.[53] The reasons for refusal were clearly stated by the Polish delegate, Dmowski, at the second meeting of the Commission on the 26th April. He pointed out that " the Allies had no executive power in Eastern Europe and that Poland had to depend on her own efforts to continue to exist and to struggle against Bolshevism." He insisted on the necessity for reaching junction with Rumania, " the only country in Eastern Europe which was seeking order and willing to assist in maintaining it." In its reply [54] of the 13th May to the proposal of General Botha's Commission to accept the draft terms of the Armistice, the Polish Delegation strongly objected to the point of view taken by the Commission that the question had only a local character. The reply stated among other things :

> " The tentative suggestions of an Armistice made towards the end of March had no result, because it became necessary to obtain adequate safeguards against the danger of Bolshevism, which was increasing amongst the Ukrainian forces. To-day this danger has become much greater, as the Bolsheviks have advanced to the frontier of Galicia, and the Bolshevik movement is making rapid progress amongst the Ruthenian troops of Galicia. The disorganization amongst these troops is proceeding rapidly to-day.
>
> " On the other hand, the reports received by the Polish Government as to the German preparations against Poland, and an entente between the Germans and the Bolshevik Government of Russia, give ground to the fear of a simultaneous attack upon Poland from the East and the West. If, at the moment of such attack, Eastern Galicia were exposed to an easy invasion by the Russian Bolshevik armies, the military situation of Poland would become hopeless—threatened on the West by German troops, pressed on the East by Russian Bolshevik armies, she would soon find herself enveloped in the South-East, and thus separated from Rumania, from whom she is awaiting military co-operation.
>
> " It is these circumstances which have influenced the Polish Commander-in-Chief to aim at an effectual junction in Eastern

Galicia of the Polish and the Rumanian armies, in order to establish an uninterrupted front with Rumania against Bolshevik invasion from the East. The Polish General Staff hope that this junction will be effected during the current month."

The Polish offensive actually began on the 14th May, and in view of the disintegration of the Ukrainian troops advanced very quickly. On the 27th May the Polish troops occupied Halicz and Stanislawow, obtaining junction with the Rumanian divisions which the previous day had occupied Kolomea. The Polish Commander-in-Chief stopped this offensive on the line Brody-Zalozce-River Zlota Lipa in order to comply with the wishes of the Allies, and the military operations could only be resumed after some weeks. On the 17th July the Polish troops reached the old Austro-Hungarian frontier on the River Zbrucz.[55]

Did the Poles make use of false pretences in order to justify their action in Eastern Galicia? Let us state first of all that the disintegration of the Ukrainian forces was fairly advanced at that time, as the quick success of the Polish offensive sufficiently proves. There were many desertions from the Ukrainian ranks, including superior officers, among them General Oskilko, Commanding Officer of the Second Ukranian Army, with two of his higher officers. He gave as " the reason for his conduct the contamination of the Ukrainian Army by Bolshevism and the necessity for quitting in order that his own life might be saved." [56] The Ukrainian troops had not sufficient support from the local population. A Ukrainian writer, Mr. Reshetar, speaks in this way of the attitude of the whole Ukrainian nation at that time : " The failure of the Ukrainians to achieve permanent independent statehood during the upheaval caused by the First World War was, in a large measure, a result of the underdevelopment of the national movement." [57] Moreover, there was no co-operation between the Ukrainians in the Russian Ukraine and those in Eastern Galicia, separated by differences of religion, civilization, social and economic conditions.[58]

In such circumstances it was an abuse of the credulity of some Western statesmen to affirm that the Ukrainians were at that time able to oppose efficient resistance to the Bolshevik advance. The tragedy of the Ukrainian national movement in the Soviet Ukraine, which at that time was approaching its end, provides the best proof of this. It was to Poland that the Ukrainians fighting against the Red Army eventually turned for assistance, and it was on Polish soil that the remnants of the defeated Ukrainian Army, with its Commander-in-Chief Ataman Petlura, found refuge. Further, it was with Petlura that the Poles in 1920 made an attempt to liberate the Soviet Ukraine from the Bolshevist yoke. The Poles always claimed that a necessary prerequisite of such co-operation was the recognition of the territorial integrity of Galicia, a province with a mixed population sharing the same fate for centuries.

At the beginning Western statesmen were unaware of the impact of the developments in Galicia on the general situation in Eastern Europe, and addressed several injunctions to the Polish Government to stop the offensive against the Ukrainian troops. A telegram sent by the President of the Peace Conference on the 27th May even went so far as to menace Poland with the stopping of all supplies and assistance should " the Polish Government refuse to accept the guidance and the decisions of the Peace Conference." [59] Moreover, the Allies forbade the use of Haller's army in Eastern Galicia, which forced the Polish Supreme Command to change the plans for military operations on the eve of the offensive.[60] But in the end better counsels prevailed, and on the 25th June the following telegram signed by the Heads of the Four Principal Governments was sent to the Polish Government :

> " With a view to protecting the persons and property of the peaceful population of Eastern Galicia against the dangers to which they were exposed by Bolshevist bands, the Supreme Council of the Allied and Associated Powers decided to authorize the forces of the Polish Republic to pursue their operations as far as the River Zbrucz.
>
> " This authorization does not, in any way, affect the decisions to be taken later by the Supreme Council for the settlement of the political status of Galicia."

On the 27th June the Supreme Council sent another telegram to the Polish Government, authorizing it " to utilize any of its military forces, including General Haller's army, in Eastern Galicia."

Problem of Eastern Galicia before the Supreme Council

The authorization to occupy the whole of Galicia, given to Poland by the Supreme Council, did not remove the question of Eastern Galicia from the agenda of the Peace Conference. The impossibility of reaching an agreement within the Supreme Council at the time of signing the Austrian Treaty at Saint-Germain-en-Laye on the 10th September, 1919, created a most strange position for Poland so far as concerned the recognition of her rights to former Austrian territories. The said Treaty stipulated in Article XCI that :

> " Austria renounces so far as she is concerned in favour of the Principal Allied and Associated Powers all rights and title over the territories which previously belonged to the former Austro-Hungarian Monarchy and which, being situated outside the new frontiers of Austria as described in Article XXVII, Part II (Frontiers of Austria), have not been assigned to any State."

On this particular point, therefore, the idea put forward by General Smuts of cession to the Principal Allied and Associated Powers of former Austrian, German and Russian territories (p. 290) was carried out, bringing about a clear discrimination between the frontiers of Poland and those of all other successor States. Francesco Tommassini, former Italian Minister to Poland, states in his book *La Risurrezione della Polonia* :

> " So Cracow was ceded to the Principal Powers! This treatment was the more harsh as the same Treaty, although leaving open the question of frontiers, recognized in Article LIX the rights of Rumania over Bukovina, a province, certainly no more Rumanian than Western Galicia was Polish, and the population of which had joined also the so-called ' Republic of Western Ukraine,' while the Treaty of Trianon by Article XLVIII assigned Carpathian Ruthenia to the Czechoslovak State, the title of which to this province was undoubtedly much weaker than that of Poland to Eastern Galicia." [61]

The question was raised by the French Delegation (see Note of 9th October, 1919, *D.B.F.P.*, First Series, Vol. I, p. 927), and put on the agenda of the Supreme Council on the 11th October, but being considered one of " secondary importance " was referred to the Commission on Polish Affairs.[62]

It is very interesting to observe the evolution of the question of Eastern Galicia at the Peace Conference, and to see how gradually, in connection with the general political situation in Eastern Europe, Western statesmen were won for the Polish point of view.

It was the Commission on Polish Affairs which first brought forward the question of the settlement of this matter by a Note signed by Cambon and presented to the Council of Foreign Ministers on the 26th April, 1919. In this Note Cambon observed that the question

> " introduces problems of general policy involving consequences of the utmost gravity. Several solutions may be considered, namely : the creation of an independent State, the establishment of an autonomous State, under the control of the League of Nations, the partition of Eastern Galicia between Poland and the Ukraine. Either of these might, owing to the attraction which Russia would undoubtedly exercise upon a weak Slav State, result in the extension of the Russian frontier to the Carpathians.
> " On the other hand, it may be thought desirable to consider the political advantage which might result from the establishment of a common frontier between Poland and Rumania while securing for Eastern Galicia adequate guarantees in the way of local autonomy." [63]

The Note put the whole problem in a nutshell : any temporary solution leaving room for bargaining in the future was bound to encourage the Russian expansion across the Carpathians towards Southern and Central Europe, while a permanent settlement of the problem recognizing the old Polish title to this province would inevitably create a serious obstacle to such moves, highly undesirable for European peace. Tommassini, in his above-quoted book, warned also against the consequences which would arise from Russia reaching the Carpathians for the " political balance " of Europe [64]— to-day it is hardly necessary to stress this point, as the consequences of the occupation of Eastern Galicia by Russia (and of much more besides) are obvious.

On the 12th June Wilson made the proposal to ask the Council of Foreign Ministers to examine with experts the question whether a plebiscite in Eastern Galicia was advisable, and in such event what should be the area of the plebiscite.[65]

On the 17th June the Commission on Polish Affairs presented a report on the question in which it reviewed all possible solutions without recommending any one in particular.[66] This report was examined by the Council of Foreign Ministers on the 18th June.[67] Two conflicting views were presented at this meeting. The Italian delegate, Sonnino, advocated a definite solution : autonomy under Polish sovereignty. According to him " a plebiscite would lead to agitation and intrigue by all the parties whose ambitions were centred on the final issue. If, therefore, the Ruthenians could be guaranteed such rights as they required under Polish sovereignty, all these disadvantages would be avoided." Cambon stated that " Galicia should not be ceded to the Ukrainians," and agreed with Sonnino that " anything which would give to the undecided population of this area the impression of an indication that the Peace Conference was expressing its final will would put a stop to unrest and disorder."

Balfour took a different view. In his memorandum submitted to the Council he recommended the appointment of a High Commissioner for Eastern Galicia under the League of Nations, " who should be instructed, while the Bolshevik peril lasts, to work in harmony with the Poles and to facilitate the use of Polish troops as military necessity may require." [68]

Lansing considered that it would be more satisfactory to " give a mandate to Poland to hold the country, under such conditions as might be fixed by the League of Nations or the Great Powers, until such time as these might decide that a plebiscite should take place."

The question was again referred to the Commission on Polish

Affairs, which in its supplementary report of the 20th June [69] to the Council of Foreign Ministers stated that " the decision to proceed in Eastern Galicia to a plebiscite after a long delay would involve a danger of very serious political consequences; it might cause neighbouring States to compete with each other with the object of attracting Eastern Galicia within their orbit "; it submitted to the Council a draft Statute for Eastern Galicia on the hypothesis of its receiving the largest measure of local autonomy within the Polish State, under conditions analogous to the connection with the Czechoslovak State of Carpathian Ruthenia.[70]

The question of the political status of Eastern Galicia was again discussed by the Council of Foreign Ministers on the 25th June.[71] It was a draft resolution submitted by Lansing that served as the basis of discussion. The resolution, as we have said, authorized the Polish Government to occupy with military forces the whole of Galicia up to the River Zbrucz and to use for this purpose Haller's troops also. Thanks to Lansing's initiative, the appointment of a High Commissioner of the League of Nations, as previously proposed by Balfour, did not materialize, and the Polish Government was authorized to establish a civil government in Eastern Galicia. However, a special agreement had to be signed between Poland and the Principal Powers " which shall be conditioned to preserve as far as possible the autonomy of the territory and the political, religious and personal liberties of the inhabitants." Moreover the possibility of holding a plebiscite after some time was not precluded, and thus the Polish administration in Galicia was to be only provisional. The Polish Government of course strongly objected to a plan assigning to Poland only a provisional administration of Eastern Galicia, seeing in this a source of perpetual unrest and intrigue. In a note of the 25th August Dmowski, on behalf of his Government, demanded the incorporation of the whole of Galicia into Poland as an integral part of the national territory.[72]

On the strength of information obtained in a conversation with the Assistant Secretary of State, Skrzynski, on the 3rd September, the British Chargé d'Affaires in Warsaw, Sir Percy Wyndham, was able to inform the Foreign Office by a telegram of the 4th September that negotiations had taken place between the Polish Government and the representative of the Ukrainians from Soviet Ukraine. An armistice had been signed between the two armies on the 1st September and the delegates of Petlura had made a declaration recognizing the Zbrucz river (pre-war frontier of Galicia) as the definite frontier between Poland and the Ukraine.[73]

At almost the same time the Commission on Polish Affairs completed its report (23rd August) containing a draft Statute for Eastern

Galicia.[74] This report was not unanimous. The majority—consisting of French, Italian and Japanese experts—wished to extend the rights of the Central Polish Government in Galicia, while the British expert insisted on the limitation of the rights of Poland and the extension of the rights of the Provincial Diet. The report was discussed on the 19th September [75] at the meeting of the Supreme Council, which later, on the 23rd September,[76] heard the Delegate of Poland, Prime Minister Paderewski. The latter objected above all to the provisional mandate of Poland in Galicia, saying among other things : " It was not easy for him to translate the feelings of a multitude of people, but intense pain had been caused to Poland by the rigour of the Council's decision to cut out of its body political a province which had been a part of Poland since the fourteenth century. . . . Poland's rights to Galicia were not based upon past history but upon the present and the future. It was not a correct statement that only the urban population was Polish and that the rural population was Ruthene. The population of the rural districts was largely Polish and in certain regions was as high as 50 per cent." He further pointed out that " neither Admiral Koltchak, as representing Russia, nor General Petlura, as representing the Ukraine, disputed Poland's claims to Eastern Galicia. . . . " The general scheme of the Treaty seemed to him to be to detach Galicia from Poland at the earliest possible moment. The temporary régime provided for the loss of Lemberg and all Eastern Galicia, a loss which Poland could not endure and survive. Poland would never forgive its delegates to the Conference should it lose Eastern Galicia. It was obliged to defend this territory as it would defend its own body. Galicia had given poets, heroes and statesmen to Poland." He asked that " the treaty be not upheld, if the Council desired to see a firm allied State in Central Europe."

It was the American Delegation that was the most impressed by Paderewski's statement. On behalf of this delegation Mr. Polk presented a memorandum on the 25th September [77] in which he proposed to delete all passages in the Statute relating to the provisional character of the Polish administration in Eastern Galicia, and to the plan of holding a plebiscite in the future. At the meeting of the Supreme Council on the 25th September [78] he stressed that " he felt that in establishing a provisional régime the Council were allowing the existence of a region in Central Europe which would become a dangerous centre of discord." He was supported by Mr. Cambon, who said that " Poland would be much more disposed to accept a more complete autonomy for Galicia if she knew that there was a question of definite organization." But the British Delegation was adamant on this point, and Sir Eyre Crowe declared that " he could not agree to the Council suppressing the temporary character of the Statute." After the meeting Sir Eyre Crowe asked Lord Curzon for new instructions by a letter of the 25th September [79] in which he stated " that as the British Delegation is likely to be isolated on this question the political expediency of opposing the American propositions is for consideration," and in a telegram of the 1st October he said, " I presume that in view of the apparent unanimity of the other delegations you will not wish me to insist on maintaining the position hitherto held by His Majesty's Government." [80] But the British Prime Minister refused to yield.[81] Sir Eyre Crowe fully realized that the British Delegation was putting itself into an awkward position. He continued to object to " the specific provision after a fixed period," and recalled that the British Government had refused the principle of automatic revision of the mandates held by it under the Covenant of the League of Nations. " We should, in the specific case of Poland," he said, " be imposing a condition which was deliberately kept out of the Covenant because it was known to be generally unacceptable and certainly so to the British Dominions." [82] The attitude of the British Government on the question of Eastern Galicia recalls the witty remark made by Nicolson in his book *Peacemaking* 1919 :

> " The Anglo-Saxon is gifted with a limitless capacity for excluding his own practical requirements from the application of the idealistic theories which he seeks to impose on others." [83]

In his telegram of the 5th November Sir Eyre Crowe warned Lord Curzon of what might be the consequences of the British refusal to accept the proposals of the majority :

> " The Peace Conference cannot ' decide ' anything against the wishes of the British plenipotentiary. If the other plenipotentiaries object to the proposal which I shall put forward, it will simply mean that no decision is arived at. Of course this involves the non-adoption of our proposal, and, in all probability, a complete deadlock."

Owing to the repeated attempts of Sir Eyre Crowe to induce his Government to change its attitude, the discussion of the question of Eastern Galicia was not resumed until the 7th November, 1919.[85] Acting in accordance with his instructions Sir Eyre Crowe was obliged to declare then that the British Government insisted on the maintenance of the provisional character of the settlement. He added that he " personally had done his best to conciliate the views of the Council with those of the British Government." The American Delegate, Polk, objected to fixing a date for Poland's mandate, as " it would mean that Galicia would be in a state of ferment, and Poland remain in uncertainty over this grave position. This case was not the same as that of other countries where a plebiscite was asked for; it would be difficult to see where Eastern Galicia would go, if not to Poland." The British proposal to give Poland a Mandate for a determined period was referred to the Polish Commission, which presented its report on the 10th November.[86] Taking into account the British objection to giving Poland a permanent title to Galicia, the report proposed a mandate for a period of twenty-five years, adding however :

> " Although recommending to the Council the adoption of this solution which, alone, under the present circumstances seems of a nature to realize the unanimity of the Delegations and to lead to a concrete result, the Commission deems it its duty to call attention to the fact that no mandate has been considered so far for the countries situated in Europe, and that Eastern Galicia profoundly differs from the territories to which the principle of the mandate has so far been applied."

Sir Eyre Crowe, informing Lord Curzon of the debates in the Polish Commission by his telegram of the 10th November,[87] pointed out that four Allied delegations strongly opposed the British proposal for a mandate under the League of Nations for a period of ten years, and the American Delegation put on record a formal declaration that its acceptance of the principle of a mandate for a limited period only is " absolutely conditional on the British agreeing to twenty-five years, failing which the American Delegation reverts to its proposal for a mandate with no time limit." The British Cabinet eventually agreed to the extension of the duration of the mandate [88] and the Polish Commission presented its new report on the 20th November [89] which was examined by the Supreme Council the same day.[90] The Polish Delegates Patek and S. Grabski were heard that day, and it is worth while to quote some of their arguments as they greatly impressed the Delegates, according to the declarations of the latter made after the Polish Delegates had left the meeting.

Patek reminded above all that : " Even during the partition Eastern Galicia had not been separated from the Polish provinces annexed to Austria. . . . " He expressed fears of the demoralizing effects of the decisions of the Council on the Polish soldiers fighting at that time against the Bolsheviks : " If the Polish troops got the impression that their leaders had deceived them when telling them a year ago that they were fighting in defence of Polish territory, it was to be feared that they would again believe themselves deceived when they were told that the Bolsheviks were the enemy to be fought." Speaking of the relationship between Poles and Ruthenians in Eastern Galicia, Patek observed that " in

Eastern Galicia the proportion of mixed marriages was more than 35 per cent. How could one speak of hatred under these conditions? " He further said :

> " The Diet of Warsaw had unanimously voted that there could be no Poland without Eastern Galicia. . . . The Polish people would not understand how its Allies could have taken from it Galicia, which had always formed part of Poland and which no one was claiming. It was important that the Council should realize the gravity of the situation in Poland ; on one side Bolshevism, on the other German revolution. In the interior a threatened famine. The Polish Army was strong and Poland counted on it as an element of order. If the Army became demoralized Poland's position would become most serious and it would be threatened with extinction."

Finally the Polish Delegate declared that " Poland was not asking her Allies to give her anything at all; she was only asking not to be deprived of the territory which she considered belonged to her as of right."

In view of the well-known British attitude, however, other members of the Council were unwilling to reopen the whole question. So on the 21st November the Statute of Eastern Galicia, with a mandate for twenty-five years for Poland, was approved by the Council.[91] The American Delegation did not wish to let the occasion pass without a reminder in a memorandum [92] of the American attitude on this matter. This memorandum, entitled " Summary of American Position regarding Eastern Galicia," recalled that the American Delegation took the view that the " only practicable solution of the immediate problem of administering Eastern Galicia is to entrust this administration to Poland. In the interests of peace it is necessary to create as solid an administration as possible; any administration that is clearly marked as ' temporary ' would fail to inspire the confidence and support which is necessary to restore normal conditions in Eastern Galicia and would foster propaganda and intrigue." The American Delegate, Mr. White, observed that the purpose of this memorandum was to put on record the American attitude in order that " in twenty years Poland should not consider America responsible."

But the child whose foster-father was undoubtedly Lloyd George was stillborn, as Poland was never asked to sign the respective agreement and the text of the Statute for Eastern Galicia was not even disclosed at that time. Lloyd George himself agreed with Clemenceau's conclusions that imposing the Statute on Poland would have been inopportune, and the whole plan was shelved. On the 22nd December, that is to say a month later, the Supreme

Council decided to suspend the execution of the resolution of the 21st November. It was quite clear at that time that it would be difficult to find a Government in Poland which might be induced to sign the agreement undermining the whole strategic and economic position of the Polish State.[94] But it was not only the resistance of the Polish nation that forced the Principal Powers to abandon the plan. Let us remember that on the 17th November Denikin's resistance in Southern Russia began to crumble, and on the 16th December Kiev fell into Russian hands. Poland remained the only bastion of the Western civilization in the East.

When Poland's Eastern frontiers were recognized by the Western Powers in March 1923, Lloyd George, the driving force of all the Allied moves on this question and the one chiefly responsible for the resolution of the 21st November, 1919, was no longer British Prime Minister. Thus no condition was attached to the recognition of Poland's sovereignty over the whole of Galicia. The Allied intervention in the question of Eastern Galicia, however, sowed the seeds of mistrust between two kindred ethnic groups in an area in which so much depended on close collaboration of all classes of the population. Any idea of autonomy for Eastern Galicia became extremely unpopular in Poland, and fairly advanced plans to this effect were dropped. Whatever one may think of the policy of excessive centralism carried out by the Polish Government in the inter-war period, a feature common to so many modern States, an unbiased observer must state that the Polish rule in Galicia preserved the very substance of the Ukrainian population, who were spared all the horrors of agricultural collectivization, expulsions of millions of men from their native soil, and the de-Christianization carried out in the inter-war period in Soviet Ukraine.

Some members of the British Delegation to the Peace Conference were well aware of the alternative referred to by us above. Sir Esme Howard, who was conversant with the local conditions, having served as the British representative in the first Inter-Allied Commission to Poland, writes in his *Memoirs* :

> " ... it was a choice between this (incorporation of Galicia in Poland) or setting up another diminutive State and ' Balkanizing ' that part of the world still more, or joining Eastern Galicia on to the Soviet Russia, which was clearly to be the fate of the Ukraine ... most of us felt that the Ruthenes of Eastern Galicia would probably be far more gently treated under Polish administration than if they were joined on to the Ukrainians over the border and subjected to the gentle system of ' liquidation '." [95]

We are therefore unable to explain Lloyd George's initatives simply by his allegations that he wished to stand by the principle of self-determination. All his moves on this question can be better explained in connection with his whole policy in Eastern Europe, a matter which is to be reviewed in the next chapter.

NOTES

[1] R. W. SETON-WATSON, *A History of the Czechs and Slovaks*, p. 321.

[1a] See handbooks prepared under the direction of the Historical Section of the Foreign Office, No. 4, *Austrian Silesia*: "The Poles occupy the rural district of Bieliitz and the districts of Teschen and Friestadt, forming 77, 76 and 63 per cent. of the population respectively. The minorities consist of Germans (21, 17 and 13 per cent.) and Czecho-Slovaks (1, 6 and 23 per cent.) ... The Poles do not differ in race or language from those adjoining districts of Galicia. ... The distribution of the different nationalities of the Duchy is thus unusually simple ... the East is predominantly Polish."

[2] *Ibidem*, p, 327.

[3] S. HARRISON THOMSON, *Czechoslovakia in European History*, p. 354.

[4] We have drawn some information contained in this account from a well-documented *History of the Polish Foreign Policy* (in Polish), written by Starzewski, (only polygraph copies).

[5] T. G. MASARYK, *The Making of a State*, p. 234.

[6] S. HARRISON THOMSON, o.c., p. 310 and p. 351.

[7] DAMIAN S. WANDYCZ, *Zapomniany List Pilsudskiego do Masaryka*, Orzel Bialy, Nos. 32-5 ; also in seperate leaflet published by the Jozef Pilsudski Institute of America, New York, 1953.

[7a] ARCHIBALD CARY COOLIDGE, *Life and Letters* by HAROLD JEFFERSON COOLIDGE and ROBERT HOWARD LORD, pp. 208-9

[7b] HOWARD, o.c., Vol. II, p. 306.

[8] *The Paris Peace Conference*, III, p. 777.

[9] *Ibidem*, pp. 818 ff.

[10] *Ibidem*, p. 836.

[11] *Ibidem*, IV, p. 607.

[12] *Ibidem*, V, pp. 677-8. See also the opinion of Lloyd George, P. MANTOUX, *Les Délibérations*, Vol. I, p. 232. Séance du 12 avril, 1919: "Dans la question de Teschen, j'incline du côté des Polonais. La population de cette région paraît être en grande majorité polonaise."

[13] *D.B.F.P.*, First Series, Vol. I, pp. 612-13, discussion. Rapport présenté au Conseil Suprême des Alliés par la Commission des Affaires Polonaises et la Commission des Affaires Tchéco-Slovaques Réunies sur la Question de Teschen et d'Orava, pp. 616 ff.

[14] *Ibidem*, pp. 624 ff.

[15] *Ibidem*, pp. 635 ff.

[16] *Ibidem*, pp. 666 ff.

[17] *Ibidem*, pp. 682 ff. Rapport au Conseil Suprême.

[18] *Ibidem*, p. 674.

[18a] For the legal aspects of the solution of the Teschen problem see P. PINK, *The Conference of Ambassadors*, pp. 87-104.

[19] R. W. SETON-WATSON, o.c., p. 328.

[20] J. BAINVILLE, article " L'Alerte de 1920," published in *L'Action Française*, 29th July, 1920 : " Quant aux Tchéco-Slovaques, il y a déjà longtemps qu'ils ont dit par la bouche de leur ministre, M. Benès, qui pendant le guerre affirmait à Paris qu'une Bohème libre serait un rempart contre l'Allemagne : la neutralité est le devoir de la Tchéco-Slovaquie, sa nécéssité vitale. Neutralité avec l'Allemagne, neutralité avec la Russie. ... Un bon Tchéco-Slovaque brûlerait l'Europe pour avoir Teschen " (J. BAINVILLE, " La Russie et la Barrière de l'Est ").

[21] HERBERT HOOVER, *The Memoirs*, p. 357.

[22] From the Czech papers in Prague (*Komunikat Wydzialu Prasowego Departmentu Stanu*, 27th April, 1918, No. 31).

[23] MASARYK, o.c. p. 371.

[24] *Ibidem*, p. 372.

[25] *P. R. F. R.*, 1918, Sup. I, Vol. I, p. 807.

[26] MASARYK, o.c., p. 378.

[27] *Ibidem*, p. 33.

[28] *Independent Bohemia*, April, 1915. See ASKENAZY, *Uwagi*, p. 465.

[29] MASARYK, o.c., p. 294.

[30] Quoted by S. HARRISON THOMSON, o.c., p. 348.

[31] MASARYK, o.c., p. 32.

[32] *Ibidem*, p. 132.

[33] *Ibidem*, p. 197.

[34] *Ibidem*, p. 106.

[35] THOMAS GARRIGUE MASARYK, *The New Europe* (The Slav Standpoint), 1918. For private circulation only, p. 71.

[36] *Ibidem*, p. 44.

[37] MASARYK, *Making of a State*, p. 384.

[38] L. FISCHER, *The Soviets in World Affairs*, p. 505. " The outstanding characteristic of Czechoslovakia's policy towards Moscow is the desire to act as intermediary between Russia and other States. As early as 1920, when Lenin sent Krassin to Copenhagen, Beneš dispatched a telegram to Krassin offering to serve as middleman between the East and the West. Thereafter, in every possible circumstance, Beneš pursued the same aim. ... Neither the East nor the West availed itself of the good offices he volunteered. Nevertheless, he continued to sue for the rôle, and as late as 1928 he wished to bring Moscow into the League of Nations."

[39] DILLON, o.c., p. 206.

[40] See a letter of Mr. Patek to Clemenceau, dated 10th December, 1919. " A la suite du premier partage de la Pologne, l'Autriche avait acquis cette partie du territoire national polonais ainsi que d'autres territoires situés plus à l'ouest qui, avec le Grande Duché de Cracovie formèrent une province autrichienne -la Galicie. L'unité de cette province au point de vue administratif, judiciare et législatif, était complète et elle à été maintenue jusqu'au dernier jour de la monarchie des

Habsbourgs. Il n'y a donc jamais eu de Galicie Orientale " (*D.B.F.P.,* First Series, Vol. III, p. 907).

[41] *Ibidem,* Vol. III, No. 699. *Report of the Commission on Polish Affairs,* No. 3, 17th June, 1919.

[41a] See handbooks prepared under the direction of the Historical Section of the Foreign Office, No. 46, *Eastern Galicia*: " In Eastern Galicia the proportion of Polish-speaking inhabitants is 39 per cent. . . . although the Poles are in minority when Eastern Galicia is considered as a single area, there are a number of districts in which they form more than half the population. This is the case in the four political districts of Sanok, Brzozow, Przemysl and Jaworz, all of which extend eastwards across the San as well as in the adjoining political district of Cieszanow, on the Northern frontier, eastwards of the San. Poles have the majority in the political district and town of Lemberg (Lwow) and again in three political districts (Tarnopol, Skalat and Trembowla)."

[42] *The Paris Peace Conference,* IV, p. 828. *D.B.F.P.,* Vol. III, pp. 844 ff.

[43] *Ibidem,* p. 849.

[44] CLYDE EAGLETON, *Excesses of Self-determination,* p. 598.

[45] See also an interesting memorandum written in 1918 by Professor Lezins of Königsberg, " Deutschland und der Osten," the summary of which was given by DR. J. SKRZYPEK (*Ukraincy w Austrji i Geneza Zamachu na Lwow-Niepodleglosc,* Vol. XIX, p. 194). According to this memorandum the frontiers of the future Ukrainian State should extend to Lublin and Siedlce and include also the greatest part of Galicia and Northern Hungary ; in the East they should include the whole Russian Ukraine and go as far as the Caucasus. Poland should be reduced to Cracow district and a part of Congress-Kingdom (the rest of it being divided between the Germans and the Ukrainians). In this way, concluded Professor Lezins, the Poles and the Hungarians, these chief trouble-makers, would be rendered innocuous.

[46] See the above quoted study of DR. SKRZYPEK, pp. 28-82, 187-224, 349-87.

[47] See a declaration by Mr. Paderewski before the Council of Four on 5th June, 1919. " On the day I left Warsaw a boy came to see me, a boy about thirteen to fourteen years old. He was in uniform, shot twice through the leg, once through the lungs, and with a deep wound in his skull. He was one of the defenders of Lemberg. Do you think that children of thirteen are fighting for annexation, for imperialists? I saw girls in the same position, also wounded through the chest, through the lungs, through the legs, also with fingers missing ; they were all defenders of Lwow. Do they fight for territory, or for oil, or for annexation, or for imperialism." Mr. Lloyd George: " Lemberg, I understand, is a Polish city " (*The Paris Peace Conference,* VI, p. 200).

[48] FILASIEWICZ, o.c., No. 290.

[48a] P. MANTOUX, *Les Délibérations,* Vol. II, p. 7, 8th May, 1919. " Lloyd George: ' Pour l'Ukraine, tout ce que j'ai appris montre qu'elle est une véritable création de l'Allemagne. M. Bark, l'ancien ministre

des finances de l'Empire russe, que j'ai rencontré hier, me disait qu'il était né lui-même en Ukraine et que personne n'avait jamais pensé sérieusement à ce pays autrement que comme à une partie de la Russie.'

" Le Président Wilson : ' Je ne suis pas tout à fait de votre avis. Je crois qu'il existe en Ukraine un désir véritable d'autonomie.'

" Lloyd George : ' D'autonomie, soit ; mais de séparation complète de la Russie, je crois que c'est un mouvement temporaire.' "

[49] *The Paris Peace Conference*, IV, pp. 849 ff. See also minutes of the meeting of the Council of Four on 30th May, 1919. " *President Wilson* read a report from a United States Officer, a Lieutenant Foster, who had visited Sämbor and Stanislau, and reported that in the districts he had visited, the peasants, who were Ukrainians by nationality, had returned to land and showed no antipathy to Poles ; the Poles had behaved with great tact and judgment, and had released all their prisoners : the Ukrainian Government, according to this report, had proved most unsatisfactory—had been unable to keep order and had made many requisitions mainly at the expense of the Polish population. The Ukrainian transport had been disorganized and the currency system hopeless. The Ukrainian troops had perpetrated many outrages on the Poles, and this officer marvelled at the restraint shown by the Polish troops. In his view, the Ukrainians were not capable of self-government, but he qualified his report by stating that he had visited only a limited part of the country, and this only applied to what he himself had seen."

[50] D. H. MILLER, XVIII, p. 274.

[51] *D. B. F. P.*, First Series, I, p. 735.

[52] *The Paris Peace Conference*, IV, p. 379. D. H. MILLER, XV, pp. 401 ff.

[53] D. H. MILLER, X, pp. 319-488. Inter-Allied Commission for the negotiation of Armistice between Poland and the Ukraine.

[54] See the report (with Appendices) presented to the Supreme Council of the Peace Conference by the Inter-Allied Commission for the Negotiation of an Armistice between Poland and the Ukraine, 15th May, 1919 (*The Paris Peace Conference*, V, pp. 783-99).

[55] A. PRZYBYLSKI, *Wojna Polska*, pp. 86 ff.

[56] From a telegram of Mr. Gibson, American Minister to Poland, forwarding a message of Prime Minister Paderewski to President Wilson, 14th May, 1919 (*The Paris Peace Conference*, V, pp. 711-12).

[57] JOHN S. RESHETAR, *The Ukrainian Revolution*, p. 319.

[58] *Ibidem*, p. 291.

[59] D. H. MILLER, *Diary*, XVIII, pp. 427-8. *D.B.F.P.*, First Series, III, p. 328.

The question of the armistice was discussed at many meetings of the Council of Four, in particular on 17th, 19th, 21st and 27th May. President Wilson at the meeting of the 27th May recalled " the old plan of the so-called sanitary cordon which the military authorities had proposed to establish against the Bolsheviks, and which had been rejected."

It shows how unrealistic were the views on the situation at that moment in Paris.

It was Lloyd George who as usual displayed the most aggressive attitude towards the Poles and said, for instance, on 21st May, that " the Poles were using Bolshevism as a cloak for their imperialism."

The insistence of the Allied Powers to stem the Polish advance nearly provoked the downfall of Paderewski's Government (see the telegram from Mr. Gibson of 14th May. *The Paris Peace Conference,* V, p. 713).

Without entering into the reasons for the outbursts of popular indignation in Poland the British Prime Minister commented this even with his usual anti-Polish bias: " We are told that the Warsaw mob would overturn Paderewski's Government if we took strong steps. If that were so it showed pretty conclusively that the Poles were quite unfitted to govern themselves."

[60] The news of the use of Haller's troops first reached the Supreme Council from Czechoslovak sources. The Czechoslovak Government took a strange view that the advance of the Polish army might favour the spreading of Bolshevism(!). " The Czechoslovak Government was concerned lest the Bolshevik forces should, owing to the diversion by the Polish attack, overwhelm the Ukrainians " (*The Paris Peace Conference,* V, p. 754).

By a telegram to Clemenceau forwarded through the French Minister in Warsaw Pilsudski as the Polish Commander-in-Chief informed the President of the Peace Conference that in view of the reservations of the Principal Powers in regard to the use of Haller's troops he ordered " a fresh regrouping in order to avoid the possibility of a conflict between Haller's troops and the Ukrainians. As a result, one part of Haller's troops was transferred to Volhynia in the direction of the Bolshevik front, and another was withdrawn from the Front and placed in reserve with a view to its transfer to the Western Front. I would particularly draw attention to the fact that these movements were extremely difficult to carry out quickly, and called for great efforts both on the part of the troops and on the part of the Commanders " (*ibidem,* VI, p. 127).

PRZYBYLSKI, o.c., p. 88, relates that these enforced changes had greatly upset the plans of the Polish High Command.

[61] FRANCESCO TOMMASINI, *La Risurrezione della Polonia,* p. 232.

[62] Poland did not sign the Treaty of Sèvres of 10th August, 1920, by which (Article I) the question of Western Galicia was settled, and consequently, Poland's sovereignty over whole Galicia was recognized by the Principal Powers only by the decision of the Council of Ambassadors of 15th March, 1923.

[63] *The Paris Peace Conference,* IV, pp. 624 ff.

[64] TOMMASINI, o.c., p. 236. " Che l'eventualità di un'annessione della Galizia Orientale costituisce una seria minaccia per l'equilibrio politico europeo e per gli interessi italiani, è intuitivo . . . non possiamo dissimularci i pericoli di una Russia panslavista che, in Galicia, raggiungesse i Carpazi, li valicasse colla Rutenia sub-carpaziana, congiungendosi

territorialmente alla Ceco-Slovakia, in cui non mancano elementi pan-slavisti, per scender poi fin nelle valle del Tibisco. Viceversa l'unione della Galizia Orientale colla Polonia avrebbe assicurato a questa una frontiera commune colla Rumania, stato latino, interessato come la Polonia, come l'Italia ad arginare un ritorno offensivo dell 'imperialismo russo.'

[65] *The Paris Peace Conference,* VI, pp. 352-3.

[66] *D. B. F. P.,* Vol. III, No. 699.

[67] *Ibidem,* No. 700.

[68] *Ibidem,* Annex A to No. 700.

[69] *Ibidem,* Annex A to 701.

[70] *Ibidem,* Sub-annex, pp. 859-61.

[71] *Ibidem,* No. 701.

[72] *Ibidem,* enclosure to No. 712. We quote the most important passage of this note. "' Une convention qui ne reconnaîtrait pas la Galicie Orientale comme partie intégrante de l'Etat polonais mais qui autoriserait seulement la Pologne d'établir dans ce pays un gouvernement civil à titre provisoire, serait une source d'encouragement pour toutes agitations et créerait des obstacles au développement pacifique du pays.

" Pour les raisons ci-dessus énoncées la Délégation polonaise considère comme une nécéssité absolue que la Galicie soit attribuée à la Pologne comme partie intégrante de l'Etat polonais."

[73] *Ibidem,* No. 715.

[74] *Ibidem,* Vol. I, pp. 742-55. Statut de la Galicie Orientale.

[75] *Ibidem,* No. 61.

[76] *Ibidem,* No. 63.

[77] *Ibidem,* p. 787.

[78] *Ibidem,* pp. 784-6.

[79] *Ibidem,* Vol. III, No. 716.

[80] *Ibidem,* No. 717.

[81] *Ibidem,* No. 723.

[82] *Ibidem,* No. 724.

[83] H. NICOLSON, *Peacemaking,* p. 193.

[84] *D. B. F. P.,* Vol. III, No. 727.

[85] *Ibidem,* Vol. II, No. 16.

[86] *Ibidem,* p. 283.

[87] *Ibidem,* Vol. III, No. 732.

[88] On 12th November, *ibidem,* No. 731.

[89] *Ibidem,* Vol. II, pp. 372-6.

[90] *Ibidem,* No. 27.

[91] *Ibidem,* No. 28.

[92] *Ibidem,* p. 383.

[93] *Ibidem,* No. 44.

[94] See, in particular, a letter from Mr. Patek to Clemenceau, dated 10th December, 1919 (*ibidem,* Vol. III, p. 906).

[95] HOWARD, o.c., Vol. II, p. 385.

POLICY OF THE WESTERN POWERS TOWARDS RUSSIA AND THE BORDERLANDS. POLISH-SOVIET WAR IN 1919. EASTERN FRONTIERS OF POLAND AT THE PEACE CONFERENCE

Two Stages in the Policy of Western Powers relating to Eastern Europe

ONE can distinguish two stages in the policy of the Western Powers in relation to Eastern Europe in the period beginning with the Armistice with Germany and ending with the conclusion of the Peace Treaty of Riga between Poland and Soviet Russia on the 18th March, 1921. In the first stage, which ended at the beginning of winter 1919, the Western Powers either underestimated the danger of Bolshevism and thought it possible to bring to an end by peaceful means the military operations in Eastern Europe, or placed their hopes in the victory of the White Russian armies and the overthrow of the Bolshevik Government by the forces fighting against it. The Allied policy—if there was one—at that time was the result of mutual compromises between the divergent views of particular governments; the unity of the Allied policy was, however, more apparent than real. Gradually the problem of Russia disappeared from the agenda of the Peace Conference, and the adjustment outside it of the different views of the Principal Powers became ever more difficult. Counting on the early reappearance of a regenerated Russia on the international stage, the Principal Powers avoided any commitments relating to the territorial settlement in Eastern Europe; they limited themselves to the recognition of the sovereignty of the Polish State over a part only of the Polish territories of the former Russian Empire "without prejudging the provisions which must in future define the Eastern frontiers of Poland" (Declaration of the Supreme Council of the 8th December, 1919), and saw the future of the Western Borderlands of Russia as more or less autonomous units of the re-established Russia.

But with the defeats of the White Russian Armies the prospects of the restoration of a Russian State friendly towards the West vanished. The great discrepancy of views as regards the attitude to be adopted towards the new order in Russia rendered impossible the maintenance of a common front of the Western Powers so far as concerned the problems of Eastern Europe. First of all the United

States, unwilling to ratify the Versailles Treaty and join the League of Nations, took refuge in a policy of isolation and pure negation. The rivalry between Great Britain and France extended also to Eastern European questions, and on the other hand the desire to reopen trade channels set aside all other considerations in the British policy towards Russia. The disruption of the common front of the victorious powers involved momentous changes in the political situation in Eastern Europe, and the neighbours of Russia had to come to terms with the Soviet State.

The main lines of a *modus vivendi* between Russia and her Western neighbours were established at that time and lasted about twenty years. The conclusion of a series of peace treaties, the last being that between Poland and Soviet Russia in March 1921, and the signing of the Russo-British Trade Agreement in the same month closed that period.

*

*   *

" There are unmistakable signs that Russia is emerging from the trouble. When that comes, she is once more the same, calm and normal, we shall make peace in Russia."—(From the speech of Lloyd George in the House of Commons, 16th April, 1919.)

" L'Occident considère généralement que le bolchevisme est le monstre qui a dénaturé la Russie loyale. Il suffit donc que le monstre fût terrassé pour que la France retrouvât l'alliée des temps anciens. Trop de signes montrent que cette illusion retarde. ... Sous le bolchevisme . . . une autre Russie a poussé. Et c'est la Russie éternelle qui se déplace, qui cherche de l'espace et de l'air dans le sens où la Russie en a toujours cherché. Il ne fallait pas trop souhaiter que la Russie depuis que les bolcheviks nous avaient abandonné au milieu de la bataille, redivînt forte et reparût dans le monde comme puissance politique."—(From an article by J. Bainville, *L'Action Française*, 30th January, 1920.)

In Chapter IV of Part I of this book (pp. 197 *et seq.*) we dealt with the beginning of the Allied intervention in Russia after the outbreak of the Bolshevik Revolution. The military reasons which had seemed to justify the Allied intervention in Russia became obsolete after the defeat of Germany. It must be said that from that time one looks in vain for a consistent policy of the Western Powers in Eastern Europe. This fact is admitted not only by the historians of this period [1] but even by Western statesmen themselves. For instance, Lord Curzon says in a letter to Balfour of the 21st August, 1919 :

" It cannot be said that an altogether consistent policy has been pursued. Even now, the principles upon which that policy rests in the last resort are in some respects in dispute. Action is taken sometimes by the representatives of the Allied and Associated Governments sitting in Paris or by the institutions which they have set up, sometimes by the Governments themselves. The situation is so complex, and the difficulties of arriving at a decision which is acceptable to all are so great that, in some instances, it would be no exaggeration to admit that there is no policy at all.

" In these circumstances, the Great Powers where they act—and too often it must be confessed that refuge is taken in inaction—adopt an uncertain line of conduct." [2]

If the drawbacks resulting from this lack of a policy were deplored by some far-sighted statesmen in the West, how much more did the peoples of Eastern Europe feel the consequences of the inaction or incoherence prevailing in the West as regards questions concerning their most vital interests. On many occasions Pilsudski spoke bitter words about the Allied policy on these matters. In an interview given to a French paper (*L'Echo de Paris*) in February 1920 he said :

" It is a misfortune for our country that the Entente cannot reach a clear and straight decision. We are left to our own devices in Eastern questions, because Europe does not know what to do. England can wait, concoct plans, watch events ; perhaps she sees some advantages in it. We, the Poles, are close neighbours of Russia. The result of our endeavours depends on our decision." [3]

French Plans of Military Intervention in Russia

Let us state first of all that from the beginning of the Peace Conference the Allied statesmen vetoed the plans devised by Foch for organizing an Allied Army, which being based mainly on Polish territory would carry on military operations against the Bolsheviks. Foch presented this plan to the Supreme Council on the 12th January, 1919, (see pp. 235 *et seq.*). It was President Wilson who first opposed the plan, taking the view that the question (of sending an Allied military corps to Poland after securing the Danzig base and the railway line Danzig-Torun) " was a part of the much larger question of checking the advance of Bolshevism to the westward. There was room for great doubt whether this advance could be checked by arms at all." He expressed a similar opinion on the 21st January : " One thing that was clear in the Russian situation was that by opposing Bolshevism with arms they were in reality serving the cause of Bolshevism." On another occasion he said that " the seeds of Bolshevism could not flourish without a soil ready to receive them. If this soil did not exist Bolshevism could be neglected." [4]   Lloyd George took a similar view, observing at the same time that Canadian and other troops from overseas were withdrawing from the European continent and that it would be impossible to raise the required army of 150,000 men consisting of volunteers only. He then put the question : " What contribution America, Italy and France would make towards the raising of this army," to which Wilson, Sonnino and Clemenceau replied on behalf of their countries that they could make no contribution for such a purpose. Foch's proposal to transform the Polish territory into the base for operations against the Bolsheviks was made not so much for the protection of Poland's interests as for the purpose of reconstituting Russia.[5] Marshal Foch himself observed that the Poles " should agree to a restricted programme ... the Polish authorities should undertake not to occupy any debatable ground." [6]

Foch's plans for gathering in Poland a heterogeneous army, including White Russians, had been presented before the opening of the Conference to the White Russian leaders and, of course, met with their full approval.[7] On the other side, the Warsaw Government had not been consulted on this issue, and it is hardly necessary to stress that the plan for sending such an army to Poland and putting it under foreign command could hardly appeal either to Pilsudski or to the Warsaw authorities. It would have meant that war would have been carried on from Polish bases by an army over which Poland had no control at all.

The Allies at the beginning made the mistake of taking for granted that in her military operations against the Bolsheviks Poland would play the part of a pawn in their game. The same mistake, by the way, was made in dealing with the Russian Borderlands. The statesmen in Paris could have been spared many disappointments if they had taken more account of the feelings and interests of the peoples of Eastern Europe. At that time Allied policy continued to be based on the division of spheres of activity in Russia between France and Great Britain on the lines of the agreement of the 23rd December, 1917, established on purely military considerations [8] (see p. 198). This agreement was still considered valid between the contracting parties at the time of the Peace Conference, as appears from many official documents of this period.

A new factor had appeared since that agreement had been signed, namely independent Poland, whose rôle was increasing during the whole period under review. France considered Poland as entering her zone of influence, while Great Britain reserved for herself the Baltic States and Caucasus. Such a division had great disadvantages for Poland, as she had to depend entirely on French assistance and military supplies and was hampered in her actions by the British Government, unwilling to extend what was considered the French zone of influence. So, when General Carton de Wiart was, at the beginning of February 1919, appointed head of the British Military Mission in Poland in the place of General Botha who became ill,

" he learnt in Paris that Poland had been earmarked as the French sphere, and the French did not allow us to forget the fact for one single instant." Remarking on the enthusiastic welcome by the Warsaw population on his arrival there, General Carton de Wiart says : " They must have expected great things from the inter-allied missions, but I am afraid they did not get much." [9]

This obsolete method of dividing spheres of interest between Great Powers, and the view that the small States should play the part of satellites of the Great appears clearly in connection with the initiative taken by Ambassador Noulens, Head of the Inter-Allied Mission to Poland, who by his telegram of the 14th February, 1919, to the Secretary-General of the Peace Conference asked that an Allied General with his Staff should be sent to Poland " as the head of the Polish Army," as in the Ambassador's opinion it " would be a guarantee that these (Polish troops) would not be employed in a way contrary to the intention of the Entente Governments." [10] At the meeting of the Supreme Council on the 11th March this initiative was supported by Lloyd George, who took the opportunity to add some comments highly disparaging to the Poles and completely unjustified as subsequent events showed :

> " The Poles had no idea of organization, they have no capacity to direct or govern. The Premier is a pianist,* the President (Pilsudski) an idealist without any practical ideas. ... A French general of position should immediately be sent to take command of the Polish forces. ... He felt confident the Polish Government would willingly accept some such arrangements, on the understanding that the President of the Republic would be the nominal head of the army with the French general as his Chief of Staff ; the latter, however, being granted full powers of action." [11]

* To Lloyd George's disparaging remarks about Paderewski as " a pianist " (incidentally, he had to revise his opinion about the Polish Prime Minister in the later stages of the Conference) many most flattering opinions of leading Western statesmen can be opposed (see above, pp. 145, 171, note 59 to Chapter II, Part II). American Secretary of State, Robert Lansing, said about Paderewski: " Everything about Mr. Paderewski and his career invites the superlative form of expression. ... Honesty of means as well as honesty of purpose was evident in his conduct as a negotiator. ... Confidence in his integrity was the natural consequence of acquaintance and intercourse with Mr. Paderewski, and it was the universality of this confidence that made him so influential with the delegates to the Peace Conference " (*The Big Four*, pp. 210-12).

Clemenceau, after Paderewski's call on 27th May, 1919, expressed the following opinion about him to General Mordacq: " J'ai trouvé en lui, me disait le lendemain M. Clemenceau, un homme très cultivé, une connaissance générale très étendue, particulièrement averti de toutes les grandes questions politiques à l'ordre du jour " (Mordacq, *Le Ministère* Clemenceau, Vol. III, p. 288).

Let us state in this connection that General Carton de Wiart, who being on the spot, was in a better position to judge the position in Poland than was Lloyd George, took the completely opposite view to the disparaging remarks on Pilsudski and the Polish abilities uttered by the British statesman. " The day after my arrival," says Carton de Wiart, " we went to pay our respects to the Chief of State, General Pilsudski. Since those days it has been my destiny to meet many of the great men of the world, but Pilsudski ranks high among them—in fact, for political sense, almost at the top." [12]

Similar opinions were held by an experienced diplomat, Sir Esme Howard, who summed up the impressions of his journey to Poland in the capacity of the British member of the first Allied Mission to Poland : " After having come in such close contact with Poland as I did during those weeks in 1919. . . . I became convinced not only that her people is capable of great things but also that its future, like ours, is inextricably bound up in a common aim, the maintenance of peace."

He observed further that Pilsudski not only " fascinated " General Carton de Wiart but also himself, and he noted in his Diary on 18th February, 1919 : " After that conversation I felt Pilsudski was a real human being whom I could understand and I had a genuine fellow-feeling for him." It was therefore on the strength of quite mistaken opinions on Poland that a resolution was passed by the Supreme Council on 11th March to ask the " Polish Government to accept General Henrys as military adviser and Chief of the Staff to the President and Commander-in-Chief of the Polish Republic, to organize the Polish forces in Poland." [13] This resolution was never

HOUSE in his preface to HOUSE-SEYMOUR, *What Really Happened at Paris* (p. 451) considers Paderewski one of the most outstanding statesmen at the Peace Conference : " There were some who towered above their fellows, and these became centres of groups from which policies and opinions radiated. Wilson, Clemenceau, Lloyd George, Orlando, Paderewski, Venizelos, Smuts, Makino, and Wellington Koo, were among the statesmen having distinct and enthusiastic followers. . . . Paderewski and Wilson had about them something of romance and spirituality lacking in others."

Professor Lord in his answer to the question at a gathering in the United States. " How valuable were Mr. Paderewski's services to Poland? " stated the following: " Mr. Paderewski is so obviously a thoroughly high-minded and disinterested patriot that he commands confidence. He was able to win even the warm friendship of Mr. Lloyd George, who was not on friendly terms with the other Poles; and through the confidence of the British Prime Minister and President Wilson and M. Clemenceau I think he gained a great many things for Poland that a statesman who was less trusted could never have secured. In general, Mr. Paderewski's services have been of inestimable value, and in his handling of negotiations with other powers I think he did what no other Pole could have done " (HOUSE-SEYMOUR, o.c., p. 451).

accepted in this form by Poland (contrary to what occurred in Czechoslovakia, where a French General actually became Commander-in-Chief of the Czechoslovak Army). The French General remained only adviser and head of a mission responsible for training, equipment and the general needs of the Polish Army.[14] Pilsudski retained his supreme command over the Polish Army, and his authority remained unimpaired.

Nevertheless, the Principal Powers continued, at least for some time, to retain the fiction of a French General assuming supreme command of the Polish Army. For instance, at the meeting of the Supreme Council on the afternoon of the 15th September, when the question was discussed of the evacuation of the Baltic Countries by Germany, it was decided to appoint as representative of the Allied Governments for this purpose General Henrys, Head of the French Military Mission in Poland. On this occasion Clemenceau observed that " General Henrys was now in command of the Polish Army and would be a suitable appointee." [15]

In these circumstances there was wide room for friction between Pilsudski and the Polish Government on the one side and the French Military Mission on the other. It was certainly not in Poland's interests to depend entirely on the French, but the aloofness of the British and Americans and the jealousy of the French of any Allied interference in Polish matters often made the position extremely delicate, as may appear from the following observation of General Carton de Wiart : " The French were hardly tactful and did not like any assistance to be given except through French channels, regarding any gesture from another country as a sign of meddling." [16]

In a memorandum written by Mr. Selby, of the British Foreign Office, dated 6th June, 1919, we find the following remark : " Poland falls to France, owing to a theory which has arisen that, since France undertook the arrangements for equipping General Haller's army, she is now responsible for meeting all other requirements." [17]

We refer to this particular question because it was very characteristic of the Allied policy that at a time when the Principal Powers were unwilling themselves to assume any direct military responsibilities in Eastern Europe and were unable to agree on any plan of constructive policy referring to this area, they raised a claim to reducing the countries of Eastern Europe to the rôle of the tools of their policy and to prescribing the line of conduct for the latter on issues on which to a great extent the very existence of these countries depended.

The outcome of the debates of the Supreme Council on Foch's proposal of the 12th January, 1919, was summarized by Churchill

DD2

in these vivid terms : " The Marshal then fell back on minor expedients and the statesmen took refuge in platitudes." [18] This remark refers in the first place to the strange proposal put forward by Lloyd George on the 16th January to bring about a " truce between warring factions in Russia." At that time Lloyd George exaggerated the strength of Bolshevik Russia, saying that " now Bolshevism is strong and has a formidable army." [19] He was to change his mind some weeks later when the star of Koltchak began to rise in Siberia. The proclamation issued on the 22nd January by the Supreme Council to Russian Groups to send representatives to the Princes Islands, Sea of Marmora, proves that at that time some Principal Powers fostered strange illusions as to the possibility of coming to terms with the Bolsheviks through negotiations. According to Dillon, " underlying the impending summons was the conviction that Bolshevism, divested of its frenzied manifestations, was a rough and ready government calumniously blackened by unscrupulous enemies, criminal perhaps, but suited in its feasible aims to the peculiar needs of a peculiar people, and therefore as worthy of being recognized as any of the others." [20]

At the time when the Principal Powers were issuing their invitation to the Russian Groups the Allied armies still stood on various points of the former Russian Empire and gave their assistance to the anti-Bolshevik forces. An Armistice in Russia at that time could only facilitate the reconquest of the territories still in the hands of the anti-Bolshevik forces, especially if the Allies agreed to withdraw their troops from Russia and stopped their assistance to the various Governments formed in that part of Europe.

Another example of the same line of policy was the unofficial mission of Mr. Bullitt, who went to Moscow on the 18th February and brought the Bolshevik proposals of the 16th March. They consisted in a short armistice pending a peace conference, recognition of all *de facto* governments established in the territory of the former Russian Empire, withdrawal of Allied troops and cessation of Allied assistance to anti-Soviet Governments, simultaneous reduction of all armies fighting in Russia to a peacetime footing, resumption of diplomatic relations, etc. But the statesmen who either took the initiative of sending this mission or approved it, had not the courage to make these proposals known to the public. President Wilson vetoed the publication of the report of the Bullitt Mission, and Lloyd George flatly denied the existence of any approach to Russia in his speech in the House of Commons on the 16th April [21] What was the alternative to the Prinkipo policy and armistice proposals? We find an answer to this question in House's cablegram of the 23rd February, 1919 :

" No foreign intervention in Soviet Russia and no foreign troops to be sent to aid of non-Bolshevik Russia unless volunteers choose to go of their own accord, but material assistance to be supplied to these Governments to enable them to hold their own in the territories which are not anxious to submit to Bolshevik rule. Russia must save herself. If she is saved by outside intervention she is not really saved. We are bound to give moral, material, and if necessary, military support to protect Poland, Finland and other such States against Bolshevik invasion." [22]

A curious note was struck by *The Times* in an article on the 1st February, " The Alternative to Prinkipo ":

" Those who favour a formal campaign in Russia are always anxious to use the troops of some other nation than their own. ... The strength of Bolshevism is at the circumference; but if by supporting them with the means of healthy life we made a ring of plenty round Russia, can it be doubted that the contact with prosperity and liberty would lead to the collapse of a political system that was identified with famine and oppression? "

We can see from the above lines that this strange illusion that the attraction of material prosperity might dispose of the Bolshevik danger was not born in our days.

The evacuation of Odessa by the French troops in the first week of April 1919 marked the end of the French plans for direct military intervention in Russia. Louis Fischer says that the French policy from that time would consist in letting " others do and die; Paris would pay—and supply the powder. This was the cordon sanitaire idea." [23]

In his masterly book, *The Russian Revolution*, W. H. Chamberlin quotes the words of Colonel Freydeberg, Chief of Staff to General Anselme, Commander of the forces of occupation in Odessa : " No French soldier who saved his life after the Marne and Verdun would want to lose it on the fields of Russia." At the same time Chamberlin points out that " few soldiers of the Allied Powers lost their lives as a result of intervention. The total British losses in North Russia, where there was more direct fighting with the Soviet troops than in other theatres of intervention, are officially stated as 983, including 327 killed." [24]

According to Wilson's biographer, R. S. Baker, the cordon sanitaire policy described by him as " the plan of a defensive line based upon strong friendly States in Eastern Europe," appealed strongly to Wilson.[25] However, as subsequent events showed, America's share in assisting the Governments fighting against the Bolsheviks was very modest. In a memorandum of General Sosnkowski, Polish Vice-Minister of War, September 1919, only food supplies from America were mentioned,[26] and when the Report of the Supreme War Council relative to aid to be given to the Polish Army was discussed by the Supreme Council on the 20th October, 1919, it was stated that the American Government would not participate in any way in furnishing supplies to Poland,[27] and the American representative, Mr. Polk, even asked whether " an army of the present size was a necessity to Poland."

Military Supplies to Poland

In these circumstances the main financial burden of the material assistance to the armies fighting against the Bolsheviks fell upon Great Britain and France. The expenditure for this purpose ran into very high figures, but the White Russian Armies took the lion's share. This refers more particularly to Great Britain, but also French expenses for White Russian Armies were much higher than for Poland.[28] As appears from an official British document, " Cost of Naval and Military Operations in Russia from the date of the Armistice to 31st October, 1919," [29] Poland had no share in the British war supplies. This is also confirmed by the above-mentioned report of General Sosnkowski, in which we read :

> " The arms, munitions and generous assistance furnished by France, have permitted her (Poland) to attain a brilliant success of very important extent. The aid furnished by the United States and Great Britain in the form of thousands of tons of supplies has saved millions of people from death by hunger."

On the other side, the new States had great difficulty in purchasing war material abroad, as shown for instance by a " Note [30] on the Supply of Armaments to the New States of Central and Eastern Europe," submitted to the Supreme Council on the 15th May, 1919 :

" So far as Great Britain is concerned, the War Office has allocated certain munitions to Russia in accordance with Allied military policy. Except for this allocation, no arms have been supplied to Europe, and up to the present we have refused to entertain any application in the case of small arms." The Note further expresses doubts as to the wisdom of competitive purchase of munitions by the new States " at the expense of the raw materials necessary for the re-establishment of their industries." The Note was discussed by the Council of Four on the 17th May,[31] when Lloyd George pointed out that the question " was closely connected with the reference to the Military Representative at Versailles to consider the size of the military forces of the new States." We remember that at that time the question of the limitation of the armaments of the new States was discussed by the Supreme Council (see pp. 286 et seq.). So while on the one side the Allied Powers saw great advantage in building up a strong barrier against Bolshevism around the Soviet dominated part of the former Russian Empire, they hesitated to provide the new States, Poland in the first place, with adequate means of defence. It was a direct consequence of the mistaken views on Bolshevism prevailing at that time in some Anglo-Saxon quarters and of the underestimation of the danger of Bolshevism for the neighbours of Russia. A very characteristic example of such misguided opinions is the confidential report of Major-General F. J. Kernan, chief American representative on the Inter-Allied Commission to Poland, to President Wilson, dated 11th April, 1919. Major-General Kernan saw in the defensive measures taken by Poland and other new States only " an outburst of intoxicated nationalism," and he makes the queer statement that " although the common report and the common talk in Poland constantly spoke of Bolshevik aggression against Poland, I could get no evidence to that effect . . . nobody is attacking Poland to-day. Quite the contrary . . Bolshevism can be eradicated by good Government and equal opportunity for all citizens, but the military disease, once fastened upon the State, is going to be difficult to eradicate." [32]

The same unrealistic view was expressed by the Italian representative, Tittoni, at the meeting of the Supreme Council on the 20th October, 1919.[33] Tittoni said that " his immediate concern was, however, not Bolshevism, for he felt that this was rapidly tending to become less dangerous." General le Rond, who appeared before the Council as the representative of the Supreme War Council, to this replied that " it was somewhat premature to dismiss the question of the danger of Bolshevism thus lightly," but Tittoni insisted that " the size of the Polish Army must be reduced as there was no way of paying it." In the course of the debate Sir Eyre Crowe remarked that " if the British were asked to make a further effort with respect to supplying the Polish Army it should be remembered what had already been done by them; for instance, the British practically alone had undertaken the complete supply of the forces in Southern Russia." This statement confirms our previous remarks relating to Great Britain limiting herself to assistance to the White Russian armies, leaving practically nothing for the Polish Army.

Thus the Allies carried out a hand-to-mouth policy in the matter of supplying Poland with the necessary means of defence, being unable to understand that Poland's effort should be sustained by them, and that that country could not depend on the supplies delivered at the last moment. As we shall see in the following chapters, such was precisely the position at the moment of the decisive battle on the Vistula. How the position was viewed by the

Allied representatives on the spot we can see from numerous telegrams sent by H.M. Envoy in Warsaw, Sir Horace Rumbold. For instance, he says in his telegram of 30th October, 1919 :

> " It is most regrettable that the French or the Allies as a whole have not yet succeeded in providing the necessary warm clothing for the Polish troops at the front. The matter is of vital importance. The winter has begun earlier than usual, and is already below freezing point. I have troubled Your Lordship (Lord Curzon) with several telegrams on this subject of equipment because I realize, in common with everybody else here, the extreme importance of the matter." [34]

In a telegram of the 7th November Sir Horace relates his conversation with Pilsudski, who bitterly complained of this lack of Allied supplies, saying that " it appears as if Poland had been left by the Allies to her own devices, both in dealing with Germany and in dealing with the Bolsheviks." [35] In his telegram of the 19th January, 1920, Sir Horace says :

> " The Polish army might, in co-operation with the Rumanian army, bring the Bolsheviks to terms. The alternative is to remain on the defensive, but in order to maintain a successful defence the Poles will undoubtedly require considerable support in the way of military equipment and railway equipment so as to improve their communications at the front. ... Looking at the problem from a general point of view, it seems clear that if the Polish barrier against Bolshevism goes, the barrier will be shifted much further west and an opportunity will be given to latent Bolshevism in Czechoslovakia to join hands with Russian Bolshevism thereby creating a very serious state of things for Central Europe and the Western Powers. ... I am of opinion that everything should be done to assist them (the Poles) to withstand a Bolshevist offensive." [36]

Let us see how this question of military supplies was viewed by a Polish writer, General T. Kutrzeba, who in his book devoted to the Polish operations against Russia in 1920,[37] writes :

> " We wished to build up as big an army as was possible, but we were affected by an acute shortage of equipment. We had not enough clothing, arms, munitions and implements. It occurred at a time when great amounts of arms and munitions were being destroyed in the disarmed Germany. Poland was fighting against the Soviets in her own interests, but indirectly by her operations she was stemming the advance of the Communist revolution against the West. One might think that in such circumstances Poland should have no difficulty in obtaining the required war material. But it was not so. We met great obstacles. Only France was

actively assisting Poland, being interested in the existence of a strong Poland as her natural future ally, and also in sustaining a war against the Soviets in the interests of a future Russia.

"England put all obstacles to our obtaining the German war material which had to be destroyed; she based herself on the formal provisions of the Peace Treaty by virtue of which this material had to be destroyed and not used even for such an important purpose as repelling the Bolshevik advance."

Although France undoubtedly gave Poland very substantial assistance in arms and war materials (the Haller Army went to Poland fully equipped by the French), it should be noted that this assistance was often tied to the fulfilment of conditions particularly onerous for a country impoverished by war destruction and long years of foreign occupation. We find an interesting account of this matter in the *Memoirs* of Mr. Bilinski,[38] a prominent Galician states-man, former Austro-Hungarian Minister of Finance, who in autumn 1919 held the post of Polish Minister of Finance. Bilinski related an incident which arose in connection with some important trans-action in Parisian luxury goods on the Polish market by a man called Bastid, a close friend of the French Foreign Minister, Pichon. Owing to the fall of the Polish mark Bastid suffered heavy losses (the rate of exchange of the Polish mark fell within a few weeks from 4 to 8 marks to the French franc). The French Envoy in Warsaw made a request in very strong terms that the Polish Treasury should give full compensaion to Bastid, paying the difference in the rate of exchange. Moreover, according to this demand all French merchants should in the future receive adequate compensation from the Polish Treasury for the fall of the Polish mark. Bilinski, an experienced financier, defined this demand as a request for " an unlimited guarantee for unknown losses of an unknown number of French citizens." When French Minister Pralon called on Mr. Bilinski in September 1919 he told him that the French Government had decided to stop delivery of the uniforms and warm clothing bought by Poland in France for the army fighting at the front until the above-mentioned request had been granted. Bilinski ends his account with the exclamation : " I love France, our only faithful ally . . . but I am afraid of commercial France."

This is only one of the many similar examples. In his memoirs entitled *Happy Odyssey* General Carton de Wiart passes a severe judgment on the conduct of some members of the French Military Mission, who abused their official position. " The French Mission," he says, " consisted of some fifteen hundred French officers, who were responsible for the training, equipment and general needs of the Polish Army. They were under the direct orders of General

Henrys and needed close supervision and very firm handling, which they did not get. Instead they indulged themselves in easy and pleasant living not at all conducive to successful military training, and found plenty of time and opportunity to meddle in trade on a big scale, but failed to further the Polish cause." [39] This judgment is however too severe, as many French officers rendered good service to the Polish Army.

Foch's plans for using Poland as a base for military operations against the Bolsheviks were revived at the end of February 1919. At the meeting of the Supreme Council on the 22nd February Balfour, referring to "very strong recommendations from the British members of the Allied Commission to Poland," proposed to put on the agenda of the next meeting the question of sending Haller Army to Poland. [40] This point was discussed by the Supreme Council at its meetings on the 24th and 25th February. Marshal Foch then expressed the opinion that prior to sending these troops the Eastern frontiers of Germany should be fixed and the Port of Danzig together with the railway lines connecting it with Poland be freed from German control. Having thus settled all outstanding questions on the Western side the Allies would be enabled " to use the resources thus made available for the solution of the Eastern question." Subsequent suggestions made by Foch prove once more that it was the question of Russia that was his primary concern.

> " The difficulties which the Allies had to face in Russia were due not only to the enormous distances, to which he had already referred, but also to the nature of the enemy that had to be dealt with. ... Now to fight against such an enemy, troops of a particular composition were required; and in great numbers, in order to cover the whole territory involved. But these troops need not be strongly organized or of superior quality. The necessary condition would be fulfilled by the employment of such armies as might be raised locally in the conditions of Eastern Europe. For instance, the Polish troops would be quite able to face the Russians provided the former were strengthened by the supply of modern appliances and engines of war. But great numbers were required, which could be obtained by mobilizing the Finns, Poles, Czechs, Rumanians and Greeks, as well as the Russian pro-Ally element still available.
>
> " These young troops, in themselves not well organized, (though better organized than the Bolsheviks), would, if placed under a unique command, yield a total force sufficient to subdue the Bolshevik forces and to occupy their territory." [41]

Foch's renewed proposal had no chance of being approved by the Supreme Council, although it no longer required the use of Allied contingents. Balfour showed all the drawbacks involved by linking the question of an immediate measure of assistance to Poland by sending there Haller Army from France, with big schemes of military operations against the Bolsheviks and the previous setlement of all outstanding political problems on which the Allies were at that time far from in agreement. Balfour said that the question he raised was " that the Polish division (or rather divisions) in France should be sent to Poland : a small and modest suggestion involving no particular question of principle at all. On that narrow foundation Marshal Foch had started out to build a great plan : stretching from the Rhine to Vladivostock, which involved the immediate conclusion of the preliminary terms of peace with Germany." He stressed that " the question of sending troops to Poland should be dissociated from the greater question of policy." According to his views, " it would be impossible to wait five or six weeks, which appeared to be the shortest time within which the preliminaries of peace could be drawn up, before sending to Poland the Polish troops which were so urgently required."

As we know, Haller Army was not sent to Poland until April (see p. 236), and consequently more than six weeks had elapsed before that army reached Polish soil and could be available for military operations. Foch's proposal took into account military considerations only; the Marshal seemed to be unaware of the big political issues raised by him, not only in relation to Germany but also, and above all, to the Russian problem. Such schemes, as subsequent events amply showed, required the establishment of a political programme which would take into account not only the interests of the future and unknown Russia but also those of Russia's neighbours, who had to bear practically all the sacrifices.

All these schemes seemed overshadowed a few weeks later by Koltchak's successes in Siberia and then by Denikin's advance in Southern and Central Russia. In his speech in the House of Commons on the 16th April, 1919, Lloyd George stated that although he considered that " to attempt a military intervention in Russia would be the greatest act of stupidity that any Government could possibly commit," he thought nevertheless that the British Government should support all the anti-Bolshevik forces in order " to arrest the flow of the lava—that is, to prevent the forcible eruption of Bolshevism into Allied lands." For that reason the British Government would support the White Russian Armies and was allegedly organizing " all the forces of the Allied countries bordering on Bolshevist territory from the Baltic to the Black Sea— Poland, Czechoslovakia and Rumania. . . . If Bolshevism attacks any of our Allies, it is our business to defend them. Therefore the British Government was supplying all these countries with the necessary equipment to set up a real barrier against an invasion by force of arms."

But it seemed that at that time Lloyd George put all his hopes in the successes of the White Russian Armies, since he said in his conclusions that " there are unmistakable signs that Russia is emerging from the trouble." He was still more emphatic on this point when the question of Koltchak's advance was discussed at the meetings of the Supreme Council at the beginning of May. At the meeting on the 7th May, Lloyd George said that " in a short time the Allied and Associated Powers might be faced with a Koltchak Government in Moscow," [42] and on the 10th May he stated that " he did not think public opinion would allow us to abandon Koltchak even if he should establish a reactionary Government, because the world would say that the establishment of order was so important." [43]

But already in mid-June Koltchak suffered his first great defeats and eventually collapsed. The Allied hopes were then placed in Denikin, who advanced at a remarkable pace in summer 1919, seizing Odessa on the 23rd August, Kiev on the 31st August, and reaching Orel, the high point in his march to Moscow, on the 14th October. Then began for him a series of defeats and his army began to crumble in mid-November. Kiev was reoccupied by the Red Army in December 1919, and Rostov, the former seat of Denikin's Government, in January 1920. We recall these dates because they are landmarks in the history of the White Russian campaign against the Red Army in 1919. Since the Allies attached great hopes to this movement and supplied the White Russian forces on a much bigger scale than other Governments established on the soil of the former Russian Empire, it is clear that the Allied policy failed on what was its main object in Russia. As the principal aim of the White Russian movement was the reconstitution of an indivisible Russian Empire, the conclusion can be drawn that the Allied policy, with some qualifications about which we shall speak later, had obviously concurred with the White Russian movement on this point. The Principal Powers, each for a different reason, undoubtedly wished for the re-establishment of the Russian Empire, friendly to the Allies, that is to say not dependent either economically or politically on Germany. The effect of this policy on the attitude of the Principal Powers towards the Borderlands and Poland in particular could be felt in all problems relating to Eastern Europe.

U.S.A. and the principle of territorial integrity of Russia

Let us note that even the United States, which viewed with the greatest distrust and suspicion the White Russian movement, fearing that it might result " in a policy of reaction and military power," [44] and which consequently gave litle support to the forces fighting against Bolshevism, and under Wilson's influence became the main protagonists of the policy of abstention,[45] unwilling even to assume any responsibility in the case of Armenia—a case particularly popular in the United States—adhered the most to the principle of safeguarding the territorial integrity of Russia (see p. 202). Lansing Secretary of State, in his memorandum for President Wilson written on the eve of the Peace Conference (26th November, 1918), states that " First of all, I would suggest we inform the French, British, Italians and Japanese that we will use our best efforts to see to it that Russia's interests are safeguarded, and that we propose to urge that Russian questions be considered as parts of a whole and not as separate problems resulting from what may prove, for the most part, temporary disintegration." [46] He stated the same views at the meeting of the Council of Foreign Ministers on the 9th May, 1919, when the policy of the Allied and Associated Powers in the region bordering the Baltic Sea was discussed. He pointed out that " at the bottom of the whole question lay a very important principle of policy. The recognition of *de facto* Governments in territories formerly Russian constituted a measure of dissection of Russia which the United States of America had carefully avoided, except in the case of Finland and Poland. In the case of Poland Russia herself had acquiesced." [47]

In the Outline of Tentative Report and Recommendations prepared by the Intelligence Section, in accordance with instructions, for the President and Plenipotentiaries, dated 21st January, 1919, the same ideas are put forward in connection with the proposed territorial settlement in Eastern Europe :

" It is recommended:

"(1)   That encouragement be given, at opportune time, to the reunion with Russia of these border regions of the South and West which have broken away and set up their own national governments, particularly the Baltic provinces and the Ukraine, if reunion can be accomplished within a federalized or genuinely democratic Russia.

"(2)   That there be excepted from the general application of the principle above mentioned Finland, Poland, the Armenians in Transcaucasia, and probably Lithuania. ... Among these exceptions the case of Lithuania is much less clear-cut than the others. If she unites with Poland, as now seems quite possible, she will naturally share Poland's independence. If not she will be in the position of the Esths and Letts rather than of the Finns and Poles." [48]

This standpoint of the United States Government became still more accentuated later when it resumed its policy of isolation. This policy was best summed up in a note of the Secretary of State, Mr. Colby, to the Italian Ambassador to the United States, Avezzana, of 10th August, 1920 : " The United States maintains unimpaired its faith in the Russian people, in their high character and their future. That they will overcome the existing anarchy, suffering and destitution we do not entertain the slightest doubt. . . . Russia's interests must be generously protected . . . all decisions of vital importance to it, and especially those concerning its sovereignty over the territory of the former Russian Empire, be held in abeyance." For this reason the United States refused to recognize the Baltic States as " separate nations independent of Russia," and " withheld its approval from the decision of the Supreme Council recognizing the independence of the so-called republics of Georgia and Azerbaijan." [49].

France and Eastern Europe

French policy in Eastern Europe was prompted by much more direct interests, in either the economic or political sphere, than was the case with the U.S.A. France could not support a vacuum in the East, and for this reason she gave all her backing to Poland, recovering her old possessions seized by Prussia by the Treaties of Partition, and to her becoming strong enough to withstand the German expansionism in Eastern Europe. But at the same time France wanted the reconstitution of a strong Russia and she tried to use Poland as a springboard for intervention against Bolshevism, which she considered an implacable enemy. The official French policy was under the influence of the White Russian statesmen of the old school, and the Quai d'Orsay never severed its connection with them. It was Pichon, Minister of Foreign Affairs, who at the first meeting of the Supreme Council on the 12th January, 1919, proposed to allow Prince Lvov and Sazonov to state unofficially their views on questions concerning Russia. Lloyd George then observed that these statesmen represented " every opinion except the prevalent opinion in Russia," and he protested " against an attempt to select representatives for some hundred million people." France agreed with great reluctance to the Prinkipo Plan, which put on the same footing various " warring factions in Russia."

The very nature of the separatist movements in Russia found little understanding in France, faithful to the principle of unity and indivisibility of her own State and fearing that the small States organized on the ruins of the Russian Empire might fall an easy prey to the revived German imperialism or become pawns in German imperialistic policy.

Some more lucid minds in France criticized the reactionary spirit prevailing in the Quai d'Orsay and stressed the necessity for appealing to the dynamic forces of young nationalisms in Eastern Europe. An eminent deputy, M. Franklin Bouillon, in the Chambre des Députés on the 29th December, 1918, recommended giving full support to the different nations of Russia claiming the recognition of their right to full self-determination. " Without mentioning Finland and Poland," he said, " there are the Esthonians, Latvians, Lithuanians and Ukrainians whom we should support and organize. They can become a most solid barrier against Germany, there are bases from which a convergent action can be carried out for the purpose of the restoration of Russia proper. . . . It has not been understood that the most efficient means of fighting Bolshevism in Russia consists in developing the national feelings of the alien nationalities of Russia." [50] But even these progressive minds saw the future of Russia as a federation of states or a Federal State believing in the possibility of agreeing the interests of Russia and the Borderlands and underestimating the secular traditions of the Russian policy of expansion at the expense of other nations. Most Frenchmen believed that a reconstituted Russia might again play the same rôle in European policy as at the time of the French-Russian Alliance—that of a counterpoise to the German imperialism, the reawakening of which was the nightmare of post-war French policy. A very characteristic example of this trend of mind can be found in an article written by a prominent French publicist, M. René Pinon, in a well-known magazine, *Revue des Deux Mondes* (15th January, 1919). The picture of the future is rose-coloured and gives a good idea of the wishful thinking of French public opinion. " After such upheavals," wrote René Pinon, " the reconstruction of Russia will be difficult and long. The Russia of the future will be really a Russian Russia and no longer a mosaic of nations. Around her independent nations will constitute their own States which will be free, using, however, their liberty for concluding pacts of alliance or federation with a Russia who, ceasing to be a danger to their independence would, on the contrary, become a safeguard of their security and an associate for their prosperity." René Pinon considered that Poland should be strong, as " only a strong Poland can maintain her existence. A small Poland such as was devised in Berlin in 1917 was forced to be subservient to Germany; a great Poland can be but an enemy of Germanism. . . . A great Poland is a necessary element for the reconstitution of a new Europe and for the security of France "; but in Pinon's opinion all the new States should and could come to an agreement with a new and strong Russia. " In the post-war Europe it is unavoidable that Poland, Rumania and Bohemia will assume a part of the important rôle played in the past by Russia. What is of capital importance for us as for our Allies is not only the existence of a strong Russia but also good harmony between that Russia and Poland. In spite of painful memories, an agreement between them based on common interests will be less difficult than one might imagine."

At that time only a very few French publicists saw the flaws in this picture. Jacques Bainville's opinions differed, perhaps, the most from those of the great majority of his compatriots. In vain he warned his country against unrealistic views on the future Russia, whether White or Red (see passages from one of his articles devoted to this subject in the introduction to this chapter).

Great Britain and Eastern Europe

Which were the aims pursued by Great Britain in Eastern Europe? We find a reference to this subject in a Memorandum by Mr. Hoare of the Foreign Office dated 22nd December, 1919 :

> " We have two main interests in the Russian problem: (1) the early establishment of stable conditions and the renewal of trade ; (2) to ensure that whatever the future of Russia may be, Bolshevism shall not hurt us." [51]

Great Britain was not so much interested in the revival of a strong Russia, as in the resumption of normal trade exchanges with Eastern Europe. Her approach to Bolshevism was also different from that of France. It should be noted, however, that there were at that time some British statesmen whose point of view on the danger of Bolshevism approached that of the French, and Winston Churchill was the most prominent of these. Like the French he was appalled by the prospect of the Bolshevik advance in Eastern Europe and the possibility of collusion between Soviet Russia and Germany. He stated his views before the Supreme Council on the 15th February, 1919, to which Clemenceau fully agreed. If the Allies abandoned Russia to her fate, he said " would it be possible to make sure that Germany would do the same? Would it be possible to make certain that Germany, either by alliance with the Bolsheviks or with the other parties at present friendly to the Allies, would not in the near future become the supreme influence in Russia? " But Churchill also shared the illusions of the French that Russia might become " a living part of Europe " and a " living partner in the League of Nations " and " a friend of the Allied Powers." [52]

On the opposite side were those to whom economic considerations seemed to be of primary importance, and who took the view that the revival of the economy of Eastern Europe, even with German assistance, should overshadow all other issues. Such were the views of Keynes, for instance, expressed in his famous pamphlet *The Economic Consequences of the Peace* :

> " I see no possible means of repairing this loss of productivity within any reasonable period of time except through the agency of German enterprise and organization. It is impossible geographically and for many other reasons for Englishmen, Frenchmen or Americans to undertake it ; we have neither the incentive nor the means for doing the work on a sufficient scale. ... It is in our interest to hasten the day when German agents and organizers will be in a position to set in train in every Russian village the impulses of ordinary economic motives. ... We may surely predict with some certainty that, whether or not the form of communism represented by the Soviet Government proves permanently suited to the Russian temperament, the revival of trade, of the comforts of life and of ordinary economic motion are not likely to promote the extreme forms of those doctrines of violence and tyranny which are the children of war and despair. ... Let us encourage and assist Germany to take again her place in Europe as a creator and organizer of wealth for her Eastern and Southern neighbours." [53]

It should be noted that Lloyd George's policy, favouring the Germans on all territorial issues between them and the Poles and consequently weakening the barrier separating Germany from Russia, seemed to reserve to Germany in the future in conjunction with Great Britain the rôle assigned to her by Keynes, (these plans collapsed at the Genoa Conference in 1922).

British policy at that time was often accused of inconsistency, as on the one side the British spent big sums on the White Russians, " the champions of the restoration of a great indivisible Russia," [54] and on the other side on the protection of the little independent States on the Baltic Sea and in the Caucasus, the very existence of which was menaced by the Great Russians. This lack of consistency was more apparent than real. In a conversation with the American Ambassador to Great Britain, Davis, on the 3rd December, 1919, Lloyd George frankly stated his views on this matter. He said that he favoured " encouraging the ultimate division of Russia into a number of independent States leaving none of sufficient size to threaten the general peace." [55]

This statement throws light on Lloyd George's policy towards Poland and the Borderlands. Great Britain wished to secure in Eastern Europe some outposts for her future economic penetration in Russia, and it explains her policy in all countries bordering the

Eastern part of the Baltic Sea (including Danzig, which remained a " thorn in the living flesh of Poland "), and in the Caucasus, encouraging their independence but at the same time leaving all doors open for any possible compromises. She was unwilling to admit the existence of any new and independent factor in this area which might check her plans. Moreover she saw in Poland a close ally of France, if not a satellite, and had little sympathy for the extension of French influence in Eastern Europe. The rivalry between the French and British appeared in a most striking manner during Denikin's campaign. Denikin depended much more on British than on French assistance, and proposals were made by the British at that time to bring about the revision of the Agreement of the 23rd December, 1917, assigning the Ukraine to the French sphere of activity.[56]

When Denikin's forces collapsed in Southern Russia economic considerations began to take first place in the British policy, and the French and British were more and more driven apart, as clearly appeared in 1920.

These general remarks on the aims pursued by the three Principal Western Powers in Eastern Europe explain the attitude of the latter towards the White Russian movement, the so-called Russian Borderlands and the problems arising from the Polish-Soviet war as well as the settlement of the Eastern frontiers of Poland.

1. THE ENTENTE POWERS AND THE WHITE RUSSIAN MOVEMENT

There is no doubt that all the anti-Bolshevik Russians of whatever shade clung to the idea of the indivisibility of Russia. On many occasions the Allies showed great interest in the question of the relations between the White Russians and the Governments established on the ruins of the Russian Empire, but they were prompted by purely military considerations rather than by the wish to impose on the Russians definite pledges in this matter. The principle of the indivisibility of Russia was not only an article of faith of the old Tsarist statesmen like Kokovtsev [57] or Sazonov, who reappeared on the international stage as the Foreign Minister of the administration of Koltchak and Denikin. To Milyukov, first Foreign Minister of the First Revolutionary Government of Prince Lvov, all the new States were an artificial creation of Germany and must disappear, jointly with the abolition of the Brest-Litovsk Treaty.[58] But even an old revolutionary, Tchaikovsky, considered by Western statesmen to be a man of liberal views, during his hearing by the Supreme Council on the 10th May, 1919,[59] gave an answer which

could hardly be considered satisfactory : " All the national group-
ings that had sprung up," he said, " had been seized by a fashion
of independence. But when they looked at the question coolly
and viewed their economic position, they were far from suggesting
any such solution. Economically, these small States were weak and
they must inevitably fall into dependence on someone else." During
the visit of Tchaikovsky and Savinkov to Warsaw in January 1920,
that is to say after the defeat of Denikin when the position of the
White Russian movement became extremely critical, Pilsudski, who
wished to ascertain the views of these leaders on future relations
between Russia and the Russian Borderlands, laid before them a
plan consisting of an alliance between all the Russian Border States,
Finland and Poland and anti-Bolshevik Russia, to combat Bolshevism. It was an idea for " a kind of League of Nations in the Near
East of Europe to combat the Bolsheviks." After an interval of two
days the two Russian leaders called again on Pilsudski and declared
that they " would prefer to call the combination of States a Federation rather than an alliance." According to Sir Horace Rumbold,
British Envoy in Warsaw, " Pilsudski had gathered clearly from
Mr. Savinkov and Mr. Tchaikovsky that they would never be
resigned to agree to complete independence of former Russian
Border States and would be prepared to grant them autonomy." [60]
This also appears clarly from the text of the telegram of Serafinov,
deputy to Sazonov, of the 5th May, 1919,[61] read by Tchaikovsky in
the course of his hearing by the Supreme Council on the 10th May
and endorsed by him :

> " Declaration as to the ends pursued by the High Command of
> the Armed Forces of Southern Russia : ... (2) Reconstitution of
> the Russian Army and of strong and indivisible Russia. ... (4)
> Institution of a decentralized government through regional
> autonomy and a large measure of local self-government."

The dispatch sent by the Heads of the Delegations of the Five
Principal Powers to Admiral Koltchak on the 26th May, 1919, is
the only document in which all the Principal Allied and Associated
Powers stated their views on " the policy they proposed to pursue
in regard to Russia."

Among the conditions laid down in this dispatch three refer to
the relations between the future democratic Russian Government on
the one side and the neighbouring States and so-called Russian
Borderlands on the other :

> " Fourthly, that the independence of Finland and Poland be
> recognized, and that in the event of the frontiers and other rela-
> tions between Russia and these countries not being settled by

EE 2

agreement, they will be referred to the abitration of the League of Nations.

" Fifthly, that if a solution of the relations between Esthonia, Latvia, Lithuania and the Caucasian and Transcaucasian territories and Russia is not speedily reached by agreement the settlement will be made in consultation and co-operation with the League of Nations, and that until such settlement is made the Government of Russia agrees to recognize these territories as autonomous and to confirm the relations which may exist between their *de facto* Governments and the Allied and Associated Governments.

" Sixthly, the right of the Peace Conference to determine the future of the Rumanian part of Bessarabia to be recognized." [62]

Let us state first of all that the Ukraine was not mentioned at all in this document, although at the same time Great Britain took the defence of the interests of the Ukrainians in Eastern Galicia against the alleged imperialism of the Poles. Only the recognition of the independence of Poland and Finland was requested, while the question of the frontiers of these two States as well as the solution of the relations between the Border States and Russia was left to settlement by agreement with some co-operation from the League of Nations.

Although the wording of this document seems to agree with the principle of national self-determination, its true meaning can appear more clearly only in connection with the policy pursued at that time by the Allied and Associated Powers in relation to the Border States and to the Eastern frontiers of Poland; we have to refer again to this document when reviewing these problems. For the time being let us observe that this document could hardly be qualified as an attempt to dismember Russia. In the event of the victory of the White Russian leaders, their voice would probably have carried great, if not preponderant, weight with the Allied and Associated Powers, and consequently with the organs of the League of Nations. It is not very likely that the League of Nations, as subsequent experience amply showed, would have been able to give sufficient protection to the small Border States against the pressure of a reconstituted Russia. The reaction of the White Russian leaders to this modest proposal was a good test of their democratic and liberal views.

Koltchak's reply, sent from Omsk on the 5th June, was rather evasive and did not contain any definite pledges on the problems raised by Points 4, 5 and 6 of the Allied conditions. Koltchak sheltered behind the authority of the future Constituent Assembly. As " Russia cannot now and cannot in future ever be anything but a democratic State " all " questions involving modifications of the territorial frontiers and of external relations must be ratified by a representative body which is the natural expression of the people's sovereignty." Koltchak expressly recognized only the independence of Poland, "considering the creation of a unified Polish State to be one of the chief of the normal and just consequences of the world war," but "the final solution of the question of delimiting the frontiers between Russia and Poland" had to be "postponed until the meeting of the Constituent Assembly." Also "the final solution of the Finnish question must belong to the Constituent Assembly."

So far as the Border States were concerned Koltchak obviously declined to agree to their independence. "We are fully disposed at once to prepare for the solution of the question concerning the fate of the national groups in Esthonia, Latvia, Lithuania, of the Caucasian and Transcaucasian countries, as we have every reason to believe that a prompt settlement will be made, seeing that the Government is assuring us from the present time the autonomy of the various nationalities. It goes without saying that the limits and conditions of these autonomous institutions will be settled separately as regards each of the nationalities concerned." Koltchak's Government was, moreover, ready to "have recourse to the collaboration and good offices of the League of Nations" should any difficulty arise in regard to the solution of these various questions." [63]

This very qualified answer to the Allied terms was given at a time when Koltchak's troops were already in full retreat and had lost any hope of reaching Moscow. Koltchak depended entirely on Allied support, and could not of course flatly reject the Allied conditions. But there is every reason to believe that the White Russian statesmen forgot nothing and learned nothing. The democratic phraseology of Koltchak's answer could not deceive anyone, and it did not prove a sincere wish to settle all outstanding questions with the neighbouring States and the Borderlands by mutual agreement and not by force. We have sufficient evidence to the contrary. According to the Foreign Office Memorandum on Siberia of December 1919 : "Admiral Koltchak stands for a 'United Indivisible Russia,' and if not Admiral Koltchak at least his immediate entourage are in favour of restoring a monarchy in Russia." [64] We also know very well the opinions of his Foreign Minister Sazonov, who according to a note of Lord Curzon of the 11th June, 1919, "when in London had not shown a complete grasp of the situation and had appeared to think that the conditions proposed (in the Allied dispatch to Koltchak) might be considerably modified or even refused without a great risk. In regard to Finland, Sazonov had said, ' The Finns are asking for a great deal, but they shall have nothing, absolutely nothing.' " [65]

If we now turn our attention to another White Russian leader,

Denikin, we find the same stiff attitude towards the liberated nationalities of the former Russian Empire. By a note of the 12th June to Brigadier Briggs he protested against the recognition by the Allies of the independence of Finland without a consultation with Russia and without taking into consideration the strategic needs of Russia.[66] In a memorandum of Nabokov to Sir R. Graham of the 8th August, 1919, in which the " guiding principles " of General Denikin and his Military and Political Advisers were laid down, we find a passage relating to the nationalities inhabiting the borders of Russia : " Under the new Russian régime they will receive the fullest measure of self-government, but as integral parts of the Russian State." We further find an assertion that " General Denikin's authority extends over 40,000,000 Russians," and by these words the existence of any alien nationality on the territory under his control was simply denied.[67]

In a report by Major Torin to the General Staff " Intelligence " of the 15th September, 1919, we find the following passages :

> " The chief point which struck me at Taganrog was the absolute determination of the Volunteers, to carry out their ' All United Russia ' policy *coûte que coûte.*
> " As regards the Caucasus, there appears to be only one point of view, namely that they were an integral part of Russia ; for the present they could stay as they were but as soon as the time came they had got to come back to Russia, peacefully if possible, but if not force would be used. . . . The same applied to Rumania. For the moment General Denikin has issued strong orders for his officers to ignore all hostile acts of the Rumanians and to co-operate with them, but stated that as soon as the moment was opportune it was his intention to declare war on her and reoccupy Bessarabia."

In a note from the Russian Embassy of the 28th October, 1919, a request was made to stop any assistance by the Allies to the Baltic States, as the wish of these " small political units " to conclude peace treaties with the Soviets (advised by the British, by the way) should be considered a sign of their demoralization and inability to defend themselves from Bolshevism." [68]

Denikin's attitude towards Poland will be expounded later in the proper place.

The consequences of the narrow-mindedness of the White Russian military and political leaders are well known. The refusal of the Esthonians to co-operate with Yudenich, the revolt against Denikin of the Cossacks of the Don, Kuban and Terek, the Ukrainian separatist movement, the lack of co-operation between Denikin and the Caucasian nations, and to some extent also the failure of the negotiations between Denikin and Pilsudski, were among the important factors in the defeat of the White Russian armies. The Bolsheviks were better propagandists and by appealing to the separatist movements in Russia they undermined the action of the White Generals. This is the common opinion of all the historians of the Russian Civil War.[69] The Bolsheviks themselves, whose promises to the oppressed nationalities of Russia turned out to be a most shameful deception, frankly confessed that this was the cause of their successes against the White Russians. In a series of articles in the Moscow *Pravda,* written after the end of the Civil War, Stalin —then Commissar for Nationalities—was quite outspoken on this matter. For instance, on the 6th–7th November, 1921, he wrote :

> " The Russian workers would have been unable to overcome Koltchak, Denikin and Wrangel without the sympathy of the opppressed masses of the Borderlands. One should not forget that the area of the operations of these rebellious generals was limited to the borderlands, inhabited mostly by non-Russian nationalities, and the latter could not but hate Koltchak, Denikin and Wrangel for their imperialistic and Russian-dictatorial policy. The Entente, which was meddling in these affairs and supported the generals, could rely only on the Russificatory elements of the Borderlands. But this only aroused the hatred of these Borderlands towards the rebellious generals and deepened their sympathy for the Soviet State." [70]

On another occasion Stalin said :

> " Do not forget that, if in the rear of Koltchak, Denikin, Wrangel and Yudenich we had not had the so-called ' aliens,' if we had not had the former oppressed peoples who undermined the rear of these generals by their sympathy with the Russian proletariat—and this, comrades, is a special factor in our growth, this silent sympathy, nobody sees it or hears it, but it decides everything—if it had not been for this sympathy we should not have beaten one of these generals." [71]

There is, of course, a great deal of exaggeration in Stalin's out-pourings as regards the " sympathy " of the " alien " nationalities for the Soviet power, because neither the Baltic nations nor the Caucasians cast their lot with the Bolsheviks, and fought for their independence against the Bolsheviks, but it is beyond question that the policy of the White Russian leaders made impossible any true co-operation between the anti-Bolshevik forces on the lines advised by Pilsudski in the above-quoted conversation with Tchaikovsky and Savinkov in Warsaw (see p. 419), that is by forming a League of Nations in the Near East of Europe, combating Bolshevism as equal partners.

2. THE ENTENTE POWERS AND THE RUSSIAN BORDERLANDS

The principle of the territorial integrity of the Russian Empire which guided the policy of the U.S.A. and France explains the very cautious approach of these States to the problem of the Eastern frontiers of Poland and the independence of the Border States. The Italian representative on various territorial commissions of the Peace Conference also shared these views.[72] The British Government was, however, favourable to the claims of the Baltic and Caucasian States. A British historian, speaking of the idea of helping the " non-Slavonic Russian Border States, both on the Baltic and in Transcaucasia," was justified in asserting that " it is to the lasting credit of Great Britain, to which country more than any other these border states looked for guidance and assistance, that this policy of interest in them as a whole commended itself to her first amongst the Great Powers, the only drawback being that it was not more extensively, opportunely and energetically carried out." [73] But the unfavourable attitude towards Poland's claims in the West and East, taken on so many occasions by Lloyd George, proves that it was not the intention of the British Government to create in Eastern Europe a strong and continuous barrier against the potential aggressors in this area. It was evident that all these border states needed a strong Poland, for if they had been isolated from her they were bound sooner or later to fall an easy prey to Russia or Germany, the more so as Great Britain did not wish to, or perhaps could not, assume the permanent duty of protecting these little states. In fact on many occasions the British Government declared that it wished to reserve the final decision on the fate of the Border States for agreement with the future Russia. For instance, in a conversation in Paris on the 11th June, 1919,[74] between Balfour and the Esthonian delegates, Messrs. Poska and Piip, the latter were told that " while His Majesty's Government regarded with the greatest sympathy the struggle of the Esthonians, and had shown their sympathy by supplying them with arms and munitions of war, yet His Majesty's Government felt strongly that no satisfactory or final settlement of the status of the Baltic States could be secured without the consent of the Russian Government, whenever a Government was set up in Russia which could be recognized by the Allied Powers. As this was not yet the case, it seemed impossible now to meet altogether the wishes of the Baltic States by recognizing their independence forthwith." The answer given by one of the Esthonian delegates, Piip, was most pertinent and fully justified by later events. He said " that it was possible that the

Esthonians, if they saw a democratic Russia was really established on a federal basis, would not be unwilling to join such a federation. But they wanted to see what the new Russia would be, and felt that they would be in a better position to negotiate with the future Russia if they could do so as one independent State with another, as was done in the case of the United States and the Swiss Confederation, where the federation was not imposed from above but entered into voluntarily by the different parties to it."

In a letter from Lord Curzon to Balfour of the 1st July, 1919, we find further confirmation of the British attitude towards the Border States :

> " At no stage in their negotiations with the latter (Border States) have the Allied Governments committed themselves to a promise of complete independence. In the communications which had been addressed by His Majesty's Government to the Esthonian, Latvian and Georgian delegations in London, the question of their future has been specially reserved for the decision of the Peace Conference." [75]

In September 1919 [76] the British Government stopped supplying the Baltic States with military material and stores and providing them with credits and limited itself to a declaration couched in guarded terms that should the existence of these States be imperilled by an invasion of Bolshevik forces, " His Majesty's Government might be prepared to make the sacrifices, which are not justified in present conditions, and to reconsider their decision as to the supply of war material." This decision, at the same time leaving to the " unfettered " judgment of these States " whether they should make any arrangement and if so of what nature, with the Soviet authorities," eventually led to the conclusion by Esthonia and Latvia of the Peace Treaties with the Soviets (respectively on the 2nd February, 1920, and 1st August of the same year, that is to say much in advance of Poland).

It was not until the 26th January, 1921, that Latvia and Esthonia obtained recognition *de jure* by the Allied Powers, and on the 22nd September were admitted to the League of Nations.

Apart from the heroic struggle for independence of these vigorous small nations, the ultimate fate of the latter depended much more on the issue of the Polish-Soviet War in 1920 than on anything else. There is no doubt that if the Bolsheviks and not the Poles had won the victory on the Vistula the independence of these nations would have been of short duration, as has been proved by the sad events of 1940 as well as by the many endeavours supported by the Soviet Union to bring about the collapse of these States by internal upheavals in the course of the inter-war period. The reconquest of the Caucasian republics by the Soviet Union is further evidence to the same effect.

The attitude of the Allies towards the national claims of the Ukrainians was as a rule negative. It was a matter of greater importance for the outcome of the Civil War than the Allied statesmen realized at that time, because Denikin's forces occupied territories the main part of which was ethnographically Ukrainian.

In a letter from Balfour to Lord Curzon of the 10th July, 1919, regarding the policy of His Majesty's Government towards Petlura and the future status of Galicia we find the statement that " the policy of His Majesty's Government has always been to assist such *Russian* forces as are engaged in fighting the Bolsheviks, and they would therefore be prepared to assist any forces under Petlura's command which might be engaged in such operations provided any practical means of doing so could be devised. It is not, however, the policy of His Majesty's Government to recognize the independence of the Ukrainian Government or to encourage separatist tendencies in the Ukraine." [77] This letter throws a peculiar light on the British policy regarding Eastern Galicia and its defence of the rights of the Ukrainians to this territory. Was it not for a future Russia that Great Britain reserved Eastern Galicia?

In a letter from Balfour to Lord Curzon of the 15th August, 1919, it was stated that " no encouragement has been given by the Peace Conference to the idea of an independent Ukrainian State, and existing information goes to show that most of the elements for the formation of such a State are lacking." [78]

In a letter from Lord Curzon to Balfour dated 21st August, 1919, we find the following remarks referring to the same question :

" The situation in the Ukraine is at present obscure. It is certain, however, that the authority of the Russian Soviet Government is not generally recognized in these areas, where an independent Ukrainian Government, under the leadership of General Petlura, claims to exercise jurisdiction. None of the Allied Governments has hitherto recognized General Petlura's authority, and there have been no dealings with his Government. His Majesty's Government have always regarded the Ukraine as an integral part of Russia, and they have felt very strongly that the utmost care should be taken to avoid any steps which might commit them to encouraging the separatist tendencies of certain sections of Ukrainian opinion. Economically, the Ukraine can never be separated from Russia, and this must always be a predominant factor in considering Russo-Ukrainian relations." [79]

What was the true position at that time in Russia? According to

Chamberlin : " Of the three governments that fought for power in Ukrainia in 1919, the Soviets, Denikin's régime, and Petlura's, the last was apparently the least objectionable to the peasants. This is the judgment of a Communist named Popov, who went on a mission to Petlura's temporary headquarters at Kamenetz-Podolsk in the autumn of 1919." But while the Allied supplies were pouring in to Denikin, eventually falling into Bolshevik hands, " Petlura was quite unable to make military headway, if only because his army lacked any adequate source of supply with munitions." [80]

All the foregoing remarks show that in their policy towards Russia the Allied Powers, although appealing to all anti-Bolshevik forces, took the utmost care to preserve the territorial integrity of Russia so far as it was possible and tried to postpone all outstanding issues until the appearance of an imaginary democratic Russia. This policy was to a great extent responsible for the failure of the intervention in Eastern European affairs, carried out mainly through the White Russian armies. It was Winston Churchill who clearly saw all the shortcomings of such a policy. " Could not the statesmen who had assembled at Paris," he said, " have pursued their task coherently? Could they not have said to Koltchak and Denikin : ' Not another cartridge unless you make terms with the Border States, recognizing their independence or autonomy as may be decided.' And having applied this superior compulsion to the Russian leaders have used their whole influence to combine the operations of all the States at war with Soviet Russia," [81] instead of which " they encouraged Koltchak and Denikin and spent both money and men in their support, they gave no encouragement to Finland, to the Baltic States or to Poland." [82]

It was the vision of the Russia of the past and the will-o'-the-wisp of a democratic Russia which never became a reality that stood in the way. Some inveterate beliefs die hard. A very characteristic example of the turn of mind of some representatives of the old " Russian " school in the Foreign Office is the following statement of a former Ambassador to the Tsarist Empire, Sir George Buchanan :

> "While the Prinkipo scheme had disheartened many of our friends and sympathizers, the recognition of the Caucasian republics and of the Baltic States, coupled with the unfounded suspicion that we were encouraging the Poles to annex territory that was ethnically Russian, was resented by many patriotic Russians. It was the fear that the Allies were intent on the dismemberment of Russia, and not intervention, that reinforced the ranks of the Red Army." [83]

Nothing is further from the truth, because the Soviets took advantage of disruptive and not of constructive forces of Russia, but the idea of the indivisibility of the former Russian Empire of the Tsars had become so deeply rooted in the West in the course of the last century that it was not so easy for Western statesmen to get rid of it.

3.   THE ENTENTE AND THE POLISH-SOVIET WAR IN 1919

There had, perhaps, been no more complicated issue among those the Western statesmen had to face in 1919-20, than that arising from the Polish-Soviet War. It can be said of this war that in the circumstances then existing it was unavoidable, and that on its outcome depended not only the final configuration of the Eastern frontier of Poland, but the whole future political position of Central and Eastern Europe. For Poland it was a struggle for survival and her existence as an independent political entity; for the Entente it was the whole of the work accomplished by the Peace Conference that was at stake. We referred above (pp. 279 ff.) to the theory of " creation " of Poland, as well as of the other so-called new States, by the peacemakers in Paris. Even those who may share such views must, however, admit that the recognition of Poland's freedom at Versailles would not have taken Poland very far if she had not successfully resisted the Bolshevik invasion in 1919-20.

It must be said first of all that in her struggle Poland found little understanding in the West for the cause she was defending. Public opinion in the West, for reasons with which we will deal later, saw a very distorted picture of the situation. We quote as a typical, although perhaps extreme, example of some misleading opinions on the subject, the following passage from Lloyd George's *The Truth about the Peace Treaties* :

> " No one gave more trouble than the Poles, having once upon a time been the most formidable military power in Central Europe —when Prussia was a starveling Duchy—there were few provinces in the vast area inhabited by a variety of races that Poland could not claim as being historically her inheritance of which she had been reft. Drunk with the new wine of liberty supplied to her by the Allies, she fancied herself once more the resistless mistress of Central Europe. Self-determination did not suit her ambitions. She coveted Galicia, the Ukraine, Lithuania and parts of White Russia. A vote of the inhabitants would have emphatically repudiated her dominion. So the rights of all peoples to select their nationhood was promptly thrown over by her leaders. They claimed that these various races belonged to the Poles through the

conquering arms of their ancestors. Like the old Norman baron who, when he was asked for the title to his land unsheathed his sword, Poland flourished the sword of her warrior Kings which had rusted in their tombs for centuries." [84]

This passionate outburst shows Lloyd George's astonishing ignorance both of the history of Eastern Europe and of the real position at that time in that area. This is not surprising, because Lloyd George did not care very much for either.

In order to ascertain the facts we must first take into consideration the aims pursued by the Bolsheviks in regard to the territories the fate of which was to be decided by the Polish-Soviet war.

Principle of national self-determination and revolutionary expansion of Bolshevism

About the end of 1918 the principle of national self-determination was readjusted by the Bolsheviks to suit their aims of revolutionary expansion (pp. 183 ff.). The Third All-Russian Congress of the Soviets in January 1918 accepted Stalin's proposal that the right of self-determination " ought to be understood as the right of self-determination not of the bourgeoisie but of the toiling masses of a given nation,"[85] and was " operative only in so far as the practical exercise of this principle was compatible with the Communist scheme of things." [86] It was rightly observed that " to those who do not accept the doctrine of the dictatorship of the proletariat the ' self-determination ' promised to the nationalists has, admittedly, been a farce, and often a tragic farce at that, if we mean by self-determination the right of a nationality to decide, by the will of numerical majority, what its political and social constitution shall be, and whether or no it shall adhere to the Soviet Union." [87] Rosa Luxemburg characterized the complete contradiction between theory and practice of the Bolshevik policy on nationalities : " It is analogous," she said, " to the Bolshevik policy with regard to peasants, whose appetite for land it is proposed to settle by permission to take direct possession of the great estates, thus securing their adhesion to the Revolution. . . . Unfortunately the calculation has been absolutely wrong in both cases." [88] In his book *The Bolshevik Revolution*,[89] Carr finds that this contradiction was only apparent, and justifies it by calling the Bolshevik doctrine of self-determination " like other doctrines of political life " . . . " conditional and dynamic "; but he admits that on the strength of the interpretation given by the Bolsheviks to this doctrine " the proletariat of the Ukraine, of White Russia and of the Baltic countries could be *assisted* to exercise the right of national determination as against the competing claims of local bourgeoisie " (my italics). Mr.

Carr's justification is based on a considerable distortion of facts. So far as the Russian Borderlands were concerned there existed there few local elements which adhered to Bolshevism. These could be found mostly in the town proletariat, which there constituted a very small minority, and it cannot even be said that it was won in its entirety to a Russian style revolution. This small minority could hardly pretend to represent the whole country, and needed *outside assistance* to assume power. Moreover, it was eventually not this part of the local proletariat that had the ultimate say in the fate of their country, but the delegates sent by the Russian Bolshevik party, frequently having no connection with the population. Never has a conquest by force been veiled by such false pretences and deceit.[90] In his well-documented book *Russia and Her Colonies*, Mr. Kolarz drew attention to the fact that " the October Revolution was based on a principle which from the outset was not acceptable to the non-Russian nationalities—the leadership of the proletariat over the peasantry. This meant in reality the leadership of the Russian working-class over the peasants of all the peoples of Russia." [91]

By his interpretation of the doctrine of self-determination Stalin remained faithful to the principles which he had upheld from the beginning of his political career. As early as 1904, still writing in a Georgian local Socialist paper, he said :

> " Proletarians will not support the so-called national movements for liberation because so far all such movements have turned only to the benefit of the bourgeoisie and have perverted and impaired the class consciousness of the proletariat." [92]

About the end of the war with Poland and of the Civil War, in *Pravda* of the 10th October, 1920, Stalin justified the Soviet policy towards the Borderlands in these terms :

> " The claim of the borderlands to secession from Russia as a form of relationship between the centre and borderlands is to be refused, not only because it contradicts the very purpose of the question consisting in establishing links between the centre and borderlands, but above all because it clashes with the interests of the toiling masses both of the centre and of the borderlands. . . . The seceded borderlands would inevitably have fallen into slavery to international imperialism. . . . It is enough to look at Georgia, Armenia, Poland, which have separated from Russia and which have preserved merely the appearance of independence, while actually having been transformed into unconditional vassals of the Entente. . . . The so-called independence of the so-called independent Georgia, Armenia, Poland, Finland, etc., is only an apparent independence covering full dependence of these so-called, let me say, independent States on that or another group of imperialists. . . .

The interests of the toiling masses said that the claim to the secession of the borderlands is, in a given stage of Revolution, deeply counter-revolutionary." [93]

Did the Bolsheviks at that time pursue a policy for establishing true federation between the peoples of the former Russian Empire, as might appear from the second proposal of Stalin, adopted by the Third All-Russian Congress of the Soviets in January 1918 : " The Russian Socialist Soviet Republic is created on the basis of a voluntary union of the peoples of Russia in the form of federation of the Soviet Socialist republics of those peoples." [94] The Constituent Assembly of the Bolshevik Delegation further declared that " it limits itself to the establishment of the fundamental basis of the federation of Soviet Republics in Russia, leaving it to the workers and peasants of every nation to take an independent decision of their own authorized Soviet Congress as to whether and on what basis they desire to participate in the federal Government and in the other federal Soviet institutions." [95] This principle was proclaimed in the Constitution of the R.S.F.S.R. of the 19th July, 1918.

According to the well-established definition of international law a federation is a " free association " [96] of States " in which the member States retain a large amount of their original independence " and in which " the field of government is divided between a general authority and regional authorities which are not subordinate to one another but co-ordinate with each other." [97]

Both the Russian Federal Soviet Republic and later the Union of Soviet Socialist Republics were established by force and not by voluntary agreement. The Webbs, whom nobody can consider prejudiced against Communism, say frankly in their fundamental book *Soviet Communism* that :

" The Union of Soviet Socialist Republics was a leonine partnership. What happened in 1922 was that the R.S.F.S.R. (Russian Socialist Federal Soviet Republic), with an elaborate parade of federal forms and a genuine concession of cultural autonomy virtually annexed to itself the three other fragments of Tsarist Russia which had been, by the Bolshevik forces with the active co-operation of a large proportion, if not the majority, of the inhabitants, cleared of hostile armies and insurgent bandits and then in effect conquered." [98]

But also the second feature of federalism, the division of power between the central and regional authorities, was already missing in the early stage of Soviet statehood, that is in the Constitution of 1918. Analysing this Constitution Professor Carr says that " what was in fact created in 1918 was a Russian republic of indefinite territorial extent ... of specifically federal machinery as distinct from the division of powers between central and local organs of government, the constitution of 1918 contained no trace whatever." [99]

There is nothing surprising in this because the Communists in their inmost conviction have always been centralists and not federalists; it suffices to remember what Lenin said in his letter to S. Shaumian in 1913 : " We stand for unconditional democratic centralization. We are opposed to federation. We are for the Jacobins against the Girondins. We oppose federation in principle; it weakens economic bonds, and is not a desirable type of State." [100] The conversion to federalism which occurred at the above-mentioned Third Congress of the Soviets was simply a change of façade dictated by pure opportunism. Nobody has explained it better than Stalin who in *Pravda* on the 11th April, 1917, said that " it is foolish to try to establish federation in Russia, because a federation there is bound to disappear." [101] Commenting on these words in 1924, Stalin said :

> " There were three reasons for the party's change of opinion on the question of federalism:
> " First, because at the time of the October upheaval several nationalities of Russia completely separated from Russia and from one another, and so federalism was a step forward from a state of dissociation of the toiling masses of those nationalities to their coming together and their reunion.
> " Second, because the very forms of federalism, elaborated in the course of the socialist construction, turned out to be not so contradictory to the aim of bringing together the toiling masses of the nationalities of Russia as might have appeared previously— even not at all contradictory to it, as further practice has shown.
> " Third, because the specific weight of the national movements appeared much greater and the way to reunion in the course of the war much harder than it might have seemed before the October Revolution." [102]

It would be difficult to find a more frank avowal that the Bolshevik Party had readjusted the idea of federalism to its practical requirements, that is to say completely perverted its whole meaning, and that there were purely opportunist and temporary reasons which prompted the Bolshevik leaders to hoist the banner of federalism to captivate the imagination of the peoples struggling for their national self-determination.

Mr. N. Basseches, in his biography of Stalin, comparing the attitude of the revolutionary and counter-revolutionary movements in Russia towards the problem of nationalities, reaches the conclusion that both these movements aimed at the reconstitution of an undivided Russia. " By 1922," he says, " it had been possible to make

an end of the apparent independence of the Soviet Republics. ...
With the theory of national territorial autonomy, and the practice
of pseudo-federalism, it recovered the Russian imperial idea." [103]

Invasion of the Borderlands by the Red Army

Against this background we must view the Bolshevik moves
towards the Borderlands at the moment of the military collapse of
Germany in November 1918. In the official Soviet publication dealing wih the Civil War we read this characteristic confession of the
aims which the Bolsheviks decided to pursue :

> " The breaking down of the German occupation faced the
> R.S.F.S.R. with the task of liberation of the occupied territories
> and establishment there of Soviet rule.
> " The pursuit of this aim forced the Soviet strategy to direct the
> whole expansion against the Baltic countries, Lithuania, Bye-
> lorussia and the Ukraine." [104]

This westward and southward drive had much more distant objec-
tives : the spread of the Bolshevik revolution towards Central
Europe, as appears from a speech made by Trotsky on the 30th
October, 1918 :

> " Free Latvia, free Poland and Lithuania, free Finland, and on
> the other side, free Ukraine will not be a wedge but a uniting link
> between Soviet Russia and the future Soviet Germany and Austria-
> Hungary. This is the beginning of a European Communist federa-
> tion—a union of the proletarian republics of Europe." [105]

In an article in *Pravda* on the 6th–9th November, 1918, Stalin
wrote :

> " Some people assert that the ' governments ' of borderlands
> fight for national freedom against the ' soulless ' imperialism of
> the Soviet Power. But it is completely untrue. Not one power in
> the world admits such a large measure of decentralization, not one
> Government in the world leaves such freedom as the Soviet Power
> does in Russia. The struggle of the ' governments ' of borderlands
> was and remains the struggle of counter-revolution against
> socialism. The national banner is hoisted only to deceive the
> masses, as it serves to cover the counter-revolutionary designs of
> the national bourgeoisie. ... It has been said that the principles of
> self-determination and defence of the fatherland have been dis-
> carded in the circumstances of the rising revolution. In fact, it is
> not the principle of self-determination that is discarded, but its
> bourgeois interpretation." [106]

Stalin did not doubt that Soviet governments would be established in the borderlands very soon. In a periodical, *Zhizn
Natsionalnostii*, on the 17th November, 1918, he wrote :

" There appear already the first signs of revolution in the occupied countries. Strikes in Finland, demonstrations in Latvia, a general strike in the Ukraine, revolutionary unrest in Finland, Poland, Latvia, are the first swallows. There is no need to say that revolution and Soviet Governments in these territories are bound to come in the nearest future." [107]

The Bolshevik intervention in the Finnish civil war, the recognition of the Finnish " Council of the People's Commissariat " with a Communist, Kullervo Manner, at its head, the signing in Moscow on the 1st March, 1918, of the agreement of " friendship " between the latter and the Council of People's Commissars of Russia, and the resulting state of war between Finland and Russia, terminated only on the 4th October, 1920, by the Peace Treaty of Tartu, may serve as an example of the Bolsheviks' interpretation of the principle of self-determination in relation to a people whose independence was solemnly proclaimed at the beginning of the Bolshevik revolution.   .

The invasion of the Ukraine after her evacuation by the German troops (Kiev was occupied by the Red Army on the 19th February, 1919), where numerous anti-Soviet risings started from April of the same year, proves that the actions of the Bolsheviks quickly belied Lenin's utterances on the unrestricted rights of the Ukrainian people to independence (see p. 183). These actions agreed much more with the centralist views on Ukrainian nationalism professed by Rosa Luxemburg than with that of Lenin. According to Rosa Luxemburg " the Ukrainian nationalism was a mere whim, a folly of a few dozen petty bourgeois intellectuals without the slightest roots in the economic, political or psychological relationship of the country . . . this ridiculous pose of a few university professors and students was inflated into a political force by Lenin and his comrades through their doctrinaire agitation concerning the ' right of self-determination '." [108]

The westward drive of the Red Army was greatly facilitated by the lack of adequate provisions in the Armistice Convention with Germany. While an Allied Commission was appointed by the Principal Powers to superintend the evacuation of the German troops in the West, no corresponding Commission was appointed in the East.[109] This brought many complications and imposed much suffering on the borderlands in their fight for national independence against the Bolsheviks, German volunteers under Von der Goltz, and White Russians. Puppet governments were first established by the Bolsheviks for each Baltic country. The Esthonian, Latvian and Lithuanian Soviet Republics were recognized by the All-Russian Soviet Central Executive Committee in December 1918, and their union with the R.S.F.S.R. proclaimed by it in Moscow on the 23rd December, 1918, with a promise to give " all aid to the workers of these countries and Ukraina in their struggle against the system of exploitation and in their defence against foreign aggression." In its issue of the 25th December, *Izvestia* commented on this decision in these words :

> " Lithuania, Latvia and Esthonia are an obstacle on the road which leads from Russia to Western Europe. Therefore they are a hindrance to our revolution, separating Soviet Russia from revolutionary Germany. This wall must be pulled down. The Red proletariat of Russia should find an opportunity for exercising influence on the revolutionary development of Germany in order, later on, when the Soviet Germany has been established, to merge with it in one united Central and Eastern European Socialist Federation. . . . Soviet Russia must secure all Baltic countries in order to create a strong revolutionary bulwark against the whole world. The conquest of the Baltic Sea and its shores will enable Soviet Russia to influence the Scandinavian States in the interests of the Socialist revolution." [110]

The offensive of the Red Army against Byelorussia, Lithuania and Poland began on the 17th November, 1918. These operations were named very characteristically " Target Vistula," which proves that they were to prepare for the drive of the Red Army into the heart of Poland. The official Soviet publication says of these operations :

> " The offensive—target Vistula—started after the withdrawal of the Germans. Its objectives were the following: (1) occupation of Byelorussia ; (2) advance in the direction of Warsaw up to the Western Bug, including the latter. The offensive movements of the Red Army towards these objectives developed successfully. Poland was busy on other fronts and because of that she could only weakly defend her frontiers." [111]

On the 9th December Minsk was occupied by the Red Army, and on the 31st December the Soviet-Republic of Byelorussia was proclaimed there, at the " North-Western Regional Conference of the Bolshevik Party " (it was formally constituted on the 19th February, 1919). But it was not the local proletariat that played a decisive rôle in it. The Chairman of the Congress was the Commander of the Western Soviet Army, a Russian, of course, Miasnikov, and the præsidium of the Conference was composed almost exclusively of Russians. Kolarz observes that at that time the Russian Communists had " such a poor opinion of the strength of the Byelorussian national consciousness that they confined the Republic to a small border strip of 20,000 square miles and 1,500,000 inhabitants. Important Byelorussian districts with the towns of Vitebsk, Gomel and Moghilev remained with the R.S.F.S.R." [112]

After the withdrawal of the German troops from Wilno the town was temporarily occupied by local Polish volunteers, but it fell into Bolshevik hands on the 5th January, 1919.[112a] The puppet Lithuanian Government which followed the Russian troops was installed in Wilno. It consisted of two Poles, two Jews and four Lithuanians; no Byelorussian was included in it as, according to Kolarz, " it was impossible to find a suitable Byelorussian in Wilno." [113]

In February 1919 the Soviet republics of Lithuania and Byelorussia decided to unite and establish federal links with the R.S.F.S.R., and thus Communist Russia was given a free hand in organizing this region. In the *Izvestia* of 9th February, Stalin explained the events which took place in Wilno and Minsk in the course of the winter 1918-19 in these sophistic terms : " In borderlands which passed through all the horrors of the occupation a leaning towards the Russian proletariat has arisen, a leaning to which must bow the governments of the borderlands in their separatist efforts." [114] He forgot to say that this " leaning," curiously enough, materialized only after the intervention of the Red Army. Did not the Chairman of the Lithuanian Soviet Government, Mr. V. S. Kapsukas-Mitskevich, confess later that the policy pursued by his government was mistaken because it gave rise to suspicion that " the Lithuanian Government was simply another occupation government maintained in power by Red Army bayonets "? [115]

There is no necessity to stress now, although the Western countries did not become aware of it until much later, that the Russian endeavours to organize the territories separating Central Poland from Russia proper presented the most serious threat to Poland's independence. This menace was greatly increased at that time by unmistakable signs of German-Russian collusion, about which we shall speak later. It suffices to remember also that a Soviet Republic was established in Hungary on the 21st March, 1919, that Communist upheavals were occurring in Germany, and that the Red Army was advancing in the Ukraine towards Galicia, in order to understand the extent to which Poland's existence was menaced.

Reasons for Polish resistance to the annexation of Borderlands by Russia

There were obvious strategic and political reasons which forced Poland to defend the populations of the provinces in which the Bolsheviks installed puppet governments of Lithuania and Byelorussia. The movements of the Red Army converged on Poland's vital centres, and it was clear that the Bolsheviks awaited only a suitable moment to launch a great attack which would open to them the way into the heart of Europe. It was urgent for Poland to push back the invaders as far as possible, as to remain in an expectant attitude would have meant suicide. Russia, occupying the border of the former Congress Kingdom and having a territorial junction with Germany in Eastern Prussia, would have weighed heavily on the whole life of Poland and become indisputable mistress of the latter within a very short time. Consequently it was a matter of life and death for Poland to put a stop to the Russian endeavours in the invaded provinces adjoining Congress Kingdom and to drive the Bolshevik outposts from that area.

Military reasons, although of very great importance, were by no means the only reasons for the Polish action undertaken for the defence of vast territories formerly belonging to the Polish-Lithuanian Commonwealth. Poland could not remain passive in face of the attempts to impose on the populations of these territories a foreign rule and way of life contrary to the traditions and wishes of the nationalities inhabiting them. Moreover, she was at that time the only country able to defend these populations against the yoke of Bolshevik occupation.

We have said above (pp. 193 ff.) that during the occupation of the former Eastern provinces of Poland the Germans very reluctantly had to admit that the numerical and cultural importance of the Polish element there surpassed their expectations. Lloyd George, who was certainly less conversant with the real conditions in these territories than were the German authorities basing their calculations on wide inquiries on the spot, was consequently completely mistaken when he asserted that the Polish claim to having a voice in the fate of that part of the former Polish-Lithuanian territories could be compared to that of a Norman baron drawing his rusty sword. Russian propaganda and historiography in the nineteenth century succeeded to a great extent in convincing Western public opinion that these provinces were ethnographically Russian, that Poland's rights to them were based only on conquest, and that the seizure of these lands by virtue of partitions was a natural process of unification of the Russian race, thus removing a great historic injustice and enabling Russia to come into closer contact with Western civilization, which after all could only be beneficial to Europe.

We find a typical example of such a turn of mind in one of the first books devoted to Poland after a long interval and published in England at the beginning of the First World War by Mr. Phillips W. Allison. We quote some characteristic statements from that book :

" The Polish-Lithuanian empire was a creation from above, the work of a series of great warriors and rulers, notably those of the dynasty of Jagello, and its cohesive force lay in their power to hold it together." [116]

" Poland, practically, morally and economically decadent, formed a barrier between Russia and the progressive civilization of Western Europe, which had to be broken down if Russia was to be brought into full contact with this civilization." [117]

Such opinions die hard, especially if they continue to serve some political purposes, and we come across them in some recent books dealing with Eastern Europe. A distinguished writer, Mr. Kolarz, who in his works unmasks the oppressive character of the Soviet rule in Eastern Europe but who wishes at the same time to preserve intact the structure of the multi-national Soviet Empire, asserts in his *Myths and Realities in Eastern Europe* [118] that " the Polish-Lithuanian State seized vast Russian territories," and he classifies the Jagellonian idea as a myth, in his view based on a mistaken belief that " the ancient Polish Kingdom was an ideal State, excelling by its democratic spirit and institutions and by its religious toleration." He quotes two sources which should prove the contrary, one being the old book of Montesquieu, *Esprit des Lois,* and the other a work by a Soviet writer, Pisheta, published in Moscow in 1940, when the Soviet Union was trying to justify her conquest of Eastern Poland thanks to connivance with Hitler. We do not pretend to present here a full story of the developments which led to the formation of the Polish-Lithuanian State. One can find ample information on this subject in the *Cambridge History of Poland.* Let us state that it is historically untrue to assert that the Polish-Lithuanian State was a work " from above," without deep roots in the consciousness of the nations which formed it. From a purely dynastic union (agreement between the Polish Queen Jadwiga and the Lithuanian Grand-Duke Jagello at Krevo on the 14th August, 1385) arose a real union based on the free agreement of the representatives of the two nations. The Treaty of Lublin in 1569 created in place of a union through the person of the monarch a real union based upon common institutions—the King and the Seym. The extinction of the Jagellonian dynasty which occurred soon afterwards did not bring to an end this union, as the latter was wholeheartedly supported by the population enjoying great political freedom. Of the constitutional law of the Polish-Lithuanian Commonwealth the *Cambridge History of Poland* says that it was " based on the maxims of liberty and equality and on government with the consent of the nation." " The attractive force of this system of government was so great that the population which for one reason or another were also subject to the King of Poland exhibited an elemental urge to enter the Polish Commonwealth as full and permanent members. The inhabitants of several neighbouring territories owing no fealty to the King of Poland likewise voluntarily entered the Union." [119] Let us remember that even the partition brought no end to the Polish-Lithuanian community, and on all great historical occasions, and especially in the risings and struggles against the Russian oppressors, the Poles and Lithuanians fought jointly for the common cause until 1863, the date of the last rising.

Two eminent American experts at the Paris Peace Conference, Mr. Haskins and Professor Lord, in their interesting study *Some Problems of the Peace Conference,* published in 1920, devote the following lines to this great page of Polish-Lithuanian history :

> " For generations Poland has spent an infinite amount of effort in organizing and civilizing these Eastern territories and in defending them against Swedes and Muscovites. . . . For most outsiders the partitions have overshadowed all the preceding period of Polish history. Such observers have fastened their eyes too exclusively upon the deplorable condition into which Poland had fallen just before her dismemberment and have concluded that her history is chiefly made up of a tissue of mistakes, sins and follies, interesting only as furnishing a terrible example of how a State ought not to be governed and of how badly a people can mismanage its national life." [120]

Contesting such one-sided views, the authors of this book state that " the old republic represented an effort to organize the vast open plain between the Baltic and the Black Sea—a region containing so many weak and under-developed races and a region so much exposed to Germanic ambitions on the one side and to Turco-Tartar onslaughts on the other—into a compact and powerful realm, which was directed indeed by the strongest and most advanced race within its borders—the Poles—but which in its better period allowed a genuine equality to the other races and expansive self-government to some of them."

> " A great enthusiasm for freedom in almost every branch of life ; the principle of the sovereignty of the nation, calling citizens to participate in the responsibilities of government ; the conception of the State as not a thing existing for itself, but as an instrument serving the wellbeing of society ; aversion to absolute monarchy, standing armies and militarism ; disinclination to undertake aggressive wars, but a remarkable tendency to form voluntary unions with neighbouring peoples—such are some of the hallmarks of the old Polish State, which make it stand out as a unique excep-

tion among the rapacious and militaristic monarchies of that age." [121]

It is in the past of this vast area which constituted the former Polish-Lithuanian Commonwealth that we can find the explanation of the capital differences between the Central-eastern region of Europe and Russia proper. This region, populated by several nationalities—Poles, Lithuanians, Ukrainians, Byelorussians—has far more features in common with Western Europe than with Eastern Europe populated by Great Russians. The eminent Polish historian Halecki, in his study *The Limits and Divisions of European History,* published in 1950, shows how mistaken and contrary to the historic truth are the views of those who divide Europe into two regions only—Western and Eastern—identifying the history and conditions of the latter with those of Russia. This misconception, according to Halecki, can only be explained by " the transitory situation of the nineteenth century in which the study of Eastern European history was started in a Germany allied with Russia." [122]

" The partition of the Polish Commonwealth between the Russian and German Empires," says Halecki, " made the third region disappear completely for more than a hundred years, creating the impression that there was nothing between Western European Germany and a new Russia, identified with ' Eastern ' Europe." [123]

The partitions of the Polish Commonwealth, often misrepresented as an exceptional case in world history (Professor Lord rightly recalls in his well-documented book *The Second Partition of Poland* that " the history of the eighteenth century is full of partitions and projects for partition; there was scarcely a State on the Continent whose dismemberment was not planned by its neighbours at one time or another during these hundred years,") [124] and credulously believed by those who seem to forget the upheavals at the end of the eighteenth and beginning of the nineteenth century. Moreover it is preposterous to assert that the partitions were due to the natural urge of the Russian nation for the unification of all the brothers of the Russian race under a common sceptre, because national impulses were alien to the mentality of the eighteenth century. The partitions were due to the lust for conquest and the accretion of material power so characteristic of the expansion of the Russian State in the course of the last centuries.[125] For many decennaries after the partitions the Russians considered their acquisitions from the Partitions as a purely Polish land, and Tsar Alexander the First promised the Poles to unite all the former Polish territories under his sceptre in one Kingdom (The Treaty of Vienna expressly refers to this intention of the Tsar to " extend " the Congress Kingdom). In a very interesting correspondence between Tsar Nicholas I and his brother Grand-Duke Constantine referring to Polish matters, the Polish character of the territories acquired by Russia in the partitions of Poland is not questioned, and the seizure of this land is represented by Constantine as an *acte de brigandage*. " I was, I am and I shall ever remain Russian," wrote Constantine, " but I am not one of those Russians, blind and stupid, who adhere to the principle that everything is allowed to them and nothing to others. Our little mother Russia takes everything amicably, treading on the throat." [126] In 1794 and 1812 the Poles had fought for the reunion of all the territories belonging to the former Polish Commonwealth and seized by Russia, casting their lot with Napoleon, and they fought for it again in 1830 and in 1863.[127] On their side the Russians after 1830 began intense Russification of these territories in order to obliterate their Western character and move westward the " Western boundaries of Russia one and indivisible." [128] The Poles had never accepted the idea that this land should be irrevocably lost to Western civilization. It is no wonder that when the hour of the liberation of Poland struck they turned their eyes to these territories, the liberation of which had been the supreme aim of their fathers. Whatever one may think of it, it was a fact which remained one of the essential factors of the policy of the liberated Poland. Haskins and Lord in their above-mentioned book said very appropriate words about these ideas which were shared by all Polish democrats and even socialists :

> " There is no need to pass judgment here upon the justice or expediency of such ideas. But they cannot be ignored ; and it certainly does not advance us towards a solution of these questions, nor is it a sign of insight or fairmindedness to brand these ideas as due simply to ' Polish imperialism ' or ' chauvinism ' or ' megalomania,' as our Liberal journals are fond of doing ; or to castigate the Poles for claiming a single unit of territory outside the area where—according to the statistics prepared by Governments hostile to them *—there is demonstrably a Polish-speaking minority." [129]

* It is really very strange that for a very long time, under the influence of some White Russian émigrés or their protectors, the opinion prevailed, particularly in Great Britain, that the number of the Polish population in the former Grand Duchy of Lithuania was insignificant. We read, for instance, in Toynbee's *Survey of International Affairs* for 1920-1923 (pp. 255-6), that " although the Polish element was larger than the Lithuanian in Vilna-City where, however (as in many Polish towns), the Poles themselves were outnumbered by the Jews, throughout the rest of the province the Polish population was numerically insignificant, though it included a

Those who, like Lloyd George, condemned the Polish action against the Bolsheviks in 1919-20 showed their complete ignorance of the position existing at that time in North-Eastern Europe, and forgot that Poland, far from being warned against undertaking any action, was on the contrary even encouraged by the Western Allies to participate in the defence of the Eastern territories menaced by the

larger proportion of the landowning class." To support this assertion the author is able to refer only to the figures of population of the Russian census of 1897. The author does not explain why the census carried out in that epoch, which was by the way the epoch of the most severe Polish persecutions in the Western provinces of old Russia, should be considered more reliable than the subsequent Russian estimates much more favourable to Poles, carried out in later periods when the police régime in Russia was to some extent relaxed, or the German census of 1916 which certainly was not carried out with pro-Polish bias. We refer to what we said about this matter above (pp. 193 ff.). Von Beckerath in his Memorandum to the German Government, dated 3rd January, 1917, emphasized that " The official Russian statistics which we have found here and which do not answer at all to the requirements of contemporary science, were certainly drawn up to the prejudice of the Poles, the number of whom has not been brought into prominence." In the district of Wilno the percentage of the Polish population which, according to the Russian statistics, was no higher than 12·1, was, according to the German figures, 74·8; in the same way in the Grodno district it mounted from 5·6 per cent. to 63·4 per cent., and in the district of Lida from 4·6 per cent. to 63·4 per cent.

May we quote in this connection the statement made by the eminent American expert of the American Delegation to the Peace Conference, Professor Lord, in answer to a question at a gathering in the United States: " What can you say of the frequent statement that the present aims of the Polish Government were imperialistic? (HOUSE-SEYMOUR, o.c., p. 452): " I should say that the statement in the main is based on inaccurate knowledge of the ethnographical situation. As heard to-day, this charge is usually made with regard to the claims of the Polish Government to certain territories in the East. In that quarter the Poles have claimed a good deal of territory which, according to the statistics of the old Russian Government, does not have a Polish majority. But these statistics of the old Russian Government, like those of the Turks, were in large part simply fabricated for political reasons. Take, for example, the case of the district of Vilna, which is so much in dispute to-day. The Russian census of 1897 affirms that the Poles made up only 20 per cent. of the population there. In 1909 the Russian estimates admitted that the Poles were 43 per cent. of the population. In 1916 the Germans, who were then occupying this region, took a census and found that 80 per cent. of the population were Polish. Last winter the Poles themselves took a census (1919) which agrees pretty well with the German one. This may illustrate how unreliable the Russian figures often are. Unfortunately the Russian statistics, particularly those of 1897, are almost the only data with which the rest of the world has hitherto been familiar; almost all the current ethnographic maps of Eastern Europe are based solely upon them, and therefore the rest of the world gets a false idea of the ethnographic character of much of the territory which the Poles are laying claim to."

Bolsheviks. Did not Great Britain at the same time help the Latvians
and Esthonians in their struggle against the Bolsheviks mainly by
the action of her fleet in the Baltic?

According to Temperley's *History of the Peace Conference of
Paris* :

> " There were three main courses possible (for Poland). The first
> was that Poland should abandon these territories to the Bolsheviks.
> But if these territories did not wish to be Bolshevik why should
> they be forced to become so, and was it not too much to ask that
> the Poles should peacefully make over to the Bolsheviks territories
> in which their compatriots constitute the greater part of the
> bourgeoisie and still possess a very great portion of the land? The
> second was that these intermediate peoples should become inde-
> pendent. But without Polish help their independence would
> immediately fall before a Bolshevik invasion, and even apart from
> that it is more than doubtful whether any of them (with the excep-
> tion of the Lithuanians who are in contact with the sea and can
> secure foreign help) is capable or even desirous of organizing or
> maintaining any kind of stable national government. The third
> course was that the Poles should take these peoples under their
> protection, should become responsible for their defence, and should
> introduce such order and institutions as were suitable for their
> needs. It is small wonder that the Poles preferred the last course
> and it is a misconception to maintain that in doing so they were
> necessarily actuated only by blind folly and criminal ambition." [130]

It might have seemed that Poland at the end of 1918 and the
beginning of 1919 would be unable to stop the advance of the Red
Army, as she was only about to start her big effort to organize
the national army consisting only of volunteers (the first call-up of
men born in 1898 was carried out on the 19th January, 1919), as
stated above in Chapter V if the First Part (pp. 239 ff.). Nor were
conditions in Poland very propitious, as it was on Polish territory
that the greatest battles on the Eastern Front had been fought, and
the country was impoverished by the predatory policy of the
occupying powers, Germany and Austria-Hungary. Moreover a
great part of these small forces was engaged in the defensive battle
around Lwow. The Warsaw Government was still being snubbed
by Western statesmen, and received no help from the West until the
arrival of the Haller Army in April 1919. An unbiased observer can
judge for himself whether Lloyd George's allegations concerning the
lack of organizing ability of the Poles were really warranted.

Beginning of hostilities between Poland and Soviet Russia

Poland was surprised by the quick withdrawal of the German
forces from the East and by the way in which the evacuation of the

German forces under the command of the notorious General Hoffman, former negotiator at Brest-Litovsk, was carried out. His
collusion with the Chiefs of the Soviet Armies is well known, being
also confirmed by himself in his *Memoirs*. The Red detachments
immediately occupied the positions vacated by the German forces,
and the latter supplied them with munitions and rolling stock. The
Poles were unable to pass through the German lines, a " corridor "
being kept by the German forces extending along the railway line
Rowno–Kowel–Brest-Litovsk–Bialystok and Grajewo. The
Northern part of this corridor was held until the last moment by the
German troops, while the Germans were withdrawing from the
Ukraine. Therefore the Poles were unable to send their troops to
relieve Wilno, which fell into Bolshevik hands on the 5th January,
1919.

The dramatic position arising from the conduct of the German
High Command is best shown by a telegram sent by Pilsudski, then
Chief of State (still unrecognized by the Entente) to Clemenceau
as President of the Peace Conference :

> " The German authorities have for some time begun a systematic
> evacuation of the territories called ' Ober Ost,' delivering them to
> the Red Army and Bolshevik bands. On the 4th January the
> Germans will evacuate Wilno, which will thus be exposed to all
> the horrors of the Bolshevik régime unless the Poles arrive in time
> to stop the advance of the Red guards and help the local popula-
> tion to organize the defence. The Polish detachments are ready to
> be sent immediately to Wilno, but the Government of Berlin has
> just given orders to General Hoffmann to refuse the right of transit
> to the Polish troops under the pretext that their presence in Wilno
> would be in contradiction to the general conditions of the Armis-
> tice concluded with the Allies. I urge you to force the German
> Government to give immediately free passage to the Polish troops
> which have for sole aim the preservation of order and stopping the
> Bolshevik invasion. Will you please order the German military
> authorities to deliver to the local Polish anti-Bolshevik organiza-
> tions a sufficient quantity of arms to organize the defence. The
> smallest delay would be disastrous for Lithuania and for Poland as
> a whole." [131]

At the same time Mr. A. Zaleski of the Polish Mission in Berne
was ordered by his government to address an appeal to the Entente
Governments to issue appropriate orders to the German Armistice
Commission at Spa. Mr. Zaleski also gave the information that the
conversations between Captain Gorka of the Polish General Staff
with the German military authorities had been broken off by the
order of the Berlin Government. In its conclusions the appeal

stated that " in view of recent events in Berlin the Polish Government supposes that the German Government desires to contribute to the development and the spread of Bolshevism in Poland and that it desires to paralyse all offensive action on the part of the Poles." [132] Thus started the sinister collaboration between German militarism and Bolshevik Russia, directed both against Poland and the Western Powers, which was to continue for many years to come.

Due to German-Bolshevik collusion, at the beginning of February 1919 Red detachments almost reached the line of the River Niemen, having for their bases Wilno, Baranowicze and Pinsk.

Allied intervention came late, too late to save Wilno from Bolshevik occupation, but an agreement was eventually reached between General Von Seeckt and the representatives of the Polish General Staff and Ministry for Foreign Affairs (on the 5th February at Bialystok). This agreement secured the departure of the German troops from the northern strip of the Ober Ost, and allowed the immediate passage of ten reinforced Polish battalions through the German lines. General Von Seeckt commented on this event in his Diary in these ironic terms : " I have just signed an agreement with Polish brothers; it should bring them into conflict with Bolsheviks, from which I expect relief for the German front." General Von Seeckt writes further about the motives for the action of the Entente in this matter : " It was not friendship for the Poles that was the reason for the action of the Entente but the fear that if we keep fighting we might gradually rebuild our army which, by the way, is our aim." [133]

As a matter of fact we know little about the manner in which this Allied intervention was carried out. We remember that the question of Bolshevism and of the Bolshevik danger to Poland in particular was discussed at several meetings of the Supreme Council in January, in connection with Marshal Foch's schemes and the appeals of the Polish Government. A very characteristic debate took place on the 22nd January when the sending of an Inter-Allied Commission to Poland was decided upon.[134] How little the Allies knew about the events in Eastern Europe at that time appears clearly from Foch's statement : " The Poles were fighting the Bolsheviks who might attack them." As a matter of fact the Polish troops came into contact with the first detachments of the Red Army only in mid-February 1919. Foch considered that the Poles should limit themselves to the action against the Bolsheviks, this being their primary task, and the representative of Italy, Sonnino, similiarly observed that the Commission which the Supreme Council was about to send to Poland " should try and induce the Poles to confine their activities to resisting the Bolsheviks." At that moment

Lloyd George intervened, saying that " he agreed to this proposal provided that under this pretence they (the Poles) did not attempt to push their conquests Eastwards and face the Congress with the capture of Kovno or Grodno." Did this mean that Lloyd George would have preferred these territories to remain under Bolshevik occupation? In the light of Lloyd George's further moves there is no doubt that Lloyd George looked with marked hostility on any advance of the Polish troops beyond the borders of the former Congress Kingdom. On the first occasion on which this question was discussed Lloyd George appeared as an adversary of the liberation from the Bolshevik yoke of the oppressed nationalities of these provinces, as only Poland could carry out this task.

Betwen the 9th and 14th February the first detachments of the Polish forces moved across the zone occupied by the Germans and occupied the line : River Niemen near Skidel, River Rozanka, Pruzany-Kobryn. On the 13th February they occupied Wolkowysk, and on the 19th February Bialystok, evacuated by the Germans. The first encounters between the Poles and Bolsheviks occurred at Bereza Kartuska (17th February) and East of Grodno (21st February).[135]

The war thus started between Poland and Soviet Russia was never officially declared, but there was nothing extraordinary in that because all the wars carried out on the soil of the former Empire of the Tsars, since the outbreak of the Bolshevik Revolution, were *de facto* wars.

There was another important feature of that war : neither party recognized the treaties of Partition on which were based the claims of the Tsars to domination over the former Eastern provinces of the Polish-Lithuanian Commonwealth.

In fact, even before the German collapse, on the 29th August, 1918, the Council of the People's Commissars issued a decree which cancelled many treaties concluded by the former Tsarist Government, Prussia, and Austria-Hungary. Articles III, IV and V of this decree concerned Polish matters. Article III is the most important of these, and runs as follows :

> " All treaties and agreements concluded by the Government of the former Russian Empire and the Government of the Kingdom of Prussia and the Austro-Hungarian Empire relating to the partitions of Poland, being contrary to the principle of self-determination and the revolutionary feelings of the Russian nation who recognize the intangible right of the Polish nation to independence and union—are irrevocably annulled."

On the strength of this decree, on the 3rd September, 1918, the Soviet Government addressed a Verbal Note to the German

Government by which, with reference to Article IV of the Additional Treaty concluded at Brest-Litovsk on the 3rd March, 1918, it announced the denunciation of the above-mentioned treaties. Whatever may have been the reasons which prompted the Soviet Government to this important step (propaganda, wish to win Polish sympathies in the event of a German collapse, or on the contrary to state that Russia was not interested in Poland), the consequence of this move was that the Soviet Government was debarred from the possibility of basing its claims to the possession of the former provinces of the Polish-Lithuanian Commonwealth on obsolete " juridical " titles.[136]

So far as the Poles were concerned they had never recognized the validity of the treaties of Partition, considering them " acts of lawless usurpation." To them *de jure* Poland still existed within the frontiers of 1772.[137] It is very interesting to note that while the Western Powers in their reply to Germany of the 16th June, 1919, called the acts of partition " one of the greatest wrongs of which history has record," "a crime the memory and result of which has for long poisoned the political life of a large portion of the continent of Europe " (see pp. 339 ff.), they never drew the necessary conclusions from this standpoint in relation to the lawless possession by Russia of portions of the former Polish territories, acquired in exactly the same way as by Germany.[138]

Consequently it was not by invoking obsolete treaties of Partition that the Soviet Government justified the invasion of the Eastern provinces of the former Polish-Lithuanian Commonwealth, but by the alleged will of the toiling masses of these areas. This point of view agreeing with the principle of self-determination, the whole meaning of which was perverted by the Bolsheviks as we stated above, appeared clearly in the exchange of telegrams between Mr. Wasilewski, then Polish Minister for Foreign Affairs, and Commissar Chicherin, in the weeks preceding the outbreak of the Polish-Soviet war.

In the preface to the collection of these diplomatic documents published in Moscow by the Soviet Government in 1920 under the name of the *Red Book,* we find the following statements referring to the guiding principles of the Soviet policy :

> " ... Soviet diplomacy is pursued in the daylight, being generated by the toiling masses and appealing to the foreign masses of foreign nations. ... In any approach to other governments, this diplomacy has always in view which might be the repercussions of each step taken by it on the consciousness of the wide masses of that country and of the government with which it deals. ... Soviet Russia does not impose on anyone its rule, its régime and its

principles—it does not bring on its bayonets those revolutionary conquests which the toiling masses of each country should win by their own efforts. It recognizes invariably that each nation should shape its fate by its own efforts." [139]

We know very well that all further actions of the Soviet Government belied this phraseology, and there is now no need to prove it, but one should keep in mind that at that time when these slogans were first launched there were many people all over the world who took them at their face value.

The Polish Government protested many times in December 1918 and January 1919 against the advance of the Red Army. In a telegram sent by Wasilewski to Chicherin on the 22nd December the Polish Government declared that it considered this advance " as a hostile act directed against our country." [140] The following day Chicherin replied that " the Soviet forces were at a considerable distance from the Polish frontier " (but what Chicherin considered to be the Polish frontiers nobody knew), and " are moreover separated from them by Lithuania and the adjoining part of the Ukraine." [141]

Wasilewski sent another telegram to Chicherin on the 30th December in which he clearly stated the Polish point of view :

> " Unfortunately, numerous facts prove the aggressive character of the policy pursued by the Russian Soviet Government whose armed forces have flooded Lithuania and Byelorussia, introducing there a Soviet administration alien to them and enslaving the nations ... the latter are debarred from the right themselves to decide their future. Considering that a part of these territories is unquestionably Polish, these measures directly affect the vital interests of the Polish nation. Further, the presence in the ranks of the Soviet Army of units composed of Poles, usurping the names of towns of the Polish Republic such as Warsaw and Sandomierz, destined, according to most trustworthy information, to occupy the territory of the Polish Republic for the purpose of raising there a social revolution, should be considered as a measure of aggression imposing on the Polish Government the duty to react in a most energetic way." [142]

As a marginal note to this last remark we have to state that from the early days of the Bolshevik Revolution the Soviet Government had organized units composed of former soldiers of the Russian army and ex-prisoners of war from the German and Austro-Hungarian armies, of Polish descent, and that Lenin himself took a lively interest in the organization of these shock-troops of the Bolshevik Revolution in Poland. Speaking at a meeting of the

Warsaw Regiment in Moscow on the 1st August, 1918, Lenin said :
" The same desire unites now the Russian and Polish Revolutionaries: the desire to secure the conquests of the first socialist revolution,
which should be followed by revolutions in other countries." [143]

At the end of the said telegram Wasilkewski expressed the fear that
in the near future the Polish Government " might have to defend by
armed force the integrity of the territory inhabited by Poles against
the invasion of the armies of the Russian Soviet Government."

In his telegram of the 7th January, 1919, Chicherin did not deny
the existence of the units composed of Poles in the ranks of the
Soviet Army, explaining this fact by " a spontaneous urge of the
Poles to enlist with the Soviet forces in order to participate in the
struggle for the liberation of the working class." So far as the
invasion of the Western borderlands was concerned, he declared
that " he did not know anything about the desire of the workers
and peasants of those countries to join the Polish Republic," and
stated emphatically that " Lithuania is an independent country, and
so is Byelorussia." [144]

In a telegram of the 10th February, Chicherin offered his good
offices to Poland in the delimitation of frontiers between her and
the " Soviet " Republics of Lithuania and Byelorussia.[145] It was
clear that the Soviet Government was hiding behind the fictitious
governments imposed by itself on Lithuania and Byelorussia. In
these circumstances the failure of the mission of Wieckowski,
sent to Moscow as a special envoy on the proposal of Prime Minister
Paderewski, was a foregone conclusion.

By a telegram of the 16th February, 1919, Mitskevich-
Kapsukas and Miasnikov, on behalf of the puppet governments
of Lithuania and Byelorussia, informed the Polish Government
that their countries had decided to unite into one Lithuanian-
Byelorussian Socialist Soviet Republic and wished " to establish the
closest possible links with other neighbours, with all existing
already on the territory of the former Russian Empire, Socialist
Soviet Republics : Russia, the Ukraine, Latvia, Esthonia, and to
found from all these republics a Federative Socialist Soviet
Republic." [146]

Chicherin supported this step by addressing to the Principal
Powers a telegram in which, declaring that his government fostered
friendly feelings towards Poland, protested against the advance of
the Polish troops " threatening the Soviet Republics of Lithuania
and Byelorussia and the Russian Soviet Republic united to them by
indissoluble friendship." [147] The purpose of all these steps was
obvious : to forestall any Polish moves and face the world with
accomplished facts.

We have stated above the reasons for which Poland could not remain an impassive observer of the events taking place in the Eastern borderlands. At that time the Polish policy was at the cross-roads. Should Poland limit herself to actions for the purpose of liberating only that part of her former territories in the East in which the Western civilization implanted by her centuries before had taken deep roots and was still to a great extent preserved, and try to save only this part from destruction by Bolshevism of all cultural values and the systematic de-Christianization as well as from the most oppressive social system mankind has ever known (this area corresponding roughly to the line of the Second Partition of Poland and later to the Treaty of Riga frontier); or should Poland conceive a bolder plan aiming at the complete political reshaping of the area separating Poland from Russia proper, that is to say encourage and assist all the efforts of the nationalities inhabiting this region to start a new life free from any foreign domination? Here we have in a nutshell two different lines of policy, one pursued first by the Polish National Committee in Paris and its indisputable leader, R. Dmowski, and another promoted by Pilsudski, and to some extent also by Paderewski.

We shall deal with the first political programme in connection with the next sub-heading of this chapter, referring to the problem of the Eastern frontiers of Poland at the Peace Conference.

Pilsudski's great plan

The second political programme, that advocated by Pilsudski, rested on premises different from those of Dmowski, but it would be quite mistaken to assume that it appeared in definite shape from the beginning of the Polish-Soviet war in 1919. Pilsudski's programme developed step by step, depending on the course of military operations. It could not be complete so long as an understanding had not been reached between Poland and the Ukrainian national movement for liberation. The "little" war in Eastern Galicia delayed for several months such an understanding, and there is much evidence that Pilsudski deplored this fratricidal struggle which could in the last instance benefit only the Russian imperialistic designs, as had been the case in the seventeenth century at the time of the Cossack revolts in Poland. Pilsudski's programme corresponded to his inmost convictions, as appears from his activity before the outbreak of the 1914 war and his attempts to bring together the nationalities of Russia in a common struggle against Tsarist oppression. In this connection we must remember the programme developed by Pilsudski during the Russo-Japanese war (see p. 109). According to Pilsudski true peace in Eastern Europe depended on the satisfaction of all well-defined national aspirations of the oppressed nationalities of Russia and the establishment of a League of free nations in the Near East of Europe (see his conversations with Tchaikovsky and Savinkov, quoted on pp. 419 ff.). But Pilsudski was not an idle dreamer or an abstract schemer. He realized that carrying out such a plan depended on the material force available and on the response of these nationalities. Let us remember here that the problem of nationalities was, besides the social problem, the most vital issue in Eastern Europe and that the Bolsheviks realized its impact far more than did the White Russian leaders and their western protectors. Hence the Bolshevik attempts to find some solutions which apparently giving satisfaction to these dynamic movements actually harnessed them to lay the foundations of a new and highly centralized Soviet State.

Nobody better defined Pilsudski's Eastern programme than one of his close collaborators, an eminent historian, Sokolnicki :

> " When the whole of Eastern Europe was still in a fluid state, when its thorough reconstruction could still be carried out, Pilsudski's designs were far-reaching. The new Poland liberated under his leadership wants freedom and rights not only for herself. She supports and strengthens all movements for independence and all aspirations for autonomous existence of all nationalities of Russia. Poland will give her assistance and help to independent Baltic States. She will show her sympathy and friendly feelings to the Caucasian Republics which were founded at that time and try to establish through them close contacts and understanding with Turkey. Such a programme, if it had met with understanding and full co-operation of the peoples concerned, would have been able to solve for a long time the problem of the Polish-Russian relations. Instead of competition between these two Powers for the ' borderlands ' a new system would have arisen, based on the independence and freedom of these new States. It was a programme of Richelieu, transplanted to a different epoch and different geographical surroundings, enabling the peaceful development of Eastern Europe for centuries." [148]

Since it was Pilsudski who was responsible for Poland's Eastern policy in his capacity of Chief of State and Commander-in-Chief of the Polish Army, we must see in all the moves of this policy his hand and initiatives. But he was not alone. He was wholeheartedly supported on this point by the whole radical wing of Polish public opinion, including the Polish Socialist Party (P.P.S.).

Louis Fischer, who at the time of writing his work *The Soviets in World Affairs* was still much impressed by Bolshevik propaganda slogans, underlines this fact although unable to find a proper explanation for it : " And strangely enough," he writes, " the most enthusiastic advocates of the federative idea, which amounted to poorly disguised imperialism, were the Polish socialists led by Pilsudski and by Ignatius Daszynski (leader of the P.P.S.)."[149]

This fact should forewarn us against jumping to hasty conclusions like that of Louis Fischer. The standpoint of the Polish Socialist Party on this matter appears clearly from a telegram sent by a prominent Socialist leader, Niedzialkowski, on behalf of the Central Executive Committee of this party to the Central Committee of the Communist Party of Russia on 4th March, 1919, that is to say at the beginning of the military operations between the Polish and Bolshevik forces. In this telegram an interesting suggestion was made referring to the method of settling outstanding territorial issues; a suggestion, by the way, recalling the proposal made by the Bolsheviks themselves in the course of the Brest-Litovsk Peace Conference (see p. 184) and discarded by them immediately after the withdrawal of the German forces. The Polish Socialist Party's proposal ran as follows :

> " So far as the question of frontiers is concerned, we wish to settle it on the basis of self-determination of the population inhabiting the disputed territories and in the first instance in Lithuania and Byelorussia. We insist on the withdrawal from these territories of all foreign troops and the carrying out of an immediate popular vote under conditions of absolute freedom. Allegations that the working class of Lithuania has already expressed its will to join Russia on a basis of federation must be considered a fiction since no popular vote has taken place in Lithuania and Byelorussia." [150]

On many other occasions, especially in the Polish Seym, Polish Socialists defended the right of self-determination of the nationalities of the Eastern borderlands. The same Socialist leader, Niedzialkowski, proposed a motion which was carried by the Seym on the 4th April, 1919, and which ran as follows :

> " The Constituent Seym, stating the primary right of the Lithuanians and Byelorussians inhabiting the territory of the former Grand Duchy of Lithuania to decide their own fate in full freedom, cannot recognize, consequently, either the Soviet Lithuanian-Byelorussian Republic subservient to Russia or the governments of the Lithuanian and Byelorussian propertied classes set up by German authorities, without the participation of the toiling masses." [151]

No wonder that the Polish Socialists were the target of the most violent attacks by Soviet propaganda, the official Russian *Red Book* calling the first Socialist Government of Moraczewski a " petty bourgeois " government. By the way, those radicals in the West who were so often led astray by this propaganda were unaware at that time that they were themselves assigned to the same category of despicable " petty bourgeois " by the Bolsheviks.

All the implications of Pilsudski's Eastern programme appeared only in 1920. For the time being we wish to show the impact of his ideas on the programme proclaimed by the Poles in the course of the struggle for liberation from the Bolshevik oppression of the North-Eastern territories formerly belonging to the Polish-Lithuanian Commonwealth.

Some passages of the Report of the Commission for Foreign Affairs of the Polish Seym, adopted at the plenary meeting of the latter on the 4th April, 1919, unquestionably bear marks of the ideas expounded above :

> " The Polish military action has nowhere in view " [states the report], " to forestall by means of arms the decisions of the Peace Conference or to incorporate into Poland any territories against the wishes of their populations, but only to defend them against foreign invasion. ... The Government should do their utmost that not only the local Polish population but also the Byelorussians and Ruthenians (Ukrainians) may be free to express their will as regards union with Poland. Remembering the bonds of a freely agreed union which for so many centuries united the Polish Nation with the Lithuanian Nation, and recognizing the right of the Lithuanians to organize a State of their own—the Government of the Republic shall firmly endeavour to establish again a free union between these two nations. The Republic cannot recognize, however, as representatives of the genuine will of the populations of these territories the Soviets imposed on them by the Bolshevik armies which, no less than in the past the armies of the former Tsardom, pursue the aim of conquest." [152]

In their advance to the East the Polish troops reached Wilno, which fell into their hands on the 19th April, 1919. Three days later Pilsudski issued a Proclamation to " the inhabitants of the former Duchy of Lithuania " [153] (which he himself dictated to the Chief of the Civil Administration). In it he spoke to his country-men as " a native of this unhappy land " (he was born not far from Wilno and spent his school years in that city), which " for over a hundred years has not known what is freedom, having suffered under a hostile oppression by Russians, Germans and Bolsheviks, who without any concern for the wishes of the population imposed on it alien patterns of life, fettered its will, often breaking lives." It was an important document (for issuing which he was censured by the right wing of Polish public opinion), because Pilsudski not only

gave his pledge that from then on the population in that land
" would live without any violence or oppression by Poland," but
stated also that instead of a military administration he would install
there a civil administration (he wished to do much more, as we
shall see later, namely to install there a Government in which all
nationalities would be represented). It should be added that until
the conclusion of the Riga Treaty Poland, unlike the Bolsheviks,
maintained a provisional administration in Eastern territories,
distinct from that of the remaining parts of Poland.

On many occasions Pilsudski advocated ideas of freedom and the
right of self-determination of the nationalities of this region. For
instance, speaking at Minsk on the 19th September, 1919, Pilsudski
opposed the Polish programme of national self-determination to the
Bolshevik methods of oppression.[154] " Once more," he said, " had
this land to endure oppression and violence coming from the East,
which under the cloak of the highest ideas of brotherhood used
terror and imposed the way of life and the laws contrary to the wishes
of the population." He then outlined the Polish programme in the
following words : " Poland does not wish to tread upon this land
with a rough, soldierly boot, or to force anyone to obey her laws. At
the very moment when I appeared here at the head of my soldiers I
gave the order according to which nothing would be imposed on this
land by violence, and this land will have its own free voice among
other lands, to decide over its own life and pass the laws which will
rule it."

In an interview granted in mid-February 1920 to a correspondent of *L'Echo de Paris*, Pilsudski said :

> " The will of the countries occupied by us is the decisive factor
> for me. I do not wish, by any means, that Poland may have great
> spaces inhabited by a hostile population. ... It will be my pride
> as a statesman and soldier to bring freedom to neighbouring
> peoples. I keep in mind the historic links which united us with
> them, and I know also that these links became even closer after the
> partitions of Poland. By liberating these oppressed peoples I wish
> to delete the last traces of the partitions.
> " To attach them by force to us—never! It would mean that we
> would retort by new acts of violence to those committed in the
> past." [155]

One might take the view that it was only brilliant oratory cloaking some sinister imperialistic designs, of which Lloyd George so
often accused the Poles. But, on the other side, the Allies were on
many occasions officially informed of the Polish desire to comply
with the wishes of the populations of the territories liberated from
the Bolshevik occupation; they opposed any Polish initiative to put

these ideas into practice and preferred to suspend any decision on the fate of these territories, looking forward to the restoration of the Russian Empire.

At the meeting of the Council of Four on the 5th June, 1919, Mr. Paderewski read the resolution of the Polish Constituent Diet, which stated among other things that

> " the Polish Republic does not intend to incorporate into the Polish State the territories of the former Grand Duchy of Lithuania solely on the basis of a decision of the Polish Constituent Assembly. The Diet recognizes the application of the principle of self-determination to the nations of the former Grand Duchy of Lithuania, as stated in the report of the Commission for Foreign Affairs, voted by the Diet on the 4th April, 1919, as well as in the proclamation of the Commander-in-Chief issued in Wilno on the 22nd April, without specifying for the time being, the way in which this principle should be applied." [156]

In a conversation between Pilsudski and Sir H. Mackinder, British High Commissioner for South Russia, on 15th December, 1919, in Warsaw, when the latter said " that British public opinion had some suspicion as to the use to which the Poles might put their victory over the Bolsheviks," Pilsudski emphatically disclaimed imperialistic desires and made the important declaration that he was willing to allow the future position of the inhabitants of the country as far back as the Conference line through Brest-Litovsk to be submitted to a plebiscite." [157]

In November 1919 Pilsudski declared to the Commission for Foreign Affairs that he intended to organize in the near future a plebiscite in the territories liberated by the Polish troops. But the disclosure of these plans met with the complete disapproval of the Western Allies, and Millerand on behalf of the Supreme Council on the 10th March, 1920, sent a note to the Polish Delegation to the Peace Conference, which, referring to Article LXXXVII of the Versailles Treaty (" the boundaries of Poland not laid down in the present Treaty will be subsequently determined by the Principal Allied and Associated Powers "), protested against holding such a plebiscite in liberated territories.[158] In the West no attempt was made at that time to ascertain the true wishes of the local population. Several time the Poles proposed a visit by members of the British Parliament to the Eastern territories so that the representatives of British public opinion might become better acquainted with the conditions of life of the population and the wishes of those who, being liberated from Bolshevik oppression, looked to Poland as " a land of promise "; but Western public opinion preferred to rely on the information spread from White Russian quarters, and last but not least by Soviet propaganda.

Poland and Ethnic Lithuania

Although defending the right of the Poles to the territories in which they had the majority, Pilsudski at the same time showed that he respected the rights of the Lithuanian nation to self-determination. The unity of the former Duchy of Lithuania was at that time the inmost wish of all Poles, who thought it should be based on the free consent and equality of rights of all nationalities in the area. It was the idea of reviving the old Polish-Lithuanian federation of both nations, an idea shared at that time not only by the Poles inhabiting historical Lithuania but also by all political parties in Poland itself. During the occupation of the Congress Kingdom by the Central Powers two important declarations were issued, on the 10th and 20th May, 1917, one by the parties of the Left, the other by the parties of the Right.[159] Both declarations rejected plans for the annexation of Lithuania by Poland, and emphasized the necessity for restoring the old historical links between Poland and Lithuania, as only in this way " might the peoples inhabiting the historic Lithuania, united freely and harmoniously to the Polish nation, find guarantees of national, cultural and economic development of all social classes." The Poles realized that should each nationality of historic Lithuania go its own way it would mean the disrupture of the unity of the former Grand Duchy, the only safeguard of their future independence.

These plans met with opposition from the young Lithuanian intelligentsia, whose ambitions were stirred by the skilful activity of the German occupants, ready to sow the seeds of hatred for their own designs (see pp. 194 ff.). It would go beyond the scope of this book to deal at length with the special conditions in which this revival of the Lithuanian nationalism after so many centuries took place. We wish only to point out that although it was true that in the past, in the course of the freely agreed union the upper strata of the Lithuanian and Byelorussian population became Polonized, this was due exclusively to the attractiveness of the Polish civilization and the Polish liberal institutions. On the other side, the peasant population of Lithuania was able to preserve its particular traditions, language and way of life, and the bulk of the Lithuanian population remained intact. One can understand the reasons for which the young Lithuanian intelligentsia feared close contact with Polish civilization, too attractive to Lithuanians eager to build up their own national State; but on the other hand, once the Lithuanians wished to keep aloof from Poland they should have recog-

nized the fact that only a part of historic Lithuania was ethnographically Lithuanian, and that other nationalities of Lithuania
should enjoy the same rights of self-determination. Apart from the
Lithuanian districts of Lithuania there were purely Polish districts
around Wilno and Grodno, adjoining ethnographic Poland, and
there were Polish-Byelorussian districts where the number of Lithuanians was negligible. The slogan of Lithuania for the Lithuanians,
first launched by the Lithuanian delegates at the Third Congress of
Nationalities at Lausanne on the 27th June, 1916, disregarded this
fact and was bound to provoke the opposition of other nationalities
of historic Lithuania.[160] It should be remembered that Wilno, which
according to the views of the Lithuanian nationalists should become
the capital of the new Lithuanian State, had only 1·9 per cent. of
Lithuanians, according to the German census of 1918 which by no
means favoured the Poles, and that the Polish character of Wilno
was recognized even by the mortal enemy of Poland, Ludendorff
(see p. 193).

The first declaration on the subject of Polish-Lithuanian relations
was made by Pilsudski on the 18th December, 1918, during the
reception of a delegation of Lithuanians living in Poland. Pilsudski
stated his views in the following manner :

> " The Poles are ready to help their sister Lithuania, but the
> Lithuanians should limit themselves to ethnographic Lithuania,
> because historic Lithuania has some districts which are purely
> Polish. So far as ethnographic Lithuania was concerned, the Poles
> have no wish to conquer it, but the Lithuanian imperialism has no
> chance of success, because it was favoured by the Germans." [161]

Pilsudski remained faithful to his programme during his whole
life, and on no occasion did the Poles encroach on the ethnographically Lithuanian territory. It is impossible to give here a full account
of Pilsudski's endeavours to establish friendly co-operation with the
Lithuanians and to revive the old free union. (We can refer here
to the relative diplomatic correspondence published in 1920 by
the Polish Ministry for Foreign Affairs.) [162] We will recall only a
few facts referring to this problem. For instance, in mid-December
1919, when the Bolsheviks approached the Wilno district, Pilsudski
proposed to organize in common with the Lithuanians the defence
of that city, but the Lithuanians refused. Before the liberation of
Wilno in April 1919 Pilsudski sent a delegation to Kaunas in order
to issue a common declaration with the Lithuanians on the restitution of the old Duchy of Lithuania. At that moment the Lithuanians
preferred to follow the advice of the Germans still occupying a great
part of the Lithuanian territory, and refused to comply with Pilsudski's suggestions. They demanded that purely Polish-Byelorussian

districts of Bialystok, Wolkowysk and Grodno be included in the Lithuanian State, which would have no connection with the Polish State. Thus began the tragic story of painful negotiations which brought no result save the weakening of the anti-Bolshevik front in Eastern Europe.

We have stated above some general facts necessary for a better understanding of the intricate issues raised by the advance of the Polish troops in the Eastern borderlands for the purpose of liberating them from Bolshevik occupation. At that time only the Poles were able to undertake this task, otherwise all the nationalities of this area, including the Lithuanians, would have undergone the same fate as the nationalities already subjugated by Red bayonets. Consequently any obstacle put in the way of this advance should be judged in the light of these indisputable facts.

Let us now see what were the reactions of the Western Powers to this surprising advance by the Polish troops in the East. These reactions depended entirely on the general policy of those powers in relation to the problem of Bolshevism and on their concern for safeguarding the interests of the future Russia after her liberation from the Bolshevik régime. On the one hand realizing the importance of Poland's resistance to Bolshevism, and on the other looking with some suspicion at any independent moves of Polish policy, the Powers were faced with a rather perplexing dilemma. It should be emphasized that in April 1919 the Polish Commission of the Peace Conference showed a marked tendency to postpone any recommendations relating to the Polish Eastern frontier beyond what was then wrongly considered the border of ethnographic Poland, that is to say that of the Congress Kingdom (see below, pp. 480 ff.). It might seem that some moves of the Entente Powers aimed to protect Lithuanian interests, but in the light of what we have said it is clear that the Allies neither believed in nor supported the final separation of the borderlands from Russia, and consequently it was more for the purpose of safeguarding the interests of the future Russia than those of Lithuania that they tried to prevent the extension of the area occupied by Polish troops. On the other side Pilsudski was aware of the political difficulties arising at the Peace Conference from the Polish advance in the East, but all he wanted to obtain from the Allies was that the liberation of Eastern territories might not be hampered by them. Nor did he wish to provoke any conflict with the Lithuanians beyond the border of ethnographic Lithuania. However, he was obliged to take into account the fact that the Lithuanians raised claims to territories with a Polish-Byelorussian majority and with practically no Lithuanian population; moreover, as Commander-in-Chief of the Polish army he had to secure lines of communication between Wilno and the rest of Poland. So when the Germans evacuated Grodno on the 28th April the town was immediately occupied by Polish troops and the Byelorussian Regiment, although organized by the Germans, went over to the Poles in spite of German endeavours to keep this regiment with the bulk of their forces in Lithuania. Thus the Poles secured possession of the railway line Warsaw–Grodno–Wilno, very important for their future operations against the Bolsheviks. Before the occupation of that town there were, however, some suggestions on the Allied side that the Polish troops should abstain from extending their zone of occupation. This appears clearly from the minutes of the Council of Foreign Ministers on the 26th April (" Lord Hardinge explained that he had seen Mr. Zaleski and he had done his utmost to persuade him to approach Mr. Paderewski in order to put a stop to all Polish operations in the direction of Grodno " [163]). It also appears clearly from a letter from Pilsudski to Paderewski dated 4th May in which he referred to the anxiety of Balfour caused by the occupation of Grodno by Polish troops.[164]

At the said meeting of the Council of Foreign Ministers it was also decided that

" the Council of Foreign Ministers should notify the Polish and Lithuanian representatives in Paris that whatever arrangements might be reached at the present moment in order to avoid hostilities in the regions of Wilno and Grodno would in no way affect the final decision. It was also agreed that the Allied and Associated Governments should notify their respective representatives in Warsaw to use their good offices with a view to an arrangement being reached between the Poles and Lithuanians in the regions of Wilno and Grodno in order to avoid hostilities."

So far as the demarcation line between Polish and Lithuanian areas was concerned, in the previous conversations in Warsaw on the 8th April between Pilsudski and the members of the Inter-Allied Commission to Poland, a proposal was made by Pilsudski to establish this line in a manner leaving on both sides an equal number of the Polish and Lithuanian minority (150,000 Poles on the Lithuanian side and 150,000 Lithuanians on the Polish side, these figures being based on the German census of 1916). This line ran : Olita–Koshedary–Czabiszki–Szyrwinty, and passed further along the road from Wilkomierz to Dunaburg, leaving the town of Wilkomierz and the road on the Lithuanian side. Sir Esme Howard, the British member of the Commission, then proposed another line which left the Northern, ethnographically Lithuanian tip of the Suwalki district on the Lithuanian side, but was less favourable to the Poles around Wilno because it did not go beyond the Wilja river to the

North of Wilno, of course leaving the town on the Polish side. On the other hand it was more favourable to the Poles in the central sector, as it ran 20 kilometres east to Kowno. Sir Esme's line was based also on ethnographical criteria, because it left an equal number of the Lithuanian and Polish minorities on each side (approximately 160,000), but it ruled out a common Polish-Latvian frontier on the Dvina river. Approximately the same line was advocated at that time by Ambassador Noulens, Chairman of the Inter-Allied Commission to Poland.[165] As we see, the Allied observers on the spot showed a much better understanding for the ethnographic and strategic position in that area than did the statesmen in Paris who looked with suspicion on anything they considered an encroachment on the integrity of the Russian territory.

As Polish-Lithuanian direct negotiations failed, the Supreme Council on the 18th June proposed a demarcation line much less favourable to the Poles than that suggested by Sir Esme Howard and the Inter-Allied Commission to Poland. The line originally proposed on the 18th June was traced parallel to the main railway line Grodno, Wilno-Dunabourg, running at a distance of a few kilometres to the West of that railway. This line did not take into consideration either military or ethnographic criteria, leaving to the Poles only some military bases and supply lines without an adequate hinterland. The line was ignored in practice, and in view of the complaints of the Lithuanians the matter was again brought before the Supreme Council on the 10th July. We can judge in what spirit from Clemenceau's statement : " The Poles had made an advance in Lithuania in defiance of the orders of the Conference. He thought that Marshal Foch should be requested on behalf of the Council to order the Poles to withdraw." [166] But when the question was submitted to a more careful study by Marshal Foch's staff, it appeared that the line of the 18th June aroused considerable objections among the Allied experts, and a new line was adopted by the Council on the 26th July which was traced further to the West, at a distance of approximately 10 kilometres from the railway line. This was later known as Foch line.[167] The main alteration concerned the area around Suwalki, Augustow and Seyny, which was evacuated by the Germans and to which Poland had indisputable rights, these districts being unquestionably ethnographically Polish. Moreover it was an area in which, according to the decision of the Polish Territorial Commission, the Poles were authorized by the Peace Conference to establish a permanent administration. But while on the one side an organ of the Peace Conference took a decision favourable to the Poles, the Supreme Council took a different one a few weeks later, which shows the extent of the confusion prevailing at the Peace Conference. At the Meeting of the Council of Foreign Ministers on the 24th May [168] a characteristic exchange of views took place, showing the spirit in which some delegates approached the whole problem. In particular it was the American Secretary of State, Lansing, the foremost advocate of the principle of the territorial integrity of Russia, who opposed the advance of the Polish troops beyond what was considered by him the border of ethnographic Poland.

Mr. Lansing: " It should be provided that the area around Suwalki and Augustow, which was Lithuanian, should be occupied only by Lithuanian troops and not by Polish troops." In his opinion, " the Poles should be prevented from occupying Lithuanian territory just as much as the Germans."

Colonel George, who appeared as the representative of Marshal Foch, observed that there were no Lithuanian troops available and that moreover " the zone to be evacuated by the Germans, including Suwalki, Augustow and Seyny, had been attributed by the Polish Territorial Commission." He further observed that " the line of demarcation was intended to protect the Polish troops on the Wilno front." But Lansing persisted in his opposition, stating peremptorily that " no Pole should be allowed to advance North of the ethnic line. The intervening region between the line of demarcation and the ethnic line would, under these conditions, be occupied by the Lithuanians," and when Colonel George repeated that " no Lithuanian troops would be available to occupy that area," Mr. Lansing said that " under those circumstances the Germans should not be withdrawn," showing the lengths to which he was ready to go provided that the Poles might not occupy the area in question. Such was the background of the decision of the Supreme Council on the 18th June line.

On what one-sided and biased information was based the opinion of Mr. Lansing appears from the debates of the Council of Five on the 26th July, when the problem of the districts of Suwalki and Seyny was again discussed in connection with the establishment of Marshal Foch line. Clemenceau stated first that the territory was mostly Lithuanian, but when the opinion of the experts was asked, " the American, British, French and Italian experts agreed that the population in these districts was mainly Polish "; Balfour then declared that " he had been given the impression that the Poles had defied the orders of the Conference, but he was prepared to accept the explanation given and to agree to the line proposed by Marshal Foch in view of the unanimous opinion that the territory which would be assigned to the Poles was Polish in character." [169]

The Allies' attitude was bound to stiffen the Lithuanian resistance to any reasonable compromise with the Poles. The full consequences of these moves of Allied policy will appear only in the subsequent period. It is interesting to note that on this point the Allies pursued the policy inaugurated by the Germans, consisting in supporting the Lithuanian nationalism against the Polish plans to bring about close co-operation between all the nationalities of this region, equally menaced by German and Russian imperialistic policy.

On the other side, in spite of the marked hostility of the Lithuanian Government towards Poland, the latter abstained from any act of external aggression against the ethnographic part of Lithuania. At the most difficult moment for Lithuania, in autumn 1919, when German-Russian troops under Bermondt took Radsivilishki and Shavli, interning the Lithuanian authorities at those places, the Polish Acting Foreign Minister gave the British Envoy in Warsaw, Sir Horace Rumbold, on the 12th October

> " a formal and spontaneous assurance that the Poles would take no advantage of the difficult situation thus created for the Lithuanians, who were at liberty to denude the Lithuanian-Polish frontier of troops if they so desired. The Polish Government would not do anything which could in any way favour the Russo-German adventurers of von der Goltz and Bermondt. Poland wished to be on the best of terms with Lithuania." [170]

In a declaration made by the same Acting Minister for Foreign Affairs to all Allied representatives and the Polish Diplomatic Missions abroad, it was emphasized that " Poland would not take an attitude hostile towards Lithuania and would not assist even indirectly the plots of German militarism." The declaration also expressed the hope that " a moment would come when the real aspirations of the Lithuanian people would find their expression in, setting up a Government which would represent the majority of the Lithuanian people and would not base its activity, as was the case with the present Lithuanian Government, exclusively on anti-Polish propaganda. The Lithuanians would then appreciate the attitude of Poland, which avoided anything which might provoke bloodshed between the Poles and the Lithuanians." [171]

It should also be pointed out that whenever the question of a plebiscite in the province of Wilno was raised by the Poles in negotiations with the Lithuanians the latter always declined such proposals, finding them " inadmissible " (see, for instance, the report of Minister Wasilewski, sent on a special mission to Kaunas, to the Polish Under-Secretary of State for Foreign Affairs, dated 17th September, 1919).[172]

Summing up, we can say that the Allies lent no support to the Polish endeavours to bring about a reasonable understanding with Lithuania, as they limited themselves to the establishment of a demarcation line between the Polish and Lithuanian forces, hampering the Poles in laying the foundations of a system of closer co-operation between two nations so near to one another by tradition, political position and common dangers. The Allies played for time, expecting the reappearance of a new Russia, a hope which did not materialize. Eventually it was the Bolsheviks who benefited from the tension which the Allies could have removed.

Evacuation of the Baltic countries by the Germans

The question of the co-operation of the Polish forces for the purpose of removing the German troops from the Baltic States was another instance in which the Allies showed the lack of any definite line of policy. At its meetings in mid-September 1919 the Supreme Council discussed the question of how far the presence of the German forces presented a danger to the Allied cause. At the meeting on the 15th September [173] Lloyd George, referring to it, said that on the one hand there " was a set of people who said that the Germans were a great force with which to meet Bolshevism," and on the other hand Paderewski took the view, on behalf of the Polish Government, that " to utilize the Germans was playing with fire." In fact Poland had for many months warned of the dangers arising from the presence of German and Russian volunteer troops in the Baltic countries.[174] Lloyd George expressed his personal opinion, agreeing with that of the Polish Government, and said that " the Germans ought to be cleared." Marshal Foch, called upon to state his views, said that " under the terms of the Armistice the Allied and Associated Powers had the right to demand the German retirement from the Baltic provinces," but he added that the sending of Allied troops to disembark in the Baltic " was out of the question." Clemenceau then recommended " restoration of the Blockade of Germany and that action should be taken on the Rhine with action in Poland," and Lloyd George agreed that the Poles might be " profitably employed in this manner." The only objection was raised by the American representative, Polk, who said that " the presence of the Polish troops might not be acceptable to the Lithuanians."

At the next meeting in the afternoon of the same day, Paderewski declared that " the Polish army was at the service of the Conference," and a resolution was carried by the Supreme Council according to which

" it was agreed that General Henrys (Head of the French Military

Mission in Poland) should be entrusted by the Allied and Associated Powers, as their representative, with control of the evacuation of the German troops. Acting in the same quality, he shall have authority to use the Polish Army in case the Germans do not comply with the demand for evacuation.

" In placing the Polish Army at the disposal of the Allies, Mr. Paderewski indicated at the same time that there should be no interference by the Polish Army with the local governments of the Baltic Provinces."

Again the only objection was raised by the American representative, Polk, who saw danger in the use of Polish troops as it might provoke a war between Poland and Germany. The day following the above-mentioned resolution by the Supreme Council Polk addressed a letter to Clemenceau in which he stated that " it would be unwise to authorize the use of the Polish troops against the German forces in Lithuania," and he asked for the postponement of any decision relating to such use.

This opinion was shared by the British War Office, as appears from the declarations of General Gough at the meeting of the Supreme Council on the 17th September, and from the War Office letter of the 30th October, 1919, countenanced by Lord Curzon.[175] At the same time the British delegates in Paris agreed with Marshal Foch that should force be required the Polish troops should be employed, and Sir Eyre Crowe declared on the 13th October to Marshal Foch that " his Government had strongly supported the proposal to employ the Polish Army and had sincerely regretted the decision of the Supreme Council objecting to this measure " due to " the American refusal to agree to this action." [176] The Latvian Government, being directly concerned in the matter, also expressed its desire for the Polish military co-operation,[177] and on the 19th October a Latvian Delegation headed by the Foreign Minister, Meierovits, went to Warsaw to negotiate with Poland the terms of such co-operation. On the 23rd October Poland recognized *de facto* the Latvian Republic. Fortunately for the Allies the Germans eventually consented to the withdrawal of their troops from the Baltic States, but a good opportunity was missed by the Allies to bring about closer co-operation between the nations of this area, combining their forces for common defence against the enemies endangering their independence. There is no doubt that the American opposition to the use of Polish troops in that area was due not so much to fear of the German reactions as to the general attitude towards the Western borderlands of Russia, whose right to independence seemed questionable to the U.S.A. at that time. So far as the opposition of the British military authorities was concerned, it can be explained by their wish to keep the Baltic countries under complete British control and the fear that the Polish troops might be the forerunners of French influence there. This opinion was mistaken, because Poland wished above all to co-operate with Great Britain in Eastern Europe and made several attempts to come to an agreement with the British on a common policy towards Russia.

Nevertheless, a few months later the Poles had an opportunity to show that they were ready to help their neighbours in difficult hours. By virtue of an agreement with the Latvian Government, reached at the end of December 1919, the Poles assisted the Latvians in the military operations on the Dvina. On the 3rd January, 1920, Polish troops entered the town of Dunaburg from the South, and the Latvian troops from the North. Poland surrendered to Latvia all Latvian territories liberated by her from the Bolsheviks, including the province of Letgalia which had an important Polish minority. A military convention was signed between Poland and Latvia on the 16th January, 1920. There is no doubt that the Polish military assistance to Latvia and the presence of the Polish forces there greatly contributed to the preservation of the independence of the Baltic States, a fact which is not denied by anyone. This Polish action should be taken in connection with the simultaneous endeavours of the Poles to establish the Baltic Union, and attempts to use the good offices of the Baltic States in the settlement of the outstanding territorial questions between Poland and Lithuania (The Baltic Conference in Helsingfors, 19th January, 1920).[178]

First agreement between Poland and Petlura

In midsummer 1919 the Polish front in the East seemed to have attained the main military targets and become stabilized, in the North on the River Berezina, further to the South in the Polesie Marshes, and in Northern Volhynia on the Rivers Ptycz and Uborts. In August an armistice was concluded between the Polish headquarters and the Ukrainians fighting under Ataman Petlura, and thus the military operations between the Poles and Ukrainians ended. Petlura, who failed to obtain from Denikin recognition of the Ukrainian independence and had to fight against Denikin and the Bolsheviks, was eventually forced to ask for Poland's protection. An agreement signed between Poland's and Petlura's representatives in October 1919 stated that the Ukraine, whose national existence was menaced, asked Poland for assistance in her struggle for liberation. The interests of the Ukrainian nation could be secured only through close union with the Polish State. The Ukrainian Government renounced its claims to Eastern Galicia and, taking into consideration the secular influence of the Polish civilization in

Western Volhynia, agreed that the part up to the River Styr should become an integral part of the Polish State. The Ukrainian army would be organized under Polish command. The Polish population in the Ukraine would enjoy full rights there and the same rights would be granted to the Ukrainians in Poland.[179] It is evident that those who considered that the national rights of the Ukrainians might have been better safeguarded under the Soviet régime bitterly criticized that agreement, regarding it as a betrayal. It is enough to refer to the opinion of Professor Carr who, speaking about this agreement, says that " Petlura cynically abandoned the Ukrainian claims to Eastern Galicia in exchange for ruling the Ukraine as a satellite unit in a Polish Empire,"(?) and that the agreement "marked the ultimate bankruptcy of Ukrainian bourgeois nationalism, since the rudimentary feelings of the Ukrainian peasantry had been stimulated mainly by hostility to the Polish landowners." [180] Did not the Bolsheviks eventually abandon the same territories to Poland? Did not the physical destruction of millions of Ukrainians by deportation and famine follow the establishment of the Soviet régime in the Ukraine? Were not the conditions of the Ukrainian minority considerably better in the Polish State than in the Soviet Union, whatever one may say about the unreasonably centralistic policy pursued by Warsaw?

The full implications of the agreement with Petlura, subsequently considerably modified in the favour of the Ukraine, did not appear until 1920. Before committing themselves to a definite line of policy the Poles wished to ascertain the views of the Western Allies on the future of Russia and the rôle assigned by them to Poland in Eastern Europe. It was above all in Great Britain that Poland tried to find support for her political plans in Eastern Europe. In the instructions sent to the Polish Minister in Great Britain, Prince Sapieha, on the 20th June, 1919, we find the first allusions to the possibility of close co-operation between Poland and Great Britain. Poland considered that Great Britain should play the first part in organizing the future Russia on Western liberal lines, and offered Great Britain her services for this purpose. At the same time she warned Great Britain against any co-operation with Germany in Russia, because in that way dangerous competition would be fostered.[181]

Pilsudski and Denikin

But at that time there was little prospect of the Polish offers being accepted by Great Britain. The successes first of Koltchak and then of Denikin in the late summer 1919 seemed to foreshadow the imminent fall of the Bolshevik régime. Pilsudski neither believed in nor desired the victory of the White Russian generals. He never shared the illusions of the West on the possibility of the White Russians regaining control of Russia. His political views on that matter Pilsudski frankly stated in an interview granted to a French newspaper, *Le Matin* (15th February, 1920). He said then that the Entente did not dare to approach the problem of Russia in a proper way, but pursued a policy of half-measures and behaved like an ostrich. He further said that "it is impossible to revive the old Russia at any price by her old statesmen. New formulas must be found. One must have the courage to realize that great changes have taken place in Eastern Europe."

As a soldier also Pilsudski had a poor opinion of the fighting value of Denikin's troops. He based his opinions on the report of his military representative, General Karnicki, sent to Denikin's headquarters at the end of September 1919. We have an interesting account in this connection in Colonel Beck's papers; he relates a conversation between Pilsudski and Minister Eden in Warsaw in April 1935.

> "Your Intelligence Service" [said Pilsudski], "based all its hopes on Denikin and Wrangel. I was asked to co-operate with them at any price. Wishing to have an idea of the value of these troops I sent there one of my generals who was far from being one of the most brilliant but who had previously served in the Russian Army, and I gave him a few weeks to inform me by telegram how much one could rely on the value of these troops and on the 'White' leaders. The said general wired me after a week that these troops were not worth much and that, moreover, they were going to pieces, and yet he was an ancient comrade of these Russian commanders. At the same time, however, the Intelligence Service based all its plans on entirely opposite conclusions. You know the rest." [182]

It was not an idea which Pilsudski had only formed after Denikin's defeats. We have a good witness on this point in the person of the British Military Attaché in Warsaw, General Carton de Wiart, who in his *Memoirs* left the following account :

> "General Briggs, who had been my commanding officer in the Imperial Light Horse, came to see me in Warsaw. He was Chief of the British Military Mission to Denikin, who commanded the White Russian troops. . . .
>
> "I took Briggs to see Pilsudski and explain the situation, and to ask him personally for his co-operation. During the interview I could see that Pilsudski was not in the least impressed by what Briggs was telling him, and when Briggs had left Pilsudski said that Denikin would fail to get to Moscow and worse still that he would be soon in the Black Sea. In view of Denikin's rapid advance this seemed a fantastic statement but Pilsudski's judgment rarely failed, and I had such confidence in him that I reported this at once to the War Office. I returned home to report and Mr. Winston

Churchill, who was then at the War Office, asked me to lunch. ... It was the first time that I had met Mr. Churchill. ... Mr. Churchill wished me to get the Poles to join in Denikin's offensive, but I repeated Pilsudski's warnings, and I remember Mrs. Winston Churchill saying: ' You had much better listen to General de Wiart.' I hastened to point out that it was not my opinion that I was giving but Pilsudski's, and that he never put me wrong." [183]

As we have said above, Pilsudski's attitude towards Denikin was based on the reports of General Karnicki's mission to Denikin. This mission arrived at Taganrog, General Denikin's headquarters, on the 26th September, 1919. It is true that it was received in a cordial and ostentatious manner, as General Denikin states in his *Memoirs* and his answer to General Kutrzeba's book, but the political results of the mission were rather poor. The allusions made by Denikin to future close relations between restored Russia and Poland aroused Polish suspicions that he would be unwilling to recognize the full independence of the Polish State, the more so as the principle of one and indivisible Russia seemed to prevail among Denikin's political advisers. Marked hostility towards all national movements for liberation, and above all to Petlura, imbued all Russian declarations, although the Polish representatives were able to ascertain on the spot the strength of the Ukrainian movement in the peasant masses.

As appears from General Karnicki's own declarations in 1936 to a Polish paper, the instructions he received from Pilsudski were the following : establishment of a demarcation line between the Polish and Denikin's troops, no political agreements, military assistance to Denikin to depend on clarification of the Russian attitude towards the future Polish-Russian territorial settlement. This did not mean, however, that a definite Polish-Russian delimitation should be negotiated with Denikin, as it was obvious that he had not sufficient authority to make such an agreement. In other words Karnicki's mission was of a purely exploratory nature. In his first reports General Karnicki already stated that Denikin's army had no reserves, that his infantry was of poor fighting value, that the soldiers were undisciplined and were prepared to fight only if allowed to plunder the civil population. In General Karnicki's opinion all Denikin's successes were due exclusively to his technical superiority and to the Allied equipment.

But it was the political programme of the White Russian leaders which aroused the greatest objections from the Poles. It was obvious that the Russians cared only for Polish military assistance and wished to impose their own terms on Poland after having reached Moscow. A very characteristic exchange of views took place on the 7th October between Major Przezdziecki, Karnicki's Chief of Staff, and Baron Nolden, Head of the Political Department at Denikin's headquarters. The latter stated that he saw the future Polish-Russian frontier as roughly corresponding to the boundaries of the former Congress Kingdom (without the district of Chelm) and without Eastern Galicia. Nolden stated that the territories of historical Lithuania were purely Russian and he rejected any idea of holding a plebiscite there. Denikin himself avoided any commitment on the future Polish-Russian territorial settlement, and General Karnicki did not press the matter further, seeing no possibility of obtaining a satisfactory answer from Denikin.[184]

If, consequently, the chances of bringing about collaboration between the Poles and White Russian generals were slender at the time of Denikin's successes, they were practically non-existent after the latter's failure to reach Moscow (Pilsudski said to Mackinder that Denikin's advance on Moscow was " in the nature of a great adventure "). Yet the Allied endeavours continued up to the end of 1919, although it was more and more evident that the White Russian movement would not be able to play the rôle assigned to it by the Western Powers. Such was above all the purpose of the visit of Mackinder to Warsaw in mid-December. During this visit Mackinder was greatly impressed by Pilsudski, of whom he said in his report that " he has an uncanny fellow-Slavonic insight into the realities of the Russian position " (let us remember here a sarcastic statement by Lloyd George about Pilsudski a few months before : " An idealist without any practical ideas "—see p. 401). In this conversation Pilsudski " expressed the opinion that at the present moment the Bolshevik military organization was superior to that of General Denikin. He asserted that General Denikin would never be able to overthrow the Bolshevik régime." [185]

In view of the falsity of the hopes of the Entente in the defeat of Bolshevism by the efforts of the White Russian generals, Pilsudski wished to ascertain whether the Western Powers saw the possibility of a third solution of the problems of Eastern Europe, that is to say neither the maintenance of the Bolshevik régime nor the restoration of a reactionary Russia. Pilsudski considered that this third solution might consist in the liberation of Eastern Europe from Bolshevism and the establishment of a new order based on the wishes of the nationalities and populations concerned. He feared that a lasting peace could hardly be attained by an agreement with the Bolsheviks, but there was no other alternative, to his mind, should the Allies continue to pursue their policy of half-measures.

Polish proposals to the Supreme Council

Such was the background of the proposals put forward by Poland before the Supreme Council on the 15th September, 1919.[186] Very characteristically it was to Great Britain that Poland turned for advice in the first instance. In a conversation between Paderewski and Lloyd George on the 14th September, the former asked the latter whether the Allied and Associated Powers would encourage the Poles sending an army of 500,000 men to Moscow. According to Lloyd George, who at that time seemed to be interested in the plan, " Mr. Paderewski's attitude had been perfectly reasonable. He said that if the Allied and Associated Powers wished the Poles to advance to Moscow he was prepared to do it. The cost, however, would amount to 30,000,000 marks a day. Later, he said he could do it for £600,000 sterling a day but this would really mean £1,000,000 a day."

This proposal should be taken in connection with a declaration made by Pilsudski to Mackinder in the above-mentioned conversation with the latter in Warsaw on the 16th December, 1919. Pilsudski said that " he regarded the Bolsheviks as being in none too good case and was decidedly of the opinion that the Polish Army alone could go to Moscow next spring, but from a political point of view he asked himself what he should do when and if he got there."

This declaration shows that the Poles did not desire to advance into the heart of Russia unless carrying out a common plan of the Allied Powers, previously agreed with them. The answer to the question whether the Allies would be prepared to grant Poland their political and financial support for such action was of vital importance to Poland. Should the answer be negative it meant that the only possibility of overthrowing the Bolshevik régime would vanish, and consequently Poland would be obliged to adjust her political plans to this contingency.

The answer was negative. It was primarily the French, who, without being aware at the time of all the implications of their attitude, opposed the Polish plan. Clemenceau took the view " that the worst thing to do was to attempt to conquer Russia by means of the Poles. If the British or French forces were operating, it was known that they were merely acting in the interest of Europe, but if the Polish troops were employed it would rally the whole of Russia against them." A similar view was taken by Marshal Foch, who said " that the Conference was faced with a very dangerous proposal from several points of view. If it were a question of action by a Great State fully settled, the matter would be different, but this was not the case with Poland : consequently, he did not think he could advise action by the Poles." Should the violence of the French reaction be ascribed to the fact that the Poles had first approached the British on that issue, and that it was Lloyd George who raised it before the Supreme Council although the French considered Poland as their zone of political influence? Did the French fear that within the framework of such a plan the British would be able to become a decisive factor in the affairs of Eastern Europe? It is difficult to say, because no French diplomatic correspondence for this period has yet been published. The British did not insist, and the Supreme Council decided to appeal to the Polish forces only should the Germans not comply with the demand for their evacuation of the Baltic countries. As we have said before, this decision was subsequently revised owing to American opposition (pp. 463 ff.).

Receiving the negative answer from the Supreme Council Paderewski asked, when invited to attend the next meeting, " what were the plans of the Allies " as " Poland could not fight indefinitely." ... " The Polish Government will settle their plans in accordance with those of the Conference. Poland cannot afford to keep up or increase her military establishments. She is a new State and is lacking in raw materials and war factories. If the decision of the Allies should be for peace he was most anxious to know this as soon as possible, for very advantageous peace terms had been offered him by the Bolsheviks." In conclusion he emphasized the importance of a rapid decision by the conference " whatever it might be."

The answer to this question was hardly satisfactory. It was given by Clemenceau, but Lloyd George agreed to it. Clemenceau said that " he would not make peace nor would he make war He suggested that Poland could carry out the first part of the proposed programme (evacuation by the Germans of the Baltic countries) and by that time the Bolshevik situation would be clarified." This ambiguous statement showed clearly that the Allied Powers had no policy at all on Eastern European questions and preferred to rely on the White Russians in whose victory they still believed. In such circumstances the rôle they assigned to the Poles was secondary, hardly corresponding to that of a military factor of the first importance. According to Churchill's definition, used in a conversation with Clemenceau, the Poles were " the left wing of Denikin's army against the Bolsheviks." [187]

Churchill, who at that time was much nearer to the French point of view that to that of the British Prime Minister so far as the problem of intervention in Russia was concerned, in his *General Survey to the Cabinet* of the 22nd September, 1919, explained which rôle should be assigned to the Poles. Stating incorrectly, first of all, " that the Polish front now stands in most places on the Russian soil " (as a matter of fact, at no time during the 1919-20 war did the Polish armies stand on territory ethnographically Russian), Churchill said that " the Poles are now inclined to suggest one of two courses to the Allies :

"(a)   That the Allies should finance a Polish army of 500,000 men which should advance into the heart of Russia and capture Moscow, or

"(b)   That the Poles should make a peace with the Bolsheviks.

" Either of these courses at the present moment would be injurious. The advance of the hereditary enemy of Russia to Moscow would rouse whatever sense of nationalism is latent in those parts of Russia under the Bolshevik international régime. Moreover, the project is not one for which any of the Allied Powers would be justified by their own public opinion in furnishing funds. On the other hand, if the Poles make a separate and precipitate peace with the Bolsheviks, the Bolshevik army opposite the Polish front, which is the third strongest Bolshevik army in the field, could swiftly be transferred to the attack of Denikin. ... It seems therefore clear that our policy at the present moment should be to persuade the Poles to carry on for a few months as they are doing, i.e. fighting and defeating the Bolsheviks on their borders where and when they can, without preparing either for a decisive advance into the heart of Russia or for a separate peace." [188]

For the time being we leave aside the question whether, from a military point of view, it was possible for the Poles to pursue a purely defensive war against the Bolsheviks, as this matter will be dealt with later in connection with similar suggestions of the Allied Powers in 1920. Let us observe only that it should suffice to look at the map to reach the conclusion that a purely defensive strategy in the geographical conditions of Eastern Europe would have placed the Poles in a position of definite inferiority, leaving to the Bolsheviks the choice of the moment and the place for a decisive battle once their concentrations had been completed behind the lines. Far more important at that time were political considerations. On the one hand the Allies wished Poland to continue her operations against the Bolsheviks, but on the other they abstained from revealing their political plans concerning Eastern Europe, and offered the Poles no serious guarantees that their rights would be safeguarded in the event of a White Russian victory. Churchill, who criticized the Allies for " the complete abeyance of any definite or decided policy " and said that " in result they made neither peace nor war," was at the same time against any policy for the dismemberment of Russia and advised that " every effort should, therefore, be made to guide affairs into a channel which leads into a federalized Russia without prejudice either to local autonomy or the principle of general unity." He did not at that time believe that Poland could withstand alone the Bolshevik armies, and placed all his hopes in the victory of Denikin's troops assisted by the Poles :

> " The idea that Poland will serve as a barrier to such danger is illusory. The idea that by standing on the defensive in the East until every other anti-Bolshevik force has been destroyed, she will be able to maintain a strong attitude towards Germany in the West is equally ill-founded. What is the wisdom of a policy which seeks to strengthen Poland by Allied money and munitions and yet calmly acquiesces in the destruction of Denikin and the consequent liberation of the main Bolshevik forces to treble and quadruple the enemies with whom Poland has to contend."

Polish approaches to Great Britain

Although advising the Poles to continue military operations against the Bolsheviks, the British Government was at the same time withdrawing its troops from Caucasus and Northern Russia, without previous warning to its Eastern Allies. This hardly facilitated the Polish position. The consequences were emphasized in a letter from L. Skrzynski, then Under Secretary of State for Foreign Affairs, to Sir Percy Wyndham, British Chargé d'Affaires in Warsaw, dated 13th August, 1919 : " This evacuation (from Murmansk) ... will result in the Bolshevik troops unexpectedly pouring to our front and prolonging our war against the Bolsheviks." [189]

The Poles had every reason to believe that Great Britain was leaving Eastern Europe to its own devices, and that she would not intervene in disputes which might arise between restored Russia and her neighbours. Relating a conversation with Prime Minister Paderewski, Sir Horace Rumbold, British Envoy to Poland, says in his telegram of the 24th October, 1919, that he " has been much struck by the manner in which the Polish Government appears to be preoccupied with the Russian question." He further says :

> " My impression is that as the Bolshevik régime seems to be nearing its end, the Poles are getting nervous about the régime which will replace it. They are uncertain whether General Denikin when he has once established himself at Moscow and overthrown the Bolshevists will develop reactionary tendencies. Such tendencies could not fail unfavourably to affect this country. The Poles have not said this to me in so many words, but that is the impression left on my mind.
>
> " The above impression will also explain why the Poles do not want to face a reconstituted Russia alone, but would like to have some understanding with, or be able to count on the support of a liberal power such as Great Britain. They would argue that France is concerned to obtain repayment of the large sums of money owing to her by Russia and will not much mind the régime set up in that country provided she recovers the debt due to her."

In these circumstances what was the advice given to the Poles by the British Envoy? In conversation with Paderewski Sir Horace told him that in his opinion

> " the Poles would eventually have to a certain extent to choose between their two great neighbours. They would naturally wish to be on good terms with all countries surrounding them but it would seem more natural that they should entertain cordial relations with Russia than with Germany. They knew the Russians well and had penetrated Russia in an economic sense before the war. Their commercial relations with their Eastern neighbours were bound to be very close for Russia will be their principal outlet." [190]

It appears from this declaration that the British diplomat was noncommittal at the moment when the chances of Denikin seemed to him to be very high. But Sir Horace's optimism and belief in an imminent collapse of Bolshevism were, as we know, not shared by Pilsudski :

> " I have since learnt " [he says], " that General Pilsudski himself selected a nonentity who has been sent to General Denikin (see p. 467) because he thought that such a person would be better able to find out what were the views of the Russian headquarters with regard to the future policy of Russia: in this question the Chief of State and Mr. Paderewski did not see eye to eye. The former is anti-Russian and not inclined to forget his exile in Siberia. Moreover he has not great faith in any Russian and doubts whether General Denikin will really get to Moscow and overthrow the Bolshevist régime."

We find more direct allusions to the possibility of a close British-Polish collaboraion in two conversations between Skrzynski and Sir Horace (Report of the British Minister of the 20th October), and the most important of all, one between Pilsudski and Sir Horace on the 6th November, 1919 (Report of the 7th November).

In the first of his conversations Skrzynski pointed out that " even when the Bolshevist régime shall have been swept away, the anti-revolutionary party will need foreign support in reorganizing Russia and starting her afresh." Taking the view that " the Russians would be incapable of discharging these functions themselves," he stated that " only two Great Powers in Europe enter into consideration as far as Poland is concerned. Those are Great Britain and Germany." He rejected collaboration with Germany and in conclusion stated " that the co-operation of Great Britain and Poland is essential in the future work of reorganizing Russia," and for this purpose he considered that it would be advantageous " if a confidential exchange of views were to take place between the two

Governments with regard to Russia." Skrzynski added that " he would not wish the Polish Government to commit themselves to any action in that country (Russia) which may in any way hamper Great Britain." [191]

A still more explicit offer of collaboration was made by Pilsudski in his conversation with Sir Horace on the 6th November. At the beginning of this conversation Pilsudski observed that " he had noticed for some time a certain obstruction on the part of Great Britain in matters which concerned Poland," at Sir Horace's request specifying : the questions of Eastern Galicia and Danzig, and the warning not to advance to Dzwinsk (Dunaburg), which would have allowed the Polish troops to link up with the Letts and Esthonians and " so form a continuous barrier against the Bolsheviks " (see p. 464). Taking the same view as Skrzynski, that even in the event of the destruction of the Bolshevik régime it would be up to foreign powers to undertake the economic and administrative reconstruction of Russia, and that " there was only one other great country (than Germany) which could take in hand the reconstruction of Russia, and that was Great Britain," he said that " he did not know what was the policy of His Majesty's Government with regard to Russia."

Stating that " Poland had nothing to fear from a material point of view from Russia, for she knew that Russia was bound to be very weak for a long time to come " and that " the Poles had no aggressive intentions towards Russia," Pilsudski observed that, on the other hand, " Poland was too weak in an economic sense to organize Russia herself. She could do so only in collaboration with another Power, meaning Great Britain."

A very important passage of this conversation referred to the question of the Eastern frontier of Poland. Pilsudski explained " that he would not be able to call upon the Polish troops to continue their present effort against the Bolsheviks if these troops felt that the territory they had recovered from the Bolsheviks was eventually to be handed back to Russia." His solution would be to ask the inhabitants of the districts at present occupied by the Polish troops under which régime they wished to come in the future (see similar suggestions made by Pilsudski in his conversation with Mackinder, p. 455).

Pilsudski further complained of inadequate Allied supplies for the Polish Army, saying that " it appeared as if Poland had been left by the Allies to her own devices, both in dealing with Germany and in dealing with the Bolsheviks. That being the case, he drew the conclusion that it was for Poland to help herself and make her own arrangements."

So far as concerned possible arrangements with the Bolsheviks, Pilsudski said that " Poland might declare that she would not interest herself in the affairs of Russia provided that the Bolsheviks left the Poles alone on their side." The British envoy defined this attitude as " an equivalent of neutrality on the part of Poland.'

Sir Horace's answer seemed to point out that Great Britain had no definite line of policy in relation to Eastern Europe.

> " I reminded General Pilsudski " [said Sir Horace], " that Great Britain had just come through a most exhausting war, during which all the energies of the Government and of the country had been diverted from the consideration of internal problems. These problems now called for solution, and for that reason alone it was not surprising that the Government had probably not had the necessary time to formulate their future policy in Eastern Europe." [192]

This conversation should be taken in connection with a very outspoken declaration by Pilsudski on the 8th October, 1919, to *The Times*. In the last passage of this interview Pilsudski said that should Poland be obliged to come to terms either with the Germans or with the Bolsheviks it would mean that she was unable to carry out her mission. Pilsudski obviously had in mind a position in which Poland, feeling abandoned by the Western Powers, would be obliged to look after her own interests exclusively, whatever might be the consequences of such an attitude for the West.

The outcome of these Polish attempts to achieve closer collaboration with Great Britain seemed completely negative, as there was no response to them from the British side.

Bolshevik peace-feelers

This explains an incident which throws interesting light on Pilsudski's policy at that time—the negotiations which took place between Polish and Bolshevik representatives in autumn 1919. A Bolshevik delegation went to Mikaszewicze, near Luck (Volhynia), staying from 9th October to 2nd December, 1919, to discuss the question of the exchange of prisoners and hostages. This delegation was headed by Dr. Julian Marchlewski, a prominent Polish Communist having wide connections with the Polish Left. The Bolsheviks obviously had far-reaching plans much beyond the official scope of the negotiations, namely the discussion of an armistice and perhaps of a peace treaty. Louis Fischer was the first writer to disclose some details of these negotiations, but he had at his disposal only Soviet sources.[193] It cannot be said that the Allies were kept completely in the dark about the Soviet intentions, because Sir Horace Rumbold tells in one of his reports that he was informed by the Under Secretary of State, Skrzynski, that the Soviet Commissioner had declared at the first meeting with the Polish Commission that he had full powers to discuss with the Poles the peace terms.[194] But the British envoy received no details of the attitude taken by the Poles in the course of the negotiations, although he was warned by Pilsudski, in the above-mentioned conversation on the 6th November, that " it was for Poland to help herself." We know the instructions given by Pilsudski to his representative, Captain Boerner, on the 3rd November, 1919, and the whole political background of the negotiations from a book published in 1937 by General Kutrzeba, who had access to Captain Boerner's Diary and papers. It appears clearly from these documents that Pilsudski did not at that time wish to discuss peace terms with the Bolsheviks, because he did not believe in the sincerity of their offers, and on the other hand he realized that in view of the attitude of the Entente Powers towards Bolshevism at that time an armistice and peace negotiations would have brought about a rupture between the Western Powers and Poland. In too many questions still unsettled Poland depended on the goodwill of the Entente Powers; it suffices to mention the plebiscite in Upper Silesia and the settlement of the statute of Danzig. Unwilling to go very far for the time being, Pilsudski wished above all to test the ground and make quite clear to Lenin that the Polish policy could not be identified with the policy of the Western Powers basing their hopes on the revival of the old Russia. He ordered Boerner to inform Lenin that the Polish troops would not advance beyond the line held by them, but at the same time he stressed Poland's community of interests with the nations fighting against the Bolsheviks for the right of self-determination. He strongly advised the Soviet Government to surrender Dzwinsk (Dunaburg) to the Latvians, and declared that he would support the Latvian claims to that city (as we know, the Polish troops helped the Latvians to liberate Dunaburg from the Bolsheviks at the beginning of January 1920). He also asked the Bolsheviks to abstain from attacking Petlura. On the other side Captain Boerner was to declare to the Soviet representative :

" Poland is not and does not wish to be the gendarme of Europe. Poland desires to defend only and exclusively her own interests. She takes her bearings in policy from what is consonant with the Polish State reason. It cannot agree with Polish interests to support Denikin in his struggle against Bolshevism."

Marchlewski went to Moscow to confer with Lenin, and returned on the 21st November. We will not go into the technical details of the negotiations, but there were some important political matters on which there was a complete disparity of views between Pilsudski and Lenin. Above all, Pilsudski refused to discuss the merits of the dispute between Petlura and the Bolsheviks, but declared that he would defend Petlura if the Bolsheviks attacked the latter.

At that stage Pilsudski interrupted the negotiations, as he saw no further advantage in continuing them, realizing that the primary aim of the Bolsheviks was to bring about the severance of the links between Poland and the Entente Powers, that is to say the political and military isolation of Poland. Moreover, there was too big a gap between Poland's attitude towards the problem of the liberation of the nationalities of Russia and that of Bolshevik Russia, bent on the subjugation of these nationalities. Also in late November 1919 Denikin had his first serious setbacks and it was obvious that Polish anticipations that he would not reach Moscow would come true.

Causes of Denikin's defeat

Denikin's failure was due above all to his own shortcomings. The view of some writers, among them L. Fischer and W. H. Chamberlin, that one of the major reasons for his defeats was the inaction on the Polish front, seems completely unwarranted. Polish military assistance to the White Russian armies in autumn 1919 could only be limited. The Polish army at that time was poorly equipped, because the bulk of the Allied supplies went to Denikin, as stated above (pp. 406 ff.). As it appears from the statement of General S. Haller, then Chief of the Polish General Staff (murdered by the Russians in Katyn in 1940), the Polish army was then in full reorganization and several divisions were immobilized in Western Poland awaiting the withdrawal of the German troops from the territories assigned to Poland by virtue of the Versailles Treaty.[195] Poland was not able to lauch a serious offensive against the Bolsheviks until spring 1920. All that the Poles could do was to undertake limited military operations on the Polesye front (against Mozyrz), and it cannot be taken for granted that such operations would have saved Denikin. Moreover, when the Bolsheviks were informed of Pilsudski's decision not to advance the Polish troops beyond the line then held, that is in mid-November 1919, Denikin's retreat had already started. It is hardly possible that the Soviet troops which could be withdrawn from the Polish front could play a decisive part in the battle. (Denikin assessed the strength of these troops at 43,000 men, but this figure, amounting to three to four divisions, is disputed by Polish writers.)

Whatever one may think of the part played by these troops on Denikin's front, we have much more evidence (if only in Mackinder's final report) to the effect that the moral and material strength of the White Russian army was greatly overestimated by Allied statesmen and military authorities, and that Pilsudski's information was much nearer the truth than that of the Allies.

It clearly appears from the foregoing that the Allies followed a quite mistaken line of policy in this whole affair. Their belief that in their policy in Eastern Europe they could refrain from agreeing their plans with the Poles was completely unrealistic; the Allied Powers were living in the past, and as Pilsudski rightly said, were pursuing an ostrich-like policy.

When other counsels prevailed it was too late. It was Mackinder who made the first serious attempt to persuade Denikin to revise his policy towards Poland, but this occurred too late, namely at a time when the Allied policy was changing radically, and nothing could have induced the Entente Powers to continue to support the cause of intervention in Russia. In his conversation with Denikin on the 10th January, 1920, Mackinder explained to Denikin that " he could not expect Poland to throw her whole weight into the war unless the principle, at any rate, on which the frontier would be fixed were accepted beforehand," consequently taking the same view as Pilsudski in his instructions for General Karnicki. " If Poland," continued Mackinder, " took any other course, what would be her position as a small State when she had helped to set up afresh a mighty Power at Moscow. I told him plainly that the attitude he had hitherto assumed would not result in business." [196]

One can hardly find a fuller justification of the attitude of the Poles towards Denikin, and it can only be regretted that an Allied representative understood the position so late. These endeavours to find a reasonable basis for co-operation between the anti-Bolshevik forces came at the moment when the Allied statesmen in Paris took the view that Denikin's cause was lost. This appears clearly from the debates of the Supreme Council on the 5th January, 1920, when Denikin's request for assistance was brought before the Council. In this request Denikin asked : " bring pressure upon Poland and Rumania to force them to give adequate help to the Russian army fighting against the Bolsheviks." The reactions of the members of the Council to this request were very characteristic, as they marked the radical change of policy of the Allied Powers on the Russian problem. Sir Eyre Crowe observed that it would be necessary to consult the military experts. " Why, for example," he said, " apply pressure on the Poles in order to ask them to help Denikin, if their assistance were not to change anything in the unfavourable situation in which that General found himself. He was personally inclined to think that Denikin's troops would continue to retreat whether the Poles intervened or not." The same attitude was taken by the Italian representative, and Clemenceau, summing up the discussion, stated that " it seemed to him that the opinion of the Council was against any pressure being applied to the Poles to make them intervene in Denikin's favour. That was also his view." [197]

So closed the first stage of the Allied policy in Eastern Europe during the Paris Peace Conference. From then on the Allied Powers had to face a new Bolshevik Russia engaged in a struggle against her neighbours on whom she was trying to impose her rule and régime. To what extent could Poland rely on Allied assistance in this new period of the history of Eastern Europe? Before we pass to this problem, which will be dealt with in the following chapters, we must devote a few words to a question closely connected with those previously reviewed, namely that of the Eastern frontier of Poland.

4. THE QUESTION OF POLAND'S EASTERN FRONTIER AT THE PARIS PEACE CONFERENCE

The Peace Conference—or rather the Supreme Council, as only the latter and its organs dealt with this matter—was in a rather awkward position when called upon to make any decision relating to Poland's Eastern frontier. If we take first the juridical titles of the Allied and Associated Powers to assign to Poland some territories which had formerly belonged to the late Russian Empire, these titles could be based only on two grounds : (1) that the Russian Empire had ceased to exist and that the sovereign rights of Russia to her former territories had become extinct; or (2) that the partitions of Poland in the eighteenth century having been an international crime, the *restitutio in integrum* of the former Polish State was the natural reparation of what was called, in the Reply of the Allied and Associated Powers to Germany on the 16th June, 1916, " one of the greatest wrongs of which history had record, a crime the memory and the result of which has for long poisoned the political life of the Continent of Europe."

If we now ask the question whether the Allied and Associated Powers exercised any executive power in Eastern Europe at the time of the Peace Conference, we have to answer in the negative, because the territories which were to be assigned to Poland had never been occupied by the Allied and Associated Powers, thus these Powers could not or did not wish to impose their will on the Bolsheviks, the latter refusing to recognize the authority of the Supreme Council to interfere in matters of Eastern Europe. On some occasions the Supreme Council exercised some pressure on Poland, but not on Soviet Russia, and this circumstance put Poland in an inferior position in comparison with the Bolsheviks. It eventually turned out that it was the outcome of the Polish-Soviet war and not the decisions of the Supreme Council that brought about the new territorial settlement in Eastern Europe.

These circumstances explain to some extent the hesitations and inability of the Supreme Council to carry out the provisions of Article LXXXVII of the Versailles Treaty (" The boundaries of Poland not laid down in the present Treaty will be subsequently determined by the Principal Allied and Associated Powers ").

Poland based her territorial claims in the East on her historical rights and on the fact that the partitions of Poland could not constitute a valid title for Russia to possess these territories. Also to be considered from the Polish point of view were the interests and the wishes of the population of this whole area, as well as the necessity for such frontiers as would render Poland completely independent of Russia, whether Bolshevik or not.[198]

In all the official documents of the Polish Delegation to the Peace Conference we find the statement that the 1772 frontier should be taken as the starting point for all decisions concerning Poland's Eastern frontier. Such, for instance, were the statements made by Mr. Dmowski at the meeting of the Supreme Council on the 29th January, 1919, and the terms of two Polish Notes to the Peace Conference relating to the future frontiers of Poland, dated 28th February and 3rd March, 1919.[199]

Although the principle of national self-determination was often put forward by the peacemakers in Paris, we know that in many instances the historical rights were given preference over all other considerations. Such was the case of the old historic frontiers of Bohemia. We find a direct reference to them in the Covering Letter addressed by the Supreme Council in Reply to the Austrian Counter-proposals dated 30th August, 1919 :

> " In general, the Allied and Associated Powers have endeavoured to determine the boundaries of the States formed out of the late Austro-Hungarian Monarchy in such an equitable way as to conduce to the lasting peace of Central Europe. *Thus they have drawn for Czechoslovakia the historical frontiers of the Crown of Bohemia.*" [200]

We can point out that also in relation to Russia the Principal Allied Powers admitted in some cases the validity of historical claims, as appears from the Treaty between the Principal Allied Powers and Rumania respecting Bessarabia, signed in Paris on 28th October, 1919 (Cmd. 1747). The preamble to this Treaty states that " from *geographic*, ethnographic, *historic* and economic points of view, the reunion of Bessarabia to Roumania is fully justified." By Article I " the high contracting parties declare that they recognize the sovereignty of Roumania " and by Article II, they " invite Russia to adhere to the present Treaty as soon as a Russian Government recognized by them all shall be in existence. They reserve the right to submit to the arbitration of the Council of the League of Nations all questions which the Russian Government may raise respecting the details of this Treaty, *it being understood that the frontiers defined in the present Treaty, as well as the sovereignty of Rumania over the territories therein comprised, cannot be called in question.*"

The historical rights of the former Russia obviously clashed with Poland's historical claims. The principles of the unity and indivisibility of Russia, as existing at the moment of the outbreak of the 1914 war, were put forward on many occasions by the Russian statesmen and ambassadors in exile, maintaining the fiction of the legal existence of the Russian Empire. For instance, the " aggrandisement " of Poland and Rumania and the " unreserved recognition " of the " so-called Baltic States," according to a note dated 17th January, 1920, addressed to the Secretary of State by Mr. Bakhmeteff, still remaining at the post of Russian Ambassador in Washington, " mean compensation at the expense of Russia by the violation of Russia's territorial integrity and of her sovereign rights." [201]

The rights of the Russian people, as superior to the rights of other nationalities of the former Russian Empire, were also often invoked by the White Russians. For instance, we read the following request in a note addressed by the Russian Political Conference to the Peace Conference on the 9th March, 1919 :

" The Powers recognize that: (*a*) all questions concerning the territories of the Russian Empire in the limits of 1914, with the exception of ethnographic Poland, (*b*) as well as the questions relative to the future States of the nationalities included in those limits, cannot be solved without the consent of the Russian people. No decisive solution could consequently be interposed on this subject so long as the Russian people is not in a position to freely manifest its will and to participate in the settlement of these questions." [202]

We can judge the reaction of the Western statesmen to the claims put forward by White Russian quarters in the light of the foregoing remarks (see pp. 424 ff. and 458 ff.). Throughout the year 1919 the Western statesmen maintained the hope that Bolshevism would collapse and that a Russian Empire could be restored on more or less the old lines. For this reason they abstained from undertaking any commitments regarding territorial issues in Eastern Europe. Apart from these political considerations we must take into account the mistaken views on the nature of Russian expansionism, due to clever Russian propaganda throughout the second part of the nineteenth century, and to the trends of public opinion in the West favourable to Russia in the course of the 1914 war. Only at the end of 1919 did Lloyd George remember that in the past British policy had had different views on Russia. He did so in order to justify the abandonment of the White Russian cause by the Allies. In his speech in the House of Commons on the 17th November, 1919, he said :

> " There was a very great statesman, a man of great imagination, who certainly did not belong to the party to which I belong, Lord Beaconsfield, who regarded a great gigantic Russia rolling onwards like a glacier towards Persia and the borders of Afghanistan and India as the greatest menace the British Empire could be confronted with." [203]

In these circumstances, whatever arguments might have been produced by the Poles at the Peace Conference in relation to the former Eastern provinces of Poland, they could have been of no avail so long as the restoration of the old Russia engrossed the minds of the peacemakers in Paris. Neither the more limited programme put forward by Dmowski and the Polish Delegation to the Peace Conference, consisting in proposals to establish Poland's Eastern frontier along the boundary of Western civilization represented by Polish influence predominating there for centuries, nor the demand to extend to all nationalities of the Eastern borderlands the right of self-determination in order to form a solid territorial barrier between Russia and Germany (such were the views expressed by Paderewski in some speeches at the Peace Conference) found a favourable reception in Paris.

It should be noted that the Polish territorial programme was presented to the Supreme Council in the first instance by a man well known to Western statesmen through his pro-Allied activity during the war, and who was imbued with a sincere conviction that Poland and Russia, both equally menaced by German imperialism, should and could reach a reasonable compromise based on respect for their mutual rights (see pp. 48 ff. and 178 ff.) and that in such a way the old historic feud between the two nations might be liquidated once for all. Roman Dmowski, leader of the Polish National Committee during the war and then a Delegate of Poland to the Peace Conference, considered that this compromise could consist in Poland renouncing her claims to her old historic frontier of 1772 and establishing a new frontier line between the two States based on the boundary between two civilizations. Like many Western statesmen he took the view that neither the Ukrainians nor the Lithuanians had attained a sufficient degree of political maturity to justify their constituting independent States. Using Wilson's well-known expression, one might say that in his view the national aspirations of these two nations were not yet well-defined (see p. 22). Speaking before the Supreme Council on the 29th January, 1919, Dmowski

> " defined a nation as a race of men capable of so organizing itself as to be able to express the collective will to organize its affairs both externally and internally. In a word, it must be able to govern itself and to oppose oppression. By this test Russia strictly speaking was not fit for admission to a League of Nations, nor were the Lithuanians advanced far enough in national unity or ideals to be included amongst the nations. The Ukrainian State at present was really organized anarchy, and the Ukrainians were not so far advanced as the Lithuanians on the road to nationality. The great need in Eastern Europe was to have established governments, able to assure order and to express their will in foreign and internal policy. It was too early to think of Lithuania or Ukraina as independent States. Therefore, it would be best that if organized as separate States they should be united in some other States, and as the Lithuanians were closely allied to the Poles he suggested Poland as the best State to which they should be united." [204]

It follows from this statement that Dmowski recognized Russia's right to the greater part of ethnographical Ukraine, this standpoint agreeing with the programme followed even before the 1914 war by the National-Democratic Party of Poland. Dmowski's attitude on this question was also influenced by the events of 1918, namely the attempts to set up a Ukrainian State as a bulwark against German expansionism in the East, directed against both Poland and Russia (see pp. 195 ff.).

A considerable part of Byelorussia, namely that with Orthodox population, should also remain within the frontiers of the Russian State according to Dmowski's plan. As the establishment of independent States between Poland and Russia was excluded by Dmowski, Poland would have a common frontier with Russia. Dmowski considered that it was necessary for the maintenance of friendly and close collaboration between these two States, against the German attempts in the future to resume the *Drang nach Osten* policy.[205]

The Polish Note of the 3rd March, 1919, proposed the establishment of the Eastern frontier of Poland in accordance with the above considerations. It should be noted that we find similar ideas to those expounded by Dmowski in the " Outline of Tentative Report and Recommendations prepared by the (American)

Intelligence Section, in Accordance with Instructions, for the President and the Plenipotentiaries," dated 21st January, 1919.[206] In this Report we read the following :

"If a new Polish State is formed it follows that the frontiers should be drawn so as to include all of the Polish majorities contiguous to the main group, in order not to leave upon the outside Polish districts that may form the centre of irredentist movement.

"The Eastern frontier assigned on the map to the Polish–Lithuanian–Catholic–White Russian complex ought to stand, because it is based primarily on the line of religious division between Catholics and Orthodox. ... It is recommended that a union of Poland and Lithuania be effected, if possible, with boundaries as shown on map 6. Poland and Lithuania are bound together by so many historic ties and common economic interests that their former political union, lasting for many centuries, should be restored. Lithuania is not strong enough to stand alone. ... It is recommended that, if this union is not effected, Poland and Lithuania be established as mutually independent States, with boundaries not as shown on map 6, but adjusted to the ethnic facts in the Wilno–Grodno–Minsk district."

The map enclosed showed the Polish frontier passing beyond Pinsk and Minsk; the possibility was foreshadowed of assigning to Poland the whole of Galicia and Volhynia. So far as the Ukraine was concerned, the Report stated that "there should be established a Ukrainian State, provided Ukrainian nationalism is strong enough to justify that decision," but at the same time recommended that "encouragement be given, at opportune time, to the reunion with Russia of those border regions of the South and West which have broken away and set up their own national governments, particularly the Baltic Provinces and the Ukraine, if reunion can be accomplished with a federalized or genuinely democratic Russia."

It should be stressed that according to the resolution adopted by the Polish Diet on the 4th April, 1919, quoted above (p. 452), the wishes of the populations concerned were to be taken into consideration in establishing the future Eastern frontier of Poland. Prime Minister Paderewski, who was an enthusiastic partisan of the principle of federation,[207] on the strength of this resolution was able to state at the meeting of the Commission on Polish Affairs on the 12th April that Poland would ensure the freedom of the Byelorussians and Ukrainians to decide whether or not they desired to stay in union with the Polish State. He also said that Poland recognized the right of the Lithuanians to found their own independent State, but at the same time making every effort to re-establish with

Lithuania a freely consented union. Pilsudski's proclamation of the 22nd April, after the liberation of Wilno, and the resolution of the Diet reaffirmed the wish of the Polish nation to respect the right of the population of the Eastern borders to decide their own future.

The following organs of the Supreme Council had within their province the study of the question of Poland's Eastern frontier : the Commission on Polish Affairs appointed by the decision of the Supreme Council of the 12th February, and the Sub-committee for the study of Poland's Eastern frontier set up by the said Commission on the 20th March, 1919.[208]

At one of the first meetings of the Commission on Polish Affairs on the 1st March, the Italian Delegate, Marquis della Torretta, of whom his compatriot Francesco Tommasini says that " he was well known for his pro-Russian feelings," [209] and who by his marriage was related to the Russian landed aristocracy,[210] protested against discussing the question of Poland's Eastern frontier at the Peace Conference. At the first meeting of the Sub-committee for the study of the Eastern frontier of Poland the same della Torretta read a declaration in which he recalled " the declarations of the Entente Powers according to which Russia remained an Allied country and which promised that the Entente Powers would make every effort to ensure the reconstitution of Russia in her unity and territorial integrity." To the question of the American delegate, Dr. Lord, whether he understood the " unity " of Russia in ethnographical or historical sense, della Torretta answered that he intended the latter. According to him the Peace Conference should take its bearings from the Declaration of the Provisional Government of Russia (which by the way had long disappeared) of 16th(29th) March, 1917 (see p. 156), which " considered the creation of an independent Polish State from all the territories where the Polish people constitute a majority of population," giving to these words a most restrictive interpretation, that is to say recognizing the right of Poland to the Congress Kingdom only (without the districts of Kholm and Suwalki).

There were many reasons why the Peace Conference did not wish to establish at that time the Eastern frontier of Poland, and the most important of these was the fact that the Eastern borders of Poland were then invaded by the Red Army and nobody could say who would eventually secure possession of them. The resolution of the Polish Commission of the 29th March, submitted to the Supreme Council on the 22nd April as Report No. 2 of the Commission,[211] consequently stated a provisional line only, as well as some principles according to which the future definitive Eastern frontier of Poland should be established. Amongst them we find reference to the said Declaration of the Russian Provisional Government (" The Announcement of the Provisional Government of Russia," which recognized the "formation of an Independent Polish State consisting of all the areas inhabited by a majority of Poles is considered the proper basis for the definition of the Eastern frontier of Poland within the territories of the future Russian Empire "). The second paragraph of the Report stated that the future frontier line should be established according to the same principles as the Western frontier of Poland. There is no need to say that in practice it would be impossible to apply the same standards to the Eastern borders of Poland, the main feature of which was the intermixture of nations, as to the Western borders where only two nations with well-defined national aspirations, Poles and Germans, faced each other. The third paragraph of the Report stated that whenever a doubt arose about the ethnic character of an area and the wishes of its population, such an area must not, for the time being, be assigned to Poland. But on the other side the Report anticipated inquiries on the spot, if possible, for the purpose of ascertaining the ethnic, linguistic and religious character of the areas outside the indisputably Polish territory, as well as the wishes of the population concerned. This paragraph constituted a concession to those members of the Commission (French and American) who considered that the final frontier line should be established further to the East.[212] It should be added that such inquiries were never made by the Commission, in spite of many proposals put forward by the Polish authorities. Moreover the provisional nature of the proposed line appeared clearly from the last paragraph of the Report : " that a final settlement of the question of the Eastern frontier of Poland should be made as soon as a Russian Government is established with which the Great Powers can deal in regard to this question."

No decision on the provisional line recommended in Report No. 2 was taken by the Supreme Council, and the Commission on Polish Affairs was only authorized on 26th April, 1919, to proceed with the examination of the frontier to be assigned to Poland in Eastern Galicia.

It followed from the last paragraph of Report No. 2 that the Allied and Associated Powers did not consider themselves fully authorized to draw the final frontier between Poland and Russia, and that they expected that direct agreement to this effect could be reached between the two States concerned. This also followed clearly from the fourth condition laid down in the dispatch sent by the Heads of the Five Principal Powers to Admiral Koltchak on the 26th May, 1919 (see p. 419). We also know the endeavours of the Allied Powers, made especially by Mackinder at Denikin's headquarters (p. 479) to induce the White Russians to state their views on the future territorial settlement with Poland.

But at the end of 1919 it appeared that the hopes of the Allied Powers for the restoration of the old Empire would not materialize and that it was more than probable that Poland would have a Bolshevik Russia as her neighbour for an indefinite period. Thus the question of the Eastern frontier of Poland appeared before the Supreme Council in a quite different form. On behalf of the Commission on Polish Affairs, presenting Report No. 6 dated 1st September at the meeting of the Supreme Council on the 25th September.[213] Laroche stated that " it was not a question of a Treaty defining the Eastern frontier of Poland, but a treaty according certain territories to Poland." Speaking of the form in which this report should be brought to the notice of the Polish Government, Polk, the American delegate, observed that " it would be possible to give Poland her choice between two solutions :

> "(a) The acceptance of the minimum line proposed in the Committee's reports, *with the assurance that this would not prejudice any future negotiations* regarding this frontier after the re-establishment of Russia or the obtaining of *satisfactory information regarding the desires of the people to the East of this frontier ;* or
> "(b) leaving the determination of this Eastern frontier entirely open until such time as Russia and Poland considered it possible to make a definite settlement."

At the same meeting the Supreme Council approved the conclusions of Report No. 6 and requested the Drafting Committee to study the means by which these decisions should be communicated to the Polish Government.

Report No. 6, which established the provisional minimum frontier afterwards improperly called the " Curzon Line," stated in these terms the reasons for which it proposed such a line :

> " At present it is impossible to foresee at what date there will come into being the regular Russian Government whose co-operation is necessary to the definitive determination of the Eastern frontiers of Poland.
> " The Commission does not, however, overlook the fact that the prolongation of the present state of uncertainty offers very serious disadvantages, both to the population and to the Polish Government. It is necessary to put an end to this uncertainty. The Eastern frontier of Poland as defined in Report No. 2 and in the present report, represents a *provisional* frontier to the extent that, *in the future other territory situated to the East of that line may be incorporated with Poland.*

" ... the Eastern frontier of Poland as described in Reports No. 2 and No. 6 of the Commission on Polish Affairs should be considered as marking the line to the West of which the Polish Government may, from now onwards, legally exercise all rights appertaining to sovereignty."

The Commission on Polish Affairs proposed that the decisions of the Supreme Council relating to the provisional frontier of Poland should take the form of an " additional Protocol to the Treaty concluded at Versailles between the Principal Allied and Associated Powers and Poland, on 28th June, 1918," but this formal character of the document was opposed by the American delegate, Polk, when the question was again reviewed by the Supreme Council on the 29th November, 1919,[214] The American delegate considered that it was not wise to " give this recognition in so formal a way by signing a protocol of this nature," and he wondered whether " it did not mean shutting the door to any future negotiations with Russia." He repeated similar objections at the next meeting on the 1st December.[215] Eventually the document approved on the 8th December took the form of a simple declaration.[216] There was no more mention of the recognition of Polish sovereignty over territories West of the provisional line, but only of the right " of the Polish Government to proceed, according to the conditions previously provided by the Treaty with Poland of 28th June, 1919, to organize a regular administration " there. This document, called " Declaration Relating to the Provisional Frontiers of Poland " provided that the decision on the matter was taken " without prejudging the provisions which must in the future define the Eastern frontiers of Poland," and also that " the rights that Poland may be able to establish over the territories situated to the East of the said line are expressly reserved."

What conclusions can be drawn from this whole story? Did the Allied and Associated Powers do what was necessary to ensure for Poland the necessary conditions in order that she might be able to play the part assigned to her a few days after the meeting of the 2nd December, namely by the Resolutions of the Inter-Allied Council held in London (11th, 12th and 13th December, 1919), stating that " a strong Poland is in the interest of the Entente Powers "? In the eyes of the Principal Powers were the interests of the populations East of the provisional frontier line less worthy of respect than to the West of it? How long were they to live in a state of uncertainty? There seems no doubt that the Principal Allied and Associated Powers wished to evade any responsibility in the reorganization of Eastern Europe. They refused to be a party to any settlement which in their opinion might prejudge the Russian interests. All their moves can be explained only by the desire to safeguard the interests of the future Russia. It was the bitter irony of fate that these endeavours eventually benefited only Bolshevik Russia.

As we shall see in the following chapters, an attempt was to be made in the course of the following year to impose on Poland this provisional line as a definitive frontier between Poland and Soviet Russia, thus completely distorting the original meaning and purpose of the Declaration of the 8th December, 1919, and considerably weakening Poland's position in her struggle against the Red imperialism.

NOTES

[1] W. C. CHAMBERLIN, *History of the Russian Revolution*, II, p. 151. " One searches in vain in the records of the time not only for a consistent Allied policy, but even for a steadfast policy on the part of the individual Allied Powers."

[2] *D.B.F.P.*, First Series, Vol. III, p. 520. See also a characteristic confession of Wilson at the meeting of the Council of Four on 20th May, 1919: " President Wilson said that he did not feel the same chagrin that he formerly felt at having no policy in regard to Russia. It had been impossible to have a policy hitherto " (*The Paris Peace Conference*, V, p. 735).

[3] PILSUDSKI, *Pisma*, V, p. 145.

[4] *The Paris Peace Conference*, III, p. 584. BAKER, *Woodrow Wilson*, I, pp. 166-7.

[5] *Istoriya Diplomats*, III, p. 35. " Frantsusov pri etom vovse ne trogali interesi Polshi. Oni ne sobiralis' otstavliyat' eiya nuzhdy."

[6] *Paris Peace Conference*, III, p. 671. Balfour also suggested that the Poles " should limit their actions to the protection of indisputable Polish territories against invasion from without." He meant by it that the Poles should abstain from any action in the Eastern part of Galicia, but in few months later he would complain that " the Allies were hampering the action of the Poles there " (see p. 373).

[7] MILYUKOV, *La Politique Extérieure des Soviets*, p. 48. " Ce secours de 150,000 soldats (de préférence grecs, roumains, polonais, etc.), dont parlait Lloyd George était promis avant le réunion de la Conférence aux chefs du mouvement russe anti-bolshevik, par les représentants militaires alliés qui jugeaient de l'état de choses sur les lieux." CHURCHILL (*Aftermath*, p. 168) mentions also Foch's proposal saying that the Marshal " contemplated forming a considerable army principally of American troops, together with Polish forces and well disposed Russian prisoners of war, for the protection of Poland and operations against the Bolsheviks."

[8] Terms of the Convention agreed at Paris on 23rd December, 1917, in *D.B.F.P.*, Vol. III, p. 369 and L. FISCHER, *The Soviets in World Affairs*, II, p. 836. Under this agreement Great Britain assumed

responsibility for the Cossacks' territories, Armenia, the Caucasus, Georgia and Kurdistan, while the French control was extended to Bessarabia, the Ukraine and Crimea.

[9] CARTON DE WIART, o.c., p. 95. HOWARD, o.c., Vol. II, p. 305: " 30th January (1919) . . . Poor Wade (Colonel Wade) keeps telegraphing that Poland lacks everything for her army, but no decisions are taken. It is really heartbreaking."

[10] D. H. MILLER, Diary, XVII, p. 29.

[11] The Paris Peace Conference, IV, p. 316.

[12] CARTON DE WIART, o.c., p. 95.

[12a] HOWARD, o.c., Vol. II, pp. 317, 331.

[13] D. H. MILLER, XVII, p. 315.

[14] A special convention was signed between the Governments of the Allied and Associated Powers and the Polish Government on 14th June, 1919, which conferred on Marshal Foch the Chief Command of the Polish forces, the same as of the other Allied forces. Thus the agreements of Doullens, Beauvais and Abbeville signed respectively on 26th March, 3rd April and 2nd May, 1918, were extended to Poland in connection with the enforcement of the Versailles Treaty. All these agreements became obsolete with the coming into force of the Peace Treaty and the cessation of the state of war with Germany. Marshal Foch asked the Supreme Council to be relieved of his duties by a letter of 15th October, 1919 (D. B. F. P., Vol. II, p. 92).

So far as Pilsudski's standpoint was concerned we can refer to the interview given by him to a correspondent of the Journal des Débats on 2nd May, 1919. Speaking about the negotiations with the French Mission under General Henrys, Pilsudski said: " These negotiations are terminated and we reached full agreement. There remain only a few details to be settled. The agreement consists in the following: The French Mission will retain the command over the French staff, but each Polish soldier crossing the Polish frontier passes under the Polish High Command. From now there will be only one army in Poland " (PILSUD-SKI, Pisma, V, p. 80).

[15] D. B. F. P., Vol. I, p. 703.

[16] CARTON DE WIART, o.c., p. 97.

[17] D. B. F. P., Vol. III, p. 365.

[18] CHURCHILL, o.c., p. 168.

[19] Winston Churchill was of different opinion at that time. See The Aftermath, p. 234: " Still I suppose that twenty or thirty thousand resolute, comprehending well-armed Europeans could, without any serious difficulty or loss, have made their way swiftly along any of the great railroads which converged on Moscow and have brought to the hard ordeal of battle any force that stood against them. But twenty or thirty thousand resolute men did not exist or could not be brought together."

[20] DILLON, o.c., p. 301.

[21] For the details of the Bullitt Mission, see D. B. F. P., III, pp. 425 ff.,

D. H. MILLER, *Diary*, VI, pp. 445 ff., DILLON, o.c., pp. 112 and 307. TEMPERLEY, o.c., Vol. VI, pp. 314 ff.

[22] HOUSE, IV, p. 359.

[23] L. FISCHER, o.c., Vol. I, p. 178. P. MANTOUX, *Les Délibérations du Conseil des Quatre*, Vol. I, séance du 25 mars, 1919, pp. 20 ff.

[24] CHAMBERLIN, o.c., Vol. II, pp. 166 and 170.

[25] BAKER, *Woodrow Wilson*, II, p. 31.

[26] *D.B.F.P.*, Vol. I, p. 859.

[27] *Ibidem*, Vol. II, p. 30. See also *The Paris Peace Conference*, VIII, p. 720: Report on Furnishing Material to the Polish Army, 15th October, 1919.

[28] According to M. Barthou's assessments presented in his speech of 28th December, 1920, at the Chambre des Députés, France spent for military assistance to the White Russian generals—952 million francs in 1919 and 500 million in 1920.

[29] Cmd. 395 of 1919. See also the instructions of Lord Curzon to Mr. Mackinder, November 1919 (*D.B.F.P.*, Vol. II, pp. 672 ff.).

[30] *The Paris Peace Conference*, V, p. 683.

[31] *Ibidem*, p. 675.

[32] R. S. BAKER, o.c., Vol. III, pp. 218 ff.

[33] *D.B.F.P.*, Vol. II, p. 31.

[34] *Ibidem*, Vol. III, p. 622.

[35] *Ibidem*, p. 634.

[36] *Ibidem*, pp. 765-6.

[37] T. KUTRZEBA, *Wyprawa Kijowska*, pp. 314-5.

[38] L. BILINSKI, *Wspomnienia i Dokumenty*, II, pp. 235 ff.

[39] CARTON DE WIART, o.c., p. 102.

[40] *The Paris Peace Conference*, IV, p. 97. D. H. MILLER, *Diary*, XV, p. 21.

[41] *The Paris Peace Conference*, IV, p. 122.

[42] *Ibidem*, V, p. 497.

[43] *Ibidem*, p. 560.

[44] *Ibidem*, p. 544.

[45] The meeting of the Supreme Council on 9th May, 1919. " President Wilson said he had always been of opinion that the proper policy of the Allied and Associated Powers was to clear out of Russia and leave it to the Russians to fight it out themselves " (*The Paris Peace Conference*, V, p. 528).

[46] *Ibidem*, Vol. I, p. 271.

[47] *Ibidem*, IV, p. 687.

[48] D. H. MILLER, *Diary*, IV, p. 219. See also R. LANSING, *The Peace Negotiations*. A memorandum of my views as to the territorial settlement 21st September, 1918." ... *Second*. The Baltic Provinces of Lithuania, Latvia and Esthonia should be autonomous States of a Russian Confederation."

[49] *P.R.F.R.*, 1920, Vol. III, pp. 463 ff. See also the appreciation of this policy by P. MILYUKOV, *Rossiya na Perelomie*, I, p. 232.

[50] *Journal Officiel*, 30 décembre, 1918. Chambre des Députés,

2-me séance du 29 décembre, 1918. Franklin Bouillon, although recommending a policy of intervention in Russia, takes the view that France could bear no substantial sacrifices for this cause: " En ce qui concerne la France, les alliés comprendront que son effort en effectifs doit être réduit au minimum. C'est à ceux qui qui ont eu le moins de sacrifices à consentir qu'il appartient d'envoyer les gros bataillons.'

[51] *D. B. F. P.,* Vol. III, pp. 735 ff.

[52] *The Paris Peace Conference,* IV, pp. 14 ff. D. H. MILLER, *Diary,* XIV, pp. 448 ff.

[53] KEYNES, *The Economic Consequences of the Peace,* p. 275.

[54] CHAMBERLIN, o.c., Vol. II, p. 151.

[55] *P. R. F. R.,* 1920, Vol. III, p. 484.

[56] See Memorandum by Mr. Selby, 6th June, 1919: " The Ukraine, when it is reconquered should properly fall within General Denikin's sphere of influence, and, consequently under our control, and we should make a strenuous endeavour to obtain a modification of the existing agreement with the French to secure the elimination of their activities in these regions forthwith " (*D.B.F.P.,* Vol. III, p. 366).

[57] Note by Sir Esme Howard of a conversation with Count Kokovtsov and Prince Trubetskoy, 3rd June, 1919: " The gist of all this is that the Russian parties of the right represented here by Messrs. Kokovtsov and Trubetskoy will evidently do all in their power to prevent Admiral Koltchak from giving any assurances respecting the nationalities " (*D. B. F. P.,* III, p. 341).

[58] *Le Temps,* 26th December, 1918. Déclarations de M. Milyukov : " Il faut que l'unité de la Russie soit réconstituée ... que les Etats artificiels ébauchés sous la protection allemande le long des frontières russes lui furent restitués."

[59] *The Paris Peace Conference,* V, pp. 544 ff.

[60] *D. B. F. P.,* III, p. 800.

[61] *The Paris Peace Conference,* V, p. 551.

[62] *D. B. F. P.,* Vol. III, p. 332.

[63] *Ibidem,* p. 363.

[64] *Ibidem,* p. 710.

[65] *Ibidem,* pp. 360-1.

[66] " Une décision de la question finlandaise en dehors de la Russie et sans égard pour ses intérêts stratégiques, ne saurait être accueillie par le peuple russe. Cette argumentation s'applique également à toutes les questions touchant à la souveraineté de l'Etat Russe, telles que la fixation de ses frontières, son régime intérieur etc." (*Ibidem,* p. 377).

[67] *Ibidem,* pp. 474 ff.

[68] *Ibidem,* p. 584.

[69] See among others: L. FISCHER, o.c., pp. 188 ff., CARR, *The Bolshevik Revolution,* p. 257. M. K. DZIEWANOWSKI, *Pilsudski's Federal Policy,* pp. 123 ff.

[70] STALIN, *Sochineniya,* V, pp. 113 ff.

[71] *Ibidem,* p. 246. English translation by CARR, o.c., p. 257.

[72] See the discussion on a draft declaration on Baltic Affairs in the

Council of the Heads of Delegations, 26th July, 1919 (*The Paris Peace Conference*, VII, p. 326).

[73] H. W. V. TEMPERLEY, o.c., Vol. VI, p. 296.

[74] *D. B. F. P.*, Vol. III, pp. 377 ff.

[75] *Ibidem*, p. 410.

[76] *Ibidem*, pp. 569 ff.

[77] *Ibidem*, pp. 424-5.

[78] *Ibidem*, pp. 494-5.

[79] *Ibidem*, p. 522. So far as the attitude of the U.S.A. towards the problem of the independence of the Ukraine was concerned, see the meeting of the Commissioners Plenipotentiary (*The Paris Peace Conference*, Vol. XI, p. 253) on 27th June, 1919. Hearing of the Ukrainian Delegation composed of Margolin, Vice-Minister of Foreign Affairs of the Ukraine under Petlura, and Mr. Paneyko, representing the Ukrainians of Galicia: " Mr. Lansing stated definitely that the United States was not in favour of independence for the Ukrainians but that it was in favour of a single Russia, in which the various portions should have a certain degree of autonomy. ... Only in the event that the Ukrainians come to an agreement with Admiral Koltchak, said Mr. Lansing, would it be possible for the United States to give to it proper support in material and technical help. ... As yet the United States had recognized no part of Russia, except the countries which should by rights remain permanently independent, such as Finland and Poland. They could not recognize even provisionally the independence of the Ukraine."

[80] CHAMBERLIN, o.c., Vol. II, p. 223. M. K. DZIERZANOWSKI, o.c., p. 121.

[81] CHURCHILL, *The Aftermath*, p. 254.

[82] *Ibidem*, p. 256.

[83] SIR GEORGE BUCHANAN, *My Mission to Russia*, Vol. II, p. 258.

[84] DAVID LLOYD GEORGE, *The Truth about the Peace Treaties*, Vol. I, p. 308.

[85] J. STALIN, *Sochineniya*, Vol. IV, pp. 31-2.

[86] T. A. TARACUZIO, *The Soviet Union and International Law*, p. 81.

[87] C. A. MACARTNEY, *National States and National Minorities*, p. 463.

[88] B. SOUVARINE, *Stalin*, p. 206.

[89] E. H. CARR, *The Bolshevik Revolution*, pp. 260 ff.

[90] C. A. MACARTNEY, o.c., p. 452. " The doctrine of the dictatorship of the proletariat justifies the proletariat in imposing its will on the bourgeoisie and forcing an entire nation to join the Soviet State, even when the numerical majority would prefer separation. This is true self-determination, since the only ' self ' for the purposes of the act is the Communist Party. It must also be remembered that Communism aspires to be worldwide and postulates the use of force in establishing its reign."

[91] W. KOLARZ, *Russia and Her Colonies*, p. 7.

[92] STALIN, o.c., Vol. I, p. 49.

[93] *Ibidem*, Vol. IV, p. 352. See also TROTSKY, Stalin, p. 261.

[94] *Ibidem,* pp. 32-3.

[95] CHAMBERLIN, o.c., Vol. I, pp. 491 ff. TARACUZIO, o.c., p. 29.

[96] G. SCELLE, Règles Générales du Droit de la Paix (*Recueil des Cours de l'Académie de Droit International de la Haye,* 1933, Vol. 46, pp. 393-400). " Le fédéralisme suppose en outre un phenomène d'association libre. C'est par la qu'il se distingue de la subordination qui à pour origine une contrainte. On l'a qualifié de procédé démocratique d'organisation sociale, par opposition, par exemple, à l'annexion ou protectorat qui peuvent laisser subsister une compétence gouvernementale, mais qui ne supposent pas le respect de l'égalité des participants et leur reconnaissance volontaire de l'intérêt commun."

[97] K. C. WHEARE, *Federal Government,* Second Edition, pp. 1-2.

[98] SIDNEY AND BEATRICE WEBB, *Soviet Communism,* p. 82.

[99] CARR, o.c., p. 140.

[100] SOUVARINE, o.c., pp. 200-1.

[101] STALIN, Vol. III, p. 25.

[102] *Ibidem,* pp. 30-1.

[103] NIKOLAUS BASSECHES, *Stalin,* p. 54.

[104] *Grazhdanskaya Voina,* Vol. III, p. 120. T. TESLAR, *Polityka Rosji Sowieckiej podczas wojny z Polska,* p. 75.

[105] CHAMBERLIN, Vol. II, p. 122.

[106] STALIN, Vol. IV, p. 161.

[107] *Ibidem,* p. 168.

[108] ROSA LUXEMBURG, *The Russian Revolution,* translated by Bertram D. Wolfe, quoted by RUTH FISCHER, *Stalin and German Communism,* pp. 49 ff.

[109] TEMPERLEY, o.c., Vol. VI, pp. 297-8.

[110] English translation by A. A. KRISTIAN, o.c., p. 34.

[111] *Grazhdanskaya Voina,* Vol. III, pp. 152-3. TESLAR, o.c., p. 77.

[112] KOLARZ, o.c., p. 153.

[112a] According to LOUIS L. GERSON, o.c., footnote 16: " The Bolshevists did not take Vilna. It was an indigenous Polish Socialist group that took this city "(!).

[113] KOLARZ, o.c., p. 108.

[114] STALIN, Vol. IV, p. 226.

[115] KOLARZ, o.c., p. 108.

[116] PHILLIPS W. ALISON, *Poland,* p. 49.

[117] *Ibidem,* p. 60. Mr. Phillips Alison even finds an excuse for the Tsarist policy of severe repressions after the Rising of 1863 as " they prevented the Poles from wasting their energies in useless political agitation " (*Ibidem,* p. 164).

[118] See pp. 100 ff. Kolarz refers to the book of PISHETA, *Osnovnyie momenty istoricheskovo razvitiya Zapadnoi Ukrainy i Zapadnoi Bielorussii,* Moscow, 1940.

[119] *The Cambridge History of Poland from the Origins to Sobieski* (editor Professor W. F. Reddaway), Cambridge, 1950, p. 433.

[120] CHARLES ROMER HASKINS and ROBERT HOWARD LORD, *Some Problems of the Peace Conference,* p. 165.

[121] *Ibidem*, pp. 166-7.

[122] O. HALECKI, *The Limits and Divisions of European History*, p. 109.

[123] *Ibidem*, p. 120.

[124] R. H. LORD, *The Second Partition of Poland*, p. 503.

[125] *Ibidem*, p. 500. "The modern conception of the 'rights of nationality' was so utterly alien to the eighteenth century, Catherine's policy was shaped on such entirely different lines, that it seems incongruous to imagine the Empress as governed by the nationalist impulse, or fired with the ambition to be the unifier of the Russian race. What she, like her contemporaries, was vastly more concerned about was material power, and the glory and profit of making territorial acquisitions."

[126] Letter to Tsar Nicholas, 30th March, 1827 (*Sbornik Ist. Obschch.*, Vol. 131, pp. 129-31), quoted in an article of M. KUKIEL, "La Révolution de 1830 et la Pologne," *Revue Internationale d'Histoire Politique et Constitutionnelle*, 1953, p. 237.

[127] B. H. SUMNER, *Survey of Russian History*, pp. 215 ff.

[128] HALECKI, o.c., p. 98.

[129] HASKINS and LORD, o.c., p. 169.

[130] TEMPERLEY, o.c., Vol. VI, p. 276.

[131] *Documents Diplomatiques Concernant les Relations Polono-Lithuaniennes* (Décembre 1918–Septembre 1920), Varsovie, 1920, p. 5.

[132] *Ibidem*, p. 5. The text in English can be found in a telegram sent by the American Minister in Switzerland to the Commission to Negotiate Peace (*The Paris Peace Conference*, Vol. II, p. 421).

[133] VON SEECKT, *Aus Meinem Leben*, Vol. II, pp. 143 ff. See also Dmowski's statement before the Council of Ten, 29th January, 1919: "The German soldiers on returning from the Eastern front committed many crimes, but their worst crime of all was the fact that they assisted the Bolsheviks leaving them their arms and ammunition, and also by allowing them to follow the Germans up in close succession" (*The Paris Peace Conference*, Vol. III, p. 776). See also the passage from letter of Pilsudski to Dluski, quoted on p. 262.

[134] *The Paris Peace Conference*, III, pp. 674-5.

[135] See the Polish War Communiqués published by S. POMARANSKI, *Pierwsza Wojna Polska*, Warsaw, 1920. Also A. PRZYBYLSKI, o.c., p. 59.

[136] J. OCHOTA, *Uniewaznienie aktow rozbiorowych przez Rosje* (Sprawy Obce, 1930).

[137] See Dmowski's statement before the Council of Ten, 29th January, 1919: "In reaching the settlement of the territory to belong to Poland, we should start from the date 1772, before the First Partition" (D. H. MILLER, *Diary*, XIV, p. 62).

[138] DR. PAUL ROTH, *Die Entstehung des polnischen Staates*, p. 21: "Die Bedeutung des Annullierungbeschlusses der russischen Sovietregierung liegt nach alledem nicht auf völkerrechtlichem, sondern auf politischem Gebiet. In Versailles hat er bei den Bestimmungen über die Errichtung des polnischen Staates und sein Gebiet keine Rolle gespielt."

[189] *Krasnaya Kniga*, Sbornik diplomaticheskikh dokumentov o russko-polskikh otnosheniyakh, 1918-1920, Moscow, 1920, pp. 3-5.

[140] *Ibidem*, p. 28.

[141] *Ibidem*, p. 29.

[142] *Ibidem*, pp. 30-1.

[143] TESLAR, o.c., p. 85.

[144] *Krasnaya Kniga*, p. 34.

[145] *Ibidem*, p. 39.

[146] *Ibidem*, pp. 41 ff.

[147] *Ibidem*, pp. 43-4.

[148] M. SOKOLNICKI, " Józef Pilsudski a Zagadnienie Rosji " (*Niepodległość*, Tome II, London, 1950, pp. 51-70).

[149] L. FISCHER, o.c., Vol. I, p. 245.

[150] *Krasnaya Kniga*, p. 45.

[151] *Documents Diplomatiques*, p. 9.

[152] See all the respective resolutions of the Polish Seym in W. KOMARNICKI, " Odbudowa Panstwowości Polskiej na Ziemiach Wschodnich " (*Rocznik Prawniczy Wileński*, Vol. III, 1929).

[153] J. PILSUDSKI, *Pisma*, Vol. V, p. 75.

[154] *Ibidem*, p. 107.

[155] *Ibidem*, p. 145.

[156] *The Paris Peace Conference*, Vol. VI, p. 200.

[157] *D.B.F.P., First Series*, Vol. III, p. 788.

[158] F. TOMMASINI, o.c., pp. 115 ff.

[159] L. WASILEWSKI, " Stosunki Polsko-Litewskie w dobie popowstaniowej " (*Niepodległość*, Vol. I, No. 1, pp. 30-59). The same author, *Les Polonais et les Lithuaniens pendant la Guerre Mondiale*, Warsaw, 1930. W. WIELHORSKI, *Polska a Litwa*, London, 1947.

[160] WIELHORSKI, o.c., p. 253. K. OKULICZ, o.c., p. 105.

[161] PILSUDSKI, *Pisma*, Vol. V, p. 41.

[162] Quoted above, No. 131.

[163] D. H. MILLER, *Diary*, Vol. XVI, pp. 133 ff. *The Paris Peace Conference*, Vol. IV, pp. 628 ff.

[164] PILSUDSKI, *Pisma*, Vol. V, pp. 81 ff.

[165] WIELHORSKI, o.c., pp. 309 ff.

[166] *D.B.F.P.*, Vol. I, p. 59.

[167] *Ibidem*, p. 203, and the map on p. 216.

[168] *The Paris Peace Conference*, Vol. IV, pp. 770 ff.

[169] *The Paris Peace Conference*, Vol. VII, pp. 315 ff.

[170] *D.B.F.P.*, Vol. III, pp. 153-4.

[171] *Documents Diplomatiques*, p. 33.

[172] *Ibidem*, pp. 33-5.

[173] *D.B.F.P.*, Vol. I, Nos. 57, 58, 59 and Appendix A to No. 59.

[174] See a Memorandum from the Polish Minister in London, 27th August, 1919: " Poland wishes to fulfil her part in protecting itself and other countries against a Bolshevik advance as well as in preventing a direct contact of Germany and Russia, most dangerous to Poland on account of her geographical position, and no less dangerous to the

Entente Powers. The co-operation of Germany in any anti-Bolshevik action can be considered at present as being solely a masked means employed by Germany to regain contact and influence Russia. Such an activity on the part of Germany is most dangerous to Poland's future and to the maintenance of peace. It also threatens the Entente Powers in their most vital interests and can be the cause of an un-called-for growth of power of Germany " (*D. B. F. P.*, Vol. III, No. 67).

[175] *Ibidem*, Vol. III, No. 188.

[177] *Ibidem*, No. 165.

[178] *Documents Diplomatiques*, pp. 35 ff.

[179] See J. STARZEWSKI, o.c., p. 60.

[180] CARR, o.c., p. 303.

[181] STARZEWSKI, o.c., p. 59a.

[182] J. BECK, *Dernier Rapport*, p. 90.

[183] CARTON DE WIART, o.c., p. 118. See also the opinion of Marshal Foch on Denikin, MANTOUX, o.c., Vol. I, p. 23. Séance du 25 mars: " Ce qu'on envoie à Denikine est perdu. Je n'attache pas à l'armée de Denikine une grande importance, parce que les armées n'existent pas par elle-mêmes. . . . Il vaut mieux encore avoir un gouvernement sans armée qu'une armée sans gouvernement."

[184] General Karnicki's interview in a Polish paper, *Torpeda*, 4th October, 1936. All other details in General Kutrzeba's series of articles, " Odpowiedz Generalowi Denikinowi " (*Gazeta Polska*, Warsaw, December, 1938). General Kutrzeba based his account on the documents filed in the Military Archives in Warsaw.

[185] Report by Sir H. Mackinder on the Situation in South Russia, 21st January, 1920 (*D. B. F. P.*, Vol. III, No. 656 and Appendices).

[186] *Ibidem*, Vol. I, Nos. 57 and 58.

[187] *The Paris Peace Conference*, Vol. IX, p. 849.

[188] CHURCHILL, o.c., pp. 251 ff.

[189] *D. B. F. P.*, Vol. III, No. 376. " C'est avec une grande anxiété que j'ai reçu l'information donnée à la Chambre des Communes sur l'évacuation projétée par les Alliés des régions de la Russie du Nord. Dans les plans des campagnes de l'Etat-Majeur Polonais la co-opération des troupes alliées à Mourman et Archangel était naturellement prise en considération. Il est évident que cette évacuation, à laquelle le Gouvernement Britannique s'est vu contraint, aura pour conséquence une affluence inattendue des troupes bolchevistes sur nôtre front et un prolongement de notre guerre avec les bolchèvisme. Un tel fait pourrait avoir des conséquences des plus fâcheuses pour nous. Je me permets donc d'attirer là-dessus la bienveillante attention de Votre Excellence en La priant de bien vouloir faire part de nos craintes au Gouverne-ment de Sa Majesté Britannique.'

[190] *Ibidem*, No. 495.

[191] *Ibidem*, No. 486.

[192] *Ibidem*, No. 522.

[193] L. FISCHER, o.c., Vol. I, pp. 234 ff.

[194] *D. B. F. P.*, Vol. III, No. 516.

195 T. KUTRZEBA, o.c., pp. 25 ff., and his articles in the *Gazeta Polska*. GENERAL S. HALLER, "Nasz stosunek do Denikina" (*Kurjer Warszawski*, 13th June, 1937).

196 *D. B. F. P.*, Vol. III, p. 779.

197 *The Paris Peace Conference*, Vol. IX, p. 784.

198 See a collective work published under the title *The Eastern Frontiers of Poland*, Paris, 1919 (The Polish Commission of works preparatory to the Peace Conference).

199 See note No. 137. The Note of the Polish Delegation of 28th February, 1919: "La reconstitution de l'Etat polonais doit être envisagée comme:

"(1) Un acte de justice et une réparation du crime des partages (1772-93-95) ;

"(2) La résultante du développement des forces nationales polonaises malgré tous les efforts destructeurs des Puissances et une conséquence de l'effondrement récent de l'Autriche-Hongrie, de la désagrégation de l'Empire russe et de la défaite de l'Allemagne ;

"(3) Une nécéssité d'établir entre l'Allemagne et la Russie un Etat fort et réellement indépendant.

"Il ressort de la première considération que le territoire de la Pologne d'avant le premier partage (1772) doit servir de point le départ pour le définition des frontières de l'Etat polonais reconstitué."

200 *The Paris Peace Conference*, Vol. VIII, p. 23.

201 *P. R. F. R.*, 1920, Vol. III, p. 446.

202 D. H. MILLER, *Diary*, XVII, pp. 408 ff.

203 *Parliamentary Debates*, House of Commons, Vol. 121, p. 723.

204 SEYDA, o.c., Vol. II, p. 429: "Polska winna graniczyć na wschodzie z Rosja, jezeli ziemie litewskie i ruskie, wobec niemozliwości utworzenia istotnie niezawislych panstw ukraińskiego i litewskiego, zamiast znajdować sie pod wplywem niemieckim, znajda sie cześciowo pod wplywem polskim, cześciowo pod Rosji." KOZICKI, *Sprawa Granic Polski na Konferencji Pokojowej w Paryzu*, 1919 r, p. 119.

205 See DMOWSKI, o.c., pp. 17-18.

206 D. H. MILLER, *Diary*, IV, Document No. 246, pp. 219 ff.

207 About Paderewski's federalist views, see SEYDA, o.c., II, p. 474 ; KOZICKI, o.c., pp. 119 ff. ; PILSUDSKI, *Pisma*, V, pp. 73 ff., VI, pp. 121 ff.

208 W. KOMARNICKI, o.c., pp. 10 ff.

209 F. TOMMASINI, o.c., p. 235: "Noto per le sue tendenze favorevoli alla restaurazione di uno stato russo imperialista."

210 S. ASKENAZY, *Uwagi*, p. 460. Torretta's wife was Baroness Barbi-Wulf, from a Russified Balt-German family.

211 D. H. MILLER, *Diary*, IX, Document No. 845.

212 TEMPERLEY, o.c., Vol. VI, p. 275. "It should be observed here, however, that the Curzon line at the time it was drawn up was only *a provisional minimum frontier* and that both the French and the Americans believed that the final frontier should be farther to the East."

213 *D. B. F. P.*, Vol. I, pp. 785 ff. Report No. 6, *ibidem*, pp. 788 ff. *The Paris Peace Conference*, Vol. VIII, pp. 350 ff. Report No. 6,

ididem, p. 374. *D.B.F.P.,* Vol. II, pp. 424-5, the text of the Protocol,
[214] *The Paris Peace Conference,* Vol. IX,, p. 370, and the Protocol,
ibidem, p. 374. *D.B.F.P.,* Vol. II, pp. 424-5, the text of the Protocol,
ibidem, p. 430.
[215] *The Paris Peace Conference,* IX, p. 393. The text of the Declaration, *ibidem,* p. 446.
[216] *D.B.F.P.,* Vol. II, p. 470.

CHANGES IN THE ALLIED POLICY TOWARDS SOVIET RUSSIA AFTER THE COLLAPSE OF THE WHITE RUSSIAN MOVEMENT

THE ENTENTE AND THE POLISH-SOVIET ARMISTICE NEGOTIATIONS

" No revolutionary class can denounce revolutionary war, for it would mean condemnation to a ridiculous pacifism. It is impossible to denounce such a war. This would mean Tolstoism and the pitifulness of the bourgeoisie ; it would mean forgetting all the science of Marxism, all the experience of European revolution."—(LENIN, *Sochineniya*, Vol. XIV, p. 309.)

THE defeats of Denikin's armies induced the principal Allied Powers to reconsider their policy towards the problems of Russia and Eastern Europe. At the end of 1919 we enter a period of great confusion and, which was still more dangerous for Europe, of the disruption of the common front of the West so far as concerned the problem of Bolshevism.

With the possibility of reconstituting old Russia ever more remote, engrossed in internal difficulties due to post-war conditions, divided on many international issues, and above all on the implementation of the provisions of the Peace Treaties, the Western Powers steered between the policy of moral condemnation of the practices of the Bolshevik régime and hopes of drawing some immediate advantages from the recognition of Soviet Russia. Much confusion arose from the tortuous policy pursued by Lloyd George, the ultimate ends of which remained obscure to insufficiently informed public opinion.

Change in British Policy towards Bolshevism

On the 17th November, 1919, Lloyd George announced in the House of Commons that H.M. Government had decided to stop supporting the anti-Bolshevik forces in Eastern Europe, adding that " the fact that the object is good is no justification for our incurring heavy obligations in carrying it out." But, turning to those members of the House of Commons " whose detestation of Bolshevism " was no deeper than his, he declared " that Bolshevism would lead to black reaction. It always had and I hate it." [1]

On the 18th December, 1919, he said in the House of Commons:

" ... there is no Russia you can make peace with ... until there be some means by which the Russian people can speak authoritatively,

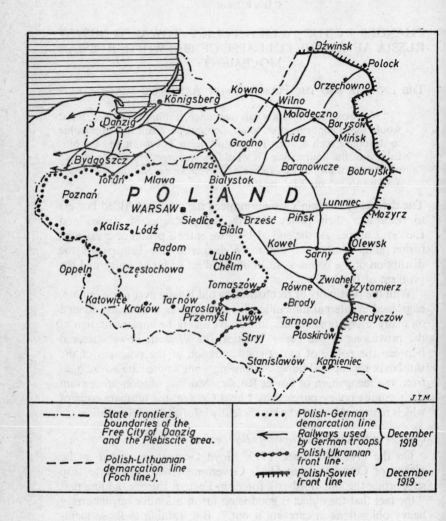

— · — · —	State frontiers, boundaries of the Free City of Danzig and the Plebiscite area.	
— — —	Polish-Lithuanian demarcation line (Foch line).	
· · · · ·	Polish-German demarcation line	December 1918
←	Railways used by German troops.	
∘∘∘∘∘	Polish Ukrainian front line.	
⊥⊥⊥⊥⊥	Polish-Soviet front line	December 1919.

Map labels: Dźwinsk, Polock, Orzechowno, Kowno, Königsberg, Wilno, Molodeczno, Borysów, Danzig, Grodno, Lida, Mińsk, Bydgoszcz, Lomza, Baranowicze, Bobrujsk, Toruń, Mlawa, Bialystok, Poznań, POLAND, Luniniec, Mozyrz, WARSAW, Brześć, Pińsk, Kalisz, Łódź, Siedlce, Biała, Kowel, Olewsk, Radom, Sarny, Lublin, Chełm, Oppeln, Częstochowa, Tomaszów, Zwiahel, Zytomierz, Katowice, Tarnów, Równe, Berdyczów, Kraków, Jaroslaw, Brody, Przemyśl, Lwów, Tarnopol, Stryj, Ploskirów, Stanislawów, Kamieniec

J.T.M.

and declare what their minds are upon this subject—I am afraid it seems a policy of despair—nothing better can be done than to pursue the policy in regard to which the Allies are in complete accord. It is a dismal prospect, but there it is ... therefore there is at present no basis for peace." [2]

We know well that Lloyd George was responsible for many decisions of the Supreme Council in the course of 1919, which might prove that at that time he was already unwilling to oppose Bolshevism by armed intervention (see above, pp. 399, 404 ff.), on this point disagreeing with the Secretary of State for War, Winston Churchill, about whom he said in a conversation with Lord Riddell: " While we were in Paris, Winston was very excited about Russia. I had to handle him firmly He was most insistent, and prepared to sacrifice both men and money." [3] Field-Marshal Sir Henry Wilson, Chief of the Imperial General Staff, noted in his diary under the 12th January, 1919, after a lunch with the Prime Minister, that " Lloyd George is opposed to knocking out Bolshevism ... this tacit agreement to Bolshevism is a most dangerous thing." [4] But Lloyd George, as we have said above, was not quite consistent in his policy and seemed to cherish some hope of the overthrow of Bolshevism at the time of the short-lived successes of the White Russian generals (see p. 411). At the end of 1919 he returned to his initial policy, although first disclosing it only in private conversations. Mr. Polk, American delegate to the Supreme Council, reported to the Secretary of State on the 29th November, 1919, the following conversation with Lloyd George :

" He (Lloyd George) said Great Britain would not give any more assistance to Denikin or Koltchak after the present supplies which had been set apart for them were exhausted. He seemed to think that their situation was serious and did not see what more could be done to help them. In his opinion the time has come to see if it is not possible *to come to an understanding with the Bolshevik Government*. ... He said that his information was that the Bolsheviks were gaining but more anxious to make peace and *were willing to recognize their international obligations.*" [5]

Davis, the American Ambassador in London, reported to the Secretary of State on the 3rd December, 1919, that Lloyd George had told him that " in order to bring peace in Russia he was not averse to treating with the Bolshevik Government and was utterly opposed to further military ventures." [6]

In a conversation between Davis and Lloyd George on the 6th February, 1920, the British Prime Minister was still more outspoken on this point :

" The Prime Minister " [reports Davis], " desires peace in Russia and thinks that the *régime of the Bolsheviks is changing color* and has given up the use of terror. He believes that a stable régime will be brought about by opening the country up to trade. *He does not credit the possibility of the Bolsheviks engaging in militaristic designs* when fighting ceases on their frontiers." [7]

In his Diary Lord Riddell notes under the date of the 6th March, 1920 :

" Spent the morning with Lloyd George. . . . He spoke of Russia. He strongly favours peace with the Russian Government. He said he had advocated this in Paris in February 1919." [8]

It would be unfair to say that the policy pursued by Lloyd George had not, from the beginning, the backing of an important section of the British public opinion, desiring a return to normal peaceful conditions within the shortest possible time. In an interesting memorandum dated the 22nd December, 1919, prepared by Hoare of the Foreign Office for H.M. Government, we find some interesting remarks on this point :

" We have two main interests in the Russian problem: (1) the early establishment of stable conditions and the renewal of trade ; (2) to ensure that whatever the future of Russia may be, Bolshevism shall not hurt us.

" A continuation of our negative policy will not advance either of these aims. The question remains whether there is at present any constructive—as opposed to negative—course of action open to us, and the answer to the question necessarily depends on what views we take on the genesis and future of Bolshevism. First to define ' Bolshevism ' for our purposes and as existing in Russia to-day, it may be described as a military tyranny which aims at the overthrow of existing civilization by means of propaganda backed by force of arms.

" As stated above there is every probability that in the course of next year Bolshevism will be established as the only Government in Russia. If that occurs, we may find ourselves compelled to fight Russia in defence of our Empire. The successful conduct of a great war depends mainly on the state of public opinion in the belligerent countries. At present it is difficult to see how public opinion could be roused to support a war with Bolshevism. There is undoubtedly a widespread feeling which may be summed up in the phrase: ' They had not been given a chance,' while the Labour Party take the point of view that, admitting Bolshevik practice in Russia to be brutal, the ' capitalist classes ' which have enjoyed our support are very little better. Neither ' atrocities propaganda ' as now conducted by *The Times* nor evidence of subversive activity in India, Egypt or elsewhere would suffice to convince the country as a whole that Bolshevism must be fought. If the fight is to come

we require both the conviction of our own people that it was inevitable and, so far as possible, the active or passive support of the
Russian people."

We find some explanation for the attitude taken by Lloyd George
in the following discreet remarks of the above-mentioned British
diplomat, contained in the last passages of his memorandum :

"The other point is connected with the unfortunate fact that the
question of our attitude towards Russia has become in a great
measure a matter of party politics. The principle of continuity in
foreign policy is in danger of being abandoned. The chances of a
general election within the next year must be reckoned with and
also the possibility that it may result in the establishment of a Government largely dependent on Labour support. Should that be the
case and should no definite Russian policy have been adopted it
will become one of the main subjects of discussion and agitation.
Such a result will be deplorable because it would adversely affect
the general situation in England and also because it would render
it more difficult for the Government of the day to induce the
French and other Allied Governments to accept their Russian
policy." [9]

In a somewhat similar position to Lloyd George was the Italian
Prime Minister, Signor Nitti, who to a still greater extent than the
British statesmen depended on politics at home. *The Times*
observed, on the occasion of the meetings of the Supreme Council in
early 1920, that

"The attitude of Signor Nitti during the sittings of the Supreme
Council in London has been a little perplexing. He has seemed on
several occasions to be eager to curry favour with the Italian politicians who are most deeply tainted with Bolshevist doctrine." [10]

In him Lloyd George found a valuable assistant for many of his
moves.

The question of Russia was reviewed at several meetings in London, Paris and other places, by the Allied Prime Ministers and
Ministers for Foreign Affairs, in winter 1919-20 and spring 1920.

At the meeting in London on 11th December, Clemenceau made
a long statement in which he stressed the necessity for giving
up all idea of further direct intervention in Russia "as all efforts
in this direction would prove wasteful in the future as in the past."
He suggested instead "a barbed wire entanglement round Russia in
order to prevent her from creating trouble outside, and in order to
stop Germany from entering into relations with Russia, whether of a
political or military character " ... " the Allies must have persever-
ance, fairness and patience." According to Clemenceau Poland was
called to play an important rôle in this policy.

" The support of Poland was the best way to check Germany. Poland occupies a first-rate strategical position. She has an army of half a million good soldiers inured to hardships and animated by a strong patriotism. Politically she is well disposed to the Allies and sufficiently armed. She only asks the Allies for help. It would be a great mistake if we did not maintain Poland in order to dam up the Russian flood and to provide a check to Germany ... our policy ... ought to be to fortify Poland in order to keep Russia in check and to contain Germany." [11]

Clemenceau also advised the British Prime Minister to change his attitude towards Poland, but with little success, because Lloyd George took the view that " the Poles had always been a very troublesome people of Europe," and stated that his views on the matter would depend upon " whether Poland was expected to attack the Bolsheviks." Nevertheless he agreed to the resolution of the Conference according to which " a strong Poland was in the interest of the Entente Powers." We shall see later which interpretation he gave to this passage of the resolution. As we have said before, Lloyd George did not believe at that time that the Bolsheviks had any aggressive designs. As a matter of fact, nobody at the Conference inquired into the conception of a " barbed wire entanglement " from the military point of view, for strangely enough the advice of the military experts was not asked on that matter at the London Conference in December 1919.

At the same time the Allies rejected the idea of close collaboration between the anti-Bolshevik States, in spite of all the Polish endeavours to win Allied support for this idea. About the same time (19th January, 1920) a Conference was held at Helsingfors, attended by the representatives of Poland, Finland, Estonia, Latvia and Lithuania, which passed a resolution

" concerning the common principle for the maintenance of their independence and made an agreement, according to which all territorial controversies between the said countries and also between them and Russia should be decided on the basis of self-determination of nations. The Conference expressed the hope that the independence and the governments of the Baltic States would in the near future be recognized *de jure*. The Conference agreed to common measures for defence against danger from the East, and also that their relations with Russia should be determined in harmony with the wishes of the Entente so far as those are in accordance with the indispensable interests of the countries concerned." [12]

Any suggestions to this effect, put forward by Poland in the first instance, were turned down by the Allied Powers. At the meeting on 11th December Lloyd George stated that he had discussed with Clemenceau the question of a " federation of the anti-Bolshevik States. This was of no use unless the Allies were prepared to support the federation, and such support meant money, guns and equipment. He and Clemenceau had come to the conclusion that this was not a very helpful expedient."

The question of the Baltic States was raised at this Conference by Balfour, who asked whether the Allies would acquiesce in their making peace with the Bolsheviks. " We ought not to encourage them not to do so," he said, " unless we could give them support and assistance. If we have to surround Russia, as it were, with a barbed wire fence, could we leave so big a gap as lay between Poland and Finland. This would be to cut off Finland and to give the Bolsheviks access to the sea. If we acquiesce in their making peace with the Bolsheviks, what steps were we to take." The answer given by Lloyd George proved that he did not see eye to eye with Balfour on the question. Lloyd George observed that " the populations of these States were very formidable people," but at the same time he said that he " did not believe that the Bolsheviks would attack them further." Nor did he think " that the Baltic States intended to make peace, but they were suspending active military operations against the Bolsheviks." When Balfour observed that " he would be very sorry to see any peace which gave Russia access to the Baltic." Lloyd George answered that " the Baltic States might offer a means of peaceful penetration into Russia. The Bolsheviks had talked much of propaganda, but he thought that civilization might also undertake its peaceful penetration." Lloyd George was hardly sincere when he expressed his hope that the Baltic States would not make peace with Russia, because the Foreign Office had already for some months taken the view that the Baltic States should have an entirely free hand in negotiating with the Soviets. This appears clearly from the instruction sent by Lord Curzon to Bosanquet, British Agent in Tallin (Reval) on the 25th September, 1919. Lord Curzon announced in this instruction that H.M. Government would be unable to continue to supply military material and stores to the Baltic States or to assume financial responsibility. The note further ran as follows :

" In these circumstances His Majesty's Government feel that they are not entitled to exercise any pressure upon the free initiative of the Baltic States and that their Governments must be at liberty to decide upon such action as may be most conducive to the preservation of their own national existence. It is for them to determine *with unfettered judgement* whether they should make any arrangement, and if so of what nature, with the Soviet authorities ; and if, as seems to be in contemplation, they decide to act in unison, the effective control of the situation should be within their power." [13]

Estonia did in fact conclude the Treaty of Peace with the Soviet Union at Tartu (Dorpat) on the 2nd February, 1920. The following dispatch of the U. S. Commissioner at Riga (Gade) of the 25th January throws light on the British endeavours preceding the conclusion of this treaty :

> " I am credibly informed that British Government has notified Esthonian Government of its satisfaction at conclusion of armistice with Bolsheviks. This being known to Latvian Government will greatly influence its present negotiations in Moscow. French here indignant." [14]

The conclusion of the peace treaty with Esthonia was much more than a purely local event; coming at the time of the final defeats of Denikin, it opened a gap in the fence with which the Allies allegedly wished to surround Bolshevik Russia, and enhanced the Bolshevik self-assurance and conviction that victory over the capitalist States was just round the corner. " The peace with Esthonia," said Lenin, " is a window to Western Europe thrown open by the Russian workers; it is an immense victory over world imperialism." [15]

Resolutions of the Supreme Council of 13th December, 1919

The official communiques issued by the Supreme Council after each meeting dealing with the problem of Russia were couched in particularly ambiguous terms covering the far-reaching differences between two opposite trends of policy : one represented by Lloyd George and the Italian Prime Minister, Nitti, wanting to resume trade with Russia as soon as possible, and the other advocated by the French Government, believing in the possibility of surrounding the Soviets with a barbed wire fence. The Supreme Council on 13th December, 1919, issued the following communiqué :

> " The Russian policy agreed to at the Conference may be summed up as follows:
>
> (1)   Not to enter into any further commitments beyond what have already been promised or, in the case of Siberia, may be decided upon between the Governments of the United States of America and Japan, as to furnishing assistance to the anti-Bolshevik elements in Russia whether in the form of troops, war material and financial aid ; the anti-Bolshevik elements still to be free to purchase war material in the Allied countries ; each power to have discretion to have on the spot all political or other missions which may either be attached to the anti-Bolshevist elements or the dispatch of which may already have been decided upon ; *and to leave Bolshevist Russia, as it were, within a ring fence.*

(2) The Conference considered that a strong Poland was in the interests of the Entente Powers and left for further consideration the question of the form and extent of the assistance to be given to her for the defence of her territories.

(3) The Conference agreed that no useful purpose would be served by attempting to summon any general conference of the representatives of the anti-Bolshevist States at the present time.

(4) As regards the Border Communities with non-Russian populations which have been struggling for freedom and self-government, the Allies will give them such assistance in defending their liberties as may be found desirable in the circumstances of each case as it arises." [16]

As subsequent developments have amply shown, each Power gave a different interpretation to these resolutions. To Lloyd George the decisions of the 13th December, 1919, were only a stepping-stone to a much bolder move for entering into trade commitments with the Soviets, opening the way to a *de facto* recognition of the Soviet State; he considered that he had scored important points for his further moves by the decision of the Allied Powers to withdraw support from the anti-Bolshevist forces in Russia and by discouraging the plans for forming a defensive league of the Border States. So far as the famous " ring fence " was concerned, he was ready to smash it at the first opportunity, and the respective passage of the resolution together with that emphasizing the rôle of Poland as a defensive bulwark of the West against Bolshevism was purely lip-service to the French point of view. The latter was expressed with particular virulence by Clemenceau at the French Chamber of Deputies on the 26th December, 1919 : " Not only shall we not make peace," he declared, " but we shall not even treat with the Soviet. We consider the Soviet Government as the most atrocious and most barbarous that has ever devastated any region of the known world." Of the British newspapers it was *The Times* which most nearly approached the French point of view. It is worthwhile to remember their warnings :

" What is the British ' real-policy ' behind this profession of national egoism and selfishness," [states the editorial of *The Times* on the 3rd January, 1920], " for this is what it amounts to when those who detest the orgies of tyranny in Russia insist that we must not lift a finger to stop them. ... We cannot disinterest ourselves any more than we can in the fire that has broken out next door. If we try, we may put off the day of reckoning, but we shall have to pay, and at a ruinous rate of interest. That is why we cannot achieve indifference to the Bolshevik victories."

Resolutions of the Supreme Council of 16th January, 1920

The next point in his Russian policy was scored by Lloyd George at the sittings of the Supreme Council in mid-January 1920, held in Paris.[17] On the 14th January the Supreme Council considered a memorandum by Lloyd George containing the suggestions relating to the re-establishment of trade with Russia. This memorandum was based on a note submitted by Mr. Wiese, a British member of the Supreme Economic Council, on " Economic Aspects of British Policy Concerning Russia." Both documents stressed the importance to the European market of Russian supplies of grain and raw materials, and advised the removal of the blockade of Russia for economic and humanitarian reasons, without asking for formal diplomatic recognition of the Soviet Government. The method recommended by Lloyd George, and by the experts invited to attend the meeting of the Supreme Council, for resuming trade with " the Russian people " (and not with the Soviet Government) by using the channel of the Russian co-operative organizations seemed to rest on the quite unwarranted assumption that the Soviet Government would grant the said bodies privileges incompatible with the Soviet régime, and for that purpose would dispense with the monopoly of foreign trade. What was more interesting from the political point of view was the illusion that by restoring normal trade relations with Russia the Soviet régime might give way to a more liberal system. Did Lloyd George really believe that the restoration of trade with Russia was the most effective way of striking a blow against Bolshevism? In recommending his scheme to the Supreme Council, he did in fact make this astonishing statement, entirely refuted by later events :

> " From the point of view of exchanges and prices, the Russian supplies were vital. The second thing was that this scheme would destroy Bolshevism. The moment trade was established with Russia, Communism would go."

Signor Nitti " entirely shared Mr. Lloyd George's views that to establish commercial relations was the proper way to beat Bolshevism."

The presentation of this scheme by Lloyd George was perfectly timed : the United States had already withdrawn from the Supreme Council and the only delegate that could vote against it, Clemenceau, was placed in a very awkward position for two reasons : (1) It was difficult for him to contest the humanitarian reasons put forward by the authors of the scheme without incurring the accusation of being the enemy of the starving Russian nation; (2) he was on the eve of the turning point of his political career, namely the elections to the Presidency of the French Republic, and he dare not provoke an open clash with other Allied representatives.

Lloyd George was also careful enough to present his plan as having allegedly no political implications. We know that the Foreign Office had not been kept informed of the deliberations of the Supreme Council on that subject, as appears from the very confidential telegram sent by Lord Curzon on the 22nd January, 1920, to Lord Hardinge, Permanent Under-Secretary of State :

> " Decision of Prime Ministers in Paris was taken by them in the absence of any Foreign Office representative. ... Prime Minister took line in private conversation that this was not the affair of Foreign Office, but of Food Ministry, who should control procedure." [18]

The Note issued on the decision of the Supreme Council on the 16th January is a most confusing document. It bears the title " Decision to permit the exchange of goods on a basis of reciprocity between the *Russian people* and Allied and Neutral Countries " and runs as follows :

> " With a view to remedying the unhappy situation of the population of the interior of Russia, which is now deprived of all manufactured products from outside Russia, the Supreme Council, after having taken note of the report of a committee appointed to consider the reopening of certain trading relations with the Russian people, has decided that it would permit the exchange of goods on the basis of reciprocity between the Russian people and Allied and neutral countries. For this purpose it decided to give facilities to the Russian co-operative organizations which are in direct touch with the peasantry throughout Russia, so that they may arrange for the import into Russia of clothing, medicines, agricultural machinery and the other necessities of which the Russian people are in sore need, in exchange for *grain, flax, etc., of which Russia has surplus supplies.*
> "*These arrangements imply no change in policy of the Allied Governments towards the Soviet Government.*"

Lloyd George tried to justify his initiative at the Supreme Council in a statement made in the House of Commons on the 10th February, 1920.[19] He admitted that " it is a fact that Bolshevism is not democracy," and that " there is no government in Russia which speaks for any definite area," the Bolsheviks having " not established the right to speak even for the whole of European Russia." Therefore, according to his view, " there is no government entitled to speak for Russia as a whole at present." But on the other side he took an extremely optimistic view so far as concerned the consequences of resuming trade with Russia. Being, as we have said

above, strongly influenced by his close advisers, especially Wiese
and Philip Kerr (afterwards Lord Lothian),[20] who were unaware
of the extent of the destruction of the Russian economy by the
long war and especially by the Bolshevik social experiment,
he recalled in his statement the Russian pre-war share in world trade
(" one-fourth of the whole export of wheat in the world, four-fifths
of the flax grown in the world was produced in Russia . . . one-third
of the total supply of imported butter to Great Britain came directly
from Russian sources," and so on), and on the strength of these pre-
war figures he drew the conclusion that " *the corn-bins of Russia
were bulging with grain. This is our report.*" This preposterous
assertion was for a very long time the target for easy criticisms by
those who took a more realistic view of the Russian economic position.

Let us compare with these assertions the official Soviet statistics
at that time. According to them, in 1920 the total industrial output
of Russia fell to 18 per cent. of the pre-war output, the area under
cultivation diminished by 18 per cent. and the production of grain by
25 per cent. The national income in 1920, according to the assessment of a Soviet statistician, decreased two and a half and possibly
three times.[21]

In these circumstances it seems that Pilsudski saw the real Russian
position in a more sober way, as appears from an interview given by
him on the 28th February to the correspondent of a French newspaper, *Le Petit Parisien* :

> " The European nations, more distant from the Bolshevik hotbed,
> can still believe in the blessings of the régime installed by Lenin.
> We, who watch it at close quarters, have formed our opinion on
> the matter. We are appalled by Bolshevism in Russia.
>
> " We know well that Russia will never be able to supply grain to
> Europe, which, as I am told, the latter expects from her. A people
> which has a surplus of grain does not die from starvation. As a
> matter of fact, in most Russian provinces the population perishes
> from hunger and according to official statistics just received by me
> the population of some provinces has diminished by 13 per cent."

Were other predictions by Lloyd George warranted by subsequent
events?

> " We can save Russia by commerce. Commerce has a sober
> influence in its operations. The simple sums in addition and sub-
> traction which it inculcates soon dispose of wild theories."

Lloyd George also had rather a detached opinion on the nature
of Russian expansionism, which he depicted in vivid colours in some
of his previous statements :

" Can Russia wage war outside its own territory? ... Poland is short of things that Russia wants. ... What would they get from the mountains of Armenia? They are starving there. Baku—they might get oil there. I agree, but that is another matter. That they could get trade. ... Trade, in my opinion, will bring an end to the ferocity and the crudities of Bolshevism surer than any other method."

It is no wonder that public opinion in the Western countries was utterly surprised by what was qualified as a reversal of the Allied attitude towards Bolshevism, coming so unexpectedly after the recent resolutions on the ring fence. There was much astonishment also that the Allies, instead of boldly facing the political problems arising from Denikin's defeats, used tortuous ways, pretending that their decisions did not imply any change of policy. Perhaps the rightest note was struck by the *New York Times* in two editorials. In the first, of 18th January, entitled " Peace by Surrender," the said paper commented in the following way on the blockade decision :

" Mr. Lloyd George having failed to kill the wolf, now offers him a juicy bone. For the first time in its history the British Empire has adopted the policy of buying off a dangerous enemy—a policy which was successfully employed by famous empires of the past, but which is unlikely to bring permanent and satisfactory peace at this time, as it is inconsistent with the habit of British foreign policy. To be sure, the surrender is veiled by a solemn assurance that we are reopening the trade, not with the Bolshevists, but the Russian co-operatives, and that our policy remains the same. But nothing can be sent to Russia without coming into possession of the Soviet Government if that Government wants it. And to say that shipment of supplies of all sorts to a Government hitherto our enemy involves no change of policy is so ridiculous that the Supreme Council can hardly have hoped anybody would believe it. " This reversal of world policy overnight is, beyond doubt, the work of Mr. Lloyd George himself. It is a characteristic specimen of those ' brilliant improvisations ' by the aid of which he has vaulted from pinnacle to pinnacle, displaying the agility of a Rocky Mountain goat, always managing to keep his majority somehow. It bears the unmistakable signature of the artist."

In its editorial of 25th January the *New York Times* pointed to the dangers which might arise for Russia's neighbours from the decisions of the Supreme Council :

" ... that peace with Soviet Russia would be an intelligible policy, though a risky one ; that aggressive warfare would be an intelligible policy, though an impossible one ; that defensive warfare would be an intelligible policy ; but *that for breaking up one front while maintaining another and supplying the Bolsheviks with means of attacking the Border States no adequate explanation is forthcoming.''* [My italics.]

There was another issue on which the Supreme Council showed that it did not possess a good grasp of the situation in Russia and that it was pursuing two different lines of policy towards the Bolsheviks, because it lifted the blockade of Soviet Russia on the one side, and on the other it took some steps which could be interpreted as giving encouragement to the peoples struggling for independence on the outskirts of the Soviet State, but without providing them with adequate means of defence. On 10th January the Supreme Council decided that the Principal Allied and Associated Powers should jointly recognize the Governments of Georgia and Azerbaijan,[22] and on 19th January it extended this decision to the Government of the Armenian State.[23] But at the same time it decided not to send to the Transcaucasian States the three divisions contemplated by the Inter-Allied Military Council, although the British delegation had taken the view, in its note of 12th January, that "owing to the collapse of Denikin Transcaucasus becomes the bridge which must be defended by the Allies," [24] and in the telegram sent to the French Ambassador in Washington for the American Government the Allied Governments declared that they

"have recognised the independence of the neighbouring States, to the list of which has just been added Georgia, Azerbaijan and Armenia, and that in the eventuality that the Bolsheviks *would refuse to make peace* with these States, and would attempt to infringe on the independence of the said communities by force, *the Allies would accord the States the fullest support in their power*." [25]

We know that within a few months Soviet Russia invaded the Caucasian republics without any opposition from the Allied Powers. Baku was taken by the Bolshevik forces at the end of April 1920, and the Azerbaijan Government was overthrown. At the moment of the ultimatum addressed by the now satellite Azerbaijan State, with the backing of Soviet Russia, to Armenia on 14th May the Armenian Delegation in Paris issued a declaration stating that " all the appeals of the Armenian Government to the Powers were in vain," and that " the Armenian Republic has not up to the present received a single cartridge from her great Allies." [26] Very soon the Bolsheviks intervened also in force in Persia, where according to a British historian " a tremendous blow was struck at British prestige." [27]

Did all these events confirm Lloyd George's anticipations that the " régime of the Bolsheviks was changing colour " and that there was no danger of " Bolsheviks engaging in militaristic designs " ?

As regards Lloyd George's illusions on this matter it is worth-while to refer to a very characteristic exchange of views which took place at the sitting of the Supreme Council on the 19th January, 1920.[28] This sitting was attended by Marshal Foch who, in connection with the debate on the recognition of the Caucasian States, was asked whether there existed a danger of the Bolsheviks attacking Poland. Marshal Foch replied that

" were the Russians to recover all its former vast area, any calamity is possible unless serious precautions are taken to meet it. In a word, it is necessary to confront a vast Bolshevik Russia with strong, united efforts. It is not by Poland alone that it must be resisted, but by every State which can collaborate in the effort. The forces that can be opposed to the Bolsheviks are those of scattered republics, organized or unorganized. Passing from Azerbaijan, by the Caucasus there are Georgia, Bessarabia, Poland, Esthonia, Latvia—all new States which may be placed in a very difficult situation if they are abandoned. If, on the contrary, they are taken in hand, it is possible to succeed in establishing a system of military forces powerful enough to hold the Bolsheviks in check."

The dialogue following this statement is particularly characteristic of the difference of approach to the whole problem between a great soldier and an astute politician, unwilling to depart from his preconceived ideas :

" *Mr. Lloyd George* : Do you propose a military entente between these different States with the object of attacking Soviet Russia, or, on the contrary, with the object of common defence in the case the Bolsheviks attack?

" *Marshal Foch* : The first thing to be done is to stop the advancing Bolshevism and to consolidate the States which have just been founded. It is a matter of establishing a defensive organization, a safety belt to protect Central Europe against the advance of the Bolsheviks. That is the goal to be reached first of all.

" *Mr. Lloyd George* : You would not then propose equipping the Polish Army to enable it to enter Russia?

" *Marshal Foch* : No, and I go further still. Even if the Polish Army were equipped it could not accomplish that task. If I were asked for my opinion I should only propose to realize an Entente between Poland, Rumania, Lithuania, Latvia, Esthonia and Finland. An entente, in the first instance, political with the object of arresting the progress of Bolshevism. That league the Transcaucasian countries would join and Bolshevism would thus be surrounded.

" *Mr. Lloyd George* : Do you know whether the Bolsheviks are preparing to attack those countries?

" *Marshal Foch* : That one cannot know till after the event.

" *Mr. Lloyd George* : Could you now mention a single one of those countries against which the Bolsheviks contemplate a military attack?

" *Marshal Foch* : When attack takes place, I shall be in a position to reply. I could not do so beforehand."

It appears clearly from this dialogue that Lloyd George did not wish to admit that the Bolsheviks had any " militaristic designs " and that he was much more preoccupied with the safety of Russia than with that of the Border States, some of which he distrusted. Nor did he understand all the implications of the Bolshevik advance for the security of Europe. Such assumptions obviously stood in the way of his policy of gradually removing all the obstacles to a *rapprochement* with the Soviet State.

Soviet peace proposals to Poland and the attitude of Western Powers

It is against this general political background that we must review the position of Poland arising from the above-mentioned resolutions of the Supreme Council and the offers of peace made to her by Soviet Russia. In consequence of the negotiations with the Bolshevik representative, Marchlewski, (see above pp. 476 ff.), and in connection with the general peace offensive, Chicherin sent a telegram to the Polish Foreign Minister on the 22nd December, 1919.[29] It was couched in very general terms, proposing " to start immediately negotiations with the aim of concluding a solid and durable peace between the two countries." According to Chicherin the obstacles to the conclusion of such a peace were put up " not by Polish interests or wishes but were due to foreign inspirations contrary to the real Polish interests." Consequently Chicherin proposed " to stop immediately military actions serving only foreign interests."

The true aim of this offer was the best understood by a keen and hostile foreign observer, General von Seeckt, recently (on 24th November, 1919) appointed Chief of the Military Department (Chief of Truppenamtes) of the new German Reich. In his diary he noted:

" There is only one positive fact to be reckoned with, namely, *that the Bolsheviks intend to start an offensive* against Poland at the beginning of February. Russia did not in fact wish a military contest with Poland, willing to devote herself to the economic reconstruction of the country. She has just defeated Denikin and Koltchak and was ready to recognize Poland, *provided the latter breaks away from the Entente.* Such is the fate of any buffer State, and consequently of Poland also, that history compels here again *to take clearly the side of one or other party.*"[30]

Poland was well aware of her responsibilities towards the Western Allies, and it was only natural that before answering Chicherin's offer she was eager to ascertain the views of the Entente Powers. For this reason only an interim reply was sent to Chicherin, stating that Poland wished to " do nothing in the matter without consulting the Allies." Similar Soviet offers to the Allied Powers remained unanswered by the latter.[31] We know that at that time the view prevailed in Allied quarters that " there is no Russia one can make peace with." Such was apparently the view of Lloyd George himself, and some members of the British Cabinet were quite outspoken on this matter. Speaking at Dundee on the 16th February, 1920, Winston Churchill said :

> " I fear that the Allied Powers may have to pay a heavy penalty in the future, and perhaps the near future, in consequence of the Bolshevist success. . . . You will say to me: ' Are you for peace with Russia? ' *My regret is we have not got a Russia with whom we can make a real peace.*
> " . . . No one knows what is coming out of the Russian cauldron, but it will almost certainly be something full of evil, full of menace for Britain, France and the United States." [32]

The position of the United States, whose recent withdrawal from the councils of the Allies was to have such disastrous consequences for the establishment of lasting peace in Europe, was put clearly in a telegram sent by Secretary of State to the Ambassador in Great Britain on the 8th January, 1920 (this telegram was repeated to the Legations at Warsaw and Prague and the Commissioner at Helsinfors) :

> " With respect to suggestions in certain quarters that the time has come to establish relations with the Russian Bolsheviki, it is the view of the Government of the United States that past experience has proved the *futility to arrive at a satisfactory understanding with them.*
> " On the other hand it is possible that the Bolshevik group will never be forcibly ousted in Russia but will give way gradually to new leaders and thus evolve into a government with which it will be possible to deal. The Government of the United States is convinced that Lenin and his immediate disciples will never permanently forego the dream of world revolution or enter loyally into amicable relations with non-Bolshevik governments." [33]

All this indicated the opinion prevailing in the Western countries that so far as they themselves were concerned they rejected as impracticable any idea of a peace treaty with Bolshevik Russia. On the other side the Chief of the State, Pilsudski, took the view that the Allies should either jointly with Poland conclude a peace treaty with

Soviet Russia or help Poland in bringing the war with the Bolsheviks to a successful end. Gibson, American Ambassador to Warsaw, notes in his report of 17th January Pilsudski's objections to a premature, separate peace with Russia :

> " The Chief of State, General Pilsudski, has told me on several occasions that while Poland is in desperate need of peace, it would be folly for him to sign any treaty with the Bolshevik radical Government as they have repeatedly shown not only their bad faith but the inability of the Central Government to compel the observance of their agreements ; that if a treaty were signed he would not be able to withdraw his army for fear the country would be overrun at any time ; that, on the other hand, he could not maintain an army on guard against a possible violation of the treaty as the morale of the troops would not stand up under such questionable policy and hardship without the belief that they were defending an endangered country." [34]

At almost the same time as Mackinder, the British High Commissioner for South Russia, was discussing with Pilsudski the question of a joint offensive by the Polish and Denikin's armies against the Bolsheviks (his conversation with Pilsudski took place on the 16th December, 1919, see above p. 469), the Supreme Council passed its famous resolution on surrounding Russia with a " barbed wire fence " (13th December). The latter seemed to assign to Poland a more passive rôle, and a very uncomfortable one indeed, of the gendarme of Europe, which although very flattering could hardly appeal to Poland as it meant that she must be on guard and stand permanently on the defensive, being neither at war nor peace with Bolshevik Russia.

From the resolution of the Supreme Council of the 13th December, 1919, Poland was allowed to infer that she could count on the assistance of the Allied Powers *for the defence of her territories.*[35] Perhaps the expression used in the resolution was a little ambiguous, but nobody in Poland could suspect at that time that Lloyd George would give it such a restrictive interpretation as he did at a later period. Let us remember here that the Supreme Council did not consider that the Eastern frontier of Poland could be defined at that time (see above, pp. 486 ff.). On the other side the passage stating that " a strong Poland was in the interest of the Entente Powers " should mean that at least nothing would be done by the Powers that might endanger or weaken the political and military position of Poland as the Western bulwark in the East. In fact it was on the extent of the political, moral and material support from these Powers to Poland that the whole political future of Central and Eastern Europe largely depended. This fact was fully realized by all the diplomatic representatives of the Western Powers in Poland, as clearly appears from their reports and reiterated demands for fulfilment of the pledges of assistance to Poland. For instance, Gibson, American Minister in Warsaw, says in his report to the Secretary of State dated 17th January, 1920 :

" It seems clearly to the interest of the Bolsheviks to embark upon the attack as soon as they can be assured of a substantial initial success. They know that discussions are under way in Paris with a view to some Allied support to the Poles. . . .

" . . . if on the other hand it is decided that no support would compel general acceptance, this would in itself constitute the best possible reason for attacking Poland. In any case we may safely assume that the Bolshevists will be accurately informed as to the measures of support Poland may expect and will govern themselves accordingly." [36]

The importance of this issue was not realized in political quarters in the West. An interesting illustration of the obstacles which Poland had to overcome in her endeavours to obtain much-needed military equipment is the discussion at the Supreme Council on the 5th January, 1920, in connection with the Polish request for authorization to buy arms and munitions in Germany.[37] It should be kept in mind that such a request had nothing unusual in it, because previously similar demands by Denikin and the Czecho-Slovak Government had been favourably received. The request of the Polish Government was supported by Marshal Foch " on account of the critical position in which Denikin's defeats may place the Polish Army." The request was opposed by the British representative, Sir Eyre Crowe, who observed that it " should be first found out whether the Poles actually lacked rifles and cartridges and whether their present claims did not conceal a desire to procure war material *at small expense.*" In his further remarks Sir Eyre emphasized " the importance attached in England to the idea of progressive disarmament; he would not, therefore, like to furnish the Poles with war material of which they (the Poles) were *not strictly in need* : if the Poles were in possession of too great a quantity of guns of German origin they would be obliged to continue to obtain German material which would be contrary to the *business interest of the Allies.*" This declaration is really astonishing, because the British Government was in possession of numerous reports from H.M. Minister in Warsaw who on many occasions stressed the necessity for supplying Poland with war material and warm clothing (see above, p. 408). Even in her critical hour Poland met British opposition to obtaining supplies from Germany, as appears from the conversation between Lord d'Abernon, sent to Warsaw on a special mission during the Red offensive, and some British generals. Lord d'Abernon notes in his diary, under the date of the 26th July, 1920 : " Conversation with English generals now stationed in Berlin and Danzig . . . the project of transferring German munitions of war to Poland is impracticable, as under the Treaty of Versailles these munitions have to be destroyed." [38] The great shortage of war material, and even of warm clothing, of the Polish army in the field was a matter of common knowledge. The Warsaw correspondent of *The Times* reported the following on the 15th February :

> " Allied officers who have visited the front of Dvinsk and the Ukraine report that few of the troops are properly clothed to face the winter weather in these regions. One of the officers in question visited an armoured train, of whom, out of a crew of sixty, only twenty had sufficient clothing to enable them to leave the train. If it were not for the general stoicism of the soldiers and their hatred of their opponents, it would be impossible to keep the army in the field, and peace or no peace, the army will have to be kept on the frontier to prevent Poland from being inundated by Bolshevist propaganda and Bolshevist paper money. ... "

The correspondent adds :

> " I should like to emphasize the fact that the rest of Europe owes a debt to the Polish army, which has been the main factor in preventing the spread of Bolshevism westwards. If English people will take out their atlases and measure the line from Dvinsk to Kamenetz-Podolsk, and ask themselves where Bolshevism would have stopped if there had been no Polish army, they will realize how great the debt is." [39]

Such was the view of all the British observers on the spot, from the British Minister in Warsaw down to the Press correspondent, while the British representative in the Supreme Council was anxious that Poland might not receive more than was strictly necessary and obviously cared more for British business interests than for the security of Poland. Clemenceau showed more understanding, because in reply to Sir Eyre's objections at the same sitting of the Supreme Council he said

> " that they (the Supreme Council) had a double reason for strengthening Poland ; she constituted the strongest rampart against Bolshevism and on the other hand on account of the stategic position she occupied she might be a decisive aid in case of difficulties with Germany. ... He did not personally see any objection to the 300,000 rifles in question being in Poland, a friendly country, rather than in Germany.'

A few days after this discussion at the Supreme Council came the reversal of the Allied policy caused by the decision of the same

Council on the reopening of certain trading relations, carried out on 16th January (see above, p. 511). This decision bewildered world opinion, and even more that of Poland, which could not understand how this new trend of policy could be agreed with the rôle assigned to Poland by the previous decision on the " barbed wire fence." From the Polish point of view this new trend of Allied policy meant beginning normal relations with Russia at the wrong end, as a much safer way for world peace would have been previously to obtain sufficient guarantees from the Bolsheviks for their abiding by the rules of international law and respecting the new political order in Eastern Europe. The new States of this region suddenly saw the dangers of Russian pressure greatly increased as the Bolsheviks obtained gratuitously valuable assets for future dealings with their neighbours. Moreover, in Paris Russia obtained from the British Prime Minister a solemn assurance that " in no circumstances whatever will there be any offensive campaign against Russia." When asked at the Press conference after the meeting in Paris which steps would be taken " if the Bolsheviks were to threaten Poland," the British Prime Minister answered rather flippantly that in such an event " something would have been done," which meant that in Lloyd George's mind trading with Russia had absolute priority over all political issues in Eastern Europe. In its editorial of the 26th January, 1920, *The Times* said :

> " We shall be equipping the Bolshevik forces for next spring, whether they attack in Poland or in other Border States, or in Asia. ... America is mystified, France is mystified, our own people are mystified, by this latest *volte-face,* which all with one accord ascribe to the personal action of the Prime Minister."

May we add to these remarks by *The Times* that the first purchases made by the Russian Trade Mission abroad after the lifting of the blockade were not food or consumer goods for the impoverished Russian population, but railway engines greatly needed by Russia for the transport of troops and war material to the front against Poland. Some of these engines actually reached Russia in the course of the offensive against Warsaw (those bought in Sweden and the U.S.A.).[40]

Signor Tommasini, the Italian Minister in Warsaw, in his book already quoted, says that the impression produced by the resolution of 16th January on the Polish public opinion was quite disastrous, and nobody there could make out from the " nebulous " terms of it which were the true aims of the Entente in Eastern Europe. In conversation with Tommasini at the end of January, Pilsudski seemed to be exasperated by the pacific recommendations lavished on Poland by the Powers which had the advantage of being far from the danger zone.[41]

The journey of Patek, then Polish Minister of Foreign Affairs, to the Western capitals in January did not help very much in disentangling the puzzle of the new policy of the Western Powers. In each capital Patek heard opposite advice. In Paris he was strongly warned against any peace negotiations with the Bolshevik Government. In London it was obvious that the British Prime Minister did not see eye to eye with other responsible British quarters, the Foreign Office and Winston Churchill, then Minister for War, in the first instance. Patek had a conversation with Lloyd George on the 26th January; we have a detailed report of this conversation in the letter from Lord Curzon to Sir H. Rumbold. As there are some omissions in the said report we had to complete it from other sources.

According to Lord Curzon's report [42] Lloyd George stated first of all that " while it was not for Britain to advise Poland, which must take full responsibility for deciding as between peace and war, the British Government did not advise war." The position has considerably changed after the White Russian generals' defeats and there " was clearly, therefore, grave risk that Poland might be left to face a Bolshevik concentration by itself." . . . " The British Government did not wish to give Poland the slightest encouragement to pursue the policy of war, because if it were to give that advice it would incur responsibilities which it could not discharge."

Lloyd George's statement could be interpreted to mean that according to him the question of war or peace depended exclusively on Poland. This impression is increased by what he said further about the Bolshevik policy. Making clear that if Poland wished to pursue the war she could not reckon on British assistance, Lloyd George tried to persuade Patek that " Bolshevism did not constitute a serious military menace outside its own borders." He did not think, in fact, that " the Bolshevik armies, in view of the great desire of the population for peace, now, constitute a military menace against any well-organized State. Their transportation and manufacturing resources were not sufficient to admit of great offensive operations." Having thus minimized the danger of Bolshevism to Poland, which it is worth while to stress in view of later events and especially of the Russian offensive in summer 1920, Lloyd George started to discuss the character of a possible peace between Poland and Russia. Lloyd George stated first of all that " the Polish armies had advanced beyond the racial boundary into considerable territories which contained large Russian majorities." Lord Curzon's report omitted the remark made at that moment by Patek (which is to be found in Patek's report to the Polish Government) :

" We were called there to save the population from Bolshevik oppression," to which Lloyd George replied : " The principle of self-determination is very attractive, indeed. If anyone is asked whether he prefers to live under the Polish or Bolshevik domination, the answer will be—of course—under the former, but this is not pertinent." But Lloyd George was unable to define which were Poland's ethnographical limits, as appears from the report of the American Ambassador, Davis, to the Secretary of State : " of these limits he professed himself in ignorance." The British Prime Minister further said that

> " if the Poles made a sincere attempt to make an equitable peace and the Bolsheviks either refused peace or, having made peace, proceeded to repudiate it, Great Britain would feel bound to assist Poland to the best of its power. ... If, on the other hand, Poland insisted on retaining within Poland areas which were indisputably Russian according to principles generally applied by the Peace Conference, and if the Bolshevik Government refused the peace on this ground and attacked Poland in order to recover Russian districts for Russia, it would be very difficult, if not impossible, for the British Government to get public opinion to support military or financial outlay in these circumstances."

It appears clearly from this declaration that Lloyd George stuck to his opinion that the territories separating Central Poland from Russia, with mixed population and containing infinitesimal Russian minorities, territories undoubtedly belonging to Western civilization and in some areas having compact Polish majorities, should go to Russia whether White or Red. A small Poland was obviously his preference, as in his view there was no place for any big State between Germany and Russia. Thus Lloyd George began to destroy the conception of a strong buffer State between Germany and Russia on the Eastern side also, having done everything possible at the Peace Conference to weaken it on the Western side. He wished to avoid anything that might stand in the way of his favourite conception of resuming at the earliest possible moment relations with Russia. (It is interesting, by the way, to quote here the opinion of Sir Esme Howard on this point : " Looking back on that time it seems to me that the Prime Minister was so obsessed with making peace with Soviet Russia that it mattered nothing to him what progress the Communist ideas might make in Eastern Europe and he was willing for all new neighbouring States to fall into the Soviet net provided he could get the temporary respite he needed." [42a]).

In fact, he insisted very much on the necessity for re-establishing normal trading exchanges with Russia, saying to the Polish Foreign Minister that " it was the best method of bringing peace and partly because Russian sources of supply and food were essential to the feeding of Europe and the bringing down of prices."

According to Curzon's report Patek asked two questions. The first was whether " the Allies guarantee any peace made with Soviet Russia, for under existing circumstances there was nothing to prevent either the Soviet Government itself, which was not a *de jure* Government under international law, or its successor from repudiating any treaty it made." This question went straight to the point because Lloyd George obviously advised Poland to do something which the Allied Governments declined to do themselves, namely to recognize the Soviet Government and to enter into normal political relations with it. Lloyd George replied that " it was impossible for the Allies to guarantee a treaty or to go beyond the general guarantees contained in the Covenant of the League of Nations. This difficulty was inherent in the existing state of affairs, and it was a question of balance between the risk of making peace with an unstable government and the risk of war." Thus Lloyd George recommended Poland to assume risks which the Allies were unwilling to assume themselves.

The second question was whether the Prime Minister's declarations were those of all the Allies. As we know, Patek had visited Paris before London and was informed by Millerand himself that the French Government would strongly object to Poland concluding a peace treaty with Russia. The British Prime Minister evaded this question. He stated only that " Signor Nitti entirely agreed with him," and so far as France was concerned " he had not discussed the question with M. Millerand because the latter had not had time to get into office."

According to Patek's report, Lloyd George stated that he would not interfere with the Polish-Soviet peace negotiations and in his view Poland could obtain more advantageous peace terms by direct negotiations with the Bolsheviks than from the Supreme Council. He said that it was a favourable circumstance that the Supreme Council did not settle the Eastern frontier of Poland as the Bolsheviks would be more generous on this point. Lloyd George also tried to convince Patek that Poland had nothing to fear from Russia because Poland was a poor country. It was quite true that Poland was at that time impoverished by long years of war and foreign occupation, but Lloyd George showed by this statement that he completely disregarded the importance of Poland from the geographical point of view and ignored the Bolshevik urge for expansion westwards for the scope of re-establishing direct connection with Germany. Patek also stated in his report that when he observed that France was opposed to an agreement between the Bolsheviks and Poland and that he had believed that the same opinion prevailed in England, because in such a case Russia would shift all her activities to Asia, Lloyd George answered that he was not afraid of Russia. " Georgia and the Baltic States can be sure of maintaining their independence."

It would be easy to point to the declarations to the contrary made by the same Lloyd George in the House of Commons a few weeks before. The events in Caucasus and Asia which were to start very soon brought, as we know, many disappointments to the British policy. Did Lloyd George at that moment already wish to compensate Russia in Central Europe at the expense of her Western neighbours in order to divert her attention from Caucasus and Asia? As a matter of fact the Soviet moves in Caucasus and Asia, the complicity between Kemal and the Soviet, at that time preoccupied many minds in Britain.

The outcome of all the Polish endeavours to obtain from the Allied and Associated Powers a coherent statement of policy towards Russia and clear advice, gave disappointing results. This circumstance is particularly stressed in many dispatches from the American Minister in Warsaw, Gibson. On the 8th February, 1920, he wrote :

> " Patek said the Polish reply (to the Soviets) would not be sent until he had received the advice of the Powers. ... He said very definitely that he felt the Powers should not evade their share of responsibility in the decision to be taken. ... So far as I can see the governing motive of the Polish agents at present is to do what the Powers desire. ... Thus far the Powers have shown a disposition to leave the entire responsibility to Poland. This is perhaps the wiser course until such time as Poland has formulated her own views. I venture respectfully but earnestly to express the opinion, however, that when the time for a decision comes the Powers cannot, in justice to themselves, cut Poland adrift without the benefit of their guidance which was never so necessary as now." [43]

On the 19th February, 1920, he wrote :

> " Patek has been hampered in his efforts to formulate a reply to the Soviet peace offer by his inability to secure a coherent statement of the course that Allied and Associated Powers desire Poland to follow.
>
> " (1) The British Minister is giving the Polish Government to understand that Lloyd George desires Poland to make peace. ...
>
> " (2) The French while making no definite promises to help are apparently encouraging a decision to fight. ...
>
> " (3) My Italian colleague is vigorously urging the Poles to refuse the peace offer. ...

" I venture to recommend that the Department endeavour to reach some understanding with the Allied Powers as to what course is desired that Poland pursues. Until some decision is reached the whole situation in our part of Europe is out of hand." [44]

On 22nd March he concluded :

" The Polish Government has not been able to secure any expression of opinion since the peace offer and the feeling has grown among all classes that Poland has been cast adrift politically and must shift for herself."

Nor was Gibson more fortunate in obtaining a clear answer from his own government. By his dispatch of the 30th January, 1920, he asked the Secretary of State for answers to the following :

" Does the Government desire

" 1. (a) that Poland resist intention of Bolshevist invasion by force of arms; (b) or that the Poles make peace with the Bolshevists?

" 2. If the former, does our Government favor material and financial support to Poland and is there early prospect of some action being taken in this regard by us? What is our policy towards inducing the other Great Powers to assume some share of the burden? " [45]

A similar question was put to the Secretary of State by the American Ambassador in Great Britain after a conversation with the Polish Minister in that country on 28th January :

" The Poles desire to act in accordance with the views of the Allies and are particularly anxious to know whether American sentiment would be offended if they yielded to necessity and made the best terms possible. This question I declined to answer stating that I would submit it for consideration." [46]

The answer of the Secretary of State to Gibson's question was completely evasive. It stated namely :

" This Government is not in a position at the present moment to take any responsibility in advising Poland to adopt a specific policy towards Bolshevist Russia. For your own information, however, I feel that it would be most unfortunate if the Polish Government should conclude from the silence of this Government in the matter that there is implied such military and economic assistance as might determine the Polish Government in refusing to enter into armistice negotiations with Bolshevist Russia." [47]

Resolutions of the Supreme Council of 27th February, 1920

The Supreme Council again dealt with the problems of Russia and the Border States at its meeting in London at the end of

February 1920. The following statement published on the 24th February summed up the conclusions reached by the Allies :

> " If the communities which border on the frontiers of Russia and whose independence or *de facto* autonomy they have recognized were to approach them and to ask for advice as to what attitude they should take with regard to Soviet Russia, the Allied Governments would reply that they cannot accept the responsibility of advising them to continue a war which may be injurious to their own interests.
>
> " Still less they advise them to adopt a policy of aggression towards Russia. If, however, Soviet Russia attacks them *inside their legitimate frontiers,* the Allies would give them every possible support.
>
> " The Allies cannot enter into diplomatic relations with the Soviet Government, in view of their past experiences, until they have arrived at the conviction that Bolshevist horrors have come to an end. . . . "

This was undoubtedly a triumph of the ideas advocated by Lloyd George, and the tenor of the above statement agreed to a great extent with the advice given by Lloyd George to Patek on 26th January. The obvious contradiction between the advice given to the Border States and the line of policy adopted by the Allies in their own dealings with the Soviet Government bewildered many people at that time. The leading French newspaper *Le Temps* wrote on 25th February : " The four Powers which refuse to enter into diplomatic relations with the Government of the Soviets then recommended the countries bordering on Russia, which are much more exposed to dangerous Bolshevist propaganda, to do just what they themselves proclaim to be impossible. It is neither logical nor safe." Lloyd George's policy aroused strong objections in some British quarters, as appears from the editorial of *The Times* of 25th February, entitled " The Bolshevist Seduction ":

> " It is impossible not to admire the profligate art with which for over a year Mr. Lloyd George has sought for his own purposes to throw a weak, ignorant and reluctant Europe into the venal arms of her Bolshevik seducer. . . . He did not hurry matters. . . . He carefully respects the remains of virtue—or the prudery of his dupe.
>
> " Yesterday's conclusions cannot fail to confirm our contemporary in its misgivings. . . . In other words, they advise them (the Border States) to make peace with the Bolshevists. This is really the gist of the chief ' conclusions ' though it is followed by the comforting, but far from precise, assurance that if Soviet Russia attacks them ' inside their legitimate frontiers ' the Allies will give them all possible support."

Pro-Russian attitude of British Labour

There is no doubt that Lloyd George's policy was at that time prompted to a great extent by reasons of British domestic policy. He obviously wished, in view of the growing disruption in the ranks of his own party, to win the support of the Labour Party, then having a strong pro-Russian bias. While the Labour leaders had shown little interest in the cause of the liberation of the populations of Eastern Europe from Bolshevik oppression, and did nothing to ascertain the position existing in the Eastern Borderlands, they made frequent journeys to Russia and returned from there fervent supporters of the Bolshevik revolution and of the achievements of the Soviet State. We must deal with this matter later, as it was during the summer offensive of the Red Army in Poland that all the implications of this pro-Russian trend within the British Labour movement became particularly dangerous. But already at that stage the pro-Russian trends in the Labour movement began to produce its effects on Lloyd George's policy. So we must deal briefly with the reasons for the pro-Russian attitude of the Labour movement in Great Britain. In his autobiography Philip Snowden said :

> " The Bolshevik Revolution had made a great impression upon the younger members of the party, who were enthused by the spectacle of a great country overthrowing the capitalist system and establishing a communist republic. Their sympathy with the Russian communists was more emotional than intellectual, and they were not in the least critical of the methods which were being employed in Russia to fortify the Revolution." [48]

The biographer of Ernest Bevin, who took such a prominent part in this pro-Russian movement of the British trade unionism, ingenuously says about him that

> " to his critics he sometimes seemed over-ready to sacrifice the interests of small groups—small nations even—to the purpose of a grand design. There is some truth in this criticism. He was impatient of minorities. He had a majority mind." [49]

F. Borkenau, at one time a prominent member of the Third International, in his book devoted to the history of this movement explains in these words the reasons for which " the British Labour movement gave more help to Russia than any other ":

> " The wave of sympathy was very strong all over the world of labour, but on the Continent, and especially in Germany and Austria, it had been balanced by the attempts to force the Continental Labour movements into the channel of Russian methods. The fight against the communists at home had forestalled the fight for the Soviet Union. In England the Communist Party had not

yet been formed. Precisely for that reason the sympathy of a large section of the British workers for the Soviet Union, strengthened by the ' labour unrest ' of the epoch, would transform itself into practical action." [50]

The British Labour movement took the view that the war of liberation going on in Eastern Europe in 1920 was but the continuation of the Allied intervention in Russia, which according to Mr. Morrison (like Bevin, beginning to take the lead of the Labour movement) should " be resisted with the full political and industrial power of the whole Trade Union movement." [51]

A manifesto on the Russian question, signed by a group of trade union officials and Labour men representing " the more moderate section of the Labour movement," appeared in the Press on the 29th January, 1920, and demanded immediate and complete peace with the Russian Government. We quote below some striking passages from this manifesto.

> " The course of least risk all round is complete peace. If it is true that the Soviet Government has really failed to reconcile its people and still impose its power, over a territory and population as great as the United States, merely by tyranny, it must be because the people are cowed and spiritless by privation and hunger. . . .
>
> " *The Polish Army is already in occupation of the Russian territory*. If its invasion of Russia is repelled by the Soviet forces, we shall undoubtedly be told that this is an attack upon Poland and that it is our duty to stand by the *State we have created*. We should then be committed to support this war, not owing to any policy sanctioned by the country, but to acts of the Polish Army instigated by obscure diplomatic intrigues." [52]

What impression was made upon some Labour leaders during their visits to Russia we may see from the following speech made by Lansbury on his return from Russia, at the Albert Hall in London on the 22nd March, 1920. Amongst other things Lansbury said that " he had personal advice that the Central Government of Russia, the Extraordinary Commission of Russia, had done more to put down terrorism and keep down murder than any other government in similar circumstances could be expected to do. . . . "

He summed up in this way his conversation with Lenin :

> " As I sat talking to Lenin and looking into his eyes, I understood the stupendous crimes of the Allies against those people and I felt ashamed of myself. Lenin's message was: ' You, Lansbury, believe in Christianity. You believe that you can bring about in England a peaceful revolution. I do not believe it, but if you can nobody will be more pleased than we in Russia.' " [53]

These views on Bolshevism were not confined in Great Britain only to the Labour movement. They were shared by the whole progressive section of the British public opinion. We can find in the *New Statesman*, which can be considered to represent the typical state of mind of those quarters, the following statements :

> (31st January, 1920.) " Obviously Soviet rule is not democratic in the Western sense of the word, but it is incomparably more democratic than anything Russia has previously known. It is not Government ' by the people ' except in a limited sense, but it would appear to be Government ' for the people ' in the fullest possible sense ; that is to say it is a government which serves no interests whatever save those which it conceives—fighting rightly or wrongly, but honestly—to be those of the mass of the Russian people."
>
> (7th February, 1920). " That is the obsession of *The Times* and Mr. Winston Churchill and their followers in this country and of their counterparts in France, with Bolshevism as the arch-enemy of the human race, as Anti-Christ, and a hundred other absurdities." ... " We are a little tired of investigating the terror and the machinations of Bolshevism."

Refusing to see any danger in Bolshevism, the pro-Soviet section of British public opinion saw in Poland an obstacle to the policy of *rapprochement* with Soviet Russia, and consequently an anti-progressive factor, serving only as a trump in the hands of those who pursued an imperialistic policy towards Russia. According to these views there was no need for a barrier between Russia and Central Europe. It is very interesting to see how much these opinions differed from those expressed by the Allied representatives in Poland, who were infinitely better placed to see all the consequences which might arise in the event of the collapse of the Polish barrier.

Sir H. Rumbold, British Minister in Warsaw, wrote in his dispatch of the 19th January, 1920 :

> " It seems clear that if the Polish barrier against Bolshevism goes, the barrier will be shifted further west and an opportunity will be given to latent Bolshevism in Czecho-Slovakia to join hands with Russian Bolshevism, thereby creating a very serious state of things for Central Europe and the Western Powers." [54]

Hugh Gibson, American Minister in Poland, wrote to the Secretary of State on the 17th January, 1920 :

> " Success in a campaign against Poland would leave the Soviet Government triumphant in Eastern Europe and a large part of Asia and would give a fresh impetus to the Bolshevik movement throughout the world." [55]

Lord d'Abernon, sent to Warsaw as the head of the British Mission at the time of the Warsaw Battle, writes in his book *The Eighteenth Decisive Battle of the World* :

> "On the essential point there is little room for doubt: had the Soviet forces overcome Polish resistance and captured Warsaw, Bolshevism would have spread throughout Central Europe and might well have penetrated the whole continent." [56]

Let us compare with this the following statement of the *New Statesman* on the most decisive moment in Polish modern history :

> (31st July, 1920). "A small nation such as Poland, placed between two Great Powers such as Russia and Germany, cannot be truly independent, but must move in the orbit of one of them or perish between the two ... the fanciful policy of making Poland 'a check and barrier,' a French policeman for Central and Eastern Europe, has broken down. Russia has arisen as a Great Power."

The *New Statesman* saw with indifference the possibility of the destruction of the Polish State and was quite outspoken on this point, although admitting that it had a very limited knowledge of the political conditions in Eastern Europe. We find in its issue of 15th May the following statement :

> "There are signs that within a very short time all English parties from the extreme Left to extreme Right are likely to be united on the Russian side. ... *It needs no close knowledge of local conditions* to realize that if Poland succeeds in all that she has set out to accomplish, even to the extent of forcing the Bolshevik Russian Government to acknowledge her conquests, a fresh war in Eastern Europe within two or three years will be not a possibility but an absolute certainty. And it seems equally certain that in such a war the sympathies of practically the entire world would be with Russia *and that Poland will be crushed and possibly even destroyed. But, perhaps, that is the only way out of the present tangle of Eastern Europe.*" [My italics.]

Perhaps the best answer to those doctrinaires who did not see all the implications of the possible Polish defeat at that time was given in the article, "A Vendetta Against Poland," which appeared in the *National Review* (August 1920). Speaking about the cause of Poland, "A Student of History" said :

> "Her cause is our cause. She stands in the path between Germany and Russia, those giants of Europe—the one for four years our deadliest foe and still unrepentant; the other, the enemy of all that the civilization of Western Europe has stood for. *Poland may be crushed to the ground and broken to pieces, but more than she will be involved in her ruin.* Let it be consummated, if we will,

without raising a finger to help or encourage her. And then let us set to work to sharpen our swords and look well to our harness, *for there will be no more hope of peace for Europe.*" [My italics.]

The resolutions of the Supreme Council of 24th February were interpreted in a different way in Paris and London, a common occurrence after each meeting of this body.

According to the British interpretation, this resolution meant that the Border States, Poland in the first place, were advised to abstain from any military initiative and to try to come to terms with the Bolshevik Government. This interpretation obviously placed the Border States in a position of inferiority towards Russia, which thus received important trump cards. Already before the meeting of the Supreme Council, Lord Curzon in his dispatch to General Keynes, British Military Representative at Denikin's headquarters, dated 9th February, 1920,[57] stated that the position had radically changed since the discussions between General Denikin's Government and Mackinder for combined offensive operations between the Poles and the Russians against the Bolsheviks, which at the time had his (Lord Curzon's) full approval. His Majesty's Government informed, consequently, the Polish Government that " if they undertake an offensive against the Bolsheviks they will not receive support " and added " for your confidential information, that the Polish Government will consider peace proposals made to them."

The following were the reasons which induced the British Government to change its policy on that matter :

(1) The evidence that " internal conditions in Poland are not such as to admit of their undertaking military operations on a large scale."

(2) The failure of Denikin, which was so complete that " it is idle to hope for any substantial recovery."

(3) The food situation in Europe, which " makes it imperative that by some means or another surplus supplies in Russia should be made available as soon as possible."

On this last point Lord Curzon remarked that " whether or not this attempt will be successful remains to be seen, but its failure is certain if all available transport in Soviet Russia has to be diverted to the movement of troops." It can be assumed from this remark that the illusory hopes of obtaining food supplies from Russia had in some minds overshadowed all political considerations. Was the position of the Allies as desperate as that of Austria at the end of 1917 when she craved for *Brotfrieden*?

France and " the barbed wire fence " policy

The French position at that time was far from clear, being a pure negation without any positive plan of action. It is true that M. Millerand, in his statement at the Chamber of Deputies on the 6th February, 1920, stressed that Poland was France's dearest ally (*une alliée particulièrement chère*) and that Poland and Rumania could count on the fullest assistance on the side of the Allied Powers (*le concours le plus complet des puissances alliées*) in the event of their being attacked by the Bolsheviks.[58] But the French Prime Minister did not answer the question asked by Deputy Cornudet as to whether France was in agreement with Great Britain so far as concerned the advice to conclude a peace treaty with the Bolsheviks given by Lloyd George to Poland.[59] Nor did Millerand state which were the ultimate aims pursued by French policy in Eastern Europe and he did not take any position on the proposal made by Deputy Gailhard-Boncel, who advised that France should follow the example of Poland (agreement between Poland and Petlura of December 1919, see above, p. 465) and recognize the independence of the Ukraine under Petlura's administration, in accordance with the principle of self-determination, the basis of the whole work of the Conference.[60]

While officially repudiating intervention in Russia, France was giving her financial support and was supplying war material to General Denikin's successor, General Wrangel. While agreeing to the advice of the Supreme Council to the Border States to abstain from any offensive, the French Government clung to the idea of the 13th December Resolution about the " barbed wire fence," and continued to warn the Poles against taking any steps which might lead to the recognition of the Soviet Government, and consequently against an armistice and peace with the Bolsheviks.

Did France at that time still hope for the collapse of the Soviet Government through external pressure? It is difficult to answer this question, but what is certainly true is that France did not believe in the possibility of establishing a lasting and orderly government in Russia under the Bolshevik administration, which she considered inefficient and wicked. Nevertheless the French Government was gradually forced to follow the lead of Great Britain for the sake of maintaining unity among the Allies, so much needed by France for the enforcement on Germany of the provisions of the Versailles Treaty.

At the sitting of the Chamber of Deputies on the 26th March, the Left Wing of the Chamber, and strangely enough also Louis Barthou, who several years later was to play such a prominent rôle in introducing Soviet Russia into the League of Nations, appealed to the Government to follow the example of the British in their policy towards Soviet Russia. Deputy Cachin advocated with the greatest vigour the Bolshevik cause, referring to the words

of Masaryk in the speech made by the latter on the occasion of his
seventy-first birthday, in which the veteran Czech statesman said
that " the Russian policy was led by the strong and deft hand of
M. Chicherin, and that it had to be expected that within a short
time excellent relations would be established with Russia." This
time Millerand was more cautious in his reply, stating only that
he did not wish to enter into any underhand dealings with Russia
and that the *political* negotiations with Russia could be conducted
only in common agreement with the Allies.[61]   In fact, on the eve
of the San Remo Conference (19th–27th April) the French representatives at the Supreme Economic Council took part in negotiations in Copenhagen with the so-called representatives of the
Russian co-operatives, but these semi-official pourparlers proved
abortive because the Soviet delegates refused to consider any question of compensation for pre-war debts. At the San Remo Conference on 16th April the Supreme Council decided to authorize
representatives of the Allied Governments to meet Krassin and
other Russian delegates (except Litvinov) in London at the
earliest date in order to discuss the resumption of peaceful trade
relations. No wonder that for many months the French Government
was opposed to surrendering any means of pressure on the Soviet
Government before reaching a compromise with it on questions of
vital importance to France. This explains to a great extent the
advice of the French Government to Poland not to take any step
which might have been considered as recognition of the Bolshevik
régime. On the other hand there is no evidence to the effect that
France wished to destroy the unity of Russia, as has been asserted
by many writers, among them L. Fischer in his important work *The
Soviets in World Affairs*.[62] Such a plan was far from the French
minds at any time, and particularly at that time. France wished to
keep alive the Polish-Bolshevik feud for her own and limited purposes, and she certainly did not encourage any plans in Eastern
Europe based on the principle of self-determination, if only for the
one simple reason that the French Right-wing politicians and the
Quai d'Orsay were unwilling to sever their links with the White
Russian leaders living in exile, who were strongly opposed to any
capital changes in the political structure of Eastern Europe, depriving
Russia of a great part of her previous conquests.

Soviet Peace offensive and propaganda

A new move towards Poland was made by the Soviet Government at the end of January 1920. It was first of all the Declaration
of the Council of People's Commissars to the Polish Government
and the Polish Nation, dated 28th January and signed by Lenin,

Chicherin and Trotsky.[63] It laid the burden of responsibility for any future military operations between Poland and Russia entirely on Poland, and tried to convince the Poles that there were " extreme imperialists among the Allies, the colleagues and agents of Churchill and Clemenceau " who were making " every effort to draw Poland into a baseless, senseless and criminal war with Soviet Russia." The Soviet Government declared that it was anxious " to prevent the new and countless disasters, sacrifices and devastations threatening the two nations." It declared that " the policy of the R.S.F.S.R. towards Poland is based not on any accidental, transient or diplomatic consideration, but on the inviolable principle of national self-determination," that " it had unconditionally recognized and recognizes without any reservation the independence and sovereignty of the Polish Republic, and that this recognition has from the first moment of the formation of the independent Polish State been the basis of all its relations with Poland."

It further stated that Soviet Russia had " no aggressive intentions whatever " and declared that the Red armies would not cross the line of the front, at that time passing near Drissa, Disna, Polotsk, Borisov, river Ptycz, Chudnov, Piliava, Derazhna and Bar. Concerning this point it should be emphasized that what the Soviet Government actually proposed was that the Red armies would not undertake any offensive operation beyond the above-stated front line, and not, as was further asserted by Soviet propaganda, the establishment of a frontier approximately along this line.

The Soviet Government also declared that it had not entered into any agreement with Germany or with any other State aimed directly or indirectly against the Poles and that " the character and spirit of the Soviet Government policy preclude the very possibility of such agreement." In the last instance it asserted that " there is no question, territorial, economic or other that might not be settled peacefully by negotiations, mutual concessions and agreement," and expressed the hope that " all questions in dispute will be settled by agreement between Russia and Poland concluded in a spirit of good neighbourliness."

A second Soviet document issued on the same day was the message from Chicherin to the workers of Allied countries against intervention.[64] According to this appeal, " Soviet Russia for its part constitutes no threat to Poland. It is ready at any moment to cease military operations and conclude an agreement for an enduring peace with Poland." The appeal stated further that " the only obstacle in the way of peace and the cessation of the countless disasters from which the toiling masses in Russia and the neighbouring countries are, together with the whole of Europe, suffering, is the reactionary, imperialistic policy of the Allied Governments." At the end Chicherin urged the workers of the Allied countries " to put an end to this policy of their Governments."

A few days later, on 2nd February, the All Russia Central Executive Committee addressed a message to the Polish Nation, signed on behalf of the Committee by its Chairman Kalinin. It tried first of all to detach Poland from the Entente, saying that the Poles had nothing to expect from " the capitalists of England and France who for a hundred years had looked impassively on the oppression of Poland by Tsardom, who during the war, until the last moment, supported and covered the deceitful policy of Tsardom towards Poland, and who now assume the rôle of the defenders of Poland." It stated that Soviet Russia was ready, at the cost of far-reaching concessions, to conclude peace with small peoples such as Estonians and Latvians " because, at present, the most valuable thing for all nations is peace." It declared that " the freedom of Poland is an indispensable condition of the free development of Russia." It would be a great mistake to believe those who assert that " the Russian Government wishes to implant Communism on Polish soil by the bayonets of the Red Army." " The reorganization of Poland in accordance with the wishes of the Polish working masses should be done by these working masses themselves." It did not abandon, however, the hope that " the toiling masses of all countries would enter the path followed already by the Russian working people." [65]

All these declarations were very clever examples of Bolshevik propaganda, and pursued two ends : first they aimed to impress the Polish people by displaying the good intentions of Russia towards Poland. Chicherin's note would be distributed in millions of copies during the Red offensive against Warsaw as a proof that the Russians had no hostile designs against Poland. But the still more important aim was to bring about the moral isolation of Poland by shifting the whole burden of responsibility for whatever might occur in the future on to the Poles. It should be observed that none of these statements contained any concrete proposal for peace, but each of them tried only to present the war between Poland and Russia as a war of the imperialist intervention of the Western countries against the Soviet State. Public opinion in the Western countries had to be won so that it might exercise pressure on Poland to induce her to accept peace on terms agreeable to the Bolsheviks. This circumstance was rightly observed in the correspondence from Warsaw which appeared in *The Times*. This correspondent stated amongst other things :

" The new Bolshevik offer can hardly be said to be a proposal of peace terms. ... The idea conveyed by the Bolshevist peace note after a study of the complete text is that it is designed to impress public opinion in Western countries, particularly in Britain." [66]

While the Bolshevik peace offensive brought many disappointments to the Soviet rulers, especially at decisive moments, so far as concerned undermining the morale of the Polish people and in particular of the Polish troops (although its influence cannot be totally disregarded—according to General Sikorski's book on the Polish-Russian campaign of 1920 the Soviet peace offer was a factor which actually disturbed some minds),[67] the principal aim of this peace offensive, that is to say the moral isolation of Poland in the coming struggle, was to a great extent attained.

The Bolshevik declarations referring to respect for Poland's independence and the peaceful designs of the Soviet State were taken at their face value, especially in the so-called progressive circles all over the world. As we shall see, this factor played an enormous part in future developments.

Difficulty of Polish position arising from lack of agreement between the Allies and impossibility of remaining on the defensive

Poland was unable to obtain any satisfactory answer to her demands addressed to the Allied Governments; she had to take this momentous decision alone, being aware that the time factor worked to her disadvantage in view of the growing tendencies in the West to resume normal relations with Russia and the gradual improvement of the military and political position of the Soviet State.

It should be emphasized that Poland had the choice between two solutions only : to carry on the war to a successful end, and consequently without any limitation of her initiative, or to conclude peace. There was no third solution, of a purely defensive war, as was desired by some people in the West, especially in France which regarded the Polish factor as only a pawn in her game. A few explanations suffice to dispose of such a solution, if only for purely military considerations.

The question of the defensive tactics recommended by the Allies to Poland arose on many occasions in 1920, last but not least after the defeat of the Bolshevik armies in Poland in August 1920. We will deal with this matter later. For the time being it would be pertinent to refer to what was said by Pilsudski in an interview given to a Polish newspaper on the 26th August, 1920 :

> " Our friends " [said Pilsudski], " wish that we might stand in the East in a purely defensive attitude. In my view it is simply preposterous. How would it be possible for a small army, poorly equipped, to hold a defensive line running for hundreds of kilo-

metres, from the Baltic Sea tothe South? Such a line must be
fortified with concrete, surrounded by barbed wire. It would
require our whole railway equipment to carry only barbed wire.
We cannot hold a purely defensive line. There are only two solutions: advance, until the enemy is completely defeated and asks for
terms, or stop on an illusory Eastern frontier and conclude peace
as quickly as possible." [68]

The question whether Poland would be able indefinitely to carry
out limited military operations was examined in a telegram from the
British Minister in Warsaw, Sir H. Rumbold, dated 19th January,
1920 :

" In my opinion it will anyhow not be possible for the Poles to
continue for any appreciable length of time their present limited
operations against the Bolsheviks. Although these operations are
not costly in men, the expenditure involved is reacting unfavour-
ably on the internal political position and financial resources of
the country and adding to its economic difficulties. The Polish
Government are therefore faced, as they have pointed out, with the
alternative of making peace now, when they can do so on advantageous terms, or as they say endeavour to prosecute the war to a
successful conclusion with the help of the Allies . . .

" Unless I am mistaken, the Poles, through either of the above
courses, hope to achieve three main points: (1) settlement of their
Eastern frontier combined with a solution of the Lithuanian and
White Russian questions in a way which they would consider satisfactory to themselves, (2) immediate economic and financial relief,
and (3) the means of effectually controlling and checking Bolshevist
propaganda in Poland.

" On the other hand if the Poles continue their present limited
operations without any definite objective, and without Allied support, even supposing the Bolshevists were to allow them to retain
the initiative in military matters, they risk eventual defeat supposing
the Bolshevists attack them with all their forces." [69]

Those who advised the Poles to stand on the defensive, and such
was the true meaning of the resolution of the Supreme Council of
24th February, seemed completely to overlook the special strategical
requirements of the Polish-Soviet war and the position of the Polish
army in the field. All military writers agree on this point that the
features of this war of movement were " swiftness, suddenness of
concentration, the tactics of surprise." [70] Cyril Falls, reviewing
this war in his outstanding work, *A Hundred Years of War*,[71] entirely
approves Pilsudski's main strategical ideas, which " were based
neither on field fortifications nor on mass," as " both were out of
the question by reason of space, terrible space, 600 miles of it, no
such space in civilized Europe." Pilsudski could not rely on what

he called " *stratégie serrée* " or " *stratégie encadrante.*" He chose instead " *stratégie de plein air* "—strategy of the open space. General W. Sikorski said in his book devoted to the Polish-Russian campaign of 1920 [72] that while passivity in general " is one of the worst blunders a commander can commit as only an offensive is able to bring about a decision," the more so in the Polish-Soviet War in which " a passive defence with badly-trained soldiers, insufficient strength and inadequate equipment would inevitably have caused the breaking of the front," consequently final defeat.

Those who held strong views on the necessity for the Poles to adopt a purely defensive position seemed to care very little for the consequences which would have resulted had the Poles followed their advice. It was Lieutenant-Colonel Guinness, who in the course of an important debate in the House of Commons on the 20th May, 1920,[73] put the whole question in a nutshell. Referring to the objections of Sir D. Maclean he observed that the latter

> " suggested that you can wage war on a system of limited responsibility. Of course, that is out of the question. In war it does not do to sit still and wait till you are attacked, and especially in the case of Russia where mobile operations cease during the winter and become possible and inevitable at the end of April when the country dries up. Initiative is everything, especially under those conditions, and the Poles very wisely forestalled their enemy."

Some advocates of Polish passivity on the Eastern Front took a rather fatalistic view, quite unwarranted as we shall see later, that the Bolsheviks were neither capable of carrying out an offensive nor had they any warlike designs. For instance so said Lord Robert Cecil, in the debate on the Address in the House of Commons on the 12th February, 1920 [74] :

> " I have *not the least idea as to what the Bolshevik policy may be*. It may be that they are going to make an aggressive war, but I agree very much with what the Prime Minister said the other day —that it is an unlikely thing in itself, and that it is very unlikely to be successful."

While the pacifist lord could take such a detached attitude on the matter, the position of those who were responsible for Poland's security was much more complicated, and they could hardly risk the fate of the nation on such unwarranted assumptions.

Did Poland desire peace in those decisive months of February–March 1920, when the Soviet-Polish peace negotiations were under discussion? The question should be thoroughly investigated in view of the great confusion still existing in historical studies dealing with it, owing to the impact of Soviet propaganda on many minds.

Poland, certainly, did not wish for peace at any price, a peace which would have jeopardized her political independence and made her subservient to Russia. Such would have been the peace if the provisional boundary set up by the Supreme Council on the 2nd December, 1919, had been adopted as a definite frontier. We have seen (p. 489) that this line was a provisional one and that it was adopted *with the assurance that this would not prejudice any further decisions.* On the impossibility of establishing the future Poland's Eastern frontier on this line all Poles agreed. In fact this line was not based on either ethnographical or strategical criteria. It would suffice to look at the map to reach the conclusion that *should Poland's frontier be established on that line she would become a satellite of Russia, as events after the Second World War have amply proved.* Nobody explained this position better than Mr. Hugh Gibson, American Minister in Warsaw, in a dispatch to the Secretary of State in September 1920,[75] in reply to the suggestions of the State Department that the Polish troops after having defeated the Red Army should stop at that line. He said that

> " there is a strong feeling that to stop at the line would be disastrous from a military point of view. This view is entertained not only by the Polish Government but by the military representatives of the Powers who are acquainted with the actual military conditions. This line, of course, was never intended as a military line, but a basic administrative boundary to the West of which the Poles could set up a permanent administration without prejudice to further acquisitions to the East. If it can be considered as a military line all its advantages obviously lie in the hands of the Bolsheviks, as they would hold the fortified positions of Brest-Litovsk and Grodno which are carefully excluded from Polish occupation, as well as the lateral railroads which are of vital importance. Furthermore this line is impossible from a defensive point of view and if broken the capital would be in imminent danger."

All the assertions of the pro-Soviet wing in the House of Commons that the line of the 8th December was Poland's definitive boundary were quite baseless, and were refuted on many occasions by representatives of the Government itself, although not always with sufficient vigour.

In an oral answer given on the 11th March, 1920, to a question by Mr. Carter, the Prime Minister stated : " The Eastern frontiers of Poland have only been fixed provisionally by the Supreme Council." [76]

In an oral answer given on the 10th May to a question by Lieutenant-Commander Kenworthy—" Whether steps have been taken by the Allied Powers to define the Eastern and South-Eastern frontiers of Poland? " Bonar Law stated : " A provisional Eastern frontier for Poland has been laid down already. It has not yet been possible for the Allies to exercise the right given them by Article 87 of the Treaty to determine these frontiers definitely." [77]

In an oral answer to the question by Mr. Lambert, of the 11th May—" By what authority the Polish forces are occupying the Lithuanian city of Vilna? "—Bonar Law stated : " By a decision of the Supreme Council of July last, Vilna was provisionally allotted to the Poles without prejudice to the final frontiers of Poland or Lithuania." [78]

In a written answer to the question by Mr. Cope, on the 17th May, Bonar Law stated : " Poland's boundaries have never been definitely fixed by the Supreme Council." [79]

Sir Halford Mackinder, former High Commissioner for South Russia, a man who was probably the best qualified in the House to speak about the matter, as he was well acquainted with the local conditions, was consequently right in saying in the House of Commons on the 20th May [80]:

> " A line was drawn by the Paris Conference, it is quite true, through Brest-Litovsk approximately from North to South. The minute of the Paris Conference—I inquired into the matter when in Paris, and also as to the understanding of it in Warsaw—made it clear that West of that line from that date onwards the Polish administration should be recognized, but that same minute made it perfectly clear that nothing definite was decided as regards territory East of that line. Therefore, though a *minimum* limit to Poland has been fixed, the Powers have fixed no *maximum* limit. Therefore, in the strict sense of the word, the Poles are perfectly justified in claiming that the Eastern frontier has not in fact been fixed by the Peace Conference, the Supreme Council or anyone else."

In the light of all these statements one can see how ambiguous were the terms of the resolution of the Supreme Council of the 24th February, promising Allied assistance to the States bordering Russia in the event of their being attacked by the latter " inside their legitimate frontiers." As events turned out, Poland did not receive this assistance even within her " minimum frontier."

As it was stated above (see pp. 450 ff.), Poland claimed for the populations living within her historical frontiers the right of national self-determination, refusing to accept the Bolshevist interpretation of this principle. Such was the meaning of the resolutions passed by the Foreign Affairs Committee of the Polish Diet, after exhaustive discussions in the presence of the Premier and Chief of the General Staff on the 23rd and 24th February, 1920. These resolutions prove that the Polish Diet was conscious of its responsibilities and wished to lay down the basis for a lasting and just peace settlement.

> " The Government and the Diet, in answer to the Note of the Russian Government, put forward the principles on the basis of which they are ready to enter into peace negotiations, and the acceptance of which would secure a permanent Eastern frontier for the Republic and its international status. ... The crimes of the partitions should be definitely effaced and the frontier between the two States should be established *in accordance with the desires and the interests of the population*. This has long been the attitude of the Government and Diet of the Polish Republic. The Polish Republic is unalterably resolved to fix its Eastern frontier *in agreement with the local population*, and has the right and duty to demand likewise that the population of those districts which are situated beyond the present boundary of the Polish administration, but belonged to Poland before 1772, be given the opportunity of *freely deciding their own future allegiance*. ... Poland must demand that the peace conditions shall be approved and ratified by a body representative of the entire Russian population."

On 26th February the Warsaw correspondent of *The Times* summed up the attitude of Poland.

> " There is still an inclination to wait on events. The Government holds the opinion that peace with the Bolsheviks is not worth having unless it is a peace which guarantees the security of Poland within her new frontiers for the future. This condition, it is considered, will not be fulfilled *unless the Entente Powers make peace at the same time*." [81]

A direct appeal for joint action with the Entente Powers was contained in an interview given by Pilsudski on the 15th February, 1920, to a correspondent of a French paper, *Le Matin* :

> " The time for concluding peace with Russia has come. It has come not only for us, *but for all States of the Entente*.
> " Nobody has dared so far to undertake this tremendous task ; there has been only a tendency to bypass this issue by half-measures. Koltchak, Denikin and others have been used as ostrich feathers behind which world diplomacy tried to seek refuge. But these were obsolete measures and, consequently, reactionary ones. It is impossible to revive old Russia at any cost. New formulas must be found. ... One must have courage to admit that enormous changes have taken place in Eastern Europe.
> " The time has come to show this courage. We must set ourselves to this task boldly. Poland offers her help to the Entente in this difficult task. We are not doing it for ambition, for the wish to play a part, but simply because we consider it is up to Poland as the

country directly interested to take the initiative on this matter. We are preparing now a plan aiming to establish a legal status for Eastern Europe."

Many Allied observers in Poland underlined the moderating influence of Pilsudski on Polish public opinion at that time. Such was, for instance, the conviction of Sir Halford Mackinder, former British High Commissioner for South Russia, who in his speech in the House of Commons on the 20th May, 1920, stated peremptorily that so long as Pilsudski was in power there was no danger of Poland pursuing imperialistic designs.

" One personal influence in Poland counts for a great deal more than any other. In this country we speak of Marshal Pilsudski as the President of the Polish Republic. In Warsaw they speak of him as the Head of State. He is much more in Poland than merely President, as we understand the term. His career in this respect is not dissimilar from that of our own Prime Minister. He is a moderating influence in Poland just because he has come up from the Left in politics, and is trusted by the people of the Left because of what he said and suffered for them in past times. He is not a reactionary. ... In my judgment so long as Marshal Pilsudski occupies the powerful position which he does in Poland, so long have you a force which will act against imperialistic ends on the part of the Poles."

In the editorial of *The Times* of the 15th February, 1920, entitled " The Bolshevists and the Poles," we find the following interesting appreciation of the moderating rôle played by Pilsudski in Poland. Stating that there were in Poland some people " intoxicated by the memory of a world which has gone," *The Times*' correspondent opposed to them

" sober thinkers, like Paderewski and Pilsudski, who have never countenanced these fantastic dreams. They have a truer sense of the position of their country. They understand that for a State which has still to lay the foundations of her own future, it will be madness to fill her neighbours with suspicion or to make them her permanent and irreconcilable enemies. They know that no Power or combination of Powers can save Poland unless, by her own wisdom and her own exertions, she makes her salvation possible. Their aim is not a conquering Poland, holding down reluctant provinces by the strong hand, but a Poland voluntarily supported by friendly States from the shores of the Baltic to the shores of the Black Sea. The principle of such policy is unexceptionable, provided that it is fairly applied with the general consent of the populations concerned, and it is gratifying to know that it commends itself to the majority of the Polish Diet."

In the light of the foregoing it appears clearly that there were two factors which had a decisive bearing on subsequent developments in the Polish-Russian peace negotiations. The first was the impossibility of Poland obtaining from the Allied Powers any clear statement on the ends pursued by Allied policy towards Eastern Europe, the second was the attitude of Russia herself, arousing more and more the suspicion that her plan consisted in gaining the time necessary to prepare a decisive offensive against Poland and subsequently enforce on her a peace treaty on Bolshevik terms.

In the meantime the voices reaching Poland from England were mostly those of advocates of the Soviet cause, who strongly influenced the British Prime Minister. These quarters, overlooking the fact that military operations had never actually stopped, wished to hamper any military initiative on the part of the Poles, at the same time justifying any Russian one. It suffices to refer to the passionate comments roused by the military operations of Polish troops at the beginning of January 1920, having a limited scope and leading to the capture of Dunaburg (Dvinsk) on 3rd January, and the establishment of the junction with the Latvians (see pp. 465 ff.). This military operation, which secured the Polish Northern flank and severed all connections between the Lithuanians and Russians, pursued no political aims of conquest,[82] because Poland immediately surrendered the ethnographically Latvian territory (in spite of the considerable Polish minority there) to the Latvians. The percentage of Russian population in that area was infinitesimal, far below the number of Poles settled there. This Latvian territory was later included in Latvia by virtue of the peace treaty between Soviet Russia and Latvia.

In spite of all these facts the *New Statesman* wrote on 31st January :

> " Meanwhile the Poles and Letts are pursuing their insane incursion into *Russian territory*. The Letts, as we stated last week, are acting at the direct instigation of the French Military Mission. The Poles also received encouragement from Paris, but they have other motives beside. . . . They are therefore not prepared to negotiate without arms in their hands. Their view is excusable—or if it be reprehensible, it is the Allied statesmen rather than the Poles who should be blamed."

In the debate on the Address on the 12th February, Lieutenant-Commander Kenworthy asserted that obviously the Bolsheviks cannot demobilize their armies unless they can be assured that they are not going to be attacked. " They have *offered very generous peace terms to Poland*(?), but apparently instead of the peace terms being received and examined, *this new advance into Russia*, which is called a raid, is taking place." [83]

On 16th February, Colonel Wedgwood asked in the House of Commons : " May we take it that His Majesty's Military Mission in Poland has had nothing to do with the attack on Dvinsk and the raid on Zitomir? " to which Mr. Churchill replied : " Certainly not. Any operations which Poland may engage in are settled by the Polish State and by the Polish Government." [84]

On 19th February Mr. Spoor asked the Prime Minister " whether any steps were taken by the Allies to prevent the attack by the Poles on Soviet Russia culminating in the capture of Dvinsk about 5th January? " to which the Prime Minister answered in a way which proved his sympathies were not on the Polish side : " His Majesty's Government have made it clear that they do not encourage and cannot support by men, money or material *an offensive by Polish troops into Russian territory.*" [85]

At the same sitting of the House, when asked about the Polish-Soviet negotiations, Lloyd George took a detached attitude, saying that " the question of peace or war with Russia is one which Poland must decide by itself." Lieutenant-Commander Kenworthy expressed some astonishment at this aloofness of the British policy, asking : " Is the Right Honourable Gentleman aware that the Polish Government stated that they were going to consult the Allies before replying? What is our attitude? " But there was no reply to this question.

Soviet designs on Poland and preparations for offensive operations

In order to ascertain the true position of all the parties concerned in the East European settlement it is only natural to investigate what were the real intentions of the Soviet Government at that time. The pro-Bolshevik wing in the Western countries based its attitude on uncritical acceptance at their face value of all official Soviet declarations, and from them exclusively it drew the belief that Soviet Russia sincerely desired peace by mutual agreement with Poland and did not intend to menace the political independence of the Polish State. Nowadays there are still writers who try to justify the Soviet policy of that period on the strength of exclusively Soviet sources, or rather of some carefully selected evidence to which they refer so far as it agrees with their purpose of defending the genuineness of the Soviet peaceful intentions. For instance, we find in a book recently published by Trotsky's apologist, Mr. Isaac Deutscher (*The Prophet Armed*), a statement which the author does not even try to prove by any evidence :

> " For many months Chicherin had in vain addressed *secret* peace offers to Warsaw urging a settlement of the frontier dispute

extremely favourable to Poland. Pilsudski ignored the advances and kept Polish opinion in the dark about them. Chicherin continued to make conciliatory proposals even at the beginning of the Polish offensive." [86] [My italics.]

This statement, by the way, confirms the general impression of any reader of the Soviet Notes quoted above, that they did not contain any concrete peace offer. To justify the Soviet attitude, Mr. Isaac Deutscher felt obliged to allege that there were some *secret* offers apart from the official notes and messages. We venture to say that such secret offers did not exist at all, and we find no reference to them in any subsequent declarations by the Soviet leaders who, on the contrary, used to assert that the concrete peace offers, namely offers of a territorial settlement, were contained in *official* declarations. As a matter of fact on many occasions the Soviet leaders tried to mislead the world public opinion as well as their own people by saying that they had proposed a much better frontier before the war operations in spring 1920 than that fixed by the Riga Treaty. Besides the wish to shift the whole burden of responsibility for the bloodshed in 1920 on Poland, there was another reason for such assertions. After the defeats in summer 1920 the Soviet leaders wished to save their face, and it was very important from that point of view to say that the Poles obtained at Riga less than the Soviet Government had spontaneously offered to them before the resumption of war operations. This was to prove that the Polish victory was by no means as complete as it may have appeared.

At a meeting on the 12th June, 1920, Lenin said :

" Referring in particular to the Polish offensive there is an opinion that the Bolsheviks presented to Poland exorbitant demands and started an offensive, while we know perfectly well that *we had fully agreed to the cession of vast territories which had been occupied by the Poles* before their starting the offensive. We valued the lives of our Red soldiers much more than the carrying on of a war for Byelorussia and Lithuania, seized by the Poles. We solemnly declared, not only on behalf of the Council of the People's Commissars but also by special message of the All-Russia Executive Committee to the Polish Government, a government of bourgeois and squires, besides an appeal to Polish workers and peasants, that we proposed peace negotiations *on the basis of the actual front line,* thus leaving Lithuania and Byelorussia, these non-Polish lands, on the Polish side ; we did believe that the Polish squires and bourgeois would be unable to keep alien lands and that by a peace treaty, disadvantageous to us, we would be able to win something more—to save the lives of our Red soldiers, because *every month we become ten times stronger* while all other governments disintegrate more and more every month. . . . " [87]

It is worth while to note first of all that in Lenin's views a peace with Poland was but a short break and that he put much trust in the impact of Soviet propaganda. But what is still more striking is his assertion that the Soviet messages contained a concrete proposal for the territorial settlement with Poland, while in fact they put forward only a declaration that the Soviet troops would not cross the actual front line.

Lenin made many similar statements after the Bolshevik defeats in summer 1920. For instance, speaking on the 2nd October he repeated that the Soviet Government had, before the spring offensive, proposed a frontier corresponding to the front line.

"We had preferred to obtain a settlement of the question of Byelorussia not by arms but exclusively by the struggle carried out *within the Polish frontiers*. We know that we could assist the liberation of the toiling masses of Poland—not, and far less, by force than by the impact of our propaganda." [88]

In a speech on the 15th October, 1920, Lenin, referring to the terms of the Riga preliminaries, said that " the line proposed by the Soviets in early 1920 passed fifty versts to the East of the Riga frontier," and he concluded : " Russia made a preliminary peace upon conditions more favourable than those proposed herself before the offensive." [89]

We find similar assertions in Trotsky's declarations. On the 13th October he wrote in the newspaper *V Puti* :

"We proposed to Pilsudski a peace treaty with much wider frontiers, that is to say embracing more Ukrainian and Byelorussian territory than the frontiers established in Riga." [90]

We find the same and even more explicit assertion in an official Soviet publication devoted to the Civil War :

" The Polish Government did not attain its main aims in the outcome of the 1920 campaign, the aims consisting in the extension of the Polish frontiers much further to the East. In accordance with the preliminaries of peace, Poland received 59,650 square kilometres and a population of 4,470,000 less than what was proposed by the Soviet Government in January 1920." [91]

Pilsudski's political adversaries in Poland also fell victims to this Soviet propaganda. Professor S. Grabski, then Chairman of the Committee for External Affairs of the Diet, writes in his book *The Polish-Soviet Frontier* :

NN2

" The Council of People's Commissars accordingly considered, in January 1920, that the Polish-Russian frontier from Dryssa to Bar (the front line) would not be injurious to ' the real interests of Russia,' notwithstanding that this line was considerably to the East of the frontier fixed by the Peace Treaty of 1921." [92]

We repeat, it suffices to read attentively the Soviet Notes to see that the Soviet Government proposed at that time *only peace negotiations* and an *armistice* along the actual front line, and not a definite territorial settlement. What was the Bolshevist conception of peace negotiations with Poland? One can easily conclude from various statements by the Soviet leaders that their plans were to carry on these negotiations on Brest-Litovsk lines, that is to say, jointly with violent propaganda aiming to disrupt the morale of the enemy, propaganda which would have taken advantage of the craving for peace throughout the world, for peace at any price, even sacrificing Poland's most vital interests, bringing about the moral isolation of Poland and making her subservient to the Bolshevik aims for the expansion of Communism in Europe. In a moment of sincerity Trotsky disclosed the Soviet intentions in this matter; he said :

" We were ready to come to terms with the Polish Government *so long as it was tolerated by the Polish toiling masses,* in order to avoid further bloodshed of the Polish and Russian workers and peasants. But the Warsaw chauvinists were afraid that if they disclosed *their robber programme and if the latter had been refuted by Soviet Russia,* the Polish soldier, whom they had misled by their lies about the defence of the homeland, would have wrathfully refused to shed his blood for the lust for power and riches of the Polish squires. In order to avoid the *dreadful ordeal of open peace negotiations* the Polish Government refused to conclude an armistice." [93]

It was Lenin who disclosed even more outspokenly the mood in which the Soviet leaders approached the future negotiations with Poland. In a report presented to the Ninth Congress of the Russian Communist Party on the 29th March, 1920, he gave a quite different picture of the proposed peace negotiations from that put forward by Soviet peace propaganda to the world. He said :

" The position is now such that Latvia has made an official peace offer to us ; Finland has sent a telegram in which a demarcation line was proposed, this being in fact the beginning of a peaceful policy. In the last instance, Poland, this Poland whose representatives in a specially ostentatious manner indulged in sabre-rattling, a Poland which has received more than any other country of trucks loaded with munitions and artillery and promises of help provided she continues to fight against Russia ; even this Poland, the unstable position of the Government of which drives her into an adventurous war, *sends us peace offers*. One must be very careful. Our policy requires a most cautious attitude. In the consciousness of the representatives of Poland themselves, of squires and bourgeois, an idea begins to make its way: ' Is it not too late, would a Soviet Republic in Poland be established before we declare ourselves for war or peace? ' They do not know what they are doing. They do not know what to-morrow may bring to them. We know that *each month gives us a gigantic increase of our forces,* and these forces will continue to grow. For this reason our international position is stronger than at any moment before. ... *We have a formal peace offer from Poland. These gentlemen are in a quite desperate position. The Polish bourgeoisie proposes peace negotiations,* knowing well that a war adventure could finish in the same way as Kornilov's affair. Knowing well that our adversary is in a *desperate position,* that he is one who does not know what he will do to-morrow, we must say to ourselves most firmly that *in spite of peace offers, a war is possible.* One cannot foresee the future ... our endeavours for peace should go hand in hand with *intense war preparations,* and we should definitely not disarm our army." [94]

So according to Lenin it was Poland who made peace offers to Russia, and not *vice versa*. It was Poland who was obliged to beg for peace. Was Soviet Russia ready to give concessions to a Government which she believed to be in a desperate position? So long as illusions of a social upheaval in Poland, illusions which later led Soviet armies to the very gates of Warsaw, persisted in Russia, it was most unlikely. There is no doubt that apart from Soviet successes against Denikin the policy of Lloyd George encouraged the Soviet leaders and made a peaceful settlement with Poland infinitely more improbable than at the time of Soviet isolation.

What also contributed to some extent to the unrelenting attitude of the Bolsheviks towards Poland was the knowledge that Poland's economic position was extremely difficult at that time and that she was not receiving adequate assistance from the Allied Powers in the rehabilitating of her economy.

Although Lenin stated in one of his above-mentioned speeches that no country in the world had received such assistance from the Allies as Poland, this was obviously said only to stir up hatred for the capitalist countries.

Gibson was right when he stated in a dispatch (see p. 519) that : " We may safely assume that the Bolsheviks will be accurately informed as to the measure of support Poland may expect and will govern themselves accordingly." In fact it appears from a manifesto of the Comintern on the Polish question, addressed on the 17th

February to the workers of the whole world, that the Bolsheviks were well acquainted with the difficult economic position of Poland and drew some pertinent conclusions from it :

> " The Polish ruling class now in power in Poland has thrown itself into the arms of the victorious powers, hoping that the latter would help it not only to strangle the revolutionary movement in Poland and deliver to the Poles a complete domination over the Lithuanians, Byelorussians and Ukrainians, but that they would also foster the reconstitution of capitalism in Poland. The Allies, although wanting an increase of the military strength of Poland did not, on the other side, show any interest in the rehabilitation of Polish industry. ... They did not give the Poles any machinery, raw materials or grain. ...
>
> " The dream that Poland, being a country without State debts, might, thanks to the support of the Allies, receive substantial credits abroad, have collapsed. For all the goods delivered by the Allies the Poles have to pay usurious prices ; the French, American and British speculators without any obstacle carry away from ruined Poland the last remnants of her national wealth." [95]

There was another circumstance contributing to the stiffening of the Soviet attitude towards Poland. On the 13th March, 1920, a Junker Revolution broke out in Germany (the so-called Kapp Putsch). The German Government fled to Stuttgart, while the German trade unions proclaimed a General Strike, which within a short time brought about the collapse of this reactionary movement. There was a possibility of forming a new government consisting of Socialists and Communists. According to Borkenau, the historian of the Third International, " this was a decisive moment in the history of the German Republic." [96] But the German Communists, relying on their own forces, turned down the offers of collaboration made to them by veteran union leader Legien, and the Communist sedition was quenched by the Reichswehr. This unrest rekindled the Bolshevik hopes for an early revolution in Germany. Lenin and Trotsky, as a matter of fact, put all their hopes in this event. As early as 1918, speaking to Raymond Robin, Lenin said :

> " The flame of the Socialist revolution may die down. But we will keep it at its height till it spreads to countries more developed. The most developed country is Germany. When you see a Council of Workers' and Soldiers' Deputies in Berlin you will know that the proletarian world revolution is born." [97]

The Ninth Congress of the Communist Party addressed to the German proletariat the following message :

> " The proletarians of Soviet Russia, like the proletarians of the

whole world, watch with excitement your heroic struggle, realizing that the victory of the German proletariat will give the signal for a world socialist revolution. We express our firm hope that you will attain the aim pursued by you and install the dictatorship of the working class." [98]

The hope of joining hands with the German proletariat across Poland certainly appealed more strongly to Bolshevist minds than a temporary truce with a Poland of " bourgeois and squires," and this factor played a great part in the Soviet policy of that period, as subsequent events have clearly shown. The Poles were well aware of this circumstance, and we find a direct reference to the bearing of the Kapp Putsch on the aggressive policy of the Soviets towards Poland in a proclamation issued by the Polish Socialist Party.[99]

Moreover, the aftermath of the Kapp Putsch brought about grave dissensions between France and Great Britain owing to the single-handed action of France in connection with the violation by Germany of the clauses of the Versailles Treaty referring to the demilitarized zone on the left bank of the Rhine. At that time the Western Powers were in complete disagreement, which diverted their attention from the problems of Eastern Europe and weakened the authority of the Supreme Council. The Soviets took it for granted that they had little to fear from that side and that they had a free hand in dealing with Poland, at least so long as these dissensions persisted.

The belief prevailing among Bolshevik leaders that it would hardly be worth while to conclude even a short truce with a " Poland of bourgeois and squires " was partly due to the influence of a small group of Polish Communists, some of whom—and amongst these the notorious head of the Cheka, Dzerzhinsky—occupied a prominent position either within the Soviet Government or within the Comintern. We have said (pp. 185 ff.) that the Social Democratic Party of the Kingdom of Poland and Lithuania, which later transformed itself into the Polish Communist Party, following the lead of Rosa Luxemburg was opposed to the programme of Poland's independence as a matter of principle. According to the Manifesto of the First Congress of the Communist International of March 1919 : " The national State which gave a tremendous impulse to capitalist evolution has become too narrow for the development of the forces of production."[100] In the history of the Polish Communist movement, written by one of its leaders, Warski, we read : " Also in 1919–20 the Polish Communist Party continued to contest the independence of Poland without taking into consideration the special conditions and its previous mistakes. The mistake on the national question was corrected only after the setbacks suffered in 1920." [101] In November 1925 Dzerzhinsky wrote : " Our mistake consisted in contesting Poland's independence. . . . Opposing this independence as a matter of principle we lost the struggle for an independent Soviet Poland." [102]

At that time there were, however, a few Polish Communists who saw the danger of the Soviet policy directed against Poland's independence, and at the meeting of the Central Executive Committee on 18th February they made a declaration in which they protested against the plan for the conquest of Poland by Soviet Russia. But they were rebuked, because according to a Bolshevik writer this declaration showed a complete lack of understanding on the part of these Polish Communists for " the revolutionary rôle of the Red Army and the revolutionary-defensive character of the war on the part of Soviet Russia." [103] The events which occurred during the Bolshevik offensive in summer 1920 prove that the Soviet Government gave its full backing to the anti-national programme of the majority of the Polish Communists.

The foregoing account has dealt with some features of the Soviet policy towards Poland at that time. But we can also find an explanation for this policy in the Soviet doctrine on war and peace, the true meaning of which was beyond the mental reach of the advocates in the West of the allegedly peace-loving policy of the Soviet State, taking advantage of every opportunity to accuse the Poles of obstructing the work of peace. In his book *The Task of the Proletariat in our Revolution*, Lenin proclaimed a ruthless struggle against " nauseating, sweet, social pacifist phrases." Taracuzio, who devoted some illuminating pages to this matter in his book, *War and Peace in Soviet Diplomacy*, stresses that the primary task of Communists is " to unveil bourgeois preparations for war and reveal to the masses at large the hypocrisy of the non-Communist politics." [104] On the other hand : " Worthy of note also is the significance attached by the Communists to the revolutionary progressiveness of wars . . . to Marxists wars like peace are an advance towards the ultimate proletarian end—the World Union of Socialist Soviet Republics." [105]

We are far from the ingenuous beliefs of some radical sections in Western countries who in 1920 were taking for granted that the Soviet State wished to attain its aims exclusively by peaceful means.

Since the " unofficial war " between Poland and Russia, due to the invasion by the Red Army of the Borderlands, still continued in 1920, the military preparations of Soviet Russia should give us the final clue to the intentions of Soviet policy.

The Russian military preparations against Poland at that time were not quite unknown in Western countries. Churchill, then Secretary of State for War, and consequently the man best conversant in Great Britain with the military position in Eastern Europe, summed up his information in a memorandum written on the 21st May, 1920 :

"In addition to a steady flow of reinforcements towards the Polish front, there have been numerous indications of an impending attack by the Bolshevists. The approximate strength of the Bolshevik armies on the Western Front has increased from 81,200 in January 1920 to 99,200 in early March, and to 133,600 by mid-April. These figures are rifles and sabres, i.e. effective fighting strength."

Churchill further remarks that during the peace negotiations between Poland and Russia

"free Bolshevik reinforcements were being concentrated on the Polish front and *there was every indication that the offensive against the Poles was about to be renewed*. The Poles therefore naturally assumed that the Soviet Government was only procrastinating and was endeavouring to create a delay in which to undermine the morale of the Polish troops and population by propaganda, while preparing for the renewed offensive.

"The Polish Government, under Marshal Pilsudski, a former revolutionary agent against the Tsarist régime, of course, understood very intimately the Russian political situation."[106] [My italics.]

Field-Marshal W. E. Ironside, in an article written for the *Encyclopædia Britannica* (Russo-Polish campaign), notes similar facts :

"The Soviet began to concentrate their troops towards the West. Inflammatory speeches in Moscow and a fierce propaganda amongst the Polish working people brought Polish public opinion to a fever heat. From seven divisions in January, the Soviet had, by March, increased the number of their troops facing the Poles to twenty divisions, with three cavalry divisions. Poland decided that *she could not wait quietly for the inevitable Soviet attack* by which she would certainly be destroyed and that she must act at once." [My italics.]

The same opinion was held by Captain C. Kuntz, at that time attached to the French Military Mission in Poland. In his book *L'offensive Militaire de l'Etoile Rouge contre la Pologne*, he stresses the importance of the reinforcement of the Red Army on the Western front and of the reorganization of railway transports by Trotsky's ruthless measures.[107]

If we now wish to compare this information with that in the possession of the Polish military authorities we can refer to the book written by General Kutrzeba, *Wyprawa Kijowska* :

> " The observation of the Polish-Russian front proved that steady and considerable reinforcement of the Soviet forces was taking place, which in military language meant that Russia was proceeding to concentrate against Poland.
>
> " In order to illustrate this assertion I give below significant figures of the growing strength of the Soviet troops against Poland, on the basis of the reports of our intelligence at that period:

1st January, 1920	4 Infantry Divisions	1 Brigade.
1st February, 1920	5 Infantry Divisions	5 Brigades.
1st March, 1920	8 Infantry Divisions	4 Brigades.
1st April, 1920	14 Infantry Divisions	3 Brigades.
15th April, 1920	16 Infantry Divisions	3 Brigades.
25th April, 1920	20 Infantry Divisions	5 Brigades.

> " One can understand the meaning of this steady and considerable reinforcement of the front against Poland if one keeps in mind that in February 1920 the general plan of the campaign against Poland was outlined by the Chief of the Department of Military Operations of the Field Staff of the Revolutionary Council, General Shaposhnikov, and that this plan was approved by the said Council as the basis for further decisions. On the 10th March, 1920, a conference was held between the C.-in-C. (Kamenev) and the C.G. of the Western Front (then Gitlis) at which the final plan for the offensive against Poland was approved. It was the same plan which in June 1920 was almost completely fulfilled by the Soviet Army." [108]

Does all this information agree with what one may find in Russian military sources?

Soviet writers are obviously at a loss when they mention the Russian military preparations on the Western Front in early spring 1920. They have to produce proof that Russia did not desire the continuation of the war against Poland, because otherwise they would have contradicted the Bolshevik peace slogans. In a book by Kakurin and Melikov, *War against the White Poles,* we find an assertion that the concentration of the Soviet forces did actually

> " begin to be carried out only from April and was completed only at the end of June. It was due not so much to the objective factors (disorganization of railway transports) as to the well-known peace-loving attitude of the Soviet Government, which has taken measures to the effect of avoiding an armed conflict with Poland, as well as to the situation on the other fronts of the Republic. In fact the decisive operations against Denikin began only on the 14th

February in Northern Caucasus and were completed on the 1st April." [109]

There is no doubt whatever that the concentration of the Soviet forces was completed only in June, which enabled the Red Army to start its offensive immediately afterwards, but this was the very reason for which Pilsudski considered it necessary to strike a blow before this date, as the consequences of the delay might have been fatal for Poland. But on the other side, the same authors contradict themselves, stating on another page of their book :

"*From the beginning of* 1920 the necessary measures were taken to put into good order and reinforce the armies on the Western Front ; thanks to the changes in the external position in connection with the actual interruption of the military operations against Finland, Estonia and, soon afterwards against Latvia, the regrouping of our forces on that front became topical in its turn." [110]

As we see, these authors make a distinction between " regrouping " and " reinforcing," and this probably accounts for the difference between the figures given by them and those which were at that time in the possession of the British, French and Polish Intelligence. According to them : " between 1st January and 1st April the Western Front was reinforced by four divisions and one brigade, and in the course of the following months by nine more infantry divisions and one cavalry brigade." [111] From these figures we can assume that the Soviet writers mentioned only those units which were moved from other distant parts of Russia. Moreover they avoid mentioning that between the 1st and 25th April many new units increased the strength of the Soviet troops on the Western Front, preferring to state a total figure for all the three following months, much below other estimates by the way.

The same authors mention, however, that Lenin had long since foreseen the necessity for reinforcing the Western Front because in his dispatch of the 11th March he urged the Revolutionary Soviet of the Caucasian Front to send as quickly as possible all available troops to the West, adding : " You will concentrate on that task." [112] Even earlier, namely in January 1920, Lenin said : " We cannot demobilize our army because we have such an enemy as Poland." [113]

Let us now consider the character of the Bolshevik military preparations. Were they simply measures of self-defence or preparations for an offensive? The concentration of Soviet forces took place almost exclusively on the Northern sector of the front. Kakurin and Melikov confirm General Kutrzeba's information that the plan for the offensive against Poland was finally approved at a conference at Smolensk on 10th March between the C.-in-C. Kamenev and the Commander of the Western Front, Gitlis. Even before, on the 26th February, Kamenev said that " the decisive blow would be struck on the sector of the Northern Front." [114]

We can find more trustworthy information than in the previous book in the official Soviet history of the Civil War, which frankly admits that owing to the Soviet preparations Pilsudski was forced to take the offensive in the Ukraine " *in order to forestall the Soviet offensive.*" [115] In connection with the choice of the sector on which the Soviet troops were concentrated, the said book emphasizes the geographic and strategic importance of the " Gate of Smolensk," through which pass the roads leading to the political and industrial centres of Poland. " In the event of our operations *in the direction of Warsaw,* the right flank of the Red Army was secure, because the adjoining territories belonged to neutral States." [116]

Moreover, we know from other sources that at that time Trotsky's warlike policy prevailed in the Politbureau. Trotsky's apologist, Mr. Isaac Deutscher, states unequivocally that " Trotsky stood for a strong-arm policy towards Poland " and that Chicherin's allegedly peaceful policy " aroused opposition within the Commissariat of Foreign Affairs, especially from Litvinov, his deputy. Trotsky intervened and firmly sided with Litvinov. He urged the Politbureau to stop (peace) overtures." [117]

But the strongest proof of the Soviet aggressive plans was provided by subsequent developments. The Soviet Army was able to launch a vigorous offensive which led it to the gates of Warsaw within a few weeks after the resumption of military operations between Poland and Russia. Considering the vastness of the Soviet territories and the disrupture of transport at that time, it is evident that the operations on such a big scale were possible only thanks to very careful and lengthy preparations planned and carried out many months in advance.

*

*   *

NOTES

[1] *Parliamentary Debates,* House of Commons, 1919, Vol. 121.

[2] *Ibidem,* Vol. 123.

[3] LORD RIDDELL'S *Intimate Diary,* p. 162.

[4] SIR C. E. CALLWELL, *Field-Marshal Sir Henry Wilson, His Life and Diaries,* Vol. II, p. 163.

[5] *P. R. F. R.,* The Paris Peace Conference, Vol. XI, p. 675.

[6] *P. R. F. R.,* 1920, Vol. III, p. 484.

[7] *Ibidem,* p. 702.

[8] LORD RIDDELL, o.c., p. 175.

[9] *D.B.F.P.*, First Series, Vol. III, p. 735-8.

[10] *The Times*, 5th March, 1920.

[11] London Conference (11th-13th December, 1919). *D.B.F.P.*, Vol. II, pp. 727-84.

[12] *P.R.F.R.*, 1920, Vol. III, pp. 643 ff. Documents Diplomatiques, No. 25.

[13] *D.B.F.P.*, Vol. III, No. 445.

[14] *P.R.F.R.*, 1920, Vol. III, p. 644.

[15] LENIN, *Sochineniya*, Vol. XXV, p. 23. Cf. the remarks of TARACUZIO, *War and Peace in Soviet Diplomacy*, on the Treaty of Tartu, as " a turning point in communist tactics " (p. 87).

[16] *The Paris Peace Conference*, Vol. IX, p. 857.

[17] *D.B.F.P.*, Vol. III, Nos. 71, 74 and Appendices 1 and 2, No. 76 and Appendix A to No. 78.

[18] *Ibidem*, Footnote 5 on p. 911.

[19] *Parliamentary Debates*, Commons, Vol. 125.

[20] *The Times*, 3rd June, 1920. " The Prime Minister's Secretary (Mr. Philip Kerr) and the British representative on the Supreme Economic Council (Mr. Wiese) are believed to be the chief advocates of the Bolshevik cause while in the Foreign Office and other departments of State the negotiations are regarded with mistrust and misgivings."

[21] P. V. SUSLOV, *Politicheskoye obezbecheniye sovetsko-polskoi kompanii* 1920 *goda*, pp. 7 ff.

[22] *D.B.F.P.*, Vol. III, p. 797.

[23] *Ibidem*, p. 925.

[24] *Ibidem*, p. 926.

[25] *Ibidem*, p. 944.

[26] *The Times*, 17th May, 1920.

[27] H. W. V. TEMPERLEY (editor), o.c., Vol. VI, p. 215.

[28] *D.B.F.P.*, Vol. III, pp. 921-2.

[29] *Krasnaya Kniga*, p. 81.

[30] VON SEECKT, *Aus meinem Leben*, Vol. II, p. 213.

[31] See the telegram by Chicherin, forwarded to the Secretary of State by the American Minister at Stockholm on 26th February, 1920 (*P.R.F.R.*, 1920, Vol. III, p. 447): " On 5th December, the Seventh All-Russian Congress solemnly proposed to all the Governments of the Allied and Associated Powers and to each of them separately that negotiations should be commenced with the view of concluding peace. We repeat once more the proposition and ask the Government of the United States of America to inform of its wishes."

[32] *The Times*, 16th February, 1920.

[33] *P.R.F.R.*, 1920, Vol. III, p. 444.

[34] *Ibidem*, pp. 371 ff.

[35] *The Times*, from Warsaw correspondent, 1st January, 1919. " Most appreciated is the mention of material assistance, for it must be obvious that Poland cannot hold the fort much longer against Bolshevism, much less undertake the offensive without the sinews of war."

[36] *P. R. F. R.*, Vol. III, pp. 371 ff.

[37] The Polish demand concerned 300,000 Mauser rifles, 8,000,000 cartridges, 1,000,000 kgm, of powder (*The Paris Peace Conference*, Vol. IX, pp. 787 ff.).

[38] LORD D'ABERNON, *The* 18*th Decisive Battle of the World*, p. 33.

[39] *The Times,* 17th February, 1920.

[40] SUSLOV, o.c., p. 8.

[41] TOMMASINI, o.c., pp. 112-13. " Scomparso il timore della vittoria dei generali reazionari russi, tutti i polacchi tornaron concordi nel sentirsi, come al tempo di Giovanni Sobieski, lo scudo della civiltà occidentale contro la barbaria orientale. Ma la citata decisione del Consiglio Supremo sembrava riconoscere che la barbaria era innocua e che quindi lo scudo diveniva superfluo. Essa fece dunque una grande e sconfortante impressione nel popolo polacco, anchè perchè, colla sua forma nebulosa, metteva in un penoso imbarrazzo chi non poteva rimanere in atteggiamenti teoretici ma doveva contare colla dura realtà. Di questo stato d'anima si fece interprete lo stesso Pilsudski in un colloquio, che ebbi con lui sulla fine di gennaio. Egli appariva esacerbato: osservava che era facile dar consigli pacifici, quando si era lontani dal pericolo, come le grandi Potenze dalla Russia."

[42] *D. B. F. P.*, Vol. III, pp. 803 ff. Patek's report, see STARZEWSKI, o.c., p. 66. The report of the American Ambassador in London (Davis) to the Secretary of State, *P.R.F.R.*, 1920, Vol. III, pp. 376 ff.

[42a] HOWARD, o.c., Vol. II, p. 297.

[43] *P. R. F. R.* , 1920, Vol. III, pp. 379 ff.

[44] *Ibidem,* pp. 380 ff.

[45] *Ibidem,* p. 382.

[46] *Ibidem,* p. 376.

[47] *Ibidem,* p. 378.

[48] VISCOUNT PHILIP SNOWDEN, *An Autobiography,* Vol. II, p. 535.

[49] FRANCIS WILLIAMS, *Ernest Bevin, Portrait of a Great Englishman.* p. 11.

[50] F. BORKENAU, *The Communist International*, p. 187.

[51] FRANCIS WILLIAMS, o.c., p. 82.

[52] *The Times,* 29th January, 1920.

[53] *The Times,* 22nd March, 1920.

[54] *D. B. F. P.*, Vol. III, No. 651.

[55] *P. R. F. R.*, 1920, Vol. III, p. 374.

[56] LORD D'ABERNON, o.c., p. 11.

[57] *D. B. F. P.*, Vol. III, No. 67.

[58] Débats Parlementaires, Chambre des Députés, *Journal Officiel* du 7 février, 1920.

[59] *Ibidem,* séance du 5 février, 1920. M. Cornudet: " La politique vis-à-vis de la Pologne n'apparaît plus tout-à-fait la même au sein de l'alliance. Si nous sommes certains que la grande amitié de la France pour la Pologne est toujours la même, si la Pologne est assurée, de nòtre part, d'un plein concours au cas elle serait attaquée par les bolsheviks, d'après les indiscretions de la presse anglaise-et je ne fais naturellement

à ces indiscrétions qu'un crédit relatif, mais tout de même, je suis obligé de m'y arrêter un instant-la Grande Bretagne aurait fait savoir à la Pologne qu'elle ne pourrait plus la secourir et qu'il fallait que la Pologne, elle aussi songeât comme l'Esthonie à une nouvelle politique vis-à-vis des Soviets."

[60] Séance de 6 février. M. de Gailhard-Boncel: " La reconnaissance de l'indépendence de l'Ukraine est conforme aux principes des nationalités."

[61] Séance du 26 mars, 1920. M. Millerand: " Le Gouvernement français ayant pris l'engagement à plusieurs reprises, de ne négocier *sur le terrain politique* avec les Soviets que le jour où d'accord avec ses alliés, il estimera que de telles negotiations sont possibles, ne fera pas seul et secrètement ce qu'il ne pourrait faire publiquement."

[62] L. FISCHER, o.c., Vol. I, p. 249: " France seemed prepared to destroy the unity of Russia through agency of the Poles."

[63] *Krasnaya Kniga*, pp. 84-5, English translation by JANE DEGRAS, *Soviet Documents on Foreign Policy*, Vol. I, pp. 179 ff.

[64] *Ibidem*.

[65] *Ibidem*, pp. 86 ff.

[66] *The Times*, 3rd February, 1920.

[67] W. SIKORSKI, *La Campagne Polono-Russe de* 1920, p. 259: " L'excellent moral des troupes fut miné secrètement par deux facteurs subtils, mais très dangereux. Le premier fut la discussion inopportune et trop bruyante de nos buts de guerre par les partis politiques polonais, que le Gouvernement de la République ne sut ni prévenir ni modérer. Le deuxième fut la propaganda savante et extraordinairement habile que les Soviets entreprirent à la fin de 1919 en faveur de la paix prétendue sincère et avantageuse pour la Pologne." Cf. also a Report of the Agents of the Political Department of the Soviet Army, dated 10th March, 1920, and quoted by SUSLOV, o.c., p. 360: " The disintegrating effect of our peace proposals can be felt even within the ranks of the most sturdy units from Posnania."

[68] J. PILSUDSKI, *Pisma*, Vol. V, p. 166.

[69] *D.B.F.P.*, Vol. III, No. 651.

[70] GENERAL MARIAN KUKIEL, *The Polish Soviet Campaign of* 1920, p. 6.

[71] CYRIL FALLS, *A Hundred Years of War*, p. 225.

[72] W. SIKORSKI, o.c., p. 278.

[73] *Parliamentary Debates*, Commons, Vol. 129.

[74] *Ibidem*, Vol. 125.

[75] *P.R.F.R.*, 1920, Vol. III, pp. 401 ff.

[76] *Parliamentary Debates*, Commons, Vol. 126.

[77] *Ibidem*, Vol. 129.

[78] *Ibidem*.

[79] *Ibidem*.

[80] *Ibidem*.

[81] *The Times*, 28th February, 1920.

[82] The following statement was issued on 25th January by the Polish

Information Committee in London: " Nothing would be more improbable than a warlike policy on the part of the Polish Republic, which endeavours to bring all the disputes arising out of the East-European upheaval to a peaceful settlement. The Polish advance on Dvinsk was of a purely defensive character in face of Trotsky's threats of future attack on Poland. The possession of the fortress and the junction of the Polish-Lettish troops has strengthened the line of defence, without complicating in the least Poland's political aims " (*The Times*, 26th January, 1920).

[83] *Parliamentary Debates*, Commons, Vol. 125.

[84] *Ibidem.*

[85] *Ibidem.*

[86] ISAAC DEUTSCHER, *The Prophet Armed*, p. 458.

[87] LENIN, *Sochineniya*, Vol. XXV, p. 294.

[88] *Ibidem*, p. 398.

[89] *Ibidem*, p. 411.

[90] L. TROTSKY, *Kak vooruzhalas' revolutsiia*, II, II, No. 134.

[91] *Grazhdanskaya Voyna*, Vol. III, p. 469.

[92] STANISLAS GRABSKI, *The Polish-Soviet Frontier*, p. 21. Similarly GENERAL SZEPTYCKI, *Front Litewsko-Bialoruski*, p. 13: "We had before us the prospects of concluding a peace treaty. ... It was a good occasion, a quite unusual one to extricate ourselves from a difficult military position, in the East."

[93] L. TROTSKY, o.c., p. 98.

[94] LENIN, *Sochineniya*, Vol. XXV, p. 100.

[95] P. V. SUSLOV, o.c., p. 10.

[96] F. BORKENAU, o.c., pp. 153 ff.

[97] WILLIAM HARD, *Raymond Robin's Own Story*, p. 2.

[98] P. V. SUSLOV, o.c., p. 6. The author states that " in March-April there existed good reasons for believing in the victory of socialism in Germany."

[99] *Ibidem*, p. 14.

[100] *The Communist International*, No. 1.

[101] WARSKI, " Social-Demokratiya Polshi i Litvy i II Siyezd R.S.D.R.P.," *Communist International*, No. 16-17, 1919.

[102] P. V. SUSLOV, o.c., p. 18.

[103] *Ibidem*, p. 18.

[104] TARACUZIO, o.c., p. 32.

[105] *Ibidem*, p. 53.

[106] W. CHURCHILL, *The Aftermath*, pp. 264 ff.

[107] C. KUNTZ, *L'offensive Militaire de l'Etoile Rouge contre le Pologne*, p. 11: "Dès février 1920, le Gouvernment des Soviets prépare, par un remaniement de l'organisation des transports militaires les opérations à entreprendre à la belle saison contre la Pologne. ... Un comité spécial actionné par Trotsky, prend la direction, des transports et du ravitaillement."

[108] T. KUTRZEBA, o.c., p. 68.

[109] N. E. KAKURIN i V. A. MELIKOV, *Voyna z belopolyakami*, p. 65.

[110] *Ibidem*, p. 14.

[111] *Ibidem*, p. 62.

[112] *Grazhdanskaya Voyna*, Vol. III, p. 317.

[113] P. V. SUSLOV, o.c., p. 25.

[114] KAKURIN i MELIKOV, o.c., pp. 71-2.

[115] *Grazhdanskaya Voyna*, Vol. III, p. 318: " Zhelaya predupredit' svoim nastupleniem udar sovetskikh voisk Pilsudski reshil nanesti svoy udar na Ukraine."

[116] *Ibidem*, pp. 309-10.

[117] I. DEUTSCHER, o.c., pp. 458 ff.

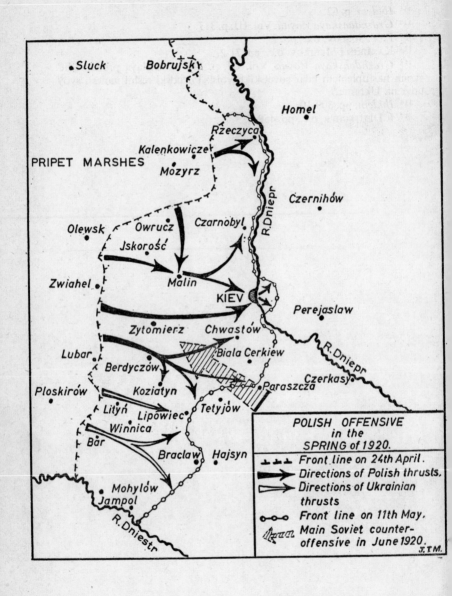

Sluck ·   Bobrujsk ·

PRIPET MARSHES

Homel ·

Rzeczyca

Kalenkowicze
Mozyrz ·

Czernihów ·

R. Dniepr

Olewsk ·   Owrucz ·   Czarnobyl
Jskorość ·

Zwiahel ·   Malin ·

KIEV

Perejaslaw ·

Żytomierz ·   Chwastów ·

Lubar ·   Biala Cerkiew ·

Berdyczów ·   R. Dniepr

Ploskirów ·   Koziatyn ·   Paraszcza ·   Czerkasy ·

Lityń ·   Lipowiec ·   Tetyjów ·
Winnica ·

Bar ·   Braclaw ·   Hajsyn ·

Mohylów ·
Jampol ·

R. Dniestr

POLISH OFFENSIVE
in the
SPRING of 1920.

- - - Front line on 24th April.
→ Directions of Polish thrusts.
⇒ Directions of Ukrainian thrusts
∘-∘-∘ Front line on 11th May.
≈≈≈ Main Soviet counter-offensive in June 1920.

J.T.M.

CHAPTER VI

THE FIRST PHASE IN THE POLISH-SOVIET WAR IN 1920

POLISH ADVANCE INTO THE UKRAINE

ABOUT the end of February, soon after the session of the Foreign Affairs Committee of the Diet and its resolutions stating Poland's peace aims (see p. 541), Pilsudski became more and more alarmed by Soviet military preparations and propaganda confirming his previous fears that the Bolsheviks, perverting the principle of self-determination, aimed at the subjugation of Poland. He felt also that the Western countries were leaving Poland to her own devices. The state of mind of the Polish leader was best expressed in an interview granted on the 28th February to a French newspaper *Le Petit Parisien,* and published in it on the 6th March :

" It is a very intricate matter for me to state my views on the problem of peace. The subject is extremely delicate. Many endeavours are at present devoted to the solution of this problem. The statements which I might give you could frustrate the decisions of the Government or obstruct them. So long as these decisions have not been published I must keep silence, as behoves me in view of the importance of the problem under consideration. I can tell you, nevertheless, that Poland wants peace as she has always been a peace-loving country. She gave proof of her feelings by not rejecting the discussions on peace. In principle, Poland does not refuse to enter into peace negotiations. But I will never stop saying that we shall not be able to negotiate or agree to the negotiations under menace. I had thought before that the Bolsheviks could negotiate with us in a peaceful spirit, without hidden intentions. So far as I am concerned, I have also desired that Poland might negotiate without hidden intentions, playing an open game. I did not wish to take advantage of our favourable position and back our arguments by force of arms. I did not wish a peace imposed by our cannons and bayonets. Unfortunately my impression of the Bolshevik behaviour is that a peace with a peaceful background is out of the question—what they desire is a peace extracted by fists, as was the case with the Esthonians. If someone puts a knife to my throat I have an unpleasant feeling. I am not a man to whom one can speak in such a manner. I can also speak with determination and get angry if someone wishes to impose his will on me by menace. I am sure that all Poland shares my opinion. We are ready to negotiate but we shall spurn all threats in the most resolute way. *We will never conclude a peace under pressure. Either a real peace, voluntarily accepted, or war.*

" I know that the Bolsheviks are concentrating big forces on our front. They make a mistake, thinking that they can frighten us and face us with an ultimatum. Our army is ready. I put my whole confidence in it. I know that should anyone menace it, it can also menace in its turn."

Two decisions taken by Pilsudski at the beginning of March showed that he was preparing for all emergencies : the first decision was military, the second political in character. First of all he decided to improve the military position of the Polish Army by a limited military operation on the Polesye front starting on the 6th March and leading to the capture of an important railway junction, Mozyrz-Kalinkowicze.

This operation provoked an immediate diplomatic reaction by the Soviet Government. On the 6th March Chicherin sent a Note to the Polish Foreign Minister, Patek,[1] stressing the peaceful intentions of the Soviet Government : " Soviet Russia, the only true and unselfish friend of endangered and insufficiently strong nations, does not jeopardize the security of the nations once oppressed by the Tsarist régime." The Note further states that the Poles have started offensive operations against the independence of the Ukrainian Republic and, consequently, Soviet forces would not in the future keep to the line proposed by the Soviet Government in its Note of the 28th January (see p. 535). This line was never, in fact, observed by the Soviet Army, and continuous local operations were carried out by it in the course of the weeks following the Note of the 28th January. Chicherin promised, however, that the Soviet troops would not undertake new offensive operations provided the Polish forces would behave in the same way. The conciliatory tone of this Note can be explained not only by the wish of Soviet Russia to appear to world opinion as a peace-loving country, but above all by the fact that the concentration of the Soviet Army on the Polish front was far from complete at that time, as stated above. The time factor was of primary importance to the Soviet Government.

The second decision taken by Pilsudski had far-reaching political consequences : negotiations with the Ukrainian leader in exile, Petlura, were pushed on and entered the decisive stage from the 10th March.

In the meantime the Polish Government was preparing its reply to the Bolshevik formal peace offer, but it wished first to ascertain the views of the Allied Governments. On the 13th March a Note was handed to the representatives of the Entente Powers, stating in general terms the Polish peace conditions. The Note is summed up in the following points :

1. Annulment of the crimes of the partitions of Poland in which Russia participated.

2. Recognition of the States established on the ruins of Russia, at that time existing *de facto.*

3. Return of the State property comprised within the Polish frontiers of 1772.

4. Participation of Poland in the gold reserves of the Russian State Bank on the basis of the balance of the 5th August, 1914, and restitution of archives and libraries.

5. Ratification of the treaty by the representatives of the supreme body of the Russian nation.

6. On her side Poland, remaining faithful to her traditions of tolerance and respect for the rights of nations, declares that she will decide the fate of the populations living to the West of the 1772 frontier in accordance with their wishes.

As a matter of fact these terms were never communicated to the Soviet Government, just as the latter never informed the Poles of the terms upon which it was ready to negotiate.

Thus the Note aimed in the first instance to ascertain the views of the friendly powers and to obtain their co-operation in the future settlement in Central-Eastern Europe. *The Times,* quoting a telegram from its Warsaw correspondent, called it a *ballon d'essai* and added that the Note would not be dispatched to Moscow before the end of the month at the earliest. " Between then and now its present form and sense may be substantially altered either in order to suit the wishes of the Letts and Rumanians or as a result of comments by one of the Allied Powers or even in deference to opinion in Poland." [2]

As we have said, the Note was actually never sent to Russia in this form, because on the 27th March Mr. Patek sent a telegram to Chicherin stating only formal acceptance by Poland of the Soviet peace offer and proposing to start peace negotiations on the 10th April in the town of Borisov. On this sector the war operations had to be stopped.

Before dealing with the further diplomatic correspondence between Poland and Russia we have to review the reactions of the Allied Powers to the programme outlined in the Polish Note to them of 13th March. In formulating the programme the Polish Government was hampered by the fact that for obvious military and political reasons it could not disclose how far the secret negotiations with Petlura had progressed. However, the Polish Note made it clear, and Polish diplomatic representatives in conversations with

Western statesmen confirmed this point, that what Poland wished was *not annexation* of the whole territory included in the old frontiers of the Polish Republic of the eighteenth century, but the *disannexation*, leaving to the populations of this whole area the opportunity of stating its wishes for the political future. The Warsaw correspondent of *The Times* [2a] realized the awkward position of the Polish Government :

> " The impression which the conditions have managed to convey abroad, namely that Poland wishes to extend her dominion in fact and not word up to the ancient frontiers of 1772, *does not correspond with the desires of a single political party in the country.* It would have been a simple matter to make this clear.
>
> " Similarly, no declaration has even been made about Poland's relations with the Ukraine. Presumably they satisfy the Ukrainians since a Ukrainian division formed with the assistance of the Polish General Staff is at present fighting with the Poles on the Podolian front, but nothing has been said to show what agreement has been come to between the Polish and Ukrainian Governments, with the result that the outside world is easily led to believe that the Poles aspire to plant the White Eagle in Kiev and turn Volhynia and Podolia again into Polish provinces." [My italics.]

At the moment when the Polish programme of negotiations with Russia reached the Allied capitals the whole attention of the latter was diverted to German problems, the aftermath of the Kapp Putsch, problems of reparations and enforcement on Germany of the provisions of the Versailles Treaty. The Western Powers did not desire any complications in the political situation in Central-Eastern Europe and shrank from the magnitude of the task outlined in the Polish Note. This programme obviously clashed with their conception of a purely defensive war on the part of Poland, and their ideas on the future of Russia. The principle of the indivisibility of Russia, of the unity of the Russian race, including the Ukrainians and Byelorussians, a poor knowledge of the real conditions in the Eastern Borderlands, illusions of advantages which might follow the resumption of trade relations with Russia—such were the factors which hampered the Western Powers from going beyond platitudinous advice. Europe wanted the return as soon as possible to peaceful conditions everywhere, whatever the price to be paid for it by later generations. It is no wonder that the Polish programme had a cool reception in Western capitals. M. Millerand, the French Prime Minister, speaking with Count Zamoyski, Polish Minister in Paris, pointed to the danger which might arise for Poland if she became too much entangled in Eastern Europe and incurred the permanent enmity of the Russia of the future (he was thinking of a regenerated Russia after the collapse of Bolshevism), as in such event Poland would be unable to play the rôle of counterweight to Germany in the East.[3]

Great Britain took a detached attitude, considering that it was entirely up to the Poles to come to an arrangement with Russia. Asked by Lieutenant-Commander Kenworthy about the contents of the Polish peace programme, Lloyd George stated in the House of Commons on 29th March :

> " His Majesty's Minister at Warsaw has received a Note from the Polish Minister for Foreign Affairs, in which were outlined certain principles on which the Polish Government propose to open negotiations with the Soviet Government. It is not for His Majesty's Government to publish this Note. ... It must be left to the Poles to make their own terms with the Soviet Government." [4]

The American Minister in Warsaw, while regretting that " the Polish (terms) are more far-reaching than Patek had led the representatives of the Powers to believe," remarked that " a new sense of independence and self-importance is evident. I cannot but feel that this growing impatience of restraint is in large measure due to the refusal of the Great Powers to guide and counsel Poland during the past two months." [5]

There is no doubt that the stiffening of the Polish attitude was due to Pilsudski's initiative. We have frequently referred to Pilsudski's plan to encourage the formation of the East of Russia-proper of a chain of independent States closely associated with Poland either by federative links or by treaties of alliance, in accordance with the principles of national self-determination. He thought this the only way to check Russian expansionism. Could this end be attained by negotiation? That was the view of Mr. Grabski, Chairman of the Foreign Affairs Committee of the Diet who soon afterwards resigned from his post, and who asserted rather unconvincingly that the Ukrainians " might be helped to gain their national liberty by negotiations and not by armed action." [6]

The Polish–Ukrainian Treaty of 21st April, 1920

Pilsudski saw that it was impossible to obtain a reasonable peace from Russia by negotiations so long as the latter felt strong and her army remained undefeated. He realized that his conception of national self-determination was poles apart from the perverted Soviet doctrine on this issue. It would be idle speculation to try to answer the question which factors carried more weight in his decisions, military or political.[7] But it can be taken for granted that he carefully weighed the pros and cons, and his plans matured only at the time when he saw the possibility of agreeing them with a prominent Ukrainian leader. Pilsudski's political adversaries often represented him as an idle dreamer engrossed by memories of the past, a knight errant of purely idealistic schemes. Mr. Grabski, who believed in the possibility of a compromise with Soviet Russia, states in his book that to all his objections to extending Polish peace aims to the Ukraine " Pilsudski for a long time had only one answer— refusal to aid a nation with whom we lived in voluntary union for five hundred years would be an indelible stain on Polish honour."

Does this picture agree with the facts? Did Pilsudski really wish to jeopardize Polish interests only for the sake of liberation from the Soviet yoke of a great neighbouring nation? First of all, he did not believe in the peaceful intentions of Soviet Russia in 1920, contrary to the opinion spread in some Western countries, England above all. He took the view that Russia wanted only to play for time, and once her military preparations were completed to negotiate " from strength," trying to impose on Poland political and military conditions which would have made her subservient to Russia. The fate of Poland, consequently, could be decided only by the sword, whatever may have been the views of her Western allies on this problem. Should Poland wait until the moment when the Soviets had completed their military preparations and launched an offensive? There was only one solution : to forestall the Soviet offensive and defeat the Red Army before it was completely ready for a decisive battle.

Apart from these paramount military considerations there were important political factors which Pilsudski took into account. He did not believe that Poland's independence could be established on a firm basis if Russia were not deprived of her conquests in Europe since the end of the eighteenth century and her frontiers pushed back to the East.[8] He kept in mind that Poland's decline began at the time of the Cossack seditions in the seventeenth century, due to some extent to the shortsighted policy of the Polish aristocracy (mainly of Ukrainian descent, by the way).[8a]

About the end of March Pilsudski reached his final conclusions. He did not refuse to enter into negotiations with Soviet Russia, but wished to carry them out as promptly as possible in order not to lose the military trumps which he still held. We know the inmost thoughts of Pilsudski at that time from a conversation on 30th March between Pilsudski and Wasilewski, former Minister for Foreign Affairs, who was appointed one of the principal plenipotentiaries to the peace conference with the Bolsheviks. Wasilewski asked Pilsudski " about some problems connected with his departure for Borisov—what is the position of the Ukraine, what are Pilsudski's plans regarding Byelorussia, what he thinks about

the possibilities of a peace treaty with the Bolsheviks." Pilsudski
gave the following answer :

> " So far as the Ukraine is concerned, we will oppose to Rakov-
> sky's (Communist leader of Soviet Ukraine) Ukraine the Ukraine
> of Petlura and we will not discuss which is the real one. Let the
> Ukrainians decide for themselves. For this scope we shall request
> the neutralization of Kiev to convene there a Constituent Assembly
> for the Ukraine within the limits recognized by us to the West of
> the Dnieper, and by the Soviets for that to the East of this river.
> It will be up to this Constituent Assembly to settle the Ukrainian
> problem." [9]

Thus if the peace conference had been held two totally opposed
principles of self-determination would have confronted each other :
one democratic, according to which the fate of a country shall be
decided by the majority of the population, and the other Communist, leaving to the town proletariat, and in fact to the Communist
party alone, the exclusive right of decision. As a matter of fact
the Bolsheviks asserted that the Ukrainians had already exercised
their right to self-determination thanks to the intervention of the Red
Army. One can hardly believe that such negotiations could be very
fruitful in view of the growing Soviet self-confidence after the
victories over the White Russian generals and the lifting of the
blockade.

On the 28th March Chicherin replied to the Polish Note of the
27th March. While accepting the date of the 10th April as the
beginning of the peace conference, he declined the Polish offer to
hold it at Borisov and proposed instead one of the Esthonian towns,
that is to say in the British zone of influence. Moreover, and this
was a far more important objection, he did not wish to agree to a
" merely local and temporary cessation of hostilities." In his view
" it was essential that hostilities cease immediately along the entire
front where Polish and Russian armies face each other." [10] We
know well what Soviet Russia expected from such a truce.

On the 1st April Patek answered Chicherin, insisting on Borisov
as the meeting place and refusing a general armistice. The hostilities
would be suspended only on the Borisov sector, but of course for
the whole period of the peace negotiations.[11]

In his reply of the 2nd April Chicherin threw the whole responsibility for the continuation of the war on the Poles, accusing them
of " having some strategic plans at the back of their minds (Hinter-
gedanken)." He proposed to hold the conference in an Esthonian
town, Moscow, Petrograd or even in Warsaw.[12] The Soviet Government's preference was obviously for places which would have provided the Soviet negotiators with a better opportunity simultane-

ously to carry out the negotiations and propaganda than a small Byelorussian borough in a remote corner of the Polish-Russian front, more suitable for straight talk and prompt elucidation of the respective intentions of the two parties.

In his reply of the 7th April Patek explained the reasons for which the Polish Government considered that it would be impracticable to negotiate a general armistice in the first instance. The establishment of the modalities of such an armistice would have required the same amount of time as the discussion of the principles on which the future peace treaty should rest. The Polish Government did not wish to interfere with the progress of the negotiations for peace by any offensive actions, having no aggressive designs. Poland, however, did not wish to be deprived of freedom of action. The Polish reserves can be better understood nowadays, when the whole world realizes how difficult it is to obtain any reliable information about what is going on behind the Russian frontier.

In his last telegram of the 8th April Chicherin insisted on a general armistice and categorically refused to hold the peace conference in Borisov. He again proposed other places, even Paris or London. Chicherin took the view that the last Polish telegram was in fact an ultimatum to which the Soviet Government refused to bow.

On the same day Chicherin, jointly with Rakovsky, President of the Soviet Ukrainian Republic, sent a telegram to the Western Foreign Ministers—Lord Curzon, Millerand, Scialoia and Colby, in which both Soviet leaders emphasized the peaceful intentions of Soviet Russia and Ukraine. A characteristic passage of this telegram showed that the Soviet Government wished to avail itself of the support of those quarters in the West to whom the resumption of trade had absolute priority over any political issue in Eastern Europe :

> " Poland carries out a war against the Soviet Republics of Russia and the Ukraine, hampering thus their peaceful activities and obstructing their exploitation of the riches of their countries and supplying their products to the countries which need them." [13]

This telegram remained *unanswered*, the Allied Governments declining to enter into any discussions with the Soviet Government on the political issues.

The Polish Government considered that the last telegram from Chicherin virtually closed the negotiations, and summed up its point of view in a press communiqué issued on the 20th April explaining the reasons for which it insisted on holding the negotiations at Borisov :

" the town of Borisov is situated along a railway line relatively un-
damaged, suitable for establishing telegraphic and telephonic connections with both Warsaw and Moscow. Thus either party would
have been able to establish and maintain communications under
their exclusive control with the respective capital. ... The negotiations for fixing the terms of an armistice ... along a front of 2,000
klm. would have required no less time than the discussion on the
main bases of a peace settlement. ... In view of the lack of sufficient guarantees for the maintenance of the terms of the armistice
disputes on this issue would have been a daily occurrence, influ-
encing the progress of negotiations and, moreover, the result would
have been that a state neither of war nor peace would have prevailed, enabling the negotiations to be prolonged *ad infinitum*. The
Polish Government rejected the proposal of an armistice but declared its readiness to start peace negotiations at once. This was
the simplest way of directly attaining the aim pursued. In order to
give proof of its goodwill and to avoid unnecessary bloodshed, the
Polish Government declared that the Polish High Command did
not intend to obstruct the negotiations by aggressive actions.

" In the meantime Soviet troops have intensified their concentration and undertaken offensive actions against the Polish front, and
a new Note has been sent by the Soviet Government in which,
instead of direct negotiations with Poland, it asked the Allied
Governments to intervene in the matter of the choice of the place
for negotiations, although previously the Soviet Government had
left to Poland the choice of a place. It is obvious that the difference
on the question of a meeting place was but a pretext for postponing
the date of the negotiations.

" The Polish Government maintains its will to conclude as soon
as possible a just peace—and once the Soviet Government reached
the conclusion that the continuation of the war and further delays
were purposeless it would meet with readiness on the part of the
Polish Government to start negotiations."

The Warsaw correspondent of *The Times* explained in the following manner the attitude of the Polish Government on this issue, in a
telegram dated the 12th April :

" Chicherin's message to the Entente Powers definitely refusing
to negotiate with the Poles at Borisov is now available. The opinion
held in official quarters is that the message is an admission by the
Bolshevists of the failure of their peace plans against Poland. Their
aim was to secure an armistice and then to protract peace negotiations, while carrying on an intensive propaganda behind the Polish
front. At the same time they were confident, once an armistice was
concluded, that the campaign would never be continued, and the
danger of the Polish army would be neutralized."

The failure of the negotiations with the Soviets forced the Polish
Government to reconsider the whole situation and gave Pilsudski

an incentive to conclude the business with the Ukrainian leaders in exile, particularly since no enlightenment came from the Western Powers. The latter did not even answer Chicherin's telegram of the 8th April addressed to them, contrary to Polish expectations. In his telegram of 15th April (published in the issue of 19th April) the Warsaw correspondent of *The Times* states that the Warsaw Government considered that " it is for the Entente to make the next move, and by the tone of their communciations to Mr. Chicherin *to judge between the Bolshevists and Poland.*" He characterized in the following way the bewilderment of the Polish public opinion in face of the ambiguous attitude of the Western countries, England in particular :

> " It is characteristic of mistrust of England which the attitude of Lloyd George has fostered in Poland that numbers of persons of average information and intelligence assumed that Britain would support the Bolshevists against Poland. Such has been the effect of raising the Russian blockade and of Mr. Lloyd George's statement to Mr. Patek of Britain's disinterestedness in relations between Poland and Soviet Russia. Whatever reply the Allies make to Mr. Chicherin *they are bound by circumstances to interest themselves in Poland for good or ill.* For this reason Mr. Patek is leaving Warsaw on Saturday next (18th April) in order to explain personally to the Entente Governments Poland's reasons for acting as she has done and her policy towards Russia. He hopes to visit San Remo, Paris and London. The Polish Government is very anxious that there should be no misunderstanding about its intentions in regard to the Eastern provinces of the old Polish Kingdom which it is endeavouring to detach from Russia."

In his telegram of 19th April (published in the issue of 21st April) the same correspondent states :

> " Poland is waiting for two things—first *enlightenment of the attitude of the Entente Powers towards Poland and the Bolshevists,* and secondly the development of the military operations which are by no means suspended. Either of these may put a new aspect upon the present state of affairs. *A pronouncement is expected from the San Remo Conference,* but even silence on the part of the Entente Powers would alter the situation and strengthen the hand of the Polish Government." [My italics.]

The exploratory steps taken by the Polish Government gave no practical result. The Allied Governments did not answer Chicherin's telegram and the San Remo Conference was mainly devoted to the settlement of the future of Turkey and the enforcement of the Versailles Treaty, both issues provoking violent clashes between the French and British. The official communiqué issued by the San Remo Conference did not even mention the Russian problem. Nevertheless it was later disclosed that at San Remo the Supreme Council empowered the Permanent Committee of the Supreme Economic Council " to make such arrangements with the Russian Delegation as are necessary to enable trade with Russia to be resumed as rapidly as possible." This decision cleared the way to the opening of negotiations in London with Krassin, Head of the Soviet Trade Delegation. Krassin arrived in London on the 26th May. Lloyd George took advantage of the difficulties of the French position in relation to Germany to wring a new concession from the French ally and score an important point in his policy of *rapprochement* with Soviet Russia. A fiction that Krassin and Litvinov were acting as the representatives of Centro-Soyuz—that is the Russian Co-operatives—could hardly be maintained. Lloyd George expected to strike a bargain with Soviet Russia in the Near East, " allowing himself to be blackmailed by troubles in Persia and Asia Minor." He sought rather a political compromise with Soviet Russia than " a barrier which he was powerless to effect in a military sense against a Bolshevik advance." [14]

In these circumstances Poland could expect nothing from the Allied councils and had to fend for herself, being left once more to her own devices. Pilsudski decided to proceed to the conclusion of the negotiations with Petlura. The Polish Cabinet discussed Ukrainian matters on 13th April and decided to submit to the Foreign Affairs Committee a draft Treaty with the Ukrainian Government in exile. The meeting started by a declaration by the Chairman, Mr. S. Grabski, that he disagreed with the policy of the Government in relation to the future of the Ukraine, and in view of that tendered his resignation. But only the National Democrats, that is to say the Right Wing of the Diet, supported Grabski's point of view. It is important to state that the Government's policy towards the Ukraine, based on the recognition of the independence of the Ukraine, was approved by the Left and Centre. Speaking of these resolutions of the Foreign Affairs Committee, the Warsaw correspondent of *The Times* in his telegram of 23rd April (*The Times* of 26th April) emphasized the support given to the Government by the overwhelming majority of Polish public opinion :

" An obscure situation was straightened out and Poland's Eastern policy reaffirmed yesterday at an important meeting of the Diet Commission on Foreign Affairs.

" It is suggested that the Government in demanding the dis-annexation of the whole of the ancient Kingdom of Poland from

Russia and helping the establishment of an independent Ukrainian State and an autonomous White Russia out of the Eastern provinces, was pursuing a policy unacceptable to the country as a whole. These assumptions were entirely refuted at yesterday's session, and the Government's policy was approved by practically every member of the Committee except the National Democrats. Mr. Grabski resigned the presidency of the Committee at the beginning of the meeting.

"The Government's position is considerably strengthened for the future, since the National Democrats have always tried to pretend that the policy towards Russia was the policy of one party, or rather of one man, Marshal Pilsudski. Yesterday's singular demonstration of unity in the opposite direction was largely caused by the feeling that Mr. Grabski, in breaking away from the Government just as peace negotiations were about to begin, placed a strong card in the hands of the Bolshevists, thereby betraying the country's interests."

Grabski himself stated in his above-mentioned book that he and his party found themselves in the minority.[15]

The resolutions of the Foreign Affairs Committee enabled the Government to conclude the Treaty with Petlura. A political agreement was signed on the 21st April, and a military one on the 24th.[16] The preamble to the Political Agreement stated that both Governments were " profoundly convinced that each people possesses the natural right to self-determination and to define its relations with neighbouring peoples," and that they were " equally desirous of establishing a basis for concordant and friendly co-existence for the welfare and development of both peoples." Article I of the treaty proclaimed the right of the Ukraine to independent political existence. Article II defined the Western frontier of the Ukraine, that is to say the frontier with Poland (which roughly coincides with that established later in the Peace Treaty of Riga). In Article III " The Polish Government recognized as Ukrainian the territories East of the frontier, as defined in Article II of the Agreement, and extending to the 1772 frontiers of Poland (prior to the partitions) and occupied at present by Poland or acquired in the future from Russia by military or diplomatic means." Thus Poland disposed only of territories to which she had a juridical title by virtue of her non-recognition of the Acts of Partition (principle of disannexation). According to the military convention the Polish and Ukrainian troops would co-operate in the future as allied forces. Poland promised her assistance to the Ukraine, but only to the West of the Dnieper. No Polish troops were to be sent to the left bank of the river, as from the Polish point of view it would have been an act of aggression against what was formally a Russian territory; it was left to the Ukrainians to liberate that part of the Ukraine by their own forces. The conventions fully safeguarded the sovereign rights of the Ukrainian State, as in the liberated Ukrainian territory the civil and military administration was to be taken over by Ukrainian authorities. After completion of their action the Polish forces were to evacuate the territory at the request of either party. This clause disposed of any suspicion that the Poles intended to occupy indefinitely the Ukrainian territory for some imperialistic designs. On the contrary Poland was eager to evacuate her forces from Ukrainian territory at the earliest possible moment, expecting the imminent Soviet offensive on the Northern front where Soviet troops were concentrating. General Kutrzeba in his book quotes the Order of the Day of Polish Headquarters of the 8th May which best reveals the Polish intentions :

" It is in the Polish interest to withdraw our troops from the occupied Ukrainian territories as soon as possible in order to establish friendly neighbourly relations with the new Ukrainian State, as it will enable us to secure the great part of our Eastern front from the imminent danger from Bolshevik forces. The Polish occupation of the Ukraine must be calculated in months and not in years. The sooner regular Ukrainian forces were formed the sooner they would go to the front line in order to liberate further parts of the Ukraine, the better it would be for the Polish State. The fewer the frictions and clashes with the Ukrainian authorities during the period of co-operation with them the better will Poland attain her ultimate end." [17]

General Kutrzeba explains that according to the calculations of the Polish General Staff twelve weeks should have sufficed for the formation of six regular Ukrainian divisions, the minimum number of troops for the task assigned to them, thus enabling the Poles to withdraw within that period.

K. Dziewanowski, in his interesting study *Pilsudski's Federal Policy* shows how preposterous were the ideas of those who suspected Poland of imperialistic designs in the Ukraine :

" To suppose that the Poles could have turned a nation more numerous, far richer, and at least potentially more powerful than themselves into a vassal state is nonsense. There is, moreover, no documentary or even indirect evidence that Pilsudski or his supporters ever harboured such intentions. What is more important, Poland had no resources with which to accomplish such an objective. She had to fight in the initial stage of the campaign with no more than 230,000 front-line soldiers against a country with overwhelmingly superior human and industrial resources. She desperately needed an ally but could not afford to support a vassal. To turn the Ukraine into a vassal State, Soviet methods of suppression and deportation were needed, and Poland was neither willing nor able to apply them." [18]

Mr. Reshetar, who belongs to the school of Ukrainian maximalists, unwittingly bestows the highest praise on the Polish-Ukrainian Agreement of 1920, saying in his book *The Ukrainian Revolution* that " the treaty was in *complete violation* of the centuries-old animosity which prevailed between the Poles and Ukrainians." [19] One can, of course, take a different view of the past, because as a matter of fact it was thanks to their belonging to the Polish-Lithuanian Commonwealth for centuries that the Ukrainians were able to preserve their nationhood, and side by side with sad events and violent conflicts there had been other, glorious memories of common struggle against Turks, Tartars and Muscovites for the defence of the common homeland, but the definition by Reshetar of the purpose of the Treaty of 1920 seems to us a very appropriate one; its aim was, in fact, to dispose of the animosity between kindred nations who so often mixed their blood and who were equally menaced by Russian imperialism. Petlura seemed to take a more realistic view of the situation :

> " He was sober enough to understand that the slogans ' Ucraina farà da se! ' and ' everything ' or ' nothing,' in practice spelled national suicide. Even the Ukrainian nationalist historians who, like Kutschabsky or Shelukin, deny Petlura the legal right to sign the agreement and call him ' a traitor,' fail to draw a constructive plan of action that could have been followed in the spring of 1920." [20]

It should be stated that at that time some quarters in Britain saw clearly the advantages which would result for Europe as a whole in the event of the success of Pilsudski's plans for liberation of the Ukraine. We shall see later that in the first stage of the 1920 campaign these views were spreading to a considerable part of British public opinion, although the pro-Soviet wing was more clamorous.

Churchill, then Secretary of State for War, in his account of 21st May stated that

> " There could be no greater advantage to the famine areas of Central Europe than the re-establishment of a peaceful State of Ukraine on a basis which permitted economic and commercial transactions to take place. . . . But on the assumption that Petlura's Government manages to set up and maintain a separate Government of a civilized type capable of liberating the corn supplies of the Ukraine, and with that territory sheltered and assisted in this task by a strong Poland, it ought not to be impossible to arrive

at satisfactory conditions for a general peace in the East in the course of the present summer." [21]

A. L. Kennedy, who observed events on the spot, writes in his book *Old Diplomacy and New* :

" If Poland were assisted to reach it (Odessa) by land South Russia would be opened up to Europe, whose most pressing need of the moment would be relieved ... a prosperous State might be established under the aegis of Poland and financed by the capital of Britain and France. The project found some support in Paris. ... They (Poles) saw that London, far from supporting them, has just received with every mark of official favour a representative of their arch-enemy Mr. Krassin." [22]

The Warsaw correspondent of *The Times,* in an article entitled " Future of the Ukraine. What the Poles Want " (*The Times,* 1st May, 1920), reviewed with sympathy the Polish plans. He wrote :

" What do the Poles hope will become of the Ukraine? At best they hope that they will be able to re-establish order West of the Dnieper and open the country for foreign trade. They hope that with a National Ukrainian non-Bolshevik Government established at Kiev, the Ukrainians will be able to make the Eastern Ukraine and the Donetz as well too hot for the Bolshevists. If they accomplish this much they hope that some power, *preferably Great Britain,* acting for the League of Nations, will back up the Kiev Government, take the railways in hand, and generally reorganize the country for production with the help of the Ukrainians, Russians and Poles who used to live there. At the worst, and if the big Powers decline to intervene and help them to stabilize the country, the Poles hope with the help of Petlura and his men to keep the Ukraine so uncomfortable for the Bolshevists that they will not be able to derive any economic advantage from it. ... It is to the credit of the Poles that they had administered the greater part of White Russia for over six months without having had any trouble to speak of with the inhabitants."

The suspicions which Pilsudski's policy towards the Ukrainian problem aroused in the Western countries were due to a great extent to the fact that, as we said before, the Ukrainians were considered in the West as a branch of an indivisible Russian nation, and as such having no right to a separate political existence. Pilsudski's adversaries in Poland, the National Democrats, seeking a permanent compromise with Russia, took the same view, as appears clearly from the speech of Dmowski before the Supreme Council on the 29th January, 1919 (see pp. 484 ff.), and Grabski's opposition to the plans of the Government within the Foreign

Affairs Committee of the Diet. The Socialist and Peasant parties
suported Pilsudski's policy and sympathized with the Ukrainian
claims to an independent political existence.

Did Petlura really represent a serious political factor in the
Ukraine? Such was the opinion of many Western observers in
Poland and Eastern Europe. For instance, the Warsaw correspon-
dent of *The Times* (15th April, 1920) says :

> " Whatever may be said about Petlura, he has more influence in
> the Ukraine than any other person, and he is capable of making
> it a very uncomfortable place for anybody else. ... It is significant
> that neither the Bolshevists nor Denikin were able to get a very
> secure hold on the country or recruit troops there."

As a matter of fact the Bolshevists themselves emphasized that
Denikin's defeats were due, to a great extent, to the hostility of
the Ukrainian peasants to his policy of a one and indivisible Russia.

In his *History of the Russian Revolution* Chamberlin states that
" the Ukrainian villages experienced the same disillusionment with
Soviet agrarian policy that the Russian villages had experienced in
1918." [23] He also says that " so serious was this problem of repressing internal revolt in Ukraina that the head of the Cheka, Dzerzhinsky, was sent to Ukraina and took over the newly-established
post of chief of military administration in the rear of the Red
Army." [24]

We also find ample evidence in Russian sources to the effect that
the Ukrainian national movement headed by Petlura was predominant in the Ukraine in 1920. In his speech at the meeting of the
Moscow Soviet on the 20th September, 1921, Trotsky stated
unequivocally that before the occupation of the Ukraine by the
Red Army " Petlura's movement (Petlurovschina) was predominant
there," and that this movement " spread not only among the
kulaks but also among the poorer classes of peasantry." [25]

The official Soviet history of the Civil War mentions the difficulties encountered by the Red Army in the Ukraine owing to " the
hostility of some strata of the population towards the Soviet
régime," and gives it as one of the reasons for which an offensive
on the Northern sector of the front, where the population was more
passive, offered more opportunities to the Soviet forces than in the
Ukraine. [26] On the eve of the Polish offensive, namely on the 23rd
April, two Galician brigades revolted and went over to the Poles, in
spite of being composed of volunteers who had previously fought
against the Poles in Eastern Galicia. This mutiny was highly
embarrassing to the Soviet High Command, as stated by the Soviet
authors, Kakurin and Melikov :

"The mutiny of two Galician brigades at a time almost coinciding with the decisive advance of the Poles on the South-Western front not only has diminished the weak Soviet forces on the Polish front, but also brought about an accidental regrouping of forces, unfavourable to us and favourable to the enemy, and diverted the army and divisional reserves of the fourteenth and partly of the twelfth Army to carry out tasks which had nothing in common with the one assigned to them originally." [27]

The very popular, extreme radical peasant leader Makhno, with whom the Bolsheviks were unable to deal, also joined the Polish forces with his peasant partisans.

There was certainly not enough dynamism in the movement for an independent Ukraine among wide strata of the population, demoralized by war and several occupations and impoverished by spoliations by Germans and Bolshevists. Many months would have been required to bring anarchic and disruptive forces under control, and the formation of regular Ukrainian units, an urgent and primary task, was not proceeding quickly enough. The Polish occupation of the Ukraine was too short for this end to be achieved, but it would be most unfair to make any definite judgment on the records of Petlura's short-lived experience. One of the main arguments of the adversaries of Pilsudski's policy was that it aimed at the disruption of Russia, and because of that aroused Russian nationalism. It is true that many Tsarist officers, among them some of the highest rank (Generals Brusilov, Polivanov), faced with the alternative of remaining for ever in forced labour camps or joining the Red Army, preferred the second solution, but on the other side there were many desertions from the Soviet Army, not only at the time of the final Polish victories when these desertions were of mass proportions, but even in the initial stages of the campaign. As a rule Soviet writers prefer to hush up these facts. According to a Soviet writer, P. V. Suslov, the desertions were limited to those counter-revolutionary elements which had not been "politically indoctrinated," but nevertheless he mentions, apart from two Galician brigades :

"separate groups of officers and other ranks who on the eve of the war with the 'White Poles' had passed to the Red Cavalry Army (Budienny Army) from Denikin or had been taken prisoner and enrolled into the Red Cavalry Army; such was the case of the 59th Regiment of the 10th Cavalry Division, formerly the Oranienburg Cossack Regiment, which passed to the Poles on the 25th May together with the Commander of the Regiment, owing to the 'inadvertency' of the Command of the Division." [28]

Moreover we have the evidence of Lord d'Abernon and of the

Allied officers, who interviewed many Russian prisoners of war after the defeat of the Red Army in the Battle on the Vistula, that there was no enthusiasm among the former Tsarist officers enrolled by the Bolshevists and that their hatred of the Bolshevik régime had by no means diminished. There was certainly much exaggeration in the view spreading in the West at that time, under the impact of Bolshevist propaganda, that the Polish offensive provoked an outburst of national feeling even among those strata of the Russian population which were hostile to Communism. The Western countries were also under the influence of the White Russian leaders in exile, those ghosts of a past gone for ever, who branded the " Polish imperialism " at the time of the Polish advance into the Ukraine. One should keep in mind that what was really at stake at that moment was not whether the Ukraine should belong to a democratic, liberal and united Russia, which has so far remained but a dream, but be liberated from Bolshevik oppression and the Red terror. The Polish-Ukrainian Convention of the 21st April did not prejudge the question of the Ukraine eventually joining a free, democratic federation of Russia, if such might be her wish. She could " freely decide her relations with neighbouring peoples." Those White Russians who allegedly supported the principle of federalism for the future Russia did not wish to admit any real federation which in the last instance should rest on the free will of the peoples concerned and not be imposed by one nation. In 1920 the Ukraine had an alternative, either to be liberated from Bolshevism or remain within the framework of a totalitarian State which after some temporary concessions had done everything to stamp out all traces of the awakening Ukrainian nationalism.

While Burtzev and Kerensky attacked Polish imperialism in the Russian emigré paper appearing in Paris, *La Cause Commune*, some true Russian liberals showed more understanding for the reality. In an open letter by a group of Russian liberals, at that time staying in Warsaw, and signed by the famous writer and philosopher, D. Merezhkovsky (who considered Bolshevism as the forces of Anti-Christ and called Pilsudski, in a moment of inspiration, " the man elected by God," " *l'élu de Dieu* "), Filosofov, Hippius and others, it was stated that Poland was fighting against Bolshevism and not against Russia. Pilsudski was not an enemy of the Russian nation, but considered that so long as Russia oppressed alien nationalities she was unable to become a genuinely democratic and constitutional country. Those who at that time opposed the liberation of the Ukraine were indifferent to her being delivered to the Bolshevist hangman.

Moreover, as explained above, it is a mistake to see in Pilsudski's policy exclusively political motives, and this mistake was current in political literature which completely ignored the bearing of military factors on Pilsudski's policy. Pilsudski was not only the political leader but also the Commander-in-Chief of the Polish Army. Poland had to defeat the Bolshevik army, as only in this way could she save herself. To defeat the Red Army it was necessary to forestall the imminent Russian offensive and begin the great battle far beyond the frontiers of Poland. Military writers emphasize that had the Soviet army not come to the gates of Warsaw in such an exhausted condition and Budienny's cavalry been partly destroyed in the course of numerous battles in the South-Eastern outskirts of Poland, Poland would have been unable to achieve such a decisive victory as was the case on the Vistula.

It appears from the foregoing that there is no reason to suppose that the Polish political and military actions in 1920 were due to external influences. The Polish war and peace aims were limited to problems considered, rightly or wrongly, as having a direct bearing on Poland's vital interests, her security against any future aggressions, from the East above all. The Poles did not wish to go to Moscow to overthrow the Bolshevik régime and install there a government more agreeable to the capitalist countries of the West.[29] The whole international position had changed since similar problems were discussed before the Supreme Council and in conversations between Pilsudski and Sir Halford Mackinder in Warsaw. Consequently it was misguided and unfair to Poland to consider the Polish-Soviet war as the continuation of Allied intervention in Russia, such an attitude often being taken by radical and socialist circles in the West under the influence of Bolshevik propaganda. Those who upheld such ideas showed exceptional ignorance of the problems of Eastern Europe and gross prejudice preventing them from fairly judging men and events. For instance, the *New Statesman* on the 20th May wrote under the curious title " Wanted Some Honest Policy " :

> " It would, however, be unfair to lay upon the Poles all the blame for this lamentable adventure of theirs. They are politically immature to a degree which is difficult for the politically educated West to comprehend. Their leaders are chauvinists almost by a man, but they are morally and intellectually at the mercy of their Western advisers. It is the French and British Governments who are mainly responsible for this war."

We know that the West failed to give any advice to Poland so far as her future relations with Russia were concerned, leaving Poland to her own devices. This fact being established beyond any doubt, there is no reason to consider the Polish-Soviet War as a war of reaction against revolution and socialism. It was in fact a war in which not social but national factors carried weight.

In his work devoted to the 1920 campaign Pilsudski derides assertions by the Commander of the Red Armies which suffered the defeat on the Vistula, Tukhachevsky, contained in a series of his lectures, "Advance beyond the Vistula."

> " M. Tukhachevsky " [wrote Pilsudski], " and also M. Sergheiev want to see in any action of mine a kind of subservience to a number of indefinable instances. They enumerate several of these instances, such as the Entente, a conspiracy of the capitalists of the whole world, a plot of imperialists, and last but not least the General Staff of the Entente, or to speak more accurately, the French General Staff. .... I had taken over command of the Polish Army as C.-in-C. of an army built up literally from nothing, I had been elected Chief of the Polish State by the unanimous vote of the Diet convened by myself, and I do not think it is a secret that both these events took place not under the influence of the Entente but against the wishes of what was then called the Entente. I do not, however, see that this should be considered something discreditable either to myself or to the Entente. So far as the political issues were concerned, as I stated before, I represented in this, unfortunately so short spring of the new life, all those who wanted to defend with their bodies a Poland emerging to new life from the quagmires of slavery. Realizing how difficult was this task I concentrated all my efforts and thoughts on this problem only, while the Entente—which is also no secret from anybody— was endeavouring much more to find a solution of the Russian problem than any settlement of Polish affairs. So far as the question of war and my own decisions were concerned, I was not willing to submit to anybody. For this reason if the military representative of France—at that time General Henrys, whom I keep in heartfelt memory—had any illusions on this point, he had to part with them." [30]

We add to Pilsudski's words what Lord d'Abernon said after his arrival in Warsaw about the heads of the French and British Military Missions there :

> " The dominant personality here is unquestionably Marshal Pilsudski, Head of the State and Commander-in-Chief of the Army. ... An ardent patriot and a man of immense courage and force of character. ... It is noticeable that he has gained a complete ascendancy over the foreign military officers who have been brought into contact with him. General Henrys is devotee and the Head of the British Military Mission, General Carton de Wiart—a man of marked independence of judgment—is fascinated by this strange Polish phenomenon." [31]

The same is the opinion of the eminent American historian, W. H. Chamberlin, who wrote that

" the Polish offensive is sometimes attributed to French influence, and France probably made no effort to restrain it. But if Pilsudski had been a mere puppet in the hands of France, French prompting, in all probability, would have caused him to launch his drive in the autumn of 1919, when Denikin's successes were at their height and the Polish action might much more easily have brought about the overthrow of the Soviet régime." [32]

The most that can be said is that the French Government, considering Bolshevism as its moral enemy, sympathized with Pilsudski's military action but not with its political ends.[33]

There were three phases in the Polish-Russian War of 1920, from the 26th April, date of the beginning of the Polish offensive, to the 20th October, when the military operations ceased altogether in view of the signing of the Armistice and the Preliminaries of Peace at Riga on the 12th October, 1920. The first phase was marked by the success of the Polish offensive in the Ukraine and the vigorous Russian attacks which followed a few weeks later; the second saw the retreat of the Polish Army, leading to the quick advance of the Red Army into the heart of Poland; the third started by the spectacular victory of the Polish Army before Warsaw and ended by the virtual destruction of the Soviet forces in the field. I shall review each of these phases in turn, dealing above all with the reactions in the West to the military developments.

Polish and Russian war aims

It is beyond the scope of this book to deal with the history of the Polish-Soviet War in 1920 from the military point of view, such a task being the province of professional military writers. Consequently we shall limit ourselves to outlining the principal facts without going into strategic and tactical considerations.

The offensive launched by the Polish Army on the 26th April took the Soviet High Command completely by surprise. The bulk of the Soviet Army was concentrating on the Northern sector, and to the nine Polish infantry divisions and one-and-a-half cavalry divisions (the Second, Third and Sixth Armies), the Russians were able to oppose smaller forces, namely seven infantry divisions and one cavalry division (Twelfth and Fourteenth Soviet Armies). The Polish offensive took fifteen days to achieve the main targets assigned to it, that is the right bank of the Dnieper; Kiev was occupied on the 7th May by the troops under General Rydz-Smigly's command.

The political aims of the offensive were made known to the population of the Ukraine by two proclamations, both issued on the 26th April, one signed by Pilsudski and the other by Ataman Petlura. Pilsudski's proclamation stated that

> "The Polish troops will clear the territories inhabited by the Ukrainian nation of foreign invaders against whom the Ukrainian people has risen in defence of its homes against violence, robbery and looting. The Polish Armies will remain in the Ukraine for the time necessary for control of the country to be taken over by a legitimate Ukrainian Government. As soon as a national government of the Ukrainian Republic has established the State authority, as soon as armed bodies of Ukrainians have taken hold of the border, being capable of defending the country against a fresh invasion, and the free Ukrainian nation has been able to decide its own fate, the Polish soldier will withdraw behind the frontier of the Polish Republic, after having fulfilled an honourable task for the cause of the freedom of nations."

Petlura's Proclamation contained a pledge to summon an Ukrainian Constituent Assembly within a short time, and confirmed that the Polish forces had come to the Ukraine by virtue of an agreement between the Polish and Ukrainian Governments and that they would withdraw to their own country after the end of the hostilities against Russia.

The Russians in their turn proclaimed their war aims. These were of a most aggressive character, aiming at the overthrow of the democratic régime in Poland and the subjugation of that State to Soviet Russia. The Bolshevik leaders appealed to Russian nationalistic feelings, and the editorial of the *Red Star* in the issue of 7th May even went so far as to call the troops of the Fifteenth Army to fight for " one, indivisible, Red Russia." [34] But this was going a bit too far, and the editors were rebuked by Trotsky for their patriotic zeal, because the Soviet leaders preferred to use more subtle methods in relation to the peoples they wished to subjugate. To the Polish agitation for an independent Ukraine they were unable to oppose anything that might arouse the Ukrainian masses (as stated by the Soviet writer Suslov, who devoted his work to what is now called psychological warfare),[35] except demagogic statements that the Poles had come to the Ukraine in order to recover land for the Polish landlords.[36]

As according to Soviet assertions the war was imposed on the Polish workers and peasants by foreign imperialists on the one side and Polish squires and bourgeois on the other, Soviet Russia set herself also the task of " liberation," namely the liberation of the Polish toiling masses from their foreign and native exploiters. In a message addressed by the All Russia Executive Committee on the 7th May to Polish workers, peasants and soldiers [37] we read the following :

> " The war is needed by the Polish squires, landlords and capital-ists, it is necessary to the bourgeois of the Entente who instigate Poland to a foolish adventure. ... The last (Soviet) Government not only did not make any attempt against Poland's existence, but on the contrary, for the sake of peace, was ready to cede to Poland considerable territories, even those where the Poles did not consti-tute a majority. ... After having crushed your squires, Soviet Russia will leave to the Polish nation the right to organize its life according to its wishes. ... It will be for you, Polish workers and peasants, to decide whether you wish to maintain the present régime or to take the factories in your own hands. ... Long live a Poland of peasants and workers!"

In the political theses entitled *Polish Front and our Tasks*, approved by the Supreme Revolutionary War Soviet on the 30th April, it was stated that " the outcome of the coming struggle leaves no room for doubt—the squires and bourgeois of Poland will be defeated. The Polish proletariat will turn its country into a Soviet Republic." [38]

In a conversation with the representatives of the Soviet press Trotsky declared that the attitude of Soviet Russia towards Poland's independence had not changed, but immediately added what he meant under this term : " This independence should not turn into a menace to our existence and peaceful work—it should be *completed* by friendly relations on the basis of co-operation and ex-change of goods." [39] A *friendly,* consequently a *Soviet* Poland.

Stalin in his letter to Lenin dated 12th June and approved by the latter, outlined in this way the future of Central-Eastern Europe con-verted into a Soviet zone of influence, which was to be brought into being twenty-five years later with the connivance of the West :

> " For the nations which formerly belonged to the old Russia, our (Soviet) type of federation may and ought to be considered as leading towards unity. The motives are obvious: either those nations had no independent existence of their own or they lost it a long time ago ; that is why they would be willing to accept with-out much friction our Soviet type of federation. The same cannot be said of nations which did not make part of the old Russia, which existed as independent States. But *if such States became Soviet States, they would have to establish some sort of relations with Russia.* I am speaking of a future Soviet Germany, Poland and Hungary. It is doubtful whether those peoples which have their own governments, their own armies, their finance, would

agree, even if they became Soviet States, to establish with us a
federal union of a type which links us now with the Bashkirs or
the Ukrainians. ... They would consider federation of our Soviet
type as diminishing their national and their State independence. ...
On the other hand, I do not doubt that for those nations a confederation would be the most acceptable form of relations with
us." [40]

As we see, the terms federation or confederation had for the Soviet
leaders a meaning quite different from the Western one, as both
forms of the union of States were to be imposed from outside. The
intentions of Soviet Russia towards Poland became quite clear in
the second period of the war, that is to say the short-lived Soviet
victories, and we shall return to this subject in the following chapter.

While the Polish-Ukrainian forces were occupying the Ukraine
the Soviets were preparing their offensive in the North according
to the plan the general lines of which had been approved as long
before as the 10th March at a conference between the Soviet
C.-in-C., Kamenev, and the Commander of the Western front, then
Gitlis (see p. 556). In view of the developments in the Ukraine the
Soviet High Command was forced to launch this offensive before
the concentration of troops had been completed. It started on the
14th May, that is to say fourteen days after the capture of Kiev, and
although achieving considerable successes until the 1st June, was
unable to attain the important strategic targets Swienciany–
Molodeczno–Minsk. The Polish counter-attack in the North started
on the 1st June, under General K. Sosnkowski's command, pushing
back the Soviet line to the Rivers Auta–Beresina, and ended on the
8th June.

But at the end of May a new danger appeared in the Ukraine :
Budienny with his cavalry army coming from Wrangel's front. The
first battle with Budienny was fought on the 29th May. In spite
of considerable losses the Poles repulsed this first attack, but on the
5th June Budienny succeeded in piercing the Polish front. The
Poles had not enough cavalry, and the Polish commanders fought
against this new enemy with obsolete tactics of the Great World
War, trying to maintain a tight front, contrary to Pilsudski's instructions. Thus the Polish Third Army was cut off in Kiev from the
bulk of the Polish forces, but was able to effect the retreat between
the 10th and 16th June. Kiev was evacuated after having been held
by the Poles for about five weeks. The Soviet offensive in the South
forced the Polish forces to retreat in Podolia and Volhynia, while a
new Soviet offensive in the North started on the 4th July from the
line Auta–Beresina, inaugurating a new series of Soviet successes,
this time directly threatening Central Poland. Thus we enter the

second phase of this war, marked by spectacular Soviet successes and the advance of the Red Army into the heart of Poland.

Attitude of the British Government and public opinion towards military and political developments in Eastern Europe

What was the attitude of the Western countries towards the military developments in Eastern Europe in this first stage of military operations marked by a series of Polish initial successes? The Soviet leaders often asserted that the Poles were carrying on the war with the assistance of their Allies, but a distinction must be made between propaganda slogans and Soviet policy, which took its bearings from the diplomatic position in the West, marked by deep fissures in the Entente.

Speaking at a meeting of glass and hardware workers in Moscow on the 29th April, Lenin struck a demagogic note, indiscriminately accusing all the Allies of giving their full assistance to the Poles : " Evidently the influence of the imperialists in France prevailed within the Polish Government. ... It is evident that Poland is receiving military support from France, England and the whole Entente." [41]

But Lenin's approach to the problem was much more sober and realistic in a later speech he made on 5th May : in this speech he made a distinction between the French and English attitude, realizing the great advantages which the Soviet diplomacy might obtain from the disputes between two principal European Powers :

"We see clearly the discrepancy between the interests of the imperialistic States. In spite of assurances by their ministers that all points in dispute should be settled by peaceful means, the imperialistic States are in fact unable to take any serious step without falling out with one another. The French need a strong Poland and a strong Russia of the Tsarist type, and they are ready to make sacrifices for this purpose, while England, taking into consideration her geographical situation, pursues different aims: the dismemberment of Russia and the *weakening of Poland* in order to establish a balance between France and Germany which might ensure the victorious imperialists the possession of colonies stolen by them in the outcome of the World War from Germany. This descrepancy of interests is patent, and whatever may be said by the representatives of the imperialist States at the San Remo Conference about their having reached full agreement, we know perfectly well that there is no such agreement between them." [42]

Thus the lack of unity between France and Britain played into Soviet hands. Neither on German problems nor on Eastern questions did the French and British see eye to eye. Lloyd George's opposition to French action after the invasion of the neutral zone by German armed forces (the aftermath of the Kapp Putsch), the disclaiming of responsibility by Great Britain in the enforcement of the economic clauses of the Versailles Treaty, the British abstention from the organization of the plebiscite in Upper Silesia, interpreted as a refusal to co-operate with France in that matter—such was one side of the picture. The other side was the difference of approach to the problems of the Middle East and Russia; France suspected that Lloyd George wanted to go far beyond purely economic subjects in his negotiations with Krassin and that Britain wished to strike a political bargain with Soviet Russia in the Middle East and Asia. In fact, immediately after his arrival in London Krassin was received by Lloyd George and other Cabinet Ministers at 10 Downing Street. According to the Paris correspondent of *The Times* this news came as " a thunderbolt to the French. .. The French may be very amenable to an official lead, but they cannot imagine for a minute that Mr. Lloyd George, Mr. Bonar Law, Lord Curzon, Sir Robert Horne and company came to Downing Street in order to receive the representative of the Russian co-operative societies with no other object than to talk about the resumption of trade with Russia." [43]

Lloyd George's speech in the House of Commons on 3rd June [44] could only confirm these suspicions, because he emphasized that " Mr. Krassin is head of a delegation representing the Russian co-operative organizations, but he is also a Minister of the Soviet Government and as such is acting in the name and under the authority of the Soviet Government." He added that " we shall also want some guarantees that there will be no attack made upon the British interests in the East," thus confirming that the conversations with Krassin would not be limited to purely economic issues.

The Krassin negotiations aroused bitter comments in the Polish press. One of the leading Polish papers, *Kurjer Warszawski,* in an editorial of 2nd June entitled " Lloyd George speaks with Lenin," said that

" it was a comedy to pretend to be carrying on negotiations with the Russian co-operatives, as the Swedish commercial treaty with Russia showed that the Soviets had nothing to export, except stolen gold. ... General Petlura is known to further the participation of Great Britain in the economic development of the Ukraine. Instead of pursuing this policy and openly helping Poland to redeem the Ukraine from anarchy, Great Britain prefers to negotiate with Lenin." [45]

The Warsaw correspondent of *The Times* wrote on 5th June (7th June issue) :

" It would be hard to exaggerate the nervousness with which our dealings with Krassin are watched from here. .... It is felt that should our government seem to support Soviet Russia, the Bolshevists will refuse the peace terms which the Polish Government is anxious to offer as soon as it can do it in favourable conditions."

The reactions in Great Britain to the military developments in Eastern Europe in the first period of Polish successes show that there was no unanimity on the political issues raised by the Polish action, either in British public opinion or even within the Cabinet. It is true that Lloyd George never departed from his latent hostility towards Poland,[46] and he manifested on many occasions his lack of faith in the final Polish victory until the end of the Battle of the Vistula. Lord Riddell noted two conversations with Lloyd George at that period which best show the feelings of the British Prime Minister towards the Poles.

On the 9th May, 1920, Lloyd George said to Lord Riddell :

" There are two nations in Europe who have gone rather mad, the French and the Poles. Unless the Poles are careful they will revive and intensify the spirit of Russian nationality. . . . The Poles are inclined to be arrogant and they will have to take care that they don't get their heads punched."[47]

On 30th May Lloyd George said to Lord Riddell that he still thought the Poles would be beaten. " The Poles have quarrelled with all their neighbours and they are a menace to the peace of Europe." So according to Lloyd George it was the Poles who presented a menace to the peace of Europe and not the Bolshevists. But at that time Lloyd George let other members of the Cabinet speak on Polish affairs. In face of the attacks on Poland by the pro-Soviet wing the British Government took a detached point of view, to use Sir Halford Mackinder's expression in his speech in the House of Commons on 20th May. When on 5th May Major Mackenzie Wood asked the Prime Minister " whether the Allies or any of them is giving moral or material support to Poland in her attack on Russia, and have the Allies exercised any pressure on Poland in the direction of peace," Mr. Bonar Law replied that the " answer to both parts of the question is negative, so far as concerns His Majesty's Government." Replying to the questions of other members of the Opposition he stated that the British Government has informed " the Poles and all other Baltic States that we could give them no advice and take no responsibility for their action," and that " if we interfere in this matter and stop Poland, we take upon ourselves the responsibility of protecting them from attack." [49]

The attitude of the British Government was put more explicitly by Lord Curzon in his reply to Lord Robert Cecil, who in the capacity of Chairman of the Executive Committee of the League of Nations Association wrote to Lord Curzon on 3rd May saying that " For months past Poland has been notoriously preparing to attack Russia." Lord Curzon in his reply dated 11th May, said :

> " Our information does not at all support the view that ' for months past Poland has been notoriously preparing to attack Russia.' Until quite recently there has been no evidence to show that the Poles have been contemplating an offensive against Russia ; *we have every reason to believe that their endeavours to open peace negotiations were genuine.* .... In any case this episode does not constitute an outbreak of war, it is merely a phase of war which has been going on for some time and has not yet been terminated. I do not see how we can invoke the intervention of the League of Nations to check an offensive by the Poles in the course of their conflict with the Bolshevists. We told them that His Majesty's Government could offer them no advice and that they must choose peace or war on their own responsibility. Having left them to choose, I hardly think that it is open to us to attempt to repress their action when they have made their choice. Such an attempt would certainly be regarded as an *intervention in favour of the Bolshevists and against our Allies*—a result which it would be difficult to defend.
>
> " Even were such intervention desirable, it seems to me that the League of Nations (which cannot exercise its full powers until its Assembly has been convoked) would be in a very difficult position in any attempt to mediate between Poland and a Russian Government which does not recognize the League's authority." [50]

Lord Curzon later, in the House of Lords on the 22nd July, made a similar statement in which he refuted the arguments of the pro-Soviet speakers : [51]

> " Poland and Soviet Russia have been sporadically engaged in military operations against each other throughout the whole of that time, and indeed, just before this advance happened, *we all knew that the Bolshevist armies were massing themselves in great force to attack Poland.* ... "

He further pointed out the preposterousness of the proposals made by irresponsible advocates of intervention by the League of Nations in view of the attitude of the Bolshevists towards the League of Nations, quoting the text of the Note of the Soviet Government of 17th July :

> " The Soviet Government considers still less admissible the interference in the cause of peace between Russia and Poland of the group of Governments called the League of Nations. ... The Soviet Government can in no way agree that one group of powers

should assume the rôle of supreme body over all the States of the
world, and, watching over the full inviolability of the sovereign
rights of the Russian labouring people, the Soviet Government
absolutely rejects the pretension of any foreign group of Powers
claiming to assume the rôle of supreme masters of the fate of other
nations. It absolutely rejects therefore every interference of this
Association in the cause of peace between Russia and Poland." [52]

As a matter of fact the British pacifists and the advocates of the
intervention of the League of Nations unconsciously took the side
of a Power which derided pacifism (see p. 552) and the League of
Nations, and by no means abhorred war as an instrument of a
policy of conquest and revolution imposed by bayonets. If the
appeals of these ingenuous enthusiasts had been heeded it would
have been only Poland who would have been hampered in her
military operations, without receiving from this body any guarantees
against foreign aggression. Even Lloyd George saw how irresponsible was the action of the groups advocating such ideas. Receiving a
deputation organized by the League to Abolish War, on 16th June,
Lloyd George declared that " Britain could not spare a battalion for
the League of Nations." The speech of the mouthpiece of the delegation, Bishop Gore, shows the spirit in which this section of British
public opinion approached the Polish-Russian relations : " The
invasion on the part of the Poles of Russian territory," said Bishop
Gore, " was exactly the thing which it was supposed the League
of Nations was to be able to check. It was to be able to say to any
nation which invaded the territory of another : ' This must not be.
If you act, you act with the knowledge that the whole combined
force of all the nations constituting the League of Nations will be
directed against you. You are an offender against the common
law.' Now nothing happened." In reply Lloyd George said :

> " We are anxious to find out exactly what the proposal is. Take
> Poland. What can we do? I agree that we could bring some
> pressure to bear on Poland. But what pressure could you bring
> to bear on Russia? The Supreme Council, which is the culprit I
> understand, tried to move the League of Nations in respect of
> Russia. The League of Nations communicated with Russia. The
> Russian Government took weeks before they even replied." (Mr.
> Balfour: " Months.") ... " What is the good of the League of
> Nations intervening in the case of a power that absolutely refuses
> to receive a deputation from another power? " [53]

It was Bonar Law's speech in the House of Commons on 20th
May which best explained the attitude of the British Cabinet as a
whole towards the Polish-Soviet War at that moment. This speech
refuted the arguments of the Opposition by showing that the stand-

point of the pro-Soviet and pacifist wing of the House in fact amounted to taking sides with Soviet Russia against Britain's ally, Poland :

" I think it is a little unfair to overlook the problem of Poland in this matter. ... All this kind of criticism leaves out of account one vital fact in dealing with Eastern Europe or any of those countries. It is no use giving advice and expressing an opinion unless you are prepared to back it. If you were to adopt the sort of attitude which has been urged upon us, we must take the responsibility of seconding men to carry out our views. Is there a man in this House who will say that the British Government or the British people can be induced to throw their armed weight into the scale? ... There is another side of that story. It is a fact that after the defeat of Denikin, the Bolshevist army on the Polish frontier was increased by more than 60 per cent."

(Lord Robert Cecil: " When was that? ").

Mr. Bonar Law: " I think it was in April. Their numbers were increased to that extent, as compared with the end of the year. The Bolshevists said they only sent the troops because they were afraid of an attack by Poland. It was possible to say that. On the other hand, the Poles said that every indication they got was that, unless they were strong, and unless they showed their strength, the Bolshevists would overrun them. That is their case. I am not going to say whether they were right or wrong, but I can imagine nothing that would be more discreditable to this Government or to the Supreme Council than to say to Poland: ' Even if you think it necessary for your safety, you are not to attack the Bolshevists.' Then suppose it had been found that the Poles were right, and the Bolshevists overran Poland, what would our position have been? It is obvious you cannot have it both ways. We cannot say to this country or that ' Do this or that because we think it is wise.' We have to do one of two things. We have to leave them to work as they think best, or we have got to take the responsibility of supporting them by arms."

Further reminding them that the Poles and Bolshevists " have never ceased to be at war," Bonar Law stated that he could not imagine

" anything which could make its (the League of Nations') future more precarious and more doubtful than if the idea were to go forth that its influence is to be thrown in at a particular time to help the Bolshevists, and not when it is going to damage them. ... What is the good of saying to Poland: ' We want to submit all this to the League of Nations,' if you cannot rely upon what you try to do being effective with the Supreme Government in Russia ? Can you rely on that ? ... Is there any sense in the suggestion that it is a practical proposal now when the first offer made by the

League of Nations to the Soviet Government (7th March) that they should receive a deputation has been refused? " [54]

This speech shows the best that the British Government had some understanding for the difficult military and political position of Poland, without however wishing to commit itself in any sense, as if the outcome of the war going on in Eastern Europe had been a matter of indifference to the West.

It may be said that it steered a middle course : it refused to censure the actions of the Poles [55] or to endorse the point of view of those who were ready to find excuses for anything the Soviet Government might do and to hamper the freedom of action of Poland only; but on the other side the British Government let the Poles fight alone against the enemy, the victory of which would have destroyed the foundations of the new political order established so painfully in Paris by Western diplomacy.

In order to see how far went the discrepancy of views on the Polish-Soviet war, it is enough to quote two voices, among so many others. On the one side *The Times,* in its editorial of 1st May, showed full understanding for the Polish point of view :

" In this country there is an impression that the Poles are engaged in an unwarrantable war of conquest. Such an impression needs much qualification. ... First and foremost, the Poles are fighting a battle for the defence of Western civilization. ... Next, their object is to create buffer regions which will protect their own Republic and with it Western Europe from future Bolshevist onslaughts. Finally, they seek to place themselves in a position to lay solidly the foundations of their resuscitated State without being harnessed by constant fears for the safety of their Western frontier."

On the opposite side we read the following editorial in the *New Statesman* on 8th May :

" The nature of the new Polish war against Russia seems hardly yet to have been realized in this country. In view of the desperate condition of all Europe East of the Rhine it can only be regarded as a crowning disaster. Officially the Allied Governments disclaim responsibility. Mr. Bonar Law stated on Tuesday (6th May) that it was only the continuation of an old war—though anybody knows that in reality it is as much a new war as if Great Britain were to send a fresh army to Archangel—and that the Allies could not interfere. Unofficially the Poles were receiving support from both France and Great Britain. The French have provided them with a ' General Staff ' picked from the ablest soldiers in France ; we are providing them with munitions of all kinds. It is an imperialist adventure pure and simple. ... It is impossible, therefore, for anyone who is concerned for the future peace of Europe to *hope for anything but an early disaster for the Polish armies*. The Supreme Council seems determined *to make us all pro-Bolshevists*." [56] [My italics.]

We shall see later how much truth there was in the assertions contained in the *New Statesman* editorial that the Allied Governments were supplying their ablest officers, arms and munitions of all kinds to Poland; we shall then be able to conclude that it was very far from the truth. For the time being let us note that in their accusations against the British Government the *New Statesman* went even farther than Lenin himself.

A fact which aroused much comment both at home and abroad was the sending by H.M. King George V of a most cordial message to Marshal Pilsudski on the occasion of the Polish National Feast of 3rd May.[57] It should be noted that never before or after has such publicity been given to the exchange of telegrams between two Heads of State on a similar occasion, unless there were special political reasons for it. The telegram of King George V appeared in the newspapers on the same day on which the capture of Kiev by the Poles was announced, and it read as follows :

" On this day when you are commemorating one of the greatest events in the illustrious history of your country, I wish to send to your Excellency, and through you to the ancient nation which you represent, the most cordial congratulations of myself and of my people, and my sincere good wishes for the future of the Polish State.

" My country has watched with the greatest sympathy the resurrection of Poland after the long period of anguish through which she has passed, and is confident that with the dawn of a new era she will enjoy unlimited prosperity and peace."

Marshal Pilsudski replied in the following terms :

" I am sincerely grateful for the good wishes which Your Majesty has graciously sent in your name and that of the great and noble British people on the occasion of our national fête. I am specially grateful for the manner in which the wishes are expressed, and can assure Your Majesty that your words will be echoed throughout Poland, and that they will contribute in strengthening the bonds of friendship between Poland and Great Britain. The cordiality of your message has been emphasized by its date, for the 3rd May remains memorable evidence of the affinity of the political conception of our two nations, and is a witness of the simultaneous growth of constitutional liberty in each of our countries."

In its June issue the *National Review* commented in these words on the telegram of King George V :

" On the anniversary of the voting of the Polish Constitution in 1791 the King sent a cordial congratulatory telegram to the great soldier at the head of the Polish State—Marshal Pilsudski. This coincided with the opening of a brilliant offensive that Marshal Pilsudski had organized in conjunction with the Ukraine against Bolshevik Russia whom the rest of the world was funking. The King's telegram was not unnaturally hailed in Poland as a God-speed to their new enterprise."

A reference to the King's telegram was made by Lieutenant-Commander Kenworthy in the House of Commons on 10th May in a manner which could be considered as a veiled criticism of this act of the Sovereign. This pro-Soviet member was eager to avail himself of any occasion to prove the British Government's share of responsibility in the military initiative of the Poles. Bonar Law emphatically denied the charge in connection with this question and similar ones put by the Opposition in order to involve British responsibility in the Polish actions. As a matter of fact no evidence can be produced to prove that the British Government had actually been informed of the imminent Polish offensive.

On 18th May Winston Churchill gave a written reply to the question put by Lieutenant-Colonel Malone, asking " whether the Secretary of State for War and Air received a warning of the Polish offensive against Soviet Russia from the missions in Poland and from other sources; and if so, when."

Winston Churchill replied :

" The British Military Mission in Warsaw, in a telegram dated 22nd April and received on the 23rd April, conjectured that some Polish offensive appeared imminent. A subsequent telegram dealing with the subject, dispatched from Warsaw on the 24th April, was received in London after the offensive had been launched. Most of the reports received have dwelt rather on the Soviet preparations for a renewal of the Soviet attack on Poland, which was delivered in great force in March, and finally checked early in April." [58]

The assertions of the Opposition that there were numerous British officers serving in Poland were also refuted by the Government, and Churchill at the request of the pro-Soviet members produced the figures, very small indeed, relating to British officers attached to the Military, Air and Naval Missions in Poland. The British officers had helped, but in organizing the armies of the Baltic States, fifteen of them having contracts with the Lithuanian Government. There was a numerous personnel in the French Military Mission in Poland under General Henrys, but this Mission was responsible only for training, equipment and the general needs of the Polish Army and had no influence on the plans for military operations. The strength of this Mission was not increased before the April offensive.

So far as military supplies were concerned, we have already said that Polish needs were covered partly by France and partly by purchases abroad by Poland, and until autumn 1919 Great Britain supplied no arms and munitions to Poland (p. 406). A new situation arose late in autumn 1919 after Denikin's defeat, as appears from the account given by Bonar Law in his speech in the House of Commons on the 17th May, 1920 :

> " In October last year when it was feared that the Russian Border States would be attacked by the Soviet Government a request was addressed by the Polish Government for assistance in their military commitments. In consequence of our commitments elsewhere the British Government were unable to give any financial assistance, but they offered to supply a certain quantity of surplus stores on condition that the cost of moving them, as well as the arrangements for transport, should be undertaken by the Polish Government. The offer was accepted. In consequence of that gift the material in question became the property of the Polish Government, and part of it is now being shipped by that Government. Beyond that no assistance has been or is being given to the Polish Government."

The British Government was quite correct in saying that it had not provided any arms or munitions to Poland for some definite military operations. It should be remembered that the British engagements on this point were made before the lifting of the blockade of Soviet Russia and before the new trend of British foreign policy due to Lloyd George. The resolution passed by the Supreme Council on the 13th December, 1919, stated expressly : " not to enter into any further commitments *beyond what have already been promised,*" and by virtue of this resolution the arms promised at that time to Denikin were delivered to him so long as his armies were fighting. What the Opposition demanded was the cancellation of a previous engagement of the Government and the laying of an embargo on what had become in fact the property of the Polish Government. In his subsequent speech in the House of Commons on 20th May Bonar Law showed the spirit in which the British Government approached the whole position of Poland at the end of 1919 :

> " It is the common knowledge of everyone who knows the inside of political affairs that there was a belief and fear that the Bolshevists, having been freed from the pressure of General Denikin, would throw their whole force on the bordering States, and they

had given reason for that belief, because in a message sent by Trotsky to the French soldiers, he said: 'We can watch this temporary advance of the feeble Polish troops without being too alarmed, when we have finished with Denikin—and the day is near —we will throw ourselves on to that front with overwhelming reserves.' [59]

" It is said that we only gave these munitions for purposes of defence. We gave them to an Ally which had been created as the result of the War, whose position had been secured by the Supreme Council. We did it to put them in a good position to defend themselves, and to make it less probable that a time might come when we might be forced against our will to intervene with armed forces in that part of the world. It is said that we should have made conditions, but we have made no conditions in other cases in which we helped our Allies. We could not make them.

" . . . It is seriously suggested that when this material was the property of the Polish Government the fact that we had given it made no difference. It is seriously suggested that they would not be allowed to make their own arrangements or that it would not be allowed to go."

It was in fact a very limited quantity of British stores, and it was a complete distortion of facts that the *New Statesman* stated in its issue of 5th May :

" We know that the Polish Army is well organized, well led and very well equipped largely with British aeroplanes, guns and munitions. We are informed also that the Poles have the advantage of being able to employ a number of new British tanks of a type greatly superior in speed and armament to any that were employed on the Western Front. *The Russian Army, on the other hand, is known to have partially demobilized.*" [My italics.]

As a matter of fact even this very limited quantity of British surplus stores could not be delivered in full because all shipments to Poland were virtually stopped owing to the action of the British trade unions. The question of the boycott of all arms shipments to Poland first arose in connection with loading arms and munitions in London docks on a merchant vessel, *The Jolly George,* on 9th May. A deputation was sent by the workers to Mr. Bevin, then their trade union leader, who told the men to stop loading at once, and issued an order to dockers in other ports not to load any arms and munitions going to Poland. [60] Lloyd George who took this matter in hand, bowed to this decision of the trade unions, and when Lieutenant-Commander Kenworthy asked him on the 17th June : " Have munitions been stopped going from this country to Poland? ", Lloyd George answered : " None are going from this country." [61]

It was much more than the stopping of any assistance by the British Government to Poland, it was a total blockade of Poland while Russia was free to make her purchases in other countries. Lieutenant-Colonel Guinness stressed this point in the debate in the House of Commons on 20th May :

> " In view of the advantage we got during the most critical days of the war by getting ammunition in America, I should have thought it was a most short-sighted policy to attempt to overthrow the well-established principle which allows belligerents to obtain munitions in neutral countries." [62]

While the British Labour Party was sending numerous delegations to Russia, none of these visited Poland to ascertain the facts from the other side, and consequently took their bearings exclusively from the Bolshevist propaganda slogans. On 27th April a delegation chosen by the Executive Committee of the Labour Party and of the Trades Union Congress, in fulfilment of the resolution passed by a special Trades Union Congress held on 10th December, 1919, left England and after staying in Russia six weeks returned to England on 30th June. This delegation consisted of Arthur Henderson, W. H. Hutchinson, Ben Turner, Ramsay MacDonald, Miss Mary Macarthur and Mrs. Philip Snowden. The latter in a book published in London in 1920, *Through Bolshevik Russia,* summed up her impressions from the visit to that country. Many assertions contained in that book were afterwards recanted by her, but at the time her book was published the ideas advocated by Mrs. Snowden greatly impressed many people. In the war between Poland and Russia she saw only imperialistic adventure, and approved unreservedly the attitude adopted by the Soviets :

> " The territory claimed by the Poles and for which they entered upon this foolish and wicked adventure is an area of about four hundred thousand square miles, containing a population which is not ten per cent. Polish. The remaining ninety per cent. do not wish to belong to the Polish Empire. The claim of the Poles to this territory is of the shadowiest description and dates back to the time when the United States of America was still a part of the British Empire. Undoubtedly, the claim upon this land rests upon the ambition of the Poles to make it a jumping-off ground for an imperialistic adventure which would establish Polish rule from Warsaw to Odessa. No Russian Government, whatever its name or quality, would accept such an arrangement and it is the most natural thing in the world that the insolent campaign of Poland should have united behind the Soviet Republic every section of the Russian people. . . . The Russians need so sorely to get on with their work of internal reconstruction that *only the most stupid blunderer*

*could for a moment imagine they were eager for spoils and con-
quest,"* [my italics],

and she added :

"one's whole sympathy is with the Russians." [63]

Another batch of the British Labour Delegation to Russia, consisting of Mr. Robert Williams, Mr. A. A. Purcell, Mr. R. C.
Wallhead, Miss Margaret Bondfield and Mr. R. Skinner, on their
return from Russia made the following statement to the newspaper
Politiken at Stockholm on the 8th June :

"From all they heard from the Soviet leaders, from Lenin to
Trotsky to Chicherin and Kamenev, and had seen with their own
eyes, Russia is under the Soviet régime, they declared, the happiest
country in the world and it was absurd to say that England had
nothing to learn from Russia. The political, economic and social
progress made since 1917 was so wonderful that it must affect any
country in Europe when better known. ... The Putilov works were
producing the finest guns in greater number than the works in
England during the war. These guns fired not only explosive shells
on the Polish positions, but bundles of tracts and pamphlets which
the enemy feared much more than bullets. ... In prison camps they
had seen Polish officers who had but one wish—namely, to serve
under the Soviet Government." [64]

A woman who played an outstanding part in the German Communist movement but later suffered the bitterest disappointments
from Soviet Russia, Ruth Fischer, wrote in her book *Stalin and the
German Communism* about the pro-Soviet sentiment among British
workers at that time that this sentiment

"was reflected in British trade union policy, but even when it was
not directly reflected, often rank-and-file pressure modified what
would otherwise have been an anti-Russian attitude. Sidney and
Beatrice Webb, Fabian Socialists, the chroniclers of the British
trade union movement, exemplify a general mood in their development into almost the *official non-Communist apologists of Soviet
Russia.*" [65]

All the consequences of the pro-Soviet attitude of British Labour
and of British Liberals and Radicals, appeared in the subsequent
period when Poland's independence seemed to be endangered to the
highest degree by the Soviet invasion. But already in this period
this attitude began to disintegrate the delicate structure of post-war
Europe and encourage all pro-Russian or pro-Soviet elements in
Central Europe, in Germany and Czechoslovakia in particular. At
the height of the Polish action in the Ukraine, Beneš, the Foreign

Minister of Czechoslovakia, sent the following telegram to Chicherin :

> " I wish Russia and the great Russian nation a beneficent peace in the shortest possible time. Since the very existence of our Republic our policy has always tended to peace, friendship and sincere co-operation with the Governments of all *truly democratic nations*." [66]

The Czech attitude greatly perplexed Western observers in Poland, as appears from the telegram of the American chargé d'Affaires in Warsaw to the Department of State, dated 12th June. Stressing the " general lack of support in the West for Poland," Mr. White drew attention to the disquieting features of Czech policy :

> " The Czechs in particular are stated to be holding up several ammunition trains destined for Poland. I understand that the Czech Government lays the responsibility for this action at the door of the railway labour union. However, if the Department shares my views that the Poles are fighting the battle of civilization against the Bolsheviks, I think it would be desirable, in view of the credit which the American nation enjoys with the Czechs, for the Department to address pointed inquiries to Prague." [67]

But these were voices crying in the wilderness. To the ideological crusade of the East the West had nothing to oppose, believing that only the resumption of trade could save civilization.[68] On 24th June the Acting Secretary of State informed the U.S. Ambassador in Great Britain " that the decision has been reached by the President that restrictions now existing on trade with Russia shall soon be removed ... probably one exception—war materials," at the same time stating that did not mean " recognition of any existing faction or of the Soviet régime." On 7th July the said restrictions were actually removed.[69] Even the attitude of France, in spite of the limited support by munitions supplies given by her to Poland, became ambiguous. About the end of June, " the germ of belief in the advantages of recognizing the Soviet Government was beginning to grow in France," and this fact is confirmed by the well-informed Radek, in his report to the Fourth Congress of the Third International.[70]

In these circumstances the first news of Polish setbacks on the Eastern front created an extremely favourable position for the Soviet Government. At the time of the Polish successes the whole attention of the Western statesmen was absorbed by other problems —Germany, Turkey, the Middle East. The meaning of the Polish-Soviet War was understood only by the very few conversant with the problems of Eastern Europe.[71] But the time came when the

Western Powers had to assume their responsibilities. It had to be decided what might be obtained from Soviet Russia by negotiations. The valuable asset of the latter was not so much her military power, as the outcome of the war showed, but internal dissensions among the Western partners, their domestic troubles, due to a great extent to labour unrest, and last but not least their unwillingness to make any sacrifices to preserve the political *status quo* in Eastern Europe. In spite of these assets Soviet Russia eventually suffered the greatest defeat in her history when her revolutionary drive was stopped at the gates of Warsaw.

NOTES

[1] *Krasnaya Kniga,* pp. 92-3.

[2] *The Times,* 23rd March, 1920.

[2a] *The Times,* 5th April, 1920.

[3] STARZEWSKI, o.c.,p. 68.

[4] *Parliamentary Debates,* Commons, Vol. 127.

[5] *P. R. F. R.,* 1920, Vol. III, p. 381.

[6] GRABSKI, o.c., p. 22. It is interesting to note that similar views were expressed at that time by the mouthpiece of the pro-Soviet wing in the House of Commons, Lieutenant-Commander Kenworthy, (*Par. Deb.,* Com., Vol. 129, 20th May, 1920): "I believe that the Ukraine could be free, not by fighting but by negotiations, and it is for negotiations that I do beg at the present time."

[7] T. KUTRZEBA, o.c., p. 248.

[8] W. H. CHAMBERLIN, o.c., Vol. II, pp. 300 ff. "Pilsudski was pursuing a lifelong dream: the permanent weakening of Russia through the detachment of the non-Russian territories of the former Tsarist Empire. The creation of a chain of new States, Finland, Latvia, Esthonia, Lithuania, to the north of Poland had undone already the work of Peter the Great and shut Russia off from access to the Baltic Sea. Far away, in the semi-oriental Caucasus, were now national Republics, Georgia, Armenia, Azerbaijan. Pilsudski's drive into Ukraine was designed to bridge the gap between these groups of little States by creating an independent Ukraine, which would be dependent on Poland, and, perhaps, an independent Cossack State in the Don and Kuban. Reduced to its frontiers of the sixteenth century, cut off from the Black and Baltic Seas, deprived of the agricultural and mineral wealth of the South and South-East Russia might easily sink to the status of second-class power, incapable of seriously threatening the newly gained independence of Poland."

[8a] Cf. CHRISTOPHER DAWSON, *Understanding Europe,* London, 1952, p. 89: "For though the Cossack revolt was a genuinely popular and even democratic movement which was inspired by the freedom of the steppes and aimed at an independent Ukrainian State, it actually resulted in the ruin of both the Ukraine and Poland to the benefit of Moscow."

[9] KUTRZEBA, o.c., p. 248.

[10] *Krasnaya Kniga*, p. 95. It is interesting to note that the Polish proposals insisting on Borisov as the meeting place were rejected only after long deliberations within the Soviet Government. This appears clearly from the reactions of the Soviet press. M. P. V. Suslov writes in this connection that " the meaning of the proposals concerning Borisov as a place in which the Conference should be held, was not immediately guessed rightly by our press. Only on 29th March *Pravda* and *Izvestia* were *forced* to look at this proposal with other eyes stating the true meaning of it in a correct sense. Thus within the space of two days the reader received two different points of view, first *Pravda* and *Izvestia* interpreted the Polish proposal as ' a new move,' as ' a stage on the way to peace,' and then they declared that this proposal was inadmissible and not proper to advance the cause of peace " (SUSLOV, o.c., p. 29).

[11] *Krasnaya Kniga*, p. 95.

[12] *Ibidem*, p. 96.

[13] *Ibidem*, p. 100.

[14] *The Times*, 1st June, 1920.

[15] S. GRABSKI, o.c., p. 23.

[16] The text of the Political Convention was published in English by JOHN S. RESHETAR, JR., *The Ukrainian Revolution*, 1917-1920, pp. 301 ff., the text of the military convention (in Polish) by T. KUTRZEBA, o.c., pp. 83 ff.

[17] T. KUTRZEBA, o.c., p. 254. In the light of this evidence the assertions of Mr. Reshetar, o.c., p. 308, seemed completely unfounded: " Following the completion of the general plan of joint operations, the evacuation of Polish forces was to commence upon the proposal of one of the signatories, but the technical execution of the evacuation was to be based on a mutual understanding between the Polish and Ukrainian Commands. This meant that Pilsudski could occupy the country for as long a period as he wished . . . this humiliating military convention."

[18] M. K. DZIEWANOWSKI, o.c., p. 286.

[19] J. S. RESHETAR, o.c., p. 303.

[20] M. K. DZIEWANOWSKI, o.c., p. 274.

[21] W. CHURCHILL, o.c., p. 266.

[22] A. L. KENNEDY, o.c., p. 319.

[23] W. H. CHAMBERLIN, Vol. II, pp. 213 ff.

[24] *Ibidem*, p. 300.

[25] L. TROTSKY, Vol. III, p. 249 and 255.

[26] *Grazhdanskaya Voyna*, Vol. III, p. 310.

[27] KAKURIN i MELIKOV, o.c., p. 944.

[28] P. V. SUSLOV, o.c., p. 35.

[29] Pilsudski stated to Mackinder during the visit of the latter to Warsaw that " he was decidedly of the opinion that the Polish Army alone could go to Moscow next spring, but from a political point of view he asked himself what he should do when and if he got there!" (*D.B.F.P.*, Vol. III, p. 788).

[30] PILSUDSKI, *Pisma*, Vol. VII, p. 152.

[31] LORD D'ABERNON, o.c., pp. 38 ff.

[32] W. H. CHAMBERLIN, o.c., Vol. II, pp. 316 ff.

[33] H. SLOVES, *La France et l'Union Sovietique*, p. 119. " Le premier mai 1920 l'abassadeur de Wrangel à Paris, M. Maklakov télegraphia en Crimée: ' Gouvernement français hostile à toute entente avec les bolchéviques. N'exerce aucune pression pour la capitulation de la Crimée. Ne participera point à une médiation pareille si d'autres l'entreprennent. Sympathise avec l'idée de défendre la Crimée et la province Taurique. Considérant bolchévisme l'ennemi principale de la Russie, *gouvernement français sympathise l'offensive polonaise* '."

[34] P. V. SUSLOV, o.c., p. 31.

[35] *Ibidem*, p. 48. " spetsiphichnomu v agitatsii poliakov i Petluri (osvobozhedieniye Ukrainy) nichevo i ne protivopostavlialos."

[36] These Soviet war-slogans are taken at their face value by Trotsky's biographer DEUTSCHER, o.c., p. 460: " Pilsudski's troops did much to stir up the anti-Polish sentiment. Their behaviour in occupied Ukraine was overbearing ; they began to establish the Polish landlords on their former domains, and they marked their victories by the shooting of prisoners of war and by pogroms."

[37] *Krasnaya Kniga*, p. 105.

[38] L. TROTSKY, o.c., Vol. II, Book II, p. 93.

[39] *Ibidem*, p. 104.

[40] English translation from *Lenin, Oeuvres Complètes* (L'année 1920) by M. K. DZIEWANOWSKI, o.c., p. 278.

[41] LENIN, *Sochineniya*, Vol. XXV, pp. 251 ff.

[42] *Ibidem*, pp. 259 ff.

[43] *The Times*, 2nd June, 1920.

[44] *Parliamentary Debates*, Commons, Vol. 129.

[45] *The Times*, 5th June, 1920.

[46] K. F. NOWAK, *Versailles*, p. 90. " In Poland he (Lloyd George) saw a nation of rebels whom he would never willingly have assisted against Britain's former ally, Russia. He still hoped that the day would come when the Bolsheviks would be overthrown ; then the old Russia would reappear in some form and he would re-enter into friendly relations with her. He had no love for the Poles."

[47] LORD RIDDELL, o.c., p. 191.

[48] *Ibidem*, p. 198.

[49] *Parliamentary Debates*, Commons, Vol. 129.

[50] *The Times*, 17th May, 1920.

[51] *Parliamentary Debates*, Lords, Vol. 41.

[52] Cf. p. 620.

[53] *The Times*, 19th June, 1920.

[54] *Parliamentary Debates*, Commons, Vol. 129.·

[55] See a characteristic intervention of the Speaker at the sitting of the House of Commons on 20th May. Interrupting the speech of Sir Donald Maclean, the Speaker declared: " We have no right or title of any sort to interfere or criticize, or have anything to say as to the motives which govern the actions of other countries," and when Sir

Donald was supported by Lord Robert Cecil, the Speaker intervened again saying: " The less we criticize or seek to interfere with the motives which govern the conduct of other States the more likely are we to arrive at, and remain in, friendly relations with them."

⁵⁶ Lord Robert Cecil expressed the fear in his speech in the House of Commons on 20th May that " if the Poles are completely successful it may mean the destruction of the Soviet Government in Russia."

⁵⁷ *The Times*, 10th May, 1920.

⁵⁸ *Parliamentary Debates*, Commons, Vol. 129.

⁵⁹ TROTSKY, *My Life*, p. 455. Referring to Bonar Law's speech, tried to refute it by an insolent remark: " All this is sheer drivel from beginning to end," and says that " such statements were the result of the entire setting "(?).

⁶⁰ FRANCIS WILLIAMS, o.c., p. 83.

⁶¹ *Parliamentary Debates*, Commons, Vol. 129.

⁶² *Ibidem*, Vol. 130.

⁶³ MRS. PHILIP SNOWDEN, *Through Bolshevik Russia*, pp. 81 ff.

⁶⁴ *The Times*, 10th June, 1920.

⁶⁵ RUTH FISCHER, *Stalin and the German Communism*, p. 559.

⁶⁶ *The Times*, 14th May, 1920.

⁶⁷ *P. R. F. R.*, 1920, Vol. II, p. 384.

⁶⁸ Speech by Mr. Maclean in the House of Commons on 20th May (*Parliamentary Debates*, Commons, Vol. 129): " It would be better if you would load these vessels with these munitions which you do not require and dump them overboard rather than to send them to Poland to be used in the wasting of more human life, which this country and all countries require to be used in an effort to build up civilization again."

⁶⁹ *P. R. F. R.*, Vol. III, p. 702.

⁷⁰ K. RADEK, *Die Liquidation des Versailler Friedens*, Hamburg, 1922, p. 24. " Auf der zu dieser Zeit zusammengetretenen Konferenz in Boulogne, war nicht nur England, sondern auch Frankreich bereit, Sovietrussland anzuerkennen, um so seinen siegreichen Vormarsch aufzuhalten."

⁷¹ A. TARDIEU, p. xxiv, Preface by Georges Clemenceau: " Il a fallu les convulsions d'une Russie désorbitée pour faire découvrir à des esprits volontairement fermés les premiers aspects de la question polonaise. Une fois de plus, l'historique vaillance de la Pologne a fait ses preuves."

CHAPTER VII

SECOND PHASE IN THE POLISH-SOVIET WAR IN 1920

SOVIET ADVANCE INTO POLAND

" On the essential point there is little doubt: had the Soviet forces overcome Polish resistance and captured Warsaw, Bolshevism would have spread throughout Central Europe and might well have penetrated the whole continent. ... To set against the propagandist zeal of the Bolsheviks, there was, on the side of Western European civilization nothing but a divided camp."— (VISCOUNT D'ABERNON, *The Eighteenth Decisive Battle of the World*, pp. 11-12.)

Polish reverses and the Spa Conference

A NEW Cabinet was formed in Poland on the 24th June by a Right-Wing politician, W. Grabski, and it was immediately faced with a very serious position at the front after the withdrawal of the Polish troops from the Ukraine and the failure to check the advance of the Russians in Volhynia. This position definitely worsened after the 5th July, when the overwhelming Soviet forces launched an offensive in the North, and the Bolsheviks forced the passages across the Auta and Beresina. The withdrawal of the Polish forces from the Dvina immediately followed, and the big territories to the North of the Pripet had to be evacuated. At the same time the stronghold of Rowno, an important railway and road junction in Volhynia, fell into Bolshevik hands. Grabski's Cabinet decided to appeal to the Supreme Council for assistance. This appeal was put on the agenda of the Conference at Spa which began on the 5th July to consider the problem of German reparations.

It should be stressed that the position of the Polish Army, although very serious, was not desperate; it is true that the Poles were in full retreat at that time along the whole Eastern front, but their resistance had not been broken and the bulk of their army remained unimpaired, as subsequent events were to show. The Western countries, whose views on war were moulded on the experiences of trench warfare in the course of the Great War, were not prepared to face the ups and downs of a war of movement. On the other side, the momentum of the Soviet offensive should have convinced those who believed in the pacific designs of the Soviet Government that the Poles had been right in their anticipation of forthcoming events and in launching at the end of April an operation far beyond the vital centres of Poland in order to forestall the Soviet initiative. However, the conclusions drawn by the Western countries were just the opposite, and the opinion prevailed that the Soviet offensive was provoked by Polish " aggressiveness," and even now we still meet with such opinions in books based almost exclusively on Soviet sources. Thus the reactions of the Western statesmen were rather unfavourable to Poland. Events took them by surprise, and they did not believe that they might be able to induce public opinion at home to make the important sacrifices necessary for the strengthening of the Polish position. Lord Riddell, one of Lloyd George's intimates, summed up his impression of the rather incoherent and inconsistent policy of Great Britain and France at that time, saying that " the difficulty is that Great Britain and France have gradually assumed the position of being responsible for the management of Europe—a task which they are not equipped to perform."

The foregoing remarks may explain what it is so difficult to understand now—that the Entente Powers, instead of taking decisions which might strengthen the position of the Poles, did just the contrary, believing that in order to ensure the success of the negotiations with Soviet Russia (and they believed that Poland could be saved only by negotiations) pressure must be exercised on the Poles to soften them and prepare them for far-reaching concessions to the Soviets. For instance, we find very characteristic statements in the Diary of Field-Marshal Sir Henry Wilson, then C.I.G.S., the principal military adviser of His Majesty's Government at Spa. Sir Henry considered that " the Poles appeared to occupy a line space 200 km. beyond their proper ethnographic frontier, that this must tend to accentuate Russian hostility and that they ought to be called upon to retire." To Foch's contention that such a retirement would ruin the morale of the Polish Army, Sir Henry rejoined that " *their morale must be risked* for the sake of getting them out of Russian territory, where they had no business to be." [1] It is astonishing that he did not realize what such a withdrawal would mean for the defence of Poland, and that it would have left that country at the mercy of Soviet Russia.

In its issue of 10th July *The Times* said, in connection with the agenda of the Spa Conference : " While the Conference at Spa is dealing with questions on its official programme, *issues of strictly minor importance* are being debated in the background. Of those the most urgent is the situation in Poland and the possibility of saving the Poles from disaster." The indifference to the fate of Poland caused bitter feeling among the Poles, as is emphasized by the following telegram from the Warsaw correspondent of *The Times*, dated 2nd July (*The Times*, 5th July, 1920) :

" The Poles fully realize that their national existence is at stake, and are only disconcerted by the attitude of the Allies, mainly England, who appear indifferent to the fate of Poland and unable to appreciate the danger facing Eastern Europe should Poland be overrun by Bolshevist armies."

It was neighbouring Rumania which realized better than the Western countries what was at stake in this great battle in Eastern Europe. One of the greatest statesmen in modern Rumanian history, Take Ionescu, then Minister for Foreign Affairs of the Kingdom of Rumania, addressed the following letter to the Supreme Council :

" I do not delude myself that my opinion might carry weight with the Conference, but I feel, nevertheless, that it is my duty as the nearest and direct witness of the dramatic events taking place on Rumania's frontier, to draw the attention of the Great Allies to the dangers which will menace Europe should Poland be defeated. The interests of Europe demand the immediate stopping of the war between Poland and Russia, as in the opposite case this whole part of Europe would be conquered by the Soviets. Europe is interested in keeping the front from the Baltic to the Black Sea, and because of that the question of Eastern Galicia must not be reopened. A Poland surrounded by an iron ring of Germany and Russia will cease to be an independent country and will be unable to play the rôle assigned to her in the European balance of power ; she can fulfil this mission only if supported by her neighbours and allies." [2]

The Polish Prime Minister, Grabski, addressed the Supreme Council at Spa on 6th July. He stated :

" Poland is a living wall against the Bolshevik invasion. In her struggle for existence, and just and lasting peace, able to secure to Poland the possession of territories inhabited by the Poles who do not wish to be separated from their mother-country, Poland is ready to accept at once a peace based on the principle of self-determination. Should the Polish Army, outnumbered by the enemy, be overwhelmed the whole of Europe will be in danger: consequently it is Poland's duty to warn the Supreme Council of this danger in order that it may make its decisions in due time. Should events force Poland to carry on the war, the material and moral assistance of the Allies will be needed. The Polish Government asks for assistance most insistently, assistance which must be *immediate and efficient,* and whichever may be the measures taken by the Supreme Council the Polish Government will be ready to accept them." [3]

Grabski was a representative of the most pro-Allied wing of Polish public opinion; his trust in the good intentions of the Entente Powers and in their readiness to come to Poland's assistance turned out to be quite unwarranted, and his Cabinet had a short life. A more representative body was set up in Poland, the Council for the Defence of the State, consisting of ten members of the Diet, of all political allegiances, six members of the Government and five representatives of the Army. It was granted full powers in matters concerning the conduct of the war and the conclusion of peace. On 24th July a Coalition Government was set up in Warsaw, with peasant leader Witos as Prime Minister, the leader of the Socialist party, Daszynski, as Vice-Premier, and Pilsudski's closest friend, General Sosnkowski, as Minister for War.

A peculiar position arose at Spa. The French made an indispensable condition of their officially concurring in any steps taken by the Supreme Council an undertaking by the Soviet Government that it would respect the engagements of previous Russian Governments. Lloyd George refused to go so far, being eager to enter into negotiations with the Soviets at any cost. The French consequently left Lloyd George a completely free hand. Count Sforza, the Italian Foreign Minister, who attended the Spa Conference and jointly with Lloyd George and Millerand took part in the confidential conversations on Polish matters, remarks in his book *Diplomatic Europe since the Treaty of Versailles* : " For his part, M. Millerand deeply desired to help Poland, but stronger than his desire was his distaste for any sort of contact with the Bolshevists, and he remained practically aloof." [4]

" Thus," H. Nicolson states in his book *Curzon, the Last Phase,* " the onus of mediation fell upon Mr. Lloyd George, who had never been guilty of pro-Polish sentiments, and whose personal record in regard to intervention against the Soviet had been comparatively clear." [5]

Did Lloyd George really wish to help the Poles at this fateful hour? The question must be answered negatively, and both his proposals and his attitude in the course of the following six weeks prove quite the contrary. What he wished to attain above all was to meet the Bolsheviks at a conference table and start political negotiations with them. He wanted to assure in advance the full success of these negotiations, and believed that the best way would be to present to the Bolsheviks such tempting offers that it would be most unlikely that they could refuse to negotiate on such advantageous terms. Consequently he decided to exert overwhelming pressure on the Poles, to ask them not to stop on their actual front line but to withdraw to the provisional line established by the Supreme Council in December 1919 and wrongly considered by him to be Poland's ethnographical frontier. He intended also to reopen the problem of Eastern Galicia, in spite of the previous decisions of the Supreme Council with the full concurrence of the United States, in order to lure the Russians with prospects of extending their frontiers in that direction also.[6] Moreover, he decided to impose on the Poles some additional conditions which had nothing to do with Polish-Russian relations, the only urgent and topical matter at that time.

Poland was consequently forced to accept that " Wilno shall without delay be relinquished to Lithuania and excluded from the zone occupied by the Red Army during the armistice," as well as to accept " the decision of the Supreme Council regarding Lithuanian frontiers, the settlement of the question of Eastern Galicia, that of Teschen, and the future Polish Treaty with Danzig."

So far as the decision of the Supreme Council on Teschen was concerned we know that it was unfavourable to Poland in spite of the attitude of the British and American delegations during the previous debates on that point (see pp. 364 ff.). The convention which Poland had to sign with Danzig deprived her of the most essential rights guaranteed by the Treaty of Versailles, especially in regard to the administration of the port. Thus Lloyd George, instead of reinforcing " the living wall against Bolshevik invasion," did his utmost to weaken it, and at Poland's expense recompensed Czechoslovakia in spite of her ambiguous behaviour in relation to the Bolsheviks. By the Treaty with Danzig that city definitely became a bastion of Germanism in the East and a " thorn in Poland's living flesh," with far-reaching consequences for the peace of the world, as events leading to the outbreak of the Second World War were to show.

In his above-mentioned book H. Nicolson related that " On 10th July Mr. Lloyd George interviewed Mr. Grabski alone. He abused the Poles for having advanced into Russian and Ukrainian territory and he ordered them to withdraw some 125 miles behind the line which they had at that moment occupied. This would bring them to their ' legitimate frontier.' Mr. Grabski inquired where that frontier lay. Mr. Lloyd George then indicated what has since been known as the ' Curzon Line ' (although Curzon himself had little to do with it)." Nicolson further adds that " it is difficult, even with the documents before us, even with full recollection of Curzon's dilemma at the time, to be certain how far the Foreign Secretary was responsible for this humiliating episode. On the one hand Lord Curzon was not present at the crucial interview between Lloyd George and Mr. Grabski. On the other hand he consented to give his name to the telegrams and Notes which resulted from that interview." [7] Count Sforza sums up his impressions of the Spa conference in the following way : " I must confess that the recollection of the Spa Conference had left me the impression of a British and especially a Lloyd Georgian policy which was rather prejudiced against Poland. . . . It was in vain that I tried to obtain more favourable terms for the Poles." [8]

Sforza's compatriot, Signor Tommasini, then Italian Minister in Warsaw, in his book *La Risurrezione di Polonia* calls the terms imposed on Poland " very hard and humiliating for that country as it had to abandon to its enemy, who every day committed the most revolting acts of cruelty against the wounded, the civil prisoners and women, the vast areas still held by its armies." [9]

> " The whole conference at the Belgian watering-place " [he says], " was dominated by Lloyd George who thus became the arbiter of the destinies of Poland and who was little favourable to Poland owing to the influence of the Jewish high finance with which he had personal ties, owing to the desire to ingratiate himself with the Labour Party sympathizing with the Bolsheviks, and owing to the pessimistic reports supplied by the British agents in Poland. In fact, my British colleague, Sir Horace Rumbold, was fully convinced that Warsaw would fall into the hands of the Soviet armies, and that Poland would be completely defeated, while General Carton de Wiart, head of the English Military Mission, concurred in and reinforced this pessimism, which although justified to a certain extent continued to persist even when certain circumstances occurred which should have qualified it." [10]

Two important points must be clarified in relation to the Agreement of 10th January, 1920, signed at Spa between Poland and the Powers.

The first concerns the future armistice line between the Polish and Russian Armies. According to this agreement :

> " an armistice shall be signed without delay, and the Polish army withdrawing to the line provisionally laid down by the Peace Conference of 8th December, 1919, as the Eastern boundary within which Poland was entitled to establish a Polish administration, whereas the Soviet armies shall stand at a distance of 50 kilometres eastwards of that line. . . . In East Galicia both armies shall stand on the line fixed at the date of the signature of the armistice."

The difference between the provisions relating to the 8th December Line and Eastern Galicia was further emphasized in the Agreement of 10th July by the fact that while, so far as the first line was concerned, " the Soviet armies should stand at a distance of 50 kilometres eastwards of that line," in Eastern Galicia " each army shall withdraw 10 kilometres in order to create a neutral zone."

This point must be kept in mind because it has been often wrongly assumed that the so-called Curzon Line extended to Eastern Galicia and that Poland agreed to such extension. This wrong assumption was drawn from an obvious topographical error in the Note sent by Lord Curzon on the following day.

The second point is that the agreement was a bilateral one, as in the event of the acceptance of its conditions by Poland the Allied Powers made definite pledges to assist Poland :

" In the event of Poland's acceptance of the above terms the British Government shall immediately send a *similar* proposal to Soviet Russia, and should she refuse an armistice the Allies shall give Poland all aid, particularly in war material, as far as would be possible in view of their own exhaustion and heavy obligations undertaken elsewhere. This aid would be given in order to enable the Polish nation to defend its independence."

Curzon's telegrams of 11th July

Implementing the Agreement of 10th July Lord Curzon, on behalf of the British Government, dispatched two telegrams to the Soviet Government on the following day. The first dealt with the resumption of the trading relations with Russia. In view of the acceptance by the Soviet Government of the principles laid down by the British Memorandum dated 1st July, the British Government agreed to carry on the negotiations for a definite trade agreement with the Soviet Russia. The second telegram dealt with Polish-Russian relations and proposed that :

"(a) An immediate armistice be signed between Poland and Soviet Russia whereby hostilities shall be suspended ; the terms of the armistice should provide on the one hand that the Polish Army shall immediately withdraw to the line provisionally laid down last year by the Peace Conference as the Eastern boundary within which Poland was entitled to establish a Polish administration."

Assuming that the said line might not be known to the Soviet authorities Lord Curzon gave a detailed description of this line committing an obvious error in this description : " This line runs approximately as follows : Grodno Vapovka, Niemirow, Brest-Litovsk, Dorohobuz, Ustilug, East of Hrubeshov, Krylow, *and then West to Rawa Ruska, East of Przemysl to the Carpathians.*" The line traced by Curzon's telegram runs, in fact, further to the South than the line established by the Supreme Council on 2nd December (8th December Line). The latter " according to its detailed description in the 8th December Declaration *ran solely across the territory of the former Russian Empire*—whereas the topographical description in Lord Curzon's note encroached upon the territory of Eastern Galicia and extended to the Carpathian Mountains." [11] The best proof that it was an error is provided by the further passage of Lord Curzon's telegram, exactly corresponding to the text of the Polish-British Agreement of 10th July: " In Eastern Galicia each army will stand on the line which they occupy at the date of the signature of the armistice."

Compared with the previous description of the line this passage makes nonsense. A Polish writer, Sworakowski, who devoted a special study to this obvious slip in Curzon's telegram, explains it by an unintentional mistake made by the British Foreign Office. In this connection Sworakowski writes the following :

> " It must be borne in mind that Great Britain's representative had signed the 10th July Agreement. Thus the condition of this agreement constituted not only an obligation on the part of Poland towards the Principal Allied and Associated Powers signatories to the agreement (as a matter of fact it was *not* signed by the representative of the United States who was not represented at Spa, my remark) of 10th July, 1920. On the other hand, one cannot without sufficient proof assume that the British Government, having obligated itself toward Poland and the other Powers, signatories to the 10th July Agreement, to act as mediator between Poland and Russia, had before twenty-four hours elapsed violated the conditions under which it had agreed to mediate. One must, therefore, dismiss the thought that the official of the Foreign Office had *consciously* introduced an error into such an important diplomatic document— an error that would allow an ambiguous interpretation of the entire note, or of its most essential constituent parts."

In this connection it is interesting to point out that the additional clause contained in the Agreement of 10th July according to which " in Eastern Galicia each army shall withdraw 10 kilometres in order to create a neutral zone " was not put in Curzon's telegram of 11th July. As Sworakowski rightly observes it was " an error of an essential nature " and " there were no reasons which could justify the omission of that additional condition in Lord Curzon's Note to the Soviet Government other than an inaccuracy in wording of the British Note of 11th July, 1920."

Unfortunately we cannot dismiss altogether the possibility of bad faith on the part of some members of Lloyd George's staff who probably abused Lord Curzon's confidence, especially in view of the fact that the next passage of Curzon's telegram referring to the conference to be held in London contained some details to which Poland had never explicitly agreed. It suffices to compare this passage with the respective text of the Agreement of 10th July quoted above :

"(b) That as soon as possible thereafter a conference sitting under the auspices of the Peace Conference should assemble in London, to be attended by the representatives of Soviet Russia, Poland, Lithuania, Latvia and Finland, with the object of negotiating a final peace between Russia and its neighbouring States. Representatives of Eastern Galicia would also be invited to London, to state their case for the purpose of this conference. Great Britain will place no restriction on the representatives which Russia may nominate, provided they undertake while in Great Britain not to interfere in the politics or the internal affairs of the British Empire or to indulge in propaganda. The British Government as a separate proposal suggests that an armistice should similarly be signed between the forces of Soviet Russia and General Wrangel on the condition that General Wrangel's forces shall immediately retire to the Crimea and that during the armistice the isthmus be a neutral zone and that General Wrangel should be invited to London to discuss the future of troops under his command and the refugees under his protection, but not as a member of that conference. The British Government would be glad of an immediate reply to this telegram, for the Polish Government has asked for the intervention of the Allies, and if time is lost a situation may develop which will make the conclusion of lasting peace far more difficult in Eastern Europe. Further, while the British Government has bound itself to give no assistance to Poland for any purpose hostile to Russia and to take no action itself hostile to Russia, it is also bound under the Covenant of the League of Nations to defend the integrity and independence of Poland within its legitimate ethnographic frontiers; if, therefore, Soviet Russia, despite its repeated declarations accepting the independence of Poland, will not be content with the withdrawal of the Polish armies from the *Russian soil* * on the condition of a mutual armistice but intends to take action hostile to Poland on its own territory, the British Government and its Allies would feel bound to assist the Polish nation to defend its existence *with all the means at their disposal*. The Polish Government has declared its willingness to make peace with Soviet Russia and to initiate negotiations for an armistice on the basis of conditions set out above directly if it is informed that Soviet Russia also agrees. The British Government, therefore, would be glad of a definite reply within a week as to whether Soviet Russia is prepared to accept the aforesaid proposal for putting an end to further unnecessary bloodshed and giving peace to Europe." [12]

Reading this lengthy document must confirm what we have said above about the aims of Lloyd George's policy. The proposal, as

* These words confirm our interpretation of the future armistice line because Eastern Galicia had never belonged to Russia, and consequently its territory could not be considered " Russian soil."

has been justly observed, was " exceedingly like the old Prinkipo proposal," and for the sake of holding such a conference Lloyd George offered Soviet Russia, before the peace negotiations had even started, vast territories called " Russian soil," although the Russian population there did not exceed 5 per cent. At the same time the right of self-determination in these Eastern borderlands was denied not only to the Poles, who in some areas constituted the majority or the largest proportion of the ethnographically mixed population and who impregnated these territories with their Western civilization, but also other nationalities such as Byelo-russians, Ukrainians and other smaller groups who had to pass under Russian domination without even being able to state their views and defend their case at the London Conference.

The Warsaw correspondent of *The Times* wired on 15th July (*The Times,* 17th July) :

" The Polish Delegates who have returned from Spa have a diffi-cult business to persuade the country, over which a wave of patriotic ardour is surging, of the necessity of accepting the terms of the armistice imposed by Mr. Lloyd George. They state that *only the knowledge that in the event of refusal they would be cut off from all supplies of ammunition from Western Europe com-pelled them to accept.* ... It is considered unfair by Poland that its army should be expected to retire before the peace-terms are discussed. Should the negotiations break down Poland would have to start again with the enemy 140 miles from Warsaw." [My italics.]

But the picture would not be complete if we did not mention what turned out to be one of the biggest frauds in modern history. The Polish delegation accepted these hard terms at Spa on the condition that a prompt and efficient Allied assistance would be given to them. Would there otherwise have been any sense in their agreeing to such humiliating and hard conditions? But instead of arms a diplomatic and military mission was sent to Poland. Lord d'Abernon, British Ambassador in Berlin, who was appointed head of the British Mission (in addition to him consisting of General Sir Percy Rad-cliffe and Sir Maurice Hankey), noted in his book *The Eighteenth Decisive Battle of the World* : " It was agreed between Mr. Lloyd George and the French Prime Minister that *the best method of assistance* was not only to dispatch munitions to Warsaw but to send an Anglo-French Mission composed of diplomatic and military elements." [13] The French Mission consisted of M. Jusserand, the French Ambassador to Washington, General Weygand and M. Vignon.

The terms of the official British decision referring to this mission were : " Proceed to Poland, in conjunction with similar French Mission, as a special Envoy to advise His Majesty's Government as to the measures to be taken with the Polish and other Governments on questions arising out of negotiations with regard to Spa conclusion of an Armistice between Poland and Soviet Russia." [14] Obviously the purpose of the mission was to exert pressure on Poland, and, if possible, to get in touch with the Soviet Government.

Did the Allies immediately send assistance to Poland? The most conclusive evidence to the contrary can be found in Field-Marshal Sir Henry Wilson's papers. In his Diary he noted under 16th July :

> " Lloyd George told me he had heard—I don't know how—that the Bolshevists were going to completely overrun Poland and come up against Germany. We had a meeting of Lloyd George, Millerand, Foch and me. Foch and I said that *it was no use pouring in more arms to Poland,* unless and until the Poles had a good government, fully representative of a united people determined to stand against invasion. Lloyd George asked if Foch would go out to Poland and steady the situation. He replied that that was a matter for M. Millerand. Millerand said he could not agree, unless the conditions put forward by the two Marshals were fulfilled, and I said it would never do to ruin the priceless asset of Foch's name in a wild scheme of this sort." [15] [My italics.]

So at the time when a prompt delivery of arms and munitions was so necessary to the Poles the Allies tried to interfere with Poland's internal affairs, and sent advice instead of arms. Did the Poles really need any encouragement in the defence of their country? The delays caused by these untimely steps might have been fatal to a nation in distress. As a matter of fact, even the French assistance to Poland so emphatically promised to the Poles by Millerand at Spa did not reach Poland before the Battle of Warsaw. The first thing stated by the Anglo-French Mission, which arrived in Warsaw at the end of July, was that " the French have not shipped any munitions to Poland since the offensive began over two months ago," [16] and for that reason it sent an urgent appeal to the Allied Governments to dispatch munitions to Poland immediately.

So far as assistance by the British Government was concerned, we are able to state most categorically that no assistance was given to Poland by it even at the time when the Red Army was at the gates of Warsaw. As we shall see later, at that time the British High Commissioner who represented there the League of Nations, acting upon the instructions of his Government closed the Port of Danzig to all ships loaded with arms and munitions for Poland.

As the best proof of the non-fulfilment by the British Government of the pledges given to Mr. Grabski at Spa we can quote the following debate in the House of Commons on 3rd August, that is at the time at which the Red Army was approaching Warsaw and Soviet intentions regarding Poland were not secret from anybody : [17]

Lieutenant-Commander Kenworthy asked the Prime Minister whether British munitions are being sent from this country or elsewhere to Poland; and whether any of the munitions at Danzig which the dockers in that city recently refused to handle are of British origin?

Mr. Bonar Law : The answer to the first part of the question is that *no British munitions are being sent to Poland by His Majesty's Government.* I have no information as to the origin of the munitions referred to in the last paragraph of the question.

Lieutenant-Commander Kenworthy : Cannot the Right Honourable Gentleman tell us whether we are sending munitions to Poland at the present time?

Mr. Bonar Law : If the Hon. Member reads the answer which I have just given he will see that *we are not sending any,* but, of course, the Hon. Member is familiar with the recent correspondence with the Soviet Government which may alter the situation.

Lieutenant-Commander Kenworthy : It is because I am familiar with the correspondence that I ask for an assurance that we have not altered our policy and are sending munitions to Poland.

Mr. Bonar Law : We are not sending any.

Mr. Palmer : Why is there so much hostility from democratic people in this House towards Poland, a nation struggling to be free?

Mr. Bonar Law : I cannot say.

On 9th August, that is five days before the battle for Warsaw began, Mr. Bonar Law, answering numerous questions put by the members of the Opposition, stated :

> " As I said the other day, *we have not sent munitions from this country,* but I did not say we will not send them. .... It was stated last week that in view of the fact that an Armistice was not being concluded and that ethnographical Poland was being invaded, we should have to consider in what way we should strengthen them in the event of the Russian Government not making peace." [18]

The position taken by the British Government on this matter changed only after the Polish victories, but no assistance was given by it to Poland before the main battle was over.

Did the British Government abide by its pledges contained in the Note of Lord Curzon of 11th July, according to which in the event of " an action hostile to Poland within its own territory " assistance would be given to Poland by the British Government and its Allies

" with all the means at their disposal " ? The answer can only be negative. Yielding to the pressure of the British Left, and considering the unpopularity in Great Britain of any measures which might involve war, the British Government gave Poland much advice, often with more or less veiled menaces, but no effective help. In defence of her independence Poland had to rely on her forces alone. She paid a heavy price in advance at Spa without receiving any counter-value.

Instead of encouraging the Poles in their resistance to the Bolsheviks the Allied decisions at Spa could only dishearten a fighting nation. Did they serve the cause of peace, as Lloyd George, ignoring everything about Russia and Bolshevism, was ready to believe? General W. Sikorski, in his book quoted above, ascribed the wild drive of the Soviet armies into the heart of Poland—which in the last instance caused their defeat—to the " debates of the Spa Conference and to the isolation of Poland which was manifest there " [19] He says that it " over-stimulated the imagination of the Soviet leaders." Thus by his defeatism and readiness to negotiate with the Bolsheviks at the cost of very big concessions granted in advance, Lloyd George ruined all prospects of peace there may have been.

Soviet–Lithuanian Peace Treaty

Before answering Lord Curzon's Note of 11th July the Soviet Government made a surprise move, creating a *fait accompli* with Lithuania by signing a peace treaty with that country on 12th July. By this treaty the Soviet Government disposed of the fate of the vast territories in which, apart from some isolated areas, Lithuanians constituted a small minority, that is to say Wilno and district, Grodno and district, and the Southern part of Suwalki district. As we have said before (pp. 446 ff.), on the 29th August, 1918, the Council of People's Commissars had denounced the treaties of partition, which by the way Poland had never considered a valid title of sovereignty, and thus the Soviet Government ceded to Lithuania territories which, even from its own point of view, did not belong to it and which at the time of the conclusion of the treaty were not even wholly occupied by the Red Army. (Wilno was not evacuated by the Poles until 14th July). Moreover, by doing this Soviet Russia violated the principle of self-determination either in the proper, that is to say democratic, meaning of this term or the Communist one, according to which this right should be exercised by the working class only. Nobody asked the local population its wishes. This move by Soviet Russia was a complete change of the policy pursued by Soviet Russia towards Lithuania. We know that at the end of 1918 Soviet Russia tried to set up a Communist government in Lithuania and that she even recognized such government as the only representative of the Lithuanian people (see pp. 435 ff.). It was only after the liberation of Wilno by the Poles in 1919 that the Soviet Government began to change its policy towards Lithuania, but still in its Note of the 8th April, 1920, to the Lithuanian Government it refused to acknowledge the Lithuanian claims to the territories of Wilno, Grodno and Suwalki, saying that "the Government of Soviet Russia accepts the ethnographical criteria for the solution of territorial problems. If the Lithuanian Government produces the ethnographical data on this question we shall be able to draw from them the appropriate conclusions and begin such political steps as may be required. If the Lithuanian Government is sure that the ethnographical data impose the union of the said towns to Lithuania, it can take for granted that the Government of Soviet Russia will accept these proposals." Such proofs the Lithuanian Government was, of course, unable to produce because it based its claims to these territories not on ethnographical criteria. The Soviet Government changed its mind at the time of the offensive of the Red Army against Poland in 1920, wishing to secure in this way Lithuania's neutrality and at the same time to obtain the full and undisturbed use of this allegedly Lithuanian territory for its military operations. All the districts " ceded " to Lithuania were occupied by Soviet troops with the consent of the Lithuanian Government, whose attitude was far from neutral. Nevertheless there is no doubt that in the event of the Soviet victory on the Vistula Lithuanian independence would not have survived, and such is also the opinion of Lithuanian writers. L. Natkevicius, in his book *Différend polono-lithuanian* (Paris 1930) states : " It was perfectly realized in Lithuania that Lithuania's turn would come after the capture of Warsaw and the proclamation of Soviet Poland." [20] The behaviour of the Soviet troops on the territory " ceded " to Lithuania is in itself the best proof of the real Bolshevist intentions. The correspondent of *The Times* discovered in Grodno after the recapture of this town by the Poles in September 1920 many anti-Lithuanian posters circulated by the Red Army, and among them a lengthy proclamation entitled: " To all working and peasant youth of Lithuania and White Russia." This contained the following interesting passage :

> " Active struggle for the overthrow of the Lithuanian bourgeois-clerical Government which has seized the reins of power in your country basing itself on the White Guards, to which, alas, not a few of the youthful proletariat shamefully adhere—such is the prime object which you must set out to attain." [21]

The fate of Lithuania and other Baltic States after the invasion of Poland by German and Bolshevik troops in September 1939 proves what was in store for these States had the Polish Army been defeated on the Vistula in 1920.

An English author who thinks rather lightly of the Lithuanian claims to independence, E. H. Carr, explains in the following words the Bolshevist policy towards Lithuania :

" Lithuania, though slightly larger and more populous than Latvia or Estonia, was an almost exclusively peasant country without a proletariat and with only a handful of intellectuals. Its claim to independence, whether under bourgeois or under Soviet auspices, rested on precarious foundations, drawing the major part of its support, moral and material, from a large Lithuanian population in the United States. The main interest of Lithuanian independence for Soviet Russia was negative. Were Lithuania not independent, it was likely to fall within the Polish orbit ; on the other hand an independent Lithuania could be a thorn in the side of Poland." [22]

In July 1920 the Peace Treaty with Lithuania served well the Bolshevik purposes in the diplomatic field also, as a proof that the settlement of the East European questions might be undertaken without any interference from the Entente Powers and, consequently, that there was no need to hold a conference with the Border States in London, as proposed in Lord Curzon's Note of 11th July.

Chicherin's reply to Curzon (17th July)

The Soviet answer to that Note was sent under Chicherin's signature on the last day stated in Curzon's Note for the reply by the Soviet Government, that is on 17th July.[23] This Note was a masterpiece of Soviet diplomacy, as it attacked the elaborate British argument at its weakest points. It began by recalling the British attitude in previous periods and emphasizing that at the time of the Polish offensive in the Ukraine " the British Government failed ... to give any evidence of a desire to preserve peace in Eastern Europe." It further assured of the peaceful intentions of the Soviet Government " whose desire to live in peace with all the States mentioned in the British communication remains unshakeable and unalterable. Even in regard to Poland, despite its wholly unjustified attack on the Soviet Republics, Soviet Russia remains as before true to the principles which it has frequently proclaimed, and the desire it has frequently expressed to establish peaceful relations with all nations." It declined, however, any foreign interference and showed a preference for direct negotiations with Poland.

" The working masses of Russia want a complete and final reconciliation with Poland, and, precisely in order to attain this object, the Soviet Government considers it necessary to remove from the scope of this reconciliation everything that might appear irrelevant and alien to the interests and wishes of the two peoples and governments." The following passage shows clearly the sort of Poland with which the Soviet Government wished to deal in the future : " In regard to peace with Poland, the Soviet Government considers it necessary to take into account, besides the interests and aspirations of the Russian working masses, *only the interests and aspirations of the Polish working masses,* and, consequently, it considers it possible to reach peace with Poland *solely by direct negotiations.*"

The Soviet Government further stated that it had already concluded peace treaties with Estonia, Georgia and quite recently with Lithuania :

> " The peace with Lithuania was unknown to the British Government when in its ultimatum of 12th July (the date of Lord Curzon's Note is always given by the Soviet Government as the 12th and not 11th July) it included Lithuania among the countries bordering on Russia with which peace was still to be concluded."

The reference to the League Covenant in Lord Curzon's Note provoked the following angry comments, which must have been disappointing for all who advocated League intervention in the Polish-Soviet War :

> " Even less tolerable to the Soviet Government is the intervention in this matter of the group of Governments called the League of Nations, to the covenant of which the British Government makes reference in justifying its ultimatum of 12th July. The so-called League of Nations has never informed the Russian Government of its establishment and its existence, and the Soviet Government has never had occasion to take any decision on recognition or non-recognition of this association. ... The Soviet Government cannot in any circumstances agree to a group of Powers taking on themselves the functions of a Supreme Court over all States on the earth, and, *standing guard over the complete inviolability of the sovereign rights of the Russian working people,* the Soviet Government categorically rejects the claims of any outside grouping of Powers to take on themselves the part of supreme arbiters of the fate of other peoples. Therefore it categorically rejects any interference whatever by this association in the matter of peace between Russia and Poland."

The Soviet Note then declared that the Soviet Government was ready to enter into direct negotiations with Poland " for an armistice or any other means of facilitating the conduct of peace negotiations."

The Soviet Note then expressed the Soviet willingness to make more advantageous offers to Poland than those laid down in the British Note, and severely criticized the decision of the Supreme Council referring to the provisional frontier of Poland :

> " The Soviet Government announces its readiness to agree to a territorial frontier more favourable to the Polish nation than that indicated by the Supreme Council in December last and which is again proposed by the British Government in its ultimatum of 12th July. The Soviet Government cannot refrain from calling attention to the fact that to a certain extent *this frontier was drawn up by the Supreme Council under the influence of counter-revolutionary Russian elements,* adherents of the bourgeoisie and the landlords, and that, for example in the Kholm district, the decision of the Supreme Council reflects the influence of these counter-revolutionary elements and *follows the anti-Polish policy of Tsarism* and the White Russian bourgoisie."

The following passage of the Note stresses once more the wish of the Soviet Government to establish in Poland a régime more amenable to Bolshevik ideas :

> " Soviet Russia is the more ready to meet the interests and wishes of the Polish people in regard to the terms of peace *the further the Polish people go in their internal life along the road which will create a firm foundation for truly fraternal relations between the working masses of Poland, Russia, the Ukraine, White Russia and Lithuania,* and will provide a guarantee that Poland will cease to serve as an instrument of aggression and intrigue against the workers and peasants of Soviet Russia and other nations."

The Note rejects the British proposal to hold a conference in London with the Border States, and suggests continuation of negotiations with Great Britain for the conclusion of a trade agreement. With this object in view the Soviet Government intends to send to London " an enlarged delegation," and states that " this object will be attained the more successfully if all new and irrelevant circumstances are set aside since they would be only to the detriment of that improvement in the relations between Russia and Great Britain which is already beginning to be made."

As a matter of fact Chicherin's Note of 17th July rejected all the proposals put forward by Lord Curzon's Note of 11th July. If British policy had been consistent there was hardly room for further negotiations at that stage. But as we shall see other counsels prevailed within the British Cabinet under Lloyd George's influence, and this reassured the Bolshevists that they had nothing to fear from that side and that they were free to pursue the invasion of Poland, undisturbed for the time being.

We can judge the real Soviet intentions at that time from its many official documents and statements, which leave no doubt that Soviet Russia aimed at the total defeat of Poland and the supplanting of all Western influence in that part of Europe, considering it an important and decisive step towards a general upheaval in Europe.

An Order issued by the Revolutionary War Council to the Polish Front, dated 2nd July (No. 1423) openly proclaimed Soviet Russia's aims :

" The time of reckoning has come. In the blood of the defeated Polish Army we will drown the criminal Government of Pilsudski. ...Turn your eyes to the West. It is in the West that the fate of the World Revolution is being decided. Across the corpse of White Poland lies the way to the world conflagration. On our bayonets we will bring happiness and peace to toiling mankind. The time of advance has come. Forward to Warsaw, Minsk, Wilno." [24]

The directives issued by the Political Department of the Red Army on 21st July stated the following in connection with the exchange of Notes with the British Government [25] :

" 2.   The English ultimatum is a new political move of diplomatic deceit, the same as with Wrangel. We are told to stop our military operations at a time when it is inconvenient to us and convenient to Poland.

" 3.   In the event of the success of the English plan we should have been involved in a long, endless war on the part of Poland. It is necessary to carry on the war until the end and *help the workers, labourers and peasants of Poland to liberate themselves from the oppression of landlords and capitalists*. At the same time *we must not say openly that we would conclude peace only with a Soviet Poland*.

" It is necessary to explain only that Soviet Russia must be given full security from new, sudden aggression by the Polish nobles ; it is necessary to emphasize on every occasion that the Polish workers who follow the lead of the present Polish Government, not only support the Polish landlords and capitalists but also all imperialists who ruin Poland, converting it into a theatre of imperialistic war and an international gendarme, while buying up its riches and preparing its complete submission to international capitalism.

" 5.   The Soviet Government, on the contrary, will not at all assail the territorial integrity of Poland. It is necessary to explain to the Poles in full detail the Note of Chicherin in which he stated that *we are ready to cede to the Polish nation much bigger territories than those promised by Lord Curzon*. ... There still exist strong national prejudices among the petty-bourgeois masses of Poland and even among the workers, and because of that this point should be emphasized particularly strongly. It is necessary to open the following prospects: *should the Polish nation establish a real Workers' State we would be ready then to make far-reaching concessions* to it, because our aim and sincere desire is to create a brotherly alliance between the working masses.

" The rôle of England shall be unmasked."

The Appeal of the All-Russian Central Executive Committee and the Ukrainian Government to the Polish workers, peasants and legionaries closely follows the lines of the above directives [26] :

" Is it then not senseless and criminal to give your life and to shed your blood for the advantage and profit of a handful of predatory magnates and stockbrokers?

" ... We are ready to give you brotherly help against your internal and *external enemies,* that is against both Polish and *foreign robbers.*

" Long live independent workers' and peasants' Poland in brotherly alliance with the workers' independent Ukraine and Russia."

Let us see now the terms in which the Soviet Government explained the motives for its refusal to accept the British proposals. In an appeal to workers, peasants and all honest citizens of Soviet Russia and Soviet Ukraine, issued in July, the policy of the Soviet Government is explained in the following terms [27] :

" England has provoked this war and England is responsible for it. ... No, England is not qualified to be a mediator and peacemaker in this bloody struggle which was brought about and fostered by her criminal bourgeoisie. We have declined the British mediation, the blood-stained craftiness of which is disguised behind peaceful phrases. ...

" Together with the representatives of the Polish nation we will establish a *frontier of Poland infinitely more correct and corresponding to the interests of the Polish nation than that drawn by Marshal Foch and his associates under the pressure of Sazonov, Maklakov and other representatives of the Great-Russian White-Guards.*

" ... The real frontier of Poland which we, Soviet Russia, will establish together with the representatives of the Polish nation, will be situated much farther to the East than that drawn in London and Paris by the imperialists equally hostile and inimical to the workers both of Poland and Russia."

It was obvious that the Soviet Government wished to dissociate the Poles from the Allies by taking advantage of the wave of indignation aroused in the Polish masses by the humiliating proposals put forward by the Spa Conference. On the other hand it was eager to know which were the real intentions of the Allied Governments towards Poland, wondering whether they were in earnest in their pledges of assistance to the Poles in the event of the rejection by it of the British proposals. How much depended on the tenor of the British answer to Chicherin's Note of 17th July appears clearly from the report of the Soviet C.-in-C. to the Chairman of the Revolutionary War Council dated 20th July [28] :

> " In accordance with your instructions referring to the operations on the Polish front in connection with the negotiations in progress, I report as follows:
>
> " Both our fronts (Byelorussian and Ukrainian) were given imperative instructions to advance *without taking into account the frontier-line* indicated in Lord Curzon's radio-telegram. . . .
>
> " Should the Poles agree to negotiations with us, it will *mean that they could not count on any serious support from anybody and that we should have complete freedom of action in our advance into Poland* ; should the Poles refuse to negotiate and should other signs appear that Poland could count on real support from the Allies, we shall take measures to safeguard us against possible dangers, without abandoning our advance into Poland."

The time factor was of primary importance to the Russians; they reckoned that they might conquer the whole of Poland within two months and that Europe would bow to this fact. [29]

Seeing his grandiose plans ruined within a week, Lloyd George did not wish to draw the necessary conclusions from the Soviet refusal and did not realize the necessity for prompt decisions. Speaking of the Cabinet meeting about the Soviet Note, Field-Marshal Sir Henry Wilson uses the following rude language :

> " (20th July). A cabinet this morning, Lloyd George presiding over some 20. We spent three hours discussing what last night's telegram meant, when it is as plain as a pikestaff—an impudent of all Frock demands. The Gadarene swine never galloped so fast as these Frocks." [30]

Curzon's Note of 20th July

Lord Curzon's Note of 20th July [31] to Chicherin gave the Soviet Government a breathing space, which it so much desired. Lord Curzon was satisfied that the Soviet Government was ready " to concede a frontier not less favourable to Poland than an ethnographical frontier originally suggested by the Supreme Council." At the same time he expressed the desire of H.M. Government that " the negotiations should be carried out in good faith and without delay; that the frontier between Russsia and Poland should correspond as far as possible to the wishes of the population concerned,*

---

* It meant that Lord Curzon himself abandoned the line whose conception was ascribed to him and that he took into consideration another line corresponding more to the wishes of the population. The so-called " Curzon Line " was consequently short-lived.

and that a permanent peace should be established between Poland and her Eastern neighbours, which would secure the cessation of hostilities and the abstention on the part of either nation from any interference in the internal policy of the other."

The Note further stated that :

" in order to bring matters to a clear issue, *the Polish Government have been urged by the Allies immediately to initiate negotiations for armistice and for peace*. If, however, despite a request for an armistice from the Polish Government, the *Soviet armies continue to advance,* the British Government and its Allies would necessarily assume that it is the intention of the Soviet Government to make war on the Polish people and will in conjunction with their Allies *give to Poland the assistance and support they have promised in that event.*

" Further they must make it clear that the negotiations for the resumption of trade between Russia and the British Empire cannot be usefully pursued if Soviet Russia invades Poland, and they have therefore telegraphed to Messrs. Kamenev and Krassin to delay their departure from Russia until an armistice has been agreed to.

Thus the Poles and the Bolsheviks were left face to face, much to the Soviet liking; pressure was to be exerted on the Poles to enter into negotiations with the Soviet Government immediately, while the promised assistance was made hypothetical, depending on the outcome of negotiations and Soviet good faith. The only practical step taken by the British Government was the proposal to postpone trade negotiations, but even that was cancelled a few days later, and Kamenev and Krassin were authorized to proceed to London. The British Minister in Warsaw was instructed by H.M. Government to advise the Poles to ask the Soviet headquarters and the Government in Moscow for an immediate armistice. Complying with these wishes, the Polish Government sent a Note to the Soviet Government on 22nd July, proposing that negotiations for an armistice should commence immediately. We shall have much to say about these negotiations later, for the time being noting only that the Soviet Government did everything possible to postpone the opening of these negotiations, each day's delay being of extreme importance for them in view of the quick advance of the Soviet armies, which had crossed the line designated by Lord Curzon in his Note of 11th July (the so-called Curzon Line) on 23rd July.

Debate in the House of Commons on 21st July

The debate in the House of Commons on 21st July [32] devoted to the Spa Conference and following the dispatch of Lord Curzon's second Note to Chicherin dated 20th July, showed to the full the perplexity and unsteadiness of Lloyd George who, fearing to confess the ruin of his policy of conciliation towards the Soviet Government, did not communicate to the House the full text of the last Soviet Note. This fact deprived him of many valid arguments in favour of a more resolute policy in relation to the Soviet Government, but he was far from proposing to draw such conclusions from the Bolshevik rejection of the British proposals. In his speech he struck some right notes, especially in the passages in which he dealt with the consequences which would inevitably follow should Poland be overcome by the Bolsheviks, but fearing the attacks of the pro-Soviet wing of the House he evaded his responsibilities as leader and preferred not to incur unpopularity and to jeopardize his political future on the Polish issue.

Lloyd George started his speech by criticizing the action of the late Polish Government, which he called " reckless and foolish," and stated that he protested against it. As a matter of fact it would be difficult to find a document attesting this last fact, and when pressed by many members of the Opposition in the course of the following debates in the Commons he was unable to produce any proof, and on the contrary stated that it would have been improper to give advice on such issues to a foreign Government. Nevertheless Lloyd George found some excuses for the action of the Polish Government : " The only excuse—and one must take it into account—was Bolshevik interference in Polish affairs. I must say this about the Bolsheviks, that they seem to resent with great intensity any interference by other countries in what they regard as their own legitimate sphere, but their policy of non-intervention never prevents them from interfering with the affairs of everyone else." He did not say this time that the Poles were urged by imperialistic aims and seemed even to excuse their policy of creating " some form of buffer States between the Soviet Government and themselves," but added that " you cannot form States in that way," without saying in what other way a buffer State might be created. Did he believe that such an end could be attained by negotiations?

Then he spoke of the importance to Europe of the existence of an independent Poland :

> " Poland—independent Poland—is essential to the whole fabric of peace. ... The second reason why we cannot disinterest ourselves in the fate of Poland is this. If the Bolsheviks overrun Poland they march right up to the frontiers of Germany, and *Sovietland, after destroying the independence and existence of a free people, extends as a great, aggressive, imperialistic power*, which has grabbed territories belonging to another race and another people—right up to the border of Germany."

Speaking of Chicherin's last Note, he called it " incoherent," although as a matter of fact it was clear enough and M. Millerand was nearer to the truth in calling it " impertinent."

He mentioned that the Bolsheviks proposed direct negotiations with Poland, drawing the attention of the House, however, to " some phrases in the document which would rather indicate that they are only prepared to discuss this matter with a proletariat government." " If that is the interpretation," he said, " it is an intolerable one. They have no right to dictate what sort of government the Poles should have. . . . Poland has chosen her own government by universal suffrage, and it is intolerable that any country from outside should come in and impose on her a government which she does not want. However, *in order to test the* bona fide *of this document we have advised the Poles to approach for an armistice with a view to peace."*

Then Lloyd George repeated once more the British pledges to Poland in a most emphatic way :

> " In our reply to Moscow we were bound to make it clear that *if,* notwithstanding the application by the Polish Government to the Russians for an armistice, *the Russian army still marches on, we shall give such assistance as it is in our power to the Polish Government."*

As appears from this declaration as well as Curzon's Note of 20th July, any measure of assistance to the Poles was being postponed, and as it turned out was never given in spite of these pledges.

Lloyd George then tried to reassure the House of the undaunted spirit of the Polish nation :

> " The Poles have a very considerable number of troops. They have no lack of brave men, for they have been historically and traditionally a brave people. . . . What they lack is equipment and especially organization. Within the last few days they have raised, I am told, a voluntary army of 300,000 men. Students from the universities, men of all ranks, have flocked to the flag. But they need equipment. France and ourselves could supply that. I think France and ourselves could supply them with the necessary means for organizing their forces. It is entirely a question whether the Poles have to defend their own independence. *It is the British interest, it is the European interest, that Poland should not be wiped out. It would be fatal to the peace of Europe that it should be wiped out, and the consequences would be disastrous beyond measure."*

But the conclusions drawn by Lloyd George from this clear statement were hardly appropriate. He stated that it was a matter of indifference to the British Government whether the peace conference should be held in London and " whether the Poles communicate direct with the Soviet Government or whether it is done indirectly." " All I say," he repeated, " is that if Poland notwithstanding this is attacked in her particular territories, *Great Britain is bound by the covenants she has entered into, she is bound by her own interests, she is bound by the interests of Europe, and by the general interests of the world, to give every assistance in her power to the party which is assailed."*

The Opposition which monopolized the floor of the House represented two shades of opinion. There were, first of all, stubborn advocates of the intervention of the League of Nations, such as Mr. Asquith and Lord Robert Cecil. Their arguments were hardly convincing to all those who knew the text of Chicherin's Note, in which the latter used such strong language in relation to the so-called League of Nations and most peremptorily dismissed any intervention of that body.

The second category of speakers consisted of Labour members who continued to brand the alleged Polish imperialism and found all kinds of excuses for the attitude of the Bolsheviks, to whom they gave all credit. It is interesting to read, from the distance of time, the arguments used by these speakers and to see the lengths to which they went in their trust in the good faith of the Bolsheviks and in the information supplied exclusively by Soviet agents. For instance, the principal Labour speaker, Mr. T. Shaw, said :

> " I hope that the Bolshevists will have more statesmanship than the League of Nations and that they will not attempt to carry the war into Polish territory. ... My hopes are centred not in the Poles but in the Russians themselves and in their common sense, in avoiding a war which inevitably will bring the Allies on their backs. ...
>
> " *If my information be of any value, and I think it is, because it comes from reliable sources,* Poland is very near revolution against her present Government, and the danger is that if the Bolshevists continue their attacks on a country divided against itself, with one-third of the population refusing to take arms of any kind and a considerable proportion of the remaining two-thirds more likely to fight against the Polish Government than with it, our troubles will increase. ...
>
> " Probably the best thing that can be done is to allow the Bolshevists to conduct their propaganda in this country quite freely. *They are men of very great frankness ; they do not hide anything under a bushel. They are not diplomatic enough to make you believe that the things they say are the things they do not mean. What they say they mean and they mean what they say.* ... I hope that the Bolshevik policy will be saner and wiser than that of

Poland and the League of Nations. That is the only hope that exists."

But Colonel Wedgwood surpassed by his pro-Soviet bias and his aggressive anti-Polish spirit anything that has ever been said in the House. Without knowing the exact text of the Note, as he alleged, he said : " I think we owe almost a debt of gratitude to the Soviet Government for the wit and humour of their reply." On the other side he rightly understood the passiveness of the British Government, and he even had some words of appreciation for this standpoint : " I am glad the Government, instead of getting on its high horse, which seems to have been expected across the channel, has dealt with this message from Moscow as if it contained the hopes of settlement, have pocketed their pride, and have sanctioned the opening of peace negotiations between Poland and Russia, if not for any reason, at any rate because of the last hope of securing peace."

He most strongly opposed supplying any assistance to Poland on the pretext that the Poles, like Denikin, Koltchak, Yudenitch, would be unable to make proper use of the material given them, and that eventually all these munitions would fall into Bolshevik hands. He saw with indifference the prospect of Poland becoming a Soviet State :

> " We ought to welcome peace even if it is a peace between Soviet Russia and Soviet Poland. What we want first of all is peace, not the repressing of Bolshevism within the boundaries of Soviet Russia, but peace ; *because every sane man knows that peace is the best cure for Bolshevism, even if Poland as well as Russia goes Bolshevik. . . . All is not lost if the Poles become Bolshevik. . . .* I do think you might get a settlement even if Poland went Red, because there is one thing quite clear: that the Russian Soviet movement is not an Imperial movement in the old sense of nationality. . . . I think it is possible to contemplate not wholly as a disaster the victory of the Russian Government over Poland which should result in the setting up of a revolutionary Government there. Poland would be reconstituted after the peace, and the people would find that Bolshevism was merely a question of one form of tyranny over another."

These revolting outpourings by those who pretended to represent the cause of democracy in the British Parliament brought to his feet Lloyd George, whom nobody could accuse of tender feelings for the Poles :

" I want to know," said Lloyd George, " what is the attitude of the Labour Party now. Has Poland the sympathy of that party in its struggle for its national existence? Not a word of sympathy with Poland was said, not a word indicating that they support Poland." About Lord Robert Cecil he said : " When he comes to Poland he seems to me to be much more concerned to find fault with the Allies than to save Poland from perishing." And again he made a pathetic declaration about Poland, which in the light of his whole policy was unfortunately only lip-service to the Polish cause : " We want to save the life of Poland. We cannot allow it to perish. It would be a disaster to the world; it would be a crime. ... I am convinced that, if the Bolsheviks advance, they will regret it. ... I do not believe what the hon. member for Preston (Mr. Shaw) said, namely that the Poles will be disunited, will break up into parties. People forget all that when their country is in danger. They did it here, and they will do it in Poland; they are doing it now. The Socialists, I am convinced, are just as enthusiastic as anyone else in ranging themselves behind the Government for the defence of their homeland. That is the material we have to deal with."

But the conclusions drawn by Lloyd George were hardly consonant with these declarations : " I am sincerely desirous that the negotiations, which I hope the Poles will initiate, will end in peace, but it is our business to prepare for the other contingency, and to see that the Poles are properly equipped. We can do that. The time may never come, and I hope it will never come. If it does come, I shall, of course, put the whole question before the House of Commons. It is obviously a matter for the House of Commons and the House has a right to be informed of it."

Mr. Thomas, answering the Prime Minister's question as to the attitude of the Labour Party with regard to Poland, stated : " So far as Russia is concerned, Russia has said nothing up to now that conflicts with the Prime Minister's view. The *Bolshevists have given no intimation or indication that they desire anything else than the independence of Poland*. That is the attitude of our party." At the end of his speech he expressed his satisfaction with the Prime Minister's assurance that " before this country is committed in any way, Parliament is to be further consulted."

It is strange that the Labour Party paid no attention to the appeals launched at that time by the Polish Socialist Party, one of the most prominent members of which, I. Daszynski, was Vice-Premier.

About that time a message was addressed by the Polish Socialist Party to " the Socialist and Labour organizations of the whole world," in which, after referring to the constant struggle of the Party in the cause of peace and to its efforts to prevent an alliance between Poland and Denikin, the following was stated :

" At present the situation is changed. The Red Russian Army is led by the Tsarist generals. The Russian militarized newspapers are full of racial hatred and threaten to dictate peace in the smouldering ruins of Warsaw. Comrades! It is not the social revolution which is threatening the gates of Poland, nor is the red flag which flutters over the divisions led by General Brussilov. Russian bayonets are endangering our independence; the Cossacks are bringing in their train murder, violence and destruction. The Soviet leaders bow before Imperialistic militarism, replacing the old principles of liberty by an appeal to annex foreign territories. In face of such a situation we act as our comrades in Belgium, France and England acted at the beginning of the World War. We say to the workers and peasants of Poland: 'Defend your Motherland.' The working classes will defend their own independence.

"We demand of you, comrades, understanding and impartiality. Remember that to-day your boycott no longer affects our Imperialists, but that it strikes at the Polish workman and hampers his strenuous efforts at self-defence. To-day your anti-Polish campaign is not a support of the Russian revolutionaries, but of the masked designs of Brussilov." [33]

Lloyd George's information about Poland's unrelenting efforts to organize the defence of the country in danger was much nearer the truth than the biased information of the democratic wing of the British public opinion. According to official statistics :

"In the critical phase from the beginning of July to 20th August, the Polish Ministry of War supplied the Commander-in-Chief with more than 172,000 officers and men, 70 new batteries, 200 gun replacements, more than a thousand machine guns and about 22,000 horses. About 140,000 new recruits were enlisted and about 80,000 volunteers enlisted at General Haller's (commander of the Volunteer Army) call." [34]

And a British historian states :

"Women also answered the call, as always the case in Poland in times of national stress ; a Legion of women was formed ; many women came forward to work beside the men in the trenches. In short the national spirit was revived, it soared to wonderful heights of devotion and self-sacrifice." [35]

But in the meantime the Red Army was rapidly advancing across the line called, since the Spa Conference, the Curzon Line, and no Allied help was forthcoming in spite of the pathetic declarations of the Western statesmen.

In this connection the Warsaw correspondent of *The Times* wrote to his paper on 26th July (*The Times*, 30th July, 1920) :

"The question must be faced by British public opinion whether the time has come to give effect to the Prime Minister's promise ' to assist the Polish nation to defend its existence with all the means at its disposal.' ... It seems singularly inept on the part of the Allied Governments to give as the limits beyond which the Bolshevists might not advance a frontier which is only marked on a few Allied maps, never previously published and naturally never communicated to the unrecognized Soviet Government. This amateur excursion of our Prime Minister into diplomacy seems to have led us into another dilemma. *Technically the Polish Government is certainly within its rights in claiming the help of the Western Powers,* and public opinion here (in Poland) takes the same view. The niceties of diplomatic delimitations are not usually studied by the public, which only understands that the line has been crossed beyond which the Allied Powers said the Bolshevists were not to go." [My italics.]

Even the *New Statesman,* in spite of its marked hostility towards Poland and its continuous criticism of the Polish policy, for a few days took the view that the Allies' duty was to help the Poles, but being frightened by this prospect recommended for the purpose ... the recognition of the Soviet Government by the Allies. We quote below some passages from this curious article entitled " The Great Unrecognized " (24th July) :

" The Allies have very little power to influence the decision. .... The game is now undeniably in the hands of the Bolshevists. .... If the Soviet Government decides to march on Warsaw in face of our protests, then we shall have no alternative but to break off the negotiations for a resumption of trade, reopen formal hostilities and give the Poles all the assistance we can. We should be bound to take this course not merely because of our Government's pledges or because of Article X of the Covenant of the League of Nations, but because it would be our plain duty to do everything in our power to avert the disaster of a Bolshevik occupation of Warsaw with the inevitable Red Terror which would be inaugurated and the equally inevitable White Terror to follow. It is one thing to tolerate the maintenance of the tyranny which the Russian Bolshevists have established in their own country ; it would be quite another thing to tolerate an attempt to establish a similar tyranny by force of arms in another land. In such a case our moral obligation to support the Poles—however richly they deserved their fate—would be scarcely less clear or strong than was our obligation to support the Belgians in 1914 ... the utmost we could hope for would be a military deadlock ... the failure of the present negotiations would be an unprecedented disaster ... we suggest that the first and most obviously sensible thing to do is to offer the Soviet Government ' recognition ' in the full and ordinary sense of that word ... on the day on which we accord official recognition to the Soviet Government our influence in Moscow will be double."

Chicherin's telegram of 24th July

Side by side with the military offensive, pursued with great vigour, the Red Army approaching the vital centres of central Poland, a diplomatic offensive was carried on by the Soviet Government with the aim of disrupting the Allied unity and nipping in the bud all stray impulses and inclinations to fulfil the pledges given to Poland at Spa. Such, undoubtedly, was the purpose of the new Note sent by Chicherin under the date of 24th July.[86] This Note was apparently of a very conciliatory nature, and to Lloyd George seemed a windfall after the days of frustration and anxiety for his political future following the rejection of the proposals contained in Lord Curzon's telegrams. The Note of 24th July stated that the Russian Government was willing " to meet the desire of the British Government as to its proposal to convene a Conference with the purpose of establishing a definite agreement between Russia and other Powers which participate in hostile actions against her or support such, and is of the opinion that the said conference ought to be composed of representatives of Russia and of the leading Powers of the Entente." The Soviet Government agreed to hold this conference in London. So far as negotiations with Poland were concerned, the Note announced that " orders had been given to the military command to meet the Polish parlementaires, and begin with pourparlers relative to armistice and peace." It was another master-stroke of Soviet diplomacy—had the Bolshevik plan succeeded it would have meant the complete isolation of Poland and her definite abandonment by the Allies. In fact the conference proposed by Chicherin was to have a different scope and composition from that initially proposed in Lord Curzon's Note of 11th July. It would not be a conference of the Border States meeting under the auspices of the Peace Conference, but a conference of the Bolsheviks and the leading Powers of the Entente, that is to say without Poland and the Border States. These States were to negotiate separately and directly with the Soviet Government, and in fact Chicherin's Note said that the pourparlers with Poland would concern both armistice and peace. The object of Chicherin's Conference would, of course, be to bring about the recognition of the Soviet régime by the Allies, a measure recommended by the *New Statesman* as the best way leading to lasting peace. It was evident that so long as this conference was being held immediate armed intervention by the Western Powers in Poland was out of the question. But Lloyd George looked at that Note from a different angle. It was a conference with the Bolsheviks that mattered above all to him, not the future of Poland. An optimistic telegram was sent from London to Lord d'Abernon in Warsaw. In his Diary he notes under 27th July : " At 3 p.m. to-day a telegram arrived from London announcing that the Soviet Government was ready to negotiate a *favourable* armistice with Poland. This news came as a surprise here and is not generally credited."[37] On what information did London base the belief that the Soviet conditions were to be favourable to Poland? The next day Lord d'Abernon notes :

> " My apprehension that the telegram from London stating that the Soviet had agreed to a London conference would lead the Poles to relax war preparations was groundless. The leading men here attach *no importance* to any Soviet acceptance of a London Conference, being convinced that the Soviet proposal would be quite unacceptable." [38] [My italics.]

Lloyd George, however, took a different view and saw in Chicherin's Note of 24th July a positive step on the part of the Bolsheviks. This appears clearly from his optimistic statements in the House of Commons on 26th July and from the first British reply made on the spur of the moment before consulting the Allies, dated also 26th. Asked by several members of the Opposition about the armistice with Poland he answered that " the situation has been changed since these questions were put down, by reason of the fact that the Soviet Government has now agreed to the request of Poland for an armistice with a view to peace. *Negotiations for the armistice have already commenced.*" As we shall see presently this statement was completely untrue. He read out the text of Chicherin's Note, which meant that he was satisfied with its tenor, as on previous occasions he had allowed publication of diplomatic correspondence with the Soviet Government, but with considerable delay, after they had been published by pro-Soviet newspapers. Then the Prime Minister added :

> "We certainly could not receive delegates from the Russian Government if they were marching upon Poland with a view to the destruction of its liberties. It was in the interest of everybody that we should stop them at once rather than send them back when they arrived here. Now I trust it will be quite unnecessary to take that step. Of course, *negotiations are proceeding at this moment for an armistice. I am hopeful of peace. That is what the world wants.*"

Speaking about Lloyd George's statements in the House of Commons, the parliamentary correspondent of *The Times* observed [39] : " The Prime Minister had his way. There will be full-blooded negotiations for peace all round and the old policy of Prinkipo is to be resurrected and sanctified by the salvation of Poland. No wonder he looked more cheerful, for his persistency was rewarded.

Less than a week ago it looked as though Poland might ruin him, for war with Russia, however just and necessary in the interest of peace, would not have been popular and would have discredited the Government. He has bluffed and won." The anticipations of the parliamentary correspondent of *The Times*, however, turned out to be premature, and it was not until after the Boulogne Conference that *The Times* became aware of the true meaning of the last Soviet Note. On 30th July *The Times* stated : " By combining deference to our desire to see them (the Bolsheviks) in London, with arrogance towards the Poles they have defeated our diplomacy at the expense of Poland."

It is true that the British Note of 26th July stated that " no trade agreement, even if completed, could have produced practical results if Soviet Russia had refused an armistice and invaded Poland, and had thus forced Great Britain and her Allies to give active support to the Polish people in defending their liberties and independence. They therefore thought it best to stop Messrs. Kamenev, Krassin and Miliutin from making a journey which would be fruitless if no armistice were arranged.

> " *In view, however, of the present reply*, they have instructed the destroyer to bring Messrs. Kamenev, Krassin and Milutin *immediately*, or if they prefer another route, the British Government will ask the Governments concerned to facilitate their journey." [40]

Thus at the beginning the Soviet manœuvre seemed to have attained its object. Great Britain was ready to accept Soviet assurances at their face value and to let the Bolshevik negotiators come, without insisting on an immediate acceptance of the armistice.

The Boulogne Conference

But the situation changed rapidly, owing to French intervention. Public opinion in France began to be impatient with M. Millerand's passiveness, and the French Prime Minister in his turn felt that his whole political future might be in danger owing to the angry attacks of the French press on his policy. A conference between Lloyd George and Millerand, the shortest on record, took place at Boulogne on 27th July. As the Paris correspondent of *The Times* observed :

> " The French are unable to regard all the diplomatic correspondence that has come from Russia in the last few days as the result of British initiative in the favourable light in which it is viewed by Mr. Lloyd George. They see in the Soviet Note the claims that the future of Poland no longer concerns the Allies, and

that at the proposed Conference the States bordering upon Russia are not to be represented." [41]

Millerand made it clear that he would agree to the proposed conference only if it were understood that " Poland and Poland alone should fill its agenda and that all the border States should participate in the discussion." Thus Millerand forced Lloyd George to revise his point of view.

Consequently a second Note was sent by the British Government as a result of the Boulogne Conference, dated 28th July, and stating the agreed policy of the two Allied Governments which was, at least verbally, more consonant with their obligations towards Poland. The Note of 28th July explained that the preceding Note had been sent

" on the assumption that an armistice is about to be concluded and that hostilities were about to cease between Soviet Russia and Poland. ... The British Government considers that, if the Allied Governments are to meet the delegates of the Soviet Government with any chance of success, the delegates of the Polish Government and of the other Border States who are concerned must be present. The Conference should have as its essential object the re-establishment of peace in Europe, and in the first place between Poland and Russia, upon conditions which would secure the independence of Poland and the legitimate interests of both countries. ... After the settlement of these questions the Conference could proceed to deal with the matters in dispute between the Government of Soviet Russia and the Allies, and to the re-establishment of normal relations between them."

On what information did Lloyd George base his optimistic belief in the chances of direct negotiations between Poland and Soviet Russia? One cannot help thinking that he considered Poland must accept any terms that the Soviet Government might offer her, and that in fact he dissociated himself entirely from Poland's destinies. All his subsequent moves fully warrant this opinion. He seemed to share the unrealistic and defeatist views of the radical wing of British public opinion. For instance, the *New Statesman* which a week before had rendered lip service to the cause of Poland's independence and liberty now was putting it entirely into Bolshevik hands. In its issue of 31st July we read the following outpourings :

" Since the Polish army seems for the time being almost to have ceased to exist as a coherent force, an armistice will no doubt be concluded. And, for our part, we do not doubt that the armistice will be followed, no matter where the negotiations are conducted, by a *moderate and satisfactory peace*. The wild reports which have been current this week concerning the nature of the terms to be offered by Moscow seem worthy of no credence. ... The Bolsheviks ... will almost certainly offer Poland quite *generous terms*. Firstly, because such terms would be in accord with their principles and their declarations—and it is a noteworthy fact that *Lenin's Government has never proved slippery or untrustful or failed to live up to its declarations*; and secondly because they are quite clever enough to realize that they have a unique opportunity of inducing Poland definitely to withdraw from the orbit of French diplomacy." [My italics.]

Mrs. Philip Snowden, in her book *Through Bolshevik Russia,* spoke with even more enthusiasm and confidence in Russian generosity :

" And now the victorious Russians are requested to stop fighting and to make peace on terms prepared for them by interested outsiders, who have helped their foes, or to prepare to have brought against them the armed power of Great Britain and, it may be, the rest of the Allies. It is a preposterous position, in which only the Russians occupy a position of credit. ... For the choice of peace on fair terms will prove the *Bolshevik Commanders superior in international morale to any European Government engaged in the recent war. A government capable of such self-control and a people of such self-denial would go down into history as marking a new epoch.* There would be a new faith in idealism born to Europe, which would help to undo the cruel wrong to Faith and Hope dealt by the treaties miscalled of Peace." [42] [My italics.]

But even immediately after the Boulogne Conference Lloyd George continued for some time to uphold an unwarranted optimism, which changed a few days later when the Soviet reply to the British Note of 28th July was not forthcoming. On 29th July, answering the question of Lord Robert Cecil " whether that advance of the Red troops has ceased," he stated : " The information that we had upon the subject of the Bolshevik advance was that it had slowed down a good deal. It does not look as if it were being pursued with very great vigour." [43]

We now turn to the direct negotiations between Poland and Russia in order to see whether the optimistic anticipations of Lloyd George and of the ingenuous advocates of the Soviet cause in Great Britain agreed with reality.

In the light of Soviet sources and many outspoken declarations of the Soviet leaders, there is no doubt whatever that the Soviet Government wished to conquer the whole of Poland, although it has been alleged that it had in mind only the liberation of the Polish working masses and that it did not intend any interference with Poland's independence. Were the Bolsheviks sincere in their declarations that they desired only to help the Polish proletariat in its struggle for liberation? Can we assume that they were so misinformed of the true feelings of the Polish masses as might appear from their declarations and appeals to the Polish proletariat? After the defeat on the Vistula Lenin tried to justify the invasion of Poland by the Red Army by hopes of the outbreak of revolution in Poland. Speaking in winter 1920 with Clara Zetkin, " who faithfully noted his words," Lenin said :

> " The Polish revolution on which we reckoned failed. The paesants and workers, stultified by the partisans of Pilsudski and Daszynski, defended their class enemies, permitted our brave Red Army soldiers to die of starvation and killed them ... all the talents of Budienny and of other revolutionary army leaders could not counterbalance our military and technical shortcomings and even less our false political reckoning; our hope in the Polish revolution." [44]

But this was a justification *post factum,* an attempt to ascribe the responsibility for the defeat to the lack of revolutionary spirit of the Polish masses. In fact, the Bolshevik leaders could have had no doubt whatever about the spirit of resistance of all strata of the Polish people against the invader. As early as 25th-26th May, 1920, Stalin wrote in *Pravda* :

> " The rear of the Polish troops differs from that of Koltchak and Denikin's, to the advantage of Poland. Unlike the rear of Koltchak and Denikin the rear of the Polish troops is uniform from the national point of view. This explains its coherence and steadfastness. The predominating feeling is ' the patriotic feeling ' (chuvstvo otchizny), which is being transmitted through numerous channels to the Polish front, creating the national unity and stubbornness in the military units." [45]

When the Second Congress of the Comintern met in Moscow in July 1920 the war with Poland was very naturally one of the most topical problems on the agenda. According to a German writer, a former Communist and member of the organization, F. Borkenau :

> " Everybody expected the quick collapse of Poland and the German Communists prepared to launch big revolutionary activity as soon as the Red cavalry appeared on Germany's Eastern frontier. These expectations are naïvely revealed in Zinoviev's opening speech. ... But in the general enthusiasm the Polish delegates remained sceptical. They were asked whether the Polish proletariat would rise at the moment of the approach of the Red Army to Warsaw. *They flatly denied it."* [46]

It is true that a provisional revolutionary " Polish Government " was set up at Bialystok, composed of Soviet stooges J. Marchlewski,

Felix Dzerzhynsky (ill-famed head of the Cheka), Felix Kohn and and Joseph Unszlicht, but it was obvious from the very beginning that its revolutionary appeals found no response in the Polish masses.[47] The prominent German Communist, Mrs. Ruth Fischer, wrote : " Polish workers and peasants remained passive, or if they acted they very often acted with Pilsudski; they preferred the status they had in the new Polish State to the possibility of a proletarian dictatorship, which would have become in actuality renewal under different circumstances of the submission to Moscow that had just been broken." [48] " The war was popular," wrote two leading Polish Communists, E. Brand and H. Walecki, in their book *Der Kommunismus in Polen,* " among broad strata of the Polish people." [49]

In his biography of Trotsky, Isaac Deutscher rightly observed that " whatever Lenin's private beliefs and motives, the Polish war was Bolshevism's first important essay in revolution by conquest. . . . If the Red Army had seized Warsaw it would have proceeded to act as the chief agent of social upheaval, as a substitute, as it were, for the Polish working classes." [50]

But no doubt can remain about the Soviet aggressive war aims in this dramatic struggle on Polish soil in summer 1920 if one becomes acquainted with the very outspoken statements of the Soviet leaders on this subject. Those Western " democrats " who thought so little of Poland's independence as something which did not concern their countries, and who deluded themselves that the peace of the world would not have suffered even if Poland had become Sovietized, did not realize that the Soviet policy saw in Poland's destruction only the first step to the destruction of the whole, still delicate, fabric of peace due to the long labours of the Western statesmen in Paris. Lenin himself disclosed the true Soviet intention at that time. In his speech at the All-Russia Conference of the Communist Party (Bolsheviks) on the 22nd September, 1920, he said :

> " The advance of our army towards Warsaw has undoubtedly shown that somewhere near it the hub of the whole system of world imperialism based on the Versailles Treaty can be found. Poland, the last bulwark against Bolshevism, being entirely in the hands of the Entente was to such an extent a powerful factor of this whole system that when the Red Army menaced this bulwark the whole system began to collapse. . . . At the approach of our army to Warsaw all Germany began to boil up." [51]

In his speech a few days later, on 2nd October, Lenin said :

> " By destroying the Polish army we are destroying the Versailles

Treaty on which nowadays the whole system of international relations is based. ... Had Poland become Soviet, had the Warsaw workers received our assistance which they awaited and welcomed(?) the Versailles Treaty would have been destroyed and with it the whole international system arising from the victories over Germany would have collapsed. The question was that after still a few days of victorious advance not only Warsaw would have been taken (and this was not so important in itself), but the whole Versailles Treaty would have been destroyed." [52]

In his well-documented book *War and Peace in Soviet Diplomacy*, Taracuzio draws the most pertinent conclusions from the above-mentioned declarations by Lenin : " In other words, not only from the political standpoint but from the military as well, the Soviet war against the Poles became a *de facto aggressive war against Poland, and against the Versailles Treaty of Peace*." [53] [My italics.]

In many speeches and writings after the Soviet defeat on the Vistula Trotsky asserted that he was against the offensive against Warsaw and for the conclusion of peace with Poland.[54] Some writers,[55] and recently Mr. Deutscher, Trotsky's apologist, wishing to preserve the infallibility of his hero for posterity, share this view. Unfortunately for them there is too much evidence to the contrary, including this document prepared by Trotsky himself entitled " Theses for the military-political campaign against Poland and the conclusion of peace with her," dated 11th August, 1920, and submitted by him to Lenin, Chicherin, Zinoviev and others, as well as to the Moscow Communist Party (published in Trotsky's book *How the Revolution Armed*). In this document we read : " If we now stop the pursuit of the retreating Polish troops we would be depriving ourselves of the fruits of our victory." [56] As a matter of fact Trotsky's dream was of a " free " (that is Communist) Poland, Finland, Latvia and Lithuania which would serve as a bridge between Soviet Russia and the future " Soviet Germany and Austria-Hungary." [57] In the opinion of contemporaries who read Trotsky's passionate declarations and speeches, it was Trotsky who pressed for the offensive. Lord d'Abernon, relating the impressions of the Polish delegation which went to Baranowicze for the armistice negotiations, wrote :

> " Private conversations with the Russians at Baranowicze gave no indication of what their terms to Poland would be, but they confirmed the view that there are two schools of thought in Russia, headed respectively by Lenin and Trotsky. The object of both is identical, viz., the widest extension of their propaganda. Lenin thinks this can be carried out during peace ; Trotsky holds that military prestige is a better advertisement." [58]

These views must be corrected in the light of historic evidence : not only Trotsky but Lenin also wished to attain these aims by a war of aggression against Poland.

But the best proof against allegedly pacific trends in Trotsky's policy is the fact that it was Trotsky who advocated most fervently the policy of *rapprochement* with Germany on the ruins of Poland. Enver wrote to General von Seeckt from Moscow on 26th August : " There is a party here which has real power, and Trotsky also belongs to this party, which is for an agreement with Germany. This party is ready to recognize the old German frontier of 1914." [59]

If we now turn to Stalin who, although at that time not among the most prominent Soviet leaders, well expressed the views prevailing within the Kremlin ruling circle, we find the following retrospective reflections on the events in summer 1920 in his article in *Pravda* of 14th March, 1923 :

> " There exist some moments when tactical successes, dazzling by their immediate effects but not corresponding to the strategical possibilities, create an ' unexpected ' position, fatal to the whole campaign. Such was the case of Denikin at the end of 1919, when carried away by the easy successes of a rapid and sensational march on Moscow he extended his front from the Volga to the Dnieper and thus prepared the ruin of his armies. The same thing occurred in 1920 when *having underestimated the strength of the national movement in Poland* and carried away by the easy successes of an impressive advance we undertook *a task beyond our forces of breaking through Warsaw to Europe*—we thus coalesced the overwhelming majority of the Polish people, created a position nullifying all the successes of the Soviet army at Minsk and Jitomir and tarnished Soviet prestige in the West." [60]

Germany and the Polish–Soviet War

As a marginal note to this story let us remember some strange and quite unrealistic suggestions at that time for winning Germany's assistance in the struggle against Soviet Russia. Winston Churchill, who was the main protagonist of this policy in England, wrote on the 26th June, 1920, that is, immediately after the first Polish set-backs :

> " In the event of the collapse of Poland, what reaction would this situation entail upon the German position? It would clearly not be possible to disarm Germany if her Eastern frontiers were in contact with a Bolshevized area." [61]

Lord Riddell relates the following conversation with Winston Churchill on the 22nd July, 1920 :

> " Talk with Winston, who was very depressed regarding the

Polish situation. He said: ' The Bolshevists are fanatics. Nothing will induce them to give up their propaganda and endeavours to create a Communist world.' He prophesies that they will attempt the formation of a Soviet Government in Poland and later on endeavour to accomplish their purpose in Germany. ' It may well be,' he continued, ' that Great Britain and France will have to call upon the Germans for their assistance.' " 62

In an article published in the *Evening News* on the 27th July, 1920, Churchill called Poland " the lynch-pin of the Versailles Treaty." The lynch-pin is loose and the Bolshevists are not alone in their desire to pull it out. Taking the view that Bolshevism is as dangerous to its civilized neighbours in peace as in war, that a Bolshevist peace is only another form of war and the subjugation of Poland either by Bolshevik arms or by Bolshevik propaganda would vitally affect British and French interests, Churchill nevertheless saw a silver lining in the overcast sky. Namely he stated that a Bolshevist conquest of Poland would offer Germany " an awful but wonderful choice : to sink into the Bolshevist welter or build a dike of virtue against the flood of Red barbarism," which in fact amounted to the abandonment of the disarmament clauses.

We call these plans unrealistic because instead of giving assistance to Poland, which continued to fight a lonely battle against Bolshevism with practically no Allied assistance, they pursued a dream, beyond any link with real facts. Illusions of the possibility of winning German assistance against Russia was to play a very important rôle in subsequent periods. Consequently it is worth while to consider the prospects of such a policy in the initial stage of this important chapter of international relations between the two wars. It was an alternative to the policy based on the enforcement of the Versailles Treaty and the defence of the new European structure set up in Paris. This alternative policy was based on the illusion that Germany might feel more attracted by the Western outlook than by the Russian, Bolshevik one. " It seemed unthinkable," writes Professor Carr, " that the German Right should enter into an alliance with the Russian Left. This overestimate of the ideological factor was very persistent, especially in the Western world." 63

The reality was quite different. In his study on *German-Russian Relations* 1921–1934, Lionel Kochan recalls Radek's article in *Izvestia* on the 5th November, 1925, in which the latter pointed out that " the victory of the German bourgeoisie over the Communist threat—such as it was—coincided with the Bolshevik victory over the Whites." In other words the German bourgoisie, having now nothing to fear from its own Communists, could co-operate with the Bolshevists, relieved of the horror that it might thereby become Communist.[64]

The German answer to the Western seducers was not long in coming. On 25th July Dr. Simons, the German Foreign Minister, actually forbade the transport of munitions across Germany from France to Poland. "German neutrality was not without benevolence on the side of Lenin," said the Stinnes-owned *Kölnische Zeitung*.[65]

Speaking in the Reichstag on 2nd August Dr. Simons expounded the German policy of neutrality. He said : " As regards the transport of arms, ammunition and military personnel through Germany we have certain duties arising out of treaties—the agreement for so-called Poland trains. We are of opinion that if the trains are to be utilized for purposes inimical to neutrality they should no longer be allowed a through passage." Replying to Churchill's suggestions, Dr. Simons declared : " As to the speech of Mr. Churchill, I will remark that the time has not yet come when we should strive to get ourselves admitted to the League of Nations. *Germany is not going to allow herself to be enticed into joining the League of Nations simply because people want to use us as mercenaries.*" [66]

It was the attitude of the German military circles that influenced more than anything else the policy of Republican Germany. Von Seeckt, who was to emerge as the " central figure in the half-secret game of Russo-German reconciliation," [67] remained firmly opposed to any proposals for co-operation with the West. In a letter written on the 31st January, 1920, von Seeckt stated his views on the matter :

" Since the future political and economic *understanding with Great-Russia was to be our fixed* (unverrückbares) *target,* we must avoid anything that might antagonize Russia. ... I would refuse to help Poland, even if there existed a danger that Poland might be swallowed by Russia. On the contrary I reckon on it and although we cannot, for the time being, help Russia in regaining the old frontiers of her Empire, we must not do anything that might prevent her from doing so. The same refers to Lithuania and Latvia." [68]

Obsessed by memories of the past and blinded by his hatred for Poland, von Seeckt was quite impervious to the idea that Russia in the future might endanger Germany's independence.

" With Poland " [he wrote on another occasion], " we come to the core of the Eastern question. Poland's existence is intolerable, incompatible with the conditions essential to Germany's life. She must disappear and she will disappear owing to her own internal weakness and by the endeavours of Russia with our assistance.

Poland is still more intolerable for Russia than for ourselves; no Russia will be able to put up with Poland. Poland can never be of any advantage to us either from the economic point of view, being incapable of any progress, or the political, being a satellite of France. Russia and Germany within the frontiers of 1914—such must be the basis of the agreement between the two powers. There is no need for our standpoint to remain a timidly concealed secret. If we make our position on that matter quite clear we shall be able to win Russia's confidence. The menace from both sides will in the long run undermine Poland's stability." [69]

Lord d'Abernon, whose pro-German feelings were secret from nobody since thanks to his endeavours the reconciliation between Germany and the Western countries could have been achieved at Locarno, deplored German short-sightedness in relation to Poland. " The Germans," he wrote, " have quite an undue contempt for Polish ability, while some of them underrate *the immense import-ance of Poland as a barrier against Russia*. ... A strong Poland would be an effective barrier. But national prejudice obscures the vision." [70] [My italics.]

We have dealt at some length with this incipient Soviet-German *rapprochement* in view of its bearing on the general policy. What we already know about this " half-secret game " fully displays the opportunism and unprincipled conduct of Soviet foreign policy, ready to collaborate with the most reactionary military circles of Germany. What is one to think in the light of this evidence of the opinions on Russia prevailing at that time among " democrats " in Western countries who were unaware that by their unrestrained campaign against Poland they fostered not the cause of peace but the revival of German and Russian imperialism, paving the way to the Second World War.

Polish–Soviet negotiations delayed by Bolshevik manœuvres

Let us review the direct Polish-Soviet negotiations in August. Lord d'Abernon, who was in the best position to judge this question, states in his book :

" It may be regarded as certain that from July 1920 all negotia-tions entered into by the Soviet under the pretext that they were preparing to make peace with Poland were little more than a blind ; they were designed with a view both to gain time for a military advance and to give an opportunity for subversive propa-ganda in Poland to bear fruit. Amongst erroneous ideas enter-tained by the Western Powers none was more dangerous than their belief that peace was possible with the Soviet. The Russian authori-ties were confident of their power to destroy the Polish army and capture Warsaw. They would treat seriously after that had been done and not before." [71]

And under the date of 29th July he noted in his Diary : " London appears to me too much inclined to believe in the possibility of an immediate arrangement with the Soviet Government. What would the Soviet gain thereby? " [72]

Let us now see the facts as they speak for themselves. Urged by the British Government to approach the Soviet Government direct (see pp. 625 ff.) the Polish Government telegraphed the Soviet Government on 22nd July, proposing that negotiations for an armistice should commence immediately. Simultaneously a telegram was sent by the Polish High Command to the Soviet High Command, proposing the date of 25th July for the opening of the armistice negotiations. In their reply to the Polish Government the Soviets acknowledged the receipt of the Polish proposal and stated that they accepted the suggestion made therein to start negotiations on 30th July.

Kamenev, member of the Soviet Delegation to Great Britain, gave another version of this incident in his letter to the British Prime Minister dated 5th August.[73] He asserted that

" on 22nd July a telegram over the signature of Prince Sapieha, the Polish Minister for Foreign Affairs, was received in Moscow, proposing in accordance with the suggestion of the Allies to open negotiations for an armistice and peace. At the same time a telegram received from General Rozwadowski, Chief of the Polish General Staff, mentioned 30th July as the date of the meeting of the delegates of both parties. On the very same day, viz., 22nd July, Mr. Chicherin on behalf of the Soviet Government informed the Polish Government of his consent to begin negotiations for armistice and peace."

The difference between the two versions concerns the date and the scope of the negotiations—whether for armistice only or for armistice and peace.

So far as the first question was concerned Lord d'Abernon observes :

" The Soviet Government deliberately delayed the meeting until 30th July under the pretext that that date had been proposed by the Polish Military Commander. The Polish Government state that no such proposal was made, the obvious interest both of Polish diplomats and Polish generals being to conclude an armistice as rapidly as possible in order to prevent a further advance of the Soviet army." [74]

A strong denial was also contained in an official communiqué of the Polish Chargé d'Affaires in London, dated 6th August, recalling that he had drawn the attention of the British Government to the discrepancy between the two dates immediately after receipt of the Soviet reply, that is on 28th July :

> " The Soviet Government, acting in accordance with its usual methods, perverted the Polish proposal by acknowledging a later date than that put forward by the Polish High Command, with the obvious aim of causing a delay in the negotiations for an armistice and of throwing the responsibility for such a delay on the Polish Government. This intention of the Soviet Government was so clear to the Polish Government that the above-stated manœuvre was communicated by me officially to His Majesty's Government on 28th July." [75]

The Polish delegation to negotiate an armistice crossed the front line on 30th July and met the Russians at Baranowicze. As Lord d'Abernon states, the Polish delegates " did not find there any Soviet Delegation with whom serious discussion was possible " [76] and the " Soviet representatives insisted that the Poles must have a mandate to make peace as well as to make an armistice. There had been no previous mention of this additional power and Chicherin's statements as to what powers were or were not usual on such occasions is so confused that it does not suggest sincerity." [77]

In this connection Kamenev states in the above-mentioned letter of 5th August :

> " It turned out, however, that *contrary to the agreement reached* by the previous exchange of messages, the Polish delegates had only been authorized to deal with military problems, and that their powers had been derived solely from the military command. It is obvious from the above-mentioned facts that such limited powers do not correspond to the tasks with which the conference of the delegates were to deal in accordance with the proposals of both the British and Russian Governments.
>
> " It goes without saying that the Russian Soviet Government have not, and never had, any desire to combine the negotiations for an armistice with negotiations for a definite peace treaty between Poland and Russia. Nevertheless, it is inevitable that negotiations for an armistice should include negotiations for certain conditions and guarantees over and above the strictly military domain."

And in the following lines Kamenev discloses for the first time the points which would be raised in these negotiations by the Soviet Government :

> " It is a matter of necessity for the Russian Government to demand the inclusion in the terms of armistice with Poland of such reasonable guarantees as will prevent all attempts on the part of Poland to use the period of armistice for the renewal of hostile acts

against Russia. Such guarantees would include partial disarmament, the cessation of recruitment of conscript soldiers as well as of voluntary enrolment, and so on. ... International law and the customs of war know of no case in which the army of one of the belligerents has suspended military operations before the conclusion of an armistice, and it is, therefore, natural that the Russian Soviet army should continue its advance, which, being purely a military operation, does not in the least prejudge the nature of the peace treaty and does not constitute an attempt against the independence and integrity of the Polish State in its ethnographic frontiers."

We shall see later, when the Soviet terms are disclosed in full, whether or not they constituted a threat to Polish independence. For the time being the point in question is whether the matter of such wide powers of the Polish delegation had or had not been put so clearly in the exchange of messages between the Polish and Soviet Governments as Kamenev's Note alleged.

In the communiqué of the Polish Legation in London of 6th August we find the following refutation of the Soviet allegations :

"The Polish Delegates were empowered to conclude an armistice. The Polish Government has not given powers to conclude the principles of a peace settlement, it being understood at the time it had been proposed to hold a peace conference presided over by the representatives of the Allied Governments in London.

"Mr. Kamenev's statement that the Polish Government has been informed by the Soviet Government that the latter would expect the Polish plenipotentiaries to be empowered to negotiate other than purely military principles, alone necessary for the conclusion of an armistice, is equally untrue. The Polish Government received no such intimation. ... In a telegram addressed to the Polish Government on 2nd August, Mr. Chicherin stated, 'The Russian Government in no way wishes to hinder the correspondence of your delegation with your Government, but only desired to attract their attention to the real tenor of our demands, which consist not only in presenting the powers of the Polish Central Government, but also in extending these powers to the right of negotiating peace.' This sentence from Mr. Chicherin's telegram clearly shows that contrary to the statement in Mr. Kamenev's letter, the Soviet Government demanded that the Polish Delegation should have powers to negotiate a peace settlement."

The Soviet manœuvre thus appears quite clearly. On the one hand that Government wished to delay the negotiations with Poland as long as possible, and on the other to deprive of any object the negotiations proposed by the Allies in London by previously imposing on Poland such terms as would prejudice the main lines of the peace settlement. In fact the above-mentioned note of

Kamenev put it quite clearly : " We are still of opinion that direct negotiations with Poland for peace would serve the interests both of the Russian and the Polish people and the Russian Soviet Government again declares that it is firm in its recognition of the freedom and independence of Poland and its willingness to grant to the Polish State wider frontiers than were indicated by the Supreme Council and mentioned in the British Note of 20th July." At the same time Kamenev tried to shift all responsibility for the delay on to Poland : " One is, indeed, justified in inferring from the conduct of the Polish delegates, who have preferred to return to Warsaw, that the Polish Government are speculating on foreign assistance and are delaying the armistice and peace negotiations in expectation of it. The Russian Government will exceedingly regret if any *false hope or exaggerated expectation on the part of the Polish Government from outside* should cause the failure of the Polish Delegation to present themselves for negotiations with the Russian delegates at the earliest possible moment." These sarcastic remarks show that the Soviet Government was not afraid of the Allied menaces and that it did not take into account any effective assistance to Poland from the Entente Governments.

At the same time the Soviet Government was cautious enough in avoiding disclosure of its terms for peace. Lord d'Abernon notes a characteristic incident relating to this :

> " During the whole of this period " [he writes], " from 11th July to 13th August, the Soviet army was pushing on. An intercepted radio message is of interest in connection with the above. It was from one Russian Army to another on 26th July, and said: 'We have arranged not to inform Poles of our armistice conditions before 4th August. You have therefore four additional days to continue fighting '." [78]

The Polish Delegation at Baranowicze was not allowed to leave that town before the 3rd August. On the day of its departure from Baranowicze the Polish Government received a proposal from the Soviet Government that negotiations should be resumed at Minsk on 4th August. It was clear that it was physically impossible for the Polish Delegation to reach Minsk by that date. It could be inferred from this that the Soviet wished to throw the responsibility for further delay in the resumption of negotiations on the Polish Government. When Prince Sapieha, Polish Foreign Minister, having agreed to the proposed meeting at Minsk, wished to transmit a message to Moscow on 5th August the Moscow radio station refused to accept it on the pretext of not being able to receive messages during the late hours of the night. The Soviet authorities fixed the hour when they would be willing to accept the radio message as 5 p.m. on 6th August. Notwithstanding this flagrant proof of wilful delay, the Polish Ministry for Foreign Affairs gave orders that the message be transmitted at the time thus fixed, but a fresh refusal was then made, on the pretext that the Moscow station was out of order owing to a weakening of current caused by bad weather. This alleged state of things did not, however, prevent direct communication between the two radio stations. Consequently it was not until 14th August that the Polish peace delegation was able to leave for Minsk; it was composed of representatives of all parties of the Diet, under the Chairmanship of a peasant leader, Jan Dabski, Under-Secretary of State for Foreign Affairs. At that time the Russians were already at the gates of Warsaw and the great historic battle which ended in the complete victory of the Poles began on the very day the Polish Delegation left for Minsk.

At the beginning of August Poland's prospects seemed very gloomy. As the Warsaw correspondent of *The Times* stated on 8th August : " Poland has had a sense of abandonment since the breakdown of the negotiations at Baranowicze. ... The Polish people may be faced with a choice between a greater Russified Poland and a small Poland under the aegis of distant and hitherto unhelpful Allies—whom, nevertheless, the bulk of the people still vastly prefers."

The proclamation of the Polish Council of National Defence shows well this feeling " of abandonment " to which the Warsaw correspondent of *The Times* alluded in his correspondence :

" In the hard struggle to found national independence fought in the last 20 months under the most adverse economic conditions, the Polish nation received her first Diet elected on the basis of universal suffrage, initiated a scheme of far-reaching social reforms, and finally nominated a government at whose head stands a peasant representative of the biggest peasant party in Poland (Witos), with next to him a leader of Polish workmen (Daszynski, leader of the Polish Socialist Party). ... If Polish freedom dies, to-morrow yours will be threatened. Think how the fall of Poland may become the commencement of a new world war. A Bolshevist victory on the Vistula threatens all Western Europe ; a new world war hangs over the world like a storm-cloud. Wake up, nations of the world. Humanity, justice and truth call you. You hesitate? Are you afraid of war? It will come to you as it came to us. When it is on your threshold it will be too late to save yourselves. Not only our but also your future is at stake to-day on the Vistula." [79]

As we said above, the British Government sent a Note to the Soviet Government, dated 28th July (see p. 636), agreed upon between France and Great Britain at the Boulogne Conference. Receiving no reply, Lord Curzon sent a new Note on 3rd August to Chicherin. This Note ran as follows :

"No reply has yet been received to the message which was sent to the Soviet authorities by the British Government, after consultation with their Allies, as far back as 29th July last, proposing a conference at London, the essential object of which should be the re-establishment of peace in Europe, and in the first place between Poland and Russia. Meanwhile, a wireless press message has just come from Moscow, stating that the Soviet Armistice Delegation had insisted, as the condition of an armistice, on the Polish Armistice Delegation being empowered also to conclude the fundamental conditions of peace, and that the Polish Delegates, not being empowered to do so, have returned to Warsaw.

"The Soviet Government should realize that if they insist upon peace conditions being settled between Poland and Russia, to the exclusion of other Powers, the bases on which it was proposed to conduct negotiations in London will have disappeared, and the project of a Conference falls to the ground. Further, it appears that the Soviet armies have now advanced far into ethnographic Poland. If advantage be taken of the delays now caused to continue this advance, His Majesty's Government will be driven to the conclusion that it is not the intention of the Soviet Government to respect the liberty and independence of Poland, and the situation contemplated in their telegram to Mr. Chicherin of 20th July will have arisen." [80]

The impression made in Poland by the above-mentioned Note was best summed up by the Warsaw correspondent of *The Times*, who wrote on 3rd August (*The Times*, 7th August) : "Gloom is settling down on Warsaw as it becomes known that in spite of the contemptuous provocation of the Soviet Government, in spite of our engagements, we have not sent an ultimatum to Russia, only another argumentative Note." And the editorial of *The Times* on 5th August repeated : "Time is the essence of the whole situation ... while the Allies are exchanging views, the Reds are marching on."

Messrs. Krassin and Kamenev, who arrived in London on 3rd August and whose presence in the British capital aroused such indignation in Poland and France, were called by Lloyd George to 10 Downing Street on 4th August for what Lloyd George called "a straight talk." Lloyd George gave an account of this conversation to the House of Commons on 5th August. He stated that he had said to the Soviet representatives that the Soviet advance on Warsaw "raised the *suspicion* that the Soviet Government was not sincere in its professed desire for peace and its declarations that it intended to respect the liberty and independence of Poland." Lloyd George further said that he had made it clear " that the *immediate* conclusion of an armistice *on fair terms* was the only course which would remove that suspicion." We shall very soon have the opportunity to see what Lloyd George meant by fair terms. On the other hand, he declared, " we have taken the effective steps to remove the obstacles in the way of transmission to Poland from Danzig of military supplies which were detained in that port." [81]

The Port of Danzig closed to transport of arms to Poland

As appears from this declaration, Lloyd George did not go very far in fulfilling the British pledges of assistance to Poland " with full means," as had been promised at Spa. However, even the steps mentioned in that declaration would have been welcomed in Poland. As Lord d'Abernon relates in his Diary, he had a conversation with Marshal Pilsudski on 25th July. In this conversation " Pilsudski said the greatest service the Mission could render to Poland was to keep the communications through Danzig open. Poland was in urgent need of supplies. But this was not all. The importance of keeping the road open was not only material but moral. He attached more importance to supplies than to military assistance in the form either of advice or foreign officers." [82]

In this Great Britain had a great opportunity to help Poland, if not herself sending munitions and arms to Poland, which she did not, as we know, at least by issuing appropriate orders to Sir Reginald Tower, Provisional Administrator and Representative of the Allied Powers then occupying Danzig (the Free City of Danzig was constituted later, namely on 5th November, 1920). Sir Reginald Tower happened to be an old British Civil Servant with a record for the stubborn defence of British interests in the overseas countries (see above, p. 336). Sir Reginald had at that time full powers in Danzig and his voice was decisive on all matters referring to the use and the administration of the port of Danzig. We shall see below in which spirit he carried out his duties.

Lord d'Abernon realized the importance of Danzig and asked for assistance from Sir Reginald Tower and General Sir Richard Haking, British Commander in that area. " The only practical course," wrote Lord d'Abernon in his Diary, " is to keep the Danzig port open, and on this I decided to concentrate. If it is achieved, Polish necessities can be met." [83] And on 29th July : " General Haking has displayed great energy at Danzig. He reports favourably regarding *possibility* of sending supplies through that port." [84]

At this fateful hour for Poland the importance of Danzig as Poland's only outlet to the sea came into particular prominence.

At no time have the words used in Temperley's *A History of the Peace Conference of Paris* been more true : " For the Polish nation the possession of Danzig, in some form or other, is a matter not of a mere economic convenience but rather a matter of life and death." [85] It must be kept in mind, however, that in this whole period Great Britain, not satisfied with having debarred Poland from the possession of Danzig, did everything to drive Poland off the sea. Many important moves by the British representatives within the bodies set up by the Peace Conference after the signature of the Versailles Treaty can serve as evidence to this effect.

The pro-German bias of the British representatives even as regards relatively minor problems relating to the Polish position on the Baltic coast appeared undisguisedly, meeting with no opposition on the French part because France had to take into account British special interests in all matters relating to maritime problems. So, for instance, when the question of allotting small German ships to new States for police duties was discussed in the Council of Heads of Delegations at the beginning of December 1919 [86] (Poland was to receive six enemy torpedo boats and the Kingdom of Serbs, Croats and Slovenes, twelve torpedo boats); it was the British representative, Sir Eyre Crowe, who objected to this proposal at the meeting of 24th December, 1919, saying that such decision might create certain difficulties between Germany and Poland, " the more especially as it was the case of giving to that latter Power German vessels actually stationed at Danzig." In these circumstances the question was referred to the naval experts who " should come to a final decision regarding the transfer to Poland of ex-Austrian torpedo boats."

But decisions more far-reaching were to come. By the resolution of the Conference of Ambassadors of 7th May, 1920, passed under British influence and approved by the Supreme Council on 11th July, 1920, at the Spa Conference " Poland could not be authorized to establish a military or naval base at Danzig." The same resolution laid down the main lines of the treaty to be concluded between Poland and the Free City of Danzig under the auspices of the Principal Powers containing a far-reaching revision of the Treaty of Versailles to Poland's detriment. This treaty, actually signed on 9th November, 1920, and known as the Treaty of Paris, according to John Brown Mason " greatly curtailed certain rights originally assigned to Poland. Instead of gaining complete control of the port and waterways, she was allowed only to share that control with Danzig on terms of equality." [87] This equality meant in fact that Poland was to depend to a great extent on the goodwill of the local authorities in Danzig acting as proxies of the German Reich.

Inevitably many disputes arose between Poland and Danzig leaving wide room for the discretionary powers of the representative of the Allied Powers. The events of summer 1920 showed to what extent Poland's access to the sea depended on the good faith of the Danzig authorities even in that early period before the Free City was formally constituted. On 22nd April, 1920, an agreement was signed between Poland and Sir Reginald Tower, acting on behalf of the Free City, by which " Danzig guaranteed all necessary facilities for any goods unloaded in the port and destined for Poland, including war materials." The war materials could be escorted by Polish military guards and it was taken for granted that previous permission from the Danzig authorities would be allowed. The provisions of this agreement were quite clear but as events turned out they did not safeguard free traffic through the port of Danzig. The unrest among the Danzig dock labourers owing to pro-Soviet agitation forced Sir Reginald Tower to ask the Allied Powers, early in July, for permission to admit Polish labour to unload the munitions and war material destined for Poland. *To this demand Sir Reginald never received a reply.*[88] On 21st July a vessel arrived in the port of Danzig with munitions which the dock workers refused to unload. There is no doubt that, apart from the pro-Soviet sympathies so common at that time among workers, the ambiguous attitude of the Western Powers towards the Polish-Soviet conflict greatly encouraged the Germans in Danzig in their open hostility towards Poland. Ian F. D. Morrow, whose book *The Peace Settlement in the German-Polish Borderlands* is more favourable to Danzig than to Poland, does not deny this circumstance. He said in this connection :

> " Poland appealed for assistance to the Supreme Council at Spa on 15th–16th July (*it occurred actually a week earlier,* my remark). Her reception had been cold. . . . How much of this was known to the Danzig working class—possibly in the form of exaggerated rumours—it is impossible to say. At least the Provisional Government of Danzig—the Municipal Council with the Burgomaster, Herr Sahm, at its head—must have had some inkling of the cold attitude adopted towards Poland by the Great Powers at this critical moment." [89]

We do not know exactly what instructions Sir Reginald Tower received at this critical moment from the Allied Powers, but as they were issued under the authority of Lloyd George we do not think that they actually enjoined Sir Reginald to take very strong measures in order to carry out the pledges of assistance to Poland. The whole attitude of Sir Reginald at this critical moment confirms our strong suspicion that he was given wide freedom of action.

Without entering into a detailed description of the events in Danzig given by other writers,[90] we state only that thanks to General Haking's intervention one vessel (the above-mentioned that arrived on 21st July provoking the strike of Danzig dock workers) was unloaded on 27th July by British troops and the munitions transported by barges to Tczew on Polish territory under Polish military escort. But all subsequent transports were stopped. Riots and demonstrations broke out in Danzig on 29th July. Instead of proclaiming martial law Sir Reginald informed the Polish Commissioner-General in Danzig, Mr. Biesiadecki, that " vessels laden with munitions would be forbidden to enter the port of Danzig. He alleged that the Allied garrison was not strong enough to control the situation in event of further riots." [91]

On 9th August a resolution was passed by the General Association of Trade Unions in Danzig which ran :

> " The meeting pledges itself never again to transmit through Free State territory war-materials intended for Poland. The Danzig workers regard it as beneath their dignity to act as policemen for Poland in its contest with the Russian proletariat. They bind themselves to ensure that no work of any kind should be anywhere carried out in furtherance of Poland's reactionary efforts and of the purposes of the war."

Thus while in Warsaw Lord d'Abernon was promising Pilsudski to do his best in order to " keep the Danzig port open," his countryman in Danzig was closing this port to the import of munitions destined for Poland. There can be no excuse for Sir Reginald Tower's behaviour—was it really beyond the strength of the greatest naval power in the world to ensure the freedom of traffic in the port of Danzig? Available forces were at that time near at hand in West- and East-Prussian plebiscite areas. Were the Polish chances of survival estimated lower by Sir Reginald than tranquility and order in the city of Danzig?

It is beyond any doubt that Sir Reginald was under exclusive German influence while staying in Danzig. With the exception of five Englishmen his whole staff consisted entirely of Germans. *The Times* observed on 29th July : " Poland lies practically at the mercy of the enemies of the Entente, and the French safeguards are disappearing in the dust of the policy pursued by Sir Reginald Tower at Danzig and behind the veil of Allied inaction." And it observed later on 20th August : " The departure of the Prussian troops left both railways to Danzig free, and the only obstacle to Poland's free communication to the sea, as guaranteed her by the Treaty of Versailles, was the scruples of the High Commissioner, Sir Reginald Tower, or of his superiors."

The American expert who visited Danzig a few weeks later as a member of the Inter-Allied Commission, Professor Lord, passed also a very strong judgment on Sir Reginald Tower's behaviour : " The Poles in Danzig are frequently mobbed; in the face of the crisis threatening her very existence last summer Poland found her one port virtually closed to her through the animosity of the Danzigers and what seems to me the very ill-advised action of the High Commissioner." [92]

As we shall see later, the position at Danzig did not change until the Polish victory on the Vistula.

Negotiations with Krassin and Kamenev

Returning now to the negotiations in London with the Soviet representatives : they took a very bad turn because in reply to the British Note of 3rd August and Lloyd George's exhortations in the talk with Messrs. Kamenev and Krassin on 4th August, Kamenev addressed a Note to Lloyd George on 5th August (to which we referred in connection with the Polish-Soviet negotiations). This Note laid all the responsibility for the delay in the Polish-Soviet direct negotiations at the door of the Polish Government, and refused to halt the advance of the Soviet armies. The Soviets declared that they would come to a direct arrangement with the Poles, thus trying again to eliminate the Allies from the negotiations.

There was another conversation between Messrs. Kamenev and Krassin on the one side and Lloyd George and Bonar Law, assisted by Sir Henry Wilson, C.I.G.S., on the other, at 10 Downing Street on Friday, 6th August, lasting several hours. In the course of this conversation Lloyd George proposed a ten-day truce between the Bolshevists and the Poles, the cease-fire being fixed as midnight Monday–Tuesday, (9th–10th August). (For the Text see Note 93.) Lloyd George's proposal contained an unusual proviso, that the Bolshevist officers should be permitted to superintend the execution of the terms behind the Polish lines (including Danzig).* In his papers Sir Henry Wilson left a most vivid account of this conference, which he attended in the capacity of military adviser :

" At 4 o'clock Lloyd George sent for me, and I remained till 10 to 9. First drawing terms of truce between the Bolshevists and Poles, and then with Lloyd George and Bonar Law, discussing these with Kamenev and Krassin. I was horrified at the almost servile way in which Lloyd George looked after Russian interests and was hostile to the Poles. Also the way in which he told the Bolshevists what he would do with our fleet ' at Helsingfors and in

* The passage relating to Danzig explains to some extent the attitude taken by Sir Reginald Tower (see above).

the Black Sea ' if he had to take action, making it quite clear that his action would be naval. The whole tone of Lloyd George shocked me very much. He was with friends in Kamenev and Krassin and together they discussed the French and the Poles." [94]

Sir Henry also noted the following incident :

" When I said that I thought we ought to put ' from G.H.Q. Russian Army ' and ' G.H.Q. Polish Army ' as it was possible the Poles would no longer be in Warsaw, the two Bolsheviks and Lloyd George burst out laughing, Kamenev having to stuff his handkerchief into his mouth. It was quite clear to me that all three knew, and that Lloyd George approved of the occupation of Warsaw by the Bolsheviks. It was an amazing five hours' meeting. It left me with a clear sense that Lloyd George is in company with friends and kindred spirits when with the Bolsheviks. All through the meeting the Bolshevists, assisted by Lloyd George, were driving a wedge between the English and the French, and Lloyd George went so far as to say that if the French did not agree to the truce terms, then he would not support Poland nor make war on the Bolsheviks. Whew! " [95]

In Lenin's speech of 15th October, 1920, we find confirmation of the fact that Lloyd George in his negotiations with Kamenev and Krassin was imprudent enough to disclose the dissensions between Great Britain and France, which could only encourage the Soviet Government in its policy of aggression. Lenin said :

" When comrade Kamenev carried out the negotiations with the English Government and declared to the British Prime Minister : ' Supposing you will do what you say, what then will France do?', the British Prime Minister replied that France would go its own way, as England could not fall into step with France." [96]

No wonder that in these circumstances the British truce proposal was rejected by the Soviet Government, by a Note of 8th August, stating that it had already proposed to meet the Poles on 11th August at Minsk, and that " in this way the cessation of hostilities and the resumption of peaceful relations between Russia and Poland will be attained in the speediest and simplest way by direct negotiations." In fact, according to Lord d'Abernon's information, " the Soviet Government sent a negotiator to the Polish front pretending that they had previously sent a radio message to the Polish Government fixing a date and hour of appointment. No such radio message was received in Warsaw, and there is no indication of any attempt to send such a message." [97] The Bolsheviks knew well that they could continue their manœuvres as they had nothing to fear from Lloyd George.

In its issue of 7th August the *New Statesman* stated :

" Who is most to blame for the delays in the armistice negotia-tions it is hard to say. ... The Russians, however, have certainly been more successful in keeping themselves in the right. ... The terms of any armistice must include either a provision for the dis-armament of the beaten side or else the fundamental political con-ditions of the future peace leaving only details to negotiations."

The prominent English Radical periodical fully concurred with the official Soviet views. It severely criticized Allied attempts to inter-fere in Polish-Russian relations :

" In the whole matter the Allies are still acting as if they possessed some inherent moral right to dictate both to Russia and Poland. ... They use threats which, as the Moscow Government very well knows, they have no power to make good ; and so they reduce themselves to impotence, sacrificing Poland's interests as well as their own for the sake of some ridiculous conception of *amour propre*—ridiculous because they cannot substantiate it."

Lord d'Abernon and M. Jusserand, respectively heads of the British and French Missions in Warsaw, took another view and urged their Governments to render immediate military assistance to Poland, Lord d'Abernon notes in his Diary under 5th August :

" Jusserand and I have telegraphed home regarding the form which military assistance from France and England might take if the action of the Soviet Government in armistice negotiations renders military assistance to Poland necessary. We are unanimous that in no case should less than two divisions be sent, together with two cavalry divisions and the administrative services necessary to make the force self-supporting. Should it prove impracticable to send an expeditionary force we suggest the occupation of Danzig by Franco-Polish troops." [98]

The Hythe Conference

The urgent appeals sent by the Allied representatives in Poland asking for immediate military assistance to that country found no response, however, as clearly appears from the proceedings of the Franco-British Conference held at Hythe on the 8th and 9th August (also called the Lympne Conference). This conference, attended by the British and French Prime Ministers assisted by their military and naval advisers, Wilson, Beatty and Foch had, in Lloyd George's view, the purpose of inducing the Poles to accept the ten-day truce proposed by him to the Soviet Government in conversation with Messrs. Krassin and Kamenev on 6th August. This proposal was strongly opposed by the French. Sir Henry Wilson notes in his Diary that in reply to it M. Millerand made a clear statement " that he would not deal with the Bolsheviks, that their word and honour were worth nothing and that they had neither honour nor laws." [99] Millerand disapproved also of " Lloyd George's absolutely indefensible decision to allow Kamenev and Krassin to remain in London after the Soviet refusal to agree to the truce terms." [100] In the meantime it had been made known that the Soviet Government rejected the British proposal and this refusal was commented on : " That the Bolshevists intended to do their best in order that they might set up a puppet Polish Soviet with which Moscow could come to such terms as it might please it to impose." [101] This intelligence obliged the Conference to discuss the question as to how pressure could be exerted on the Bolsheviks. The naval and military advisers, however, received a mandate to envisage only a naval blockade in the Baltic and Black Seas, and not direct military assistance to Poland. In order to help Poland it was suggested that there should be " the sending of some assistance to Wrangel and the Don Cossacks "(!). But Lord Beatty took the view that a blockade would not be possible without holding Danzig or Helsingfors, while General Haking wired from Danzig that in order to be able to hold Danzig he would have to have at his disposal four battalions and some guns. To this Sir Henry remarked : " Of course, we have not four battalions. And so the whole Versailles Treaty continues to crash and even these idiotic and self-satisfied Frocks are beginning to see this." The mistake made at Versailles in depriving Poland of Danzig, due to Lloyd George's initative, thus became patent. It is interesting to note that to assist Poland in this critical hour the Western Allies could not spare even four battalions, an insignificant force compared to the big armies which had fought on the Western Front during the Great War. Eventually an agreement was laboriously patched up between the Allies on the text of a telegram to the Polish Government, but as Sir Henry noted, " Millerand and Foch were profoundly dissatisfied, alarmed and suspicious."

We know from French sources that the French delegates wished to obtain something more tangible at Hythe, namely a guarantee for the Western frontiers of Poland but they met with refusal not only from Lloyd George but also Lord Curzon and A. J. Balfour, who accompanied him. The British negotiators requested that the scope of the Hythe Conference be limited strictly to problems arising from what they then thought imminent, namely " the Polish collapse." M. Bardoux, who at that time had close contacts with the Quai d'Orsay, sums up the result of the Hythe Conference in these two concise sentences : " Aucune sécurité ne fut donnée. Aucune garantie ne fut envisagée." [102]

The text of the telegram sent to the Polish Government by the Hythe Conference reads as follows :

"The French and British Governments make the following declaration to the Polish Government:

"They consider that at forthcoming negotiations at Minsk Polish Government should do its utmost to conclude an armistice and, if necessary, preliminary peace, on terms which will secure independence of Poland within its ethnographic frontiers.

"If, however, the Russian Soviet Government insists on terms which infringe legitimate independence of Poland and *Polish Government rejects them,* French and British Government will:

"1. Take all the steps they can to interrupt contacts between Russia and the outside world and put pressure on Russia by other means to respect independence of Poland.

"2. Supply Polish Army with military material for twenty-two divisions and military advice, but *they cannot in any circumstances send Allied troops over and above missions already there.*

"3. Do their utmost to keep open communications between Poland and Allies.

"On the other hand, provided that Poland:

"1. Makes a public declaration that it is its intention to fight to the end for its independence against Soviet attacks ;

"2. Appoints Commander-in-Chief who shall have no other functions and will accept effective assistance of Allied Officers ;

"3. Will accept and act on military advice tendered by Allies ;

"4. Maintain Polish Army at strength of twenty-two divisions completed as far as possible to their normal effective ;

"5. Defend at all costs line of the Vistula in case the line held at this moment by Polish armies cannot be maintained." [103]

What was the real meaning of this misbegotten fruit of British-French diplomatic compromise at Hythe? At that time, when the battle was already raging in the Warsaw suburbs, the two Allied countries poured on Poland good advice, and continued to make their assistance dependent on the outcome of the Soviet-Polish negotiations which at that time had not even begun, and although the intentions of the Soviet Government towards Poland were largely known. Lord d'Abernon, who was the best judge of the situation, wrote in this connection :

"The Soviet endeavoured to draw the maximum advantage from what they believed to be their military superiority. They did so with so thin a veneer of pacific intention that no one but a friend with a telescope to his blind eye could have been deceived by it. The whole Middle East was amazed at the apparent simplicity of large sections of public opinion in Western Europe, and their incomprehensible blindness to quite obvious facts."

But it was the second part of the Hythe communiqué which was bound to raise the strongest objections from the Polish point of view. Did the Poles really need to make a public declaration as to

their intention to fight, at a moment when the whole Polish nation
was passing through a patriotic fever following the passionate
appeals of the Council of National Defence? While Pilsudski was
preparing his great strategic plan, conceived against the advice of
General Weygand, Allied statesmen tried to remove Pilsudski
from his post or to make him subservient to foreign military
advisers whose authority in Poland was greatly impaired by the lack
of any assistance on a large scale by the Western Powers. Lord
d'Abernon saw all the implications of such proposals stating that
" any change in the Supreme Command might be dangerous." The
spirit of the Allied recommendations was best summed up by an
official commentary after the Hythe Conference : " The issue must
depend in a great measure upon the Poles themselves and upon
their power, with the assistance indicated(?), to repel the Russian
attack." [104] If so, what was the use of Allied advice?

Labour unrest in Great Britain

Returning to London, Lloyd George was faced with a great
constitutional crisis caused by Labour unrest. We can state now,
in the light of all the evidence produced in this book, that the fears
of British Labour, which brought about this crisis, rested on quite
erroneous assumptions. In fact the British Government, which
assumed the main burden of responsibility as regards the diplomatic
developments connected with the Polish-Soviet war, had been
surrendering one position after another since 11th July, and had
decided to avoid any step which might lead to British-Soviet hostilities. It exerted pressure on the Poles, only uttering ineffectual
threats towards Soviet Russia, which was well aware of the fact
that Poland could not count on any real assistance from the Western
countries. So the conflict which arose at that time between British
Labour and Lloyd George did not concern the substance of the
Polish-Soviet dispute, in spite of all the lip-service given to the
Polish cause by Lloyd George in the course of his conversations
with the Labour leaders, but exclusively constitutional issues,
because the action of Labour meant in fact an encroachment upon
the privileges of the Parliamentary Government in Great Britain.

Reviewing this crisis later, Lenin said :

" The English Mensheviks have always been opposed to Bolshevism and direct revolution, advocating co-operation with the
bourgeoisie. Now the old leaders of the English workers have
changed their mind and while they have in the past been against the
dictatorship of the working-class they pass to our side. ... It is a
great break with the past for the whole English policy, having

the same meaning for England as for us the February (March) Revolution ... the whole British bourgeois press wrote that 'Councils of Action' were 'Soviets.' And it was right because although they did not call themselves Soviets they were in fact exactly the same." [105]

As early as 24th July Ernest Bevin, speaking at a Labour demonstration at Bridgwater, and referring to Russia, said, " The politicians were undecided whether to plunge us into another war or not." If any attempt were made to do so, he hoped every worker and trade unionist would follow the lead of those who were pre- pared to say " no more sacrifices of human life." [106]

" An Appeal to the British Nation " was issued in the first days of August by a group of Labour Party members, signed by George Lansbury, J. R. Clynes, Arthur Henderson, Miss Margaret Bond- field and others, stating that " the war party in this country are using their most supreme efforts to put themselves into the saddle and involve us in a war against Russia and those who might become her Allies, which will drive us over the precipice of bankruptcy, on the edge of which we now stand." Branding the Poles as aggres- sors and imperialists, the appeal concluded with these words :

" We think the workers would be thoroughly justified in refusing labour services in a war which was purely in support of a nation that had attempted conquest, spoliation and self-aggrandisement. ... We have to warn the responsible Government ... that labour in this country will not co-operate in a war as the allies of Poland." [107]

A joint conference of the T.U.C. Parliamentary Committee, the National Executive Committee and the Parliamentary Labour Party was called and met on 9th August " in an atmosphere of acutest tension." The Conference at Hythe alarmed the Labour leaders to the highest degree, as they thought that " Marshal Foch was instruc- ted to draw up plans for large-scale military intervention." We know that was far from being true. The Labour Conference declared that such a war would be " an intolerable crime against humanity."

" It warned the Government that the whole industrial power of the organized workers would be used to defeat any attempt to engineer a conflict between the Allied Powers and Soviet Russia on the issue of Poland and set up a Council of Action to mobilize resistance. ... Bevin was asked to become the organizer and spokesman of the Council of Action." [108]

On 10th August the delegates of the Council of Action, E. Bevin, J. R. Clynes, Colonel Wedgwood and A. A. Purcell, called at 10 Downing Street. We reproduce below some extracts from a detailed account of his interview, as they show best the position adopted by both parties on the Polish issue [109] :

" *The Prime Minister.* I am not going to make any statement, I am going to listen to your statement. The statement I have to make I must make to the House of Commons this afternoon, because I promised to make it to them, and we have not had a Soviet established in this country yet.

"*Mr. Ernest Bevin.* We believe that hidden forces at work, especially in Paris, have been responsible for the prolongation of this terrible conflict with Russia. ... We believe that the hidden forces —these reactionary forces—have been endeavouring to manœuvre the diplomatic situation so as to make Russia appear in the wrong, so as to find excuse to declare war with all the force of the Allies against her. ... We have no hesitation in putting our cards on the table, that if war with Russia is carried on directly in support of Poland or indirectly in support of General Wrangel, there will be a match set to an explosive material the result of which none of us can foresee to-day ...

" *The Prime Minister.* ... does it mean that if the independence of Poland is really menaced, if it is really destroyed, and if Bolshevist Russia does for Poland what their Tsarist predecessors did a century and a half ago, we cannot send a single pair of boots there, otherwise Labour will strike? That is what I want to know.

" *Ernest Bevin.* Our answer is this—that the hypothesis does not hold good, that the independence of Poland is not at stake.

" *The Prime Minister.* How do you know? I do not know now what the conditions are. I think I am entitled to an answer to that question.

" *Ernest Bevin.* The public declarations of Russia up to now in Kamenev's letter, and in all declarations we have seen, is that they are not challenging the independence of Poland.

" *The Prime Minister* asked again whether, if Soviet Russia did what Tsarist Russia did, Labour in this country would not permit the Government to send a single pair of boots to people who were fighting for their liberty?

" *Ernest Bevin.* Labour will consider its position when that occasion arises.

" *The Prime Minister.* Very well, that is quite good enough for me.

" *Ernest Bevin.* But I want to make this perfectly clear, that that condition has not arisen.

" *The Prime Minister.* No. You need not make that clear to me, because *I agree with you. I do not think it has arisen,* but it will arise one way or the other when the terms are known.

" *Ernest Bevin.* But supposing the Polish people themselves agree upon a Constitution which did not suit the Allied Powers?

" *The Prime Minister.* What have we to do with that? That is their business, not ours.

" *Ernest Bevin.* Is it their business?

" *The Prime Minister.* Certainly. What have we to say to that?

I do not care what the Constitution is. If they like to have a Mikado there that is their business.

"*Ernest Bevin.* That is what we wanted to know.

"*The Prime Minister.* Not if it is done by force, you understand ; only if it is done by their choice.

"*Ernest Bevin.* I am talking about their own determination.

"*The Prime Minister.* Certainly. We would have absolutely nothing to say to it, and I have made it absolutely clear."

After the interview Lloyd George sent a letter to Bevin in which he stated, amongst other things, the following :

"I should like, however, to call your attention to the fact that obstacles have apparently been constantly placed by the Russian Soviet authorities in the way of the rapid conclusion of an armistice. Despite the constant efforts of the Polish Government to get into touch with Moscow by wireless, of which we have full information from our representatives in Warsaw, the Russian authorities for days refused to accept the Polish wireless and took no steps to notify the Polish Government that they were ready to receive the Polish peace and armistice delegation in time to open negotiations on the 11th.

"I am sure that you will agree with me in thinking that the prospects of peace between Russia and this country depend on the way in which the Polish peace is made, and I trust that the Labour movement will make it clear to Russian opinion that just as we have pressed for a square deal for Russia, so they also insist on *a square deal for Poland.*" [110]

Was Lloyd George sincere in his declarations about the necessity of a " square deal " for Poland, or were his angry remarks prompted rather by the fear that Labour was stealing his thunder by recommending a policy which he had decided to follow himself—to force Poland to surrender by using his full pressure to make her feel obliged to accept, apparently by her own choice, the Soviet terms which in fact amounted to complete loss of her independence. The events which took place within the next few days gave ample evidence that Lloyd George wished to evade all responsibility for the future destinies of Poland and, considering the Polish cause definitely lost, was unwilling to stake his political future on that issue.

Debate in the House of Commons (10th August)

The most important debate on the Polish-Soviet war took place in the House of Commons on 10th August, in an atmosphere of great tension.[111] The galleries were full, the Duke of York listened from a seat over the clock, and not far from him were the American Ambassador and Messrs. Kamenev and Krassin.

Lloyd George's speech fully displayed his great gifts as a parliamentary debater. In spite of all caustic remarks about Soviet Russia and her system of government, which was bound to please the Right Wing of the Coalition, he reassured all the members by saying that whatever steps might be taken by the Government they would not involve the country in a war with Russia. He began his speech by stating that he was still hopeful of peace although at the same time adding that " the conditions may arise which will render it necessary for the Government to take certain steps." He then abused the Poles for their " attack upon Russia," this time finding no extenuating circumstances and forgetting all that had been said about the conditions which produced this action by members of his own Cabinet (see p. 592). At the time of his speech did Lloyd George know the terms which the Soviet Government was to propose to Poland? As a matter of fact these terms were already known in rough outline on the second day of the Lympne Conference, and their tenor was given by the *Daily Herald*. Many passages from Lloyd George's speech may give rise to the suspicion that he wished to prepare the public opinion of his country to approve of these terms, which he read to the House in winding up the debate. His allusions to the Polish attack on Russia thus served to justify the Soviet terms for armistice, disclosed a few hourse later. " The Soviet Government are entitled in our judgment," he said, " in any conditions of peace to take these two facts in account (Polish attack and warning of the Allies). . . . I mean that they are entitled in any conditions of peace to demand such guarantees as would be exacted by any power against the repetition of an attack of that kind." He made a distinction, however, between " guarantees exacted from a defeated nation against a repetition of an act of aggression and any terms which involve the destruction of the national independence of a people." He stressed once more the " importance of the independence of Poland and its existence as an independent nation, as an essential part of the structure of European peace." Referring to " suspicious delays in the start of the Polish-Soviet negotiations " which he ascribed to a deliberate policy of the Soviet Government, he defined the attitude of the Allied Governments in relation to the Polish-Soviet negotiations which were about to begin at Minsk in the light of the resolutions of the Lympne Conference. " If Poland accepts the terms the Allies will certainly not intervene either to prevent or upset that arrangement. . . . If they negotiate an agreement at Minsk we do not propose to intervene to upset any arrangement which is acceptable to the Poles. It is their affair. I sincerely trust that it will be peace." The failure of the Minsk Conference may be due to two causes, according to Lloyd George : " because the Poles refuse conditions which in the circumstances, having regard to the commencement of the conflict and to the military position, the Soviet are in the judgment of every fair-minded man entitled to exact from them, then the Allies could not support Poland." The other alternative was " supposing the Bolsheviks insist upon terms absolutely inconsistent with the independence and existence of Poland as a free nation, and the Poles reject them and are prepared to fight for their independence, then undoubtedly a very serious situation will arise." Let us dwell for a moment on this second contingency. According to Lloyd George's statement, the judgment on what was incompatible with Poland's independence was left not to the Poles themselves but to the Western statesmen. This left the door open for any arbitrary judgment and the evasion of all responsibility for further developments. In fact, such was Lloyd George's master plan. He kept this card in his hand, and as we shall see he used it when the moment came to state whether the Bolshevik terms were or were not in agreement with Poland's independence. When these terms were disclosed a few hours later, Lloyd George refused to consider them as incompatible with Poland's independence.

By what means was Poland to be assisted in the second alternative? Lloyd George had to refer on this issue to the resolutions of the Lympne Conference, covering himself by his interpretation of the Covenant of the League of Nations. According to Lloyd George's interpretation the Covenant " does not contemplate, necessarily, military action in support of the imperilled nation. It contemplates economic pressure; it contemplates support for the struggling people, and, when it is said that if you give any support at all to Poland it involves a great war with which we have been so painfully acquainted within the last few years, that is inconsistent with the whole theory of the Covenant of the League of Nations." Much could be said about this interpretation of the Covenant of the League of Nations; the experience of sanctions ordered later by the League of Nations in the case of the Italian-Abyssinian war proved, however, that economic sanctions are ineffective unless the Powers taking part in the collective action were ready to face all the consequences which might arise if the aggressor State considered these measures as acts of war. According to a Report by a group of members of the Royal Institute of International Affairs, published in 1938 :

> " The distinction between economic and military sanctions is difficult to draw. A State which is being subjected to economic pressure may think to free itself from strangulation by striking at one of the Powers which is co-operating against it. It is manifestly impossible for the States applying economic sanctions to ascertain beforehand how far it is possible to go without running the

danger, for to desist from applying sanctions at the aggressor's behest at the point at which they are beginning to prove effective is to ensure in advance that economic pressure will fail of its effects." [112]

If Lloyd George thought of such economic sanctions as would not have involved war, it means, consequently, that narrowing the British obligations towards Poland he was ready to desist from them should they meet with military resistance from Soviet Russia. In any case, exactly one month after the Spa Conference the British pledges were considerably watered down, if one keeps in mind the assurances made there that the Allies would assist the Poles " with all means " should the so-called Curzon Line be crossed by Soviet armies. Lloyd George further said that " No Allied troops can be sent to Poland. . . . There are troops at Danzig which will be essential for communications with Poland, but we are sending no Allied troops. We have made it clear to this country. . . . On the assumption that the Bolshevik Government imposes conditions which are incompatible with the notion of freedom and are exclusive . . . the Allies out of the stores at their disposal will help to equip the Polish people for their own defence . . . next the Poles will be supplied with the necessary military advice and guidance . . . the economic pressure . . . by naval action or by international action or by both."

Lloyd George was aware of the fact that such a blockade would require the assistance of other States in order to be effective, and he made an allusion to a possible co-operation of the United States : " America," he said, " was a strong protagonist of Polish independence. No man took such an active and determined, and, I may say, zealous part in setting up Polish independence and the Polish nation as President Wilson." It is necessary to state that before such international action could be undertaken Poland could have been completely overrun by the Soviet Army. All that was said before about the deceptive results of the Lympne Conference holds true in relation to the interpretation of its resolutions by Lloyd George. In fact Poland was left face to face with the Soviet Government without any effective support from her Allies, undergoing double pressure—from Russia and from her friends. The lip-service of Lloyd George to the cause of Polish independence could not deceive anyone. " The Poles are a brave people," he said, " there is no braver people in Europe, they have always made fine soldiers, and some of the greatest military achievements in the history of Europe stand to their credit—but they have got their difficulties." According to Lloyd George's distorted views on Poland these difficulties were due to " the unskilled and very largely unskilled labour of statesmanship in Poland." So it was not the geographical position, not the imperialistic urges of her neighbours, but " the unskilled labour of statesmanship " that caused the vicissitudes of Polish history.

It is interesting to note that Lloyd George's speech met with unanimous approval on both sides of the House, apart from the Labour objections to his criticisms of the Soviet Government, and even the parliamentary correspondent of *The Times* wrote : " The Prime Minister never spoke better than to-day on Poland." [113] The French Press, however, took the opposite view, and almost unanimously criticized this speech. *Le Temps* observed that Mr. Lloyd George preached repentance rather than resistance to the Poles, and asked whether the attitude of the British Government was not likely to encourage the Bolshevists to increase the claims that they would make upon Poland and to redouble their propaganda for world revolution.[114] The French Press also considered that Lloyd George once again showed his hostility towards the Poles by making sarcastic remarks on the policy of that country, and regretted that he condemned Poland on the ground that she had attacked Russia, pointing out that the Bolshevist offensive could not possibly have been prepared in the few weeks which elapsed between the Polish operations in the Ukraine and the offensive of the Red Army.

The fact remains that the Commons approved Lloyd George's policy of non-intervention on the whole, and although the *New Statesman's* comment (14th August) that " not a single voice raised in the debate in favour of Poland " was not quite exact, another of its assertions was quite true, namely that " none was against the policy which Lloyd George announced."

In the first instance the pacifists and advocates of the intervention of the League of Nations were quite satisfied with Lloyd George's statements this time. Mr. Asquith, speaking against " all steps of belligerent kind," observed that " if the negotiations break down the question which of the parties is in the wrong is a question about which obviously there must remain a very great latitude for difference of opinion. It is not a clear-cut thing," and expressed his trust in Soviet sincerity; he referred to the peace treaties recently concluded by Russia with Esthonia, Lithuania and Latvia, and stated that " in none of these treaties they (the Russians) ostensibly interfered in any way either with the independence of the State concerned, or with the form of its government."

Lord Robert Cecil was also satisfied and said : " The course of this Debate has allayed a large part of the anxiety with which, I confess, I entered this House," and observed : " If Russia insists —as she has right, in the circumstances, to insist—on making peace herself, and conducting the negotiations direct with Poland, that is a demand which, in the circumstances, you cannot refuse; and that being so, the less you say about it, until you see what the proposed terms are, the better off you are. It is far better that we should keep ourselves entirely clear ... if that peace really involves the destruction of Poland, that will be the time for intervention."

It was the Labour members, of course, who most abused the Poles and showed once more their inmost belief in the genuinely pacific intentions of Soviet Russia.

Mr. Malone said : " People who have been to Russia know quite well that religion is free in Russia to-day ... it is really rather ludicrous to talk about lack of Christianity in Russia. ... I believe Russia is just as religious and as Christian as we in this country, and probably more so."

Lieutenant-Commander Kenworthy disclosed that he knew the Soviet peace terms (as Lloyd George must have known them at the time he was making his speech), and he said that " if the Poles refuse them through sheer jingoism there will not be one shred of excuse for us continuing a blockade or veiled war against Soviet Russia ... the excuse of defending the integrity and freedom of Poland has gone." In concluding his speech he challenged his opponents, saying, " Not one hon. Member dare stand up here and make a speech in favour of war against the Bolsheviks, not one Member of the Conservative Party, whose feelings are well-known, will support publicly the taking of action against Russia, because they are afraid of their constituents."

Mr. Neil Maclean said : " We have nothing whatever to do with Bolshevik Russia and Poland in their quarrels ... if the Government make any attempt to send munitions, material, or to lend naval assistance to Poland in the fight against Russia, the people of this country will rise against it."

Those members of the House who did not share the views of either pacifist or Labour members limited themselves to criticism of the policy of the Government in the past and of the attitude of Labour towards Soviet Russia. Said Mr. Billing : " We have said to the Bolsheviks that if they did a certain thing—and they did it— we would do a certain thing, but we did not do it." He addressed to the Labour members the following question :

" I ask the Labour Party if they were satisfied that Russia's aims were imperialistic and military, and that she was marching into Poland with the idea of imposing on Poland, as victors can impose upon the vanquished, any form of rule they choose, what would be their position then? Would they still say to the Government ' You must not interfere ' ? Would they wait till the Russians got to

Berlin, or would they wait till they entered the gates of Paris or the Channel ports? "

Another member of the House took a line similar to that of Billing, Lieutenant-Colonel Hurst, but his conclusions hardly agreed with his statements, proving that Lloyd George met no serious opposition from any side of the House. We quote below some striking passages from his speech, because they reflected the state of mind of the moderate section of British public opinion, of which the *New Statesman* (14th August) said not without reason : " Everyone in England wants a settlement and peace."

Lieutenant-Colonel Hurst said, among other things :

" Everyone will welcome the Prime Minister's declaration that no British life should be sacrificed in the struggle between Poland and Russia. At the same time, though, we want peace with honour ; and British honour and British interests are likely bound up with the maintenance of the independence of Poland. ... It is very remarkable that those members of the Independent Liberal Party who have spoken, and who are always such slaves of maxims and catch-words, have no word of praise whatever for the rights and liberties of little nations. ... There are three ways in which it is clear that public opinion on this great subject is at present very uninformed and very unenlightened. ... First of all it is quite obvious that a very large section of society believes that Bolshevism represents a perfect type of democracy. .... Secondly, and this is an even more important point, the Government has come to a decision which happens to be more or less in accord with the views of the spokesmen of organized labour, so far as the maintenance of peace is concerned, and the abstention from sending armed forces to Russia. ... No party in England, no class in England wants war, and if the Government has sought peace and has ensured it, let it be set to the credit of the Government and of the country, and do not let public opinion be misguided to believe that that decision has been come to because the Government has found it necessary to surrender to the spokesman of this uninformed, ill-instructed democracy represented by the Labour Party."

This last remark entirely agrees with what has been said here about Lloyd George's policy, which in fact followed a line parallel to that advocated by Labour. The *New Statesman* was right in observing :

" We do not think it is possible to over-estimate the importance of the action taken by British Labour this week in connection with the Russo-Polish crisis. .... It served, of course, to strengthen Mr. Lloyd George's hand, but ... his personal views on this particular subject are scarcely distinguishable from those of Labour."

Lloyd George's next move brought him still nearer to the standpoint of British Labour. In winding up the debate Lloyd George announced that a document had come into his hands, signed by Kamenev, and he read it out to the House. This document contained the terms of Armistice and Preliminaries of Peace, which were to be submitted to the Polish Delegates at Minsk. At the beginning of his Note Kamenev made the reservation that "these terms may be *supplemented by details of secondary moment.*" As appeared later, the document omitted some important clauses, and this fact provided Lloyd George with a good opportunity to state, after the Polish victory, that he had been deliberately misled by Kamenev. We give below the full text of Kamenev's terms, and beside it that submitted by the Soviet Delegation to the Polish Delegation at Minsk on the 19th August.

After having read out Kamenev's letter, Lloyd George stated that he did not think it would be fair for him, " when the delegates of both sides are meeting, perhaps to-morrow or the day after, to express an opinion which might embarrass the discussion," but he added that " we have given our preliminary impression to the Polish Government. Beyond that I do not think it would be fair to go." At the same time he said that " this creates a new situation." We shall see later that he went much further and his intervention in this matter provoked a wave of indignation in Poland and an acute crisis in French-English relations.

KAMENEV'S LETTER [115]

SOVIET PEACE TERMS AT MINSK [116]

1. The R.S.F.S.R. and the Ukrainian S.S.R. unconditionally recognize the independence of the Polish Republic and solemnly confirm the unconditional right of the Polish people to order their life and to establish the form of their Government at their own discretion.

2. The R.S.F.S.R. and the Ukrainian S.S.R. renounce all indemnities.

4. The final frontier of the independent State of Poland shall in the main be identical with the line indicated in the Note of Lord Curzon of Kedleston of 20th July, but additional

3. The definite frontier of the Polish Republic coincides basically with the line indicated in Lord Curzon's Note of 12th July, with a rectification to the East in Poland's

territory shall be given to Poland on the East in the region of Bialystok and Kholm.

1. The strength of the Polish army shall be reduced to one annual contingent up to 50,000 men and the command and administration of the army to an aggregate of 10,000 men.

2. The demobilization will take place within one month.

3. All arms, over and above such as may be required for the needs of the army as reduced above, as well as *of the Civic militia,* shall be handed over to Soviet Russia and the Ukraine.

4. All war industries shall be demobilized.

favour in the Bialystok and Kholm (Chelm) district.

4. The Polish Republic undertakes to limit all its armed forces without exception to a number not greater than 50,000, composed of only one age group and no more than 10,000 men on the staff and in military administration. *These armed forces are to be supplemented by a civil militia, to be organized among the workers, to maintain order and safeguard the security of the population.*

5. Immediately after signing the armistice agreement and the preliminary peace the Government of the Polish Republic will begin demobilization and carry it through within one month.

6. The Polish Republic will retain only such armaments and military enquipment as are required to meet the needs of the armed forces referred to in Clause 4. All other arms and military equipment until their transfer to the R.S.F.S.R. and the Ukrainian S.S.R. within a month from the signature of the preliminary peace treaty, are at the disposal of the Control Commissions of the R.S.F.S.R. and the Ukrainian S.S.R. *From the arms and equipment thus received the R.S.F.S.R. and Ukrainian S.S.R. will return an appropriate quantity to the militia provided for in Clause 4.*

7. The Polish Republic will cease to manufacture arms and military equipment and will begin to dismantle war

5. No troops or war material shall be allowed to come from abroad.

On the other hand:

1. Parallel with the demobilization, the Russian and Ukrainian troops shall withdraw from the Polish front.

3. The Armistice line shall be *status quo* but not further East than the one indicated in the Note of Lord Curzon of Kedleston of 20th July. The Polish Army shall withdraw to a distance of 20 versts from that line, the zone between the two lines being neutral.

2. Upon the termination of these operations, the number of Russian troops on the Russian front line *shall be considerably reduced and fixed at a figure to be agreed upon.*

industries, and will complete the dismantling within a period to be determined by the mixed commissions.

8. The Polish Republic undertakes not to admit on its own territory and not to receive from Foreign States, organizations and groups, assistance in the form of men, horses, arms and military equipment, and to prohibit on its own territory organizations hostile to the R.S.F.S.R. and the Ukrainian S.S.R. and States allied to them setting themselves up as the Governments of the R.S.F.S.R. and the Ukrainian S.S.R. or parts thereof.

9. Hostilities will cease within 72 hours of the signing of the armistice and the troops of the R.S.F.S.R. and Ukrainian S.S.R. will remain on the line they then occupy, but not to the East of the line indicated in Lord Curzon's Note of 12th July; the *Polish troops will withdraw 50 versts West of the Russian and Ukrainian armies and the area between the two will form a neutral zone in which a Polish civilian administration will be established under the control of mixed commissions and of special trade union commission. The withdrawal of the Polish Army will also be supervised by a mixed commission.*

10. *Pari passu* with the demobilization of the army of the Polish Republic and the transfer of military surplus to the R.S.F.S.R. and the Ukrainian S.S.R., Russia and Ukrainian troops will withdraw to the

7. The families of all Polish citizens killed, wounded or incapacitated in the war shall be given land free.

6. The line Wolkowysk–Bialystok–Grajewo shall be placed at the disposal of Russia for commercial transit from and to the Baltic.

rear, and when Polish demobilization is completed and equipment deposited in the neutral zone, their total number will not exceed 200,000.

11. The Polish Republic undertakes to restore to the districts formerly occupied and now abandoned by their armies, railway stock and communications equipment, cattle and agricultural equipment, finished industrial products and other property and valuables and other structures destroyed or wilfully damaged by its troops.

12. The Polish Republic undertakes to pass legislation for the free division of the land, granting it in the first instance to the families of Polish citizens killed, wounded or incapacitated in the war or as a result of the war.

13. The Polish Republic grants to the R.S.F.S.R. and Ukrainian S.S.R. *unconditional rights of free transit through its territory for passengers and all goods,* and that part of the Wolkowysk – Bialystok – Grajewo railway which passes through Polish territory is to remain in the full possession and at the disposal of the R.S.F.S.R.

14. *The Polish Republic undertakes to proclaim a full political and military amnesty.*

15. *The Polish Republic undertakes immediately on the signature of the preliminary peace treaty to publish the treaty and all the material and documents relating to the war between the Polish Republic and the Russian and Ukrainian Socialist Soviet Republics.*

There are obvious differences between the two texts, which show the best how much one could rely on Kamenev's assurances that there would be additions of " secondary moment only." The new terms produced at Minsk undoubtedly further aggravated the very harsh conditions for peace laid down in Kamenev's letter : the character of the civic militia as the instrument of civil war and Sovietization of Poland became clear enough, the extension of the neutral zone to 50 versts meant that the Polish army had to abandon Warsaw and the most important line of defence on the Vistula river. One wonders for what purpose the Soviet Government introduced these new clauses, the initial terms announced by Kamenev to Lloyd George having been quite sufficient for the complete subjugation of Poland within a few weeks. Seven days separate Kamenev's letter from the final statement of the Soviet peace terms at Minsk. In the meantime it became quite clear that Great Britain would remain passive whatever might be done by the Soviet Government, as British public opinion was opposed to any step which might involve the country in war with Russia. This fact created a sense of complete impunity in Moscow, and the Russian leaders thought there was no longer any need to restrain their actions and that they could speed up the process of subjugating Poland. Consequently they dotted the i's and crossed the t's. The anticipations of the French Press after Lloyd George's speech of 10th August that " the attitude of the British Government was likely to encourage the Bolsheviks to increase their claims " thus came true within a few days. A great part of the responsibility for the Soviet breach of trust which later helped Lloyd George to divert the attention of world opinion from his own capital errors should thus be assumed by the British Prime Minister himself.

Did Kamenev's terms agree with Poland's independence, which according to Lloyd George was " an essential part of the structure of European peace "? There can be no hesitation in answering this question in the negative. The Soviet terms could not be acceptable to a still undefeated nation which a few days later scored a signal victory. Instead of encouraging Polish resistance Lloyd George did everything possible to weaken it, advising the Poles to surrender their country to the Russian invader. Let us quote Lord d'Abernon's words in relation to Kamenev's terms, transmitted from London in order to be forwarded to the Polish Government : " These terms were so extravagant that I cannot conceive any Polish Government taking them into consideration. I should have expected London to have refused them without further parley." [117] But London not only did not refuse to accept these terms but went much further. Lloyd George communicated to Poland Kamenev's armistice proposal and made it quite clear that should Poland not agree to it the British Government would take no further interest in her fate. That was the true sense of the British communication to Warsaw, whatever may have been the interpretation given to it later.

On 14th August an official communiqué published in London through the Press Association announced :

" The statement has been made that Mr. Lloyd George advised the Poles that ' the Russian terms are fair and ought to be accepted.' This is not accurate. The communication addressed to Warsaw was decided upon at a meeting of the Cabinet. It did not advise the Poles to accept the Bolshevist terms. It was only an intimation that if the terms communicated to His Majesty's Government were *bona fide,* the British Government was of opinion that the British people would not approve of a declaration of war—in order to obtain better terms for Poland." [118]

Replying to Chicherin's Note, Balfour stated on behalf of the British Government, in a Note to Chicherin dated 1st September :

" Mr Chicherin is in error in supposing that the British Government ever ' recognized ' that ' the limitation of the Polish army to 50,000 men was just a term of peace.' The British Government never expressed any such opinion. What they said was that this term of peace would not be considered either by the British Government or the British people as a sufficient ground for active intervention." [119]

The impression created in Poland by the British communication was disastrous. Lord d'Abernon notes in his Diary that " it was a disagreeable surprise " both to himself and to the Polish Government. " It fell like a bombshell here. Previous news both from London and Paris had convinced the Poles that they would obtain full support from the West unless reasonable terms were offered with genuine security for execution. ... The fact that any such basis has been thought possible in London has not improved the position of the British section of the Anglo-French Mission."

A dramatic conversation took place in Warsaw between the Polish Minister for Foreign Affairs, Prince Sapieha, and the British Minister.[120] Prince Sapieha declared that Poland would not accept any humiliating conditions and would refuse to disarm. The British advice would not be made known to the Polish Cabinet in order that Great Britain might withdraw from the position stated in the Note. Poland did not need to state publicly that she would defend herself because she was determined to fight tooth and nail even if abandoned by her allies.

Crisis in British–French relations

The British decision also provoked the biggest crisis in Anglo-

French relations since the Versailles Treaty. Paris took the view that the British initiative violated the agreement so laboriously reached at Lympne. The French Government thought that before any of the Allies could advise Poland to accept the terms offered by the Bolsheviks the Allies should consider whether or not they constituted any guarantee for the peace of Europe or for Poland's independence. *The Times* in its editorial of 13th August said :

> " The British Government Note reached Poland at a moment when her last hour efforts were being made to prepare for the defence of Warsaw, and the reports of M. Jusserand (Head of the French Mission) and M. Panafieu (French Minister in Warsaw) show how deplorable is the impression it has made upon the Poles. Lord d'Abernon was as surprised as the rest of his colleagues at the taking of such isolated action, and members of the Inter-Allied Mission sent there to advise their Governments may well wonder why they took the trouble to journey to Warsaw."

The French Minister in Warsaw was instructed to inform the Polish Government that France had decided to grant her unreserved support to Poland in her struggle. The French Government considered that the Soviet conditions for armistice and preliminary peace aimed at the complete annihilation of Poland's independence. At the same time the French Government decided to recognize as *de facto* Government the Government of South Russia (Wrangel), and gave instructions to its representatives in London not to have any relations with Messrs. Kamenev and Krassin. France sent a High Commissioner to General Wrangel's headquarters at Sebastopol and promised him all her material assistance.

British refusal to intervene in the Polish–Soviet War

The decision of the British Government to refuse any assistance to Poland was maintained throughout this whole period until the Polish victory became obvious, and British pressure on Poland found expression in, amongst other things, the closing by Sir Reginald Tower of the port of Danzig to the transit of arms and munitions to Poland. There was no lack of information, however, that the Russians intended to destroy Poland's independence. On 11th August in the Commons Colonel Gretton observed :

> " It was stated that Mr. Kamenev makes the reservation that these terms may be ' supplemented ' by details ' of secondary moment.' Since then there is clear indication in some of the communications in the Press that part of the ' supplementary details ' referred to is that the Polish people will be required to set up a Soviet Government in Warsaw." [121]

But the British Government remained unmoved, being under

constant pressure from the Radical wing and organized Labour. On 14th August the *New Statesman* declared :

> " If the Poles refuse the Russian terms (as published) the British Government will have no alternative but to wash its hands of them and pursue its negotiations with Messrs. Kamenev and Krassin. If the Poles accept, then still more surely these negotiations will go on. The only event that could lead to the breaking of relations with the Bolshevik representatives is the production by Russia at the last moment of fresh terms so onerous that Poland could not be advised to accept them. And that does not seem to be at all likely."

" The Council of Action " addressed the following letter to Lloyd George on 11th August :

> " The Committee of the Council of Action who have been appointed to represent the Labour movement, and who met you as a deputation yesterday, held a meeting this morning and gave careful consideration to the position arising from the published terms of peace from Soviet Russia to Poland. These published terms set forth clearly the point you made yesterday re the independence of Poland, and in view of your declaration of non-interference we now presume that further interference with Russia by the Allies on behalf of Poland or General Wrangel will not be proceeded with." [122]

An Emergency Conference was held on 13th August, in the Central Hall, Westminster, with a concourse of 1,044 delegates, 689 of them representing trade unions and the remainder local Labour parties.

The Chairman, W. Adamson, M.P., Chairman of the Parliamentary Labour Party, quoting various Soviet pronouncements, declared amidst cheers that " the independence of Poland was never at stake."

Ernest Bevin who, according to his biographer, " worked furiously drawing up detailed plans for a nation-wide stoppage of work if the Government persisted in the course of action(?) " [123] stated at the Emergency Conference that " the Russian terms were not only fair, but generous. What was going to be the attitude of the Labour movement if Poland refused the generous peace terms that had been offered? "

J. R. Clynes stated that " in every document since Russia had first to declare her attitude towards Poland, Polish independence had been absolutely guaranteed, and no Government, therefore, should frame its policy on a contrary assumption."

Tom Shaw declared that much as he disliked the Bolshevist

system " the Bolsheviks were immensely superior to our Government in candour, truth and in doing things in the light of day."

One of the resolutions carried by the Emergency Conference stated that " The Conference of Trade Unions and Labour representatives hails with satisfaction the Russian Government's declaration in favour of the complete independence of Poland as set forth in their Peace Terms to Poland, and realizing the gravity of the international situation, pledges itself to resist any and every form of military and naval intervention against the Soviet Government."

The Emergency Conference authorized the Council of Action " to call for any and every form of withdrawal of labour which circumstances may require." [124]

At the last sitting of the Commons, just before the adjournment, on the 16th August,[125] Bonar Law summed up the position of the Government on the Polish-Soviet war. He said that if the terms proposed by Russia did not go beyond what had been published the British Government would not interfere.

> " Nothing would make us interfere, except interference with the internal arrangements of Poland. ... The Soviet Government has stated in the most categorical way that they do not intend to impose such conditions, and only yesterday Mr. Kamenev sent to the Prime Minister a letter in which he said ' the terms submitted by us will not be altered.' ... In these circumstances the British Government will take no action. There will be no occasion to call the House of Commons together."

Asquith praised the policy of the Government in warm words, saying that "the Government have taken a perfectly proper course ... they did, as I understand, clearly indicate to the Soviet Government that if the terms as published be not enlarged, or modified in a sense which points to an ulterior intention to undermine the actual independence of Poland, and Poland chooses to refuse them, she does so on her own responsibility, and this country at any rate will not give her any assistance direct or indirect ... that is a very satisfactory assurance and I take note of it with gratification."

There is no need to say that the Labour members also approved of the policy of the Government and once more showed complete indifference to the fate of Poland. Sexton was the most outspoken of them, saying that the British workers " are not concerned about Russia or Poland. I do not suppose they are concerned for a moment about the independence of Poland. What they are concerned about is that under no circumstances shall this or any other Government compel them to go to war with any country. This is the feeling that has united the Trade Union movement in this country."

Mr. Thomas said : " I agree entirely to the independence of

Poland, but if Poland refuses what this Government has already said would be a reasonable and fair peace, then it is the business of Great Britain ... to have nothing more to do with Poland, but to fully recognize Russia in every respect."

Another Labour member, Spencer, said : " One thing that has been abundantly and amply clear during the whole of this year, and before the year commenced, is the desire of the Soviet Government to maintain the independence of Poland," but he also observed : " If Poland falls there is not a man in this House who can say that some form of Soviet Government will not be established in Poland."

The feelings of the House were best summed up by the Parliamentary correspondent of *The Times* (17th August) : " The House adjourned over the week-end in the hope that our difference with France might be smoothed out and peace made safe for Poland."

General conclusions

Closing our review of the diplomatic developments in the period commencing with the Polish reverses at the end of June and ending with the battle on the Vistula—the outcome of which so much disappointed the friends of Soviet Russia in the West—we must draw some general conclusions from the attitude of the Western Powers to the Polish-Soviet war. The reader is aware that we have dealt above all with the British policy during that period, for one simple reason that the onus of mediation fell on Great Britain and in particular on Lloyd George. The eminent British writer Hilaire Belloc, in his letter to the *New Statesman* dated 31st July, rightly observed : " To desire the destruction of Poland is one thing; to prophesy it is another; to depend on it as a certainty and to base a whole policy on it a third—more dangerously practical in its result than the other two." These words can justly be applied to Lloyd George's whole policy on that issue. The verdict of history can hardly find any extenuating circumstances for Lloyd George's conduct. Let us quote some British judgments of the line adopted by the British Prime Minister in that period. A. L. Kennedy writes in his study *Old Diplomacy and New* :

" Mr. Lloyd George frequently led Poland to expect that British aid would be forthcoming. In his speech in the House of Commons on 21st July he said that ' the Allies had come to the conclusion that steps must be taken to arrest the destruction of Poland.' In reply to Moscow it had been made clear that if the Russians marched on despite a Polish application for an armistice, the Allies would have to assist Poland. ' The Poles need equipment. This France and Britain would supply,' ' Our interests coincide with our duty,' ' We cannot let Poland perish.'

" These words can hardly be called ambiguous. Yet they were empty phrases. When the Polish troops, at the behest of the British Prime Minister at Spa, had receded 125 miles from the position which they originally held ; when the Bolshevist forces had passed, without any question or possibility of doubt over the line beyond which they had been forbidden by the Allies to go ; when the clear case had arisen for intervention, Britain did not intervene. ... As a consequence of our inaction the political credit of Britain suffered grievous depreciation in Central Europe. Mr. Lloyd George would certainly have risked his position if he had definitely assisted Poland ; but the good name of the country is more important than the continuance in office of any particular Prime Minister. ... Having once promised aid, it would have been more statesmanlike to make clear to his countrymen the obligation to intervene, and to Poland that such assistance would only take the form of supplies, equipment, ammunition and stores. More than that the Poles need never have been led to expect : and to make such supply was within the compass of Britain's strength, however exhausted by long effort." [126]

H. Nicolson writes in his biography of Lord Curzon :

" The British Government confined their support to the dispatch of a mission of inquiry. ... Our credit in Central Europe was seriously damaged by these events. The credit of France was justifiably enhanced. We had promised full assistance in certain eventualities and had, when these eventualities occurred, refused to furnish it. ... Those traditions (of British policy) enjoin that Great Britain should neither threaten nor promise in the cases in which her threats or her promises cannot with complete certainty be fulfilled. In the Polish crisis of 1920 there was no such certainty. Great Britain therefore should have indulged in neither threats nor promises. She indulged in both. And both were falsified." [127]

One may see in Lloyd George's policy some traces of the traditions of the Manchester school, which exalted the principle of non-intervention in foreign affairs " putting peace before any other consideration whatsoever ... untrammelled by any considerations of self-interest, prejudice or jealousy of any particular foreign State." [128] But what was perhaps pertinent in other circumstances became quite obsolete in post-war times, when Great Britain could not escape her responsibilities in Europe in view of the danger that a great part of the European continent might otherwise be organized against her.[129] Only the Polish victory on the Vistula saved Great Britain from this danger for the long period of twenty years. Unfortunately, as H. Nicolson rightly observed, the Western democracies, and especially the British Empire, did not at that time possess " an enlightened or continuous will for power." [130]

Lord d'Abernon, who observed events at close quarters from Warsaw, was more aware of it than the Western Governments.

"I hold" [he writes], "that a crushing defeat of the Bolshevik army is not only desirable but is an indispensable condition to any real peace with the Bolsheviks. If without inflicting a military defeat we patch up some kind of trade agreement with Moscow the value of any engagements taken by them will be nil. No agreement will be worth the paper on which it is written. A striking military success is an indispensable preliminary to serious negotiations. Unless their military prestige is shattered their propaganda will undermine the position in many countries of Central Europe." [131]

Many reverses in Lloyd George's policy were due also to his mistaken opinions and prejudices against the Poles, unfortunately rather common at that time in England on account of intense German and Russian propaganda (whether White or Red). In its interesting article entitled "The New Poland," which appeared in the issues of 13th and 14th February, 1920, *The Times* gave an interesting picture of the opinions on Poland which prevailed at that time in England :

"The Poles are classed in England as a romantic and unpractical people, who can never come to complete agreement among themselves about anything, who have never been able to govern themselves properly and never will. They are credited with having the artistic temperament developed to an unusual degree for a whole nation, with being good fighters, good patriots and good conspirators, and those are about all the virtues they are admitted to possess."

Even the immense efforts made by the Poles within the short period since the armistice in building up a great State and organizing a big army, which withstood the Soviet attacks much better than the White Russian armies led by experienced Tsarist generals, brought little change in these opinions about the Poles. Lloyd George, as we know (p. 279), took the view that Poland was "a creation" of the Versailles Treaty, and he gave the Poles little credit for their achievements.

"In between Russia and Germany stands Poland" [wrote *The Times*]. "It was cast by the Entente chiefs for the rôle of barrier-state, and the Poles rose to the occasion to such good purpose that, as though by magic, a State as large as Germany, with a population equal to that of Italy, has arisen out of the ruins of the Russian and Austrian Empires. The whole thing has happened so simply and with *so little effort by the Entente Powers* as to support the primitive theory of the Peace Conference that, to create a State, it is merely necessary to mark out frontiers enclosing a number of persons speaking the same language" [my italics].

Very few Western statesmen had the opportunity to ascertain personally the immense task carried out by the Poles within a short time. Among them this evidence of the late President of the United States, Herbert Hoover, who went twice to Poland during this period in the capacity of Head of the Relief Mission, is particularly noteworthy. In his speech in America, which appeared as an article in the *National Review* in London in April 1920 under the title " Inspiration of Poland," we read the following :

> " It requires but a short review of the situation that existed ten months ago within the present boundaries of Poland, in contrast to its position to-day, to appreciate the gigantic strides that have been made in the making of the great edifice of the independence of Poland. ... Yet, eight months after the arrival of Pilsudski in Warsaw, I found in Poland a vigorous Government ... an army of five hundred thousand well-drilled, well-equipped and spirited troops. ... Poland after ten months was a democracy with a government for the people and by the people, in a country that had no government for one hundred and fifty years but a government of foreign oppressors. Poland to-day must hold the front-line of Europe against Bolshevik invasion. In the midst of her economic misery she must maintain an army of five hundred thousand men, fighting on a front of fifteen hundred miles, as the outpost of Europe. Yet the people of Poland are fired by an emotion of freedom that will carry her over another year of suffering."

But Lloyd George continued to disparage " the labour of statesmanship " in Poland, and instead of encouraging the forces of resistance against Bolshevism in the interest of all Europe, from the beginning of the resumption of military operations between the Poles and the Russians took the view that the Poles would inevitably be beaten and preferred to win the favour of the potential victors, that is to say of the Bolsheviks. General Sir Henry Wilson censured Lloyd George's conduct in these severe words :

> " Lloyd George's foreign policy has been beneath contempt. He has tried, luckily with little success, to make love to Kamenev and Krassin and the Bolsheviks. He fairly carted the Poles during the Bolshevik advance on Warsaw. He has nearly quarrelled with the French. ... He has made enemies of all countries and friends of none." [132]

Lloyd George's policy was criticized at that time even by some members of his Cabinet, as appears from the following account of Sir Henry Wilson :

> " I had two long talks with Winston ; he enumerated the different steps from Prinkipo to to-day when, although pretending to uphold

the integrity of Poland, we did nothing to ensure it and even prevented arms and stores passing through Danzig. The whole thing is
most perplexing and worse, and my often recurring suspicions of
Lloyd George crowd in on me to-night." [133]

The disclosure in August 1920 by the British Government made
public by it after the Bolshevik defeat on the Vistula, referring to
raising funds in Russia for the support of the *Daily Herald* [134] proves
that the pro-Soviet and anti-Polish campaign in Great Britain was
largely subsidized by the Soviet Government. The intercepted telegrams between Litvinov and Chicherin, published by the British
Government, provided sufficient evidence of this fact.   Philip
Snowden in his autobiography recalls the facts relating to this
incident :

"The *Daily Herald* indignantly denied that it had received any
money from Bolshevik sources. However, three weeks later, when
it was known that the police were making inquiries, the *Herald*
came out with a fantastic story that one of its directors, Mr. Francis
Meynell, ' without the knowledge of his colleagues had collected
£75,000 to be held in trust for the Third International and to be
offered to the *Daily Herald* if the need arose.'

"A week later the British Government issued a communiqué
which stated that Mr. Kamenev, the Soviet representative in
London, had informed his Government that £40,000 worth of
diamonds had in fact been sold and that the proceeds had been
paid over to the *Daily Herald*. The communiqué further stated
that the British Government had evidence that the statement that
Mr. Meynell acted on his own initiative was incorrect, and that
Mr. Edgar Lansbury, the son of Mr. George Lansbury, the Editor
of the *Daily Herald,* had, in fact, received part of the notes given
for the jewels. When the transaction could no longer be denied
the Editor of the *Daily Herald* asked his readers if the money
should be accepted. The Trade Unions who were financially
supporting the paper dissociated themselves from the whole affair,
of which they had no knowledge previous to the exposure. What
became of the money has never been cleared up satisfactorily.
The whole transaction was a very sordid business and left a very
bad impression." [135]

It was only after the Polish victory on the Vistula that the British
Government decided to make these disclosures,[136] feeling that it had
regained full freedom of action in relation to foreign agents working
on British soil. After his departure Kamenev was not readmitted to
England. It is well established that he worked in close contact with
the Council of Action and indulged in many acts of interference
with British domestic policy. Speaking about his mission to London
after his return to Russia, in the Bolshoi Theatre in Moscow he

declared quite openly : " At present the bourgeois parliament has by no means the monopoly of power in England. There exists a duality of powers—on one side the Parliament, on the other the Council of Action." [137] The defeat of the Red Army in distant Poland thus helped Great Britain to avoid a grave constitutional and social crisis.

Strangely enough, the City of London also fostered many illusions about Russia, and we have to refer here to all that was said previously about the exaggerated hopes in the revival of trade with Russia and " saving Russia by commerce." It explains the reserved attitude of the Conservative Party in the course of the debates on the Polish-Soviet War in the House of Commons. The *New Statesman* was right when, speaking of the debate on 10th August, it observed : " The City shares, though on different grounds, the views of Labour." It suffices to read all Liberal and some Conservative papers of that time, apart from *The Times* and *Morning Post*, to draw the same conclusions. While Kamenev informed and inspired the Council of Action another member of the delegation, Leonid Krassin, lured the City with bright prospects of big Soviet orders. Mrs. Krassin, in the biography of her husband, writes that in spite of the interruptions in the commercial negotiations the Soviet Delegation was not idle. She writes : " The Delegation contrived, however, during these intervals to establish contacts with the commercial circles of the City with a view to refloating the old Anglo-Russian concerns. It was hoped that they would be able to place orders at once with several firms, such as Vickers, Marconi, Armstrong, etc." [138]

If we pass now to the second Allied Power, France, we have to state that politically France followed the lead of Lloyd George for many weeks.[139] Fearing to disrupt her alliance with Great Britain, and placing the problem of German reparations above all other political considerations, she sacrificed Polish interests until the Boulogne Conference (p. 635) when she became aware that the unfavourable outcome of the Polish-Soviet war might endanger her whole position in Europe. At the Boulogne Conference France for the first time checked Lloyd George's initiative, which would have led to the complete isolation of Poland. But later, at the Lympne Conference, Millerand was not bold enough, and concurred in the drafting of a telegram to Poland which involved interference in Polish domestic policy by the attempt to remove Pilsudski from the Supreme Command of the Polish Army at the time when he was preparing a plan for the offensive against Russia.

It was not until 11th August that France, at the risk of rupturing her alliance with Great Britain, granted her unconditional and full moral and political support to Poland. But at the same time she made a grave mistake in recognizing Wrangel's administration as *de facto* Government, which introduced an unnecessary complication in her relations with Great Britain and made more difficult Anglo-French co-operation on the Polish issue, the only issue which mattered at that moment. In fact, as soon as the Polish campaign was over, in spite of extremely heavy losses on the Polish front, the Soviet armies were able to overcome Wrangel's resistance within a few weeks. On 6th October they broke through the fortified lines at Perekop, and on 31st October the whole of Wrangel's army left Crimea. It proved that Wrangel's forces had no chance whatever of playing any part in the developments in Eastern Europe.

The political and moral assistance of France at the most critical moment undoubtedly constituted a very valuable asset for Poland, who deeply resented her political isolation at a time when she was defending all Europe against the Communist invasion. Unfortunately the material assistance of France was late in coming, being delayed first for administrative reasons, secondly because of the closing of transit through Germany and Czechoslovakia. Moreover France dared not impose her policy on the High Commissioner at Danzig. It was not until 23rd August that the French cruiser *Geydon*, convoying a French steamer loaded with arms and munitions for Poland, disregarded the orders of Sir Reginald Tower prohibiting the unloading of munitions for Poland in Danzig. Thus the French supplies did not reach Poland on a big scale before the Battle of Warsaw. But the political benefits for France arising from the attitude she eventually took were very substantial, and for many years assured to France a very strong political position in Central and Eastern Europe.

What was the attitude to the intricate problems arising from the Polish-Soviet War taken by a Power which had so many times upheld the Polish cause during the Great War and immediately after it, that is to say the United States? After repudiation of the Covenant of the League of Nations and the refusal to ratify the Versailles Treaty, America kept aloof from any political entanglements throughout the world, and limited herself to proclaiming some principles, without taking any steps to enforce them other than by diplomatic Notes. These principles were : non-recognition of the Bolshevik régime, sympathy for the independence of Poland, unity of the former Russian Empire. For the above reasons the United States declined to concur in any policy which would be contrary to these principles, and refused to have anything to do with the proposals put forward by the Spa Conference relating to holding a conference with Russia and the Border States in London. This appears clearly from the dispatch sent by the Secretary of State to the American Ambassador in London (Davis) dated 2nd August [140] :

> " As this Government desires that the integrity of Poland be maintained, it sympathizes with arrangements for a Polish-Russian armistice, but for the present at least it does not see its way clear to take part in plans to extend armistice negotiations so as to bring about a general European Conference involving the recognition of the Bolshevik Government and a settlement of the Russian problem in a way that would almost inevitably be based on a partition of Russia. ... As the Department thinks that a real solution of the actual problem will be delayed and complicated by the dismemberment of Russia, it has been persistent in refusing to recognize the Baltic States as independent States apart from Russia. ... A decision arrived at in any international conference to recognize as independent governments the factions which now exercise some degree of control over territory which was part of Imperial Russia, and to establish their relationship and boundaries, is not advisable and will seriously prejudice the future of Russia and an enduring peace. Dispositions of this sort must prove to be temporary and without doubt would fall when faced by a restored Russia resolved to vindicate its territorial integrity and unity."

The same ideas were developed in a letter addressed by the Acting Secretary of State, dated 23rd August, 1920,[141] in reply to the demand for recognition put forward by Mr. Jonas Vileisis, agent of the Lithuanian Government in Washington, in a Note of 9th August :

> " This Government has held constantly to the belief that Russia —the Russia of 1917—must herself be a party to any readjustments of her frontiers. The American people sympathizes with the desire of non-Russian people along the border for the largest possible measure of self-government, but it believes that any attempt to reach a permanent settlement of the complicated problems involved, without a consultation and cordial consent of a government generally recognized as representing the great Russian people, will be futile. Unless all parties in interest can reach an amicable agreement among themselves there is no hope for permanent tranquillity."

We have previously referred to the evolution of the policy of the United States in relation to the problems of Eastern Europe after the signature of the Versailles Treaty (pp. 414 ff.), and in particular to the Note of the Secretary of State, Colby, to the Italian Ambassador in Washington, Signor Avezzana, dated 10th August, 1920. It clearly appears from that Note that the attitude of the

United States was based on the belief that the Bolshevik régime was bound to collapse sooner or later. No wonder that this policy was applauded by all the reactionary forces of old Russia, whose rôle was finished for ever. It was General Wrangel who on the eve of his final defeat addressed these words of appreciation to Colby, through the special agent of the Department of State in the South of Russia, Admiral McCully [142] :

> " The declaration of policy recently made by the Government of the United States corresponds entirely to the political programme of General Wrangel, both as regards the part dealing with the preservation of the unity and territorial integrity of Russia and as regards the part relative to Poland. General Wrangel already deemed it his duty to express to the Federal Government on that occasion his sincerest appreciation."

The Note of Colby had this unexpected result that it enabled the Soviet Government, which itself so perverted the true meaning of the principle of self-determination, to step forward as a champion of this principle in international relations. In a statement handed to Colby by the Bolshevik agent in America, L. Martens, on the 4th October, 1920, Chicherin had a relatively easy task in refuting the assertions of Colby :

> " Mr. Colby imagines that the other oppressed nationalities of Tsarist Russia were not annexed by force and that the aspirations of the Georgian, Azerbaijanian, Lithuanian, Latvian, Esthonian and Ukrainian peoples for independence in the form of either secession or State sovereignty and federation with Russia are illegal. The discrimination on the part of the American Government in favour of some nationalities as against the others is unintelligible, being probably due to lack of information concerning national conditions in Eastern Europe. ... The Soviet Government unwaveringly upholds the right of national self-determination of the working people of every nationality, including the right of secession and of forming separate States. This is the cornerstone on which it wishes to establish friendly relations with the new border States." [143]

The lack of any comprehension for the national problems in Eastern Europe, due to mistaken analogies with the problems facing the Western hemisphere, also provoked strong protests from the liberated Border States. For instance, we quote this dispatch of Meierovits, Latvian Foreign Minister, of 14th October :

> " The Republics of Esthonia, Latvia and Lithuania have never willingly adhered to the Empire of the Tsars. On the contrary, these States have repeatedly, even lately, manifested by the voice of their constituent assemblies elected on the most democratic

principles of the world their unshakable will to have an independent political existence, and their reintegration by force into the
Russian Empire would be a violation of the natural rights of the
people."

The Latvian Foreign Minister stated, moreover, that the Baltic
States would never willingly accept a federation between them and
Russia, " which would have for its result the oppression and slavery
of the Baltic States." [144]

Colby's Note admitted only three exceptions to the principle of
preserving the territorial status of the Russian Empire of 1917 :
Poland, Finland and Armenia. " This Government," said Colby's
Note, " believes in a united, free and autonomous Polish State, and
the people of the United States are earnestly solicitous for the maintenance of Poland's political independence and territorial integrity.
From this attitude we will never depart, and the policy of this
Government will be directed to the employment of all available
means to render it effectual." But at the same time the American
Government concurred with the views of all those who wished to
confine Poland in the East to the boundaries of the Congress Kingdom, thus leaving the spoils of all three partitions of Poland with
Russia. At this tragic moment for Poland the United States Government showed more preoccupation for the maintenance of the boundaries of the old Russian Empire than for the rights of the peoples
who wanted to free themselves from the Bolshevik oppression.

Under the influence of British policy and the pressure of their own
workers, misled by the slogans of Soviet propaganda, some small
States also concurred in the blockade of Poland, although officially
proclaiming their strict neutrality. For instance, the Belgian Government prohibited not only all export of arms and munitions but also
of food to Poland, and stopped all transit of goods sent to Poland
across Belgian territory.[145]

The attitude of Czechoslovakia, the close neighbour of Poland
and, one might have thought, menaced by the same dangers as
Poland, showed the best the extent to which Czechoslovakia was
infected at that time by the Communist virus. We have spoken
before of the pro-Russian orientation of the Czechoslovak leaders
(pp. 369 ff.). No wonder that the Czechoslovak Government
welcomed Colby's Note. In a Note handed by J. Masaryk, then
Czechoslovak Chargé d'Affaires in Washington (the same Masaryk
who after the Second World War had to pay with his life
for his pro-Russian illusions) we read : " The Czechoslovak
Government agrees with the principles as formulated in this document " and express " the conviction that restored and reunited
Russia will again resume her mighty position among the nations of

the world." The Czechoslovak Government further stated that it had observed " the strictest neutrality in every respect in all present conflicts involving Russia." [146] But in fact the Czechoslovak attitude was far from neutral, because it went far beyond the obligations imposed by neutrality : it concurred in the blockade of Poland by virtually stopping all transit across its territory to Poland, which as we have noted provoked strong indignation among the Western diplomatic observers in Poland (p. 600). In fact, Czechoslovakia was not only pro-Russian but distinctly pro-Bolshevik. Lord d'Abernon summed up his observations on the Czechoslovak attitude in the course of the Polish-Soviet war : " I am convinced that the Czech population, apart from its leaders, is more friendly to the Bolshevists than to the Poles." [147]

On his way to Warsaw Lord d'Abernon stopped at Prague and had a conversation with President Masaryk on 24th July. According to Lord d'Abernon's account :

> " Masaryk not only did consider the capture of Warsaw by the Bolshevik Army a matter of certainty but he warned against organizing any military assistance to the Poles on two grounds : it was certain to be completely ineffective in a military sense, and it was liable to destroy the authority of the Western Powers in the subsequent negotiations for peace. By openly siding with the Poles in their hopeless position we would do them no good and we should do ourselves much harm." [148]

Returning to London after the Polish victory, Lord d'Abernon again stopped at Prague, and on 27th August he had lunch with Masaryk and the principal Ministers. Beneš this time spoke of forming " a group between Czechoslovakia, Serbia and Roumania," and said, " If we add Poland to this we can be indifferent to any attack from the Soviets or from Germany, and we can also keep Hungary quiet." Lord d'Abernon observed : " What a difference victory makes! A month ago the atmosphere was secretly hostile to Poland; to-day exactly the reverse. Had the Anglo-French Mission followed the advice given at Prague in July, we should have abstained from any action at Warsaw." [149]

Summing up, we can say that the Polish victory on the Vistula, the consequences of which assured peace in Europe for nearly twenty years, was won not only without the material assistance of the West but even against the advice and in spite of the blockade imposed by the West.

NOTES

[1] SIR C. E. CALWELL, *Field-Marshal Sir Henry Wilson*, Vol. II, p. 248.
[2] J. STARZEWSKI, *Zarys Dziejow*, p. 71.
[3] *Ibidem*, p. 71.

[4] COUNT SFORZA, *Diplomatic Europe*, p. 21.

[5] H. NICOLSON, *Curzon, The Last Phase*, p. 203.

[6] See *The Times*, 22nd July (from the Warsaw correspondent): " In reference to Eastern Galicia, I learn from one of the principal Polish delegates at Spa that Mr. Lloyd George began by claiming the reopening of the whole question. When it was demonstrated that the question was settled by the Supreme Council in December 1919, and that the inhabitants must not get the impression that no decisions of the Supreme Council are ever final, the British Prime Minister exclaimed that, anyhow, the representatives of Eastern Galicia must be present at the London Conference. They will, therefore, it is presumed, attend in a consultative capacity, but not as contracting parties."

[7] H. NICOLSON, pp. 204 and 207.

[8] COUNT SFORZA, o.c., p. 21.

[9] H. TOMMASINI, o.c., pp. 121-2.

[10] *Ibidem*, p. 120.

[11] W. SWORAKOWSKI. An error regarding Eastern Galicia in Curzon's Note to the Soviet Government. *Journal of Central European Affairs*, Vol. IV, No. 1, April 1944.

[12] The text of this Note was published in all English papers on 15th July.

[13] LORD D'ABERNON, o.c., p. 16.

[14] *Ibidem*, p. 17.

[15] SIR C. E. CALWELL, o.c., Vol. II, p. 253.

[16] *The Times*, 30th July, 1920.

[17] *Parliamentary Debates*, Commons, Vol. 132.

[18] *Ibidem*, Vol. 133.

[19] W. SIKORSKI, o.c., p. 47.

[20] W. WIELHORSKI, o.c., p. 326.

[21] *The Times*, 5th October, 1920.

[22] E. H. CARR, *The Bolshevik Revolution*, p. 314.

[23] English translation of the Note in JANE DEGRAS, o.c., Vol. I, pp. 194 ff.

[24] P. V. SUSLOV, o.c., p. 72.

[25] *Ibidem*, p. 80.

[26] J. DEGRAS, o.c., Vol. I, pp. 189-90.

[27] L. TROTSKY, *Kak vooruzhalas' Revolutsiya*, Vol. II, pp. 157 ff.

[28] KAKURIN-MELIKOV, o.c., p. 210.

[29] *Ibidem*, pp. 206 ff.

[30] SIR C. E. CALWELL, Vol. II, p. 253.

[81] The text appeared in *The Times*, 26th July, 1920.

[82] *Parliamentary Debates*, Commons, Vol. 132.

[33] *The Times*, 26th July, 1920.

[34] M. KUKIEL, *The Polish-Soviet Campaign of 1920*, p. 14.

[35] R. MACHRAY, *The Poland of Pilsudski*, p. 107.

[86] *The Times*, 27th July, 1920. The text of this Note was also read out by Mr. Lloyd George in the House of Commons on 26th July (*Parliamentary Debates*, Commons, Vol. 132).

[37] LORD D'ABERNON, o.c., p. 37.

[38] *Ibidem*, pp. 42-3.

[39] *The Times*, 27th July, 1920.

[40] *The Times*, 30th July.

[41] *The Times*, 28th July.

[42] MRS. PHILIP SNOWDEN, o.c., pp. 83 ff.

[43] *Parliamentary Debates*, Commons, Vol. 132. Cf. *The Times* editorial " The Fate of Poland," 30th July: " This statement does not tally with the news from other sources. . . . Be this as it may, the Prime Minister himself is unable to deny that the armistice is still unsigned, that the advance is still continuing, and that it has already been prosecuted beyond the Polish frontier as laid down at Versailles and as confirmed at Spa."

[44] L. FISCHER, o.c., Vol. I, p. 270. The quotation is from CLARA ZETKIN'S book, *Lenin*.

[45] STALIN, *Sochineniya*, Vol. IV, p. 323.

[46] F. BORKENAU, o.c., p. 194. Cf. TROTSKY *My Life*, p. 457: " Some of our Polish comrades, such as the late J. Marchlewski, weighed the situation very soberly."

[47] The appeal of the Provisional Soviet for Poland to the labouring population of Poland: " The works and mines must be wrested from the hands of the capitalists, speculators and money-lenders, and become the property of the people represented by the Workers' Committees. The land and forests must be handed over as the property of the people and at the direction of the people. The landowners must be driven away, and property managed by poorer peasants. The land committees of the working peasants will remain untouched. . . . When, throughout all Poland, the bloody Government which dragged the country into a criminal war is overthrown, the Soviet of Workers' deputies of the towns and villages will form a Polish Socialist Soviet Republic."

[48] R. FISCHER, o.c., p. 136.

[49] Quoted *Ibidem*, p. 422.

[50] I. DEUTSCHER, o.c., p. 470. Tukhachevsky's definition of the Revolution from without in his lectures at the Military Academy in Moscow. " There can be no doubt that, if we had been able to tear away from the Polish bourgeoisie its army of nobility and middle classes, the revolution of the working classes would have become a reality. And this conflagration would not have stopped at the Polish frontier. Like a wild mountain torrent it would have swept over Western Europe. *The Red Army will never forget this principle of revolution from without.*"

[51] LENIN, *Sochineniya*, Vol. XXV, p. 377.

[52] *Ibidem*, p. 398.

[53] TARACUZIO, o.c., p. 101.

[54] TROTSKY, *My Life*, pp. 457 ff. " Lenin fixed his mind on carrying the war to an end, up to the entry into Warsaw, to help the Polish workers overthrow Pilsudski's Government and seize the power. . . . I demanded an immediate armistice, before the army should grow too exhausted. I was supported, as far as I can remember now, only by

Rykov." TROTSKY, *Stalin*, pp. 327-8. " Although the war with Poland had thus been imposed on the Red Army, the aim of the Soviet Government was not only to repulse the attack, but to carry the Bolshevik Revolution itself into Poland and thus force open a door for Communism into all Europe. ... I was opposed to the march on Warsaw because, considering the weakness of our forces, it could end successfully only on condition of an immediate insurrection in Poland itself and there was absolutely no assurance of that. I have expounded the essence of the conflict in my autobiography."

[55] RUTH FISCHER, o.c., p. 135. SOUVARINE, o.c., p. 246.

[56] TROTSKY, o.c., Vol. II, pp. 164-5.

[57] CHAMBERLIN, o.c., Vol. II, pp. 219 and 303.

[58] LORD D'ABERNON, o.c., p. 245.

[59] Quoted by E. H. CARR, *German-Soviet Relations*, p. 36.

[60] STALIN, o.c., Vol. V, p. 167.

[61] W. CHURCHILL, *The Aftermath*, p. 266.

[62] LORD RIDDELL, o.c., p. 222.

[63] E. H. CARR, o.c., p. 16.

[64] LIONEL KOCHAN, o.c., p. 18.

[65] *Ibidem*, pp. 35-7.

[66] *The Times*, 4th August, 1920.

[67] GEORGE W. F. HALLGARTEN, *General von Seeckt and Russia*, 1920-1922, p, 24.

[68] VON SEECKT, o.c., Vol. II, p. 252.

[69] *Ibidem*, p. 316.

[70] LORD D'ABERNON, o.c., pp. 66-7.

[71] *Ibidem*, p. 27.

[72] *Ibidem*, p. 44.

[73] *The Times*, 7th August.

[74] LORD D'ABERNON, o.c., p. 101-2.

[75] *The Times*, 7th August.

[76] LORD D'ABERNON, o.c., p. 54.

[77] *Ibidem*, p. 102.

[78] *Ibidem*, p. 103.

[79] *The Times*, 11th August.

[80] The Note was read out by Lloyd George in the House of Commons on 5th August, 1920 (*Parliamentary Debates*, Commons, Vol. 132).

[81] *Ibidem*.

[82] LORD D'ABERNON, p. 32.

[83] *Ibidem*, p. 33.

[84] *Ibidem*, p. 43.

[85] TEMPERLEY, o.c., Vol. VI, p. 258.

[86] *The Paris Peace Conference*, Vol. IX, pp. 469, 535, 637, 672, 679.

[87] JOHN BROWN MASON, *The Danzig Dilemma*, p. 118.

[88] IAN F. D. MORROW, o.c., p. 69.

[89] *Ibidem*.

[90] MORROW, MASON and T. BIEROWSKI, *La Ville Libre de Dantzig et la guerre polono-bolchévique de* 1920.

[91] MORROW, p. 71.

[92] HOUSE-SEYMOUR, o.c., p. 82.

[93] Memorandum presented by Mr. Lloyd George on 6th August to Messrs. Kamenev and Krassin, and which was cabled to Moscow:
" 1. That a truce should be declared for ten days from midnight, 9th-10th August, and that orders would be issued from Moscow and Warsaw at that time that the Soviet Army on the Polish front shall halt upon the line on which they then stand, and cease fighting on conditions: (a) That Poland does not take advantage of the cessation of pressure upon her to re-equip her armies or to move troops or munitions of war, and the Soviet armies shall not utilize the interval to strengthen their front; (b) that the Allies shall undertake that during the period between the cessation of hostilities and the signature of peace they will take no steps to send troops to Poland or to supply the Polish armies with any war material; (c) that the Allies will take the necessary steps to arrange for a Russian Soviet representative to be present at Danzig and at any other point of entry into Poland in order to satisfy the Soviet Government that no war material is being supplied to Poland on the understanding that they shall not undertake any form of political propaganda.
" 2. That immediately on the cessation of hostilities Russian and Polish armistice delegates will meet to define the line of demarcation between the Soviet and the Polish armies until the conclusion of an armistice as a preliminary to peace negotiations " (The Times, 9th August, 1920).

[94] SIR C. E. CALWELL, o.c., Vol. II, p. 256.

[95] Ibidem, pp. 256-7.

[96] LENIN, o.c., Vol. XXV, p. 415.

[97] LORD D'ABERNON, o.c., p. 103.

[98] Ibidem, pp. 59-60.

[99] SIR C. E. CALWELL, o.c., Vol. II, p. 257.

[100] Ibidem, p. 258.

[101] The Times, 9th August, 1920.

[102] J. BARDOUX, De Paris à Spa, p. 363.

[103] LORD D'ABERNON, p. 68.

[104] The Times, 10th August.

[105] LENIN, o.c., Vol. XXV, pp. 420-4.

[106] The Times, 26th July.

[107] The Times, 7th August.

[108] FRANCIS WILLIAMS, o.c., pp. 83 ff.

[109] Ibidem, pp. 84 ff. The Times, 11th August.

[110] The Times, 13th August.

[111] Parliamentary Debates, Commons, Vol. 133.

[112] International Sanctions. A report by a group of members of the Royal Institute of International Affairs, p. 18.

[113] The Times, 11th August.

[114] Le Temps, 11th August.

[115] Parliamentary Debates, Commons, Vol. 133.

[116] English translation in JANE DEGRAS, o.c., Vol. I, pp. 201 ff.

[117] LORD D'ABERNON, o.c., pp. 73-4.

[118] *The Times*, 14th August.

[119] *The Times*, 3rd September, 1920.

[120] J. STARZEWSKI, o.c., p. 77.

[121] *Parliamentary Debates*, Commons, Vol. 133.

[122] *The Times*, 12th August.

[123] FRANCIS WILLIAMS, o.c., p. 86.

[124] The account given by *The Times*, 14th August, and FRANCIS WILLIAM'S book.

[125] *Parliamentary Debates*, Commons, Vol. 133.

[126] A. L. KENNEDY, o.c., pp. 333-4.

[127] H. NICOLSON, o.c., pp. 206 ff.

[128] A. A. W. RAMSAY, *Idealism and Foreign Policy*, p. 57.

[129] E. H. CARR, *Conditions of Peace*, p. 200. " Great Britain, for good or evil, is involved in the affairs of Europe ; and those who desire the maintenance of British power must accept the inevitability of British commitments in Europe. An attempt to escape from her responsibilities will now for the first time—a thing which has never been possible before —unite the greater part of the Continent against her."

[130] H. NICOLSON, o.c., p. 4.

[131] LORD D'ABERNON, o.c., p. 73.

[132] SIR C. E. CALWELL, o.c., Vol. II, p. 275.

[133] *Ibidem*, p. 258.

[134] *The Times*, 19th August, 1920.

[135] VISCOUNT PHILIP SNOWDEN, o.c., p. 538.

[136] Cf. Sir Henry Wilson's Diary (CALWELL, o.c., Vol. II, p. 258). " I sent for Sir Basil Thomson ; he told me some curious things. He was publishing in America and in *Le Temps* certain wireless messages which showed the connection between the *Daily Herald* and the Bolsheviks. At a Cabinet meeting it was decided that Curzon should write to Kamenev and say that it appeared that he was carrying on a propaganda, and asking for his reasons. After the Cabinet had gone away Lloyd George sent for Curzon, and put so many conditions on to the letter that finally Curzon said he would not write the letter and did not." It is a convincing proof that only after the Polish victory the British Cabinet took more decisive steps.

[137] LENIN, o.c., Vol. XXV, p. 636 (footnote No. 193).

[138] LUBOV KRASSIN, *Leonid Krassin, His Life and Work*, p. 123.

[139] J. BARDOUX, o.c., p. 300.

[140] *P. R. F. R.*, 1920, Vol. III, pp. 461-2.

[141] *Ibidem*, pp. 658-9.

[142] *Ibidem*, pp. 616 ff.

[143] *Ibidem*, p. 474.

[144] *Ibidem*, pp. 664-6.

[145] J. BARDOUX, o.c., p. 385. " Le 17 juin et le 28 juillet (1920) le Conseil des Ministres belges adoptant, dans le conflit russo-polonais le point de vue britannique, refusait au gouvernement polonais l'autorisa-

tion d'acheter en Belgique des armements et des *vivres* et interdisait tout transit de munition. La décision fut confirmée le 17 août."

146 *P. R. F. R.*, 1920, Vol. III, pp. 472-3.
147 LORD D'ABERNON, o.c., p. 48.
148 *Ibidem*, pp. 20-1.
149 *Ibidem*, pp. 112-13.

CHAPTER VIII

THIRD PHASE IN THE POLISH-SOVIET WAR IN 1920

DEFEAT OF THE SOVIET ARMIES
SETTLEMENT OF THE POLISH EASTERN FRONTIER

" The error in the strategic calculations in the Polish war had great historical consequences. The Poland of Pilsudski came out of the war unexpectedly strengthened. On the contrary, the development of the Polish revolution received a crushing blow. The frontier established by the Riga Treaty cut off the Soviet Republic from Germany, a fact that later was of great importance in the lives of both countries. Lenin, of course, understood better than anyone else the significance of the ' Warsaw ' mistake and returned to it more than once in thought and word."—(TROTSKY, *My Life*, p. 459.)

ON the 6th August Pilsudski issued his historic Order of the Day, establishing the plan for what was called the Warsaw Battle. Pilsudski planned a bold counter-offensive against the left flank of the Soviet Army approaching Warsaw (it reached the Warsaw suburbs on the 13th August). As the bulk of the Polish armies (First and Fifth Armies) had to stand up to the Soviet attacks on Warsaw and under General Sikorski in the North to cover the left flank of the Polish army and participate in a pincers movement in later stages of the offensive only five divisions could be spared for the counter-blow in the South. It was not an easy task to disengage those forces from military operations and to regroup them to the South of the capital on the River Wieprz. However, this task was carried out very efficiently. These five divisions, under the personal command of Pilsudski, had to disrupt the rear of the Soviet army attacking Warsaw. The position arising from these operations was best explained by Pilsudski himself in a Press interview on the 26th August : " The Bolshevists played a hazardous game. They abnormally extended their forces from East to West in the shape of a long sausage. The idea was not bad at all : it might have succeeded. I had to reply to it by taking risks myself. I pushed my divisions from the South to the North-west and North and cut their lines at several places, and the Soviet army was disrupted." [1]   In view of the worsening of the position at Warsaw, Pilsudski decided

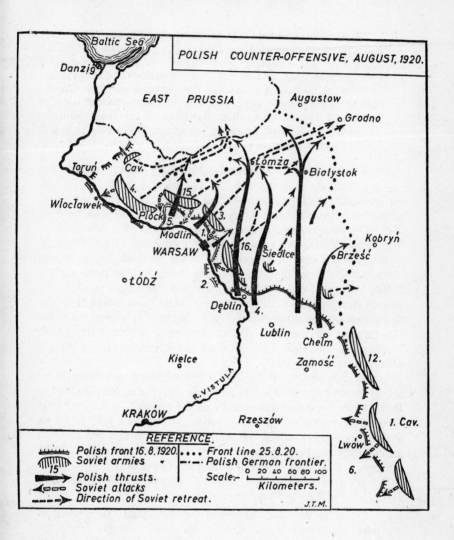

POLISH COUNTER-OFFENSIVE, AUGUST, 1920.

Baltic Sea
Danzig
EAST PRUSSIA
Augustow
o Grodno
Toruń
Cav.
Słomża
Białystok
Włocławek
15
Płock
3.
Modlin
1.
Kobryń
WARSAW
16.
Siedlce
Brześć
ŁÓDŹ
2.
Dęblin
4.
Lublin
3.
Chełm
Zamość
12
Kielce
R. VISTULA
KRAKÓW
Rzeszów
1. Cav.
Lwów
6.

REFERENCE.
Polish front 16.8.1920. •••• Front line 25.8.20.
15 Soviet armies — Polish German frontier.
Polish thrusts. Scale:- 0 20 40 60 80 100
Soviet attacks Kilometers.
Direction of Soviet retreat.
J.T.M.

to advance the date of his counter-stroke by one day, starting it on the 16th August instead of the 17th.

The well-known British military writer, Cyril Falls, says of these operations :

> " The result exceeded his (Pilsudski's) rosiest hopes. The widely spread Russian covering force dispersed and evaporated. Pilsudski thought he was dreaming. Five divisions in all advancing on a hundred-mile front, and virtually no opposition ... the novel and unorthodox methods and ideas of Pilsudski must exercise fascination upon the student. This man was an amateur, a civilian who had learnt what he knew about war from his experience with the ' Legions.' ... He had, however, brought an immensely powerful intellect and an objective mind to bear on its problems." [2]

Field-Marshal W. E. J. Ironside, describing this offensive in the *Encyclopædia Britannica,* states : " The pace of the Polish pursuit was remarkable. From 16th August to 25th August the advanced units of the Second Polish Army had covered 200 miles as the crow flies. The Fourth Army averaged 25 m. a day in their advance. .... The victory of the Poles was due to the adoption of a determined offensive based upon a sound plan." [3] On the 18th August it was already quite clear that the Warsaw Battle had become a great Polish victory. Lord d'Abernon, who on this occasion identified himself entirely with the Poles, writing " *Our* flank attack from the South-east surprised the enemy," was able to send a telegram to his Government on the 19th August informing it that " the Polish counter-offensive against the left flank of the Russian army has completely reversed position." [4]

Let us state first of all that it is well established, as confirmed by all the above-mentioned military writers, that the whole plan for the Battle of Warsaw was due entirely to the Polish C.-in-C., and that General Weygand, whom many people in the West held to be its author, for reasons which we shall state later, in fact put forward a quite different plan, more orthodox and more consonant with the principles of strategy followed during the Great War.

Referring to this question, General Sikorski states in his book *La Campagne Polono-Russe* :

> " General Weygand intervened for the retreat. He advised to establish a fixed front, strong and distant enough, inside the country, enabling considerable reserves to be built up in order to use them on both flanks. General Weygand, like General Henrys, Head of the Permanent French Military Mission in Poland, took the view that our capital was in great danger of being outflanked from the North and advised building up a strong army on our northern flank. The C.-in-C. of the Polish Army, on the contrary,

carried out a plan for a counter-offensive on one flank, using for this purpose the reserves drawn from the right flank of the front." [5]

General Weygand himself, in an interview given to M. Paul Genty, the correspondent of a Paris paper *L'Information,* said in reply to the remark that some Poles proclaimed him the " Saviour of Warsaw ":

> " That is not the case, and I beg you to fix French opinion on that important point. This is a purely Polish victory. The preliminary operations were carried out in accordance with Polish plans by Polish generals. My task, like that of other officers of the French Mission, has been only to make certain suggestions in regard to the details of execution, and in this we have done what we could. But we have done no more, as it is heroic Poland which has saved itself." [6]

Marshal Foch also testified in his preface to General Sikorski's book that the plan for the Battle of Warsaw was Polish. [7]

In his article " The Polish-Soviet Campaign," General Kukiel states : " The conception matured in the mind of the Polish Commander-in-Chief after long and strenuous reflection," [8] and in another article, " General Weygand's Drama," published in a Polish military review *Bellon*a in 1949, drawing parallels between General Weygand's strategic conceptions in the course of the Second World War and those advocated by him in Warsaw in 1920, expounded the differences between the plans of the offensive against the Red Army established by Pilsudski on the one side and by Weygand on the other. [9]

M. Leon Noel, French Ambassador in Warsaw, who made special inquiries on that particular question among the French generals, received from the latter full confirmation of the fact that the plan for the Warsaw Battle was entirely due to the Polish Supreme Command. [10]

Lord d'Abernon, who watched the military operations from Warsaw, expresses a similar opinion :

> " The precise authorship of the Polish plan of defence is not known, but statements made both by Weygand and Pilsudski point to the conclusion that the boldest measures included in the scheme were due to the personal initiative of Pilsudski." [11]

Cyril Falls connects the whole plan of campaign with Pilsudski's strategical conceptions : " The strategy of space." " Use of space," he writes, " had won him earlier victories in White Russia and the Ukraine, it won Tukachevsky his greatest successes, even though he planned to win them by mass; it won Pilsudski his ' crowning mercy ' on the Vistula." [12]

Robert Machray, in his book *The Poland of Pilsudski,* describes in these words the French contribution to the victory : " The Poles gladly recognized the value of Weygand's advice, and particularly his help in organizing the defence of Warsaw; they also admitted that French officers and under-officers assisted them, their real significance being far more moral than material." [13]

If we insist so much on this point it is above all on account of the political implications arising from the allegations that the victory on the Vistula was primarily due to French help and assistance.[14] A psychological factor undoubtedly played a certain part in the assertions that in the occurrence another victory was scored by French generals. One should keep in mind that the prestige of French commanders and the French General Staff was very high after the victorious outcome of the Great War, ascribed mainly to French strategy. The theory fostered by the Left that Poland was but a puppet in French hands (it was even asserted that French colonial troops were used on the Polish front) [15] also contributed greatly to such allegations. Nobody could believe that the Poles could disregard the advice of experienced French generals. In fact there was constant friction between General Weygand and the Polish Headquarters, to which Lord d'Abernon refers often in his book. Marshal Pilsudski also, in his study of the 1920 war, mentions that there was a certain tension in the relations between General Weygand and General Rozwadowski, Chief of the Polish General Staff, who avoided any personal contacts, keeping in touch only by letters.

There was another reason, connected with French domestic policy, which contributed to building up the legend about the decisive influence of French policy and strategy on the outcome of the campaign in 1920. M. Millerand's partisans were advancing his candidature to the post of President of the French Republic, which had become vacant owing to the prolonged illness of M. Deschanel. M. Millerand's credit in the country had suffered greatly on account of his passive attitude from Spa to Boulogne and of his still following the lead of Lloyd George at the Lympne Conference. The Warsaw victory was just the windfall his partisans needed, and in their praise of his statesmanlike and far-sighted attitude in the Polish-Soviet conflict they lost all sense of proportion. *Le Temps* wrote on the eve of the Presidential elections (23rd September) : " In the recent Polish crisis he (M. Millerand) defended almost single-handed the honour of Western Europe." Millerand was elected President of the Republic on the 23rd September. Speaking of this event the Paris correspondent of *The Times* underlines the bearing of the Warsaw victory on his election :

" The triumph of French policy in Poland is a tremendous asset
for M. Millerand. Without that triumph he might have been called
upon to accomplish miracles at Geneva, for the somewhat jingo
majority of the Chamber has been increasingly displeased with the
results of Boulogne, Hythe and Spa. Poland spells glory to French
eyes, and General Weygand has probably been the best possible,
if unconscious, Presidential election agent to an unconscious
candidate, M. Millerand." [16]

To show how far some of Millerand's partisans went in exagger-
ating the part played by him in that occurrence it suffices to
quote the following statements contained in a book written by a
well-known French political writer, M. J. Bardoux : " M. Millerand
will remain as the chief author of this recovery of the Polish front,
of this increase of French prestige and the maintenance of European
peace. . . . By saving Warsaw he saved peace and exalted France." [17]
The Allied Governments were well aware of the fact that by their
passive attitude in that occurrence they had lost many trump cards,
and that their advice to Poland, aiming to influence her military
and political decisions, could not carry much weight with a country
which resented its isolation in a critical period of its existence. There
were very few in the West, therefore, who stated unequivocally that
the Polish victory was won against Allied advice, as was done by
General Radcliff, Director of Military Operations at the War Office.
In his book Lord d'Abernon tells us that " General Radcliff holds
that the Polish Army has won a victory as dramatic as any in
history. All honour to Poland for her achievements, the merit of
which is enhanced by the fact that the battle was fought while the
Polish Government was being urged by more than one friendly
power to accept the conditions offered by the Soviets." [18]
But even Lord d'Abernon, in spite of all his impartiality and
comprehension of Poland's position, one may even say admiration
for the greatness of the Polish efforts, was not quite free from a
feeling that he also had contributed to the Polish victory, and
obviously exaggerated the rôle of the Allied Mission in Warsaw. He
writes : " Had there been no Mission, or had we been unsuccessful
in establishing communication between Warsaw and Dantzig(?), or
again, had we failed to inspire the Polish Government with reliance
on support to be expected from the Western Powers, I have little
doubt that Tukhachevsky's view would have been justified and that
the Polish Army, driven back so far, would have been incapable of
serious resistance and impotent to prevent the Bolshevik troops from
capturing Warsaw." [19] Let us remark, first of all, that the Mission
was unsuccessful in establishing communications between Warsaw
and Danzig before the decisive battle, as we have stated, and

secondly that the Polish nation had the feeling of being abandoned by its Western Allies in spite of the presence of the Allied Mission in Warsaw, because the Allied Governments took no heed of the warnings and requests of the latter. Moreover, on the eve of the Warsaw Battle the British Government stated in unequivocal terms that it washed its hands of the Polish business, while the French assurances of unconditional assistance came very late, namely at the moment when the Polish divisions in the South were already re-grouping for their decisive operations under Pilsudski's command.

The news of the Polish victory on the Vistula was greeted with immense relief by all those who feared the consequences which would inevitably have followed if the Soviet troops had advanced deep into Central Europe, joining hands with the subversive forces in Germany, Czechoslovakia and other countries in which Communist elements awaited that moment to overthrow the " capitalist " governments. Churchill wrote enthusiastically :

> " Warsaw like Paris is saved. The ponderous balances have adjusted themselves to a new decision. Poland, like France, is not to perish but to live. Europe, her liberties and her glory, are not to succumb to Kaiserism and to Communism. ... The frontiers of Asia and the conditions of the Dark Ages had advanced from the Urals to the Pripet Marshes. But there it was written ' so far and no farther '." [20]

Attempts of the Western Powers to stop the advance of Polish Armies

But these feelings were not shared by all to the same extent, in some quarters not being free from a certain anxiety that the Poles might exploit their victory for " imperialistic " purposes.

In the first place it was very natural that those who had asserted since the end of June that the Polish army was non-existent,[21] that a revolution was near in Poland, and that the Russian forces were irresistible, were greatly disappointed by the news from Warsaw. In the beginning they simply refused to believe it. For instance, the New Statesman wrote on 21st August :

> " A flood of telegrams is reporting a great Polish victory. If they were all to be accepted at their face value it would appear that the whole of the Red armies in Poland were in imminent danger of destruction. ... Such things, however, do not happen ... it would be unwise to assume that the Polish victory amounts to much more than the withdrawal of scattered groups of Red cavalry:. ... The French are stated to be bringing all possible moral pressure to bear upon the Poles to induce them to refuse the Russian terms. The saving of Warsaw will undoubtedly reinforce that tendency, and is so far unfortunate. On the other hand, it is impossible to wish that the Polish capital should be handed over to the tender

Western opinion
of Poland...

America's lack
of
support

mercies of the Red soldiery. . . . We do not think that anyone can
any longer entertain any serious doubts as to the sincerity of the
intentions of the Russian Government towards Poland. The President of the Russian delegation at Minsk has declared that all the
discussions of the Conference are to be public, and full permission
for foreign Press correspondents to attend has been given. That
can only mean that the Russians intend to make a good impression
upon the democrats of the world, or, in other terms, that they
intend to negotiate on very generous lines with full respect for the
independence of Poland and with none of the alleged 'secret'
conditions. Nevertheless, the prospects of the Conference do not
at the moment seem to be bright, for if the French can prevent it—
and unfortunately they probably can—the Polish representatives
will not be reasonable. *With such a people, absolutely crushing
defeat seems to be an indispensable preliminary to serious negotiations. The Russians may be obliged to go on until Warsaw falls"*
[my italics].

A week later the *New Statesman* began to correct its views on the
Polish success on the Vistula, but refused to consider the Russian
defeat as final. On 28th August the *New Statesman* stated :

" It is clear that the Poles have won a great victory, that most
of them believe it to be a decisive victory, and that the militarist-
chauvinist elements in Warsaw are seated more firmly than ever
in the saddle. . . . A few days of military success have revived the
old imperialistic dreams. The military recovery of the Russians is
only a question of date. . . . If they can get peace in no other way
the Russians will go to Warsaw . . . these ' hysterical children ' (the
Poles) propose to ' dictate peace ' . . . as it is the war will probably
have to go on until the Russians are once more victorious . . . the
only useful step which the British Government can take—since it
has naturally little influence in victorious Warsaw—seems to be the
immediate recognition of the Russian Government."

Some moves by the American Government, probably in concert
with the British Government, deserve special consideration in the
weeks following the victory on the Vistula. As the Washington
correspondent of *The Times* stated on 22nd August, " the Americans are overjoyed at the turn of events in Poland," but added that
" it would be a mischievous misrepresentation to assert that ' the
Americans would unreservedly support the Poles to whatever
purpose they put their victory '." [22] In fact, the *New York World,*
the chief Wilsonian organ, stated : " There would be no more fool-
hardy policy for the Poles than to make of the present situation an
excuse for seeking to carry the war against Russia to a successful
end. It would be a suicidal project. . . . It should gladly renounce
the career of imperialistic conquest into which it was lured by
fatuous leaders."

In fact, immediately after the Warsaw battle American diplomacy made a move aiming to prevent the Poles from carrying the war " to a successful end." On 21st August the American Chargé d'Affaires in Poland, White, was instructed by the State Department to deliver to the Polish Minister for Foreign Affairs a Note, the most striking passages of which are given below [23] :

" The United States applauds the steadfast gallantry of the Polish Army in the defence of Warsaw and is sympathetic with all necessary measures which Poland may take to preserve its political and territorial integrity." At the same time the American Government advised, however, that " every reasonable effort be made to terminate the present bloodshed." Faithful to its policy of defending the territorial integrity of the old Russian Empire, the American Government took the view that Poland should limit its military operations and territorial claims to what was then called " the Curzon Line," considering any operation carried out beyond that line as an act of aggression against Russia.   " The American Government is of the opinion that the Polish advance into Russia tended to create a national sentiment in that country. ... To prevent a recurrence of the present situation, the United States Government believes that the Polish Government might well take the opportunity afforded by the favourable turn of events to declare its intention to abstain from any aggression against Russian territorial integrity, to state that its policy is not directed against the restoration of a strong and united Russia, and that pending a direct agreement as to its Eastern frontier, Poland will remain within the boundary indicated by the Peace Conference."

The above Note should, of course, be taken in close connection with the previous official announcements of the American policy on Russia referred to above (see pp. 685 ff.).

According to the dispatch of Mr. White,[24] who handed the Note to the Polish Minister for Foreign Affairs on 24th August, the latter " does not acknowledge that the Peace Conference boundary corresponds with the ethnographic frontier of Poland, by reason of the large Polish populations situated East of that line. He indeed notes a strong tendency on the part of Lloyd George to insist that Poland respects it but as in the course of the six weeks which had elapsed since the British Premier had made such a line the basis of an armistice proposal he had neither done anything to cause it to be respected by the Reds nor given aid to the defenders, he had no right to insist that Poland which had triumphed by its own effort should be held to a strict observance."

The reply from the Polish Minister for Foreign Affairs to the said Note from the Department of State, handed by the Polish

Minister, Prince Lubomirski, to the Secretary of State on 30th August,[25] states the main reasons for which Poland was unable to agree with the American point of view :

" Poland desired a just, lasting and equitable peace, and has not altered her attitude in consequence of her recent victory. . . . Peaceful relations between Poland and Russia will be easily established if the real spirit of justice and sound common sense dictates to both the mutual territorial concessions which, based upon the wish of the local populations, the economic necessities and national right, will create a state of things that will render impossible a feeling of suffered wrong and future reclamations.

" The Polish Government, however, has the honour to draw the attention of the United States Government to the circumstance that the provisional Eastern frontier laid down by the Peace Conference has not been respected by the Bolshevik Government. In spite of the diplomatic intervention of our Allies, the Red Army has for a whole month advanced and ravaged territory which is admitted by all as being ethnographically Polish.

" Notwithstanding the sympathetic attitude of our Allies, the Polish nation had to face the danger alone, and political events proved that it must in the first place rely upon its own military strength. If military operations necessitated measures to prevent a renewed invasion of Poland, it could hardly be considered fair that the artificial boundaries that do not bind one opponent should interfere with the military operations of the other."

Military developments in Poland and the reasons stated in the Polish reply induced the U.S. Government to moderate its advice to Poland to keep strictly to the so-called Curzon Line, as appears from the instructions [26] sent by the Acting Secretary of State, Davis, to the Ambassador in France, Wallace (repeated to the American Missions in London, Rome, Berlin and Warsaw) dated 31st August.

" 1. It is clearly understood by the State Department that any just Polish claim to territory East of the line set up by the Supreme Council of the Peace Conference on 8th December, 1919, is not prejudiced by that decision at a time when Russia also can be heard."

But on the other hand the Department of State insisted that " It is the view of this Department that Poland should not try to establish any Civil administration East of the line fixed by the Peace Conference pending the determination in the future of a definite boundary . . . " The Department refused to accept any strategical reasons for the further military operations carried out in what was qualified as " Russian territory ": " It is of especial importance that a veiled excuse for further invasion of Russian territory be not found in a strategic consideration."

It is very interesting to note that the Department continued to insist that the Poles should abstain from occupying Wilno : " It is the special wish of the Department to avoid such Polish-Lithuanian difficulty as might arise if Poland occupied Vilna. The Department believes that the issue of the possession of Vilna in the future ought not to be raised now and should not be prejudiced by occupation of the city by the armed forces of Poland." Since it was well known that the U.S. Government refused to recognize the independence of Lithuania as well as of the other Baltic States, it can be assumed that it reserved that city for a future, indefinite Russia. Apart from the merits of the American requests, with which we shall deal later, it should be noted that these requests were not accompanied by any promises by the United States in the event of the American advice turning out to be inadequate, unrealistic or not corresponding to the Polish security and interests.

This point was put quite unequivocally by the State Department :

" Considering the conditions in which Poland finds itself and the fact that the American Government cannot promise to render Poland material assistance if she should continue to contest, it is the view of the Department that the Poles should adopt any reasonable measures to end the present conflict."

This standpoint of the American Government deprived its policy of the most valuable argument in international policy. Were the Poles to take it for granted that the Americans knew better than themselves what was the best way of ending the conflict with Russia, and that the foreign Powers knew better than themselves the local conditions? It should be remembered that Bonar Law said in the House of Commons on 5th May (see p. 589) : " If we interfere in this matter and stop Poland we take upon ourselves the responsibility of protecting Poland from attack." The U.S. Government was not ready to assume this responsibility at any time in the course of the Polish-Soviet war.

A survey of the military operations after the Warsaw Battle should convince any unbiased student that Poland would have incurred disaster and probably have been finally defeated if she had followed the advice of her friends. In fact, the Warsaw Battle had not yet definitely broken Rusian resistance nor removed any danger of a further Russian offensive. It is true that in the operations called the Warsaw Battle the Poles took 65,000 prisoners, 231 guns, more than a thousand machine guns, 10,000 wagons of ammunition and war material, and that 30,000 Russian soldiers who escaped across the German frontier were disarmed and interned in East

Prussia, Tukhachevsky's total losses amounting to 150,000 men during July-August, but the Third and Fifteenth Bolshevik armies escaped encirclement and were regrouping further East. It was only the general offensive started on 12th September that led to the destruction of the Twelfth and Fourteenth Bolshevik armies and to the reoccupation of the whole of Galicia, Volhynia and Northern Polesye, and the Battle of Niemen—more important even than the Warsaw Battle—which started on 20th September led to the destruction of the Third Soviet Army, being followed by the Battle of Szczara in which the Fifteenth Soviet Army was destroyed : all these battles were fought far beyond the artificial boundary called the Curzon Line. The war correspondent of *The Times*, giving an account of the Battle of Niemen, wrote :

> " The Bolshevik forces had concentrated enormous forces on the North-west Polish front, those defending Grodno consisting of 20 per cent. of Communists. . . . The Polish offensive was merely a forestallment of the Bolshevik offensive. Events have shown that it was started none too early. Delay might have been fatal." [27]

Without all these battles it is hardly imaginable that the Bolsheviks would have agreed so quickly to conclude an armistice and the preliminaries of peace. It was only by bringing the war to a successful end against the warnings of her Western friends that Poland was able to secure peace for herself and all Europe for nearly twenty years. This fact is largely confirmed by different official Soviet statements.

On the 15th October Lenin stated that " the position of the Soviet Republic is extremely difficult, and this has forced us to speed up the conclusion of peace before the winter campaign." [28] In a speech on the 20th November he said that " after brilliant victories we have suffered a tremendous defeat (gromadnoye porazheniye) at Warsaw." [29] But it is in Trotsky's autobiography that we find the most convincing proofs to the effect that only the disruption of the Soviet armies could have brought about the armistice and peace. He writes that " the catastrophe before Warsaw assumed extraordinary proportions," and states the position arising from the defeat in the following terms :

> " Our armies were rolled back four hundred kilometres and more. After the brilliant victories of the days before no one would be reconciled to the situation. On my return from the Wrangel front I found Moscow fostering a second Polish war. Now even Rykov went over to the other camp. ' Once started,' he was saying, ' we must carry it through to the end.' The Command of the Western front was encouraging hope ; sufficient reserves had come up, the artillery had been replenished, and so on and so forth. The

wish was father to the thought. 'What have we on the Western front,' I rejoined. ' Only morally defeated units into which we have now poured raw human dough. One cannot fight with such an army. Or to be more exact, with an army like this, one might be able to engage in defensive operations while retreating and preparing a new army in the rear ; but it would be senseless to think such an army is capable of rousing itself to a victorious advance along a road strewn with its own fragments ' ... Though Lenin formally defended the continuation of the war, this time he did it without his former conviction and insistence. ... He proposed that we put off deciding the question until I could visit the Western front and get a direct impression of the condition of our armies after the retreat. ... The lower I went on the military ladder, from an army to a division, a regiment, a company, the more I realized the impossibility of an offensive war." [30]

We have stated above the reasons for which a purely defensive strategy, as advised by the Western Allies, could not be applied to the Polish-Soviet front (see p. 537). To hold indefinitely a long front line and leave the initiative entirely to the Bolsheviks would inevitably bring disaster to Poland. Had the Poles not advanced beyond the so-called Curzon Line it would have meant that two important key positions, Grodno and Brest-Litovsk would have remained in Russian hands only a short distance from Poland's vital centres. It would also have meant that the Pripet Marshes,[31] the importance of which cannot escape the notice of any student of the geographical features of the Eastern front, would have been left behind the Russian forces, enabling them to strike at Poland from either North or South.

The position of Poland was understood better by the diplomatic representatives of the Western countries in Poland than by their governments. The following report from Gibson to the Secretary of State dated 2nd September best shows the difficult position in which Poland was placed owing to the unreasonable, unrealistic and often discordant advice poured on Poland by the West :

" Prince Sapieha has described to me at considerable length his negotiations with the Bolsheviks and the Powers. The constant inconsistencies and fluctuations of the various Powers in their dealings with Poland would be laughable if they were not tragic in their toll of human life and unhappiness. ... The Chief of Staff, Prime Minister, Minister of Foreign Affairs, my colleagues and others with whom I have talked express complete discouragement at the impossibility of finding a course for Poland to follow which will be agreeable for all her Allies. Everyone connected with the question longs for some concerted policy and I feel that the war weariness and anxiety for peace are such that any reasonable policy could now be enforced. It is, however, impossible to coerce Poland into being reasonable through conflicting advice and in the absence of material support.

"There is a strong feeling that *to stop at the line indicated in your telegram* 363 *(Curzon Line) would be disastrous from a military point of view.* This view is entertained not only by the Polish Government but by the military representatives of the Powers who are acquainted with the actual military conditions. *This line, of course, was never intended as a military line,* but as a basic administrative boundary to the West of which the Poles could set up a permanent administration *without prejudice to further acquisitions in the East.* If it can be considered as a military line all its advantages obviously lie in the hands of the Bolsheviks as they would hold the fortified positions of Brest-Litovsk and Grodno which are carefully excluded from Polish occupation as well as the lateral railroads which are of vital importance. Furthermore, *this line is impossible from a defensive point of view* and if broken the capital would be in imminent danger. General Weygand has recommended that the Poles should occupy the former German line above referred to (running east of Dubno, Pinsk, Nowogrodek, etc.). Military Intelligence Division can furnish details on this line. Weygand advised against the occupation of Wilno as this would make too long a line and would produce a salient difficult to hold. It is evident that any public announcement that the Polish advance would stop at the Curzon Line would be a distinct advantage to the Bolsheviks as it would constitute an assurance that they might withdraw to the East and there unhindered organize a drive for the annihilation of Wrangel, returning at their leisure for a fresh attack on Poland. Even with the forces they now possess they could, if not harassed, organize within a short time to strike the Poles at any given point thereby creating a serious situation and perhaps a renewal of the crisis from which we are now emerging.

"Sapieha stated that in the natural course of military operations it will be probably necessary to disregard the advice not to pass beyond the Curzon Line. He said this without resentment but made it clear that in the opinion of the Government this was a matter of self-preservation." [32]

If we now turn to France, who at the risk of breaking her alliance with Great Britain at the last moment before the Warsaw victory rallied to the Polish cause in the struggle between the Poles and the Bolsheviks, her attitude towards Poland after the victory was not free from contradictions and ambiguity. Like the United States, France stood firmly for the integrity of the Russian Empire believing in the early collapse of the Soviet régime in Russia, as this agreed with her desire for the reappearance of Russia as a great European Power and necessary factor of peace and the balance of power policy.

France did not wish Poland to stand in the way of such a policy in the future, and was ready to sacrifice Poland's interests for such a hypothetical contingency. Millerand gave his full approval to the principles announced in Colby's letter to Signor Avezzana.[33] But France went even further in that direction than did the United States, because she did not wish to await events passively. She put her hopes in Wrangel, whose administration was even recognized by France as a *de facto* Government and who in fact became France's protégé. Consequently she continued to look at East European problems from the old point of view of the French-Russian alliance, and identified herself with the views of the White Russian emigrés enjoying a privileged position at the Quai d'Orsay How unreal and built on sand were these views may appear from the following passage of the declaration of General Weygand, made on the eve of his departure from Poland on 27th August to the Warsaw correspondent of *Le Temps* : " We should not neglect an important and cheering factor. A cautious, sagacious and lucky captain, Wrangel continues his action. He has at his disposal well-disciplined and hardened forces and war material." A few days after the Polish-Russian armistice the forces of this " lucky " captain had hurriedly to evacuate the Crimea, causing many dreams to vanish.

France realized, however, that it would be preposterous to interfere with the Polish-Russian military operations and to ask the Poles not to cross an imaginary line which had never been respected by the Bolsheviks. But the French had no understanding for the particular features of the war in the East, requiring swiftness of action and " open air " strategy. Taking their pattern from the experiences of the Great War in the West, and fearing the political implications of the Polish military operations, the French advised Poland to establish a defensive line along the old Russo-German front of 1915 and to stop there. General Weygand clearly stated his point of view on the plan for future military operations in the above-mentioned declaration to *Le Temps* :

> " The Polish army should continue to advance, but cautiously, and carefully cover the line along which it will pass the winter. . . . From the political point of view the Polish Government, taught by the experience of distant operations, will in my view profit by establishing this line far enough from the capital for the purpose of its protection but not pushing it to the point which might produce new misunderstandings with friendly Powers."

This advice, however, was disregarded by Pilsudski who, as we knew, took the view that only the destruction of the Soviet armies and a complete victory could remove the danger of a further Soviet offensive and bring an armistice and peace settlement with Soviet Russia.

On the other side, the French Government instructed its representatives in Warsaw to call the attention of the Polish Government to the decision taken by the Supreme Council in December 1919, establishing the provisional boundary of Polish civil administration, and took the view that Poland should adhere to it in a general sense, although reserving her right for the future to claim some territories to the East of that line. We do not go into the merits of the French demand, as we have explained the Polish position on this issue many times before. What interests us here is the obvious contradiction between the strategical and political advice given by France to Poland. Did France suggest that Poland should conclude a peace treaty on the basis of the Curzon Line? Let us state first of all that in the French view this line had nothing to do with Eastern Galicia, the fate of which was decided by another decision of the Supreme Council. The mouthpiece of the French Government, *Le Temps,* put it quite clearly in its editorial of 22nd August, stating that " it is well understood that the fate of Eastern Galicia should not be brought again to discussion, as it has been settled by the Supreme Allied Council after toilsome debates." A different point of view prevailed at that time in relation to Wilno Reserving the whole of Lithuania for the future Russian Empire, the French preferred that city to be occupied by the Lithuanians rather than by the Poles.[34] But it was not the wish to defend a small people against its bigger neighbour that carried weight in such a resolution, because by accepting at their face value the pre-war Russian statistics France considered that all territories beyond the Curzon Line were indisputably Russian (Curzon Line—a line based allegedly on statistics*, *Le Temps* asserted at that time).[35] France watched with anxiety the Polish policy of liberation aiming at the recognition of the right of national self-determination of the populations beyond the Curzon Line. In France's opinion Poland should limit her territorial claims in the East in order to concentrate her whole attention on the German problem.[36] To many French people the Polish aspirations in the East were but dreams of expansion, capable of provoking an outburst of Russian nationalism, strengthening the position of Bolshevism.[37] In the French view Bolshevism was a passing phenomenon and French policy should pay no attention to it in pursuing the defence of some principles. In its editorial of 21st August (" Pologne et la Russie ") *Le Temps* gave the following definition of the French policy towards Poland and Russia :

* See the footnote on pp. 441-2.

" Our ideas, either on the reconstruction of Russian integrity or on future relations between Poland and Russia, should not depend on what the Bolshevists might say or do. We have our principles."

But such a purely theoretical approach to the urgent political issues could hardly be maintained in the long run, because it was impossible to disregard the fact that Poland could not take such a detached point of view. It was, however, obvious in 1920 that France wished only a temporary settlement in Eastern Europe, considering that the final solution of all territorial and political questions should be postponed until the moment when a " legitimate " Russian Government, established after the collapse of Bolshevism, might concur in it. The French could not, of course, openly dissuade the Poles from coming to terms with the Bolshevik Government, as they were anxious not to endanger again the Franco-British unity temporarily disrupted after the incident preceding the Warsaw Battle, but they were at the same time afraid that the consequences of anything more than a temporary arrangement between Warsaw and Moscow might be disastrous for General Wrangel. It was this complex situation that prevented the French Government from clearly stating its position on the question of armistice and peace between Poland and Soviet Russia. But they had to depart eventually from their detached attitude. This evolution of the French policy found its best expression in the editorial of *Le Temps* on 21st September, which read as follows :

" What Moscow seeks to obtain is not the peace but a truce. Consequently, whatever may be her wish for peace and sincere desire for a fair settlement, Poland has a duty towards herself and the others to obtain all the guarantees of security that are imperative in view of her geographical position between a revolutionary Russia armed to the teeth and a hostile Germany who has not yet disarmed."

The persistence in France of belief in the early collapse of Bolshevism and the reappearance in Russia of a system of government more acceptable from the Western point of view undoubtedly did much harm to the stabilization of peace in Eastern Europe. It was, in fact, not until 1923 that France, jointly with other Western Powers, recognized the Polish Eastern frontiers, which enabled Poland to play the part assigned to her by her geographical position. Winston Churchill gave the best definition of the rôle of Poland in post-Versailles Europe, arising from the victory on the Vistula :

" The intention of those who framed the Treaty of Versailles had been to create in Poland a living, healthy, vigorous organism which should form a serviceable barrier between Germany and Russia and between Russian Bolshevism—as long as it might last —and the rest of Europe. The ruin and collapse of Poland and its incorporation as a whole in the Russian political group would sweep away this barrier and would bring Russia and Germany into direct and immediate contact." [38]

The historian must wonder at the obstacles Poland's friends put in the way of her becoming "a living, healthy and vigorous organism."

The moral and political position of the British Government after the Polish victory at Warsaw was considerably weakened, as stated above. It turned out that this Government had completely miscalculated the chances of Poland's resistance and was working on the wrong assumption—that Russia was entitled to dictate the conditions of peace to her Western neighbour. On 21st August the London correspondent of *Le Temps* described in the following terms the state of mind in London at that time :

"One has the definite feeling that the Polish victory is beginning to produce its effect here. The political quarters and even British public opinion show now the wish to liberate themselves from a kind of terror exercised upon them by the English Bolsheviks and also from the influence of Kamenev and Krassin. Those closely connected with the Foreign Office begin to see how imprudent it was to take the final victory of Bolshevism for granted." [39]

But at the same time the correspondent of *Le Temps* noted that " all the English papers express the desire that the Poles might conclude the peace with the Bolsheviks as soon as possible."

In order to re-establish unity between the Great Powers and clear himself of the accusation of partiality for the Bolsheviks, Lloyd George interrupted his Swiss holiday and made one of those *volte faces* which astonished world public opinion. Some revision of his policy was, of course, a necessary prerequisite for his regaining the political initiative in Eastern European matters, and one cannot deny that the astute Welsh politician showed in this case a great skill and gifts of an excellent tactician, when necessary ready to abjure the ideas advocated by him only a few days before.

The Lucerne Communiqué

On 22nd and 23rd August Lloyd George had a conference with the Italian Prime Minister, Giolitti, at Lucerne, and the result of these conversations was made known by a communiqué in which the new policy of the British Prime Minister was outlined. [40]

The first part of this communiqué dealt with the necessity for establishing peace in Eastern Europe on the following lines :

"In their conversations to-day and yesterday Signor Giolitti and Mr. Lloyd George discussed the general political situation, and more particularly the bearing thereon of recent events in Eastern Europe.

" This exchange of views has established that complete agreement exists between the British and Italian Governments as to the vital and paramount need for the re-establishment of peace throughout the world at the earliest possible moment.

" The first guarantee of such a peace is to be found in the various Treaties of Peace which have already been signed, and the way in which these Treaties are carried out. The victors in the war should display a spirit of moderation in their enforcement and the vanquished a spirit of loyalty in their execution."

In relation to this part of the communiqué let us observe that it pursued two aims at the same time : first to win the support of France, who could only be pleased by an express reference to the execution of the peace treaties; second, to exhort the Poles not to exploit their victory and to limit their demands.

The following part of the communiqué deals in particular with Eastern Europe :

" Before peace is fully established, however, there remain a number of important questions to be decided, the majority of which are indissolubly connected with the march of events in the territories of the former Russian Empire. Until peace is established between Russia and the rest of the world an atmosphere of disturbance and unsettlement will continue to menace the world. For that reason the British and Italian Governments have been taking steps, *in the face of much misrepresentation,* to restore communication between Russia and the world outside.

" It is, therefore, with profound regret that they have just heard that the Soviet Government have, in spite of their repeated assurances to the contrary, given officially on their behalf by their representative in London, sought to impose on Poland conditions incompatible with national independence. The Government of Poland is based on the choice of the whole adult male population of the country without distinction of class, and this so-called Civil Army to be drawn from one class only which is referred to in the fourth condition of the Soviet terms, is only an indirect method to overthrow by violence the democratic constitution and substitute for it the despotism of a privileged few who may have absorbed the doctrines of Bolshevism.

" We cannot help apprehending that when the detailed conditions of the composition and direction of this force, kept back as they are now until Poland demobilizes her army, are revealed later on they will be found to be moulded on the plan of the Russian Red Army. For one nation to insist as a condition of peace with another that the force organized for the protection of life, property and good order in the latter country shall be drawn only from one class of its citizens to the exclusion of all others, is an unwarranted infringement of the liberty and independence and self-respect of that country. To have added such condition after Mr. Kamenev's pledges to the British Government that nothing which was not of a secondary order was omitted from his summary of the terms is a gross breach of faith, and *negotiation of any kind with a Government which so lightly treats its word becomes difficult, if not impossible.*

" The Soviet Government rejected a suggestion made by the British Government for the making of a truce *under conditions which would have guaranteed Russian territory against any acts of aggression,* and continued its career of invasion of ethnographic Poland with a view of conquering that country by force of arms for Soviet institutions.

" If the Soviet Government, notwithstanding the punishment which its aggression is encountering, still refuses to withdraw this sinister proposal, but continues the war inside Polish territory in order to force its acceptance on the Polish people, no free Government can either acknowledge or deal with the Soviet oligarchy.

" What has befallen in this short war the invaders on national rights, whether in Russia or in Poland, ought to teach wisdom to aggressors. The world, East and West, is crying for peace, but it is only obtainable on the basis of full recognition of the liberties of nations. The British and Italian Governments are alarmed at the indefinite prolongation of the present state of conflict amongst nations. To the people engaged these antagonisms can bring nothing but ever-increasing misery. To the peoples of the world at large they involve continued unrest.

" Until these conflicts cease the betterment of agriculture and industry and the interchanges of commodities of different lands and climates on which the economic life of nations depends cannot come into full operation."

We wish to observe the following in relation to this part of the Lucerne communiqué. First of all, it was rather artificial to establish such a neat distinction between paragraph 4 of the Soviet conditions and the rest; the new wording of paragraph 4 was, of course, a proof of the bad faith of a Government which enjoyed such credit among the British and other Western radicals for its loyalty and honesty, but, as we have seen, the Soviet conditions whether territorial-political or military were unacceptable as a whole from the Polish point of view, as they would have converted Poland into a defence-less and inviable semi-independent State subservient to Moscow. To insist on a change in this paragraph in particular amounted to the admission of all the other conditions as a fair and reasonable basis for a future Russo-Polish settlement.

Secondly, although in spite of his formal pledges Lloyd George did not take any measures to ensure respect for the integrity of what he called " ethnographical Poland," he again appeared as the

champion of the integrity of Russia, obviously considering all terri-
tories beyond the " Curzon Line " as indisputably Russian territory.
He therefore put on the same level the invasion of Poland by the
Red Army in summer 1920 and the military operations of the Polish
Army beyond the " Curzon Line." The parallel drawn by the
Lucerne communiqué between the two " aggressions " shows that
in spite of all his bitter disappointments with the Soviet Govern-
ment Lloyd George continued to advocate the idea of a small
Poland with such frontiers in the East as would make it impossible
for her ever to become " a living, healthy and vigorous organism."

Moreover there was an obvious contradiction between the
assertion of the communiqué that " negotiation of any kind " with
the Soviet Government " becomes difficult if not impossible " and
the urgent demands for an early peace between Poland and Russia,
that is to say a peace without any adequate guarantees for Poland,
preventing her from bringing the military operations then in full
swing to a successful end.

There was only one issue on which Lloyd George seemed to have
totally reversed his policy, namely in the question of the Polish
rights in Danzig. A special communiqué issued on the first day of
the Lucerne Conference dealt with that matter :

> " Mr. Lloyd George and Signor Giolitti have made proposals to
> the French Government for Allied action for the purpose of
> securing Poland her full rights under the Treaty of Versailles, to
> the free use and service, without any restriction, of the port of
> Danzig and its communications as provided by the Treaty of
> Versailles." [41]

It was the irony of fate that it was Lloyd George who, single-
handed, had at the Paris Conference opposed the surrender of
Danzig to Poland and whose nominee, Sir Reginald Tower, at
Danzig prevented the unloading of arms and munitions for Poland
at the most critical hour of the Polish-Soviet war, had to reverse now
his whole policy by taking a rather belated step in the right direction. His move recalls an old French saying, " courir au secours
du vainqueur."

In this connection The Times, in its editorial of 24th August
dealing with the rights of Poland in Danzig, observed :

> " The Danzig compromise was come to against the deliberate
> advice of the experts. It was the irreductible minimum which could
> be offered to Poland, but, such as it is, she should not find it with-
> held in her hour of need. We are only glad to note that Mr. Lloyd
> George, the ' only begetter ' of the arrangement, has agreed with
> Sgr. Giolitti that Allied action be taken for the purpose of securing
> Poland her full rights."

It is interesting to note that at the Press conference at Lucerne Lloyd George laid great emphasis on the decision relating to Danzig :

" In reply to a question whether the use of British troops to disembark munitions for Poland would not be an act of hostility to Russia, the Prime Minister said that the Treaty of Versailles must be carried out, and that it was the business of the Allies to see that Treaty was respected. Poland has an absolute right to freedom and communications through Danzig and Danzig had secured its freedom only on this condition. If the freedom of Danzig interfered with this liberty, it would be the first business of the Allies to see that Poland received her supplies. Whether these were food or munitions made no difference."

Lord d'Abernon in Warsaw received on 25th August a " strong telegram from Lloyd George " in which the latter stated

" that the object of the Treaty of Versailles in this regard (free communications through the Port of Danzig) was to secure to Poland without any restriction the free use and service of the port for Polish imports and exports. The High Commissioner is instructed to do everything possible to secure this. If the Danzig dockers refuse to unload the ships, any suitable labour is to be employed under the protection of the Allied Powers. British and French men-of-war and Allied military forces at Danzig will render all support and if necessary the Allied contingents will be reinforced. The English Admiralty has been instructed to secure the presence of a suitable naval force at Danzig." [42]

In fact, on 27th August a British squadron consisting of two small armoured cruisers and some auxiliary vessels arrived at Danzig, where two other British vessels and two French armoured cruisers had already anchored. The British Ambassador in Washington was able to inform the Secretary of State on 27th August that " an adequate British naval force is being dispatched to Danzig to afford such assistance as may be possible to the High Commissioner with a view to securing Poland's communications with the sea, in accordance with the Article CIV of the Treaty of Versailles." [43]

The American Chargé d'Affaires in Warsaw also informed the Secretary of State on 29th August that " Consul at Danzig telegraphs 25th that as a result of energetic action taken by Great Britain and France ammunition for Poland is being forwarded to its destination by the Free City." [44]

There were some obvious reasons why Lloyd George suddenly made such an unexpected and ostentatious display of his intention to enforce the provisions of the Versailles Treaty relating to the rights of Poland in Danzig. It seems that he wished first of all to liquidate the open conflict with the French in Danzig, where on 23rd August the French cruiser *Guyedon* and a French steamer with munitions for Poland arrived, while Sir Reginald declared that he would not let the *Guyedon* enter the port. Not only the specific Polish rights guaranteed by the Versailles Treaty, but the binding force of the peace treaties was directly challenged by the strange behaviour of Sir Reginald Tower. We know that the French were particularly sensitive on this point. Lloyd George understood perfectly that he had nothing to gain by continuing his quarrel with the French and that only through the re-establishment of the united front with the friends across the channel could Great Britain recover a part of its prestige in Eastern Europe. Moreover there was no chance whatever that the British voice would count for very much in Poland so long as Great Britain continued to tolerate the obvious violation of the Peace Treaty, of which she was one of the principal signatories. British good faith and loyalty could be questioned so long as the authority of international law was not restored in Danzig.

A few days after the Warsaw Battle the Polish Government sent to Danzig the Under-Secretary of State for Foreign Affairs, M. Dabrowski, in order to ascertain the actual state of affairs in that city. In a statement to the correspondent of *The Times* M. Dabrowski summed up his impressions in the following words :

> " The situation which has arisen can be called absurd. Poland, by her supreme efforts, has beaten the enemy at the gate of Warsaw, thus not only saving her national existence but consolidating the Treaty of Versailles ... at this moment Poland's only port, guaranteed to her by the Treaty of Versailles, has been closed to her by German Bolshevists in Danzig." [45]

On 31st August came an Inter-Allied Commission, composed of Sir Maurice Hankey, Lord d'Abernon and M. Jusserand, to make necessary inquiries and recommendations.

The decisions of the Lucerne Conference relating to Polish rights in Danzig can hardly be considered a concession to Poland, but simply the enforcement of the Peace Treaty provisions. But by restoring the legal order in Danzig Lloyd George hoped to be able to exert some pressure on Poland, jointly with France and the United States, in order to induce the Polish Government to " moderate " its terms of peace with Soviet Russia. Consequently the opening of the port of Danzig was to serve as proof of the British readiness to support Poland. This line of conduct is best shown by the editorial of *The Times*, " Duty of the Allies," of 26th August. Abandoning its previous standpoint, sympathizing with the wishes of the Poles to obtain a durable settlement of the problems of Eastern Europe based on the principle of national self-determination, *The Times* took the view that the early conclusion of peace was the most urgent matter and therefore advised the Poles to reduce their claims and show " moderation " in the coming negotiations with Russia.

> " There lies before these statesmen a clear course of conduct " [stated the said editorial of *The Times*], " the sentiment of the peoples they represent will sustain them in the action they have agreed to take in support of Poland. They have the right, and the consent of responsible public opinion, to open for that country (Poland) the door which was promised her at Danzig and to make available for her the material and the expert guidance needed to secure her safety as a nation. In so doing, they will be forwarding the cause of justice and serving the interests of Europe and the world. What is equally important *they will thus establish a claim to be heard by Poland, which should be asserted in the discussion of peace terms*. The people of France, Italy, America and Great Britain have, we feel sure, convictions in this matter which are as reasonable as they are emphatic. Their sympathy goes to Poland in her demand for freedom from interference within her own borders—the ethnographic borders assigned by the Supreme Council. They will help her to help herself in the fight to secure this freedom, but no more. If, in the flush of military success, the Polish Government should formulate demands which go beyond the intentions of the Supreme Council, much of the sympathy which they now enjoy in Allied countries—and on which, in the last resort, they must rely to make their position stable—would be lost." [My italics.]

The Lucerne communiqué was immediately challenged by the Labour Committee of Action, which on 25th August issued a statement [46] saying that " the Lucerne Note must be read as a move in the direction of war and a reactionary policy in which the civic militia is being used as a pretext." The Committee saw nothing extraordinary and menacing to Polish independence in the Soviet proposal relating to the civic militia, and expressed its indignation that " the French Government has definitely advised the Poles to reject the Russian peace terms (the Committee obviously took the wrong view that the Poles had acted exclusively upon French advice in that matter) which the Prime Minister has previously described as reasonable."

The Committee put forward the following requests :

> " The reported refusal by the Poles of the Russian peace terms at once brings Mr. Lloyd George's *bona fide* to a test. Will he apply to the Poles the same peremptory methods which he applied to the Russians(?) when they seemed to transgress beyond what he had stated to be a reasonable policy? Further than this, the Council of Action is convinced that it is necessary to have an immediate

opening of the peace negotiations between Britain and Russia, to cease all support of Poland, and to withdraw at once all British warships from Russian waters."

Uncritically taking all the Soviet statements at their face value, the British Labour Party turned a deaf ear to all arguments coming from the other party, that is to say the Poles, even if they were Polish Socialists. On 31st August the *Daily Herald* published the statement of the Polish cause sent by the Executive Committee of the Polish Socialist Party to the Executive of the Labour Party in which statement the Polish Socialists objected to " many fantastic tales and inexact rumours which had accumulated about the question of Poland." The statement then gave the history of the war with Russia, started by the Red Army which, after the occupation of Wilno in January 1919, advanced " into the former Congress Kingdom, occupying parts of the Sokolka and Bielsk districts which already at that time were formally a recognized part of the Polish Republic." The statement recalled that " the Polish population inhabiting in compact mass the districts of Oszmiana, Wilno, Lida, Troki, Grodno and Wolkowyszki (in the former provinces of Wilno and Grodno) were dissatisfied with the Bolshevik occupation and turned towards Poland with the demand for help." The Polish Socialist Party then laid down its " programme of democratic peace " based on the principle of national self-determination, and expressed its " utmost sympathy with the efforts of the Ukrainian people." It stood for " the solution of the common frontier of Poland, Lithuania, White Ruthenia, Ukraina and Russia on the basis of the self-determination of peoples through freely expressed decision of the peoples interested."

This document in which the Polish Socialist Party, having a long record of the struggle for the rights of the Polish working people against Tsarism, expounded the principles of a democratic peace, was called by the *Daily Herald* " a disingenuous document." In the conflict between the democratic principle of national self-determination as represented by the Polish Socialist Party and the perverted one as carried out in practice by the Soviet Union, the preference of the *Daily Herald* was entirely for the Soviet one. The *Daily Herald* stated emphatically that " Russia . . . has proved in the cases of Esthonia and Latvia, and Lithuania and Georgia and Azerbaijan that it believes not merely in preaching but in practising self-determination." In the editorial entitled " A Reply to the Poles " on 3rd September the *Daily Herald,* by its vile attack on the Polish Socialists, proved that it took its inspiration exclusively from Moscow. According to this editorial the authors of the memorandum of the Polish Socialist Party " are mere agents of Pilsudski. . . .

This party has always voiced the interests of the Nationalists and Imperialist petty bourgeois. It would be absurd to take seriously the Socialism and Democracy of these people. ... When a party whose past and present have been of the character described, attempts to criticize the policy of the Russian workmen and peasants, the result, naturally, shows nothing but hypocritical stupidity."

Even those who are but little conversant with the development of democracy in Poland cannot ignore the enormous part played by the Polish Socialist Party in this respect. The pro-Soviet Labourites only echoed Soviet opinions, and one can find in Lenin's books exactly the same opinions about the Polish Socialist Party as those expressed by the *Daily Herald*. Said Lenin : " The war is carried on by Polish adventurers, S.R.'s, the Polish Socialist Party, men in looking at whom one may best observe the same that one sees among the S.R.'s; revolutionary phraseology, boasting, patriotism, chauvinism, clownery and empty words." [47] It is well known that Bolshevism always considered the democratic socialists their worst enemies because they were backed by the working masses, and Lenin's opinion of the Polish Socialist Party is not surprising. What is surprising is that the members of the British Labour Party allowed themselves to be so infatuated by Bolshevik propaganda.

There was an obvious contradiction between the advice of moderation poured on Poland by Great Britain and the growing tension in Anglo-Russian relations after the Lucerne meeting, as reflected by the attacks of the British Press on the " Minsk treachery " and Bolshevik bad faith, as well as the Notes exchanged at that time between the two Governments. In reply to the Lucerne communiqué, Chicherin addressed a Note to London dated 25th August,[48] in which, recalling that " the British Government has recognized the limitation of the Polish Army to 50,000 as a just term of peace," he presented the armistice clause relating to the civic militia as " a concession to Poland " because the Soviet Government admitted in this way " a supplementary armed force " for Poland. Chicherin ironically observed that " if the British Government indeed thinks that workers must by nature be animated with the doctrines of Bolshevism, such a point of view will undoubtedly be welcomed by those who look forward to the spreading of Bolshevism in Britain." Balfour, who replied to this amazing statement by a Note dated 1st September,[49] denied that the British Government " ever recognized that the limitation of the Polish Army to 50,000 men was a just term of peace," and declared that " to present civic militia as a concession to Poland is a jest and so far neither requires nor deserves a reply."

The revelations concerning Soviet subsidies to the *Daily Herald* through Kamenev, a member of the so-called Soviet Trade Mission, and the proofs that the latter was endeavouring to carry out political propaganda, induced the British Government to inform Kamenev, on the eve of his departure in September to visit Moscow, that he would not be allowed to return to London.

Summing up the attitude of the Allied and Associated Powers towards the Polish-Soviet armistice negotiations, we can state that neither the military nor the political advice given by them was of much help to the Polish Government in its endeavours to find a satisfactory solution of the Polish-Russian conflict. The unity of the Allied and Associated Powers was reconstituted around a purely negative programme,[50] interfering with the Polish counter-offensive and with the carrying out of the programme aiming to secure a durable peace based on mutual compromise and the satisfaction of Poland's vital interests on her Eastern frontier.

The Minsk Conference

The negotiations for the armistice and preliminaries of peace started, as we have said, during the Battle of Warsaw. The Polish delegation under the chairmanship of Dabski left Warsaw for Minsk on the 14th August (see p. 649). The instructions given to this delegation were of the most general nature, considering that the result of the Warsaw Battle could not be known, but in any case the delegation was ordered to reject any humiliating terms, and especially unilateral disarmament of Poland.

The conditions in which this delegation had to work at the beginning prove that the Soviet authorities wished to exert moral pressure on the Polish delegates and to prepare them to agree to peace " by surrender " (as we know, called by Soviet sympathizers in the West " of a most generous kind "). We find a description of these first days at the Minsk Conference in S. Grabski's book [51] :

> " The Bolshevik authorities did not make the Polish delegation's path easy. We only arrived at Minsk on the third day, when the retreat of the Soviet armies had already begun. Everything possible was done to prevent us from learning the result of the battle. We were accommodated in a house with a garden surrounded by a high board-fence. Outside were sentries who did not allow the local population to come into the least contact with us. We were not allowed to go out into the town. We were *de facto* interned. The Russian newspapers which reached Minsk contained no war news at all. We had, indeed, a portable wireless transmitter and receiving set, which we had brought with us for communication with our government in Warsaw. But at the hours appointed for our talks ' atmospherics ' invariably caused such disturbances as to

make communications impossible. But from all this we drew the conclusion that things must be going badly for the Bolsheviks at the front. And five days after our arrival one of our wireless operators succeeded in catching part of a war communiqué broadcast from Warsaw. From it we learned that the Bolshevik armies were in full retreat, having lost hundreds of guns and tens of thousands of prisoners. However, the Bolshevik delegation expected that we should be disheartened by the treatment received on the way to Minsk and after our arrival; so on 19th August, its chairman, Danishevsky, laid before us the draft of a peace treaty which would have made Poland into a political vassal of the Soviet Union.

" The Polish delegation asked for time to prepare its answer. In order to make us still further inclined (as it was thought) to make concessions, the next day, 20th August, a manifesto by General Tukhachevsky, Commander-in-Chief of the Soviet Army, was posted in the streets of Minsk, accusing the Polish delegation of having ' disturbed the peace in the most disgraceful manner. The Polish delegation, composed exclusively of spies and counter-espionage agents, is attempting to utilize its position for purposes of espionage.' To increase the effect of this proclamation the commandant of the local Cheka came to the chairman of the Polish delegation and informed him that he would defend us to the best of his ability against the indignant populace, but doubted whether he would succeed. The same day, however, we got the above-mentioned fragment of the Warsaw broadcast. So at the next meeting of the peace conference our chairman first and foremost lodged a strong protest against General Tukhachevsky's insulting manifesto, and then declared that we absolutely rejected the Soviet proposals, which were designed to destroy the sovereignty of the Polish Republic and impose upon it the unilateral will of the Soviet Union, as though it were victor and Poland vanquished; whereas in point of fact it was the other way round. Having seen that we must know the true state of things at the front, Danishevsky changed his tone, expressed his regret for General Tukhachevsky's tactless procedure, and affirmed that his draft treaty was not final, but merely a basis for discussion."

We complete this account by giving some details relating to the declarations of the chairman of each delegation. Danishevsky in fact produced on 19th August the text of the Russian armistice and peace proposals which we have already analysed; as we know, this text contained many important additions to that published in London and considered by Lloyd George to be a " reasonable " basis for negotiations. Moreover, Danishevsky's declaration contained violent attacks against the Entente Powers and Great Britain in particular. The Soviet Government, he stated, rejected the English offers of mediation because England was an interested party, being a member of the same association of imperialistic powers (League of Nations) as the Polish Republic, and because of the part played by the Entente Powers in preparing and supporting the war policy of the Polish Government of " landlords." [52]

Dabski, chairman of the Polish Delegation, replied on 19th August. He recalled the origins of the Polish-Soviet hostilities and outlined the Polish peace programme in accordance with the principles proclaimed on several occasions in the course of the war by the Polish Government and Diet.

We give below the full text of this declaration, as it explains in the best way the position of the Polish Government as regards the important problems arising between Poland and Russia :

" The Delegation of the Polish Republic has arrived at Minsk for the purpose of fixing the conditions of armistice and of peace, which will put an end to the war between Poland and the Soviet Republic. The war was imposed on Poland when the Government of the Soviets, after having taken at the end of 1918 the lands of Lithuania and White Ruthenia, and after having imposed the Soviet régime on them, directed the troops on to the ethnographic territory of Poland with the clear object of marching on Warsaw and imposing a Soviet régime on Poland against the will of her people. The Polish Republic, menaced in its liberty and its recently won independence, was compelled to resist the Soviet invasion.

" Our troops occupied territories formerly attached to Poland, not with an imperialistic object but in view of the self-determination of peoples. The population of these countries in manifold petitions asked to be reunited to Poland. On his entry into Wilno Marshal Pilsudski announced that the people of Lithuania would decide their own fate. Poland helped Latvia to deliver Dunaburg (Dvinsk), and immediately restored it to the Latvian Republic in conformity with its wishes. The Polish Diet has prepared peace conditions which proclaim the oblivion of the past for Russia and Poland and Russia's renunciation of the Tsar's sanguinary inheritance, and has proposed basing the question of White Ruthenia and Lithuania and the Ukraine on the will of the population.

" When that hope failed Polish troops arrived in the Ukraine and Poland, in the name of the principles above-mentioned, recognized the Ukraine's right to independence and guaranteed her self-determination. The facts above-mentioned clearly prove that the relations between Poland and the other nations have always been based on the principles of the recognition of the rights of all peoples to liberty and self-determination, and also of the dependence of the choice of a régime on the will of the majority of the people.

" The Diet and the Republic of Poland, composed in a great measure of peasants and workmen, which has shown its democratic character by voting the Agrarian Reform Law and the Eight Hours Working Day Law, has given proof of the direction it intends to give Poland's policy. At the commencement of 1919 the Diet published a declaration saying that Poland was making war solely to ensure her liberty and her frontiers.

" As to the purely Russian territories, Poland was not able to apply imperialism to them, for the foot of the Polish soldier never touched Russian soil. The Government of the Soviet Republic acted in the opposite sense ; taking advantage of the weakening of Poland, it invaded purely Polish territories and menaced Warsaw. It published manifestos and proclamations announcing the introduction of the Soviet régime into Poland, notwithstanding the protestations of the Polish population. The Soviet Government did all that, although the fate of the war was not yet decided.

" The Government of Poland sincerely desires peace with the Soviet Republic in the interests of the two nations and of humanity, exhausted by a prolonged war. This peace will be possible and durable if it is just and if it is the result of an agreement between the two nations, in which mutual consideration will be given to the following points: The political and economic interests, the sovereignty and complete independence of the Republic of Poland within *the frontiers indispensable for her political and economic development, the guarantee that Russia will not interfere in the internal questions of Poland ;* such are the principal conditions of our peace terms.

" In the future Poland has no intention of interfering in the internal affairs of other nations, and it fully recognizes the principle that every people has a right to govern itself, according to its desire. In the hope that these principles will be admitted and that a durable, just and honourable peace will result therefrom for both nations, the Polish delegation approaches the negotiations for establishing the armistice conditions and the principles of the peace." [53]

Dabski's declaration stated only some general principles on which in the opinion of the Polish delegation the future peace settlement should rest. It was quite natural that it could go no further, considering that the delegation knew very little about the military operations and, being practically interned, was debarred from any contact with the Warsaw Government. The Soviet Government wished to take full advantage of this position, and by skilful propaganda in the West tried to enlist the support of public opinion in Western countries, representing the Poles as " unreasonable " and obstructing the way to peace. Its endeavours were greatly facilitated by the anti-Polish prejudice which, as we know, was not confined to " fellow-travellers."

The Soviet Trade Mission in London was not inactive, continually communicating to the Press various telegrams from Moscow, giving biased and untrue information about Polish " unreasonableness." At the same time the endeavours of the Mission were directed to minimizing the Polish successes in order to convince public opinion in the West that if the Poles refused to accept the Soviet terms the war would be carried on until the final Soviet victory. For instance, on 24th August several telegrams from Chicherin were issued by Kamenev to the London Press. One of them stated that the Polish delegation at Minsk refused to accept the Soviet terms and that the Polish answer contained only "criticism and nothing resembling positive proposals." [54] The Soviet authorities expressed astonishment that the Poles refused limitation of armaments and that they described the workers' militia as impossible to discuss, like the handing over of the railway Bialystok–Grajewo. Knowing that the Curzon Line had become popular in the West, the Soviet authorities announced indignantly that the Poles refused to accept the Eastern frontier fixed by the Supreme Council, although not long before they had criticized it themselves as being drawn under the influence of Russian reactionary elements. About the Polish successes one of the telegrams from Chicherin stated : "Polish and French wireless spread false news about Polish victories. In reality Russian forces are intact, retreat was executed in full order. Polish radios about great victory are fable." [55] In a Note delivered by Kamenev to Balfour on 8th September we read :

> "It seems as if Mr. Balfour labours under the illusion that a radical change has occurred in the military situation as between Russia and Poland. What has in reality occurred is the unsuccessful result of one particular operation which, at most, means a delay in the attainment of the object of the campaign. ... Our relative strength with regard to Poland is the same as before : it has even altered to our advantage, owing to the reinforcements sent to the front."

This fable of Polish unreasonableness can be observed in many public utterances in the West. Even Winston Churchill, who hailed the victory on the Vistula as the victory of European civilization, was not free from these prejudices, as appears from the following words of his :

> "From the ruins there emerged this prisoner of the eighteenth century, long cut off from light and air, limbs dislocated by the rack, with a nature as gifted, a heart as proud, and *a head as it seemed as impractical as ever*. Adversity had not broken the spirit of Poland ; had it taught her wisdom? " [56] [Our italics.]

Lord d'Abernon in his Diary complains of the persistence of these prejudices in England, which were revived by the negotiations in Minsk :

> "The English papers continue to harbour the delusion that the Poles are not willing to make peace except upon extravagant terms.

This is quite untrue. Even after the astonishing victory of the last few days Poland is not unreasonable, and desires above everything a durable peace safeguarding her independence and giving security.

"All my conversations with Prince Sapieha confirm the view that the Polish authorities will be moderate and sensible as to terms of peace. They are tired of war, and I do not find any of the light-headed aggressiveness which is supposed to be incurable in the Polish national character." [57]

On 22nd August Lord d'Abernon noted in his Diary :

"It looks as though the Poles may capture, destroy or drive the whole Russian force over the German frontier. I have just written to Curzon in this sense, and have added what I feel strongly, namely, my admiration for Polish moderation in the light of so great a success." [58]

It was obvious that at Minsk the Soviet authorities could not for long maintain their unrealistic attitude and claim that the Poles should accept the humiliating terms as if nothing had happened in the meantime. For a few days Danieshevsky continued, nevertheless, to contest the Polish arguments and deliver propaganda speeches. In a declaration of 23rd August Danishevsky asserted that the Soviet régime was introduced in Lithuania, White Ruthenia and elsewhere by the working peoples of those countries, although admitting that "some units of our army co-operated with these young republics at their request." According to him, the Ukraine, White Ruthenia and Latvia had themselves already decided their fate. He thus put on the same level the countries which liberated themselves by fighting against the Russian invaders and the countries subjugated by the Soviet State. According to him it was wrong to compare the policy pursued by R.S.F.S.R. with the Tsarist policy towards Poland. He admitted that the Tsars interfered with the internal policy of Poland, but "the Russian Soviet Republic has abjured such methods and it is unimaginable that being a workers' State it could carry on a similar policy." All these palavers, so reminiscent of the Brest-Litovsk Peace Conference, served no purpose, and the Soviet Government became aware of it. To save the situation they sent to Minsk the well-known Jewish Communist Radek, who was able to ascertain in semi-official conversations that the Poles did not wish to interfere with Russian domestic affairs or to carry on the war indefinitely for the interests of other Powers. Consequently it was decided by common agreement to transfer the negotiations to a neutral country, namely to Riga, where they were to be resumed in mid-September (the first meeting was held on 21st September). Thus closed the Minsk Conference, which showed how Soviet Russia treated the representatives of a country which she considered defeated. " Dirty and disgusted, Messrs. Dabski and Grabski arrived at Brest-Litovsk on 28th August," announced a Reuter telegram giving the account of the bad treatment of the Polish delegation at Minsk.

In order to reassure the world about the peaceful intentions of Poland the Prime Minister, Witos, in a declaration of 26th August stated the reasons for which the Polish delegation had been unable to remain at Minsk. Amongst other things he said :

> " the firm decision of the Polish Government to reach an equitable solution of the conflict with the Bolshevist Government has at no time undergone any change. We did not wage and are not waging war against the Russian nation, we have no desire to appropriate foreign territories ; on the contrary, we consider that friendly relations with the Russian nation are one of the principal conditions for the definite pacification of Eastern Europe.
>
> "These efforts will, however, remain vain if the communications between the Polish Government and its delegation in Minsk continue to be impaired by technical difficulties regarding the exchange of radio-telegrams and the journeys of couriers." [59]

Position of Poland on the eve of the Riga Conference

In spite of continuous military successes on the Eastern front, the general political and economic position of Poland on the eve of the Riga negotiations was extremely difficult. Serious complications were arising in Upper Silesia in connection with the preparations for the plebiscite and the clashes between the Polish population and the German administration. The danger of armed intervention by the Reich seemed quite near, and it was fully warranted, as appears from the information from German sources, published during and after the Second World War. We know that von Seeckt was preparing a plan of military operations with the object of reoccupying Poznan by German troops, while in the West the Germans intended to withdraw behind the River Weser.[60] So the plebiscite in Upper Silesia, which Poland owed to Lloyd George, weighed heavily on Poland, hampering her freedom of movement in the East. The necessity for withdrawing the greater part of the Polish troops from the East (according to the plan of the Polish General Staff, sixteen divisions were to be moved to the Polish-German frontier, only twelve remaining in the East [61]) became every day more urgent.

On the other side the withdrawing Bolshevik troops let the Lithuanians enter the city of Wilno (on 24th August). The Polish Foreign Minister, Sapieha, by a telegram of 31st August [62] requested the Lithuanian Government to withdraw the Lithuanian forces from the Wilno area beyond the demarcation line established by the decision of the Supreme Council of 26th July, 1919 (the so-called Foch Line, see p. 460). The Lithuanian Government refused, and the Allied Powers were not willing to give their support to the Polish request, in spite of its being based on a previous decision of the Supreme Council.

All the implications of the Upper Silesia and Wilno questions will appear in the later period, and I hope to be able to deal with them in another book, but the bearing of these two problems on Polish-Soviet negotiations was considerable.

The position of Poland at the beginning of September 1920 was best described by the American Minister in Poland, Gibson, in his dispatch to the Secretary of State dated 2nd September [63] :

" Polish opinion appears convinced that peace to-day would only be a truce of more or less indefinite duration. Conditions here are such, however, that the Government feels Poland must have such a peace even at the cost of sacrificing Wrangel. The country is exhausted by warfare, her whole energy is being devoted to military operations, many of the civil functions of the Government have practically ceased, and bankruptcy seems inevitable unless the population can soon be returned to productive work."

The Polish Foreign Minister, Sapieha, declared to Gibson that " he assumed the office of Foreign Minister for the avowed purpose of making an early peace," but he " stated, however, that his difficult position has been further weakened by the adoption of restrictions placed upon Poland by the Powers."

" There is a general feeling " [continued Gibson in his dispatch], " not only among radicals but even among the most pro-Ally elements who are trying to keep Poland upon the right path, that the country has had to bear the full brunt of carrying on the war and that far from receiving active help has been actually hampered by her Allies not only as regards the actual fighting but in the various other important questions. The Bolsheviks are offering frontiers far to the East of anything proposed by the Allies, and at Minsk the Bolshevist representative openly jeered at the Poles for their hesitation ; radical elements here are harping upon the fact that Poland was being treated more generously by her enemies than by her friends, that the Allies were doing nothing for Poland and the only evidence of their interest was in the form of restrictions which, if observed, would lead to the annihilation of her independence.'

At the end of this dispatch Gibson added that " we have an exceptional opportunity to secure adjustments which would contribute materially to the maintenance of peace in this part of the world. This opportunity can be exploited only if the Allies promptly formulate *a concerted policy based upon an understanding of the political and military necessities of the situation.*"

This and similar appeals by the Western diplomatic representatives in Poland to their Governments remained without any response however. The Western Governments were unable to formulate a concerted policy based on realities in relation to Eastern Europe; they limited themselves to pure negation : no general peace negotiations with Soviet Russia, much advice to Poland without assuming any responsibility for future developments.

Polish peace programme

Poland therefore had to negotiate armistice and peace with Soviet Russia alone, without any diplomatic support from the Western countries. Having agreed to direct Polish-Soviet negotiations after the refusal of the Soviet Government to attend the London Conference proposed by Lloyd George after Spa, the Allied and Associated Powers had deprived themselves of any right to interfere in the said negotiations when the respective positions of the two partners underwent a radical change thanks to the Polish victories. As a matter of fact, Poland hardly needed counsels of moderation, because although resolute to carry the war to a successful end the Polish Government was prepared to use great restraint in its territorial claims and to reach a peace settlement with Russia by mutual concessions. This meant, firstly, that the plans for assistance to the Ukrainians in their struggle for liberation had to be abandoned, as following these plans would have involved the prolongation of war operations against Russia for an indefinite period, a contingency which had to be excluded, as it would have over-taxed Poland's strength, particularly as no Western assistance could be counted upon for such an endeavour. Secondly, Poland deliberately and spontaneously reduced the extent of her territorial claims upon the lines stated below, although the Bolsheviks, eager to avoid a winter campaign, were prepared for much bigger territorial concessions (especially in the North, in the Minsk area). Such a decision on the part of Poland involved the abandonment of the previous plans for the liberation from Russian domination of those non-Russian populations (including one and a half million Poles) who for centuries have shared the fate of Poland and have lived with her in the shadow of Western civilization, and which were then passing definitely under the most oppressive and tyrannic rule of the Soviet State. The extent of these self-imposed sacrifices by Poland was scarcely realized at that time in the West which, under the influence of Russian propaganda, took the view that Polish claims rested exclusively on obsolete historic titles (one could assert as well that Poland's claim to independence rested on obsolete historic title.

One of the principal Polish negotiators of Riga, the man who

was undoubtedly the author of the Polish territorial programme produced there by the Polish delegation, S. Grabski, whose hostility
towards Pilsudski's programme on the Ukrainian question was noted
above (see pp. 573 ff.), explains in his book the criteria on which the
new Polish territorial programme was based.

> " The Polish frontier Committee " [he says], " considered that if
> the peace treaty concluded by us was to be really a basis for good
> neighbourly relations it should not be the product of a trial of
> strength, or of the exploitation of a temporary military superiority
> of one side or the other, but should embody a reasonable com-
> promise between the actual, permanent, vital interests of both
> parties. Consequently we decided to formulate not several variants
> but a single project for the equitable demarcation of a frontier
> in the territory taken from Poland by the former Russian Empire
> at the time of the three partitions." [64]

Grabski further explains that the Polish frontier Committee took
into account above all the results of the elections to the former
Russian Duma and the national composition of the zemstvas
(Russian local self-government bodies) and municipal councils. The
Committee also based itself on religious criteria, accepting the
principle that " only that part of White Ruthenia should be incorporated in Poland where the Catholic population was in the
majority." In this connection let us remember that one of the first
programmes of Poland's Eastern frontiers, drafted by the American
Peace Delegation, was inspired by similar denominational criteria
(see p. 485). " We were scrupulous," states Grabski, " in counting
only White Ruthenian Catholics in the area in question, so as not to
make up a majority by including Poles, and we did not press for the
incorporation in Poland of even so strong a centre of Polish culture
as Minsk, which always elected Poles to the Duma and to the presidency of the municipal council." Summing up, Grabski recalls that
in the territories included into Poland by virtue of this programme
" according to the census of 1931 there were 2,090,000 Catholics
and 1,690,000 Orthodox in the voievodships of Bialystok, Wilno
and Nowogrodek. ... Russia could not put forward any serious
claim, political or religious, to this territory, which embraced 78,000
sq. kilometres and had a population of 3,686,000 in 1931. For the
seventeen members by which it was represented in the Duma, the
Russians, at the only free elections in 1906, elected only three. And
according to the official Russian statistics the Russian language was
used in daily life by scarcely 5 per cent. of the population of the
government of Wilno; by 5·08 per cent. of that of Grodno; and by
4·39 per cent. of that of Minsk." So far as the South-eastern border
of Poland was concerned, the Polish delegation decided not to push

" the southernmost sector of the frontier further East than the old frontier of Galicia, which had belonged to Poland from the middle of the fourteenth century and had never belonged to Russia."

The primary condition of security for Poland was the linking of the two above-mentioned areas in the North and in the South by a defensive line running from the North-eastern corner of Eastern Galicia to the part of White Ruthenia claimed by Poland (railway line Brody–Rowno–Sarny–Luniniec–Baranowicze, with a security strip sixty to seventy kilometres wide).

Thus, in spite of the complete defeat of the Russian armies, Poland put forward a programme which can be considered the strict minimum required by her vital national and defensive interests.

Grabski was right in stating that " The Polish delegation did not make its territorial claims dependent on the development of military operations. And there was no difference over this question between the representatives of the six parliamentary parties and the representatives of the High Command." [65]

Pilsudski himself realized the necessity for taking into account the crisis through which the Polish nation was passing after the bitter experiences of summer 1920. In his lecture on the problem of Wilno delivered on the 24th August, 1923, Pilsudski said in this connection :

" The Bolshevik invasion of Poland ended by their great defeat. The Bolshevik army was so disrupted that I met practically no military obstacle in reaching whichever line I might have wished. But I was stopped then in the advance by the lack of moral strength of the nation. So the Riga negotiations started." [66]

It is hardly necessary to stress the importance of the factor of the moral and political isolation of Poland in her lonely struggle against Soviet Russia. The blockade imposed on Poland by the West, even in the purely defensive phase of the war with Soviet Russia, had a great demoralizing effect on the Polish people. Consequently Pilsudski took the view that the future frontiers with Russia should be established in such a way as would secure Poland the best possible conditions for defence. About this time he said to one of his close friends (with special reference to the abandonment of Minsk) : " I do not wish any debatable frontier questions in the future between us and Russia." [67] This point should be particularly noted, because it meant that Poland henceforth passed to a purely defensive position in relation to Soviet Russia. She remained in this position until the outbreak of the Second World War, refusing to be associated in any plans aiming at the upheaval of the territorial status of Eastern Europe as established by the Riga Treaty. Thus Poland became a stabilizing factor of peace in Eastern Europe, incurring the hostility of all those forces in Central and Eastern Europe which aimed at a general upheaval and followed the policy of territorial and political expansion.

The Riga Peace Conference

It is beyond the scope of this book to give a detailed account of the negotiations between Poland and Russia at Riga, the first stage of which ended by the signature of armistice and the preliminaries of peace on 12th October in that city. The final peace treaty was signed on the 18th March, 1921. I shall limit myself to some points illustrating the respective positions of the contracting parties and the attitude of the Western Powers towards these negotiations.

Let us remember once more that Poland started these negotiations without having secured the firm diplomatic and moral support of the Western Governments, which were more preoccupied about safeguarding the interests of the future Russia than about the satisfaction of the legitimate claims of Poland to such terms of peace as might create the conditions for her survival as a really independent State between Germany and Russia. There is no doubt that such an attitude on the part of the Western countries considerably strengthened the position of the Soviet delegation, and might have rendered the conclusion of peace impossible if the Soviet armies had not been utterly defeated.

On the eve of these negotiations Pilsudski referred to this ambiguous attitude of the Western countries in an interview granted to *Le Temps* (15th September) : " I am under the impression that the Soviet delegates will be adamant on all territorial, political and economic issues. You see, they have many reasons to consider themselves authorized to put excessive conditions." The extent to which the pro-Soviet wing in the West upheld the Russian standpoint appears from the following assertions of the *New Statesman,* disappointed in its hopes for a final Russian victory (18th September) :

> " The Riga negotiations are about to open under none too favourable auspices.
> " The Poles, it is evident, are only taking the negotiations seriously at all under pressure from their Western friends, and they will probably seek to prolong them indefinitely—unless the impending Russian counter-offensive is extremely successful, which is not very likely. Russia, it is reported, intends on the partial disarmament of the Poles—as in common prudence she obviously must, in view of the widely expressed opinion of the Poles that in any case the peace will only be a truce—and that is a condition which Poland seems by no means in a temper to accept."

The negotiations at Riga started by the Russian request that the Polish delegation should recognize the full powers of the Ukrainian

Soviet Republic.[68] It was a *conditio sine qua non*. At the meeting of the Conference on 24th September the Chairman of the Soviet delegation, Joffe, read out the declaration of the All-Russian Executive Committee [69] which, apart from attacks on the imperialistic policy of the Entente allegedly solely interested in the continuation of the war, contained the proposal for the recognition by Poland and Russia of the " independence " of the Ukraine, Byelorussia and Lithuania, and " the independence " of Eastern Galicia in which, according to this declaration, " the Soviet régime has not yet been installed."

The Polish delegation put forward its programme in a declaration [70] made on the same day (24th September). Following the instructions of the Council of National Defence the declaration stated that :

" The establishment of the frontier between the parties in the territories detached from the Polish Republic by the former Russian Empire should be based on equal regard by both parties for the following principles:

" (a) The termination of the struggle between Poland and Russia for the territories in dispute between them, and the establishment of a basis for good neighbourly relations. The State frontier should not be determined by reference to historical claims, but by a just harmonization of the vital interests of both the negotiating parties.

" (b) The just solution of the question of nationality in the said territories in accordance with democratic principles.

" (c) The permanent assurance of each of the negotiating parties against the possibility of attack by the other. As Poland desires a freely negotiated peace and has no wish to dictate its conditions, it proposes to the other party a common determination of the frontier on the basis of the above principles."

The Polish delegation peremptorily refused to discuss the question of Eastern Galicia with Russia, and declined to enter into a theoretical discussion of the Soviet conception of national self-determination which, according to the Polish delegation, " is reduced in Soviet practice to local self-government and to the dictatorship of one party installed by force with the assistance of the Red Army."

In spite of this apparent deadlock due to a quite different approach to the problem of national self-determination, both parties were anxious to reach an agreement. Although on the 28th September Joffe proposed the same frontier line as that put forward by the Soviet delegation at Minsk, four days later he extended this line much further to the East, to the railway line Brody–Rowno–Sarny–Luniniec–Baranowicze, a frontier which did not differ very much from that eventually determined in the final agreement. Joffe requested, however, that the said railway line should be left in Soviet hands. The following day Dabski proposed a frontier line including the above-mentioned railway and a " security strip " sixty to seventy kilometres wide. He declared at the same time : " I do not wish to proceed in the usual way by suggesting a frontier line further to the East and then gradually withdrawing it westwards until I have reached the maximum we are prepared to yield. I prefer at once to describe the line beyond which we are in no case prepared to withdraw."

According to the account of one of the principal Polish delegates, Grabski :

" On 3rd October a conversation took place between Mr. Joffe, Mr. Dabski, deputies Barlicki, Kiernik and myself. Mr. Joffe asked me how I justified the claim that the railway line should be given to Poland rather than to Russia. I replied that Russia, with its population of 150 millions, would never need to fear aggression on the part of Poland with its 30 millions ; whereas the numerically stronger Russia might some day display aggressive tendencies against Poland, in which case not Russia but Poland would need the best possible defensive line together with the strategically important railway behind it. Continuing, Mr. Joffe asked what guarantee we could give him that Poland would not itself be pushed into war with the Soviet Union by the Western capitalist world. To this my answer was as follows: ' The best and surest guarantee of the action of States is given by a consideration of their interests. Now, the interests of Poland do not allow it to join in any kind of military co-operation with Germany. And the idea that Great Britain or France would ever send armies to Poland and join in a common expedition against Moscow is ridiculous. Further, if Poland concludes a treaty with Soviet Russia outlining the frontier it desires, it will not be so foolish as to overthrow the government in Russia which signed the treaty and set up another government there which would not feel bound by the treaty.' Mr. Joffe then informed me that in view of these explanations he would put our frontier proposal before the Council of People's Commissars. Two days later, on 5th October, he informed us that the Council of People's Commissars had empowered him to accept our proposal in its entirety, if the Polish delegation would agree to reduce their claim to a share of the gold of the former Imperial Bank of Russia."

Grabski concludes his account :

" Russia apparently had more interest in keeping the largest possible reserve of gold than in keeping the territories claimed by us, where Polish culture was undoubtedly predominant." [71]

Contrary to Western expectations it was consequently not the establishment of the frontier line which constituted the stumbling block, but the Soviet claim to speak in the name of the Ukrainians and Byelorussians. In a private conversation with Dabski on 1st October,[72] Joffe explained quite outspokenly the true motives of Russian policy. Abandoning the Russian claim to discuss at the Conference the problem of Eastern Galicia, the Soviet delegate stated that this question was raised for purely tactical reasons in order to forestall any Polish initiative on the question of the recognition of the Petlura Government. Joffe added that the problem of the Ukraine was primarily of economic importance to Russia, as she needed the Ukrainian grain. Russia could not tolerate any but a " friendly " government in the Ukraine. According to Joffe, the fact that the Poles supported the independence of the Ukraine proved that Polish policy was taking its bearings from France, who needed the Ukraine for her expansion(?).

Joffe added that although Russia was in a very difficult position and was anxious to avoid a winter campaign, she was not prepared to give up her claim to negotiate in the name of the Ukraine and White Ruthenia, as otherwise she " would have ruined her moral prestige in the eyes of the world proletariat." It was not, of course, the principle of the independence of White Ruthenia (Byelorussia) and the Ukraine that raised objection on the Polish side. This principle was invariably defended by the Polish Government and Diet from the beginning of the Polish-Russian conflict at the end of 1918. It was only the Russian interpretation of this principle and the claim that the national self-determination of these two nations was carried out in practice by the Soviet Government that met with Polish opposition. As a matter of fact the Soviet delegation had not one Byelorussian in its ranks, and the Ukrainian negotiators consisted only of members of the Communist Party.

In his declaration on 4th October,[73] Dabski stated once more that the Polish Government was unable to consider the régimes installed by the Soviet armies in the Ukraine and White Ruthenia as the genuine and free expression of the will of the populations. The Polish declaration further stated that the Soviet Government had given no guarantee of the independence of these two countries whose Northern and Eastern frontiers (that is their frontiers with Russia and the frontiers with each other) had not been determined. Thus Poland had to establish frontiers with the States the territorial status of which was completely indefinite. Moreover, Russia had taken no step to ascertain the wishes of the population in a truly democratic manner, that is by enabling the meeting of constituent assemblies elected by a democratic suffrage; a preliminary condition of holding such assemblies was the withdrawal of foreign troops (was not this request put forward by the Soviet delegation at Brest-Litovsk in the negotiations with the Central Powers? See p. 184).

We pass over other difficulties arising in the course of the Riga negotiations and relating to different clauses of the armistice and the preliminary peace—together with this main political claim referred to for a few days they blocked the way to a definite agreement. It should be remembered, moreover, that since the end of September, in connection with the advance of Polish troops towards the territories ceded to Lithuania by the Russians and evacuated by them in their retreat, as well as the action of General Zeligowski, leading to the reoccupation of Wilno by the Poles, Poland's relations with the Western Powers had become strained because of the attitude of the latter in that connection. It was obvious that the Western Powers again appeared as the protagonists of the integrity of the Russian Empire, and such an attitude could only be welcome to Soviet Russia because it was she, and in fact she alone, who could derive real benefits from it.

In this connection the Warsaw correspondent of *The Times* noted (7th October) the wave of indignation in Poland about the position taken at that time by Great Britain : " British intervention to persuade the Poles not to occupy Wilno has again brought forth a storm of angry comments both privately and in the Press. At the same time Polish correspondents at Riga profess to trace British influence behind the tactics of the Bolshevist delegation." It would, however, be very difficult to find proof of such assertions, but it is an indisputable fact that the Polish position was made very difficult owing to the indifference or more or less veiled hostility towards any extension of the Polish territory beyond what was wrongly considered as the legitimate limit of the Polish interests.

But whatever may have been the attitude of the Western Powers it became ever more obvious that each negotiating party at Riga had an urgent interest in stopping hostilities and coming to an arrangement. The Riga correspondent of *The Times* was able to inform his paper on the 6th October (*The Times,* 7th October) that the territorial questions were virtually settled between the parties :

> " The boundary line thus throughout its length is well to the East of the German trench line of 1915-16. It is obviously drawn on the strength of the present military position to leave the strategic advantages in Polish hands.
>
> " A point which will perhaps find yet more favour in Polish eyes is that, by getting into contact with Latvia, Poland separates Lithuania from Russia. Lithuania will not in future be able to act as a corridor between Russia and Germany. If Poland can succeed in carrying out the rôle of a buffer State between these powerful countries, it may be the gain of Europe."

In its editorial, " Poland and Soviet Russia," the following day

(*The Times,* 8th October), the leading London newspaper drew practical conclusions from the new position arising at Riga :

> " ... our policy has been so mismanaged as to lead the Poles to think that we are hostile to their claims as a nation. ... When Poland's fortunes were at their lowest, our Government, by rashly advising her Government to make peace on terms which were imperfectly apprehended here, seemed to be deserting her in what was the moment of her great danger. ... If, as we hope, a satis-factory peace is made with Russia, we should have a breathing-space in which to reform our policy ; conceive it deliberately on sounder lines which will recognize the place that Poland holds in Eastern Europe. ... The settlement, whatever it is, should be such as to enable Poland to play her part worthily in the politics of Eastern Europe."

The armistice and the preliminaries of peace between Poland and Soviet Russia (and Soviet Ukraine) were signed at Riga on 12th October. Both parties agreed on a rather ambiguous formula for the recognition of the " independence " of the Ukraine and White Ruthenia (Byelorussia), and a frontier between Poland on the one side and the Ukraine and Byelorussia on the other was established (there was formally no common frontier between Poland and Russia). The future final treaty should be based on the principles : durable, honourable and resting on mutual agreement.

The negotiations for a definite treaty were resumed at Riga after a month's interval, on the 17th November, 1920, and lasted several months until 18th March, the date of the signature. Many political events took place in the meantime, the most important being the signature of the French-Polish alliance on the 19th February and of the Polish-Rumanian alliance on the 3rd March, 1921. On the other side, events in Upper Silesia in connection with the plebiscite and the marked hostility of Lloyd George towards Poland absorbed much Polish attention and considerably weakened the Polish posi-tion at Riga.

In spite of many obstacles the pacification of the Polish-Russian relations was brought to a successful end, although without the con-currence of the Western Powers. It is interesting to note that both Poland and Russia considered the Riga settlement at the time of its signature a just and fair solution of all the debatable questions between the two countries.

The Chairman of the Polish delegation, Dabski, made the follow-ing declaration after the signature of the final treaty on 18th March :

> " The Peace Treaty which we have just signed marks the begin-ning and forms the foundation of a new period in the life and

development of the Polish and Russian nations. After a century of Polish struggle for independence, after two years of a severe war, there comes a period of peace and mutual collaboration. ... We have endeavoured to settle all problems in a spirit of fairness and justice, making concessions not only in order to reach agreement but also to facilitate our future relations."

The Polish Prime Minister, Witos, speaking at the moment of ratification of the Treaty by the Diet on 14th April, 1921 stated :

" The Treaty of Riga is the first peace treaty concluded by the resuscitated Polish State after a victorious war. It is the first act of great international importance by our Republic. It is the fruit of the sacrifices of the Polish nation which bought its independence with them. The Treaty of Riga is the best proof of the goodwill, spirit of moderation and really democratic intentions of the Polish nation and Government. In spite of our military successes we have started negotiations with the firm intention of concluding peace. We have not tried in any way to exploit our favourable military situation and overcome the adversary, but on the contrary we have tried to come to an arrangement with him."

The Bolshevik leaders appreciated the work of Riga in the same spirit, as appears from the declaration of Joffe, Chairman of the Soviet delegation, after the signature of the Treaty on 18th March :

" We have signed a treaty satisfying the vital, just and indispensable interests of the Polish nation. ... None of the peace treaties which have been concluded by Russia and (Soviet) Ukraine allow the preparation for a new war, because there is no question that has remained unsolved. Nor does it settle any question by a simple proportion of force, as it occurred in the past, to the detriment of the nation with which the peace was concluded. As the nations have received everything that was necessary for them, they watch and will watch in the future that the peace be durable."

In spite of many pessimistic predictions at the time of the signature of the Treaty of Riga, peace in Eastern Europe was assured by it for nearly twenty years, and its collapse was due not to any defect of the Treaty itself but to the work of outside factors inherent in the nature of aggressive imperialisms.

*
* *

In the Order of the Day issued to the Polish armies on the 18th October, 1920, on the occasion of the termination of the war with Russia, Pilsudski made an allusion to the unfriendly feelings which the new Poland had to overcome on her way to liberation and asserting her claims to political independence.

" From the first moment of free life Poland had been surrounded
by many grasping hands stretched towards her—many efforts have
also been devoted to keep her, since her existence cannot be prevented, in a powerless state so that she might remain simply a place
for the plots of the whole world." [74]

These bitter words of the first Chief of the restored Polish State
contain much truth, as the reader of this book, I presume, can see
for himself. Speaking about this curious phenomenon of hostility
towards Poland from the first months of her reappearance on the
international stage, the *National Review* (August 1920) of London,
in an excellent article entitled " The Vendetta against Poland,"
referred to on a previous occasion said the following :

" Here was a nation which had kept its spiritual existence in
being during more than a century of servitude and butchery, now
at last come into its own again. Here was a people which had
refused to bear willingly an alien yoke and to merge itself into the
number of its conquerors, which had risen like the phœnix from its
ashes at the appointed time, and was busily restoring its own submerged national life and the ruins of its land and home. . . .

The path of the new State was throughout beset by thorns
thoughtfully laid in her way by all her friends. For some reason
or other Poland was not only denied most of what she demanded
as essential to her future existence, but held up to the world as a
greedy and rapacious nation for wanting to exist at all."

The decision of the Conference of Ambassadors (15th March, 1923)

Two full years had to elapse before the Western Powers recognized the Eastern frontiers of Poland established by the Riga Treaty.
This procrastinating attitude was due to the lack of any definite and
concerted policy on matters concerning Eastern Europe. One of the
keenest observers of the political developments in that part of the
world, Signor Tommasini, Italian Minister in Warsaw, notes in this
connection :

" An unbiased survey of the situation should have induced the
Great Powers since the spring 1921 to take a position towards the
Treaty of Riga, and thus eliminate any contradictions which might
still have existed between the said treaty and Article LXXXVII of
the Treaty of Versailles. So long as this did not happen Poland
was bound to remain in a precarious position, being fatally
weakened through the impossibility of achieving the political con-
solidation and exploiting economically the territories recognized
as Polish by the Soviet Government." [75]

But before the Western Powers took this step many unrealistic
ideas on Eastern Europe were to be removed : hopes in the early
fall of the Bolshevist régime in Russia and in its evolution on the

lines desired by the democratic countries, the French illusions on the possibility of the revival of Old Russia, Lloyd George's plans about winning German collaboration for the restoration of Russian economy collapsed at the Genoa Conference, and above all the inveterate, unjustified pessimism about Poland's ability to maintain peace and order in the Eastern outskirts of Western civilization.

The diplomatic history of the recognition of Poland's Eastern frontiers belongs to a later period and, as I hope, will be dealt with by me in another book following this one.

We will note simply that on 15th March, 1923, the Conference of Ambassadors (British Empire, France, Italy and Japan) decided " to assign to Poland who accepts the decision all rights of sovereignty over the territories situated within the frontiers defined above " (exactly corresponding to the frontier established at Riga so far as the frontier with Soviet Russia was concerned and to the line established by the Council of the League of Nations in February 1923 as regards the frontier with the Lithuanian Republic).[76]

The Polish Government notified the above decision to all Governments with which Poland maintained diplomatic relations. The United States Government recognized Poland's sovereignty over her Eastern provinces on 5th April, 1923. With it the plan of Poland's mandate for twenty-five years in Eastern Galicia was finally abandoned, and to the question put to the Prime Minister by Sir John Simon in the House of Commons on 20th March, 1923, as to whether the decision regarding the future status of Eastern Galicia was provisional or final, Bonar Law, the Prime Minister answered that it was final.[77]

Debate in the House of Lords (16th May, 1923)

Let us state at the end of this long story that it was Lord Curzon with whose name another short-lived line was connected, who not only concurred with the decision of the Ambassador's Conference, being at that time Secretary of State for Foreign Affairs, but vigorously defended it in the House of Lords on 16th May, 1923.[78]

The debate on the matter was introduced by Lord Treowan, who declared that he had stayed in Poland for some weeks in autumn 1922. His words of appreciation of the Polish efforts ought to be remembered on this occasion :

> " But one thing about which I was able to satisfy myself completely was that whether the frontier was demarcated or not by frontier posts, whether it was recognized or not by the Great Powers signatory to the Treaty of Versailles, Marshal Pilsudski had realized his conception of a moral frontier extending throughout this region, on the Eastern side of which there was nothing but

rapine and chaos, whilst on the Western side there was law and
order, peace and protection for life and property. Of that I can
speak from my personal knowledge.

" ... I was so much struck by the extraordinary development
that has taken place in a country which I knew well some thirty
years ago, when it was no longer a nation—the development, that
is, which has taken place in the short period that it has existed as
a free and independent State. The Government, which has been
submitted to a great deal of criticism both here and abroad, has
certainly shown wisdom in its general lines of policy, that of
conciliating the minorities which exist within its boundary, of
setting up that which did not exist in the former days to which I
have alluded, a thoroughly national system of education and of
developing and restoring its old system of internal communications which had been wrecked during the war. That is a very
notable record for a Government which has only existed for two
years with peace.

" Another remarkable thing was the zeal and earnestness with
which all classes were working for the reparation of the destruction
by war—the reparation of a devastated condition the like of which
I have not seen in any country of Europe, not even in the most
devastated regions of France. One could not fail to realize that for
a nation which had set itself to its task so nobly that was the great
condition of success, and that peace could only be assured when
the frontiers of the country were established and guaranteed by
international compact."

Lord Treowan did not spare his criticism of the politicians who
showed such unjustifiable hesitation in assisting Poland's efforts by
the recognition of her frontiers :

"Article LXXXVII of the Treaty of Versailles empowered the
principal signatories of the Treaty to define through their representatives at some future time what those frontiers might be. In
other words, representatives to be appointed at some unspecified
time would at some unspecified date declare what certain statesmen had in their mind when they decreed the creation of a united
and independent Polish State with free access to the sea. ...

" ... The minds of politicians are not easily fathomed, and after
the lapse of five years, during which some of these politicians may
have exercised the common right, which we all have, of changing
our minds, it became increasingly difficult to ascertain what was
really intended. And it became the more difficult, inasmuch as
upon the results of this investigation of politicians' minds depended
the establishment of a solid and just peace and the dominance in
Europe of the rule by right."

Lord Curzon's reply showed that he availed himself of the
" common right of changing his mind." He stated that " the circum-

stances have advanced " within last six months. " The long uncertainty upon this frontier," he said, " was telling so heavily upon
both parties that all were anxious to arrive at a solution, and accordingly the matter was finally referred to the Ambassadors' Conference." Lord Curzon defended in the first instance the final settlement of the question of Eastern Galicia stating the following :

> " *It would have been impossible for many reasons—political,*
> *economic and strategic—to place Eastern Galicia in the borders*
> *of the Russian State,* and there was the less necessity for any such
> solution because the Russian and Ukrainian Governments had
> themselves disowned any such settlement and had ceded any claim
> that they might have been held to possess. That alternative there-
> fore could be dismissed. The second alternative was to have
> Eastern Galicia to stand alone. Anybody who is at all familiar
> with local conditions will at once recognize that so small a State,
> divided in the manner that I have described, could not possibly
> have acquired such stability as would enable it to maintain an
> independent existence."

Lord Curzon associated himself with the words of sympathy
towards Poland expressed by Lord Treowan and declared :

> " I am myself strongly hopeful that under the conditions which I
> have described this afternoon a brighter future, a future resting
> upon surer foundations, lies before the Polish State than could
> have been predicted a few years ago, and the friends of Poland—
> namely the noble Lord himself—can now, I think, look forward
> with reasonable confidence to the future."

A Polish writer who after some years remembered Lord Curzon's
declaration in 1923, rightly observed that " it is untrue from the
historical point of view to call the provisional line " (referred to by
Lord Curzon in his Note to the Soviet Government of 11th July)
by his name, since it was the frontier established by the Riga Treaty
that was eventually recognized by him as one more adequate to
Poland's political, economic and strategic requirements.[79]

Soviet Pledges to Poland

Let us recall here that the integrity of this frontier has been
proclaimed by Soviet Russia in many diplomatic instruments,
such as the Protocol between Estonia, Latvia, Poland, Rumania and
the Union of Soviet Socialist Republics, for the immediate entry
into force of the Treaty of Paris of 27th August, 1928, regarding
renunciation of war as an instrument of national policy, signed in
Moscow, 9th February, 1929 [80]; the Pact of Non-Aggression between
Poland and the Union of Soviet Socialist Republics, signed in
Moscow, 25th July, 1932 [81]; the Convention for the Definition of

Aggression, signed in London, 3rd July, 1933,[82] and in the last instance the Protocol signed in Moscow, 5th May, 1934, between Poland and the Union of Soviet Socialist Republics, prolonging until 31st December, 1945, the Pact of Non-Aggression of 25th July, 1932.[83] In all these instruments any act of violence against the integrity and inviolability of the territory or the political independence of the contracting parties was defined as an act of aggression.

NOTES

[1] J. PILSUDSKI, *Pisma*, Vol. V, pp. 165 ff. As disclosed by Colonel J. Kowalewski (Na czym polegal, " Nonsens strategiczny," Kampanii, 1920 r. *Polish Daily*, London, 15th August, 1953), the Polish Headquarters were well informed of the existing gap between the Northern and Southern groups of the Soviet armies, from the intercepted and decoded Soviet telegrams.

[2] C. FALLS, o.c., p. 225.

[3] *Encyclopædia Britannica*, Russo-Polish Campaign.

[4] LORD D'ABERNON, o.c., p. 90.

[5] W. SIKORSKI, o.c., p. 62.

[6] *L'Information*, 21st August, 1920. General Weygand made a similar statement in a public lecture at Bruxelles.

[7] W. SIKORSKI, o.c., p. 6. Preface by Marshal Foch: " Ce sera la bataille de Vistule. Elle sera conduite suivant les directives établies le 6 août par le Haut Commandement Polonais."

[8] M. KUKIEL, " The Polish-Soviet Campaign," *Slavonic Review*, 1928, and as a separate leaflet in Scottish-Polish Society Publications, No. 1.

[9] Cf. also " Dramat Generala Weyganda," *Bellona*, April-June, 1949.

[10] LEON NOEL, *L'Agression allemande contre la Pologne*, p. 17. " Quel qu'ait étè en circonstance le rôle du général Weygand, venu pour apporter au jeune Etat-Major polonais les conseils de son expérience, il semble bien que la paternité du plan de campagne qui determina le désastre russe appartienne à Pilsudski seul. Interrogé par moi sur ce point le général Debeney m'a repondu affirmativement, en ajoutant: ' C'était très bien.' Cf. also GENERAL CAMON, *La manœuvre libératice de Maréchal Pilsudski contre les Bolchéviks*, août 1920, Paris, 1934 ; GÉNÉRAL H. MORDACQ, *Les Légendes de la Grande Guerre*, Paris, 1935.

[11] LORD D'ABERNON, o.c., p. 81.

[12] C. FALLS, o.c., p. 285.

[13] R. MACHRAY, o.c., p. 117.

[14] Cf. P. N. MILUKOV, *La Politique Extérieure des Soviets*, p. 82. " L'Armée Rouge qui s'approchait deja jusqu' à l'enceinte de Varsovie, fut rejetée vers le Boug, par l'Armée polonaise sous le commandement français."

[15] See Lenin's speech on 15th October, 1920 (*Sochineniya*, Vol. XXV, p. 413). " Not long ago we had the information that the black troops, it is to say the French colonial troops, had appeared on the Polish front.

It means that the war was carried out by France who was assisted by England and America."

This preposterous information was widely circulated by the pro-Soviet groups in Great Britain, as it appears from the debate at the House of Commons on 20th July, 1920 (*Parliamentary Debates,* Commons, Vol. 132):

" Sir F. Hall asked the Lord Privy Seal if the Government are taking any steps to put a stop to the anti-Polish campaign in this country which takes the form of unfounded reports as to the use of coloured troops, the commission of atrocities, and other mis-statements, and whether the Government has any evidence to confirm the suspicion that the circulation of such reports is the work of persons in political circles in this country who are compensated for their anti-Polish service from German and Russian sources."

Mr. Bonar Law: " It is quite true that there is an organized anti-Polish campaign which circulates many unfounded reports, but it is not possible to prosecute for false statements as to the things which are alleged to have happened in foreign countries beyond the personal knowledge of any witness in this country."

[16] *The Times,* 29th August, 1920.

[17] J. BARDOUX, o.c., p. 365. See also another passage on p. 385: " Jamais victoire n'a été plus oportune, que nous devons au sang froid de M. Millerand et à la claire intelligence du général Weygand." It is interesting to note that, so far as M. Millerand himself was concerned, he took a dignified attitude on this occurrence. Cf. his article " Au secours de la Pologne " in the *Revue de France,* 15th August, 1932, in which, quoting General Weygand's declarations, he stated that " the whole honour of the victory " belonged to " the glorious Marshal Pilsudski."

[18] LORD D'ABERNON, o.c., p. 114.

[19] *Ibidem,* p. 122.

[20] W. CHURCHILL, *The Aftermath,* pp. 270-2.

[21] See p. 636 of the book. Tukhachevsky himself, as states C. Falls in his above-mentioned book, fell victim of his own propaganda (see p. 226): " He constantly announced that one army or another had ' disintegrated ' or that it had been destroyed. In the Battle of the Vistula he tells us plaintively, he found ' quite a different army '." In the earlier stages of the war Tukhachevsky was more sober in his views on the Polish Army. See *Grazhdanskaya Voyna,* Vol. III, p. 316: " After the first battles with Polish troops Tukhachevsky summed up his impressions in the following words: ' The enemy forces are conducted in an excellent way. The team-work of staffs and the manner in which the troops are manœuvred is remarkable from the point of view of the preparation and carrying out of tasks on the scale of the regular war of movement. The tactical preparation is also good. The single units-divisions, regiments, battalions manœuvre in a splendid manner. It proves the tactical cohesion of their parts and the high standard of commanders.' In conclusion the Commander of the Western Front stated that ' the Polish

Army has a European flavour (ot polskoi armii zakhvatyvayet evropeismom)."

[22] *The Times,* 23rd August, 1920.

[23] *P. R. F. R.,* 1920, Vol. III, pp. 391 ff.

[24] *Ibidem,* p. 392.

[25] *Ibidem,* pp. 397-8.

[26] *Ibidem,* p. 399.

[27] *The Times,* 5th October, 1920.

[28] LENIN, o.c., Vol. XXV, p. 426.

[29] *Ibidem,* p. 481.

[30] L. TROTSKY, *My Life,* pp. 458 ff.

[31] The importance of the Pripet Mashes from the military point of view has been stressed by many military writers. Cf. W. SIKORSKI, o.c., p. 20, quoting the Memoirs of one of the most prominent generals in the 1830-31 War, General Pradzynski: " Il y eut toujours deux théâtres de guerre distincts des guerres russo-polonaises ; cela provenait de l'étendue de la frontière et de la nature du terrain, nettement scindé par tout le système de Pripet', de ses affiuents et de ses marais de Polésie. Ce système et ses rares passages jouent un rôle capital dans toutes les guerres polonaises car *celui qui en maître peut avec un seul groupement de forces intervenir tour à tour sur chaque théâtre avec sa masse et battre l'adversaire coupé en deux tronçons sans liaison.* La Polésie a encore un autre avantage considérable ; celui qui l'occupe, s'il est faible et réduit à la défensive peut occuper une position de flanc et arrêter ainsi la progression d'un ennemi supérieur."

[32] *P. R. F. R.,* 1920, Vol. III, pp. 401 ff.

[33] *Ibidem,* pp. 469-70. The French Chargé d'Affaires to the Secretary of State 14th August, 1920: " The President of the Council and Minister of Foreign Affairs ... is in entire agreement with the Federal Government as regards the principles formulated in this document " (Note to Signor Avezzana).

See also *Le Temps,* editorial, 21 août, 1920: " La France n'a jamais encouragé personne à entamer le territoire de la Russie tel que le définit la note americaine."

[34] *Le Temps,* 27 août, 1920 (editorial): " Dans l'ensemble le ligne du 8 décembre doit être maintenue. Il ne faut pas oublier qu'elle à été acceptée à Spa par le chef du gouvernement polonais M. Grabski ... quel front pourra atteindre l'armée polonaise, si la guerre continue— la ligne sur laquelle s'etaient installées les armées austro-allemandes. Toutefois, il paraît désirable que l'armée polonaise ne réoccupe pas la région de Wilno."

[35] *Le Temps,* 21 août, editorial " Pologne et Russie.": " A mesure que les Polonais avancent, des voix de plus en plus nombreuses vont leur demander jusqu' où ils ont l'intention d'aller. Des amis trop entreprenants leur conseilleront de ne pas s'arrêter avant d'avoir abattu le gouvernement des Soviets. Des adversaires obstinés leur enjoindront de ne franchir sous aucun pretexte *la ligne du partage des statistiques.* Ces propos de l'arrière n'ont en eux-mêmes qu'une mince valeur. On est en

guerre et les mouvements d'une armée qui repousse un envahisseur dépendent avant tout de la situation militaire. Mais à côté de la situation militaire, il faut toujours songer à la situation politique. C'est là, dans le domaine politique, que l'intérêt de la paix générale et l'intérêt particulier de la Pologne commandent, l'une et l'autre, d'éviter certains dangers."

[36] *Le Temps*, 23 août, editorial " les conditions de la Pologne ": " Que la Pologne gouverne bien son propre territoire national: les populations voisines chez qui sévira le bolchevisme, ne tarderont pas à faire des comparaisons assez efficaces."

[37] J. BARDOUX, o.c., p. 367. " Il ne reste plus que les clauses territoriales, sur lesquelles l'accord est facile, si la chimère orientale ne reprend pas possession des imaginations embrasées." *Ibidem*, p. 359. " Et il semble qu'il eût été facile de condamner des rêves chimériques et les imprévoyances coupables d'un parti austro-polonais(?)."

[38] W. CHURCHILL, o.c., p. 263.

[39] *Le Temps*, 22 août, 1920.

[40] *The Times*, 24th August, 1920.

[41] *Ibidem*.

[42] LORD D'ABERNON, o.c., p. 105.

[43] *P. R. F. R.*, 1920, Vol. III, p. 395.

[44] *Ibidem*, p. 396.

[45] *The Times*, 23rd August, 1920.

[46] *The Times*, 26th August, 1920.

[47] LENIN, o.c., Vol. XVII, p. 223.

[48] *The Times*, 27th August, 1920.

[49] *The Times*, 3rd September, 1920.

[50] *Le Temps*, 25 août, 1920, editorial " l'Union des Alliés ": " La victoire de la Pologne a reserré l'union des alliés. ... Mr. Lloyd George and Mr. Giolitti souhaitent en revanche, que la Pologne respecte les droits nationaux de la Russie. Tel est aussi le désir de la France ... il faut se garder d'encourager les revendications polonaises au delà de la limite fixée au mois de décembre," (1919).

[51] S. GRABSKI, o.c., pp. 24-5.

[52] J. DABSKI, *Pokoj Ryski*, pp. 29 ff.

[53] The English text of this declaration was published in *The Times*, 30th August.

[54] *The Times*, 26th August.

[55] *The Times*, 9th September.

[56] W. CHURCHILL, o.c., p. 262.

[57] LORD D'ABERNON, o.c., p. 91. See also the account of the conversations with M. Millerand in Paris on 1st September, p. 115: " From conversations with French officials I gather that to some extent they share the apprehension felt in London that the Poles will be unreasonable about their Eastern frontier. I have endeavoured to dispel anxiety on this head as I have always found Prince Sapieha moderate and sensible on the subject."

[58] *Ibidem*, pp. 98-9.

[59] *The Times*, 27th August.

[60] VON SEECKT, o.c., Vol. II, pp. 295 ff.

[61] See the report of the Polish liaison officer at Marshal Foch's H.Q. dated 14th September, 1920 (*Niepodległość*, Vol. II, London, pp. 215 ff.).

[62] *Documents Diplomatiques* concernant les relations polono-lithuaniennes (Dec. 1918-Sept. 1920), p. 45.

[63] *P. R. F. R.*, 1920, Vol. III, pp. 402 ff.

[64] S. GRABSKI, o.c., pp. 29 ff.

[65] *Ibidem*.

[66] J. PILSUDSKI, *Pisma*, Vol. IV, p. 124.

[67] M. SOKOLNICKI, " Pilsudski a zagadnienie Rosji " (*Niepodległość*, London, Vol. II, 1950, p. 65).

[68] J. DABSKI, o.c., p. 78.

[69] *Ibidem*, p. 80. Also *Grazhdanskaya Voyna*, Vol. III, p. 468.

[70] J. DABSKI, o.c., p. 83. S. GRABSKI, o.c., p. 29.

[71] S. GRABSKI, o.c., pp. 34-5.

[72] J. DABSKI, o.c., p. 105.

[73] *Ibidem*, pp. 99-100.

[74] J. PILSUDSKI, *Pisma*, Vol. V, p. 175.

[75] F. TOMMASINI, o.c., p. 134.

[76] League of Nations, Treaty Series, Vol. X, pp. 260-5.

[77] *Parliamentary Debates*, Commons, 1923, Vol. 161, 20th March. *Parliamentary Debates*, Commons, 1923, Vol. 164, 16th May, 1923.

[78] *Parliamentary Debates*, Lords, 1923, Vol. 54, 16th May.

[79] WACLAW KOMARNICKI, " Lord Curzon o wschodnich granicach Polski " (*Wiadomości*, No. 41/132, 10th October, 1948).

[80] *Polish-Soviet Relations* 1918-1943, Official Documents, issued by the Polish Embassy in Washington, 1944, No. 6.

[81] *Ibidem*, No. 7.

[82] *Ibidem*, No. 8.

[83] *Ibidem*, No. 9.

A SELECTED BIBLIOGRAPHY

THE author is unable to give a full list of books relating to the problems reviewed by him, as this would require a special volume. He confined himself to stating those sources on which he mostly relied and those books to which a special reference was made in the text. State Papers and the articles in newspapers are not included in this list; they are to be found under the respective chapters (see also the Index).

A. Diplomatic Correspondence, Official or Semi-official Publications and Other Primary Sources

Akty i Dokumenty, dotyczące sprawy Granic Polski na Konferencji Pokojowej w Paryzu (Acts and Documents relating to the Problem of the Polish Frontiers at the Peace Conference). Paris, 1920. Polish Delegation, Peace Conference.

ALDROVANDI, CONTE LUIGI MARESCOTTI. *Guerra Diplomatica; ricordi e frammenti di diario* (1914-1919). A. Mondadori, Milano, 1936.

ALDROVANDI, CONTE LUIGI MARESCOTTI, *Nuovi ricordi e frammenti di diario*. A. Mondadori, Milano, 1938.

BAKER, R. S. *Woodrow Wilson, Life and Letters,* Vol. VIII, Armistice, New York, 1934.

BAKER, R. S. *The Public Papers of Woodrow Wilson.* Authorized edition, six vols. Edited with William E. Dodd, 1925-1927.

BROWN SCOTT, J. *President Wilson's Foreign Policy. Messages, Addresses, Papers.* New York, 1918.

Centr-Arkhiv, Russko-Polskiye Otnosheniya v period mirovoi voyny (Preface by M. G. Valetsky). Moscow-Leningrad, 1926.

DEGRAS, JANE. *Soviet Documents on Foreign Policy.* Vol. I (1917-1924). Oxford University Press, 1951.

Documents on British Foreign Policy (quoted *D.B.F.P.*). First series, Vols. I-III.

Documents Diplomatiques Concernant les Relations Polono-Lithuaniennes. Décembre 1918-Septembre 1920. Ministère des Affaires Etrangères, Varsovie, 1920.

Documents Diplomatiques Secrets Russes, 1914-1917, d'après les archives du Ministère des Affaires Etrangères à Petrograd traduit du Russe, par J. Polonsky, Payot, Paris, 1928.

Documents and Statements relating to Peace Proposals and War Aims, with an Introduction by G. Lowes Dickinson. London, George Allen & Unwin, 1919.

FILASIEWICZ, S. *La Question Polonaise pendant la Guerre Mondiale. Recueil des Actes Diplomatiques, Traités et Documents concernant la Pologne.* Tome Deuxième, Paris, 1920.

GOOCH AND TEMPERLEY. *British Documents on the Origin of the War*, 1898-1914. Eleven vols. H.M. Stationery Office, London, 1926-1938.

Grazhdanskaya Voyna. Three vols. Gosizdat, Moscow, 1930.

Die Grosse Politik der Europäischen Kabinette, 1871-1914. Forty vols. Deutsche Verlagsgesellschaft für Politik und Geschichte, Berlin, 1922-1927.

Handbooks prepared under the direction of the Historical Section of the Foreign Office. H.M. Stationery Office, London, 1920. No. 4, Austrian Silesia ; No. 40, Upper Silesia ; No. 43, Poland—General Sketch of History, 1569-1815 ; No. 44, Russian Poland, Lithuania and White Russia ; No. 45, Prussian Poland ; No. 46, Austrian Poland.

Journal Officiel, Chambre des Députés, 1918-1920. Paris.

KAKURIN, N. E., and MELIKOV, V. A., *Voyna z belopolyakami*. Gosizdat, Moscow, 1925.

KLUCHNIKOV, U. B., and SABANIN, A. (compiled by), *International Politics in Modern Times. Recent International Policy in Treaties, Notes and Declarations*. Publication of the Commissariat of Foreign Affairs, Moscow, 1926.

KRASNAYA, KNIGA. *R.S.F.S.R. Narodnyi Komissariyat Innostrannykh Del, Sbornik Diplomaticheskikh dokumentov o russko-polskikh othosheniyakh*, 1918-1920. Moscow, 1920.

KRAUS, HERBERT, und RÜDIGER, GUSTAV. *Urkunden zum Friedensvertrage von Versailles vom 28 Juni*, 1919 (Kommentar zum Friedensvertrage herausgegeben von Prof. Dr. Walter Schücking). Two vols. Berlin, 1920.

MANTOUX, PAUL. *Les Délibérations du Conseil des Quatre* (24 mars-28 juin, 1919). *Notes de l'Officier Interprète*. Editions du Centre National de la Recherche Scientifique. Two vols. Paris, 1955.

MERLOT, A. *Recueil Analitique des actes de l'armée polonaise* (*Juin 1917-Septembre* 1918). Paris, 1918.

MERLOT, A. *L'Armée polonaise. Constitution en France et organisation* (*Juin 1917-Avril* 1919). Paris, 1919.

MERMEIX (GABRIEL TERRAIL). *Le Combat des Trois. Notes et Documents sur la Conférence de la Paix. Fragments d'Histoire*, 1914-1919, No. 8). Paris, 1922.

MILLER, DAVID HUNTER. *My Diary at the Conference of Paris*. Twenty-one vols. New York, 1924.

Papers Relating to the Foreign Relations of the United States (quoted *P.R.F.R.*). United States Printing Office, Department of State. *The Lansing Papers*, 1914-1920. Two vols. Washington, 1939. *The Paris Peace Conference*. Eleven vols. Washington, 1942. *Russia*, 1918. Three vols. Washington, 1931. 1917, *Vol. I, Suppl.* 1 *and* 2 ; 1918, *Vol. I, Suppl.* 1 ; 1919, *Vol. II* ; 1920, *Vol. III*.

Parliamentary Debates (see the Index).

POMARANSKI, S. *Pierwsza Wojna Polska* (Polish War Communiqués). Warszawa, 1920.

Proceedings of the Brest-Litovsk Peace Conference (*The Peace Negotiations between Russia and the Central Powers*, 21 *November*, 1917-3 *March*, 1918). Washington, Government Printing Office, 1918.

*Reichstag-*12 *Ausschuss*. (*Beilage zu den stenographischen Berichten über die öffentlichen Verhandlungen des Untersuchungsausschusses*). *Ursachen des Zusammenbruchs*. Gutachten des Obersten a. D. Schwerfeger, des Generals der Infanterie a. D. von Kuhl und des Geheimrates Professor Hans Delbrück. Berlin, 1923.

Sbornik sekretnykh dokumentov iz arkhiv byvshavo Min. In. Del. Izdaniye Nar. Kom. In. Del, Moscow, 1917.

SCOTT, JAMES BROWN. *Official statements of War Aims and Peace Proposals, December* 1916 *to November* 1918. Washington, 1921.

SUSLOV, P. V. *Politicheskoye obezpecheniye sovetsko-polskoi kampanii* 1920 *goda*. Gosizdat, Moscow-Leningrad, 1930.

Der Waffenstillstand, 1918-1919. *Das Dokumenten Material der Waffenstillstands-Verhandlungen von Compiegne, Spa, Trier und Brüssel*. Herausgegeben im Auftrage der Deutschen Waffenstillstands-Kommission, Berlin, 1928.

B. Memoirs, Diaries, Works of Authors who took part in the Events described, and Other Secondary Sources

D'ABERNON, LORD. *The* 18*th Decisive Battle of the World*. London, 1931.

Affaires de Pologne. La Proclamation du Généralissime Russe et l'Opinion Française. Paris, 1915.

BAKER, R. S. *Woodrow Wilson and World Settlement*. London, 1923.

BARDOUX, JACQUES. *De Paris à Spa. La Bataille Diplomatique pour la Paix Française* (*Février* 1919 - *Octobre* 1920). Paris, 1921.

BENEŠ, DR. EDUARD. *Der Aufstand der Nationen ;* also in English, *My War Memoirs*. London, 1928.

BERNSTORFF, COUNT. *My Three Years in America*. London, 1920.

BERTIE, *The Diary of Lord Bertie of Thame,* 1913-1918. Two vols. London, 1924.

V. BETHMANN-HOLLWEG, TH. *Betrachtungen zum Weltkriege,* 2 *Teil, Während des Krieges*. Berlin, 1921.

V. BETHMANN-HOLLWEG'S *Kriegsreden*. Herausgegeben und historisch-kritisch eingeleitet von Dr. Friedrich Thimme, Stuttgart und Berlin, 1919.

BILIŃSKI, L. *Wspomnienia i Dokumenty*. Two vols. Warsaw, 1924.

BONSAL, S. *Suitors and Suppliants, The Little Nations at Versailles*. New York, 1946.

BONSAL, S. *Unfinished Business*. New York, 1944.

BORKENAU, F. *The Communist International*. London, 1938.

BUCHANAN, SIR GEORGE. *My Mission to Russia and other Diplomatic Memoirs*. Two vols. London, 1923.

BÜLOW, FÜRST VON. *Deutsche Politik*. Berlin, 1916.

BURIAN, GRAF STEPHAN. *Drei Jahre aus der Zeit meiner Amtsführung im Kriege*. Berlin, 1923.

CALLWELL, MAJOR-GENERAL, SIR C. E. *Field-Marshal Sir Henry Wilson, His Life and Diaries.* Two vols. London, 1927.

CARTON DE WIART, LIEUTENANT-GENERAL. *Happy Odyssey.* London, 1950.

CHERNOV, V. *The Great Russian Revolution.* New Haven, Yale University Press, 1936.

CHOULGIN, ALEXANDRE. *L'Ukraine contre Moscou* (1917). Félix Alcan, Paris, 1935.

CHURCHILL, WINSTON. *The Aftermath.* First published in London, 1929.

CLEMENCEAU, G. *Grandeur and Misery of Victory.* George G. Harrap, London, 1930.

CONRAD VON HOETZENDORFF. *Aus Meiner Dienstzeit* (1906-1918). Five vols. Wien, 1921-1923.

COOLIDGE, ARCHIBALD CARY. *Life and Letters,* by Harold Jefferson Coolidge and Robert Howard Lord. Houghton Mifflin Co., 1932.

CRAMMON, VON A. *Unser österreichisch-ungarischer Bundesgenosse im Weltkriege.* Berlin-Wien, 1920.

CZERNIN, COUNT. *Im Weltkriege.* Berlin-Wien, 1919.

DABSKI, JAN. *Pokój Ryski. Wspomnienia. Pertraktacje. Tajne Uklady z Joffem. Listy.* Warsaw, 1931.

DANIELS, JOSEPHUS. *The Wilson Era, Years of Peace,* 1910-1917. Chapel Hill, University of North Carolina Press, 1944-1946.

DANIELS, JOSEPHUS. *The Wilson Era: Years of War and After. Ibidem,* 1946.

DELBRÜCK, HANS. *Ludendorffs Selbstporträt.* Berlin, 1922.

DMOWSKI, ROMAN. *Polityka Polska i Odbudowanie Państwa.* Second edition. Warsaw, 1926.

ERZBERGER, M. *Erlebnisse im Weltkrieg.* Berlin, 1920.

FOCH, FERDINAND. *Mémoires pour servir à l'histoire de la guerre.* Two vols. Paris, 1931.

GERARD, JAMES W. *My Four Years in Germany.* London-New York, 1917.

GOURKO, BASIL. *Memories and Impressions of War and Revolution in Russia* 1914-1917. London, 1918.

GRABSKI, STANISLAW. *The Polish-Soviet Frontier.* London, 1943.

HAIG, DOUGLAS, EARL. *The Private Papers of Douglas Haig,* 1914-1919. Edited by Robert Blake, London, 1952.

HARD, WILLIAM. *Raymond Robin's Own Story.* New York and London, 1920.

HASKINS (CHARLES HOMER), and LORD (ROBERT HOWARD). *Some Problems of the Peace Conference.* Harvard University Press, Cambridge, 1920.

HELFFERICH. *Der Weltkrieg,* Berlin, 1920. Vol. I, *Die Vorgeschichte des Krieges ;* Vol. II, *Vom Kriegsausbruch bis zum uneingeschränkten U-Bootkrieg* ; Vol. III, *Vom Eingreifen Amerikas bis zum Zusammenbruch.*

HINDENBURG. *Aus Meinem Leben.* Berlin, 1920 ; also in English, *Out of my Life.* New York, 1921.

HOFFMANN, GENERAL. *Krieg der versäumten Gelegenheiten*, München, 1924.

HOLOWKO, T. *Przez Dwa Fronty*. Two vols. Warsaw, 1931.

HOOVER, HERBERT. *The Memoirs of Herbert Hoover*. Two vols. New York, 1952.

HOUSE, E. M. *The Intimate Papers of Colonel House*. Arranged as a narrative by Charles Seymour. Four vols. London, 1926-1928.

HOUSE, E. M. *Paderewski : The Paradox of Europe*. Harper's Magazine, 152, 1925.

HOUSE, E. M., and SEYMOUR, CH. *What Really Happened at Paris*. London, 1921.

HOWARD, SIR ESME W. (Lord Howard of Penrith). *Theatre of Life*. Vol. II. London, 1936.

HUTTEN-CZAPSKI, BOHDAN. *Sechzig Jahre Politik und Gesellschaft*. Two vols. Berlin, 1936.

KELLOG, VERNON. *Herbert Hoover, The Man and His Work*. New York and London, 1920.

KELLOG, VERNON. *Paderewski, Pilsudski and Poland. Two Patriots who sank their Political Differences to save their Country*. World's Work, 38, 1919.

KESSLER, COUNT HARRY. *Germany and Europe*. Yale University Press, 1923.

KOZICKI, STANISLAW. *Sprawa Granic Polski na Konferencji Pokojowej w Paryzu 1919 r.* Warsaw, 1921.

KOZLOWSKI, L. *Russkaya Revolutsiiya i nezavisimost' Polshi* (translated from Polish). Paris, 1922.

Krassin, Leonid, His Life and Work. By his wife LUBOV KRASSIN. London, 1929.

KUNTZ, CHARLES AUGUSTE HENRI. *L'Offensive militaire de l'Etoile Rouge contre la Pologne*. Paris, 1922.

LANSING, R. *The Big Four and Others at the Peace Conference*. Hutchinson & Co., London, 1922.

LANSING, R. *The Peace Negotiations. A Personal Narrative*. Constable & Co., London, 1921.

LANSING, R. *War Memoirs*. Indianopolis-New York, 1935.

LENIN, V. I. *Sochineniya*, Partizdatskvkp(b). Moscow, 1935.

LLOYD GEORGE, D. *War Memoirs*. Five vols. London, 1935-1936.

LLOYD GEORGE, D. *The Truth about the Peace Treaties. Memoirs of the Peace Conference*. London, 1938.

LOCKHART, R. H. B. *Memoirs of a British Agent*. Putnam, London and New York, 1932.

LUDENDORFF, ERICH. *Meine Kriegserrinnerungen, 1914-1918*. Berlin, 1919.

LUDENDORFF, ERICH. *The General Staff and its Problems. The History of the Relations between the High Command and the German Imperial Government as revealed by official documents* (English translation).

MANTEYR, G. DE (ed). *Austria's Peace Offer*, 1916-17, with the introductory letter by Prince Sixte de Bourbon. London, 1927.

MASARYK, THOMAS GARRIGUE. *The New Europe (The Slav Standpoint)*, 1918 (for private circulation).

MASARYK, THOMAS GARRIGUE. *The Making of a State. Memoirs and Observations*. An English version by H. W. Steed, London, 1927.

MILYUKOV, P. *Istoriya Vtoroi Russkoi Revolutsii*. Sofia, 1921.

MILYUKOV, P. *Russlands Zusammenbruch*. Two vols. Obelisk Verlag, Berlin, 1926.

MILYUKOV, P. *Rossiya na Perelome*. Paris, 1927.

MILYUKOV, P. *La Politique Extérieure des Soviets*. Paris, 1934.

MILYUKOV, P. *Aleksander Lednicki*. January-March, Vol. XVIII. Przegląd Wspólczesny, Warsaw, 1939.

MORDACQ, GÉNÉRAL HENRI. *Le Ministère Clemenceau. Journal d'un témoin*. Four vols. Plon, Paris, 1931.

MORDACQ, GÉNÉRAL HENRI. *L'Armistice du 11 novembre 1918. Récit d'un témoin*. Plon, Paris, 1937.

NAUMANN, FRIEDRICH. *Central Europe*, with an Introduction by W. J. Ashley. London, 1916.

NAUMANN, FRIEDRICH. *Was wird aus Polen?* Berlin, 1917.

NICOLSON, H. *Peacemaking* 1919. London, 1933.

NICOLSON, H. *Curzon : The Last Phase*, 1919-1925. *A Study in Postwar Diplomacy*. London, 1934.

NOULENS, JOSEPH. *Mon Ambassade en Russie Soviétique, 1917-1919.* Paris, 1933.

PADEREWSKI, I. J. *The Paderewski Memoirs*. Collins, London, 1939.

PALÉOLOGUE, MAURICE. *La Russie des Tsars pendant la Grand Guerre.* Three vols. Paris, 1921.

PERSHING, GENERAL. *My Experiences in the World War*. Two vols. London, 1931.

PILSUDSKI, J. *Pisma Zbiorowe*. Ten vols. Warsaw, 1937-1938.

POINCARÉ, RAYMOND. *Au service de la France*. Vol. X. Paris.

RADEK, K. *Die Liquidation des Versailler Friedens. Bericht an den 4 Kongress der Kommunistischen Internationale*. Hamburg, 1922.

REED, JOHN. *The Days that Shook the World*. London, 1934.

RIBOT, ALEXANDRE. *Lettres à un ami. Souvenirs de ma vie publique.* Paris, 1924.

RIBOT, ALEXANDRE. *Journal et correspondances inédites*, Paris 1914-1922. Paris, 1936.

RIDDELL (LORD). *Intimate Diary of the Peace Conference and After* (1918-1923). London, 1933.

SADOUL, JACQUES. *Notes sur la Révolution Bolchevique*. Paris, 1920.

SAVINKOV, B. *Memoirs of a Terrorist*. New York, 1931.

SAZONOV. *Vospominaniya*. Paris, 1927.

SEECKT, HANS VON. *Aus meinem Leben* (herausgegeben von General-Leutenant Friedrich von Rabenau, 1918-1936). Leipzig, 1941.

SEYDA, MARJAN. *Polska na Przelomie Dziejów. Fakty i Dokumenty.* Two vols. Poznan, 1927-1931.

SFORZA, CARLO. *Diplomatic Europe since the Treaty of Versailles.* Institute of Politics Publications, New Haven, 1928.

SHOTWELL, JAMES T. *At the Paris Peace Conference.* New York, 1937.

SNOWDEN, MRS. PHILIP. *Through Bolshevik Russia.* London, 1920.

SNOWDEN, VISCOUNT PHILIP. *An Autobiography.* Two vols. London, 1934.

SOKOLNICKI, M. *W sluzbie Komendanta. Kultura* 12/74, 1953.

SOSNOWSKI, JERZY JAN. *Prawda Dziejowa.* Warsaw, 1925.

STALIN, I. V. *Marxism and the National and the Colonial Question.* Martin Lawrence Ltd., London.

STALIN, I. V. *Sochineniya.* Partizdatsk VKP(b), Moscow, 1946.

STEED, HENRY WICKHAM. *Through Thirty Years. A Personal Narrative.* Two vols. London, 1924.

STRESEMANN, GUSTAV. *His Diaries, Letters and Papers.* Three vols. English translation 1935-1940. Edited and translated by Erich Sexton.

SZEPTYCKI, S. *Front Litewsko-Bialoruski.* Cracow, 1925.

TEMPERLEY, H. W. (ed). *A History of the Peace Conference of Paris.* Published under the auspices of the Institute of International Affairs. Six vols. London, 1920-1921.

TIRPITZ, ALFRED. *Errinnerungen.* Leipzig, 1920.

TOMMASINI, FRANCESCO. *La Risurrezione della Polonia.* Treves, Milano, 1925.

TROTSKY, LEON. *Kak vooruzhalas' revolutsiya.* Three vols. Moscow, 1924.

TROTSKY, LEON. *My Life.* New York, 1930.

TROTSKY, LEON. *Stalin.* Hollis and Carter, London, 1947.

TUMULTY, JOSEPH P. *Woodrow Wilson as I Knew Him.* William Heinemann, London, 1922.

WIELICZKA, Z. *Od Prosny po Rawicz. Wspomnienia z powstania wielkopolskiego,* 1918-1919. Poznan, 1931.

WIELICZKA, Z. *Wielkopolska a Prusy w dobie powstania* 1918-1919. Poznan, 1932.

WILCOX, E. H. *Russia's Ruin.* London, 1919.

WILLIAM, MRS. HAROLD (Mrs. Ariadna Tyrkóva). *From Liberty to Brest-Litovsk.* London, 1919.

WILSON, MRS. EDITH BOLLING. *My Memoir.* The Bobbs-Merrill Co., 1938-1939.

Wspomnienia Legjonowe. Two vols. Instytut Badania Najnowszej Historji Polskiej. Warsaw, 1924-1925.

C. Historical and General Works

ALEXINSKY, GREGOIRE. *La Russie et la Guerre.* Paris, 1915.

ALBERTINI, LUIGI. *The Origins of the War of* 1914. Two vols. Oxford University Press, London.

ANONYM (BOBRZYNSKI, M.) *Wskrzeszenie Państwa Polskiego.* Two vols. Cracow, 1920-1925.

APPUHN, CHARLES. *La Politique Allemande pendant la Guerre*. Publication de la Société de l'Histoire de la Guerre. Paris, 1926.

ASKENAZY, S. *Uwagi*. Warsaw, 1924.

ASKENAZY, S. *Danzig and Poland*. London, 1921.

BAILEY, THOMAS. *Woodrow Wilson and His Great Betrayal*. New York, 1945.

BAILEY, THOMAS. *Wodrow Wilson and the Lost Peace*. New York, 1944.

BAINVILLE, JACQUES. *La Russie et la Barrière de l'Est*. Paris, 1937.

BASILY, N. DE. *Russia Under Soviet Rule. Twenty Years of Bolshevik Experiment*. London, 1938.

BASSECHES, N. *Stalin* (translated from German). London and New York, 1952.

BECK, J. *Dernier Rapport. Politique Polonaise, 1926-1939*. Neuchâtel, 1952.

BEMIS, SAMUEL FLAG. *A Diplomatic History of the United States*. New York, 1936.

BEREZOWSKI, C. *Powstanie Państwa Polskiego w świetle Prawa Narodów*. Warsaw, 1934.

BERNHARD, LUDWIG. *Die Polenfrage. Der Nationalitätenkampf der Polen*. Dritte, neubearbeitete Auflage, München und Leipzig, 1920.

BIEROWSKI, THADDÉE. *La Ville Libre de Dantzig et la guerre polono-bolchévique de 1920*. Danzig, 1932.

BIRDSALL, PAUL. *Versailles Twenty Years After*. London, 1941.

BIRKENHEAD, LORD. *Turning Points in History*. Hutchinson & Co., London, 1930.

BLOCISZEWSKI. *La restauration de la Pologne et la diplomatie européenne. Revue Générale de Droit International Public*, 1921, pp. 1-83 ; 1924, pp. 89-144 ; 1926, pp. 387-483.

BLUM, JOHN M. *Joe Tumulty and the Wilson Era*. Boston and Cambridge, 1951.

BUELL, RAYMOND LESLIE. *Poland : Key to Europe*. London, 1939.

BUKOWIECKI, ST. *Rola czynników wewnętrznych w utworzeniu nowej państwowości Polski. Niepodległość*. Vol. II, 1930.

BULLITT, WILLIAM C. *The Great Globe Itself*. London, 1947.

BUNYAN, JAMES. *Intervention, Civil War and Communism in Russia*. Baltimore, 1936.

Cambridge History of Poland. Vol. I, *From the Origins to Sobieski* (ed. Professor W. F. Reddaway), Cambridge, 1950 ; Vol. II, *From Augustus II to Pilsudski* (1697-1935), Cambridge, 1941.

CAMON, GÉNÉRAL. *La Manœuvre libératrice du Maréchal Pilsudski contre les Bolchéviks août 1920*. Paris, 1929.

CARDWELL, ANN SU. *Poland and Russia. The Last Quarter Century*. New York, 1944.

CARR, EDWARD HALLETT. *The Bolshevik Revolution* (1917-1923). Three vols. London, 1950.

CARR, EDWARD HALLETT. *Twenty Years Crisis*. Second edition. London, 1946.

CARR, EDWARD HALLETT. *Conditions of Peace*. London, 1942.

CHAMBERLIN, W. H. *History of the Russian Revolution*, 1917-1921. Two vols. London, 1935.

CHAMBERS, P. FRANK. *The War Behind the War*, 1914-1918. *A History of the Political and Civilian Fronts*. London, 1939.

CHÉRADAME, ANDRÉ. *L'Allemagne, la France et la Question d'Autriche*. Deuxième édition. Paris, 1902.

CREEL, GEORGE. *The War, the World and Wilson*. Harper and Brothers, New York and London, 1920.

CZERWINSKI, W. *Le Problème de l'indépendance économique de la Pologne*. Paris, 1932.

DABROWSKI, S. *Les Empires Centraux et la Lutte pour le recrutement polonais pendant l'occupation* (1914-1918). Préface de M. le Général Niessel. Paris, 1924.

DABROWSKI, J. *Wielka Wojna*, 1914-1918. Warsaw, 1937, Two vols.

DEUTSCHER, I. *Stalin, a Political Biography*. London, 1949.

DEUTSCHER, I. *The Prophet Armed : Trotsky*, 1879-1921. Oxford University Press, 1954.

DILLON, E. J. *The Peace Conference*. London, 1919.

DODD, WILLIAM E. *Woodrow Wilson and His Work*. New and revised edition, New York, 1932.

DONALD, SIR ROBERT. *The Polish Corridor and the Consequences*. Thornton Butterworth Ltd., London, 1929.

DUGDALE, E. C. BLANCHE. *Arthur James Balfour*. Three vols. London, 1936.

DZIEWANOWSKI, M. K. *Pilsudski's Federal Policy*, 1919-1921. *Journal of Central European Affairs*. Vol. X, No. 2-3, July-October, 1950.

EAGLETON, CLYDE. *Excesses of Self-determination*. *Foreign Affairs*. Vol. XXXI, No. 4, July, 1953.

FALLS, CYRIL. *A Hundred Years of War*. Gerald Duckworth, London, 1953.

FAY, SIDNEY BRADSHAW. *The Origins of the World War*. Second edition. revised. New York, 1935.

FEILING, KEITH. *The Life of Neville Chamberlain*. Macmillan, London, 1946.

FEINBERG, N. *La Question des Minorités à la Conférence de la Paix de 1919-1920*. Paris, 1929.

FELDMAN, J. *Bismarck a Polska*. Second edition. Warsaw, 1947.

FISCHER, L. *The Soviets in World Affairs*. Two vols. Jonathan Cape, London, 1930.

FISCHER, RUTH. *Stalin and German Communism*. Harvard University Press, Cambridge, 1948.

FISHER, H. A. L. *The Value of Small States*. Oxford Pamphlets 1914, No. 17. Oxford University Press.

FISHER, H. H. *America and the New Poland*. The Macmillan Company, New York, 1928.

FISHER, H., and BUNYAN, J. *The Bolshevik Revolution*, 1917-1918. Stanford, 1934.

GERSON, LOUIS L. *Woodrow Wilson and the Rebirth of Poland.* Yale University Press, New Haven, 1953.

GLAISE-HORSTENAU, EDMOND VON. *The Collapse of the Austro-Hungarian Empire.* Translated by Ian F. D. Morrow. London, 1930.

GLEASON, JOHN HOWES. *The Genesis of Russophobia in Great Britain.* Harvard University Press, Cambridge, 1950.

GOOCH, G. P. *Before the War. Studies in Diplomacy.* London and New York, 1936-1938.

GORSKI, ANTOINE. *La Pologne et la Guerre.* Paris, 1922.

GORECKI, R. *Poland and Her Economic Development.* London, 1935.

GRUMBACH, S. *Das annexionistische Deutschland.* Lausanne, 1917. Also in an English version: *Germany's Annexionist Aims.* London, 1917.

HALECKI, OSKAR. *The Limits and Divisions of European History.* London and New York, 1950.

HALECKI, OSKAR. *Problems of Polish Historiography. The Slavonic and East European Review,* 1941-1943.

HALÉVY, E. *The World Crisis of* 1914-1918. Oxford, 1930.

HANC, JOSEPH. *Eastern Europe.* London, 1943.

HARRIS, H. WILSON. *The Peace in Making.* The Swartmore Press Ltd., London, 1920.

HARRISON, THOMSON S. *Czechoslovakia in European History.* Princeton University Press, 1953.

HUDDLESTON, SISLEY. *Peace-Making at Paris.* Fisher Unwin Ltd., London, 1919.

JANOWSKI, O. I. *The Jews and Minority Rights,* 1898-1919. London, 1933.

KEETON, G. W. *National Sovereignty and International Order.* London Institute of World Affairs. Monographs, Series No. 49, London, 1939.

KENNEDY, A. L. *Old Diplomacy and New* (1876-1922). With an Introduction by Sir Valentine Chirol. London, 1922.

KEYNES, JOHN MAYNARD. *The Economic Consequences of the Peace.* London, 1919.

KEYNES, JOHN MAYNARD. *A Revision of the Treaty.* London, 1922.

KLIMAS, P. *Le Développement de l'Etat Lithuanien.* Paris, 1919.

KOLARZ, WALTHER. *Myths and Realities in Eastern Europe.* London, 1946.

KOLARZ, WALTHER. *Russia and Her Colonies.* London, 1952.

KOMARNICKI, W. *Odbudowa Państwowości Polskiej na Ziemiach Wschodnich, Rocznik Prawniczy Wileński.* Vol. III, 1929.

KRISTIAN, A. A. *The Right to Self-Determination and the Soviet Union.* Boreas Publishing Co. Ltd. (East and West No. 6), 1952.

KUKIEL, M. *The Polish-Soviet Compaign of* 1920. *Slavonic Review,* 1928 ; also as a leaflet in Scottish-Polish Society Publications, No. 1.

KUMANIECKI, K. W. *Odbudowa Państwowości Polskiej. Najwazniejsze Dokumenty.* Warsaw-Cracow, 1924.

KUTRZEBA, ST. *Polska Odrodzona.* Fourth edition. Warsaw, 1935.

KUTRZEBA, ST. *Polskie Prawo Polityczne wedlug Traktatów*. Two vols. Cracow, 1923.

KUTRZEBA, T. *Wyprawa Kijowska*, 1920. Warsaw, 1937.

LANDAU, ROM. *Ignace Paderewski, Musician and Statesman*. Thomas Y. Crowell, New York, 1934.

LAWRENCE, DAVID. *The True Story of Woodrow Wilson*. New York, 1924.

LHOPITAL, COMMANDANT. *Foch, Armistice et la Paix*. Paris, 1938.

LINK, ARTHUR S. *Woodrow Wilson and the Progressive Era*, 1910-1917. Harper and Brothers, New York, 1954.

LINK, ARTHUR S. *Wilson, the Road to the White House*. Princeton University Press, 1947.

LIPINSKI, W. *Walka Zbrojna o Niepodległość Polski*. Second edition. Warsaw, 1935.

LORD, ROBERT HOWARD. *The Second Partition of Poland*. Harvard University Press, Cambridge, 1915.

LUCKAU, ALMA. *The German Delegation at the Peace Conference*. Columbia University Press, New York, 1941.

MACARTNEY, C. A. *National States and National Minorities*. Royal Institute of International Affairs, London, 1934.

MACHRAY, ROBERT. *Poland 1914-1931*. London, 1932.

MACHRAY, ROBERT. *The Poland of Pilsudski*. London, 1936.

MACKINDER, H. J. *Democratic Ideals and Reality*. London, 1919. (Pelican edition, 1944.)

MAIR, L. P. *The Protection of Minorities. The Working and Scope of the Minorities Treaties under the League of Nations*. Christophers, London, 1928.

MANTOUX, ETIENNE. *The Carthaginian Peace, or the Economic Consequences of Mr. Keynes*. Oxford University Press, 1946.

MARGUERITTE, VICTOR (preface). *Les Alliés contre la Russie avant, pendant et après la guerre mondiale*. Paris, 1926.

MARRIOTT, SIR J. A. R. *Federalism and the Problem of Small States*. London, 1943.

MASON, JOHN BROWN. *The Danzig Dilemma. A Study in Peacemaking by Compromise*. Stanford University Press, California and London, 1946.

MAURICE, SIR FREDERIC. *The Armistice of 1918*. Royal Institute of Foreign Affairs, London, 1943.

MICHOU, G. *L'Alliance franco-russe*, 1891-1917. Paris, 1927.

MILLIN, SARAH GERTRUD. *General Smuts*. Two vols. London, 1936.

MORDACQ, GENERAL H. *Les Légendes de la Grande Guerre*. Flammarion, Paris, 1935.

MORROW, IAN F. D. (assisted by L. M. Sieveking). *The Peace Settlement in the German-Polish Borderlands. A Study of Conditions To-day in the Pre-war Prussian Provinces of East and West Prussia*. Issued under the auspices of the Royal Institute of International Affairs. Oxford University Press, 1936.

MURRAY, GILBERT. *Self-determination of Nationalities. Journal of British Institute of International Affairs,* Vol. I-11, 1922-1923.

NAMIER, L. B. *Facing East.* Hamish Hamilton, London, 1947.

NOBLE, GEORGE BERNARD. *Policies and Opinions at Paris,* 1919. *Wilsonian Diplomacy, the Versailles Peace, and French Public Opinion.* The Macmillan Company, New York.

NOTTER, HARTLEY. *The Origins of the Foreign Policy of Woodrow Wilson.* Baltimore, 1937.

NOWAK, KARL FRIEDRICH. *The Collapse of Central Europe.* London, 1924.

NOWAK, KARL FRIEDRICH. *Versailles.* London, 1928.

OKULICZ, K. *Podzial Ziem Wielkiego Księstwa Litewskiego* (Alma Mater Vilnensis). London, 1953.

PHILLIPS, W. ALISON. *Poland.* London, 1915.

PINGAUD, ALBERT. *Histoire Diplomatique de la France pendant la Grande Guerre.* Three vols. Paris, 1938-1940.

PINK, P. *The Conference of Ambassadors* (Paris 1920-1931). *Geneva Studies.* Vol. XII, No. 4-5, February, 1942.

PINON R. *La reconstruction de l'Europe Orientale. Revue des Deux Mondes,* 15th January, 1919.

POTEMKIN, V. P. (ed.). *Istoriya Diplomatsii.* Three vols. Moscow, 1941-1945.

PRZYBYLSKI, A. *Wojna Polska,* 1919-1921. Warsaw, 1930.

RAMSAY, A. W. *Idealism and Foreign Policy. A Study of the Relations of Great Britain with Germany and France,* 1860-1878. London, 1925.

RECKE, WALTHER. *Die Wiederaufrichtung Polens in Versailles.* Berlin, 1928.

RENOUVIN, PIERRE. *Les origines immédiates de la guerre.* Publications de la Société de l'Histoire de la Guerre. Paris, 1927.

RENOUVIN, PIERRE. *La crise européene et la Grande Guerre* (1904-1918). Deuxième édition, Paris, 1939.

RENOUVIN, PIERRE. *Les engagements de l'alliance franco-russe. Revue d'Histoire de la Guerre Mondiale.* Vol. XII, 1934.

RESHETAR, JOHN S. Jr. *The Ukrainian Revolution,* 1917-1920. *A Study in Nationalism.* Princeton, New Jersey, 1952.

ROTH, P. *Die politische Entwicklung in Kongresspolen während der deutschen Okkupation.* Leipzig, 1919.

ROTH, P. *Die Entstehung des polnischen Staates, eine völkerrechtlichex-politische Untersuchung.* Berlin, 1926.

RUDIN, HARRY. *Armistice 1918.* Yale University Press, New Haven, 1944.

SALISBURY, ROBERT, MARQUESS OF. *Essays,* 1861-1864. First published in the *Quarterly Review,* London, 1905.

SCHÄFER, W. *Die Schuld an der Wiederherstellung Polens.* Berlin, 1919.

SCHMITT, B. E. *The Coming of the War,* 1914. Two vols. New York and London, 1930.

SCHWERTFEGER, B. *Der Weltkrieg der Dokumente. Zehn Jahre Kriegsschuldforschung und Ihr Ergebnis.* Berlin, 1929.

SETON-WATSON, R. W. *Masaryk in England.* Cambridge University Press, 1943.

SETON-WATSON, R. W. *A History of the Czechs and Slovaks.* London and New York, 1943.

SIKORSKI, WLADYSLAW (or Ladislas). *La Campagne Polono-Russe de 1920.* Préface de M. le Maréchal Foch. Paris, 1928. (French edition of the Polish work, *On the Vistula and the Wkra.* Lwow, 1928.)

SKRZYPEK, J. *Ukraińcy w Austrji podczas Wielkiej Wojny. Geneza Zamachu na Lwow. Niepodległość,* Vol. XIX.

SLOCOMBE, GEORGE. *A History of Poland.* Revised and enlarged edition. Thomas Nelson and Sons, Ltd., London, 1941.

SLOVES, H. *La France et l'Union Soviétique.* Paris, 1935.

SMOGORZEWSKI, K. *Abrégé d'une bibliographie relative aux relations Germano-polonaises* Problèmes Politiques de la Pologne Contemporaine, II (Supplément). Paris, 1933.

SMOGORZEWSKI, K. *La Pologne restaurée.* Préface de M. Auguste Gauvain. Paris, 1927.

SMOGORZEWSKI, K. *Joseph Pilsudski et les Activistes polonais pendant la guerre.* Extrait de la *Revue des Questions Historiques.* Paris 1930.

SMOGORZEWSKI, K. *L'Union Sacrée Polonaise. Le Gouvernement de Varsovie et le "Gouvernement" Polonais de Paris* (1918-1919). Publications de la Société de l'Histoire de la Guerre, Paris, 1929.

SMOGORZEWSKI, K. *La Pologne et la Guerre à travers les Livres Polonais.* Paris, 1929.

SMOGORZEWSKI, K. *Poland's Access to the Sea.* George Allen and Unwin, London, 1934.

SMOGORZEWSKI, K. *Poland, Germany and the Corridor.* Williams and Norgate, London, 1930.

SOKOLNICKI, M. *Polska w Pamiętnikach Wielkiej Wojny.* Warsaw, 1925.

SOKOLNICKI, M. *Sprawa Polska na terenie międzynarodowym* (1914-1918). *Niepodległość,* Vol. I. London.

SOUVARINE, BORIS. *Stalin. A Critical Survey of Bolshevism.* New York and London.

SROKOWSKI, K. *N. K. N. Zarys Historji Naczelnego Komitetu Narodowego.* Cracow, 1923.

STACHIEWICZ, JULIAN. *Niemieckie Plany Organizacji Wojska Polskiego w Czasie Wielkiej Wojny Swiatowej. Niepodległość,* Vol. I, 1933.

STARZEWSKI, J. *Zarys Dziejów Polskiej Polityki Zagranicznej* (1914-1939). London, 1944.

STIEVE, F. *Izvolsky and the World War.* London, 1926.

STRAKHOVSKY, L. J. *The Origins of American Intervention in North Russia* (1918). Princeton University Press, 1937.

SUMNER, B. H. *Survey of Russian History.* First published, London, January, 1944.

SWORAKOWSKI, W. *An Error regarding Eastern Galicia in Curzon's Note to the Soviet Government. Journal of Central European Affairs.* Vol. IV, No. 1, April, 1944.

TARACUZIO, *The Soviet Union and International Law.* New York, 1935.

TARACUZIO. *War and Peace in Soviet Diplomacy.* Macmillan, New York, 1940.

TESLAR, T. *Polityka Rosji Sowieckiej podczas wojny z Polską.* Warsaw, 1937.

TIMS, R. W. *Germanizing Prussian Poland (The H.K.T. Society and the Struggle for the Eastern Marches in the German Empire).* New York, 1941.

TOYNBEE, ARNOLD J. *The World After the Peace Conference* (being an epilogue to the *History of the Peace Conference of Paris* and a prologue to the *Survey of International Affairs* 1920-1923). London, 1925.

TOYNBEE, ARNOLD J. *Survey of International Affairs,* 1920-1923. London, 1926.

TREVELYAN, G. M. *History of England.* London, 1937.

VALLENTIN, ANTONIA. *Stresemann.* London, 1931.

VICTOROFF-TOPOROFF, V. (ed.). *La Première Année de la Révolution Russe (Mars 1917 to Mars 1918).* Berne and Paris, 1919.

VOLKMANN, MAJOR ERICH OTTO. *Der grosse Krieg, 1914-1918.* Berlin, 1922.

WASILEWSKI, L. *Stosunki Polsko-Litewskie w dobie po-powstaniowej. Niepodległość,* Vol. I, No. 1, 1933.

WEBB, SIDNEY, and BEATRICE. *Soviet Communism: A New Civilization?* London, 1935.

WHEARE, K. C. *Federal Government.* Second edition. Oxford University Press, London, 1951.

WHEELER-BENNETT, JOHN W. *Brest Litovsk. The Forgotten Treaty.* London, 1938.

WIELHORSKI, W. *Polska a Litwa. Stosunki wzajemne w biegu dziejów.* The Polish Research Centre. London, 1947.

WILLIAMS, FRANCIS. *Ernest Bevin, Portrait of a Great Englishman.* London, 1952.

INDEX